CONTRIBUTORS

Introductions and Special Essays

William L. Andrews
University of North Carolina
Chapel Hill

Alice A. Deck
University of Illinois
Urbana/Champaign

David Dorsey
Clark Atlanta University

Mari Evans
Formerly at
Cornell University

Robert E. Fox
Southern Illinois University
Carbondale

David Adams Leeming
Formerly at
University of Connecticut

Arnold Rampersad
Princeton University

John Edgar Tidwell
University of Miami
Oxford, Ohio

Cheryl A. Wall
Rutgers University

Advisers and Reviewers

William L. Andrews
University of North Carolina
Chapel Hill

Carole Boyce Davies
SUNY, Binghamton

David Dorsey
Clark Atlanta University

Robert E. Fox
Southern Illinois University
Carbondale

Henry Louis Gates, Jr.
Harvard University

David Adams Leeming
Formerly at
University of Connecticut

Phil W. Petrie
Freelance Writer and Editor
Clarksville, Tennessee

Arnold Rampersad
Princeton University

John Edgar Tidwell
University of Miami
Oxford, Ohio

Christopher van Wyk
SACHED
Johannesburg, South Africa

Cheryl A. Wall
Rutgers University

Instructional Materials

Constance Burts Jackson
Communication and Media Arts
High School
Detroit, Michigan

Sterling C. Jones, Jr.
Program Supervisor of
Academic Task Force/Gifted
and Talented Education
Detroit Public Schools

Yvonne Robinson Jones
Shelby State Community
College
Memphis, Tennessee

Barbara Smith Palmer
Locke High School
Los Angeles, California

Phil W. Petrie
Freelance Writer and Editor
Clarksville, Tennessee

Nancy Timmons
Assistant Superintendent of
Administrative Services
Fort Worth Independent
School District

Shirley W. Tinsley
Formerly at
Northwestern High School
Detroit, Michigan

Mary Toskos
Formerly
Supervisor of English
Flushing High School
New York

*We wish to thank the following
people in the Detroit Public
Schools, who served as a special
committee to assist in the planning
of this program:*

Barbara Bowen Coulter
Formerly
Director of Communication Arts

Constance Burts Jackson
Teacher
Communication and Media Arts
High School

Sterling C. Jones, Jr.
Program Supervisor of
Academic Task Force/Gifted
and Talented Education

Jewel Lenard, Teacher
Formerly at
Cooley High School

Viola Palmer
English Department Head
Cass Technical High School

Shirley W. Tinsley, Teacher
Formerly at
Northwestern High School

AFRICAN AMERICAN LITERATURE

Voices in a Tradition

HOLT, RINEHART AND WINSTON
Harcourt Brace & Company
Austin • New York • Orlando • Atlanta • San Francisco • Boston • Dallas • Toronto • London

ACKNOWLEDGMENTS

We wish to thank the following people, who participated in field testing and reviewing of prepublication materials:

Marion Amery
Madison Park High School/
Humphrey Center
Boston, MA

Mary Ayala
Cleveland High School
Portland, OR

Chana Bass
Catonsville High School
Baltimore, MD

Linnea Beal
Kettering High School
Detroit, MI

Joyce Bellinger
Independence High School
Columbus, OH

Brenda Browder
Reading Coordinator
Kellerman School
Chicago, IL

Louis Endel
MacArthur High School
Houston, TX

Portia Garrett
Eastern Sr. High School
Washington, D.C.

Vincent Garrity
Central High School
Detroit, MI

Gwendolyn Grant
Dundalk High School
Baltimore, MD

Teresa Knight
Westinghouse High School
Chicago, IL

Eva Miller
Sheffield High School
Memphis, TN

Maxine Mitchell
Weaver High School
Hartford, CT

Evelyn Shepherd
Longfellow Academy
Dallas, TX

Jeanette Swenson
Cleveland High School
Portland, OR

Judy Thomas
Storey Middle School
Dallas, TX

Alan Tucker
Parkdale High School
Riverdale, MD

Carmen Walston
Boys and Girls High School
Brooklyn, NY

Catherine Webb
Mt. Vernon Jr. High School
Los Angeles, CA

Jacqueline Wells
Storey Middle School
Dallas, TX

Rita Woods
Andrew Jackson High School
Cambria Heights, New York

Frederick Yudin
Ingraham High School
Seattle, WA

CREDITS

EDITORIAL

Project Director:
Fannie Safier

Managing Editor:
Richard Sime

Senior Book Editor:
Laura Baci

Editorial Staff:
Daniela Guggenheim, Bobbi Hernandez, Marc Ottaviani

Editorial Support:
Mark Koenig

Editorial Permissions:
Lee Noble

PRODUCTION, DESIGN, AND PHOTO RESEARCH

Director:
Athena Blackorby

Art Director:
Betty Mintz

Designer:
Ruth Riley

Layouts:
Tony Hom/Harry Chester, Inc.

Photo Research:
Cindy Joyce, Mary Monaco

Maps:
R. R. Donnelley & Sons Cartographic Services

Unit Designs:
Brian Pinckney, Kirchoff/Wohlberg

Cover Design:
Michael Mendelsohn/Harry Chester, Inc.

Cover: *The Lovers (Somali Friends)* by Loïs Mailou Jones, casein on canvas, 1950. Courtesy of The Estate of Thurlow E. Tibbs, Jr., photography by Mary S. Rezny

Table of Contents _____

UNIT ONE
PASSAGES

UNIT TWO
THE AFRICAN LITERARY TRADITION

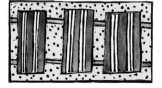

UNIT THREE
THE BEGINNINGS OF AFRICAN AMERICAN LITERATURE

Contents   vii

UNIT FOUR

RECONSTRUCTION TO RENAISSANCE

UNIT FIVE
THE HARLEM RENAISSANCE

Introduction
Cheryl A. Wall, Rutgers University   267

UNIT SIX

FROM RENAISSANCE TO MID-FORTIES

CONTEMPORARY AFRICAN AMERICAN LITERATURE

UNIT SEVEN
CONTEMPORARY SHORT STORIES

UNIT EIGHT
CONTEMPORARY NONFICTION

UNIT TEN

CONTEMPORARY DRAMA

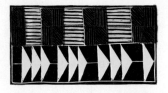

UNIT ELEVEN

CONTEMPORARY AFRICAN LITERATURE

UNIT TWELVE
THE NOVEL

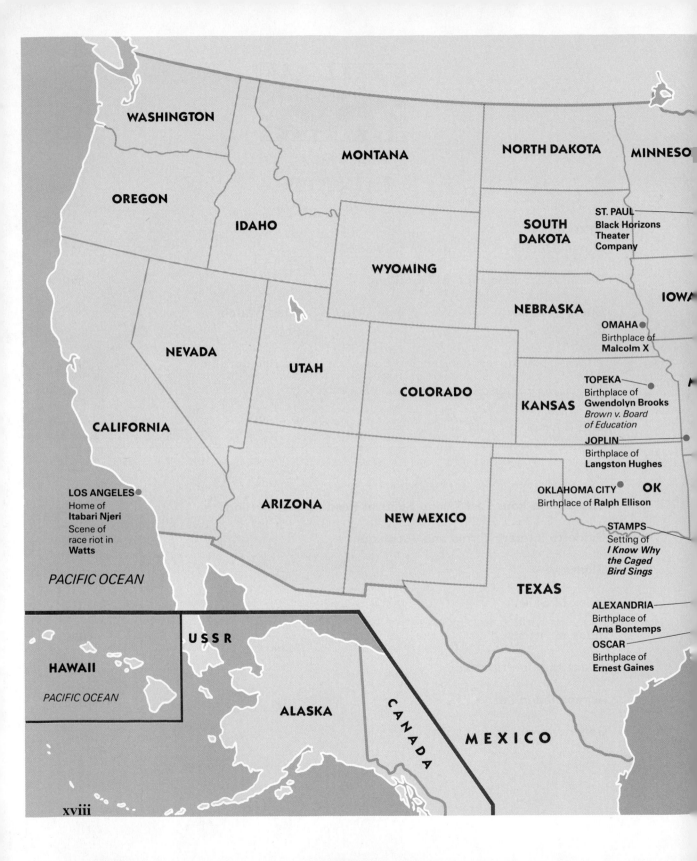

WASHINGTON

OREGON

IDAHO

MONTANA

NORTH DAKOTA

MINNESO

SOUTH DAKOTA

ST. PAUL
Black Horizons
Theater
Company

WYOMING

NEVADA

UTAH

COLORADO

NEBRASKA

IOWA

OMAHA ●
Birthplace of
Malcolm X

TOPEKA
Birthplace of
Gwendolyn Brooks
*Brown v. Board
of Education*

KANSAS

CALIFORNIA

ARIZONA

NEW MEXICO

JOPLIN
Birthplace of
Langston Hughes

LOS ANGELES ●
Home of
Itabari Njeri
Scene of
race riot in
Watts

OKLAHOMA CITY ●
Birthplace of Ralph Ellison

OK

PACIFIC OCEAN

TEXAS

STAMPS
Setting of
*I Know Why
the Caged
Bird Sings*

ALEXANDRIA
Birthplace of
Arna Bontemps

OSCAR
Birthplace of
Ernest Gaines

HAWAII

PACIFIC OCEAN

USSR

ALASKA

CANADA

MEXICO

xviii

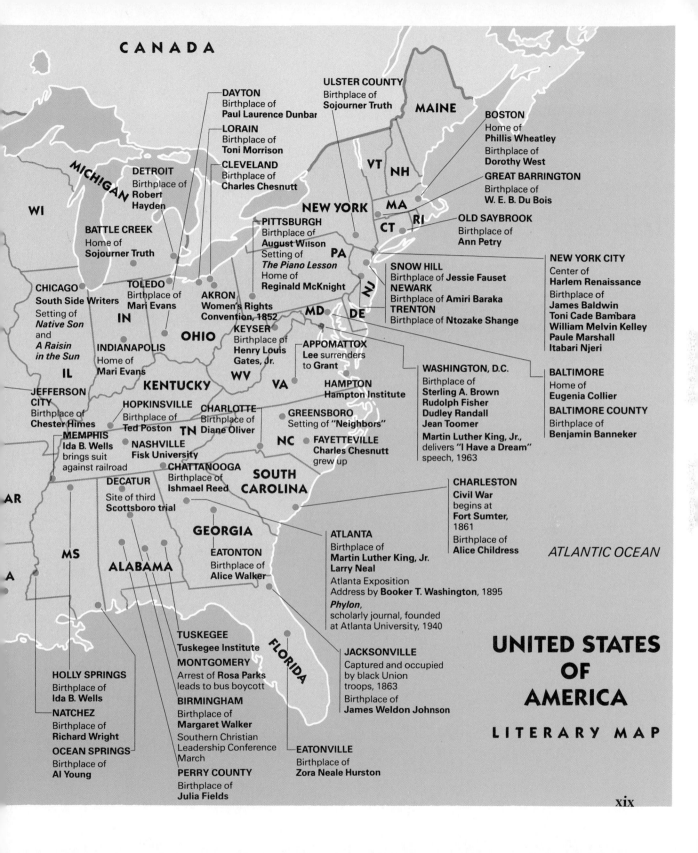

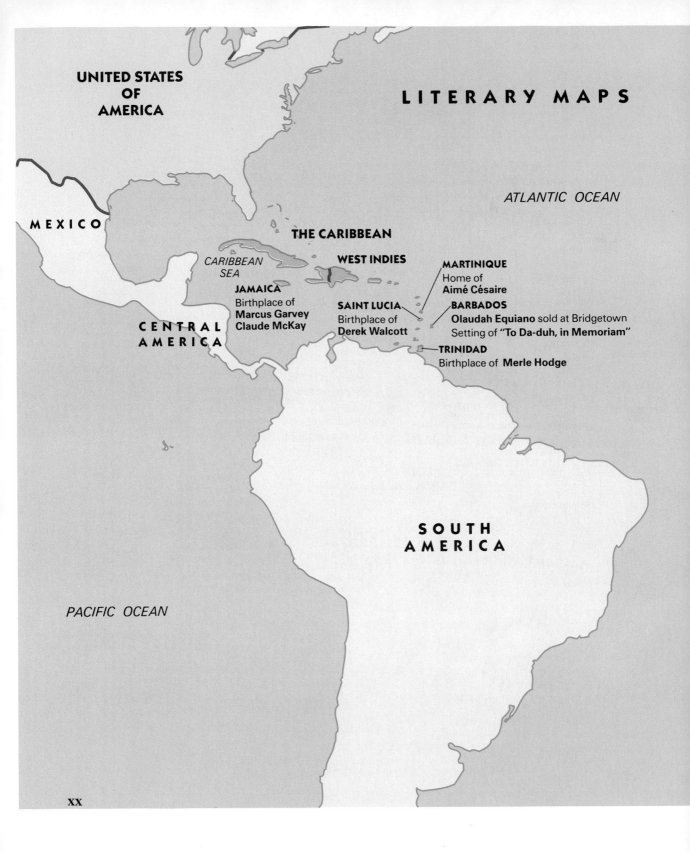

LITERARY MAPS

UNITED STATES OF AMERICA

MEXICO

ATLANTIC OCEAN

THE CARIBBEAN

CARIBBEAN SEA

WEST INDIES

JAMAICA
Birthplace of
Marcus Garvey
Claude McKay

SAINT LUCIA
Birthplace of
Derek Walcott

MARTINIQUE
Home of
Aimé Césaire

BARBADOS
Olaudah Equiano sold at Bridgetown
Setting of **"To Da-duh, in Memoriam"**

TRINIDAD
Birthplace of **Merle Hodge**

CENTRAL AMERICA

SOUTH AMERICA

PACIFIC OCEAN

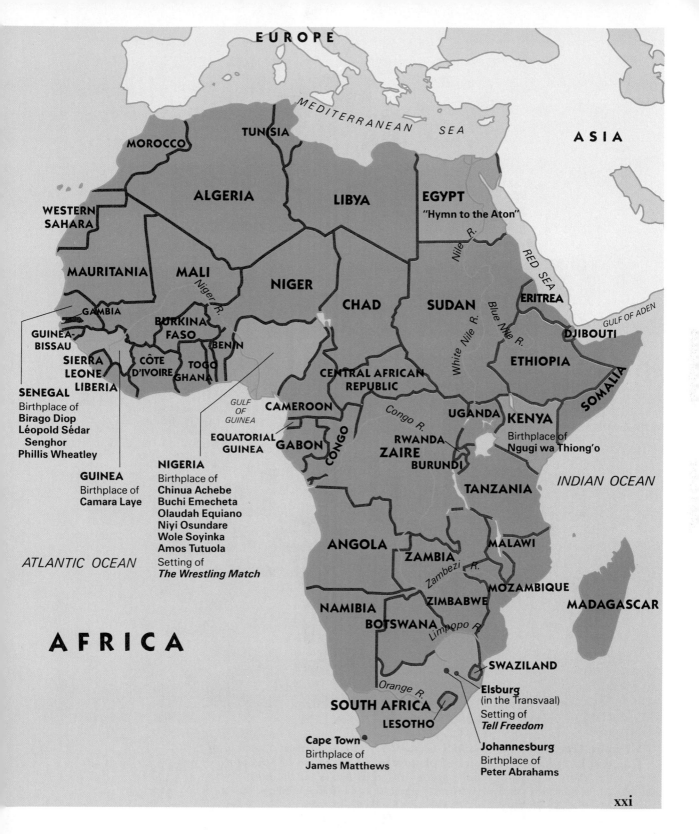

EUROPE

MEDITERRANEAN SEA

ASIA

MOROCCO

TUNISIA

ALGERIA

LIBYA

EGYPT
"Hymn to the Aton"

WESTERN
SAHARA

Nile R.

RED SEA

MAURITANIA

MALI

NIGER

Niger R.

CHAD

SUDAN

ERITREA

GULF OF ADEN

DJIBOUTI

White Nile R.

Blue Nile R.

ETHIOPIA

GAMBIA

BURKINA
FASO

BENIN

GUINEA-
BISSAU

SIERRA
LEONE

CÔTE
D'IVOIRE

TOGO

GHANA

LIBERIA

SOMALIA

CENTRAL AFRICAN
REPUBLIC

SENEGAL
Birthplace of
**Birago Diop
Léopold Sédar
  Senghor
Phillis Wheatley**

GULF
OF
GUINEA

CAMEROON

Congo R.

UGANDA

KENYA

Birthplace of
Ngugi wa Thiong'o

EQUATORIAL
GUINEA

GABON

RWANDA

ZAIRE

CONGO

BURUNDI

GUINEA
Birthplace of
Camara Laye

NIGERIA
Birthplace of
**Chinua Achebe
Buchi Emecheta
Olaudah Equiano
Niyi Osundare
Wole Soyinka
Amos Tutuola**
Setting of
The Wrestling Match

TANZANIA

INDIAN OCEAN

ATLANTIC OCEAN

ANGOLA

ZAMBIA

MALAWI

Zambezi R.

MOZAMBIQUE

MADAGASCAR

AFRICA

NAMIBIA

ZIMBABWE

BOTSWANA

Limpopo R.

SWAZILAND

Orange R.

Elsburg
(in the Transvaal)
Setting of
Tell Freedom

SOUTH AFRICA

LESOTHO

Cape Town
Birthplace of
James Matthews

Johannesburg
Birthplace of
Peter Abrahams

Family Tree, *quilt by Wini McQueen, 1987. This quilt uses a variety of techniques, including the transfer of photographs to cloth, to tell the story of a family. Note how photographs are arranged as leaves on the tree.*
Part of the exhibition "Stitching Memories," organized by the Williams College Museum of Art; on loan from the Museum of Arts and Sciences, Macon, Georgia

Unit One

Passages

In New York City's Harlem,
a runner strolls down Broadway,
practicing her breathing exercises
for the May Day races.

A poet from Georgia
remembers a sister who
opened her mind to new
experiences and interests.

A boy performing in the
annual school play in a
Kentucky town adds some
unrehearsed action to the
script.

A girl sent to live with
her grandmother in
Stamps, Arkansas,
discovers a "Fun House
of Things" in the family
store.

A girl from the island of
Trinidad recalls what it was
like to attend "Big School."

In South Africa, a child
experiences the oppression
and cruelty of apartheid.

These are some of the experiences you will share when you read
the selections in this unit. The young people who appear in these
selections have grown up in different places, some in American
cities and small towns, and others in distant lands. While there
may be differences in their cultural backgrounds, you will find that
like young people all over the world they have similar concerns
about who they are and what they wish to become.

About the Author

Toni Cade Bambara (1939–1995)

Sandra L. Swans/The Schomburg Center for Research in Black Culture/New York Public Library

Toni Cade Bambara (bäm-bä'rä), a New Yorker who grew up in Harlem, Brooklyn, and Jersey City, began writing when she was very young. She attended Queens College, where she studied theater arts and English, and she received her master's degree from the City College of New York. Bambara took her last name from a signature in a sketchbook she found in her great-grandmother's trunk. (Bambara is the name of a people of northwest Africa who are noted for their delicate wood carvings.) She worked as a social investigator, a film writer and producer, and a college teacher of English. In the 1960s and 1970s she became active in civil rights issues. She edited two anthologies: *The Black Woman* (1970) and *Tales and Stories for Black Folks* (1971). In the introduction to the second collection, she explained that her main aim was to teach young African Americans the value of one of their great traditions—telling stories. She published two collections of her own stories: *Gorilla, My Love* (1972), from which "Raymond's Run" is taken, and *The Sea Birds Are Still Alive* (1977). In addition she wrote two novels, *The Salt Eaters* (1980) and *If Blessing Comes* (1987). She also produced scripts for television and film.

One critic has written that in all of Toni Cade Bambara's stories "there is an undercurrent of caring for one's neighbors that sustains black Americans." In her fiction Bambara used black-speech styles and focused on the lives and relationships of African Americans. Poet Lucille Clifton has said this about the stories in *Gorilla, My Love:* "She has captured it all, how we really talk, how we really are; and done it with love and respect. I laughed until I cried, then laughed again."

Before You Read

Raymond's Run

Using What You Know

Older brothers and sisters often have to look after a younger child. What difficulties can such a situation cause for a teenager? Are there also satisfactions in taking care of another family member? Think about these questions as you get to know a character named Squeaky.

Literary Focus: Characterization

A writer can develop a character in any combination of ways:

1. by giving a physical description of the character
2. by commenting directly on the character
3. by showing the character's actions and speech
4. by revealing the character's thoughts
5. by telling what others think of the character

When writers *tell* what characters are like through description or comment, they are using **direct characterization**. When writers *show* what characters are like through their actions, their words, their thoughts, and the reactions of other characters, they are using **indirect characterization**.

Setting a Purpose

Squeaky, the main character in "Raymond's Run," has grown up in Harlem in New York City and prides herself on being tough and streetwise. As you read, note how Squeaky reveals herself through her actions, her thoughts, and her words. How does she show that she cares a lot about her family, her neighborhood, and the people who live in the inner city?

Raymond's Run

Toni Cade Bambara

I don't have much work to do around the house like some girls. My mother does that. And I don't have to earn my pocket money by hustling; George runs errands for the big boys and sells Christmas cards. And anything else that's got to get done, my father does. All I have to do in life is mind my brother Raymond, which is enough.

Sometimes I slip and say my little brother Raymond. But as any fool can see he's much bigger and he's older too. But a lot of people call him my little brother cause he needs looking after cause he's not quite right. And a lot of smart mouths got lots to say about that too, especially when George was minding him. But now, if anybody has anything to say to Raymond, anything to say about his big head, they have to come by me. And I don't play the dozens[1] or believe in standing around with somebody in my face doing a lot of talking. I much rather just knock you down and take my chances even if I am a little girl with skinny arms and a squeaky voice, which is how I got the name Squeaky. And if things get too rough, I run. And as anybody can tell you, I'm the fastest thing on two feet.

There is no track meet that I don't win the first place medal. I used to win the twenty-yard dash when I was a little kid in kindergarten. Nowadays, it's the fifty-yard dash. And tomorrow I'm subject to run the quarter-meter relay all by myself and come in first, second, and third. The big kids call me Mercury[2] cause I'm the swiftest thing in the neighborhood. Everybody knows that—except two people who know better, my father and me. He can beat me to Amsterdam Avenue with me having a two fire-hydrant headstart and him running with his hands in his pockets and whistling. But that's private information. Cause can you imagine some thirty-five-year-old man stuffing himself into PAL[3] shorts to race little kids? So as far as everyone's concerned, I'm the fastest and that goes for Gretchen, too, who has put out the tale that she is going to win the first-place medal this year. Ridiculous. In the second place, she's got short legs. In the third place, she's got freckles. In the first place, no one can beat me and that's all there is to it.

I'm standing on the corner admiring the weather and about to take a stroll down Broadway so I can practice my breathing

---

1. **play the dozens:** The players trade insults about a family member.

2. **Mercury:** the messenger god in classical mythology. He wore winged sandals and was known for his speed.
3. **PAL:** Police Athletic League.

exercises, and I've got Raymond walking on the inside close to the buildings, cause he's subject to fits of fantasy and starts thinking he's a circus performer and that the curb is a tightrope strung high in the air. And sometimes after a rain he likes to step down off his tightrope right into the gutter and slosh around getting his shoes and cuffs wet. Then I get hit when I get home. Or sometimes if you don't watch him he'll dash across traffic to the island in the middle of Broadway and give the pigeons a fit. Then I have to go behind him apologizing to all the old people sitting around trying to get some sun and getting all upset with the pigeons fluttering around them, scattering their newspapers and upsetting the waxpaper lunches in their laps. So I keep Raymond on the inside of me, and he plays like he's driving a stage coach which is O.K. by me so long as he doesn't run me over or interrupt my breathing exercises, which I have to do on account of I'm serious about my running, and I don't care who knows it.

Now some people like to act like things come easy to them, won't let on that they practice. Not me. I'll high-prance down 34th Street like a rodeo pony to keep my knees strong even if it does get my mother uptight so that she walks ahead like she's not with me, don't know me, is all by herself on a shopping trip, and I am somebody else's crazy child. Now you take Cynthia Procter for instance. She's just the opposite. If there's a test tomorrow, she'll say something like, "Oh, I guess I'll play handball this afternoon and watch television tonight," just to let you know she ain't thinking about the

Raymond's Run 5

test. Or like last week when she won the spelling bee for the millionth time, "A good thing you got 'receive,' Squeaky, cause I would have got it wrong. I completely forgot about the spelling bee." And she'll clutch the lace on her blouse like it was a narrow escape. Oh, brother. But of course when I pass her house on my early morning trots around the block, she is practicing the scales on the piano over and over and over and over. Then in music class she always lets herself get bumped around so she falls accidently on purpose onto the piano stool and is so surprised to find herself sitting there that she decides just for fun to try out the ole keys. And what do you know—Chopin's[4] waltzes just spring out of her fingertips and she's the most surprised thing in the world. A regular prodigy. I could kill people like that. I stay up all night studying the words for the spelling bee. And you can see me any time of day practicing running. I never walk if I can trot, and shame on Raymond if he can't keep up. But of course he does, cause if he hangs back someone's liable to walk up to him and get smart, or take his allowance from him, or ask him where he got that great big pumpkin head. People are so stupid sometimes.

So I'm strolling down Broadway breathing out and breathing in on counts of seven, which is my lucky number, and here comes Gretchen and her sidekicks: Mary Louise, who used to be a friend of mine when she first moved to Harlem from Baltimore and got beat up by everybody till I took up for her on account of her mother and my mother used to sing in the same choir when they were young girls, but people ain't grateful, so now she hangs out with the new girl Gretchen and talks about me like a dog; and Rosie, who is as fat as I am skinny and has a big mouth where Raymond is concerned and is too stupid to know that there is not a big deal of difference between herself and Raymond and that she can't afford to throw stones. So they are steady coming up Broadway and I see right away that it's going to be one of those Dodge City[5] scenes cause the street ain't that big and they're close to the buildings just as we are. First I think I'll step into the candy store and look over the new comics and let them pass. But that's chicken and I've got a reputation to consider. So then I think I'll just walk straight on through them or even over them if necessary. But as they get to me, they slow down. I'm ready to fight, cause like I said I don't feature a whole lot of chit-chat, I much prefer to just knock you down right from the jump and save everybody a lotta precious time.

"You signing up for the May Day races?" smiles Mary Louise, only it's not a smile at all. A dumb question like that doesn't deserve an answer. Besides, there's just me and Gretchen standing there really, so no use wasting my breath talking to shadows.

"I don't think you're going to win this time," says Rosie, trying to signify[6] with her hands on her hips all salty, completely forgetting that I have whupped her behind many times for less salt than that.

"I always win cause I'm the best," I say straight at Gretchen who is, as far as I'm concerned, the only one talking in this ventriloquist-dummy routine. Gretchen smiles, but it's not a smile, and I'm thinking that girls never really smile at each other because they don't know how and don't want to know how

4. **Chopin** (shō′păn′): Frédéric François Chopin (1810–1849), a Polish composer and pianist.

5. **Dodge City:** the setting of an old television series called *Gunsmoke.* The episodes often contained showdown scenes between the marshal and the gunslingers.
6. **signify:** here, using gestures as a kind of insult.

and there's probably no one to teach us how, cause grown-up girls don't know either. Then they all look at Raymond who has just brought his mule team to a standstill. And they're about to see what trouble they can get into through him.

"What grade you in now, Raymond?"

"You got anything to say to my brother, you say it to me, Mary Louise Williams of Raggedy Town, Baltimore."

"What are you, his mother?" sasses Rosie.

"That's right, Fatso. And the next word out of anybody and I'll be *their* mother too." So they just stand there and Gretchen shifts from one leg to the other and so do they. Then Gretchen puts her hands on her hips and is about to say something with her freckle-face self but doesn't. Then she walks around me looking me up and down but keeps walking up Broadway, and her side-kicks follow her. So me and Raymond smile at each other and he says, "Gidyap" to his team and I continue with my breathing exercises, strolling down Broadway toward the ice man on 145th with not a care in the world cause I am Miss Quicksilver herself.

I take my time getting to the park on May Day because the track meet is the last thing on the program. The biggest thing on the program is the May Pole dancing, which I can do without, thank you, even if my mother thinks it's a shame I don't take part and act like a girl for a change. You'd think my mother'd be grateful not to have to make

Photograph of 125th Street in Harlem.
Richard Hutchings/Photo Researchers

me a white organdy dress with a big satin sash and buy me new white baby-doll shoes that can't be taken out of the box till the big day. You'd think she'd be glad her daughter ain't out there prancing around a May Pole getting the new clothes all dirty and sweaty and trying to act like a fairy or a flower or whatever you're supposed to be when you should be trying to be yourself, whatever that is, which is, as far as I am concerned, a poor Black girl who really can't afford to buy shoes and a new dress you only wear once a lifetime cause it won't fit next year.

I was once a strawberry in a Hansel and Gretel pageant when I was in nursery school and didn't have no better sense than to dance on tiptoe with my arms in a circle over my head doing umbrella steps and being a perfect fool just so my mother and father could come dressed up and clap. You'd think they'd know better than to encourage that kind of nonsense. I am not a strawberry. I do not dance on my toes. I run. That is what I am all about. So I always come late to the May Day program, just in time to get my number pinned on and lay in the grass till they announce the fifty-yard dash.

I put Raymond in the little swings, which is a tight squeeze this year and will be impossible next year. Then I look around for Mr. Pearson, who pins the numbers on. I'm really looking for Gretchen if you want to know the truth, but she's not around. The park is jam-packed. Parents in hats and corsages and breast-pocket handkerchiefs peeking up. Kids in white dresses and light-blue suits. The parkees unfolding chairs and chasing the rowdy kids from Lenox as if they had no right to be there. The big guys with their caps on backwards, leaning against the fence swirling the basketballs on the tips of their fingers, waiting for all these crazy people to clear out the park so they can play. Most of the kids in my class are carrying bass drums and glockenspiels[7] and flutes. You'd think they'd put in a few bongos or something for real like that.

Then here comes Mr. Pearson with his clipboard and his cards and pencils and whistles and safety pins and fifty million other things he's always dropping all over the place with his clumsy self. He sticks out in a crowd because he's on stilts. We used to call him Jack and the Beanstalk to get him mad. But I'm the only one that can outrun him and get away, and I'm too grown for that silliness now.

"Well, Squeaky," he says, checking my name off the list and handing me number seven and two pins. And I'm thinking he's got no right to call me Squeaky, if I can't call him Beanstalk.

"Hazel Elizabeth Deborah Parker," I correct him and tell him to write it down on his board.

"Well, Hazel Elizabeth Deborah Parker, going to give someone else a break this year?" I squint at him real hard to see if he is seriously thinking I should lose the race on purpose just to give someone else a break. "Only six girls running this time," he continues, shaking his head sadly like it's my fault all of New York didn't turn out in sneakers. "That new girl should give you a run for your money." He looks around the park for Gretchen like a periscope in a submarine movie. "Wouldn't it be a nice gesture if you were . . . to ahhh . . ."

I give him such a look he couldn't finish putting that idea into words. Grownups got a lot of nerve sometimes. I pin number seven to myself and stomp away, I'm so burnt. And

7. **glockenspiels** (glŏk′ən-spēlz′): musical instruments played with small, light hammers.

I go straight for the track and stretch out on the grass while the band winds up with "Oh, the Monkey Wrapped His Tail Around the Flag Pole," which my teacher calls by some other name. The man on the loudspeaker is calling everyone over to the track and I'm on my back looking at the sky, trying to pretend I'm in the country, but I can't, because even grass in the city feels hard as sidewalk, and there's just no pretending you are anywhere but in a "concrete jungle" as my grandfather says.

The twenty-yard dash takes all of two minutes cause most of the little kids don't know no better than to run off the track or run the wrong way or run smack into the fence and fall down and cry. One little kid, though, has got the good sense to run straight for the white ribbon up ahead so he wins. Then the second-graders line up for the thirty-yard dash and I don't even bother to turn my head to watch cause Raphael Perez always wins. He wins before he even begins by psyching the runners, telling them they're going to trip on their shoelaces and fall on their faces or lose their shorts or something, which he doesn't really have to do since he is very fast, almost as fast as I am. After that is the forty-yard dash which I use to run when I was in first grade. Raymond is hollering from the swings cause he knows I'm about to do my thing cause the man on the loudspeaker has just announced the fifty-yard dash, although he might just as well be giving a recipe for angel food cake cause you can hardly make out what he's sayin for the static. I get up and slip off my sweat pants and then I see Gretchen standing at the starting line, kicking her legs out like a pro. Then as I get into place I see that ole Raymond is on line on the other side of the fence, bending down with his fingers on the ground just like he knew what he

was doing. I was going to yell at him but then I didn't. It burns up your energy to holler.

Every time, just before I take off in a race, I always feel like I'm in a dream, the kind of dream you have when you're sick with fever and feel all hot and weightless. I dream I'm flying over a sandy beach in the early morning sun, kissing the leaves of the trees as I fly by. And there's always the smell of apples, just like in the country when I was little and used to think I was a choo-choo train, running through the fields of corn and chugging up the hill to the orchard. And all the time I'm dreaming this, I get lighter and lighter until I'm flying over the beach again, getting blown through the sky like a feather that weighs nothing at all. But once I spread my fingers in the dirt and crouch over the Get on Your Mark, the dream goes and I am solid again and am telling myself, Squeaky you must win, you must win, you are the fastest thing in the world, you can even beat your father up Amsterdam if you really try. And then I feel my weight coming back just behind my knees then down to my feet then into the earth and the pistol shot explodes in my blood and I am off and weightless again, flying past the other runners, my arms pumping up and down and the whole world is quiet except for the crunch as I zoom over the gravel in the track. I glance to my left and there is no one. To the right, a blurred Gretchen, who's got her chin jutting out as if it would win the race all by itself. And on the other side of the fence is Raymond with his arms down to his side and the palms tucked up behind him, running in his very own style, and it's the first time I ever saw that and I almost stop to watch my brother Raymond on his first run. But the white ribbon is bouncing toward me and I tear past it, racing into the distance till my feet with a mind of their own start digging up footfuls of dirt and brake me short. Then all the kids standing on the side pile on me, banging me on the back and slapping my head with their May Day programs, for I have won again and everybody on 151st Street can walk tall for another year.

"In first place . . ." the man on the loudspeaker is clear as a bell now. But then he pauses and the loudspeaker starts to whine. Then static. And I lean down to catch my breath and here comes Gretchen walking back, for she's overshot the finish line too, huffing and puffing with her hands on her hips taking it slow, breathing in steady time like a real pro and I sort of like her a little for the first time. "In first place . . ." and then three or four voices get all mixed up on the loudspeaker and I dig my sneaker into the grass and stare at Gretchen who's staring back, we both wondering just who did win. I can hear old Beanstalk arguing with the man on the loudspeaker and then a few others running their mouths about what the stopwatches say. Then I hear Raymond yanking at the fence to call me and I wave to shush him, but he keeps rattling the fence like a gorilla in a cage like in them gorilla movies, but then like a dancer or something he starts climbing up nice and easy but very fast. And it occurs to me, watching how smoothly he climbs hand over hand and remembering how he looked running with his arms down to his side and with the wind pulling his mouth back and his teeth showing and all, it occurred to me that Raymond would make a very fine runner. Doesn't he always keep up with me on my trots? And he surely knows how to breathe in counts of seven cause he's always doing it at the dinner table, which drives my brother George up the wall. And I'm smiling to beat the band cause if I've lost this race, or if me and Gretchen tied, or even if I've won, I can always retire as a runner and begin a whole new career as a coach with Raymond as my champion. After all, with a little more study I can beat Cynthia and her phony self at the spelling bee. And if I bugged my mother, I could get piano lessons and become a star. And I have a big rep as the baddest thing around. And I've got a roomful of ribbons and medals and awards. But what has Raymond got to call his own?

So I stand there with my new plans, laughing out loud by this time as Raymond jumps down from the fence and runs over with his teeth showing and his arms down to the side, which no one before him has quite mastered as a running style. And by the time he comes over I'm jumping up and down so glad to see him—my brother Raymond, a great runner in the family tradition. But of course everyone thinks I'm jumping up and down because the men on the loudspeaker have finally gotten themselves together and compared notes and are announcing "In first place—Miss Hazel Elizabeth Deborah Parker." (Dig that.) "In second place—Miss Gretchen P. Lewis." And I look over at Gretchen wondering what the "P" stands for. And I smile. Cause she's good, no doubt about it. Maybe she'd like to help me coach Raymond; she obviously is serious about running, as any fool can see. And she nods to congratulate me and then she smiles. And I smile. We stand there with this big smile of respect between us. It's about as real a smile as girls can do for each other, considering we don't practice real smiling every day, you know, cause maybe we too busy being flowers or fairies or strawberries instead of something honest and worthy of respect . . . you know . . . like being people.

Responding to the Selection
Raymond's Run by Toni Cade Bambara

Identifying Facts

1. Why is Raymond called Squeaky's little brother even though he is bigger and older than she is?
2. Who is George?
3. Who is Squeaky's strongest competitor in the May Day races?
4. What does Squeaky practice as she walks down Broadway?
5. What does Squeaky dream about before the race?

Interpreting Meanings

1. Why is Squeaky so protective of her brother Raymond? Do you admire her for defending him when she meets Gretchen and her friends?
2. What is Squeaky's attitude toward pretty clothes and dancing? Do you think this attitude will change?
3. Why do you think racing is so important to Squeaky?
4. Why does Squeaky call Cynthia Procter "phony"? What does her irritation at Cynthia show about herself?
5. Do you think Squeaky is as tough as she claims to be? Consider her decision about Raymond and her feelings about Gretchen at the end of the story.
6. What change can you see in Squeaky after the race? Why do you think the story is called "Raymond's Run"?

Literary Elements
Analyzing a Character

You learn a great deal about Squeaky from what she says and does and from what she thinks. How do you know, for example, that she is loyal? that she is honest? How does she show courage in facing problems? Where does she reveal that she is generous?

You can begin to put together a portrait of Squeaky. What other evidence can you add to this list? What additional qualities can you name? Write your answers on the special sheet that your teacher will distribute to you.

Loyalty	*Squeaky refuses to let others make fun of Raymond.*
Honesty	*She admits that she needs to practice her running and spelling.*
Courage	*When she meets the hostile girls on the street, she refuses to back down.*
Generosity	*She is willing to admit that Gretchen is a good runner.*

Language and Vocabulary

Understanding Informal Expressions

The story is told in language that a character like Squeaky might actually use. On page 4 Squeaky says

> And I don't play the dozens or believe in standing around with somebody in my face doing a lot of talking.

In speaking or writing more formally, one might express the idea in this way:

> I don't make a habit of trading insults and I don't believe in wasting time arguing.

Locate some quotations from the story in which Squeaky uses informal expressions. Rewrite each quotation, substituting more formal words for the informal expressions. Use a dictionary if you need help.

Descriptive Writing

Using Action Words in Description

Description is the kind of writing that creates pictures of persons, places, things, or actions. Description tells how something sounds, looks, smells, tastes, or feels.

In this passage from the story, Squeaky describes her movements during the race. Note how she uses action words in her description:

> . . . the pistol shot *explodes* in my blood and I am off and weightless again, *flying* past the other runners, my arms *pumping* up and down and the whole world is quiet except for the crunch as I *zoom* over the gravel in the track.

You have probably seen many different indoor and outdoor races. You may have watched track events in the Olympics as they were televised. Perhaps you have taken part in a race.

Recall a race in which you were a contestant or a spectator. What is your most vivid memory of the events? In a single paragraph, re-create that experience for your classmates, using action words.

Prewriting Strategies

Begin by listing words you could use to describe a runner's movements. For example:

streak	spring
flash	bound
tear	leap
whiz	accelerate
dash	overtake
fly	burn the ground
charge	tear up the road

Think of some comparisons you could use:

like a bird	quick as lightning
like a flash	run like the wind
like an arrow	

Compose an opening sentence that will capture your reader's interest. For example:

At the start of the hundred-meter race, I was trailing, but as we neared the finish line I began to overtake the front runner.

Speaking and Listening

Re-Creating a Narrator's Voice

When you read a story, do you "listen" to the different voices of the characters? Do you imagine how these people would sound if you could hear them speak?

Choose a short passage from the story in which you "hear" Squeaky's voice. You might select one or two paragraphs from the opening, Squeaky's reactions to Cynthia Procter, her description of the race, and so on. Practice reading the passage until you feel you have Squeaky's personality down pat. Then read it aloud to a partner or to a small group. Compare your reading with the interpretations of other students. Do you get new ideas from listening to your classmates read?

Telling a Personal Account

Have you ever been in a situation where you had to protect someone who couldn't defend himself or herself? Share your experience with your classmates. When you tell your story, explain the circumstances and relate the events in the order in which they happened.

Critical Thinking

Using Methods of Comparison and Contrast

Seeing relationships in literary works increases your enjoyment and understanding of what you read. To **compare** is to look for ways in which things are alike. To **contrast** is to look for ways in which they are different.

Read the following poem by Lucille Clifton. Then recall Bambara's story "Raymond's Run," which takes place in a neighborhood in Harlem. What do both writers emphasize about life in the inner city? Do you think Squeaky would agree or disagree with the feelings of the speaker in this poem?

In the Inner City
Lucille Clifton

In the inner city
or
like we call it
home
we think a lot about uptown
and the silent nights
and the houses straight as
dead men
and the pastel lights
and we hang on to our no place
happy to be alive
and in the inner city
or
like we call it
home

About the Author

Alice Walker (b. 1944)

LGI

 Alice Walker was born to sharecroppers in Eatonton, Georgia. She attended Spelman College and graduated from Sarah Lawrence College in 1965. The following year she won *The American Scholar* essay contest with a work called "The Civil Rights Movement: How Good Was It?"

Walker has helped to register voters in Georgia, and she has worked with the Head Start program in Mississippi. She has also worked for the welfare department in New York City. She has had several teaching appointments, as writer-in-residence and as lecturer in literature.

Walker has written poetry, short stories, essays, novels, and biography. She has also edited the work of Langston Hughes, Zora Neale Hurston, and other writers. She has won many honors, including the Rosenthal Award of the American Academy of Arts and Letters for her short stories, *In Love and Trouble* (1973); the Lillian Smith Award of the Southern Regional Council for her poems *Revolutionary Petunias* (1973); a Guggenheim Fellowship (1977–1978); a Pulitzer Prize and an American Book Award for *The Color Purple* (1982). To date she has published four novels, five volumes of poetry, two collections of short stories, three collections of essays, and two books for children.

In her fiction black women are the central characters. They are often subjected to violence and cruelty, but they survive and triumph over adversity. Walker uses the word *womanist* to refer to the liberation of black women. Walker's essay "In Search of Our Mothers' Gardens" (1974) celebrates African American women's expression through such arts as quilting, cooking, gardening, and storytelling.

Before You Read

For My Sister Molly Who in the Fifties

Using What You Know

By using language in creative ways, poets make readers respond imaginatively to their poems. For example, poets do not always use complete sentences or complete thoughts. What are some other characteristics you associate with poetry?

Background

This poem is from the collection *Revolutionary Petunias.* Alice Walker has called it "a pretty real poem" about a brilliant and beloved sister "who saw me grow." *Fifties* refers to the 1950s, when Alice Walker was a young girl. You need to read this poem's title as its opening line.

Literary Focus: Imagery

Imagery is language that appeals to your senses. An image may help you *see, smell, taste, hear,* or *feel* something in your imagination. Good images make experiences more intense for readers. Walker's poem opens with a *visual* image in which she describes a rooster made of vegetables. Be alert to other images that appeal to the different senses.

Setting a Purpose

This poem should make you ask several questions. Why do some lines have only one word? Why has the poet left spaces between words in line 38 and elsewhere?

For My Sister Molly Who in the Fifties

Alice Walker

Once made a fairy rooster from
Mashed potatoes
Whose eyes I forget
But green onions were his tail
And his two legs were carrot sticks   5
A tomato slice his crown.
Who came home on vacation
When the sun was hot
and cooked
and cleaned   10
And minded least of all
The children's questions
A million or more
Pouring in on her
Who had been to school   15
And knew (and told us too) that certain
Words were no longer good
And taught me not to say us for we
No matter what "Sonny said" up the
road.   20

FOR MY SISTER MOLLY WHO IN THE FIFTIES
Knew Hamlet° well and read into the night
And coached me in my songs of Africa
A continent I never knew
But learned to love   25
Because "they" she said could carry

22. **Hamlet:** a famous play
by William Shakespeare.

16   ALICE WALKER

Seated Woman, *gouache by Charles Sebree, 1940.*
Countee Cullen Art Collection at Hampton University Museum, Hampton, Virginia

A tune
And spoke in accents never heard
In Eatonton.
Who read from *Prose and Poetry*   30
And loved to read "Sam McGee from Tennessee"°
On nights the fire was burning low
And Christmas wrapped in angel hair
And I for one prayed for snow.

31. **"Sam McGee . . ."**: a poem by Robert Service. The actual title is "The Cremation of Sam McGee."

For My Sister Molly Who in the Fifties   17

WHO IN THE FIFTIES   35
Knew all the written things that made
Us laugh and stories by
The hour   Waking up the story buds
Like fruit. Who walked among the flowers
And brought them inside the house   40
And smelled as good as they
And looked as bright.
Who made dresses, braided
Hair. Moved chairs about
Hung things from walls   45
Ordered baths
Frowned on wasp bites
And seemed to know the endings
Of all the tales
I had forgot.   50

WHO OFF INTO THE UNIVERSITY
Went exploring   To London and
To Rotterdam°

Prague° and to Liberia°
Bringing back the news to us   55
Who knew none of it
But followed
crops and weather
funerals and
Methodist Homecoming;   60
easter speeches,
groaning church.

WHO FOUND ANOTHER WORLD
Another life   With gentlefolk
Far less trusting   65
And moved and moved and changed
Her name
And sounded precise
When she spoke   And frowned away
Our sloppishness.   70

53. Rotterdam (rŏt′ər-dăm′):
a city in the Netherlands.

54. Prague (präg): an important center of learning in
Czechoslovakia. **Liberia**
(lī-bîr′ē-ə): a country in western Africa, founded in the
nineteenth century as a
home for former slaves from
the United States.

WHO SAW US SILENT
Cursed with fear   A love burning
Inexpressible
And sent me money not for me
But for "College."   75
Who saw me grow through letters
The words misspelled   But not
The longing   Stretching
Growth
The tied and twisting   80

Tongue
Feet no longer bare
Skin no longer burnt against
The cotton.

WHO BECAME SOMEONE OVERHEAD   85
A light   A thousand watts
Bright and also blinding
And saw my brothers cloddish
And me destined to be
Wayward   90
My mother remote   My father
A wearisome farmer
With heartbreaking
Nails.

FOR MY SISTER MOLLY WHO IN THE FIFTIES   95
Found much
Unbearable
Who walked where few had
Understood   And sensed our
Groping after light   100
And saw some extinguished
And no doubt mourned.

FOR MY SISTER MOLLY WHO IN THE FIFTIES
Left us.

Responding to the Selection

For My Sister Molly Who in the Fifties by Alice Walker

Interpreting Meanings

1. In this poem the narrator tells about an older sister who changed her life. How did Molly awaken the children's imaginations? How did she teach the narrator to love both her African and her American heritages?

2. How did Molly encourage the narrator to develop her mind? What does the phrase "tied and twisting tongue" (lines 80–81) tell you about the narrator? What change is indicated in lines 82–84?

3. Molly is associated with light. What does the image of bright and blinding light in lines 85–87 tell you about her? Compare this image with that of the family groping after light in lines 99–101. What contrast is intended?

4. Look at the spaces that appear in line 38 and elsewhere. Do these spaces suggest a gap between Molly and her family? Do they suggest some kind of separation, or do they express a break in thought? What do the spaces in lines 77–78 suggest?

5. Why do you think Molly left the family?

Literary Elements

Analyzing Imagery

What images in the poem are associated with Molly's summer vacations? with the Christmas holidays? Can you find images in the poem that appeal to the senses of smell and touch?

Writer's Journal

Recalling a Personal Experience

A **journal** is a record of happenings. Many writers use journals to keep ideas for future use. One advantage to keeping a journal is that you can write down your reactions as they happen, when your memory of events is most accurate.

You are the subject of your journal. What happens is important, of course, but what is even more important is how the experience affects you. When you write in your journal, tell what happened. Also tell what you thought and felt.

Prewriting Strategies

If you do not already have a journal, begin keeping one. Use a notebook or folder for your journal entries and date each entry.

Recall an experience that helped you learn about yourself or about other people. Include what happened, where and when it happened, the people who were involved, and your thoughts and feelings.

Someday you may want to use this incident to write a short story or poem. Try to include all the important details.

Speaking and Listening

Reading Poetry Aloud

Practice reading Walker's poem aloud, paying attention to meaning and sound. Present an oral reading that expresses the moods and emotions in the poem.

About the Author

Ted Poston (1906–1974)

 Theodore Roosevelt Augustus Major Poston was born in Hopkinsville, in southwest Kentucky. He attended the Booker T. Washington Grammar School and Crispus Attucks High School. At fifteen Poston worked for the *Hopkinsville Contender,* his family's newspaper. After graduating from Tennessee Agricultural and Industrial College (now Tennessee State University) in Nashville, he went to New York City, where he began a long, successful career as a journalist. He worked as a reporter for the *Amsterdam News.* He later took a job with the *New York Post* and became one of the few African Americans to work full time for a New York daily paper.

Poston was described as "a first-rate reporter who had a unique ability to extract information from persons of all walks of life." During his life he received a number of awards for outstanding reporting and for his contributions to interracial and interfaith understanding.

Poston was active in covering civil rights stories and often took great risks. In "My Most Humiliating Jim Crow Experience" (1944), he tells of being the only black reporter covering the third Scottsboro trial in Decatur, Alabama. The Scottsboro case was a notorious example of racism that attracted wide attention. In 1931 nine black teenagers had been convicted of attacking two white women, and eight of them were sentenced to death. The Supreme Court overturned this conviction in 1932, and a new series of trials began. The defendants were never acquitted

Ben Martin/Time Magazine

but eventually obtained their freedom—the last one in 1950. To protect his identity as a Northern reporter, Poston used an assumed name and false identification papers. He was nearly discovered, however, and had a narrow escape.

Poston's talent for writing extended to fiction. "The Revolt of the Evil Fairies," the autobiographical short story included here, first appeared in the *New Republic* in 1942.

Before You Read

The Revolt of the Evil Fairies

Using What You Know

We usually associate the word *prejudice* with intolerance of a particular race or creed. Prejudice can also exist, however, within a minority group that is the victim of discrimination. Have you ever experienced or witnessed favoritism within a family or a community? Can you explain why some members of a racial or ethnic minority might be given special treatment?

Literary Focus: Cause and Effect in Plot

In a short story, a single cause can often lead to an effect, and that effect becomes the cause of still another effect, and so forth until there is an entire connected chain of events. Recognizing **cause-and-effect relationships** helps you to follow the **plot,** or sequence of events, and to understand the reasons for the characters' actions. What is the cause—a situation, an event, a reason, a motive—that sets things going in this story? What are the outcomes?

Setting a Purpose

The events in this story take place in a small Southern town in the early part of the century, many years before the Civil Rights Movement challenged segregation in schools and other public places. As you read, determine how students putting on the annual school play are affected by the attitudes of the community.

The Revolt of the Evil Fairies

Ted Poston

The grand dramatic offering of the Booker T. Washington Colored Grammar School was the biggest event of the year in our social life in Hopkinsville, Kentucky. It was the one occasion on which they let us use the old Cooper Opera House, and even some of the white folks came out yearly to applaud our presentation. The first two rows of the orchestra were always reserved for our white friends, and our leading colored citizens sat right behind them—with an empty row intervening, of course.

Mr. Ed Smith, our local undertaker, invariably occupied a box to the left of the house and wore his cutaway coat[1] and striped breeches. This distinctive garb was usually reserved for those rare occasions when he officiated at the funerals of our most prominent colored citizens. Mr. Thaddeus Long, our colored mailman, once rented a tuxedo and bought a box too. But nobody paid him much mind. We knew he was just showing off.

The title of our play never varied. It was always Prince Charming and the Sleeping Beauty, but no two presentations were ever

the same. Miss H. Belle LaPrade, our sixth-grade teacher, rewrote the script every season, and it was never like anything you read in the storybooks.

Miss LaPrade called it "a modern morality play[2] of conflict between the forces of good and evil." And the forces of evil, of course, always came off second best.

The Booker T. Washington Colored Grammar School was in a state of ferment from Christmas until February, for this was the period when parts were assigned. First there was the selection of the Good Fairies and the Evil Fairies. This was very important, because the Good Fairies wore white costumes and the Evil Fairies black. And strangely enough most of the Good Fairies usually turned out to be extremely light in complexion, with straight hair and white folks' features. On rare occasions a darkskinned girl might be lucky enough to be a Good Fairy, but not one with a speaking part.

There never was any doubt about Prince Charming and the Sleeping Beauty. They were always lightskinned. And though nobody ever discussed those things openly, it

---

1. **cutaway coat:** a man's formal coat, with the front edges cut away from the waist.

2. **morality play:** a kind of drama popular in the Middle Ages, in which the characters represented virtues and vices.

A photograph of the Booker T. Washington Colored Grammar School in Hopkinsville, Kentucky, taken in 1954.
Pennyroyal Area Museum

was an accepted fact that a lack of pigmentation was a decided advantage in the Prince Charming and Sleeping Beauty sweepstakes.

And therein lay my personal tragedy. I made the best grades in my class, I was the leading debater, and the scion[3] of a respected family in the community. But I could never be Prince Charming, because I was black.

In fact, every year when they started casting our grand dramatic offering my family started pricing black cheesecloth at Franklin's Department Store. For they knew that I would be leading the forces of darkness and skulking back in the shadows—waiting to be vanquished in the third act. Mamma had

experience with this sort of thing. All my brothers had finished Booker T. before me.

Not that I was alone in my disappointment. Many of my classmates felt it too. I probably just took it more to heart. Rat Joiner, for instance, could rationalize the situation. Rat was not only black; he lived on Billy Goat Hill.[4] But Rat summed it up like this:

"If you black, you black."

I should have been able to regard the matter calmly too. For our grand dramatic offering was only a reflection of our daily community life in Hopkinsville. The yallers[5] had the best of everything. They held most of the

3. **scion** (sī′ən): descendant.

4. **Billy Goat Hill:** apparently, a rundown part of the community.
5. **yallers:** a term for light-skinned blacks.

teaching jobs in Booker T. Washington Colored Grammar School. They were the Negro doctors, the lawyers, the insurance men. They even had a "Blue Vein Society,"[6] and if your dark skin obscured your throbbing pulse you were hardly a member of the elite.

Yet I was inconsolable the first time they turned me down for Prince Charming. That was the year they picked Roger Jackson. Roger was not only dumb; he stuttered. But he was light enough to pass for white, and that was apparently sufficient.

In all fairness, however, it must be admitted that Roger had other qualifications. His father owned the only colored saloon in town and was quite a power in local politics. In fact, Mr. Clinton Jackson had a lot to say about just who taught in the Booker T. Wash-

ington Colored Grammar School. So it was understandable that Roger should have been picked for Prince Charming.

My real heartbreak, however, came the year they picked Sarah Williams for Sleeping Beauty. I had been in love with Sarah since kindergarten. She had soft light hair, bluish-gray eyes, and a dimple which stayed in her left cheek whether she was smiling or not.

Of course Sarah never encouraged me much. She never answered any of my fervent love letters, and Rat was very scornful of my one-sided love affairs. "As long as she don't call you a black baboon," he sneered, "you'll keep on hanging around."

After Sarah was chosen for Sleeping Beauty, I went out for the Prince Charming role with all my heart. If I had declaimed boldly in previous contests, I was matchless now. If I had bothered Mamma with rehearsals at home before, I pestered her to death

6. **"Blue Vein Society":** a society of blacks who gave themselves airs because their skin color was light enough to show blue veins.

this time. Yes, and I purloined my sister's can of Palmer's Skin Success.[7]

I knew the Prince's role from start to finish, having played the Head Evil Fairy opposite it for two seasons. And Prince Charming was one character whose lines Miss LaPrade never varied much in her many versions. But although I never admitted it, even to myself, I knew I was doomed from the start. They gave the part to Leonardius Wright. Leonardius, of course, was yarrler.

The teachers sensed my resentment. They were almost apologetic. They pointed out that I had been such a splendid Head Evil Fairy for two seasons that it would be a crime to let anybody else try the role. They reminded me that Mamma wouldn't have to buy any more cheesecloth because I could use my same old costume. They insisted that the Head Evil Fairy was even more important than Prince Charming because he was the one who cast the spell on Sleeping Beauty. So what could I do but accept?

I had never liked Leonardius Wright. He was a goody-goody, and even Mamma was always throwing him up to me. But, above all, he too was in love with Sarah Williams. And now he got a chance to kiss Sarah every day in rehearsing the awakening scene.

Well, the show must go on, even for little black boys. So I threw my soul into my part and made the Head Evil Fairy a character to be remembered. When I drew back from the couch of Sleeping Beauty and slunk away into the shadows at the approach of Prince Charming, my facial expression was indeed something to behold. When I was vanquished by the shining sword of Prince Charming in the last act, I was a little hammy perhaps—but terrific!

The attendance at our grand dramatic offering that year was the best in its history. Even the white folks overflowed the two rows reserved for them, and a few were forced to sit in the intervening one. This created a delicate situation, but everybody tactfully ignored it.

When the curtain went up on the last act, the audience was in fine fettle.[8] Everything had gone well for me too—except for one spot in the second act. That was where Leonardius unexpectedly rapped me over the head with his sword as I slunk off into the shadows. That was not in the script, but Miss LaPrade quieted me down by saying it made a nice touch anyway. Rat said Leonardius did it on purpose.

The third act went on smoothly, though, until we came to the vanquishing scene. That was where I slunk from the shadows for the last time and challenged Prince Charming to mortal combat. The hero reached for his shining sword—a bit unsportsmanlike, I always thought, since Miss LaPrade consistently left the Head Evil Fairy unarmed— and then it happened!

Later I protested loudly—but in vain— that it was a case of self-defense. I pointed out that Leonardius had a mean look in his eye. I cited the impromptu[9] rapping he had given my head in the second act. But nobody would listen. They just wouldn't believe that Leonardius really intended to brain me when he reached for his sword.

Anyway, he didn't succeed. For the minute I saw that evil gleam in his eye—or was it my own?—I cut loose with a right to the chin, and Prince Charming dropped his shining sword and staggered back. His astonishment lasted only a minute, though, for he

7. **Palmer's Skin Success:** a commercial product for lightening skin color.

8. **in fine fettle:** in good spirits.
9. **impromptu** (ĭm-prŏmp′tōō): unrehearsed.

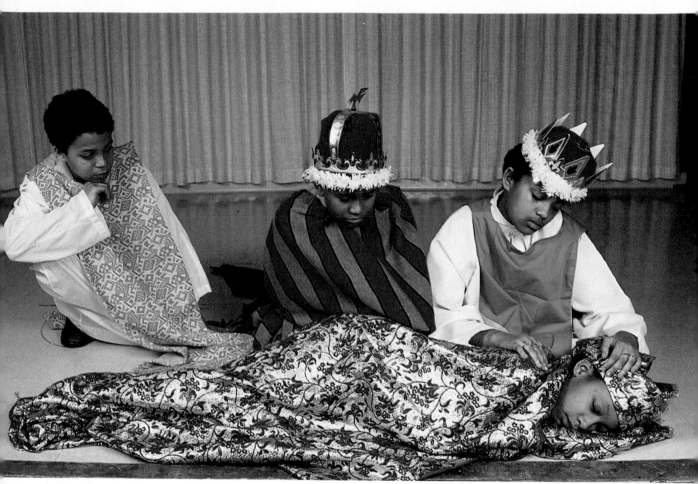

lowered his head and came charging in, fists flailing. There was nothing yellow about Leonardius but his skin.

The audience thought the scrap was something new Miss LaPrade had written in. They might have kept on thinking so if Miss LaPrade hadn't been screaming so hysterically from the sidelines. And if Rat Joiner hadn't decided that this was as good a time as any to settle old scores. So he turned around and took a sock at the male Good Fairy nearest him.

When the curtain rang down, the forces of Good and Evil were locked in combat. And Sleeping Beauty was wide awake and streaking for the wings.

They rang the curtain back up fifteen minutes later, and we finished the play. I lay down and expired according to specifications but Prince Charming will probably remember my sneering corpse to his dying day. They wouldn't let me appear in the grand dramatic offering at all the next year. But I didn't care. I couldn't have been Prince Charming anyway.

The Revolt of the Evil Fairies   27

Responding to the Selection

The Revolt of the Evil Fairies by Ted Poston

Identifying Facts

1. How was the audience segregated at the annual school play?
2. Name the three leading roles in the play.
3. What was the narrator's personal tragedy?
4. What caused a fight to break out in the third act?
5. How did Rat Joiner "settle old scores"?

Interpreting Meanings

1. The narrator says that the "grand dramatic offering was only a reflection of our daily community life." How did the "yallers" have the best of everything in the community? How did they also have the best of everything in the school play?
2. Why did the narrator keep on trying out for the part of Prince Charming?
3. What impression do you get of Rat Joiner? What might have been the "old scores" for which he got even?
4. What was the direct cause of the revolt of the Evil Fairies? What may have been a long-standing and indirect cause?
5. Although the story makes the reader think seriously about the effects of discrimination, the author's **tone,** or attitude, is often humorous. What examples of humor can you find in the narrative?

Language and Vocabulary

Recognizing Levels of Language

Standard English can be **formal** or **informal.** Informal standard English is the language used most of the time in writing and speaking. It is conversational or **colloquial** (kə-lō'kwē-əl). Formal standard English is more elegant and elaborate. It is used in scholarly books and on formal occasions such as public speaking. **Slang** is highly informal, colorful language that tends to be humorous and fresh.

Poston uses a mixture of different levels of language, often for humorous or satiric effect. When he describes the pretensions of the local undertaker, Ed Smith, who over-dresses for the school play, Poston uses deliberately elegant words such as *garb* and *officiated*:

This distinctive *garb* was usually reserved for those rare occasions when he *officiated* at the funerals of our most prominent colored citizens.

At the climax of the story, when the narrator hits Prince Charming, Poston uses informal language appropriate for the occasion:

I cut loose with a right to the chin . . .

How would you describe the language used by Rat Joiner? What do you think is the author's intention in making Rat Joiner's speech different from that of the narrator?

Recognizing Analogies

The word *analogy* means "likeness" or "partial resemblance" between things. People often draw an analogy between the human body and a machine.

When the word *analogy* is used in vocabulary study, it refers to a special kind of question that involves two pairs of words. You must first determine the relationship between the words in the first pair. Then you must look for the same relationship in the second pair.

Here is one type of analogy question. It has a special format and uses special symbols.

delay : postpone :: purloin : _____
a. criticize b. end c. steal d. promise

The two dots (:) stand for "is to"; the four dots (::) stand for "as." The example, therefore, reads "Delay *is to* postpone *as* purloin *is to* _____." Since the first two words, *delay* and *postpone,* are synonyms, the correct answers is **c.** The word that has the same meaning as *purloin* is *steal.*

Analogy questions may test synonym and antonym relationships, understanding of grammatical relationships, cause-and-effect relationships, sequential relationships, and the like.

Complete the following analogies.

Synonym
1. purloin : steal :: obscure : _____
   a. interrupt   **c.** recite
   b. conceal   **d.** deny

Antonym
2. poverty : wealth :: ferment : _____
   a. rest   **c.** disorder
   b. movement   **d.** scarcity

Grammatical Relationship
3. proclaim : proclamation :: intervene :

_____
   a. interference   **c.** intervention
   b. convene   **d.** intervening

Action and Object Relationship
4. call : meeting :: declaim : _____
   a. attack   **c.** protest
   b. recite   **d.** speech

Expository Writing

Developing a Paragraph by Cause and Effect

One method of developing a paragraph is to use **cause and effect.** There are two ways to organize such a paragraph. One way is to state the cause in the topic sentence and then give the effects. Another way is to state the effect in the topic sentence and then discuss the causes.

Think of some action that produced positive results for an individual, a community, or an entire country. Then use the cause-and-effect method of organizing details to construct your paragraph.

Prewriting Strategies

Begin by stating the cause in a complete sentence. Then list the effects. For example:

Cause

The city has approved a plan that will provide funds for a day-care center in our community.

Effects

1. Working parents can now arrange to have preschool children cared for every working day.
2. Children are carefully supervised in small groups.
3. The day-care center gives jobs to qualified individuals.

The second way of developing your paragraph is to begin with the effect and then state the causes:

Effect

Efforts by students and faculty have resulted in a cleaner and more attractive school cafeteria.

Causes

1. Students earn merit points for working on clean-up squads.

2. A student-faculty committee chooses posters and original art to display in the cafeteria.
3. Additional carts for stacking trays and additional waste bins have reduced overcrowding in aisles.

For additional help in planning your paper see the **Writer's Guide** on pages 65–66.

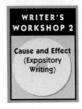

Speaking and Listening

Dramatizing a Scene

Imagine a scene from the script of the play: casting a spell on Sleeping Beauty, challenging Prince Charming to mortal combat, and so on. Make up the dialogue for the scene and assemble a group of actors to present it before the class.

About the Author
Maya Angelou (b. 1928)

"Growing up is painful for the Southern Black girl," writes Maya Angelou (än'jə-lo͞o') in her introduction to *I Know Why the Caged Bird Sings,* the first of her autobiographical books. Born Marguerite Johnson, in St. Louis, she was sent to live with her grandmother in a town in Arkansas after her parents' marriage ended. Years later, she vowed never to return to what she called the "grim, humiliating South." Except for a brief visit as a teenager, she kept her promise until she was forty years old.

Her love of dance led Angelou to study with a famous teacher in New York City. Also a talented actress and singer, she soon toured Europe in a production of *Porgy and Bess,* a folk opera about life on the Charleston waterfront. After teaching dance in Paris and Tel Aviv, she returned to the United States to work for the Civil Rights Movement. For a while, she lived in Cairo and Ghana, writing for newspapers.

Angelou is best known for her autobiographies, but she has also written poetry, screenplays, magazine articles, and a ten-part television series for National Educational Television, dealing with Africanisms in United States culture. She was highly acclaimed for her role in the television series *Roots.*

Angelou has presented her poetry on stage. One reviewer has described her "electrifying stage presence" in this way: "An-

Wide World Photos

gelou's statuesque figure, dressed in bright colors (and sometimes, African designs), moves exuberantly, vigorously to reinforce the rhythm of the lines, the tone of the words."

In 1982 Angelou received a lifetime appointment as Reynolds Professor of American Studies at Wake Forest University in Winston-Salem, North Carolina. Besides teaching, she devotes a good deal of time each day to reading and writing.

Angelou was chosen to read her poem "On the Pulse of Morning" at the inauguration of President Clinton in January 1993. She was the first African American and the first woman poet to do so.

Maya Angelou   31

Before You Read

from I Know Why the Caged Bird Sings

Using What You Know

In the following selection, Maya Angelou describes her early years, after she was sent to live in Stamps, Arkansas. Have you ever traveled to another city, town, or country? What were some of the things you had to get used to? Did you find it interesting to meet new people and to learn about new places and customs?

Literary Focus: Setting

When most of us begin reading stories, we read mainly to find out *what happened.* A careful reader eventually discovers, though, that *when and where* the events happened can sometimes be just as important. **Setting** is the time and place in which a narrative occurs. To give readers a sense of place, writers generally use description, but dialogue can also make a setting come to life. Note how Angelou gives you a feeling for the speech and the customs of the people in her small rural town.

Setting a Purpose

Angelou grew up in a Southern town that suffered from poverty and the effects of racism. Despite years of hardship and struggle, however, she has become a dancer, an actress, a producer, and a writer who has lived in places all over the world. As you read, ask yourself what you might gain from reading about the life of a person like Maya Angelou.

I Know Why the Caged Bird Sings

Maya Angelou

1

When I was three and Bailey four, we had arrived in the musty little town, wearing tags on our wrists which instructed—"To Whom It May Concern"—that we were Marguerite and Bailey Johnson, Jr., from Long Beach, California, en route to Stamps, Arkansas, c/o Mrs. Annie Henderson.

Our parents had decided to put an end to their calamitous marriage, and Father shipped us home to his mother. A porter had been charged with our welfare—he got off the train the next day in Arizona—and our tickets were pinned to my brother's inside coat pocket.

I don't remember much of the trip, but after we reached the segregated southern part of the journey, things must have looked up. Negro passengers, who always traveled with loaded lunch boxes, felt sorry for "the poor little motherless darlings" and plied us with cold fried chicken and potato salad.

Years later I discovered that the United States had been crossed thousands of times by frightened Black children traveling alone to their newly affluent parents in Northern cities, or back to grandmothers in Southern towns when the urban North reneged on its economic promises.

The town reacted to us as its inhabitants had reacted to all things new before our coming. It regarded us a while without curiosity but with caution, and after we were seen to be harmless (and children) it closed in around us, as a real mother embraces a stranger's child. Warmly, but not too familiarly.

We lived with our grandmother and uncle in the rear of the Store (it was always spoken of with a capital s), which she had owned some twenty-five years.

Early in the century, Momma (we soon stopped calling her Grandmother) sold lunches to the sawmen in the lumberyard (east Stamps) and the seedmen at the cotton gin (west Stamps). Her crisp meat pies and cool lemonade, when joined to her miraculous ability to be in two places at the same time, assured her business success. From being a mobile lunch counter, she set up a stand between the two points of fiscal interest and supplied the workers' needs for a few years. Then she had the Store built in the heart of the Negro area. Over the years it became the lay center of activities in town. On Saturdays, barbers sat their customers in the shade on the porch of the Store, and troubadours[1] on their ceaseless crawlings

---

1. **troubadours** (trōō′bə-dôrz): poet-musicians of southern France and northern Italy during the eleventh, twelfth, and thirteenth centuries. Loosely, any strolling poet-musician.

Cigar-box fiddler Scott Dunbar.
© 1996 Roland L. Freeman

through the South leaned across its benches and sang their sad songs of The Brazos[2] while they played juice harps[3] and cigar-box guitars.

The formal name of the Store was the Wm. Johnson General Merchandise Store. Customers could find food staples, a good variety of colored thread, mash for hogs, corn for chickens, coal oil for lamps, light bulbs for the wealthy, shoestrings, hair dressing, balloons, and flower seeds. Anything not visible had only to be ordered.

Until we became familiar enough to belong to the Store and it to us, we were locked up in a Fun House of Things where the attendant had gone home for life.

Each year I watched the field across from the Store turn caterpillar green, then gradually frosty white. I knew exactly how long it would be before the big wagons would pull into the front yard and load on the cotton

2. **The Brazos** (brä′sōs′): a district in central Texas around the Brazos River.
3. **juice harps:** *jew's-harps*, musical instruments held in the mouth and plucked.

pickers at daybreak to carry them to the remains of slavery's plantations.

During the picking season my grandmother would get out of bed at four o'clock (she never used an alarm clock) and creak down to her knees and chant in a sleep-filled voice, "Our Father, thank you for letting me see this New Day. Thank you that you didn't allow the bed I lay on last night to be my cooling board, nor my blanket my winding sheet. Guide my feet this day along the straight and narrow, and help me to put a bridle on my tongue. Bless this house, and everybody in it. Thank you, in the name of your Son, Jesus Christ, Amen."

Before she had quite arisen, she called our names and issued orders, and pushed her large feet into homemade slippers and across the bare lye-washed wooden floor to light the coal-oil lamp.

The lamplight in the Store gave a soft make-believe feeling to our world which made me want to whisper and walk about on tiptoe. The odors of onions and oranges and kerosene had been mixing all night and wouldn't be disturbed until the wooded slat was removed from the door and the early morning air forced its way in with the bodies of people who had walked miles to reach the pickup place.

"Sister, I'll have two cans of sardines."

"I'm gonna work so fast today I'm gonna make you look like you standing still."

"Lemme have a hunk uh cheese and some sody crackers."

"Just gimme a coupla them fat peanut paddies." That would be from a picker who was taking his lunch. The greasy brown paper sack was stuck behind the bib of his overalls. He'd use the candy as a snack before the noon sun called the workers to rest.

In those tender mornings the Store was

full of laughing, joking, boasting and bragging. One man was going to pick two hundred pounds of cotton, and another three hundred. Even the children were promising to bring home fo' bits and six bits.[4]

The champion picker of the day before was the hero of the dawn. If he prophesied that the cotton in today's field was going to be sparse and stick to the bolls like glue, every listener would grunt a hearty agreement.

The sound of the empty cotton sacks dragging over the floor and the murmurs of waking people were sliced by the cash register as we rang up the five-cent sales.

If the morning sounds and smells were touched with the supernatural, the late afternoon had all the features of the normal Ar-

kansas life. In the dying sunlight the people dragged, rather than their empty cotton sacks.

Brought back to the Store, the pickers would step out of the backs of trucks and fold down, dirt-disappointed, to the ground. No matter how much they had picked, it wasn't enough. Their wages wouldn't even get them out of debt to my grandmother, not to mention the staggering bill that waited on them at the white commissary downtown.

The sounds of the new morning had been replaced with grumbles about cheating houses, weighted scales, snakes, skimpy cotton and dusty rows. In later years I was to confront the stereotyped picture of gay song-singing cotton pickers with such inordinate rage that I was told even by fellow Blacks that my paranoia was embarrassing. But I had seen the fingers cut by the mean little

4. **fo' bits and six bits:** (colloquial) four bits and six bits. "Bit" is an old-fashioned term for an amount equal to 12 1/2 cents, usually spoken of as *two bits*, *four bits*, etc.

cotton bolls, and I had witnessed the backs and shoulders and arms and legs resisting any further demands.

Some of the workers would leave their sacks at the Store to be picked up the following morning, but a few had to take them home for repairs. I winced to picture them sewing the coarse material under a coal-oil lamp with fingers stiffening from the day's work. In too few hours they would have to walk back to Sister Henderson's Store, get vittles and load, again, onto the trucks. Then they would face another day of trying to earn enough for the whole year with the heavy knowledge that they were going to end the season as they started it. Without the money or credit necessary to sustain a family for three months. In cotton-picking time the late afternoons revealed the harshness of Black Southern life, which in the early morning had been softened by nature's blessing of grogginess, forgetfulness and the soft lamp-light.

Weighing the half-pounds of flour, excluding the scoop, and depositing them dust-free into the thin paper sacks held a simple kind of adventure for me. I developed an eye for measuring how full a silver-looking ladle of flour, mash, meal, sugar or corn had to be to push the scale indicator over to eight ounces or one pound. When I was absolutely accurate our appreciative customers used to admire: "Sister Henderson sure got some smart grandchildrens." If I was off in the Store's favor, the eagle-eyed women would say, "Put some more in that sack, child. Don't you try to make your profit offa me."

Cotton pickers in Pulaski County, Arkansas, 1935.
Ben Shahn/Library of Congress

Then I would quietly but persistently punish myself. For every bad judgment, the fine was no silver-wrapped Kisses, the sweet chocolate drops that I loved more than anything in the world, except Bailey. And maybe canned pineapples. My obsession with pineapples nearly drove me mad. I dreamt of the days when I would be grown and able to buy a whole carton for myself alone.

Although the syrupy golden rings sat in their exotic cans on our shelves year round, we only tasted them during Christmas. Momma used the juice to make almost-black fruit cakes. Then she lined heavy soot-encrusted iron skillets with the pineapple rings for rich upside-down cakes. Bailey and I received one slice each, and I carried mine around for hours, shredding off the fruit until nothing was left except the perfume on my fingers. I'd like to think that my desire for pineapples was so sacred that I wouldn't allow myself to steal a can (which was possible) and eat it alone out in the garden, but I'm certain that I must have weighed the possibility of the scent exposing me and didn't have the nerve to attempt it.

Until I was thirteen and left Arkansas for good, the Store was my favorite place to be. Alone and empty in the mornings, it looked like an unopened present from a stranger. Opening the front doors was pulling the ribbon off the unexpected gift. The light would come in softly (we faced north), easing itself over the shelves of mackerel, salmon, tobacco, thread. It fell flat on the big vat of lard and by noontime during the summer the grease had softened to a thick soup. Whenever I walked into the Store in the afternoon, I sensed that it was tired. I alone could hear the slow pulse of its job half done. But just before bedtime, after numerous people had walked in and out, had argued over their bills, or joked about their neighbors, or just dropped in "to give Sister Henderson a 'Hi y'all,'" the promise of magic mornings returned to the Store and spread itself over the family in washed life waves.

Momma opened boxes of crispy crackers and we sat around the meat block at the rear of the Store. I sliced onions, and Bailey opened two or even three cans of sardines and allowed their juice of oil and fishing boats to ooze down and around the sides. That was supper. In the evening, when we were alone like that, Uncle Willie didn't stutter or shake or give any indication that he had an "affliction." It seemed that the peace of a day's ending was an assurance that the covenant[5] God made with children, Negroes and the crippled was still in effect.

Throwing scoops of corn to the chickens and mixing sour dry mash with leftover food and oily dish water for the hogs were among our evening chores. Bailey and I sloshed down twilight trails to the pig pens, and standing on the first fence rungs we poured down the unappealing concoctions to our grateful hogs. They mashed their tender pink snouts down into the slop, and rooted and grunted their satisfaction. We always grunted a reply only half in jest. We were also grateful that we had concluded the dirtiest of chores and had only gotten the evil-smelling swill on our shoes, stockings, feet and hands.

In Stamps the custom was to can everything that could possibly be preserved. During the killing season, after the first frost, all neighbors helped each other to slaughter hogs and

5. **covenant:** a solemn agreement or compact, such as the promises made by God to the Hebrews, as recorded in the Bible.

I Know Why the Caged Bird Sings 37

even the quiet, big-eyed cows if they had stopped giving milk.

The missionary ladies of the Christian Methodist Episcopal Church helped Momma prepare the pork for sausage. They squeezed their fat arms elbow deep in the ground meat, mixed it with gray nose-opening sage, pepper and salt, and made tasty little samples for all obedient children who brought wood for the slick black stove. The men chopped off the larger pieces of meat and laid them in the smokehouse to begin the curing process. They opened the knuckle of the hams with their deadly-looking knives, took out a certain round harmless bone ("it could make the meat go bad") and rubbed salt, coarse brown salt that looked like fine gravel, into the flesh, and the blood popped to the surface.

Throughout the year, until the next frost, we took our meals from the smokehouse, the little garden that lay cousin-close to the Store and from the shelves of canned foods. There were choices on the shelves that could set a hungry child's mouth to watering. Green beans, snapped always the right length, collards, cabbage, juicy red tomato preserves that came into their own on steaming buttered biscuits, and sausage, beets, berries and every fruit grown in Arkansas.

But at least twice yearly Momma would feel that as children we should have fresh meat included in our diets. We were then given money—pennies, nickels, and dimes entrusted to Bailey—and sent to town to buy liver. Since the whites had refrigerators, their butchers bought the meat from commercial slaughterhouses in Texarkana[6] and sold it to the wealthy even in the peak of summer.

6. **Texarkana:** a city on the border between Texas and Arkansas.

Crossing the Black area of Stamps which in childhood's narrow measure seemed a whole world, we were obliged by custom to stop and speak to every person we met, and Bailey felt constrained to spend a few minutes playing with each friend. There was a joy in going to town with money in our pockets (Bailey's pockets were as good as my own) and time on our hands. But the pleasure fled when we reached the white part of town. After we left Mr. Willie Williams' Do Drop Inn, the last stop before whitefolksville, we had to cross the pond and adventure the railroad tracks. We were explorers walking without weapons into man-eating animals' territory.

In Stamps the segregation was so complete that most Black children didn't really, absolutely know what whites looked like. Other than that they were different, to be dreaded, and in that dread was included the hostility of the powerless against the powerful, the poor against the rich, the worker against the worked for and the ragged against the well dressed.

I remember never believing that whites were really real.

2

On Sunday mornings Momma served a breakfast that was geared to hold us quiet from 9:30 A.M. to 3 P.M. She fried thick pink slabs of home-cured ham and poured the grease over sliced red tomatoes. Eggs over easy, fried potatoes and onions, yellow hominy and crisp perch fried so hard we would pop them in our mouths and chew bones, fins and all. Her cathead biscuits were at least three inches in diameter and two inches thick. The trick to eating catheads was to get the butter on them before they got cold—then they were delicious. When, unluckily, they were allowed to get cold, they tended to a gooeyness, not unlike a wad of tired gum.

We were able to reaffirm our findings on the catheads each Sunday that Reverend Thomas spent with us. Naturally enough, he was asked to bless the table. We would all stand; my uncle, leaning his walking stick against the wall, would lean his weight on the table. Then Reverend Thomas would begin. "Blessed Father, we thank you this morning . . ." and on and on and on. I'd stop listening after a while until Bailey kicked me and then I cracked my lids to see what had promised to be a meal that would make any Sunday proud. But as the Reverend droned on and on and on to a God who I thought must be bored to hear the same things over and over again, I saw that the ham grease had turned white on the tomatoes. The eggs had withdrawn from the edge of the platter to bunch in the center like children left out in the cold. And the catheads had sat down on themselves with the conclusiveness of a fat woman sitting in an easy chair. And still he talked on. When he finally stopped, our appetites were gone, but he feasted on the cold food with a non-talking but still noisy relish.

In the Christian Methodist Episcopal Church the children's section was on the right, cater-cornered from the pew that held those ominous women called the Mothers of the Church. In the young people's section the benches were placed close together, and when a child's legs no longer comfortably fitted in the narrow space, it was an indication to the elders that that person could now move into the intermediate area (center church). Bailey and I were allowed to sit with the other children only when there were informal meetings, church socials or the like. But on the Sundays when Reverend Thomas preached, it was ordained that we occupy the first row, called the mourners' bench. I thought we were placed in front because Momma was proud of us, but Bailey assured me that she just wanted to keep her grandchildren under her thumb and eye.

Reverend Thomas took his text from Deuteronomy.[7] And I was stretched between loathing his voice and wanting to listen to the sermon. Deuteronomy was my favorite book in the Bible. The laws were so absolute, so clearly set down, that I knew if a person truly wanted to avoid hell and brimstone, and being roasted forever in the devil's fire, all she had to do was memorize Deuteronomy and follow its teaching, word for word. I also liked the way the word rolled off the tongue.

Bailey and I sat alone on the front bench, the wooden slats pressing hard on our behinds and the backs of our thighs. I would have wriggled just a bit, but each time I looked over at Momma, she seemed to threaten, "Move and I'll tear you up," so, obedient to the unvoiced command, I sat still. The church ladies were warming up behind me with a few hallelujahs and Praise the Lords and Amens, and the preacher hadn't really moved into the meat of the sermon.

It was going to be a hot service.

On my way into church, I saw Sister Monroe, her open-faced gold crown[8] glinting when she opened her mouth to return a neighborly greeting. She lived in the country and couldn't get to church every Sunday, so she made up for her absences by shouting so hard when she did make it that she shook the whole church. As soon as she took her seat,

7. **Deuteronomy** (dōō′tə-rŏn′ə-mē): the fifth Book of the Bible, in which the law of Moses is summarized.
8. **crown:** a covering for a tooth made of an artificial substance such as porcelain or gold.

I Know Why the Caged Bird Sings   39

Hallelujah, *graphite drawing by Raymond Lark.*
Lent by Dr. Curtis W. Branch; Photo courtesy Edward Smith

40 MAYA ANGELOU

all the ushers would move to her side of the church because it took three women and sometimes a man or two to hold her.

Once when she hadn't been to church for a few months (she had taken off to have a child), she got the spirit and started shouting, throwing her arms around and jerking her body, so that the ushers went over to hold her down, but she tore herself away from them and ran up to the pulpit. She stood in front of the altar, shaking like a freshly caught trout. She screamed at Reverend Taylor. "Preach it. I say, preach it." Naturally he kept on preaching as if she wasn't standing there telling him what to do. Then she screamed an extremely fierce "I said, preach it" and stepped up on the altar. The Reverend kept on throwing out phrases like home-run balls and Sister Monroe made a quick break and grasped for him. For just a second, everything and everyone in the church except Reverend Taylor and Sister Monroe hung loose like stockings on a washline. Then she caught the minister by the sleeve of his jacket and his coattail, then she rocked him from side to side.

I have to say this for our minister, he never stopped giving us the lesson. The usher board made its way to the pulpit, going up both aisles with a little more haste than is customarily seen in church. Truth to tell, they fairly ran to the minister's aid. Then two of the deacons, in their shiny Sunday suits, joined the ladies in white on the pulpit, and each time they pried Sister Monroe loose from the preacher he took another deep breath and kept on preaching, and Sister Monroe grabbed him in another place, and more firmly. Reverend Taylor was helping his rescuers as much as possible by jumping around when he got a chance. His voice at one point got so low it sounded like a roll of thunder, then Sister Monroe's "Preach it" cut through the roar, and we all wondered (I did, in any case) if it would ever end. Would they go on forever, or get tired out at last like a game of blindman's bluff that lasted too long, with nobody caring who was "it"?

I'll never know what might have happened, because magically the pandemonium spread. The spirit infused Deacon Jackson and Sister Willson, the chairman of the usher board, at the same time. Deacon Jackson, a tall, thin, quiet man, who was also a part-time Sunday school teacher, gave a scream like a falling tree, leaned back on thin air and punched Reverend Taylor on the arm. It must have hurt as much as it caught the Reverend unawares. There was a moment's break in the rolling sounds and Reverend Taylor jerked around surprised, and hauled off and punched Deacon Jackson. In the same second Sister Willson caught his tie, looped it over her fist a few times, and pressed down on him. There wasn't time to laugh or cry before all three of them were down on the floor behind the altar. Their legs spiked out like kindling wood.

Sister Monroe, who had been the cause of all the excitement, walked off the dais, cool and spent, and raised her flinty voice in the hymn, "I came to Jesus, as I was, worried, wound, and sad, I found in Him a resting place and He has made me glad."

The minister took advantage of already being on the floor and asked in a choky little voice if the church would kneel with him to offer a prayer of thanksgiving. He said we had been visited with a mighty spirit, and let the whole church say Amen.

Responding to the Selection

from **I Know Why the Caged Bird Sings** by Maya Angelou

Identifying Facts

1. What conditions made it necessary for so many black children to travel alone across the United States?
2. What did most of the people in Stamps do for a living?
3. What was Momma's business before she opened the Store?
4. How did Angelou make an adventure out of working at the Store?
5. How did the men and women of Stamps help one another to prepare for winter?

Interpreting Meanings

1. What is the mood of the Store in the morning? How does it change in the evening? What does the passage reveal about black Southern life at this time?
2. How does Angelou react to stereotyped images of the cotton pickers? What does her reaction reveal about her attitude toward the workers?
3. Angelou clearly admired and loved her grandmother. Which details show that Momma was industrious and hard-working? Which details show that she was a good homemaker? How do we know that she was concerned about the conduct and well-being of the children?
4. Throughout the autobiography, Angelou talks about Bailey. How does she feel about her brother?

Literary Elements

Understanding Setting

Setting is a very important element of Angelou's autobiography. She devotes many pages to describing the small rural community of Stamps. She includes details about the countryside, the Store, the people, and even the food they ate.

About the Store Angelou writes, "Customers could find food staples, a good variety of colored thread, mash for hogs, corn for chickens, coal oil for lamps, light bulbs for the wealthy, shoestrings, hair dressing, balloons, and flower seeds. Anything not visible had only to be ordered." What does this passage reveal about the lives of the people? What does it show about the significance of the Store?

Find other passages that describe something about the community of Stamps. What does Angelou show about the interactions of the people and their daily activities? How was she affected by the sights and sounds of her childhood?

Recognizing Simile and Metaphor

To describe the appeal of the Store in the early mornings, Angelou writes that "it looked like an unopened present from a stranger. Opening the front doors was pulling the ribbon off the unexpected gift." She could have said simply "I enjoyed the Store in the morning," but the comparison she uses is more interesting and vivid.

Language which is not intended to be understood in a strict literal sense is known as **figurative language. Simile** is a form of figurative language in which two essentially unlike things are compared, with the use of a term such as *like, as,* or *than* ("it looked *like* an unopened present"). **Metaphor** is a comparison of two unlike things that does not use terms such as *like, as,* and *than* ("Opening the front doors was pulling the ribbon off . . .").

Determine whether each of the following quotations uses a simile or a metaphor, and explain the comparison in each:

> Until we became familiar enough to belong to the Store and it to us, we were locked up in a Fun House of Things where the attendant had gone home for life.

> We were explorers walking without weapons into man-eating animals' territory.

> The eggs had withdrawn from the edge of the platter to bunch in the center like children left out in the cold.

> And the catheads had sat down on themselves with the conclusiveness of a fat woman sitting in an easy chair.

> She stood in front of the altar, shaking like a freshly caught trout.

> The Reverend kept on throwing out phrases like home-run balls . . . .

> His voice . . . got so low it sounded like a roll of thunder.

The selection has several other examples of figurative language. See if you can find them.

Language and Vocabulary

Explaining Word Origins

Many English words developed very gradually from other languages, especially Greek, Latin, and the old Germanic tongues. If you look in an unabridged dictionary, you will see that the word *paranoid* comes from the Greek *para,* meaning "beside" and *nous,* meaning "the mind." The term refers to a mental disorder characterized by suspicion and feelings of persecution.

Look up the following words in an unabridged dictionary and explain their meanings:

paragraph
paralegal
parallel
paramilitary
parasite

Descriptive Writing

Using Specific Details in Description

Reread the passage where Angelou describes her grandmother's early morning rising. She could have said simply, "Grandmother got on her knees and prayed and . . . walked across the floor." Instead she writes,

I Know Why the Caged Bird Sings 43

"... grandmother would ... *creak* down to her knees and *chant* in a *sleep-filled* voice ..."

"... she pushed her *large* feet into *homemade* slippers and across the *bare lye-washed wooden* floor."

How does each italicized word add to the image being created? Since Grandmother rose at four o'clock every morning without the help of an alarm clock, and issued orders even before completely rising to her feet, she must have been a strong, industrious woman. What do you learn about her from the words of her prayer?

Look over the selection for other instances where words and details create an image that is interesting and vivid.

Write a paragraph in which you describe the physical appearance and personality of a real or an imaginary individual. Use vivid words and specific details.

Speaking and Listening

Relating a Personal Experience

Angelou writes, "In later years I was to confront the stereotyped picture of gay song-singing cotton pickers with such inordinate rage that I was told even by fellow Blacks that my paranoia was embarrassing." She describes the harsh lives of these people— their dragging tiredness, their hard toil which leaves them poorer than before, fin-gers "cut" and "stiffening from the day's work." Her detailed description makes the image of the struggling cotton pickers so convincing that the reader understands her anger at those who show such insensitivity.

Think about an experience you had as a child that still affects you deeply— something that still makes you sad or happy or angry or proud whenever you are reminded of it. Tell the class about the experience. Use specific details and descriptive language so that your listeners will understand and share your feelings and emotions.

Critical Thinking

Understanding Allusion

Sometimes a piece of writing contains a reference to another published work. This is called **allusion**. The word *allude* means "to refer to something in a casual or indirect way."

Angelou took her title for *I Know Why the Caged Bird Sings* from the following poem.

Sympathy
Paul Laurence Dunbar

I know what the caged bird feels, alas!
When the sun is bright on the upland
    slopes;
When the wind stirs soft through the
    springing grass
And the river flows like a stream of glass;
When the first bird sings and the first bud
    opes,
And the faint perfume from its chalice
    steals—
I know what the caged bird feels!

I know why the caged bird beats his wing
Till its blood is red on the cruel bars;
For he must fly back to his perch and cling
When he fain would be on the bough
    a-swing;
And a pain still throbs in the old, old scars
And they pulse again with a keener sting—
I know why he beats his wing!

I know why the caged bird sings, ah me,
When his wing is bruised and his bosom
    sore,—
When he beats his bars and would be
    free;
It is not a carol of joy or glee,
But a prayer that he sends from his heart's
    deep core,
But a plea, that upward to Heaven he flings—
I know why the caged bird sings!

According to Dunbar, how does the caged bird feel? Why does Maya Angelou identify with the songbird?

About the Author

Merle Hodge (b. 1944)

Junia Brown

 Merle Hodge was born on the island of Trinidad in the West Indies. Her father was an immigration officer. She attended Bishop Anstey's High School, where she won the Trinidad and Tobago Girls' Island Scholarship in 1962. She went to University College in London, where she studied French and earned her undergraduate and graduate degrees. She traveled widely in Europe before returning to Trinidad. Hodge spent several years teaching at the junior secondary level in Trinidad and lecturing at the University of the West Indies in Jamaica. In 1979 she took a job as director of the development of curriculum in Grenada, and she also worked with adult education programs. She now lives in Trinidad, where she does free-lance writing and lecturing.

The novel *Crick Crack, Monkey* was published in 1970. It deals with the childhood of Tee, whose father has emigrated to England and left her in the care of two aunts. Her early years are spent with Tantie, her father's sister, and this period is filled with warm and happy experiences. When Tee wins a scholarship to a girls' school in Trinidad, she goes to live with Aunt Beatrice, her mother's sister. Tee enters a middle-class world that is formal, artificial, and pretentious. Aunt Beatrice's daughters treat her as an intruder. She becomes isolated, and she loses touch with her earlier self. She comes to feel that because of her dark skin and background, she will never be accepted in Aunt Beatrice's world. At the end of the novel, Tee leaves for England, her conflicts still unresolved.

In addition to *Crick Crack, Monkey,* Hodge has written stories, reviews, articles, and a young adult novel, *For the Life of Laetitia* (1993). She has also translated poems by Léon Damas, a French Guyanese poet.

Before You Read

from Crick Crack, Monkey

Using What You Know

Recall your first day at school. Were you excited about going? Were you also uneasy? Did your first day turn out as you expected? Compare your experiences with those of your classmates. Keep your memories in mind as you read about Tee's experiences.

Background

Today the islands of Trinidad and Tobago make up a republic in the West Indies, but when Merle Hodge was growing up, they were a British colony. The schools she attended were patterned after English schools. In *Crick Crack, Monkey,* Tee, the narrator, looks forward to attending "Big-school." Once there, however, she is disappointed. The children are expected to be obedient and to perform their tasks mechanically. Hodge makes us aware of the children's confusion and boredom at the same time that she lets us laugh at their absurd lessons.

Literary Focus: Satire

A **satire** is a literary work that points up weaknesses in human nature. Satire can be gentle and humorous, or it can be harsh and bitter. Satire can make you laugh even while it causes you to think seriously about some failing in an individual or in society.

Setting a Purpose

In this selection, the narrator satirizes one of her teachers, who is always referred to as *Sir.* As you read, ask yourself how the portrait of the teacher points up certain weaknesses in Tee's schooling.

Crick Crack, Monkey

Merle Hodge

We ascended into Third Standard.[1] Sir received us on high with a lengthy booming harangue,[2] clearing his throat and pacing grandly to and fro with his hands joined behind his back or tapping the whip against his leg, rocking on his heels, now and then half-sitting on a corner of the table as he twirled his mustache, pausing for long seconds at a time with his head cocked on one side as if to savour the echo of what he had said before. We were further over-whelmed, as well as vaguely flattered, by the incomprehensibility of his utterances.[3]

This performance proved to be a regular feature. Sir was given to discoursing on things called "Seemliness" and "Constancy" and "Veracity" and others. We had to sit as immobile as furniture, for a falling pencil, a sneeze or a fidgeting child made him forget what it was he was going to say, and by the time he had finished roaring with anger he had also forgotten where it was he had broken off, so that he was obliged to begin several paragraphs back, or sometimes from the very beginning.

Across the top of the blackboard was a permanent inscription in multicoloured chalk: THE DISCIPLE IS NOT GREATER THAN THE MASTER. It was written in flowery letters which Sir spent ages repairing when they became the slightest bit faded, stepping back and holding his head on one side to admire each curl he performed. Offenders were sentenced to writing out this row of words a hundred times, an exercise which did not add to anyone's enlightenment as to their significance.

The inscription was also our model text when we had Penmanship. Painfully we copied letter by letter—necks strained upward to their absolute limit of elasticity and eyes narrowed, then a nervous pencil gripped with such intensity that often the letter appeared on the following page, and finger-joints were sore for a long time afterwards. Sir moved about among us with his hands clasped behind his back, wagging the whip. Often the whip descended with terrible sud-

---

1. **Third Standard:** *Standard* refers to a grade or class in British and colonial schools. First Standard is the lowest of the graded classes.
2. **harangue** (hə-răng'): an emotional speech.
3. **incomprehensibility** (ĭn′kŏm-prĭ-hĕn′sə-bĭl′ə-tē) **of his utterances** (ŭt′ər-əns-əs): The children did not understand what he was saying.

Women of Tustic Grove, Jamaica, *collage by Phoebe Beasley.*

denness upon a back hunched tensely over its copy-book;[4] Sir did not brook[5] "upstartedness" in the young, nor letters that did not bear a suitable likeness to the model script.

Sir called his whip "Fire and brimstone" or "The wrath of God." He and the whip were inseparable—he used it to point things out on the blackboard; he waved it in the air or tapped on the table with it during his speeches; it lay across the table in front of him as he sat and read to us tales of unvanquished knights with valiant swords and trusty steeds; with it he liberally dispensed both the wrath of God and fire and brimstone. But there were times when he relinquished it.

From time to time there blew a silence across the whole floor. Sometimes it started out of a commotion of one kind or another in a class. Often it was purely accidental and unaccountable, "an angel passing." But sometimes it spread from one of the two doors at either end of the floor, where Mr. Thomas[6] had suddenly appeared, or the Reverend had come to smile on us and pat random heads. Then it was that Sir edged backwards and eased the whip onto his chair or slid it under papers on his table, or on a few desperate occasions it slithered to the floor.

And when either of them appeared in the middle of a roaring, then a curious process took place before us. Sir's eyes shooting crimson out of his head seemed to scurry in behind eyelids lowered a little like shutters, his forehead flattened itself, the bristling mustache lay down, and the roaring tailed off as his mouth was seen to roll swiftly out across his face like a mat.

We looked forward to Mr. Thomas visiting our class. Sir drilled us regularly and violently in the Art of Noiselessly Rising from our seats: one afternoon a week we spent getting up and sitting down, getting up and sitting down without interruption (sometimes the recess bell rang and the rest of the floor drained away from around our class still bobbing up and down) while Sir stamped about and roared and banged the whip on the table and on our desks and on us until we could "gently rise up as with one will" (the little choir-boys of Westminster Abbey[7] of six, seven and eight years were trained to do this, he had read or imagined, so there was no possible alternative open to us) instead of making a "din and sore confusion that calls to mind Coriaca Market on a Sunday morning."

We looked forward to Mr. Thomas visiting our class. For as he approached not only did Sir relinquish the whip, but fiercely beaming at us he motioned to us to stand up, whereupon without fail Mr. Thomas impatiently waved us down again, but already we had started up in the most joyful pandemonium[8] of scraping, banging benches, rulers and books and pencils clattering to the floor, shuffling feet (those with shoes coming into full play), before we slowly crashed to our seats again in a relayed thunder.

And all the while Sir smiling for all he was worth—the smile only became wavy around the edges as Mr. Thomas began to move away, and not until he was through the door and out of sight for some time did Sir begin to roar. Mr. Thomas had so much to think about that he sometimes forgot things and had to come up the steps again to say something he had remembered on the way down.

4. **copy-book:** a book used for teaching penmanship.
5. **brook:** stand for.
6. **Mr. Thomas:** head of the school.

7. **Westminster Abbey:** a famous church in London, where English kings and queens are crowned.
8. **pandemonium** (păn′də-mō′nē-əm): noise; commotion.

Responding to the Selection
from **Crick Crack, Monkey** by Merle Hodge

Identifying Facts

1. What object did Sir use to discipline students?
2. What model did the children use to learn penmanship?
3. When Sir read to the class, what kind of stories did he read?
4. How were children prepared for Mr. Thomas's visits?

Interpreting Meanings

1. Although the other teachers were addressed by name, Sir was addressed only by a title. What conclusions can you draw about him from this detail?
2. Describe Sir's regular "performance." What do you think was his purpose—to gain students' respect or to frighten them?
3. Why do you suppose Sir talked about things the children did not understand? Judging from the inscription that he placed on the blackboard, what was his attitude toward the children?
4. What "curious process" took place in Sir's behavior when Mr. Thomas or the Reverend appeared? How do you know that Sir's smiling on these occasions was false?
5. Why do you suppose Sir chose to read stories of the past rather than stories more closely related to the children's experience?

6. Sir tried unsuccessfully to train the children to rise from their seats noiselessly. How does this incident show what was wrong with his teaching? How does it show what was wrong with the system of schooling?

Literary Elements
Understanding the Purpose of Satire

The aim of **satire** is to hold up to ridicule the weaknesses and wrongdoings of individuals or institutions. The satirist's weapon is laughter. By making a character's actions seem foolish, the satirist influences the reader to condemn or dismiss these actions.

Sir is shown to be an absurd figure—a ranting bully who frightens children and who demands obedience to the rules, even if they make no sense. He is also a hypocrite who hides his whip when outsiders are present.

Read aloud the passage describing the "curious process" that changes Sir's appearance. How does this passage show his hypocrisy?

Language and Vocabulary
Analyzing Word Structure

Many words in English are made up of separate word elements. A **prefix** is an element joined to the beginning of a word or to a word base to create a new word. The prefix in– can mean "not," "lacking," or "without." When it is joined to the word *separable,* we get a new word, *inseparable,* which means "not capable of being separated."

This prefix sometimes changes its form. When it is joined to the word *legal,* a word beginning with the letter **l,** the **in–** changes to **il–** to form the word *illegal.* When it is joined to the word *mobile,* which begins with the letter **m,** the **in–** changes to **im–** to form *immobile.* When the prefix is joined to a word beginning with the letter **r,** such as *responsible,* the **in–** changes to **ir–**: *irresponsible.*

Another prefix that carries the meaning of "not" is **un–**. When **un–** is joined to the word *vanquished,* meaning "defeated," we get a new word, *unvanquished,* meaning "not defeated."

Some words in the following list take the prefix **in–** and some take **un–**. Form new words by adding the correct prefix to each one. Give the definition of each new word and check your work in a dictionary.

active	eventful
American	familiar
attentive	formal
believable	fortunate
capable	literate
defensible	mature
direct	perfect

real	relevant
reasonable	significant
regular	visible

LANGUAGE WORKSHOP

LW 9 Ch 9:59
LW 10 Ch 10:47
Adding Prefixes and Suffixes

Writer's Journal
Recalling a Personal Experience
Recall one of your earliest experiences in school, for example, the day when you learned to write your name or the day you began using finger paints.

In your entry include

what happened
where and when it happened
the people who were involved
your thoughts and feelings

Speaking and Listening
Interpreting Sayings
Reread the inscription Sir wrote across the top of the blackboard. Then consider the following saying by Amos Bronson Alcott:

The true teacher defends his pupils against his own personal influences. He inspires self-trust. . . . He will have no disciple.

Be prepared to discuss the concepts of teaching contained in both sayings.

About the Author
Peter Abrahams (b. 1919)

 Peter Lee Abrahams was born in the slums of Vrededorp (frĕd'ə-dôrp) outside Johannesburg, South Africa. His father was an Ethiopian and his mother was a "Cape Colored," a term used in South Africa as a classification for persons of mixed racial descent. At the age of five he went to live in the Transvaal (trăns-văl', trănz-) with his aunt and uncle. In the autobiographical novel *Tell Freedom* (1954), he relates experiences from this period of his life.

Because Abrahams was classified as colored, he had little control over his life. Illiteracy was the norm in the slums where he grew up, and he was nine or ten years old before he learned to read. Reading was the key that opened the door to choices for him—choices that brought about change and growth. He attended school whenever he could manage to go between menial jobs. In 1939 he worked as a stoker on a ship to earn his passage to England, where he began to write articles for newspapers and radio scripts for the BBC (British Broadcasting Corporation). Abrahams has written short stories and poems, but his reputation chiefly rests on his novels. *Mine Boy* (1946), *The Path of Thunder* (1948), and subsequent novels called attention to the racial barriers plaguing blacks in South Africa.

When Abrahams wrote *Tell Freedom,* apartheid (ə-pärt'hīt', -hāt') was the official government policy of South Africa. Apartheid was instituted in 1948 when the Nationalist Party, made up chiefly of Boers (descen-

dants of Dutch settlers), gained control of the government. The official policy of apartheid was one of discrimination against nonwhites that affected education, jobs, and housing.

In 1990 Nelson Mandela, the president of the African National Congress and the head of South Africa's antiapartheid movement, was freed after more than a quarter century of imprisonment. The era of apartheid ended in 1994 when Mandela was elected president. The effects of apartheid, however, can still be felt throughout the country.

Before You Read

from **Tell Freedom**

Using What You Know

On May 10, 1994, Nelson Mandela, a leader of the antiapartheid movement, was elected president of the new South Africa. Consider what you have learned about recent developments in South Africa from news broadcasts, newspaper articles, and classroom discussions. What problems remain for the postapartheid society?

Literary Focus: Theme

Theme is the basic meaning or the main idea of a literary work. Theme expresses a point of view about life or gives you some insight into human beings and their actions. A writer does not generally state theme directly but allows characters and events to reveal theme indirectly.

Setting a Purpose

As you read, think about the underlying meaning of this selection. Focus on the narrator and his conflicts. Does he undergo some change or does he gain some new understanding? What statement do you think the author is making? Does he give you new insights into the effects of apartheid on family life?

Tell Freedom

Peter Abrahams

Wednesday was crackling[1] day. On that day the children of the location[2] made the long trek to Elsberg siding[3] for the squares of pig's rind that passed for our daily meat. We collected a double lot of cow dung the day before; a double lot of *moeroga*.[4]

I finished my breakfast and washed up. Aunt Liza was at her wash-tub in the yard. A misty, sickly sun was just showing. And on the open veld[5] the frost lay thick and white on the grass.

"Ready?" Aunt Liza called.

I went out to her. She shook the soapsuds off her swollen hands and wiped them on her apron. She lifted the apron and put her hand through the slits of the many thin cotton dresses she wore. The dress nearest the skin was the one with the pocket. From this she pulled a sixpenny piece.[6] She tied it in a knot in the corner of a bit of coloured cloth.

"Take care of that. . . . Take the smaller

piece of bread in the bin but don't eat it till you start back. You can have a small piece of crackling with it. Only a small piece, understand?"

"Yes, Aunt Liza."

"All right."

I got the bread and tucked it into the little canvas bag in which I would carry the crackling.

" 'Bye Aunt Liza." I trotted off, one hand in my pocket, feeling the cloth where the money was. I paused at Andries's home.

"Andries!" I danced up and down while I waited. The cold was not so terrible on bare feet if one did not keep still.

Andries came trotting out of their yard. His mother's voice followed; desperate and plaintive:

"I'll skin you if you lose the money!"

"Women!" Andries said bitterly.

I glimpsed the dark, skinny woman at her wash-tub as we trotted across the veld. Behind, and in front of us, other children trotted in two's and three's.

There was a sharp bite to the morning air I sucked in; it stung my nose so that tears came to my eyes; it went down my throat like an icy draught; my nose ran. I tried breathing through my mouth but this was worse. The cold went through my shirt and shorts;

1. **crackling:** crisp pork rind left after roasting or frying.
2. **location:** a segregated area where the narrator and his family are required to live.
3. **Elsberg:** a village in the Transvaal, a province in South Africa; **siding:** a short section of a railroad track or a sidetrack used for unloading or bypassing. (Also spelled *Elsburg*.)
4. *moeroga*: wild spinach.
5. **veld** (vĕlt): an open grassy field with almost no trees or bushes.
6. **sixpenny piece:** a coin equal to sixpence in British money.

my skin went pimply and chilled; my fingers went numb and began to ache; my feet felt like frozen lumps that did not belong to me, yet jarred and hurt each time I put them down. I began to feel sick and desperate.

"Jesus God in heaven!" Andries cried suddenly.

I looked at him. His eyes were rimmed in red. Tears ran down his cheeks. His face was drawn and purple, a sick look on it.

"Faster," I said.

"Think it'll help?"

I nodded. We went faster. We passed two children, sobbing and moaning as they ran. We were all in the same desperate situation. We were creatures haunted and hounded by the cold. It was a cruel enemy who gave no quarter.[7] And our means of fighting it were pitifully inadequate. In all the mornings and evenings of the winter months, young and old, big and small, were helpless victims of the bitter cold. Only towards noon and the early afternoon, when the sun sat high in the sky, was there a brief respite. For us, the children, the cold, especially the morning cold, assumed an awful and malevolent personality. We talked of "It." "It" was a half-human monster with evil thoughts, evil intentions, bent on destroying us. "It" was happiest when we were most miserable. Andries had told me how "It" had, last winter, caught and killed a boy.

Hunger was an enemy too, but one with whom we could come to terms, who had many virtues and values. Hunger gave our *pap*,[8] *moeroga*, and crackling, a feast-like quality. We could, when it was not with us, think and talk kindly about it. Its memory could even give moments of laughter. But the cold of winter was with us all the time. "It"

7. **gave no quarter**: showed no mercy.
8. *pap* (păp): tasteless food.

never really eased up. There were only more bearable degrees of "It" at high noon and on mild days. "It" was the real enemy. And on this Wednesday morning, as we ran across the veld, winter was more bitterly, bitingly, freezingly, real than ever.

The sun climbed. The frozen earth thawed, leaving the short grass looking wet and weary. Painfully, our feet and legs came alive. The aching numbness slowly left our fingers. We ran more slowly in the more bearable cold.

In climbing, the sun lost some of its damp look and seemed a real, if cold, sun. When it was right overhead, we struck the sandy road which meant we were nearing the siding. None of the others were in sight. Andries and I were alone on the sandy road on the open veld. We slowed down to a brisk walk. We were sufficiently thawed to want to talk.

"How far?" I said.

"A few minutes," he said.

"I've got a piece of bread," I said.

"Me too," he said. "Let's eat it now."

"On the way back," I said. "With a bit of crackling."

"Good idea. . . . Race to the fork."

"All right."

"Go!" he said.

We shot off together, legs working like pistons. He soon pulled away from me. He reached the fork in the road some fifty yards ahead.

"I win!" he shouted gleefully, though his teeth still chattered.

We pitched stones down the road, each trying to pitch further than the other. I won and wanted to go on doing it. But Andries soon grew weary with pitching. We raced again. Again he won. He wanted another race but I refused. I wanted pitching, but he

Little Willie, *serigraph by Raymond Lark.*
Photo courtesy Edward Smith

refused. So, sulking with each other, we reached the pig farm.

We followed a fenced-off pathway round sprawling white buildings. Everywhere about us was the grunt of pigs. As we passed an open doorway, a huge dog came bounding out, snarling and barking at us. In our terror, we forgot it was fenced in and streaked away. Surprised, I found myself a good distance ahead of Andries. We looked back and saw a young white woman call the dog to heel.

"Damn Boer[9] dog," Andries said.

"Matter with it?" I asked.

"They teach them to go for us. Never get caught by one. My old man's got a hole in his bottom where a Boer dog got him."

I remembered I had outstripped him.

"I won!" I said.

"Only because you were frightened," he said.

"I still won."

"I'll knock you!"

"I'll knock you back!"

A couple of white men came down the path and ended our possible fight. We hurried past them to the distant shed where a queue[10] had already formed. There were grown-ups and children. All the grown-ups, and some of the children, were from places other than our location.

The line moved slowly. The young white man who served us did it in leisurely fashion, with long pauses for a smoke. Occasionally he turned his back.

At last, after what seemed like hours, my turn came. Andries was behind me. I took the sixpenny piece from the square of cloth and offered it to the man.

"Well?" he said.

"Sixpence crackling, please."

Andries nudged me in the back. The man's stare suddenly became cold and hard. Andries whispered into my ear.

"Well?" the man repeated coldly.

"Please *baas*,"[11] I said.

"What d'you want?"

"Sixpence crackling, please."

"What?"

Andries dug me in the ribs.

"Sixpence crackling, please *baas*."

"What?"

"Sixpence crackling, please *baas*."

"You new here?"

"Yes, *baas*." I looked at his feet while he stared at me.

At last he took the sixpenny piece from me. I held my bag open while he filled it with crackling from a huge pile on a large canvas sheet on the ground. Turning away, I stole a fleeting glance at his face. His eyes met mine, and there was amused, challenging mockery in them. I waited for Andries at the back of the queue, out of the reach of the white man's mocking eyes.

The cold day was at its mildest as we walked home along the sandy road. I took out my piece of bread and, with a small piece of greasy crackling, still warm, on it, I munched as we went along. We had not yet made our peace so Andries munched his bread and crackling on the other side of the road.

"Dumb fool!" he mocked at me for not knowing how to address the white man.

Hurling curses at each other, we reached the fork.

---

9. **Boer** (bo͞or, bōr): Boers are descendants of Dutch colonists. The term *Afrikaner* (ăf'rĭ-kä'nər) is often used for a South African of Dutch ancestry.

10. **queue** (kyo͞o): a line of people.

11. *baas* (bäs, bôs): an Afrikaans word that came from the Dutch word for "master" or "boss," used to address a white man.

Andries saw them first and moved over to my side of the road.

"White boys," he said.

There were three of them. Two of about our own size and one slightly bigger. They had school bags and were coming toward us up the road from the siding.

"Better run for it," Andries said.

"Why?"

"No, that'll draw them. Let's just walk along, but quickly."

"Why?" I repeated.

"Shut up," he said.

Some of his anxiety touched me. Our own scrap was forgotten. We marched side by side as fast as we could. The white boys saw us and hurried up the road. We passed the fork. Perhaps they would take the turning away from us. We dared not look back.

"Hear them?" Andries asked.

"No."

I looked over my shoulder.

"They're coming," I said.

"Walk faster," Andries said. "If they come closer, run."

"Hey, *klipkop*!"

"Don't look back," Andries said.

"Hottentot!"[12]

We walked as fast as we could.

"Bloody kaffir!"[13]

Ahead was a bend in the road. Behind the bend were bushes. Once there, we could run without them knowing it till it was too late.

"Faster," Andries said.

They began pelting us with stones.

"Run when we get to the bushes," Andries said.

The bend and the bushes were near. We would soon be there.

A clear young voice carried to us:

"Your fathers are dirty baboons!"

"Run!" Andries called.

A violent, unreasoning anger suddenly possessed me. I stopped and turned.

"You're a liar!" I screamed it.

The foremost boy pointed at me:

"An ugly baboon!"

In a fog of rage I went towards him.

"Liar!" I shouted. "My father was better than your father!"

I neared them. The bigger boy stepped between me and the one I was after.

"My father was better than your father! Liar!"

The big boy struck me a mighty clout on the side of the face. I staggered, righted myself, and leapt at the boy who had insulted my father. I struck him on the face, hard. A heavy blow on the back of my head nearly stunned me. I grabbed at the boy in front of me. We went down together.

"Liar!" I said through clenched teeth, hitting him with all my might.

Blows rained on me, on my head, my neck, the side of my face, my mouth, but my enemy was under me and I pounded him fiercely, all the time repeating:

"Liar! Liar! Liar!"

Suddenly, stars exploded in my head. Then there was darkness.

I emerged from the darkness to find Andries kneeling beside me.

"God man! I thought they'd killed you."

I sat up. The white boys were nowhere to be seen. Like Andries, they'd probably thought me dead and run off in panic. The inside of my mouth felt sore and swollen. My nose was tender to the touch. The back of my head ached. A trickle of blood dripped from

12. **Hottentot** (hät′n-tät′): The original inhabitants of South Africa were the Khoi (koi), a nomadic people, also called Hottentots. Here the name is used as an insulting term.

13. **kaffir** (kăf′ər): a term for black South Africans, used scornfully.

my nose. I stemmed it with the square of coloured cloth. The greatest damage was to my shirt. It was ripped in many places. I remembered the crackling. I looked anxiously about. It was safe, a little off the road on the grass. I relaxed. I got up and brushed my clothes. I picked up the crackling.

"God, you're dumb!" Andries said. "You're going to get it!"

I was too depressed to retort. Besides, I knew he was right. I was dumb. I should have run when he told me to.

"Come on," I said.

One of many small groups of children, each child carrying his little bag of crackling, we trod the long road home in the cold winter afternoon.

There was tension in the house that night. When I got back Aunt Liza had listened to the story in silence. The beating or scolding I expected did not come. But Aunt Liza changed while she listened, became remote and withdrawn. When Uncle Sam came home she told him what had happened. He, too, just looked at me and became more remote and withdrawn than usual. They were waiting for something; their tension reached out to me, and I waited with them, anxious, apprehensive.

The thing we waited for came while we were having our supper. We heard a trap pull up outside.

"Here it is," Uncle Sam said and got up.

Aunt Liza leaned back from the table and

Transkei, a territory in South Africa.
Bettmann Newsphotos

put her hands in her lap, fingers intertwined, a cold, unseeing look in her eyes.

Before Uncle Sam reached it, the door burst open. A tall, broad, white man strode in. Behind him came the three boys. The one I had attacked had swollen lips and a puffy left eye.

"Evening *baas*," Uncle Sam murmured.

"That's him," the bigger boy said, pointing at me.

The white man stared till I lowered my eyes.

"Well?" he said.

"He's sorry, *baas*," Uncle Sam said quickly. "I've given him a hiding he won't forget soon. You know how it is, *baas*. He's new here, the child of a relative in Johannesburg and they don't all know how to behave there. You know how it is in the big towns, *baas*." The plea in Uncle Sam's voice had grown more pronounced as he went on. He turned to me. "Tell the *baas* and young *basies* how sorry you are, Lee."

I looked at Aunt Liza and something in her lifelessness made me stubborn in spite of my fear.

"He insulted my father," I said.

The white man smiled.

"See Sam, your hiding couldn't have been good."

There was a flicker of life in Aunt Liza's eyes. For a brief moment she saw me, looked at me, warmly, lovingly, then her eyes went dead again.

"He's only a child, *baas*," Uncle Sam murmured.

"You stubborn too, Sam?"

"No, *baas*."

"Good. . . . Then teach him, Sam. If you and he are to live here, you must teach him. Well . . .?"

"Yes, *baas*."

Uncle Sam went into the other room and returned with a thick leather thong. He wound it once round his hand and advanced on me. The man and boys leaned against the door, watching. I looked at Aunt Liza's face. Though there was no sign of life or feeling on it, I knew suddenly, instinctively, that she wanted me not to cry.

Bitterly, Uncle Sam said:

"You must never lift your hand to a white person. No matter what happens, you must never lift your hand to a white person. . . ."

He lifted the strap and brought it down on my back. I clenched my teeth and stared at Aunt Liza. I did not cry with the first three strokes. Then, suddenly, Aunt Liza went limp. Tears showed in her eyes. The thong came down on my back, again and again. I screamed and begged for mercy. I grovelled at Uncle Sam's feet, begging him to stop, promising never to lift my hand to any white person. . . .

At last, the white man's voice said:

"All right, Sam."

Uncle Sam stopped. I lay whimpering on the floor. Aunt Liza sat like one in a trance.

"Is he still stubborn, Sam?"

"Tell the *baas* and *basies* you are sorry."

"I'm sorry," I said.

"Bet his father is one of those who believe in equality."

"His father is dead," Aunt Liza said.

"Good night, Sam."

"Good night, *baas*. Sorry about this."

"All right, Sam." He opened the door. The boys went out first, then he followed. "Good night, Liza."

Aunt Liza did not answer. The door shut behind the white folk, and, soon, we heard their trap moving away. Uncle Sam flung the thong viciously against the door, slumped down on the bench, folded his arms on the table, and buried his head on his arms. Aunt Liza moved away from him, came on the floor beside me and lifted me into her large lap. She sat rocking my body. Uncle Sam began to sob softly. After some time, he raised his head and looked at us.

"Explain to the child, Liza," he said.

"You explain," Aunt Liza said bitterly. "You are the man. You did the beating. You are the head of the family. This is a man's world. You do the explaining."

"Please, Liza. . . ."

"You should be happy. The whites are satisfied. We can go on now."

With me in her arms, Aunt Liza got up. She carried me into the other room. The food on the table remained half-eaten. She laid me on the bed on my stomach, smeared fat on my back, then covered me with the blankets. She undressed and got into bed beside me. She cuddled me close, warmed me with her own body. With her big hand on my cheek, she rocked me, first to silence, then to sleep.

For the only time of my stay there, I slept on a bed in Elsberg.

When I woke the next morning Uncle Sam had gone. Aunt Liza only once referred to the beating he had given me. It was in the late afternoon, when I returned with the day's cow dung.

"It hurt him," she said. "You'll understand one day."

That night, Uncle Sam brought me an orange, a bag of boiled sweets, and a dirty old picture book. He smiled as he gave them to me, rather anxiously. When I smiled back at him, he seemed to relax. He put his hand on my head, started to say something, then changed his mind and took his seat by the fire.

Aunt Liza looked up from the floor where she dished out the food.

"It's all right, old man," she murmured.

"One day . . ." Uncle Sam said.

"It's all right," Aunt Liza repeated insistently.

Responding to the Selection

Identifying Facts

1. Identify the setting of this narrative, giving the place and time of year.
2. What difficulty does the narrator have in getting the crackling?
3. Why is the narrator, not Andries, beaten by the white boys?
4. How is the narrator punished for lifting his hand to a white person?
5. How does Uncle Sam show his remorse?

Interpreting Meanings

1. According to the narrator, why is the cold a worse enemy than hunger?
2. The narrator is new to Elsberg. What does he learn at the siding? How does this incident prepare you for the conflict with the white boys?
3. In the scene with the bullies, which boy—the narrator or Andries—shows greater maturity in his choice of actions? Why?
4. Aunt Liza and Uncle Sam react differently when the white man bursts into their home. How does Sam try to protect the boy? How does Liza show her defiance?
5. Although the narrator is beaten and humiliated, do you feel at the end of the selection that he is a winner rather than a loser? In what way is he admirable?
6. What do you think the title *Tell Freedom* means?

Literary Elements

Expressing Theme

Theme is seldom stated directly in a literary work. Most of the time you have to state it for yourself after you have thought about the characters and events.

There is no single correct way to state a theme. However, your statement has to express the underlying idea of a selection, and it has to account for all the important things that happen.

Consider the following statements. Which do you think is the better expression of the selection's theme?

A young boy who stubbornly stands up for himself is punished severely for his defiance.

A young boy's mistreatment and humiliation gives us insight into the nature of apartheid and its assault on an individual's will and dignity.

Language and Vocabulary

Getting Meaning from Context

When you meet an unfamiliar word in your reading, you may be able to work out its meaning by looking at the **context,** that is, the sentence or passage in which the word appears. The word *malevolent* means "malicious" or "showing ill will." What words in this passage give you clues to its meaning?

For us, the children, the cold, especially the morning cold, assumed an awful and *malevolent* personality. We talked of "It." "It" was a half-human monster with evil thoughts, evil intentions, bent on destroying us.

Using context clues, determine the meaning of the following italicized words. Check your answers in the Glossary.

But Aunt Liza changed while she listened, became *remote* and withdrawn (p. 60).
They were waiting for something; their tension reached out to me, and I waited with them, anxious, *apprehensive* (p. 60).

Narrative Writing

Writing a Dialogue

Interaction between characters in a short story or a novel is frequently revealed through **dialogue**. When you write dialogue, you need to begin a new paragraph every time the speaker changes. Note where the punctuation appears in this passage:

"How far?" I said.
"A few minutes," he said.
"I've got a piece of bread," I said.
"Me too," he said. "Let's eat it now."

Invent a brief dialogue for two characters in a story you have read. Keep in mind that the dialogue should show how the characters

feel and that the language should be suitable to the situation.

LANGUAGE WORKSHOP

LW 9 Ch 8:54
LW 10 Ch 9:42
Punctuating Quotations

Speaking and Listening

Presenting an Argument

Argumentation refers to the use of reasons to support or to disprove a position. An **argument,** in this sense, is not simply a statement based on a difference of opinion. An argument is an orderly sequence of ideas that aims to persuade a reader or a listener that your conclusion is correct. Before you present an argument, you must gather your evidence, examine it carefully, and then make a generalization based on *all* the evidence.

Take a position on this issue:

Are the narrator's actions—his fight with the white boys and his statement to the white man—due to innocence and ignorance, or do his actions indicate that he has chosen to rebel against the existing state of affairs?

List the reasons supporting your conclusion. Then consider the argument for the *other* point of view and try to find reasons against that position. Refer to your notes when you present your argument to the class.

Writer's Guide

The Writing Process

Writing is often spoken of as a **process.** The word *process* refers to a series of actions or some method of doing something in a number of steps. The **writing process** involves thinking, making decisions, and rethinking. It consists of several important stages or phases: **prewriting, writing, evaluating** and **revising, proofreading,** and **publishing.**

In this process a number of things come before the actual writing of a paper. In **pre-writing,** the writer decides what to say and how to say it. Prewriting activities include

    choosing and limiting a topic
    identifying purpose and audience
    gathering ideas
    organizing ideas
    arriving at a central idea for the paper

Some people can plan all their writing in their heads. Others need to put their ideas down on note cards or on a sheet of paper. Some people work best from an outline.

In **writing,** the writer uses notes or an outline to compose sentences and paragraphs. In **evaluating** and **revising,** the writer judges the draft and considers how the content, organization, and style might be improved. Then the writer reworks the draft, adding or deleting ideas, rearranging sentences, rephrasing for greater clarity. For **proofreading** and **publishing,** the writer checks the revised version for errors in spelling, punctuation, and grammar. The writer produces a clean, error-free manuscript and shares it with his or her audience.

In actual practice, writing is seldom so orderly. Few writers move in a straight line from one stage to another. Movement back and forth is to be expected. Writers often find that even after they have rewritten a paper several times, they want to add new material or change the order of ideas.

LANGUAGE WORKSHOP

LW 10 Ch. 8
Writing
Effectively

Writer's Guide

GUIDELINES FOR EVALUATING A PAPER

CONTENT

Purpose
1. Do the ideas and details support the main purpose: to describe, to tell a story, to explain, or to persuade?

Audience
2. Will the intended reader find the paper interesting or useful?

Development
3. Is there enough information or detail?

ORGANIZATION

Order
4. Does the paper have a beginning, middle, and end?
5. Are similar ideas grouped together?
6. Is the order clear?

Transitions
7. Are sentences joined by connecting words so that ideas flow smoothly?

STYLE

Tone
8. Is the language serious enough or light enough for the writer's purpose?

Sentence Structure
9. Is there enough variety in sentence length and structure?

Word Choice
10. Are words precise and is there variety?

Checklist for Proofreading

1. Every sentence begins with a capital letter and ends with a punctuation mark.
2. All words are spelled correctly.
3. Names of specific persons, places, and things are capitalized.
4. All sentences are complete and grammatically correct.

Writing an Autobiographical Narrative

An autobiographical narrative may cover a short or long period of time, and it may be a collection of incidents rather than a single incident. The writer gives the action a specific setting and generally tells the events in chronological order. Often the writer makes the narrative lively by including dialogue, description, and thoughts and feelings expressed in figurative language.

In your notebook or your journal or on a special sheet of paper that your teacher provides, follow this plan for writing an autobiographical narrative.

Prewriting/ Thinking

Draw a time line representing your life. Place an X at four points representing experiences that brought about changes (growth) in your life, and label each experience.

Birth ___X_____X_____X_____X_____ Now
         started   *went*   *broke my*   *had my*
         school   *camping*   *leg*   *first date*

Select *one* of the experiences and think about it. Use the **Prewriting Worksheet** to develop your ideas.

PREWRITING WORKSHEET

My **purpose** is *(to inform? to entertain? to explain? to convince?)*

My **audience** is *(my classmates? my teacher? my parents?)*

Actions that were part of my experience (expressed in verb phrases)

Observations about the participants and the surroundings

Thoughts and **feelings** during the experience

Words spoken by people or topics discussed

Writing an Autobiographical Narrative

Choose the actions, observations, thoughts, feelings, conversations, and discussions to be used in your narrative. Cross out all others.

Writing

Focus on telling what happened. Do not be too concerned with details of word choice, grammar, or mechanics. Save these matters for your revision. Have a classmate help you edit your first draft. Use the **Checklist** to evaluate your editing.

Evaluation/ Revision Checklist

Place a check in front of the items that apply to your edited paper.

_____ 1. My purpose and audience for this narrative are clear.

_____ 2. My narrative is easy to follow because the order of events is clear.

_____ 3. My narrative includes observations about the participants and the surroundings.

_____ 4. My narrative includes thoughts and feelings expressed during the experience.

_____ 5. My narrative includes dialogue and/or topics of discussion.

_____ 6. My narrative includes an opening sentence that identifies the autobiographical experience.

_____ 7. My narrative includes an effective opening that captures the reader's attention.

_____ 8. My narrative uses transitions to make connections between ideas clear.

_____ 9. My narrative uses precise language and specific details.

_____10. My narrative contains sentences that vary in length and structure.

Proofreading and Publishing

Ask a classmate to check your revision for accuracy and then prepare a final copy. Proofread carefully for errors in spelling, punctuation, grammar, and capitalization. Then share your paper with your audience.

WRITER'S WORKSHOP 2

Autobiographical Incident (Narrative Writing)

UNIT REVIEW

▶I. Interpreting New Material

Ted Thai/Time Magazine

Toni Morrison was born in Lorain, Ohio, a small town near the shores of Lake Erie, in 1931. She has said, "I am from the Midwest so I have a special affection for it. My beginnings are always there." Lorain is the setting for *The Bluest Eye,* a novel about a black girl growing into womanhood.

Morrison attended Howard and Cornell universities. She has taught at several colleges, and she has worked as an editor. Morrison is primarily a novelist, but she has also written drama, essays, and reviews. In addition to *The Bluest Eye,* her first novel, she has written *Sula* (1973), *Song of Solomon* (1977), *Tar Baby* (1981), *Beloved* (1987), and *Jazz* (1991). She received the National Book Critics Circle Award for *Song of Solomon* and the Pulitzer Prize for *Beloved.* In 1993 she became the first African American woman to win the Nobel Prize in Literature.

A. Read the following passage carefully before answering the questions.

from *The Bluest Eye*
Toni Morrison

This disrupter of seasons was a new girl in school named Maureen Peal. A high-yellow dream child with long brown hair braided into two lynch ropes that hung down her back. She was rich, at least by our standards, as rich as the richest of the white girls, swaddled in comfort and care. The quality of her clothes threatened to derange Frieda and me. Patent-leather shoes with buckles, a cheaper version of which we got only at Easter and which had disintegrated by the end of May. Fluffy sweaters the color of lemon drops tucked into skirts with pleats so orderly they astounded us. Brightly colored knee socks with white borders, a brown velvet coat trimmed in white rabbit fur, and a matching muff. There was a hint of spring in her sloe green eyes, something summery in her complexion, and a rich autumn ripeness in her walk.

She enchanted the entire school. When teachers called on her, they smiled encouragingly. Black boys didn't trip her in the halls; white boys didn't stone her, white girls didn't suck their teeth when she was assigned to be their work partners; black girls stepped aside when she wanted to use the sink in the girls' toilet, and their eyes genuflected under sliding lids. She never had to search for anybody to eat with in the cafeteria—they flocked to the table of her choice, where she opened fastidious lunches, shaming our jelly-stained bread with egg-salad sandwiches cut into four dainty squares, pink-frosted cupcakes, sticks of celery and carrots, proud, dark apples. She even bought and liked white milk.

Frieda and I were bemused, irritated, and fascinated by her. We looked hard for flaws to restore our equilibrium, but had to be content at first with uglying up her name, changing Maureen Peal to Meringue Pie. Later a minor epiphany was ours when we discovered that she had a dog tooth—a charming one to be sure—but a dog tooth nonetheless. And when we found out that she had been born with six fingers on each hand and that there was a little bump where each extra one had been removed, we smiled. They were small triumphs, but we took what we could get—snickering behind her back and calling her Six-finger-dog-tooth-meringue-pie. But we had to do it alone, for none of the other girls would co-operate with our hostility. They adored her.

When she was assigned a locker next to mine, I could indulge my jealousy four times a day. My sister and I both suspected that we were secretly prepared to be her friend, if she would let us, but I knew it would be a dangerous friendship, for when my eye traced the white border patterns of those Kelly-green knee socks, and felt the pull and slack of my brown stockings, I wanted to kick her. And when I thought of the unearned haughtiness in her eyes, I plotted accidental slammings of locker doors on her hand.

1. This passage reveals as much about the narrator as it does about Maureen Peal. How would you describe the narrator's feelings about the new girl in school?
2. Why would a friendship with Maureen Peal be "dangerous"?
3. Why do you suppose none of the other students react to Maureen as the narrator and Frieda do?
4. The narrator says she and Frieda experienced "a minor epiphany" when they discovered a flaw in Maureen. From clues in the passage, what do you think the word *epiphany* means?
5. This passage is rich in figurative language and imagery. What does the phrase "dream child" suggest? How does the narrator use the seasons to create an impression of Maureen?

B. Choose one of these assignments for a short essay.

1. Using Morrison's passage as a model, relate an experience in which you felt envious of a stranger or someone close to you. In your essay, explain why this person caused you to feel envy.
2. Invent a scene between the narrator and Maureen. Imagine the action taking place in a specific setting—in the cafeteria, at the lockers, in class. Write the narrative and dialogue for the scene, if you wish.

▶▶II. For Discussion

The title of this unit is **Passages.** As you know, the word *passage* refers to movement from one place to another. It also refers to change or progress from one condition or state to another. Growing up is a kind of passage or transition from childhood to adulthood.

Which selections in this unit have had the greatest meaning for you? Are there some characters you have felt close to because their thoughts and feelings are like your own? Discuss your responses to the experiences you have read about.

▶▶▶III. For Writing

The selections in this unit all have something to say about young people's experiences in the real world and in the world of the imagination. For example, Squeaky, in "Raymond's Run," lives in a big city, but before a race she always dreams of being lifted up like a feather and blown across the sky. In *I Know Why the Caged Bird Sings,* the narrator's imagination changes a country store into a "Fun House of Things."

Choose one or more of the selections in this unit and think of the contrast between the everyday world and the world that is created in the mind. In your opinion, does the imagination add an important element to everyday life? Does imagination help young people grow in some way? Write a short paper presenting your ideas.

The African Literary Tradition

INTRODUCTION BY **Robert Elliot Fox**

Southern Illinois University at Carbondale

A Literary Art with a Long History

In 1986, Wole Soyinka, a Nigerian, became the first African author to win the Nobel Prize for Literature. This honor brought increasing world attention to the literary art of a continent that had been known primarily for its sculpture, music, and dance. Yet not many years earlier, in England, Soyinka had to present the Cambridge University lectures that became the book *Myth, Literature and the African World* (1976) in the anthropology department because the department of English did not recognize the existence of African literature! Chinua Achebe's *Things Fall Apart* (1958)—one of the best African novels, and until recently, one of the few to achieve a wide recognition—was often taught in sociology or anthropology courses because it was valued for the insights it offered non-Africans concerning a traditional African worldview. The literary qualities it possesses were ignored or considered to be secondary. The fact is, however, that literary art of high quality, whether in written or spoken form, does exist in Africa and indeed has a very long history. It goes back at least as far as the ancient Egyptians.

Benin horn player, bronze, c. 1550–1680. Hornblowers accompanied the Oba, or king, in royal processions.
Lee Boltin

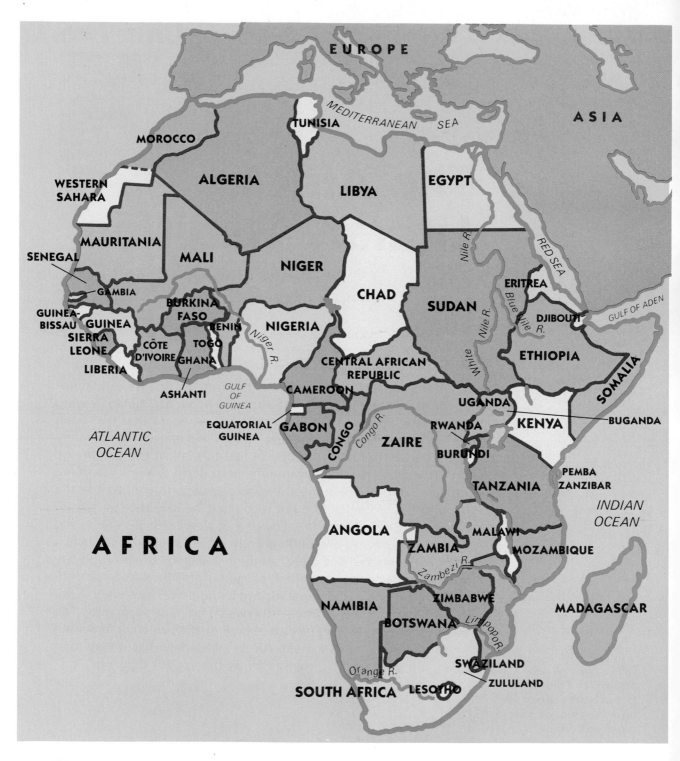

EUROPE

ASIA

MEDITERRANEAN SEA

TUNISIA

MOROCCO

WESTERN SAHARA

ALGERIA

LIBYA

EGYPT

RED SEA

GULF OF ADEN

MAURITANIA

MALI

NIGER

CHAD

SUDAN

ERITREA

DJIBOUTI R.

Nile R.

Blue Nile

White Nile R.

SENEGAL

GAMBIA

GUINEA-BISSAU

GUINEA

SIERRA LEONE

LIBERIA

BURKINA FASO

CÔTE D'IVOIRE

GHANA

ASHANTI

BENIN

TOGO

NIGERIA

Niger R.

GULF OF GUINEA

CAMEROON

CENTRAL AFRICAN REPUBLIC

ETHIOPIA

SOMALIA

UGANDA

KENYA

BUGANDA

EQUATORIAL GUINEA

GABON

CONGO

Congo R.

ZAIRE

RWANDA

BURUNDI

ATLANTIC OCEAN

TANZANIA

PEMBA

ZANZIBAR

INDIAN OCEAN

AFRICA

ANGOLA

ZAMBIA

MALAWI

MOZAMBIQUE

Zambezi R.

NAMIBIA

ZIMBABWE

MADAGASCAR

BOTSWANA

Limpopo R.

Orange R.

SWAZILAND

ZULULAND

SOUTH AFRICA

LESOTHO

MAP STUDY

As you read the material in this unit, you may wish to refer to the map on page 74 in order to locate the following lands:

Ashanti (ə-shănt'ē), a region in central **Ghana** (gän'ə), a country in western Africa.

Buganda (byo͞o-găn'də), a region in **Uganda** (yo͞o-găn'də), a country in eastern Africa.

Burkina Faso (bo͞or-kē'nə fä'sō): a country in western Africa.

Cameroon (kăm'ə-ro͞on'), a country in west-central Africa.

Egypt (ē'jəpt): a country in northeastern Africa.

Ethiopia (ē'thē-ō'pē-ə), a country in north-eastern Africa.

The Gambia (găm'bē-ə): a country on the west coast of Africa.

Ghana (gän'ə): a country in western Africa, on the Gulf of Guinea.

Guinea (gĭn'ē): a coastal region in western Africa; also a country in west-central Africa.

Kenya (kēn'yə), a country in east-central Africa.

Madagascar (măd'ə-găs'kər), an island country in the Indian Ocean, off the coast of southeastern Africa.

Mali (mä'lē): a country in western Africa.

Mauritania (môr'ĭ-tā'nē-ə), a country in northwestern Africa.

Niger (nī'jər), a country in west-central Africa.

Nigeria (nī-jîr'ē-ə), a country in west-central Africa, bounded on the north by **Niger**.

Pemba (pĕm'bə): an island in the Indian Ocean, off the northeastern coast of **Tanzania.**

Senegal (sĕn'ĭ-gôl'), a country in western Africa, on the Atlantic Ocean.

Sierra Leone (sē-ĕr'ə lē-ōn'), a country in western Africa, on the Atlantic.

Somalia (sō-mä'lē-ə), a country in East Africa, on the Gulf of Aden and the Indian Ocean.

Tanzania (tăn'zə-nē'ə), a country in east-central Africa, on the Indian Ocean.

Togo (tō'gō'): a country in western Africa, on the Gulf of Guinea.

Uganda (yo͞o-găn'də): a country in eastern Africa.

Zaire (zī'îr), a country in equatorial Africa.

Zanzibar (zăn'zə-bär'): an island off the coast of eastern Africa, part of **Tanzania.**

Zululand (zo͞o'lo͞o-lănd'): a region in Natal, a province in northeastern **South Africa.**

THE LITERATURE OF ANCIENT EGYPT

Cuneiform clay block showing list of Sumerian kings, c. 1820 B.C.
Ashmolean Museum, Oxford

The Invention of Writing

Writing is approximately five thousand years old. One ancient form of writing is that of the Sumerians of Mesopotamia (měs'ə-pə-tā'mē-ə), a region of the Near East coinciding with present-day Iraq. This form of writing is known as **cuneiform** (kyo͞o'nē-ə-fôrm'), meaning "wedge-shaped," a name derived from the wedgelike appearance of the signs made in clay with a sharp instrument called a stylus. Cuneiform writing evolved from an earlier form of writing known as **pictographic** because it used symbols that had the appearance of actual things.

One of the earliest writing systems was developed in Egypt and is known as **hieroglyphic** (hī'ər-ə-glĭf'ĭk) writing. Originally, it, too, was pictographic. The symbols were all derived from plants and animals of the Nile, thus proving that this writing was of purely African origin. Eventually, this writing system evolved two cursive forms—**hieratic** (hī'ə-răt'ĭk) and **demotic** (dǐ-mŏt'ĭk). Hieratic, which developed toward the end of the Old Kingdom (2705–2250 B.C.), reduced the pictorial hieroglyphs to a few easy strokes (something like the difference between handwriting and printed letters). **Demotic,** an abbreviated or shorthand form of hieratic, appeared during the New Kingdom (1550–1070 B.C.).

Painted relief from tomb of Queen Nefertari of Thebes.
Brian Brake/Photo Researchers

76

Bas-relief from the Eighteenth Dynasty, B.C., showing scribes holding scrolls of papyrus. The papyrus was made by soaking, pressing, and drying thin slices of the pith of the papyrus plant. Museo Archeologico, Florence, Italy.
Scala/Art Resource, NY

Unlike the ancient Mesopotamians, the Egyptians did not need to rely on clay tablets. They had ink; they had pens or brushes made from reed; and they had papyrus sheets on which to write. These sheets were pasted together and rolled up, forming scrolls. Writing was highly valued by the Egyptians; they described it as "words of the god," since it was supposed to have been invented by Thoth (thōth), the Egyptian god of wisdom.

Once writing was invented, **scribes,** who copied texts, became powerful and indispensable. For this reason, the Egyptians believed that to be a scribe was the finest of all professions, and an ancient papyrus declares that "a book is more valuable than a house . . . more beautiful than a palace." But skill in oratory was also highly prized. Consider the pharaoh who advised his son to become a master of language because "there is power in the tongue, and speech is mightier than war." In fact, the Egyptian hieroglyph for "mouth" represents the creative force. This is very similar to ideas to be found in both the Old and New Testaments. In Genesis, we read, "And God *said,* 'Let there be light,'" while the Gospel According to John tells us that "In the beginning was the *Word.*"

The Literature of Ancient Egypt   77

Types of Literature

Egyptian literature was of two types, religious and secular, with religious literature predominating. The oldest religious texts are inscribed on the walls of the tombs of kings of the Fifth and Sixth dynasties of the Old Kingdom. These are known as the **Pyramid Texts,** and they make up the oldest version of the *Book of the Coming Forth by Day,* which has come to be called the *Book of the Dead.* This work contains spells, prayers, and incantations that the dead were required to repeat in order to ward off dangers and ensure success on their journey to the Kingdom of Osiris (ō-sī′rĭs) in the next world. According to Egyptian belief, only those who had been judged by the gods to have lived righteous lives could attain everlasting life in heaven. Religious devotion was important, but immortality was assured only by a good character and a life lived in harmony with the divine order (*maat*).

The **Sarcophagus** or **Coffin Texts,** dating from the Middle Kingdom (2035–1668 B.C.), were inscribed on the inside of stone coffins. By the time of the New Kingdom, the texts were being written on papyrus rolls and buried with the mummified bodies of the deceased. These, too, are part of the *Book of the Dead.* Other burial texts dating from the New Kingdom are the *Book of Gates* and the *Book of He-who-is-in-the-Underworld.*

Hymns to the gods constitute a large portion of Egyptian religious literature. One of the most famous is the Pharaoh Akhenaton's "Hymn to the Sun," also called "Hymn to the Aton," which dates from the New Kingdom.

Among the forms of secular literature are autobiography, which developed during the Fifth Dynasty (Old Kingdom), and narrative tales, among the oldest of which are the story of *King Cheops and the Magician,* the *Tale of the Shipwrecked Sailor,* and the *Story of Sinuhe.*

Although the Egyptians clearly possessed different types of literature, the only one for which they had a specific term was the **instruction** or **teaching.** *The Instruction of Ptahhotep* is one fine example, thought to date from the Old Kingdom. Many of the instructions are in the form of proverbs.

A section of a scroll from the Book of the Dead, Eighteenth Dynasty, c. 1550–1291 B.C. *The Louvre.*
Giraudon/Art Resource, NY

Before You Read

from **The Hymn to the Aton**

Using What You Know

A **hymn** is any song of praise. Often, the term refers specifically to songs honoring God. For example, the English poet John Donne wrote "A Hymn to God the Father," affirming his faith in the mercy of God. Think of some hymns you have read or sung. Share the titles with your classmates. Do these hymns have certain characteristics in common?

Background

The **praise song** is one of the chief forms in the African poetic tradition. "The Hymn to the Aton" is a praise song celebrating the power of Aton, the sun. The poem is attributed to the Pharaoh Akhenaton ("He who is devoted to Aton"), who was a religious reformer as well as a poet. During his reign, from about 1367 to 1350 B.C., Egypt underwent a great many changes. Akhenaton worshipped Aton as the sole god and abandoned the official state religion of the god Amon.

In this translation, parentheses are inserted around words or phrases that have been added for clarity. Italics are used where the translation of the original text is uncertain. Square brackets indicate text that has been restored.

Setting a Purpose

As you read, note the strong feeling for nature and for the benevolence of the sun god expressed in the poem's imagery.

The Hymn to the Aton

Pharaoh Akhenaton
TRANSLATED BY John A. Wilson

Thou appearest beautifully on the horizon of heaven,
Thou living Aton, the beginning of life!
When thou art risen on the eastern horizon,
Thou hast filled every land with thy beauty.
Thou art gracious, great, glistening, and high over every land; 5
Thy rays encompass the lands to the limit of all that thou hast
    made:
As thou art Re,° thou reachest to the end of them;
(Thou) subduest them (for) thy beloved son.°
Though thou art far away, thy rays are on earth;
Though thou art in *their* faces, *no one knows thy* going.   10

When thou settest in the western horizon,
The land is in darkness, in the manner of death.
They sleep in a room, with heads wrapped up,
Nor sees one eye the other.
All their goods which are under their heads might be stolen, 15
(But) they would not perceive (it).
Every lion is come forth from his den;
All creeping things, they sting.
Darkness *is a shroud,* and the earth is in stillness,
For he who made them rests in his horizon.   20

At daybreak, when thou arisest on the horizon,
When thou shinest as the Aton by day,
Thou drivest away the darkness and givest thy rays.
The Two Lands° are in festivity *every day,*
Awake and standing upon (their) feet,   25
For thou hast raised them up.
Washing their bodies, taking (their) clothing,
Their arms are (raised) in praise at thy appearance.
All the world, they do their work. . . .

7. Re (rā): the best-known name of the sun god. By day, he crosses the sky in a boat; by night he goes to the underworld. He is usually shown as having the head of a falcon and wearing a solar disc as a crown.

8. beloved son: Akhenaton.

24. Two lands: Upper and Lower Egypt. The Nile flows from the south to the north. Lower Egypt is northern Egypt, the lands around the delta. Upper Egypt is southern Egypt.

How manifold it is, what thou hast made!   30
They are hidden from the face (of man).
O sole god, like whom there is no other!
Thou didst create the world according to thy desire,
Whilst thou wert alone:
All men, cattle, and wild beasts,   35
Whatever is on earth, going upon (its) feet,
And what is on high, flying with its wings. . . .

The world came into being by thy hand,
According as thou hadst made them.
When thou hast risen they live,   40
When thou settest they die.
Thou art lifetime thy own self,
For one lives (only) through thee.
Eyes are (fixed) on beauty until thou settest.
All work is laid aside when thou settest in the west.   45
(But) when (thou) risest (again),
[*Everything is*] made to flourish for the king . . .
Since thou didst found the earth
And raise them up for thy son,
Who came forth from thy body: 50
the King of Upper and Lower Egypt, . . . Akh-en-
Aton, . . . and the Chief Wife of the King . . . Nefert-iti,°
living and youthful forever and ever.

52. **Nefert-iti** (nĕf′ər-tē′tē).

**Akhenaton and Sun-god
Aton,** *relief, c. 1350* B.C.
Cairo Museum/Archiv/Photo
Researchers

Responding to the Selection

from **The Hymn to the Aton** by Pharaoh Akhenaton

Interpreting Meanings

1. This hymn opens with an **apostrophe** (ə-pŏs'trə-fē), a figure of speech in which the Aton is addressed directly, as if present. In this opening passage, the rising of the sun is associated with beauty. What is associated with the setting of the sun in the next stanza?
2. What characteristics of the god are praised in this hymn?
3. In line 33 the poet says, "Thou didst create the world according to thy desire." According to the poet, what is the purpose of creation?
4. This hymn was probably composed to be recited. What makes the poem effective for oral presentation?

Descriptive Writing

Observing a Scene

In "The Hymn to the Aton," the poet celebrates the beauty of the natural world at daybreak and after sunset as a sign of divine goodness.

Description is a form of writing that has many purposes. It can be used to express one's thoughts and feelings; it can be used to make a narrative vivid and interesting; it can be used to explain something; it can be used to influence a reader's opinion.

Write a paragraph describing a familiar scene at sunrise or at sunset. Make sure that your purpose for writing is clear. Are you writing to share your impressions with your readers or to help them experience what you have observed? Are you writing to demonstrate the beauty of the world around you?

Prewriting Strategies

Begin with careful observation. Note details of sight and sound.

Sight	Sound
_____	_____
_____	_____
_____	_____

Write an opening sentence in which you state the main impression of your description. For example:

At sunset in my back yard, you can get a spectacular view of the city's skyline.

WRITER'S
WORKSHOP 2

Observational
Writing
(Descriptive
Writing)

THE ORAL TRADITION

The Development of Writing Systems in Africa

The earliest kind of writing that developed in Africa was in the form of hieroglyphs, which were pictures or symbols used to represent objects and ideas. Arabic language and alphabet were introduced into Africa by the seventh century as a result of the spread of Islam, and European languages were introduced as a result of exploration and colonization. Beginning in the nineteenth century, European missionaries began to record African languages using the Roman alphabet, paving the way for written African literature in indigenous, or native, languages. At the same time, the teaching of English, French, and Portuguese to the Africans prepared the ground for African writing in these languages.

Initially, literature written in indigenous African languages mainly served a religious purpose, whether Christian or Muslim. It drew upon the oral tradition from the start, however, and soon became concerned with problems of contemporary life.

The Egyptian god Thoth. Relief from the Temple of Amon, Eighteenth Dynasty, c. 1570 B.C.
SEF/Art Resource

The Importance of the Spoken Word

Although writing has long been known there—whether one considers the very early development of writing in Ancient Egypt, or the spread of writing in Arabic or European languages—Africa remains a continent in which the spoken word is paramount. Even today, the average literacy rate for all of Africa is about 34 percent, and in certain countries it goes below 10 percent. Most literature in modern Africa therefore remains oral.

Oral cultures are primarily cultures of memory. The invention of writing and the spread of literacy changed this, as is made clear in a tale about the Egyptian god Thoth, who was the scribe of the gods. When he presented his invention of writing to the god-king Ammon, Thoth claimed that it would make the Egyptian people wiser and improve their memories. Ammon, however, disagreed, arguing that reliance on writing would promote forgetfulness because people would no longer need to use their memories. This tale emphasizes the fact that speech, alive and immediate, takes precedence over writing. In societies where writing is unknown or rare, people are bound by the spoken word. In a very real sense, the individual *is* his or her word. Writing can store information, but *in oral cultures, people are information.* Moreover, writing is "fixed" in a way that speech can never be. Once a work has been written down, the creativity that went into its composition is complete; but a story that is told, although its plot or message may be unchanged, may be told differently by different storytellers, or told differently at different times by the same storyteller. Being unwritten, no tale has a final version to which each narrator must be faithful. The creative process in a speech context is therefore an ongoing one.

Storytelling in the African Community

Storytellers have always been crucial to the life of the community in Africa. They did not simply entertain; they served as the chroniclers of tradition, the custodians of history, the guardians of their society's values and beliefs. Stories were used to educate children about their people's customs and they are still used today to supplement Western-style education.

A boy from Yaou Village in Côte d'Ivoire (Ivory Coast), learning to play a drum.
Marc & Evelyne Bernheim/
Woodfin Camp

A storyteller at Yaou Village, Côte d'Ivoire (Ivory Coast).
Marc & Evelyne Bernheim/
Woodfin Camp

Stories are usually told at night, so that they do not interfere with the necessary labors of the daylight hours. Storytelling in traditional African cultures is an important feature of what is known as "moonlight play," in which children and adults gather in the village square for singing and dancing, exchange of riddles, and the recitation of poems and tales. One crucial aspect of this event is its atmosphere of freedom. Performers are allowed to satirize social misbehavior, regardless of the people involved. This is both a safety valve for the release of anger and resentment, and at the same time a means of "policing" the community by publicly exposing and criticizing rudeness and misdeeds.

Storytelling itself involves more than simply the use of words; it includes song, dance, mime, drums and other instruments. In Africa, instruments—especially drums—are not only associated with the voice in the sense of providing accompaniment for a singer or narrator, they can actually "talk" by copying the tones as well as the rhythms of speech. Each instrument has its own voice, which can interact with other voices, human and instrumental. The audience actively participates in the performance. By this means, the

The Oral Tradition 85

Theater troupe at Mbaki Club, Oshogbo, West Nigeria.
Marc & Evelyne Bernheim/
Woodfin Camp

community celebrates and reinforces its solidarity and cohesion. The audience may also respond to the narrative, making comments, and even corrections, where appropriate. Indeed, the audience is the most important element controlling an oral performance. The oral artist's goal is to instruct and entertain the audience. He is ever receptive to reactions of its members, since they are the critics and judges of the value and skill of the performance. In Africa, art *is* life, not something apart from life; it is a running commentary on how things are, and how they ought to be.

The exchange or dialogue between a singer or storyteller and the audience emphasizes the interdependent relationship that exists between an individual and African society as a whole. This dialogue is known as **call-and-response,** and it is also important in African American culture. The best examples are the interaction between preacher and congregation in black churches, and between a soloist and the ensemble in jazz performances. In both cases, the leader strives for a certain technical skill and originality while the group supports and challenges the leader to inspire them by reaching for higher heights.

The Griot and His Counterparts: Experts in Oral Performance

The word **griot** (grē′ō), a French term of unknown origin, has become popular throughout West Africa as a name for an expert in oral performance. According to D. T. Niane, in his preface to the epic *Sundiata,* griots in ancient Africa were preservers of tradition—''speaking documents''—whereas in contemporary Africa they are often professional musicians. In fact, it appears that the functions associated with the term *griot* are quite various, including poet, genealogist, historian, spokesperson, teacher, musician, singer, and entertainer. Each African ethnic group has its own term for such people. The Yoruba (yō′rōō-bä), for instance, distinguish be-

A griot of Dogon tribe, Mali.
Jason Laure

Griot and elders of Dogon tribe, Mali, are shown at dawn, reading fox prints in order to tell a fortune.
Jason Laure

(Opposite page)
A Kenya harpist.
Marc & Evelyne Bernheim/
Woodfin Camp

tween *akéwì,* a composer of poetry, either oral or written, and *asun-rárà,* a professional singer of *oríkì* (praise poetry) and historical, genealogical, and didactic verse. The Hausa (hou′sə) call their traditional bards *maroka.* They engage in both praise-singing and satire—and praise is likely to change to criticism if they are insufficiently rewarded! Among the Xhosa (kō′sä) people, the tribal poet is called *imbongi,* and in the past, he was closely associated with a chief, whose praises it was the imbongi's task to sing. At the same time, however, the imbongi had the right to criticize the chief by voicing the collective opinion of the people in order to moderate a chief's improper behavior. The imbongi was able both to arouse loyalty to the chief and to remind the chief of his obligations to his people.

In Uganda (yōō-găn′də), the poet-musicians who play the *nanga* (a seven-stringed instrument upon which every type of tune can be played) are both loved and feared—loved because of their skill in composing songs that touch people's hearts, and feared because of their satirical skill. The late Ugandan poet Okot p'Bitek, whose own writings drew heavily on oral tradition, claimed that nanga players can figuratively "kill" people with their songs through ridicule. The great American poet Walt Whitman understood this power when he said in his Preface to *Leaves of Grass* (1855) that a great poet "can make every word he speaks draw blood." Some African American authors have also adopted this strategy of using words as weapons. One example is to be found in "Black Art" by Amiri Baraka (LeRoi Jones), where the poet summons his poem to "attack" an adversary: "Put it on him, poem. Strip him naked / to the world!"

Nanga players not only compose their own songs, they are also capable of taking other people's compositions and transforming them so that they sound original. This is similar to the often drastic reworkings that black American jazz musicians perform on tunes written by nonjazz composers. As a good example, listen to Lerner and Loewe's song "My Favorite Things," from the *Sound of Music,* and then listen to John Coltrane's instrumental version on the album *My Favorite Things* (Atlantic 1361–2).

Among the Gikuyu (kē-kōō′yōō) people of Kenya, the griot is called *gicaandi.* In his novel *Devil on the Cross* (1982), Ngugi wa Thiong'o, one of contemporary Africa's most important writers, casts his narrator in the role of a gicaandi who is called upon to tell a tale exposing the injustices in his society. His voice becomes that of his people, on whose behalf he speaks (remember that this is also one of the roles of the Xhosa imbongi). Ngugi is emphasizing that the traditional function of the storyteller remains vital today, and he is also demonstrating that the oral tradition can be embraced successfully by the written tradition. A book, in other words, may "speak." This is made very clear in Ngugi's novel *Matagari* (1989). Here, there is an invocation to the "reader-listener." We are reminded that the story may be read *by* those who are literate and read *to* those who are not. The narrator invites us to participate by imagining that the story takes place in the country or moment of our choice. In this way, Ngugi asks for our involvement and assures us that his story is broadly relevant and intended for everyone.

The Power of the Word

The extent to which the power of the word—especially the word of criticism or dissent—is still feared in Africa and elsewhere helps to explain why oral performers as well as writers have been feared and hated by those in power. Ngugi, for example, was jailed and is now in exile. On the other hand, the power of the word has been used by the powerful on their own behalf, for griots and their counterparts in Africa are used by individuals and political parties to sing their praises, not only at public gatherings, but also on radio and television! This use of modern media reminds us that today, oral performers in Africa have the chance to reach a wider audience than ever before possible, but at the same time, they are becoming increasingly divorced from that audience in terms of direct contact and the intimacy and reinforcement which such contact ensures.

The Value of the Oral Tradition

In literate societies, we are accustomed to relying on libraries as places for storing knowledge, yet it is clear that oral tradition contains much of great value that may be lost if steps are not taken soon to preserve it. Indeed, one African scholar has said that every time an elder dies, it is like a library burning. There is a very real sense in which knowing each other, as the Somali novelist Nuruddin Farah has said, means *listening* to one another. This is not only true within a given society, it is equally true across cultures. In our reading, let us pay attention to the way in which the voices of other peoples *speak* to us, challenging our assumptions and inviting our understanding.

In the words of Swahili poet-novelist Shaaban Robert: "In the saying which goes, 'What there is in Pemba is in Zanzibar as well,' take away Pemba and Zanzibar and say, 'What is in Europe is in Africa as well'; take away Europe and say, 'What is in Africa is in Asia as well'; take away Africa and say, 'What is in Asia is in America as well'; take away Asia and say, 'What is in America is in Australia as well.' The created word repeats itself within the nations of human beings in order to show their common origin and their great unity."

PROVERBS

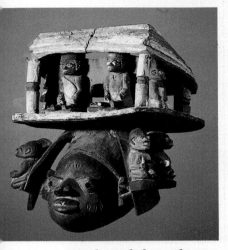

Yoruba Gelede mask,
Yoruba.
Marc & Evelyne Bernheim/
Woodfin Camp

The word **proverb** comes from the Latin *proverbium* (*pro* meaning "in front of, on behalf of" and *verbium* meaning "word"), suggesting that a proverb takes the place of ordinary words. There is an Ibo (ē'bō') saying that reinforces this idea: "Proverbs are the palm-oil with which words are eaten." Just as food often tastes better with a sauce, so words, too, are easier to digest with the "seasoning" of proverbs. Thus the Somali (sō-mä'lē) say that proverbs "put spice into speech."

Proverbs are important in all traditional societies. They are kernels of wisdom, moral and philosophical precepts reduced to a few very carefully crafted words or phrases. Their brevity aids in memorization, so that everything important and relevant in daily life can be recollected easily and passed on from person to person, generation to generation. A well-chosen proverb can have a far weightier impact than a good deal of ineffective talk, which is why the Yoruba say, "Proverbs are the horses of words [ideas]. When a word is lost, we use a proverb to look for it."

Modern African writers such as Chinua Achebe are quite adept in their use of proverbs as a means of conveying the deep reality of the African experience. Some Swahili (swä-hē'lē) short stories and novels are built around the essence of a single, unifying proverb. What is especially interesting about this use of proverbs in such works is its suggestion of a movement from the written language back to the oral, a reminder that African literature may really best be described as **lit/orature,** an interlock between two coexisting traditions.

Before You Read

African Proverbs

Using What You Know

Think of famous sayings you know that express some wisdom or lesson about human experience. For example, "A stitch in time saves nine" gives some commonsense advice about taking care of problems before they get out of hand. Working in small groups, draw up lists of common sayings that state some truth about life in easily remembered form. Retain these lists for comparison with the African selections.

Literary Focus: Proverbs

A **proverb** is a short, traditional statement—generally one sentence—expressing a general truth about life. Proverbs are common throughout the world and have been in existence for thousands of years. One famous collection is the Book of Proverbs in the Old Testament. Proverbs are like **morals,** the lessons that are attached to fables.

Setting a Purpose

As you read the African proverbs, note the point of view toward experience and behavior. Which of these proverbs resemble sayings you are familiar with? Which proverbs offer a striking contrast to familiar American sayings?

African Proverbs

ASHANTI

Only when you have crossed the river, can you say the crocodile has a lump on his snout.

One falsehood spoils a thousand truths.

When a man is wealthy, he may wear an old cloth.

Hunger is felt by a slave and hunger is felt by a king.

The ruin of a nation begins in the homes of its people.

When the cock is drunk, he forgets about the hawk.

By the time the fool has learned the game, the players have dispersed.

He who cannot dance will say: "The drum is bad."

It is the fool's sheep that break loose twice.

No one tests the depth of a river with both feet.

BUGANDA

He who hunts two rats, catches none.

When the master is absent, the frogs hop into the house.

CAMEROON

By trying often, the monkey learns to jump from the tree.

Knowledge is better than riches.

Male figure.
Bamum peoples, Fumban,
Grassfields region, Cameroon
wood, brass, cloth, glass
beads, cowrie shells 160 cm
(63 in).
Photograph by Franko Khoury,
National Museum of African Art,
Eliot Elisofon Photographic Archives,
Smithsonian Institution

ETHIOPIA

He who learns, teaches.

Confiding a secret to an unworthy person is like carrying grain in a bag with a hole.

The fool speaks, the wise man listens.

Advise and counsel him; if he does not listen, let adversity teach him.

KENYA

Do not say the first thing that comes to your mind.

Because a man has injured your goat, do not go out and kill his bull.

Absence makes the heart forget.

Home affairs are not talked about on the public square.

MADAGASCAR

Indecision is like the stepchild: if he doesn't wash his hands, he is called dirty; if he does, he is wasting the water.

The end of an ox is beef, and the end of a lie is grief.

Cross the river in a crowd and the crocodile won't eat you.

MAURITANIA

One must talk little, and listen much.

If you watch your pot, your food will not burn.

A cutting word is worse than a bowstring: a cut may heal, but the cut of the tongue does not.

NIGER

A wise man who knows his proverbs can reconcile difficulties.

Ashes fly back into the face of him who throws them.

NIGERIA

Fine words do not produce food.

Not to know is bad; not to wish to know is worse.

SENEGAL

It is better to travel alone than with a bad companion.

To spend the night in anger is better than to spend it in repentance.

SIERRA LEONE

To try and to fail, is not laziness.

SOMALIA

A thief is always under suspicion.

Wisdom does not come overnight.

TANZANIA

Do not mend your neighbor's fence before looking to your own.

ZAIRE

You do not teach the paths of the forest to an old gorilla.

Two birds disputed about a kernel, when a third swooped down and carried it off.

To love someone who does not love you, is like shaking a tree to make the dew drops fall.

ZULULAND

The horse who arrives early gets good drinking water.

Responding to the Selections

African Proverbs

Interpreting Meanings

1. Which African proverbs suggest parallels to the following sayings?

   When the cat's away, the mice will play.
   People who live in glass houses should not throw stones.
   The early bird catches the worm.
   You can't teach an old dog new tricks.
   Speech is silver but silence is golden.
   Out of sight, out of mind.
   Think before you speak.
   If at first you don't succeed, try, try again.
   A bird in hand is worth two in the bush.
   Don't wash your dirty linen in public.
   There is safety in numbers.

2. Which African proverbs suggest the *opposite* of these sayings?

   Absence makes the heart grow fonder.
   A watched pot never boils.
   Clothes make the man.
   Sticks and stones may break my bones, but words will never harm me.
   Where ignorance is bliss, 'tis folly to be wise.

Creative Writing

Composing a Fable
Choose one of the African proverbs and invent a fable to accompany it. Here is an example.

A young man who hoped to become a rock star set out for the big city with an electric guitar, a pocketful of dreams, and a wallet containing his life savings. When he got off the bus, he asked a stranger to direct him to a hotel.

"Hotels in this city are expensive," the stranger replied. "I know a place where you can get a room at a reasonable price."

The would-be musician was delighted with the stranger's suggestion and allowed himself to be escorted to a cheap lodginghouse in a rundown part of the city. There he was met by another man who introduced himself as the room clerk. The young man was shown to a room and invited to make himself comfortable.

Before leaving, the stranger said, "I know a place where you can get a good dinner for very little money. But it is not safe to carry a great deal of money with you on the streets. Why don't you lock your money in your suitcase until you return?"

The young man did as he was advised. Dinner was, indeed, quite good and moderately priced. When he returned to the lodginghouse later that evening, he found that his guitar, his suitcase, and his money were gone, and that the room clerk and the stranger were nowhere to be found. He then realized that he had been the victim of a scam.

Moral: By the time the fool has learned the game, the players have disappeared.

FOLK TALES

Monkey, glazed earthen-ware, New Kingdom, Eighteenth Dynasty.
The Brooklyn Museum, 48.181
Charles Edwin Wilbour Fund

The novel is the only major literary form that has no real counterpart in African oral tradition; the nearest equivalent is the **folk tale.** Nigerian author Amos Tutuola's novels, such as *The Palm-Wine Drinkard* (1952) and *My Life in the Bush of Ghosts* (1954), written in English, and the novels of D. O. Fagunwa, who wrote in Yoruba, are based on the folklore and traditional beliefs of the Yoruba people.

Most African folk tales involve animal characters. The best known of these are Ananse the Spider, Tortoise, Elephant, Monkey, and Hare. So popular are these characters that one researcher has collected more than two hundred stories dealing with Tortoise in Nigeria alone.

These animal tales traveled from Africa to the New World in the oral tradition that the slaves carried with them on the **middle passage,** the route across the Atlantic from West Africa to the West Indies and America. Ananse became established as the principal figure in the folklore of the Caribbean, but he is largely unknown in the United States. Here, it is Hare, otherwise known as Brer Rabbit, who is the central character in black folk tales. Monkey, meanwhile, inhabits both regions, making mischief in Caribbean folklore as well as in the Signifying Monkey stories of the black oral tradition of the United States.

Among the Yoruba, the folk tale has several components. First is a **riddling section** that serves as an introduction. The narrator, after announcing that he is about to tell a folk tale, may ask, "What fell into the river without making a sound?" A member of the audience will then say, "I know the answer." "Say it." "A needle." "Try this one. A single thread that runs from heaven to earth." "I can tell what it is." "Do so." "The rain." After a few more riddles, there will be a short dialogue between narrator and audience during which the story itself is introduced. "Shall I tell you an interesting tale?" "Yes, tell us. We are listening." "My story is about the tortoise and his in-law the snail. Once upon a time . . ." During the actual telling of the tale, there will be a song or two in which the narrator functions as soloist and the audience acts as the chorus (the call-and-response mode referred to earlier). The tale finally concludes with a closing formula that points out the moral, since these stories almost always have a particular lesson they are intended to teach.

Before You Read

Spider's Bargain with God

Using What You Know

The characters in myths and folk tales include animals who speak and behave very much like human beings. One character who became popular in African American folk tales was Brer Rabbit. What stories do you know about him? Can you name some other animal characters who act like people?

Literary Focus: The Trickster

One type of character that turns up in folklore of different lands is the **trickster**. In Norse myths, he is Loki, the god of fire, who is associated with mischief. The Norse gods use his cunning to outwit their enemies. In African American folklore, Brer Rabbit often uses trickery to get the better of other characters who are bigger and stronger. Among the Ashanti people of Ghana, Anansi (or Ananse), the Spider, is the trickster hero. In Caribbean folklore, he turns up as Nancy.

Setting a Purpose

As you read this tale from Ghana, note how Ananse uses wit and deceit to trick others. Why do you think he was such a popular figure?

Spider's Bargain with God

A Tale from Ghana

Kwaku Ananse, the spider, went to Sky God Nana Nyamee and asked whether he could buy the stories told about Him so they would be told about Ananse instead. Nana Nyamee said, "Yes, provided you bring me the following things in payment."

Ananse said, "I am willing. Just name them."

Nana Nyamee said, "Bring me a live leopard, a pot full of live bees, and a live python." Ananse was afraid, but nevertheless he agreed to provide them. He went home and sat down and thought and thought.

At last he took a needle and thread, and set out toward the forest where the leopard lived. When he got to the stream where Leopard got his water, he sat down, took out the needle and thread, and sewed his eyelids together. He waited. When he heard the footsteps of Leopard coming to fetch water, he began to sing to himself: "Hmm. Nana Nyamee is wonderful. He sewed my eyes and took me to his palace. Then I began to see wonderful things, and I have been singing of them ever since. Beautiful women, palaces, rich and delicious food, and a wonderful life."

Leopard came up to him and asked Ananse, "What were you singing about?"

He replied, "Hmm. Nana Nyamee is wonderful. He sewed my eyes and took me to his palace. Then I began to see wonderful things, and I have been singing of them ever since. Beautiful women, palaces, rich and delicious food, and a wonderful life."

Leopard said, "Eh, Ananse, what is it, are you dreaming?" "No," said Ananse, "there is a beautiful woman here."

Leopard said, "Please Ananse, sew my eyes shut, too, and lead me to Nana Nyamee so that I, too, may see all the wonderful things."

"No, I know you, Leopard, when you see her and all those other beautiful creatures you will kill them and eat them up."

"No, No, No," Leopard growled. "I shall not. Rather, I shall thank you."

Ananse took his needle and thread and sewed Leopard's eyes and led him to Nana Nyamee's palace. He said, "Nana Nyamee, here is the first installment. Keep it."

Next day Ananse took an earthenware pot and went to a place where he knew there were honey bees. As he came near the place he sang, "Oh bees! Oh bees!"

The bees said, "Ananse, what is all this murmuring about?"

Ananse replied, "I have had an argument

The carved finial of a "linguist's stick," carried by a counselor and spokesman of an Akan chief in southern Ghana. The finial shows a spider on its web. Ananse, the bringer of wisdom to the Akan, is a metaphor for the chief and his advisers.
© Doran H. Ross

with Nana Nyamee. He says all of you together won't fill this pot, but I say you will, and so I came to find out."

They said, "Oho, that is easy," and they flew into the pot, buzz, buzz, buzz, until the pot was full, and every bee had flown into it. Then Ananse quickly sealed the pot and carried it off to Nana Nyamee as his second installment.

For two days he could not think how to get the third—a live python. But at last he hit on a plan. He went to the forest and cut a long stick, a stick as long as a tree. He carried this off to the forest, singing to himself, "I am right, he is wrong! He is wrong, I am right."

When Python saw him he said, "Ananse, what are you grumbling about?"

He answered, "How lucky I am to meet you here. I have had a long and bitter argument with Nana Nyamee. I have known you for a long time, and I know your measurements both when you are coiled, and when

you are fully stretched out. Nana Nyamee thinks very little of you. He thinks you are only a little longer than the green mamba, and no longer than the cobra. I strongly disagree with him, and to prove my point I brought this pole to measure you."

Python was very angry, and he began stretching himself out to his greatest length along the stick.

And Ananse said, "You are moving! You are moving! Let me tie you to the stick so I can get the measurement exactly right."

And Python agreed. As Ananse tied Python up he sang a little song, and when he had Python securely fastened to the stick, Ananse carried him off to Nana Nyamee.

Nana Nyamee was very pleased with Ananse and forthwith beat the gong throughout the world that all stories should be told about Ananse.

This is how Ananse became the leading figure in all Ananse stories.

Responding to the Selection

Interpreting Meanings

1. The rivalry between Ananse and the Sky God appears in many tales. Why do you think Ananse wants to buy the Sky God's stories? What does this show about Ananse's character?
2. In many folk tales and fairy tales, the hero or heroine needs to accomplish tasks that appear to be impossible. What are the three tasks set for Ananse? What tricks does he use to succeed?
3. How does Ananse rely on the weaknesses of other animal characters in order to outwit them?
4. Why do you suppose people of different cultures find the trickster hero admirable?
5. What other stories do you know in which the hero or heroine must accomplish seemingly impossible tasks? Do any of these characters depend on the use of cunning or deceit?

Literary Elements

Recognizing the Trickster Figure

The animal trickster is a popular figure in West African folk tales. In one cycle of tales, the trickster hero is Hare. Elsewhere the trickster is Tortoise or Spider. Similar stories are told about all these characters.

The folk tales of the Ashanti people of Ghana are called *Anansesem,* or spider tales. The selection you have just read explains how Ananse became the owner of all the tales that are told.

Although Ananse is always referred to as a spider, he thinks and behaves as though he were human. He is almost always shown to be lacking in moral principles. He can be mischievous and wicked, selfish and cruel, shrewd and greedy. In a number of tales, he is punished when he is caught in some outrageous action. Usually, however, he manages to triumph over creatures that are larger and stronger by outwitting them.

Speaking and Listening

Telling a Trickster Tale

In African American folklore, the Signifying Monkey is a trickster figure who enjoys making mischief. Consider some popular trickster figures in cartoons and television programs. Choose one character and relate an episode showing how he or she outwits others by means of cunning and trickery.

Before You Read

Olode the Hunter Becomes an Oba

Using What You Know

The ancient Greeks told a story about Orpheus, a poet and musician, who could make trees and rocks move with his singing. He loved his wife so much that after she died, he won her release from the land of the dead by charming the king and the queen of the underworld with his music. There was one condition, however, to her release. Orpheus had to lead his wife out of the underworld without once looking at her face. When they were nearly at the end of their journey, he turned to look at her and she vanished forever.

There are many tales in which an individual is tested and fails through some weakness. Give examples of other stories that use this theme. Can you explain why such a theme would appear in the tales of many different lands?

Literary Focus: The Moral

Harold Courlander, who retells the tale of Olode, calls it a "morality tale." Its object is to teach a lesson. The **moral** of a story is not always stated directly but must be inferred from the characters and their actions.

Setting a Purpose

As you read this tale from Nigeria, determine the lesson that it teaches. Try to state that moral in your own words.

Bronzplatte (bronze relief), Benin. This relief shows a Benin archer taking aim at an ibis on a tree branch above him.
Museum für Völkerkunde, Staatliche Museen Preussischer Kulturbesitz, Berlin

Olode the Hunter Becomes an Oba°

Harold Courlander
WITH Ezekiel A. Eshugbayi

There was a hunter in the land. Bad luck dogged him. He had nothing in the world except the hut he lived in on the edge of the village, his gun, and a single cloth to wrap around his loins. He was so poor that he had never been able to take a wife. His relatives, some had gone away; some had died. He was alone. In the village, people did not even acknowledge that he had a name. They merely called him Olode, meaning hunter.

Olode went hunting one day. He followed the tracks of the game, but he caught nothing. He went deeper and deeper into the forest. He went farther than he had ever gone before. Because the trees were large and the foliage dense, it was dark. Olode struggled through the thick underbrush and waded through swamps. He found no game. He was discouraged. He sat down to rest. He closed his eyes for a moment. When he opened them, he saw a fierce-looking manlike creature standing before him. He sprang to his feet. But the creature said: "Put away the gun. I am Oluigbo, King of the Bush." Olode

° **Oba:** king.

"Olode the Hunter Becomes an Oba" from *Olode the Hunter and Other Tales from Nigeria* by Harold Courlander with Ezekiel A. Eshugbayi. Copyright © 1968 by Harold Courlander. Reprinted by permission of the *Estate of Harold Courlander.*

Olode the Hunter Becomes an Oba   103

put his gun away. Oluigbo said: "You, man, what brings you here?"

Olode said: "I am a hunter. I followed the game tracks. There was no game to be found. I am hungry. I must find meat. I must have skins to sell. Therefore, I pressed into the bush. I arrived at this place."

Oluigbo said: "Indeed, you are poor. It meets the eye."

They talked. They smoked together. Olode spoke of his misery. "I am alone. I have no son. I have no wife. My family, they are scattered and gone. Good fortune, it eludes me. I have no ointment for the sores on my legs. It is this way with me."

Oluigbo said: "Yes, it is visible. Say no more."

They smoked in silence. The King of the Bush arose at last. He put out the fire from his pipe. He said: "Hunter, to the most miserable person there must come at least one good thing. Therefore, follow me."

Olode arose. He followed Oluigbo to a great tree standing among smaller trees. Oluigbo said: "Throw down the gun." Olode threw it down. Oluigbo said: "Throw down your loincloth." Olode threw it down. Then Oluigbo struck the great tree with his hand. A door opened. "Enter," Oluigbo said. Olode entered. The door closed. Olode found himself at the gate of a large town. People were waiting for him. They welcomed him with dancing and hand-clapping. They brought clothing for him and covered his naked body. They placed him in a carrying chair and carried him into the town. A servant held a large red parasol over his head to shield him from the sun. A drummer went ahead of the procession beating out signals that said: "The Oba, our king, has arrived."

They carried Olode to the king's compound. There was a wall, and inside were many houses. The procession stopped, and the elders of the town came and touched their foreheads in the dust. One of them, the oldest, said: "Olode, we receive you as our new Oba. The town and the land around it are yours. You are our father. You will dispense justice. You will dispense charity. You will govern. All things that belong to an Oba are yours. Only one thing is forbidden."

To Olode it seemed like a dream. He said: "What is forbidden?"

The old man answered: "Inside the third house there is a carved door. The room behind it must never be entered. Do you accept the condition?"

"I accept," Olode said.

There was feasting, dancing, and music. An animal was sacrificed. Olode was proclaimed Oba. Messengers went out beating iron gongs to announce the event everywhere.

The days came, one after another. Olode did the things that a king is expected to do. He ruled. He dispensed charity. He collected taxes. He judged the lawsuits that were brought to him. He ate. Poverty fell away from him. He chose a wife. He had children. All was well with Olode.

But now that all was well, he remembered how it used to be, when he could not buy even a small gourd of palm wine. So he ordered that palm wine be brought. He drank much of it. When it was gone he called for more. He came to think only of palm wine. Instead of caring for the people, he drank. The days went on. Olode forgot everything but his drinking. When he walked he staggered from drunkenness.

Bronze head of an Oba, Court of Benin, Bini tribe, c. 1550–1680.
Lee Boltin

And one day he entered the third house and stood in front of the carved door. He said: "Am I not the Oba? Who can forbid anything to a king? Is not the land mine? And everything in the land? Is not this house mine? Therefore, the door is mine. I will open it."

He pushed against the door. It opened. It was dark beyond. Olode stepped across the threshold. The door closed behind him. He looked back. There was nothing there, no house, no town. All around him there was nothing but forest. He saw that he was naked. On the ground at his feet were his gun and his old ragged loincloth. He put the ragged cloth around him. He searched for the town. It was not there.

So it was that Olode the hunter found good fortune and lost it.

There is a saying among the people:

"The hunting dog must listen to the hunter's horn,
Otherwise the forest will devour him."

Thus it was with Olode. He did not listen. He accepted the condition when he became king. Then in drunkenness he went through the forbidden door. The forest devoured him.

Responding to the Selection
Olode the Hunter Becomes an Oba

Interpreting Meanings

1. Why does the King of the Bush help Olode?
2. Olode is told that he must never enter the room in the third house but is not told why this is forbidden. Why do you think he is not given a reason?
3. What causes Olode to fail the test?
4. Do you feel that his punishment is deserved?
5. Interpret the saying that appears at the end of the story. What **moral** do you think this tale is intended to teach?
6. To what modern-day situations might you apply the lesson in this tale?

Creative Writing

Writing a Tale

Create a modern-day version of the "forbidden door" story. The "forbidden door" can, of course, be something other than the entrance to a room. It might be a locked box; it might be a book; it might be a computer program or anything else that can be entered or opened.

Before You Read

Osebo's Drum

Using What You Know

In many fables and myths, characters are tripped up by their own weaknesses, such as vanity or pride. Aesop tells of a hungry fox who sees a crow fly off to the branch of a tree, holding a piece of cheese in its beak. The fox flatters the crow into singing, and as the bird begins to caw, the cheese drops to the ground and the fox snaps it up.

Think of some other stories that use a similar situation. How is it used, for example, in some animated cartoons that you have seen?

Literary Focus: Myths of Explanation

Some myths give explanations for natural occurrences, such as the rising and setting of the sun, the cycle of the seasons, the origin of thunder, and so on. Many mythologies offer an explanation for the way human beings obtained fire. In some African myths, Dog is the hero who is responsible for bringing fire to the earth. According to one account, Dog steals fire from the sky gods and in so doing burns his tail. The fire from his tail sets light to the grass, and people then come to gather the flames.

Setting a Purpose

As you read this tale from Ghana, think of other explanation stories you have read or heard about. Is the turtle in this tale a trickster hero?

Osebo's Drum

Harold Courlander
WITH Albert Kofi Prempeh

Osebo, the leopard, once had a great drum which was admired by all animals and gods. Although everyone admired it, no one ever hoped to own it, for Osebo was then the most powerful of animals on earth, and he was feared. Only Nyame, the Sky God, had ambitions to get the drum from the leopard.

It happened one time that Nyame's mother died, and he began the preparations for a spectacular funeral. He wondered what he could do to make the ceremony worthy of his family. People said to him: "For this ceremony we need the great drum of Osebo."

And Nyame said: "Yes, I need the drum of Osebo."

But Nyame didn't know how he could get the drum. At last he called the earth animals before him, all but the leopard himself. Nyame's stool was brought out, and he sat upon it, while his servants held over his head the many-colored parasol which is called the rainbow. He said to the animals:

"For the funeral ceremonies I need the great drum of the leopard. Who will get it for me?"

Esono, the elephant, said: "I will get it." He went to where the leopard lived and tried to take the drum, but the leopard drove him away. The elephant came back to the house of the Sky God, saying: "I could not get it."

Then Gyata, the lion, said: "I will get the drum." He went to the place of the leopard and tried to take the drum, but the leopard drove him off. And Gyata, the lion, returned to the house of the Sky God, saying: "I could not get it."

Adowa, the antelope, went, but he couldn't get it. Odenkyem, the crocodile, went, but he couldn't get it. Owea, the tree bear, went, but he couldn't get it. Many animals went, but the leopard drove them all away.

Then Akykyigie, the turtle, came forward. In those days the turtle had a soft back like other animals. He said to the Sky God: "I will get the drum."

When people heard this, they broke into a laugh, not even bothering to cover their mouths. "If the strong creatures could not get Osebo's drum," they said, "how will you, who are so pitifully small and weak?"

The turtle said: "No one else has been able to bring it. How can I look more foolish than the rest of you?"

And he went down from the Sky God's house, slowly, slowly, until he came to the

Bronze statue of leopard, Benin, c. 1750.
Lee Boltin

place of the leopard. When Osebo saw him coming, he cried out: "Are you too a messenger from Nyame?"

The turtle replied: "No, I come out of curiosity. I want to see if it is true."

The leopard said: "What are you looking for?"

"Nyame, the Sky God, has built himself a great new drum," the turtle said. "It is so large that he can enter into it and be completely hidden. People say his drum is greater than yours."

Osebo answered: "There is no drum greater than mine."

Akykyigie, the turtle, looked at Osebo's drum, saying: "I see it, I see it, but it is not so large as Nyame's. Surely it isn't large enough to crawl into."

Osebo said angrily: "Why is it not large enough?" And to show the turtle, Osebo crawled into the drum.

The turtle said: "It is large indeed, but your hind quarters are showing."

The leopard squeezed further into the drum.

The turtle said: "Oh, but your tail is showing."

The leopard pulled himself further into

the drum. Only the tip of his tail was out.

"Ah," the turtle said, "a little more and you will win!"

The leopard wriggled and pulled in the end of his tail.

Then the turtle plugged the opening of the drum with an iron cooking pot. And while the leopard cried out fiercely, the turtle tied the drum to himself and began dragging it slowly, slowly, to the house of Nyame, the Sky God. He dragged for a while; then he stopped to beat the drum as a signal that he was coming.

When the animals heard the great drum of Osebo, they trembled in fear, for they thought surely it was Osebo himself who was playing. But when they saw the turtle coming, slowly, slowly, dragging the great drum behind him, they were amazed.

The turtle came before the Sky God and said: "Here is the drum. I have brought it. And inside the drum is Osebo himself. What shall I do with him?"

Inside the drum Osebo heard, and he feared for his life. He said: "Let me out, and I will go away in peace."

The turtle said: "Shall I kill him?"

The animals all said: "Yes, kill him!"

But Osebo called out: "Do not kill me; allow me to go away. The drum is for the Sky God, and I won't complain."

So the turtle removed the iron pot which covered the opening in the drum. Osebo came out frightened. He came hurriedly. And he came out backwards, tail first. Because he couldn't see where he was going, he fell into the Sky God's fire, and his hide was burned in many little places by the hot embers. He leaped from the fire and hurried away. But the marks of the fire, where he was burned, still remain, and that is why all leopards have dark spots.

The Sky God said to the turtle: "You have brought the great drum of Osebo to make music for the funeral of my mother. What can I give you in return?"

The turtle looked at all the other animals. He saw that they were jealous of his great deed. And he feared that they would try to abuse him for doing what they could not do. So he said to Nyame: "Of all things that could be, I want a hard cover the most."

So the Sky God gave the turtle a hard shell to wear on his back. And never is the turtle seen without it.

Responding to the Selection
Osebo's Drum

Interpreting Meanings

1. Which animals fail to return with Osebo's drum? Why is the turtle able to succeed where they fail?
2. How does the turtle trick the leopard?
3. What explanation is given for the leopard's spots?
4. Why does the turtle ask for a hard shell?
5. How does the turtle in this tale remind you of the character of Ananse in "Spider's Bargain with God"?

Creative Writing

Writing an Explanation Story
Make up a story explaining some natural occurrence. Begin by considering one of these questions or another of your own:

Why does the elephant have a long trunk?
Why does the spider have eight legs?
Why does the kangaroo have a pouch?
Why can you sometimes see the moon during the day?

Before You Read

Nana Miriam

Using What You Know

In many television programs and in films, a character is exposed to some chemical substance or dangerous rays that bring about an extraordinary change. An early version of change through scientific experimentation is Robert Louis Stevenson's tale of Dr. Jekyll and Mr. Hyde. What are some current examples of this idea? Why do you think the idea of magical change appeals to the imagination?

Literary Focus: Metamorphosis

In myths and legends, characters often undergo sudden and magical transformations. A girl who is skilled in weaving is transformed into a spider; a woman grieving for her children is transformed into stone; a giant takes the form of a dragon to guard his gold. This kind of change is called **metamorphosis** (mĕt′ə-môr′fə-sĭs).

Setting a Purpose

What does this myth tell you about the characteristics valued by the Songai (sông′hī)?

Nana Miriam

TOLD BY **Hans Baumann**

Fara Maka was a man of the Songai tribe, who lived by the River Niger. He was taller than the other men and he was also stronger. Only he was very ugly. However, no one thought that important, because Fara Maka had a daughter who was very beautiful. Her name was Nana Miriam and she too was tall and strong. Her father instructed her in all kinds of things. He went with her to the sandbank and said, "Watch the fish!" And he told her the names of all the various kinds. Everything there is to know about fish he taught her. Then he asked her, "What kind is the one swimming here, and the other one over there?"

"This is a so-and-so," replied Nana Miriam. "And that is a such-and-such."

"Male or female?" asked Fara Maka.

"I don't know," said Nana Miriam.

"This one is a female, and so is the other one," explained Fara Maka. "But the third one over there is a male." And each time he pointed to a different fish.

That was how Nana Miriam came to learn so much. And in addition she had magic powers within her, which no one suspected. And because her father also taught her many magic spells, she grew stronger than anyone else in the Land of Songai.

Beside the great river, the Niger, there lived a monster that took the form of a hippopotamus. This monster was insatiable.[1] It broke into the rice fields and devoured the crops, bringing famine to the Songai people. No one could tackle this hippopotamus, because it could change its shape. So the hunters had all their trouble for nothing and they returned to their villages in helpless despair. Times were so bad that many died of hunger.

One day, Fara Maka picked up all his lances and set out to kill the monster. When he saw it, he recoiled in fear, for huge pots of fire were hung around the animal's neck. Fara Maka hurled lance after lance, but each one was swallowed by the flames. The hippopotamus monster looked at Fara Maka with scorn. Then it turned its back on him and trotted away.

Fara Maka returned home furious, wondering whom he could summon to help him. Now there was a man of the Tomma tribe who was a great hunter. His name was Kara-Digi-Mao-Fosi-Fasi, and Fara Maka asked him if he would hunt the hippopotamus with his one hundred and twenty dogs. "That I will," said Kara-Digi-Mao-Fosi-Fasi.

---

1. **insatiable** (ĭn-sā′shə-bəl): not capable of being satisfied.

So Fara Maka invited him and his one hundred and twenty dogs to a great banquet. Before every dog, which had an iron chain around its neck, was placed a small mound of rice and meat. For the hunter, however, there was a huge mound of rice. None of the dogs left a single grain of rice uneaten, and neither did Kara-Digi-Mao-Fosi-Fasi. Well fortified, they set out for the place where the monster lived.

As soon as the dogs picked up the scent, Kara-Digi-Mao-Fosi-Fasi unchained the first one. The chain rattled as the dog leaped forward towards its quarry. One chain rattled after the other, as dog after dog sprang forward to attack the hippopotamus. But the hippopotamus took them on one by one, and it gobbled them all up. The great hunter Kara-Digi-Mao-Fosi-Fasi took to his heels in terror. The hippopotamus charged into a rice field and ate that too.

When Fara Maka heard from the great hunter what had happened, he sat down in the shadow of a large tree and hung his head.

"Haven't you been able to kill the hippopotamus?" Nana Miriam asked him.

"No," said Fara Maka.

"And Kara-Digi-Mao-Fosi-Fasi couldn't drive it away either?"

"No."

"So there is no one who can get the better of it?"

"No," said Fara Maka.

"Then I'll not delay any longer," said Nana Miriam. "I'll go to its haunts[2] and see what I can see."

"Yes, do," said her father.

Nana Miriam walked along the banks of the Niger, and she soon found the hippopotamus eating its way through a rice field. As

2. **haunts:** place that it inhabits.

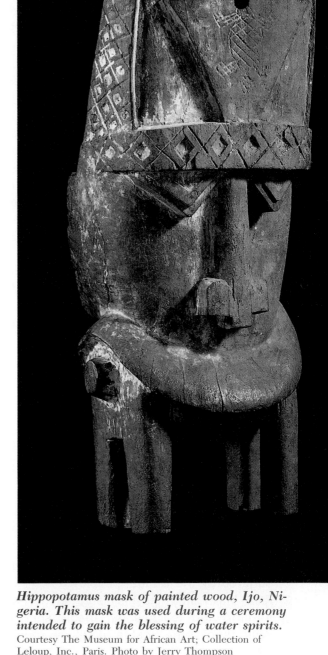

Hippopotamus mask of painted wood, Ijo, Nigeria. This mask was used during a ceremony intended to gain the blessing of water spirits.
Courtesy The Museum for African Art; Collection of Leloup, Inc., Paris. Photo by Jerry Thompson

Nana Miriam   115

soon as it saw the girl it stopped eating, raised its head and greeted her.

"Good morning," replied Nana Miriam.

"I know why you have come," said the hippopotamus. "You want to kill me. But no one can do that. Your father tried, and he lost all his lances. The great hunter Kara-Digi-Mao-Fosi-Fasi tried, and all his dogs paid with their lives for his presumption. And you are only a girl."

"We'll soon see," answered Nana Miriam. "Prepare to fight with me. Only one of us will be left to tell the tale."

"Right you are!" shouted the hippopotamus and with its breath it set the rice field afire. There it stood in a ring of flame through which no mortal could pass.

But Nana Miriam threw magic powder into the fire, and the flames turned to water.

"Right!" shouted the hippopotamus, and a wall of iron sprang up making a ring around the monster. But Nana Miriam plucked a magic hammer from the air, and shattered the iron wall into fragments.

Now for the first time the hippopotamus felt afraid, and it turned itself into a river that flowed into the Niger.

Again Nana Miriam sprinkled her magic powder. At once the river dried up and the water changed back into a hippopotamus. It grew more and more afraid and when Fara Maka came up to see what was happening, the monster charged him blindly. Nana Miriam ran after it, and when it was only ten bounds away from her father, she seized it by its left hind foot and flung it across the Niger. As it crashed against the opposite bank, its skull was split and it was dead. Then Fara Maka, who had seen the mighty throw, exclaimed, "What a daughter I have!"

Very soon, the whole tribe heard what had happened, and the Dialli, the minstrel folk,[3] sang the song of Nana Miriam's adventure with the hippopotamus, which used to devastate the rice fields. And in the years that followed, no one in the Land of the Songai starved any more.

3. **minstrel folk:** storytellers.

Responding to the Selection
Nana Miriam

Interpreting Meanings

1. What explanation is given for the famine suffered by the Songai people?
2. Fara Maka instructs his daughter, Nana Miriam, and teaches her magic spells. Why, then, is he unable to kill the monster?
3. How does Nana Miriam use magic and physical prowess to overcome the monster?
4. Most myths and legends focus on the adventures of a hero. In what way is Nana Miriam like the heroes of other tales?

Language and Vocabulary

Learning Words from a Greek Root

The word *hippopotamus* comes from two Greek words: *hippos,* meaning "horse," and *potamos,* meaning "river." The word *hippopotamus* means "horse of the river."

The root *hippo* appears in several English words. Use a college dictionary to determine the meaning of each of these words. Tell how its meaning is related to *hippos.*

hippocampus   hippodrome   hippogriff

Creative Writing

Writing a Story About Metamorphosis

Choose some natural object and write an original story explaining how and why someone was transformed into the object. Your story can be humorous if you wish. Here are some suggestions:

a computer terminal
a compact disk player
a traffic signal

Critical Thinking

Drawing Inferences

When you draw an inference, you come to a conclusion on the basis of certain facts or evidence. In reading you are continually drawing inferences. Some inferences are simple. They depend on a single detail or statement. Other inferences are more complex. You need to put together several clues in order to reach a logical conclusion.

Read the following poem several times. Then answer the questions that follow it.

Song for the Sun That Disappeared Behind the Rainclouds
Translated by **Ulli Beier**

The fire darkens, the wood turns black.
The flame extinguishes, misfortune upon
us.
God sets out in search of the sun.
The rainbow sparkles in his hand,
the bow of the divine hunter.
He has heard the lamentations of his children.
He walks along the milky way, he collects
the stars.
With quick arms he piles them into a basket,
piles them up with quick arms
like a woman who collects lizards
and piles them into her pot, piles them up
until the pot overflows with lizards,
until the basket overflows with light.

1. What conclusion can you draw from the first two lines of the poem?
2. What characteristics of the god can you infer from this poem?
3. What conclusion can you draw about the god's search?

THE EPIC IN AFRICA

An **epic** is a long narrative poem relating the deeds of a hero. Whether one talks of the *Gilgamesh* of the Babylonians, the *Iliad* and *Odyssey* of the ancient Greeks, the Anglo-Saxon *Beowulf,* the German *Nibelungenlied,* the French *Chanson de Roland,* John Milton's *Paradise Lost,* or even a contemporary work such as Derek Walcott's *Omeros,* which fuses the traditions of the *Iliad* and the *Odyssey* with a Caribbean vision, the epic is one of the oldest, most enduring literary forms. Until recently, Africa generally was believed to have no epic tradition, but in the last twenty years, much scholarly work has been done which demonstrates beyond doubt that the epic does in fact exist in Africa.

Probably the best known African epic is that of Sundiata, a thirteenth-century leader who was the founder of the Empire of Mali (mä'lē). This epic exists in many versions; it is common to the Mande (män'dä') peoples of West Africa, including the regions of Gambia, Guinea, Burkina Faso (bōōr-kē'nə fä'sō), Mali, and Senegal (sĕn'ĭ-gôl'). Mamoudou Kouyaté's version, carefully edited by D. T. Niane, is the most widely available one.

The epic of Askia Mohammed, ruler of the Songhay (sông' hī) Empire from 1493 to 1528, also exists in oral tradition in numerous versions, as well as in the written accounts of Arab chroniclers. The African novelist Yambo Ouologuem used both oral and written sources, yet cast the narrative in the style of a griot when he wrote *Bound to Violence.* Masizi Kunene's epic *Emperor Shaka the Great* (London, 1979), while written, is based upon oral tradition, much of it retained in the author's own family.

Askia Mohammed, Sundiata, and Shaka (1795–1828, founder of the Zulu Empire) are all historical people who, however, have become legendary, so that much of what is related about them in these epics cannot be taken to be "real." The purpose of these poems is not so much historical as celebratory and instructive. The Sundiata epic, for example, would be performed for the king and his attendants before battle as encouragement and an incitement to bravery and prowess. The warriors would be stirred to rival the epic hero and his achievements. The story of Sundiata (or other extraordinary personage) would also make a listener examine his own life and ask himself if he had done his utmost.

Before You Read

from **Sundiata**

Using What You Know

A *document* is anything that serves as proof. Usually, it refers to written or printed material. What kinds of documents do historians rely upon to draw their conclusions? Do historians ever rely on interviews or tapes? What do you think a "speaking document" might be?

Background

The subtitle of *Sundiata* is *An Epic of Old Mali.* The Mali Empire was an area in West Africa that included most of the present-day lands of Gambia, Guinea, Senegal, and Mali (see map). The Mali Empire flourished from A.D. 1235 to 1500.

Sundiata Keita is credited with consolidating the kingdom of Mali. Between 1235 and 1240 he conquered the Soso (or Sosso) people and built a new city, Niani, as the capital of his kingdom.

Literary Focus: The Epic

An **epic** is a long narrative work, usually about a great warrior or hero. Epics tend to include history, legend, and myth. An epic reflects the values of the society that produced it.

The oldest epics we know are **primary** epics, which belong to the oral tradition. They were composed and recited for many years before they were finally written down.

The characters in epics tend to be larger than life. The language is generally dignified. It is common for the hero of an epic to have an unusual childhood and to be destined for greatness at an early age. Often the hero must undertake a perilous journey and face dangerous adventures.

Setting a Purpose

The narrator of *Sundiata* is a **griot,** an oral historian (see page 87). Note how he establishes his credentials as a "speaking document." Why is he qualified to tell the story of Sundiata?

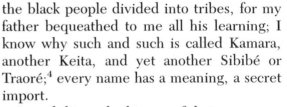

Sundiata

TRANSLATED BY **D. T. Niane**

The Words of the Griot Mamoudou Kouyaté

I am a griot. It is I, Djeli Mamoudou Kouyaté, son of Bintou Kouyaté and Djeli Kedian Kouyaté, master in the art of eloquence. Since time immemorial the Kouyatés have been in the service of the Keita princes[1] of Mali; we are vessels[2] of speech, we are the repositories which harbour secrets many centuries old. The art of eloquence has no secrets for us; without us the names of kings would vanish into oblivion, we are the memory of mankind; by the spoken word we bring to life the deeds and exploits of kings for younger generations.

I derive my knowledge from my father Djeli Kedian, who also got it from his father; history holds no mystery for us; we teach to the vulgar just as much as we want to teach them, for it is we who keep the keys to the twelve doors of Mali.[3]

I know the list of all the sovereigns who succeeded to the throne of Mali. I know how the black people divided into tribes, for my father bequeathed to me all his learning; I know why such and such is called Kamara, another Keita, and yet another Sibibé or Traoré;[4] every name has a meaning, a secret import.

I teach kings the history of their ancestors so that the lives of the ancients might serve them as an example, for the world is old, but the future springs from the past.

My word is pure and free of all untruth; it is the word of my father; it is the word of my father's father. I will give you my father's words just as I received them; royal griots do not know what lying is. When a quarrel breaks out between tribes it is we who settle the difference, for we are the depositaries[5] of oaths which the ancestors swore.

Listen to my word, you who want to know; by my mouth you will learn the history of Mali.

---

1. **Keita princes:** a dynasty of rulers in Mali.
2. **vessels:** here, people who are agents or receptacles for something.
3. **twelve doors of Mali:** Mali was originally composed of twelve provinces.
4. **Kamara . . . Traoré:** names of Mandingo tribes. Mali at first was a confederation of tribes.
5. **depositaries** (dĕ-päz′ə-tĕr′ēz): trustees, people who are entrusted with something.

By my mouth you will get to know the story of the ancestor of great Mali, the story of him who, by his exploits, surpassed even Alexander the Great;[6] he who, from the East, shed his rays upon all the countries of the West.

Listen to the story of the son of the Buffalo, the son of the Lion.[7] I am going to tell you of Maghan Sundiata, of Mari-Djata, of Sogolon Djata, of Naré Maghan Djata; the man of many names against whom sorcery could avail nothing.

6. **Alexander the Great:** a famous military conqueror of the fourth century B.C., whose empire extended from the Mediterranean to India.
7. **son . . . Lion:** According to D. T. Niane, Sundiata's mother had a buffalo as a totem; the lion is the totem and ancestor of the Keita. Through his mother, Sundiata is son of the Buffalo, and through his father, he is son of the Lion.

Sundiata is the rightful heir of the king of Mali, but after his father's death, he is forced into exile by his father's first wife, who wants the throne for her own son. Sundiata soon becomes a master hunter and a powerful warrior. His mother, Sogolon, prepares him for the time when his destiny will be fulfilled and he will reclaim the kingdom of Mali. In the climax of the epic, he battles Soumaoro Kante, the evil sorcerer king of Sosso, who has invaded Mali.

Terra-cotta statue of a man from Ancient Jenné in Mali Empire, twelfth–fourteenth centuries, A.D.
Photograph © 1995 The Detroit Institute of Arts, Founders Society Purchase. Eleanor Clay Ford Fund for African Art

FROM

Krina

Sundiata went and pitched camp at Dayala in the valley of the Niger. Now it was he who was blocking Soumaoro's road to the south. Up till that time, Sundiata and Soumaoro had fought each other without a declaration of war. One does not wage war without saying why it is being waged. Those fighting should make a declaration of their grievances to begin with. Just as a sorcerer ought not to attack someone without taking him to task for some evil deed, so a king should not wage war without saying why he is taking up arms.

Soumaoro advanced as far as Krina, near the village of Dayala on the Niger and decided to assert his rights before joining battle. Soumaoro knew that Sundiata also was a sorcerer, so, instead of sending an embassy, he committed his words to one of his owls. The night bird came and perched on the roof of Djata's tent and spoke. The son of Sogolon in his turn sent his owl to Soumaoro. Here is the dialogue of the sorcerer kings:

"Stop, young man. Henceforth I am the king of Mali. If you want peace, return to where you came from," said Soumaoro.

"I am coming back, Soumaoro, to recapture my kingdom. If you want peace you will make amends to my allies and return to Sosso where you are the king."

"I am king of Mali by force of arms. My rights have been established by conquest."

"Then I will take Mali from you by force of arms and chase you from my kingdom."

"Know, then, that I am the wild yam of the rocks; nothing will make me leave Mali."

"Know, also that I have in my camp seven master smiths who will shatter the rocks. Then, yam, I will eat you."

"I am the poisonous mushroom that makes the fearless vomit."

"As for me, I am the ravenous cock, the poison does not matter to me."

"Behave yourself, little boy, or you will burn your foot, for I am the red-hot cinder."

"But me, I am the rain that extinguishes the cinder; I am the boisterous torrent that will carry you off."

"I am the mighty silk-cotton tree that looks on from high on the tops of other trees."

"And I, I am the strangling creeper that climbs to the top of the forest giant."

"Enough of this argument. You shall not have Mali."

"Know that there is not room for two kings on the same skin, Soumaoro; you will let me have your place."

"Very well, since you want war I will wage war against you, but I would have you know that I have killed nine kings whose heads adorn my room. What a pity, indeed, that your head should take its place beside those of your fellow madcaps."[8]

"Prepare yourself, Soumaoro, for it will be long before the calamity that is going to crash down upon you and yours comes to an end."

Sosso was a magnificent city. In the open plain her triple rampart with awe-inspiring towers reached into the sky. The city comprised a hundred and eighty-eight fortresses and the palace of Soumaoro loomed above the whole city like a gigantic tower. Sosso had but one gate; colossal and made of iron, the work of the sons of fire. Noumounkeba[9]

8. **madcaps:** impulsive or rash people.
9. **Noumounkeba:** a tribal chief who is directing the defense of the city.

hoped to tie Sundiata down outside of Sosso, for he had enough provisions to hold out for a year.

The sun was beginning to set when Sogolon-Djata appeared before Sosso the Magnificent. From the top of a hill, Djata and his general staff gazed upon the fearsome city of the sorcerer-king. The army encamped in the plain opposite the great gate of the city and fires were lit in the camp. Djata resolved to take Sosso in the course of a morning. He fed his men a double ration and the tam-tams beat all night to stir up the victors of Krina.

At daybreak the towers of the ramparts were black with sofas.[10] Others were positioned on the ramparts themselves. They were the archers. The Mandingoes[11] were masters in the art of storming a town. In the front line Sundiata placed the sofas of Mali, while those who held the ladders were in the second line protected by the shields of the spearmen. The main body of the army was to attack the city gate. When all was ready, Djata gave the order to attack. The drums resounded, the horns blared and like a tide the Mandingo front line moved off, giving mighty shouts. With their shields raised above their heads the Mandingoes advanced up to the foot of the wall, then the Sossos began to rain large stones down on the assailants. From the rear, the bowmen of Wagadou[12] shot arrows at the ramparts. The attack spread and the town was assaulted at all points. Sundiata had a murderous reserve; they were the bowmen whom the king of the Bobos had sent shortly before Krina. The archers of Bobo are the best in the world. On one knee the archers fired flaming arrows over the ramparts. Within the walls the thatched huts took fire and the smoke swirled up. The ladders stood against the curtain wall and the first Mandingo sofas were already at the top. Seized by panic through seeing the town on fire, the Sossos hesitated a moment. The huge tower sur-

A rider on horseback, terra cotta, eleventh–fifteenth centuries, A.D., found near Jenné, Inland Niger Delta region, Mali.
Dr. Leon Wallace

10. **sofas:** infantrymen.
11. **Mandingoes:** inhabitants of Mali.
12. **Wagadou:** a name for Old Ghana.

Sundiata   123

mounting the gate surrendered, for Fakoli's[13] smiths had made themselves masters of it. They got into the city where the screams of women and children brought the Sossos' panic to a head. They opened the gates to the main body of the army.

Then began the massacre. Women and children in the midst of fleeing Sossos implored mercy of the victors. Djata and his cavalry were now in front of the awesome tower palace of Soumaoro. Noumounkeba, conscious that he was lost, came out to fight. With his sword held aloft he bore down on Djata, but the latter dodged him and, catching hold of the Sosso's braced arm, forced him to his knees whilst the sword dropped to the ground. He did not kill him but delivered him into the hands of Manding Bory.[14]

Soumaoro's palace was now at Sundiata's mercy. While everywhere the Sossos were begging for quarter,[15] Sundiata, preceded by Balla Fasséké,[16] entered Soumaoro's tower. The griot knew every nook and cranny of the palace from his captivity and he led Sundiata to Soumaoro's magic chamber.

When Balla Fasséké opened the door to the room it was found to have changed its appearance since Soumaoro had been touched by the fatal arrow. The inmates of the chamber had lost their power. The snake in the pitcher was in the throes of death, the owls from the perch were flapping pitifully about on the ground. Everything was dying in the sorcerer's abode. It was all up with the power of Soumaoro. Sundiata had all Soumaoro's fetishes[17] taken down and before the palace were gathered together all Soumaoro's wives, all princesses taken from their families by force. The prisoners, their hands tied behind their backs, were already herded together. Just as he had wished, Sundiata had taken Sosso in the course of a morning. When everything was outside of the town and all that there was to take had been taken out, Sundiata gave the order to complete its destruction. The last houses were set fire to and prisoners were employed in the razing of the walls. Thus, as Djata intended, Sosso was destroyed to its very foundations.

Yes, Sosso was razed to the ground. It has disappeared, the proud city of Soumaoro. A ghastly wilderness extends over the places where kings came and humbled themselves before the sorcerer king. All traces of the houses have vanished and of Soumaoro's seven-storey palace there remains nothing more. A field of desolation, Sosso is now a spot where guinea fowl and young partridges come to take their dust baths.

Many years have rolled by and many times the moon has traversed the heaven since these places lost their inhabitants. The bourein,[18] the tree of desolation, spreads out its thorny undergrowth and insolently grows in Soumaoro's capital. Sosso the Proud is nothing but a memory in the mouths of griots. The hyenas come to wail there at night, the hare and the hind come and feed on the site of the palace of Soumaoro, the king who wore robes of human skin.

Sosso vanished from the earth and it was Sundiata, the son of the buffalo, who gave these places over to solitude. After the destruction of Soumaoro's capital the world knew no other master but Sundiata.

13. **Fakoli:** Soumaoro's nephew. Soumaoro made an enemy of him by abducting his wife.
14. **Manding Bory:** Sundiata's brother.
15. **quarter:** mercy.
16. **Balla Fasséké:** Sundiata's griot.
17. **fetishes:** objects believed to have magical power.
18. **bourein:** a dwarf shrub.

Responding to the Selection

Interpreting Meanings

1. According to the griot, what different functions does he perform?
2. What reason does he give for teaching history to kings?
3. Explain the griot's statement that "the future springs from the past."
4. Before the two armies fight, their leaders hold a contest in which each one boasts that he will be victor. What is the purpose of this "war of mouths"? What claims does each one make for his powers?
5. After the city of Sosso is taken, Sundiata and his griot enter Soumaoro's magic chamber. What evidence do they find that the sorcerer has lost his power?
6. Why do you think Sundiata chose to destroy the city of Sosso rather than occupy it?

Literary Elements

Characteristics of the Epic

Sundiata was a real person who ruled the Mali Empire in the thirteenth century and helped to make it a wealthy empire. He built the city of Niani, which became the capital of the Mali Empire. In the epic he is transformed into a hero who is larger than life and who has certain magical powers as well as great physical prowess.

Like other traditional epics, *Sundiata* tells how the fate of a people depends on the actions of the hero.

Like heroes in other epics, Sundiata is forced to undertake a long journey and to meet with many adventures before he fulfills his destiny.

In traditional epics such as the *Iliad* and the *Odyssey,* there are supernatural beings in the form of gods and goddesses. In *Sundiata,* the supernatural element exists in the form of sorcery.

Sundiata shares with other epics great battle scenes and catalogs of the chief characters, whose lines of descent are carefully reported by the griot.

An epic generally uses a grand style and formal language.

Expository Writing

Researching the Background of the Epic

Choose one of these topics for a brief report.

Locate several sources that contain information about the historical Sundiata. Consult encyclopedias and textbooks. If there are no entries under *Sundiata,* try *Mali, Old Mali,* or *Mali Empire.* Determine how Sundiata influenced history and find out what happened during the reigns of his successors. Share your findings with the class.

Learn as much as you can about the *griot* and other professional singers and historians. Refer to pages 87–90.

Writing About Literature

You can write about many different topics in literature, but whatever topic you choose to write about, the object is the same: to clarify your own thinking and to reach conclusions that you can share with your readers. Most writing of this kind is **expository**, or **informative**. The purpose of exposition is to provide information or to explain related facts and ideas. Here you will find suggestions for developing an informative essay about a literary topic.

Sometimes you can understand a single literary work more fully if you are familiar with other literary works of the same type. All of the myths and folk tales you have read in this unit are entertaining as literature and give you interesting information about the traditions of individual people.

Prewriting Strategies

One way to approach analysis of literature is to **classify** or group characteristics that selections share in common. One plan might look like this:

Selection	Function	Details
"Spider's Bargain with God"	To tell a good story	The story of a spider, Ananse, who enjoys playing tricks on more powerful creatures is entertaining and appealing.
	To explain origin of certain stories	Tale explains why many stories are about Ananse. 1. Ananse wants to buy the Sky God's stories. 2. Sky God agrees to sell him stories in exchange for a live leopard, live bees, and a live python.
	To show value of wit and cleverness	Ananse tricks all the creatures he intends to bring to the Sky God. 1. Ananse convinces the leopard to have his eyes sewn shut. 2. Ananse tricks bees into getting into a pot. 3. Ananse fools the python and ties him to a stick.

Using the special form provided by your teacher or a separate sheet of paper, complete the outline for these tales. Fill in as many columns as you can for each selection.

Selection	Function	Details
"Olode the Hunter" "Osebo's Drum" "Nana Miriam"		

Writing

The chart shown on page 128 can help you organize your essay. Your **introduction** should give the titles of the works you intend to discuss. It should also state your **thesis**, the main point or points you wish to make. This is how one thesis might be stated:

> These three tales show that the stories were entertaining. They also gave explanations for natural occurrences and showed which human characteristics were admired.

The **body** of your essay should develop your main idea. Each of the columns on the chart might be used for a separate paragraph. Your **conclusion** should summarize or restate your findings.

Each paragraph in the body of your essay should be devoted to one idea. For example, each paragraph on the function of the tales might discuss one purpose: explaining natural occurrences, setting standards for behavior, and so on.

State the main idea of each paragraph in a **topic sentence**. The topic sentence is often the first sentence in the paragraph. Choose appropriate **transitional expressions** to connect the ideas within each paragraph. These are words and phrases that show the relationships between ideas. Some transitional expressions are *besides, in the same way, although, on the contrary, consequently, as a result, finally,* and *at once.*

Use this plan to outline the main idea of each paragraph.

Writing About Literature

INTRODUCTION
Paragraph 1   State your thesis, or main idea.
_____
_____

BODY
Paragraph 2   State the main idea of the paragraph and list sup-
                     porting details.
_____
_____

Details   _____
                     _____

Paragraph 3   State the main idea of the paragraph and list sup-
                     porting details.
_____
_____

Details   _____
                     _____

Repeat this pattern as often as you need to.

CONCLUSION
Final   This paragraph should bring together your main
Paragraph   ideas.
_____
_____

Refer to the **Guidelines** on page 66 to evaluate and revise your essay. Then proofread and prepare a final copy.

WRITER'S WORKSHOP 2

Interpretation (Expository Writing)

UNIT REVIEW

▶I. Interpreting New Material

A. The following story is from Ghana. Read it carefully before answering the questions.

Talk

Once, not far from the city of Accra on the Gulf of Guinea, a country man went out to his garden to dig up some yams to take to market. While he was digging, one of the yams said to him:

"Well, at last you're here. You never weeded me, but now you come around with your digging stick. Go away and leave me alone!"

The farmer turned around and looked at his cow in amazement. The cow was chewing her cud and looking at him.

"Did you say something?" he asked.

The cow kept chewing and said nothing, but the man's dog spoke up.

"It wasn't the cow who spoke to you," the dog said. "It was the yam. The yam says leave him alone."

The man became angry because his dog had never talked before, and he didn't like his tone, besides. So he took his knife and cut a branch from a palm tree to whip his dog. Just then the palm tree said:

"Put that branch down!"

The man was getting very upset about the way things were going, and he started to throw the palm branch away, but the palm branch said:

"Man, put me down softly!"

He put the branch down gently on a stone, and the stone said:

"Hey, take that thing off me."

This was enough, and the frightened farmer started to run for his village. On the way he met a fisherman going the other way with a fish trap on his head.

"What's the hurry?" the fisherman asked.

"My yam said, 'Leave me alone!' Then the dog said, 'Listen to what the yam says!' When I went to whip the dog with a palm branch the tree said, 'Put that branch down!' Then the palm branch said, 'Do it softly!' Then the stone said, 'Take that thing off me!'"

"Is that all?" the man with the fish trap asked. "Is that so frightening?"

"Well," the man's fish trap said, "did he take it off the stone?"

"Wah!" the fisherman shouted. He threw the fish trap on the ground and began to run with the farmer, and on the trail they met a weaver with a bundle of cloth on his head.

"Where are you going in such a rush?" he asked them.

"My yam said, 'Leave me alone!'" the farmer said. "The dog said, 'Listen to what the yam says!' The tree said, 'Put that branch down!' The branch said, 'Do it softly' And the stone said, 'Take that thing off me!'"

"And then," the fisherman continued, "the fish trap said, 'Did he take it off?'"

"That's nothing to get excited about," the weaver said, "no reason at all."

"Oh yes it is," his bundle of cloth said. "If it happened to you, you'd run too!"

"Wah!" the weaver shouted. He threw his bundle on the trail and started running with the other men.

They came panting to the ford in the river and found a man bathing.

"Are you chasing a gazelle?" he asked them.

The first man said breathlessly:

"My yam talked to me, and it said, 'Leave me alone!' And my dog said, 'Listen to your yam!' And when I cut myself a branch the tree said, 'Put that branch down!' And the branch said, 'Do it softly!' And the stone said, 'Take that thing off me!'"

The fisherman panted:

"And my trap said, 'Did he?'"

The weaver wheezed:

"And my bundle of cloth said, 'You'd run too!'"

"Is that why you're running?" the man in the river asked.

"Well, wouldn't you run if you were in their position?" the river said.

The man jumped out of the water and began to run with the others. They ran down the main street of the village to the house of the chief. The chief's servants brought his stool out, and he came and sat on it to listen to their complaints. The men began to recite their troubles.

"I went outside to my garden to dig yams," the farmer said, waving his arms. "Then everything began to talk! My yam said, 'Leave me alone!' My dog said, 'Pay attention to your yam!' The tree said, 'Put that branch down!' The branch said, 'Do it softly!' And the stone said, 'Take it off me!'"

"And my fish trap said, 'Well, did he take it off?'" the fisherman said.

"And my cloth said, 'You'd run too!'" the weaver said.

"And the river said the same," the bather said hoarsely, his eyes bulging.

The chief listened to them patiently, but he couldn't refrain from scowling.

"Now this really is a wild story," he said at last. "You'd better all go back to your work before I punish you for disturbing the peace."

So the men went away, and the chief shook his head and mumbled to himself, "Nonsense like that upsets the community."

"Fantastic, isn't it?" his stool said. "Imagine a talking yam!"

1. This tale is based on a single joke. Why does the story get funnier each time the joke is repeated?

2. A **tall tale** is a humorous story that stretches facts beyond belief. In American folklore, heroes like Paul Bunyan, the giant logger, are capable of superhuman actions. How does this story resemble the tall tale?

B. Choose one of these assignments for a short essay.

1. Many folk tales warn about the danger or foolishness of speaking too much or talking when it is best to be silent. Recall some fairy tales or legends that illustrate the need for common sense in speech.

2. Rewrite the story "Talk" with a contemporary American setting.

▶▶II. For Discussion

This unit has focused chiefly on the importance of the oral tradition in African literature and indirectly on the influence of that tradition on African American literature. Think of the ways that the oral tradition is important in your life. Consider the **call-and-response** dialogue between a preacher and the congregation and the interaction between a soloist and the ensemble in a jazz performance. Where else is there an exchange between a singer or storyteller and the audience?

▶▶▶III. For Writing

This unit has included several examples of literature in the oral tradition, including myths, tales, legends, and proverbs. Which selections did you enjoy the most? Write a brief essay expressing your opinion.

WRITER'S WORKSHOP 2

Interpretation (Expository Writing)

Asante Spokesman's Staff. *Among the Asante of Ghana, each chief has a spokesman, who carries an official staff. The staffs are topped with elaborate carvings, such as the one shown here. This carving represents a proverb that reminds chiefs and the people of their rights and duties. It shows two figures seated at a table, one of whom is watching the other eat. The observer might represent the people who watch the chief and his appetites (or desires) carefully.*
William Kohler

Unit Review 131

The Beginnings of African American Literature

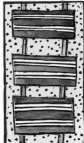

INTRODUCTION BY **William L. Andrews**

University of North Carolina at Chapel Hill

Slavery in the New World

In 1517 Bartolomé de las Casas, a Spanish missionary to the Caribbean island of Hispaniola, decided that his country's mistreatment of the Indian peoples of New Spain had become so bad that some way had to be found to protect them. His solution was to recommend that Africans be imported to the Spanish colonies to relieve the overworked Indians. Thus the African slave trade in the New World began. Before the slave trade was abolished in the late nineteenth century, approximately ten million human beings had been brought to North and South America against their will, to be subjected to one of the most inhuman systems of social and economic oppression the world has ever seen.

The Europeans who developed the institution of slavery in the New World were not the first to practice and justify the bondage of one person to another. Slavery existed throughout the ancient world, and in Africa itself the enslavement of those conquered in war was widespread. But the Europeans of the sixteenth and seventeenth centuries introduced the idea of enslavement as the natural and proper condition for particular *races* of people. Because of

Underground Railroad, 1982, a quilt made by an interracial group of senior citizens from Oberlin, Ohio. The episodes in the quilt tell the story of the Underground Railroad and how Oberlin helped fugitive slaves.
Oberlin Senior Citizens, Inc.

Slave ship.
William Loren Katz

their physical and cultural differences from Europeans, the Africans were presumed to be mentally and morally inferior. As a result, they were forced to become human cogs in the vast machinery of economic exploitation that the European colonial powers created to enrich themselves at the expense of the New World.

The first black people who came to North America were not slaves, however, but explorers. Among the most famous were Estevanico, who opened up what is now New Mexico and Arizona for Spanish settlement, and Jean Baptiste Point du Sable, who founded a trading post on the southern shore of Lake Michigan, from which the city of Chicago grew. The first Africans in British North America were brought to work as laborers; they arrived in 1619 at Jamestown, Virginia. Only twenty in number, including at least three women, these people had survived the horrendous **"middle passage"** from their homeland to America, a voyage so harsh that it is estimated that one in eight Africans died in transit without ever reaching the slave markets of the New World. At first

Black Child, *oil by Philip Thomas Cole Tilyard, c. 1825.*
New York State Historical Association, Cooperstown, New York

the black people brought to Virginia were not considered slaves. They were classed as indentured servants who could become free if they worked satisfactorily for their masters for a specified number of years. But by 1700 the growing plantation economy of Virginia demanded a work force that was cheaper than free labor and more easily controlled. By establishing the institution of **chattel slavery,** in which a black person became not just a temporary servant but the lifetime property of his or her white master, the tobacco, cotton, and rice planters of British North America ensured their rise to economic and political pre-eminence over the southern half of what would become the United States.

In the summer of 1776, more than a year after the outbreak of the Revolutionary War, many representatives of the Southern planter elite joined with delegates from the Northern colonies of British North America to debate a Declaration of Independence from England. It is one of history's greatest ironies that while these men were justifying their revolution against England by claiming the "inalienable rights" of humankind to "life, liberty, and the pursuit of happiness," they denied the same rights to black Americans. Thomas Jefferson, author of the Declaration of Independence and one of America's strongest advocates for freedom and equality, was himself the owner of more than one hundred slaves. Future presidents George Washington and James Madison were also Virginia slaveholders.

African American Writers in the Revolutionary Era

African Americans of the Revolutionary era were acutely aware of the contradictions between their country's political ideals and its actual practice. The earliest black writers of the United States appealed to their readers to follow the Christian gospel of the universal brotherhood of humanity. Through these writers, the social conscience of African American Christianity inspired the early antislavery movement in Europe and America.

The first widely read autobiography by a former slave, *The Interesting Narrative of the Life of Olaudah Equiano* (1789), urged its white readers to rethink their stereotypes of blacks as subhuman and whites as God's chosen. Recalling the day he first saw white men, Equiano provides a vivid picture of European slave traders as brutal savages. By comparison, their African victims seem innocent and civilized. After giving the English-speaking world its first detailed eyewitness account of the slave trade, Equiano demanded to know if the God of the Christians taught whites to steal human beings and sell children away from their parents. Benjamin Banneker, a Maryland mathematician and almanac-maker, agreed with Equiano's belief that Christianity and slavery were opposed. In an open letter to Thomas Jefferson, Banneker asked why the principles of the Declaration of Independence should not apply to every American since "one universal Father hath given Being to us all." Phillis Wheatley, who published her first poetry while a slave in pre-Revolutionary Boston, accepted the popular view of her time that enslavement and conversion to Christianity had been a blessing in disguise for "pagan" Africans like herself. Yet she insisted on the essential spiritual equality of all Christians, regardless of color. She also became convinced that "civil and religious liberty" were "so inseparably united," that there could be "little or no enjoyment of one without the other."

The writings of Equiano, Banneker, and Wheatley did not change the mind of America about the rights their country denied to African Americans. Although some slaves received their freedom in exchange for military service in the Revolutionary War, the laws of the new republic did not challenge the widespread belief that slavery was economically necessary and morally justified. Nevertheless, though the writings of Equiano, Banneker, and Wheatley did not lead to social or political reforms, their examples were important. Simply by writing effectively in the literary forms that whites respected, the early black writers of the United States forced many of their readers to reconsider long-standing prejudices. Because not all Africans had a written language, whites had assumed they were uncivilized and intellectually deficient. But after Wheatley's achievement in poetry, Banneker's in mathematics and astronomy, and Equiano's in autobiography, many Americans realized that blacks had the same intellectual and creative abilities as whites and deserved the same opportunities to develop them.

Sectional Conflicts over Slavery

At the beginning of the nineteenth century, more than a million African Americans lived in the United States, making up about twenty percent of the total population. The states of the North gradually abolished slavery, but the blacks who lived there still had to endure much racial discrimination and injustice. In the South,

The Schomburg Center for Research in Black Culture/New York Public Library

NEGROES FOR SALE

A CARGO OF *very ftout* Men and Women, *in good order and fit for immediate fervice, juſt imported from the Windward Coaſt of Africa, in the Ship* TWO BROTHERS. *Conditions are one half Cafh or Produce the other half payable the firſt of January next, giving Bond and Security if required.*

May 19, 1784 *John Mitchell*

622

One half of a "magic lantern" slide, showing a plantation scene in Georgia, 1850.
Culver Pictures

The first issue of the Liberator, *an abolitionist newspaper, appeared in January 1831. The initials on the banner are those of the publisher, William Lloyd Garrison, a leader in the antislavery movement.*
Massachusetts Historical Society

where the large majority of black people lived, slavery flourished. The South's political leadership pressed for the extension of slavery into the territories of the West and the islands of the Caribbean. But those in the North who believed in **"free soil"** opposed the introduction of slavery into new states such as Ohio, Indiana, and Illinois. The United States Congress was kept busy devising compromises to balance the power of the slave and free states so that conflict between the two sections would not split the country apart. But each compromise only intensified the feeling in both the South and the North that the opposition was gaining an unfair share of power.

In the 1830s a new generation of reformers announced their absolute and uncompromising opposition to slavery. Led by William Lloyd Garrison, these **abolitionists,** as they called themselves, demanded the immediate abolition of slavery throughout the United States and its territories. Free blacks in the North lent their support to Garrison's American Anti-Slavery Society. They edited newspapers, held conventions, circulated petitions, and invested money of their own in protest actions designed to advance the cause of black Americans. The antislavery movement thus gave a

Frontispiece from David Walker's **Appeal,** *1829.*
William Loren Katz

ready outlet and strong purpose for black speakers and writers of the early nineteenth century. The two great themes of African American literature during the crisis decades from 1830 to 1865 became the institution of slavery and the destiny of blacks in freedom.

As the conflict over slavery grew in the United States, pro-slavery propagandists went on the offensive, arguing that slavery was justified in the Bible and a blessing to both master and servant. Antislavery activists counterattacked, determined to win the war of words by proving how evil slavery really was. One of their most effective weapons was the testimony of those who best knew the bone-chilling facts about the inhumanity of slavery—former slaves themselves. Abolitionists began interviewing black runaways from the South while helping them get to the North or to Canada on the **Underground Railroad.** These interviews were published in antislavery newspapers. When abolitionists discovered gifted fugitive slaves living in the Northern states, they urged them to enlist in the antislavery cause as traveling platform speakers. Such public activity was dangerous for fugitive slaves because it enabled slavecatchers to locate and track them down. Yet to men like Frederick Douglass, William Wells Brown, and James Pennington, the chance to change America's mind about slavery was worth the individual risk. They became some of antislavery's most eloquent speakers, traveling thousands of miles in the United States and in Europe to raise money and a swelling tide of opposition to American slavery. Not surprisingly, the autobiographies that these men wrote sold in the tens of thousands, making them international best-sellers in their own time.

Slave Narratives

The *Narrative of the Life of Frederick Douglass, An American Slave* (1845) gave its readers not only a remarkably accurate picture of slavery but also a compelling portrait of African American humanity. What makes Douglass's narrative such an outstanding contribution to American autobiographical literature is its careful tracing of the growth of selfhood in a Maryland slave boy, which in turn empowers him to rebel against his master and seize his own liberty. Douglass realized that a slave narrator had to be more than just an eyewitness to the brutality of slavery. He or she had to be an I-witness to the selfhood of the slave. The personal focus of autobiography could become a potent weapon against racist myths that treated blacks as lacking the essential uniqueness that makes every human being a person. Many blacks followed Douglass's literary example, with the result that some of the most memorable writing done by African Americans before emancipation is autobiographical.

Slave narratives by males stressed the author's heroic struggle for what Douglass called "my manhood." Formerly enslaved women, such as Sojourner Truth and Harriet A. Jacobs, spoke and wrote of their equally heroic efforts to preserve their self-respect as women in spite of slavery's attempts to turn them into its helpless, hopeless victims. Female slave narrators joined with women abolitionists to urge white women in the North to take a public stand against slavery, regardless of those who would condemn such public activism as unladylike. To many men as well as women, the model of antislavery heroism was Harriet Tubman, a fugitive slave who became famous as a fearless and successful conductor of runaways along the Underground Railroad. Although she left no autobiographical record, the example of the woman known as "the Moses of her people" has inspired books, poems, and plays by black and white writers since the mid-nineteenth century.

(left) *Sojourner Truth, 1864.*
Sophia Smith Collection, Smith College

(right) **Harriet,** *lithograph by Elizabeth Catlett, 1975, showing Harriet Tubman leading fugitive slaves to freedom.*
Hampton University Museum, Hampton, Virginia. © 1998 Elizabeth Catlett/Licensed by VAGA, New York, NY

First African American Literary Renaissance

Through the slave narrative, African Americans entered the world of prose and dramatic literature in the 1850s. In 1853 William Wells Brown, a well-known fugitive slave narrator, authored the first black American novel, which he entitled *Clotel; or The President's Daughter.* It tells the tragic story of a beautiful light-skinned African American, the daughter of Thomas Jefferson and his slave mistress, who dies trying to save her own daughter from slavery. Five years later Brown also published the first African American play, *The Escape; or A Leap for Freedom,* based on scenes and themes familiar to readers of fugitive slave narratives. In 1859, Martin R. Delany, a black journalist and physician who would later serve as a major in the Federal army during the Civil War, wrote *Blake; or The Huts of America,* a novel whose hero plots a slave revolt in the South. In the same year the first African American women's fiction also appeared: "The Two Offers," a short story by Frances Ellen Watkins Harper, and *Our Nig; or Sketches from the Life of a Free Black,* an autobiographical novel by Harriet E. Wilson. Harper was renowned in the mid-nineteenth century black community as the poetic voice of her people, a writer who spoke to the needs of slaves and free people alike in verse that was direct, impassioned, and poignant. She and James M. Whitfield, author of a volume of angry protest poetry entitled *America, and Other Poems* (1853), helped ensure that the 1850s would be known as the first African American literary renaissance (rĕn'ĭ-säns'), when the potential of black American writers in a wide variety of poetic as well as prose forms would be clearly asserted.

The Oral Tradition

Behind the achievements of individual African American writers during the antislavery period lies the communal consciousness of millions of slaves. Their expression in song and story has given form and substance to literature by black people ever since they began writing in English. In his *Narrative* Frederick Douglass recalls having received his first glimmering of the awful evil of slavery by listening to the work songs of his fellow slaves in Maryland. Later in his life he revealed that the familiar plantation spiritual "Run to Jesus" had first suggested to him the thought of making his escape from slavery. The genius of the spirituals rested in their double meaning. When slaves sang "I thank God I'm free at las',"

(top) *William Wells Brown.*
William Loren Katz

(below) *Major Martin R. Delany.*
William Loren Katz

only they knew whether they were referring to freedom from sin or from slavery. Even in those spirituals that express a powerful yearning for deliverance in heaven from earthly burdens, one can hear a powerful complaint against the institutions that forced black people to believe that only in the next world would they find justice.

A second great fund of Southern black folklore, the animal tales, tells us much about the slaves' commonsense understanding of human psychology and everyday justice in this world. Although many of these tales explain in comic fashion how the world came to be as it is, many more concentrate on the exploits of trickster figures, most notably Brer Rabbit, who use their wits to overcome stronger animal antagonists. Tales that celebrate the trickster, whether in animal or human form, are universal in human folklore. Still the popularity of Brer Rabbit in the folklore of the slaves attests to the enduring faith of black Americans in the power of mind over matter. The spirit of Brer Rabbit lived in every slave who deceived his master with a smile of loyalty while stealing from his storehouse and making plans for an escape.

Brer Rabbit and Brer Fox, an illustration for the 1895 edition of Uncle Remus.
The Granger Collection, New York

African Americans and the Union Cause

In 1860 the first avowedly antislavery candidate for President, Abraham Lincoln of the Republican party, was elected in one of the bitterest campaigns ever waged in the United States. The South regarded Lincoln as its enemy and began making plans for secession from the republic to form its own separate nation. Lincoln promised the South that as President he would not demand the abolition of slavery, but he warned the secessionists that he would not allow them to split the Union apart. When South Carolina bombarded Federal troops at Fort Sumter in Charleston on April 12, 1861, Lincoln issued a call for 75,000 volunteers to help put down what Northern politicians called the Southern rebellion. During the next five years, while the American Civil War raged on, African Americans played an increasingly important role in the Union cause. At first black men were forbidden to serve in the Union army. They had to wait until the summer of 1862 before Lincoln would listen to advisers like Frederick Douglass and permit free blacks in liberated portions of Louisiana and South Carolina to form regiments. When two South Carolina regiments, combining both free blacks and former slaves, captured and occupied Jacksonville, Florida, in March of 1863, Lincoln decided the time was right for full-scale recruitment of black soldiers for the army. By the

Black troops during the Civil War.
Library of Congress

war's end, more than 186,000 blacks had served in the artillery, cavalry, engineers, and infantry as well as in the United States Navy. Black troops left a notable record of valor in major battles throughout the South in the last two years of the war even though

TIME LINE **THE BEGINNINGS OF AFRICAN AMERICAN LITERATURE**

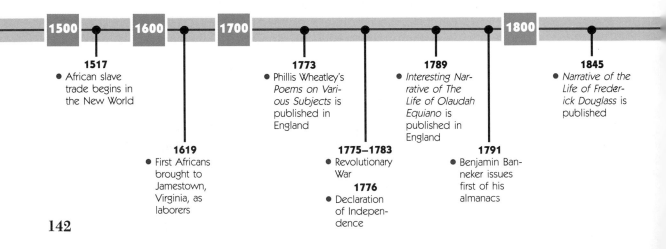

1500

1517
- African slave trade begins in the New World

1600

1619
- First Africans brought to Jamestown, Virginia, as laborers

1700

1773
- Phillis Wheatley's *Poems on Various Subjects* is published in England

1775–1783
- Revolutionary War

1776
- Declaration of Independence

1789
- *Interesting Narrative of The Life of Olaudah Equiano* is published in England

1791
- Benjamin Banneker issues first of his almanacs

1800

1845
- *Narrative of the Life of Frederick Douglass* is published

they were routinely paid less than the wages white soldiers received. More than 38,000 African Americans gave their lives for the Union cause.

Although Northern whites joined the Union army for many varied reasons, blacks fought for one overriding purpose—to bring an end to slavery. For more than a year after the outbreak of hostilities, African Americans waited for their president to link the Union cause with the extinction of slavery. When Lincoln issued the Emancipation Proclamation in September of 1862, which declared all slaves in the rebellious states to be free as of January 1, 1863, blacks in the North felt that, at long last, their country had committed itself to an ideal worth dying for. Few African Americans criticized Lincoln for failing to declare freedom for the slaves in the border states, such as Kentucky and Maryland, that had not joined the Southern confederacy. The black American leadership understood that the Emancipation Proclamation was a military measure, designed as much to undermine the South's ability to wage war as to liberate the slaves. But when the final surrender came at Appomattox, Virginia, on April 9, 1865, blacks were ready to see enacted into law the end of slavery and the beginning of a new era of freedom and opportunity for every African American. On December 6, 1865, the Thirteenth Amendment to the United States Constitution, which abolished "slavery and involuntary servitude" throughout the country, was ratified by the newly united states of America, including eight from the former Confederacy. But the long-anticipated era of freedom, equality, and opportunity for all would prove much more difficult to bring into reality.

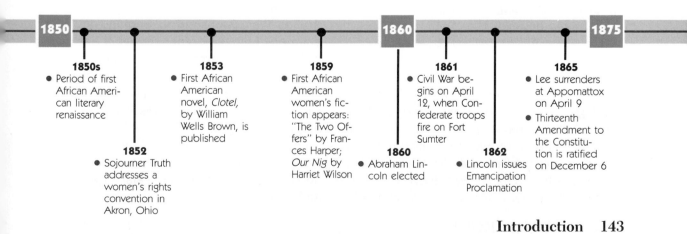

1850

1850s
- Period of first African American literary renaissance

1852
- Sojourner Truth addresses a women's rights convention in Akron, Ohio

1853
- First African American novel, *Clotel,* by William Wells Brown, is published

1859
- First African American women's fiction appears: "The Two Offers" by Frances Harper; *Our Nig* by Harriet Wilson

1860

1860
- Abraham Lincoln elected

1861
- Civil War begins on April 12, when Confederate troops fire on Fort Sumter

1862
- Lincoln issues Emancipation Proclamation

1865
- Lee surrenders at Appomattox on April 9
- Thirteenth Amendment to the Constitution is ratified on December 6

1875

Introduction 143

About the Author

Olaudah Equiano (1745–1797)

Oil painting of Olaudah Equiano, in the style of Sir Joshua Reynolds.
Royal Albert Memorial Museum, Exeter

 Olaudah Equiano (ĕk-wä′nō), who later became known as Gustavus Vassa, was born in a part of West Africa that is now in Nigeria. In the opening chapter of his autobiography, he describes the customs and beliefs among his people, the Ibo. When he was eleven, he was kidnapped by native traders and sold into slavery. Eventually he was transported to Barbados by a slave ship. From there he was taken to a Virginia plantation. A British naval officer bought him and gave him the name Gustavus Vassa. Equiano served the English cause in the Seven Years' War, but instead of being freed by his master, as he had been promised, he was sold again and taken to the West Indies. He finally was able to buy his freedom in 1766, when he was twenty-one. He then worked as a sailor and led an exciting and adventurous life. His travels included an expedition to the Arctic.

Equiano had his mind set on returning to Africa but never realized his dream. He finally settled in England, where he became active in the antislavery movement. In 1781, the captain of the *Zong,* which was transporting more than 400 slaves from Africa to Jamaica, threw overboard a third of the slave cargo in order to collect the insurance. Equiano was instrumental in bringing this atrocity to the attention of British naval authorities.

The Interesting Narrative of the Life of Olaudah Equiano, or Gustavus Vassa, the African was published in England in 1789. The book enjoyed great success. It has been called the first great black autobiography. Equiano's *Narrative* contains one of the earliest descriptions of African life by an African. Equiano is a careful observer; his autobiography is filled with vivid details. His account of the voyage to Barbados on a slave ship, included here, is a gripping and horrifying description of the slave trade in all its brutality.

Before You Read

from **The Interesting Narrative of the Life of Olaudah Equiano**

Using What You Know

Suppose you wanted to research the early years of the slave trade in the New World. What kinds of evidence would you look for? What records might you consult? Where would you get firsthand accounts of slavery?

Background

Slave trading was big business in the eighteenth century, when Olaudah Equiano was kidnapped by African raiders and sold to Europeans for transportation to Barbados. Slaves were needed for the sugar plantations of the Caribbean. After trading posts were established on the African coasts, ships filled with goods from Europe arrived at these posts, and the goods were exchanged for slaves. Sometimes it was difficult to find enough slaves to fill a ship, and traders had to call at several different places to purchase their slave cargo. After the traders loaded their ships, they began the dreaded voyage to America, referred to as the "middle passage." On a map, trace the route these ships followed from West Africa to the Caribbean.

Literary Focus: Slave Narratives

An **autobiography** is a person's account of his or her own life. Equiano wrote in a period that produced many outstanding autobiographies, including Benjamin Franklin's. Equiano's *Narrative* is the forerunner of a number of **slave narratives,** so-called because they were written by ex-slaves. These writers included William Wells Brown, Frederick Douglass, Henry Bibb, and Harriet A. Jacobs.

Setting a Purpose

As you read Equiano's account of his enslavement, determine why his autobiography has become an important source for the study of American slavery.

The Interesting Narrative of the Life of Olaudah Equiano   145

The Interesting Narrative of the Life of Olaudah Equiano

Olaudah Equiano

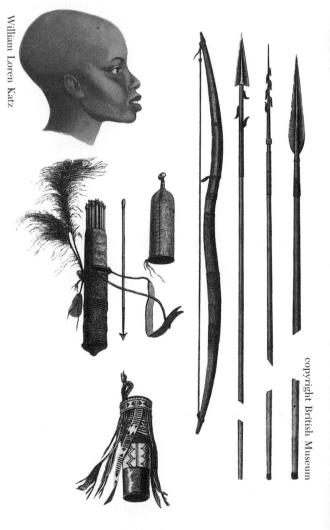

William Loren Katz

copyright British Museum

I hope the reader will not think I have trespassed on his patience, in introducing myself to him with some account of the manners and customs of my country. They had been implanted in me with great care, and made an impression on my mind, which time could not erase, and which all the adversity and variety of fortune I have since experienced, served only to rivet and record; for, whether the love of one's country be real or imaginary, a lesson of reason or an instinct of nature, I still look back with pleasure on the first scenes of my life, though that pleasure has been for the most part mingled with sorrow.

I have already acquainted the reader with the time and place of my birth. My father, besides many slaves, had a numerous family, of which seven lived to grow up, including myself and a sister, who was the only daughter. As I was the youngest of the sons, I became, of course, the greatest favourite with my mother, and was always with her, and she used to take particular pains to form my mind. I was trained up from my earliest years in the art of war: my daily exercise was shooting and throwing javelins; and my mother adorned me with emblems, after the manner of our greatest warriors. In this way I grew up till I was turned the age of eleven, when an end was put to my happiness in the following manner:—When the grown people in the neighbourhood were gone far in the fields to labour, the children generally assembled together in some of the neighbours' premises to play; and some of us often used to get up into a tree to look out for any assailant, or kidnapper, that might come upon us. For they sometimes took those opportunities of our parents' absence, to attack and carry off as many as they could seize. One day, as I was watching at the top of a tree in our yard, I saw one of those people come into the yard of our next neighbour but one, to kidnap, there being many stout young people in it. Immediately on this I gave the alarm of the rogue, and he was surrounded by the stoutest of them, who entangled him with cords, so that he could not escape till some of the grown people came and secured him.

But alas! ere long it was my fate to be thus attacked, and to be carried off, when none of the grown people were nigh. One day, when all our people were gone out to their work as usual, and only I and my sister were left to mind the house, two men and a woman got over our walls, and in a moment seized us both; and without giving us time to cry out, or to make any resistance, they stopped our mouths and ran off with us into the nearest wood. Here they tied our hands, and continued to carry us as far as they could, till night came on, when we reached a small house, where the robbers halted for refreshment and spent the night. We were then unbound, but were unable to take any food; and being quite overpowered by fatigue and grief, our only relief was some sleep, which allayed our misfortune for a short time. The next morning we left the house, and continued travelling all the day. For a long time we had kept the woods, but at last we came into a road which I believed I knew. I had now some hopes of being delivered; for we had advanced but a little way before I discovered some people at a distance, on which I began to cry out for their assistance; but my cries had no other effect than to make them tie me

Procession to Ijo, *c. 1840*.

faster and stop my mouth; they then put me into a large sack. They also stopped my sister's mouth, and tied her hands; and in this manner we proceeded till we were out of sight of these people.

When we went to rest the following night, they offered us some victuals; but we refused it; and the only comfort we had was in being in one another's arms all that night, and bathing each other with tears. But alas! we were soon deprived of even the small comfort of weeping together. The next day proved one of greater sorrow than I had yet experienced; for my sister and I were then separated, while we lay clasped in each other's arms. It was in vain that we besought[1] them not to part us; she was torn from me, and immediately carried away, while I was left in a state of distraction not to be described. I cried and grieved continually; and for several days did not eat any thing but what they forced into my mouth. At length, after many days' travelling, during which I often changed masters, I got into the hands of a chieftain, in a pleasant country. This man had two wives and some children, and they all used me extremely well, and did all they could to comfort me; particularly the first wife, who was something like my mother. Although I was a great many days' journey from my father's house, yet these people spoke exactly the same language with us. This first master of mine, as I may call him, was a smith, and my principal employment was working his bellows, which were the same kind as I had seen in my vicinity. They were in some respects not unlike the stoves here in gentlemen's kitchens; and were covered over with leather, and in the middle of that leather a stick was fixed, and a person

stood up and worked it, in the same manner as is done to pump water out of a cask with a hand pump. I believe it was gold he worked, for it was of a lovely bright yellow colour, and was worn by the women on their wrists and ankles.

Equiano attempts to escape, but he loses hope of finding his way home and returns to his master's house.

Soon after this my master's only daughter and child by his first wife, sickened and died, which affected him so much that for some time he was almost frantic, and really would have killed himself, had he not been watched and prevented. However, in a small time afterwards he recovered, and I was again sold. I was now carried to the left of the sun's rising, through many dreary wastes and dismal woods, amidst the hideous roaring of wild beasts. The people I was sold to used to carry me very often, when I was tired, either on their shoulders or on their backs. I saw many convenient well-built sheds along the road, at proper distances, to accommodate the merchants and travellers. They lie in those buildings along with their wives, who often accompany them; and they always go well armed.

From the time I left my own nation I always found somebody that understood me till I came to the sea coast. The languages of different nations did not totally differ, nor were they so copious as those of the Europeans, particularly the English. They were therefore easily learned; and while I was journeying thus through Africa, I acquired two or three different tongues. In this manner I had been travelling for a considerable time, when one evening, to my great surprise, whom should I see brought to the

1. **besought:** begged.

house where I was, but my dear sister? As soon as she saw me she gave a loud shriek, and ran into my arms. I was quite overpowered: neither of us could speak; but for a considerable time, clung to each other in mutual embraces, unable to do any thing but weep. Our meeting affected all who saw us; and indeed I must acknowledge, in honour of those sable destroyers of human rights, that I never met with any ill treatment, or saw any offered to their slaves, except tying them, when necessary, to keep them [from] running away.

When these people knew we were brother and sister, they indulged us to be together; and the man, to whom I supposed we belonged, lay with us, he in the middle, while she and I held one another by the hands across his breast all night; and thus for a while we forgot our misfortunes in the joy of being together. But even this small comfort was soon to have an end, for scarcely had the fatal morning appeared, when she was again torn from me for ever! I was now more miserable, if possible, than before. The small relief which her presence gave me from pain was gone, and the wretchedness of my situation was redoubled by my anxiety after her fate, and my apprehensions lest her sufferings should be greater than mine, when I could not be with her to alleviate them. . . .

I did not long remain after my sister. I was again sold, and carried through a number of places, till, after travelling a considerable time, I came to a town called Tinmah, in the most beautiful country I had yet seen in Africa. It was extremely rich, and there were many rivulets which flowed through it, and supplied a large pond in the centre of the town, where the people washed. Here I first saw and tasted cocoa nuts, which I thought

Currency and weights of Akan people, from Ghana and Côte d'Ivoire (Ivory Coast), showing cowrie shells. National Museum of African Art, Smithsonian Institution, Washington, D.C.
Aldo Tutino/Art Resource, NY

superior to any nuts I had ever tasted before; and the trees, which were loaded, were also interspersed among the houses, which had commodious shades adjoining, and were in the same manner as ours, the insides being neatly plastered and whitewashed. Here I also saw and tasted, for the first time, sugarcane. Their money consisted of little white shells, the size of the fingernail. I was sold for one hundred and seventy-two of these, by a merchant who lived at this place. I had been about two or three days at his house, when a wealthy widow, a neighbour of his came there one evening, and brought with her an only son, a young gentleman about my own age and size. Here they saw me; and, having taken a fancy to me, I was bought of the merchant, and went home with them. Her house and premises were situated close to one of those rivulets I have mentioned, and were the finest I ever saw in Africa; they were very extensive, and she had a number of slaves to attend her. The next day I was washed and perfumed, and when mealtime came, I was led into the presence of my mistress, and ate and drank before her with her son. This filled me with astonishment; and I could scarcely avoid expressing my surprise that the young gentleman should suffer me, who was bound, to eat with him who was free; and not only so, but that he would not at any time either eat or drink till I had taken first, because I was the eldest, which was agreeable to our custom. Indeed every thing here, and their treatment of me, made me forget that I was a slave. The language of these people resembled ours so nearly, that we understood each other perfectly. They had also the very same customs as we. There were likewise slaves daily to attend us, while my young master and I, with other boys, sported with our darts, and bows and arrows, as I had been used to do at home. In this resemblance to my former happy state, I passed about two months; and now I began to think I was to be adopted into the family, and was beginning to be reconciled to my situation, and to forget by degrees my misfortunes, when all at once the delusion vanished; for, without the least previous knowledge, one morning, early, while my dear master and companion was still asleep, I was awakened out of my reverie to fresh sorrow, and hurried away even amongst the uncircumcised.

Thus, at the very moment I dreamed of the greatest happiness, I found myself most miserable; and it seemed as if fortune wished to give me this taste of joy, only to render the reverse more poignant. The change I now experienced was as painful as it was sudden and unexpected. It was a change indeed from a state of bliss to a scene which is inexpressible by me, as it discovered to me an element I had never before beheld, and of which till then had no idea; and wherein such instances of hardship and cruelty continually occurred, as I can never reflect on but with horror.

During his journey to the coast, Equiano notes the manners and customs of different peoples. After six or seven months of captivity, he arrives at the sea.

The first object that saluted[2] my eyes when I arrived on the coast was the sea, and a slave ship, which was then riding at anchor, and waiting for its cargo. These filled me with astonishment, that was soon converted into terror, which I am yet at a loss to describe, and much more the then feelings of my mind when I was carried on board. I was immediately handled and tossed up to see if I was sound, by some of the crew; and I was now persuaded that I had got into a world of bad spirits, and that they were going to kill me. Their complexions too, differing so much from ours, their long hair, and the language they spoke, which was very different from any I had ever heard, united to confirm me in this belief. Indeed such were the horrors of my views and fears at the moment, that if ten thousand worlds had been my own, I would have freely parted with them all to have exchanged my condition with the meanest slave in my own country. When I looked round the ship too, and saw a large furnace or copper boiling and a multitude of black people, of every description, chained together, every one of their countenances expressing dejection and sorrow, I no longer doubted of my fate; and, quite overpowered with horror and anguish, I fell motionless on the deck, and fainted. When I recovered a little, I found some black people about me, who I believed were some of those who brought me on board, and had been receiving their pay: they talked to me in order to cheer me, but all in vain. I asked them if we

2. **saluted:** here, met.

were not to be eaten by those white men with horrible looks, red faces, and long hair. They told me I was not: and one of the crew brought me a small portion of spirituous[3] liquor in a wine glass; but, being afraid of him, I would not take it out of his hand. One of the blacks therefore took it from him and gave it to me, and I took a little down my palate, which, instead of reviving me, as they thought it would, threw me into the greatest consternation at the strange feeling it produced, having never tasted any such liquor before.

Soon after this the blacks who brought me on board went off, and left me abandoned to despair. I now saw myself deprived of all chance of returning to my native country, or even the least glimpse of gaining the shore, which I now considered as friendly; and I even wished for my former slavery, in preference to my present situation, which was filled with horrors of every kind, still heightened by my ignorance of what I was to undergo. I was not long suffered to indulge my grief. I was soon put down under the decks,

3. **spirituous** (spĭr′ĭ-chōō-əs): containing alcohol.

Cross-section of a slave ship.
The Schomburg Center for Research in Black Culture/New York Public Library

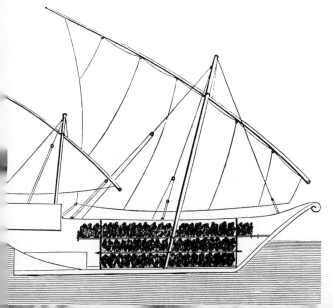

and there I received such a salutation to my nostrils as I had never experienced in my life; so that, with the loathsomeness of the stench, and with my crying together, I became so sick and low that I was not able to eat, nor had I the least desire to taste any thing. I now wished for the last friend, death, to relieve me; but soon, to my grief, two of the white men offered me eatables; and, on my refusing to eat, one of them held me fast by the hands, and laid me across, I think, the windlass,[4] and tied my feet, while the other flogged me severely. I had never experienced any thing of this kind before, and although, not being used to the water, I naturally feared that element the first time I saw it, yet nevertheless, could I have got over the nettings, I would have jumped over the side, but I could not; and besides the crew used to watch us very closely, who were not chained down to the decks, lest we should leap into the water. I have seen some of these poor African prisoners most severely cut for attempting to do so, and hourly whipped for not eating. This indeed was often the case with myself. In a little time after, amongst the poor chained men, I found some of my own nation, which in a small degree gave ease to my mind. I inquired of these what was to be done with us. They gave me to understand we were to be carried to these white people's country to work for them. I was then a little revived, and thought if it were no worse than working, my situation was not so desperate. But still I feared I should be put to death, the white people looked and acted, as I thought, in so savage a manner; for I had never seen among any people such instances of brutal cruelty:

4. **windlass** (wĭnd′ləs): a device for raising something such as an anchor.

151

and this is not only shewn towards us blacks, but also to some of the whites themselves. One white man in particular I saw, when we were permitted to be on deck, flogged so unmercifully with a large rope near the foremast, that he died in consequence of it; and they tossed him over the side as they would have done a brute. This made me fear these people the more; and I expected nothing less than to be treated in the same manner. I could not help expressing my fearful apprehensions to some of my countrymen; I asked them if these people had no country, but lived in this hollow place, the ship. They told me they did not, but came from a distant one. "Then," said I, "how comes it, that in all our country we never heard of them?" They told me, because they lived so very far off. I then asked, where their women were: had they any like themselves. I was told they had. "And why," said I, "do we not see them?" They answered, because they were left behind. I asked how the vessel could go. They told me they could not tell; but that there was cloth put upon the masts by the help of the ropes I saw, and then the vessel went on; and the white men had some spell or magic they put in the water, when they liked, in order to stop the vessel. I was exceedingly amazed at this account, and really thought they were spirits. I therefore wished much to be from amongst them, for I expected they would sacrifice me; but my wishes were in vain, for we were so quartered that it was impossible for any of us to make our escape.

While we stayed on the coast I was mostly on deck; and one day, to my great astonishment, I saw one of these vessels coming in with the sails up. As soon as the whites saw it, they gave a great shout, as which we were amazed; and the more so as the vessel appeared larger by approaching nearer. At last she came to an anchor in my sight, and when the anchor was let go, I and my countrymen who saw it, were lost in astonishment to observe the vessel stop, and were now convinced it was done by magic. Soon after this the other ship got her boats out, and they came on board of us, and the people of both ships seemed very glad to see each other. Several of the strangers also shook hands with us black people, and made motions with their hands, signifying, I suppose, we were to go to their country; but we did not understand them. At last, when the ship, in which we were, had got in all her cargo, they made ready with many fearful noises, and we were all put under deck, so that we could not see how they managed the vessel.

But this disappointment was the least of my grief. The stench of the hold,[5] while we were on the coast, was so intolerably loathsome, that it was dangerous to remain there for any time, and some of us had been permitted to stay on the deck for the fresh air; but now that the whole ship's cargo were confined together, it became absolutely pestilential. The closeness of the place, and the heat of the climate, added to the number in the ship, being so crowded that each had scarcely room to turn himself, almost suffocated us. This produced copious perspirations, so that the air soon became unfit for respiration, from a variety of loathsome smells, and brought on a sickness among the slaves, of which many died, thus falling victims to the improvident avarice, as I may call it, of their purchasers. This deplorable situation was again aggravated by the galling of the chains, now become insupportable; and

5. **hold:** the interior below the decks of a ship.

the filth of necessary tubs, into which the children often fell, and were almost suffocated. The shrieks of the women, and the groans of the dying, rendered it a scene of horror almost inconceivable. Happily, perhaps, for myself, I was soon reduced so low here that it was thought necessary to keep me almost continually on deck; and from my extreme youth, I was not put in fetters. In this situation I expected every hour to share the fate of my companions, some of whom were almost daily brought upon deck at the point of death, and I began to hope that death would soon put an end to my miseries. Often did I think many of the inhabitants of the deep much more happy than myself; I envied them the freedom they enjoyed, and as often wished I could change my condition for theirs. Every circumstance I met with served only to render my state more painful, and heighten my apprehensions and my opinion of the cruelty of the whites. One day they had taken a number of fishes; and when they had killed and satisfied themselves with as many as they thought fit, to our astonishment who were on the deck, rather than give any of them to us to eat, as we expected, they tossed the remaining fish into the sea again, although we begged and prayed for some as well as we could, but in vain; and some of my countrymen, being pressed by hunger, took an opportunity, when they thought no one saw them, of trying to get a little privately; but were discovered, and the attempt procured for them some very severe floggings.

One day, when we had a smooth sea and moderate wind, two of my wearied countrymen, who were chained together, (I was near them at the time) preferring death to such a life of misery, somehow made through the nettings and jumped into the sea; immediately another quite dejected fellow, who on account of his illness was suffered to be out of irons also followed their example; and I believe many more would very soon have done the same, if they had not been prevented by the ship's crew, who were instantly alarmed. Those of us who were the most active were in a moment put down under the deck; and there was such a noise and confusion amongst the people of the ship as I never heard before, to stop her and get the boat out to go after the slaves. However, two of the wretches were drowned; but they got the other, and afterward flogged him unmercifully, for thus attempting to prefer death to slavery. In this manner we continued to undergo more hardships than I can now relate, hardships which are inseparable from this accursed trade. Many a time we were near suffocation from the want of fresh air, being deprived thereof for days together. This, and the stench of the necessary tubs, carried off many.

During our passage I first saw flying fishes, which surprised me very much: they used frequently to fly across the ship, and many of them fell on the deck. I also now first saw the use of the quadrant.[6] I had often with astonishment seen the mariners make observations with it, and I could not think what it meant. They at last took notice of my surprise: and one of them, willing to increase it, as well as to gratify my curiosity, made me one day look through it. The clouds appeared to me to be land, which disappeared as they passed along. This heightened my wonder, and I was now more persuaded than ever that I was in another world, and that every thing about me was magic. At last we came in

6. **quadrant** (kwŏd′rənt): an instrument for measuring altitudes.

The Interesting Narrative of the Life of Olaudah Equiano   153

sight of the island of Barbadoes,[7] at which the whites on board gave a great shout, and made many signs of joy to us. We did not know what to think of this, but as the vessel drew nearer we plainly saw the harbour, and other ships of different kinds and sizes; and we soon anchored amongst them off Bridge Town.[8] Many merchants and planters now came on board, though it was in the evening. They put us in separate parcels, and examined us attentively. They also made us jump, and pointed to the land, signifying we were to go there. We thought by this we should be beaten by these ugly men, as they appeared to us; and, when soon after we were all put down under the deck again, there was much dread and trembling among us, and nothing but bitter cries to be heard all the night from these apprehensions, insomuch that at last the white people got some old slaves from the land to pacify us. They told us we were not to be eaten, but to work, and were soon to go on land, where we should see many of our country people. This report eased us much; and, sure enough, soon after we landed, there came to us Africans of all languages.

We were conducted immediately to the merchant's yard, where we were all pent up together like so many sheep in a fold, without regard to sex or age. As every object was new to me, every thing I saw filled me with surprise. What struck me first was that the houses were built with bricks in stories, and were in every other respect different from those I had seen in Africa; but I was still more astonished at seeing people on horseback. I did not know what this could mean; and indeed I thought these people full of nothing but magical arts. While I was in this astonishment one of my fellow prisoners spoke to a countryman of his about the horses, who said they were the same kind they had in their country. I understood them, though they were from a distant part of Africa, and I thought it odd I had not seen any horses there; but afterwards, when I came to converse with different Africans, I found they had many horses amongst them, and much larger than those I then saw.

We were not many days in the merchants' custody before we were sold after the usual manner, which is this:—On a signal given, such as the beat of a drum, the buyers rush at once into the yard where the slaves are confined, and make choice of that parcel they like best. The noise and clamour with which this is attended, and the eagerness visible in the countenances of the buyers, serve not a little to increase the apprehensions of the terrified Africans, who may well be supposed to consider them the ministers of that destruction to which they think themselves devoted. In this manner, without scruple, are relations and friends separated, most of them never to see each other again. I remember in the vessel in which I was brought over, in the man's apartment, there were several brothers, who, in the sale, were sold in different lots; and it was very moving on this occasion to see their distress and hear their cries at parting. O, ye nominal[9] Christians! might not an African ask you, "learned you this from your God, who says unto you, Do unto all men as you would men should do unto you? Is it not enough that we are torn from our country and friends, to toil for your luxury and lust of gain? Must every tender

7. **Barbadoes** (bär-bā′dōs): Barbados, an island country in the West Indies.
8. **Bridge Town:** Bridgetown, capital of Barbados.

9. **nominal:** in name only.

feeling be likewise sacrificed to your avarice? Are the dearest friends and relations now rendered more dear by their separation from the rest of their kindred, still to be parted from each other, and thus prevented from cheering the gloom of slavery, with the small comfort of being together, and mingling their sufferings and sorrows? Why are parents to lose their children, brothers their sisters, or husbands their wives? Surely this is a new refinement in cruelty, which, while it has no advantage to atone for it, thus aggravates distress, and adds fresh horrors even to the wretchedness of slavery."

Responding to the Selection

from The Interesting Narrative of the Life of Olaudah Equiano

Identifying Facts

1. How are Equiano and his sister carried off?
2. What kind of work does Equiano do for his first master, the chieftain?
3. How is Equiano able to communicate with the different people he lives with?
4. What does he think will happen to him when he sees the boiler on board the ship?
5. Why is Equiano allowed to stay on deck during the journey?

Interpreting Meanings

1. What do you learn about Equiano's life before his capture? How does his happy childhood make the story of his enslavement even more moving?
2. Why does Equiano make a point of saying that he never met with any ill treatment from the African traders?
3. Equiano says that until he came to the sea coast, he always found somebody who understood him. How does the similarity in languages help to explain communication among the slaves after their arrival in America?
4. How were the slaves punished by the sailors? Why do you think he includes the flogging of a white man in his descriptions of "brutal cruelty"?
5. Equiano is curious about everything he sees. Why does he think the quadrant works by magic? Why is he puzzled by the people on horseback in Barbados?
6. Equiano describes a slave auction in which several brothers are sold in different lots. Why does he consider this aspect of slavery "a new refinement in cruelty"? Whom do you think Equiano is thinking of as "nominal Christians"?

Developing Sentence Sense

Analyzing a Long Sentence

Equiano tends to combine ideas into long sentences. In reading these sentences, look for relationships between the different units of thought.

> Here I first saw and tasted cocoa nuts, which I thought superior to any nuts I had ever tasted before; and the trees, which were loaded, were also interspersed among the houses, which had commodious shades adjoining, and were in the same manner as ours, the insides being neatly plastered and whitewashed.

There are three main parts to this description: the cocoa nuts, the trees, and the houses. Look at how the words *which* and *and* connect the units of thought:

Here I first saw and tasted cocoa nuts,
↑
which I thought superior to any nuts I had ever tasted before;

and the trees,
↑
which were loaded, were also interspersed among the houses,
↑
which had commodious shades adjoining, and were in the same manner as ours, the insides [of the houses] being neatly plastered and whitewashed.

Choose another long sentence in the selection and analyze its parts.

LANGUAGE WORKSHOP

LW 9 Ch 7
LW 10 Ch 7
Sentences

Writer's Journal
Writing an Autobiographical Narrative

Select an experience that brought about a change in your life and write about it. Be sure to include actions, observations, thoughts, feelings, and conversations in enough detail to allow readers to feel they are a part of your experience.

If you like, think about a time when you had to leave the comfort and security of home to go to a new place and meet strangers. How did you feel? What did you expect? Were there any surprises? If so, were they negative or positive? What did you learn from the experience? Share your writing with your classmates.

Speaking and Listening
Evaluating a Written Narrative

A **critique** is a critical examination of some work. Choose a partner. Exchange and critique your written narratives. Take turns discussing the strengths and weaknesses of your papers. At the conclusion of your discussion, be prepared to revise your narratives and submit a final draft to the teacher.

About the Author

Benjamin Banneker (1731–1806)

 When Benjamin Banneker was born, there were few free blacks in Baltimore County, Maryland. Banneker went to a one-room, interracial school run by a Quaker. He quickly showed an interest in mathematics and in mechanical things. When he was twenty-two, he constructed a clock entirely of wood, without any model except a pocket watch. This remarkable clock continued to work until the end of his life.

Banneker formed a friendship with George Ellicott, a Quaker, who lent Banneker books on mathematics and astronomy. Within a short time, Banneker was able to predict a solar eclipse. He decided to work on an almanac. In colonial times, the almanac was an important book in every household. It contained practical information about many subjects as well as proverbs and poems. In order to write an almanac, Banneker had to establish the position of the sun, moon, and planets each year. Then he could make calculations about eclipses, weather conditions, and the like. Banneker issued his almanacs from 1791 to 1802. He sent a manuscript copy of his first almanac to Thomas Jefferson, who was then Secretary of State, along with a letter that has become a classic document.

A few years earlier, in 1787, Jefferson had published his *Notes on the State of Virginia,* in which he expressed the opinion that blacks were inferior to whites in reason and in imagination. In his letter, Banneker called for the abolition of slavery and for a more enlightened attitude toward blacks.

The Granger Collection, New York

In 1791, Banneker received an appointment as a surveyor for a plot of land on the Potomac River. He helped define the boundaries and lay out the streets for what would become the District of Columbia. Banneker spent the last years of his life at his home in Maryland, where he worked on his almanacs. He continued his investigations, recording his observations of nature, mathematical puzzles, and astronomical calculations in a journal. Two days after Banneker's death, his house caught fire and the clock that he had made so many years earlier was destroyed in the flames.

Benjamin Banneker   157

Before You Read

from Letter to Thomas Jefferson

Using What You Know

Think of a time when you wished to change someone's point of view about an issue that was important to you. How did you go about trying to convince that person? What arguments did you use? What was the outcome? Share that experience with a partner.

Literary Focus: Argument

The words **argument** and **persuasion** are often used interchangeably, but there is a distinction between the two. **Persuasion** is a type of speaking or writing that is intended to make its audience accept a certain opinion, or perform some action, or do both. An **argument** consists of the reasons and evidence used to explain the speaker's or writer's opinions. Thus, a persuasive speech or essay may contain one or more arguments.

Different kinds of arguments may be used in persuasive writing. In general, a sound argument is supported by facts, logical reasoning, and other kinds of reliable evidence.

Setting a Purpose

Sidenotes have been provided with this selection to help you understand and appreciate Banneker's intent and meaning. As you read the excerpt from Banneker's letter, note how he uses facts, his own testimony, and logical reasoning to appeal to Jefferson's intellect. How does he also appeal to Jefferson's emotions?

Letter to Thomas Jefferson

Benjamin Banneker

Maryland, Baltimore County
Near Ellicotts' Lower Mills, August 19th, 1791

Thomas Jefferson, Secretary of State.

Sir:—I am fully sensible of the greatness of that freedom, which I take with you on the present occasion, a liberty which seemed to me scarcely allowable, when I reflected on that distinguished and dignified station in which you stand, and the almost general prejudice and prepossession[1] which is so prevalent in the world against those of my complexion.

Banneker is aware that his writing a letter to such an important person as Jefferson might be interpreted as boldness.

I suppose it is a truth too well attested to you, to need a proof here, that we are a race of beings who have long laboured under the abuse and censure of the world, that we have long been considered rather as brutish than human, and scarcely capable of mental endowments.

A long-standing prejudice against African Americans is that their intellectual ability is inferior to that of whites.

Sir, I hope I may safely admit, in consequence of that report which hath reached me, that you are a man far less inflexible in sentiments of this nature than many others, that you are measurably friendly and well disposed towards us, and that you are willing and ready to lend your aid and assistance to our relief, from those many distresses and numerous calamities, to which we are reduced.

Jefferson has a reputation for being fair-minded and sympathetic to the situation of African Americans.

Now, sir, if this is founded in truth, I apprehend[2] you will readily embrace every opportunity to eradicate that train of absurd and false ideas and opinions, which so generally prevails with respect to us, and that your sentiments are concurrent with mine, which are that one universal Father hath given Being to us all, and that he hath not only made us all of one flesh, but that he hath also without

Banneker asks Jefferson to help get rid of unfavorable attitudes toward African Americans. He reminds Jefferson of his own belief that all human beings have been created equal by God.

1. **prepossession:** an attitude formed beforehand; bias.
2. **apprehend:** here, believe.

partiality afforded us all the same sensations, and endued[3] us all with the same faculties,[4] and that however variable we may be in society or religion, however diversified in situation or colour, we are all of the same family, and stand in the same relation to him.

Sir, if these are sentiments of which you are fully persuaded, I hope you cannot but acknowledge, that it is the indispensable duty of those who maintain for themselves the rights of human nature, and who profess the obligations of Christianity, to extend their power and influence to the relief of every part of the human race, from whatever burden or oppression they may unjustly labour under, and this I apprehend a full conviction of the truth and obligation of these principles should lead all to.

Sir, I have long been convinced that if your love for yourselves and for those inesteemable[5] laws, which preserve to you the rights of human nature, was found on sincerity, you could not but be solicitous that every individual of whatever rank or distinction, might with you equally enjoy the blessings thereof, neither could you rest satisfied, short of the most active diffusion of your exertions in order to their promotions from any state of degradation to which the unjustifiable cruelty and barbarism of men have reduced them.

Sir, I freely and cheerfully acknowledge that I am of the African race, and in that colour which is natural to them of the deepest dye, and it is under a sense of the most profound gratitude to the Supreme Ruler of the universe that I now confess to you that I am not under that state of tyrannical thraldom[6] and inhuman captivity to which too many of my brethren are doomed; but that I have abundantly tasted of the fruition of those blessings which proceed from that free and unequalled liberty with which you are favoured and which, I hope you will willingly allow you have received from the immediate hand of that Being, from whom proceedeth every good and perfect gift.

Sir, suffer me[7] to recall to your mind that time in which the arms and tyranny of the British Crown were exerted with every powerful effort in order to reduce you to a State of Servitude, look back I entreat you on the variety of dangers to which you were exposed; reflect on that time in which every human aid appeared unavailable, and in which even hope and fortitude wore the aspect of inability to the conflict and you cannot but be led to a serious and

> Banneker says Jefferson has a duty to use his power and influence to help relieve those who suffer from oppression.

> Banneker asks for a test of Jefferson's sincerity in extending to all human beings the rights that he enjoys.

> Banneker identifies himself as a free black who has enjoyed the blessings of liberty.

> Banneker recalls the pre-Revolutionary period, when the colonists were subject to the tyranny of British rule.

3. **endued** (ĕn-dyo͞od′): endowed; provided.
4. **faculties:** powers or abilities.
5. **inesteemable:** inestimable; invaluable (archaic).
6. **thraldom** (thrôl′dəm): servitude.
7. **suffer me:** permit me.

160   BENJAMIN BANNEKER

grateful sense of your miraculous and providential preservation; you cannot but acknowledge that the present freedom and tranquility which you enjoy you have mercifully received and that it is the peculiar blessing of Heaven.

This sir, was a time in which you clearly saw into the injustice of a state of slavery and in which you had just apprehensions of the horrors of its condition, it was now, sir, that your abhorrence thereof was so excited, that you publickly held forth this true and valuable doctrine, which is worthy to be recorded and remembered in all succeeding ages. "We hold these truths to be self-evident, that all men are created equal, and that they are endowed by their creator with certain unalienable[8] rights, that among these are life, liberty and the pursuit of happiness."

He quotes from Jefferson's famous document on human rights, the Declaration of Independence.

Here, sir, was a time in which your tender feelings for yourselves had engaged you thus to declare, you were then impressed with proper ideas of the great valuation of liberty and the free possession of those blessings to which you were entitled by nature; but, sir, how pitiable is it to reflect that although you were so fully convinced of the benevolence of the Father of mankind and of his equal and impartial distribution of those rights and privileges which he had conferred upon them, that you should at the same time counteract his mercies in detaining by fraud and violence so numerous a part of my brethren under groaning captivity and cruel oppression, that you should at the same time be found guilty of that most criminal act which you professedly detested in others with respect to yourselves.

Banneker points out that Jefferson, a strong advocate for freedom and equality, is guilty of allowing the institution of slavery to continue.

Sir, I suppose that your knowledge of the situation of my brethren is too extensive to need a recital here; neither shall I presume to prescribe methods by which they may be relieved, otherwise than by recommending to you and all others to wean yourselves from those narrow prejudices which you have imbibed[9] with respect to them and as Job[10] proposed to his friends, "put your souls in their souls stead," thus shall your hearts be enlarged with kindness and benevolence towards them, and thus shall you need neither the direction of myself or others, in what manner to proceed herein.

Banneker recommends that Jefferson and others free themselves of their prejudices and view African Americans with compassion.

Benjamin Banneker

Massachusetts Historical Society

8. **unalienable** (ŭn-āl′yə-nə-bəl): not to be separated.
9. **imbibed** (ĭm-bībd′): absorbed into the mind as ideas or principles.
10. **Job** (jōb): a well-known Biblical figure who endured great suffering but never lost his faith in God.

Letter to Thomas Jefferson   161

Thomas Jefferson's reply to Banneker's letter, 1791.
Massachusetts Historical Society

Responding to the Selection

from **Letter to Thomas Jefferson** by Benjamin Banneker

Identifying Facts

1. According to Banneker, what was the general attitude toward African Americans in his time?
2. Why does Banneker believe Jefferson would be an ally to his cause?
3. Locate Banneker's references to the Declaration of Independence.
4. What does Banneker ask Jefferson to do?

Interpreting Meanings

1. Banneker opens his letter by drawing a contrast between his own position and the "distinguished and dignified station" of Jefferson, who was then Secretary of State. Why is it important for Banneker to stress the difference in their ranks? What argument does he later use to convince Jefferson that these differences should not matter?

2. What are the "absurd and false ideas and opinions" that Banneker wishes Jefferson to help wipe out? Why does he think that Jefferson would be in a position to sway public opinion?
3. What is Banneker's purpose in drawing a comparison between the tyranny of the British Crown and the enslavement of African Americans?
4. How persuasive do you think Banneker is? Where do you feel he presents his position most effectively?

Literary Elements

Understanding Argument from Analogy

One common kind of reasoning is the **argument from analogy**. An **analogy** draws a comparison between two different things by noting their points of similarity. For example, the body is often compared to a machine because there are certain resemblances in structure and function.

Argument from analogy compares two things and concludes that because certain things are apparently similar, the two things will be similar in some additional way.

In his letter, Banneker notes certain similarities between the oppression of the colonies under British rule and the "inhuman captivity" of black Americans. What points of resemblance does he find? What conclusion does he draw from this comparison?

Language and Vocabulary

Using Context Clues

Locate the following words in Banneker's letter and examine the passage in which each one appears. See if you can define each word by using context clues. Discuss your definitions with a partner and see if you agree. Then check your answers in the Glossary or in a dictionary.

prevalent (p. 159)	fruition (p. 160)
endowments (p. 159)	fortitude (p. 160)
concurrent (p. 159)	providential (p. 161)
solicitous (p. 160)	abhorrence (p. 161)
tyrannical (p. 160)	prescribe (p. 161)

Persuasive Writing

Writing a Letter to Solicit Support

Select an issue you feel strongly about. Where do you stand? What arguments would you use to influence a change in public policy? Draft a letter to a public official in which you ask for that person's support. You may wish to refer to your responses for **Using What You Know.**

Speaking and Listening

Reading a Letter Aloud

In groups of four or five, have each person read aloud the letter drafted to a public official. Each group can select the best letter to be read to the entire class.

About the Author

Phillis Wheatley (1753?–1784)

Phillis Wheatley, one of the earliest American poets and the first black writer to publish a book of poetry, was born in Africa, probably in Senegal (sĕn'ĭ-gôl'), in the early 1750s. She was kidnapped when she was only five or six years old and taken to Boston in a slave ship. In 1761 she was sold to John Wheatley, a prosperous merchant-tailor. The Wheatleys raised her as a Christian. She quickly became a favorite and was given an opportunity few slaves had: she was taught to read and write.

Phillis Wheatley wrote her first poem, "To the University of Cambridge in New England," in 1767, when she was about fourteen.

"On the Death of the Reverend Mr. George Whitefield," published in 1770, made her famous.

From her earliest years, Phillis Wheatley was physically frail. In 1773 the Wheatleys gave her her freedom and sent her to London to receive medical care. There she met Benjamin Franklin and other notable figures. She became known as the "Sable Muse." In London she published *Poems on Various Subjects, Religious and Moral.*

Phillis Wheatley returned to Boston in 1773. During the pre-Revolutionary period, she wrote poems supporting the American cause. One poem was addressed to George Washington, who had been put in command of the American armies. Washington wrote to Wheatley and invited her to visit him at the Continental Army camp.

In 1774 Mrs. Wheatley died. Within a short time the other Wheatleys died and Phillis's fortunes took a turn for the worse. She married John Peters, a free black, in 1778. The marriage was ill-fated. At one point she was forced to do washing in a lodging house while Peters sat in jail for debt. Around 1784 two of her three children died. Her own health quickly deteriorated and she died later that year, when she was about thirty.

Phillis Wheatley's poetry was written for a white audience and imitates the style of eighteenth-century English writers. Yet in several of her poems she reveals what it was like to be black and a slave. One of those poems, "On Being Brought from Africa to America," is reprinted here.

Before You Read

On Being Brought from Africa to America

Using What You Know

Recall a time when you expected the worst and things actually worked out in your favor. Using what you learned from your experience, what could you teach someone else? Jot down your responses and share them with others.

Background

Phillis Wheatley's poetry reflects her extensive reading. She acquired what was equal to a college education. She knew Christian scripture. She studied geography and astronomy. She also knew ancient history and mythology. In the eighteenth century, an educated person read the Latin classics. Wheatley studied the work of Virgil, Ovid, and Horace, great Roman writers. She also read the great English poets. She particularly admired the poetry of Alexander Pope, who had done a translation of the Greek epic the *Iliad,* by Homer. Her own verse is written in **couplets**—a form that Pope excelled in. A **couplet** is a pair of rhyming lines that generally forms a complete unit of thought. Much eighteenth-century literature is **didactic**—that is, it is intended to teach, to present a moral or religious statement.

Setting a Purpose

As you read the following poem, ask yourself what is Wheatley's message to her readers. What is her attitude toward being both black and Christian?

On Being Brought from Africa to America

Phillis Wheatley

'Twas mercy brought me from my pagan land,
Taught my benighted soul to understand
That there's a God, that there's a Saviour too:
Once I redemption neither sought nor knew.
Some view that sable race with scornful eye:
"Their colour is a diabolic dye."
Remember, Christians, Negroes black as Cain
May be refined and join the angelic strain.

Responding to the Selection

On Being Brought from Africa to America by Phillis Wheatley

Interpreting Meanings

1. What is Wheatley's attitude toward Africa and her heritage? Why does she feel that being brought to America was merciful?
2. In the Bible, Cain was the eldest son of Adam and Eve, who became jealous of his brother, Abel, and murdered him. Why does Wheatley refer to Cain in line 7?
3. What prejudices against African Americans does she protest? How does she defend her race in the last four lines of the poem?
4. What is Wheatley's message to the Christian readers of her poem?

Writing About Literature

Expressing an Opinion

At the end of Chapter 2 in his autobiography, Olaudah Equiano protests against "nominal Christians," who close their eyes to the suffering of slaves. Judging from Wheatley's poem, would she agree with Equiano's statements about Christians who do not show mercy and charity? Reread the passage in Equiano's narrative, and then write a brief essay expressing your opinion.

About the Author
Sojourner Truth (1797?–1883)

Although Sojourner Truth was illiterate all of her life, she became one of the most eloquent orators of her time. She was an important figure in the antislavery movement and in the struggle for women's rights.

The woman who became known as Sojourner Truth was born a slave in Ulster County, New York, and was called Isabella. By her own account, she bore thirteen children, most of whom were sold into slavery. After she escaped to freedom in 1827, she took her last name, Van Wagener, from the family that sheltered her. She had her youngest son and daughter with her when she took work as a household servant in New York City around 1829. Here she came under the influence of an evangelical preacher. She began to experience mystical visions. In one of these visions, she received her new name, "Sojourner Truth." Her mission thereafter was to travel throughout the country, determined to speak the truth.

During her travels in Massachusetts, Sojourner Truth met George W. Benson, who was related to the well-known newspaper editor William Lloyd Garrison, a leader in the antislavery movement. She became an ardent abolitionist and toured the West, moving audiences with her speeches and gospel songs. She was sought after as a speaker at many meetings, but she also attended many meetings where she had not been asked to participate, often interrupting the proceedings to speak out. In 1850, a book about her life appeared: *The Narrative of Sojourner Truth,* an autobiography that was written

down by Olive Gilbert. The sales provided money for her travels.

In 1851, a women's rights convention was held in Akron, Ohio. Many members of the clergy were opposed to women's rights. Sojourner Truth, who had not been invited, suddenly appeared. During the second day of the convention, various speakers argued for the superior rights and principles of men, using the Bible to defend their position. Then Sojourner Truth arose and walked to the platform, where she addressed the group. The famous speech she delivered, "Ain't I a Woman?," is reprinted here.

During the postwar period, Sojourner Truth became active in the cause of women's suffrage. She continued to lecture until the end of her life. She died at her home in Battle Creek, Michigan.

Sojourner Truth 167

Before You Read

Ain't I a Woman?

Using What You Know _____

Consider the position of women in this country in the nineteenth century. What rights did they have to property? to education? to the vote? Can you explain why many people who were active in the antislavery movement would be active in the crusade for women's rights?

Background _____

Women's rights was an unpopular issue in 1851, when Sojourner Truth attended the convention held in Akron, Ohio. One of the speakers argued that men were entitled to superior rights and privileges because they had superior intellects. Another said that if God had wanted women to have equality, he would have made that clear through Jesus Christ. A third speaker pointed to the trouble that had been caused by Eve. In her speech, which was delivered without any preparation, Sojourner Truth answered each of these arguments.

Literary Focus: Aphorism _____

An **aphorism** (ăf'ə-rĭz'əm) is a brief, easily remembered statement expressing some wise or clever observation about life. One of Benjamin Franklin's well-known aphorisms is, "If you would know the value of money, try to borrow some." Speakers often use aphorisms to emphasize a point or to summarize an argument.

Setting a Purpose _____

As you read, note how Sojourner Truth makes use of logic and humor to deflate the arguments of men's superiority. How does she use aphorism? What other persuasive techniques do you recognize?

Ain't I a Woman?

Sojourner Truth

Well, children, where there is so much racket there must be something out of kilter. I think that 'twixt the negroes of the South and the women at the North, all talking about rights, the white men will be in a fix pretty soon. But what's all this here talking about?

That man over there says women need to be helped into carriages, and lifted over ditches, and to have the best place everywhere. Nobody ever helps me into carriages, or over mud-puddles, or gives me any best place. And ain't I a woman? Look at me! Look at my arm! I have ploughed and planted, and gathered into barns, and no man could head me! And ain't I a woman? I could work as much and eat as much as a man—when I could get it—and bear the lash as well! And ain't I a woman? I have borne thirteen children, and seen most sold off to slavery, and when I cried out with my mother's grief, none but Jesus heard me! And ain't I a woman?

Then they talk about this thing in the head; what's this they call it? [Intellect, someone whispers.] That's it, honey. What's that got to do with women's rights or negro's rights? If my cup won't hold but a pint, and yours holds a quart, wouldn't you be mean not to let me have my little half-measure full?

Then that little man in black there, he says women can't have as much rights as men, 'cause Christ wasn't a woman! Where did your Christ come from? Where did your Christ come from? From God and a woman! Man had nothing to do with Him.

If the first woman God ever made was strong enough to turn the world upside down all alone, these women together ought to be able to turn it back, and get it right side up again! And now they is asking to do it, the men better let them.

Obliged to you for hearing me, and now old Sojourner ain't got nothing more to say.

Responding to the Selection

Ain't I a Woman? by Sojourner Truth

Interpreting Meanings

1. Sojourner Truth's first point is directed against the statement that women need to be treated with special consideration. How does she expose the hypocrisy of this position? Which of her arguments do you consider most effective?
2. What **aphorism** does Sojourner Truth use to refute the argument about intellect? Why does she think that the matter of intellect is not relevant?
3. Where in the speech does Sojourner Truth use humor to undercut the arguments for men's superiority?
4. One of the speakers had commented that Eve, the first woman, brought pain and suffering into the world. How does Sojourner Truth overturn this argument?

Speaking and Listening

Interpreting a Speech

Plan to deliver Sojourner Truth's speech to an audience. Study the speech to determine the tone of each part. Where will you indicate humor? Where will you indicate indignation or anger? Remember that this speech was composed **impromptu** (without preparation), in response to other speakers at the convention. How can you make your own delivery sound spontaneous? If you wish, record the speech and have a partner listen with you to help you with your presentation.

Sojourner Truth and Abraham Lincoln.
The Schomburg Center for Research in Black Culture/New York Public Library

About the Author
Frederick Douglass (1818–1895)

 Frederick Douglass, who became an orator, writer, statesman, and diplomat, began life as a slave on a Maryland plantation. While he was still a baby, he was separated from his mother. He never knew his exact age. His strength of character surfaced early. Though he was denied a formal education, Douglass taught himself to read and write. In 1838 he escaped to New York and then to New Bedford, Massachusetts.

In 1841 Douglass spoke at an abolitionist meeting in Massachusetts. His gifts as an orator were recognized immediately. One historian has written, "He was endowed with the physical attributes of an orator: a magnificent, tall body, a head crowned with a mass of hair, deep-set, flashing eyes, a firm chin, and a rich, melodious voice." In 1845 he went abroad, where he helped win British support for the abolition of slavery in America. After he returned to the United States in 1847, Douglass worked for the Underground Railroad, helping runaway slaves escape to the North. He began publishing the *North Star,* which became the most influential black newspaper of its time.

During the Civil War, he helped raise black troops for the Union cause, and later in life he was appointed American Consul General to Haiti.

Douglass worked tirelessly for the betterment of black Americans. He believed that education and civil rights were the keys to "the treasures of freedom."

Douglass's critics protested that a man of such eloquence could not possibly have

National Portrait Gallery, Smithsonian Institution

been a slave. He responded with the *Narrative of the Life of Frederick Douglass, an American Slave* (1845), a highly acclaimed autobiography, which showed his detractors that he had in fact endured the hardships of slavery, survived, and triumphed.

Douglass wrote three accounts of his life. The *Narrative* told the story of his life from early childhood until he escaped from bondage. He published an enlarged version of his autobiography called *My Bondage and My Freedom* in 1855, which included his achievements after joining the abolitionists in 1841. During his sixties, he brought out *Life and Times of Frederick Douglass* (1881), which added the events of his career before and after the Civil War. In addition to these works, he produced editorials, speeches, and orations.

Frederick Douglass 171

Before You Read

from Narrative of the Life of Frederick Douglass, an American Slave

Using What You Know _____

Think of an experience that was a "turning point" in your life, some event or series of events that brought about an important change. Briefly recall in writing what happened. Was there some crucial decision you had to make? What did you finally decide to do? How did you come to that conclusion? What was the outcome? Share your writing with a partner.

Literary Focus: Conflict _____

Conflict is a struggle between opposing forces or points of view or individuals. Conflict can be **internal** or **external**. A conflict that takes place within an individual's own mind is an **internal conflict**. **External conflict** can take one of these forms:

1. A person against another person
2. A person against some element of society—its laws or traditions
3. A person against some natural force—an animal or some disaster such as a flood or fire
4. A person against fate or some uncontrollable power

There may be more than one kind of conflict in a narrative.

Setting a Purpose _____

As you read, determine why Douglass considered this episode a "turning point." What conflicts did he experience? How did this experience change his life?

Narrative of the Life of Frederick Douglass, An American Slave

Frederick Douglass

I have already intimated that my condition was much worse, during the first six months of my stay at Mr. Covey's,[1] than in the last six. The circumstances leading to the change in Mr. Covey's course toward me form an epoch in my humble history. You have seen how a man was made a slave; you shall see how a slave was made a man. On one of the hottest days of the month of August, 1833, Bill Smith, William Hughes, a slave named Eli, and myself, were engaged in fanning wheat. Hughes was clearing the fanned wheat from before the fan. Eli was turning, Smith was feeding, and I was carrying wheat to the fan. The work was simple, requiring strength rather than intellect; yet, to one entirely unused to such work, it came very hard. About three o'clock of that day, I broke down; my strength failed me; I was seized with a violent aching of the head, attended with extreme dizziness; I trembled in every limb. Finding what was coming, I nerved myself up, feeling it would never do to stop work. I stood as long as I could stagger to the hopper with grain. When I could stand no longer, I fell, and felt as if held down by an immense weight. The fan of course stopped; every one had his own work to do; and no one could do the work of the other, and have his own go on at the same time.

Mr. Covey was at the house, about one hundred yards from the treading-yard where we were fanning. On hearing the fan stop, he left immediately, and came to the spot where we were. He hastily inquired what the matter was. Bill answered that I was sick, and there was no one to bring wheat to the fan. I had by this time crawled away under the side of the post and rail-fence by which the yard was enclosed, hoping to find relief by getting out of the sun. He then asked where I was. He was told by one of the hands. He came to the spot, and, after looking at me awhile, asked me what was the matter. I told him as well as I could, for I scarce had strength to speak. He then gave me a savage kick in the side, and told me to get up. I tried to do so,

1. **stay at Mr. Covey's:** In 1833 Douglass was hired out as a field hand to a man named Edward Covey, who had a reputation for breaking slaves.

Douglass Flogged by Covey, *engraving from an almanac.*
William Loren Katz

but fell back in the attempt. He gave me another kick, and again told me to rise. I again tried, and succeeded in gaining my feet; but, stooping to get the tub with which I was feeding the fan, I again staggered and fell. While down in this situation, Mr. Covey took up the hickory slat with which Hughes had been striking off the half-bushel measure, and with it gave me a heavy blow upon the head, making a large wound, and the blood ran freely; and with this again told me to get up. I made no effort to comply, having now made up my mind to let him do his worst. In a short time after receiving this blow, my head grew better. Mr. Covey had now left me to my fate. At this moment I resolved, for the first time, to go to my master,[2] enter a complaint, and ask his protection. In order to do this, I must that afternoon walk seven miles; and this, under the circumstances, was truly a severe undertaking. I was exceedingly feeble; made so as much by the kicks and blows which I received, as by the severe fit of sickness to which I had been subjected. I, however, watched my chance, while Covey was looking in an opposite direction, and started for St. Michael's.[3] I succeeded in getting a considerable distance on my way to the woods, when Covey discovered me, and called after me to come back, threatening what he would do if I did not come. I disregarded both his calls and his threats, and made my way to the woods as fast as my feeble state would allow; and thinking I might be overhauled by him if I kept the road, I walked through the woods, keeping far enough from the road to avoid detection, and near enough to prevent losing my way. I had not gone far before my little strength again failed me. I could go no farther. I fell down, and lay for a considerable time. The blood was yet oozing from the wound on my head. For a time I thought I should bleed to death; and think now that I should have done so, but that the blood so matted my hair as to stop the wound. After lying there about three quarters of an hour, I nerved myself up again, and started on my way, through bogs and briers, barefooted and bareheaded, tearing my feet sometimes at nearly every step; and after a journey of about seven miles, occupying some five hours to perform it, I arrived at master's store. I then presented an appearance enough to affect any but a heart of iron. From the crown of my head to my feet, I was covered with blood. My hair was all clotted with dust and blood; my shirt was stiff with blood. My legs and feet were torn in sundry places with briers and thorns, and were also covered with blood. I suppose I looked like a

2. **my master:** Thomas Auld, son-in-law of Douglass's first master.

3. **St. Michael's:** in Talbot County, Maryland.

man who had escaped a den of wild beasts, and barely escaped them. In this state I appeared before my master, humbly entreating him to interpose his authority for my protection. I told him all the circumstances as well as I could, and it seemed, as I spoke, at times to affect him. He would then walk the floor, and seek to justify Covey by saying he expected I deserved it. He asked me what I wanted. I told him, to let me get a new home; that as sure as I lived with Mr. Covey again, I should live with but to die with him; that Covey would surely kill me; he was in a fair way for it. Master Thomas ridiculed the idea that there was any danger of Mr. Covey's killing me, and said that he knew Mr. Covey; that he was a good man, and that he could not think of taking me from him; that, should he do so, he would lose the whole year's wages; that I belonged to Mr. Covey for one year, and that I must go back to him, come what might; and that I must not trouble him with any more stories, or that he would himself *get hold of me*. After threatening me thus, he gave me a very large dose of salts, telling me that I might remain in St. Michael's that night, (it being quite late,) but that I must be off back to Mr. Covey's early in the morning; and that if I did not, he would *get hold of me*, which meant that he would whip me. I remained all night, and, according to his orders, I started off to Covey's in the morning, (Saturday morning,) wearied in body and broken in spirit. I got no supper that night, or breakfast that morning. I reached Covey's about nine o'clock; and just as I was getting over the fence that divided Mrs. Kemp's fields from ours, out ran Covey with his cowskin, to give me another whipping. Before he could reach me, I succeeded in getting to the cornfield; and as the corn was very high, it afforded me the means

of hiding. He seemed very angry, and searched for me a long time. My behavior was altogether unaccountable. He finally gave up the chase, thinking, I suppose, that I must come home for something to eat; he would give himself no further trouble in looking for me. I spent that day mostly in the woods, having the alternative before me—to go home and be whipped to death, or stay in the woods and be starved to death. That night, I fell in with Sandy Jenkins, a slave with whom I was somewhat acquainted. Sandy had a free wife who lived about four miles from Mr. Covey's; and it being Saturday, he was on his way to see her. I told him my circumstances, and he very kindly invited me to go home with him. I went home with him, and talked this whole matter over, and got his advice as to what course it was best for me to pursue. I found Sandy an old adviser. He told me, with great solemnity, I must go back to Covey; but that before I went, I must go with him into another part of the woods, where there was a certain *root*, which, if I would take some of it with me, carrying it *always on my right side*, would render it impossible for Mr. Covey, or any other white man, to whip me. He said he had carried it for years; and since he had done so, he had never received a blow, and never expected to while he carried it. I at first rejected the idea, that the simple carrying of a root in my pocket would have any such effect as he had said, and was not disposed to take it; but Sandy impressed the necessity with much earnestness, telling me it could do no harm, if it did no good. To please him, I at length took the root, and, according to his direction, carried it upon my right side. This was Sunday morning. I immediately started for home; and upon entering the yard gate, out came Mr. Covey on his way to meeting.

He spoke to me very kindly, bade me drive the pigs from a lot near by, and passed on towards the church. Now, this singular conduct of Mr. Covey really made me begin to think that there was something in the *root* which Sandy had given me; and had it been on any other day than Sunday, I could have attributed the conduct to no other cause than the influence of that root; and, as it was, I was half inclined to think the *root* to be something more than I at first had taken it to be. All went well till Monday morning. On this morning, the virtue of the *root* was fully tested. Long before daylight, I was called to go and rub, curry, and feed, the horses. I obeyed, and was glad to obey. But whilst thus engaged, whilst in the act of throwing down some blades from the loft, Mr. Covey entered the stable with a long rope; and just as I was half out of the loft, he caught hold of my legs, and was about tying me. As soon as I found what he was up to, I gave a sudden spring, and as I did so, he holding to my legs, I was brought sprawling on the stable floor. Mr. Covey seemed now to think he had me, and could do what he pleased; but at this moment—from whence came the spirit I don't know—I resolved to fight; and, suiting my action to the resolution, I seized Covey hard by the throat; and as I did so, I rose. He held on to me, and I to him. My resistance was so entirely unexpected, that Covey seemed taken all aback. He trembled like a leaf. This gave me assurance, and I held him uneasy, causing the blood to run where I touched him with the ends of my fingers. Mr. Covey soon called out to Hughes for help. Hughes came, and, while Covey held me, attempted to tie my right hand. While he was in the act of doing so, I watched my chance, and gave him a heavy kick close under the ribs. This kick fairly sickened

Hughes, so that he left me in the hands of Mr. Covey. This kick had the effect of not only weakening Hughes, but Covey also. When he saw Hughes bending over with pain, his courage quailed. He asked me if I meant to persist in my resistance. I told him I did, come what might; that he had used me like a brute for six months, and that I was determined to be used so no longer. With that, he strove to drag me to a stick that was lying just out of the stable door. He meant to knock me down. But just as he was leaning over to get the stick, I seized him with both hands by his collar, and brought him by a sudden snatch to the ground. By this time, Bill came. Covey called upon him for assistance. Bill wanted to know what he could do. Covey said, "Take hold of him, take hold of him!" Bill said his master hired him out to work, and not to help whip me; so he left Covey and myself to fight our own battle out. We were at it for nearly two hours. Covey at length let me go, puffing and blowing at a great rate, saying that if I had not resisted, he would not have whipped me half so much. The truth was, that he had not whipped me at all. I considered him as getting entirely the worst end of the bargain; for he had drawn no blood from me, but I had from him. The whole six months afterwards, that I spent with Mr. Covey, he never laid the weight of his finger upon me in anger. He would occasionally say, he didn't want to get hold of me again. "No," thought I, "you need not; for you will come off worse than you did before."

This battle with Mr. Covey was the turning-point in my career as a slave. It rekindled the few expiring embers of freedom, and revived within me a sense of my own manhood. It recalled the departed self-confidence, and inspired me again with a determination to be free. The gratification afforded by the triumph was a full compensation for whatever else might follow, even death itself. He only can understand the deep satisfaction which I experienced, who has himself repelled by force the bloody arm of slavery. I felt as I never felt before. It was a glorious resurrection, from the tomb of slavery, to the heaven of freedom. My long-crushed spirit rose, cowardice departed, bold defiance took its place; and I now resolved that, however long I might remain a slave in form, the day had passed forever when I could be a slave in fact. I did not hesitate to let it be known of me, that the white man who expected to succeed in whipping, must also succeed in killing me.

From this time I was never again what might be called fairly whipped, though I remained a slave four years afterwards. I had several fights, but was never whipped.

It was for a long time a matter of surprise to me why Mr. Covey did not immediately have me taken by the constable to the whipping post, and there regularly whipped for the crime of raising my hand against a white man in defence of myself. And the only explanation I can now think of does not entirely satisfy me; but such as it is, I will give it. Mr. Covey enjoyed the most unbounded reputation for being a first-rate overseer and negro-breaker. It was of considerable importance to him. That reputation was at stake; and had he sent me—a boy about sixteen years old—to the public whipping-post, his reputation would have been lost; so, to save his reputation, he suffered me to go unpunished.

Frederick Douglass speaking at an abolitionist meeting in Tremont Temple, December 3, 1860. The meeting was broken up by a Boston mob and the police.
The Granger Collection, New York

Responding to the Selection

from **Narrative of the Life of Frederick Douglass, an American Slave**

Identifying Facts

1. Why was Douglass working for Covey?
2. Why was he unable to complete his work in fanning the wheat?
3. What was his master's reaction to his complaint?
4. What advice did Sandy give Douglass?
5. Douglass was not punished for beating Covey. What explanation does he give?

Interpreting Meanings

1. Why does Douglass consider his experience with Covey to be an *epoch,* or memorable event, in his history?
2. Sandy gives Douglass a root to carry in his pocket. How does this episode **foreshadow,** or hint at, what is to come?
3. Trace the stages of the **conflict** between Douglass and Covey. What events build toward the **climax** in the stable, where Douglass fights Covey?
4. At what point is there a change in Douglass's attitude? What do you think is chiefly responsible for the change?
5. Douglass calls the battle with Covey the turning point in his career as a slave. Explain what he means.
6. Toward the end of the episode, Douglass says, "I now resolved that, however long I might remain a slave in form, the day had passed forever when I could be a slave in fact." How do you interpret the distinction between "form" and "fact"?
7. What impression do you form of Douglass from this selection? Despite the terrible cruelty that he suffered, did you find his account of "how a slave was made a man" uplifting?

Literary Elements

Identifying Conflicts

The major conflict in Douglass's narrative is the **external conflict** between Douglass and Covey, which is resolved when Covey is beaten. What other conflicts occur in the narrative? How are these other conflicts related to the major conflict? Is Douglass's conflict with Covey simply a struggle between two individuals, or does the struggle have some greater significance? Support your conclusions with evidence from the selection. Share your findings with your classmates.

Language and Vocabulary

Recognizing Parallelism in Style

In addition to being a great champion of human rights, Douglass was an impressive writer. One technique he uses with particular effectiveness in the *Narrative* is **parallelism.**

The term **parallelism** refers to the use of phrases, clauses, or sentences that are similar in structure or in meaning. When parallelism is used skillfully, it has great emotional impact. The lines and thoughts seem to balance one another. For example, note how the two clauses in this sentence illustrate parallel structure. What is inverted in the second clause?

> You have seen how a man was made a slave; you shall see how a slave was made a man.

Find other examples of parallelism in the selection. Compare your findings with those of other members in the class.

Narrative Writing

Telling About a Turning Point

Douglass calls his conflict with Covey a "turning point" that changed him forever. Douglass not only relates the events but also interprets their significance for us. He lets us know what happened to him, what he thought, and how he felt.

Consider some event in your own life that might be termed a "turning point." Follow this plan in developing your narrative. Use the form provided by your teacher or a separate sheet of paper for your notes.

Prewriting Strategies

1. Identify the episode and state how it caused some change in your circumstances, your thinking, or your feelings.

2. List the series of events in **chronological order,** or the order in which they happened. Use the **5W-How?** questions (**Who? What? When? Where? Why?** and **How?**)

3. Add descriptive details to help re-create the events. Choose words that will bring characters and actions to life.

Precise Verbs	Specific Modifiers
_____	_____
_____	_____

Writing

Begin with a sentence that will capture your reader's attention. In telling the story, include only those events that relate to the main action. Vary sentences so that they don't all begin the same way. Use transitions (*then, next, at a later time*) to connect your ideas.

Consult the **Writer's Guide** on pages 65–66 for evaluating, revising, and proofreading your paper.

Creative Writing

Writing a Play or Poem

Frederick Douglass was "transformed." Prepare to "transform" his story from an autobiography to another form of literature. Rewrite this episode from the *Narrative* as a play or poem.

Critical Thinking

Investigating a Subject

In his *Narrative,* Frederick Douglass tells how he resisted Covey's attempts to break his spirit by fighting back. Was Douglass's resistance an unusual action or was resistance to slavery widespread in the period before the Civil War? How would you go about getting information to answer this question?

You first need to determine how relevant material might be indexed in the library's catalog or in reference books. For example, the information you are seeking might be available under any of these general topics:

Slavery in the United States
Runaway Slaves
Underground Railroad
Revolts of Slaves

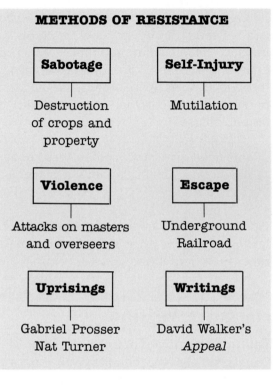

METHODS OF RESISTANCE

Sabotage
Destruction of crops and property

Self-Injury
Mutilation

Violence
Attacks on masters and overseers

Escape
Underground Railroad

Uprisings
Gabriel Prosser
Nat Turner

Writings
David Walker's *Appeal*

What other topics can you add to this list?

Note those titles that seem clearly related to the subject of your investigation. Often, a chapter in a trustworthy history book or other reference work can be a good guide to further investigation. In *From Slavery to Freedom,* John Hope Franklin and Alfred A. Moss, Jr., organize some pertinent information under the heading "The Slave's Reaction to Bondage."

During the early stages of your investigation, you might find it helpful to organize the material into areas for further study, such as these:

Many other items can be added to this chart.

As you read your sources, take notes in your own words. When you are satisfied that you have a good grasp of your subject, share your findings with other members of the class. Some students may be interested in pursuing their investigations into other places in the Western Hemisphere where the institution of slavery existed: Haiti, Jamaica, Brazil, for example.

African American Folk Tales

Storytelling is an important part of every culture and as natural as life itself. Long before there was writing, stories were passed on orally from one storyteller to another. The term **folklore** is used for the traditional songs, myths, legends, fables, folk tales, proverbs, and riddles composed by unknown authors and passed down from generation to generation. Folklore reveals a great deal about the culture that created it.

A rich tradition of storytelling existed for centuries in West Africa. This tradition, which the slaves brought with them, became the basis for storytelling on the American continent. Sharing a common cultural heritage from Africa, the slaves sought to make sense of their new environment and to find expression for their own conception of life and its meaning.

One kind of folk tale is the animal tale, also called the **beast fable,** in which human characteristics are attributed to animals. Brer Rabbit is the hero of many African American folk tales. (*Brer,* used before a name, means "brother.") He is cunning and uses his wits in order to get the better of stronger animals. He does not live by the slave master's code of right and wrong, but by an outlaw code. As one scholar has pointed out, "A man on short rations is bound to steal chickens. The only moral code he can afford to entertain is one that helps him to survive." One of the most famous Brer Rabbit tales is the story of the briar patch. Brer Rabbit is trapped by Brer Fox, who considers different ways of killing his captive: burning, hanging, drowning, and skinning him. Brer Rabbit outwits Brer Fox by saying, whatever you do, don't throw me in the briar patch. Naturally Brer Fox does exactly that and Brer Rabbit gains his freedom, shouting that he was born and bred in a briar patch.

Another kind of tale centers on the **trickster,** who is generally a slave called John or Jack. He is often caught by Ole Master in some lie or in some wrongdoing, and he tries to get out of trouble by outsmarting his owner. Sometimes he manages to avoid a whipping and even to gain his freedom. These tales often poke fun at the storytellers as well as at the slave masters.

Stories of exaggeration, sometimes called "lies," give humorous explanations for the beginnings of things, for example, "why" the possum has no hair on his tail. Zora Neale Hurston later collected a number of these "lies" and published them in *Mules and Men* (1935).

There are a number of other kinds of folk tales, including conjure stories, preacher tales, and legends of various kinds.

The importance of the oral tradition to the survival of African American culture cannot be overestimated. The slaves were forbidden by law to learn how to read and write. Therefore, their culture had to be shared and preserved through word of mouth. The art of storytelling that evolved influenced the literature that was to come after emancipation and continues to influence literature today.

Before You Read

Folk Tales from **Mules and Men**

Using What You Know

Think of some of the great storytellers you know—entertainers, teachers, friends, preachers, relatives—who can make a story come to life when they perform it for an audience. What are the characteristics that good storytellers share? What effects can storytellers get from speaking that they cannot get from writing? Compare your responses with those of your classmates.

Background

Zora Neale Hurston became interested in folk traditions when she was studying anthropology in college. She received a fellowship to study the oral traditions in her native state of Florida. She made field trips and collected oral narratives, which she later published in *Mules and Men* (1935). A number of the tales she collected date back to slavery times. As you will see, Hurston carefully represents the speech patterns of her tale-tellers.

Setting a Purpose

Although most tales have been recorded by folklorists and now appear in written form, the reader needs to remember that they were created for speaking and that the storyteller performed them face to face with an audience. As you read, note how the tales catch the style of oral telling.

Mules and Men

Zora Neale Hurston

How Jack O'Lanterns Came to Be

It was slavery time, Zora, when Big Sixteen was a man. They called 'im Sixteen 'cause dat was de number of de shoe he wore. He was big and strong and Ole Massa looked to him to do everything.

One day Ole Massa said, "Big Sixteen, Ah b'lieve Ah want you to move dem sills Ah had hewed out down in de swamp."

"I yassuh, Massa."

Big Sixteen went down in de swamp and picked up dem 12 × 12's and brought 'em on up to de house and stack 'em. No one man ain't never toted a 12 × 12 befo' nor since.

So Ole Massa said one day, "Go fetch in de mules. Ah want to look 'em over."

Big Sixteen went on down to de pasture and caught dem mules by de bridle but they was contrary and balky and he tore de bridles to pieces pullin' on 'em, so he picked one of 'em up under each arm and brought 'em up to Old Massa.

He says, "Big Sixteen, if you kin tote a pair of balky mules, you kin do anything. You kin ketch de Devil."

"Yassuh, Ah kin, if you git me a nine-pound hammer and a pick and shovel!"

Ole Massa got Sixteen de things he ast for and tole 'im to go ahead and bring him de Devil.

Big Sixteen went out in front of de house and went to diggin'. He was diggin' nearly a month befo' he got where he wanted. Then he took his hammer and went and knocked on de Devil's door. Devil answered de door hisself.

"Who dat out dere?"

"It's Big Sixteen."

"What you want?"

"Wanta have a word wid you for a minute."

Soon as de Devil poked his head out de door, Sixteen lammed him over de head wid dat hammer and picked 'im up and carried 'im back to Old Massa.

Ole Massa looked at de dead Devil and hollered, "Take dat ugly thing 'way from here, quick! Ah didn't think you'd ketch de Devil sho 'nuff."

So Sixteen picked up de Devil and throwed 'im back down de hole.

Way after while, Big Sixteen died and went up to Heben. But Peter looked at him and tole 'im to g'wan 'way from dere. He was too powerful. He might git outa order and there wouldn't be nobody to handle 'im. But he had to go somewhere so he went on to hell.

Soon as he got to de gate de Devil's children was playin' in de yard and they seen 'im and run to de house, says, "Mama, mama! Dat man's out dere kilt papa!"

So she called 'im in de house and shet de door. When Sixteen got dere she handed 'im a li'l piece of fire and said, "You ain't comin' in here. Here, take dis hot coal and g'wan off and start you a hell uh yo' own."

So when you see a Jack O'Lantern in de woods at night you know it's Big Sixteen wid his piece of fire lookin' for a place to go.

How the Snake Got Poison

Well, when God made de snake he put him in de bushes to ornament de ground. But things didn't suit de snake so one day he got on de ladder and went up to see God.

"Good mawnin', God."

"How do you do, Snake?"

"Ah ain't so many, God, you put me down there on my belly in de dust and everything trods upon me and kills off my generations. Ah ain't got no kind of protection at all."

God looked off towards immensity and thought about de subject for awhile, then he said, "Ah didn't mean for nothin' to be stompin' you snakes lak dat. You got to have some kind of a protection. Here, take dis poison and put it in yo' mouf and when they tromps on you, protect yo' self."

So de snake took de poison in his mouf and went on back.

So after awhile all de other varmints went up to God.

"Good evenin', God."

"How you makin' it, varmints?"

"God, please do somethin' 'bout dat snake. He's layin' in de bushes there wid poison in his mouf and he's strikin' everything dat shakes de bush. He's killin' up our genera-

tions. Wese skeered to walk de earth."

So God sent for de snake and tole him:

"Snake, when Ah give you dat poison, Ah didn't mean for you to be hittin' and killin' everything dat shake de bush. I give you dat poison and tole you to protect yo'self when they tromples on you. But you killin' everything dat moves. Ah didn't mean for you to do dat."

De snake say, "Lawd, you know Ah'm down here in de dust. Ah ain't got no claws to fight wid, and Ah ain't got no feets to git me out de way. All Ah kin see is feets comin' to tromple me. Ah can't tell who my enemy is and who is my friend. You gimme dis protection in my mouf and Ah uses it."

God thought it over for a while then he says:

"Well, snake, I don't want yo' generations all stomped out and I don't want you killin' everything else dat moves. Here take dis bell and tie it to yo' tail. When you hear feets comin' you ring yo' bell and if it's yo' friend, he'll be keerful. If it's yo' enemy, it's you and him."

So dat's how de snake got his poison and dat's how come he got rattles.

Biddy, biddy, bend my story is end.

Turn loose de rooster and hold de hen.

How the Possum Lost the Hair off His Tail

Yes, he did have hair on his tail one time. Yes, indeed. De possum had a bushy tail wid long silk hair on it. Why, it useter be one of de prettiest sights you ever seen. De possum struttin' 'round wid his great big ole plumey tail. Dat was 'way back in de olden times before de big flood.

But de possum was lazy—jus' like he is

today. He sleep too much. You see Ole Nora[1] had a son named Ham and he loved to be playin' music all de time. He had a banjo and a fiddle and maybe a guitar too. But de rain come up so sudden he didn't have time to put 'em on de ark. So when rain kept comin' down he fretted a lot 'cause he didn't have nothin' to play. So he found a ole cigar box and made hisself a banjo, but he didn't have no strings for it. So he seen de possum stretched out sleeping wid his tail all spread 'round. So Ham slipped up and shaved de possum's tail and made de strings for his banjo out de hairs. When dat possum woke up from his nap, Ham was playin' his tail hairs down to de bricks and dat's why de possum ain't got no hair on his tail today. Losin' his pretty tail sorta broke de possum's spirit too. He ain't never been de same since. Dat's how come he always actin' shame-faced. He know his tail ain't whut it useter be; and de possum feel mighty bad about it.

1. **Old Nora:** Noah was ordered to build an ark so that he and his family might survive the flood (Genesis 6–9).

How the 'Gator Got Black

Ah'm tellin' dis lie on de 'gator. Well, de 'gator was a pretty white varmint wid coal black eyes. He useter swim in de water, but he never did bog up in de mud lak he do now. When he come out de water he useter lay up on de clean grass so he wouldn't dirty hisself all up.

So one day he was layin' up on de grass in a marsh sunnin' hisself and sleepin' when Brer Rabbit come bustin' cross de marsh and run right over Brer 'Gator before he stopped. Brer 'Gator woke up and seen who it was trompin' all over him and trackin' up his pretty white hide. So he seen Brer Rabbit, so he ast him, "Brer Rabbit, what you mean by runnin' all cross me and messin' up my clothes lak dis?"

Brer Rabbit was up behind a clump of bushes peerin' out to see what was after him. So he tole de 'gator, says: "Ah ain't got time to see what Ah'm runnin' over nor under. Ah got trouble behind me."

'Gator ast, "Whut is trouble? Ah ain't never heard tell of dat befo'."

Brer Rabbit says, "You ain't never heard tell of trouble?"

Brer 'Gator tole him, "No."

Rabbit says: "All right, you jus' stay right where you at and Ah'll show you whut trouble is."

He peered 'round to see if de coast was clear and loped off, and Brer 'Gator washed Brer Rabbit's foot tracks off his hide and went on back to sleep agin.

Brer Rabbit went on off and lit him a li'dard knot[1] and come on back. He set dat marsh afire on every side. All around Brer 'Gator de fire was burnin' in flames of fire. De 'gator woke up and pitched out to run, but every which a way he run de fire met him.

He seen Brer Rabbit sittin' up on de high ground jus' killin' hisself laughin'. So he hollered and ast him:

"Brer Rabbit, whut's all dis goin' on?"

"Dat's trouble, Brer 'Gator, dat's trouble youse in."

De 'gator run from side to side, round and round. Way after while he broke thru and hit de water "ker ploogum!" He got all cooled off but he had done got smoked all up befo' he got to de water, and his eyes is all red from de smoke. And dat's how come a 'gator is black today—cause de rabbit took advantage of him lak dat.

1. **li'dard knot:** a kind of wood used in torches.

Responding to the Selections

Folk Tales from **Mules and Men**

Indentifying Facts

1. How does Big Sixteen get his name?
2. Why does the snake ask for protection?
3. How does the possum lose the hair on his tail?
4. What does Brer Rabbit teach Brer 'Gator?

Interpreting Meanings

1. The story of Big Sixteen is one of the stories told in a "lying contest," where the storyteller uses humorous exaggeration to explain the origins of things. What does Big Sixteen have in common with other folk heroes?
2. The storyteller says that God put the snake in the bushes to "ornament" the ground. What does this word reveal about the speaker's tone? Can you find other touches of sly humor in the tales?
3. Brer Rabbit is often pictured as a trickster. How does he fool Brer 'Gator? Why do you think his qualities of deceit and cunning made Brer Rabbit a popular hero?

Creative Writing

Writing an Original Tale

Create your own fanciful story about how something came to be. Brainstorm a list of everyday objects or characteristics; for example, how the cat got whiskers, how the peacock got his tail, why the kangaroo has a pouch, why the earth has only one moon. Select one or two of the items and then invent characters and events. If you wish, tell your own version of one of Hurston's tales.

You might prefer to write a trickster tale, telling how the tables were turned on someone or how someone was outsmarted.

In groups of four or five, tell your tales. Select the best ones to be presented to the whole class.

Speaking and Listening

Presenting a Story Aloud

Recall some interesting bit of personal history, such as how your family came to settle in your home town or how a friend or relative became famous. Share the story with a partner.

Holding a Contest

People who catch fish for sport often exaggerate stories about the fish that got away. As a result, any story that exaggerates the truth has come to be called a "fish story." Hold your own contest of fish stories. You might want to have a panel of judges decide on the best entry.

Spirituals

 The spirituals developed among slaves in the South before the Civil War, but the songs were not written or collected until the 1860s. The first systematic collection of spirituals, *Slave Songs of the United States,* appeared in 1867. This book helped to introduce the songs to a wide audience. In 1871, a group of students from Fisk University, in Tennessee, went on tour, singing slave songs they had learned from their parents, in order to raise money for their school. These Jubilee Singers became famous, and after appearing in New York, carried the tour to Europe.

Spirituals are a form of **folk literature,** like the ballads. There are no known composers of these songs, and since they were transmitted by word of mouth, many of them have come down in several different versions. In *The Book of Negro Folklore,* Sterling A. Brown describes how they might have been composed:

> It is unlikely that any group of worshipers and singers, as a group, composed spirituals. Single individuals with poetic ingenuity, a rhyming gift, or a good memory "composed" or "remembered" lines, couplets, or even quatrains out of a common storehouse. The group would join in with the refrain or the longer chorus. When one leader's ingenuity or memory was exhausted, another might take up the "composition."

Even though individuals may have composed the spirituals, the ideas and language came from the group, from the "common storehouse" of images and idioms. As the songs were passed down by word of mouth, lines would be changed and new stanzas would be added.

Many spirituals had a double meaning. They expressed a desire for spiritual salvation. At the same time, they expressed a desire for freedom on earth. According to accounts by fugitive slaves, the spiritual "Go Down, Moses" became a censored song. Parallels between the slavery of the Israelites and the oppression of the Southern slaves were evident to the slaveholders. Certain religious leaders of the Bible, like Moses, became popular in spirituals. Harriet Tubman, a conductor on the Underground Railroad who brought many runaway slaves to freedom, was to become known as the Moses of her people.

Some spirituals were known as "signal" songs. They were used to carry messages that overseers would not understand. "Follow the Drinking Gourd," for instance, told the fugitive slaves to follow the Big Dipper in the night sky, which pointed to the North Star, the way to freedom.

Many writers have paid tribute to these beautiful and moving songs. In his poem "O Black and Unknown Bards," James Weldon Johnson says that the spirituals were born of oppression but became a poetry of hope, both for spiritual salvation and for freedom on earth.

Before You Read

Spirituals

Using What You Know

Compile a list of the occasions on which you join in group singing: when the congregation sings hymns during a religious service, when the national anthem is played, when the school assembly sings Christmas carols, and the like. How does singing within a group help to bind the individual members closer together? Does group singing also provide a release for strong feelings?

Literary Focus: Allusion

An **allusion** is a reference in one work of literature to another work of literature or to a particular event, person, or place. An allusion is used to call up certain associations. Literature contains many allusions to the Bible. In her poem "On Being Brought from Africa to America," Phillis Wheatley expects her readers to understand her allusion to Cain, a figure who appears in Genesis. As you read the spirituals, you will see that they are rich in Biblical allusions.

Setting a Purpose

The spirituals have no known composer and were put together from a "common storehouse" of language and ideas. Keep in mind that the songs express the thoughts and feelings of a community of people.

Spirituals

Go Down, Moses

Go down, Moses,
Way down in Egyptland
Tell old Pharaoh
To let my people go.

When Israel was in Egyptland   5
Let my people go
Oppressed so hard they could not stand
Let my people go.

Go down, Moses,
Way down in Egyptland   10
Tell old Pharaoh
"Let my people go."

"Thus saith the Lord," bold Moses said,
"Let my people go;
If not I'll smite your first-born dead 15
Let my people go."

Go down, Moses,
Way down in Egyptland,
Tell old Pharaoh,
"Let my people go!"   20

Swing Low, Sweet Chariot

Swing low, sweet chariot,
Coming for to carry me home,
Swing low, sweet chariot,
Coming for to carry me home.

I looked over Jordan and what did I see   5
Coming for to carry me home,
A band of angels, coming after me,
Coming for to carry me home.

If you get there before I do,
Coming for to carry me home,   10
Tell all my friends I'm coming too,
Coming for to carry me home.

Swing low, sweet chariot,
Coming for to carry me home,
Swing low, sweet chariot,   15
Coming for to carry me home.

Steal Away

Steal away, steal away, steal away to Jesus,
Steal away, steal away home,
I ain't got long to stay here.

My Lord, He calls me,
He calls me by the thunder,   5
The trumpet sounds within-a my soul,
I ain't got long to stay here.

Steal away, steal away, steal away to Jesus,
Steal away, steal away home,
I ain't got long to stay here.   10

Green trees a-bending,
Po' sinner stands a-trembling
The trumpet sounds within-a my soul,
I ain't got long to stay here.

Steal away, steal away, steal away
    to Jesus, 15
Steal away, steal away home,
I ain't got long to stay here.

I Got a Home in Dat Rock

I got a home in dat rock,
Don't you see?
I got a home in dat rock,
Don't you see?
Between de earth an' sky, 5
Thought I heard my Saviour cry,
You got a home in dat rock,
Don't you see?

Poor man Laz'rus, poor as I,
Don't you see? 10
Poor man Laz'rus, poor as I,
Don't you see?
Poor man Laz'rus, poor as I,
When he died he found a home on high,
He had a home in dat rock, 15
Don't you see?

Rich man Dives, he lived so well,
Don't you see?
Rich man Dives, he lived so well,
Don't you see? 20
Rich man Dives, he lived so well,
When he died he found a home in Hell,
He had no home in dat rock,
Don't you see?

God gave Noah de Rainbow sign, 25
Don't you see?
God gave Noah de Rainbow sign,
Don't you see?
God gave Noah de Rainbow sign,
No more water but fire next time, 30
Better get a home in dat rock,
Don't you see?

I Thank God I'm Free at Las'

Free at las', free at las',
I thank God I'm free at las'.
Free at las', free at las',
I thank God I'm free at las'.

Way down yonder in de graveyard walk, 5
I thank God I'm free at las'.
Me an' my Jesus gwineter meet an' talk,
I thank God I'm free at las'.

On-a my knees when de light pass by,
I thank God I'm free at las'. 10
Thought my soul would arise and fly,
I thank God I'm free at las'.

Some o' dese mornin's bright and fair,
I thank God I'm free at las'.
Gwineter meet my Jesus in de middle of
    de air, 15
I thank God I'm free at las'.

Writing Description

Writers such as Olaudah Equiano and Frederick Douglass use **description** to relive part of their own lives, to inform readers, to convince others to share their views and even to take action against injustice. In writing description, they use specific details that appeal to their readers' senses—sight, hearing, taste, touch, and smell. Good description creates one overall effect or main impression about a scene, a character, or an object.

In the following passage, Douglass describes his appearance when he arrives at his master's store. Note that Douglass arranges the details of his description in order, beginning with the crown of his head and ending with his feet.

> I then presented an appearance enough to affect any but a heart of iron. From the crown of my head to my feet, I was covered with blood. My hair was all clotted with dust and blood; my shirt was stiff with blood. My legs and feet were torn in sundry places with briers and thorns, and were also covered with blood. I suppose I looked like a man who had escaped a den of wild beasts, and barely escaped them.

1. How does Douglass's description make you feel?
2. What specific details in the description make you feel this way?

Equiano describes the horrors of the ship's hold in this passage from his autobiography:

> The stench of the hold, while we were on the coast, was so intolerably loathsome, that it was dangerous to remain there for any time, and some of us had been permitted to stay on the deck for the fresh air; but now that the whole ship's cargo were confined together, it became absolutely pestilential. The closeness of the place, and the heat of the climate, added to the number in the ship, being so crowded that each had scarcely room to turn himself, almost suffocated us. This produced copious perspirations, so that the air soon became unfit for respiration, from a variety of loathsome smells, and brought on a sickness among the slaves, of which many died, thus falling victims to the improvident avarice, as I may call it, of their purchasers.

1. In this passage, Equiano informs us that the hold of the ship was crowded and suffocating. What information does he give us about the slaves?
2. What words and details does Equiano use to make you feel the horror of his experience?

Writing Description

Writing a Descriptive Passage

Write one or two paragraphs describing a memorable moment in your life. The moment may be a happy one. Use specific details that appeal to the senses—sight, hearing, taste, touch, and smell. Arrange the details in a logical order, such as left to right, near to far, or order of importance. Try to create an overall effect or main impression.

Prewriting Strategies

1. Begin by trying to remember all the sights, sounds, smells, tastes, and textures of the time you are describing. You may use a diagram like this one to help you. Use the form that your teacher provides or a separate sheet of paper.

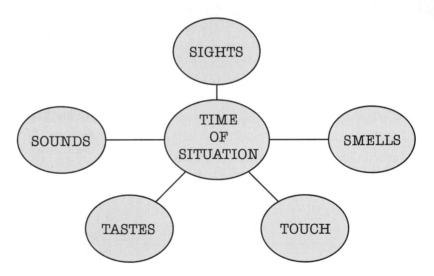

2. What main impression do you want the details to create?
3. Eliminate any details that interfere with the main impression.
4. Arrange the remaining details in an order that your reader can follow.

_____

_____

_____

_____

Writing the First Draft

Use your notes to write a first draft. One way to begin your description is to write a sentence that clearly states the main impression.

Evaluating and Revising

As you revise, try to vary your sentences so that they don't all begin the same way. Use connecting expressions such as *beside, alongside, in the middle,* and so on, to help your ideas flow smoothly. Use the following **Checklist** to edit your paper.

1. Does every sentence support the main impression?
2. Have you included enough details to develop your main impression?
3. Have you arranged the details in a clear and logical order?
4. Have you used transitional expressions to connect ideas?
5. Have you used precise words?

Writing the Final Draft

Use the **Checklist** on page 66 to proofread your paper and to prepare a final copy.

WRITER'S
WORKSHOP 2

Observational
Writing
(Descriptive
Writing)

▶I. Interpreting New Material

A. The following episode is from a slave narrative called *Incidents in the Life of a Slave Girl* by Harriet A. Jacobs. Although the author uses fictional names for her characters, the narrative is a true story. At the time of these events, Harriet Jacobs's grandmother had been freed. Jacobs's children had been bought and were living in the grandmother's house. Jacobs, however, was a runaway slave. She spent seven years hiding in a garret in her grandmother's house rather than yield to her master's demands.

The Loophole of Retreat from
Incidents in the Life of a Slave Girl
Harriet A. Jacobs

A small shed had been added to my grandmother's house years ago. Some boards were laid across the joists at the top, and between these boards and the roof was a very small garret, never occupied by any thing but rats and mice. It was a pent roof,[1] covered with nothing but shingles, according to the southern custom for such buildings. The garret was only nine feet long and seven wide. The highest part was three feet high, and sloped down abruptly to the loose board floor. There was no admission for either light or air. My uncle Phillip, who was a carpenter, had very skilfully made a concealed trap-door, which communicated with the store-room. He had been doing this while I was waiting in the swamp. The storeroom opened upon a piazza. To this hole I was conveyed as soon as I entered the house. The air was stifling; the darkness total. A bed had been spread on the floor. I could sleep quite comfortably on one side; but the slope was so sudden that I could not turn on the other without hitting the roof. The rats and mice ran over my bed; but I was weary, and I slept such sleep as the wretched may, when a tempest has passed over them. Morning came. I knew it only by the noises I heard; for in my small den day and night were all the

1. **pent roof:** a roof sloping on only one side.

same. I suffered for air even more than for light. But I was not comfortless. I heard the voices of my children. There was joy and there was sadness in the sound. It made my tears flow. How I longed to speak to them! I was eager to look on their faces; but there was no hole, no crack, through which I could peep. This continued darkness was oppressive. It seemed horrible to sit or lie in a cramped position day after day, without one gleam of light. Yet I would have chosen this, rather than my lot as a slave, though white people considered it an easy one; and it was so compared with the fate of others. I was never cruelly over-worked; I was never lacerated with the whip from head to foot; I was never so beaten and bruised that I could not turn from one side to the other; I never had my heel-strings cut to prevent my running away; I was never chained to a log and forced to drag it about, while I toiled in the fields from morning till night; I was never branded with hot iron, or torn by bloodhounds. On the contrary, I had always been kindly treated, and tenderly cared for, until I came into the hands of Dr. Flint. I had never wished for freedom till then. But though my life in slavery was comparatively devoid of hardships, God pity the woman who is compelled to lead such a life!

My food was passed up to me through the trap-door my uncle had contrived; and my grandmother, my uncle Phillip, and aunt Nancy would seize such opportunities as they could, to mount up there and chat with me at the opening. But of course this was not safe in the daytime. It must all be done in darkness. It was impossible for me to move in an erect position, but I crawled about my den for exercise. One day I hit my head against something, and found it was a gimlet.[2] My uncle had left it sticking there when he made the trap-door. I was as rejoiced as Robinson Crusoe[3] could have been at finding such a treasure. It put a lucky thought into my head. I said to myself, "Now I will have some light. Now I will see my children." I did not dare to begin my work during the daytime, for fear of attracting attention. But I groped round; and having found the side next the street, where I could frequently see my children, I stuck the gimlet in and waited for evening. I bored three rows of holes, one above another; then I bored out the interstices between. I thus succeeded in making one hole about an inch long and an inch broad. I sat by it till late into the night, to enjoy the little whiff of air that floated in. In the morning I watched for my children. The first person I saw in the street was Dr. Flint. I had a shuddering, superstitious feeling that it was a bad omen. Several familiar faces passed by. At last I heard the merry laugh of children, and presently two sweet little faces were looking up at me, as though they knew I was there, and were conscious of the joy they imparted. How I longed to *tell* them I was there!

My condition was now a little improved. But for weeks I was tormented by hundreds

2. **gimlet** (gĭm'lĭt): a hand tool used to bore holes.
3. **Robinson Crusoe**: a character in an eighteenth-century novel who is shipwrecked and who survives on a small tropical island for many years through his ingenuity.

of little red insects, fine as a needle's point, that pierced through my skin, and produced an intolerable burning. The good grandmother gave me herb teas and cooling medicines, and finally I got rid of them. The heat of my den was intense, for nothing but thin shingles protected me from the scorching summer's sun. But I had my consolations. Through my peeping-hole I could watch the children, and when they were near enough, I could hear their talk. Aunt Nancy brought me all the news she could hear at Dr. Flint's. From her I learned that the doctor had written to New York to a colored woman, who had been born and raised in our neighborhood, and had breathed his contaminating atmosphere. He offered her a reward if she could find out any thing about me. I know not what was the nature of her reply; but he soon after started for New York in haste, saying to his family that he had business of importance to transact. I peeped at him as he passed on his way to the steamboat. It was a satisfaction to have miles of land and water between us, even for a little while; and it was a still greater satisfaction to know that he believed me to be in the Free States. My little den seemed less dreary than it had done. He returned, as he did from his former journey to New York, without obtaining any satisfactory information. When he passed our house next morning, Benny was standing at the gate. He had heard them say that he had gone to find me, and he called out, "Dr. Flint, did you bring my mother home? I want to see her." The doctor stamped his foot at him in a rage, and exclaimed, "Get out of the way, you little damned rascal! If you don't, I'll cut off your head."

Benny ran terrified into the house, saying, "You can't put me in jail again. I don't belong to you now." It was well that the wind carried the words away from the doctor's ear. I told my grandmother of it, when we had our next conference at the trap-door; and begged of her not to allow the children to be impertinent to the irascible old man.

Autumn came, with a pleasant abatement of heat. My eyes had become accustomed to the dim light, and by holding my book or work in a certain position near the aperture I contrived to read and sew. That was a great relief to the tedious monotony of my life. But when winter came, the cold penetrated through the thin shingle roof, and I was dreadfully chilled. The winters there are not so long, or so severe, as in northern latitudes; but the houses are not built to shelter from cold, and my little den was peculiarly comfortless. The kind grandmother brought me bed-clothes and warm drinks. Often I was obliged to lie in bed all day to keep comfortable; but with all my precautions, my shoulders and feet were frostbitten. O, those long, gloomy days, with no object for my eye to rest upon, and no thoughts to occupy my mind, except the dreary past and the uncertain future! I was thankful when there came a day sufficiently mild for me to wrap myself up and sit at the loophole to watch the passers by. Southerners have the habit of stopping and talking in the streets, and I heard many conversations not intended to meet my ears. I heard slave-hunters planning how to catch some poor fugitive. Several times I heard allusions to Dr. Flint, myself, and the history of my children, who, perhaps, were playing near the gate. One would say, "I wouldn't move my little finger to catch her, as old Flint's property." Another would say, "I'll catch *any* nigger for the reward. A man ought to have what belongs to him, if he *is* a damned brute." The opinion was often expressed that I was in the Free States. Very rarely did any one suggest that I might be in the vicinity. Had the least suspicion rested on my grandmother's house, it would have been burned to the ground. But it was the last place they thought of. Yet there was no place, where slavery existed, that could have afforded me so good a place of concealment.

1. How did Jacobs communicate with the members of her family?
2. How did she pass the time while she was in hiding?
3. What precautions did she take to keep her hiding place secret?
4. Why do you think Jacobs called her hiding place "the loophole of retreat"?

B. **In a brief essay discuss your impression of Harriet Jacobs's character from what she reveals in this passage.**

▶▶II. For Discussion _____

The introduction to the unit states that "some of the most memorable writing done by African Americans before emancipation is autobiographical." Which of the autobiographical selections in this unit did you find most effective? Which scenes or descriptions gave you the greatest insight into the writer's thoughts and feelings? Share your impressions with your classmates.

▶▶▶III. For Writing _____

When Benjamin Banneker wrote his letter to Jefferson in 1791, he pointed out the long-standing prejudice against African Americans as people "scarcely capable of mental endowments." As the literature in this unit testifies, black Americans of the period had the same intellectual and creative abilities as whites. Write a postscript to Banneker's letter in which you note the achievements of African American literature in the period before the Civil War. Be sure to refer to specific writers and specific works.

Museum purchase with funds provided by Mrs. Leon D. Bonnet, San Diego Museum of Art.

Sharecroppers, *oil by Robert Gwathmey, 1939.*

Unit Four

Reconstruction to Renaissance

INTRODUCTION BY **William L. Andrews**

University of North Carolina at Chapel Hill

Southern Reconstruction

From 1865 to the end of the century, the United States tried to weave together into a new pattern the threads of its social, political, and economic life that had been cut by the Civil War. African Americans placed great confidence in the leadership of President Lincoln to heal the country's wounds and help the four million emancipated slaves of the South make a new start in a new land of freedom. But Lincoln was assassinated less than a week after the South surrendered in the spring of 1865. His successor to the presidency, Andrew Johnson of Tennessee, favored Lincoln's announced policy of leniency toward the South. Johnson restored the citizenship of the large majority of Southern white males regardless of whether they had taken up arms against the Union. The president expected the Southern states to accept the new laws of the land, but as a Southerner himself, he was sympathetic to the South's desire for "home rule." Thus he was willing to give the Southern states a chance to work out many of their problems themselves rather than force them to knuckle under to the much-resented Yankees and their conquering army.

Johnson was right in assuming that the states of the former Confederacy would never try to bring back slavery. But he did not anticipate the notorious **"black codes"** that the legislatures of the Southern states created in 1865 and 1866 to reassert white control over blacks. Under these laws, the rights of blacks to own property were restricted; the rights of blacks to vote were denied; and the

Introduction   201

Freedmen in Richmond, Virginia.
Library of Congress

power of white employers over black workers remained almost as absolute as that which slaveowners had held over their slaves. To the United States Congress of 1865 the Southern states elected the former vice president of the Confederacy, four Confederate generals, five Confederate colonels, six members of the Confederate president's cabinet, and fifty-eight members of the congress of the defeated Confederacy. In the eyes of the Republican leaders of the United States Congress, the passage of the "black codes" and the election of former rebels to the national legislature seemed clear evidence that the South had no intention of reforming itself. Determined to seize control of Southern affairs from the president, the so-called **Radical Republicans,** led by Congressman Thaddeus Stevens and Senator Charles Sumner, proposed a new program of **Southern Reconstruction** in 1866.

The new congressional action gave much power to the **Freedmen's Bureau,** an agency of the federal government designed to aid war refugees, establish schools, supervise contracts between white employers and black employees, and help former slaves buy land confiscated in the war. The Congress also passed a civil rights bill for blacks in 1866. Although President Johnson opposed these measures, he could not prevent the Radical Republicans, their ranks swelled by the election of 1866, from overriding his vetoes. On the strength of their numbers, the Radical Republicans forced into law the Reconstruction Act of 1867 and took control of reforms in the South for the next decade.

The First Vote, *freedmen voting in the South, colored engraving, 1867.*
The Granger Collection, New York

Under Congressional Reconstruction, the ex-Confederacy was divided into five military districts. The Freedmen's Bureau, backed by the United States Army, was given renewed power to aid the ex-slaves and protect their welfare. Martial law was declared in much of the South to put down lawlessness and mob rule caused by groups like the Ku Klux Klan, a secret society founded in 1866 to restore white supremacy. The black codes were abolished and the civil rights of African Americans were guaranteed. New representatives to Congress and new state legislatures were elected by the full male citizenry of each Southern state. To black leaders like Frederick Douglass, who believed that the right to vote was the cornerstone on which the freedpeople's prosperity was to be built, the new Reconstruction policy seemed to promise a bright future for African Americans in the South.

Few Economic Gains for African Americans

Unfortunately, Reconstruction in the South did not change significantly the economic power of whites over blacks. Many ex-slaves believed that the federal government would divide the land seized from the great plantation owners of the South and award "forty acres and a mule" to blacks who wished to become independent farmers. Instead, most of the land remained in the hands of whites, and freedmen and women found themselves compelled to work it for slim wages or shares of whatever they could harvest. This arrangement kept black agricultural workers, who composed the large majority of Southern African Americans, at the mercy of whites. Blacks who moved to urban centers in search of better opportunities generally met strong resistance from white workers, who saw African Americans as competitors for jobs already made scarce by the depressed Southern economy.

By 1870, however, some parts of the Southern agricultural economy, headed by cotton, were well on the way to recovery. Within ten years the South would be producing more cotton than it ever had in the best years of the slavery era. Southern planters and politicians realized that the agricultural resources and cheap labor of their region would be very attractive to Northern industrialists. But before Northern business interests would invest capital and create new industries in the South, they wanted assurances that the so-called "Negro problem" was well on its way to solution. To white conservatives this meant only one thing—a restoration of white supremacy in the social, political, and economic life of the South.

Black families after the Civil War.
Collection of The New-York Historical Society

Negro Exodus. *After the Civil War, many African Americans moved to urban centers.*
Judith Mara Gutman

The End of Reconstruction

A revived Democratic party in the South, representing the interests of influential planters, campaigned successfully throughout the early 1870s for the elimination of black political power. The Democrats blamed black elected officials in particular and the Republican party in general for the problems of Reconstruction. Though history has proved much of this blame groundless, most white Southerners—and many influential Northerners—were ready to believe that the best way to end racial conflict and promote economic development in the South was to put aside the Radical Republicans' experiment in democracy and equality. By 1876, Republican leaders themselves, more interested in maintaining political power than crusading for radical principle, agreed. When the hotly disputed presidential election of 1876 went to an electoral commission for a final decision, the Republicans made a political deal with the South. They promised to end Reconstruction in exchange for Southern support of their candidate. When Rutherford B. Hayes entered the White House in 1877, he paid his political debt to the Democrats by withdrawing all federal troops from the South. This signaled the North's abandonment of Southern blacks to a new generation of Southern masters.

The period from 1880 to 1915 has been called by one important historian the "decades of disappointment." Another scholar has termed this period the low point, or "nadir," of African American history. During this time the United States Supreme Court ruled that the most far-reaching civil rights legislation passed during Reconstruction was unconstitutional. The states of the former Confederacy systematically altered their constitutions so that blacks were denied the right to vote. When the Supreme Court ruled in 1896 in favor of the South's "separate but equal" racial doctrine,° the federal government put its stamp of approval on state laws requiring cradle-to-grave segregation of the races. Realizing that they could no longer expect support from the federal government in their struggle for dignity and opportunity in the South, many blacks concluded that self-reliance, self-help, and racial solidarity were their last best hopes. These people saw Booker T. Washington as their champion and adopted his autobiography, *Up from Slavery* (1901), as their guidebook to a better life.

Washington's Program of Reconciliation and Cooperation

In 1895, the year of the death of Frederick Douglass, Booker T. Washington, principal of the Tuskegee (təs-kē′gē) Institute in Alabama, gave an address at the Cotton States Exposition in Atlanta that catapulted him to national leadership of black America. In his speech Washington suggested that the best way to ensure progress and peace in the South was for whites to respect the blacks' desire for improved economic opportunities and for blacks to respect the whites' desire for social separation of the races. Washington believed that blacks could regain their rights in the South only by accepting the existing political situation and working gradually to change it by proving themselves valuable, productive members of society who deserved fair and equal treatment before the law. He wrote *Up from Slavery* to illustrate the good that a black man could do for himself and his people if given a chance to obtain an education and engage in useful, productive work. Wash-

---

° In the case of Plessy v. Ferguson, the Court ruled that laws segregating people because of their race were not unconstitutional. This ruling remained in effect until 1954.

The Tuskegee Institute faculty council, November 1902. Booker T. Washington (center, front row); George Washington Carver (standing, extreme right).
The Granger Collection, New York

ington's autobiography became an inspiring success story to many African Americans who believed in the ideas of rugged individualism and "pulling oneself up by one's own bootstraps" that were so popular throughout the United States in the post-Civil War era. When the "sage of Tuskegee" wrote that individual merit, not racial identity, was the standard on which a person would rise or fall, he reminded his white readers of traditional American ideas of fair play and justice—ideas that had declined in the racially charged atmosphere of turn-of-the-century America.

The Rise of Activism

Soon after *Up from Slavery* appeared, William Edward Burghardt Du Bois, a professor of sociology at Atlanta University, challenged the basic assumption on which Washington's program was founded. In his landmark collection of essays, *The Souls of Black Folk* (1903), Du Bois asked how could civil rights ever be gained by giving them up? How could black Americans expect to be treated with respect if they showed such paltry self-respect as to barter their civil rights for a little economic gain? In Du Bois's view, Washington's program of reconciliation and cooperation between the

In June 1905, a group under the leadership of W. E. B. Du Bois met at Niagara Falls, Canada, to draw up a program of action. This photograph was taken in July 1905, against a Niagara Falls backdrop. Du Bois is in the middle row, second from the right.
The Schomburg Center for Research in Black Culture/New York Public Library

W. E. B. Du Bois.
The Schomburg Center for Research in Black Culture/New York Public Library

races in the South had a noble aim, but its priorities were backward. Economic opportunity and the power that comes from prosperity and property-owning could not come *before* blacks regained the vote and the other civil rights that made them equal before the law with whites. Du Bois urged blacks to make agitation for their political and civil rights their first goal. He launched the **Niagara Movement** in 1905, an early civil rights organization that came to fruition in 1910 as the **National Association for the Advancement of Colored People.** As editor of *The Crisis,* the official journal of the NAACP, Du Bois became the most influential African American intellectual of his era. By the time of Booker T. Washington's death in 1915, the tide of African American public opinion had begun to turn toward Du Bois's social and political activism.

Portrayal of African Americans in Literature

A poet and novelist himself, Du Bois had strong beliefs about the role of literature in the struggle against racial injustice during his era. He urged black creative writers to confront the social and economic problems that plagued African Americans and to take a moral stand on the injustices of the day. He knew that white readers were used to finding blacks stereotyped in popular fiction as simple "happy darkies." Du Bois was also aware that whites considered the culture and values of blacks, especially in the South, to be quaint and shallow, a far cry from the ideals of whites. He called on black fiction writers to portray the higher as well as the lower classes of African American life, the "talented tenth" as well as the rank and file of black people, to emphasize the variety and complexity of African American society. Reacting to the "happy darky" image, many black novelists of the late nineteenth and early twentieth centuries focused on African Americans who were neither happy with their lot in life nor dark in complexion. These light-skinned, high-minded, upwardly mobile figures were intended to serve as advertisements for black America at its best. In the hands of a skillful writer like Charles W. Chesnutt, the middle-class heroes and heroines of black fiction were convincingly and justly presented to a reading audience that was often genuinely moved by their social and moral struggles. When less experienced black writers of protest examined the plight of the "talented tenth," however, they made their heroes and heroines so admirable and sympathetic that they seemed hardly human at all. Given the tremendous amount of negative propaganda directed at African Americans during this time, it is not surprising that many black fiction writers concentrated on creating positive propaganda about their people through **idealization**—the representation of people as better than they usually are. Nevertheless, by the 1920s a new generation of black writers was ready to challenge the literature of idealization with a new brand of **realism,** which aimed at representing the everyday experience of ordinary people.

African American Poetry

African American poetry between the end of the Civil War and the beginning of World War I also displayed a tension between idealization and realism, which appears most obviously in the work of the most famous black poet of the era, Paul Laurence Dunbar. Written in the picturesque dialect of the African American folk, Dunbar's most popular verse (at least in his own time) deals with the everyday life of rural blacks in the South. He celebrates the simple pleasures of "down home" living and the fulfillment of blacks in their own communities, apart from and seemingly unmindful of the world of whites. Dunbar's dialect poetry has often been praised for its success in evoking the robust spirit of Southern black folk life. Yet Dunbar knew all too well that writing dialect poetry was very much a mixed blessing for a black poet. The danger was that whites would assume that writing in black dialect was all a black poet *could* do. Whites might also think that because a dialect poet could describe so convincingly the good side of life among Southern black folk, there really was no bad side. These are some of the reasons Dunbar and many of his contemporaries in African American poetry worked so hard to write in standard English and to express themselves on a wide range of subjects of long-standing concern to the great Romantic poets of an earlier generation. Too often Dunbar's standard English verse strains to produce a fairly conventional statement about a subject far removed from the daily concerns of most black (or white) people. But this was a fault he shared with many other poets of his time, white as well as black. At his best, in poems like "We Wear the Mask" and "Sympathy," Dunbar spoke frankly and eloquently to the problems of being a black artist in a white supremacist era.

Women Writers of the Period

Between the Civil War and the First World War, African American literature expanded and diversified in many ways. In fiction, poetry, drama, and autobiography, steadily growing numbers of blacks expressed their outrage over the present and their dreams for the future. Women came increasingly to the fore, led by the much-revered Frances Ellen Watkins Harper and the fiery journalist and women's rights activist Ida B. Wells, who exemplified the crusading spirit passed on from the days of antislavery agitation.

TIME LINE **RECONSTRUCTION TO RENAISSANCE**

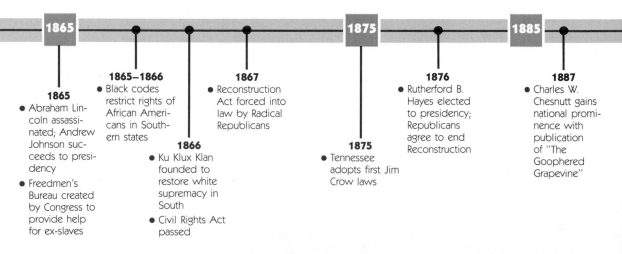

1865

1865
- Abraham Lincoln assassinated; Andrew Johnson succeeds to presidency
- Freedmen's Bureau created by Congress to provide help for ex-slaves

1865–1866
- Black codes restrict rights of African Americans in Southern states

1866
- Ku Klux Klan founded to restore white supremacy in South
- Civil Rights Act passed

1867
- Reconstruction Act forced into law by Radical Republicans

1875

1875
- Tennessee adopts first Jim Crow laws

1876
- Rutherford B. Hayes elected to presidency; Republicans agree to end Reconstruction

1885

1887
- Charles W. Chesnutt gains national prominence with publication of "The Goophered Grapevine"

Wells embodied the commitment of African American writers to the ideals of freedom and equality. Recalling her journalistic campaign against lynching in the 1890s, Wells revealed in her autobiography three decades later that she had resolved that "one had better die fighting against injustice than to die like a dog or a rat in a trap." Because of writers like Wells, the torch lit by the likes of Douglass survived decades of reaction and despair to light a new dawn for the "New Negro" of the 1920s and the Harlem Renaissance.

Emancipation, *lithograph by Phoebe Beasley.*

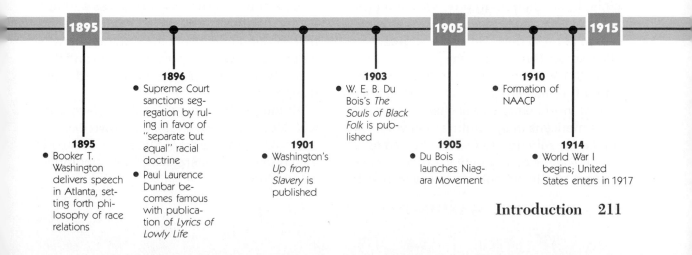

1895

1895
- Booker T. Washington delivers speech in Atlanta, setting forth philosophy of race relations

1896
- Supreme Court sanctions segregation by ruling in favor of "separate but equal" racial doctrine
- Paul Laurence Dunbar becomes famous with publication of *Lyrics of Lowly Life*

1901
- Washington's *Up from Slavery* is published

1903
- W. E. B. Du Bois's *The Souls of Black Folk* is published

1905

1905
- Du Bois launches Niagara Movement

1910
- Formation of NAACP

1914
- World War I begins; United States enters in 1917

1915

Introduction   211

About the Author

Booker T. Washington (1856–1915)

Library of Congress/Wide World Photos

 Between the end of the Civil War and the outbreak of World War I, Booker T. Washington emerged as the dominant figure in the history of African Americans. The period from 1895 to 1915, the year of his death, is often referred to as the Age of Booker T. Washington.

He was born a slave at Hale's Ford, Virginia. In his autobiography, Washington recalls that his most intense desire as a child was to learn to read. He endured great hardships to achieve his dream.

In 1881 Washington was offered the position of principal at Tuskegee Institute, a school in Alabama established to train African Americans in agricultural and vocational trades. Washington found that he had to win over the white community in order to make a success of the school. He believed that the best way to strengthen the position of his people was through industrial education.

At the Atlanta Exposition in 1895, Washington delivered an address that has become known as the "Atlanta Compromise." In this speech he accepted segregation as the price of racial harmony and economic advancement: "In all things that are purely social we can be as separate as the five fingers, yet one as the hand in all things essential to mutual progress." Washington's philosophy appealed to most whites in the North and the South and to most blacks of his time, who wanted an opportunity for economic self-development. Washington became known as the "Moses of his race."

W. E. B. Du Bois, who became one of Washington's severest critics, believed that Washington's faith in industrial education was too narrow in its objectives. Du Bois felt what was needed was a curriculum of higher learning that stressed a wide knowledge of the world and its arts. He was also alarmed at Washington's policy of submission on civil rights. It is now clear that Washington was a sincere and dedicated man who was perhaps overly optimistic. He failed to understand that the kind of educational program he was emphasizing was already outmoded and that many of the occupations he stressed were disappearing.

Although Washington's ideas have met with vigorous opposition in our own day, his autobiography, *Up from Slavery,* is acknowledged to be a masterpiece of autobiographical writing.

Before You Read

Boyhood Days from Up from Slavery

Using What You Know

Imagine yourself in the position of an ex-slave on a plantation in the South after emancipation. You have never been taught to read and write. You have never been to school because there are no schools for you. You have no training in any occupation. You have never lived anywhere but on the plantation. What will you do? How will you live? What decisions will you now have to make for yourself? Share your answers with your classmates.

Consider the adjustments that had to be made by newly freed slaves. How would these conditions have contributed to the problems of Reconstruction?

Literary Focus: Autobiography

Washington's autobiography is one of a number of life stories to appear after the Civil War that stressed the American dream of success. Readers enjoyed stories about America as a land of opportunity for those who were willing to work hard. These books also served as an inspiration to others. The black biographies and autobiographies showed that it was possible to gain success through industry and fortitude. Note the emphasis that Washington places on aspiration and racial pride.

Setting a Purpose

Booker T. Washington published *Up from Slavery* in 1901, when he was at the height of his career and a nationally known figure. As you read, determine his **purpose** in presenting the facts of his life. Do you feel that he is writing primarily to encourage others through his example or to defend his beliefs? Or has he some other purpose?

Up from Slavery

Booker T. Washington

Boyhood Days

After the coming of freedom there were two points upon which practically all the people on our place were agreed, and I find that this was generally true throughout the South: that they must change their names, and that they must leave the old plantation for at least a few days or weeks in order that they might really feel sure that they were free.

In some way a feeling got among the coloured people that it was far from proper for them to bear the surname of their former owners, and a great many of them took other surnames. This was one of the first signs of freedom. When they were slaves, a coloured person was simply called "John" or "Susan." There was seldom occasion for more than the use of one name. If "John" or "Susan" belonged to a white man by the name of "Hatcher," sometimes he was called "John Hatcher," or as often "Hatcher's John." But there was a feeling that "John Hatcher" or "Hatcher's John" was not the proper title by which to denote a freeman; and so in many cases "John Hatcher" was changed to "John S. Lincoln" or "John S. Sherman," the initial "S" standing for no name, it being simply a part of what the coloured man proudly called his "entitles."

As I have stated, most of the coloured people left the old plantation for a short while at least, so as to be sure, it seemed, that they could leave and try their freedom on to see how it felt. After they had remained away for a time, many of the older slaves, especially, returned to their old homes and made some kind of contract with their former owners by which they remained on the estate.

My mother's husband, who was the stepfather of my brother John and myself, did not belong to the same owners as did my mother. In fact, he seldom came to our plantation. I remember seeing him there perhaps once a year, that being about Christmas time. In some way, during the war, by running away and following the Federal soldiers, it seems, he found his way into the new state of West Virginia. As soon as freedom was declared, he sent for my mother to come to the Kanawha Valley, in West Virginia. At that time a journey from Virginia over the mountains to West Virginia was rather a tedious and in some cases a painful undertaking. What little clothing and few household goods we had were placed in a cart, but the children walked the greater portion of the distance, which was several hundred miles.

I do not think any of us had been very far

Crossing the Bridge, *oil by John Biggers, 1942.*

from the plantation, and the taking of a long journey into another state was quite an event. The parting from our former owners and the members of our own race on the plantation was a serious occasion. From the time of our parting till their death we kept up a correspondence with the older members of the family, and in later years we have kept in touch with those who were the younger members. We were several weeks making the trip, and most of the time we slept in the open air and did our cooking over a log fire out of doors. One night I recall that we camped near an abandoned log cabin, and my mother decided to build a fire in that for cooking, and afterward to make a "pallet" on the floor for our sleeping. Just as the fire had

gotten well started a large black snake fully a yard and a half long dropped down the chimney and ran out on the floor. Of course we at once abandoned that cabin. Finally we reached our destination—a little town called Malden, which is about five miles from Charleston, the present capital of the state.

At that time salt-mining was the great industry in that part of West Virginia, and the little town of Malden was right in the middle of the salt-furnaces. My stepfather had already secured a job at a salt-furnace, and he had also secured a little cabin for us to live in. Our new house was no better than the one we had left on the old plantation in Virginia. In fact, in one respect it was worse. Notwithstanding the poor condition of our

Up from Slavery   215

plantation cabin, we were at all times sure of pure air. Our new home was in the midst of a cluster of cabins crowded closely together, and as there were no sanitary regulations, the filth about the cabins was often intolerable. Some of our neighbours were coloured people, and some were the poorest and most ignorant and degraded white people. It was a motley mixture. Drinking, gambling, quarrels, fights, and shockingly immoral practices were frequent. All who lived in the little town were in one way or another connected with the salt business. Though I was a mere child, my stepfather put me and my brother at work in one of the furnaces. Often I began work as early as four o'clock in the morning.

The first thing I ever learned in the way of book knowledge was while working in this salt-furnace. Each salt-packer had his barrels marked with a certain number. The number allotted to my stepfather was "18." At the close of the day's work the boss of the packers would come around and put "18" on each of our barrels, and I soon learned to recognize that figure wherever I saw it, and after a while got to the point where I could make that figure, though I knew nothing about any other figures or letters.

From the time that I can remember having any thoughts about anything, I recall that I had an intense longing to learn to read. I determined, when quite a small child, that, if I accomplished nothing else in life, I would in some way get enough education to enable me to read common books and newspapers. Soon after we got settled in some manner in our new cabin in West Virginia, I induced my mother to get hold of a book for me. How or where she got it I do not know, but in some way she procured an old copy of Webster's "blue-back" spelling-book, which contained the alphabet, followed by such mean-ingless words as "ab," "ba," "ca," "da." I began at once to devour this book, and I think that it was the first one I ever had in my hands. I had learned from somebody that the way to begin to read was to learn the alphabet, so I tried in all the ways I could think of to learn it—all of course without a teacher, for I could find no one to teach me. At that time there was not a single member of my race anywhere near us who could read, and I was too timid to approach any of the white people. In some way, within a few weeks, I mastered the greater portion of the alphabet. In all my efforts to learn to read my mother shared fully my ambition, and sympathized with me and aided me in every way that she could. Though she was totally ignorant, so far as mere book knowledge was concerned, she had high ambitions for her children, and a large fund of good, hard, common sense which seemed to enable her to meet and master every situation. If I have done anything in life worth attention, I feel sure that I inherited the disposition from my mother.

In the midst of my struggles and longing for an education, a young coloured boy who had learned to read in the state of Ohio came to Malden. As soon as the coloured people found out that he could read, a newspaper was secured, and at the close of nearly every day's work this young man would be surrounded by a group of men and women who were anxious to hear him read the news contained in the papers. How I used to envy this man! He seemed to me to be the one young man in all the world who ought to be satisfied with his attainments.

About this time the question of having some kind of a school opened for the coloured children in the village began to be discussed by members of the race. As it would be the first school for Negro children that had ever been opened in that part of Virginia, it was, of course, to be a great event, and the discussion excited the widest interest. The most perplexing question was where to find a teacher. The young man from Ohio who had learned to read the papers was considered, but his age was against him. In the midst of the discussion about a teacher, another young coloured man from Ohio, who had been a soldier, in some way found his way into town. It was soon learned that he possessed considerable education, and he was engaged by the coloured people to teach their first school. As yet no free schools[1] had been started for coloured people in that section, hence each family agreed to pay a certain amount per month, with the understanding that the teacher was to "board 'round"—that is, spend a day with each family. This was not bad for the teacher, for each family tried to provide the very best on the day the teacher was to be its guest. I recall that I looked forward with an anxious appetite to the "teacher's day" at our little cabin.

This experience of a whole race beginning to go to school for the first time, presents one of the most interesting studies that has ever occurred in connection with the development of any race. Few people who were not right in the midst of the scenes can form any exact idea of the intense desire which the people of my race showed for an education. As I have stated, it was a whole race trying to go to school. Few were too young, and none too old, to make the attempt to learn. As fast as any kind of teachers could be secured, not only were day-schools filled, but night-schools as well. The great ambition of the older people was to try to learn to read the Bible before they died. With this end in

1. **free schools:** The Freedmen's Bureau promoted education and set up and supervised schools.

view, men and women who were fifty or seventy-five years old would often be found in the night-school. Sunday-schools were formed soon after freedom, but the principal book studied in the Sunday-school was the spelling-book. Day-school, night-school, Sunday-school, were always crowded, and often many had to be turned away for want of room.

The opening of the school in the Kanawha Valley, however, brought to me one of the keenest disappointments that I ever experienced. I had been working in a salt-furnace for several months, and my stepfather had discovered that I had a financial value, and so, when the school opened, he decided that he could not spare me from my work. This decision seemed to cloud my every ambition. The disappointment was made all the more severe by reason of the fact that my place of work was where I could see the happy children passing to and from school, mornings and afternoons. Despite this disappointment, however, I determined that I would learn something, anyway. I applied myself with greater earnestness than ever to the mastering of what was in the "blue-back" speller.

My mother sympathized with me in my disappointment, and sought to comfort me in all the ways she could, and to help me find a way to learn. After a while I succeeded in making arrangements with the teacher to give me some lessons at night, after the day's work was done. These night lessons were so welcome that I think I learned more at night than the other children did during the day. My own experiences in the night-school gave me faith in the night-school idea, with which, in after years, I had to do both at Hampton and Tuskegee. But my boyish heart was still set upon going to the day-

Schoolchildren before log schoolhouse in rural Virginia, c. 1895.
Students of all ages studied in a one-room school.
Valentine Museum, Richmond, Virginia

school, and I let no opportunity slip to push my case. Finally I won, and was permitted to go to the school in the day for a few months, with the understanding that I was to rise early in the morning and work in the furnace till nine o'clock, and return immediately after school closed in the afternoon for at least two more hours of work.

The schoolhouse was some distance from the furnace, and as I had to work till nine o'clock, and the school opened at nine, I found myself in a difficulty. School would always be begun before I reached it, and sometimes my class had recited. To get around this difficulty I yielded to a temptation for which most people, I suppose, will condemn me; but since it is a fact, I might as well state it. I have great faith in the power and influence of facts. It is seldom that any-

thing is permanently gained by holding back a fact. There was a large clock in a little office in the furnace. This clock, of course, all the hundred or more workmen depended upon to regulate their hours of beginning and ending the day's work. I got the idea that the way for me to reach school on time was to move the clock hands from half-past eight up to the nine o'clock mark. This I found myself doing morning after morning, till the furnace "boss" discovered that something was wrong, and locked the clock in a case. I did not mean to inconvenience any body. I simply meant to reach that schoolhouse in time.

When, however, I found myself at the school for the first time, I also found myself confronted with two other difficulties. In the first place, I found that all of the other children wore hats or caps on their heads, and I had neither hat nor cap. In fact, I do not remember that up to the time of going to school I had ever worn any kind of covering upon my head, nor do I recall that either I or anybody else had even thought anything about the need of covering for my head. But, of course, when I saw how all the other boys were dressed, I began to feel quite uncomfortable. As usual, I put the case before my mother, and she explained to me that she had no money with which to buy a "store hat," which was a rather new institution at that time among the members of my race and was considered quite the thing for young and old to own, but that she would find a way to help me out of the difficulty. She accordingly got two pieces of "homespun" (jeans) and sewed them together, and I was soon the proud possessor of my first cap.

The lesson that my mother taught me in this has always remained with me, and I have tried as best I could to teach it to others. I have always felt proud, whenever I think of the incident, that my mother had strength of character enough not to be led into the temptation of seeming to be that which she was not—of trying to impress my schoolmates and others with the fact that she was able to buy me a "store hat" when she was not. I have always felt proud that she refused to go into debt for that which she did not have the money to pay for. Since that time I have owned many kinds of caps and hats, but never one of which I have felt so proud as of the cap made of the two pieces of cloth sewed together by my mother. I have noted the fact, but without satisfaction, I need not add, that several of the boys who began their careers with "store hats" and who were my schoolmates and used to join in the sport that was made of me because I had only a "homespun" cap, have ended their careers in the penitentiary, while others are not able now to buy any kind of hat.

My second difficulty was with regard to my name, or rather *a* name. From the time when I could remember anything, I had been called simply "Booker." Before going to school it had never occurred to me that it was needful or appropriate to have an additional name. When I heard the school-roll called, I noticed that all of the children had at least two names, and some of them indulged in what seemed to me the extravagance of having three. I was in deep perplexity, because I knew that the teacher would demand of me at least two names, and I had only one. By the time the occasion came for the enrolling of my name, an idea occurred to me which I thought would make me equal to the situation; and so, when the teacher asked me what my full name was, I calmly told him "Booker Washington,"[2] as if I had been called by that name all my life; and by that name I have since been known. Later in life I found that my mother had given me the name of "Booker Taliaferro" soon after I was born, but in some way that part of my name seemed to disappear, and for a long while was forgotten, but as soon as I found out about it I revived it, and made my full name "Booker Taliaferro Washington." I think there are not many men in our country who have had the privilege of naming themselves in the way that I have.

More than once I have tried to picture myself in the position of a boy or man with an honoured and distinguished ancestry which I could trace back through a period of hundreds of years, and who had not only inherited a name, but fortune and a proud family homestead; and yet I have sometimes had

2. Washington was his stepfather's first name.

the feeling that if I had inherited these, and had been a member of a more popular race, I should have been inclined to yield to the temptation of depending upon my ancestry and my colour to do that for me which I should do for myself. Years ago I resolved that because I had no ancestry myself I would leave a record of which my children would be proud, and which might encourage them to still higher effort.

The world should not pass judgment upon the Negro, and especially the Negro youth, too quickly or too harshly. The Negro boy has obstacles, discouragements, and temptations to battle with that are little known to those not situated as he is. When a white boy undertakes a task, it is taken for granted that he will succeed. On the other hand, people are usually surprised if the Negro boy does not fail. In a word, the Negro youth starts out with the presumption against him.

The influence of ancestry, however, is important in helping forward any individual or race, if too much reliance is not placed upon it. Those who constantly direct attention to the Negro youth's moral weaknesses, and compare his advancement with that of white youths, do not consider the influence of the memories which cling about the old family homesteads. I have no idea, as I have stated elsewhere, who my grandmother was. I have, or have had, uncles and aunts and cousins, but I have no knowledge as to what most of them are. My case will illustrate that of hundreds of thousands of black people in every part of our country. The very fact that the white boy is conscious that, if he fails in life, he will disgrace the whole family record, extending back through many generations, is of tremendous value in helping him to resist temptations. The fact that the individual has behind and surrounding him proud family

history and connection serves as a stimulus to help him to overcome obstacles when striving for success.

The time that I was permitted to attend school during the day was short, and my attendance was irregular. It was not long before I had to stop attending day-school altogether, and devote all of my time again to work. I resorted to the night-school again. In fact, the greater part of the education I secured in my boyhood was gathered through the night-school after my day's work was done. I had difficulty often in securing a satisfactory teacher. Sometimes, after I had secured some one to teach me at night, I would find, much to my disappointment, that the teacher knew but little more than I did. Often I would have to walk several miles at night in order to recite my night-school lessons. There was never a time in my youth, no matter how dark and discouraging the days might be, when one resolve did not continually remain with me, and that was a determination to secure an education at any cost.

Soon after we moved to West Virginia, my mother adopted into our family, notwithstanding our poverty, an orphan boy, to whom afterward we gave the name of James B. Washington. He has ever since remained a member of the family.

After I had worked in the salt-furnace for some time, work was secured for me in a coal-mine which was operated mainly for the purpose of securing fuel for the salt-furnace. Work in the coal-mine I always dreaded. One reason for this was that any one who worked in a coal-mine was always unclean, at least while at work, and it was a very hard job to get one's skin clean after the day's work was over. Then it was fully a mile from the opening of the coal-mine to the face of the

Young coal miners in Gary, West Virginia.

coal, and all, of course, was in the blackest darkness. I do not believe that one ever experiences anywhere else such darkness as he does in a coal-mine. The mine was divided into a large number of different "rooms" or departments, and, as I never was able to learn the location of all these "rooms," I many times found myself lost in the mine. To add to the horror of being lost, sometimes my light would go out, and then, if I did not happen to have a match, I would wander about in the darkness until by chance I found some one to give me a light. The work was not only hard, but it was dangerous. There was always the danger of being blown to pieces by a premature explosion of powder, or of being crushed by falling slate. Accidents from one or the other of these causes were frequently occurring, and this kept me in constant fear. Many children of the tenderest years were compelled then, as is now true I fear, in most coal-mining districts, to

Up from Slavery   221

spend a large part of their lives in these coal-mines, with little opportunity to get an education; and, what is worse, I have often noted that, as a rule, young boys who begin life in a coal-mine are often physically and mentally dwarfed. They soon lose ambition to do anything else than to continue as a coal-miner.

In those days, and later as a young man, I used to try to picture in my imagination the feelings and ambitions of a white boy with absolutely no limit placed upon his aspirations and activities. I used to envy the white boy who had no obstacles placed in the way of his becoming a Congressman, Governor, Bishop, or President by reason of the accident of his birth or race. I used to picture the way that I would act under such circumstances; how I would begin at the bottom and keep rising until I reached the highest round of success.

In later years, I confess that I do not envy the white boy as I once did. I have learned that success is to be measured not so much by the position that one has reached in life as by the obstacles which he has overcome while trying to succeed. Looked at from this standpoint, I almost reach the conclusion that often the Negro boy's birth and connection with an unpopular race is an advantage, so far as real life is concerned. With few exceptions, the Negro youth must work harder and must perform his task even better than a white youth in order to secure recognition. But out of the hard and unusual struggle which he is compelled to pass, he gets a strength, a confidence, that one misses whose pathway is comparatively smooth by reason of birth and race.

From any point of view, I had rather be what I am, a member of the Negro race, than be able to claim membership with the most favoured of any other race. I have always been made sad when I have heard members of any race claiming rights and privileges, or certain badges of distinction, on the ground simply that they were members of this or that race, regardless of their own individual worth or attainments. I have been made to feel sad for such persons because I am conscious of the fact that mere connection with what is known as a superior race will not permanently carry an individual forward unless he has individual worth, and mere connection with what is regarded as an inferior race will not finally hold an individual back if he possesses intrinsic, individual merit. Every persecuted individual and race should get much consolation out of the great human law, which is universal and eternal, that merit, no matter under what skin found, is in the long run, recognized and rewarded. This I have said here, not to call attention to myself as an individual, but to the race to which I am proud to belong.

Responding to the Selection

from **Up from Slavery** by Booker T. Washington

Identifying Facts

1. What two actions did the ex-slaves on plantations feel they had to take?
2. At first, Washington was not permitted to attend school. Why not?
3. Why did he move the hands of the office clock?
4. How did Washington get his full name?
5. What kinds of work did he do?

Interpreting Meanings

1. Washington's desire for an education was shared by many of the black people in Malden. How did they cooperate in order to open a school for their children? In what way was the "whole race trying to go to school"?
2. Washington clearly feels that he owes his success to the qualities he inherited from his mother. How did she help him to realize his ambition? Why does he feel that she had great "strength of character"?
3. Washington compares his own situation with that of children who enjoy the privileges of "an honoured and distinguished ancestry." Why does he feel that inherited advantages can be a disadvantage? Do you agree with his conclusions?
4. "Years ago I resolved that because I had no ancestry myself I would leave a record of which my children would be proud, and which might encourage them to still higher effort." What does this statement reveal about the self-image of ex-slaves in Washington's time? Why do you suppose he makes no mention of his African heritage?
5. Washington comes to the conclusion that "success is to be measured not so much by the position that one has reached in life as by the obstacles which he has overcome while trying to succeed." Explain what he means. Do you agree or disagree with this statement?
6. After reading this excerpt from his autobiography, how would you describe Washington's character? Can you understand why he was referred to as the "Moses of his race"?

Literary Elements

Understanding a Writer's Purpose

A writer's purpose is revealed not only in direct statements but also in the details and examples chosen and the words used to express ideas and feelings.

Booker T. Washington might have called his autobiography *The Story of My Life.* Instead he chose to call it *Up from Slavery.* What does the title suggest about his purpose in writing this book?

What do you think he is attempting to communicate to his readers by emphasizing the difficulties he faced in getting an education?

Up from Slavery 223

Why does he include the incident of turning the clock hands ahead?

Why does he give so much emphasis to the cap made from homespun?

What do you consider Washington's major purpose in writing his autobiography? Be prepared to give reasons for your answer.

Narrative Writing

Relating an Anecdote

An **anecdote** is a very short narrative dealing with a single incident, used to illustrate a point, to explain an idea, or to reveal something about a person. One of the anecdotes Washington uses to impress readers with his eagerness to attend school involves turning ahead the clock hands in the office of the salt furnace. What other anecdotes does he include? What is his purpose in telling these anecdotes?

Think of someone you know well and try to remember a brief anecdote that reveals some characteristic about that person. Write the anecdote, making it as entertaining or as informative as you can. You may follow this plan if you wish.

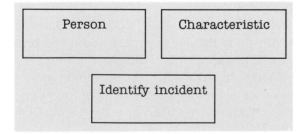

Use the 5 **W–How?** questions (**who? what? when? where? why?** and **how?**) to list events of the incident.

Events

Plan an opening sentence that captures your reader's attention.

Opening Sentence

Critical Thinking

Recognizing Two Sides of a Controversy

The following poem represents a **debate** in verse. The poet, Dudley Randall, has imagined a contest between Booker T. Washington and W. E. B. Du Bois.

In a formal debate, each speaker has a chance to speak twice. In the first round of speeches, each speaker tries to build up an argument by presenting reasons. In the second round of speeches, each speaker tries to answer the objections of the other side.

After reading the poem, make a list of each speaker's main points. Then determine which position you think is more convincing. Note that "Mister Charlie" (line 4) refers to a white farmer.

Booker T. and W. E. B.
Dudley Randall

"It seems to me," said Booker T.,
"It shows a mighty lot of cheek
To study chemistry and Greek
When Mister Charlie needs a hand
To hoe the cotton on his land,⠀⠀⠀⠀⠀5
And when Miss Ann looks for a cook,
Why stick your nose inside a book?"

"I don't agree," said W. E. B.,
"If I should have the drive to seek
Knowledge of chemistry or Greek,⠀⠀⠀10
I'll do it. Charles and Miss can look
Another place for hand or cook.
Some men rejoice in skill of hand,
And some in cultivating land,
But there are others who maintain,⠀⠀15
The right to cultivate the brain."

"It seems to me," said Booker T.,
"That all you folks have missed the boat
Who shout about the right to vote,
And spend vain days and sleepless
⠀⠀⠀nights⠀⠀⠀⠀⠀⠀⠀⠀⠀⠀⠀⠀⠀⠀20
In uproar over civil rights.
Just keep your mouths shut, do
⠀⠀⠀not grouse,
But work, and save, and buy a house."

"I don't agree," said W. E. B.,
"For what can property avail⠀⠀⠀⠀25
If dignity and justice fail?
Unless you help to make the laws,
They'll steal your house with
⠀⠀⠀trumped-up clause.
A rope's as tight, a fire as hot,
No matter how much cash you've
⠀⠀⠀got.⠀⠀⠀⠀⠀⠀⠀⠀⠀⠀⠀⠀⠀⠀30
Speak soft, and try your little plan,
But as for me, I'll be a man."

"It seems to me," said Booker T.—

"I don't agree,"
Said W. E. B.⠀⠀⠀⠀⠀⠀⠀⠀⠀⠀35

Use the form distributed by your teacher or a separate sheet of paper to complete these lists.

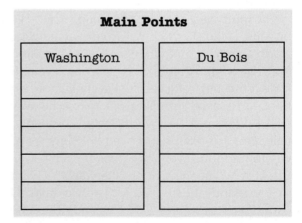

Main Points

Washington	Du Bois

About the Author

Charles W. Chesnutt (1858–1932)

Charles Waddell Chesnutt excelled in short fiction. "As a writer of satirical tales," one critic notes, "Chesnutt was by far the most accomplished literary artist of the Age of Washington."

Chesnutt was born in Cleveland, Ohio. His parents, who had come from Fayetteville, North Carolina, met while they were traveling north by wagon train. They settled in Cleveland for a time but returned to Fayetteville when Chesnutt was eight years old. While he was still a pupil at the Howard School, he began teaching. In 1883 he moved to New York, where he found work as a reporter for a Wall Street news agency. Soon afterward he went to Cleveland and took a job with a railroad company. He remained in Cleveland, where he became quite successful as a lawyer and a court stenographer and where he realized his literary ambitions.

It has been said that Chesnutt never belonged completely either to a Southern or a Northern world. During the seventeen years spent in North Carolina, he came to understand the problems of Southern Reconstruction. During his years in Cleveland, he came to know the values of the rising middle class of black Americans.

Chesnutt first came to the attention of readers in 1887 when his story "The Goophered Grapevine" was published. "The Goophered Grapevine" is one of Chesnutt's **conjure tales**—stories of magic and witchcraft fashioned out of the tales he had heard from freed slaves. The word *goopher* means "spell." The story describes the weird life and death of a slave who eats from a bewitched grapevine. The story also reveals the greed and ruthlessness of chattel slavery.

Chesnutt published two collections of stories in 1899, *The Conjure Woman* and *The Wife of His Youth and Other Stories of the Color Line.* The stories in the second collection deal with problems caused by racial prejudice. In "The Wife of His Youth," the main character, Mr. Ryder, is courting a young widow who is part of an exclusive set. His wife, from whom he has been separated for twenty-five years, appears and Ryder is forced to choose between the two women. He decides finally to acknowledge his past and to renounce the widow.

In addition to short stories, Chesnutt wrote novels, poems, and essays. He also wrote a biography of Frederick Douglass.

Before You Read

The Bouquet

Using What You Know

What does the word *aristocracy* mean? Who were the members of the *Southern aristocracy* in the decades before the Civil War? What attitudes and values do you associate with the members of this social class? Think of books and films that have helped to create your impressions of the age.

Literary Focus: Irony

The term **irony** generally refers to the difference or contrast between appearance and reality. Two basic kinds of irony are **irony of situation** and **verbal irony**. A situation is ironic if events turn out to be different from what is expected. Imagine, for example, laughing at someone who is wearing one brown and one blue sock. Then you look down at your own feet and discover that your shoes don't match! **Verbal irony** refers to saying what one does *not* mean. If you refer to a run-down car as a "limousine," you are using verbal irony.

Irony has many uses in literature. Essentially, it shows us that life is unpredictable and that our actions don't always have their intended result.

Setting a Purpose

As you read, note how Chesnutt uses irony to comment on the attitudes and values of his characters.

The Bouquet

Charles W. Chesnutt

1

Mary Myrover's friends were somewhat surprised when she began to teach a colored school. Miss Myrover's friends are mentioned here, because nowhere more than in a Southern town is public opinion a force which cannot be lightly contravened. Public opinion, however, did not oppose Miss Myrover's teaching colored children; in fact, all the colored public schools in town—and there were several—were taught by white teachers, and had been so taught since the State had undertaken to provide free public instruction for all children within its boundaries. Previous to that time, there had been a Freedman's Bureau[1] school and a Presbyterian missionary school, but these had been withdrawn when the need for them became less pressing. The colored people of the town had been for some time agitating their right to teach their own schools, but as yet the claim had not been conceded.

The reason Miss Myrover's course created some surprise was not, therefore, the fact that a Southern white woman should teach a colored school; it lay in the fact that up to this time no woman of just her quality had taken up such work. Most of the teachers of colored schools were not of those who had constituted the aristocracy of the old régime;[2] they might be said rather to represent the new order of things, in which labor was in time to become honorable, and men were, after a somewhat longer time, to depend, for their place in society, upon themselves rather than upon their ancestors. Mary Myrover belonged to one of the proudest of the old families. Her ancestors had been people of distinction in Virginia before a collateral branch[3] of the main stock had settled in North Carolina. Before the war, they had been able to live up to their pedigree; but the war brought sad changes. Miss Myrover's father—the Colonel Myrover who led a gallant but desperate charge at Vicksburg[4]—had fallen on the battlefield, and his tomb in the white cemetery was a shrine for the family. On the Confederate Memorial Day, no other grave was so profusely deco-

1. **Freedman's Bureau:** a bureau established by the War Department in March, 1865, to handle the needs of emancipated slaves.

2. **old régime** (rā-zhēm'): former system of government; here, the South before the Civil War.
3. **collateral branch:** having an ancestor in common but descended from a different line.
4. **Vicksburg:** city on the Mississippi River, captured by General Grant in 1863. Grant's object was to control the Mississippi River and split the Confederacy.

rated with flowers, and, in the oration pronounced, the name of Colonel Myrover was always used to illustrate the highest type of patriotic devotion and self-sacrifice. Miss Myrover's brother, too, had fallen in the conflict; but his bones lay in some unknown trench, with those of a thousand others who had fallen on the same field. Ay, more, her lover, who had hoped to come home in the full tide of victory and claim his bride as a reward for gallantry, had shared the fate of her father and brother. When the war was over, the remnant of the family found itself involved in the common ruin,—more deeply involved, indeed, than some others; for Colonel Myrover had believed in the ultimate triumph of his cause, and had invested most of his wealth in Confederate bonds, which were now only so much waste paper.

There had been a little left. Mrs. Myrover was thrifty, and had laid by a few hundred dollars, which she kept in the house to meet unforeseen contingencies. There remained, too, their home, with an ample garden and a well-stocked orchard, besides a considerable tract of country land, partly cleared, but productive of very little revenue.

With their shrunken resources, Miss Myrover and her mother were able to hold up their heads without embarrassment for some years after the close of the war. But when things were adjusted to the changed conditions, and the stream of life began to flow more vigorously in the new channels, they saw themselves in danger of dropping behind, unless in some way they could add to their meagre income. Miss Myrover looked over the field of employment, never very wide for women in the South, and found it occupied. The only available position she could be supposed prepared to fill, and which she could take without distinct loss of caste, was that of a teacher, and there was no vacancy except in one of the colored schools. Even teaching was a doubtful experiment; it was not what she would have preferred, but it was the best that could be done.

"I don't like it, Mary," said her mother. "It's a long step from owning such people to teaching them. What do they need with education? It will only make them unfit for work."

"They're free now, mother, and perhaps they'll work better if they're taught something. Besides, it's only a business arrangement, and doesn't involve any closer contact than we have with our servants."

"Well, I should say not!"sniffed the old lady. "Not one of them will ever dare to presume on your position to take any liberties with us. I'll see to that."

Miss Myrover began her work as a teacher in the autumn, at the opening of the school year. It was a novel experience at first. Though there had always been negro servants in the house, and though on the streets colored people were more numerous than those of her own race, and though she was so familiar with their dialect that she might almost be said to speak it, barring certain characteristic grammatical inaccuracies, she had never been brought in personal contact with so many of them at once as when she confronted the fifty or sixty faces—of colors ranging from a white almost as clear as her own to the darkest livery of the sun—which were gathered in the schoolroom on the morning when she began her duties. Some of the inherited prejudice of her caste, too, made itself felt, though she tried to repress any outward sign of it; and she could perceive that the children were not altogether responsive; they, likewise, were not entirely free from antagonism. The work was unfamiliar to her. She was not physically very strong, and at the close of the first day went home with a splitting headache. If she could have resigned then and there without causing comment or annoyance to others, she would have felt it a privilege to do so. But a night's rest banished her headache and improved her spirits, and the next morning she went to her work with renewed vigor, fortified by the experience of the first day.

Miss Myrover's second day was more satisfactory. She had some natural talent for organization, though hitherto unaware of it, and in the course of the day she got her classes formed and lessons under way. In a week or two she began to classify her pupils in her own mind, as bright or stupid, mischievous or well behaved, lazy or industrious, as the case might be, and to regulate her discipline accordingly. That she had come of a long line of ancestors who had exercised authority and mastership was perhaps not without its effect upon her character, and enabled her more readily to maintain good order in the school. When she was fairly broken in, she found the work rather to her liking, and derived much pleasure from such success as she achieved as a teacher.

It was natural that she should be more attracted to some of her pupils than to others. Perhaps her favorite—or, rather, the one she liked best, for she was too fair and just for conscious favoritism—was Sophy Tucker. Just the ground for the teacher's liking for Sophy might not at first be apparent. The girl was far from the whitest of Miss Myrover's pupils; in fact, she was one of the darker ones. She was not the brightest in intellect, though she always tried to learn her lessons. She was not the best dressed, for her mother was a poor widow, who went out washing and scrubbing for a living. Perhaps the real

tie between them was Sophy's intense devotion to the teacher. It had manifested itself almost from the first day of the school, in the rapt look of admiration Miss Myrover always saw on the little black face turned toward her. In it there was nothing of envy, nothing of regret; nothing but worship for the beautiful white lady—she was not especially handsome, but to Sophy her beauty was almost divine—who had come to teach her. If Miss Myrover dropped a book, Sophy was the first to spring and pick it up; if she wished a chair moved, Sophy seemed to anticipate her wish; and so of all the numberless little services that can be rendered in a schoolroom.

Miss Myrover was fond of flowers, and liked to have them about her. The children soon learned of this taste of hers, and kept the vases on her desk filled with blossoms during their season. Sophy was perhaps the most active in providing them. If she could not get garden flowers, she would make excursions to the woods in the early morning, and bring in great dew-laden bunches of bay, or jasmine, or some other fragrant forest flower which she knew the teacher loved.

"When I die, Sophy," Miss Myrover said to the child one day, "I want to be covered with roses. And when they bury me, I'm sure I shall rest better if my grave is banked with flowers, and roses are planted at my head and at my feet."

Miss Myrover was at first amused at Sophy's devotion; but when she grew more accustomed to it, she found it rather to her liking. It had a sort of flavor of the old régime, and she felt, when she bestowed her kindly notice upon her little black attendant, some of the feudal condescension[5] of the mistress toward the slave. She was kind to

5. **feudal condescension** (kŏn′dĭ-sĕn′shən): that is, willingly coming down to the level of someone considered an inferior.

Sophy, and permitted her to play the rôle she had assumed, which caused sometimes a little jealousy among the other girls. Once she gave Sophy a yellow ribbon which she took from her own hair. The child carried it home, and cherished it as a priceless treasure, to be worn only on the greatest occasions.

Sophy had a rival in her attachment to the teacher, but the rivalry was altogether friendly. Miss Myrover had a little dog, a white spaniel, answering to the name of Prince. Prince was a dog of high degree, and would have very little to do with the children of the school; he made an exception, however, in the case of Sophy, whose devotion for his mistress he seemed to comprehend. He was a clever dog, and could fetch and carry, sit up on his haunches, extend his paw to shake hands, and possessed several other canine accomplishments. He was very fond of his mistress, and always, unless shut up at home, accompanied her to school, where he spent most of his time lying under the teacher's desk, or, in cold weather, by the stove, except when he would go out now and then and chase an imaginary rabbit round the yard, presumably for exercise.

At school Sophy and Prince vied with each other in their attentions to Miss Myrover. But when school was over, Prince went away with her, and Sophy stayed behind; for Miss Myrover was white and Sophy was black, which they both understood perfectly well. Miss Myrover taught the colored children, but she could not be seen with them in public. If they occasionally met her on the street, they did not expect her to speak to them, unless she happened to be alone and no other white person was in sight. If any of the children felt slighted, she was not aware of it, for she intended no slight; she had not been

Schoolteacher Laura Natilda Towne.

brought up to speak to negroes on the street, and she could not act differently from other people. And though she was a woman of sentiment and capable of deep feeling, her training had been such that she hardly expected to find in those of darker hue than herself the same susceptibility—varying in degree, perhaps, but yet the same in kind—that gave to her own life the alternations of feeling that made it most worth living.

Once Miss Myrover wished to carry home a parcel of books. She had the bundle in her hand when Sophy came up.

"Lemme tote yo' bundle fer yer, Miss Ma'y?" she asked eagerly. "I'm gwine yo' way."

The Bouquet 231

"Thank you, Sophy," was the reply. "I'll be glad if you will."

Sophy followed the teacher at a respectful distance. When they reached Miss Myrover's home, Sophy carried the bundle to the doorstep, where Miss Myrover took it and thanked her.

Mrs. Myrover came out on the piazza as Sophy was moving away. She said, in the child's hearing, and perhaps with the intention that she should hear: "Mary, I wish you wouldn't let those little darkeys follow you to the house. I don't want them in the yard. I should think you'd have enough of them all day."

"Very well, mother," replied her daughter. "I won't bring any more of them. The child was only doing me a favor."

Mrs. Myrover was an invalid, and opposition or irritation of any kind brought on nervous paroxysms[6] that made her miserable, and made life a burden to the rest of the household, so that Mary seldom crossed her whims. She did not bring Sophy to the house again, nor did Sophy again offer her services as porter.

One day in spring Sophy brought her teacher a bouquet of yellow roses.

"Dey come off 'n my own bush, Miss Ma'y," she said proudly, "an' I didn't let nobody e'se pull 'em, but saved 'em all fer you, 'cause I know you likes roses so much. I'm gwine bring 'em all ter you as long as dey las'."

"Thank you, Sophy," said the teacher; "you are a very good girl."

2

For another year Mary Myrover taught the colored school, and did excellent service. The children made rapid progress under her tuition, and learned to love her well; for they saw and appreciated, as well as children could, her fidelity to a trust that she might have slighted, as some others did, without much fear of criticism. Toward the end of her second year she sickened, and after a brief illness died.

Old Mrs. Myrover was inconsolable. She ascribed her daughter's death to her labors as teacher of negro children. Just how the color of the pupils had produced the fatal effects she did not stop to explain. But she was too old, and had suffered too deeply from the war, in body and mind and estate, ever to reconcile herself to the changed order of things following the return of peace; and, with an unsound yet perfectly explainable logic, she visited some of her displeasure upon those who had profited most, though passively, by her losses.

"I always feared something would happen to Mary," she said. "It seemed unnatural for her to be wearing herself out teaching little negroes who ought to have been working for her. But the world has hardly been a fit place to live in since the war, and when I follow her, as I must before long, I shall not be sorry to go."

She gave strict orders that no colored people should be admitted to the house. Some of her friends heard of this, and remonstrated.[7] They knew the teacher was loved by the pupils, and felt that sincere respect from the humble would be a worthy tribute to the proudest. But Mrs. Myrover was obdurate.

"They had my daughter when she was alive," she said, "and they've killed her. But she's mine now, and I won't have them come near her. I don't want one of them at the funeral or anywhere around."

---

6. **paroxysms** (păr′ək-sĭz′əmz): sudden attacks or spasms.

7. **remonstrated** (rĭ-mŏn′strāt′əd): objected.

For a month before Miss Myrover's death Sophy had been watching her rosebush—the one that bore the yellow roses—for the first buds of spring, and, when these appeared, had awaited impatiently their gradual unfolding. But not until her teacher's death had they become full-blown roses. When Miss Myrover died, Sophy determined to pluck the roses and lay them on her coffin. Perhaps, she thought, they might even put them in her hand or on her breast. For Sophy remembered Miss Myrover's thanks and praise when she had brought her the yellow roses the spring before.

On the morning of the day set for the funeral, Sophy washed her face until it shone, combed and brushed her hair with painful conscientiousness, put on her best frock, plucked her yellow roses, and, tying them with the treasured ribbon her teacher had given her, set out for Miss Myrover's home.

She went round to the side gate—the house stood on a corner—and stole up the path to the kitchen. A colored woman, whom she did not know, came to the door.

"W'at yer want, chile?" she inquired.

"Kin I see Miss Ma'y?" asked Sophy timidly.

"I don't know, honey. Ole Miss Myrover say she don't want no cullud folks roun' de house endyoin' dis fun'al. I'll look an' see if she's roun' de front room, whar de co'pse is. You sed down heah an' keep still, an' ef she's upstairs maybe I kin git yer in dere a minute. Ef I can't, I kin put yo' bokay 'mongs' de res', whar she won't know nuthin' erbout it."

A moment after she had gone, there was a step in the hall, and old Mrs. Myrover came into the kitchen.

"Dinah!" she said in a peevish tone; "Dinah!"

Receiving no answer, Mrs. Myrover peered around the kitchen, and caught sight of Sophy.

"What are you doing here?" she demanded.

"I—I'm-m waitin' ter see de cook, ma'am," stammered Sophy.

"The cook isn't here now. I don't know where she is. Besides, my daughter is to be buried today, and I won't have any one visiting the servants until the funeral is over. Come back some other day, or see the cook at her own home in the evening."

She stood waiting for the child to go, and under the keen glance of her eyes, Sophy, feeling as though she had been caught in some disgraceful act, hurried down the walk and out of the gate, with her bouquet in her hand.

"Dinah," said Mrs. Myrover, when the cook came back, "I don't want any strange people admitted here today. The house will be full of our friends, and we have no room for others."

"Yas'm," said the cook. She understood perfectly what her mistress meant; and what the cook thought about her mistress was a matter of no consequence.

The funeral services were held at St. Paul's Episcopal Church, where the Myrovers had always worshiped. Quite a number of Miss Myrover's pupils went to the church to attend the services. The building was not a large one. There was a small gallery at the rear, to which colored people were admitted, if they chose to come, at ordinary services; and those who wished to be present at the funeral supposed that the usual custom would prevail. They were therefore surprised, when they went to the side entrance, by which colored people gained access to the gallery stairs, to be met by an usher who barred their passage.

The Bouquet   233

"I'm sorry," he said, "but I have had orders to admit no one until the friends of the family have all been seated. If you wish to wait until the white people have all gone in, and there's any room left, you may be able to get into the back part of the gallery. Of course I can't tell yet whether there'll be any room or not."

Now the statement of the usher was a very reasonable one; but, strange to say, none of the colored people chose to remain except Sophy. She still hoped to use her floral offering for its destined end, in some way, though she did not know just how. She waited in the yard until the church was filled with white people, and a number who could not gain admittance were standing about the doors. Then she went round to the side of the church, and, depositing her bouquet carefully on an old mossy gravestone, climbed up on the projecting sill of a window near the chancel.[8] The window was of stained glass, of somewhat ancient make. The church was old, had indeed been built in colonial times, and the stained glass had been brought from England. The design of the window showed Jesus blessing little children. Time had dealt gently with the window, but just at the feet of the figure of Jesus a small triangular piece of glass had been broken out. To this aperture Sophy applied her eyes, and through it saw and heard what she could of the services within.

Before the chancel, on trestles draped in black, stood the sombre casket in which lay all that was mortal of her dear teacher. The top of the casket was covered with flowers; and lying stretched out underneath it she saw Miss Myrover's little white dog, Prince. He had followed the body to the church, and, slipping in unnoticed among the mourners, had taken his place, from which no one had the heart to remove him.

The white-robed rector read the solemn service for the dead, and then delivered a brief address, in which he dwelt upon the uncertainty of life, and, to the believer, the certain blessedness of eternity. He spoke of Miss Myrover's kindly spirit, and, as an illustration of her love and self-sacrifice for others, referred to her labors as a teacher of the poor ignorant negroes who had been placed in their midst by an all-wise Providence, and whom it was their duty to guide and direct in the station in which God had put them. Then the organ pealed, a prayer was said, and the long cortége[9] moved from the church to the cemetery, about half a mile away, where the body was to be interred.

When the services were over, Sophy sprang down from her perch, and, taking her flowers, followed the procession. She did not walk with the rest, but at a proper and respectful distance from the last mourner. No one noticed the little black girl with the bunch of yellow flowers, or thought of her as interested in the funeral.

The cortége reached the cemetery and filed slowly through the gate; but Sophy stood outside, looking at a small sign in white letters on a black background:—

"*Notice.* This cemetery is for white people only. Others please keep out."

Sophy, thanks to Miss Myrover's painstaking instruction, could read this sign very distinctly. In fact, she had often read it before. For Sophy was a child who loved beauty, in a blind, groping sort of way, and had sometimes stood by the fence of the cemetery and looked through at the green mounds and

---

8. **chancel** (chăn′səl): space around the altar.

9. **cortége** (kôr-tĕzh′): funeral procession.

shaded walks and blooming flowers within, and wished that she might walk among them. She knew, too, that the little sign on the gate, though so courteously worded, was no mere formality; for she had heard how a colored man, who had wandered into the cemetery on a hot night and fallen asleep on the flat top of a tomb, had been arrested as a vagrant and fined five dollars, which he had worked out on the streets, with a ball-and-chain attachment, at twenty-five cents a day. Since that time the cemetery gate had been locked at night.

So Sophy stayed outside, and looked through the fence. Her poor bouquet had begun to droop by this time, and the yellow ribbon had lost some of its freshness. Sophy could see the rector standing by the grave, the mourners gathered round; she could faintly distinguish the solemn words with which ashes were committed to ashes, and dust to dust. She heard the hollow thud of the earth falling on the coffin; and she leaned against the iron fence, sobbing softly, until the grave was filled and rounded off, and the wreaths and other floral pieces were disposed upon it. When the mourners began to move toward the gate, Sophy walked slowly down the street, in a direction opposite to that taken by most of the people who came out.

When they had all gone away, and the sexton had come out and locked the gate behind him, Sophy crept back. Her roses were faded now, and from some of them the petals had fallen. She stood there irresolute,[10] loath to leave with her heart's desire unsatisfied, when, as her eyes sought again the teacher's last resting-place, she saw lying beside the new-made grave what looked like a small

10. **irresolute** (ĭ-rĕz′ə-lōōt′): indecisive.

bundle of white wool. Sophy's eyes lighted up with a sudden glow.

"Prince! Here, Prince!" she called.

The little dog rose, and trotted down to the gate. Sophy pushed the poor bouquet between the iron bars. "Take that ter Miss Ma'y, Prince," she said, "that's a good doggie."

The dog wagged his tail intelligently, took the bouquet carefully in his mouth, carried it to his mistress's grave, and laid it among the other flowers. The bunch of roses was so small that from where she stood Sophy could see only a dash of yellow against the white background of the mass of flowers.

When Prince had performed his mission he turned his eyes toward Sophy inquiringly, and when she gave him a nod of approval lay down and resumed his watch by the graveside. Sophy looked at him a moment with a feeling very much like envy, and then turned and moved slowly away.

Mel Wright

Responding to the Selection

The Bouquet by Charles W. Chesnutt

Identifying Facts

1. Why does Mary Myrover accept a teaching job?
2. Why does Mrs. Myrover object to educating black children?
3. How does Sophy become the teacher's favorite student?
4. Why is Sophy unable to enter the cemetery?
5. How does Prince help Sophy deliver the flowers?

Interpreting Meanings

1. Although the old master-servant relationship ended with the Civil War, many Southern whites were unable to accept the change in their position. How does the characterization of Mrs. Myrover reveal the prejudices of the "old aristocracy"?
2. We are told that Mary Myrover shared some of the "inherited prejudice of her caste," although she tried to repress it. How does her treatment of Sophy show that these old tendencies persist?
3. Sophy's absolute devotion to Mary Myrover is compared to that of Prince, "a dog of high degree." What do you think is intended by this comparison?
4. Sophy is not permitted to join the mourners at the funeral. How does the rejection of her offering—the bouquet—emphasize the degrading effects of racism?

5. What do you think is the author's attitude toward the Myrovers? Does he give you insight into the way Southern women "of quality" viewed themselves? Is his treatment of Sophy sympathetic or ironic?

Literary Elements

Explaining Irony

Irony often points up the absurdity or insensitivity of certain actions or beliefs. Early in the story, Mrs. Myrover questions the value of educating black children: "What do they need with education? It will only make them unfit for work." Since we generally think of education as developing a person's knowledge, skills, and character, the idea that education makes one unfit for work is ironic. This irony is a way of commenting on Mrs. Myrover and others of her class who think that blacks should always do menial labor.

In establishing the background of the story, the narrator refers to "the new order of things, in which labor was in time to become honorable, and men were, after a somewhat longer time, to depend, for their place in society, upon themselves rather than upon their ancestors." What does this statement reveal about attitudes toward work of the "old régime"? In what way is the word *honorable* ironic?

Explain the irony in this statement: "Prince was a dog of high degree, and would have very little to do with the children of the school . . ."

Language and Vocabulary

Using Context Clues

Determine the meaning of each italicized word from context clues. Then check your answers in the Glossary at the back of the textbook.

1. "Miss Myrover's friends are mentioned here, because nowhere more than in a Southern town is public opinion a force which cannot be lightly *contravened.*"
2. "On the Confederate Memorial Day, no other grave was so *profusely* decorated with flowers."
3. "Mrs. Myrover was thrifty, and had laid by a few hundred dollars, which she kept in the house to meet unforeseen *contingencies.*"
4. "If she could not get garden flowers, she would make *excursions* to the woods in the early morning, and bring in great dew-laden bunches of bay, or jasmine, or some other fragrant forest flower . . ."

Creative Writing

Composing a News Story

Imagine that you are a reporter covering Mary Myrover's funeral for a local newspaper. The opening paragraph of your news story—the **lead**—should contain the most important information.

Many news stories include the **5W–How** questions in the lead. **Who?** and **what?** are the first questions to be answered. **When?** and **where?** come next in importance. Then **why?** and **how?** are used to explain what is going on. The rest of the news article fills in the details of the story.

Answer each of these questions, using the information in the story.

WHO? _____
WHAT? _____
WHEN? _____
WHERE? _____
WHY? _____
HOW? _____

Now combine these facts into one or two sentences for your lead, which will give a summary of the action. In the rest of your article, give more information about the **5 W–How** questions. Include information not given in the lead, and include comments by any people you have interviewed.

About the Author

Ida B. Wells (1862–1931)

Oscar B. Willis/The Schomburg Center for Research in Black Culture/New York Public Library

Ida B. Wells was born a slave in Holly Springs, Mississippi, six months before the signing of the Emancipation Proclamation. She became a teacher, a lecturer, and a journalist. From the start of her career, she fought against racial discrimination. When she was twenty-two, she moved to Memphis, Tennessee, and became part owner and reporter for *Free Speech,* a local newspaper. After she investigated the lynching of three black grocers and exposed the white men who were responsible, her printing press was wrecked and she was driven out of Memphis.

In 1894 she moved to Chicago and married Ferdinand L. Barnett, a lawyer and journalist. Even while caring for a growing family, Wells continued her role as a crusader for the rights of blacks, women, and humanity. In 1898 she led a delegation to President McKinley to protest the lynching of a black postmaster. She helped found the NAACP, organized club movements for black women, and promoted political activism for African Americans.

Her autobiography, *Crusade for Justice,* is aptly titled, for like the crusaders of old, she carried her banners for freedom and equality for all people into untraveled territories. In his foreword to her autobiography, John Hope Franklin states, ''Few documents written by an American woman approach this one either in importance or interest.''

Before You Read

from **Crusade for Justice**

Using What You Know

In 1881 Tennessee passed a law that required blacks to travel in separate railroad cars. This law became known as a **Jim Crow law.** Many other Jim Crow laws were written by the Southern states to enforce discrimination. Even before the laws were written, however, Jim Crow practices were in effect. What were some of the ways African Americans were affected by Jim Crow laws? Do you know of any individuals who fought against discrimination in the Jim Crow era?

Literary Focus: Tone

The term **tone** refers to a writer's attitude toward characters and events and toward the reader. A writer's tone can be serious and straightforward, ironic, humorous, indignant, or it may shift several times within a single work. Understanding a writer's tone is important because if you don't understand tone, you might miss the writer's point.

Setting a Purpose

As you read, determine Wells's **tone** toward the events she is reporting. Do you feel that she has represented the facts accurately and objectively? Do you find any shifts in her tone? If so, what might be her purpose?

Crusade for Justice

Ida B. Wells

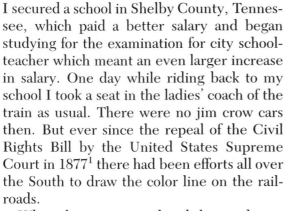

I secured a school in Shelby County, Tennessee, which paid a better salary and began studying for the examination for city school-teacher which meant an even larger increase in salary. One day while riding back to my school I took a seat in the ladies' coach of the train as usual. There were no jim crow cars then. But ever since the repeal of the Civil Rights Bill by the United States Supreme Court in 1877[1] there had been efforts all over the South to draw the color line on the railroads.

When the train started and the conductor came along to collect tickets, he took my ticket, then handed it back to me and told me that he couldn't take my ticket there. I thought that if he didn't want the ticket I wouldn't bother about it so went on reading. In a little while when he finished taking tickets, he came back and told me I would have to go in the other car. I refused, saying that the forward car was a smoker, and as I was in the ladies' car I proposed to stay. He tried to drag me out of the seat, but the moment he caught hold of my arm I fastened my teeth in the back of his hand.

I had braced my feet against the seat in front and was holding to the back, and as he had already been badly bitten he didn't try it again by himself. He went forward and got the baggageman and another man to help him and of course they succeeded in dragging me out. They were encouraged to do this by the attitude of the white ladies and gentlemen in the car; some of them even stood on the seats so that they could get a good view and continued applauding the conductor for his brave stand.

By this time the train had stopped at the first station. When I saw that they were determined to drag me into the smoker, which was already filled with colored people and those who were smoking, I said I would get off the train rather than go in—which I did. Strangely, I held on to my ticket all this time, and although the sleeves of my linen duster had been torn out and I had been pretty roughly handled, I had not been hurt physically.

I went back to Memphis and engaged a colored lawyer to bring suit against the railroad for me. After months of delay I found he had been bought off by the road, and as he was the only colored lawyer in town I had to

1. **repeal . . . 1877:** This ruling occurred in 1883.

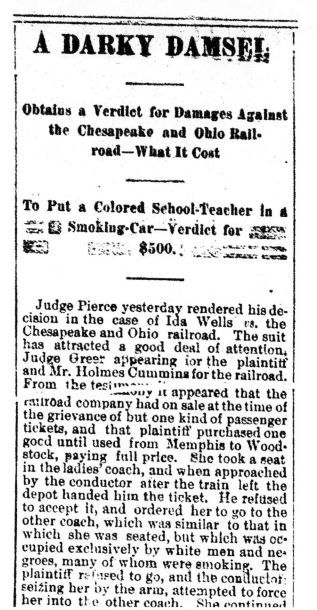

A DARKY DAMSEL.

Obtains a Verdict for Damages Against the Chesapeake and Ohio Railroad—What It Cost

To Put a Colored School-Teacher in a Smoking-Car—Verdict for $500.

Judge Pierce yesterday rendered his decision in the case of Ida Wells *vs.* the Chesapeake and Ohio railroad. The suit has attracted a good deal of attention. Judge Greer appearing for the plaintiff and Mr. Holmes Cummins for the railroad. From the testimony it appeared that the railroad company had on sale at the time of the grievance of but one kind of passenger tickets, and that plaintiff purchased one good until used from Memphis to Woodstock, paying full price. She took a seat in the ladies' coach, and when approached by the conductor after the train left the depot handed him the ticket. He refused to accept it, and ordered her to go to the other coach, which was similar to that in which she was seated, but which was occupied exclusively by white men and negroes, many of whom were smoking. The plaintiff refused to go, and the conductor seizing her by the arm, attempted to force her into the other coach. She continued

The Memphis Daily Appeal, December 25, 1884.

get a white one. This man, Judge Greer, kept his pledge with me and the case was finally brought to trial in the circuit court. Judge Pierce, who was an ex-union soldier from Minnesota, awarded me damages of five hundred dollars. I can see to this day the headlines in the *Memphis Appeal* announcing DARKY DAMSEL GETS DAMAGES.

The railroad appealed the case to the state's supreme court, which reversed the findings of the lower court, and I had to pay the costs. Before this was done, the railroad's lawyer had tried every means in his power to get me to compromise the case, but I indignantly refused. Had I done so, I would have been a few hundred dollars to the good instead of having to pay out over two hundred dollars in court costs.

It was twelve years afterward before I knew why the case had attracted so much attention and was fought so bitterly by the Chesapeake and Ohio Railroad. It was the first case in which a colored plaintiff in the South had appealed to a state court since the repeal of the Civil Rights Bill by the United States Supreme Court. The gist of that decision was that Negroes were not wards of the nation but citizens of the individual states, and should therefore appeal to the state courts for justice instead of to the federal court. The success of my case would have set a precedent which others would doubtless have followed. In this, as in so many other matters, the South wanted the Civil Rights Bill repealed but did not want or intend to give justice to the Negro after robbing him of all sources from which to secure it.

The supreme court of the nation had told us to go to the state courts for redress of grievances; when I did so I was given the brand of justice Charles Sumner[2] knew Negroes would get when he fathered the Civil Rights Bill during the Reconstruction period.

2. **Charles Sumner:** United States senator from Massachusetts. He championed civil rights for freed slaves.

Responding to the Selection

from **Crusade for Justice** by Ida B. Wells

Interpreting Meanings

1. Why did Wells's lawsuit attract so much attention?
2. According to Wells, what was the significance of the state supreme court's decision?
3. Wells states that if she had been willing to compromise the case, she could have avoided paying court costs. Why do you think she refused to give in? Do you consider her actions foolish or admirable?
4. In their conclusion, the state supreme court ruled, "We think it is evident that the purpose of the defendant in error was to harass with a view to this suit, and that her persistence was not in good faith to obtain a comfortable seat for the short ride." Comment on this ruling. How does it reveal the "brand of justice" black Americans received during the Reconstruction period?

Literary Elements

Recognizing Tone

When Wells describes the humiliating experience of being dragged from the ladies' car, she says that the viewers applauded the conductor "for his brave stand." Do you think she is serious about the word *brave* or is she being ironic? What does she really mean to say about the conductor's actions?

Reread the last paragraph of the excerpt aloud. What tone of voice should you use to get across Wells's meaning? What tone will you use for the phrase "brand of justice"?

Expository Writing

Explaining Origins of Terms

Jim Crow, as you have seen, is a term used to refer to many different kinds of discrimination faced by African Americans. The term **Uncle Tom** describes an African American who submits to whites instead of insisting on his rights. Consult a history book or a reference work to learn the origin of each term. In a brief report, explain how each term came to have its present-day meaning. Be sure to identify your source and to enclose in quotation marks any language that you copy from your source.

Speaking and Listening

Conducting an Interview

Choose a figure from past or present history who has fought to defend civil rights. Collect information about that person's life that you will use in an interview. Working with a partner or with a small group, present a talk show in which one student poses as the celebrity while another student takes the role of the talk show's host.

About the Author
W. E. B. Du Bois (1868–1963)

 Martin Luther King, Jr., called Du Bois (dōō bois') "one of the most remarkable men of our time," and the novelist John Oliver Killens claims that "he was the greatest American intellectual of the twentieth century."

William Edward Burghardt Du Bois was born in Great Barrington, Massachusetts. He went to Fisk University in Nashville, Tennessee, and then to Harvard and the University of Berlin. He was the first black person to receive a Ph.D. in American history from Harvard University.

The Souls of Black Folk, which many readers consider his masterpiece, was published in 1903. This work consists of fourteen chapters that blend history, sociology, economic theory, fiction, and political commentary. Here Du Bois announced that "the problem of the Twentieth Century is the problem of the color line." One of his most influential ideas was his adaptation of Ralph Waldo Emerson's concept of a "double-consciousness" to the psychological experience of African Americans, who are described as a people with "two souls," one "American" and one "Negro."

In one essay, "Of Mr. Booker T. Washington and Others," Du Bois challenged Washington's counsel to accept the status quo in exchange for economic cooperation from whites. Du Bois rejected Washington's position. He urged higher education for "the talented tenth" and advocated full political and civil rights for African Americans.

Du Bois became a leader in the Niagara Movement, which demanded equal rights

W. E. B. Du Bois, *pastel by Winold Reiss,* c. 1925 (detail).

for black and white Americans. Between 1910 and 1930 Du Bois edited *The Crisis,* the journal of the National Association for the Advancement of Colored People, an organization he helped to found. He became involved in the international Pan African movement, which sought an independent and united black Africa, free of white colonial powers. In 1940 he founded *Phylon,* a scholarly journal, at Atlanta University.

Du Bois became increasingly disillusioned with the struggle to break down racial barriers in the United States. He left the United States in 1961 for Ghana, where he died in 1963.

A prolific writer, Du Bois left a rich legacy of scholarly books and articles, poetry, fiction, autobiography, and essays.

Before You Read

The Song of the Smoke

Using What You Know

During the last decades of the nineteenth century, the United States emerged as a highly industrialized nation. Cities offered economic opportunities but also presented many problems. What kinds of jobs were available to African Americans who moved from the farms to cities? What difficulties did they face in finding employment and housing?

Literary Focus: Personification

Personification is a form of figurative language in which some object or some idea is spoken of as if it were alive or had human feelings. In the expression "Money talks," *money,* a thing, is given the human characteristic of speech. Poets make particular use of personification. In a famous ode to Autumn, John Keats treats the season as if it were a woman. Give some examples of personification used in everyday situations.

Setting a Purpose

Note how Du Bois uses personification in his poem. Who is the speaker? Is this a poem about the anguish of the black experience or is it about racial pride?

The Song of the Smoke

W. E. B. Du Bois

I am the Smoke King
I am black!
I am swinging in the sky,
I am wringing worlds awry;°
I am the thought of the throbbing mills,   5
I am the soul of the soul-toil kills,
Wraith° of the ripple of trading rills;
Up I'm curling from the sod,
I am whirling home to God;
   I am the Smoke King   10
   I am black.

I am the Smoke King,
I am black!
I am wreathing broken hearts,
I am sheathing love's light darts;   15
   Inspiration of iron times
   Wedding the toil of toiling climes,°
   Shedding the blood of bloodless crimes—
Lurid lowering° 'mid the blue,
Torrid towering toward the true,   20
   I am the Smoke King,
   I am black.

I am the Smoke King,
I am black!
I am darkening with song,   25
I am hearkening to wrong!
   I will be black as blackness can—
   The blacker the mantle, the mightier the man!
   For blackness was ancient ere whiteness began.
I am daubing° God in night,   30
I am swabbing Hell in white:
   I am the Smoke King
   I am black.

4. **awry** (ə-rī′): out of line.

7. **Wraith** (rāth): ghost or specter.

17. **climes**: regions.

19. **lowering** (lou′ər-ĭng): appearing dark and threatening.

30. **daubing** (dôb′ĭng): covering; smearing.

Unity, *mixed media by Herman*
"Kofi" Bailey, 1961.
Collection of Dr. Samella Lewis

  I am the Smoke King
  I am black!   35
I am cursing ruddy morn,
I am hearsing° hearts unborn: **37. hearsing** (hûrs'ĭng):
    Souls unto me are as stars in a night,   shrouding.
    I whiten my black men—I blacken my white!
    What's the hue of a hide to a man in his might? 40
Hail! great, gritty, grimy hands—
Sweet Christ, pity toiling lands!
    I am the Smoke King
    I am black.

Responding to the Selection

The Song of the Smoke by W. E. B. Du Bois

Interpreting Meanings

1. Who is the speaker in the poem? How do you know?
2. In addition to its color, what other characteristics of smoke are referred to in the poem?
3. There are several references in the poem to the dehumanizing effects of industrialization. Locate and explain as many of these as you can.
4. What do you think is meant by the reversals of color in lines 30–31 and 39?
5. Explain the meaning of this line: "The blacker the mantle, the mightier the man." Where else in the poem is a similar idea expressed?
6. What conclusions does the speaker come to?

Literary Elements

Understanding Devices of Repetition

Repetition gives us pleasure in reading and listening to poetry. It also emphasizes and communicates meaning.

One of the most common kinds of repetition is **rhyme**. Another kind of repetition is **alliteration** (ə-lĭt′ə-rā′shən), the repetition of consonant sounds, usually at the beginning of words or on stressed syllables. Still another kind of repetition is the **refrain**, a single line or group of lines that recur throughout a poem.

Examine the rhyme in this pair of lines:

I am **wreathing** broken **hearts**,
I am **sheathing** love's light **darts**;

What ideas are linked through these rhymes? Where else in the poem do you find this rhyme pattern?

Note the repetition of the initial **m** sound in line 28:

The blacker the **m**antle, the **m**ightier the **m**an

What does the alliteration emphasize? Find other examples of alliteration in the poem.

Which lines are repeated throughout the poem? What is emphasized by this refrain? Does the repetition build up to a climax in the poem?

Language and Vocabulary

Recognizing Denotative and Connotative Meanings

The literal (or "dictionary") definition of a word is called its **denotation. Connotation** refers to the emotions and associations that a word arouses. For example, the word *hide* literally means "the skin of an animal." In line 40, however, the word *hide* refers to a human being, and here the word carries with it all the associations of a thick, tough animal skin. Why do you suppose Du Bois chose to use this word?

Writers use the connotative meanings of words to arouse feelings and moods. Consider the meanings of the word *mantle* in line 28:

WORD	DENOTATION	CONNOTATION
mantle	cloak	something that covers and enfolds or conceals

Using this chart as a model, give the denotative and connotative meanings of at least three words selected from the poem. Check your answers in a dictionary.

Creative Writing

Personifying an Object

Poets have written imaginatively from the point of view of many different objects. One poet wrote a long poem with a cloud as speaker. Another poet gave the grass a character.

Choose some object or idea to personify. Then write a short story or poem from the point of view of that object. Imagine, for example, that your TV set has a personality and powers of observation. What story might it tell about its viewers?

You might complete this outline, noting details from the vantage point of your TV set.

Identification
Model _____

Dimensions _____

Where Kept _____

Viewers' Habits
Who Watches Me and When _____

_____

Favorite Programs _____

_____

You can add specific episodes. What happens, for instance, when there is a conflict over what to watch?

Speaking and Listening

Reciting a Poem

Prepare a reading of Du Bois's poem, using choral responses for the refrains. If someone in your class plays a guitar, you might want to have musical accompaniment for the reading.

About the Author

Paul Laurence Dunbar (1872–1906)

Paul Laurence Dunbar was the first African American poet to achieve national recognition. He has been called the "poet laureate of the Negro race."

Dunbar was born in Dayton, Ohio, the son of former slaves. He began writing while still in high school. The only black student in his class, he became class president and class poet. He hoped to study law but he had no money. He supported himself by working as an elevator operator while he continued to write.

Dunbar's first collection of poems, *Oak and Ivy,* was published in 1893, with the assistance of Orville Wright, who had been his classmate. The volume included some dialect poems as well as poems in standard English. "Sympathy," one of his best-known works, appeared in this collection (see page 45).

At the Chicago World's Fair in 1893, he assisted Frederick Douglass at the Haiti Pavilion. Douglass considered Dunbar to be "the most promising black man of his time."

In his second verse collection, *Majors and Minors* (1895), Dunbar wrote in several styles. He included his standard English poems under the heading of "Majors" and his dialect works under the heading of "Minors." *Lyrics of Lowly Life* (1896), a third volume, sold extremely well.

Dunbar won high praise from the critic William Dean Howells. Dunbar soon realized, however, that he was not valued primarily for the poems he considered his major work. His readers, who were chiefly whites, pre-

William Loren Katz

ferred poems that reinforced the stereotypes of contented blacks living in harmony on Southern plantations. He said:

> You know, of course, that I didn't start as a dialect poet. I simply came to the conclusion that I could write it as well, if not better than anybody else I knew of, and that by doing so I should gain a hearing, and now they don't want me to write anything but dialect.

Dunbar wrote short stories and novels, but he is best remembered as a poet. Today his reputation rests mainly on the poems he wrote in standard English.

Dunbar was always frail and in the spring of 1899, already suffering from tuberculosis, he developed pneumonia. He continued to work even though he knew he was incurably ill. The *Complete Poems* was published in 1913, seven years after his death.

Paul Laurence Dunbar 249

Before You Read

We Wear the Mask; The Debt; Life's Tragedy; Douglass

Using What You Know

A mask, as you know, is a cover of some kind used to disguise the face. The word *mask* is also used in a figurative sense for something that conceals one's feelings or intentions from view. Have you ever put on an act to protect your real feelings and thoughts? Why was it important to cover up your real self? Think of how other people use "masks" as defenses or as false faces. Share your responses with your classmates.

Literary Focus: The Lyric

A **lyric** is a poem that expresses the speaker's thoughts and feelings. Originally, the lyric was a poem sung to the accompaniment of an instrument called the lyre. We still use this meaning when we call the words of a song its *lyrics.* A lyric is generally short. It can express a range of personal and subjective emotions. Lyric poetry takes many different forms, including **songs, hymns, sonnets,** and **elegies.** The lyric is particularly suitable to autobiographical subjects.

Setting a Purpose

Dunbar wrote these lyrics many years ago, a generation after the end of slavery. What emotions and ideas does he express? Why do these poems still appeal to us?

We Wear the Mask

Paul Laurence Dunbar

We wear the mask that grins and lies,
It hides our cheeks and shades our eyes,—
This debt we pay to human guile;
With torn and bleeding hearts we smile,
And mouth with myriad° subtleties.   5

5. **myriad** (mĭr′ē-əd): innumerable.

Why should the world be over-wise,
In counting all our tears and sighs?
Nay, let them only see us, while
   We wear the mask.

We smile, but, O great Christ, our
   cries   10
To thee from tortured souls arise.
We sing, but oh the clay is vile
Beneath our feet, and long the mile;
But let the world dream otherwise,
   We wear the mask.   15

Les Fétiches (Fetishes), *oil by Loïs Mailou Jones, 1938.*
The National Museum of American Art, Smithsonian Institution, Washington, D.C./Art Resource, NY

The Debt

Paul Laurence Dunbar

This is the debt I pay
Just for one riotous day,
Years of regret and grief,
Sorrow without relief.

Pay it I will to the end—   5
Until the grave, my friend,
Gives me a true release—
Gives me the clasp of peace.

Slight was the thing I bought,
Small was the debt I thought,   10
Poor was the loan at best—
God! but the interest!

Ralph Morse, Life Magazine
© Time, Inc.

Life's Tragedy

Paul Laurence Dunbar

It may be misery not to sing at all
    And to go silent through the brimming day.
It may be sorrow never to be loved,
    But deeper griefs than these beset the way.

To have come near to sing the perfect song   5
   And only by a half-tone° lost the key,
There is the potent sorrow, there the grief,
   The pale, sad staring of life's tragedy.

To have just missed the perfect love,
   Not the hot passion of untempered youth,   10
But that which lays aside its vanity
   And gives thee, for thy trusting worship, truth—

This, this it is to be accursed indeed;
   For if we mortals love, or if we sing,
We count our joys not by the things we have,   15
   But by what kept us from the perfect thing.

6. **half-tone:** the smallest interval in a musical scale, as between a white key and a black key on a piano.

Douglass

Paul Laurence Dunbar

Ah, Douglass, we have fall'n on evil days,
   Such days as thou, not even thou didst know,
   When thee, the eyes of that harsh long ago
Saw, salient,° at the cross of devious ways,
And all the country heard thee with amaze.   5
   Not ended then, the passionate ebb and flow,
   The awful tide that battled to and fro;
We ride amid a tempest of dispraise.

Now, when the waves of swift dissension swarm,
   And Honor, the strong pilot, lieth stark,°   10
Oh, for thy voice high-sounding o'er the storm,
   For thy strong arm to guide the shivering bark,°
The blast-defying power of thy form,
   To give us comfort through the lonely dark.

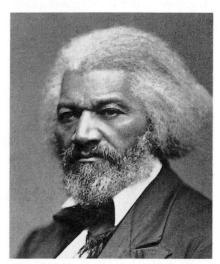

National Archives

4. **salient** (sā′lê-ənt): easily seen.

10. **stark:** stiff as a corpse.

12. **bark:** boat.

Responding to the Selections

Four Poems by Paul Laurence Dunbar

Interpreting Meanings

We Wear the Mask

1. In your own words explain what "the mask" refers to.
2. Who are the wearers of the mask? What emotions does the mask conceal?
3. *Guile* is the use of deceptive words or actions to cover up one's true intentions. Whose guile is referred to in line 3?
4. Why doesn't the speaker want the world to see "our tears and sighs"?
5. In the last stanza, what feelings are revealed?
6. Why does the speaker choose the point of view of "we" rather than "I"?

The Debt

1. A *debt* is something that is owed, usually money. What other kinds of debts are there?
2. Consider the debt the speaker refers to as a **metaphor** that stands for something else, such as a moral obligation. What, then, might the "one riotous day" represent? What would the "interest" be?

Life's Tragedy

1. In lines 15–16 the speaker says that life's tragedy lies in not being satisfied with "the things we have" and in longing for the things that remain out of reach. Why does the speaker feel that this situation is tragic?
2. What distinction does the speaker draw between perfect and imperfect love?

3. In stanza 2 Dunbar uses an **image** from music to suggest the grief of life's tragedy. Explain the image and tell whether or not it is effective.
4. What might have led the speaker to feel as he does? Do you think the poem expresses the feelings of a disappointed lover?

Douglass

1. Frederick Douglass was a great orator who became a powerful spokesperson for the abolition of slavery (see page 171). Where does Dunbar refer to Douglass's leadership in the antislavery movement? Why does he feel that Douglass's spirit is needed?
2. Dunbar wrote this poem long after the slaves had been emancipated. What do you think he is referring to as "evil days" in line 1?
3. How does the poet use the **metaphor** of a ship caught in a storm to describe the crisis of the times? What words or phrases does he use to sustain the comparison throughout the poem?

Literary Elements

Understanding the Structure of a Sonnet

A **sonnet** is one kind of lyric. A sonnet has fourteen lines. The lines are generally written in **iambic pentameter** (that is, a typical line has ten syllables with every second syllable accented):

To give us comfort through the lonely dark

Sonnets vary in structure and **rhyme scheme**. The rhyme scheme is indicated by a different letter of the alphabet for each new rhyme:

Ah, Douglass, we have fall'n on evil
days,   a
　Such days as thou, not even thou
　didst know,   b
　When thee, the eyes of that harsh
　long ago   b
Saw, salient, at the cross of devious
ways,   a
And all the country heard thee with
amaze.   a
　Not ended then, the passionate ebb
　and flow,   b
　The awful tide that battled to and
　fro;   b
We ride amid a tempest of dispraise.   a

Now, when the waves of swift dissension
swarm,   c
　And Honor, the strong pilot, lieth
　stark,   d
Oh, for thy voice high-sounding o'er
the storm,   c
　For thy strong arm to guide the
　shivering bark,   d
The blast-defying power of thy form,   c
　To give us comfort through the
　lonely dark.   d

The words *swarm, storm,* and *form* are not **exact rhymes** but are **approximate rhymes**, since the final sounds of the words are similar.

Two well-known types of sonnets are the **English** (or **Shakespearean**) and the **Italian** (or **Petrarchan**). Dunbar uses the Italian sonnet form in his tribute to Douglass.

The Italian sonnet consists of two parts—an **octave** of eight lines and a **sestet** of six lines. In some sonnets the first eight lines state a problem or ask a question. The final six lines offer a solution or answer the question. Examine Dunbar's poem. What idea is expressed in the first eight lines? What idea is expressed in the last six lines?

Language and Vocabulary
Noting Archaic Meanings of Words
A writer's choice of words is known as **diction**. Diction can be formal or informal.

An **archaism** (är'kē-ĭs'əm) is a word or expression that is no longer in common use. In the past, poets used archaisms to re-create a particular historical period or to give their work a more dignified style.

In "Douglass," Dunbar uses two archaic verb forms. The word *didst* in line 2 is an old form of the past tense of *do*. Locate another archaic verb form in the poem.

For many years the pronoun *thou* was used in speaking to someone familiar. *Thou* is still retained in religious use and occasionally in poetry. Locate two other old pronoun forms in the poem. Which words have replaced them?

Writing About Literature

Paraphrasing a Poem

A **paraphrase** is a summary or restatement of a piece of work. When you paraphrase a poem, you restate its language and ideas in your own words. A paraphrase helps to clarify meaning. It restates images and figures of speech in plain language. It puts unusual constructions into normal word order.

Consider lines 4–5 of "We Wear the Mask":

With torn and bleeding hearts we smile,
And mouth with myriad subleties.

Note that the order of words in line 4 is **inverted**, or turned around. First place the words in an order that represents a more natural form of speech:

We smile with torn and bleeding hearts

It is obvious that "torn and bleeding hearts" is a **metaphor**. Substitute a phrase that expresses the poet's idea, for example, "painful feelings" or "profound unhappiness."

The word *mouth* as a verb means "to speak." The phrase *myriad subleties* might be restated as "countless indirect, elusive statements."

A free paraphrase of the lines might be

We hide our painful feelings by smiling, and our speech is filled with countless indirect and elusive statements.

Write a paraphrase of the entire poem.

Speaking and Listening

Giving an Oral Interpretation

Select one of Dunbar's poems for oral presentation to the class. Here are some guidelines to help you prepare your reading:

1. Read the poem several times silently until you understand what the poet is saying.
2. Check the pronunciation of all unfamiliar words.
3. Note the words and phrases that are most expressive of meaning.
4. Decide if the poem calls for a slow, deliberate reading, a fast, lively reading, or some other movement.
5. Follow the punctuation clues and read units of thought, not separate lines.
6. Avoid a singsong reading.
7. Prepare a brief introduction to the poem.
8. Practice reading the poem to a partner or to a small group.

Critical Thinking

Comparing Two Treatments of a Metaphor

Some metaphors have unlimited possibilities and are used over and over again by writers. The metaphor of a ship in a storm has appealed to the imagination of many different poets. It was used by the English poet Sir Thomas Wyatt to express the unhappiness of a lover whose emotions are out of control.

Walt Whitman, an American poet, wrote the following poem in 1865, six months after the end of the Civil War. He was deeply moved by Lincoln's assassination and wrote this **elegy**, a poem of mourning, lamenting the President's death. Note how Whitman uses the metaphor of a ship and its captain. Compare his treatment of the metaphor with that of Dunbar's "Douglass."

O Captain! My Captain!
Walt Whitman

O Captain! my Captain! our fearful trip is done,
The ship has weathered every rack,° the prize we sought is won,
The port is near, the bells I hear, the people all exulting,
While follow eyes the steady keel, the vessel grim and daring;
   But O heart! heart! heart!   5
     O the bleeding drops of red,
       Where on the deck my Captain lies,
         Fallen cold and dead.

O Captain! my Captain! rise up and hear the bells;
Rise up—for you the flag is flung—for you the bugle trills,   10
For you bouquets and ribboned wreaths—for you the shores
   a-crowding,
For you they call, the swaying mass, their eager faces turning;
   Here Captain! dear father!
     This arm beneath your head!
       It is some dream that on the deck   15
         You've fallen cold and dead.

My Captain does not answer, his lips are pale and still,
My father does not feel my arm, he has no pulse nor will,
The ship is anchored safe and sound, its voyage closed and done,
From fearful trip the victor ship comes in with object won;   20
   Exult O shores! and ring O bells!
     But I with mournful tread
       Walk the deck my Captain lies,
         Fallen cold and dead.

2. **rack:** here an upheaval caused by a storm.

Library of Congress

O Captain! My Captain! 257

Before You Read

John Henry

Using What You Know

American folk tales include stories about famous heroes and heroines. You may have heard of Paul Bunyan, the giant logger of the northern lumber camps, or Pecos Bill, the Texas cowhand who was rescued by coyotes, and his girl, Slue-Foot Sue. Can you identify Mike Fink, Casey Jones, or Stackalee? What do all of these legendary figures have in common?

Background

Like many other heroes and heroines of legend, John Henry was probably a real person. It is believed that he worked for the Chesapeake and Ohio Railroad in the 1870s. The railroad was building the Big Ben Tunnel in West Virginia. John Henry's job was to pound holes for explosives into the rock by using a long-handled hammer. The story goes that one day his foreman brought a steam drill to the site and bragged that it could dig a hole faster than twenty drillers using hammers. According to legend, John Henry challenged the foreman to a contest. He won the contest but died from exhaustion. The version of the story that appears here is from *The Book of Negro Folklore*, edited by Langston Hughes and Arna Bontemps.

Literary Focus: Folk Ballad

A **folk ballad** or **popular ballad** is a song that tells a story and that has been transmitted from one generation to another by word of mouth. The folk ballad may have been composed by a single author, but the identity of that person in unknown. Since each singer who learns the song tends to introduce changes, there are variant forms for many ballads.

Setting a Purpose

As you read, note the importance of dialogue and action. What kind of information is *not* given in the story?

John Henry

Some say he's from Georgia,
Some say he's from Alabam,
But it's wrote on the rock at the Big Ben
    Tunnel,
John Henry's a East Virginia Man,
John Henry's a East Virginia Man.   5

John Henry he could hammah,
He could whistle, he could sing,
He went to the mountain early in the
    mornin'
To hear his hammah ring,
To hear his hammah ring.   10

John Henry went to the section boss,
Says the section boss what kin you do?
Says I can line a track, I kin histe a jack,
I kin pick and shovel, too,
I kin pick and shovel, too.   15

John Henry went to the tunnel
And they put him in lead to drive,
The rock was so tall and John Henry so
    small
That he laid down his hammah and he
    cried,
That he laid down his hammah and he
    cried.   20

The steam drill was on the right han' side,
John Henry was on the left,
Says before I let this steam drill beat me
    down,
I'll hammah myself to death,
I'll hammah myself to death.   25

Oh the cap'n said to John Henry,
I bleeve this mountain's sinkin' in.
John Henry said to the cap'n, Oh my!
Tain't nothin' but my hammah suckin'
    wind,
Tain't nothin' but my hammah suckin'
    wind.   30

John Henry had a pretty liddle wife,
She come all dressed in blue.
And the last words she said to him,
John Henry I been true to you,
John Henry I been true to you.   35

John Henry was on the mountain,
The mountain was so high,
He called to his pretty liddle wife,
Said Ah kin almos' touch the sky,
Said Ah kin almos' touch the sky.   40

Who gonna shoe yoh pretty liddle feet,
Who gonna glove yoh han',
Who gonna kiss yoh rosy cheeks,
An' who gonna be yoh man,
An' who gonna be yoh man?   45

Papa gonna shoe my pretty liddle feet,
Mama gonna glove my han',
Sistah gonna kiss my rosy cheeks,
An' I ain't gonna have no man,
An' I ain't gonna have no man.   50

Then John Henry he did hammah,
He did make his hammah soun',
Says now one more lick fore quittin' time,
An' I'll beat this steam drill down,
An' I'll beat this steam drill down.   55

The hammah that John Henry swung,
It weighed over nine poun',
He broke a rib in his left han' side,
And his intrels fell on the groun',
And his intrels fell on the groun'.   60

All the women in the West
That heard of John Henry's death,
Stood in the rain, flagged the east bound
    train,
Goin' where John Henry dropped dead,
Goin' where John Henry dropped dead. 65

They took John Henry to the White
    House,
And buried him in the san',
And every locomotive come roarin' by,
Says there lays that steel drivin' man,
Says there lays that steel drivin' man.   70

His Hammer in His Hand, *oil by Palmer Hayden, from the John*
Henry series, 1944–1954.
From the Collection of The Museum of African American Art (L.A.), Palmer C. Hayden
Collection, Gift of Miriam A. Hayden

Responding to the Selection

Interpreting Meanings

1. Why do you think John Henry challenges the steam driller? How can this contest be viewed as a heroic act?
2. How does the dialogue between John Henry and his wife **foreshadow** the tragedy?
3. How does John Henry die? Why is he given a hero's burial?
4. The legend of John Henry is said to **symbolize**, or stand for, the contest between human beings and machines. Do you agree with this interpretation? Give reasons for your answer.

Literary Elements

Recognizing Characteristics of the Ballad

The **folk ballad** has the following characteristics:

1. The theme is often tragic.
2. The poem usually has a strong dramatic effect.
3. The story is told through dialogue and action.
4. The narrative moves quickly with minimal detail or characterization.
5. The language is simple and is often in dialect.
6. The poem has rhyme and often one or more refrains.
7. The ballad uses abrupt transitions.

Remember that the folk ballads had to be recalled from memory. Which of these characteristics do you think would help singers to memorize the poems?

Creative Writing

Developing a Script

Form a small group. Write a radio or television script, giving your version of the legend of John Henry. You will need to invent dialogue for your characters. Be sure to include the setting when you write the script. Present the play to the class.

Speaking and Listening

Interpreting a Ballad

Practice reading "John Henry." You can take all the speaking parts yourself. Determine how you will speak the lines for the narrator, John Henry, his wife, and the captain. How will you handle lines 69–70?

Writing a Report

The purpose of **exposition** is to give information or to explain something. Most of the writing you do in your classes is expository.

The following paragraph from the unit introduction is an example of exposition. Note that the paragraph states and supports a **main idea**.

Unfortunately, Reconstruction in the South did not change significantly the economic power of whites over blacks. Many ex-slaves believed that the federal government would divide the land seized from the great plantation owners of the South and award "forty acres and a mule" to blacks who wished to become independent farmers. Instead, most of the land remained in the hands of whites, and freedmen and women found themselves compelled to work it for slim wages or shares of whatever they could harvest. This arrangement kept black agricultural workers, who composed the large majority of Southern African Americans, at the mercy of whites. Blacks who moved to urban centers in search of better opportunities generally met strong resistance from white workers, who saw African Americans as competitors for jobs already made scarce by the depressed Southern economy.

1. Which sentence states the main idea of the paragraph?
2. What details, examples, or reasons support the main idea?

Writing a Report

A research report is one kind of expository essay. In choosing a topic for a report, consult with your teacher, who can guide you in limiting your topic and in finding reference sources. For example, suppose you were interested in learning about African American journalism. You would have to narrow your topic so that it could be covered adequately in a short paper. Some possible topics for research might be

Early African American Newspapers
The Importance of African American Newspapers in the
    Antislavery Crusade
Frederick Douglass's *North Star*
Ida B. Wells's Campaign Against Lynching

Here are some other topics that can be narrowed for research. Choose one of these topics or another approved by your teacher for a short research paper:

The Black Codes
The Freedmen's Bureau
The Niagara Movement

The NAACP
Civil Rights Acts in
the Nineteenth Century

Prewriting Strategies

1. Limit your topic so that you can deal with it adequately in a short paper. Be sure you can find the information you need in printed and electronic sources.
2. As you gather information, keep a record of each source.
3. Use note cards or separate sheets of paper to take notes as you read. Use quotation marks for exact quotations. Most notes should be summarized or paraphrased in your own words.
4. Organize your cards according to major headings.
5. Use the headings to develop an outline.

Writing a First Draft

1. Begin with a **thesis statement** that identifies your topic and states the purpose of your paper.
2. Use your outline to help you develop each paragraph.
3. Support each main idea with details, examples, or reasons.
4. Vary the style of your sentences.

Evaluating and Revising

1. Is there enough factual information to develop the topic?
2. Did you begin with a thesis statement?
3. Have you used your own words wherever possible?
4. Have you identified the source of every direct quotation?
5. Does each paragraph discuss only one main idea?
6. Are your ideas arranged in a logical order?
7. Have you used transitional expressions?

Writing the Final Draft

1. Check your paper for errors in grammar, usage, and mechanics.
2. Prepare a final copy and check it for accuracy.

LANGUAGE WORKSHOP

LW 10 Ch 12
The Research Paper

WRITER'S WORKSHOP 2

Informative Report (Expository Writing)

UNIT REVIEW

▶I. Interpreting New Material

In his own day Dunbar was better known for his poetry in black dialect than for his poetry in standard English. A reaction to his dialect verse set in during the 1920s. Some African American writers felt that this poetry presented racist stereotypes based upon minstrel traditions.

In recent years Dunbar's achievement in dialect verse has been reassessed. Many readers have come to the conclusion that in his representation of black folk language and tradition he transcended the negative images associated with dialect verse to create an authentic black poetic diction.

A. Read the following poem carefully before answering the questions.

When Malindy Sings
Paul Laurence Dunbar

G'way an' quit dat noise, Miss Lucy—
  Put dat music book away;
What's de use to keep on tryin'?
  Ef you practise twell you're gray,
You cain't sta't no notes a-flyin'   5
  Lak de ones dat rants and rings
F'om de kitchen to de big woods
  When Malindy sings.

You ain't got de nachel o'gans
  Fu' to make de soun' come right,   10
You ain't got de tu'ns an' twistin's
  Fu' to make it sweet an' light.
Tell you one thing now, Miss Lucy,
  An' I'm tellin' you fu' true,
When hit comes to raal right singin',   15
  'T ain't no easy thing to do.

Easy 'nough fu' folks to hollah,
  Lookin' at de lines an' dots,
When dey ain't no one kin sence it,
  An' de chune comes in, in spots;   20
But fu' real melojous music,
  Dat jes' strikes yo' hea't and clings,
Jes' you stan' an' listen wif me
  When Malindy sings.

Ain't you nevah hyeahd Malindy?   25
  Blessed soul, tek up de cross!
Look hyeah, ain't you jokin', honey?
  Well, you don't know whut you los'.
Y' ought to hyeah dat gal a-wa'blin',
  Robins, la'ks, an' all dem things,   30
Heish dey moufs an' hides dey faces
  When Malindy sings.

Fiddlin' man jes' stop his fiddlin',
  Lay his fiddle on de she'f;
Mockin'-bird quit tryin' to whistle,   35
  'Cause he jes' so shamed hisse'f.
Folks a-playin' on de banjo
  Draps dey fingahs on de strings—
Bless yo' soul—fu'gits to move 'em,
  When Malindy sings.   40

She jes' spreads huh mouf and hollahs,
  "Come to Jesus," twell you hyeah
Sinnahs' tremblin' steps and voices,
  Timid-lak a-drawin' neah;
Den she tu'ns to "Rock of Ages,"   45
  Simply to de cross she clings,
An' you fin' yo' teahs a-drappin'
  When Malindy sings.

Who dat says dat humble praises
  Wif de Master nevah counts?   50

Heish yo' mouf, I hyeah dat music,
  Ez hit rises up an' mounts—
Floatin' by de hills an' valleys,
  Way above dis buryin' sod,
Ez hit makes its way in glory   55
  To de very gates of God!

Oh, hit 's sweetah dan de music
  Of an edicated band;
An' hit 's dearah dan de battle's
  Song o' triumph in de lan'.   60
It seems holier dan evenin'
  When de solemn chu'ch bell rings,
Ez I sit an' ca'mly listen
  While Malindy sings.

Towsah, stop dat ba'kin', hyeah me!   65
  Mandy, mek dat chile keep still;
Don't you hyeah de echoes callin'
  F'om de valley to de hill?
Let me listen, I can hyeah it,
  Th'oo de bresh of angel's wings,   70
Sof' an' sweet, "Swing Low, Sweet Chariot,"
  Ez Malindy sings.

1. Who do you think is the speaker? What might be the relationship of the speaker to Miss Lucy? to Towsah and Mandy? to Malindy?
2. What contrast does the speaker draw between the singing of Malindy and of Miss Lucy?
3. Where does the speaker use exaggeration in order to praise Malindy's gift of song?

B. Select one of the following assignments and write a brief essay.
1. Dunbar inherited a dialect tradition that had many negative images of black people. Tell whether the use of dialect in "When Malindy Sings" presents a positive or negative view of black folk traditions and language.
2. Imagine this poem written in standard English rather than in dialect. Explain what the poem might lose if it were changed in this way.

▶▶ II. For Discussion _____

During the fifty-year period after the Civil War, the expectations of African Americans for equality were shattered by oppression, unjust laws, black codes, hypocrisy, and poverty. How have the selections in this unit helped you understand the conditions that existed both in the South and in the North during this period? Which selections helped you understand why Reconstruction failed? What conclusions can you draw about the conditions or experiences of African Americans during and after Reconstruction?

▶▶▶ III. For Writing _____

Select one of the writers represented in this unit and discuss that writer's major concerns. Then, imagine how that writer might react to events if he or she were alive today.

Rise Shine for Thy Light Has Come, *gouache by Aaron Douglas, c. 1930.*
Gallery of Art, Howard University

266

The Harlem Renaissance

INTRODUCTION BY **Cheryl A. Wall**
Rutgers University

A New Identity

Langston Hughes remembered it as the time "when the Negro was in vogue." He referred to the legendary period between the end of World War I and the onset of the Great Depression when African American art and artists seemed to claim the attention of the world. This period, designated a **"renaissance"** (rĕn′ĭ-säns′) by the artists themselves, was a turning point in African American cultural history. It retains tremendous symbolic as well as literary significance for us today.

One of the important figures in this renaissance was Alain Locke. As the title of his landmark anthology, *The New Negro* (1925), proclaimed, black Americans were claiming a new identity. Three generations after slavery had been legally abolished, the group of young black writers who contributed to *The New Negro* declared themselves spiritually emancipated. They had thrown off the psychological chains of the past; their writing would redefine their heritage and celebrate their new identity. Black culture would be reborn, as the word *renaissance* denoted.

Perhaps the most distinguishing characteristic of the New Negro as opposed to the old was that the New Negro was an urban figure. One of the most significant developments in twentieth-century African American history was the so-called **Great Migration.** This term refers to the movement of blacks from the rural South to the Northern urban centers. It lasted fifty years. In 1910, three fourths of the black American population lived in the rural

A family arriving in Chicago from the rural South, c. 1920.

South; by 1960, three fourths of this population was urban and the majority lived outside the Southern states.

The Harlem Renaissance had its origins in the urban migrations of black people during and immediately following World War I. Hundreds of thousands of blacks left the rural South as economic conditions worsened and political oppression grew intolerable. In the decade before 1920, there had been a lynching on the average of one every six days; the Ku Klux Klan, an organization that terrorized blacks throughout the South, had been reactivated in 1915. The North promised jobs, housing, and educational opportunities on a scale undreamed of by most black Southerners. The war increased demand for American products, and Northern manufacturers were badly in need of unskilled and semi-skilled labor. At

The Prodigal Son, *an illustration for* God's Trombones, *by Aaron Douglas, 1927.*
Henry W. and Albert A. Berg Collection / New York Public Library

the same time, the war stopped the flow of European immigrants to the United States. Northern factories were eager to hire whoever was available. Not only could blacks hope to earn a decent wage, they could live in much better conditions, and their children could attend good schools. Few rural communities in the South provided year-round schooling, and almost none offered public high schools for blacks. So men and women as individuals, as families, and sometimes as whole communities made the journey North.

For many, the final destination was Harlem, an attractive New York City neighborhood that had recently opened its doors to blacks. To those who settled there, Harlem was more than a neighborhood; they called it the Mecca of the New Negro, the Culture Capital of the Black World, the City of Refuge, and the Promised Land. The reality did not live up to the dream; blacks soon faced overcrowded conditions and unequal employment opportunities in Harlem. Nevertheless, with the largest population of urban blacks anywhere in the world and located in New York City, the cultural capital of the United States, Harlem became the center of African American political and cultural life. In recognition of this fact, scholars have given the title **Harlem Renaissance** to the period as a whole.

A Community of Black Writers and Artists

According to Langston Hughes, Harlem during the 1920s "was like a magnet for the Negro intellectual, pulling him from everywhere." Aspiring writers flocked to the community. Jessie Fauset from Philadelphia; Rudolph Fisher from Washington; Zora Neale Hurston from Florida; Wallace Thurman from Utah and California; Claude McKay from Jamaica, West Indies; Hughes himself from Missouri and Kansas: all came to Harlem to make their fortunes.

The growth of a community of writers in Harlem marked an important development in African American literary history. Black writers had begun publishing their work in the United States in the eighteenth century. Several, such as the poets Phillis Wheatley and Paul Laurence Dunbar, the autobiographer and orator Frederick Douglass, and the novelist Charles Chesnutt, had achieved considerable fame. But never before had there been a real community of black writers—men and women who read and encouraged one another's work. Soon, in addition to being their home, Harlem became a rich source of material for these writers. Numerous novels and short stories were set against the backdrop of Harlem, and a school of Harlem fiction and poetry evolved. Even though writers moved in and out of the community, and several did their most significant work in other places, Harlem retained a hold on black writers' imaginations.

The Harlem Renaissance was not important to literature alone. Black people were innovators in music, theater, and art as well. Although blacks had long been active in each of these fields, never before had their work been so widely known or so influential.

In the 1920s, for example, Negro spirituals were performed on the concert stage by such artists as Marian Anderson, Roland Hayes, and Paul Robeson. Spirituals were probably the best-known form of music created by black Americans. Slaves had sung spirituals like ''Go Down, Moses,'' ''Swing Low, Sweet Chariot,'' and ''Sometimes I Feel like a Motherless Child,'' and their haunting melodies had gained admirers throughout the world. Some African Americans rejected these songs because they associated them with slavery, but most learned to appreciate spirituals anew in the 1920s. The period gave birth as well to a new form of religious music called gospel. This music borrowed some of its lyrics from spirituals; the accompaniment sounded like the blues.

Through the magic of phonograph recordings and the newly invented radio, blues and jazz were transmitted across America. Few

Louis Armstrong's Hot Five Band. Armstrong is seated at the piano.
Frank Driggs Collection

An autographed photograph of Josephine Baker, on tour with Shuffle Along, 1923.
Frank Driggs Collection

whites listened to the blues, and many blacks considered it "the devil's music." But others stood in line to buy phonograph records by blues singers and to hear them perform in tent shows and at all-black theaters and nightclubs. The twenties were the heyday of the so-called classic blues singers such as Bessie Smith, whose fans crowned her the Empress of the Blues. More often played than sung, jazz was the most important musical development of the period. Trumpeter Louis Armstrong, pianist and bandleader Duke Ellington, and Fletcher Henderson, who is credited with starting the first "big band," were among the major innovators. Jazz became so popular among white Americans that the decade was dubbed the **Jazz Age**.

In theater, almost every Broadway season from 1921 to 1929 saw the opening of a new black production, beginning with the legendary musical *Shuffle Along,* which introduced Josephine Baker, a singer and actress who would later become an international star. *Chocolate Dandies,* a second musical written by the same team of Noble Sissle and Eubie Blake, introduced the Charleston, which became the most popular dance in America. Serious dramas of black life were less popular, but significant. White playwrights seemed eager to explore black themes. Eugene O'Neill, perhaps the greatest American dramatist, featured black subjects in two of his plays: *The Emperor Jones* (1920) and *All God's Chillun Got Wings* (1924).

In Europe, African sculpture and design had already begun to influence such leading artists as Georges Braque, Henri Matisse, and Pablo Picasso. Their paintings defined "modern art." Yet much of what made them appear "modern" was influenced by the traditional art of Africa. African American artists, notably the painter Aaron Douglas and the sculptor Richmond Barthé, produced pieces using African motifs.

Dilemma of the Black Artist

Writers and intellectuals welcomed these developments, even as they analyzed their meaning. What was distinctive about black American art? What gave it such broad appeal? Could the art's popularity be used to uplift the conditions of a people, most of whom continued to suffer poverty and oppression? Were black artists obligated to make their art a means of protest against racism? If they were, would they produce art or propaganda? The question troubled serious writers more than it did popular performers. As

The Ascent of Ethiopia, oil by Loïs Mailou Jones, 1932. The painting suggests the legacy of ancestral art. In the foreground, an Egyptian pharaoh looks out at images of contemporary black art, music, and dance.
Photo by Tom Jenkins

Countee Cullen wondered in his poem "Yet Do I Marvel," could a black artist be devoted to beauty and protest at the same time?

Even more fundamental questions arose, some of which echoed issues that black writers had raised for centuries. The issue of identity remained central. Who were black Americans? W. E. B. Du Bois had defined the dilemma of black American identity in *The Souls of Black Folk* in 1903: "One ever feels his twoness—an American, a

Negro: two souls, two thoughts, two unreconciled strivings, two warring ideals in one dark body, whose dogged strength alone keeps it from being torn asunder." During the Renaissance, writers again voiced this dilemma. They explored their relationship to Africa. They questioned what it meant to be black in America. If, on the one hand, they protested the cruel treatment blacks suffered on account of their race, on the other, they proclaimed the beauty of blackness. Blackness was, however, not just a color. It was a state of mind, the reflection of that determined strength to which Du Bois referred.

Literary Contributions of Women

For women, the questions of identity were complicated by sexism. To be black and a woman was to be doubly oppressed. Yet many of the proclamations of race pride seemed to assume that the New Negro was a man. The leaders most in the public eye were men; so were the best-known writers. Only recently have scholars documented the literary contributions of women. Jessie Fauset is notable for the four novels she published as well as for her work as literary editor of *The Crisis,* the most widely read black journal of the period. Nella Larsen's two novels, *Quicksand* and *Passing,* were published just one year apart, in 1928 and 1929; they consider the situation of educated, middle-class black women. After decades of neglect, the work of folklorist and novelist Zora Neale Hurston was rediscovered in the 1970s. She is now considered one of the most important writers of the period.

A New Mood in Literature

A significant event of the literary renaissance was the publication in 1919 of Claude McKay's impassioned sonnet "If We Must Die." Its defiant stand immediately distinguished it from the protest poems of an earlier generation. McKay's poem achieved an immediate popularity and its readers recognized in its tone the voice of a New Negro. Written in response to the so-called "Red Summer" of 1919, which had seen the outbreak of racial rioting across the United States, the poem called for militancy and self-defense regardless of the odds.

McKay's poem was radical in its content and theme, but certainly not in its form. Most of McKay's militant poems, such as "America" and "The White House," use the Shakespearean sonnet

(Above) *Jessie Fauset.*
The Schomburg Center for Research in Black Culture/New York Public Library

(Below) *Cover of* The Crisis, *the journal of the NAACP.*
The Schomburg Center for Research in Black Culture/New York Public Library

form. Other writers found different models. James Weldon Johnson was inspired by African American spirituals and sermons. Younger poets, notably Hughes and Sterling Brown, drew on such African American oral traditions as blues, tall tales, and work songs to give shape to visions as radical as McKay's.

The new mood in literature reflected the increasing political activism of blacks. This activism had helped give birth to the National Association for the Advancement of Colored People (NAACP) and to service organizations such as the National Urban League and the National Association of Colored Women's Clubs. It had given birth as well to the first effective mass movement among African Americans, the Universal Negro Improvement Association (UNIA) founded by Marcus Garvey. With the stirring slogan, "One God! One Aim! One Destiny!," Garvey had drawn hundreds of thousands of followers to his program of racial advancement and self-help. Garvey believed that blacks could never achieve equality in the United States without the establishment of an African nation whose influence would gain respect and protection for blacks throughout the world.

In addition to the force of their ideas and language, these social and political organizations gave writers practical support. Many published their first efforts in journals such as *The Crisis,* sponsored by the NAACP and edited by Du Bois; *Opportunity,* sponsored by the Urban League; *The Messenger,* edited by labor leaders A. Philip Randolph and Chandler Owen; and *Negro World,* edited by Marcus Garvey.

The Relationship to Africa

Garveyism, with its emphasis on racial pride and the slogan "Back to Africa," was rarely treated directly in literature. The popularity of the UNIA peaked in 1920. A citizen of Jamaica, Garvey was deported in 1927. Nevertheless, the movement and the man left a mark on literary history. McKay, though not a Garveyite, was committed to Pan Africanism, an international movement that worked for an independent and united black Africa. His novels *Home to Harlem, Banjo,* and *Banana Bottom* explored the cultural bonds that united people of African descent in Africa, the Caribbean, and the United States.

While Garvey was awakening black Americans to their African heritage, the scholar W. E. B. Du Bois was organizing Pan African conferences in Paris, Brussels, and London, which established

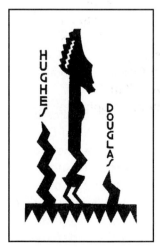

Cover for Opportunity, *October 1926.*
The Schomburg Center for Research in Black Culture/New York Public Library

Marcus Garvey (in uniform) and his attendants, shown in a film by William Greaves.
Bettmann Newsphotos

important political links among black intellectuals throughout the world. The interest excited by this activity was reflected in poetry. For example, in "The Negro Speaks of Rivers," a poem later dedicated to Du Bois, Hughes traced black history to Africa. Fittingly, the poem's refrain echoed "Deep River," an African American spiritual: "My soul has grown deep like the rivers." In "Afro-American Fragment," Hughes expressed the difficulty of grasping the reality of Africa, past or present:

So long,
So far away
Is Africa

Exploring the Southern Past

Another past was closer at hand. Jean Toomer was among those who explored the legacy of slavery and attempted to discover its meaning both for blacks who remained in the South and for those who had migrated to Northern cities. The poem "Song of the

Introduction   275

Son," in *Cane* (1923), Toomer's volume of poetry, prose, and drama, presents a speaker who returns to the South in search of his roots. The speaker arrives just in time to claim his legacy: "An everlasting song, a singing tree/Caroling softly souls of slavery."

Toomer was not alone in exploring the Southern past and in asking what was being lost as blacks rushed to fashion new lives in Northern cities. Rudolph Fisher treated the issue humorously in a series of short stories, including "Miss Cynthie," which held out the hope that cultural values could be adapted and preserved.

Innovations in Language and Literary Forms

Those cultural values were reflected most profoundly in the language writers chose to use. No writers were more dedicated to adapting traditional oral forms like folk tales, spirituals, and blues in their writing than Langston Hughes and Zora Neale Hurston. Their interest raised concern among those who felt that standard English was the only language for literature. Others believed that black writers should stress the similarities, not the differences, between black and white Americans. History has proved these critics wrong. Today, Hughes and Hurston are admired for their vision and courage. Their innovations in language and literary form have been highly influential in the development of modern African American literature.

TIME LINE **HARLEM RENAISSANCE**

c. 1910–1920 • Great Migration begins

1915

1920

1916
• Marcus Garvey founds New York chapter of UNIA

1917
• US enters World War I

1919
• Pan African Congress meets in Paris under leadership of W. E. B. Du Bois
• Claude McKay's poem "If We Must Die" is published
• "Red Summer" begins period of interracial strife

1921
• *Shuffle Along* opens

1923
• Jean Toomer's *Cane* is published

1924
• Paul Robeson appears in *All God's Chillun Got Wings*

276

A Midwesterner, Hughes knew little of the South; he celebrated the lives of Northern blacks in poetry, fiction, and drama. Throughout his long career, Hughes achieved enormous popularity among black Americans who responded enthusiastically to the images of themselves mirrored in Hughes's poetry and prose. Hughes caught the inflection of their speech; he saw the struggle and despair, nobility and joy in their experience. He was always sensitive to the rhythms of their music: drawing inspiration from the spirituals and the blues, reading his poems in the 1920s to the accompaniment of jazz bands, and in later life, composing gospel plays. In the process Hughes invented new literary forms, such as blues and jazz poetry.

Born in the all-black town of Eatonville, Florida, Zora Neale Hurston was one of the few Renaissance figures to know firsthand the culture of rural black Southerners. The stories, superstitions, and songs of her childhood remained a vital part of her adult imagination, and they influenced everything she wrote. Hurston gained new insight into these expressions when she studied anthropology at Barnard College. In 1927 she left New York to travel the back roads of the South. The folklore she collected was published in *Mules and Men,* in 1935. It was the first book of African American folklore published by a black person. In *Mules and Men,* as well as in her short stories and her first two novels, *Jonah's Gourd Vine* (1934) and *Their Eyes Were Watching God* (1937), Hurston recreated the world she had known in Eatonville. For her it was a world of promise and possibility, whose customs and folkways

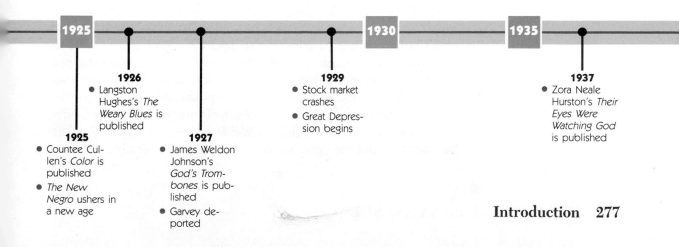

1925
● Countee Cullen's *Color* is published
● *The New Negro* ushers in a new age

1926
● Langston Hughes's *The Weary Blues* is published

1927
● James Weldon Johnson's *God's Trombones* is published
● Garvey deported

1929
● Stock market crashes
● Great Depression begins

1937
● Zora Neale Hurston's *Their Eyes Were Watching God* is published

Introduction   277

Zora and Langston, collage by Phoebe Beasley. Included in the artist's collage are famous photographs of the writers by Carl Van Vechten.

were creative and memorable. Drawing on Southern black speech patterns, Hurston shaped a language in her fiction that was rich in wit and metaphor.

The End of an Era

Their Eyes Were Watching God is Hurston's masterpiece. The novel traces a woman's search for self-fulfillment. Through the recovery of her cultural heritage, she discovers her truest self. By the time the novel was written, the Depression had dashed the optimism with which the Renaissance was launched. Blacks were suffering new indignities of economic exploitation and racism. Harlem was becoming a symbol of disillusionment rather than hope. But, in terms of literary history, *Their Eyes Were Watching God* may be said to fulfill the promise of the Harlem Renaissance.

About the Author

James Weldon Johnson (1871–1938)

The poet and novelist James Weldon Johnson was one of the first African Americans to break through many of the barriers restricting blacks. After graduating from Atlanta University, he went on to excel in many fields. He was a teacher in Georgia, a school principal in Florida, a songwriter in New York, a diplomat in Venezuela and Nicaragua, and an executive secretary of the National Association for the Advancement of Colored People (NAACP). He was also an attorney and the first African American to be admitted to the Florida bar since Reconstruction.

Johnson began his literary career as a songwriter. He collaborated with his brother, John Rosamond Johnson, a composer, to produce a comic opera and more than two hundred songs, many of them hits. Their most famous composition, "Lift Every Voice and Sing," was first sung by a chorus of five hundred children on February 12, 1900, to celebrate the birthday of Abraham Lincoln. It has come to be known as the "national anthem" of black Americans.

In 1912, his first novel, *The Autobiography of an Ex-Coloured Man,* was published anonymously. This was one of the first novels to present a frank picture of the discrimination suffered by blacks in the United States.

Fifty Years and Other Poems was published in 1917, and his best-known book of poetry, *God's Trombones,* was published in 1927. *God's Trombones* is subtitled *Seven Negro Sermons in Verse.* Johnson used the rhythms, imagery, and oratorical style of tra-

Oil pastel by Winold Reiss, c. 1925 (detail).

National Portrait Gallery, Smithsonian Institution

ditional Southern preachers, rather than dialect, in this experiment in free verse.

Johnson was also a pioneering editor of anthologies. He wanted to demonstrate and document the contributions that blacks had made to American culture, and so he collected and published *The Book of American Negro Poetry* in 1922. Johnson and his brother edited two collections of spirituals.

His autobiography, *Along This Way,* appeared in 1933. In 1934 he published *Negro Americans, What Now?,* an assessment of the American racial situation.

Johnson died in a train-car collision in 1938. He is remembered as an individual of many talents and as a leading figure in the Harlem Renaissance. His words continue to inspire people all over the world.

James Weldon Johnson   279

Before You Read

O Black and Unknown Bards

Using What You Know

The word *bard,* which today may be used as another name for a poet, originally referred to ancient poets who composed and sang works celebrating the legends and history of their tribes. Johnson's poem is addressed to the unknown poets who composed spirituals.

Earlier in this book, you read that the spirituals were a powerful form of poetry. Born of oppression, they expressed the desire for both spiritual salvation and earthly freedom. Why do you think spirituals are still sung today? Are they songs of sadness or songs of hope?

Literary Focus: Allusion

In literature, an **allusion** is a reference to a historical or literary figure, event, or text. Many book titles are allusions. The title of James Baldwin's novel *Go Tell It on the Mountain* is an allusion to a well-known spiritual. Because they tap into the reader's knowledge, allusions are a way of enriching the meaning of a piece of writing. They work best when they refer to works readers are likely to know.

Setting a Purpose

In this poem, Johnson alludes to a number of spirituals. As you read, see how many you recognize. What associations do you have with each one? Does knowing the spirituals Johnson refers to make reading his poem a more intense experience for you?

O Black and Unknown Bards

James Weldon Johnson

O black and unknown bards of long ago,
How came your lips to touch the sacred fire?
How, in your darkness, did you come to know
The power and beauty of the minstrel's lyre?°
Who first from midst his bonds lifted his eyes?   5
Who first from out the still watch, lone and long,
Feeling the ancient faith of prophets rise
Within his dark-kept soul, burst into song?

Heart of what slave poured out such melody
As "Steal away to Jesus"? On its strains   10
His spirit must have nightly floated free,
Though still about his hands he felt his chains.
Who heard great "Jordan roll"? Whose starward eye
Saw chariot "swing low"? And who was he
That breathed that comforting, melodic sigh,   15
"Nobody knows de trouble I see"?

What merely living clod, what captive thing,
Could up toward God through all its darkness grope,
And find within its deadened heart to sing
These songs of sorrow, love and faith, and hope?   20
How did it catch that subtle undertone,
That note in music heard not with the ears?
How sound the elusive reed° so seldom blown,
Which stirs the soul or melts the heart to tears.

4. minstrel's lyre: In the Middle Ages, wandering poets called minstrels went from place to place, reciting poetry and accompanying themselves on musical instruments. The lyre is associated with poetry and song.

23. reed: a wind instrument made from the hollow stem of a plant, associated with poetry and song.

Not that great German master in his dream   25
Of harmonies that thundered amongst the stars
At the creation, ever heard a theme
Nobler than "Go down, Moses." Mark its bars
How like a mighty trumpet-call they stir
The blood. Such are the notes that men have sung   30
Going to valorous deeds; such tones there were
That helped make history when Time was young.

There is a wide, wide wonder in it all,
That from degraded rest and servile toil
The fiery spirit to the seer should call   35
These simple children of the sun and soil.
O black slave singers, gone, forgot, unfamed,
You—you alone, of all the long, long line
Of those who've sung untaught, unknown, unnamed,
Have stretched out upward, seeking the divine.   40

You sang not deeds of heroes or of kings;
No chant of bloody war, no exulting pean°
Of arms-won triumphs; but your humble strings
You touched in chord with music empyrean.°
You sang far better than you knew; the songs   45
That for your listeners' hungry hearts sufficed
Still live,—but more than this to you belongs:
You sang a race from wood and stone to Christ.

42. **pean** (pē'ən): a song of praise or joy, also spelled *paean.*
44. **empyrean** (ĕm'pə-rē'ən): heavenly.

Responding to the Selection

O Black and Unknown Bards by James Weldon Johnson

Interpreting Meanings

1. In the first three stanzas, Johnson expresses his sense of wonder through a series of questions. What four questions does he ask in lines 1–8? Restate the questions, using your own words.

2. Some early societies believed that poets were inspired by the gods and that they possessed a divine gift. Where in the first stanza does Johnson allude to this belief?

3. In the second stanza, Johnson asks another series of questions. Which of them does he answer?

4. The third stanza opens with a question that embeds the answer within the question. What is the question? the answer?
5. The *reed* (line 23) refers to a musical instrument, the pipe of reeds, associated with shepherd poets. Why do you think Johnson says that this reed is "elusive"?
6. In lines 22–23, Johnson refers to a sound that is *not* heard with the ears. Can you explain how a song might be *felt* rather than heard?
7. In the fourth stanza, Johnson alludes to the orchestral works of a composer. What point does he make in lines 28–30?
8. In line 33 Johnson uses the phrase "wide, wide wonder." How does the sound of the phrase emphasize the poet's idea? How does he repeat the technique in line 38? What does the poet emphasize in line 39 in the phrase "untaught, unknown, unnamed"?
9. In the final stanza, Johnson contrasts the poems of the black and unknown bards with the works of other bards. Find lines that show the contrast. Explain the meaning of the last four lines.

Literary Elements
Understanding Inversion
Sometimes, in order to emphasize an idea or to make rhyming easier, a poet will reverse the normal order of words: "Home I go" rather than "I go home"; "To you, I say" rather than "I say to you." This reversal of the normal order of words is called **inversion.** A poet can emphasize a word or an idea by placing it at the beginning or at the end of the line.

Examine the order of words in lines 17–18 and 34–36. What would be a more natural order for the words in these lines? What emphasis is created by inversion?

Writer's Journal
Responding to the Poem
Johnson wonders how the slaves, who were uneducated and downtrodden, could have created and sung the spirituals. How do you think they found the inspiration to do so? Think about the difficult times in your own life. Write one or more paragraphs telling how you deal with troublesome times. Where do you find hope and inspiration?

Johnson talks about "music heard not with the ears." Have you ever "heard" a song in a deeper way? Describe the song, when you heard it, how you felt, and why it moved you.

Speaking and Listening
Presenting a Spiritual
Choose one of the spirituals named in Johnson's poem or another spiritual you like. Plan to read it aloud. If you wish, have a group of students sing the spiritual to the class.

Before You Read

The Creation

Using What You Know

In the preface to *God's Trombones,* Johnson says that his book of poems was inspired by memories of old-time preachers. Perhaps you have heard preachers who are fine orators. Recall their speaking styles. What do you remember about their voices? their language? their emotion? Did any of them have a sense of humor? Share your memories with your classmates.

Literary Focus: Biblical Allusion

An **allusion** is a reference in one work to a historical event or to another literary work. A **Biblical allusion** is a reference to an event or character or passage in the Bible. In their sermons, preachers often use texts from the Scriptures. Johnson's poem "The Creation" alludes to events in the Book of Genesis.

Setting a Purpose

"The Creation" takes the form of a sermon. As you read, note how the preacher's delivery lends drama to the account. Pay particular attention to the verbs and descriptive words he uses.

The Creation

(A Negro Sermon from GOD'S TROMBONES)

James Weldon Johnson

And God stepped out on space,
And he looked around and said:
I'm lonely—
I'll make me a world.

And far as the eye of God could see   5
Darkness covered everything,
Blacker than a hundred midnights
Down in a cypress swamp.

Then God smiled,
And the light broke,   10
And the darkness rolled up on one side,
And the light stood shining on the other,
And God said: That's good!

Then God reached out and took the light in His hands,
And God rolled the light around in His hands   15
Until He made the sun;
And He set that sun a-blazing in the heavens.
And the light that was left from making the sun
God gathered it up in a shining ball
And flung it against the darkness,   20
Spangling the night with the moon and stars.
Then down between
The darkness and the light
He hurled the world;
And God said: That's good!   25

Then God himself stepped down—
And the sun was on His right hand,
And the moon was on His left;
The stars were clustered about His head,
And the earth was under His feet.   30
And God walked, and where He trod
His footsteps hollowed the valleys out
And bulged the mountains up.

Then He stopped and looked and saw
That the earth was hot and barren.   35
So God stepped over to the edge of the world
And He spat out the seven seas—
He batted His eyes, and the lightnings flashed—
He clapped His hands, and the thunders rolled—
And the waters above the earth came down,   40
The cooling waters came down.

Then the green grass sprouted,
And the little red flowers blossomed,
The pine tree pointed his finger to the sky,
And the oak spread out his arms,   45
The lakes cuddled down in the hollows of the ground,
And the rivers ran down to the sea;
And God smiled again,
And the rainbow appeared,
And curled itself around His shoulder.   50

Then God raised His arm and He waved His hand
Over the sea and over the land,
And He said: Bring forth! Bring forth!
And quicker than God could drop His hand,
Fishes and fowls   55
And beasts and birds
Swam the rivers and the seas,
Roamed the forests and the woods,
And split the air with their wings.
And God said: That's good!   60

The Creation, *oil on masonite by Aaron Douglas, 1935.*
Photo by Jarvis Grant; Courtesy Gallery of Art, Howard University

JAMES WELDON JOHNSON

Then God walked around,
And God looked around
On all that He had made.
He looked at His sun,
And He looked at His moon,   65
And He looked at His little stars;
He looked on His world
With all its living things,
And God said: I'm lonely still.

Then God sat down—   70
On the side of a hill where He could think;
By a deep, wide river He sat down;
With His head in His hands,
God thought and thought,
Till He thought: I'll make me a man!   75

Up from the bed of the river
God scooped the clay;
And by the bank of the river
He kneeled Him down;
And there the great God Almighty   80
Who lit the sun and fixed it in the sky,
Who flung the stars to the most far corner of the night,
Who rounded the earth in the middle of His hand;
This Great God,
Like a mammy bending over her baby,   85
Kneeled down in the dust
Toiling over a lump of clay
Till He shaped it in His own image;

Then into it He blew the breath of life,
And man became a living soul.   90
Amen. Amen.

Responding to the Selection

The Creation by James Weldon Johnson

Interpreting Meanings

1. In the poem, God is shown to have human qualities. What human characteristic is stressed in the opening lines? What examples of other human qualities are found throughout the poem?
2. Johnson chooses verbs carefully. In the opening line, he writes, "God stepped out on space." The verb *stepped* is more precise than *walked* or *moved.* Note also that Johnson uses "*on* space" rather than "*in* space." Why is the word *on* a better choice?
3. In lines 6–8, darkness covers everything. What **simile** conveys the concept of total darkness?
4. How does God bring forth light? What do you infer about God's power in lines 9 and 13?
5. Reread lines 14–25. Describe in your own words what God does with the light. How does he create night?
6. In lines 26–60, God finishes the universe. List the things he creates and tell how he creates them. Which verbs does Johnson use effectively in this passage?
7. Why is God still unsatisfied with his creation? How does the creation of human beings differ from the creation of the world? How do lines 84–90 show God's love and tenderness?
8. The poem captures the style of a dynamic preacher who is also a skilled orator. Point out examples of strong **rhythms** and **repetition** in the poem.

Literary Elements

Recognizing Free Verse

"The Creation" is written in **free verse**. Free verse is poetry that doesn't have a definite stanza form, rhyme scheme, or meter. Free verse achieves its effects through strong rhythms and other poetic techniques, such as **imagery, figurative language, parallelism,** and **repetition**.

Free verse is particularly effective when it captures the rhythms of the speaking voice, as in "The Creation." Look back at the poem. What examples can you find of repetition? of parallel ideas and phrases? Read aloud lines 34–41. How does the poet capture the natural rhythm of the preacher's voice?

Language and Vocabulary

Analyzing Strong Verbs and Precise Modifiers

In line 20 Johnson says God *flung* the light against the darkness. The verb *fling* means "to throw with force." Why is *flung* a better choice than *threw*?

Johnson uses a number of strong verbs that convey a sense of action. Find three other examples. Substitute your own verbs to see how meaning changes.

Johnson also uses precise modifiers that help you visualize action. In line 35 he describes the earth as *barren*. Why is this a better descriptive word than *bare* or *dry*? Find three other precise modifiers.

Descriptive Writing

Interpreting a Painting

Aaron Douglas (1899–1979), one of the outstanding artists of the Harlem Renaissance, painted *The Creation* in 1935. The painting represents the dramatic moment when God creates man in his own image.

What elements of the story can you identify in the painting (page 287)? How has Douglas represented the heavens and the earth? Why do you suppose the hand of God is stretched out toward man?

Write a brief essay in which you tell what you see in Douglas's painting. Does he capture the great wonder of the Creation in his art? In planning and developing your paper, follow the instructions for descriptive writing on pages 193–195.

Speaking and Listening

Reading Poetry Aloud

Read **The Author Comments** (page 291), in which Johnson describes the characteristics of the old-time preacher. Imagine that you are such a preacher. Select one of the sections in Johnson's poem, rehearse it carefully, and read it to the class in the style described by Johnson. Your audience can respond as a congregation might.

The Preacher, *drawing by Charles White, 1952.*
Collection of the Whitney Museum of American Art, Photograph © 1996 the Whitney Museum of American Art

The Author Comments

 The old-time preacher was generally a man far above the average in intelligence; he was, not infrequently, a man of positive genius. The earliest of these preachers must have virtually committed many parts of the Bible to memory through hearing the scriptures read or preached from in the white churches which the slaves attended. They were the first of the slaves to learn to read, and their reading was confined to the Bible, and specifically to the more dramatic passages of the Old Testament. A text served mainly as a starting point and often had no relation to the development of the sermon. Nor would the old-time preacher balk at any text within the lids of the Bible. There is the story of one who after reading a rather cryptic passage took off his spectacles, closed the Bible with a bang and by way of preface said, "Brothers and sisters, this morning—I intend to explain the unexplainable—find out the undefinable—ponder over the imponderable—and unscrew the inscrutable."[1]

The old-time Negro preacher of parts was above all an orator, and in good measure an actor. He knew the secret of oratory, that at bottom it is a progression of rhythmic words more than it is anything else. Indeed, I have witnessed congregations moved to ecstasy by the rhythmic intoning of sheer incoherencies. He was a master of all the modes of eloquence. He often possessed a voice that was a marvelous instrument, a voice he could modulate from a sepulchral whisper to a crashing thunder clap. His discourse was generally kept at a high pitch of fervency, but occasionally he dropped into colloquialisms and, less often, into humor. He preached a personal and anthropomorphic[2] God, a sure-enough heaven and a red-hot hell. His imagination was bold and unfettered. He had the power to sweep his hearers before him; and so himself was often swept away. At such times his language was not prose but poetry. It was from memories of such preachers there grew the idea of this book of poems.

—God's Trombones

---

1. **inscrutable** (ĭn-skroo′tə-bəl): mysterious; difficult to understand.

2. **anthropomorphic** (ăn′thrə-pə-môr′fĭk): suggesting human form or human characteristics.

Before You Read

Lift Every Voice and Sing

Using What You Know

In *I Know Why the Caged Bird Sings,* Maya Angelou recalls that at her graduation ceremony in Stamps, Arkansas, the students sang "Lift Every Voice and Sing," the song that has come to be known as the "Negro national anthem." Although she had sung that song many times before, she had never really listened to its words until she was a member of the proud graduating class of her school.

Are there songs so familiar to you that you sing them without thinking about their meaning? If you have sung or listened to others sing "Lift Every Voice and Sing," what emotions did you experience? Have you paid attention to what the words say?

Literary Focus: Anthem

An **anthem** is a song of praise or devotion, such as "The Star-Spangled Banner," our national anthem. An anthem can also be a type of religious song chanted by a chorus in alternating parts. Johnson wrote "Lift Every Voice and Sing" to celebrate the birthday of Abraham Lincoln, and his brother set the words to music.

Setting a Purpose

Even if this poem is familiar to you, read it as if you were discovering its ideas for the first time. How do you think the Johnson brothers wanted you to feel as you read or sing the poem?

Lift Every Voice and Sing

James Weldon Johnson

Lift every voice and sing
Till earth and heaven ring,
Ring with the harmonies of Liberty;
Let our rejoicing rise
High as the listening skies,   5
Let it resound loud as the rolling sea.
Sing a song full of the faith that the dark past has taught us,
Sing a song full of the hope that the present has brought us,
Facing the rising sun of our new day begun
Let us march on till victory is won.   10

Stony the road we trod,
Bitter the chastening rod,
Felt in the days when hope unborn had died;
Yet with a steady beat,
Have not our weary feet   15
Come to the place for which our fathers sighed?
We have come over a way that with tears has been watered,
We have come, treading our path through the blood of the slaughtered,
Out from the gloomy past,
Till now we stand at last   20
Where the white gleam of our bright star is cast.

God of our weary years,
God of our silent tears,
Thou who has brought us thus far on the way;
Thou who has by Thy might   25
Led us into the light,
Keep us forever in the path, we pray.
Lest our feet stray from the places, our God, where we met Thee,
Lest, our hearts drunk with the wine of the world, we forget Thee;
Shadowed beneath Thy hand,   30
May we forever stand.
True to our God,
True to our native land.

Lift Every Voice and Sing, *cast plaster by Augusta Savage, 1939. This work, which no longer exists, was commissioned for the 1939 New York World's Fair. The singers, in choir robes, are arranged to suggest a harp.*

The singers form a procession from an outstretched hand, which forms part of the harp's frame.

Photo by Carl Van Vechten; Beinecke Rare Book Library, Yale University Library. Permission granted by the Estate of Carl Van Vechten, Joseph Solomon, Executor

Responding to the Selection

Lift Every Voice and Sing by James Weldon Johnson

Interpreting Meanings

1. Assuming that Johnson is writing about African Americans, to what does "dark past" (line 7) probably refer? How does it relate to the "victory" in line 10?
2. In line 11, what is the "stony" road? Who are the "we" referred to in this line?
3. In the second stanza, Johnson talks about the days "when hope unborn had died." What does this phrase mean? The stanza ends with a reference to "the white gleam of our bright star." What do you think the *star* stands for?
4. The third stanza is a prayer. How does this stanza express faith in God? How does it also express hope for the future?
5. Johnson wrote this poem in 1900, almost a century ago. How relevant is it to the concerns of present-day African Americans? Are there any conditions mentioned in the poem that have not changed?

Language and Vocabulary

Understanding Diction

A writer's choice of words is known as **diction.** A writer chooses words for their precise meanings and for their **connotations,** or associations. In "Lift Every Voice and Sing," Johnson chooses words that are suitable for the dignity of his subject. The words *resound* (line 6), *chastening* (line 12), and *treading* (line 18) are not used in everyday, casual conversation. They are appropriate, however, for the formal tone of the poem. Look these words up in a dictionary. Write down the definitions that match how the words are used in the poem. Then select two of the words and write a sentence of your own for each one. Be sure you understand what the word means before you write your sentence.

Writer's Journal

Responding to the Poem

Not all people agree that "Lift Every Voice and Sing" should be called the national anthem of African Americans. What do you think? Is there another song that you would consider a better choice? In your journal, state your opinion and give reasons for your position. In defending your answer, take into account that an anthem is a song of praise or gladness.

Speaking and Listening

Singing the Poem

Since this poem is usually sung, the class or a group of students might wish to sing it. In doing so, pay attention to the meaning of the words.

About the Author

Claude McKay (1889–1948)

James Latimer Allen/The Schomburg Center for Research in Black Culture/New York Public Library

 Claude McKay was born in Sunny Ville, Jamaica, in the West Indies. His love for his island home inspired his first two books of poetry, *Songs of Jamaica* and *Constab Ballads,* which were published in 1912. Most of these poems are in Jamaican dialect.

McKay's literary interests were nurtured by two individuals: his elder brother, who was a schoolteacher, and an Englishman named Walter Jekyll, who was a neighbor. They provided McKay with books of European poetry and philosophy. He especially admired the English Romantic poets.

Like many of his compatriots, McKay saw the United States as a "golden land of education and opportunity." He quit his apprenticeship to a cabinetmaker and wheelwright in Jamaica to enroll at the Tuskegee Institute in Alabama. After two months, he transferred to Kansas State College. This experience, however, left him disillusioned when he realized that, even in the United States, blacks did not have the same opportunities as whites.

In 1914 McKay moved to New York to pursue a literary career. He worked at menial jobs to support himself while he continued writing. In 1917 two of his sonnets were published in *The Seven Arts* literary magazine. They were well received and soon he had other work published.

McKay's best-known poems are militant and angry sonnets, such as "If We Must Die," which urges people to fight against injustice. That poem was written in the summer of 1919, when race riots convulsed the nation. It expresses black America's mood of desperation and defiance.

In 1922 McKay published his most important collection of poems, *Harlem Shadows.* McKay also wrote novels, including *Home to Harlem* (1928). This novel was the first best-seller by a black author and won the Harmon Foundation Gold Medal Award for Literature.

Throughout his life, McKay traveled widely, living for extended periods in England, Russia, Germany, France, and Morocco. His travels may have led him to the title of his 1937 autobiography, *A Long Way from Home.*

Before You Read

The Tropics in New York; Baptism; If We Must Die; America

Using What You Know

Some poems are intensely personal. In such poems, the speaker, who usually is the poet, expresses thoughts or feelings about a particular situation or person. Think of some poems you have read in this book or elsewhere that reveal the speaker's personal thoughts and feelings. Identify the poems and briefly recall how they affected you.

Literary Focus: The Lyric

The **lyric** is a poem that expresses personal thoughts and feelings. It is generally brief. Many lyrics are songs that are rich in musical devices.

One type of lyric is the **sonnet,** a fourteen-line poem that follows a specific pattern of rhyme and meter. If you have read Paul Laurence Dunbar's "Douglass" (page 253), then you have seen an example of the **Italian,** or **Petrarchan,** sonnet. This is one major sonnet form. Another major sonnet form is the **English,** or **Shakespearean,** sonnet. Poets are continually experimenting with the sonnet form, inventing new patterns for it. Some poets have written **sonnet sequences** in which a series of sonnets are linked together.

Setting a Purpose

As you read, note how McKay uses traditional lyric forms for his "revolutionary passions and words."

Four Poems by Claude McKay 297

The Tropics in New York

Claude McKay

Bananas ripe and green, and ginger-root,
   Cocoa in pods and alligator pears,
And tangerines and mangoes and grape fruit,
   Fit for the highest prize at parish fairs,

Set in the window, bringing memories   5
   Of fruit-trees laden by low-singing rills,
And dewy dawns, and mystical blue skies
   In benediction over nun-like hills.

My eyes grew dim, and I could no more gaze;
   A wave of longing through my body swept,   10
And, hungry for the old, familiar ways,
   I turned aside and bowed my head and wept.

Still Life, *oil on canvas by Margaret Burroughs, c. 1943.*
In the Collection of the Corcoran Gallery of Art, Washington, D.C. Gift of Thurlow Evans Tibbs, Jr. Evans Tibbs Collection

Baptism

Claude McKay

Into the furnace let me go alone;
Stay you without in terror of the heat.
I will go naked in—for thus 'tis sweet—
Into the weird depths of the hottest zone.
I will not quiver in the frailest bone,   5
You will not note a flicker of defeat;
My heart shall tremble not its fate to meet,
My mouth give utterance to any moan.
The yawning oven spits forth fiery spears;
Red aspish° tongues shout wordlessly my name.   10
Desire destroys, consumes my mortal fears,
Transforming me into a shape of flame.
I will come out, back to your world of tears,
A stronger soul within a finer frame.

10. **aspish:** like the asp, a small, poisonous snake.

Man, *drawing for the spirituals series by Charles White, 1958.*
Heritage Gallery, collection of Harry Belafonte

If We Must Die

Claude McKay

If we must die, let it not be like hogs
Hunted and penned in an inglorious spot,
While round us bark the mad and hungry dogs,
Making their mock at our accursed lot.
If we must die, O let us nobly die,   5
So that our precious blood may not be shed
In vain; then even the monsters we defy
Shall be constrained to honor us though dead!
O kinsmen! we must meet the common foe!
Though far outnumbered let us show us brave,   10
And for their thousand blows deal one deathblow!
What though before us lies the open grave?
Like men we'll face the murderous, cowardly pack,
Pressed to the wall, dying, but fighting back!

America

Claude McKay

Although she feeds me bread of bitterness,
And sinks into my throat her tiger's tooth,
Stealing my breath of life, I will confess
I love this cultured hell that tests my youth!
Her vigor flows like tides into my blood,   5
Giving me strength erect against her hate.
Her bigness sweeps my being like a flood.
Yet as a rebel fronts° a king in state,°
I stand within her walls with not a shred
Of terror, malice, not a word of jeer.   10
Darkly I gaze into the days ahead,
And see her might and granite wonders there,
Beneath the touch of Time's unerring hand,
Like priceless treasures sinking in the sand.

8. **fronts:** confronts. **in state:** on his throne.

Responding to the Selections

Four Poems by Claude McKay

Interpreting Meanings

The Tropics in New York

1. Throughout his life, McKay carried with him a love for Jamaica. What sights remind him of his island home?
2. What quality of his homeland is emphasized in the second stanza?
3. How would you describe the poet's feelings in the third stanza?
4. Explain the title of the poem, referring to details in the poem.

Baptism

1. What meaning do you usually associate with the word *baptism*? How is the poet's baptism different?
2. The furnace is clearly a **metaphor**. What do you think it represents? How is the poet changed by going into the furnace?
3. Whom do you think the poet is speaking to? Why does he choose to go into the furnace alone?
4. A *baptism by fire* is any introductory experience that is an ordeal, such as a soldier's first experience in combat. What ordeal is the poet describing in this poem? How is he strengthened by it?
5. Have you ever had any experience that you might compare to this trial by fire?

If We Must Die

1. Who are the "kinsmen" the poet addresses in line 9? What does he feel can be gained through their resistance?
2. One **metaphor** compares the violence of the mob to the viciousness of a pack of dogs. What other comparisons does the poet make?
3. Why do you think people are so moved by the ideas in this poem?

America

1. In this poem McKay expresses mixed feelings about America. What are the poet's conflicting emotions?
2. Which lines show that he views prejudice and unfair restraints as challenges?
3. What do you think the "priceless treasures" are?
4. What does he predict for America in lines 11–14? Do you agree with this prediction?

Literary Elements

Understanding Sonnet Structure

"If We Must Die" and "America" are examples of the **English,** or **Shakespearean,** sonnet. This form, made famous by William Shakespeare, is made up of three **quatrains** (four-line stanzas) and a concluding **couplet** (two rhyming lines). The **rhyme scheme** is *abab cdcd efef gg.* In a typical sonnet, each quatrain deals with one aspect of the basic idea, and the couplet ties up the argument or draws a conclusion. The rhyme in the poem helps to reinforce the poet's ideas.

"Baptism" is an example of the **Italian,** or **Petrarchan,** sonnet. This form, made famous by Francesco Petrarch, is made up of two parts: an **octave** (eight lines) and a **sestet** (six lines). It is generally rhymed *abbaabba cdecde.* The rhyme is closely related to the poet's ideas. The octave sometimes raises a question or problem and the sestet resolves it. In other cases, the octave states one part of a comparison and the sestet completes it.

Examine the structure of "If We Must Die." How does each quatrain develop one part of the basic idea? What conclusion does the poet draw in the couplet?

Language and Vocabulary

Understanding Connotation

In addition to their **denotative,** or literal, meanings, words have **connotative,** or suggested, meanings. Think of the word *mob,* for example. Literally, it refers to a large or disorderly crowd. However, the word evokes a range of associations beyond its literal meaning, so that *mob* takes on connotations of violence, destructiveness, and terror.

In line 8 of "The Tropics in New York," McKay uses the word *benediction.* The dictionary defines this word as "a short blessing" or "an expression of good wishes." As used by the poet, what does the word *bene-diction* suggest? How is this meaning reinforced by the words *mystical* (line 7) and *nun-like* (line 8)?

Writer's Journal

Re-creating the Past

In "The Tropics in New York," McKay describes his *nostalgia*—his longing for "the old, familiar ways" of his homeland. Have you ever yearned to return to some place where you once lived or to relive some past experiences? Write about your own nostalgia, re-creating the past through specific details and words that carry strong emotional associations. Share your entry with others if you wish.

Speaking and Listening

Reciting a Poem

Choose one of McKay's poems to read aloud. Prepare carefully by looking up unfamiliar words and checking their pronunciations. Follow clues to phrasing in the punctuation and meaning of the lines.

About the Author
Jean Toomer (1894–1967)

 Jean Toomer was an influential writer whose reputation rests on a single book, *Cane.* Critics find *Cane* difficult to categorize because of its mixture of fiction, poetry, and drama. From the time it was published, in 1923, it has been hailed as a masterpiece.

Toomer was born in Washington, D.C. His childhood was unhappy. His father deserted his mother soon after their marriage, and his mother died when he was still a child. He grew up under the stern eye of his grandfather. After Toomer graduated from high school, he attended several colleges and universities, but he never stayed long enough to earn a degree. He then tried out a number of jobs without success. He returned to Washington, where he began writing poems and short stories.

Toomer was inspired to write *Cane* after spending some months teaching in a small, segregated school in Sparta, Georgia, in 1921. The beauty of the land and the haunting melodies of the folk songs sparked Toomer's imagination, and he captured both that beauty and the ugliness produced by racial oppression and poverty in *Cane.*

Cane consists of three parts. The first third of the book is set in rural Georgia. The characters experience frustration and tragedy, but despite this, their lives are touched by beauty. The second part of *Cane* is set in Washington and Chicago. In this urban setting, the characters find their lives corrupted by the materialism of the cities. In the final section of the novel, a black intellectual re-

Oil pastel by Winold Reiss, c. 1925 (detail).
National Portrait Gallery, Smithsonian Institution

turns to the South in a search for his roots, but fails in his quest. The entire work is distinguished by the music of its language and its haunting imagery.

Cane's critical success did not please Toomer. Neither did his identification as a "Negro" writer. Toomer's racial heritage was mixed; he defined himself as "an American, neither white nor black, rejecting these divisions, accepting all people as people."

After *Cane* was published, Toomer dropped from public view. He continued to write to advance his political and spiritual beliefs, but little of his work was published. He died a forgotten man in 1967, the same year that *Cane* was reprinted for the first time.

Before You Read

Beehive; November Cotton Flower; Reapers

Using What You Know

The objects of the natural world have inspired poets from earliest times. Poets respond to nature in different ways. Some delight in its beauty; others view nature as a symbol of the human spirit.

Have you ever been moved by some aspect of nature, such as a sunset, a snowfall, a flock of migrating birds? Have you ever thought of yourself as part of nature? Listen closely to what your classmates reveal about their experiences and then add something of your own.

Literary Focus: Alliteration

Alliteration (ə-lĭt′ə-rā′shən) is a form of repetition that is used in both poetry and prose. The term generally refers to the repetition of a consonant sound or cluster of sounds in a group of words related in meaning: "**s**afe and **s**ound"; "**th**ick and **th**in." Although most alliteration occurs at the beginning of words, it may occur within words as well.

One purpose of alliteration is to gain emphasis. Many advertising jingles use alliteration, and manufacturers use it as an aid to memory. Can you give examples of some catchy names or slogans that use alliteration?

In poetry, alliteration is one of the techniques used to create musical sounds. In "The Creation," Johnson writes

So God **s**tepped over to the edge of the world
And He **s**pat out the **s**even **s**eas—

Read these lines aloud and listen to their music.

Setting a Purpose

Toomer had a wonderful ear for language. As you read these poems, note how the music of the lines enhances the meaning of the words. What do you think is Toomer's attitude toward nature?

Beehive

Jean Toomer

Within this black hive tonight
There swarm a million bees;
Bees passing in and out the moon,
Bees escaping out the moon,
Bees returning through the moon,   5
Silver bees intently buzzing,
Silver honey dripping from the swarm of bees
Earth is a waxen cell of the world comb,
And I, a drone,
Lying on my back,   10
Lipping honey,
Getting drunk with silver honey,
Wish that I might fly out past the moon
And curl forever in some far-off farmyard flower.

November Cotton Flower

Jean Toomer

Boll-weevil's° coming, and the winter's cold,
Made cotton-stalks look rusty, seasons old,
And cotton, scarce as any southern snow,
Was vanishing; the branch,° so pinched and slow,
Failed in its function as the autumn rake;   5
Drouth° fighting soil had caused the soil to take
All water from the streams; dead birds were found
In wells a hundred feet below the ground—
Such was the season when the flower bloomed.
Old folks were startled, and it soon assumed   10
Significance. Superstition saw
Something it had never seen before:
Brown eyes that loved without a trace of fear,
Beauty so sudden for that time of year.

1. **Boll-weevil:** a beetle whose larvae feed on cotton bolls.

4. **branch:** a stream.

6. **Drouth:** same as *drought* (drout), a period of dryness.

Harvest Talk, *charcoal drawing by Charles White, 1953.*
The Heritage Gallery, Los Angeles

Reapers

Jean Toomer

Black reapers with the sound of steel on stones
Are sharpening scythes.° I see them place the hones°
In their hip-pockets as a thing that's done,
And start their silent swinging, one by one.
Black horses drive a mower through the weeds,
And there, a field rat, startled, squealing bleeds.
His belly close to ground. I see the blade,
Blood-stained, continue cutting weeds and shade.

2. **scythes** (sī*th*z): tools with long blades, used for mowing or reaping. **hones:** hard stones used to sharpen cutting tools.

Responding to the Selections

Three Poems by Jean Toomer

Interpreting Meanings

Beehive

1. The poet describes a beehive by moonlight. What do you think the phrases "Silver bees" (line 6) and "Silver honey" (line 7) mean?
2. What picture does the poet want you to see in lines 3–5?
3. A honeycomb is made up of beeswax cells where the insects store their honey and their eggs. What **metaphor** does Toomer use in line 8?
4. In line 9, the speaker extends the metaphor to himself. A drone is a male bee that has no sting and gathers no honey. How does Toomer capture these characteristics in lines 9–14? What wish is expressed in these lines?
5. This poem contains no rhyme, but it is rich in musical devices. Read aloud the lines that you think contain the most effective examples of **repetition**.

November Cotton Flower

1. What has caused the cotton to wither?
2. In lines 4–5 the stream is said to function "as the autumn rake." What does this comparison suggest?
3. How do people react to the unexpected blooming of the flower?
4. The last line of the poem refers to the sudden appearance of beauty in a harsh and barren setting. What might this dramatic event symbolize? Think about line 13 in answering the question.
5. What words in the poem are linked through **alliteration**?

Reapers

1. Which details give you a vivid picture of what the reapers are doing?
2. Which images in the poem create an ominous or menacing mood?
3. Identify as many examples of **alliteration** as you can. Which ideas are emphasized through alliteration?

Before You Read

Song of the Son

Using What You Know

The word *home* has a special meaning for most people. It refers not only to the place where one grew up but also to the place where one lives or to a place associated with happiness and love. After a long absence from home, people often begin to appreciate what they once took for granted. Some people will return home after many years because they wish to reestablish their roots. Why, in our own times, have so many African Americans who grew up in Northern cities returned to places in the South where their parents and grandparents once lived?

Literary Focus: Assonance

Closely related to alliteration as a device of repetition is **assonance** (ăs′ə-nəns), a similarity in the vowel sounds of neighboring words. For example, in line 1 of "Beehive," Toomer uses assonance in repeating both the short **i** and long **i** sounds:

> Within this black hive tonight

We are not always aware of assonance as we read poetry, but it contributes to the music of a poem in subtle ways. Listen for it and you will find how skillfully Toomer and other poets choose sounds for precise effects.

Setting a Purpose

A theme that recurs in African American literature is the recognition and celebration of one's heritage. As you read this poem, determine the poet's attitude toward his people and their past. How do the various devices of repetition help to emphasize his main ideas?

Song of the Son

Jean Toomer

Pour O pour that parting soul in song,
O pour it in the sawdust glow of night,
Into the velvet pine-smoke air tonight,
And let the valley carry it along.
And let the valley carry it along.   5

O land and soil, red soil and sweet-gum tree,
So scant of grass, so profligate° of pines,
Now just before an epoch's° sun declines
Thy son, in time, I have returned to thee,
Thy son, I have in time returned to thee.   10

In time, for though the sun is setting on
A song-lit race of slaves, it has not set;
Though late, O soil, it is not too late yet
To catch thy plaintive soul, leaving, soon gone,
Leaving, to catch thy plaintive soul soon gone.   15

O Negro slaves, dark purple ripened plums,
Squeezed, and bursting in the pine-wood air,
Passing, before they stripped the old tree bare
One plum was saved for me, one seed becomes

An everlasting song, a singing tree,   20
Caroling softly souls of slavery,
What they were, and what they are to me,
Caroling softly souls of slavery.

7. **profligate** (prŏf′lĭ-gĭt, –gāt):
lavish; extravagant.
8. **epoch** (ĕp′ək): a particular
period of history.

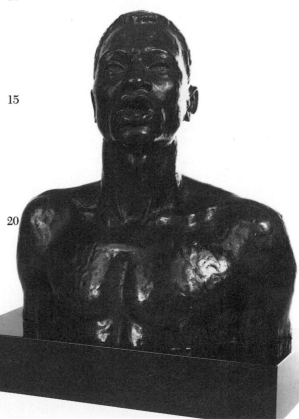

Singing Slave,
sculpture by Richmond Barthé.
Art and Artifacts Division/
The Schomburg Center for Research in
Black Culture/New York Public Library

Song of the Son 309

Responding to the Poem

Song of the Son by Jean Toomer

Interpreting Meanings

1. In line 9, the speaker says he has returned "in time." In line 13, he says, "it is not too late yet." How do you interpret these phrases? What is changing?
2. What does the speaker celebrate in his heritage?
3. How does he feel he has been touched by the soul of his people? How does he feel his heritage will be preserved?
4. What do you think the "plum" in line 19 refers to?
5. Recall Johnson's poem "O Black and Unknown Bards" (page 281). How does each poet interpret the meaning of the songs sung by slaves?
6. Note the use of similar vowel sounds in the title, which links the words *song* and *son.* Where else does the poet use **assonance** to connect or to emphasize ideas?

Literary Elements

Understanding Devices of Repetition

Note how Toomer uses both **alliteration** and **assonance** in the last line of "Song of the Son":

Caroling softly souls of slavery.

Four of the five words contain a short **o** sound, and three of the words begin with the consonant **s.** Note also how the sound I appears within four of the words. These devices contribute to the rich music of the poem.

Other kinds of repetition are **refrain** and **rhyme.** The **refrain,** a common element in ballads, can refer to a word, a phrase, a line, or group of lines repeated at regular intervals in a poem or song, often at the end of each stanza.

Rhyme is the repetition of sounds, usually at the ends of lines of poetry. The most common kind of rhyme is **end rhyme,** where the rhyming words come at the ends of lines. Rhyme that occurs within a line is called **internal rhyme.** Rhyme can be **exact** (*air/bare*) or **partial** (*lone/done*). Remember that rhyme depends on *sound,* not spelling. The words *air* and *bare* don't look alike, but when you say them aloud, they rhyme perfectly. The words *lone* and *done,* on the other hand, look as if they should rhyme exactly, but when you pronounce the words, you find that the vowel sound is different. The pattern of rhymes in a poem is known as its **rhyme scheme.**

In "Song of the Son," Toomer uses one rhyme scheme in stanzas 1–3 and another pattern in stanzas 4–5. His pattern in the first three stanzas is to rhyme the first line with lines 4 and 5, and to rhyme lines 2 and 3. We show the rhyme scheme in this way:

abbaa

The letter *a* represents the first rhyme word, which is *song.* This rhyme is repeated in *along* in lines 4 and 5. The letter *b* represents the second rhyme word, which is *night*. It rhymes with the end word in line 3. Work out the rhyme schemes Toomer uses in stanzas 4 and 5. Use a different letter for each new rhyme in the poem.

Language and Vocabulary

Understanding Related Words

In line 8 of "Song of the Son," Toomer speaks about a declining *epoch*. An epoch is a particular period of history considered memorable in some way. Other words that are used to identify historical periods are *era*, *age*, and *period*. Are these words used as synonyms, or do they have distinct meanings? Before answering the question, check the meaning of each word in a college or an unabridged dictionary.

Writer's Journal

Writing About a Special Place

When Toomer went to teach at a small school in rural Georgia, he said that he felt he was a Negro "body and soul." He later wrote, "My seed was planted in *myself* down there. Roots have grown and strengthened."

Write a brief entry about the place where you feel the most yourself. If you wish, compose a poem or a song.

Speaking and Listening

Expressing an Opinion

Which of Toomer's poems did you like the best? Prepare a short talk telling the class why you selected it. Use specific examples from the poem in explaining your preference.

About the Author

Langston Hughes (1902–1967)

Oil pastel by Winold Reiss, c. 1925 (detail).

Langston Hughes is the most famous writer of the Harlem Renaissance, but much of the work for which he is internationally known was published long after the Renaissance ended. In 1921, he published his lyric ''The Negro Speaks of Rivers,'' and he soon earned the title ''poet laureate of Harlem.'' By the end of his life, he had made many outstanding contributions not only as a poet, but also as a writer of fiction, playwright, autobiographer, humorist, translator, and anthologist. Writers in Africa and the Caribbean, notably Léopold Sédar Senghor, Aimé Césaire, and Nicolás Guillén, testified to the importance of Hughes's influence on their work.

Hughes was from the Midwest. He was born in Joplin, Missouri, and grew up in Kansas and Ohio. He came to New York City to attend Columbia University, a school he had chosen because it was located near Harlem.

The Weary Blues, his first book of poetry, was published in 1926. (See Jessie Fauset's review of this work on page 376.) Hughes drew on blues and jazz to invent new poetic forms that would express the reality and vitality of urban black life. His first work of prose fiction, *Not Without Laughter,* appeared in 1930. In 1934 he published a collection of short stories, *The Ways of White Folks.* The masterful *Montage of a Dream Deferred* (1951) was perhaps his greatest evocation of Harlem life and his most successful experiment with jazz poetry. Hughes wrote several gospel plays, including *Black Nativity* (1961) and *Tambourines to Glory* (1963).

In later life, Hughes gained fame for his ''Simple'' stories, which feature a black Everyman, Jesse B. Semple, who became known as *Simple.* Hughes edited numerous anthologies, including *An African Treasury* (1960), *The Best Short Stories by Negro Writers* (1967), and *The Poetry of the Negro* (1949), coedited with Arna Bontemps

In his work, Hughes chose to identify with ordinary people. He once said that his poetry deals with ''workers, roustabouts, and singers, and job hunters . . . people up today and down tomorrow, working this week and fired the next, beaten and baffled, but determined not to be wholly beaten.''

Before You Read

When the Negro Was in Vogue from **The Big Sea**

Using What You Know

Most people are affected by fashions, whether they are talking about hairstyles, clothes, automobiles, or foods. Think about some of the fashion trends you have seen in recent years.

The phrase "in vogue" means "in style" or "popular." What do you think it means for an entire people to be in vogue?

Background

During the 1920s, Harlem was the center of black literary, musical, and cultural activity. It was the scene of a vibrant African American community whose contributions to the arts were worldwide. Black music was copied by white musicians as far away as France, and rich whites flocked to Harlem to listen to African American intellectuals and to learn black dances. The term **Harlem Renaissance** was coined to describe this period.

For a time, it seemed to many African Americans that their time in the sun was at hand. Unlike some of his peers, Langston Hughes realized that this period of racial harmony and understanding was but a phase that would run its course like any other fashion.

Literary Focus: Irony

The term **irony** refers to a contrast between what is stated and what is really meant, or between what is expected to happen and what actually does happen. In this excerpt from his autobiography, Hughes points up the ironic contrasts between appearance and reality. What seemed to be a breakthrough toward prosperity and racial equality was merely a "vogue," a passing trend. By using the word *vogue,* he ironically suggests that interest in black life and art was no more than a short-lived fad.

Setting a Purpose

As you read, note Hughes's attitude toward his subject and his readers. Is he serious and straightforward? Is he amused? angry?

The Big Sea

Langston Hughes

When the Negro Was in Vogue

The 1920's were the years of Manhattan's black Renaissance. It began with *Shuffle Along, Running Wild,* and the Charleston.[1] Perhaps some people would say even with *The Emperor Jones,* Charles Gilpin, and the tom-toms at the Provincetown.[2] But certainly it was the musical revue, *Shuffle Along,* that gave a scintillating send-off to that Negro vogue in Manhattan, which reached its peak just before the crash of 1929,[3] the crash that sent Negroes, white folks and all rolling down the hill toward the Works Progress Administration.[4]

Shuffle Along was a honey of a show. Swift, bright, funny, rollicking, and gay, with a dozen danceable, singable tunes. Besides, look who were in it: The now famous choir director, Hall Johnson, and the com-

poser, William Grant Still, were a part of the orchestra. Eubie Blake and Noble Sissle wrote the music and played and acted in the show. Miller and Lyles were the comics. Florence Mills skyrocketed to fame in the second act. Trixie Smith sang "He May Be Your Man But He Comes to See Me Sometimes." And Caterina Jarboro, now a European prima donna, and the internationally celebrated Josephine Baker[5] were merely in the chorus. Everybody was in the audience— including me. People came back to see it innumerable times. It was always packed.

To see *Shuffle Along* was the main reason I wanted to go to Columbia. When I saw it, I was thrilled and delighted. From then on I was in the gallery of the Cort Theatre every time I got a chance. That year, too, I saw Katharine Cornell in *A Bill of Divorcement,* Margaret Wycherly in *The Verge,* Maugham's *The Circle* with Mrs. Leslie Car-

---

1. **Charleston:** a lively dance in 4/4 time, popular during the 1920s (from the name of the seaport in South Carolina).
2. **The Emperor Jones . . . Provincetown:** *The Emperor Jones,* by Eugene O'Neill, a drama featuring a black cast, made use of tom-toms. The role of Brutus Jones was first played by Charles Gilpin (1878–1930), and the play was produced by the Provincetown Players in Greenwich Village.
3. **crash of 1929:** The Great Depression of the 1930s followed the Wall Street crash in October, 1929.
4. **Works Progress Administration:** a federal agency established to provide relief and employment.

5. **Josephine Baker:** an African American singer and dancer (1906–1975) who became a famous entertainer in Paris.

A scene from Shuffle Along.
White Studio Collection, Performing Arts Research Center/New York Public Library at Lincoln Center

A floor show at the Cotton Club in Harlem.

ter, and the Theatre Guild production of Kaiser's *From Morn Till Midnight*. But I remember *Shuffle Along* best of all. It gave just the proper push—a pre-Charleston kick—to that Negro vogue of the 20's, that spread to books, African sculpture, music, and dancing.

Put down the 1920's for the rise of Roland Hayes, who packed Carnegie Hall, the rise of Paul Robeson in New York and London, of Florence Mills over two continents, of Rose McClendon in Broadway parts that never measured up to her, the booming voice of Bessie Smith and the low moan of Clara on

thousands of records, and the rise of that grand comedienne of song, Ethel Waters, singing: "Charlie's elected now! He's in right for sure!" Put down the 1920's for Louis Armstrong and Gladys Bentley[6] and Josephine Baker.

White people began to come to Harlem in

6. **Roland Hayes . . . Gladys Bentley:** Hayes was a well-known interpreter of songs and spirituals; Robeson was a widely acclaimed actor and singer; Mills was a star of musical comedy; McClendon was a noted actress; Bessie Smith was a vocalist known as "Empress of the Blues"; Clara Smith was a popular blues singer; Waters was a pioneer recording artist and an actress; Armstrong was a brilliant trumpet player; Bentley was a famous nightclub singer.

droves. For several years they packed the expensive Cotton Club on Lenox Avenue. But I was never there, because the Cotton Club was a Jim Crow club[7] for gangsters and monied whites. They were not cordial to Negro patronage, unless you were a celebrity like Bojangles.[8] So Harlem Negroes did not like the Cotton Club and never appreciated its Jim Crow policy in the very heart of their dark community. Nor did ordinary Negroes like the growing influx of whites toward Harlem after sundown, flooding the little cabarets and bars where formerly only colored people laughed and sang, and where now the strangers were given the best ringside tables to sit and stare at the Negro customers—like amusing animals in a zoo.

The Negroes said: "We can't go downtown and sit and stare at you in your clubs. You won't even let us in your clubs." But they didn't say it out loud—for Negroes are practically never rude to white people. So thousands of whites came to Harlem night after night, thinking the Negroes loved to have them there, and firmly believing that all Harlemites left their houses at sundown to sing and dance in cabarets, because most of the whites saw nothing but the cabarets, not the houses.

Some of the owners of Harlem clubs, delighted at the flood of white patronage, made the grievous error of barring their own race, after the manner of the famous Cotton Club. But most of these quickly lost business and folded up, because they failed to realize that a large part of the Harlem attraction for downtown New Yorkers lay in simply watching the colored customers amuse themselves. And the smaller clubs, of course, had

no big floor shows or a name band like the Cotton Club, where Duke Ellington usually held forth, so, without black patronage, they were not amusing at all.

Some of the small clubs, however, had people like Gladys Bentley, who was something worth discovering in those days, before she got famous, acquired an accompanist, specially written material, and conscious vulgarity. But for two or three amazing years, Miss Bentley sat, and played a big piano all night long, literally all night, without stopping—singing songs like "The St. James Infirmary," from ten in the evening until dawn, with scarcely a break between the notes, sliding from one song to another, with a powerful and continuous underbeat of jungle rhythm. Miss Bentley was an amazing exhibition of musical energy—a large, dark, masculine lady, whose feet pounded the floor while her fingers pounded the keyboard—a perfect piece of African sculpture, animated by her own rhythm.

But when the place where she played became too well known, she began to sing with an accompanist, became a star, moved to a larger place, then downtown, and is now in Hollywood. The old magic of the woman and the piano and the night and the rhythm being one is gone. But everything goes, one way or another. The '20's are gone and lots of fine things in Harlem night life have disappeared like snow in the sun—since it became utterly commercial, planned for the downtown tourist trade, and therefore dull.

The lindy-hoppers[9] at the Savoy even began to practice acrobatic routines, and to do absurd things for the entertainment of the whites, that probably never would have en-

---

7. **Jim Crow club:** a segregated nightclub.
8. **Bojangles:** nickname for Bill Robinson (1878–1949), a famous tap dancer.

9. **lindy-hoppers:** The lindy, a jitterbug dance, originated in Harlem. It was named for Charles Lindbergh's transatlantic "hop" in 1927.

The Big Sea   317

A room in a Harlem tenement.

tered their heads to attempt merely for their own effortless amusement. Some of the lindy-hoppers had cards printed with their names on them and became dance professors teaching the tourists. Then Harlem nights became show nights for the Nordics.[10]

Some critics say that that is what happened to certain Negro writers, too—that they ceased to write to amuse themselves and began to write to amuse and entertain white people, and in so doing distorted and over-colored their material, and left out a great many things they thought would offend their American brothers of a lighter complexion. Maybe—since Negroes have writer-

10. **Nordics:** people of northern Europe, here used for all whites.

racketeers, as has any other race. But I have known almost all of them, and most of the good ones have tried to be honest, write honestly, and express their world as they saw it.

All of us know that the gay and sparkling life of the so-called Negro Renaissance of the '20's was not so gay and sparkling beneath the surface as it looked. Carl Van Vechten, in the character of Byron in *Nigger Heaven*, captured some of the bitterness and frustration of literary Harlem that Wallace Thurman later so effectively poured into his *Infants of the Spring*—the only novel by a Negro about that fantastic period when Harlem was in vogue.

It was a period when, at almost every Harlem uppercrust dance or party, one would be

318 LANGSTON HUGHES

introduced to various distinguished white celebrities there as guests. It was a period when almost any Harlem Negro of any social importance at all would be likely to say casually: "As I was remarking the other day to Heywood—," meaning Heywood Broun.[11] Or: "As I said to George—," referring to George Gershwin.[12] It was a period when local and visiting royalty were not at all uncommon in Harlem. And when the parties of A'Lelia Walker, the Negro heiress, were filled with guests whose names would turn any Nordic social climber green with envy. It was a period when Harold Jackman, a handsome young Harlem school teacher of modest means, calmly announced one day that he was sailing for the Riviera for a fortnight, to attend Princess Murat's yachting party. It was a period when Charleston preachers opened up shouting churches as sideshows for white tourists. It was a period when at least one charming colored chorus girl, amber enough to pass for a Latin American, was living in a penthouse, with all her bills paid by a gentleman whose name was banker's magic on Wall Street. It was a period when every season there was at least one hit play on Broadway acted by a Negro cast. And when books by Negro authors were being published with much greater frequency and much more publicity than ever before or since in history. It was a period when white writers wrote about Negroes more successfully (commercially speaking) than Negroes did about themselves. It was the period (God help us!) when Ethel Barrymore appeared in blackface in *Scarlet Sister Mary*! It was the period when the Negro was in vogue.

I was there. I had a swell time while it lasted. But I thought it wouldn't last long. (I remember the vogue for things Russian, the season the Chauve-Souris first came to town.) For how could a large and enthusiastic number of people be crazy about Negroes forever? But some Harlemites thought the millennium had come. They thought the race problem had at last been solved through Art plus Gladys Bentley. They were sure the New Negro would lead a new life from then on in green pastures of tolerance created by Countee Cullen, Ethel Waters, Claude McKay, Duke Ellington, Bojangles, and Alain Locke.[13]

I don't know what made any Negroes think that—except that they were mostly intellectuals doing the thinking. The ordinary Negroes hadn't heard of the Negro Renaissance. And if they had, it hadn't raised their wages any. As for all those white folks in the speakeasies[14] and night clubs of Harlem—well, maybe a colored man could find *some* place to have a drink that the tourists hadn't yet discovered.

Then it was that house-rent parties began to flourish—and not always to raise the rent either. But, as often as not to have a get-together of one's own, where you could do the black-bottom[15] with no stranger behind you trying to do it, too. Non-theatrical, non-intellectual Harlem was an unwilling victim of its own vogue. It didn't like to be stared at by white folks. But perhaps the downtowners never knew this—for the cabaret owners, the entertainers, and the speakeasy proprietors treated them fine—as long as they paid.

11. **Heywood Broun:** American journalist, essayist, and novelist (1888–1939).
12. **George Gershwin** (gûrsh′wĭn): American composer (1898–1937).

13. **Alain Locke:** editor of *The New Negro* and a leader of the literary movement.
14. **speakeasies:** *Speakeasy* was a slang term for a place where alcoholic drinks were sold illegally.
15. **black-bottom:** a lively dance, popular in the late 1920s.

Responding to the Selection

When the Negro Was in Vogue from **The Big Sea** by Langston Hughes

Identifying Facts

1. Which black musical revue helped start the Negro vogue of the 1920s?
2. Why did some black owners of Harlem clubs bar members of their own race?
3. Why did Hughes never go to the Cotton Club?
4. Why did house-rent parties become popular?
5. How long did the vogue last?

Interpreting Meanings

1. Hughes identifies the beginning of the Harlem Renaissance with a famous musical revue. What characteristics in this show made it so special?
2. Why did many residents of Harlem resent the white people who began to arrive after sundown? According to Hughes, what did these white patrons want to see?
3. Why did the desire to entertain white audiences ruin certain performers?
4. How was Harlem "an unwilling victim of its own vogue"?
5. Langston Hughes says he expected that whites would soon tire of blacks: "For how could a large and enthusiastic number of people be crazy about Negroes forever?" Do you detect **irony** in this question? How do you think Hughes wants readers to respond to this comment?

Expository Writing

Investigating a Subject

Select one of the following subjects for a brief research report.

Dances of the 1920s
Bill ("Bojangles") Robinson
Eubie Blake
Marian Anderson
Duke Ellington
Roland Hayes
The Wall Street Crash of 1929

Prewriting Strategies

Make a list of the questions you wish to have answered about the subject. Consult the library catalog or an encyclopedia in order to find sources for your report. After you have read one or two articles about your subject, narrow your topic. For example, you might decide to concentrate on three or four dances of the 1920s, or you might decide to focus on the early career of Eubie Blake during the period of the Harlem Renaissance.

Speaking and Listening

Listening to Music of the 1920s

Your school or public library may contain collections of recordings by artists of the Harlem Renaissance. Listen to a recording made by one of the black bands or soloists of the period. Compare the sound of the music with music by contemporary artists.

Before You Read

The Negro Speaks of Rivers

Using What You Know

Have you ever had an idea come to you suddenly? Perhaps you have had only the germ of an idea. Then, as you turned it over in your mind, it began to take shape. What are the steps you go through in your own mind before putting your thoughts on paper? Have you ever lost an idea because you failed to write it down?

Literary Focus: The Speaker

The **speaker** of a poem is not necessarily the poet. In "The Creation," by James Weldon Johnson, the speaker is an old-time folk preacher invented by the poet. The speaker of a poem may be a character, an animal, or even an inanimate object. Your knowledge of who or what the speaker is helps you understand what the poem is about.

Setting a Purpose

In this excerpt from his autobiography, *The Big Sea,* Hughes talks about the birth of a poem. You can observe how he transformed the kernel of an idea into something rich and evocative. As you read, determine who is the speaker in the poem.

I had been in to dinner early that afternoon on the train. Now it was just sunset, and we crossed the Mississippi, slowly, over a long bridge. I looked out the window of the Pullman at the great muddy river flowing down toward the heart of the South, and I began to think what that river, the old Mississippi, had meant to Negroes in the past—how to be sold down the river was the worst fate that could overtake a slave in times of bondage. Then I remembered reading how Abraham Lincoln had made a trip down the Mississippi on a raft to New Orleans, and how he had seen slavery at its worst, and had decided within himself that it should be removed from American life. Then I began to think about other rivers in our past—the Congo, and the Niger, and the Nile in Africa—and the thought came to me: "I've known rivers," and I put it down on the back of an envelope I had in my pocket, and within the space of ten or fifteen minutes, as the train gathered speed in the dusk, I had written this poem, which I called "The Negro Speaks of Rivers":

The Negro Speaks of Rivers   Langston Hughes

I've known rivers:
I've known rivers ancient as the world and older than the flow
    of human blood in human veins.

My soul has grown deep like the rivers.

I bathed in the Euphrates° when dawns were young.
I built my hut near the Congo and it lulled me to sleep.
I looked upon the Nile and raised the pyramids above it.
I heard the singing of the Mississippi when Abe Lincoln went
    down to New Orleans, and I've seen its muddy bosom
    turn all golden in the sunset.
I've known rivers:
Ancient, dusky rivers.

My soul has grown deep like the rivers.

4. **Euphrates** (yōō-frāt′ēz): a river in southwest Asia that is associated with several ancient civilizations.

No doubt I changed a few words the next day, or maybe crossed out a line or two. But there are seldom many changes in my poems, once they're down. Generally, the first two or three lines come to me from something I'm thinking about, or looking at, or doing, and the rest of the poem (if there is to be a poem) flows from those first few lines, usually right away. If there is a chance to put the poem down then, I write it down. If not, I try to remember it until I get to a pencil and paper; for poems are like rainbows: they escape you quickly.

Responding to the Selection

The Negro Speaks of Rivers by Langston Hughes

Interpreting Meanings

1. What are the four rivers named in this poem? Explain why Hughes chose each of them.
2. What feeling for the richness of black experience is expressed through the imagery of rivers? What is implied in lines 4–7?
3. Who is the **speaker** in the poem? Does the speaker represent something more significant than an individual?
4. In the poem, Hughes emphasizes the great age of rivers. What is he saying about his own people?
5. Point out examples of **repetition,** and explain why the poet uses this device.

Writer's Journal

Responding to the Poem
How were you affected by Hughes's poem? Did it make you think about your ancestry in a new way? Discuss your reaction. If you wish, share your response with your classmates.

Speaking and Listening

Dramatizing a Poem
Present "The Negro Speaks of Rivers" as a group reading. Have a narrator read all but the refrains, which can be read by a chorus.

Before You Read

Harlem; Dreams; I, Too; Mother to Son

Using What You Know

Young people are often stripped of their dreams before they reach adulthood, sometimes with devastating results for them and for society. Do you know any young people who have succeeded against great odds by holding fast to their dreams?

Literary Focus: Figurative Language

Figurative language is language that is not meant to be taken literally. All figurative language depends on a comparison between two or more things that are basically different. For example, if you call someone "an angel," you don't mean the person is a supernatural being with wings and a halo. You mean that the person is like an angel in beauty or in goodness.

The main form of figurative language is **metaphor**. Metaphor identifies two things directly. When Toomer says "Earth is a waxen cell of the world comb," he is using a metaphor.

Simile, another common form of figurative language, makes its comparison by using a specific word, such as *like* or *as.* When Hughes says that "poems are *like* rainbows," he is using a simile.

A special form of figurative language is **personification,** which is speaking of a nonliving thing as if it were human. When Hughes refers to the "muddy bosom" of the Mississippi, he implies that the river is a person.

A **symbol** is something that stands for itself and for something more as well. The dove, for example, is a common symbol for peace. Poets often create their own symbols.

Poets appeal to your imagination through these different forms of figurative language.

Setting a Purpose

The stronger our feelings, the stronger the language we use. As you read these poems, pay attention to Hughes's use of words. How does he use figurative language to convey feelings?

Harlem

Langston Hughes

What happens to a dream deferred?

    Does it dry up
    like a raisin in the sun?
    Or fester like a sore—
    And then run?   5
    Does it stink like rotten meat?
    Or crust and sugar over—
    like a syrupy sweet?

    Maybe it just sags
    like a heavy load.   10

    Or does it explode?

Daydreaming, *oil by Raymond Lark.*
From the private collection of
James and Mary Moran Estates, New Jersey and Florida;
Photo courtesy Edward Smith

Dreams

Langston Hughes

Hold fast to dreams
For if dreams die
Life is a broken-winged bird
That cannot fly.

Hold fast to dreams
For when dreams go
Life is a barren field
Frozen with snow.

I, Too

Langston Hughes

I, too, sing America.

I am the darker brother.
They send me to eat in the kitchen
When company comes,
But I laugh,   5
And eat well,
And grow strong.

Tomorrow,
I'll be at the table
When company comes.   10
Nobody'll dare
Say to me,
"Eat in the kitchen,"
Then.

Besides,   15
They'll see how beautiful I am
And be ashamed—

I, too, am America.

Mother to Son

Langston Hughes

Well, son, I'll tell you:
Life for me ain't been no crystal stair.
It's had tacks in it,
And splinters,
And boards torn up,   5
And places with no carpet on the floor—
Bare.
But all the time
I'se been a-climbin' on,
And reachin' landin's,   10
And turnin' corners,
And sometimes goin' in the dark
Where there ain't been no light.
So boy, don't you turn back.
Don't you set down on the steps   15
'Cause you finds it's kinder hard.
Don't you fall now—
For I'se still goin', honey,
I'se still climbin',
And life for me ain't been no crystal stair.   20

Responding to the Selections

Four Poems by Langston Hughes

Interpreting Meanings

Harlem
1. The first line talks of "a dream deferred." How do you react when something you want is postponed or put off?
2. What dream is Hughes referring to?
3. Although the poem is phrased as a series of questions, Hughes is actually making a statement. What happens to dreams that are deferred? Point out specific words that tell you.
4. What do you think the last line means?

Dreams
1. What advice does this poem offer?
2. Why do you think Hughes uses the **metaphor** of the bird and the field for broken dreams?
3. **Diction** refers to a writer's choice of language. How does the diction of "Dreams" compare with that of "Harlem"? How is the language in each poem suitable for its subject?

I, Too
1. Who is the **speaker** in this poem?
2. Is "the kitchen" in line 3 meant literally or figuratively? What do you think "the table" in line 9 represents?
3. Compare the opening and closing lines. What word has Hughes changed in the closing line? What do you think is the importance of this change?
4. Is this poem also about dreams? Give your interpretation of its meaning.

Mother to Son
1. This poem is based on a single **metaphor,** which is first stated in line 2. What does the word *crystal* suggest? By contrast, what kind of staircase is the speaker describing?
2. What kind of life has the mother lived?
3. In which line does the mother first give her son advice? How does she encourage him?
4. This poem is an example of how plain speech is made into poetry. Why are **images** like *tacks, splinters,* and *boards torn up* appropriate for the mother's experience?
5. How does the **repetition** of the word *and* suggest the climb up a long staircase? Why do you think the word *bare* is on a line by itself?
6. Is this a poem about holding fast to dreams? Explain.

Literary Elements

Analyzing an Extended Metaphor
A **metaphor,** as you know, draws a comparison between two different things. Sometimes a metaphor continues for several lines or throughout an entire poem. In "Mother to Son," a person's progress through life is compared to climbing a staircase. The entire poem develops this comparison. Such a metaphor is called an **extended metaphor.**

Analyze the extended metaphor in the poem. What might the "tacks" (line 3), "splinters" (line 4), "boards torn up" (line 5) represent? the "bare" places "with no carpet" (lines 6–7)? What might the landings (line 10), the turned corners (line 11), and the darkness (lines 12–13) stand for?

What is the extended metaphor in "I, Too"?

Language and Vocabulary

Responding to Connotative Language

Poets rely on the **connotative,** or suggestive, meanings of words as well as on their **denotative,** or literal, meanings. For the poem "Harlem," Hughes has chosen words with strong emotional associations. The phrase "dry up" in line 2 has a negative connotation, as does *sags* in line 9. The word *sugar* usually has a positive connotation, but in the poem it suggests something unpleasant. Choose five words in the poem that convey strong feelings. In a dictionary, find the exact meaning of each word, and tell what connotations it has as used in the poem.

Writer's Journal

Describing a Dream for the Future

Think of a dream you have for your future. Describe your dream and tell how you plan to make it a reality. If you like, discuss your ideas with some of your classmates. Ask for additional suggestions so that you can avoid having your dream deferred.

Speaking and Listening

Reading Poetry Aloud

The language we use in everyday life has a rhythm and music of its own. "Mother to Son" uses plain speech to create certain poetic effects of great beauty. Before reading the poem aloud, look carefully at the clues to interpretation. For example, look at the punctuation in the opening line. Which of these pauses would receive stronger emphasis? Which words in the poem would need to be stressed? Which lines should be spoken gently or sadly? Have a partner listen to you read to see if you have captured the character of the speaker.

The comma has great significance in poetry since line divisions do not always indicate places to pause. The comma helps the reader in constructing meaning, since it signals pauses. Read the first line of "I, Too" aloud as if there were no commas. Then re-read it, pausing at the commas. How does the meaning of the line become clearer? Read the entire poem aloud, following the punctuation for clues in phrasing the poet's thoughts.

Before You Read

Seeing Double from **Simple Speaks His Mind;**
Two Sides Not Enough from **Simple Stakes a Claim**

Using What You Know

Do you know someone whose thinking is always different from yours? Do you find that person's ideas amusing? annoying? stimulating? Have you ever tried to disagree with or refute that person's arguments? What happened?

Literary Focus: The Sketch

A **sketch** is a short narrative that is like a short story but simpler in construction. It usually presents a single scene and has only slight character development. Its tone is generally informal. Hughes created the fictional character Jesse B. Semple (known as "Simple") in the 1940s. The Simple sketches became so popular that eventually they filled four volumes.

Setting a Purpose

Simple is a humorous sage. He has not had much formal education, but he is a wise person who is able to drive home his points with good-humored wit. As you read, ask yourself why Simple has become known as a spokesperson for the black experience.

Simple Speaks His Mind

Langston Hughes

Seeing Double

"I wonder why it is we have two of one thing, and only one of others."

"For instance?"

"We have two lungs," said Simple, "but only one heart. Two eyes, but only one mouth. Two—"

"Feet, but only one body," I said.

"I was not going to say *feet*," said Simple. "But since you have taken the words out of my mouth, go ahead."

"Human beings have two shoulders but only one neck."

"And two ears but only one head," said Simple.

"What on earth would you want with two heads?"

"I could sleep with one and stay awake with the other," explained Simple. "Just like I got two nostrils, I would also like to have two mouths, then I could eat with one mouth while I am talking with the other. Joyce always starts an argument while we are eating, anyhow. That Joyce can talk and eat all at once."

"Suppose Joyce had two mouths, too," I said. "She could double-talk you."

"I would not keep company with a woman that had two mouths," said Simple. "But I would like to have two myself."

"If you had two mouths, you would have to have two noses also," I said, "and it would not make much sense to have two noses, would it?"

"No," said Simple, "I reckon it wouldn't. Neither would I like to have two chins to have to shave. A chin is no use for a thing. But there is one thing I sure would like to have two of. Since I have—"

"Since you have two eyes, I know you would like to have two faces—one in front and one behind—so you could look at all those pretty women on the street both going and coming."

"That would be idealistic," said Simple, "but that is *not* what I was going to say. You always cut me off. So you go ahead and talk."

"I know you wish you had two stomachs," I said, "so you could eat more of Joyce's good cooking."

"No, I do *not* wish I had two stomachs," said Simple. "I can put away enough food in one belly to mighty near wreck my pocket-book—with prices as high as a cat's back in a dogfight. So I do not need two stomachs. Neither do I need two navels on the stomach I got. What use are they? But there is one thing I sure wish I had two of."

"Two gullets?" I asked.

"Two gullets is *not* what I wish I had at all," said Simple. "Let me talk! *I wish I had two brains.*"

"Two brains! Why?"

"So I could think with one, and let the other one rest, man, that's why. I am tired of trying to figure out how to get ahead in this world. If I had two brains, I could think with one brain while the other brain was asleep. I could plan with one while the other brain was drunk. I could think about the Dodgers[1] with one, and my future with the other. As it is now, there is too much in this world for one brain to take care of alone. I have

thought so much with my one brain that it is about wore out. In fact, I need a rest right now. So let's drink up and talk about something pleasant. Two beers are on me tonight. Draw up to the bar."

"I was just at the bar," I said, "and Tony has nothing but bottles tonight, no draft."

"Then, daddy-o, they're on *you*," said Simple. "I only got two dimes—and one of them is a Roosevelt dime[2] I do not wish to spend. Had I been thinking, I would have remembered that Roosevelt dime. When I get my other brain, it will keep track of all such details."

---

1. **Dodgers:** a professional baseball team called the Brooklyn Dodgers, now known as the Los Angeles Dodgers.

2. **Roosevelt dime:** The image of Franklin D. Roosevelt was created for the coin in 1944 by Selma Burke, an African American sculptor.

FROM ———————————————

Simple Stakes a Claim

Langston Hughes

Two Sides Not Enough

"A man ought to have more than just two sides to sleep on," declared Simple. "Now if I get tired of sleeping on my left side, I have nothing to turn over on but my right side."

"You could sleep on your back," I advised.

"I snores on my back."

"Then why not try your stomach?"

"Sleeping on my stomach, I get a stiff neck—I always have to keep my head turned toward one side or the other, else I smothers. I do not like to sleep on my stomach."

"The right side, or the left side, are certainly enough sides for most people to sleep on. I don't know what your trouble is. But, after all, there are two sides to every question."

"That's just what I am talking about," said Simple. "Two sides are not enough. I'm tired of sleeping on either my left side, or on my right side, so I wish I had two or three more sides to change off on. Also, if I sleep on my left side, I am facing my wife, then I have to turn over to see the clock in the morning to find out what time it is. If I sleep on my right side, I am facing the window so the light wakes me up before it is time to get up. If I sleep on my back, I snores, and disturbs my wife. And my stomach is out for sleeping, due to reasons which I mentioned. In the merchant marines, sailors are always talking about the port side and the starboard side of a ship. A human should have not only a left side and a right side, but also a port side and a starboard side."

"That's what left and right mean in nautical terms," I said. "You know as well as I do that a ship has only two sides."

"Then ships are bad off as a human," said Simple. "All a boat can do when a storm comes up, is like I do when I sleep—toss from side to side."

"Maybe you eat too heavy a dinner," I said, "or drink too much coffee."

"No, I am not troubled in no digestion at night," said Simple. "But there is one thing that I do not like in the morning—waking up to face the same old one-eyed egg Joyce has fried for breakfast. What I wish is that there was different kinds of eggs, not just white eggs with a yellow eye. There ought to be blue eggs with a brown eye, and brown eggs with a blue eye, also red eggs with green eyes."

"If you ever woke up and saw a red egg with a green eye on your plate, you would think you had a hang-over."

"I would," said Simple. "But eggs *is* monotonous! No matter which side you turn an egg on, daddy-o, it is still an egg—hard on one side and soft on the other. Or, if you turn it over, it's hard on both sides. Once an egg gets in the frying pan, it has only two sides, too. And if you burn the bottom side, it

comes out just like the race problem, black and white, black and white."

"I thought you'd get around to race before you got through. You can't discuss any subject at all without bringing in color. God help you! And in reducing everything to two sides, as usual, you oversimplify."

"What does I do?"

"I say your semantics[1] make things too simple."

"My which?"

"Your verbiage."

"My what?"

"Your words, man, your words."

"Oh," said Simple. "Well, anyhow, to get back to eggs—which is a simple word. For breakfast I wish some other birds besides chickens laid eggs for eating, with a different kind of flavor than just a hen flavor. Whatever you are talking about with your *see-antics*,[2] Jack, at my age a man gets tired of the same kind of eggs each and every day—just like you get tired of the race problem. I would like to have an egg some morning that tastes like a pork chop."

"In that case, why don't you have pork chops for breakfast instead of eggs?"

"Because there is never no pork chops in my icebox in the morning."

"There would be if you would put them there the night before."

"No," said Simple, "I would eat them up the night before—which is always the trouble with the morning after—you have practically nothing left from the night before—except the race problem."

1. **semantics** (sə-măn′tĭks): a branch of language study that deals with the meanings of words.
2. *see-antics:* a deliberate mispronunciation of *semantics,* with a play on the word *antics,* which means "playful actions or pranks."

Simple Stakes a Claim   333

Responding to the Selections

Seeing Double; Two Sides Not Enough by Langston Hughes

Interpreting Meanings

1. How does the name Jesse B. Semple suggest a character description? What are some possibilities?
2. What do you think of Simple's idea about needing two brains?
3. What comparison does Simple draw between cooking eggs and the "race problem"?
4. Simple is accused of reducing everything to two sides and oversimplifying. Do you agree?
5. What can you tell about the educational background of the two speakers from their language? How do you know that Hughes has made this distinction deliberately?

Creative Writing

Writing a Sketch

Now that you have met Simple, write your own sketch. Write about Simple or create your own character. Try to make your creation reflect the language, customs, and attitudes of some section of society.

Speaking and Listening

Dramatizing a Sketch

Since the two Simple stories are in dialogue, two students might act out the parts. For an effective reading, each performer should use the correct tone and emphasis suitable for the characters.

About the Author

Countee Cullen (1903–1946)

Throughout his life, Countee (coun'tā) Cullen fought against being labeled a "Negro poet." He often said that he wanted to be known as a man of literature, accepted by scholars and writers because of his skill, not because of his race. At the same time, however, he was drawn to the subject of his racial heritage: "Somehow I find my poetry of itself treating of the Negro, of his joys and his sorrows—mostly of the latter—and of the heights and depths of emotion I feel as a Negro." A number of his poems show his emotional involvement with his race. In "Heritage," for instance, he tries to answer the question "What is Africa to me?" In "From the Dark Tower," he speaks of a time when black people will realize their hopes for a better life. In "Incident," he expresses his rage at racial injustice. Even the titles of some of Cullen's volumes of poetry, such as *Color,* (1925), *The Ballad of the Brown Girl* (1927), and *Copper Sun* (1927) show his concern with racial themes.

Cullen was born Countee LeRoy Porter. His place of birth is unknown; it may have been Baltimore, New York City, or Louisville. His parents are also unknown. Brought up probably by a grandmother, he was taken in by Frederick A. Cullen, the pastor of a large Harlem church, who perhaps adopted him.

Cullen began publishing poetry while still a high school student. His first book, *Color,* appeared when he was twenty-two. He won

Oil pastel by Winold Reiss, c. 1925 (detail).

many fellowships and honors, and he published books in quick succession. No Harlem Renaissance poet was more popular than Cullen during the period.

Cullen viewed poetry in very traditional ways. Nearly all of his work is written in standard verse forms with fixed meters and rhyme schemes. He believed poetry should celebrate truth and beauty, as did the work of the poet he most admired, the English Romantic John Keats.

Countee Cullen   335

Before You Read

From the Dark Tower

Using What You Know

Poets often use images that have traditional associations. Langston Hughes does this with the imagery of rivers in "The Negro Speaks of Rivers." Think of some poems you have read that use traditional images, such as those of the night, the sea, and the seasons. Why do you suppose poets often use images of planting and harvesting?

Literary Focus: Rhythm and Meter

In music, the term **rhythm** refers to the regular "beat" of a song. There is rhythm, as well, in the way we talk, in the natural rise and fall of the voice and the alternation between stressed and unstressed syllables. Say this line aloud:

I **turned** a**side** and **bowed** my **head** and **wept.**

Did you stress the syllables printed in boldface?

Poets use rhythm deliberately as a way of emphasizing meaning. When poetry has a regular rhythmic pattern, we say it has **meter.**

Setting a Purpose

As you read Cullen's poem aloud, note its strong rhythm. Which words are stressed? How does the rhythm of the poem emphasize its meaning?

From the Dark Tower
(To Charles S. Johnson)

Countee Cullen

We shall not always plant while others reap
The golden increment° of bursting fruit,
Not always countenance,° abject and mute,
That lesser men should hold their brothers cheap;
Not everlastingly while others sleep   5
Shall we beguile their limbs with mellow flute,
Not always bend to some more subtle brute;
We were not made eternally to weep.

The night whose sable breast relieves the stark,
White stars is no less lovely being dark,   10
And there are buds that cannot bloom at all
In light, but crumple, piteous, and fall;
So in the dark we hide the heart that bleeds,
And wait, and tend our agonizing seeds.

2. **increment** (ĭn'krə-mənt): increase, growth.
3. **countenance** (koun'tə-nəns): to show approval; tolerate.

Sharecropper, *woodcut by Elizabeth Catlett, 1970.*
Courtesy of the Estate of Thurlow E. Tibbs, Jr., © 1997 Elizabeth Catlett/Licensed by VAGA, New York, NY

Responding to the Selection

From the Dark Tower by Countee Cullen

Interpreting Meanings

1. In your own words, explain what the poet is saying in the first two lines.
2. How is darkness used as a **metaphor** in the poem?
3. In lines 11–12, the poet refers to a flower that appears only in the dark. What do you think this metaphor means?
4. The poem begins and ends with **images** of planting and tending seeds. Is the waiting referred to in the final lines of the poem a sign of defeat, of victory, or of something else?
5. Examine the structure of the sonnet. What idea is expressed in the **octave,** the first eight lines of the poem? What idea is expressed in the **sestet,** the remaining six lines?
6. What is Cullen's **tone** in this poem? Is he angry? defiant?
7. What do you think the title of the poem means?

Literary Elements

Analyzing Meter

Meter refers to the regular pattern of rhythm—that is, of stressed and unstressed syllables in a line of verse. The analysis of a poem's meter is called **scansion**.

Meter is measured in units called **feet.** A **foot** is made up of one stressed syllable and, usually, one or two unstressed syllables. A line of poetry is scanned by dividing it into feet and marking the stressed and unstressed syllables:

> We shall/ not al/ways plant/ while
> oth/ers reap/

When this line is read aloud, we naturally stress alternating syllables. The sign (ˇ) means the syllable is unstressed. The sign (ʹ) means the syllable receives stress.

This line is made up of five metrical feet. Each foot is an **iamb**—that is, a poetic foot consisting of one unstressed syllable followed by a stressed syllable. We say that the entire line is written in **iambic pentameter,** or five iambs. The word **pentameter** means "five metrical feet."

Work out the metrical pattern of the remaining lines of Cullen's poem. Where does the pattern vary?

Language and Vocabulary

Recognizing Precise Meanings

Many words have more than one meaning. You often must use context clues to determine which meaning the writer intends. In line 3 of the poem, Cullen uses the word *countenance*. This is not the word that means "face" or "expression." In Cullen's poem, the word *countenance* is a verb. It means "to show approval" or "to tolerate."

What is the meaning of the word *cheap* in line 4? Consult a dictionary to find the precise meaning that Cullen is using.

Writing About Literature

Interpreting a Poem

Poets can say a great deal in few words. The **epigram** is a very short poem, often witty or satiric. Note how every word is essential in this epigram.

For a Lady I Know
Countee Cullen

She even thinks that up in heaven
   Her class lies late and snores,
While poor black cherubs rise at seven
   To do celestial chores.

Write an interpretation of the poem.

Prewriting Strategies

1. Check the meaning of any unfamiliar words, such as *cherubs* (line 3) and *celestial* (line 4).
2. Restate in your own words what the poem says. Make sure you understand all references. Who, for example, is *she* in line 1 and what is *her class* in line 2?
3. Determine the **tone** of the poem. For example, is it satirical? bitter? sympathetic?
4. In a paragraph, state your conclusions.

Critical Thinking

Analyzing a Poem

The following poem by Countee Cullen is one of his best-known works. The last two lines may be the most famous lines of any poetry associated with the Harlem Renaissance. Read the poem slowly and carefully. After you have read it, stop and think about it, and then read it again. The steps outlined on page 340 will help you analyze this sonnet.

Yet Do I Marvel
Countee Cullen

I doubt not God is good, well-meaning,
   kind,
And did He stoop to quibble could tell why
The little buried mole continues blind,
Why flesh that mirrors Him must some day
   die,
Make plain the reason tortured Tantalus° 5
Is baited by the fickle fruit, declare
If merely brute caprice dooms Sisyphus°
To struggle up a never-ending stair.
Inscrutable° His ways are, and immune
To catechism° by a mind too strewn   10
With petty cares to slightly understand
What awful brain compels His awful° hand.
Yet do I marvel at this curious thing:
To make a poet black, and bid him sing!

5. **Tantalus** (tăn′tə-ləs): a character in Greek mythology whose punishment in the underworld was to stand in water that always receded when he tried to drink and under branches of fruit he could never reach. 7. **Sisyphus** (sĭs′ə-fəs): a character in Greek mythology who was doomed forever to roll a heavy stone uphill, only to have it roll down again. 9. **Inscrutable** (ĭn-skrōōt′ə-bəl): beyond understanding. 9–10. **immune . . . catechism** (kăt′ə-kĭzm): not open to question or dispute. 12. **awful:** here, awe-inspiring.

1. *Look at the title.* What does it tell you about the subject of the poem or theme?

2. *Look for complete thoughts, instead of reading line by line.* Read the poem aloud, paying attention to punctuation or following meaning. Where will you pause in reading lines 1, 6, and 14?

3. *Make sure you know the meanings of all the words in the poem.* Refer to a dictionary when the meaning of a word is not clear from context. For example, what is the meaning of the phrase "brute caprice" in line 7?

4. *Identify the speaker of the poem.* Is the voice in the poem that of Cullen or a fictional character created by the poet?

5. *Note the effects of specific words, images, and figures of speech.* What are the connotations of key words in the poem? What feelings do they suggest? Note comparisons used by the poet. Point out and explain symbols and allusions.

6. *Listen for sound effects.* What words, if any, are repeated? What ideas are emphasized by devices of repetition?

7. *Examine the structure of the poem.* In the first eight lines of this sonnet, Cullen names some things that he does not understand. What point is he making through these examples? What conclusion does he come to in lines 9–12? To whom is he referring in the last line of the poem?

8. *Express the meaning of the poem in your own words.* What experience do you think the poet wishes to share with the reader? What do you think he may have felt or thought? How does the poem make you feel?

Before You Read

Using What You Know

Think of a specific incident in which a community has worked to create racial harmony. Was the effort successful or unsuccessful? What role does society play in determining how people of different races view one another?

Literary Focus: Imagery

Imagery refers to words or phrases that appeal to the senses. Most images are visual; that is, they appeal to the reader's sense of sight. Images can appeal to the other senses as well: touch, taste, smell, hearing. Sometimes, the term imagery is also used to signify **figurative language.**

The use of imagery enables us to re-create in our own minds what the writer imagines. In this way, we share the writer's sensations and participate actively in the experience.

Setting a Purpose

The following poems might be considered companion works illustrating contrasting views of race relations. In reading, note how Cullen uses imagery to depict both scenes. If you can "see" these pictures, then you and the poet have connected.

Tableau°
(For Donald Duff)

Countee Cullen

Locked arm in arm they cross the way,
  The black boy and the white,
The golden splendor of the day,
  The sable pride of night.

From lowered blinds the dark folk stare,   5
  And here the fair folk talk,
Indignant that these two should dare
  In unison to walk.

Oblivious to look and word
  They pass, and see no wonder   10
That lightning brilliant as a sword
  Should blaze the path of thunder.

°**tableau** (tăb'lō): a striking dramatic scene or picture.

Incident
(For Eric Walrond)

Countee Cullen

Once riding in old Baltimore,
  Heart-filled, head-filled with glee,
I saw a Baltimorean
  Keep looking straight at me.

Now I was eight and very small,   5
  And he was no whit bigger,
And so I smiled, but he poked out
  His tongue, and called me, "Nigger."

I saw the whole of Baltimore
  From May until December;   10
Of all the things that happened there
  That's all that I remember.

The Wall, *oil by Hughie Lee-Smith, 1989.*
Collection of Byron T. Atkinson; Courtesy June Kelly Gallery.
© Hughie Lee-Smith/Licensed by VAGA, New York, NY

Responding to the Selections

Tableau; Incident by Countee Cullen

Interpreting Meanings

1. A *tableau* is a vivid or striking picture. Why is this word a good title for Cullen's poem?
2. What **metaphors** are used in the first stanza to describe the two boys?
3. What is the reaction of members of the community, both black and white, to their friendship?
4. How do the boys react to community opinion? Read aloud the lines that support your answer.
5. What do you think is meant by the last two lines?
6. "Incident" is another lyric about two boys. In what way are the poems alike in form and content? How are they different?

7. Why is it significant that both boys are quite young?
8. How is the black boy affected by the experience?

Writer's Journal

Responding to Poetry

The two poems you have just read show two sides of race relations. One poem offers promise for a better tomorrow while the other paints a dismal picture for the future. Which lyric more closely reflects your opinion? Will young people lead the way to improved race relations, or will they accept the racial bias of past generations? If you wish, share your entry with others in the class.

About the Author

Zora Neale Hurston (1891–1960)

"Jump at de sun." In her autobiography, *Dust Tracks on a Road* (1942), Zora Neale Hurston recalls her mother urging her eight children to aim high. "We might not land on the sun, but at least we would get off the ground."

Zora Neale Hurston was born on January 7, 1891, according to most recent accounts—no birth records survive. Her family lived in Eatonville, Florida, the first incorporated black township in the United States, which she described as "the first attempt at organized self-government on the part of Negroes in America." Eatonville had a charter, a mayor, a council, and a marshal. This town gave Hurston a rich source of African American cultural tradition.

Her father, the Reverend John Hurston, was mayor of Eatonville for three terms, and his family experienced no poverty. Hurston was about nine when her mother died. Her father quickly remarried, and her opposition to her stepmother caused the relationship with her father to deteriorate. She left home to take a job as a wardrobe girl to a repertory company touring the South. She left the troupe in Baltimore, Maryland, eighteen months later and completed her high school studies at Morgan Academy. She attended Howard University in Washington, D.C., and then transferred to Barnard College in New York City, where she became interested in black folk traditions. After graduation, she returned to the South to study the oral traditions in Florida. Her research resulted in her book *Mules and Men* (1935).

Photograph by Carl Van Vechten. Berg Collection/New York Public Library. Permission granted by the Estate of Carl Van Vechten, Joseph Solomon, Executor

Hurston wrote plays, novels, short stories, and articles. Her second novel, *Their Eyes Were Watching God* (1937), is her most widely read book. Hurston's reputation declined in the 1940s. During the last decade of her life, she worked as a maid and tried without success to have her manuscripts published. She died a pauper in Fort Pierce, Florida, on January 28, 1960. She was buried in the Garden of the Heavenly Rest, the town's segregated cemetery. Langston Hughes once described her in this way: "She was full of side-splitting anecdotes, humorous tales, and tragicomic stories, remembered out of her life in the South as a daughter of a traveling minister of God."

Zora Neale Hurston 345

Before You Read

from **Dust Tracks on a Road**

Using What You Know

In this episode from her autobiography, Hurston recalls one of her earliest contacts with white people. Two strangers visit her school and take a liking to her. They are curious about her, and she, in turn, is curious about them. She tells how the pleasure of reading gives them something in common.

Can you remember which books you enjoyed reading most when you were younger? Did you like stories of fantasy and adventure more than stories about everyday life? Did books help you learn about the world? Do you think books can help to bring together people of different backgrounds?

Literary Focus: Tone

In order to understand a literary work, you often must figure out the writer's tone. **Tone** is the attitude a writer takes toward a subject, a character, or a reader. The tone of a work may be serious or humorous, solemn or lighthearted, sarcastic, affectionate, playful, cynical, bitter, or angry. The tone of a work can also vary. Misunderstanding tone can lead you to the wrong conclusions about a writer's intentions.

Setting a Purpose

As you read, determine Hurston's attitude toward the events she is recalling. Does she make you laugh? Does she make you share her enthusiasm for reading? Does the title of her autobiography give you a clue to her tone?

Dust Tracks on a Road

An Autobiography

Zora Neale Hurston

I used to take a seat on top of the gate-post and watch the world go by. One way to Orlando[1] ran past my house, so the carriages and cars would pass before me. The movement made me glad to see it. Often the white travelers would hail me, but more often I hailed them, and asked, "Don't you want me to go a piece of the way with you?"

They always did. I know now that I must have caused a great deal of amusement among them, but my self-assurance must have carried the point, for I was always invited to come along. I'd ride up the road for perhaps a half-mile, then walk back. I did not do this with the permission of my parents, nor with their foreknowledge. When they found out about it later, I usually got a whipping. My grandmother worried about my forward ways a great deal. She had known slavery and to her my brazenness was unthinkable.

"Git down offa dat gate-post! You li'l sow, you! Git down! Setting up dere looking dem white folks right in de face! They's gowine[2] to lynch you, yet. And don't stand in dat doorway gazing out at 'em neither. Youse too brazen to live long."

Nevertheless, I kept right on gazing at them, and "going a piece of the way" whenever I could make it. The village seemed dull to me most of the time. If the village was singing a chorus, I must have missed the tune.

Perhaps a year before the old man[3] died, I came to know two other white people for myself. They were women.

It came about this way. The whites who came down from the North were often brought by their friends to visit the village school. A Negro school was something strange to them, and while they were always sympathetic and kind, curiosity must have been present, also. They came and went, came and went. Always, the room was hurriedly put in order, and we were threatened with a prompt and bloody death if we cut one caper while the visitors were present. We always sang a spiritual, led by Mr. Calhoun himself. Mrs. Calhoun always stood in the back, with a palmetto[4] switch in her hand as a squelcher. We were all little angels for the duration, because we'd better be. She would cut her eyes and give us a glare that meant

1. **Orlando:** Eatonville is about five miles from Orlando.
2. **gowine:** Southern dialect for "going."

3. **old man:** a white farmer who knew the family and had befriended Zora Neale.
4. **palmetto** (păl-mĕt'ō): a palm tree with fan-shaped leaves.

Kingsborough Community College, The City University of New York.
Courtesy Estate of Romare Bearden./The Romare Howard Bearden
Foundation, NY

School Bell Time, *from the Profile/Part I: The Twenties Series,*
collage by Romare Bearden, 1978.

trouble, then turn her face towards the visitors and beam as much as to say it was a great privilege and pleasure to teach lovely children like us. They couldn't see that palmetto hickory in her hand behind all those benches, but we knew where our angelic behavior was coming from.

Usually, the visitors gave warning a day ahead and we would be cautioned to put on shoes, comb our heads, and see to ears and fingernails. There was a close inspection of every one of us before we marched in that morning. Knotty heads, dirty ears and fingernails got hauled out of line, strapped and sent home to lick the calf over again.

This particular afternoon, the two young ladies just popped in. Mr. Calhoun was flustered, but he put on the best show he could.

He dismissed the class that he was teaching up at the front of the room, then called the fifth grade in reading. That was my class.

So we took our readers and went up front. We stood up in the usual line, and opened to the lesson. It was the story of Pluto and Persephone.[5] It was new and hard to the class in general, and Mr. Calhoun was very uncomfortable as the readers stumbled along, spelling out words with their lips, and in mumbling undertones before they exposed them experimentally to the teacher's ears.

Then it came to me. I was fifth or sixth down the line. The story was not new to me, because I had read my reader through from

5. **Pluto and Persephone** (pər-sĕf'ə-nē): In classical mythology, Pluto was the god of the dead and ruler of the underworld. Persephone was his wife and queen of the underworld.

348   ZORA NEALE HURSTON

lid to lid, the first week that Papa had bought it for me.

That is how it was that my eyes were not in the book, working out the paragraph which I knew would be mine by counting the children ahead of me. I was observing our visitors, who held a book between them, following the lesson. They had shiny hair, mostly brownish. One had a looping gold chain around her neck. The other one was dressed all over in black and white with a pretty finger ring on her left hand. But the thing that held my eyes were their fingers. They were long and thin, and very white, except up near the tips. There they were baby pink. I had never seen such hands. It was a fascinating discovery for me. I wondered how they felt. I would have given those hands more attention, but the child before me was almost through. My turn next, so I got on my mark, bringing my eyes back to the book and made sure of my place. Some of the stories I had reread several times, and this Greco-Roman myth was one of my favorites. I was exalted by it, and that is the way I read my paragraph.

"Yes, Jupiter[6] had seen her (Persephone). He had seen the maiden picking flowers in the field. He had seen the chariot of the dark monarch pause by the maiden's side. He had seen him when he seized Persephone. He had seen the black horses leap down Mount Aetna's[7] fiery throat. Persephone was now in Pluto's dark realm and he had made her his wife."

The two women looked at each other and then back to me. Mr. Calhoun broke out with a proud smile beneath his bristly moustache, and instead of the next child taking up

where I had ended, he nodded to me to go on. So I read the story to the end, where flying Mercury, the messenger of the Gods, brought Persephone back to the sunlit earth and restored her to the arms of Dame Ceres,[8] her mother, that the world might have springtime and summer flowers, autumn and harvest. But because she had bitten the pomegranate[9] while in Pluto's kingdom, she must return to him for three months of each year, and be his queen. Then the world had winter, until she returned to earth.

The class was dismissed, and the visitors smiled us away and went into a low-voiced conversation with Mr. Calhoun for a few minutes. They glanced my way once or twice and I began to worry. Not only was I barefooted, but my feet and legs were dusty. My hair was more uncombed than usual, and my nails were not shiny clean. Oh, I'm going to catch it now. Those ladies saw me, too. Mr. Calhoun is promising to 'tend to me. So I thought.

Then Mr. Calhoun called me. I went up thinking how awful it was to get a whipping before company. Furthermore, I heard a snicker run over the room. Hennie Clark and Stell Brazzle did it out loud, so I would be sure to hear them. The smart-aleck was going to get it. I slipped one hand behind me and switched my dress tail at them, indicating scorn.

"Come here, Zora Neale," Mr. Calhoun cooed as I reached the desk. He put his hand on my shoulder and gave me little pats. The ladies smiled and held out those flower-look-

---

6. **Jupiter:** king of the gods.
7. **Mount Aetna** (ĕt′nə): volcanic mountain in Sicily.

8. **Ceres** (sîr′ēz′): goddess of agriculture.
9. **pomegranate** (päm′grăn′ĭt): a round fruit containing many seeds. In some versions of the myth, Persephone was required to spend one month in Pluto's kingdom for each seed she had eaten.

ing fingers towards me. I seized the opportunity for a good look.

"Shake hands with the ladies, Zora Neale," Mr. Calhoun prompted and they took my hand one after the other and smiled. They asked if I loved school, and I lied that I did. There was *some* truth in it, because I liked geography and reading, and I liked to play at recess time. Whoever it was invented writing and arithmetic got no thanks from me. Neither did I like the arrangement where the teacher could sit up there with a palmetto stem and lick me whenever he saw fit. I hated things I couldn't do anything about. But I knew better than to bring that up right there, so I said yes, I *loved* school.

"I can tell you do," Brown Taffeta gleamed. She patted my head, and was lucky enough not to get sandspurs in her hand. Children who roll and tumble in the grass in Florida are apt to get sandspurs in their hair. They shook hands with me again and I went back to my seat.

When school let out at three o'clock, Mr. Calhoun told me to wait. When everybody had gone, he told me I was to go to the Park House, that was the hotel in Maitland,[10] the next afternoon to call upon Mrs. Johnstone and Miss Hurd. I must tell Mama to see that I was clean and brushed from head to feet, and I must wear shoes and stockings. The ladies liked me, he said, and I must be on my best behavior.

The next day I was let out of school an hour early, and went home to be stood up in a tub full of suds and be scrubbed and have my ears dug into. My sandy hair sported a red ribbon to match my red and white checked gingham dress, starched until it could stand alone. Mama saw to it that my shoes were on the right feet, since I was careless about left and right. Last thing, I was given a handkerchief to carry, warned again about my behavior, and sent off, with my big brother John to go as far as the hotel gate with me.

First thing, the ladies gave me strange things, like stuffed dates and preserved ginger, and encouraged me to eat all that I wanted. Then they showed me their Japanese dolls and just talked. I was then handed a copy of *Scribner's Magazine*, and asked to read a place that was pointed out to me. After a paragraph or two, I was told with smiles, that that would do.

I was led out on the grounds and they took my picture under a palm tree. They handed me what was to me then a heavy cylinder done up in fancy paper, tied with a ribbon, and they told me goodbye, asking me not to open it until I got home.

My brother was waiting for me down by the lake, and we hurried home, eager to see what was in the thing. It was too heavy to be candy or anything like that. John insisted on toting it for me.

My mother made John give it back to me and let me open it. Perhaps, I shall never experience such joy again. The nearest thing to that moment was the telegram accepting my first book. One hundred goldy-new pennies rolled out of the cylinder. Their gleam lit up the world. It was not avarice that moved me. It was the beauty of the thing. I stood on the mountain. Mama let me play with my pennies for a while, then put them away for me to keep.

That was only the beginning. The next day I received an Episcopal hymn-book bound in white leather with a golden cross stamped into the front cover, a copy of *The Swiss*

10 **Maitland:** a city close to Eatonville.

Family Robinson,[11] and a book of fairy tales.

I set about to commit the song words to memory. There was no music written there, just the words. But there was to my consciousness music in between them just the same. "When I survey the Wondrous Cross" seemed the most beautiful to me, so I committed that to memory first of all. Some of them seemed dull and without life, and I pretended they were not there. If white people liked trashy singing like that, there must be something funny about them that I had not noticed before. I stuck to the pretty ones where the words marched to a throb I could feel.

A month or so after the young ladies returned to Minnesota, they sent me a huge box packed with clothes and books. The red coat with a wide circular collar and the red tam pleased me more than any of the other things. My chums pretended not to like anything that I had, but even then I knew that they were jealous. Old Smarty had gotten by them again. The clothes were not new, but they were very good. I shone like the morning sun.

But the books gave me more pleasure than the clothes. I had never been too keen on dressing up. It called for hard scrubbings with Octagon soap suds getting in my eyes, and none too gentle fingers scrubbing my neck and gouging in my ears.

In that box were *Gulliver's Travels, Grimm's Fairy Tales, Dick Whittington*,[12]

Greek and Roman Myths, and best of all, *Norse Tales*.[13] Why did the Norse tales strike so deeply into my soul? I do not know, but they did. I seemed to remember seeing Thor swing his mighty short-handled hammer as he sped across the sky in rumbling thunder, lightning flashing from the tread of his steeds and the wheels of his chariot. The great and good Odin, who went down to the well of knowledge to drink, and was told that the price of a drink from that fountain was an eye. Odin drank deeply, then plucked out one eye without a murmur and handed it to the grizzly keeper, and walked away. That held majesty for me.

Of the Greeks, Hercules[14] moved me most. I followed him eagerly on his tasks. The story of the choice of Hercules as a boy when he met Pleasure and Duty, and put his hand in that of Duty and followed her steep way to the blue hills of fame and glory, which she pointed out at the end, moved me profoundly. I resolved to be like him. The tricks and turns of the other Gods and Goddesses left me cold. There were other thin books about this and that sweet and gentle little girl who gave up her heart to Christ and good works. Almost always they died from it, preaching as they passed. I was utterly indifferent to their deaths. In the first place I could not conceive of death, and in the next place they never had any funerals that amounted to a hill of beans, so I didn't care how soon they rolled up their big, soulful, blue eyes and kicked the bucket. They had no meat on their bones.

But I also met Hans Andersen[15] and Rob-

---

11. **The Swiss Family Robinson**: a famous story for children by the Swiss writer Johann David Wyss (1743–1818). It tells of a family shipwrecked on an uninhabited island.

12. **Gulliver's . . . Whittington**: *Gulliver's Travels*, by the English writer Jonathan Swift (1667–1745); *Grimm's Fairy Tales*, German folk tales collected by the Grimm brothers in the nineteenth century; *Dick Whittington*, a story about a poor orphan who became mayor of London in the fifteenth century.

13. **Norse Tales**: the mythology of Scandinavia. Odin is the ruler of the gods. Thor, his son, is god of thunder.

14. **Hercules**: a hero of extraordinary strength who performed twelve extraordinary labors.

15. **Hans Andersen**: Hans Christian Andersen (1805–1875), Danish author of fairy tales.

ert Louis Stevenson.[16] They seemed to know what I wanted to hear and said it in a way that tingled me. Just a little below these friends was Rudyard Kipling[17] in his *Jungle Books.* I loved his talking snakes as much as I did the hero.

I came to start reading the Bible through my mother. She gave me a licking one afternoon for repeating something I had overheard a neighbor telling her. She locked me in her room after the whipping, and the Bible was the only thing in there for me to read. I happened to open to the place where David was doing some mighty smiting, and I got interested. David went here and he went

16. **Robert Louis Stevenson:** Scottish author (1850–1894) who wrote adventure stories such as *Treasure Island* and *Kidnapped.*
17. **Rudyard Kipling:** English writer (1865–1936), whose *Jungle Books* tell the adventures of Mowgli, an Indian boy who is raised among the animals in a forest.

there, and no matter where he went, he smote 'em hip and thigh. Then he sung songs to his harp awhile, and went out and smote some more. Not one time did David stop and preach about sins and other things. All David wanted to know from God was who to kill and when. He took care of the other details himself. Never a quiet moment. I liked him a lot. So I read a great deal more in the Bible, hunting for some more active people like David. Except for the beautiful language of Luke and Paul, the New Testament still plays a poor second to the Old Testament for me. The Jews had a God who laid about Him when they needed Him. I could see no use waiting until Judgment Day to see a man who was just crying for a good killing, to be told to go and roast. My idea was to give him a good killing first, and then if he got roasted later on, so much the better.

Responding to the Selection
from **Dust Tracks on a Road** by Zora Neale Hurston

Identifying Facts

1. Why did Zora like to take a seat on top of the gate post?
2. How were children disciplined at the village school?
3. How did Zora come to the attention of the white ladies who visited her school?
4. What did the cylinder contain?
5. Why did Zora like the stories about David?

Interpreting Meanings

1. One of the first things the author reveals about herself is that her grandmother considered her "brazen." Why did her grandmother worry about Zora's "forward ways"? Despite the whippings she received, why did Zora persist in making friends of travelers?
2. Why was Zora fascinated by the two ladies who visited her school? How do you account for their interest in Zora?

3. Zora liked the book of Norse tales because they held "majesty" for her. What do you think she means by this word?
4. Zora preferred characters with "meat on their bones." Explain what this expression means.
5. How do you know that Zora was intelligent and highly inquisitive? What other characteristics does she reveal?
6. We all make discoveries and choices, gain insights, and learn about the world as we grow up. How did Zora, a girl isolated in an all-black town, accomplish this?
7. **Tone** is the attitude or point of view a writer takes toward a subject or an audience. How do you think Hurston feels about her childhood in Eatonville? Do you think her memories are realistic or distorted?
8. This selection is filled with humorous touches. Which of these did you like the best?

Literary Elements

Understanding Tone

One way to understand **tone** in literature is to think of it as the writer's "voice." If the writer were speaking aloud, you would be able to tell many things from the sound of his or her voice. When you read, however, you must draw conclusions from other evidence. *How* a particular writer says things—his or her **style**—is often a key to tone. The words and expressions chosen, the length of the sentences, the use of rhythm, and other elements reveal tone.

Look back at the paragraph in which Hurston talks about her grandmother (page 347). Does this speech make you laugh?

In describing the children's preparations for visitors, Hurston says that children who failed inspection were "sent home to lick the calf over again." How would the tone be different if she had written "sent home to be washed a second time"?

Tone is also apparent in the way a writer's personality fills a work. Reread Hurston's description of the books about little girls who die virtuously (page 351). Describe her tone in this passage: "they never had any funerals that amounted to a hill of beans, so I didn't care how soon they rolled up their big, soulful, blue eyes and kicked the bucket. They had no meat on their bones."

Toward the end of the selection, Hurston tells about her discovery of the Bible. As a child, what was her attitude toward the stories of David? Can you give some examples of his "mighty smiting"? Do you think her discussion of a "good killing" is meant to be taken seriously or humorously?

Language and Vocabulary

Determining the Meanings of Expressions

In our language words are often joined together in expressions that take on special meanings. On page 347, Hurston says that the children were threatened if they "cut one caper." The word *caper* used alone means "a leap" or "a prank" (in slang it refers to "a robbery"). The expression "to cut a caper" means "to play tricks."

Determine the meaning of the following expressions in the selection. If you consult a dictionary, be sure to look under all the key words in a phrase.

"on my mark" (page 349)
"catch it" (page 349)
"amounted to a hill of beans" (page 351)
"kicked the bucket" (page 351)
"plays a poor second" (page 352)

Expository Writing

Explaining a Title

In Chapter 3 of her autobiography, Zora Neale Hurston says that as a baby, once she learned to walk she took to wandering:

> I always wanted to go. I would wander off in the woods all alone, following some inside urge to go places. This alarmed my mother a good deal. She used to say that she believed a woman who was an enemy of hers had sprinkled "travel dust" around the doorstep the day I was born.

Consider the title of Zora Neale Hurston's autobiography. What do the words *dust, tracks,* and *road* suggest? From what you learn about her in the selection, in what way was her life a journey and she a traveler? In a brief paragraph tell what you think the title of the book means. Also tell if you think the title is well chosen.

Writer's Journal

Recalling a Personal Experience

If you have started a journal, respond to Hurston's narrative by recalling the books you liked best when you were younger. Did you have a favorite book? Can you tell why you enjoyed it?

Speaking and Listening

Telling About a Performance

Review Hurston's description of the day in school when she and her fifth grade classmates had to read to visitors. Then think of a place and time when you had to perform before strangers. Give the circumstances and tell how you felt during and after the performance. Follow Hurston's example in making your account detailed and vivid.

About the Author

Rudolph Fisher (1897–1934)

 During his short life, Rudolph Fisher achieved distinction in two careers, medicine and literature. He was born in Washington, D.C., but grew up in Harlem and in Providence, Rhode Island. After completing his studies at Brown University, he returned to Washington and entered Howard University Medical School. He then moved to New York and established a successful practice as a radiologist.

While still a medical student, Fisher published his first short story, "The City of Refuge," in the *Atlantic Monthly.* The theme of this story and of many later writings is the conflict between the Southern black migrant's dream of life in the urban North and the city's harsh realities. Fisher treats this theme with humor as well as with sympathy.

In addition to short stories, Fisher published two novels, *The Walls of Jericho* (1928) and *The Conjure-Man Dies* (1932). *The Conjure-Man Dies* was the first detective novel to be written by an African American.

"Miss Cynthie," the story reprinted here, is one of Fisher's last works. Many critics consider it to be the best of Fisher's stories. Music is an important element in the story and is used to set up a contrast between the values of traditional Southern folk and urban black society. According to one scholar, Fisher's stories "reveal his love for the people of Harlem and the diversity of talents they represent. They also help us to understand the quality of life of Harlem during the Renaissance period." The divisions in the story have been added by the editors.

The Schomburg Center for Research in Black Culture/New York Public Library

Rudolph Fisher 355

Before You Read

Miss Cynthie

Using What You Know

Throughout this unit you have seen photographs of Harlem taken during the period of the Renaissance. You have read Langston Hughes's first-hand observations of people and places in Harlem. Make a list of adjectives you would use to describe the atmosphere of Harlem in the 1920s. After you have read "Miss Cynthie," you might want to go back and revise your list.

Literary Focus: Foreshadowing

Foreshadowing is an important device in short stories and in plays. Foreshadowing is the use of hints or clues to suggest what action is to come. It helps to build **suspense.** Often, a writer will give you information about a character early in a story so that you are prepared for what that character will do later on. An active reader is aware of clues and frequently can guess what will happen.

Setting a Purpose

As you read, try to predict how the characters will behave. Watch for clues. See how your predictions compare with the story's ending.

Miss Cynthie

Rudolph Fisher

1

For the first time in her life somebody had called her "madam." She had been standing, bewildered but unafraid, while innumerable Red Caps[1] appropriated piece after piece of the baggage arrayed on the platform. Neither her brief seventy years' journey through life nor her long two days' travel northward had dimmed the live brightness of her eyes, which, for all their bewilderment, had accurately selected her own treasures out of the row of luggage and guarded them vigilantly.

"These yours, madam?"

The biggest Red Cap of all was smiling at her. He looked for all the world like Doc Crinshaw's oldest son back home. Her little brown face relaxed; she smiled back at him.

"They got to be. You all done took all the others."

He laughed aloud. Then—"Carry 'em in for you?"

She contemplated his bulk. "Reckon you can manage it—puny little feller like you?"

Thereupon they were friends. Still grinning broadly, he surrounded himself with her impedimenta,[2] the enormous brown extension-case on one shoulder, the big straw suitcase in the opposite hand, the carpetbag[3] under one arm. She herself held fast to the umbrella.

"Always like to have sump'm in my hand when I walk. Can't never tell when you'll run across a snake."

"There aren't any snakes in the city."

"There's snakes everywhere, chile."

They began the tedious hike up the interminable platform. She was small and quick. Her carriage was surprisingly erect, her gait astonishingly spry. She said:

"You liked to took my breath back yonder, boy, callin' me 'madam.' Back home everybody call me 'Miss Cynthie.' Even my own chillun. Even their chillun. Black folks, white folks too. 'Miss Cynthie.' Well, when you come up with that 'madam' o' yourn, I say to myself, 'Now, I wonder who that chile's a-grinnin' at?' 'Madam' stand for mist'ess o' the house, and I sho' ain' mist'ess o' nothin' in this hyeh New York."

1. **Red Caps:** baggage porters.

2. **impedimenta** (ĭm-pĕd′ə-mĕn′tə): things that slow progress, such as suitcases.
3. **carpetbag:** an old-fashioned type of traveling bag, made of carpeting.

"Well, you see, we call everybody 'madam.'"

"Everybody?—Hm." The bright eyes twinkled. "Seem like that'd worry me some—if I was a man."

He acknowledged his slip and observed, "I see this isn't your first trip to New York."

"First trip any place, son. First time I been over fifty mile from Waxhaw.[4] Only travelin' I've done is in my head. Ain' seen many places, but I's seen a passel[5] o' people. Reckon places is pretty much alike after people been in 'em awhile."

"Yes, ma'am. I guess that's right."

"You ain' no reg'lar bag-toter, is you?"

"Ma'am?"

"You talk too good."

"Well, I only do this in vacation-time. I'm still in school."

"You is? What you aimin' to be?"

"I'm studying medicine."

"You is?" She beamed. "Aimin' to be a doctor, huh? Thank the Lord for that. That's what I always wanted my David to be. My grandchile hyeh in New York. He's to meet me hyeh now."

"I bet you'll have a great time."

"Mussn't bet, chile. That's sinful. I tole him 'fo' he left home, I say, 'Son, you the only one o' the chillun what's got a chance to amount to sump'm. Don' th'ow it away. Be a preacher or a doctor. Work yo' way up and don' stop short. If the Lord don' see fit for you to doctor the soul, then doctor the body. If you don' get to be a reg'lar doctor, be a tooth-doctor. If you jes' can't make that, be a foot-doctor. And if you don' get that fur, be a undertaker. That's the least you must be. That ain' so bad. Keep you acquainted with the house of the Lord. Always mind the house o' the Lord—whatever you do, do like a church-steeple: aim high and go straight.'"

"Did he get to be a doctor?"

"Don' b'lieve he did. Too late startin', I reckon. But he'd done succeeded at sump'm. Mus' be at least a undertaker, 'cause he started sendin' the homefolks money, and he come home las' year dressed like Judge Pettiford's boy what went off to school in Virginia. Wouldn't tell none of us 'zackly what he was doin', but he said he wouldn' never be happy till I come and see for myself. So hyeh I is." Something softened her voice. "His mammy died befo' he knowed her. But he was always sech a good chile—" The something was apprehension. "Hope he *is* a undertaker."

They were mounting a flight of steep stairs leading to an exit-gate, about which clustered a few people still hoping to catch sight of arriving friends. Among these a tall young brown-skinned man in a light grey suit suddenly waved his panama and yelled, "Hey, Miss Cynthie!"

Miss Cynthie stopped, looked up, and waved back with a delighted umbrella. The Red Cap's eyes lifted too. His lower jaw sagged.

"Is that your grandson?"

"It sho' is," she said and distanced him for the rest of the climb. The grandson, with an abandonment that superbly ignored onlookers, folded the little woman in an exultant, smothering embrace. As soon as she could, she pushed him off with breathless mock impatience.

"Go 'way, you fool, you. Aimin' to squeeze my soul out my body befo' I can get a look at this place?" She shook herself into the semblance of composure. "Well. You don't look hungry, anyhow."

4. **Waxhaw:** a village in South Carolina.
5. **passel** (păs'əl): a group or large number.

Parade Along Seventh Avenue, c. 1924 by James VanDerZee.
Courtesy Donna VanDerZee

"Ho-ho! Miss Cynthie in New York! Can y'imagine this? Come on. I'm parked on Eighth Avenue."

The Red Cap delivered the outlandish luggage into a robin's egg-blue open Packard[6] with scarlet wheels, accepted the grandson's dollar and smile, and stood watching the car roar away up Eighth Avenue.

Another Red Cap came up. "Got a break, hey, boy?"

"Dave Tappen himself—can you beat that?"

"The old lady hasn't seen the station yet—starin' at him."

"That's not the half of it, bozo.[7] That's Dave Tappen's grandmother. And what do you s'pose she hopes?"

"What?"

"She hopes that Dave has turned out to be a successful undertaker!"

"Undertaker? Undertaker!"

They stared at each other a gaping moment, then doubled up with laughter.

"Look—through there—that's the Chrysler Building.[8] Oh, hell-elujah! I meant to bring you up Broadway—"[9]

"David—"

"Ma'am?"

"This hyeh wagon yourn?"

6. **Packard:** an expensive automobile.
7. **bozo** (bō′zō): a fellow; man (slang).

8. **Chrysler Building:** a skyscraper in New York City.
9. **Broadway:** street known as New York's main theater and entertainment section.

"Nobody else's. Sweet buggy, ain't it?"

"David—you ain't turned out to be one of them moonshiners,[10] is you?"

"Moonshiners—? Moon—Ho! No indeed, Miss Cynthie. I got a better racket 'n that."

"Better which?"

"Game. Business. Pick-up."

"Tell me, David. What is yo' racket?"

"Can't spill it yet, Miss Cynthie. Rather show you. Tomorrow night you'll know the worst. Can't you make out till tomorrow night?"

"David, you know I always wanted you to be a doctor, even if 'twasn' nothin' but a foot-doctor. The very leas' I wanted you to be was a undertaker."

"Undertaker! Oh, Miss Cynthie!—with my sunny disposition?"

"Then you ain' even a undertaker?"

"Listen, Miss Cynthie. Just forget 'bout what I am for awhile. Just till tomorrow night. I want you to see for yourself. Tellin' you will spoil it. Now stop askin', you hear?—because I'm not answerin'—I'm surprisin' you. Now don't expect anybody you meet to tell you. It'll mess up the whole works. Understand? Now give the big city a break. There's the elevated train going up Columbus Avenue. Ain't that hot stuff?"

Miss Cynthie looked. "Humph!" she said. "Tain' half high as that trestle two mile from Waxhaw."

2

She thoroughly enjoyed the ride up Central Park West. The stagger lights, the extent of the park, the high, close, kingly dwellings, remarkable because their stoves cooled them in summer as well as heated them in winter, all drew nods of mild interest. But what gave her special delight was not these: It was that David's car so effortlessly sped past the head-long drove of vehicles racing northward.

They stopped for a red light; when they started again their machine leaped forward with a triumphant eagerness that drew from her an unsuppressed "Hot you, David! That's it!"

He grinned appreciatively. "Why , you're a regular New Yorker already."

"New Yorker nothin'! I done the same thing fifty years ago—befo' I knowed they was a New York."

"What!"

"Deed so. Didn' I use to tell you 'bout my young mare, Betty? Chile, I'd hitch Betty up to yo' grandpa's buggy and pass anything on the road. Betty never knowed what another horse's dust smelt like. No 'ndeedy. Shuh, boy, this ain' nothin' new to me. Why that broke-down Fo'd yo' uncle Jake's got ain' nothin' but a sorry mess. Done got so slow I jes' won' ride in it—I declare I'd rather walk. But this hyeh thing, now, this is right nice." She settled back in complete, complacent comfort, and they sped on, swift and silent.

Suddenly she sat erect with abrupt discovery.

"David—well—bless my soul!"

"What's the matter, Miss Cynthie?"

Then he saw what had caught her attention. They were traveling up Seventh Avenue now, and something was miraculously different. Not the road; that was as broad as ever, wide, white gleaming in the sun. Not the houses; they were lofty still, lordly, disdainful, supercilious. Not the cars; they continued to race impatiently onward, innumerable, precipitate,[11] tumultuous. Something

---

10. **moonshiners:** people who make and sell liquor illegally.

11. **precipitate** (prĭ-sĭp′ət-āt): rushing headlong.

else, something at once obvious and subtle, insistent, pervasive, compelling.

"David—this mus' be Harlem!"

"Good Lord, Miss Cynthie—!"

"Don' use the name of the Lord in vain, David."

"But I mean—gee!—you're no fun at all. You get everything before a guy can tell you."

"You got plenty to tell me, David. But don' nobody need to tell me this. Look a yonder."

Not just a change of complexion. A completely dissimilar atmosphere. Sidewalks teeming with leisurely strollers, at once strangely dark and bright. Boys in white trousers, berets, and green shirts, with slickened black heads and proud swagger. Bareheaded girls in crisp organdie dresses, purple, canary, gay scarlet. And laughter, abandoned strong Negro laughter, some falling full on the ear, some not heard at all, yet sensed—the warm life-breath of the tireless carnival to which Harlem's heart quickens in summer.

"This is it," admitted David. "Get a good eyeful. Here's One Hundred and Twenty-fifth Street—regular little Broadway. And here's the Alhambra,[12] and up ahead we'll pass the Lafayette."[13]

"What's them?"

"Theatres."

"Theatres? Theatres. Humph! Look, David—is that a colored folks church?" They were passing a fine gray-stone edifice.

"That? Oh. Sure it is. So's this one on this side."

"No! Well, ain' that fine? Splendid big church like that for colored folks."

12. **Alhambra:** a theater.
13. **Lafayette:** a theater in Harlem that presented musicals, sketches, and plays.

Taking his cue from this, her first tribute to the city, he said, "You ain't seen nothing yet. Wait a minute."

They swung left through a side-street and turned right on a boulevard. "What do you think o' that?" And he pointed to the quarter-million-dollar St. Mark's.[14]

"That a colored church, too?"

"'Tain' no white one. And they built it themselves, you know. Nobody's hand-me down gift."

She heaved a great happy sigh. "Oh, yes, it was a gift, David. It was a gift from on high." Then, "Look a hyeh—which a one you belong to?"

"Me? Why, I don't belong to any—that is, none o' these. Mine's over in another section. Y'see, mine's Baptist. These are all Methodist. See?"

"M-m. Uh-huh. I see."

They circled a square and slipped into a quiet narrow street overlooking a park, stopping before the tallest of the apartment houses in the single commanding row.

Alighting, Miss Cynthie gave this imposing structure one sidewise, upward glance, and said, "Y'all live like bees in a hive, don't y'?—I boun' the women does all the work, too." A moment later, "So this is a elevator? Feel like I'm glory-bound sho' nuff."

Along a tiled corridor and into David's apartment. Rooms leading into rooms. Luxurious couches, easy-chairs, a brown-walnut grand piano, gay-shaded floor lamps, panelled walls, deep rugs, treacherous glass-wood floors—and a smiling golden-skinned girl in a gingham house-dress, approaching with outstretched hands.

"This is Ruth, Miss Cynthie."

"Miss Cynthie!" said Ruth.

14. **St. Mark's:** a Methodist Episcopal church.

Couple in Raccoon Coats, 1932 by James VanDerZee.
Courtesy Donna VanDerZee

They clasped hands. "Been wantin' to see David's girl ever since he wrote us 'bout her."

"Come—here's your room this way. Here's the bath. Get out of your things and get comfy. You must be worn out with the trip."

"Worn out? Worn out? Shuh. How you gon' get worn out on a train? Now if 'twas a horse, maybe, or Jake's no-count Fo'd—but a train—didn' but one thing bother me on that train."

"What?"

"When the man made them beds down, I jes' couldn' manage to undress same as at home. Why, s'posin' sump'm bus' the train open—where'd you be? Naked as a jay-bird in dew-berry time."

David took in her things and left her to get comfortable. He returned, and Ruth, despite his reassuring embrace, whispered:

"Dave, you cain't fool old folks—why don't you go ahead and tell her about yourself? Think of the shock she's going to get—at her age."

David shook his head. "She'll get over the shock if she's there looking on. If we just told her, she'd never understand. We've got to railroad her into it. Then she'll be happy."

"She's nice. But she's got the same ideas as all old folks—"

"Yea—but with her you can change 'em.

Specifically if everything is really all right. I know her. She's for church and all, but she believes in good times too, if they're right. Why, when I was a kid—" He broke off. "Listen!"

Miss Cynthie's voice came quite distinctly to them, singing a jaunty little rhyme:

Oh I danced with the gal with the hole in
*   her stockin',*
And her toe kep' a-kickin' and her heel
*   kep' a-knockin'—*

Come up, Jesse, and get a drink o' gin,
'Cause you near to the heaven as you'll
*   ever get ag'in.*

"She taught me that when I wasn't knee-high to a cricket," David said.

Miss Cynthie still sang softly and merrily:

Then I danced with the gal with the dimple
*   in her cheek,*
And if she'd a' kep' a-smilin', I'd a' danced
*   for a week—*

3

"God forgive me," prayed Miss Cynthie as she discovered David's purpose the following night. She let him and Ruth lead her, like an early Christian martyr, into the Lafayette Theatre. The blinding glare of the lobby produced a merciful self-anaesthesia, and she entered the sudden dimness of the interior as involuntarily as in a dream—

Attendants outdid each other for Mr. Dave Tappen. She heard him tell them, "Fix us up till we go on," and found herself sitting between Ruth and David in the front row of a lower box. A miraculous device of the devil, a motion-picture that talked, was just ending. At her feet the orchestra was assembling. The motion-picture faded out amid a scattered round of applause. Lights blazed and the orchestra burst into an ungodly rumpus.

She looked out over the seated multitude, scanning row upon row of illumined faces, black faces, white faces, yellow, tan, brown, bald heads, bobbed heads, kinky and straight heads; and upon every countenance, expectancy—scowling expectancy in this case, smiling in that, complacent here, amused there, commentative elsewhere, but everywhere suspense, abeyance, anticipation.

Half a dozen people were ushered down the nearer aisle to reserved seats in the second row. Some of them caught a glimpse of David and Ruth and waved to them. The chairs immediately behind them in the box were being shifted. "Hello, Tap!" Miss Cynthie saw David turn, rise, and shake hands with two men. One of them was large, bald and pink, emanating good cheer; the other short, thin, sallow with thick black hair and a sour mien. Ruth also acknowledged their greeting. "This is my grandmother," David said proudly. "Miss Cynthie, meet my managers, Lou and Lee Goldman." "Pleased to meet you," managed Miss Cynthie. "Great lad, this boy of yours," said Lou Goldman. "Great little partner he's got, too," added Lee. They also settled back expectantly.

"Here we go!"

The curtain rose to reveal a cotton-field at dawn. Pickers in blue denim overalls, bandanas, and wide-brimmed straws, or in gingham aprons and sun-bonnets, were singing as they worked. Their voices, from clearest soprano to richest bass, blended in low concordances, first simply humming a series of harmonies, until, gradually, came words, like figures forming in mist. As the sound grew, the mist cleared, the words came round and full, and the sun rose bringing

The extraordinary success of **Shuffle Along** *led to many extravagant musical productions during the Harlem Renaissance.*

light as if in answer to the song. The chorus swelled, the radiance grew, the two, as if emanating from a single source, fused their crescendos, till at last they achieved a joint transcendence[15] of tonal and visual brightness.

"Swell opener," said Lee Goldman.

"Ripe," agreed Lou.

David and Ruth arose. "Stay here and enjoy the show, Miss Cynthie. You'll see us again in a minute."

"Go to it, kids," said Lou Goldman.

"Yea—burn 'em up," said Lee.

15. **transcendence** (trăn-sĕn′dəns): surpassing ordinary limits.

Miss Cynthie hardly noted that she had been left, so absorbed was she in the spectacle. To her, the theatre had always been the antithesis of the church. As the one was the refuge of righteousness, so the other was the stronghold of transgression. But this first scene awakened memories, captured and held her attention by offering a blend of truth and novelty. Having thus baited her interest, the show now proceeded to play it like the trout through swift-flowing waters of wickedness. Resist as it might, her mind was caught and drawn into the impious subsequences.

The very music that had just rounded out

White Collection, Research Center for the Performing Arts/New York Public Library at Lincoln Center

so majestically now distorted itself into ragtime.[16] The singers came forward and turned to dancers; boys, a crazy, swaying background, threw up their arms and kicked out their legs in a rhythmic jamboree; girls, an agile, brazen foreground, caught their skirts up to their hips and displayed their copper calves, knees, thighs, in shameless, incredible steps. Miss Cynthie turned dismayed eyes upon the audience, to discover that mob of sinners devouring it all with fond satisfaction. Then the dancers separated and with final abandon flung themselves off the stage in both directions.

Lee Goldman commented through the applause, "They work easy, them babies."

"Yea," said Lou. "Savin' the hot stuff for later."

Two black faced cotton-pickers appropriated the scene, indulging in dialogue that their hearers found uproarious.

"Ah'm tired."

"Ah'm hongry."

"Dis job jes' wears me out."

"Starves me to death."

"Ah'm so tired—you know what Ah'd like to do?"

16. **ragtime:** a type of American music, popular from about 1890 to 1915 and characterized by strong syncopation in fast, even time.

Miss Cynthie 365

"What?"

"Ah'd like to go to sleep and dream I was sleepin'."

"What good dat do?"

"Den I could wake up and still be 'sleep."

"Well y' know what Ah'd like to do?"

"No. What?"

"Ah'd like to swaller me a hog and a hen."

"What good dat do?"

"Den Ah'd always be full o' ham and eggs."

"Ham? Shuh. Don't you know a hog has to be smoked 'fo' he's a ham?"

"Well, if I swaller him, he'll have a smoke all around him, won' he?"

Presently Miss Cynthie was smiling like everyone else, but her smile soon fled. For the comics departed, and the dancing girls returned, this time in scant travesties on their earlier voluminous costumes—tiny sunbonnets perched jauntily on one side of their glistening bobs,[17] bandanas reduced to scarlet neck-ribbons, waists mere brassieres, skirts mere gingham sashes.

And now Miss Cynthie's whole body stiffened with a new and surpassing shock; her bright eyes first widened with unbelief, then slowly grew dull with misery. In the midst of a sudden great volley of applause her grandson had broken through that bevy of agile wantons and begun to sing.

He too was dressed as a cotton-picker, but a Beau Brummell[18] among cotton-pickers; his hat bore a pleated green band, his bandana was silk, his overalls blue satin, his shoes black patent leather. His eyes flashed, his teeth gleamed, his body swayed, his arms waved, his words came fast and clear. As he sang, his companions danced a concerted tap, uniformly wild, ecstatic. When he stopped singing, he himself began to dance, and without sacrificing crispness of execution, seemed to absorb into himself every measure of the energy which the girls, now merely standing off and swaying, had relinquished.

"Look at that boy go," said Lee Goldman.

"He ain't started yet," said Lou.

But surrounding comment, Dave's virtuosity, the eager enthusiasm of the audience were all alike lost on Miss Cynthie. She sat with stricken eyes watching this boy whom she'd raised from a babe, taught right from wrong, brought up in the church, and endowed with her prayers, this child whom she had dreamed of seeing a preacher, a regular doctor, a tooth-doctor, a foot-doctor, at the very least an undertaker—sat watching him disport himself for the benefit of a sinsick, flesh-hungry mob of lost souls, not one of whom knew or cared to know the loving kindness of God; sat watching a David she'd never foreseen, turned tool of the devil, disciple of lust, unholy prince among sinners.

For a long time she sat there watching with wretched eyes, saw portrayed on the stage David's arrival in Harlem, his escape from "old friends" who tried to dupe him; saw him working as a trap-drummer[19] in a night-club, where he fell in love with Ruth, a dancer; not the gentle Ruth Miss Cynthie knew, but a wild and shameless young savage who danced like seven devils—in only a girdle and breast-plates; saw the two of them join in a song and dance act that eventually made them Broadway headliners, an act presented *in toto*[20] as the pre-finale of the show. And not any of the melodies, not any of the

---

17. **bob:** a woman's short haircut.
18. **Beau Brummell:** a fancy dresser. George Bryan Brummell (1778–1840) was an English gentleman famous for his fashionable dress and manners.

19. **trap-drummer:** a player on the snare drum.
20. *in toto:* in its entirety.

sketches, not all the comic philosophy of the tired-and-hungry duo, gave her figure a moment's relaxation or brightened the dull defeat in her staring eyes. She sat apart, alone in the box, the symbol, the epitome of supreme failure. Let the rest of the theatre be riotous, clamoring for more and more of Dave Tappen, "Tap," the greatest tapster of all time, idol of uptown and downtown New York. For her, they were lauding simply an exhibition of sin which centered about her David.

"This'll run a year on Broadway," said Lee Goldman.

"Then we'll take it to Paris."

Encores and curtains with Ruth, and at last David came out on the stage alone. The clamor dwindled. And now he did something quite unfamiliar to even the most consistent of his followers. Softly, delicately, he began to tap a routine designed to fit a particular song. When he had established the rhythm, he began to sing the song:

> Oh I danced with the gal with the hole in her stockin',
> And her toe kep' a-kickin' and her heel kep' a-knockin'
>
> Come up, Jesse, and get a drink o' gin,
> 'Cause you near to the heaven as you'll ever get ag'in—

As he danced and sang this song, frequently smiling across at Miss Cynthie, a visible change transformed her. She leaned forward incredulously, listened intently, then settled back in limp wonder. Her bewildered eyes turned on the crowd, on those serried[21] rows of shriftless sinners.[22] And she found in

21. **serried** (sĕr'ēd): pressed or crowded together.
22. **shriftless sinners:** unrepentant sinners.

their faces now an overwhelmingly curious thing: a grin, a universal grin, a gleeful and sinless grin such as not the nakedest chorus in the performance had produced. In a few seconds, with her own song, David had dwarfed into unimportance, wiped off their faces, swept out of their minds every trace of what had seemed to be sin; had reduced it all to mere trivial detail and revealed these revelers as a crowd of children, enjoying the guileless antics of another child. And Miss Cynthie whispered her discovery aloud:

"Bless my soul! They didn't mean nothin' . . . They jes' didn' see no harm in it—"

> Then I danced with the gal with the dimple in her cheek,
> And if she'd a' kep' a-smilin' I'd a' danced for a week—
>
> Come up, Jesse—

The crowd laughed, clapped their hands, whistled. Someone threw David a bright yellow flower. "From Broadway!"

He caught the flower. A hush fell. He said:

"I'm really happy tonight, folks. Y'see this flower. Means success, don't it? Well, listen. The one who is really responsible for my success is here tonight with me. Now what do you think o'that?"

The hush deepened.

"Y'know folks, I'm sump'm like Adam—I never had no mother. But I've got a grandmother. Down home everybody calls her Miss Cynthie. And everybody loves her. Take that song I just did for you. Miss Cynthie taught me that when I wasn't knee-high to a cricket. But that wasn't all she taught me. Far back as I can remember, she used to always say one thing: 'Son, do like a church steeple—aim high and go straight.' And for doin' it—" he grinned, contemplating the flower—"I get this."

He strode across to the edge of the stage that touched Miss Cynthie's box. He held up the flower.

"So y'see folks, this isn't mine. It's really Miss Cynthie's." He leaned over to hand it to her. Miss Cynthie's last trace of doubt was swept away. She drew a deep breath of revelation; her bewilderment vanished, her redoubtable composure returned, her eyes lighted up; and no one but David, still holding the flower toward her, heard her sharply whispered reprimand:

"Keep it, you fool you. Where's yo' manners—givin' 'way what somebody give you?"

David grinned:

"Take it, tyro.[23] What you tryin' to do—crab my act?"

23. **tyro** (tī'rō): a beginner, an amateur.

Thereupon, Miss Cynthie, smiling at him with bright, meaningful eyes, leaned over without rising from her chair, jerked a tiny twig off the stem of the flower, then sat decisively back, resolutely folding her arms, with only a leaf in her hand.

"This'll do me," she said.

The finale didn't matter. People filed out of the theatre. Miss Cynthie sat awaiting her children, her foot absently patting time to the orchestra's jazz recessional. Perhaps she was thinking, "God moves in a mysterious way," but her lips were unquestionably forming the words:

—*danced with the gal—hole in her
    stockin'—*
—*toe kep' a-kickin'—heel kep'
    a-knockin'—*

Responding to the Selection

Miss Cynthie by Rudolph Fisher

Identifying Facts

1. How are Dave and Miss Cynthie related?
2. What does Miss Cynthie assume is Dave's profession?
3. What does Miss Cynthie enjoy most about the trip uptown?
4. Who is Ruth?
5. What kind of dancing is Dave's specialty?

Interpreting Meanings

1. What qualities in Miss Cynthie's character are apparent early in the story? Why do you think Dave is so devoted to her?
2. What are some early indications that she would not approve of Dave's work?
3. How does Dave overcome Miss Cynthie's disapproval?
4. How is music used in the story to set up a contrast between the values of traditional Southern folk and of urban blacks?

5. This story is famous for evoking the atmosphere of Harlem during the Renaissance. Reread the passage on page 361 describing the street scene. Why does Fisher call it a "tireless carnival"?

Language and Vocabulary
Recognizing Word Analogies
Word **analogies** are based on different relationships. To match the correct items, you must first identify the relationship. What is the relationship in this analogy question?

composure : calmness :: edifice : _____
  a. tranquility   **c.** building
  b. appearance   **d.** arrogance

The words in the first pair, *composure* and *calmness*, are **synonyms**. Therefore you must look for a word that means the same thing as *edifice.* The correct answer is **c.**

In the following analogy items, first determine how the first two words are related. Then examine the answer choices for the closest match.

1. impious : reverent :: tedious : _____
  a. agreeable   **c.** boring
  b. interesting   **d.** bulky

2. distort : truth :: contemplate : _____
  a. honesty   **c.** disport
  b. demand   **d.** scene

Descriptive Writing
Painting a Picture in Words
Fisher's story gives you the flavor of Harlem in the 1920s. In a brief composition, describe an urban or a rural scene that you know well. You might select a busy intersection or you might write about a wooded area. In your paper, try to "paint" a picture with words so that your readers can share your impressions. Follow the suggestions on pages 193–195 in planning and developing your paper.

Speaking and Listening
Reading Dialogue
With a partner, rehearse one of the passages of dialogue in the story. Re-create Miss Cynthie's speech accurately. Be sure to convey the personalities of the characters in your reading.

Miss Cynthie 369

Before You Read

Backwater Blues; Preaching Blues

Using What You Know

In this unit, you have seen references to great blues singers, such as Ma Rainey and Bessie Smith. What other blues singers can you name? Can you also name instrumentalists who have been well-known interpreters of the blues?

Background

In *Blues People,* LeRoi Jones (now known as Amiri Baraka) notes that blues music is directly related to the African American experience. He makes the point that the blues emerged from the slaves' work songs, which had origins in West Africa. Blues grew out of the shouts and hollers of the field workers and out of spirituals. These songs took the form of African **call-and-response** singing (see page 86). The blues later became the music of professional singers who often sang with a band.

Literary Focus: Blues Poetry

The blues deal with a wide range of subjects: natural disasters, superstitions, jailhouses, locomotives, and the like. Perhaps best known are the blues dealing with love in its various aspects.

The blues do not conform to any strict pattern. Many blues lyrics consist of three-line stanzas. The second line of each stanza repeats the first. The third line is often a response to the first two:

Backwater blues done caused me to pack my things and go.
Backwater blues done caused me to pack my things and go.
'Cause my house fell down and I can't live there no more.

Setting a Purpose

Many people have called attention to the personal nature of blues-singing. As you read these lyrics, note how each song takes an individual form, expressing the strong feelings of the singer.

Backwater Blues

Bessie Smith

When it rains five days and the skies turn dark as night,
When it rains five days and the skies turn dark as night,
Then trouble's takin' place in the lowlands at night.

I woke up this mornin', can't even get out of my door
I woke up this mornin', can't even get out of my door   5
That's enough trouble to make a poor girl wonder where
    she want to go.

Then they rowed a little boat about five miles 'cross the farm.
Then they rowed a little boat about five miles 'cross the farm.
I packed all my clothes, throwed them in and they rowed me
    along.

When it thunders and lightnin', and the wind begins to blow,   10
When it thunders and lightnin', and the wind begins to blow,
There's thousands of people ain't got no place to go.

Then I went and stood upon some high old lonesome hill.
Then I went and stood upon some high old lonesome hill.
Then I looked down on the house where I used to live.   15

Backwater blues done caused me to pack my things and go.
Backwater blues done caused me to pack my things and go.
'Cause my house fell down and I can't live there no more.

(Moan) . . . . I can't move no more,
(Moan) . . . . I can't move no more,   20
There ain't no place for a poor old girl to go.

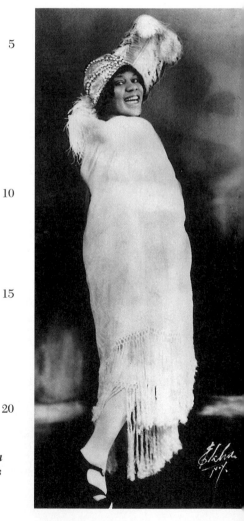

Bessie Smith, about 1925. Columbia Records gave her the title "Empress of the Blues."
Bettmann Newsphotos

Preaching Blues

Robert Johnson

Mmmmmm mmmm
Got up this morning
The blues, walking like a man
Got up this morning
The blues walking like a man   5
Worried blues:
Give me your right hand

    And the blues grabbed mama's child
       And tore it all upside down
    Blues grabbed mama's child   10
       And they tore me all upside down
    Travel on, poor Bob,
       Just can't turn you 'round

The blu-u-ues
Is a low down shaking chill   15
      (yes)(I'm preaching 'em now)
Mmmm-mmmm
Is a low down shaking chill
You ain't never had 'em, I
Hope you never will   20

Well the blues
Is a aching old heart disease
      (Do it now.
       You gonna do it?
       Tell me all about it.)   25
The blues
Is a low down aching heart disease
And like consumption
Killing me by degrees

Now if it starts to raining 30
Gonna drive,
        gonna drive my blues
Now if it's startin' a-raining
I'm gonna drive my blues away
Going to the steel rig 35
Stay
    out
        there
            all
                day 40

Responding to the Selections
Backwater Blues; Preaching Blues

Interpreting Meanings

1. Many blues deal with disasters, such as floods. What circumstances are described in "Backwater Blues"? How does the song make you sympathize with the suffering of people made homeless by the flood?
2. How does the singer in "Preaching Blues" define the blues? How does he hope to escape the blues?

Expository Writing

Investigating a Subject
The blues have been very influential. They have contributed to the development of jazz, and they have influenced classical music as well as rock music.

Select a subject about the blues for study. Here are some suggested topics:

Ancestors of the Blues
The Influence of Blues on Jazz
W. C. Handy, "Father of the Blues"
Classic Blues Singers

In order to narrow your subject, begin with a general article on the blues in an encyclopedia or history of music. Then locate specific references that relate to your topic. Make a list of questions to help you research your topic. Be sure to include your sources when you hand in your report.

Writing Literary Analysis:

Analyzing a literary work can help you discover a great deal about its meaning as well as its techniques. When you write an essay of literary analysis, you share your understanding and appreciation of a specific work or group of works with your audience.

The rules that govern other compositions apply to the essay of literary analysis. You should open with an **introduction** that identifies the author and title of the work you are discussing. Your introduction should also state your purpose. You should present your analysis in the **body** of the paper. Then end with a **conclusion** that summarizes your ideas.

One kind of literary analysis is the **explication**. An explication is the careful study of ideas, structure, and language in a literary work. Sometimes, it is a line-by-line examination of a text. Explication is often used to analyze the content and technique of poetry, but it may be used with prose as well.

When you explicate a poem, you take it apart in order to see how the elements of **imagery, figurative language, symbol, rhyme,** and **rhythm** are combined to create meaning and feeling. You examine the organization of the poet's ideas into **stanzas** or into special forms such as the **sonnet.** This kind of close critical analysis can help you understand your own response to a poem, and as you come to a deeper understanding of the poem, even to change your response.

Choose one of the poems you have studied in this unit or in another unit for explication.

Prewriting Strategies

1. Read the poem carefully, following the steps outlined on page 340. Remember to read the poem aloud so that you respond to sound as well as to sense.
2. **Paraphrase** the poem, restating in your own words what every line or every stanza says. Rephrase each figure of speech in your own words.
3. Record your responses to each of these questions:

   Who is the **speaker?**
   What kind of poem is it (**hymn, sonnet,** etc.)?
   What is the **subject** of the poem?
   How does the poet use **imagery** and **figurative language?**
   How do devices of sound (**rhyme, alliteration, rhythm,** etc.) add to meaning?
   What is the poet's **tone?**
   What is the **central meaning** of the poem?
   How does the poem make you feel?

4. Find quotations that will support your analysis of the poem.

Explicating a Poem

Writing a First Draft

1. In your opening paragraph, identify the poem by title and author. Tell what kind of poem it is. Tell who the speaker is and state the subject of the poem.
2. In paragraph 2, paraphrase the poem, pointing out and explaining the major images, figures, and symbols.
3. In paragraph 3, describe the devices of sound and tell how they contribute to the meaning of the poem.
4. In paragraph 4, describe the tone of the poem.
5. In paragraph 5, state the central meaning of the poem and give your personal response.

Evaluating and Revising

Use this **Checklist** for revision:
1. Have you identified the poem by title and author?
2. Have you identified the speaker and the subject?
3. Have you identified what kind of poem it is?
4. Have you given a paraphrase of the poem?
5. Have you analyzed the poet's use of language?
6. Have you discussed devices of sound?
7. Have you cited quotations correctly?
8. Have you concluded with a statement of the overall meaning of the poem and your personal response?

Writing the Final Draft

Ask a classmate to help you proofread your paper. Then prepare a final copy.

WRITER'S WORKSHOP 2

Interpretation (Expository Writing)

UNIT REVIEW

▶I. Interpreting New Material

A. The following excerpt is part of a review of Langston Hughes's *The Weary Blues* by Jessie Fauset, one of the leading literary figures of the Harlem Renaissance. Read the excerpt carefully before answering the questions.

A Review of *The Weary Blues*
from *The Crisis,* March 1926
Jessie Fauset

Very perfect is the memory of my first literary acquaintance with Langston Hughes. In the unforgettable days when we were publishing *The Brownies' Book*[1] we had already appreciated a charming fragile conceit[2] which read:

Out of the dust of dreams,
Fairies weave their garments;
Out of the purple and rose of old memories,
They make purple wings.
No wonder we find them such marvelous things.

Then one day came "The Negro Speaks of Rivers." I took the beautiful dignified creation to Dr. Du Bois and said: "What colored person is there, do you suppose, in the United States who writes like that and yet is unknown to us?" And I wrote and found him

1. *The Brownies' Book:* a magazine for children that Fauset edited.
2. **conceit:** here, an imaginative and striking metaphor.

to be a Cleveland high school graduate who had just gone to live in Mexico. Already he had begun to assume that remote, so elusive quality which permeates most of his work. Before long we had the pleasure of seeing the work of the boy, whom we had sponsored, copied and recopied in journals far and wide. "The Negro Speaks of Rivers" even appeared in translation in a paper printed in Germany.

Not very long after Hughes came to New York and not long after that he began to travel and to set down the impressions, the pictures, which his sensitive mind had registered of new forms of life and living in Holland, in France, in Spain, in Italy and in Africa.

His poems are warm, exotic and shot through with color. Never is he preoccupied with form. But this fault, if it is one, has its corresponding virtue, for it gives his verse, which almost always is imbued with the essence of poetry, the perfection of spontaneity. And one characteristic which makes for this bubbling-like charm is the remarkable objectivity which he occasionally achieves, remarkable for one so young, and a first step toward philosophy. Hughes has seen a great deal of the world, and this has taught him that nothing matters much but life. Its forms and aspects may vary, but living is the essential thing. Therefore make no bones about it,—"make the most of what you too may spend."

Some consciousness of this must have been in him even before he began to wander for he sent us as far back as 1921:

Shake your brown feet, honey,
Shake your brown feet, chile,
Shake your brown feet, honey,
Shake 'em swift and wil'— . . .
Sun's going down this evening—
Might never rise no mo'.
The sun's going down this very night—
Might never rise no mo'—
So dance with swift feet, honey,
(The banjo's sobbing low) . . .
The sun's going down this very night—
Might never rise no mo'.

Now this is very significant, combining as it does the doctrine of the old Biblical exhortation,[3] "eat, drink and be merry for tomorrow ye die," Horace's "Carpe diem,"[4] the German "Freut euch des Lebens"[5] and Herrick's[6] "Gather ye rosebuds while ye may." This is indeed a universal subject served Negro-style and though I am no great lover of any dialect I hope heartily that Mr. Hughes will give us many more such combinations.

3. **exhortation** (ĕg'zôr-tā'shən): urgent appeal. The phrase appears in Ecclesiastes 8:15.
4. **Horace's "Carpe diem"**: The Roman poet Horace (65–8 B.C.) urged people to make the most of the present. The phrase *carpe diem* means "seize the day" in Latin.
5. **"Freut . . . Lebens"**: "Enjoy life."
6. **Herrick:** Robert Herrick (1591–1674), an English lyric poet.

1. What qualities in Hughes's poetry does Fauset admire?
2. How does Hughes's poem combine the doctrines cited by Fauset? What new element does Hughes add to the "universal subject"?

B. Do you agree that Hughes is not concerned with form and that his verse has "the perfection of spontaneity"? Examine other poems by Hughes. Cite specific evidence to support your position.

►►II. For Discussion

During the Harlem Renaissance, some writers, such as Toomer and Cullen, chose to use standard literary English. Other writers, such as Hughes and Hurston, often based their styles on the characteristics of black speech. Choose good examples of both kinds of writing. Be prepared to tell why you think so.

►►►III. For Writing

In *The Souls of Black Folk,* W. E. B. Du Bois wrote about the "double self" of African Americans: "One ever feels his twoness,—an American, a Negro; two souls, two thoughts, two unreconciled strivings; two warring ideals in one dark body, whose dogged strength alone keeps it from being torn asunder." How is that dual allegiance shown in the works you have read in this unit? For example, how is this theme expressed in "America" (page 300) and "I, Too" (page 326)? Develop your ideas in an essay.

WRITER'S WORKSHOP 2

Interpretation (Expository Writing)

Harriet and Leon, *oil by Allan Rohan Crite, 1941.*
The Boston Athenaeum/Gift of the artist

From Renaissance to Mid-Forties

INTRODUCTION BY **John Edgar Tidwell**

Miami University
Oxford, Ohio

A Period of Disillusionment

What did it mean to be black in the fifteen years following the Stock Market Crash of 1929? How did African Americans view the world? What special political, social, economic, and cultural events influenced or altered the character of black life?

For most black Americans, this was a period of disillusionment. Alain Locke, who in 1925 had edited *The New Negro,* the anthology that had proclaimed a new identity for blacks, began to question whether he had shaped a lasting cultural movement. He wondered whether the Harlem Renaissance had become little more than a "fad." *The New Negro*'s announcement of spiritual renewal and vitality had proven to be a rather fragile concept for a cultural program. Blacks themselves discovered that instead of fleeing Egypt (or the South) for the Promised Land (the North), their escape to the North merely substituted one site of bondage for another. The flight from boll weevils, sharecropping, the Ku Klux Klan, and lynching only resulted in their enslavement by underemployment or unemployment, overcrowded tenement housing, poor medical conditions, and covert, or concealed, racism. Only incidentally, then, did the Stock Market Crash alter the character of black life in urban America. By 1929, the whole nation began to experience what many historians feel blacks had suffered for many years—a severe economic depression.

The Quest for Racial Equality

After gaining the right to vote during Reconstruction, African Americans in the South lost it with the Hayes-Tilden "compromise" of 1876. In order to get Rutherford B. Hayes elected to the presidency, the Republicans had to make certain concessions, which reconciled the white people of the North and the South at the expense of racial equality for black citizens. The voting rights of Southern blacks were only partially regained by 1929. Faith in the Republican Party—inspired by Lincoln's emancipation of the slaves—turned to disillusionment. Black voters began joining the ranks of the Democrats. In Franklin Delano Roosevelt, who was elected in 1932, African Americans identified not just a Democratic president but a compassionate friend, whose **"New Deal"** of relief and recovery programs would be extended to them. Roosevelt consulted an informal assembly of government officials called the **"Black Cabinet"** for guidance on policies relating to African Americans. These appointees, who included such prominent African Americans as Robert C. Weaver and Mary McLeod Bethune, worked hard to secure equal rights. But, as John Hope Franklin writes in *From Slavery to Freedom,* "to secure employment for blacks on the basis of ability and training rather than color" became a difficult task for the cabinet.

A variation of this problem is recorded in an unprecedented study of race relations in the United States, *An American Dilemma: The Negro Problem and Modern Democracy* (1944), by Gunnar Myrdal (mîr'däl), a Swedish sociologist. The title of this book suggests a moral dilemma, a conflict between the American creed of equality for all, on the one hand, and the denial of those values to specific racial groups and individuals, on the other. "Count us in," replied the contributors to *What the Negro Wants* (1944), "and we shall prove our worth. We shall refute the implication that Jim Crow segregation had made us into so many crazed maniacs."

For a few blacks, the Communist Party promised an opportunity to be "counted in," because its policy of racial inclusion set aside *racial* differences in favor of *class* differences. An indication of the party's radical policies is found in its making James W. Ford, a black man, its vice-presidential candidate in 1932, 1936, and 1940. In addition, its International Labor Defense helped bring worldwide attention to the case of the Scottsboro boys, one of the most important civil rights cases in United States history. But the party's

President Roosevelt, whose photograph appears top right, was admired for his New Deal programs.
Aaron Siskind/The Schomburg Center for Research in Black Culture/New York Public Library

avowed atheism and the shift to a Soviet-centered political policy eroded the support of blacks.

The quest for racial equality in labor unions had limited success. "In an effort to keep whites employed during the Depression," writes Franklin, "labor unions maintained their exclusion policies on a stricter basis than ever." But with the birth of the Congress of Industrial Organizations in 1936, membership for African Americans became more generally available. The Federal Writers' Project, beginning in the late 1930s, provided work for some unem-

Introduction 381

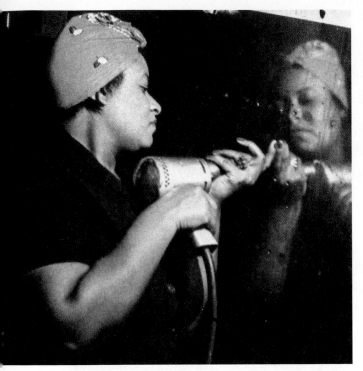 

(Left) *A woman riveter at Nashville, Tennessee, 1942.*
The Granger Collection, New York

(Right) *A skilled worker bending steel plates to fit the sidings of American warships. This is one of a series of pictures made by the Office of Emergency Management to show that no American workers in defense industries would be subject to discrimination.*
Bettmann Newsphotos

ployed black writers. The American Guide Series, a project that compiled guidebooks to towns, counties, and states, became one of the best sources for authentic representations of black life, by guarding against racial stereotyping. Perhaps the most significant gesture toward resolving the conflict between race and employment was Roosevelt's famous Executive Order 8802, issued on June 25, 1941, which banned discrimination against workers in defense industries on the basis of race, creed, or color. To a group reluctant to support or fight for freedoms denied them at home, the executive order provided new incentives. Although there was discrimination in the armed forces, more than a million African American men and women saw service during World War II, and many of them served their country with distinction.

Problems Facing African American Writers

African American writers were confronted by two pressing issues. First, they had to face the "dilemma of a divided audience." On the one hand, white readers, used to literature filled with black racial stereotypes, expected a continuing literary tradition of brute Negroes, contented slaves, wretched freedmen, and exotic-primitive figures. In contrast, black readers, wishing to see these stereotypes refuted, expected not just positive racial images but idealized versions of black life. Between these two extremes stood black writers, wondering if either audience would accept their versions of truth.

Second, and even more problematic for writers, was the urge to have their work judged according to "a single standard of criticism." Evaluating *black* literature as *literature,* they believed, would remove a stigma associated with their writing—that of race. Most white literary critics held on to the belief that black literature was less sophisticated and less accomplished than white literature. By adopting "a single standard of criticism" for writing according to expectations set forth by whites, blacks hoped their writing would no longer be excluded or ignored and that they would be integrated into the American literary mainstream.

Literature as Social Protest

While the Harlem Renaissance, under Alain Locke's direction, tended to idealize black folk values, writers in the 1930s tended to use literature as a means of social protest. They attempted to distinguish good writing from mere propaganda aimed at promoting social reforms. Most writers chose to represent life without sentimentalizing or idealizing it. Their attempt to depict the everyday life and speech of ordinary people is called **realism.**

In fiction, few would match the success of Arna Bontemps's "A Summer Tragedy" in escaping pure propaganda. Thematically, this story lays bare the despair and hopelessness produced by the sharecropping system. After forty-five years, stroke-ridden Jeff Patton and his blind wife Jennie remain enslaved to a horrific economic system. By presenting realistic detail, the story builds convincingly, not sentimentally, toward its climax.

Originally published as "Almos' a Man" (1940), Richard Wright's "The Man Who Was Almost a Man" is also committed to realism. The story is made more believable because its point of view enables the reader to share Dave's experiences. Using the language of black farmers also ensures a greater realism. Thematically, this story takes up a favorite Wright subject—a character's deliberate flight away from overwhelming conditions.

Wright's imaginative power was foreshadowed in *Uncle Tom's Children* (1938), a collection of short fiction that presents a disturb-

Langston Hughes, c. 1927.
James Latimer Allen/The Schomburg Center for Research in Black Culture/New York Public Library

ing picture of Southern black life. "Big Boy Leaves Home" is especially terrifying as it details graphically the horror of a lynching. Curiously, though, Wright felt he only succeeded in writing "a book which even bankers' daughters could read and weep over and feel good."

The novel *Native Son* (1940) would not make this mistake. The story of Bigger Thomas is a socially realistic depiction of black life, in all its anger, pain, and suffering. Bigger finds himself trapped helplessly under the control of unseen forces. His is a life of bitter futility and hopelessness, determined by whimsical but cruel economic forces.

Wright's **naturalism**—the precise and objective depiction of environmental and social conditions—opened the door for many other writers. Their prominence and skill, however, never equalled Wright's achievement. Known as members of the "School of Richard Wright," William Attaway, Chester Himes, and Ann Petry labored diligently but under Wright's long shadow. In "Black Laughter," for example, Himes illustrates the excesses of naturalism. Himes is almost consumed by anger. The sullenness brought out in a look from whites, the rebuff by the white coatroom attendant, the black couple's obstructed view of the entertainment—these become motivation for the characters' behavior and show Himes's preoccupation with social protest.

Ann Petry, by contrast, has been unfairly lumped in the School of Wright, as her novel *The Street* reveals. True, the principal aim of her fiction, as she said, was "to show how simply and easily the environment can change the course of a person's life." But even this estimate has recently been revised by critics. Lutie Johnson, the novel's main character, has come to be seen as less a pawn of social circumstance than a strong, dignified survivor of destructive forces.

African American Poetry

African American poetry of this period, like the fiction, struggles to reconcile social protest and the requirements of literary form. Thematically, poetry was often concerned with conflicts between the oppressor and the oppressed: landlords versus sharecroppers or factory owners versus workers and labor organizers. The subject matter required a form consistent with the expression of political agitation. Free verse was the form of choice. Despite its freedom from metrical and rhythmic requirements, free verse is technically

A picture dramatization of a scene in Native Son.
Hart Preston, Life Magazine
© Time, Inc.

demanding and makes use of repetition, natural speech rhythms, parallelism, and image patterns. Margaret Walker, in ''For My People,'' was quite successful in joining subject matter and form.

Divided into verse paragraphs, ''For My People'' is connected by the repetition, with some variation, of the phrase ''For My People.'' The poem is both oral and oracular—that is, prophetic. It has the sense of public speaking, perhaps in imitation of a Baptist preacher's sermon. But its sweep is panoramic—suggesting an infinitely rich but varied history of African America. The poem concludes

Slum Song, *oil by Hughie Lee-Smith, 1944.*
Photo by Herb Dreiwitz; Courtesy of the Afro-American Collection, Golden State Mutual Life Insurance Company. © Hughie Lee-Smith / Licensed by VAGA, New York, NY

TIME LINE **FROM RENAISSANCE TO MID-FORTIES**

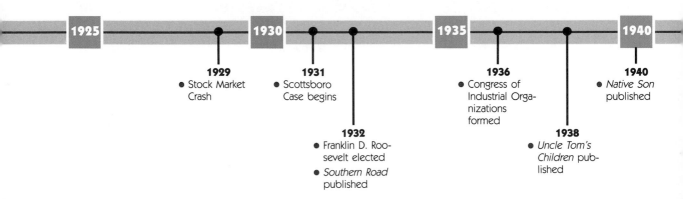

1925

1930

1935

1940

1929
● Stock Market Crash

1931
● Scottsboro Case begins

1932
● Franklin D. Roosevelt elected
● *Southern Road* published

1936
● Congress of Industrial Organizations formed

1938
● *Uncle Tom's Children* published

1940
● *Native Son* published

with a call—a call for the emergence of a world permitting all people to live freely, without restraint.

In Bontemps's "A Black Man Talks of Reaping," the speaker becomes a black Everyman, who chronicles the plight of blacks through history. In "Southern Mansion," all of nature is alive to the bitter irony of masters meeting their mistresses while slaves drag their chains, the symbols of their bondage.

In "Strange Legacies," Sterling Brown captures the heroic tradition in black poetry. In contrast to the stereotypes that reduced black people to contented slaves, brute Negroes, and exotic-primitive figures, "Strange Legacies" reclaims the dignity and humanity of blacks by juxtaposing the heroism of legendary figures like Jack Johnson and John Henry with that of unsung heroes—like the "old nameless couple in Red River Bottom." In this way, the poem thematically plays up courage, stoicism, and determination as enduring qualities of black life. The democratic verse of other modern poets, such as Edwin Arlington Robinson, Robert Frost, and Edgar Lee Masters, pointed the way. And just as Carl Sandburg said "yes" to his people—his Chicago hog butchers and stackers of wheat—Brown said "yes" to black people, celebrating the distinguished in otherwise undistinguished black lives.

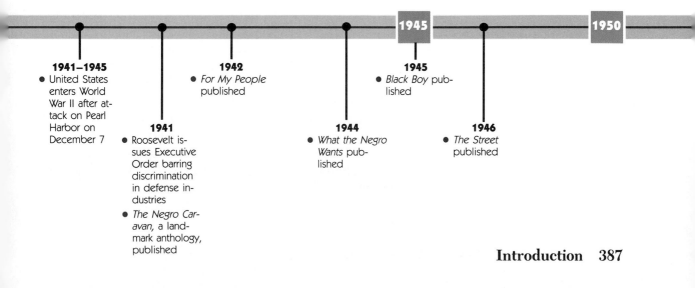

1941–1945
- United States enters World War II after attack on Pearl Harbor on December 7

1941
- Roosevelt issues Executive Order barring discrimination in defense industries
- *The Negro Caravan,* a landmark anthology, published

1942
- *For My People* published

1944
- *What the Negro Wants* published

1945

1945
- *Black Boy* published

1946
- *The Street* published

1950

Black Writers and the American Literary Tradition

By 1940, black writers would begin to ask: "What is American literature, and what role do blacks have in defining it?" In textbooks of American literature, African Americans were present as subjects but seldom as authors. Black writers now began to ask hard questions of American literature anthologies: "Which authors have been included and excluded and why?"

One anthology, V. F. Calverton's *An Anthology of American Negro Literature* (1929), had focused on the special contributions made by blacks to the development of a uniquely American literature, one freed from European influence. According to this view, the only claim American literature could make to originality was the response of blacks to the horrors of slavery—the spirituals, blues, jazz, and folklore. American literature would have to understand and include these "cultural products" if it wished to define itself as genuinely American. The question of inclusion was addressed differently by *Readings from Negro Authors: For Schools and Colleges* (1931), edited by Otelia Cromwell, Lorenzo Dow Turner, and Eva B. Dykes. By making considerations of literary form the purpose of their anthology, the editors attempted to transcend racial concerns.

In 1941, Sterling A. Brown, Arthur P. Davis, and Ulysses Lee edited *The Negro Caravan,* a landmark anthology. Formal and folk literatures by African American authors became fundamental ingredients helping to make up the *American* literary tradition. *The Negro Caravan* preserved the names of black American writers who had been ignored or omitted from the canon of American literature. It also made nontraditional genres, such as speeches, pamphlets, letters, and essays of all sorts, bear the prestige of novel, short story, poem, play, biography, and autobiography.

No longer could American literature be a literature devoted solely to "major" figures who were white. Emerson, Twain, Hemingway, and Faulkner were indeed major figures, but the challenge was to embrace Dunbar, Chesnutt, Hughes, Hurston, Wright, and many others within the literary tradition. Indeed, the literature of African Americans could no longer be viewed as something separate and apart; it had to be seen as part and parcel of the American literary tradition.

About the Author

Sterling A. Brown (1901–1989)

As a poet, critic, editor, and teacher, Sterling A. Brown was dedicated to the study of African American folk language and literature. In his poetry, he celebrated the black experience, using the speech of the people. His first book of poetry, *Southern Road* (1932), was hailed as a breakthrough.

Brown was born in Washington, D.C. He won a scholarship to Williams College in 1918 and graduated Phi Beta Kappa in 1922. After receiving his master's degree from Harvard in 1923, Brown took a number of teaching jobs in the South. There he began writing poetry in earnest. Having discovered in American poetry the drama of ordinary lives and the everyday speech of people, he began creating memorable portraits of Southern black folk. He also experimented with work songs, ballads, blues, and spirituals to find new poetic forms to contain their experiences.

In 1929, he returned to Washington and began teaching at Howard University. *Southern Road* was published in 1932. Despite his successful representation of the lives, lore, and language of black folk in this work, Brown was unable to find a publisher for his second volume, *No Hiding Place*. Nevertheless, he continued writing about literature and produced several important studies. One of Brown's most valuable contributions to American literary scholarship was his role as senior editor of *The Negro Caravan* (1941), the first comprehensive anthology of African American literature.

Brown did not receive the widespread rec-

Scurlock photo; Courtesy of the Prints and Photographs Collection, Moorland-Springarn Research Center, Howard University

ognition he deserved until the late sixties when the Black Arts Movement on college campuses drew attention to his work. Several of his important critical works were reissued, and in 1980 *The Collected Poems of Sterling A. Brown* was published.

"Strange Legacies," the poem reprinted here, is characteristic of Brown's best work. It is a celebration of the heroic quality in black people—the well-known and the unknown—who, despite overwhelming pressures and odds, still exhibit unusual strength and an extraordinary capacity for survival.

Sterling A. Brown   389

Before You Read

Strange Legacies

Using What You Know _____

What is a *legacy*? In your notebook or on the chalkboard, write a sentence defining the word. Are there legacies besides property or money? Is there a legacy that someone has left you? If so, tell why you value it.

Literary Focus: Vernacular _____

When Brown began writing poetry, many critics and poets wished to avoid dialect. They felt that it tended to reinforce certain stereotypes about African Americans. Brown's interest in black folk literature led him to develop a style that replaced the limitations of traditional dialect. It was based on the patterns and rhythms of language as it is actually spoken. The term used for the everyday spoken language of a people is **vernacular** (vər-năk'yə-lər).

In his introduction to the first edition of Brown's *Southern Road* (1932), James Weldon Johnson praised Brown for "adopting as his medium the common, racy, living speech of the Negro in certain phases of *real* life."

Setting a Purpose _____

As you read, think about the meaning of Brown's title. What are the "legacies" he refers to? Why are they "strange"?

Strange Legacies

Sterling A. Brown

One thing you left with us, Jack Johnson.°
One thing before they got you.

You used to stand there like a man,
Taking punishment
With a golden, spacious grin;
Confident.
Inviting big Jim Jeffries, who was boring in:
"Heah ah is, big boy; yuh sees whah Ise at.
Come on in. . . ."

Thanks, Jack, for that.   10

John Henry,° with your hammer;
John Henry, with your steel driver's pride,
You taught us that a man could go down like a man,
Sticking to your hammer till you died.
Sticking to your hammer till you died.   15

Brother,
When, beneath the burning sun
The sweat poured down and the breath came thick,
And the loaded hammer swung like a ton
And the heart grew sick;   20
You had what we need now, John Henry.
Help us get it.

So if we go down
Have to go down
We go like you, brother,   25
'Nachal' men. . . .

5

1. **Jack Johnson:** John Arthur Johnson (1878–1946), the first African American boxer to hold the heavyweight title. In 1910, he knocked out Jeffries in the fifteenth round.

11. **John Henry:** legendary hero celebrated in ballads for his strength as a steel driving man.

Old nameless couple in Red River Bottom,°
Who have seen floods gutting out your best loam,
And the boll weevil chase you
Out of your hard-earned home,   30
Have seen the drought parch your green fields,
And the cholera° stretch your porkers out dead;
Have seen year after year
The commissary° always a little in the lead;

Even you said   35
That which we need
Now in our time of fear,—
Routed your own deep misery and dread,
Muttering, beneath an unfriendly sky,
"Guess we'll give it one mo' try.   40
Guess we'll give it one mo' try."

27. **Red River Bottom:** Tenant farmers and sharecroppers in the South were hard hit by floods, soil exhaustion, and the boll weevil, which destroyed the bolls of cotton plants.

32. **cholera** (kăl'ər-ə): an intestinal disease.

34. **commissary** (kŏm'ĭ-sĕr'ē): a store where food and supplies are sold.

392 STERLING A. BROWN

Responding to the Selection

Strange Legacies by Sterling A. Brown

Interpreting Meanings

1. Brown wrote this poem when many Americans were facing great economic hardship. African Americans on farms in the South were particularly hard hit. What has happened to the couple in Red River Bottom? Why are they described as "nameless" (line 27)?
2. Jack Johnson was a real person. John Henry may have been a real person but belongs to legend (see page 258). Why do you think the speaker admires these heroes?
3. Why does the speaker link the "nameless couple" with these two heroic figures?
4. Who is speaking in lines 23–26 and 40–41? How do you know?
5. Explain the title of the poem.

Expository Writing

Explaining a Legacy

In a brief essay, tell what legacy has been left by a famous African American writer, religious leader, scientist, artist, teacher, or politician. Make a list of names and then narrow your choice. Use a biographical dictionary to get a list of sources. Find out if these articles and books are available in your school or public library by consulting the catalog.

Make a list of the questions you wish to have answered about your subject. Remember that your focus is the *legacy* the person has handed down.

WRITER'S WORKSHOP 2

Informative Report (Expository Writing)

(Opposite page)
They Were Very Poor,
oil by Jacob Lawrence,
panel #10 from
The Migration Series.
(1940–1941; text and title
revised by the artist, 1993).
Tempera on gesso on composition board, 12 × 18". The Museum of Modern Art, New York. Gift of Mrs. David M. Levy. Photograph © 1998 The Museum of Modern Art, New York

About the Author

Arna Bontemps (1902–1973)

Marion Palfi/The Schomburg Center for Research in Black Culture/New York Public Library

 Arna Bontemps (bän-täm') had a brilliant career as writer, editor, critic, teacher, and librarian. He was born in Alexandria, Louisiana, and grew up in California. He graduated from Pacific Union College in 1923 and moved to New York City, where he came to know Langston Hughes, Countee Cullen, and other leaders of the Harlem Renaissance.

Bontemps began his literary career as a poet. During the 1920s he had his work published in magazines. He won several prizes for his early poetry.

In 1931, he moved to rural Alabama, where he and his family lived in a decaying plantation house. This house, which had a local reputation for being haunted, appears in "Southern Mansion," one of the poems re-printed here. His brief stay in the South also inspired "A Summer Tragedy," his best-known story. It was later collected with other of his "Alabama Tales" and published in *The Old South* (1973).

Bontemps became associated with a second literary movement, which was centered in Chicago. Here he met Richard Wright and Margaret Walker, who were members of a group called the South Side Writers Group. Under the influence of this group, Bontemps's writing became more radical. His novel *Black Thunder* (1936) treats the slave rebellion of Gabriel Prosser, and *Drums at Dusk* (1939) deals with the insurrection of Toussaint L'Ouverture, in Haiti.

Bontemps became interested in writing for children. He produced a number of novels and poetry anthologies for young readers, including *Golden Slippers* (1941). In 1949, he and Langston Hughes coedited *Poetry of the Negro, 1746–1949.* In collaboration with Hughes, he produced *The Book of Negro Folklore* (1958), which contains an introductory essay on African American folk literature. *American Negro Poetry* (1963) contains an essay on black poetry from its beginnings in the eighteenth century to modern times. In 1969, Bontemps edited *Great Slave Narratives,* which contains an informative essay on the history of the slave narrative.

For many years, Bontemps served as librarian at Fisk University, in Nashville, Tennessee. He taught at the University of Illinois in Chicago and at Yale University in New Haven, Connecticut.

Before You Read

A Black Man Talks of Reaping; Southern Mansion

Using What You Know

In 1931, Arna Bontemps left New York City and took his family to northern Alabama. The critic Robert Bone has suggested that Bontemps was in search of his Southern roots: "He felt compelled to visit the ancestral soil, to stand where slaves had stood, and to dwell for a time in the haunted mansion of the past."

If you have read Jean Toomer's "Song of the Son" (page 309), discuss the speaker's feelings toward the past. What spiritual strength did Toomer find in his Southern heritage?

Literary Focus: The Stanza

A **stanza** is a group of lines forming a unit in a poem. Usually stanzas in a poem have a single pattern—each stanza follows the same rhyme pattern and each one contains the same number of lines. Some poems, however, have **variable stanzas,** where the pattern changes.

Some stanza forms have been used so often that they are identified by name. The **couplet,** for example, consists of a pair of rhymed lines. A stanza of three lines is called a **triplet** (or **tercet**). The **quatrain,** a four-line stanza, is the most common stanza in English. The Shakespearean sonnet, as you have seen, is composed of three quatrains and a concluding couplet.

Setting a Purpose

As you read, note the stanza forms Bontemps uses. How does each stanza develop a unit of thought?

A Black Man Talks of Reaping

Arna Bontemps

I have sown beside all waters in my day.
I planted deep, within my heart the fear
That wind or fowl would take the grain away.
I planted safe against this stark, lean year.

I scattered seed enough to plant the land   5
In rows from Canada to Mexico,
But for my reaping only what the hand
Can hold at once is all that I can show.

Yet what I sowed and what the orchard yields
My brother's sons are gathering stalk and root,   10
Small wonder then my children glean in fields
They have not sown, and feed on bitter fruit.

FSA photo by Dorothea Lange/The Schomburg Center for Research in Black Culture/ New York Public Library

Southern Mansion

Arna Bontemps

Poplars are standing there still as death
And ghosts of dead men
Meet their ladies walking
Two by two beneath the shade
And standing on the marble steps.   5

There is a sound of music echoing
Through the open door
And in the field there is
Another sound tinkling in the cotton:
Chains of bondmen dragging on the ground.   10

The years go back with an iron clank,
A hand is on the gate,
A dry leaf trembles on the wall.
Ghosts are walking.
They have broken roses down   15
And poplars stand there still as death.

Responding to the Selections

Two Poems by Arna Bontemps

Interpreting Meanings

A Black Man Talks of Reaping

1. This poem alludes to a verse in the Bible: "Whatsoever a man soweth, that shall he also reap" (Galatians 6:7). How is the situation described in the poem different from what is stated in the Bible?
2. What is the speaker allowed to harvest, according to lines 7–8?
3. What do you think the speaker means in lines 9–10 when he says that his "brother's sons" are reaping the harvest?
4. You have seen that poets often use images of planting and reaping as **metaphors**. What do you think the references to "grain," "seed," and "bitter fruit" mean?
5. Describe the **stanza form**. What idea is developed in each stanza?
6. How would you describe the speaker's **tone?** Is it bitter? ironic?

Southern Mansion

1. Who are the ghosts referred to in stanza 1? Who are the ghosts in stanza 3?
2. What contrast in sounds is described in stanza 2? What is the meaning of these sounds?
3. Which words and details in stanza 3 create an ominous, or menacing, mood?
4. Describe the **stanzas** in the poem. What idea is developed in each one?

Writing About Literature

Comparing Images

Countee Cullen's poem "From the Dark Tower" (page 337) opens and closes with images of tending seeds. "A Black Man Talks of Reaping" uses a similar image. Compare the ideas expressed in the poems. How does each poet use the image of planting and tending seeds to develop this theme?

Before You Read

A Summer Tragedy

Using What You Know

A **tragedy** is a literary work in which the central character or characters meet an unhappy end. Give an example of a tragic work you have read or seen in performance.

Recall the "old nameless couple" in Red River Bottom in Sterling Brown's poem "Strange Legacies" (page 391). What catastrophes have they faced? Would you consider their story tragic? Give reasons for your answer.

Literary Focus: Foreshadowing

Foreshadowing is a device used in fiction and in drama. It refers to the use of clues that hint at what is to come. A well-crafted story often suggests at the beginning what the outcome of events may be. Foreshadowing is primarily a plot device, but it may also contribute to mood.

Foreshadowing helps to create **suspense**, the state of uncertainty or curiosity about the outcome. A skillful writer can provide clues without giving the plot away.

Setting a Purpose

As you read, identify the forces that overwhelm the central characters. What details or symbolic elements foreshadow the end of the story?

A Summer Tragedy

Arna Bontemps

Old Jeff Patton, the black share farmer,[1] fumbled with his bow tie. His fingers trembled and the high stiff collar pinched his throat. A fellow loses his hand for such vanities after thirty or forty years of simple life. Once a year, or maybe twice if there's a wedding among his kinfolks, he may spruce up; but generally fancy clothes do nothing but adorn the wall of the big room and feed the moths. That had been Jeff Patton's experience. He had not worn his stiff-bosomed shirt more than a dozen times in all his married life. His swallow-tailed coat lay on the bed beside him, freshly brushed and pressed, but it was as full of holes as the overalls in which he worked on weekdays. The moths had used it badly. Jeff twisted his mouth into a hideous toothless grimace as he contended with the obstinate bow. He stamped his good foot and decided to give up the struggle.

"Jennie," he called.

"What's that, Jeff?" His wife's shrunken voice came out of the adjoining room like an echo. It was hardly bigger than a whisper.

"I reckon you'll have to he'p me wid this heah bow tie, baby," he said meekly. "Dog if I can hitch it up."

Her answer was not strong enough to reach him, but presently the old woman came to the door, feeling her way with a stick. She had a wasted, dead-leaf appearance. Her body, as scrawny and gnarled as a string bean, seemed less than nothing in the ocean of frayed and faded petticoats that surrounded her. These hung an inch or two above the tops of her heavy unlaced shoes and showed little grotesque piles where the stockings had fallen down from her negligible legs.

"You oughta could do a heap mo' wid a thing like that'n me—beingst as you got yo' good sight."

"Looks like I oughta could," he admitted. "But ma fingers is gone democrat[2] on me. I get all mixed up in the looking glass an' can't tell wicha way to twist the devilish thing."

Jennie sat on the side of the bed and old Jeff Patton got down on one knee while she tied the bow knot. It was a slow and painful ordeal for each of them in this position. Jeff's bones cracked, his knee ached, and it was only after a half dozen attempts that Jennie worked a semblance of a bow into the tie.

---

1. **share farmer:** someone who works someone else's land in order to get a share of the crop.

2. **gone democrat:** a wonderful example of black folk idiom that, in this case, refers to independence and therefore inability to control the movement of the fingers; each is doing what it wants to do.

Library of Congress

"I got to dress maself now," the old woman whispered. "These is ma old shoes an' stockings, and I ain't so much as unwrapped ma dress."

"Well, don't worry 'bout me no mo', baby," Jeff said. "That 'bout finishes me. All I gotta do now is slip on that old coat 'n ves' an' I'll be fixed to leave."

Jennie disappeared again through the dim passage into the shed room. Being blind was no handicap to her in that black hole. Jeff heard the cane placed against the wall beside the door and knew that his wife was on easy ground. He put on his coat, took a battered top hat from the bedpost and hobbled to the front door. He was ready to travel. As soon as Jennie could get on her Sunday shoes and her old black silk dress, they would start.

Outside the tiny log house, the day was warm and mellow with sunshine. A host of wasps were humming with busy excitement in the trunk of a dead sycamore. Gray squirrels were searching through the grass for hickory nuts and blue jays were in the trees, hopping from branch to branch. Pine woods stretched away to the left like a black sea.

A Summer Tragedy   401

Among them were scattered scores of log houses like Jeff's, houses of black share farmers. Cows and pigs wandered freely among the trees. There was no danger of loss. Each farmer knew his own stock and knew his neighbor's as well as he knew his neighbor's children.

Down the slope to the right were the cultivated acres on which the colored folks worked. They extended to the river, more than two miles away, and they were today green with the unmade cotton crop. A tiny thread of a road, which passed directly in front of Jeff's place, ran through these green fields like a pencil mark.

Jeff, standing outside the door, with his absurd hat in his left hand, surveyed the wide scene tenderly. He had been forty-five years on these acres. He loved them with the unexplained affection that others have for the countries to which they belong.

The sun was hot on his head, his collar still pinched his throat, and the Sunday clothes were intolerably hot. Jeff transferred the hat to his right hand and began fanning with it. Suddenly the whisper that was Jennie's voice came out of the shed room.

"You can bring the car round front whilst you's waitin'," it said feebly. There was a tired pause; then it added, "I'll soon be fixed to go."

"A'right, baby," Jeff answered. "I'll get it in a minute."

But he didn't move. A thought struck him that made his mouth fall open. The mention of the car brought to his mind, with new intensity, the trip he and Jennie were about to take. Fear came into his eyes; excitement took his breath. Lord, Jesus!

"Jeff . . . O Jeff," the old woman's whisper called.

He awakened with a jolt. "Hunh, baby?"

A slave cabin.

"What you doin'?"

"Nuthin. Jes studyin'. I jes been turnin' things round'n round in ma mind."

"You could be gettin' the car," she said.

"Oh yes, right away, baby."

He started round to the shed, limping heavily on his bad leg. There were three frizzly chickens in the yard. All his other chickens had been killed or stolen recently. But the frizzly chickens had been saved somehow. That was fortunate indeed, for these curious creatures had a way of devouring "Poison" from the yard and in that way protecting against conjure[3] and black luck and spells. But even the frizzly chickens seemed now to be in a stupor. Jeff thought they had some ailment; he expected all three of them to die shortly.

The shed in which the old T-model Ford stood was only a grass roof held up by four corner poles. It had been built by tremulous hands at a time when the little rattletrap car had been regarded as a peculiar treasure. And, miraculously, despite wind and downpour it still stood.

Jeff adjusted the crank and put his weight upon it. The engine came to life with a sputter and bang that rattled the old car from ra-

3. **conjure:** magic.

Log Cabin Quilt, *anonymous, silk appliqué, c. 1870s. The log cabin*
pattern was a traditional design.
Private Collection. Part of the exhibition "Stitching Memories," organized by Williams College Museum of Art

diator to taillight. Jeff hopped into the seat and put his foot on the accelerator. The sputtering and banging increased. The rattling became more violent. That was good. It was good banging, good sputtering and rattling, and it meant that the aged car was still in running condition. She could be depended on for this trip.

Again Jeff's thought halted as if paralyzed. The suggestion of the trip fell into the machinery of his mind like a wrench. He felt dazed and weak. He swung the car out into the yard, made a half turn and drove around to the front door. When he took his hands off the wheel, he noticed that he was trembling violently. He cut off the motor and climbed to the ground to wait for Jennie.

A few minutes later she was at the window, her voice rattling against the pane like a broken shutter.

"I'm ready, Jeff."

He did not answer, but limped into the house and took her by the arm. He led her slowly through the big room, down the step and across the yard.

"You reckon I'd oughta lock the do'?" he asked softly.

They stopped and Jennie weighed the question. Finally she shook her head.

"Ne' mind the do'," she said. "I don't see no cause to lock up things."

"You right," Jeff agreed. "No cause to lock up."

Jeff opened the door and helped his wife into the car. A quick shudder passed over him. Jesus! Again he trembled.

"How come you shaking so?" Jennie whispered.

"I don't know," he said.

"You mus' be scairt, Jeff."

"No, baby, I ain't scairt."

He slammed the door after her and went around to crank up again. The motor started easily. Jeff wished that it had not been so responsive. He would have liked a few more minutes in which to turn things around in his head. As it was, with Jennie chiding him about being afraid, he had to keep going. He swung the car into the little pencil-mark road and started off toward the river, driving very slowly, very cautiously.

Chugging across the green countryside, the small battered Ford seemed tiny indeed. Jeff felt a familiar excitement, a thrill, as they came down the first slope to the immense levels on which the cotton was growing. He could not help reflecting that the crops were good. He knew what that meant, too; he had made forty-five of them with his own hands. It was true that he had worn out nearly a dozen mules, but that was the fault of old man Stevenson, the owner of the land. Major Stevenson had the odd notion that one mule was all a share farmer needed to work a thirty-acre plot. It was an expensive notion, the way it killed mules from overwork, but the old man held to it. Jeff thought it killed a good many share farmers as well as mules, but he had no sympathy for them. He had always been strong, and he had been taught to have no patience with weakness in men. Women or children might be tolerated if they were puny, but a weak man was a curse. Of course, his own children—

Jeff's thought halted there. He and Jennie never mentioned their dead children any more. And naturally he did not wish to dwell upon them in his mind. Before he knew it, some remark would slip out of his mouth and that would make Jennie feel blue. Perhaps she would cry. A woman like Jennie could not easily throw off the grief that comes from losing five grown children within two years. Even Jeff was still staggered by the blow. His memory had not been much good recently. He frequently talked to himself. And, although he had kept it a secret, he knew that his courage had left him. He was terrified by the least unfamiliar sound at night. He was reluctant to venture far from home in the daytime. And that habit of trembling when he felt fearful was now far beyond his control. Sometimes he became afraid and trembled without knowing what had frightened him. The feeling would just come over him like a chill.

The car rattled slowly over the dusty road. Jennie sat erect and silent, with a little absurd hat pinned to her hair. Her useless eyes seemed very large, very white in their deep sockets. Suddenly Jeff heard her voice, and he inclined his head to catch the words.

"Is we passed Delia Moore's house yet?" she asked.

"Not yet," he said.

"You must be drivin' mighty slow, Jeff."

"We might just as well take our time, baby."

There was a pause. A little puff of steam was coming out of the radiator of the car. Heat wavered above the hood. Delia Moore's house was nearly half a mile away. After a moment Jennie spoke again.

"You ain't really scairt, is you, Jeff?"

"Nah, baby, I ain't scairt."

"You know how we agreed—we gotta keep on goin'."

Jewels of perspiration appeared on Jeff's forehead. His eyes rounded, blinked, became fixed on the road.

"I don't know," he said with a shiver. "I reckon it's the only thing to do."

"Hm."

A flock of guinea fowls, pecking in the road, were scattered by the passing car. Some of them took to their wings; others hid under bushes. A blue jay, swaying on a leafy twig, was annoying a roadside squirrel. Jeff held an even speed till he came near Delia's place. Then he slowed down noticeably.

Delia's house was really no house at all, but an abandoned store building converted into a dwelling. It sat near a crossroads, beneath a single black cedar tree. There Delia, a cattish old creature of Jennie's age, lived alone. She had been there more years than anybody could remember, and long ago had won the disfavor of such women as Jennie. For in her young days Delia had been gayer, yellower and saucier than seemed proper in those parts. Her ways with menfolks had been dark and suspicious. And the fact that she had had as many husbands as children did not help her reputation.

"Yonder's old Delia," Jeff said as they passed.

"What she doin'?"

"Jes sittin' in the do'," he said.

"She see us?"

"Hm," Jeff said. "Musta did."

That relieved Jennie. It strengthened her to know that her old enemy had seen her pass in her best clothes. That would give the old she-devil something to chew her gums and fret about, Jennie thought. Wouldn't she have a fit if she didn't find out? Old evil Delia! This would be just the thing for her. It would pay her back for being so evil. It would also pay her, Jennie thought, for the way she used to grin at Jeff—long ago when her teeth were good.

The road became smooth and red, and Jeff could tell by the smell of the air that they were nearing the river. He could see the rise where the road turned and ran along parallel to the stream. The car chugged on monotonously. After a long silent spell, Jennie leaned against Jeff and spoke.

A Summer Tragedy   405

"How many bale o' cotton you think we got standin'?" she said.

Jeff wrinkled his forehead as he calculated.

"'Bout twenty-five, I reckon."

"How many you make las' year?"

"Twenty-eight," he said. "How come you ask that?"

"I's jes thinkin'," Jennie said quietly.

"It don't make a speck o' difference though," Jeff reflected. "If we get much or if we get little, we still gonna be in debt to old man Stevenson when he gets through counting up agin us. It's took us a long time to learn that."

Jennie was not listening to these words. She had fallen into a trance-like meditation. Her lips twitched. She chewed her gums and rubbed her gnarled hands nervously. Suddenly she leaned forward, buried her face in the nervous hands and burst into tears. She cried aloud in a dry cracked voice that suggested the rattle of fodder on dead stalks. She cried aloud like a child, for she had never learned to suppress a genuine sob. Her slight old frame shook heavily and seemed hardly able to sustain such violent grief.

"What's the matter, baby?" Jeff asked awkwardly. "Why you cryin' like all that?"

"I's jes thinkin'," she said.

"So you the one what's scairt now, hunh?"

"I ain't scairt, Jeff. I's jes thinkin' 'bout leavin' eve'thing like this—eve'thing we been used to. It's right sad-like."

Jeff did not answer, and presently Jennie buried her face again and cried.

The sun was almost overhead. It beat down furiously on the dusty wagon-path road, on the parched roadside grass and the tiny battered car. Jeff's hands, gripping the wheel, became wet with perspiration; his forehead sparkled. Jeff's lips parted. His mouth shaped a hideous grimace. His face suggested the face of a man being burned. But the torture passed and his expression softened again.

"You mustn't cry, baby," he said to his wife. "We gotta be strong. We can't break down."

Jennie waited a few seconds, then said, "You reckon we oughta do it, Jeff? You reckon we oughta go 'head an' do it, really?"

Jeff's voice choked; his eyes blurred. He was terrified to hear Jennie say the thing that had been in his mind all morning. She had egged him on when he had wanted more than anything in the world to wait, to reconsider, to think things over a little longer. Now she was getting cold feet. Actually there was no need of thinking the question through again. It would only end in making the same painful decision once more. Jeff knew that. There was no need of fooling around longer.

"We jes as well to do like we planned," he said. "They ain't nothin' else for us now—it's the bes' thing."

Jeff thought of the handicaps, the near impossibility, of making another crop with his leg bothering him more and more each week. Then there was always the chance that he would have another stroke, like the one that had made him lame. Another one might kill him. The least it could do would be to leave him helpless. Jeff gasped—Lord, Jesus! He could not bear to think of being helpless, like a baby, on Jennie's hands. Frail, blind Jennie.

The little pounding motor of the car worked harder and harder. The puff of steam from the cracked radiator became larger. Jeff realized that they were climbing a little rise. A moment later the road turned abruptly and he looked down upon the face of the river.

"Jeff."

A Ford automobile, 1910.
Brown Brothers

"Hunh?"

"Is that the water I hear?"

"Hm. Tha's it."

"Well, which way you goin' now?"

"Down this-a way," he said. "The road runs 'long 'side o' the water a lil piece."

She waited a while calmly. Then she said, "Drive faster."

"A'right, baby," Jeff said.

The water roared in the bed of the river. It was fifty or sixty feet below the level of the road. Between the road and the water there was a long smooth slope, sharply inclined. The slope was dry, the clay hardened by prolonged summer heat. The water below, roaring in a narrow channel, was noisy and wild.

"Jeff."

"Hunh?"

"How far you goin'?"

"Jes a lil piece down the road."

"You ain't scairt, is you, Jeff?"

"Nah, baby," he said trembling. "I ain't scairt."

"Remember how we planned it, Jeff. We gotta do it like we said. Brave-like."

"Hm."

Jeff's brain darkened. Things suddenly seemed unreal, like figures in a dream. Thoughts swam in his mind foolishly, hysterically, like little blind fish in a pool within a dense cave. They rushed, crossed one another, jostled, collided, retreated and rushed again. Jeff soon became dizzy. He shuddered violently and turned to his wife.

"Jennie, I can't do it. I can't." His voice broke pitifully.

She did not appear to be listening. All the grief had gone from her face. She sat erect, her unseeing eyes wide open, strained and frightful. Her glossy black skin had become dull. She seemed as thin, as sharp and bony, as a starved bird. Now, having suffered and endured the sadness of tearing herself away from beloved things, she showed no anguish. She was absorbed with her own thoughts, and she didn't even hear Jeff's voice shouting in her ear.

Jeff said nothing more. For an instant there was light in his cavernous brain. The great chamber was, for less than a second,

A Summer Tragedy   407

peopled by characters he knew and loved. They were simple, healthy creatures, and they behaved in a manner that he could understand. They had quality. But since he had already taken leave of them long ago, the remembrance did not break his heart again. Young Jeff Patton was among them, the Jeff Patton of fifty years ago who went down to New Orleans with a crowd of country boys to the Mardi Gras doings. The gay young crowd, boys with candy-striped shirts and rouged-brown girls in noisy silks, was like a picture in his head. Yet it did not make him sad. On that very trip Slim Burns had killed Joe Beasley—the crowd had been broken up. Since then Jeff Patton's world had been the Greenbriar Plantation. If there had been other Mardi Gras carnivals, he had not heard of them. Since then there had been no time; the years had fallen on him like waves. Now he was old, worn out. Another paralytic stroke (like the one he had already suffered) would put him on his back for keeps. In that condition, with a frail blind woman to look after him, he would be worse off than if he were dead.

Suddenly Jeff's hands became steady. He actually felt brave. He slowed down the motor of the car and carefully pulled off the road. Below, the water of the stream boomed, a soft thunder in the deep channel. Jeff ran the car onto the clay slope, pointed it directly toward the stream and put his foot heavily on the accelerator. The little car leaped furiously down the steep incline toward the water. The movement was nearly as swift and direct as a fall. The two old black folks, sitting quietly side by side, showed no excitement. In another instant the car hit the water and dropped immediately out of sight.

A little later it lodged in the mud of a shallow place. One wheel of the crushed and upturned little Ford became visible above the rushing water.

Responding to the Selection

A Summer Tragedy by Arna Bontemps

Identifying Facts

1. What kind of crop has Jeff Patton worked all his life?
2. Who is Major Stevenson?
3. Why is Jeff no longer able to take care of his wife?
4. Why does Jennie want Jeff to drive past Delia Moore's house?
5. What memory does Jeff recall before he pulls off the road?

Interpreting Meanings

1. Despite years of hard work, why is Jeff Patton still in debt?
2. What is Jeff's feeling for the land?
3. At what point in the story did you realize the purpose of the trip?
4. How does Bontemps show the love between Jeff and Jennie?
5. What happens during the journey that makes it possible for Jeff and Jennie to accept their deaths?

6. Throughout the story we are kept aware of the beauty of the summer day. Why is it significant that this human tragedy occurs in summer rather than in another season?

Literary Elements

Noting Techniques of Foreshadowing and Suspense
At the opening of the story, we know that Jeff Patton and his wife are dressing for a special occasion. The first indication that this is not a happy occasion comes when Jeff thinks of the car:

> The mention of the car brought to his mind, with new intensity, the trip he and Jennie were about to take. Fear came into his eyes; excitement took his breath.

These sentences create suspense. The reader wonders: What is the trip they are about to take and why is he frightened?

Reread the story and list the clues that foreshadow the sad end of the characters.

Language and Vocabulary

Learning Alternative Pronunciations
Many words in English have more than one acceptable pronunciation. The noun *grimace*, for instance, can be pronounced in two ways. Listen to the difference as you pronounce both:

grĭ-mās′
grĭm′ĭs

If a dictionary gives you two pronunciations of a word, the first pronunciation is generally the preferred one.

Use your dictionary to find alternative pronunciations of these words: *altitude, applicable, exquisite, hemoglobin, incomparable.* Can you add any words to this list?

Writer's Journal

Responding to the Ending of the Story
How did you feel at the end of Bontemps's story? Did you feel that you had been prepared for the outcome? Did the ending have a strong impact for you?

Speaking and Listening

Explaining Vivid Comparisons
Bontemps's descriptions of his characters contain many striking comparisons, such as:

> She had a wasted, dead-leaf appearance. Her body, as scrawny and gnarled as a string bean, seemed less than nothing in the ocean of frayed and faded petticoats that surrounded her.

Choose one descriptive passage to read aloud. Then in your own words, explain the figures of speech Bontemps has used.

About the Author

Richard Wright (1908–1960)

Gordon Parks/Library of Congress

 Richard Wright (rīt) was born on a cotton plantation near Natchez, Mississippi. His father deserted the family when Wright was five years old. A few years later, his mother became ill. The children were placed with different relatives and for a time Wright and his brother were in an orphanage. Before the age of twelve, Wright did not have a single full year of formal schooling. After ninth grade—his last year of school—Wright moved to Memphis, Tennessee, where he began writing. He later moved to Chicago and then to New York City. In 1947, he left the United States for Paris, where he lived until his death.

When he was growing up, Wright was always poor and almost always hungry. The deprivations he suffered extended to his education. The schools he attended did little to encourage him. He was unable to get the books he wanted to read. Once, in order to borrow some books from a library in Memphis, he forged a note from a white borrower. Few American writers have had to overcome so many handicaps—poverty, racial prejudice, inadequate education, and a disrupted family life.

Wright's literary career began after he moved to Chicago. There he became involved in radical politics. In a short time, he joined the Communist party and began writing for leftist magazines. His interest turned to fiction and by the time he left for New York, he had begun *Uncle Tom's Children.*

Wright's first major success came in 1940, when his novel *Native Son* was published. It became the first book written by an African American to be chosen for the Book-of-the-Month Club.

Wright's ideas brought him into conflict with the ideology of Communism, and in 1944 he withdrew from the party. *Black Boy,* the story of his early life in the South, appeared in 1945 and became a bestseller. Many readers consider this book to be his masterpiece. *American Hunger,* the continuation of his autobiography, was published posthumously, in 1977.

After Wright moved to France, he continued to write fiction and nonfiction. At the time of his death, he was working on *Eight Men* (published in 1961). This collection includes the story reprinted here, "The Man Who Was Almost a Man," a work first published in 1940 under the title "Almos' a Man."

Before You Read

From **Black Boy**

Using What You Know

The following episode is from Chapter 7 of *Black Boy.* Here Wright tells about the first story he ever wrote and notes the reactions of various people to his efforts. Wright tells not only what happened to him but also what he thought and how he felt.

Think about your own memories of a particular time in your life. Which of these memories do you recall the best? Why do some memories remain strong while others fade?

Literary Focus: Autobiography

Black Boy is an **autobiography,** Wright's own story of his life. Autobiography is one kind of **nonfiction,** that is, writing that deals with real events and real people. The autobiographer must limit what can be told. In this episode from *Black Boy,* for example, Wright does not tell what happened to him every day of his fifteenth year. He chooses a specific incident that shows how his life was shaped by the struggle to realize a dream.

Setting a Purpose

Put yourself in Wright's place as you read. See if you can tell why this particular episode made an impression on him.

Black Boy
A Record of Childhood and Youth
Richard Wright

The eighth grade days flowed in their hungry path and I grew more conscious of myself; I sat in classes, bored, wondering, dreaming. One long dry afternoon I took out my composition book and told myself that I would write a story; it was sheer idleness that led me to it. What would the story be about? It resolved itself into a plot about a villain who wanted a widow's home and I called it *The Voodoo of Hell's Half-Acre.* It was crudely atmospheric, emotional, intuitively psychological, and stemmed from pure feeling. I finished it in three days and then wondered what to do with it.

The local Negro newspaper! That's it . . . I sailed into the office and shoved my ragged composition book under the nose of the man who called himself the editor.

"What is that?" he asked.

"A story," I said.

"A news story?"

"No, fiction."

"All right. I'll read it," he said.

He pushed my composition book back on his desk and looked at me curiously, sucking at his pipe.

"But I want you to read it *now*," I said.

He blinked. I had no idea how newspapers were run. I thought that one took a story to an editor and he sat down then and there and read it and said yes or no.

"I'll read this and let you know about it tomorrow," he said.

I was disappointed; I had taken time to write it and he seemed distant and uninterested.

"Give me the story," I said, reaching for it.

He turned from me, took up the book and read ten pages or more.

"Won't you come in tomorrow?" he asked. "I'll have it finished then."

I honestly relented.

"All right," I said. "I'll stop in tomorrow."

I left with the conviction that he would not read it. Now, where else could I take it after he had turned it down? The next afternoon, en route[1] to my job, I stepped into the newspaper office.

"Where's my story?" I asked.

"It's in galleys,"[2] he said.

"What's that?" I asked; I did not know what galleys were.

"It's set up in type," he said. "We're publishing it."

1. **en route** (ən rōōt'): on the way.
2. **galleys:** printer's proofs taken from type.

In 1945, Life *magazine presented a picture-dramatization of*
Black Boy. *Here, an actor is shown as the fifteen-year-old Richard,*
writing his first story.

George Karger,
Life Magazine © Time, Inc.

"How much money will I get?" I asked, excited.

"We can't pay for manuscript," he said.

"But you sell your papers for money," I said with logic.

"Yes, but we're young in business," he explained.

"But you're asking me to *give* you my story, but you don't *give* your papers away," I said.

He laughed.

"Look, you're just starting. This story will put your name before our readers. Now, that's something," he said.

"But if the story is good enough to sell to your readers, then you ought to give me some of the money you get from it," I insisted.

He laughed again and I sensed that I was amusing him.

"I'm going to offer you something more valuable than money," he said. "I'll give you a chance to learn to write."

I was pleased, but I still thought he was taking advantage of me.

"When will you publish my story?"

"I'm dividing it into three installments," he said. "The first installment appears this week. But the main thing is this: Will you get news for me on a space rate basis?"

"I work mornings and evenings for three dollars a week," I said.

Black Boy   413

"Oh," he said. "Then you better keep that. But what are you doing this summer?"

"Nothing."

"Then come to see me before you take another job," he said. "And write some more stories."

A few days later my classmates came to me with baffled eyes, holding copies of the *Southern Register* in their hands.

"Did you really write that story?" they asked me.

"Yes."

"Why?"

"Because I wanted to."

"Where did you get it from?"

"I made it up."

"You didn't. You copied it out of a book."

"If I had, no one would publish it."

"But what are they publishing it for?"

"So people can read it."

"Who told you to do that?"

"Nobody."

"Then why did you do it?"

"Because I wanted to," I said again.

They were convinced that I had not told them the truth. We had never had any instruction in literary matters at school; the literature of the nation or the Negro had never been mentioned. My schoolmates could not understand why anyone would want to write a story; and, above all, they could not understand why I had called it *The Voodoo of Hell's Half-Acre*. The mood out of which a story was written was the most alien thing conceivable to them. They looked at me with new eyes, and a distance, a suspiciousness came between us. If I had thought anything in writing the story, I had thought that perhaps it would make me more acceptable to them, and now it was cutting me off from them more completely than ever.

At home the effects were no less disturbing. Granny came into my room early one morning and sat on the edge of my bed.

"Richard, what is this you're putting in the papers?" she asked.

"A story," I said.

"About what?"

"It's just a story, granny."

"But they tell me it's been in three times."

"It's the same story. It's in three parts."

"But what's it about?" she insisted.

I hedged, fearful of getting into a religious argument.

"It's just a story I made up," I said.

"Then it's a lie," she said.

"Oh, Christ," I said.

"You must get out of this house if you take the name of the Lord in vain," she said.

"Granny, please . . . I'm sorry," I pleaded. "But it's hard to tell you about the story. You see, granny, everybody knows that the story isn't true, but . . ."

"Then why write it?" she asked.

"Because people might want to read it."

"That's the Devil's work," she said and left.

My mother also was worried.

"Son, you ought to be more serious," she said. "You're growing up now and you won't be able to get jobs if you let people think that you're weak-minded. Suppose the superintendent of schools would ask you to teach here in Jackson, and he found out that you had been writing stories?"

I could not answer her.

"I'll be all right, mama," I said.

Uncle Tom, though surprised, was highly critical and contemptuous. The story had no point, he said. And whoever heard of a story by the title of *The Voodoo of Hell's Half-Acre*? Aunt Addie said that it was a sin for anyone to use the word "hell" and that what

The editor of the local Negro newspaper runs Richard's story.
George Karger, Life Magazine © Time, Inc.

was wrong with me was that I had nobody to guide me. She blamed the whole thing upon my upbringing.

In the end I was so angry that I refused to talk about the story. From no quarter, with the exception of the Negro newspaper editor, had there come a single encouraging word. It was rumored that the principal wanted to know why I had used the word "hell." I felt that I had committed a crime. Had I been conscious of the full extent to which I was pushing against the current of my environment, I would have been frightened altogether out of my attempts at writing. But my reactions were limited to the attitude of the people about me, and I did not speculate or generalize.

I dreamed of going north and writing books, novels. The North symbolized to me all that I had not felt and seen; it had no relation whatever to what actually existed. Yet, by imagining a place where everything was possible, I kept hope alive in me. But where had I got this notion of doing something in the future, of going away from home and accomplishing something that would be recognized by others? I had, of course, read my Horatio Alger[3] stories, my pulp stories,[4] and I knew my Get-Rich-Quick Wallingford[5] series from cover to cover, though I had sense enough not to hope to get rich; even to my naïve imagination that possibility was too remote. I knew that I lived in a country in which the aspirations of black people were limited, marked-off. Yet I felt that I had to go somewhere and do something to redeem my being alive.

3. **Horatio Alger:** an American writer (1832–1899) known for stories in which penniless boys achieve fame and fortune.
4. **pulp stories:** sensational stories.
5. **Get-Rich-Quick Wallingford:** a character in a series of stories by George R. Chester. He makes a fortune through financial schemes.

I was building up in me a dream which the entire educational system of the South had been rigged to stifle. I was feeling the very thing that the state of Mississippi had spent millions of dollars to make sure that I would never feel; I was becoming aware of the thing that the Jim Crow laws[6] had been drafted and passed to keep out of my consciousness; I was acting on impulses that southern senators in the nation's capital had striven to keep out of Negro life; I was beginning to dream the dreams that the state had said were wrong, that the schools had said were taboo.

Had I been articulate about my ultimate aspirations, no doubt someone would have told me what I was bargaining for; but nobody seemed to know, and least of all did I. My classmates felt that I was doing something that was vaguely wrong, but they did not know how to express it. As the outside world grew more meaningful, I became more concerned, tense; and my classmates and my teachers would say: "Why do you ask so many questions?" Or: "Keep quiet."

I was in my fifteenth year; in terms of schooling I was far behind the average youth of the nation, but I did not know that. In me was shaping a yearning for a kind of consciousness, a mode of being that the way of life about me had said could not be, must not be, and upon which the penalty of death had been placed. Somewhere in the dead of the southern night my life had switched onto the wrong track and, without my knowing it, the locomotive of my heart was rushing down a dangerously steep slope, heading for a collision, heedless of the warning red lights that blinked all about me, the sirens and the bells and the screams that filled the air.

6. **Jim Crow laws:** laws that discriminated against African Americans.

Responding to the Selection

From **Black Boy** by Richard Wright

Identifying Facts

1. What reason does Wright give for beginning the story?
2. Where was the story published?
3. What did Wright get for his story instead of money?
4. Who encouraged him to keep writing?

Interpreting Meanings

1. Wright is telling this experience as a grown man looking back on his boyhood. What does he now think of the story he wrote? Why do you think the newspaper editor decided to publish the story?
2. Wright says that he thought his writing the story would make him "more acceptable" to his classmates. How did they react when his story appeared in print? Were you surprised by their reactions?
3. Why did the members of Wright's family try to discourage him from writing? Do you think their attitudes are understandable?
4. This episode from Wright's boyhood made a powerful impression upon him because it helped him understand other people as well as himself. What did he learn about others and about himself?
5. In the last paragraph, Wright says that his life had "switched onto the wrong track." According to his family and classmates, what would have been the "right track"? Why do you think Wright says that he was heading for "a collision"?
6. After reading this excerpt from Wright's autobiography, what impression do you have of him?

Language and Vocabulary

Finding Multiple Meanings of Words

Many words in our language have **multiple meanings**; that is, a single word can do several different jobs. The word *quarter,* for instance, is commonly used for a coin worth twenty-five cents. The word *quarter* has a different meaning, however, in this sentence:

From no *quarter,* with the exception of the Negro newspaper editor, had there come a single encouraging word.

In Wright's sentence, the word *quarter* means "some person or group." The word *quarter* has still another meaning when it is used in the phrase "to quarter soldiers." In this instance, its meaning is "to provide lodgings." In hunting, "to quarter" is to range over a field, as hounds do in searching for game.

The word *galley* also has several meanings. Using a dictionary, tell what the word *galley* means in each of the following sentences:

1. In ancient times a *galley* was propelled by oars and sails.
2. A proofreader checks *galley* proof before type is made up into pages.
3. The flight attendants were working in the airplane's *galley.*

Developing Sentence Sense

Understanding Verb Relationships
In the following sentences, Richard Wright expresses an imagined condition:

> **Had** I **been** conscious of the full extent to which I was pushing against the current of my environment, I **would have been frightened** altogether out of my attempts at writing.

The combination of the verb phrases **had been** and **would have been frightened** is a signal to the reader that what Wright is talking about never actually happened. If he had realized what he was up against, he would have been too frightened to continue writing. Since he was not aware of the obstacles, he continued to write.

Locate another sentence in which Wright expresses an imagined condition. Then tell in your own words what Wright means.

LANGUAGE
WORKSHOP

LW 9 Ch 3:15
LW 10 Ch 3:10
Verb Tenses

Writing About Literature

Interpreting a Statement
Sometimes a piece of writing contains a single sentence or a short passage that states the author's main idea. Toward the end of the chapter, Wright says that he had "a dream which the entire educational system of the South had been rigged to stifle." What do you think this statement means? What was Wright's dream? Think about the word *stifle.* How did Wright feel that he was kept from achieving his ambition? Write a paragraph interpreting the statement.

Speaking and Listening

Reading Dialogue Aloud
Dialogue is the talk or conversation between two characters. Dialogue tends to make writing more realistic and more lively. When dialogue appears in biography or fiction, the speaker's words are enclosed in quotation marks.

Wright uses dialogue throughout *Black Boy* to re-create scenes from his past. Choose a partner and read aloud one of the passages of dialogue in the selection. Try to get inside the characters as you re-create their thoughts and feelings.

Before You Read

The Man Who Was Almost a Man

Using What You Know

Young people are often eager to be treated as grownups, to have the independence and status of adults. Sometimes, however, they are given adult responsibilities before they are ready for them. How can young people show that they are mature enough to handle such responsibilities as managing their own money or driving the family car? Thinking about this question will help you understand the problems of the boy in Wright's story.

Literary Focus: Point of View

Point of view refers to the vantage point from which a story is told. There are several different ways to present a story.

When the **narrator,** the person telling the story, is a character in the story, we say the story is told from the **first-person point of view.** Squeaky, the narrator in "Raymond's Run" (page 4), tells the story from her point of view. She is the "I" in the story, a character as well as the narrator.

The narrator can be someone who stands outside the story and who observes what all the characters are doing, thinking, and feeling. We refer to this vantage point as **third-person point of view.** Sometimes, a writer chooses to tell a story from the vantage point of only one character. This is called **limited third-person point of view.** This point of view is effective when the writer wants us to get inside the character's head and to experience what he or she is seeing, doing, and feeling.

Setting a Purpose

As you read, note how Wright gets you into the mind of Dave Saunders so that you are conscious of what he sees, feels, and thinks. Does this point of view bring you closer to the character, or does it create distance from him?

The Man Who Was Almost a Man

Richard Wright

1

Dave struck out across the fields, looking homeward through paling light. Whut's the use talkin wid em niggers in the field? Anyhow, his mother was putting supper on the table. Them niggers can't understan nothing. One of these days he was going to get a gun and practice shooting, then they couldn't talk to him as though he were a little boy. He slowed, looking at the ground. Shucks, Ah ain scareda them even ef they are biggern me! Aw, Ah know whut Ahma do. Ahm going by ol Joe's sto n git that Sears Roebuck catlog n look at them guns. Mebbe Ma will lemme buy one when she gits mah pay from ol man Hawkins. Ahma beg her t gimme some money. Ahm ol ernough to hava gun. Ahm seventeen. Almost a man. He strode, feeling his long loose-jointed limbs. Shucks, a man oughta hava little gun aftah he done worked hard all day.

He came in sight of Joe's store. A yellow lantern glowed on the front porch. He mounted steps and went through the screen door, hearing it bang behind him. There was a strong smell of coal oil and mackerel fish. He felt very confident until he saw fat Joe walk in through the rear door, then his courage began to ooze.

"Howdy, Dave! Whutcha want?"

"How yuh, Mistah Joe? Aw, Ah don wanna buy nothing. Ah jus wanted t see ef yuhd lemme look at tha catlog erwhile."

"Sure! You wanna see it here?"

"Nawsuh. Ah wans t take it home wid me. Ah'll bring it back termorrow when Ah come in from the fiels."

"You plannin on buying something?"

"Yessuh."

"Your ma lettin you have your own money now?"

"Shucks. Mistah Joe, Ahm gittin t be a man like anybody else!"

Joe laughed and wiped his greasy white face with a red bandanna.

"Whut you plannin on buyin?"

Dave looked at the floor, scratched his head, scratched his thigh, and smiled. Then he looked up shyly.

"Ah'll tell yuh, Mistah Joe, ef yuh promise yuh won't tell."

"I promise."

"Waal, Ahma buy a gun."

"A gun? Whut you want with a gun?"

"Ah wanna keep it."

"You ain't nothing but a boy. You don't need a gun."

"Aw, lemme have the catlog, Mistah Joe. Ah'll bring it back."

Joe walked through the rear door. Dave was elated. He looked around at barrels of sugar and flour. He heard Joe coming back.

The Man Who Was Almost a Man 421

He craned his neck to see if he were bringing the book. Yeah, he's got it. Gawddog, he's got it!

"Here, but be sure you bring it back. It's the only one I got."

"Sho, Mistah Joe."

"Say, if you wanna buy a gun, why don't you buy one from me? I gotta gun to sell."

"Will it shoot?"

"Sure it'll shoot."

"Whut kind is it?"

"Oh, it's kinda old . . . a left-hand Wheeler. A pistol. A big one."

"Is it got bullets in it?"

"It's loaded."

"Kin Ah see it?"

"Where's your money?"

"Whut yuh wan fer it?"

"I'll let you have it for two dollars."

"Just two dollahs? Shucks, Ah could buy tha when Ah git mah pay."

"I'll have it here when you want it."

"Awright, suh. Ah be in fer it."

He went through the door, hearing it slam again behind him. Ahma git some money from Ma n buy me a gun! Only two dollahs! He tucked the thick catalogue under his arm and hurried.

"Where yuh been, boy?" His mother held a steaming dish of black-eyed peas.

"Aw, Ma, Ah jus stopped down the road t talk wid the boys."

"Yuh know bettah t keep suppah waitin."

He sat down, resting the catalogue on the edge of the table.

"Yuh git up from there and git to the well n wash yosef! Ah ain feedin no hogs in mah house!"

She grabbed his shoulder and pushed him. He stumbled out of the room, then came back to get the catalogue.

"Whut this?"

"Aw, Ma, it's jusa catlog."

"Who yuh git it from?"

"From Joe, down at the sto."

"Waal, thas good. We kin use it in the outhouse."

"Naw, Ma." He grabbed for it. "Gimme ma catlog, Ma."

She held onto it and glared at him.

"Quit hollerin at me! Whut's wrong wid yuh? Yuh crazy?"

"But Ma, please. It ain mine! It's Joe's! He tol me t bring it back t im termorrow."

She gave up the book. He stumbled down the back steps, hugging the thick book under his arm. When he had splashed water on his face and hands, he groped back to the kitchen and fumbled in a corner for the towel. He bumped into a chair; it clattered to

the floor. The catalogue sprawled at his feet. When he had dried his eyes he snatched up the book and held it again under his arm. His mother stood watching him.

"Now, ef yuh gonna act a fool over that ol book, Ah'll take it n burn it up."

"Naw, Ma, please."

"Waal, set down n be still!"

He sat down and drew the oil lamp close. He thumbed page after page, unaware of the food his mother set on the table. His father came in. Then his small brother.

"Whutcha got there, Dave?" his father asked.

"Jusa catlog," he answered, not looking up.

"Yeah, here they is!" His eyes glowed at blue-and-black revolvers. He glanced up, feeling sudden guilt. His father was watching him. He eased the book under the table and rested it on his knees. After the blessing was asked, he ate. He scooped up peas and swallowed fat meat without chewing. Buttermilk helped to wash it down. He did not want to mention money before his father. He would do much better by cornering his mother when she was alone. He looked at his father uneasily out of the edge of his eye.

"Boy, how come yuh don quit foolin wid tha book n eat yo suppah?"

"Yessuh."

"How you n ol man Hawkins gitten erlong?"

"Suh?"

"Can't yuh hear? Why don yuh lissen? Ah ast yu how wuz yuh n ol man Hawkins gittin erlong?"

"Oh, swell, Pa. Ah plows mo lan than anybody over there."

"Waal, yuh oughta keep yo mind on whut yuh doin."

"Yessuh."

He poured his plate full of molasses and sopped it up slowly with a chunk of cornbread. When his father and brother had left the kitchen, he still sat and looked again at the guns in the catalogue, longing to muster courage enough to present his case to his mother. Lawd, ef Ah only had tha pretty one! He could almost feel the slickness of the weapon with his fingers. If he had a gun like that he would polish it and keep it shining so it would never rust. N Ah'd keep it loaded, by Gawd!

"Ma?" His voice was hesitant.

"Hunh?"

"Ol man Hawkins give yuh mah money yit?"

"Yeah, but ain no usa yuh thinking bout throwin nona it erway. Ahm keepin tha money sos yuh kin have cloes t go to school this winter."

He rose and went to her side with the open catalogue in his palms. She was washing dishes, her head bent low over a pan. Shyly he raised the book. When he spoke, his voice was husky, faint.

"Ma, Gawd knows Ah wans one of these."

"One of whut?" she asked, not raising her eyes.

"One of these," he said again, not daring even to point. She glanced up at the page, then at him with wide eyes.

"Nigger, is yuh gone plumb crazy?"

"Aw, Ma—"

"Git outta here! Don yuh talk t me bout no gun! Yuh a fool!"

"Ma, Ah kin buy one fer two dollahs."

"Not ef Ah knows it, yuh ain!"

"But yuh promised me one—"

"Ah don care whut Ah promised! Yuh ain nothing but a boy yit!"

"Ma, ef yuh lemme buy one Ah'll *never* ast yuh fer nothing no mo."

The Man Who Was Almost a Man   423

"Ah tol yuh t git outta here! Yuh ain gonna toucha penny of tha money fer no gun! Thas how come Ah has Mistah Hawkins t pay yo wages t me, cause Ah knows yuh ain got no sense."

"But, Ma, we needa gun. Pa ain got no gun. We needa gun in the house. Yuh kin never tell what might happen."

"Now don yuh try to maka fool outta me, boy! Ef we did hava gun, yuh wouldn't have it!"

He laid the catalogue down and slipped his arm around her waist.

"Aw, Ma, Ah done worked hard alla summer n ain ast yuh fer nothin, is Ah, now?"

"Thas whut yuh spose t do!"

"But Ma, Ah wans a gun. Yuh kin lemme have two dollahs outta mah money. Please, Ma. I kin give it to Pa . . . Please, Ma! Ah loves yuh, Ma."

When she spoke her voice came soft and low.

"Whut yu wan wida gun, Dave? Yuh don need no gun. Yuh'll git in trouble. N ef yo pa jus thought Ah let yuh have money t buy a gun he'd hava fit."

"Ah'll hide it, Ma. It ain but two dollahs."

"Lawd, chil, whut's wrong wid yuh?"

"Ain nothin wrong, Ma. Ahm almos a man now. Ah wans a gun."

"Who gonna sell yuh a gun?"

"Ol Joe at the sto."

"N it don cos but two dollahs?"

"Thas all, Ma. Jus two dollahs. Please, Ma."

She was stacking the plates away; her hands moved slowly, reflectively. Dave kept an anxious silence. Finally, she turned to him.

"Ah'll let yuh git tha gun ef yuh promise me one thing."

"Whut's tha, Ma?"

"Yuh bring it straight back t me, yuh hear? It be fer Pa."

"Yessum! Lemme go now, Ma."

She stooped, turned slightly to one side, raised the hem of her dress, rolled down the top of her stocking, and came up with a slender wad of bills.

"Here," she said. "Lawd knows yuh don need no gun. But yer pa does. Yuh bring it right back t me, yuh hear? Ahma put it up. Now ef yuh don, Ahma have yuh pa lick yuh so hard yuh won fergit it."

"Yessum."

He took the money, ran down the steps, and across the yard.

"Dave! Yuuuuuh Daaaaave!"

He heard, but he was not going to stop now. "Naw, Lawd!"

2

The first movement he made the following morning was to reach under his pillow for the gun. In the gray light of dawn he held it loosely, feeling a sense of power. Could kill a man with a gun like this. Kill anybody, black or white. And if he were holding his gun in his hand, nobody could run over him; they would have to respect him. It was a big gun, with a long barrel and a heavy handle. He raised and lowered it in his hand, marveling at its weight.

He had not come straight home with it as his mother had asked; instead he had stayed out in the fields, holding the weapon in his hand, aiming it now and then at some imaginary foe. But he had not fired it; he had been afraid that his father might hear. Also he was not sure he knew how to fire it.

To avoid surrendering the pistol he had not come into the house until he knew that they were all asleep. When his mother had tiptoed to his bedside late that night and demanded the gun, he had first played possum; then he had told her that the gun was hidden outdoors, that he would bring it to her in the morning. Now he lay turning it slowly in his hands. He broke it, took out the cartridges, felt them, and then put them back.

He slid out of bed, got a long strip of old flannel from a trunk, wrapped the gun in it, and tied it to his naked thigh while it was still loaded. He did not go in to breakfast. Even though it was not yet daylight, he started for Jim Hawkins' plantation. Just as the sun was rising he reached the barns where the mules and plows were kept.

"Hey! That you, Dave?"

He turned. Jim Hawkins stood eying him suspiciously.

"What're yuh doing here so early?"

"Ah didn't know Ah wuz gittin up so early, Mistah Hawkins. Ah wuz fixin t hitch up ol Jenny n take her t the fiels."

"Good. Since you're so early, how about plowing that stretch down by the woods?"

"Suits me, Mistah Hawkins."

"O.K. Go to it!"

He hitched Jenny to a plow and started across the fields. Hot dog! This was just what he wanted. If he could get down by the woods, he could shoot his gun and nobody would hear. He walked behind the plow, hearing the traces creaking, feeling the gun tied tight to his thigh.

When he reached the woods, he plowed two whole rows before he decided to take out the gun. Finally, he stopped, looked in all directions, then untied the gun and held it in his hand. He turned to the mule and smiled.

"Know whut this is, Jenny? Naw, yuh wouldn know! Yuhs jusa ol mule! Anyhow, this is a gun, n it kin shoot, by Gawd!"

He held the gun at arm's length. Whut t hell, Ahma shoot this thing! He looked at Jenny again.

"Lissen here, Jenny! When Ah pull this ol trigger, Ah don wan yuh t run n acka fool now!"

Jenny stood with head down, her short ears pricked straight. Dave walked off about twenty feet, held the gun far out from him at arm's length, and turned his head. Hell, he told himself, Ah ain afraid. The gun felt loose in his fingers; he waved it wildly for a moment. Then he shut his eyes and tightened his forefinger. Bloom! A report half deafened him and he thought his right hand was torn from his arm. He heard Jenny whinnying and galloping over the field, and he found himself on his knees, squeezing his fingers hard between his legs. His hand was numb; he jammed it into his mouth, trying to warm it, trying to stop the pain. The gun lay at his feet. He did not quite know what had happened. He stood up and stared at the gun as though it were a living thing. He gritted his teeth and kicked the gun. Yuh almos broke mah arm! He turned to look for Jenny; she was far over the fields, tossing her head and kicking wildly.

"Hol on there, ol mule!"

When he caught up with her she stood trembling, walling her big white eyes at him. The plow was far away; the traces had broken. Then Dave stopped short, looking, not believing. Jenny was bleeding. Her left side was red and wet with blood. He went closer. Lawd, have mercy! Wondah did Ah shoot this mule? He grabbed for Jenny's mane. She flinched, snorted, whirled, tossing her head.

"Hol on now! Hol on."

Then he saw the hole in Jenny's side, right between the ribs. It was round, wet, red. A crimson stream streaked down the front leg, flowing fast. Good Gawd! Ah wuzn't shootin at tha mule. He felt panic. He knew he had to stop that blood, or Jenny would bleed to death. He had never seen so much blood in all his life. He chased the mule for half a mile, trying to catch her. Finally she stopped, breathing hard, stumpy tail half arched. He caught her mane and led her back to where the plow and gun lay. Then he stooped and grabbed handfuls of damp black earth and tried to plug the bullet hole. Jenny shuddered, whinnied, and broke from him.

"Hol on! Hol on now!"

He tried to plug it again, but blood came anyhow. His fingers were hot and sticky. He rubbed dirt into his palms, trying to dry them. Then again he attempted to plug the bullet hole, but Jenny shied away, kicking her heels high. He stood helpless. He had to do something. He ran at Jenny; she dodged him. He watched a red stream of blood flow down Jenny's leg and form a bright pool at her feet.

"Jenny . . . Jenny," he called weakly.

His lips trembled. She's bleeding t death! He looked in the direction of home, wanting to go back, wanting to get help. But he saw the pistol lying in the damp black clay. He had a queer feeling that if he only did something, this would not be; Jenny would not be there bleeding to death.

When he went to her this time, she did not move. She stood with sleepy, dreamy eyes; and when he touched her she gave a low-pitched whinny and knelt to the ground, her front knees slopping in blood.

"Jenny . . . Jenny. . ." he whispered.

For a long time she held her neck erect; then her head sank, slowly. Her ribs swelled with a mighty heave and she went over.

Dave's stomach felt empty, very empty. He picked up the gun and held it gingerly between his thumb and forefinger. He buried it at the foot of a tree. He took a stick and tried to cover the pool of blood with dirt— but what was the use? There was Jenny lying with her mouth open and her eyes walled and glassy. He could not tell Jim Hawkins he had shot his mule. But he had to tell something. Yeah, Ah'll tell em Jenny started gittin wil n fell on the joint of the plow. . . . But that would hardly happen to a mule. He walked across the field slowly, head down.

3

It was sunset. Two of Jim Hawkins' men were over near the edge of the woods digging a hole in which to bury Jenny. Dave was surrounded by a knot of people, all of whom were looking down at the dead mule.

"I don't see how in the world it happened," said Jim Hawkins for the tenth time.

The crowd parted and Dave's mother, father, and small brother pushed into the center.

"Where Dave?" his mother called.

"There he is," said Jim Hawkins.

His mother grabbed him.

"Whut happened, Dave? Whut yuh done?"

"Nothin."

"C mon, boy, talk," his father said.

Dave took a deep breath and told the story he knew nobody believed.

"Waal," he drawled. "Ah brung ol Jenny down here sos Ah could do mah plowin. Ah plowed bout two rows, just like yuh see." He stopped and pointed at the long rows of up-turned earth. "Then somethin musta been wrong wid ol Jenny. She wouldn ack right a-tall. She started snortin n kickin her heels. Ah tried t hol her, but she pulled erway, rearin n goin in. Then when the point of the plow was stickin up in the air, she swung erroun n twisted herself back on it . . . She stuck herself n started t bleed. N fo Ah could do anything, she wuz dead."

"Did you ever hear of anything like that in all your life?" asked Jim Hawkins.

There were white and black standing in the crowd. They murmured. Dave's mother came close to him and looked hard into his face. "Tell the truth, Dave," she said.

"Looks like a bullet hole to me," said one man.

"Dave, whut yuh do wid the gun?" his mother asked.

The crowd surged in, looking at him. He jammed his hands into his pockets, shook his head slowly from left to right, and backed away. His eyes were wide and painful.

"Did he hava gun?" asked Jim Hawkins.

"By Gawd, Ah tol yuh tha wuz a gun wound," said a man, slapping his thigh.

His father caught his shoulders and shook him till his teeth rattled.

"Tell what happened, yuh rascal! Tell whut . . ."

Dave looked at Jenny's stiff legs and began to cry.

"Whut yuh do wid tha gun?" his mother asked.

"Whut wuz he doin wida gun?" his father asked.

"Come on and tell the truth," said Hawkins. "Ain't nobody going to hurt you . . ."

His mother crowded close to him.

"Did yuh shoot tha mule, Dave?"

Dave cried, seeing blurred white and black faces.

"Ahh ddinn gggo tt sshooot hher . . . Ah ssswear ffo Gawd Ahh ddin . . . Ah wuz a-tryin t sssee ef the old gggun would sshoot—"

"Where yuh git the gun from?" his father asked.

"Ah got it from Joe, at the sto."

"Where yuh git the money?"

"Ma give it t me."

"He kept worryin me, Bob. Ah had t. Ah tol im t bring the gun right back t me . . . It was fer yuh, the gun."

"But how yuh happen to shoot that mule?" asked Jim Hawkins.

"Ah wuzn shootin at the mule, Mistah Hawkins. The gun jumped when Ah pulled the trigger . . . N fo Ah knowed anythin Jenny was there a-bleedin."

Somebody in the crowd laughed. Jim Hawkins walked close to Dave and looked into his face.

"Well, looks like you have bought you a mule, Dave."

"Ah swear fo Gawd, Ah didn go t kill the mule, Mistah Hawkins!"

"But you killed her!"

All the crowd was laughing now. They stood on tiptoe and poked heads over one another's shoulders.

"Well, boy, looks like yuh done bought a dead mule! Hahaha!"

"Ain tha ershame."

"Hohohohoho."

Dave stood, head down, twisting his feet in the dirt.

"Well, you needn't worry about it, Bob," said Jim Hawkins to Dave's father. "Just let the boy keep on working and pay me two dollars a month."

"Whut yuh wan fer yo mule, Mistah Hawkins?"

Jim Hawkins screwed up his eyes.

"Fifty dollars."

"Whut yuh do wid tha gun?" Dave's father demanded.

Dave said nothing.

"Yuh wan me t take a tree n beat yuh till yuh talk!"

The Man Who Was Almost a Man   427

"Nawsuh!"

"Whut yuh do wid it?"

"Ah throwed it erway."

"Where?"

"Ah . . . Ah throwed it in the creek."

"Waal, c mon home. N firs thing in the mawnin git to tha creek n fin tha gun."

"Yessuh."

"Whut yuh pay fer it?"

"Two dollahs."

"Take tha gun n git yo money back n carry it t Mistah Hawkins, yuh hear? N don fergit Ahma lam you black bottom good fer this! Now march yosef on home, suh!"

Dave turned and walked slowly. He heard people laughing. Dave glared, his eyes welling with tears. Hot anger bubbled in him. Then he swallowed and stumbled on.

That night Dave did not sleep. He was glad that he had gotten out of killing the mule so easily, but he was hurt. Something hot seemed to turn over inside him each time he remembered how they had laughed. He tossed on his bed, feeling his hard pillow. N Pa says he's gonna beat me . . . He remembered other beatings, and his back quivered. Naw, naw, Ah sho don wan im t beat me tha way no mo. Dam em all! Nobody ever gave him anything. All he did was work. They treat me like a mule, n then they beat me. He gritted his teeth. N Ma had t tell on me.

Well, if he had to, he would take old man Hawkins that two dollars. But that meant selling the gun. And he wanted to keep that gun. Fifty dollars for a dead mule.

He turned over, thinking how he had fired the gun. He had an itch to fire it again. Ef other men kin shoota gun, by Gawd, Ah kin! He was still, listening. Mebbe they all sleepin now. The house was still. He heard the soft breathing of his brother. Yes, now!

He would go down and get that gun and see if he could fire it! He eased out of bed and slipped into overalls.

The moon was bright. He ran almost all the way to the edge of the woods. He stumbled over the ground, looking for the spot where he had buried the gun. Yeah, here it is. Like a hungry dog scratching for a bone, he pawed it up. He puffed his black cheeks and blew dirt from the trigger and barrel. He broke it and found four cartridges unshot. He looked around; the fields were filled with silence and moonlight. He clutched the gun stiff and hard in his fingers. But, as soon as he wanted to pull the trigger, he shut his eyes and turned his head. Naw, Ah can't shoot wid mah eyes closed n mah head turned. With effort he held his eyes open; then he squeezed. *Blooooom!* He was stiff, not breathing. The gun was still in his hands. Dammit, he'd done it! He fired again. *Blooooom!* He smiled. *Blooooom! Blooooom! Click, click.* There! It was empty. If anybody could shoot a gun, he could. He put the gun into his hip pocket and started across the fields.

When he reached the top of a ridge he stood straight and proud in the moonlight, looking at Jim Hawkins' big white house, feeling the gun sagging in his pocket. Lawd, ef Ah had just one mo bullet Ah'd taka shot at tha house. Ah'd like t scare ol man Hawkins jusa little . . . Jusa enough t let im know Dave Saunders is a man.

To his left the road curved, running to the tracks of the Illinois Central. He jerked his head, listening. From far off came a faint *hoooof-hoooof; hoooof-hoooof; hoooof-hoooof.* . . . He stood rigid. Two dollahs a mont. Les see now . . . Tha means it'll take bout two years. Shucks! Ah'll be dam!

He started down the road, toward the

tracks. Yeah, here she comes! He stood beside the track and held himself stiffly. Here she comes, erroun the ben . . . C mon, yuh slow poke! C mon! He had his hand on his gun; something quivered in his stomach. Then the train thundered past, the gray and brown box cars rumbling and clinking. He gripped the gun tightly; then he jerked his hand out of his pocket. Ah betcha Bill wouldn't do it! Ah betcha . . . The cars slid past, steel grinding upon steel. Ahm ridin yuh ternight, so hep me Gawd! He was hot all over. He hesitated just a moment; then he grabbed, pulled atop of a car, and lay flat. He felt his pocket; the gun was still there. Ahead the long rails were glinting in the moonlight, stretching away, away to somewhere, somewhere where he could be a man . . .

Responding to the Selection

The Man Who Was Almost a Man by Richard Wright

Identifying Facts

1. Why does Dave stop at Joe's store on his way home?
2. Who is Jim Hawkins?
3. Why does Dave take the gun with him when he goes to work in the morning?
4. How does Dave kill the mule?
5. Where does he bury the gun?

Interpreting Meanings

1. What can you infer has happened to Dave before the beginning of the story? Refer to details in the first paragraph that tell you.
2. Why is Dave eager to own a gun?
3. Dave's mother says that Dave has no sense. Do the events in the story show that she is right?
4. How does Dave try to explain the accident?
5. How is he publicly humiliated?
6. Why does Dave decide to run away? Is this decision in keeping with his character?
7. Throughout the story, Dave refers to himself as "almost a man." Has he achieved manhood by the end of the story? Explain your answer.

Literary Elements

Understanding Point of View

We know more about Dave than we know about any other character in the story. Because the story is told from his point of view, we know his thoughts and feelings about the things that happen. We understand his resentments, his fears, his lack of confidence, his humiliation, and his restlessness. We also see things that he is not aware of: his immaturity, his lack of responsibility, and his false bravery.

What does the story gain from having Dave reveal himself through his own words? Do you think the story would have been as effective if Wright had chosen to report the conversations in standard English?

Creative Writing

Imagining a Sequel

At the end of Wright's story, Dave gets on a train that will take him "somewhere where he could be a man." What do you imagine will happen to Dave? Consider all the evidence you have about him from relationships with his parents, his employer, and other field hands. Has he learned anything from the accident? Continue Dave's story in a sequel.

About the Author
Chester Himes (1909–1984)

 Chester Himes was born in Jefferson City, Missouri. He grew up in the South and Midwest. After graduating from high school in Cleveland, Ohio, he entered Ohio State University. When he was expelled for disciplinary reasons, he drifted into a life of crime. He was arrested for armed robbery and sent to Ohio State Penitentiary. In prison he witnessed a catastrophic fire, riots, and beatings. He began to write stories about these experiences, which were accepted for publication in several magazines.

After he was paroled, in 1936, Himes worked for the Federal Writers' Project. He left for the West Coast in 1941. He hoped to find work in the government shipyards in California but met with frustration and discrimination in employment practices. He wrote about these experiences in his first two novels, *If He Hollers Let Him Go* (1945) and *The Lonely Crusade* (1947). He then wrote several autobiographical novels, including *Cast the First Stone* (1952), thought by some readers to be a classic prison novel.

These early novels did not sell well. Discouraged, Himes decided to leave for Europe in 1953. He was living in Paris, penniless and desperate, when he was approached by a French publisher who wanted him to write a detective novel set in Harlem. The book he wrote became a great success and launched his "Harlem Domestic" series. The novels in this series deal with the adventures of two black detectives, "Coffin" Ed Johnson and "Grave Digger" Jones. Out of this series

The Schomburg Center for Research in Black Culture/New York Public Library

came *Cotton Comes to Harlem* (1965), which was produced as a film in 1970.

Some readers have objected to these novels because of their violence and their negative portrayal of inner city life. Others feel that these detective novels contain some of Himes's best work.

Himes often resembles Wright in his intense anger at racial oppression. Himes believed that African Americans are too often denied an acceptable place in American society. "Black Laughter," the story included here, portrays a pair of black Americans trying to fit into the white world and to enjoy experiences that were once closed to them.

Chester Himes   431

Before You Read

Black Laughter

Using What You Know _____

Almost everyone at some time feels uncomfortable or out of place in unfamiliar surroundings or in a group of strangers. How do people act when they feel uneasy? Do all people act the same way?

Literary Focus: Internal Conflict _____

A **conflict** is a struggle between opposing forces. In literature, conflict may take several forms. Conflicts in which individuals struggle against something outside themselves are known as **external conflicts**. Conflict may occur between two or more characters, between a character and nature, or between a character and society. When a conflict takes place within a character's mind, it is called **internal conflict**.

There may be more than one conflict in a narrative. A story usually ends when its main conflict is resolved. In some stories, however, the conflict is not resolved and there is no definite conclusion.

Setting a Purpose _____

As you read the story, ask yourself what the title refers to. Does it give you a clue to the main character's conflict?

Black Laughter

Chester Himes

F. Roy Kemp

The dimly lit stairway was encased in mirrors. They saw several reflections of themselves at the same time. Their dark brown faces looked back in the gloom. Their expressions were serious and unsmiling, as if they were going to view the body of a friend. Bubber climbed jerkily. But the girl moved with a sinuous grace. Her body sang a melody but her face was carved in cold disdain. A white couple coming down the stairway looked at them and smiled, but at sight of their dark sullen scowls hurriedly looked away.

At the top an attendant met them. "Check your coat, sir."

Both immediately began taking off their coats.

"Over this way, please," the atttendant said.

Dumbly they followed him to the checkroom. The checkroom girl looked startled when Bubber handed over his girl friend's coat. "Oh, you'd better keep yours," she said to the girl. The girl snatched her coat and gave the checkroom girl a cold, defiant look.

"Come on," Bubber whispered tensely, pulling her toward the entrance to the dining room.

The floor show had not started and couples were on the dance floor. The girl shook her shoulders in time with the music but her face did not relax. Bubber felt a sudden rush of nervous energy, a wild, crazy desire to laugh; he didn't know why.

"Two?" The headwaiter was suddenly before them, smiling mechanically.

Bubber slanted him a look, then suddenly he grinned, a white blossom of teeth in his smooth black face. "You kiddin'?"

The headwaiter led them down an aisle. At the back they crossed over and turned again at the far side, moving down the far aisle until they came to a vacant table in the corner behind one of the mirrored pillars. The headwaiter pulled out the table so they could squeeze into the wall seats and a waiter came and gave them menus. Bubber began tightening inside. He didn't like the table; he didn't want to sit there. He wanted to protest but he didn't want to start any trouble. He knew if he started any trouble and the man made him angry he'd get up and hit him. He didn't want to do that. He wouldn't look up. In silence he stared down at the menu, trying to control the wild, crazy frustration which surged through him. The waiter poised impatiently with pencil and pad.

"I should like to have a steak," the girl said. Her voice, usually softly melodic, was stilted to a sharpness now.

Bubber noticed the white people at the next table cast her a furtive look. "I'm gonna have fried chicken," he said defiantly.

"Anything to drink?" the waiter asked.

"I think I should like a pink lady," she said.

"Whiskey for me," Bubber said.

"Any special kind of whiskey?"

"Yeah, good whiskey." Abruptly he grinned again. The waiter looked startled, then grinned in return.

When the waiter left they tried to see the dancers. Half of the dance floor was obscured by the side wall of the pantry, the remainder by the mirrored pillar.

"Less dance," he said.

She turned to the white couple at the table beside her and said coldly, "Excuse me."

He lifted the table out into the aisle and they arose and he lifted it back. On the dance floor they did intricate steps to the solid beat of the Negro orchestra, looking away from each other with glazed eyes and frozen faces. When the dance ended they turned to go back. They had not said a word to each other.

"Excuse me," she said to the white couple again.

He lifted out the table; they sat down; he lifted it back. The lights were dimmed for the floor show as the waiter served their drinks. Neither of them could see anything at all of what took place in the show. Suddenly they heard a staccato voice. It came so quickly they did not understand the joke. A wave of laughter rolled over them. He gave a loud burst of laughter. A split second afterward she let out a brittle giggle. The laughter of the others had ceased and the staccato voice had begun again. Heads turned to look at them. He felt ashamed, embarrassed.

"Don't laugh so loud," she whispered tensely.

"Who laughing loud?"

"Hush up and listen to the man."

The next time the audience laughed he remained silent. Her laughter trilled out in time with the others but lasted an instant too long. He turned to look at her. She picked up her drink and sipped it.

Now they could hear the sound of tap dancing. He leaned one way then another trying to see the floor.

"Quit shoving me 'gainst these folks," she said in a tense whisper.

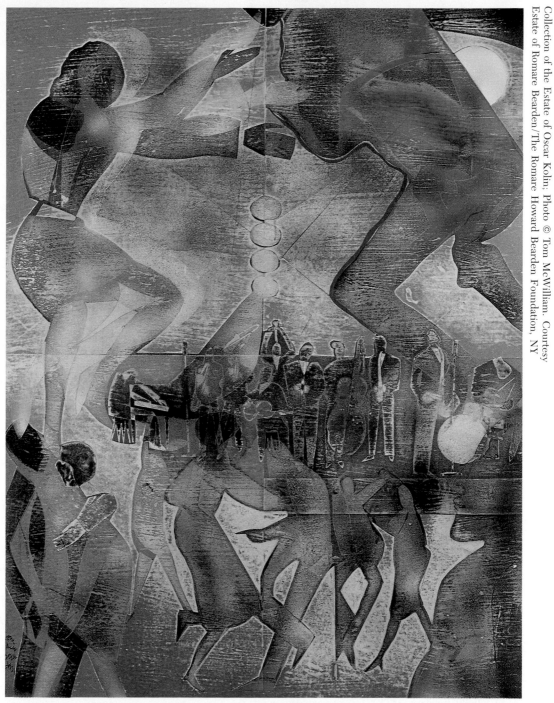

At the Savoy, *oil by Romare Bearden, from the* Of the Blues *series.*

Bill "Bojangles" Robinson and chorus, c. 1936.

"Look at that ol' boy dancin'," he said loudly.

She gave him a push with her hip. Aloud she replied, "He surely can dance."

"He mos' good as ol' Bill[1] was," he said.

"He's all right but he not that good," she said.

The tap dancing ended and the staccato voice introduced two comedians. Now the laughter came in sharp bursts and rolling waves. They tried to time their laughter with that of the others. But first he laughed too long; then she laughed too late. The jokes had little point without sight of the comedi-ans and more often than not the words were drowned in the laughter. Bubber felt a sudden hatred for himself for having to pretend that he was amused. He hated her also; he knew that she was also pretending. He felt cringing and cowardly. The desire to be angry became stifling within him, but there was no one to be angry with but himself.

When the girl laughed again he turned on her furiously, "What you laughin' at?"

She looked at him in surprise. "At what he said; it was funny." She didn't know that he had stopped pretending; she didn't know what had happened to him.

"Wan't nobody else laughin'," he muttered.

"They got through laughin'."

---

1. **ol' Bill:** Bill Robinson (1878–1949), a famous African American tap dancer, often called "Bojangles." He danced in nightclubs, on the stage, and in motion pictures.

"Then what you laughin' for after ev'ybody else done got through?"

"I laughs when I want to laugh."

"Shhh—" he said.

The waiter approached with their order. During the remainder of the floor show they ate their dinner in silence. It was dark in the corner and they could barely see what they ate. It didn't make much difference anyway, the food was unseasoned and tasteless. They didn't discover the salt and pepper and condiments behind the bread basket until they had finished eating. The waiter had gone off and they could not summon him. The meal was wasted.

Just as they were finished the floor show ended and the lights were raised. The bus boy came over and cleared the table. The waiter approached. He gave Bubber a broad, friendly grin.

"Would you like dessert?"

Bubber looked sullen. He didn't return the waiter's grin. "Naw," he said.

"I don't think I do either," the girl said.

"It's free," the waiter said confidentially, leaning forward. "It goes with the meal."

"Naw, I don't want nothin'," Bubber maintained.

The waiter looked at the girl again. She looked away with cold disdain. The waiter motioned for the bus boy to fill their water glasses and went off to add up the check.

Next to them the couple was preparing to leave. Bubber looked around. The dining room was emptying rapidly. He made up his mind to get a better table and stay through the next show. Beckoning to the waiter, he got set to ask for another table. He was grinning. But just before he got out the words the waiter presented him with the check. Anger rushed over him in a blinding wave. *Hadn' seen nuthin'—food wan't no good— now the waiter was throwin' them out!* he thought. He had to hold himself in hard.

"Like the show?" the waiter asked congenially.

Bubber swallowed. "Fine," he said loudly. "Great show, man." His voice sounded so jubilant the waiter looked suddenly happy.

Bubber tipped him two dollars and felt better than he had since his arrival. As he and the girl left, going down the stairway and standing outside on the sidewalk, waiting for a taxi, they kept talking about what a funny show it was. They laughed so loudly that people turned to look at them.

Responding to the Selection

Black Laughter by Chester Himes

Identifying Facts

1. Why is Bubber unhappy with his table in the nightclub?
2. What entertainment does the nightclub offer?
3. Why does Bubber want to stay through the next show?
4. How does he feel when the waiter gives him the bill?

Literary Elements

Understanding Conflict

The author focuses on Bubber's **conflict** by drawing contrasts between his inner feelings and outward behavior. Reread the passage in which Bubber and his girlfriend are seated at a corner table in the nightclub. How are Bubber's feelings described? How does he control himself? Locate passages that show Bubber's **internal conflict**. What **external conflicts** are there in the story?

Interpreting Meanings

1. What can you infer about the feelings of Bubber and his girlfriend from the opening paragraph of the story? Why do you suppose that their expressions are "serious and unsmiling"?
2. Why do you think Bubber grins and smiles even though he feels angry and frustrated?
3. Why are the characters trying so hard to enjoy themselves?
4. What do you think the title of the story means? How is the laughter of the couple different from the laughter of other people in the club?
5. Why does Bubber feel better as he gets ready to leave the club?
6. Recall Paul Laurence Dunbar's poem "We Wear the Mask" (page 251). Are the two people in this story wearing a kind of mask? Explain your answer.

Language and Vocabulary

Getting Meaning from Context

The **context** of a word is the sentence or paragraph in which the word appears. If you were not familiar with the verb *poise*, you could use clues in this sentence to get its meaning:

> The waiter *poised* impatiently with pencil and pad.

The context suggests that the waiter is standing still, waiting to take the couple's order. The verb *poise* here means "to hover" or "to remain in a particular place, waiting to do something."

Use context clues to figure out the meanings of the italicized words in these sentences from the story. Check your answers in the Glossary or in a dictionary.

1. "Bubber climbed jerkily. But the girl moved with a *sinuous* grace."

2. "Bubber noticed the white people at the next table cast her a *furtive* look."
3. "The waiter had gone off and they could not *summon* him."
4. "She looked away with cold *disdain*."
5. "His voice sounded so *jubilant* the waiter looked suddenly happy."

Narrative Writing

Writing from a Different Point of View

Imagine that you are sitting at a table in the nightclub, where you can watch Bubber and his girlfriend and overhear what they are saying. Tell what you observe. Remember that as an outside observer you cannot read the minds of the characters. You can, however, interpret their thoughts and feelings from what they do, what they say, and how they act.

Speaking and Listening

Understanding Nonverbal Communication

People communicate not only through words but also through body language. Facial expressions, gestures, and movements are all forms of **nonverbal communication**. Discuss the story from the point of view of nonverbal elements. How are the attitudes and emotions of the characters conveyed without words?

About the Author
Margaret Walker (1915–1998)

Carl Van Vechten, Henry W. and Albert A. Berg Collection/New York Public Library. Permission granted by the Estate of Carl Van Vechten, Joseph Solomon, Executor

 Margaret Walker was born in Birmingham, Alabama. In the introduction to *Jubilee,* her novel, she says that she grew up in a "talking" family. The history of her people became an important part of her life at an early age.

Walker attended Northwestern University, in Evanston, Illinois. After graduation, in 1937, she went to Chicago, where she worked for the Federal Writers' Project. She became part of the literary circle that included Richard Wright. After four years, she left for the University of Iowa to pursue graduate study. The poems in her first volume of poetry, *For My People* (1942), were her master's thesis.

For My People won the Yale Younger Poets Series Award. The title poem had originally appeared in *Poetry* magazine in 1937 and had created a sensation. No African American writer had yet produced poetry like this. It was new not only in its expression of racial consciousness and protest, but also in its style. Eugenia Collier has called "For My People" Walker's "signature poem." It is the work most often associated with her name. "It speaks to us, in our own words and rhythms, of our history, and it radiates the promise of our future."

Jubilee, a historical novel published in 1966, tells the story of a slave family and is based on the stories Walker first heard told by her maternal grandmother. She did extensive research while she was raising a family, teaching full time, and taking a Ph.D. at the University of Iowa.

Walker was a social worker, a reporter, and a magazine editor. She taught at many colleges and from 1968 until her retirement in 1979 was the director of the Institute for the Study of the History, Life, and Culture of Black People at Jackson State University, Jackson, Mississippi.

Before You Read

For My People

Using What You Know

Margaret Walker once said, "Writers should not write exclusively for black or white audiences, but most inclusively. After all, it is the business of all writers to write about the human condition, and all humanity must be involved in both the writing and the reading."

Choose some selections you have read that illustrate this idea of **universality** in literature. For example, why would Winston Churchill have chosen to read Claude McKay's sonnet "If We Must Die" (page 299) during the war years, when England faced its greatest crisis? Why is McKay's poem relevant to all people?

Literary Focus: The Catalog

In this textbook, you have seen examples of **free verse,** poetry that does not use regular rhyme or fixed line length and rhythm (see page 16). Free verse tends to be more conversational than traditional verse forms. Instead of rhyme and fixed meter, free verse uses **repetition, balance, parallelism,** and other techniques to achieve subtle effects.

One technique often used in free verse is that of the **catalog,** a long list of things, peoples, or events. Poets use catalogs to suggest largeness and inclusiveness. Note how Margaret Walker uses catalogs in her poem.

Setting a Purpose

As you read, ask whether this poem, which is a celebration of African American people, can speak to all people, "all the adams and eves."

Shel Hershorn/Black Star

For My People

Margaret Walker

For my people everywhere singing their slave songs repeatedly:
    their dirges and their ditties and their blues and jubilees,
    praying their prayers nightly to an unknown god, bending
    their knees humbly to an unseen power;

For my people lending their strength to the years, to the gone   5
    years and the now years and the maybe years, washing ironing
    cooking scrubbing sewing mending hoeing plowing digging
    planting pruning patching dragging along never gaining never
    reaping never knowing and never understanding;

For my playmates in the clay and dust and sand of Alabama   10
    backyards playing baptizing and preaching and doctor and jail
    and soldier and school and mama and cooking and playhouse
    and concert and store and hair and Miss Choomby and
    company;

For the cramped bewildered years we went to school to   15
    learn to know the reasons why and the answers to and the
    people who and the places where and the days when, in
    memory of the bitter hours when we discovered we were
    black and poor and small and different and nobody cared and
    nobody wondered and nobody understood;   20

For the boys and girls who grew in spite of these things to be
man and woman, to laugh and dance and sing and play and
drink their wine and religion and success, to marry their
playmates and bear children and then die of consumption and
anemia and lynching;   25

For my people thronging 47th Street in Chicago and Lenox
Avenue in New York and Rampart Street in New Orleans, lost
disinherited dispossessed and happy people filling the cabarets
and taverns and other people's pockets needing bread and
shoes and milk and land and money and something—   30
something all our own;

For my people walking blindly spreading joy, losing time being
lazy, sleeping when hungry, shouting when burdened,
drinking when hopeless, tied and shackled and tangled among
ourselves by the unseen creatures who tower over us   35
omnisciently and laugh;

For my people blundering and groping and floundering in the
dark of churches and schools and clubs and societies,
associations and councils and committees and conventions,
distressed and disturbed and deceived and devoured by   40
money-hungry glory-craving leeches, preyed on by facile
force of state and fad and novelty, by false prophet and holy
believer;

For my people standing staring trying to fashion a better way
from confusion, from hypocrisy and misunderstanding, trying   45
to fashion a world that will hold all the people, all the faces, all
the adams and eves° and their countless generations;

47. adams and eves: Adam
and Eve were the first man
and woman (Genesis 2:7,
3:20). Walker here uses their
names for a new race of
people.

Let a new earth rise. Let another world be born. Let a bloody
peace be written in the sky. Let a second generation full of
courage issue forth; let a people loving freedom come to   50
growth. Let a beauty full of healing and a strength of final
clenching be the pulsing in our spirits and our blood. Let the
martial songs be written, let the dirges disappear. Let a race
of men now rise and take control.

Responding to the Poem

For My People by Margaret Walker

Interpreting Meanings

1. "For My People" is divided into ten free verse stanzas. How do the first nine stanzas give an overview of African American experience? Which stanzas deal with Southern rural experiences? with urban experiences?
2. In the second stanza, the poet catalogs the burdens of her people. Why do you think she runs these tasks together without commas to separate them?
3. In stanzas 3–5, Walker follows the lives of children as they grow to adulthood. What comment does she make on their schooling? What truth do the children realize about themselves? How are their lives as adults cut short?
4. How does the poet use **alliteration** for emphasis in stanza 8?
5. How does the final stanza mark a new beginning?

Literary Elements

Recognizing Techniques of Free Verse

Instead of regular rhyme and rhythm, **free verse** makes use of other techniques that provide order and structure. Margaret Walker uses free verse paragraphs as stanzas in her poem.

Walker uses **parallelism** and **alliteration** as unifying elements. Explain the effect of parallelism in these phrases:

"the gone years and the now years and the maybe years" (lines 5–6)
"never gaining never reaping never knowing and never understanding" (lines 8–9)
"and nobody cared and nobody wondered and nobody understood" (lines 19–20)

Which words are linked through alliteration in the opening stanza?

Language and Vocabulary

Differentiating Types of Songs

In the first stanza of "For My People," Margaret Walker lists different kinds of songs, including *dirges, ditties, blues,* and *jubilees.* Check the meaning of each of these words in a dictionary.

Speaking and Listening

Interpreting a Poem

Richard K. Barksdale, a scholar, has discussed "For My People" as oral poetry: "In reading it aloud, one must be able to breathe and pause, pause and breathe preacher-style. . . . This is the kind of verbal music found in a well-delivered down-home folk sermon."

Prepare a reading of the poem. How will you handle the lengthy catalogs? If this poem is planned for choral presentation, which voices will read the different stanzas?

Before You Read

Lineage; Childhood

Using What You Know _____

Several different words are used for one's ancestry. For example, what is a *family tree*? What is meant by the word *pedigree*? How does that word differ from *lineage*? You might consult a dictionary for the precise meanings of these words. Then consider why Margaret Walker used one of these words as the title of her poem.

Literary Focus: Diction _____

The term **diction** refers to a writer's choice of words. A writer's diction can be formal or informal. In choosing the "right words," writers must think of their subject and their audience.

The following poems contain no words or phrases that readers would consider formal or abstract. Note the effectiveness of simple, everyday language such as "soap and onions and wet clay" and "the swing of dinner buckets in their hands."

Setting a Purpose _____

As you read, note that the poet has chosen words with rich **connotations,** or associations. Which phrases do you find particularly moving?

Lineage

Margaret Walker

My grandmothers were strong.
They followed plows and bent to toil.
They moved through fields sowing seed.
They touched earth and grain grew.
They were full of sturdiness and singing.   5
My grandmothers were strong.

My grandmothers are full of memories
Smelling of soap and onions and wet clay
With veins rolling roughly over quick hands
They have many clean words to say.   10
My grandmothers were strong.
Why am I not as they?

Harriet Tubman, *painting by Jacob Law-rence, series #7.*
Hampton University Museum, Hampton, Virginia

Childhood

Margaret Walker

When I was a child I knew red miners
dressed raggedly and wearing carbide lamps.
I saw them come down red hills to their camps
dyed with red dust from old Ishkooda mines.
Night after night I met them on the roads,   5
or on the streets in town I caught their glance;
the swing of dinner buckets in their hands,
and grumbling undermining all their words.

I also lived in low cotton country
where moonlight hovered over ripe haystacks,   10
or stumps of trees, and croppers' rotting shacks
with famine, terror, flood, and plague near by;
where sentiment and hatred still held sway
and only bitter land was washed away.

Responding to the Selections

Lineage; Childhood by Margaret Walker

Interpreting Meanings

Lineage

1. What qualities does Walker admire in her ancestors?
2. Where is the opening line repeated? What idea is emphasized by this repetition?

Childhood

1. What images does the speaker remember vividly?
2. What contrast is intended between "ripe haystacks" and "croppers' rotting shacks"?
3. What does the last line imply?
4. Compare the **tone** of this poem with that of "Strange Legacies" (page 391). What difference do you find?
5. A **slant rhyme** or **imperfect rhyme** is a rhyme that is not quite exact. The words *glance* and *hands* have the sound **an** in common, but the final consonant sounds are different. Which rhymes in the poem are imperfect?

Writing a Character Analysis

A writer develops a character through **direct** and **indirect methods of characterization**:

1. by giving a physical description of the character
2. by commenting directly on the character
3. by showing the character's actions and speech
4. by revealing the character's thoughts
5. by telling what others think of the character

When you analyze a character in a literary work, you draw on the most significant details of characterization in order to reach conclusions about a specific figure. You also make judgments about the writer's development of the character. For example, one of the things you must determine is if the character is **believable**. A character's actions have to be consistent. Just as a real person does not change without cause, a character who is depicted as cruel and stingy cannot suddenly become kind and generous. The writer has to establish **motivation** for a character's behavior so that there is a clear **cause-and-effect** relationship between what happens to the character and what the character does.

Prewriting Strategies

1. Gather ideas for your character analysis and group your details. The following diagram might be used to analyze the character of Dave in "The Man Who Was Almost a Man" (page 420):

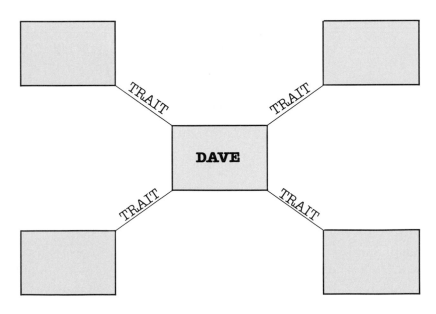

2. In each box, list one of the principal **traits** revealed through some method of characterization, such as description, commentary, actions, thoughts, dialogue, or other characters' reactions. For example, if you were to choose *immaturity* as one of Dave's traits, what supporting evidence could you cite?
3. Using the information in your diagram, write a **thesis statement** that sums up your idea of the character.

Thesis Statement _____

Writing a First Draft

1. In your first paragraph, identify the character, give the title and author of the selection, and include your thesis statement.
2. In succeeding paragraphs, develop your thesis statement. Support your thesis with details you have gathered in your analysis of the character.
3. In your concluding paragraph, summarize your ideas and give your own response to the character. For example, what is your impression of Dave? What do you think will happen to him?

Evaluating and Revising

1. Have you included the title and author?
2. Have you included a thesis statement?
3. Have you cited enough supporting evidence? Have you used direct quotations as part of your evidence?
4. Have you summed up your idea of the character?

Writing a Final Draft

Ask a classmate to check your revision for accuracy and then prepare a final copy. Proofread carefully.

WRITER'S
WORKSHOP 2

Interpretation
(Expository
Writing)

Writing a Character Analysis   449

►I. Interpreting New Material

Ann Petry, February 6, 1946.
Wide World Photos

Ann Petry (1908–1997) was born in Old Saybrook, Connecticut, and worked as a pharmacist in her family's drugstore before moving to New York City and embarking on a literary career. She wrote novels, short stories, children's books, and biographies. The following selection is from her best-known book, *The Street* (1946). The novel, which is set in New York City, has been called an example of "classic American realism."

A. Read the selection carefully before answering the questions.

from *The Street*

Ann Petry

There was a cold November wind blowing through 116th Street. It rattled the tops of garbage cans, sucked window shades out through the top of opened windows and set them flapping back against the windows; and it drove most of the people off the street in the block between Seventh and Eighth Avenues except for a few hurried pedestrians who bent double in an effort to offer the least possible exposed surface to its violent assault.

It found every scrap of paper along the street—theater throwaways, announcements of dances and lodge meetings, the heavy waxed paper that loaves of bread had been wrapped in, the thinner waxed paper that had enclosed sandwiches, old envelopes, newspapers. Fingering its way along the curb, the wind set the bits of paper to dancing high in the air, so that a barrage of paper swirled into the faces of the people on the street. It even took time to rush into doorways and areaways and find chicken bones and pork-chop bones and pushed them along the curb.

It did everything it could to discourage the people walking along the street. It found all the dirt and dust and grime on the sidewalk and lifted it up so that the dirt got into their noses, making it difficult to breathe; the dust got into their eyes and blinded them; and the grit stung their skins. It wrapped newspaper around their feet entangling them until the people cursed deep in their throats, stamped their feet, kicked at the paper. The wind blew it back again and again until they were forced to stoop and dislodge the paper with their hands. And then the wind grabbed their hats, pried their scarves from around their necks, stuck its fingers inside their coat collars, blew their coats away from their bodies.

1. What details does Petry use to create a vivid picture of the setting in these opening paragraphs?

2. **Personification,** as you have seen, is a literary device that assigns human characteristics to some inanimate thing. How does Petry give the wind a malevolent, or vicious, character?

3. What impression do you get of the neighborhood from this excerpt?

B. **Write a brief essay analyzing Petry's use of language in this passage. How does she create a realistic urban setting? Take into consideration her vivid images and figurative language.**

▶▶II. For Discussion

The unit introduction states that "writers in the 1930s tended to use literature as a means of social protest." Consider several selections you have read in this unit. How do they call attention to the problems facing African Americans during this time?

▶▶▶III. For Writing

How do the authors represented in this unit emphasize characteristics of dignity, courage, and determination as qualities of black Americans? Choose two or more selections that deal with heroic or admirable characters. Write a brief essay responding to the question. Cite specific evidence from the selections.

WRITER'S
WORKSHOP 2

Interpretation
(Expository
Writing)

452

Contemporary African American Literature

INTRODUCTION BY **Arnold Rampersad**

Princeton University

The Changing Face of African American Literature

The decade of the 1930s was one of the most troubled periods in American history. Following the crash of Wall Street in October 1929, the national economy gradually slid into the Great Depression, which lasted throughout the thirties. In this time of widespread unemployment and poverty, one casualty was certainly the outstanding African American cultural movement of the 1920s, the Harlem Renaissance. The movement withered with the dramatic decline of money available to support the young writers, artists, and musicians who were at its heart. Although many of these creative figures continued to produce works of art, their mood was far less celebratory and far less optimistic about the future of African Americans within the nation as a whole.

Out of these difficult circumstances came the appearance in 1940 of Richard Wright's astonishing novel *Native Son.* A main selection of the influential Book-of-the-Month Club, which virtually guaranteed the widest sales of any book by a black author in the history of publishing, *Native Son* had a dramatic impact. According to one important literary critic, the nation was changed "forever." *Native Son* is the story of a young black man, Bigger Thomas, made violent and unfeeling by the harshness of poverty

Challenge, collage by Loïs Mailou Jones, 1969. Hirshhorn Museum and Sculpture Garden, Smithsonian Institution, Museum Purchase, 1977. Photograph by Lee Stalsworth

and racism in his community in Chicago. Hired as a chauffeur by a wealthy white family, he soon kills his employer's daughter and then his girlfriend. Eventually, Bigger is sentenced to death. In acknowledging responsibility for his acts of violence, however, he comes face to face for the first time with the most fundamental questions concerning his dignity and humanity, as well as his identity as a black man in America.

In 1940, *Native Son* tore away some of the veils that had obscured many important truths about racism in the United States. The novel probed the dehumanizing effect of racism on blacks and whites alike. It exposed the hypocrisy of many whites who pretended to be interested in the welfare of blacks, and the timidity or cowardice of many blacks who offered themselves as leaders of their race. It depicted the hatred of blacks by many whites, and the hatred of whites by many blacks. The novel also illuminated in a significant way the underlying importance of economic conditions to American racism. By his harshly realistic exploration of these and other issues, Richard Wright changed the face of African American literature and emerged as the most important writer of his age.

New Economic and Social Opportunities

Ironically in light of its emphasis on poverty and oppression, *Native Son* appeared during World War II (1939–1945), which not only brought an end to the economic depression but also saw an increase in economic and social opportunities for blacks. The mighty industrial effort required by the military attracted a flood of black migrants from the South to the urban North. One result was that the vast majority of blacks no longer lived in the South, as they had since slavery. The urgent need for workers also led to actions by the President of the United States that curtailed segregation in certain manufacturing sectors. However, the armed forces in general remained segregated.

As usual, progress did not come without tensions and strains, as the destructive and deadly Harlem Riot of 1943 showed. The dramatic pressures affecting blacks in the Northern cities, in spite of the new economic and social opportunities, were vividly reflected also in the changes that swept over music in the 1940s. The harmonious, even sweet strains of swing, characteristic of the thirties and the first years of the war, especially in the hands of white band-

Tommy Potter, Charlie Parker, Dizzy Gillespie, and John Coltrane at Birdland in New York City, 1951.
Frank Driggs Collection

Billie Holiday, 1948.
William Gottlieb

leaders such as Artie Shaw and Glenn Miller, gave way to a new kind of music, invented and developed by black musicians. This new form, **bebop,** was distinguished by elements of distortion and dissonance never featured before in popular music. The most gifted and influential of the new musicians, who established themselves mainly in New York, included Charlie Parker, Dizzy Gillespie, and Thelonious Monk, as well as the jazz singers Ella Fitzgerald and Billie Holiday.

Accomplishments in Literature

In literature, a few older writers, especially Langston Hughes and Arna Bontemps, continued to publish a great deal of fine work. Perhaps most notably, Hughes's Jesse B. Semple, or "Simple," a character developed as part of the writer's weekly newspaper column, gave witty, wry voice to the moods and attitudes, hopes and fears of a changing Harlem. Brilliant younger writers also appeared. Chester Himes started his long successful career as a novelist by showing in his *If He Hollers Let Him Go* (1945) the clear influence of Wright. (That year, Wright himself added to his fame

Introduction   455

with his autobiography, *Black Boy,* a bestseller that was also widely praised.) Ann Petry published her outstanding novel *The Street* (1946). Ralph Ellison worked throughout much of this decade on a novel, *Invisible Man,* in which he deliberately blended African American folk motifs with unconventional fictional techniques. Published in 1952, *Invisible Man* won the prestigious National Book Award and the most sustained acclaim for a black novelist since *Native Son.* Among poets, Gwendolyn Brooks and Robert Hayden laid the foundations of their distinguished careers by a similar merging of their concern for black America with the standards and practices of innovative American and European poets. In 1950, when Brooks won the Pulitzer Prize for her *Annie Allen* (1949), she became the first black American to be so honored.

A Renewed Effort Against Jim Crow

These accomplishments in literature reflected a growing confidence on the part of many blacks. In fact, with the end of the war in 1945, the stage had been set for a renewed effort against **Jim Crow**—as segregation was called—through legal and other challenges mounted by a variety of groups. The most prominent of these bodies was the National Association for the Advancement of Colored People, which had been fighting for over three decades for black civil rights in the courts and elsewhere. After the war, at a time when the most urgent problem facing the nation appeared to be communism and the Cold War against the Soviet Union, the campaign for civil rights through the courts of law proceeded fairly peacefully. A number of smaller legal victories culminated in 1954 in the landmark Supreme Court decision known as **Brown v. Board of Education of Topeka, Kansas.** In this decision, the court held that racially segregated educational facilities, such as all-black high schools, are inherently unequal. In making its decision, the court relied in part on the testimony of psychologists who held that segregation encouraged feelings of inferiority and even self-hatred in black children.

The Brown decision was widely hailed as the most important public act on behalf of blacks in the United States since Abraham Lincoln issued the Emancipation Proclamation in 1863, during the Civil War. A mood of optimism about race relations swept many blacks and whites, who had long waited for the courts to confirm

Linda Brown in a segregated public school in Topeka, Kansas, a year before the Supreme Court's landmark decision.
Carl Iwasaki, Life Magazine
© Time, Inc.

the injustice of segregation. However, the sense of victory was short-lived. Whatever the Supreme Court ruled or intended, segregation continued to exist across the South, and in some parts of the North, as it had done from the earliest days of the country. The Brown decision had been specifically about schools. Although it seemed logically to apply to almost every other public area, such as restaurants, beaches, buses and trains, and the like, white Southerners in particular did not rush to apply it elsewhere. Indeed, they did not rush to carry out the decision even as it applied to public education. Citing the constitutional rights of states, several leaders declared their intention to defy the Supreme Court and the Federal government.

Introduction   457

Rosa Parks seated in the front of a city bus in Montgomery, Alabama, in December 1956, a year after her arrest.

Bettmann Newsphotos

Eight-year-old Nichelle Morgan facing her first day in an all-white school in Milwaukee, September 1976.

© Brent Jones

The Civil Rights Movement

Encouraged by the court decision, blacks and whites committed to integration began a campaign of open challenge to Jim Crow. This action, called the **Civil Rights Movement,** and the reaction to it, helped to make the decade following 1954 the most turbulent in Southern history since the Civil War. The Civil Rights Movement represented for the most part a combination of the efforts of certain groups in particular: the NAACP, which emphasized matters of law; the Southern Christian Leadership Conference, led by the Reverend Martin Luther King, Jr.; its more youthful and increasingly more radical offshoot, the Student Nonviolent Coordinating Committee, in which Stokely Carmichael was perhaps most prominent; and the Congress of Racial Equality, also youth-oriented, directed by James Farmer.

Starting with challenges to local laws that required blacks to sit in the back of buses, then spreading to insist on the desegregation of lunch counters, the fight against Jim Crow continued on an ever widening front. These efforts were met squarely almost everywhere by the forces of white supremacy. The result was a period of bloody strife, marked by marches and counter-demonstrations, bombings and beatings, lynchings and lawsuits. Slowly but steadily, however, the Jim Crow barriers began to fall across the South. To many people, the culmination of the Civil Rights Movement came in August 1963, with the **March on Washington for Jobs and Freedom.** Perhaps a quarter of a million people, black and white, gathered at the Lincoln Memorial and heard Martin Luther King, Jr., deliver his most celebrated address. With its inspired refrain, "I have a dream," this speech captured the idealism and pacifist zeal of the movement in its most dynamic years.

The Concept of Black Power

The defeat of segregationist laws and practices, decisively achieved in most, though not all, public places by the mid-1960s, did not mean the end of the struggle for justice on the part of black Americans. Indeed, the Civil Rights Movement, which had been dominated from the start by the principle of nonviolence, especially as stated by Dr. King, gave way to what was in some respects

Martin Luther King, Jr., touring Baltimore, Maryland, after winning the Nobel Peace Prize in December 1964.
Leonard Freed/Magnum Photos

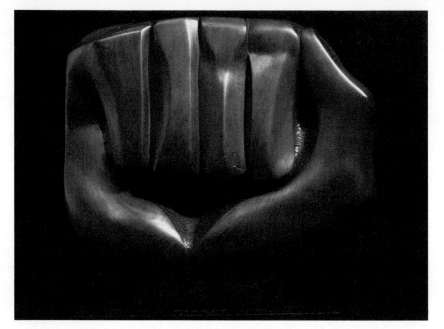

(Right) **Black Unity,** *wood sculpture by Elizabeth Catlett, 1968.* Collection of the artist. © 1998 Elizabeth Catlett/Licensed by VAGA, New York, NY

(Below) *Dr. King and Malcolm X at the Capitol, March 26, 1964.* Wide World Photos

a radically different and opposed campaign. In 1965, Stokely Carmichael, dissatisfied with the pace of progress and by the goals of the movement, first proclaimed and promoted the concept of **Black Power.** This concept played down questions of morality and legality, and instead put the focus of attention on the need for blacks to oppose whites in every way possible. Blacks must also acquire the positions and other material resources that would give them authority over their lives.

Black power was not altogether new as an idea in black American intellectual history. Marcus Garvey, for one, had offered a similar idea in the early 1920s. Never before, however, had it been invoked so sweepingly, and with such success. Perhaps the greatest hero in the eyes of believers in black power was Malcolm X. In his celebrated *Autobiography* (1964–1965), as told to Alex Haley, Malcolm recounts his passage from a troubled youth, marred by the murder of his father by whites, to a life of crime and vice that landed him in jail. From this state he is saved spiritually and intellectually by his conversion to the Nation of Islam faith. At the same time, he gains an intense sense of racial pride and a fierce determination to lead his fellow blacks. To many younger blacks, Malcolm's most memorable call was for blacks to win their freedom "by any means necessary." He hated practices such as "conking"

Coreen Simpson

(Below) *Photograph taken during the Baltimore riot in 1968, following the assassination of Martin Luther King, Jr.*
Michael Sullivan/Black Star

or hair-straightening for men, which he associated with a lack of self-love among blacks, and he encouraged the recognition of the natural beauty of blacks. "Black Is Beautiful" became the slogan of the age, and the insistence on **Black Pride** replaced in many young people feelings of shame and doubt fostered first by slavery, and then by generations of segregation and other forms of racism.

Black power threw onto the defensive the more established and conservative bodies, such as the NAACP and the National Urban League, as well as church groups and various liberal organizations. Its racial radicalism drove many whites from positions of leadership in civil rights organizations, and often from membership in them. Its militant spirit, offended by continuing conditions of poverty and racism, contributed to a series of civil disturbances and insurrections or riots in cities across the country. The first major uprising, marked by several deaths and extensive property damage through arson and looting, occurred in 1965 in Watts, Los Angeles. In 1968, the murder of Martin Luther King, Jr., caused the black populations in several American cities to explode in similar rage. By 1968, too, the deep unpopularity of the Vietnam War further heightened the drama of the struggle by blacks for greater freedom and opportunity.

Creativity in the Arts

James Baldwin.
Bettmann Newsphotos

Significantly, this age of widespread civil disturbances was also an era of renewed creativity in the arts. The excitement generated by the combined force of the Civil Rights and Black Power movements led to some extent to a rekindling of the renaissance spirit of the 1920s—although in radically different ways. The most prominent writers of the 1960s were probably James Baldwin and LeRoi Jones (later Amiri Baraka). Baldwin's first important works, especially the essays in *Notes of a Native Son* (1955) and *Nobody Knows My Name* (1961), had been among the first African American writing to disturb the false calm that had settled over the country with the Supreme Court decision of 1954. In the 1960s, his impact was even greater. His best-selling novel *Another Country* (1962) and his ominous book of essays on American race relations, *The Fire Next Time* (1963), addressed the racial issue with new force. LeRoi Jones, who first made a name for himself in the mainly white "Beat" artistic circles of Greenwich Village in New York, shattered many conventions for the depiction of racial themes with plays such as *Dutchman, The Slave,* and *The Toilet,* all of which appeared in 1964. Also a gifted poet and essayist, Jones (Baraka) became the main figure in the **Black Arts Movement**. This movement emphasized separation from whites, who were often barred from productions and other gatherings. Several of Jones's poems openly insulted and vilified whites.

In addition to Baraka's verse came an outpouring of books in the sixties and early seventies by a group of writers such as Don L. Lee, Nikki Giovanni, Sonia Sanchez, Audre Lorde, Carolyn Rodgers, and June Jordan. Some of the best books were published by Dudley Randall's Broadside Press of Detroit, as blacks attempted to end their old dependence on white publishers. In autobiography, in addition to *The Autobiography of Malcolm X* came other major texts. Perhaps the most beautiful was Maya Angelou's *I Know Why the Caged Bird Sings* (1970), which describes Angelou's escape from a childhood scarred by abuse and parental abandonment. Claude Brown's *Manchild in the Promised Land* (1965) depicted its hero's upward climb from juvenile delinquency in Harlem. Anne Moody's *Coming of Age in Mississippi* (1969) traced her path from a conventional Southern girlhood into the dangerous civil rights struggle. Moody also gave a glimpse of the disappointments that weakened the movement and set the stage for the next important moment in black culture.

Wall of Dignity, *Detroit, Michigan, mural by Bill Walker and Eugene Edaw, 1968.*

Colin L. Powell, Chairman of the Joint Chiefs of Staff, 1990.
Dennis Brack/Black Star

A Double Record: Conflicting Developments

By the end of the 1970s, African American culture had clearly reached both a new plateau of accomplishment and a familiar place of continuing doubt and confusion as it redefined itself within the changing United States. On the one hand, blacks could point with pride, as marks of their progress since 1954, to factors such as the rise in the number of powerful elected officials. Within a few years, African Americans, often as part of interracial coalitions, won the mayoralties of Atlanta, Los Angeles, New Orleans, Detroit, Philadelphia, Baltimore, Chicago, and New York. Still later came the election of a black as governor of the state of Virginia. Where once the armed forces had been segregated, a black man was appointed to the highest military position, the chairmanship of the Joint Chiefs of Staff. On the other hand, there were unmis-

Introduction 463

Coretta King and Jesse Jackson leading the Twentieth Anniversary March on Washington, 1983.
Dennis Brack/Black Star

(Opposite page)
(Top left) *Michael Jordan.*
AP/Wide World Photos

(Top right) *Aretha Franklin.*
© Paul Natkin/Outline

(Bottom left) *Eddie Murphy in* Coming to America.
Sygma

(Bottom right) *Bill Cosby.*
George Bennett/Outline Press

takable signs of the development of what was increasingly being called a **black underclass.** This term referred to a large section of the African American community that appeared to be falling economically and educationally to the bottom of the national culture. Many government programs designed to assist the poor, such as those started by President Lyndon Johnson in his War on Poverty in the mid-1960s, had been abolished. Illicit drugs, a factor in black culture at least since the 1920s, now began to take on the character of an epidemic. In the wake of poverty and drugs came a staggering increase in crimes of theft and violence that made many neighborhoods unsafe and undesirable.

In contrast to this underclass was another large section of the black community that had continued to capitalize on the attainment of increased rights and opportunities. In some respects, the most vivid symbol of this group was the success of certain figures in sports and entertainment whose popularity seemed to have no limit. On television, Bill Cosby's version of the black family became the most watched American weekly television show. In the arts, too, there was remarkable success even as poetry, so important to

Introduction **465**

August Wilson after winning the Pulitzer Prize for **The Piano Lesson,** *1990.*
Bettmann Newsphotos

TIME LINE **CONTEMPORARY AFRICAN AMERICAN LITERATURE**

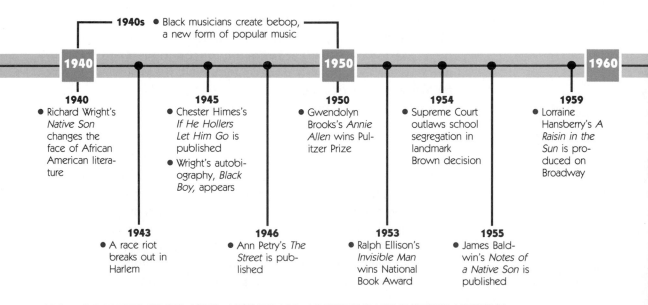

1940s ● Black musicians create bebop, a new form of popular music

1940

1950

1960

1940
● Richard Wright's *Native Son* changes the face of African American literature

1945
● Chester Himes's *If He Hollers Let Him Go* is published
● Wright's autobiography, *Black Boy,* appears

1950
● Gwendolyn Brooks's *Annie Allen* wins Pulitzer Prize

1954
● Supreme Court outlaws school segregation in landmark Brown decision

1959
● Lorraine Hansberry's *A Raisin in the Sun* is produced on Broadway

1943
● A race riot breaks out in Harlem

1946
● Ann Petry's *The Street* is published

1953
● Ralph Ellison's *Invisible Man* wins National Book Award

1955
● James Baldwin's *Notes of a Native Son* is published

Clara Hale. She cared for hundreds of drug-dependent infants at Hale House in Harlem.
Thomas Hoepker/
Magnum Photos

the culture of the 1960s, gave way to an emphasis on fiction, especially the novel. Writers such as Toni Morrison, Alice Walker, John E. Wideman, David Bradley, and Gloria Naylor enjoyed national and even international success. In drama, August Wilson won critical acclaim for his series of plays, including *Fences* and *The Piano Lesson.* Rita Dove won the Pulitzer Prize for poetry in 1987 for *Thomas and Beulah.* African American women writers especially emerged as a group to be read, studied, and followed. From the 1920s and 1930s, the novelist and folklore specialist Zora Neale Hurston emerged as a cultural heroine. African American Studies, an area marked by vitality but also by much confusion and controversy in its formative years in the 1960s, began to enjoy a more settled and accomplished place in American colleges. In 1993 Toni Morrison became the first African American woman to win the Nobel Prize in Literature.

This double sense, of accomplishment and optimism, on the one hand, and of disappointment and failure, on the other, seems to influence most judgments of black America today. Perhaps it is accurate to say that this has always been the case in the history of the African American community, as blacks struggle as a people to find their fair and just place in the American community as a whole.

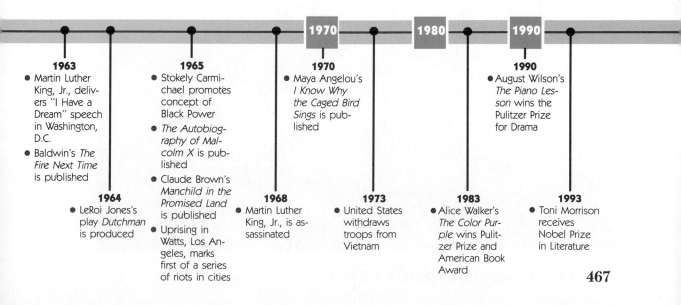

1963
- Martin Luther King, Jr., delivers "I Have a Dream" speech in Washington, D.C.
- Baldwin's *The Fire Next Time* is published

1964
- LeRoi Jones's play *Dutchman* is produced

1965
- Stokely Carmichael promotes concept of Black Power
- *The Autobiography of Malcolm X* is published
- Claude Brown's *Manchild in the Promised Land* is published
- Uprising in Watts, Los Angeles, marks first of a series of riots in cities

1968
- Martin Luther King, Jr., is assassinated

1970
- Maya Angelou's *I Know Why the Caged Bird Sings* is published

1973
- United States withdraws troops from Vietnam

1983
- Alice Walker's *The Color Purple* wins Pulitzer Prize and American Book Award

1990
- August Wilson's *The Piano Lesson* wins the Pulitzer Prize for Drama

1993
- Toni Morrison receives Nobel Prize in Literature

467

Unit Seven

Contemporary Short Stories

The purpose of any short story is to stir our imaginations. Some stories are written chiefly to entertain us—to engage and hold our interest and to make time pass pleasantly. Other stories are written to provide both entertainment and insight. These stories not only give us enjoyment but also deepen our understanding of other people and of ourselves.

A short story, by definition, is **fiction**. It is not a record of actual facts, as a biography is. Some stories are based on personal experiences; however, the writer is free to create characters, actions, and settings.

In some stories, particularly stories of adventure and mystery, the most important element may be **plot,** the sequence of related events that make up the action of the story. In other stories, such as science fiction, **setting,** or the time and place of the events, will be of greatest interest. Generally, the short-story writer focuses on **characters** and **theme,** the underlying meaning of the story.

Every story is told from a particular **point of view**. The narrator may be a character in the story or an outside observer. The way a story is told can control our response to characters and events.

Some of the short stories in this unit involve relationships among family members. In "The Rockpile," by James Baldwin, an accident brings into focus the tensions and strains dividing members of a family. In William Melvin Kelley's "Brother Carlyle," we become aware of powerful and destructive impulses that parents do not wish to acknowledge in their child. In Paule Marshall's "To Da-duh, in Memoriam," we see a conflict not only between generations but between different cultures and values.

The Banjo Lesson, *oil by Henry Ossawa Tanner, 1893.*
Hampton University Museum, Hampton, Virginia; Photo by Mike Fischer

Introduction 469

Historically, African Americans have struggled against racial injustice. That struggle is shown in several stories in this unit. In Ernest Gaines's "Robert Louis Stevenson Banks, aka Chimley," the characters take steps to reverse a lifelong humiliation. In Diane Oliver's "Neighbors," a family must decide how to act in the struggle for school desegregation. The narrator in Reginald McKnight's story "The Kind of Light That Shines on Texas" attends a recently desegregated school, where he attempts to fit in.

African Americans have shown an ability to survive with beauty and with dignity. We see an old lady planting flowers as an affirmation of life in Eugenia Collier's "Marigolds." We see acceptance and celebration of the African American heritage in Alice Walker's "Everyday Use." We find humor and an indomitable spirit in Alice Childress's "The Pocketbook Game."

A Black Look at a Black Book: Malcolm, Marcus and Martin, *acrylic on canvas by Varnette P. Honeywood, 1975.*
© Varnette P. Honeywood, 1975 SPH

About the Author
James Baldwin (1924–1987)

 James Arthur Baldwin, a major American writer, produced a considerable body of work, including novels, essays, short stories, poetry, and plays. He was born and raised in Harlem. He began writing in high school and was editor of his school magazine. When he was fourteen, Baldwin was appointed youth minister at Fireside Pentecostal Assembly. Within a few years, he lost the desire to preach, but the oratorical style of that ministry found its way into his writings.

After graduating from high school in 1942, Baldwin wrote at night and supported himself by working at odd jobs during the day. With Richard Wright's assistance, he received a Eugene F. Saxton Fellowship in 1945. Prestigious magazines began accepting his essays and short stories. In 1948 he moved to Paris. Baldwin remained in Europe until 1957. During this period, his first and best-known novel, *Go Tell It on the Mountain,* was published. This loosely autobiographical novel concerns a Harlem teenager's conflict with his repressive stepfather and the boy's religious conversion. Both of these experiences paralleled experiences in Baldwin's own life.

Notes of a Native Son, a collection of essays, appeared in 1955. Baldwin's national reputation as a writer and as a spokesperson for African American concerns was firmly established when his two books of essays, *Nobody Knows My Name* (1961) and *The Fire Next Time* (1963), were published. Literary critic Irving Howe once declared that

Gastaud/SIPA Press

Baldwin was one of "the two or three greatest essayists this country has ever produced."

Much of Baldwin's fiction is autobiographical. One of the major themes in Baldwin's fiction is black family life. The characters in "The Rockpile" also appear in *Go Tell It on the Mountain.*

James Baldwin 471

Before You Read

The Rockpile

Using What You Know

In the opening paragraphs of this story, you will read about children who are sitting on a *fire escape,* watching the street below. Many apartment houses in cities were once equipped with metal stairways attached to the outside of buildings. These structures provided tenants with a kind of terrace or tiny balcony. Have you seen such fire escapes? Where might you find illustrations to share with the class?

Literary Focus: Plot

The term **plot** refers to the sequence of related events that make up a story. Whatever the characters do or whatever happens to them forms the plot. Plot depends upon cause-and-effect relationships.

Conflict is generally the key element in plot. Conflict may take several forms. It may be **external** or **internal.** A plot may have more than one conflict, and there may be several conflicts related to one main conflict. The **climax** of a story is its high point or **turning point.** The story ends when there is a **resolution** of the major conflict and the outcome is clear.

As a plot progresses, the author may keep us in **suspense** about the course of events so that our interest is held. The author sometimes uses **foreshadowing** as a plot device, dropping hints about what is to come. An author will sometimes interrupt a narrative with a **flashback,** which tells about events that happened at an earlier time.

Setting a Purpose

As you read "The Rockpile," be aware of how events are related. Is there a clear cause-and-effect sequence? What are the major conflicts and where does the climax of the story occur?

The Rockpile

James Baldwin

Constantine Manos/Magnum Photos

Across the street from their house, in an empty lot between two houses, stood the rockpile. It was a strange place to find a mass of natural rock jutting out of the ground; and someone, probably Aunt Florence, had once told them that the rock was there and could not be taken away because without it the subway cars underground would fly apart, killing all the people. This, touching on some natural mystery concerning the surface and the center of the earth, was far too intriguing an explanation to be challenged, and it invested the rockpile, moreover, with such mysterious importance that Roy felt it to be his right, not to say his duty, to play there.

Other boys were to be seen there each afternoon after school and all day Saturday and Sunday. They fought on the rockpile. Sure footed, dangerous, and reckless, they rushed each other and grappled on the heights, sometimes disappearing down the other side in a confusion of dust and screams and upended, flying feet. "It's a wonder they don't kill themselves," their mother said, watching sometimes from the fire escape. "You children stay away from there, you hear me?" Though she said "children" she was looking at Roy, where he sat beside John on the fire escape. "The good Lord knows," she continued, "I don't want you to come home bleeding like a hog every day the Lord sends." Roy shifted impatiently, and continued to stare at the street, as though in this gazing he might somehow acquire wings. John said nothing. He had not really been spoken to: he was afraid of the rockpile and of the boys who played there.

Each Saturday morning John and Roy sat on the fire escape and watched the forbidden street below. Sometimes their mother sat in the room behind them, sewing, or dressing their younger sister, or nursing the baby, Paul. The sun fell across them and across the fire escape with a high, benevolent indifference; below them, men and women, and boys and girls, sinners all, loitered; sometimes one of the church-members passed and saw them and waved. Then, for the moment that they waved decorously back, they were intimidated. They watched the saint, man or woman, until he or she had disappeared from sight. The passage of one of the redeemed made them consider, however vacantly, the wickedness of the street, their own latent wickedness in sitting where they sat; and made them think of their father, who came home early on Saturdays and who would soon be turning this corner and entering the dark hall below them.

But until he came to end their freedom, they sat, watching and longing above the street. At the end of the street nearest their house was the bridge which spanned the Harlem River and led to a city called the Bronx;[1] which was where Aunt Florence lived. Nevertheless, when they saw her coming, she did not come from the bridge, but from the opposite end of the street. This,

weakly, to their minds, she explained by saying that she had taken the subway, not wishing to walk, and that, besides, she did not live in *that* section of the Bronx. Knowing that the Bronx was across the river, they did not believe this story ever, but, adopting toward her their father's attitude, assumed that she had just left some sinful place which she dared not name, as, for example, a movie palace.

In the summertime boys swam in the river, diving off the wooden dock, or wading in from the garbage-heavy bank. Once a boy, whose name was Richard, drowned in the river. His mother had not known where he was; she had even come to their house, to ask if he was there. Then, in the evening, at six o'clock, they had heard from the street a woman screaming and wailing; and they ran to the windows and looked out. Down the street came the woman, Richard's mother, screaming, her face raised to the sky and tears running down her face. A woman walked beside her, trying to make her quiet and trying to hold her up. Behind them walked a man, Richard's father, with Richard's body in his arms. There were two white policemen walking in the gutter, who did not seem to know what should be done. Richard's father and Richard were wet, and Richard's body lay across his father's arms like a cotton baby. The woman's screaming filled all the street; cars slowed down and the people in the cars stared; people opened their windows and looked out and came rushing out of doors to stand in the gutter, watching. Then the small procession disappeared within the house which stood beside the rockpile. Then, *"Lord, Lord, Lord!"* cried Elizabeth, their mother, and slammed the window down.

One Saturday, an hour before his father

1. **Harlem River . . . Bronx:** The Harlem River separates Manhattan Island from the Bronx, which is the only New York City borough connected to the mainland.

would be coming home, Roy was wounded on the rockpile and brought screaming upstairs. He and John had been sitting on the fire escape and their mother had gone into the kitchen to sip tea with Sister McCandless. By and by Roy became bored and sat beside John in restless silence; and John began drawing into his schoolbook a newspaper advertisement which featured a new electric locomotive. Some friends of Roy passed beneath the fire escape and called him. Roy began to fidget, yelling down to them through the bars. Then a silence fell. John looked up. Roy stood looking at him.

"I'm going downstairs," he said.

"You better stay where you is, boy. You know Mama don't want you going downstairs."

"I be right *back*. She won't even know I'm gone, less you run and tell her."

"I ain't *got* to tell her. What's going to stop her from coming in here and looking out the window?"

"She's talking," Roy said. He started into the house.

"But Daddy's going to be home soon!"

"I be back before *that*. What you all the time got to be so *scared* for?" He was already in the house and he now turned, leaning on the windowsill, to swear impatiently, "I be back in *five* minutes."

John watched him sourly as he carefully unlocked the door and disappeared. In a moment he saw him on the sidewalk with his friends. He did not dare to go and tell his mother that Roy had left the fire escape because he had practically promised not to. He started to shout, *Remember, you said five minutes!* but one of Roy's friends was looking up at the fire escape. John looked down at his schoolbook: he became engrossed again in the problem of the locomotive.

Bob Adelman/Magnum Photos

The Rockpile   475

When he looked up again he did not know how much time had passed, but now there was a gang fight on the rockpile. Dozens of boys fought each other in the harsh sun: clambering up the rocks and battling hand to hand, scuffed shoes sliding on the slippery rock; filling the bright air with curses and jubilant cries. They filled the air, too, with flying weapons: stones, sticks, tin cans, garbage, whatever could be picked up and thrown. John watched in a kind of absent amazement—until he remembered that Roy was still downstairs, and that he was one of the boys on the rockpile. Then he was afraid; he could not see his brother among the figures in the sun; and he stood up, leaning over the fire-escape railing. Then Roy appeared from the other side of the rocks; John saw that his shirt was torn; he was laughing. He moved until he stood at the very top of the rockpile. Then, something, an empty tin can, flew out of the air and hit him on the forehead, just above the eye. Immediately, one side of Roy's face ran with blood, he fell and rolled on his face down the rocks. Then for a moment there was no movement at all, no sound, the sun, arrested,[2] lay on the street and the sidewalk and the arrested boys. Then someone screamed or shouted; boys began to run away, down the street, toward the bridge. The figure on the ground, having caught its breath and felt its own blood, began to shout. John cried, "Mama! Mama!" and ran inside.

"Don't fret, don't fret," panted Sister McCandless as they rushed down the dark, narrow, swaying stairs, "don't fret. Ain't a boy been born don't get his knocks every now and again. *Lord!*" they hurried into the sun. A man had picked Roy up and now walked slowly toward them. One or two boys sat silent on their stoops; at either end of the street there was a group of boys watching. "He ain't hurt bad," the man said, "wouldn't be making this kind of noise if he was hurt real bad."

Elizabeth, trembling, reached out to take Roy, but Sister McCandless, bigger, calmer, took him from the man and threw him over her shoulder as she once might have handled a sack of cotton. "God bless you," she said to the man, "God bless you, son." Roy was still screaming. Elizabeth stood behind Sister McCandless to stare at his bloody face.

"It's just a flesh wound," the man kept saying, "just broke the skin, that's all." They were moving across the sidewalk, toward the house. John, not now afraid of the staring boys, looked toward the corner to see if his father was yet in sight.

Upstairs, they hushed Roy's crying. They bathed the blood away, to find, just above the left eyebrow, the jagged, superficial scar. "Lord, have mercy," murmured Elizabeth, "another inch and it would've been his eye." And she looked with apprehension toward the clock. "Ain't it the truth," said Sister McCandless, busy with bandages and iodine.

"When did he go downstairs?" his mother asked at last.

Sister McCandless now sat fanning herself in the easy chair, at the head of the sofa where Roy lay, bound and silent. She paused for a moment to look sharply at John. John stood near the window, holding the newspaper advertisement and the drawing he had done.

"We was sitting on the fire escape," he said. "Some boys he knew called him."

"When?"

"He said he'd be back in five minutes."

2. **arrested:** here used in the sense of halted motion.

"Why didn't you tell me he was downstairs?"

He looked at his hands, clasping his notebook, and did not answer.

"Boy," said Sister McCandless, "you hear your mother a-talking to you?"

He looked at his mother. He repeated: "He said he'd be back in five minutes."

"He said he'd be back in five minutes," said Sister McCandless with scorn, "don't look to me like that's no right answer. You's the man of the house, you supposed to look after your baby brothers and sisters—you ain't supposed to let them run off and get half-killed. But I expect," she added, rising from the chair, dropping the cardboard fan, "your Daddy'll make you tell the truth. Your Ma's way too soft with you."

He did not look at her, but at the fan where it lay in the dark red, depressed seat where she had been. The fan advertised a pomade for the hair and showed a brown woman and her baby, both with glistening hair, smiling happily at each other.

"Honey," said Sister McCandless, "I got to be moving along. Maybe I drop in later tonight. I don't reckon you going to be at Tarry Service tonight?"

Tarry Service was the prayer meeting held every Saturday night at church to strengthen believers and prepare the church for the coming of the Holy Ghost on Sunday.

"I don't reckon," said Elizabeth. She stood up; she and Sister McCandless kissed each other on the cheek. "But you be sure to remember me in your prayers."

"I surely will do that." She paused, with her hand on the door knob, and looked down at Roy and laughed. "Poor little man," she said, "reckon he'll be content to sit on the fire escape *now*."

Elizabeth laughed with her. "It sure ought

to be a lesson to him. You don't reckon," she asked nervously, still smiling, "he going to keep that scar, do you?"

"Lord, no," said Sister McCandless, "ain't nothing but a scratch. I declare, Sister Grimes, you worse than a child. Another couple of weeks and you won't be able to *see* no scar. No, you go on about your housework, honey, and thank the Lord it weren't no worse." She opened the door; they heard the sound of feet on the stairs. "I expect that's the Reverend," said Sister McCandless, placidly, "I *bet* he going to raise cain."[3]

"Maybe it's Florence," Elizabeth said. "Sometimes she get here about this time." They stood in the doorway, staring, while the steps reached the landing below and began again climbing to their floor. "No," said Elizabeth then, "that ain't her walk. That's Gabriel."

"Well, I'll just go on," said Sister McCandless, "and kind of prepare his mind." She pressed Elizabeth's hand as she spoke and started into the hall, leaving the door behind her slightly ajar. Elizabeth turned slowly back into the room. Roy did not open his eyes, or move; but she knew that he was not sleeping; he wished to delay until the last possible moment any contact with his father. John put his newspaper and his notebook on the table and stood, leaning on the table, staring at her.

"It wasn't my fault," he said. "I couldn't stop him from going downstairs."

"No," she said, "you ain't got nothing to worry about. You just tell your Daddy the truth."

He looked directly at her, and she turned to the window, staring into the street. What was Sister McCandless saying? Then from

<hr/>

3. **raise cain:** to make trouble (slang).

her bedroom she heard Delilah's thin wail and she turned, frowning, looking toward the bedroom and toward the still open door. She knew that John was watching her. Delilah continued to wail, she thought, angrily, *Now that girl's getting too big for that*, but she feared that Delilah would awaken Paul and she hurried into the bedroom. She tried to soothe Delilah back to sleep. Then she heard the front door open and close—too loud, Delilah raised her voice, with an exasperated sigh Elizabeth picked the child up. Her child and Gabriel's, her children and Gabriel's: Roy, Delilah, Paul. Only John was nameless and a stranger, living, unalterable testimony to his mother's days in sin.

"What happened?" Gabriel demanded. He stood, enormous, in the center of the room, his black lunchbox dangling from his hand, staring at the sofa where Roy lay. John stood just before him, it seemed to her astonished vision just below him, beneath his fist, his heavy shoe. The child stared at the man in fascination and terror—when a girl down home she had seen rabbits stand so paralyzed before the barking dog. She hurried past Gabriel to the sofa, feeling the weight of Delilah in her arms like the weight of a shield, and stood over Roy, saying:

"Now, ain't a thing to get upset about, Gabriel. This boy sneaked downstairs while I had my back turned and got hisself hurt a little. He's alright now."

Roy, as though in confirmation, now opened his eyes and looked gravely at his father. Gabriel dropped his lunchbox with a clatter and knelt by the sofa.

"How you feel, son? Tell your Daddy what happened?"

Roy opened his mouth to speak and then, relapsing into panic, began to cry. His father held him by the shoulder.

"You don't want to cry. You's Daddy's little man. Tell your Daddy what happened."

"He went downstairs," said Elizabeth, "where he didn't have no business to be, and got to fighting with them bad boys playing on that rockpile. That's what happened and it's a mercy it weren't nothing worse."

He looked up at her. "Can't you let this boy answer me for hisself?"

Ignoring this, she went on, more gently: "He got cut on the forehead, but it ain't nothing to worry about."

"You call a doctor? How you know it ain't nothing to worry about?"

"Is you got money to be throwing away on doctors? No, I ain't called no doctor. Ain't nothing wrong with my eyes that I can't tell whether he's hurt bad or not. He got a fright more'n anything else, and you ought to pray God it teaches him a lesson."

"You got a lot to say *now*," he said, "but I'll have *me* something to say in a minute. I'll be wanting to know when all this happened, what you was doing with your eyes *then*." He turned back to Roy, who had lain quietly sobbing eyes wide open and body held rigid: and who now, at his father's touch, remembered the height, the sharp, sliding rock beneath his feet, the sun, the explosion of the sun, his plunge into darkness and his salty blood; and recoiled, beginning to scream, as his father touched his forehead. "Hold still, hold still," crooned his father, shaking, "hold still. Don't cry. Daddy ain't going to hurt you, he just wants to see this bandage, see what they've done to his little man." But Roy continued to scream and would not be still and Gabriel dared not lift the bandage for fear of hurting him more. And he looked at Elizabeth in fury: "Can't you put that child down and help me with this boy? John, take your baby sister from

Boy Thinking, *pen and ink wash by Oliver B. Johnson.*

your mother—don't look like neither of you got good sense."

John took Delilah and sat down with her in the easy chair. His mother bent over Roy, and held him still, while his father, carefully—but still Roy screamed—lifted the bandage and stared at the wound. Roy's sobs began to lessen. Gabriel readjusted the bandage. "You see," said Elizabeth, finally, "he ain't nowhere near dead."

"It sure ain't your fault that he ain't dead." He and Elizabeth considered each other for a moment in silence. "He came mightly close to losing an eye. Course, his eyes ain't as big as your'n, so I reckon you don't think it matters so much." At this her face hardened; he smiled. "Lord, have mercy," he said, "you think you ever going to learn to do right? Where was you when all this happened? Who let him go downstairs?"

"Ain't nobody let him go downstairs, he just went. He got a head just like his father, it got to be broken before it'll bow. I was in the kitchen."

"Where was Johnnie?"

"He was in here."

"Where?"

"He was on the fire escape."

"Didn't he know Roy was downstairs?"

"I reckon."

"What you mean, you reckon? He ain't got your big eyes for nothing, does he?" He looked over at John. "Boy, you see your brother go downstairs?"

"Gabriel, ain't no sense in trying to blame Johnnie. You know right well if you have trouble making Roy behave, he ain't going to listen to his brother. He don't hardly listen to me."

"How come you didn't tell your mother Roy was downstairs?"

John said nothing, staring at the blanket which covered Delilah.

"Boy, you hear me? You want me to take a strap to you?"

"No, you ain't," she said. "You ain't going to take no strap to this boy, not today you ain't. Ain't a soul to blame for Roy's lying up there now but you—you because you done spoiled him so that he thinks he can do just anything and get away with it. I'm here to tell you that ain't no way to raise no child. You don't pray to the Lord to help you do better than you been doing, you going to live to shed bitter tears that the Lord didn't take his soul today." And she was trembling. She moved, unseeing, toward John and took Delilah from his arms. She looked back at Gabriel, who had risen, who stood near the sofa, staring at her. And she found in his face not fury alone, which would not have surprised her; but hatred so deep as to become insupportable in its lack of personality. His eyes were struck alive, unmoving, blind with malevolence—she felt, like the pull of the earth at her feet, his longing to witness her perdition.[4] Again, as though it might be propitiation,[5] she moved the child in her arms. And at this his eyes changed, he looked at Elizabeth, the mother of his children, the helpmeet given by the Lord. Then her eyes clouded; she moved to leave the room; her foot struck the lunchbox lying on the floor.

"John," she said, "pick up your father's lunchbox like a good boy."

She heard, behind her, his scrambling movement as he left the easy chair, the scrape and jangle of the lunchbox as he picked it up, bending his dark head near the toe of his father's heavy shoe.

4. **perdition** (pər-dĭsh′ən): damnation.

5. **propitiation** (prō-pĭsh′ē-ā′shən): an act that appeases.

Responding to the Selection

The Rockpile by James Baldwin

Identifying Facts

1. What is the rockpile?
2. How does Roy disobey his mother?
3. How is Roy injured?
4. Who tells the boys' father what happened?
5. Who is blamed for Roy's behavior?

Interpreting Meanings

1. How are the brothers contrasted? Why is Roy attracted to the rockpile? Why is John afraid of it?
2. We are told that the boys spend each Saturday morning sitting on the fire escape and watching the "forbidden street below." Why is the street "forbidden" to them? What dangers are there for children playing in the neighborhood?
3. Before Gabriel appears, his presence is clearly felt. How do you know that his children fear him?
4. Why is John unable to answer Gabriel's questions? How does Elizabeth try to protect John?
5. This story centers on the conflicts within a family. Roy's accident on the rockpile brings these conflicts to a head. What do you think is the major conflict in the story?
6. Reread the last sentence of the story. Why do you think the story ends with the image of the child's head bending over his father's shoe?

Literary Elements

Analyzing Conflict

Conflict is the struggle between two forces. A story can have several conflicts. These conflicts can be physical (the fight between the boys on the rockpile) or emotional (should John have told his mother that Roy had sneaked out of the house?). List the conflicts in "The Rockpile" that you would describe as emotional.

Developing Sentence Sense

Understanding Sentence Organization

Here is the opening sentence of Baldwin's story:

> Across the street from their house, in an empty lot between two houses, stood the rockpile.

How does Baldwin organize the parts of his sentence to emphasize the rockpile? Suppose he had written this instead:

> The rockpile stood across the street from their house, in an empty lot between two houses.

The information in both constructions is the same. What is lost in the second sentence?

Examine the following description of Gabriel:

He stood, enormous, in the center of the room, his black lunchbox dangling from his hand, staring at the sofa where Roy lay.

What makes this description of Gabriel ominous, or threatening? Suppose Baldwin had written this:

An enormous man, he stood in the center of the room with his lunchbox dangling from his hand. He was staring at the sofa where Roy lay.

Why is this description less effective?

Choose another sentence in the story and analyze the relationship of its parts. A good example is the last sentence in the story.

Writing About Literature
Analyzing a Title
Writers generally choose titles carefully. A title is an important clue not only to what the reader can expect, but also to what the work means.

Why do you think Baldwin calls his story "The Rockpile"? To answer this question, you need to determine what importance this object has in the story.

Prewriting Suggestions
Make a list of all references to the rockpile. For example, in the opening paragraph, Baldwin emphasizes its strangeness. Note that he uses the words *mystery, intriguing,* and *mysterious* to suggest that the rockpile has a **symbolic,** as well as a literal, meaning.

Note how the rockpile is important to the plot of the story. How does it help to define the contrasting characters of the brothers? How does the rockpile, huge and immovable, emphasize the helplessness of the characters?

Speaking and Listening
Identifying with a Character
Have you ever had to take care of a younger brother or sister or another child whose parents were away? What happened if the child did something against the family's rules? How did you handle the situation?

In light of your own experiences, was John right to keep quiet about his brother's disobedience? What might you have done in his place? Discuss your reaction to his decision with your classmates.

About the Author
Eugenia Collier (b. 1928)

 In 1996 Eugenia Collier retired as chairperson of the Department of English and Language Arts at Morgan State University in Baltimore, Maryland. Collier had taught English at Howard University and Baltimore Community College and had been head of the Department of Languages, Literature and Journalism at Coppin State College in Baltimore.

Collier grew up in Baltimore. After completing her public school education there, she matriculated at Howard University, in Washington, D.C., where she received a bachelor's degree. She went on to obtain a master's degree at Columbia University in New York City. She returned to her native state of Maryland to earn a Ph.D. in American Civilization at the University of Maryland, College Park.

Collier has coedited a two-volume anthology of African American writings. She has published literary criticism in such scholarly journals as *Phylon* and the *CLA Journal.* She has also been an editor of *Impressions in Asphalt,* an anthology of literature for young readers.

Although much of Collier's time is spent in scholarly work, her bent is toward imaginative writing. "I've always wanted to be a creative writer," Collier told a New York City edi-

Charles S. Collier

tor, when asked about her writing. "I won a contest sponsored by the Afro-American newspaper when I was twelve years old. Creative writing is my passion."

Collier's prizewinning short story "Marigolds" first appeared in *Negro Digest* in November of 1969. *Breeder and Other Stories* appeared in 1994.

Before You Read

Marigolds

Using What You Know

In a well-known essay called "In Search of Our Mothers' Gardens," Alice Walker talks about generations of black women whose creative spirit was expressed in their daily lives. Speaking of her mother's love for beauty, Walker says she "adorned with flowers whatever shabby house we were forced to live in." Have you ever taken care of a garden or planted flowers? Why do you think people enjoy growing flowers?

Literary Focus: Setting and Mood

Setting in a narrative is the general scene of the action—when and where the story takes place. Sometimes, setting is so important that the story depends on it. If you have read "Miss Cynthie" (page 357), you may recall how Fisher uses the sights and sounds of Harlem during the Renaissance to build his story. "Marigolds" takes place during the Great Depression, when life was difficult for most Americans and especially bad for African Americans.

Setting can help to establish the **mood,** or **atmosphere,** of a story. A story that takes place during a carnival, for example, would have a mood quite different from that of a story set on a deserted island.

Setting a Purpose

As you read "Marigolds," pay close attention to the descriptions of setting. What do you think the marigolds represent to the narrator?

Marigolds

Eugenia Collier

When I think of the home town of my youth, all that I seem to remember is dust—the brown, crumbly dust of late summer—arid, sterile dust that gets into the eyes and makes them water, gets into the throat and between the toes of bare brown feet. I don't know why I should remember only the dust. Surely there must have been lush green lawns and paved streets under leafy shade trees somewhere in town; but memory is an abstract painting[1]—it does not present things as they are, but rather as they *feel*. And so, when I think of that time and that place, I remember only the dry September of the dirt roads and grassless yards of the shanty-town[2] where I lived. And one other thing I remember, another incongruency[3] of memory—a brilliant splash of sunny yellow against the dust— Miss Lottie's marigolds.

Whenever the memory of those marigolds flashes across my mind, a strange nostalgia comes with it and remains long after the picture has faded. I feel again the chaotic emotions of adolescence, illusive as smoke, yet as real as the potted geranium before me now. Joy and rage and wild animal gladness and shame become tangled together in the multicolored skein of 14-going-on-15 as I recall that devastating moment when I was suddenly more woman than child, years ago in Miss Lottie's yard. I think of those marigolds at the strangest times; I remember them vividly now as I desperately pass away the time waiting for you, who will not come.

I suppose that futile waiting was the sorrowful background music of our impoverished little community when I was young. The Depression that gripped the nation was no new thing to us, for the black workers of rural Maryland had always been depressed. I don't know what it was that we were waiting for; certainly not for the prosperity that was "just around the corner," for those were white folks' words, which we never believed. Nor did we wait for hard work and thrift to pay off in shining success as the American Dream promised, for we knew better than that, too. Perhaps we waited for a miracle, amorphous[4] in concept but necessary if one were to have the grit to rise before dawn each day and labor in the white man's vineyard until after dark, or to wander about in

the September dust offering one's sweat in return for some meager share of bread. But God was chary with miracles in those days, and so we waited—and waited.

We children, of course, were only vaguely aware of the extent of our poverty. Having no radios, few newspapers, and no magazines, we were somewhat unaware of the world outside our community. Nowadays we would be called "culturally deprived" and people would write books and hold conferences about us. In those days everybody we knew was just as hungry and ill-clad as we were. Poverty was the cage in which we all were trapped, and our hatred of it was still the vague, undirected restlessness of the zoo-bred flamingo who knows that nature created him to fly free.

As I think of those days I feel most poignantly the tag-end of summer, the bright dry times when we began to have a sense of shortening days and the imminence of the cold.

By the time I was 14 my brother Joey and I were the only children left at our house, the older ones having left home for early marriage or the lure of the city, and the two babies having been sent to relatives who might care for them better than we. Joey was three years younger than I, and a boy, and therefore vastly inferior. Each morning our mother and father trudged wearily down the dirt road and around the bend, she to her domestic job, he to his daily unsuccessful quest for work. After our few chores around the tumble-down shanty, Joey and I were

486   EUGENIA COLLIER

free to run wild in the sun with other children similarly situated.

For the most part, those days are ill-defined in my memory, running together and combining like a fresh water-color painting left out in the rain. I remember squatting in the road drawing a picture in the dust, a picture which Joey gleefully erased with one sweep of his dirty foot. I remember fishing for minnows in a muddy creek and watching sadly as they eluded my cupped hands, while Joey laughed uproariously. And I remember, that year, a strange restlessness of body and of spirit, a feeling that something old and familiar was ending, and something unknown and therefore terrifying was beginning.

One day returns to me with special clarity for some reason, perhaps because it was the beginning of the experience that in some inexplicable[5] way marked the end of innocence. I was loafing under the great oak tree in our yard, deep in some reverie which I have now forgotten, except that it involved some secret, secret thoughts of one of the Harris boys across the yard. Joey and a bunch of kids were bored now with the old tire suspended from an oak limb which had kept them entertained for awhile.

"Hey, Lizabeth," Joey yelled. He never talked when he could yell. "Hey, Lizabeth, let's go somewhere."

I came reluctantly from my private world. "Where you want to go? What you want to do?"

The truth was that we were becoming tired of the formlessness of our summer days. The idleness whose prospect had seemed so beautiful during the busy days of spring now had degenerated to an almost desperate effort to fill up the empty midday hours.

"Let's go see can we find some locusts on the hill," someone suggested.

Joey was scornful. "Ain't no more locusts there. Y'all got 'em all while they was still green."

The argument that followed was brief and not really worth the effort. Hunting locust trees wasn't fun any more by now.

"Tell you what," said Joey finally, his eyes sparkling. "Let's us go over to Miss Lottie's."

The idea caught on at once, for annoying Miss Lottie was always fun. I was still child enough to scamper along with the group over rickety fences and through bushes that tore our already raggedy clothes, back to where Miss Lottie lived. I think now that we must have made a tragicomic spectacle, five or six kids of different ages, each of us clad in only one garment—the girls in faded dresses that were too long or too short, the boys in patchy pants, their sweaty brown chests gleaming in the hot sun. A little cloud of dust followed our thin legs and bare feet as we tramped over the barren land.

When Miss Lottie's house came into view we stopped, ostensibly[6] to plan our strategy, but actually to reinforce our courage. Miss Lottie's house was the most ramshackle of all our ramshackle homes. The sun and rain had long since faded its rickety frame siding from white to a sullen gray. The boards themselves seemed to remain upright not from being nailed together but rather from leaning together like a house that a child might have constructed from cards. A brisk wind might have blown it down, and the fact that it was still standing implied a kind of enchantment that was stronger than the ele-

---

5. **inexplicable** (ĭn-ĕk′splĭ-kə-bəl): that cannot be explained or understood.

6. **ostensibly** (ŏ-stĕn′sə-blē): seemingly or apparently.

Maudell Sleet's Magic Garden, *collage by Romare Bearden, 1978.*
From the Profile/Part 1: The Twenties *series.*

488 EUGENIA COLLIER

ments. There it stood, and as far as I know is standing yet—a gray rotting thing with no porch, no shutters, no steps, set on a cramped lot with no grass, not even any weeds—a monument to decay.

In front of the house in a squeaky rocking chair sat Miss Lottie's son, John Burke, completing the impression of decay. John Burke was what was known as "queer-headed." Black and ageless, he sat, rocking day in and day out in a mindless stupor, lulled by the monotonous squeak-squawk of the chair. A battered hat atop his shaggy head shaded him from the sun. Usually John Burke was totally unaware of everything outside his quiet dream world. But if you disturbed him, if you intruded upon his fantasies, he would become enraged, strike out at you, and curse at you in some strange enchanted language which only he could understand. We children made a game of thinking of ways to disturb John Burke and then to elude his violent retribution.

But our real fun and our real fear lay in Miss Lottie herself. Miss Lottie seemed to be at least a hundred years old. Her big frame still held traces of the tall, powerful woman she must have been in youth, although it was now bent and drawn. Her smooth skin was a dark reddish-brown, and her face had Indian-like features and the stern stoicism[7] that one associates with Indian faces. Miss Lottie didn't like intruders either, especially children. She never left her yard, and nobody ever visited her. We never knew how she managed those necessities which depend on human interaction— how she ate, for example, or even whether she ate. When we were tiny children, we thought Miss Lottie was a witch and we

made up tales, that we half believed ourselves, about her exploits. We were far too sophisticated now, of course, to believe the witch-nonsense. But old fears have a way of clinging like cobwebs, and so when we sighted the tumble-down shack, we had to stop to reinforce our nerves.

"Look, there she is," I whispered, forgetting that Miss Lottie could not possibly have heard me from that distance. "She's fooling with them crazy flowers."

"Yeh, look at 'er."

Miss Lottie's marigolds were perhaps the strangest part of the picture. Certainly they did not fit in with the crumbling decay of the rest of her yard. Beyond the dusty brown yard, in front of the sorry gray house, rose suddenly and shockingly a dazzling strip of bright blossoms, clumped together in enormous mounds, warm and passionate and sungolden. The old black witch-woman worked on them all summer, every summer, down on her creaky knees, weeding and cultivating and arranging, while the house crumbled and John Burke rocked. For some perverse reason, we children hated those marigolds. They interfered with the perfect ugliness of the place; they were too beautiful; they said too much that we could not understand; they did not make sense. There was something in the vigor with which the old woman destroyed the weeds that intimidated us. It should have been a comical sight—the old woman with the man's hat on her cropped white head, leaning over the bright mounds, her big backside in the air—but it wasn't comical, it was something we could not name. We had to annoy her by whizzing a pebble into her flowers or by yelling a dirty word, then dancing away from her rage, revelling in our youth and mocking her age. Actually, I think it was the flowers we

7. **stoicism** (stō′ĭ-sĭz′əm): repression of feeling.

wanted to destroy, but nobody had the nerve to try it, not even Joey, who was usually fool enough to try anything.

"Y'all git some stones," commanded Joey now, and was met with instant giggling obedience as everyone except me began to gather pebbles from the dusty ground. "Come on, Lizabeth."

I just stood there peering through the bushes, torn between wanting to join the fun and feeling that it was all a bit silly.

"You scared, Lizabeth?"

I cursed and spat on the ground—my favorite gesture of phony bravado.[8] "Y'all children get the stones, I'll show you how to use 'em."

I said before that we children were not consciously aware of how thick were the bars of our cage. I wonder now, though, whether we were not more aware of it than I thought. Perhaps we had some dim notion of what we were, and how little chance we had of being anything else. Otherwise, why would we have been so preoccupied with destruction? Anyway, the pebbles were collected quickly, and everybody looked at me to begin the fun.

"Come on, y'all."

We crept to the edge of the bushes that bordered the narrow road in front of Miss Lottie's place. She was working placidly, kneeling over the flowers, her dark hand plunged into the golden mound. Suddenly "zing"—an expertly aimed stone cut the head off one of the blossoms.

"Who out there?" Miss Lottie's backside came down and her head came up as her sharp eyes searched the bushes. "You better git!"

We had crouched down out of sight in the bushes, where we stifled the giggles that insisted on coming. Miss Lottie gazed warily across the road for a moment, then cautiously returned to her weeding. "Zing"— Joey sent a pebble into the blooms, and another marigold was beheaded.

Miss Lottie was enraged now. She began struggling to her feet, leaning on a rickety cane and shouting. "Y'all git! Go on home!" Then the rest of the kids let loose with their pebbles, storming the flowers and laughing wildly and senselessly at Miss Lottie's impotent rage. She shook her stick at us and started shakily toward the road crying, " Git 'long! John Burke! John Burke, come help!"

Then I lost my head entirely, mad with the power of inciting such rage, and ran out of the bushes in the storm of pebbles, straight toward Miss Lottie chanting madly, "Old witch, fell in a ditch, picked up a penny and thought she was rich!" The children screamed with delight, dropped their pebbles and joined the crazy dance, swarming around Miss Lottie like bees and chanting, "Old lady witch!" while she screamed curses at us. The madness lasted only a moment, for John Burke, startled at last, lurched out of his chair, and we dashed for the bushes just as Miss Lottie's cane went whizzing at my head.

I did not join the merriment when the kids gathered again under the oak in our bare yard. Suddenly I was ashamed, and I did not like being ashamed. The child in me sulked and said it was all in fun, but the woman in me flinched at the thought of the malicious attack that I had led. The mood lasted all afternoon. When we ate the beans and rice that was supper that night, I did not notice my father's silence, for he was always silent these days, nor did I notice my mother's absence, for she always worked until well into

8. **bravado** (brə-vä′dō): false bravery.

evening. Joey and I had a particularly bitter argument after supper; his exuberance[9] got on my nerves. Finally I stretched out upon the pallet in the room we shared and fell into a fitful doze.

When I awoke, somewhere in the middle of the night, my mother had returned, and I vaguely listened to the conversation that was audible through the thin walls that separated our rooms. At first I heard no words, only voices. My mother's voice was like a cool, dark room in summer—peaceful, soothing, quiet. I loved to listen to it; it made things seem all right somehow. But my father's voice cut through hers, shattering the peace.

"Twenty-two years, Maybelle, 22 years," he was saying, "and I got nothing for you, nothing, nothing."

"It's all right, honey, you'll get something. Everybody out of work now, you know that."

"It ain't right. Ain't no man ought to eat his woman's food year in and year out, and see his children running wild. Ain't nothing right about that."

"Honey, you took good care of us when you had it. Ain't nobody got nothing nowadays."

"I ain't talking about nobody else, I'm talking about *me*. God knows I try." My mother said something I could not hear, and my father cried out louder, "What must a man do, tell me that?"

"Look, we ain't starving. I git paid every week, and Mrs. Ellis is real nice about giving me things. She gonna let me have Mr. Ellis's old coat for you this winter——"

"Damn Mr. Ellis's coat! And damn his money! You think I want white folks' leavings? Damn, Maybelle"—and suddenly he sobbed, loudly and painfully, and cried help-

lessly and hopelessly in the dark night. I had never heard a man cry before. I did not know men ever cried. I covered my ears with my hands but could not cut off the sound of my father's harsh, painful, despairing sobs. My father was a strong man who could whisk a child upon his shoulders and go singing through the house. My father whittled toys for us and laughed so loud that the great oak seemed to laugh with him, and taught us how to fish and hunt rabbits. How could it be that my father was crying? But the sobs went on, unstifled, finally quieting until I could hear my mother's voice, deep and rich, humming softly as she used to hum to a frightened child.

The world had lost its boundary lines. My mother, who was small and soft, was now the strength of the family; my father, who was the rock on which the family had been built, was sobbing like the tiniest child. Everything was suddenly out of tune, like a broken accordion. Where did I fit into this crazy picture? I do not now remember my thoughts, only a feeling of great bewilderment and fear.

Long after the sobbing and the humming had stopped, I lay on the pallet, still as stone with my hands over my ears, wishing that I too could cry and be comforted. The night was silent now except for the sound of the crickets and of Joey's soft breathing. But the room was too crowded with fear to allow me to sleep, and finally, feeling the terrible aloneness of 4 A.M., I decided to awaken Joey.

"Ouch! What's the matter with you? What you want?" he demanded disagreeably when I had pinched and slapped him awake.

"Come on, wake up."

"What for? Go 'way."

I was lost for a reasonable reply. I could

---

9. **exuberance** (ĭg-zoo'bər-əns): enthusiasm; high spirits.

not say, "I'm scared and I don't want to be alone," so I merely said, "I'm going out. If you want to come, come on."

The promise of adventure awoke him. "Going out now? Where to, Lizabeth? What you going to do?"

I was pulling my dress over my head. Until now I had not thought of going out. "Just come on," I replied tersely.

I was out the window and halfway down the road before Joey caught up with me.

"Wait, Lizabeth, where you going?"

I was running as if the Furies[10] were after me, as perhaps they were—running silently and furiously until I came to where I had half-known I was headed: to Miss Lottie's yard.

The half-dawn light was more eerie than complete darkness, and in it the old house was like the ruin that my world had become— foul and crumbling, a grotesque caricature.[11] It looked haunted, but I was not afraid because I was haunted too.

"Lizabeth, you lost your mind?" panted Joey.

I had indeed lost my mind, for all the smoldering emotions of that summer swelled in me and burst—the great need for my mother who was never there, the hopelessness of our poverty and degradation, the bewilderment of being neither child nor woman and yet both at once, the fear unleashed by my father's tears. And these feelings combined in one great impulse toward destruction.

"Lizabeth!"

I leaped furiously into the mounds of marigolds and pulled madly, trampling and pulling and destroying the perfect yellow blooms. The fresh smell of early morning and of dew-soaked marigolds spurred me on as I went tearing and mangling and sobbing while Joey tugged my dress or my waist crying, "Lizabeth, stop, please stop!"

And then I was sitting in the ruined little garden among the uprooted and ruined flowers, crying and crying, and it was too late to undo what I had done. Joey was sitting beside me, silent and frightened, not knowing what to say. Then, "Lizabeth, look."

I opened my swollen eyes and saw in front of me a pair of large calloused feet; my gaze lifted to the swollen legs, the age-distorted body clad in a tight cotton night dress, and then the shadowed Indian face surrounded by stubby white hair. And there was no rage in the face now, now that the garden was destroyed and there was nothing any longer to be protected.

"M-miss Lottie!" I scrambled to my feet and just stood there and stared at her, and that was the moment when childhood faded and womanhood began. That violent, crazy act was the last act of childhood. For as I gazed at the immobile face with the sad, weary eyes, I gazed upon a kind of reality which is hidden to childhood. The witch was no longer a witch but only a broken old woman who had dared to create beauty in the midst of ugliness and sterility. She had been born in squalor and lived in it all her life. Now at the end of that life she had nothing except a falling-down hut, a wrecked body, and John Burke, the mindless son of her passion. Whatever verve there was left in her, whatever was of love and beauty and joy that had not been squeezed out by life, had been there in the marigolds she had so tenderly cared for.

Of course I could not express the things

---

10. **Furies:** In classical mythology, the Furies were three spirits who pursued and punished wrongdoers.
11. **grotesque** (grō-tĕsk´) **caricature:** a distorted exaggeration.

that I knew about Miss Lottie as I stood there awkward and ashamed. The years have put words to the things I knew in that moment, and as I look back upon it, I know that that moment marked the end of innocence. People think of the loss of innocence as meaning the loss of virginity, but this is far from true. Innocence involves an unseeing acceptance of things at face value, an ignorance of the area below the surface. In that humiliating moment I looked beyond myself and into the depths of another person. This was the beginning of compassion, and one cannot have both compassion and innocence.

The years have taken me worlds away from that time and that place, from the dust and squalor of our lives and from the bright thing that I destroyed in a blind childish striking out at God-knows-what. Miss Lottie died long ago and many years have passed since I last saw her hut, completely barren at last, for despite my wild contrition[12] she never planted marigolds again. Yet, there are times when the image of those passionate yellow mounds returns with a painful poignancy.[13] For one does not have to be ignorant and poor to find that his life is barren as the dusty yards of our town. And I too have planted marigolds.

12. **contrition:** remorse.
13. **poignancy** (poin′yən-sē): distress.

Responding to the Selection
Marigolds by Eugenia Collier

Identifying Facts

1. How old is the narrator at the time of the story?
2. What is the narrator's name?
3. Who is John Burke?
4. How do the children taunt Miss Lottie?
5. How does the narrator feel after she ruins Miss Lottie's garden?

Interpreting Meanings

1. What is your impression of the narrator's home town from the opening passages of the story?
2. According to the narrator, why were the children so "preoccupied with destruction"? How does their treatment of Miss Lottie make her a sympathetic character?
3. The narrator describes the marigolds as

"warm and passionate and sun-golden."
Yet she hated them. Explain.

4. After the narrator hears her father cry, she says, "The world had lost its boundary lines." How does this experience mark a **turning point** in the story?

5. How is the destruction of Miss Lottie's garden related to the narrator's feelings of despair?

6. What insight does she get into Miss Lottie and into herself? How is she changed by these insights?

7. At the end of the story, the narrator says that she, too, has planted marigolds. What do you think the marigolds represented for Miss Lottie? What do they represent for the narrator?

Literary Elements

Relating Setting to Theme and Character

The description of setting may be a key to the author's **theme**—the underlying idea of the story. In "Marigolds," the barren setting is a reflection of something that mars the lives of the narrator, her family, and the other people in her home town. The description of setting may also indicate the state of mind of characters in the story.

Locate passages in which the descriptions of setting give you information about the narrator's state of mind or give you insight into the story's theme.

Language and Vocabulary
Forming New Words by Adding Suffixes

The word *unsuccessful* has three parts. The core or base of the word—*success*—is its **root**. Attached to the root are two **affixes**. The affix that appears before the root—**un**—is a **prefix** meaning "not." The affix that follows the root—**ful**—is a **suffix** meaning "marked by." By combining the meanings of the different parts we arrive at the definition for *unsuccessful:* "not marked by success."

Suffixes called **derivational suffixes** not only can change meaning but can also change a word's part of speech. When the suffix **–less,** meaning "without," is added to a noun, it forms an adjective:

grass (noun) + less (suffix) = grassless (adjective), meaning "without grass"

Another suffix that changes a noun to an adjective is **–ful,** meaning "full of, marked by":

sorrow + ful = sorrowful, meaning "full of sorrow"

A noun-forming suffix is **–ness,** which means "quality of or state of being":

idle (adjective) + ness = idleness (noun), meaning "state of being idle"

The suffix **–ly** can be used to form an adjective or an adverb. When added to a noun, it forms an adjective:

friend (noun) + ly = friendly (adjective), meaning "like a friend"

More frequently, however, it is used to form an adverb from an adjective:

vivid (adjective) + ly = vividly (adverb), meaning "in a vivid way or manner"

When –**ly** is added to an adjective ending in **y,** the **y** is changed to an **i:**

weary + ly = wearily

When added to an adjective ending in **ble,** the **e** changes to **y:**

horrible + ly = horribly

Find examples of words in the story that contain all these different suffixes. Give the part of speech and the meaning for each word.

LANGUAGE
WORKSHOP

LW 9 Ch 9:59
LW 10 Ch 10:47
**Adding Prefixes
and Suffixes**

Descriptive Writing

Describing a Setting
Choose a photograph or fine art illustration in this book that shows a street or country scene. Examine the details of setting carefully. What is your general impression of the scene? What specific details create this impression? Write one or two paragraphs describing this setting.

Prewriting Strategies
1. Use precise details and modifiers. Make a list of these. Note how Collier uses precise details to describe a deteriorating house:

. . . a *gray rotting thing* with *no porch, no shutters, no steps,* set on a *cramped lot* with *no grass, not even any weeds*—a monument to decay.

2. Follow a logical order. You can use spatial order, beginning at one side of the picture and moving toward the other, or you can work from specific details toward a general impression, as Collier does in the above description.
3. For additional suggestions, see **Writing Description** on pages 193–195.

Speaking and Listening

Responding to the Story
Mari Evans, a well-known poet whose work you will read in Unit Nine, has said that literature can have a "healing" function. For example, it can make us understand that mean and violent actions are often the result of having experienced meanness and violence in one's own past. By reading, we can gain insight into such experience and learn not to seek relief from pain by causing it for others.

Do you think "Marigolds" might be considered a "healing" story? Has it helped you understand the narrator's destructive actions? Has it given you greater compassion for both the narrator and Miss Lottie?

Marigolds 495

The Author Comments

How I Wrote "Marigolds"

 When I talk with people about "Marigolds," someone usually asks me whether the story is autobiographical. I am always pleased with the question, because it means that I must have done my job well—convinced the reader that the incidents in the story are actually happening. However, I always end up admitting that Lizabeth and I are two very different people. I was born and bred in the city of Baltimore, and my family never had the economic problems of Lizabeth's. In some ways we are different in temperament: I was never as daring as Lizabeth, never a leader among my peers. However, I hope that through her I captured an experience which most young people have—the painful passage from childhood to adulthood, a passage which can be understood only in retrospect. Also, I was tapping into another deeply human experience: hoping desperately for something (planting marigolds) and then having that hope destroyed.

I wrote "Marigolds" at a time of profound unhappiness. One night I had a tremendous urge to write. I wrote nonstop until the story was finished—about twenty-four hours. Later I sent "Marigolds" (along with a fee I could hardly afford) to a well-advertised literary agency, which returned the story (not the fee) with a note saying that it had no plot, no conflict, and no hope of publication. Discouraged, I put "Marigolds" away. Five years later, doing research for a project on black writing of the 1960s, I read stories in *Negro Digest* which were similar in subject matter to "Marigolds." I submitted my story, and *Negro Digest* published it. It won the Gwendolyn Brooks Prize for Fiction, it was selected for inclusion in an anthology of black fiction, and since then it has been included in a number of collections. Of all the fiction I have written, "Marigolds" remains my favorite.

—Eugenia Collier

About the Author

Paule Marshall (b. 1929)

 Paule Marshall was born in Brooklyn, New York, which became the setting for her first novel, *Brown Girl, Brownstones* (1959). She attended Brooklyn College and Hunter College. She has worked as a librarian, as a magazine staff writer, and as a lecturer on black literature at several universities.

Marshall's writings reflect her background as the daughter of Barbadian immigrants. She concentrates on the culturally distinct world of the Caribbean Islands and of Caribbean immigrants. In an essay called "From the Poets in the Kitchen" (1983), Marshall tells how she was influenced by the language and culture she received from her mother and her mother's West Indian friends. Marshall once said about her novel *Brown Girl, Brownstones,* "I was so caught up in the need to get down on paper before it was lost the whole sense of a special kind of community, what I call Bajan (Barbadian) Brooklyn, because even as a child I sensed there was something special and powerful about it."

Marshall has written three other novels: *The Chosen Place, the Timeless People* (1969), *Praisesong for the Widow* (1983), and *Daughters* (1991). Her short stories appear in two collections: *Soul Clap Hands and Sing* (1961) and *Reena and Other Stories* (1983).

Charles Stewart/Wide World

For her skill as a storyteller, Marshall has received the Rosenthal Award from the National Institute of Arts and Letters, a Guggenheim fellowship, a MacArthur Fellowship, and grants from the Ford Foundation and the National Endowment for the Arts.

Before You Read

To Da-duh, in Memoriam

Using What You Know

In this story, the narrator and her family, who live in New York City, visit relatives in Barbados, an island in the West Indies. As you might expect, the characters discover a great many differences between life on a Caribbean island and life in a big American city.

If you live in a city, imagine what it might be like to spend a month or more in a rural area. If you live in the country, imagine what life in a big city might be. Share your thoughts and experiences with your classmates.

Background

Until 1966, when it received its independence, Barbados was a colony of Great Britain. Long before independence, many Barbadians left the island in search of greater economic opportunity. Some went to Panama to work on the Panama Canal. These immigrants to Panama would send money home to their relatives. This money became known as "Panama money." Other Barbadians went to England, to Canada, and to the United States.

Literary Focus: Types of Characters

Characters in fiction are sometimes described as **static** or **dynamic.** Characters that remain the same throughout a literary work are called **static characters.** They do not develop or change in any significant way. Characters that undergo some basic change in personality or in outlook are called **dynamic characters.**

Often, when you read a story, you have one impression of a character at the outset. As you learn more about the character, your impressions change.

Setting a Purpose

Note how your impressions of the main characters develop during the course of the story.

To Da-duh, in Memoriam°

Paule Marshall

"... Oh Nana! all of you is not involved in this evil business Death,
Nor all of us in life."
—From "At My Grandmother's Grave," by Lebert Bethune

I did not see her at first I remember. For not only was it dark inside the crowded disembarkation shed in spite of the daylight flooding in from outside, but standing there waiting for her with my mother and sister I was still somewhat blinded from the sheen of tropical sunlight on the water of the bay which we had just crossed in the landing boat, leaving behind us the ship that had brought us from New York lying in the offing.[1] Besides, being only nine years of age at the time and knowing nothing of islands I was busy attending to the alien sights and sounds of Barbados,[2] the unfamiliar smells.

I did not see her, but I was alerted to her approach by my mother's hand which suddenly tightened around mine, and looking up I traced her gaze through the gloom in the shed until I finally made out the small,

Danny Lyon/Magnum Photos

° **in memoriam** (ĭn′mə-môr′ē-əm): in memory of, a Latin phrase used as an inscription on a gravestone.
1. **in the offing:** at some distance but still in sight.
2. **Barbados** (bär-bā′dōs): country in the West Indies. It was a British colony until 1966, when it became independent.

purposeful, painfully erect figure of the old woman headed our way.

Her face was drowned in the shadow of an ugly rolled-brim brown felt hat, but the details of her slight body and of the struggle taking place within it were clear enough—an intense, unrelenting struggle between her back which was beginning to bend ever so slightly under the weight of her eighty-odd years and the rest of her which sought to deny those years and hold that back straight, keep it in line. Moving swiftly toward us (so swiftly it seemed she did not intend stopping when she reached us but would sweep past us out the doorway which opened onto the sea and like Christ walk upon the water!), she was caught between the sunlight at her end of the building and the darkness inside—and for a moment she appeared to contain them both: the light in the long severe old-fashioned white dress she wore which brought the sense of a past that was still alive into our bustling present and in the snatch of white at her eye; the darkness in her black high-top shoes and in her face which was visible now that she was closer.

It was as stark and fleshless as a death mask, that face. The maggots might have already done their work, leaving only the framework of bone beneath the ruined skin and deep wells at the temple and jaw. But her eyes were alive, unnervingly so for one so old, with a sharp light that flicked out of the dim clouded depths like a lizard's tongue to snap up all in her view. Those eyes betrayed a child's curiosity about the world, and I wondered vaguely seeing them, and seeing the way the bodice of her ancient dress had collapsed in on her flat chest (what had happened to her breasts?), whether she might not be some kind of child at the same time that she was a woman, with fourteen children, my mother included, to prove it. Perhaps she was both, both child and woman, darkness and light, past and present, life and death—all the opposites contained and reconciled in her.

"My Da-duh," my mother said formally and stepped forward. The name sounded like thunder fading softly in the distance.

"Child," Da-duh said, and her tone, her quick scrutiny of my mother, the brief embrace in which they appeared to shy from each other rather than touch, wiped out the fifteen years my mother had been away and restored the old relationship. My mother, who was such a formidable figure in my eyes, had suddenly with a word been reduced to my status.

"Yes, God is good," Da-duh said with a nod that was like a tic. "He has spared me to see my child again."

We were led forward then, apologetically because not only did Da-duh prefer boys but she also liked her grandchildren to be "white," that is, fair-skinned; and we had, I was to discover, a number of cousins, the outside children of white estate managers and the like, who qualified. We, though, were as black as she.

My sister being the oldest was presented first. "This one takes after the father," my mother said and waited to be reproved.

Frowning, Da-duh tilted my sister's face toward the light. But her frown soon gave way to a grudging smile, for my sister with her large mild eyes and little broad winged nose, with our father's high-cheeked Barbadian cast to her face, was pretty.

"She's goin' be lucky," Da-duh said and patted her once on the cheek. "Any girl child that takes after the father does be lucky."

She turned then to me. But oddly enough she did not touch me. Instead leaning close, she peered hard at me, and then quickly drew back. I thought I saw her hand start up as though to shield her eyes. It was almost as if she saw not only me, a thin truculent child who it was said took after no one but myself, but something in me which for some reason she found disturbing, even threatening. We looked silently at each other for a long time there in the noisy shed, our gaze locked. She was the first to look away.

"But Adry," she said to my mother and her laugh was cracked, thin, apprehensive. "Where did you get this one here with this fierce look?"

"We don't know where she came out of, my Da-duh," my mother said, laughing also. Even I smiled to myself. After all I had won the encounter. Da-duh had recognized my small strength—and this was all I ever asked of the adults in my life then.

"Come, soul," Da-duh said and took my hand. "You must be one of those New York terrors you hear so much about."

She led us, me at her side and my sister and mother behind, out of the shed into the sunlight that was like a bright driving summer rain and over to a group of people clustered beside a decrepit lorry.[3] They were our relatives, most of them from St. Andrews although Da-duh herself lived in St. Thomas,[4] the women wearing bright print dresses, the colors vivid against their darkness, the men rusty black suits that encased them like straitjackets. Da-duh, holding fast to my hand, became my anchor as they circled round us like a nervous sea, exclaiming, touching us with calloused hands, embracing us shyly. They laughed in awed bursts: "But look Adry got big-big children" / "And see the nice things they wearing, wrist watch

and all!" / "I tell you, Adry has done all right for sheself in New York. . . ."

Da-duh, ashamed at their wonder, embarrassed for them, admonished them the while. "But oh Christ," she said, "why you all got to get on like you never saw people from 'Away' before? You would think New York is the only place in the world to hear wunna. That's why I don't like to go anyplace with you St. Andrews people, you know. You all ain't been colonized."

We were in the back of the lorry finally, packed in among the barrels of ham, flour, cornmeal and rice and the trunks of clothes that my mother had brought as gifts. We made our way slowly through Bridgetown's[5] clogged streets, part of a funereal procession of cars and open-sided buses, bicycles and donkey carts. The dim little limestone shops and offices along the way marched with us, at the same mournful pace, toward the same grave ceremony—as did the people, the women balancing huge baskets on top their heads as if they were no more than hats they wore to shade them from the sun. Looking over the edge of the lorry I watched as their feet slurred the dust. I listened, and their voices, raw and loud and dissonant in the heat, seemed to be grappling with each other high overhead.

Da-duh sat on a trunk in our midst, a monarch amid her court. She still held my hand, but it was different now. I had suddenly become her anchor, for I felt her fear of the lorry with its asthmatic motor (a fear and distrust, I later learned, she held of all machines) beating like a pulse in her rough palm.

As soon as we left Bridgetown behind though, she relaxed, and while the others

3. **lorry** (lôr′ē): a motor truck.
4. **St. Andrews . . . St. Thomas:** parishes in Barbados.

5. **Bridgetown:** the capital of Barbados.

To Da-duh, in Memoriam 501

An open-sided bus in Barbados.

Dennis Stock/Magnum Photos

around us talked she gazed at the canes standing tall on either side of the winding marl road. "C'dear," she said softly to herself after a time. "The canes this side are pretty enough."

They were too much for me. I thought of them as giant weeds that had overrun the island, leaving scarcely any room for the small tottering houses of sunbleached pine we passed or the people, dark streaks as our lorry hurtled by. I suddenly feared that we were journeying, unaware that we were, toward some dangerous place where the canes, grown as high and thick as a forest, would close in on us and run us through with their stiletto blades. I longed then for the familiar: for the street in Brooklyn where I lived, for my father who had refused to accompany us ("Blowing out good money on foolishness," he had said of the trip), for a game of tag with my friends under the chestnut tree outside our aging brownstone house.

"Yes, but wait till you see St. Thomas canes," Da-duh was saying to me. "They's canes father, bo," she gave a proud arrogant nod. "Tomorrow, God willing, I goin' take you out in the ground and show them to you."

True to her word Da-duh took me with her the following day out into the ground. It was a fairly large plot adjoining her weathered board and shingle house and consisting of a small orchard, a good-sized canepiece and behind the canes, where the land sloped abruptly down, a gully. She had purchased it with Panama money sent her by her eldest son, my uncle Joseph, who had died working on the canal. We entered the ground along a trail no wider than her body and as devious and complex as her reasons for showing me her land. Da-duh strode briskly ahead, her slight form filled out this morning by the layers of sacking petticoats she wore under her working dress to protect her against the damp. A fresh white cloth, elaborately arranged around her head, added to her height, and lent her a vain, almost roguish air.

Her pace slowed once we reached the orchard, and glancing back at me occasionally over her shoulder, she pointed out the various trees.

"This here is a breadfruit," she said. "That one yonder is a papaw. Here's a guava. This is a mango. I know you don't have anything like these in New York. Here's a sugar apple." (The fruit looked more like artichokes than apples to me.) "This one bears limes. . . ." She went on for some time, intoning the names of the trees as though they were those of her gods. Finally, turning to me, she said, "I know you don't have anything this nice where you come from." Then, as I hesitated: "I said I know you don't have anything this nice where you come from. . . ."

"No," I said and my world did seem suddenly lacking.

Da-duh nodded and passed on. The orchard ended and we were on the narrow cart road that led through the canepiece, the canes clashing like swords above my cowering head. Again she turned and her thin muscular arms spread wide, her dim gaze embracing the small field of canes, she said— and her voice almost broke under the weight of her pride, "Tell me, have you got anything like these in that place where you were born?"

"No."

"I din' think so. I bet you don't even know that these canes here and the sugar you eat is one and the same thing. That they does throw the canes into some damn machine at the factory and squeeze out all the little life in them to make sugar for you all so in New York to eat. I bet you don't know that."

"I've got two cavities and I'm not allowed to eat a lot of sugar."

But Da-duh didn't hear me. She had turned with an inexplicably angry motion and was making her way rapidly out of the canes and down the slope at the edge of the field which led to the gully below. Following her apprehensively down the incline amid a stand of banana plants whose leaves flapped like elephants ears in the wind, I found myself in the middle of a small tropical wood—a place dense and damp and gloomy and tremulous with the fitful play of light and shadow as the leaves high above moved against the sun that was almost hidden from view. It was a violent place, the tangled foliage fighting each other for a chance at the sunlight, the branches of the trees locked in what seemed an immemorial struggle, one both necessary and inevitable. But despite the violence, it was pleasant, almost peaceful in the gully, and beneath the thick undergrowth the earth smelled like spring.

This time Da-duh didn't even bother to ask her usual question, but simply turned and waited for me to speak.

"No," I said, my head bowed. "We don't have anything like this in New York."

To Da-duh, in Memoriam   503

"Ah," she cried, her triumph complete. "I din' think so. Why, I've heard that's a place where you can walk till you near drop and never see a tree."

"We've got a chestnut tree in front of our house," I said.

"Does it bear?" she waited. "I ask you, does it bear?"

"Not anymore," I muttered. "It used to, but not anymore."

She gave the nod that was like a nervous twitch. "You see," she said. "Nothing can bear there." Then, secure behind her scorn, she added, "But tell me, what's this snow like that you hear so much about?"

Looking up, I studied her closely, sensing my chance, and then I told her, describing at length and with as much drama as I could summon not only what snow in the city was like, but what it would be like here, in her perennial summer kingdom.

". . . And you see all these trees you got here," I said. "Well, they'd be bare. No leaves, no fruit, nothing. They'd be covered in snow. You see your canes. They'd be buried under tons of snow. The snow would be higher than your head, higher than your house, and you wouldn't be able to come down into this here gully because it would be snowed under. . . ."

She searched my face for the lie, still scornful but intrigued. "What a thing, huh?" she said finally, whispering it softly to herself.

"And when it snows you couldn't dress like you are now," I said. "Oh no, you'd freeze to death. You'd have to wear a hat and gloves and galoshes and ear muffs so your ears wouldn't freeze and drop off, and a heavy coat. I've got a Shirley Temple coat with fur on the collar. I can dance. You wanna see?"

Before she could answer I began, with a dance called the Truck which was popular back then in the 1930's. My right forefinger waving, I trucked around the nearby trees and around Da-duh's awed and rigid form. After the Truck I did the Suzy-Q, my lean hips swishing, my sneakers sidling zigzag over the ground. "I can sing," I said and did so, starting with "I'm Gonna Sit Right Down and Write Myself a Letter," then without pausing, "Tea For Two," and ending with "I Found a Million Dollar Baby in a Five and Ten Cent Store."

For long moments afterwards Da-duh stared at me as if I were a creature from Mars, an emissary from some world she did not know but which intrigued her and whose power she both felt and feared. Yet something about my performance must have pleased her, because bending down she slowly lifted her long skirt and then, one by one, the layers of petticoats until she came to a drawstring purse dangling at the end of a long strip of cloth tied round her waist. Opening the purse she handed me a penny. "Here," she said half-smiling against her will. "Take this to buy yourself a sweet at the shop up the road. There's nothing to be done with you, soul."

From then on, whenever I wasn't taken to visit relatives, I accompanied Da-duh out into the ground, and alone with her amid the canes or down in the gully I told her about New York. It always began with some slighting remark on her part: "I know they don't have anything this nice where you come from," or "Tell me, I hear those foolish people in New York does do such and such. . . ." But as I answered, recreating my towering world of steel and concrete and machines for her, building the city out of words, I would feel her give way. I came to know the signs of her surrender: the total stillness that would come over her little hard dry form, the probing gaze that like a surgeon's knife sought to cut through my skull to get at the images there, to see if I were lying; above all, her fear, a fear nameless and profound, the same one I had felt beating in the palm of her hand that day in the lorry.

Over the weeks I told her about refrigerators, radios, gas stoves, elevators, trolley cars,[6] wringer washing machines, movies, airplanes, the cyclone at Coney Island,[7] sub-

6. **trolley cars:** electric streetcars.
7. **cyclone at Coney Island:** a roller coaster located in a famous amusement park in Brooklyn.

Inge Morath/Magnum Photos

ways, toasters, electric lights: "At night, see, all you have to do is flip this little switch on the wall and all the lights in the house go on. Just like that. Like magic. It's like turning on the sun at night."

"But tell me," she said to me once with a faint mocking smile, "do the white people have all these things too or it's only the people looking like us?"

I laughed. "What d'ya mean," I said. "The white people have even better." Then: "I beat up a white girl in my class last term."

"Beating up white people!" Her tone was incredulous.

"How you mean!" I said, using an expression of hers. "She called me a name."

For some reason Da-duh could not quite get over this and repeated in the same hushed, shocked voice, "Beating up white people now! Oh, the lord, the world's changing up so I can scarce recognize it anymore."

One morning toward the end of our stay, Da-duh led me into a part of the gully that we had never visited before, an area darker and more thickly overgrown than the rest, almost impenetrable. There in a small clearing amid the dense bush, she stopped before an incredibly tall royal palm which rose cleanly out of the ground, and drawing the eye up with it, soared high above the trees around it into the sky. It appeared to be touching the blue dome of sky, to be flaunting its dark crown of fronds right in the blinding white face of the late morning sun.

Da-duh watched me a long time before she spoke, and then she said, very quietly, "All right, now, tell me if you've got anything this tall in that place you're from."

I almost wished, seeing her face, that I could have said no. "Yes," I said. "We've got buildings hundreds of times this tall in New York. There's one called the Empire State Building[8] that's the tallest in the world. My class visited it last year and I went all the way to the top. It's got over a hundred floors. I can't describe how tall it is. Wait a minute. What's the name of that hill I went to visit the other day, where they have the police station?"

"You mean Bissex?"

"Yes, Bissex. Well, the Empire State Building is way taller than that."

"You're lying now!" she shouted, trembling with rage. Her hand lifted to strike me.

"No, I'm not," I said. "It really is, if you don't believe me I'll send you a picture postcard of it soon as I get back home so you can see for yourself. But it's way taller than Bissex."

All the fight went out of her at that. The hand poised to strike me fell limp to her side, and as she stared at me, seeing not me but the building that was taller than the highest hill she knew, the small stubborn light in her eyes (it was the same amber as the flame in the kerosene lamp she lit at dusk) began to fail. Finally, with a vague gesture that even in the midst of her defeat still tried to dismiss me and my world, she turned and started back through the gully, walking slowly, her steps groping and uncertain, as if she were suddenly no longer sure of the way, while I followed triumphant yet strangely saddened behind.

The next morning I found her dressed for our morning walk but stretched out on the Berbice chair in the tiny drawing room where she sometimes napped during the afternoon heat, her face turned to the window beside her. She appeared thinner and suddenly indescribably old.

"My Da-duh," I said.

"Yes, nuh," she said. Her voice was listless and the face she slowly turned my way was, now that I think back on it, like a Benin[9] mask, the features drawn and almost distorted by an ancient abstract sorrow.

"Don't you feel well?" I asked.

"Girl, I don't know."

"My Da-duh, I goin' boil you some bush tea,"[10] my aunt, Da-duh's youngest child,

---

8. **Empire State Building:** the tallest building until 1972. The World Trade Center in New York and the Sears Tower in Chicago are taller.

9. **Benin** (bĕ-nēn'): formerly a kingdom in West Africa, now part of Nigeria.

10. **bush tea:** tea made from a certain weed or wild plant.

A belt mask of ivory, Benin, Nigeria, c. 1550.
Lee Boltin

who lived with her, called from the shed roof kitchen.

"Who tell you I need bush tea?" she cried, her voice assuming for a moment its old authority. "You can't even rest nowadays without some malicious person looking for you to be dead. Come girl," she motioned me to a place beside her on the old-fashioned lounge chair, "give us a tune."

I sang for her until breakfast at eleven, all my brash irreverent Tin Pan Alley[11] songs, and then just before noon we went out into

---

11. **Tin Pan Alley:** a district of New York City associated with musicians, songwriters, and publishers of popular music.

the ground. But it was a short, dispirited walk. Da-duh didn't even notice that the mangoes were beginning to ripen and would have to be picked before the village boys got to them. And when she paused occasionally and looked out across the canes or up at her trees it wasn't as if she were seeing them but something else. Some huge, monolithic[12] shape had imposed itself, it seemed, between her and the land, obstructing her vision. Returning to the house she slept the entire afternoon on the Berbice chair.

She remained like this until we left, languishing away the mornings on the chair at the window gazing out at the land as if it were already doomed; then, at noon, taking the brief stroll with me through the ground during which she seldom spoke, and afterwards returning home to sleep till almost dusk sometimes.

On the day of our departure she put on the austere, ankle length white dress, the black shoes and brown felt hat (her town clothes she called them), but she did not go with us to town. She saw us off on the road outside her house and in the midst of my mother's tearful protracted farewell, she leaned down and whispered in my ear, "Girl, you're not to forget now to send me the picture of that building, you hear."

By the time I mailed her the large colored picture postcard of the Empire State Building she was dead. She died during the famous '37 strike[13] which began shortly after we left. On the day of her death England sent planes flying low over the island in a show of force—so low, according to my aunt's letter, that the downdraft from them

---

12. **monolithic** (măn′ə-lĭth′ĭk): like a single large block of stone.
13. **famous '37 strike:** Economic conditions became so bad in 1937 that there were riots in Barbados.

shook the ripened mangoes from the trees in Da-duh's orchard. Frightened, everyone in the village fled into the canes. Except Da-duh. She remained in the house at the window so my aunt said, watching as the planes came swooping and screaming like monstrous birds down over the village, over her house, rattling her trees and flattening the young canes in the field. It must have seemed to her lying there that they did not intend pulling out of their dive, but like the hard-back beetles which hurled themselves with suicidal force against the walls of the house at night, those menacing silver shapes would hurl themselves in an ecstasy of self-immolation[14] onto the land, destroying it utterly.

When the planes finally left and the villag-ers returned they found her dead on the Berbice chair at the window.

She died and I lived, but always, to this day even, within the shadow of her death. For a brief period after I was grown I went to live alone, like one doing penance, in a loft above a noisy factory in downtown New York and there painted seas of sugar-cane and huge swirling Van Gogh suns[15] and palm trees striding like brightly-plumed Tutsi[16] warriors across a tropical landscape, while the thunderous tread of the machines downstairs jarred the floor beneath my easel, mocking my efforts.

14. **self-immolation** (ĭm′ə-lā′shən): self-sacrifice.

15. **Van Gogh** (văn gō′, văn gôкн′) **suns:** Vincent Van Gogh, a Dutch artist, painted canvases that contained brilliant yellows and oranges.
16. **Tutsi:** Watusi (wä-too′sē) or Watutsi, an African people known for their tallness.

Responding to the Selection
To Da-duh, in Memoriam by Paule Marshall

Identifying Facts

1. How old is the narrator when she visits Da-duh?
2. How long has the narrator's mother been away from Barbados?
3. Why does Da-duh reward the narrator with a penny?
4. What is the final conflict between the narrator and Da-duh?
5. What does the narrator promise to send Da-duh?

Interpreting Meanings

1. This story traces a complex relationship between a child and the matriarch, or head, of a family. Why do you think Da-duh is drawn to the narrator, rather than to the other children?
2. Why is Da-duh frightened by the narrator's stories of New York? How does she try to hold on to what is familiar in her own world?
3. At what point is it clear that Da-duh has lost the contest with her grandchild?

4. At the end of the story, the narrator says that she has lived in the shadow of Da-duh's death. How do you interpret this statement?

5. The **setting** of a story can be established through language and customs, as well as through descriptions of place. The author records several examples of Barbadian speech, such as this one: "Adry has done alright for *sheself.*" Locate other expressions that give you the flavor of the setting.

Literary Elements

Analyzing Methods of Characterization

Find examples in the story where the author uses **direct characterization** to present Da-duh to the reader. Which descriptions and comments give you insight into Da-duh's personality?

Find examples of **indirect characterization**. Which actions and speeches reveal key aspects of Da-duh's character?

Is Da-duh a **static** or a **dynamic character**? Do you think she is one-sided (a **flat character**), or do you think she is complex (a **round character**)? Give reasons for your answers.

Explaining Similes

How would you describe a snowball to a person who lived in the tropics and had never seen one? If you say that a snowball is round *like* a ball and cold *like* ice cream, then you are using a **simile.** You are making a comparison between two unlike things and using a word of comparison, such as *like* or *as.* We use similes in everyday speech. Some similes are clichés (klē-shāz'), that is, expressions that have been used so often that they are no longer fresh: "pretty *as* a picture"; "fast *as* lightning"; "run *like* the wind."

Marshall's narrator describes Da-duh's face in this way: "It was as stark and fleshless as a death mask, that face." What comparison is she making? Examine the Benin mask on page 507. Why is this comparison effective?

Locate three or more similes in the story. Explain the comparison in each one.

Language and Vocabulary

Understanding Related Words

The phrase "in memoriam" comes from Latin. It means "in memory of."

In a dictionary, find the meanings of the following words and tell how they are related in meaning. Be sure to look at the information the dictionary gives you about the origin and development of each word. This information is often enclosed in brackets within the entry.

immemorial
memorable
memorabilia
memorialize

Writing About Literature

Responding to the Author's Comment

Read Paule Marshall's comment on her story. In what way was the narrator's relationship with her grandmother that of a rival? What was the power struggle between them? How does the story deal with "the relationship of western civilization and the Third World?" Why does Marshall feel that her existence depends upon the spirit of her ancestors?

Explore your ideas in a short essay. Refer to the story in your discussion.

Speaking and Listening

Holding an Interview

Do you have any relatives or friends who have lived in the Caribbean? If so, ask them to tell you about their experiences growing up on the islands. What was school like? What kinds of foods did they enjoy? What special holidays or festivals were held? What do they miss? Share this information with your classmates.

The Author Comments

 This is the most autobiographical of the stories, a reminiscence largely of a visit I paid to my grandmother (whose nickname was Da-duh) on the island of Barbados when I was nine. Ours was a complex relationship—close, affectionate yet rivalrous. During the year I spent with her a subtle kind of power struggle went on between us. It was as if we both knew, at a level beyond words, that I had come into the world not only to love her and to continue her line but to take her very life in order that I might live.

Years later, when I got around to writing the story, I tried giving the contest I had sensed between us a wider meaning. I wanted the basic theme of youth and old age to suggest rivalries, dichotomies of a cultural and political nature, having to do with the relationship of western civilization and the Third World . . . .

She's an ancestor figure, symbolic for me of the long line of black women and men—African and New World—who made my being possible, and whose spirit I believe continues to animate my life and work. I wish to acknowledge and celebrate them. I am, in a word, an unabashed ancestor worshipper.

—Paule Marshall

About the Author

Ernest J. Gaines (b. 1933)

 Ernest James Gaines was born in Oscar, Louisiana. Most of his childhood was spent at the old slave quarters on the River Lake Plantation, where five generations of his family had lived. In his fiction, Gaines re-creates an imaginary plantation region that he calls Bayonne, based on the area where he was raised. He once told an interviewer that his experiences growing up included "working in the fields, going fishing in the swamps with the older people, and, especially, listening to the people who came to my aunt's house."

When he was fifteen, Gaines moved from Louisiana to Vallejo, California. He attended San Francisco State College and Stanford University.

His first novel, *Catherine Carmier,* was published in 1964. It was followed by *Of Love and Dust,* in 1967, and then by *The Autobiography of Miss Jane Pittman,* in 1971. This novel, which was adapted for television, tells the story of an African American woman who is born a slave and lives until the time of the Civil Rights Movement in the 1960s. Many readers consider this book to be Gaines's greatest novel. It was awarded a gold medal for fiction by the Commonwealth Club of California. This award was also given to *A Gathering of Old Men* (1983), which deals with the changes affecting the South and with the passing of old traditions and values. His most recent novel, *A Lesson Before Dying,* was published in 1993.

Wide World Photos

In addition to novels, Gaines has written short stories. His first collection, *Bloodline,* was published in 1968. "Robert Louis Stevenson Banks, aka Chimley" appeared in the *Georgia Review* and was later included in the novel *A Gathering of Old Men.* This story illustrates one of Gaines's major themes— survival with dignity in the face of tremendous hardships.

Ernest J. Gaines   511

Before You Read

Robert Louis Stevenson Banks, aka Chimley

Using What You Know

The characters in this story are from a rural area in Louisiana. In their dialogue, they use certain **regionalisms**. A **regionalism** is a word or phrase associated with a specific geographical region. For example, the characters refer to a certain kind of sunfish, the crappie, as a *sackalay*. This word actually comes from a French word, *sac-à-lait*. Can you think of regionalisms that you use in everyday speech?

Literary Focus: Point of View

The vantage point from which a story is told is called its **point of view**. There are two basic points of view. In the **first-person point of view**, the story is told by one of the characters in his or her own words. This is the "I" vantage point. In the **third-person point of view**, the narrator tells the story from the vantage point of an observer who stands outside the action. Sometimes this narrator is **omniscient**, or all-knowing. At other times, the author limits the observations of the narrator to only one character. This is called **limited third-person point of view.**

A writer chooses point of view carefully in order to control the reader's reaction to the narrative.

Setting a Purpose

What can you tell about the characters in this story from their speech? Why do you think Gaines has chosen to tell this story in first person?

Robert Louis Stevenson Banks

aka° Chimley

Ernest J. Gaines

Me and Mat was down there fishing. We goes fishing every Tuesday and every Thursday. We got just one little spot now. Ain't like it used to be when you had the whole river to fish on. The white people, they done bought up the river now, and you got nowhere to go but that one little spot. Me and Mat goes there every Tuesday and Thursday. Other people uses it other days, but on Tuesday and Thursday they leaves it for us. We been going to that one little spot like that every Tuesday and Thursday the last ten, 'leven years. That one little spot. Just ain't got nowhere else to go no more.

We had been down there—oh, 'bout a hour. Mat had caught eight or nine good-size perches, and me about six— throw in a couple of sackalays[1] there with the bunch. Me and Mat was just sitting there taking life easy, talking low. Mat was sitting on his croker sack,[2] I was sitting on my bucket. The fishes we had caught, we had them on a string in the water, keeping them fresh. We

°**aka:** also known as, used before an alias.
1. **sackalay:** a type of freshwater fish; a white crappie.
2. **croker sack:** a bag made of coarse material called *crocus cloth*. It is similar to burlap.

was just sitting there talking low, talking 'bout the old days.

Then that oldest boy of Berto, that sissy one they called Fue, come running down the riverbank and said Clatoo said Miss Merle said that young woman at Marshall, Candy, wanted us on the place right away. She wanted us to get twelve-gauge shotguns and number five shells and she wanted us to shoot, but keep the empty shells and get there right away.

Me and Mat looked at him standing there sweating—a great big old round-face, sissy-looking boy, in blue jeans and a blue gingham shirt, the shirt wet from him running.

Mat said, "All that for what?"

The boy looked like he was ready to run some more. Sweat just pouring down the side of his face. He was one of them great big old sissy-looking boys—round, smooth, sissy-looking face.

He said: "Something to do with Mathu, and something to do with Beau Boutan dead in his yard. That's all I know, all I want to know. Up to y'all now, I done done my part. Y'all can go and do like she say or y'all can go home, lock y'all doors, and crawl under the bed like y'all used to. Me, I'm leaving."

He turned.

"Where you going?" Mat called to him.

"You and no Boutan'll ever know," he called back.

"You better run out of Louisiana," Mat said to himself.

The boy had already got out of hearing reach—one of them great big old sissy boys, running hard as he could go up the riverbank.

Me and Mat didn't look at each other for a while. Pretending we was more interested in the fishing lines. But it wasn't fishing we was thinking about now. We was thinking about what happened to us after something like this did happen. Not a killing like this. I had never knowed in all my life where a black man had killed a white man in this parish. I had knowed about fights, about threats, but not killings. And now I was thinking about what happened after these fights, these threats, how the white folks rode. This what I was thinking, and I was sure Mat was doing the same. That's why we didn't look at each other for a while. We didn't want to see what the other one was thinking. We didn't want to see the fear in the other one's face.

"He works in mysterious ways, don't He?" Mat said. It wasn't loud, more like he was talking to himself, not to me. But I knowed he was talking to me. He didn't look at me when he said it, but I knowed he was talking to me. I went on looking at my line.

"That's what they say," I said.

Mat went on looking at his line awhile. I didn't have to look and see if he was looking at his line. We had been together so much, me and him, I knowed what he was doing without looking at him.

"You don't have to answer this 'less you want to, Chimley," he said. He didn't say that loud, neither. He had just jerked on the line, 'cause I could hear the line cut through the water.

"Yeah, Mat?" I said.

He jerked on the line again. Maybe it was a turtle trying to get at the bait. Maybe he just jerked on the line to do something 'stead of looking at me.

"Scared?" he asked. His voice was still low. And he still wasn't looking at me.

"Yes," I said.

He jerked on the line again. Then he pulled in a sackalay 'bout long and wide as my hand. He rebaited the hook and spit on the bait for luck and throwed the line back out in the water. He didn't look at me all this time. I didn't look at him, either. Just seen all this out the corner of my eyes.

"I'm seventy-one, Chimley," he said after the line had settled again. "Seventy-one and a half. I ain't got too much strength left to go crawling under that bed like Fue said."

"I'm seventy-two," I said. But I didn't look at him when I said it.

We sat there awhile looking out at the lines. The water was so clean and blue, peaceful and calm. I coulda sat there all day long looking out there at my line.

"Think he did it?" Mat asked.

I hunched my shoulders. "I don't know, Mat."

"If he did it, you know we ought to be there, Chimley," Mat said.

I didn't answer him, but I knowed what he was talking about. I remembered the fight Mathu and Fix had out there at Marshall store. It started over a Coke bottle. After Fix had drunk his Coke, he wanted Mathu to take the empty bottle back in the store. Mathu told him he wasn't nobody's servant. Fix told him he had to take the bottle back in the store or fight.

A bunch of us was out there, white and black, sitting on the garry[3] eating gingerbread and drinking pop. The sheriff, Guidry, was there, too. Mathu told Guidry if Fix started anything, he was go'n protect himself. Guidry went on eating his gingerbread and drinking pop like he didn't even hear him.

When Fix told Mathu to take the bottle back in the store again, and Mathu didn't, Fix hit him—and the fight was on. Worst fight I ever seen in my life. For a hour it was toe to toe. But when it was over, Mathu was

3. **garry:** a covered porch, usually without railings (from *gallery*).

up, and Fix was down. The white folks wanted to lynch Mathu, but Guidry stopped them. Then he walked up to Mathu, cracked him 'side the jaw, and Mathu hit the ground. He turned to Fix, hit him in the mouth, and Fix went down again. Then Guidry came back to the garry to finish his gingerbread and pop. That was the end of that fight. But that wasn't the last fight Mathu had on that river with them white people. And that's what Mat was talking about. That's what he meant when he said if Mathu did it we ought to be there. Mathu was the only one we knowed had ever stood up.

I looked at Mat sitting on the croker sack. He was holding the fishing pole with both hands, gazing out at the line. We had been together so much I just about knowed what he was thinking. But I asked him anyhow.

"'Bout that bed," he said. "I'm too old to go crawling under that bed. I just don't have the strength for it no more. It's too low, Chimley."

"Mine ain't no higher," I said.

He looked at me now. A fine-featured brown-skin man. I had knowed him all my life. Had been young men together. Had done our little running around together. Had been in a little trouble now and then, but nothing serious. Had never done what we was thinking about doing now. Maybe we had thought about it. Sure, we had thought about it. But we had never done it.

"What you say, Chimley?" he said.

I nodded to him.

We pulled in the lines and went up the bank. Mat had his fishes in the sack; mine was in the bucket.

"She wants us to shoot first," I said. "I wonder why."

"I don't know," Mat said. "How's that old gun of yours working?"

Ivan Massar/Black Star

"Shot good last time," I said. "That's been a while, though."

"You got any number five shells?" Mat asked.

"Might have a couple round there," I said. "I ain't looked in a long time."

"Save me one or two if you got them," Mat said. "Guess I'll have to borrow a gun, too. Nothing round my house work but that twenty-gauge and that old rifle."

"How you figure on getting over there?" I asked him.

"Clatoo, I reckon," Mat said. "Try to hitch a ride with him on the truck."

"Have him pick me up, too," I said.

When we came up to my gate, Mat looked at me again. He was quite a bit taller than me, and I had to kinda hold my head back to look at him.

"You sure now, Chimley?" he said.

"If you go, Mat."

"I have to go, Chimley," he said. "This can be my last chance."

I looked him in the eyes. Lightish-brown eyes. They was saying much more than he had said. They was speaking for both of us, though, me and him.

"I'm going, too," I said.

Mat still looked at me. His eyes was still saying more than he had said. His eyes was saying: We wait till now? Now, when we're old men, we get to be brave?

I didn't know how to answer him. All I knowed, I had to go if he went.

Mat started toward his house, and I went on in the yard. Now, I ain't even stepped in the house good 'fore that old woman started fussing at me. What I'm doing home so early for? She don't like to be cleaning fishes this time of day. She don't like to clean fishes till evening when it's cool. I didn't answer that old woman. I set my bucket of fishes on the table in the kitchen; then I come back in the front room and got my old shotgun from against the wall. I looked through the shells I kept in a cigar box on top of the armoire[4] till I found me a number five. I blowed the dust off, loaded the old gun, stuck it out the window, turnt my head just in case the old gun decided to blow up, and I shot. Here come that old woman starting right back on me again.

"What's the matter with you, old man? What you doing shooting out that window, raising all that racket for?"

4. **armoire** (är-mwär'): a large wardrobe or clothespress.

"Right now, I don't know what I'm doing all this for," I told her. "But, see, if I come back from Marshall and them fishes ain't done and ready for me to eat, I'm go'n do me some more shooting around this house. Do you hear what I'm saying?"

She tightened her mouth and rolled her eyes at me, but she had enough sense not to get too cute. I got me two or three more number five shells, blowed the dust off them, and went out to the road to wait for Clatoo.

Responding to the Selection

Robert Louis Stevenson Banks by Ernest J. Gaines

Identifying Facts

1. What message does Fue bring?
2. Where does Fue go after he delivers his message?
3. Who has been killed?
4. Who is suspected of killing him?
5. What decision do Mat and Chimley make?

Interpreting Meanings

1. Chimley and Mat recall some things that happened in the past which affect the decision they make in the present. What trouble had Mathu gotten into at the Marshall store? What trouble is he in now?
2. Fue says that in the past, the men would go home and "crawl under the bed" when there was trouble. What can you infer about race relations in the "old days"? How are Mat and Chimley determined not to repeat the past?
3. Mat and Chimley decide to go to the defense of Mathu after talking things over carefully. Why is it significant that they make their decision slowly and deliberately rather than in anger or in haste?
4. In the opening paragraph, Chimley says, "Just ain't got nowhere else to go no more." What different meanings might this statement have?
5. What does Mat mean when he says, "This can be my last chance" (page 516)?
6. The author has Chimley tell the story in his own voice, using language that is natural to him. How does this technique make the characters convincing?

Literary Elements

Understanding Point of View
First-person point of view tells what the narrator knows and feels. This point of view can make the events seem real and can bring the reader close to the narrator.

First-person point of view is also limited. The narrator can report what other characters say and do, but not what they think and feel. In Gaines's story, for example, Chimley doesn't know what has actually happened to get Mathu into trouble. He can only speculate about what has occurred. He doesn't know why the men have been asked to fire their shotguns and then bring both the guns and the empty shells with them. The first-person point of view can be used effectively to keep information from the reader, thus increasing the element of suspense.

Examine some of the stories you have read that are written in first-person point of view. Tell why the authors might have chosen this point of view rather than third-person.

Language and Vocabulary
Understanding Regional Differences
In different areas of the United States, there are differences not only in pronunciation but also in vocabulary. For example, what do you call a paper container used to carry groceries? If you live in the East, you probably call it a *bag* or *sack.* In some rural areas of the South, it is called a *tote.* No one of these names is more correct than another. The language you use depends on custom.

Just as there are regional differences in pronunciation and vocabulary, there are differences in **idiom**—the way words are joined together to form expressions. In New York, you may hear "We stood *on* line," whereas in other parts of the country, you might hear "We stood *in* line."

Expressions of time vary, too. Which of these do you use?

A quarter till nine
A quarter to nine
A quarter of nine

What are some characteristics of rural Southern speech that you recognize in Gaines's story?

Creative Writing
Using Different Points of View
Take a well-known story, such as a nursery rhyme, a fable, or a fairy tale, and tell it from a first-person point of view. Then retell it from a third-person point of view. For example, you might tell the story of Hansel and Gretel from the vantage point of one of the children *or* the witch. Then, you might retell it from the point of view of an observer who does not play any part in the action. How does the story change when the point of view changes?

Speaking and Listening
Comparing Styles
Reread some of the stories in this book that reproduce the actual language of characters. Some stories you might consider are "Raymond's Run" (page 4), "Miss Cynthie" (page 357), and "The Man Who Was Almost a Man" (page 420). Tell what these stories achieve by representing the authentic speech of their characters.

About the Author
William Melvin Kelley (b. 1937)

 Early in his career, William Melvin Kelley wrote: "I am not a sociologist or a politician or a spokesman. Such people try to give answers. A writer, I think, should ask questions. He should depict people, not symbols or ideas disguised as people." Kelley's aim has been to treat his characters as individual human beings and not as representatives of a group.

Kelley was born in New York City. He attended Harvard University, where he studied under the direction of two notable writers: Archibald MacLeish and John Hawkes. Kelley's first novel, *A Different Drummer,* was published in 1962, when he was twenty-five. The title emphasizes the importance of individuality in Kelley's work. It comes from the famous lines of Henry David Thoreau: "If a man does not keep pace with his companions, perhaps it is because he hears a different drummer. Let him step to the music which he hears." For this book, Kelley received awards from both the John Hay Whitney and the Rosenthal Foundations.

Kelley has written three other novels: *A Drop of Patience* (1965), *dem* (1967), and *Dunfords Travels Everywheres* (1970). "Brother Carlyle" is one of the stories in *Dancers on the Shore,* a collection of stories that won the *Transatlantic Review* Award in 1964. Most of the stories in this collection were written before Kelley reached his mid-twenties.

Eyely Foto

Before You Read

Brother Carlyle

Using What You Know

In *I Know Why the Caged Bird Sings,* Maya Angelou writes that as a child she loved chocolate drops more than anything in the world, except Bailey, her brother (see page 37). In literature as well as in life, there are many instances of powerful bonds between the children in a family. Can you give any examples? There are also many cases of rivalry and anger between children. Can you name some famous instances?

Literary Focus: Tone

Tone is the attitude a writer takes toward the subject, characters, and readers of a literary work. Tone can be light or serious; it can be mocking or bitter; it can be romantic or ironic. Within a single story, the author's tone may shift. Generally, however, a story has one predominant tone. It is important to grasp the tone of a story in order to understand the author's intention.

Setting a Purpose

As you read, determine the author's attitude toward his characters. How do you think he wants you to respond to Carlyle?

Brother Carlyle

William Melvin Kelley

Irene Bedlow leaned out the kitchen window, reeled in the line's knot, and started to pin out her clothes. Then over the unoiled pulley's screeching, she heard her young son scream. He was somewhere in the alley, between her building and the next.

"Carlyle, what you doing to Mance?" She attempted to bend her voice around to him. "Carlyle, you hear?" There was no answer, but someone had begun to pound on the apartment door. Drying her hands on her apron, she shuffled through the apartment, down the dark hallway, heard her slippers scraping on the wooden floor.

"Oh-Lass, won't you come open the door?" Irene opened the door to the fat West Indian woman who occupied the alley apartment and who now stood before her in a pink nightgown. "Oh-Lass, child, they burning your babe alive!" Missus Neilberry was crying. Tears streamed over her cheeks, catching in the deep crevices on her chins. "They burning your child alive!"

Somewhere inside her, Irene felt slightly ill, but by the time she noticed it, she was on the second floor landing, had almost cascaded into old, black Mister Doozen coming back from his daily walk. Already she had lost one slipper, and the front door pulled the other from her when it slammed on her foot.

Mance's shoes were starting to steam. He was bound to the clothes pole in the alley with thick black wire, and was all but obscured by white smoke surging up from the pile of paper and trash burning at his feet. Carlyle, her older son, sat beside the fire sweating, pretending to warm his hands. The members of his club stood around, hands in pockets, in a state of mixed bewilderment, fear, and excitement, not certain, now, they were doing a good thing.

Irene lunged into the midst of smoke and flame and with bare feet kicked the fire from under Mance. She untied his hands, which despite the heat were damp and cold. When she led him out of the smoke, the other boys had disappeared, leaving Carlyle sitting as before, only now biting his fingernails.

"Carlyle?" She spoke to him almost afraid, for this was not the first time he had done such things, and she knew he would again have some valid excuse and that her protestations would have no effect. "Why'd you—"

"Awh, Mama," Mance, his breath returned, interrupted. "They was letting me join the club. You got to prove you brave before they let you in." He was pulling her apron and jumping up and down.

Carlyle smiled.

She looked down at Mance and opened her mouth, but no words came. She drew

Blue Wall, *batik by Leo F. Twiggs, 1969.*
Collection of the artist

her hand across her forehead. Mance moved away from her and sat next to Carlyle. She started up the alley.

"What time we eating, Mama?" asked Mance to her back.

"Pretty soon now, dear." She sighed and turned the corner.

Upstairs again, standing over the stove, the jellied air of the gas burners rising to her face, she began to think. She knew she was not smart, was not a doctor of the minds of children, but one thing was certain: Something must be done with Carlyle. Tonight, as she had on other occasions, she would mention this to her husband. Perhaps this time he would understand.

Her husband lumbered down the block just as the sun fell into the river. The boys came upstairs with him; today was allowance day. Supper was ready. They sat, said grace, and began to eat.

"What you boys been doing today?" He speared a pork chop with his fork. He was big, dark as the inside of a chimney. During the day he built skyscrapers.

"I got into Carlyle's club, Papa." Mance spoke through a mouth of mashed potatoes.

"Don't talk with your mouth full-up," her husband snapped. Then softly, "That's real good. Your brother helped you, I bet."

Mance nodded.

"That's good. You take good care of your brother, Junior." He grinned proudly at Carlyle. "That's what the Lord says. Ain't that right, Irene?"

"Yes, that's right." She sipped iced tea, and looked away.

Her answer seemed somehow unsatisfactory to her husband, and he was silent for a short while. "Well, I guess you boys'll be wanting your money."

Carlyle nodded.

"Here's a dollar each. Go celebrate your being club members." He handed the two dollars to Carlyle. The boys excused themselves and disappeared, leaving behind half-eaten dinners and the door's slam.

Irene twirled the ice around the bottom of her glass, staring blankly. When her husband started to sip loudly from his tea, she looked up. He watched his tea as he drank and did not see her. For a second she weighed speaking to him at all. She realized it would probably bring on an argument; he would misconstrue and distort her words. Maybe sometime, she thought, he will listen and understand. She put down her glass. "That boy try to kill his brother today."

"What boy?" he asked, cracking ice in his jaws.

"Junior."

"Damn it—there you go again—about how bad Junior is. Why don't you like him?" His voice started to expand in volume. Missus Neilberry would hear him. Tomorrow the whole house would be discussing her latest argument. He leaned forward and planted his fists on either side of the glass.

"I ain't got nothing against him. But he did set Mance afire."

He blinked, fell backward, and laughed. "You know how funny that sound? Maybe he pretend to set him afire, but they brothers and he wasn't about harming him." He stopped, then added for emphasis. "Not one bit." He pounded the table. His glass tipped; he did not notice. He laughed again.

"But it true." She leaned on the table, reached for his hand, tried to find her husband's eyes, but his laughing head would not stay still. When he stopped, he was angry.

"I sick of you babying Mance. You think I don't love him much because he my second

born. Woman, you know better. Still, you always leaping on that."

"Just ask Mance when he gets home." She felt tears coming to her eyes, but dammed them back. "You just ask him." She slumped, folded her arms, and stared at her lap.

"All right. I do just that. And if you wrong, you stop this mess!" He got up and stalked into the living room to read his paper.

When the boys returned, Carlyle was carrying a large box. He went straight to his room, which Mance shared with him, and Irene heard him open the closet door and put the box on the top shelf. He came into the living room and joined Mance, who was standing in the middle of the room.

"What you boys get?" Her husband looked up from his paper.

"A cowboy costume," answered Mance. Irene noticed he seemed a trifle perplexed, as if he were not quite sure what they had bought, who had bought it, or who would use it. "I gave my money to Carlyle. He said I'd only buy some junk and you wouldn't like that much. He said I could wear it sometimes." He breathed deeply. "I could wear it if I was good and minded."

Her husband sat quietly for a moment, then smiled at her. "See there, woman? How could that boy do anything but love his brother to give his money to him? And Junior, he taking care to see this boy ain't being foolish."

Carlyle sat next to his father, and the man put his arm around his shoulder.

"I guess you right." She got up. She went quietly into the bedroom and undressed, placing her house coat neatly on the one chair in the room. She lay on the bed, and through the wall she could hear Carlyle and her husband laughing. After a few seconds, Mance joined in.

Responding to the Selection

Brother Carlyle by William Melvin Kelley

Identifying Facts

1. How does Irene Bedlow find out that Mance is in danger?
2. What test does Mance have to pass to get into Carlyle's club?
3. What does Irene tell her husband after the boys leave?
4. What happens to Mance's allowance money?

Interpreting Meanings

1. Why is Carlyle's mother afraid to question him about the fire?
2. Why do you think Mance always defends his brother's actions? What does this suggest about Carlyle?
3. How do you know that the parents have had other arguments about Carlyle and Mance?
4. Irene Bedlow feels that her husband favors Carlyle. Do you agree?
5. The story is called "Brother Carlyle," yet Carlyle never speaks. What effect is created by his silence?
6. Kelley makes a point of telling us at the end of the story that Carlyle and the father laugh and then Mance joins in. Does Mance really think something is funny, or does he join in for a different reason?
7. What do you see in Carlyle's character that his father does not see and does not wish to accept?

Literary Elements

Recognizing Irony

Irony involves a contrast between appearance and reality—between what appears to be true and what really is true. In the light of what happens in the story, why is each of these statements ironic?

"Your brother helped you, I bet."
"You take good care of your brother, Junior."
"How could that boy do anything but love his brother to give his money to him?"

Writing About Literature

Comparing Characters

Think about the brothers in "The Rockpile" (page 473). Are they similar in some way to Carlyle and Mance? In what ways are the mothers alike? Are there similarities in the fathers? Write a brief essay comparing the characters in the two stories.

Speaking and Listening

Expressing an Opinion

Why does Carlyle treat his younger brother as he does? Is there a clue to his behavior in the father's treatment of the two boys? Discuss your ideas with your classmates.

About the Author

Diane Oliver (1943–1966)

 Diane Alene Oliver was born in Charlotte, North Carolina. She attended the University of North Carolina at Greensboro from 1961 to 1964. During that time, the fight for desegregation was in full force. On February 1, 1960, four students from the Agricultural and Technical College in Greensboro, a predominantly African American institution, had protested segregated facilities by sitting at lunch counters forbidden to them by tradition and by law. This incident launched the **sit-in movement,** which spread rapidly. It was in this climate that Oliver attended college in Greensboro. Her short story "Neighbors" reflects the tension and violence associated with school integration during this period.

At the university, Oliver served as feature editor and managing editor of the student magazine, *The Carolinian.* After graduation she was a guest editor for *Mademoiselle* magazine. In 1966, she attended the famous Writer's Workshop at the University of Iowa. That summer she was killed in an automobile accident. The University of Iowa conferred the Master of Fine Arts degree on her posthumously.

During her lifetime, Oliver's short stories were published in *Red Clay Reader, Negro Digest, The Sewanee Review,* and *New Writing of the Sixties.* "Neighbors" appeared in *The Sewanee Review* in the spring of 1966, and was selected for inclusion in *Prize Stories 1967: The O. Henry Awards.*

Before You Read

Neighbors

Using What You Know

Have you heard your parents or other adults discuss the Civil Rights Movement? What are some of the things they have talked about? How did they participate?

Background

After the Civil War, many Southern states adopted **Jim Crow** laws. These laws were used to segregate the races in public schools, in housing, in transportation, in restaurants, and in public facilities. This kind of segregation is called **de jure** (by law) segregation. Segregated schools existed in some places even where there were no laws requiring it. This kind of segregation is called **de facto** segregation (developed by custom rather than by law).

African American parents and organizations such as the NAACP fought to end segregation in the schools. A breakthrough came in the 1954 case of **Brown v. Board of Education of Topeka,** in which the Supreme Court ruled against de jure segregation in public schools. Even though *Brown* was a victory, it took many years and many conflicts for things to change.

Literary Focus: Theme

The **theme** of a story is its underlying idea, the central insight that the work gives us about people and about life. Theme is sometimes expressed directly. Most of the time, however, theme is expressed indirectly. You have to **infer** the meaning of the story from its other elements.

Setting a Purpose

This story deals with one family, but the issues it raises go beyond the experiences of the characters. As you read, ask yourself what comment the author is making on the struggle for freedom.

526　DIANE OLIVER

Neighbors

Diane Oliver

The bus turning the corner of Patterson and Talford Avenue was dull this time of evening. Of the four passengers standing in the rear, she did not recognize any of her friends. Most of the people tucked neatly in the double seats were women, maids and cooks on their way from work or secretaries who had worked late and were riding from the office building at the mill. The cotton mill was out from town, near the house where she worked. She noticed that a few men were riding too. They were obviously just working men, except for one gentleman dressed very neatly in a dark grey suit and carrying what she imagined was a push-button umbrella.

He looked to her as though he usually drove a car to work. She immediately decided that the car probably wouldn't start this morning so he had to catch the bus to and from work. She was standing in the rear of the bus, peering at the passengers, her arms barely reaching the over-head railing, trying not to wobble with every lurch. But every corner the bus turned pushed her head toward a window. And her hair was coming down too, wisps of black curls swung between her eyes. She looked at the people around her. Some of them were white, but most of them were her color. Looking at the passengers at least kept her from thinking of tomorrow. But really she would be glad when it came, then everything would be over.

She took a firmer grip on the green leather seat and wished she had on her glasses. The man with the umbrella was two people ahead of her on the other side of the bus, so she could see him between other people very clearly. She watched as he unfolded the evening newspaper, craning her neck to see what was on the front page. She stood, impatiently trying to read the headlines, when she realized he was staring up at her rather curiously. Biting her lips she turned her head and stared out of the window until the downtown section was in sight.

She would have to wait until she was home to see if they were in the newspaper again. Sometimes she felt that if another person snapped a picture of them she would burst out screaming. Last Monday reporters were already inside the pre-school clinic when she took Tommy for his last polio shot. She didn't understand how anyone could be so heartless to a child. The flashbulb went off right when the needle went in and all the picture showed was Tommy's open mouth.

The bus pulling up to the curb jerked to a stop, startling her and confusing her thoughts. Clutching in her hand the paper bag that contained her uniform, she pushed her way toward the door. By standing in the back of the bus, she was one of the first people to step to the ground. Outside the bus, the evening air felt humid and uncomfortable and her dress kept sticking to her. She looked up and remembered that the weatherman had forecast rain. Just their luck—why, she wondered, would it have to rain on top of everything else?

As she walked along, the main street seemed unnaturally quiet but she decided her imagination was merely playing tricks. Besides, most of the stores had been closed since five o'clock.

She stopped to look at a reversible raincoat in Ivey's window, but although she had a full time job now, she couldn't keep her mind on clothes. She was about to continue walking when she heard a horn blowing. Looking around, half-scared but also curious, she saw a man beckoning to her in a grey car. He was nobody she knew but since a nicely dressed woman was with him in the front seat, she walked to the car.

"You're Jim Mitchell's girl, aren't you?" he questioned. "You Ellie or the other one?"

She nodded yes, wondering who he was and how much he had been drinking.

"Now honey," he said leaning over the woman, "you don't know me but your father does and you tell him that if anything happens to that boy of his tomorrow we're ready to set things straight." He looked her straight in the eye and she promised to take home the message.

Just as the man was about to step on the gas, the woman reached out and touched her arm. "You hurry up home, honey, it's about dark out here."

Before she could find out their names, the Chevrolet had disappeared around a corner. Ellie wished someone would magically appear and tell her everything that had happened since August. Then maybe she could figure out what was real and what she had been imagining for the past couple of days.

She walked past the main shopping district up to Tanner's where Saraline was standing in the window peeling oranges. Everything in the shop was painted orange and green and Ellie couldn't help thinking that poor Saraline looked out of place. She stopped to wave to her friend who pointed the knife to her watch and then to her boyfriend standing in the rear of the shop. Ellie nodded that she understood. She knew Sara wanted her to tell her grandfather that she had to work late again. Neither one of them could figure out why he didn't like Charlie. Saraline had finished high school three years ahead of her and it was time for her to be getting married. Ellie watched as her friend stopped peeling the orange long enough to cross her fingers. She nodded again but she was afraid all the crossed fingers in the world wouldn't stop the trouble tomorrow.

She stopped at the traffic light and spoke to a shrivelled woman hunched against the side of a building. Scuffing the bottom of her sneakers on the curb she waited for the woman to open her mouth and grin as she usually did. The kids used to bait her to talk, and since she didn't have but one tooth in her whole head they called her Doughnut Puncher. But the woman was still, the way everything else had been all week.

From where Ellie stood, across the street from the Sears and Roebuck parking lot, she could see their house, all of the houses on the single street white people called Welfare Row. Those newspaper men always made her angry. All of their articles showed how rough the people were on their street. And the reporters never said her family wasn't on welfare, the papers always said the family lived on that street. She paused to look across the street at a group of kids pouncing on one rubber ball. There were always white kids around their neighborhood mixed up in the games, but playing with them was almost an unwritten rule. When everybody started going to school nobody played together any more.

She crossed at the corner ignoring the cars at the stop light and the closer she got to her street the more she realized that the newspaper was right. The houses were ugly, there were not even any trees, just patches of scraggly bushes and grasses. As she cut across the sticky asphalt pavement covered with cars she was conscious of the parking lot floodlights casting a strange glow on her street. She stared from habit at the house on the end of the block and except for the way the paint was peeling they all looked alike to her. Now at twilight the flaking grey paint had a luminous glow and as she walked down the dirt sidewalk she noticed Mr. Paul's pipe smoke added to the hazy atmosphere. Mr. Paul would be sitting in that same spot waiting until Saraline came home. Ellie slowed her pace to speak to the elderly man sitting on the porch.

"Evening, Mr. Paul," she said. Her voice sounded clear and out of place on the vacant street.

"Eh, who's that?" Mr. Paul leaned over the rail. "What you say, girl?"

"How are you?" she hollered louder. "Sara said she'd be late tonight, she has to work." She waited for the words to sink in.

His head had dropped and his eyes were facing his lap. She could see that he was disappointed. "Couldn't help it," he said finally. "Reckon they needed her again." Then as if he suddenly remembered he turned toward her.

"You people be ready down there? Still gonna let him go tomorrow?"

She looked at Mr. Paul between the missing rails on his porch, seeing how his rolled up trousers seemed to fit exactly in the vacant banister space.

"Last I heard this morning we're still letting him go," she said.

Mr. Paul had shifted his weight back to the chair. "Don't reckon they'll hurt him," he mumbled, scratching the side of his face. "Hope he don't mind being spit on though. Spitting ain't like cutting. They can spit on him and nobody'll ever know who did it," he said, ending his words with a quiet chuckle.

Ellie stood on the sidewalk grinding her heel in the dirt waiting for the old man to finish talking. She was glad somebody found something funny to laugh at. Finally he shut up.

"Goodbye, Mr. Paul," she waved. Her voice sounded loud to her own ears. But she knew the way her head ached intensified noises. She walked home faster, hoping they had some aspirin in the house and that those men would leave earlier tonight.

From the front of her house she could tell that the men were still there. The living room light shone behind the yellow shades, coming through brighter in the patched places. She thought about moving the geranium pot from the porch to catch the rain but changed her mind. She kicked a beer can under a car parked in the street and stopped to look at her reflection on the car door. The tiny flowers of her printed dress made her look as if she had a strange tropical disease. She spotted another can and kicked it out of the way of the car, thinking that one of these days some kid was going to fall and hurt himself. What she wanted to do she knew was kick the car out of the way. Both the station wagon and the Ford had been parked in front of her house all week, waiting. Everybody was just sitting around waiting.

Suddenly she laughed aloud. Reverend Davis' car was big and black and shiny just like, but no, the smile disappeared from her face, her mother didn't like for them to say things about other people's color. She looked around to see who else came, and saw Mr. Moore's old beat up blue car. Somebody had torn away half of his NAACP sign. Sometimes she really felt sorry for the man. No matter how hard he glued on his stickers somebody always yanked them off again.

Ellie didn't recognize the third car but it had an Alabama license plate. She turned around and looked up and down the street, hating to go inside. There were no lights on their street, but in the distance she could see the bright lights of the parking lot. Slowly she did an about face and climbed the steps.

She wondered when her mama was going to remember to get a yellow bulb for the porch. Although the lights hadn't been turned on, usually June bugs and mosquitoes swarmed all around the porch. By the time she was inside the house she always felt like they were crawling in her hair. She pulled on the screen and saw that Mama finally had made Hezekiah patch up the holes. The globs of white adhesive tape scattered over the screen door looked just like misshapen butterflies.

She listened to her father's voice and could tell by the tone that the men were discussing something important again. She rattled the door once more but nobody came.

"Will somebody please let me in?" Her voice carried through the screen to the knot of men sitting in the corner.

"The door's open," her father yelled. "Come on in."

"The door is not open," she said evenly. "You know we stopped leaving it open." She was feeling tired again and her voice had fallen an octave[1] lower.

"Yeah, I forgot, I forgot," he mumbled walking to the door.

She watched her father almost stumble across a chair to let her in. He was shorter

1. **octave** (ŏk′tĭv): a tone that is eight full tones above or below another tone on the musical scale.

than the light bulb and the light seemed to beam down on him, emphasizing the wrinkles around his eyes. She could tell from the way he pushed open the screen that he hadn't had much sleep either. She'd overheard him telling Mama that the people down at the shop seemed to be piling on the work harder just because of this thing. And he couldn't do anything or say anything to his boss because they probably wanted to fire him.

"Where's Mama?" she whispered. He nodded toward the back.

"Good evening, everybody," she said looking at the three men who had not looked up since she entered the room. One of the men half stood, but his attention was geared back to something another man was saying. They were sitting on the sofa in their shirt sleeves and there was a pitcher of ice water on the window sill.

"Your mother probably needs some help," her father said. She looked past him trying to figure out who the white man was sitting on the end. His face looked familiar and she tried to remember where she had seen him before. The men were paying no attention to her. She bent to see what they were studying and saw a large sheet of white drawing paper. She could see blocks and lines and the man sitting in the middle was marking a trail with the eraser edge of the pencil.

The quiet stillness of the room was making her head ache more. She pushed her way through the red embroidered curtains that led to the kitchen.

"I'm home, Mama," she said, standing in front of the back door facing the big yellow sun Hezekiah and Tommy had painted on the wall above the iron stove. Immediately she felt a warmth permeating her skin. "Where is everybody?" she asked, sitting at the table where her mother was peeling potatoes.

"Mrs. McAllister is keeping Helen and Teenie," her mother said. "Your brother is staying over with Harry tonight." With each name she uttered, a slice of potato peeling tumbled to the newspaper on the table. "Tommy's in the bedroom reading that Uncle Wiggily book."

Ellie looked up at her mother but her eyes were straight ahead. She knew that Tommy only read the Uncle Wiggily book by himself when he was unhappy. She got up and walked to the kitchen cabinet.

"The other knives dirty?" she asked.

"No," her mother said, "look in the next drawer."

Ellie pulled open the drawer, flicking scraps of white paint with her fingernail. She reached for the knife and at the same time a pile of envelopes caught her eye.

"Any more come today?" she asked, pulling out the knife and slipping the envelopes under the dish towels.

"Yes, seven more came today," her mother accentuated each word carefully. "Your father has them with him in the other room."

"Same thing?" she asked picking up a potato and wishing she could think of some way to change the subject.

The white people had been threatening them for the past three weeks. Some of the letters were aimed at the family, but most of them were directed to Tommy himself. About once a week in the same handwriting somebody wrote that he'd better not eat lunch at school because they were going to poison him.

They had been getting those letters ever since the school board made Tommy's name public. She sliced the potato and dropped the pieces in the pan of cold water. Out of all those people he had been the only one the board had accepted for transfer to the elementary school. The other children, the members said, didn't live in the district. As she cut the eyes out of another potato she thought about the first letter they had received and how her father just set fire to it in the ashtray. But then Mr. Belk said they'd better save the rest, in case anything happened, they might need the evidence for court.

She peeped up again at her mother, "Who's that white man in there with Daddy?"

"One of Lawyer Belk's friends," she answered. "He's pastor of the church that's always on television Sunday morning. Mr. Belk seems to think that having him around will do some good." Ellie saw that her voice was shaking just like her hand as she reached for the last potato. Both of them could hear Tommy in the next room mumbling to himself. She was afraid to look at her mother.

Suddenly Ellie was aware that her mother's hands were trembling violently. "He's so little," she whispered and suddenly the knife slipped out of her hands and she was crying and breathing at the same time.

Ellie didn't know what to do but after a few seconds she cleared away the peelings and put the knives in the sink. "Why don't you lie down?" she suggested. "I'll clean up and get Tommy in bed." Without saying anything her mother rose and walked to her bedroom.

Ellie wiped off the table and draped the dishcloth over the sink. She stood back and looked at the rusting pipes powdered with whitish film. One of these days they would have to paint the place. She tiptoed past her

mother who looked as if she had fallen asleep from exhaustion.

"Tommy," she called softly, "come in and get ready for bed."

Tommy sitting in the middle of the floor did not answer. He was sitting the way she imagined he would be, cross-legged, pulling his ear lobe as he turned the ragged pages of *Uncle Wiggily at the Zoo.*

"What you doing, Tommy?" she said squatting on the floor beside him. He smiled and pointed at the picture of the ducks.

"School starts tomorrow," she said, turning a page with him. "Don't you think it's time to go to bed?"

"Oh Ellie, do I have to go now?" She looked down at the serious brown eyes and the closely cropped hair. For a minute she wondered if he questioned having to go to bed now or to school tomorrow.

"Well," she said, "aren't you about through with the book?" He shook his head. "Come on," she pulled him up, "you're a sleepy head." Still he shook his head.

"When Helen and Teenie coming home?"

"Tomorrow after you come home from school they'll be here."

She lifted him from the floor thinking how small he looked to be facing all those people tomorrow.

"Look," he said breaking away from her hand and pointing to a blue shirt and pair of cotton twill pants, "Mama got them for me to wear tomorrow."

While she ran water in the tub, she heard him crawl on top of the bed. He was quiet and she knew he was untying his sneakers.

"Put your shoes out," she called through the door, "and maybe Daddy will polish them."

"Is Daddy still in there with those men?

Mama made me be quiet so I wouldn't bother them."

He padded into the bathroom with bare feet and crawled into the water. As she scrubbed him they played Ask Me A Question, their own version of Twenty Questions. She had just dried him and was about to have him step into his pajamas when he asked: "Are they gonna get me tomorrow?"

"Who's going to get you?" She looked into his eyes and began rubbing him furiously with the towel.

"I don't know," he answered. "Somebody I guess."

"Nobody's going to get you," she said, "who wants a little boy who gets bubblegum in his hair anyway—but us?" He grinned but as she hugged him she thought how much he looked like his father. They walked to the bed to say his prayers and while they were kneeling she heard the first drops of rain. By the time she covered him up and tucked the spread off the floor the rain had changed to a steady downpour.

When Tommy had gone to bed her mother got up again and began ironing clothes in the kitchen. Something, she said, to keep her thoughts busy. While her mother folded and sorted the clothes Ellie drew up a chair from the kitchen table. They sat in the kitchen for a while listening to the voices of the men in the next room. Her mother's quiet speech broke the stillness of the room.

"I'd rather," she said making sweeping motions with the iron, "that you stay home from work tomorrow and went up with your father to take Tommy. I don't think I'll be up to those people."

Ellie nodded. "I don't mind," she said, tracing circles on the oil cloth covered table.

"Your father's going," her mother continued. "Belk and Reverend Davis are too. I think that white man in there will probably go."

"They may not need me," Ellie answered.

"Tommy will," her mother said, folding the last dish towel and storing it in the cabinet.

"Mama, I think he's scared," the girl turned toward the woman. "He was so quiet while I was washing him."

"I know," she answered sitting down heavily. "He's been that way all day." Her brown wavy hair glowed in the dim lighting of the kitchen. "I told him he wasn't going to school with Jakie and Bob any more but I said he was going to meet some other children just as nice."

Ellie saw that her mother was twisting her wedding band around and around on her finger.

"I've already told Mrs. Ingraham that I wouldn't be able to come out tomorrow." Ellie paused. "She didn't say very much. She didn't even say anything about his pictures in the newspaper. Mr. Ingraham said we were getting right crazy but even he didn't say anything else."

She stopped to look at the clock sitting near the sink. "It's almost time for the cruise cars to begin," she said. Her mother followed Ellie's eyes to the sink. The policemen circling their block every twenty minutes was supposed to make them feel safe, but hearing the cars come so regularly and that light flashing through the shade above her bed only made her nervous.

She stopped talking to push a wrinkle out of the shiny red cloth, dragging her finger along the table edges. "How long before those men going to leave?" she asked her mother. Just as she spoke she heard one of the men saying something about getting some sleep. "I didn't mean to run them

away," she said smiling. Her mother half-smiled too. They listened for the sound of motors and tires and waited for her father to shut the front door.

In a few seconds her father's head pushed through the curtain. "Want me to turn down your bed now, Ellie?" She felt uncomfortable staring up at him, the whole family looked drained of all energy.

"That's all right," she answered. "I'll sleep in Helen and Teenie's bed tonight."

"How's Tommy?" he asked looking toward the bedroom. He came in and sat down at the table with them.

They were silent before he spoke. "I keep wondering if we should send him." He lit a match and watched the flame disappear into the ashtray, then he looked into his wife's eyes. "There's no telling what these fool white folks will do."

Her mother reached over and patted his hand. "We're doing what we have to do, I guess," she said. "Sometimes though I wish the others weren't so much older than him."

"But it seems so unfair," Ellie broke in, "sending him there all by himself like that. Everybody keeps asking me why the MacAdams didn't apply for their children."

"Eloise." Her father's voice sounded curt. "We aren't answering for the MacAdams, we're trying to do what's right for your brother. He's not old enough to have his own

534 DIANE OLIVER

say so. You and the others could decide for yourselves, but we're the ones that have to do for him."

She didn't say anything but watched him pull a handful of envelopes out of his pocket and tuck them in the cabinet drawer. She knew that if anyone had told him in August that Tommy would be the only one going to Jefferson Davis they would not have let him go.

"Those the new ones?" she asked. "What they say?"

"Let's not talk about the letters," her father said. "Let's go to bed."

Outside they heard the rain become heavier. Since early evening she had become accustomed to the sound. Now it blended in with the rest of the noises that had accumulated in the back of her mind since the whole thing began.

As her mother folded the ironing board they heard the quiet wheels of the police car. Ellie noticed that the clock said twelve-ten and she wondered why they were early. Her mother pulled the iron cord from the switch and they stood silently waiting for the police car to turn around and pass the house again, as if the car's passing were a final blessing for the night.

Suddenly she was aware of a noise that sounded as if everything had broken loose in her head at once, a loudness that almost shook the foundation of the house. At the same time the lights went out and instinctively her father knocked them to the floor. They could hear the tinkling of glass near the front of the house and Tommy began screaming.

"Tommy, get down," her father yelled.

She hoped he would remember to roll under the bed the way they had practiced. She was aware of objects falling and breaking as she lay perfectly still. Her breath was coming in jerks and then there was a second noise, a smaller explosion but still drowning out Tommy's cries.

"Stay still," her father commanded. "I'm going to check on Tommy. They may throw another one."

She watched him crawl across the floor, pushing a broken flower vase and an iron skillet out of his way. All of the sounds, Tommy's crying, the breaking glass, everything was echoing in her ears. She felt as if they had been crouching on the floor for hours but when she heard the police car door slam, the luminous hands of the clock said only twelve-fifteen.

She heard other cars drive up and pairs of heavy feet trample on the porch. "You folks all right in there?"

She could visualize the hands pulling open the door, because she knew the voice. Sergeant Kearns had been responsible for patrolling the house during the past three weeks. She heard him click the light switch in the living room but the darkness remained intense.

Her father deposited Tommy in his wife's lap and went to what was left of the door. In the next fifteen minutes policemen were everywhere. While she rummaged around underneath the cabinet for a candle, her mother tried to hush up Tommy. His cheek was cut where he had scratched himself on the springs of the bed. Her mother motioned for her to dampen a cloth and put some petroleum jelly on it to keep him quiet. She tried to put him to bed again but he would not go, even when she promised to stay with him for the rest of the night. And so she sat in the kitchen rocking the little boy back and forth on her lap.

Ellie wandered around the kitchen but the

light from the single candle put an eerie glow on the walls making her nervous. She began picking up pans, stepping over pieces of broken crockery and glassware. She did not want to go into the living room yet, but if she listened closely, snatches of the policemen's conversation came through the curtain.

She heard one man say that the bomb landed near the edge of the yard, that was why it had only gotten the front porch. She knew from their talk that the living room window was shattered completely. Suddenly Ellie sat down. The picture of the living room window kept flashing in her mind as a wave of feeling invaded her body making her shake as if she had lost all muscular control. She slept on the couch, right under that window.

She looked at her mother to see if she too had realized, but her mother was looking down at Tommy and trying to get him to close his eyes. Ellie stood up and crept toward the living room trying to prepare herself for what she would see. Even that minute of determination could not make her control the horror that she felt. There were jagged holes all along the front of the house and the sofa was covered with glass and paint. She started to pick up the picture that had toppled from the book shelf, then she just stepped over the broken frame.

Outside her father was talking and, curious to see who else was with him, she walked across the splinters to the yard. She could see pieces of the geranium pot and the red blossoms turned face down. There were no lights in the other houses on the street. Across from their house she could see forms standing in the door and shadows being pushed back and forth. "I guess the MacAdams are glad they just didn't get involved." No one heard her speak, and no one came

over to see if they could help; she knew why and did not really blame them. They were afraid their house could be next.

Most of the policemen had gone now and only one car was left to flash the revolving red light in the rain. She heard the tall skinny man tell her father they would be parked outside for the rest of the night. As she watched the reflection of the police cars returning to the station, feeling sick on her stomach, she wondered now why they bothered.

Ellie went back inside the house and closed the curtain behind her. There was nothing anyone could do now, not even to the house. Everything was scattered all over the floor and poor Tommy still would not go to sleep. She wondered what would happen when the news spread through their section of town, and at once remembered the man in the grey Chevrolet. It would serve them right if her father's friends got one of them.

Ellie pulled up an overturned chair and sat down across from her mother who was crooning to Tommy. What Mr. Paul said was right, white people just couldn't be trusted. Her family had expected anything but even though they had practiced ducking, they didn't really expect anybody to try tearing down the house. But the funny thing was the house belonged to one of them. Maybe it was a good thing her family were just renters.

Exhausted, Ellie put her head down on the table. She didn't know what they were going to do about tomorrow, in the day time they didn't need electricity. She was too tired to think any more about Tommy, yet she could not go to sleep. So, she sat at the table trying to sit still, but every few minutes she would involuntarily twitch. She tried to steady her hands, all the time listening to her

mother's sing-songy voice and waiting for her father to come back inside the house.

She didn't know how long she lay hunched against the kitchen table, but when she looked up, her wrists bore the imprints of her hair. She unfolded her arms gingerly, feeling the blood rush to her fingertips. Her father sat in the chair opposite her, staring at the vacant space between them. She heard her mother creep away from the table, taking Tommy to his room.

Ellie looked out the window. The darkness was turning to grey and the hurt feeling was disappearing. As she sat there she could

Neighbors 537

begin to look at the kitchen matter-of-factly. Although the hands of the clock were just a little past five-thirty, she knew somebody was going to have to start clearing up and cook breakfast.

She stood and tipped across the kitchen to her parents' bedroom. "Mama," she whispered, standing near the door of Tommy's room. At the sound of her voice, Tommy made a funny throaty noise in his sleep. Her mother motioned for her to go out and be quiet. Ellie knew then that Tommy had just fallen asleep. She crept back to the kitchen and began picking up the dishes that could be salvaged, being careful not to go into the living room.

She walked around her father, leaving the broken glass underneath the kitchen table. "You want some coffee?" she asked.

He nodded silently, in strange contrast she thought to the water faucet that turned with a loud gurgling noise. While she let the water run to get hot she measured out the instant coffee in one of the plastic cups. Next door she could hear people moving around in the Williams' kitchen, but they too seemed much quieter than usual.

"You reckon everybody knows by now?" she asked, stirring the coffee and putting the saucer in front of him.

"Everybody will know by the time the city paper comes out," he said. "Somebody was here last night from the *Observer*. Guess it'll make front page."

She leaned against the cabinet for support watching him trace endless circles in the brown liquid with the spoon. "Sergeant Kearns says they'll have almost the whole force out there tomorrow," he said.

"Today," she whispered.

Her father looked at the clock and then turned his head.

"When's your mother coming back in here?" he asked, finally picking up the cup and drinking the coffee.

"Tommy's just off to sleep," she answered. "I guess she'll be in here when he's asleep for good."

She looked out the window of the back door at the row of tall hedges that had separated their neighborhood from the white people for as long as she remembered. While she stood there she heard her mother walk into the room. To her ears the steps seemed much slower than usual. She heard her mother stop in front of her father's chair.

"Jim," she said, sounding very timid, "what we going to do?" Yet as Ellie turned toward her she noticed her mother's face was strangely calm as she looked down on her husband.

Ellie continued standing by the door listening to them talk. Nobody asked the question to which they all wanted an answer.

"I keep thinking," her father said finally, "that the policemen will be with him all day. They couldn't hurt him inside the school building without getting some of their own kind."

"But he'll be in there all by himself," her mother said softly. "A hundred policemen can't be a little boy's only friends."

She watched her father wrap his calloused hands, still splotched with machine oil, around the salt shaker on the table.

"I keep trying," he said to her, "to tell myself that somebody's got to be the first one and then I just think how quiet he's been all week."

Ellie listened to the quiet voices that seemed to be a room apart from her. In the back of her mind she could hear phrases of a hymn her grandmother used to sing, something about trouble, her being born for trouble.

"Jim, I cannot let my baby go." Her mother's words, although quiet, were carefully pronounced.

"Maybe," her father answered, "it's not in our hands. Reverend Davis and I were talking day before yesterday how God tested the Israelites, maybe he's just trying us."

"God expects you to take care of your own," his wife interrupted. Ellie sensed a trace of bitterness in her mother's voice.

"Tommy's not going to understand why he can't go to school," her father replied. "He's going to wonder why, and how are we going to tell him we're afraid of them?" Her father's hand clutched the coffee cup. "He's going to be fighting them the rest of his life. He's got to start sometime."

"But he's not on their level. Tommy's too little to go around hating people. One of the others, they're bigger, they understand about things."

Ellie still leaning against the door saw that the sun covered part of the sky behind the hedges and the light slipping through the kitchen window seemed to reflect the shiny red of the table cloth.

"He's our child," she heard her mother say. "Whatever we do, we're going to be the cause." Her father had pushed the cup away from him and sat with his hands covering part of his face. Outside Ellie could hear a horn blowing.

"God knows we tried but I guess there's just no use." Her father's voice forced her attention back to the two people sitting in front of her. "Maybe when things come back to normal, we'll try again."

He covered his wife's chunky fingers with the palm of his hand and her mother seemed to be enveloped in silence. The three of them remained quiet, each involved in his own thoughts, but related, Ellie knew, to the same thing. She was the first to break the silence.

"Mama," she called after a long pause, "do you want me to start setting the table for breakfast?"

Her mother nodded.

Ellie turned the clock so she could see it from the sink while she washed the dishes that had been scattered over the floor.

"You going to wake up Tommy or you want me to?"

"No," her mother said, still holding her father's hand, "let him sleep. When you wash your face, you go up the street and call Hezekiah. Tell him to keep up with the children after school, I want to do something to this house before they come home."

She stopped talking and looked around the kitchen, finally turning to her husband. "He's probably kicked the spread off by now," she said. Ellie watched her father, who without saying anything walked toward the bedroom.

She watched her mother lift herself from the chair and automatically push in the stuffing underneath the cracked plastic cover. Her face looked set, as it always did when she was trying hard to keep her composure.

"He'll need something hot when he wakes up. Hand me the oatmeal," she commanded, reaching on top of the icebox for matches to light the kitchen stove.

Responding to the Selection

Neighbors by Diane Oliver

Identifying Facts

1. What kind of work does Ellie do?
2. What does she expect to see in the evening newspapers?
3. What threats do the unsigned letters contain?
4. Why is Tommy the only child who has been accepted for transfer to the elementary school?
5. What decision does the family come to after the explosion?

Interpreting Meanings

1. How do the opening paragraphs of the story build **suspense**? What indications are there that something important, and perhaps dangerous, is going on?
2. Why is Tommy's father intent on sending him to school despite the threats? Do Tommy's mother and sister agree with his reasons?
3. Why are the police who are patrolling the house unable to prevent the bomb attack? How does this incident break down the family's resolve?
4. Evaluate the family's decision. Do you think they were wise to wait until "things come back to normal"?
5. What do you think this story says about the struggle for equal rights? What does it say about the price people may have to pay for freedom?

Literary Elements

Stating a Theme

The statement of a **theme** is not the same thing as the subject of a story or a summary of its plot. The statement of theme shows the *significance* of the events—what they reveal about human nature.

Which of these statements do you think best expresses the theme of "Neighbors"? Defend your choice.

> To parents, a child's safety is more important than school desegregation.
> In the struggle for freedom, the victims may be those who are the weakest and most innocent.

Writing About Literature

Explaining a Title

Why do you think Diane Oliver chose the title "Neighbors" for this story? Think of your associations with the word *neighbor.* Is her use of the word ironic in some way? Give your interpretation of the title in a brief essay.

Speaking and Listening

Defending a Position

Discuss the arguments for desegregation that are given in the story. What arguments can you add to this list? Which of these arguments do you consider strongest?

About the Author

Alice Walker (b. 1944)

 Alice Walker once told an interviewer, "I am preoccupied with the spiritual survival, the survival *whole* of my people. But beyond that, I am committed to exploring the oppressions, the insanities, the loyalties, and the triumphs of the black woman." In Walker's work, black women are almost always the main characters, and they triumph over the harsh realities of their lives through sheer force of character.

Walker was born in Eatonton, Georgia, the eighth child of sharecroppers. She attended Spelman College, where she became active in the Civil Rights Movement, and Sarah Lawrence College, where she took her B.A. in 1965. Her first book, *Once,* a collection of poems, appeared in 1968. She has since written several volumes of poetry, short stories, and essays, as well as novels. She has also edited writings by Zora Neale Hurston, whom she greatly admires. Her most famous work is *The Color Purple* (1982), which received a Pulitzer Prize and an American Book Award.

Walker uses the word "womanist" to refer to herself and her writing. One of her definitions of "womanist" is "a black feminist or feminist of color . . . usually referring to outrageous, audacious, courageous or *willful* behavior."

At the center of Walker's work is the importance of the heritage that has been passed on to black women by their maternal ances-

George Steinmetz

tors. Walker identifies strongly with the South and with the plain black women who have expressed their creativity through such arts as gardening, cooking, and quilt making. The craft of quilt making, which creates something beautiful and useful from bits and pieces of ordinary cloth, provides the key idea for Walker's story "Everyday Use."

Before You Read

Everyday Use

Using What You Know

In recent years, Americans have taken a great interest in their family histories and backgrounds. Many black Americans have discovered their African roots. What advantages do you see in having close ties to the culture and traditions of one's ancestors? For an American, what conflicts might grow out of having loyalties to another land and its people?

Literary Focus: Symbols

The term **symbol** is often used for a printed or written sign that stands for something else. The plus sign used in mathematics stands for addition; the letters of the alphabet stand for sounds.

More often, however, a symbol is an object, a person, or an event that has more than one meaning. The American flag, for example, has its own meaning—it is a piece of cloth with a specific design. At the same time, it stands for something greater than itself—it is a symbol of the United States.

In literature you find many familiar symbols: spring stands for youth or rebirth; a journey stands for one's passage through life. In addition to these common symbols, writers create their own symbols. In "Everyday Use," Walker's characters seem to be talking about some ordinary quilts. By the end of the story, however, the reader knows that the quilts really represent something more significant than bed coverings. Understanding what these quilts **symbolize,** or stand for, will give you a better understanding of Walker's theme.

Setting a Purpose

As you read, consider what the characters think about their past—their African roots and their Southern roots. How do they interpret the meaning of *heritage*? How do the quilts represent the family's heritage? Does the story make you think about your own heritage in a new way?

542   ALICE WALKER

Everyday Use

for your grandmama

Alice Walker

I will wait for her in the yard that Maggie and I made so clean and wavy yesterday afternoon. A yard like this is more comfortable than most people know. It is not just a yard. It is like an extended living room. When the hard clay is swept clean as a floor and the fine sand around the edges lined with tiny, irregular grooves, anyone can come and sit and look up into the elm tree and wait for the breezes that never come inside the house.

Maggie will be nervous until after her sister goes: she will stand hopelessly in corners, homely and ashamed of the burn scars down her arms and legs, eying her sister with a mixture of envy and awe. She thinks her sister has held life always in the palm of one hand, that "no" is a word the world never learned to say to her.

You've no doubt seen those TV shows where the child who has "made it" is confronted, as a surprise, by her own mother and father, tottering in weakly from backstage. (A pleasant surprise, of course: What would they do if parent and child came on the show only to curse out and insult each other?) On TV mother and child embrace and smile into each other's faces. Sometimes the mother and father weep, the child wraps them in her arms and leans across the table to tell how she would not have made it without their help. I have seen these programs.

Sometimes I dream a dream in which Dee and I are suddenly brought together on a TV program of this sort. Out of a dark and soft-seated limousine I am ushered into a bright room filled with many people. There I meet a smiling, gray, sporty man like Johnny Carson who shakes my hand and tells me what a fine girl I have. Then we are on the stage and Dee is embracing me with tears in her eyes. She pins on my dress a large orchid, even though she has told me once that she thinks orchids are tacky flowers.

In real life I am a large, big-boned woman with rough, man-working hands. In winter I wear flannel nightgowns to bed and overalls during the day. I can kill and clean a hog as mercilessly as a man. My fat keeps me hot in zero weather. I can work outside all day, breaking ice to get water for washing; I can eat pork liver cooked over the open fire minutes after it comes steaming from the hog. One winter I knocked a bull calf straight in the brain between the eyes with a sledge hammer and had the meat hung up to chill before nightfall. But of course all this does not show on television. I am the way my

daughter would want me to be: a hundred pounds lighter, my skin like an uncooked barley pancake. My hair glistens in the hot bright lights. Johnny Carson has much to do to keep up with my quick and witty tongue.

But that is a mistake. I know even before I wake up. Who ever knew a Johnson with a quick tongue? Who can even imagine me looking a strange white man in the eye? It seems to me I have talked to them always with one foot raised in flight, with my head turned in whichever way is farthest from them. Dee, though. She would always look anyone in the eye. Hesitation was no part of her nature.

"How do I look, Mama?" Maggie says, showing just enough of her thin body enveloped in pink skirt and red blouse for me to know she's there, almost hidden by the door.

"Come out into the yard," I say.

Have you ever seen a lame animal, perhaps a dog run over by some careless person rich enough to own a car, sidle up to someone who is ignorant enough to be kind to him? That is the way my Maggie walks. She has been like this, chin on chest, eyes on ground, feet in shuffle, ever since the fire that burned the other house to the ground.

Dee is lighter than Maggie, with nicer hair and a fuller figure. She's a woman now,

544   ALICE WALKER

though sometimes I forget. How long ago was it that the other house burned? Ten, twelve years? Sometimes I can still hear the flames and feel Maggie's arms sticking to me, her hair smoking and her dress falling off her in little black papery flakes. Her eyes seemed stretched open, blazed open by the flames reflected in them. And Dee. I see her standing off under the sweet gum tree she used to dig gum out of; a look of concentration on her face as she watched the last dingy gray board of the house fall in toward the red-hot brick chimney. Why don't you do a dance around the ashes? I'd wanted to ask her. She had hated the house that much.

I used to think she hated Maggie, too. But that was before we raised the money, the church and me, to send her to Augusta to school. She used to read to us without pity; forcing words, lies, other folks' habits, whole lives upon us two, sitting trapped and ignorant underneath her voice. She washed us in a river of make-believe, burned us with a lot of knowledge we didn't necessarily need to know. Pressed us to her with the serious way she read, to shove us away at just the moment, like dimwits, we seemed about to understand.

Dee wanted nice things. A yellow organdy dress to wear to her graduation from high school; black pumps to match a green suit she'd made from an old suit somebody gave me. She was determined to stare down any disaster in her efforts. Her eyelids would not flicker for minutes at a time. Often I fought off the temptation to shake her. At sixteen she had a style of her own: and knew what style was.

I never had an education myself. After second grade the school was closed down. Don't ask me why: in 1927 colored asked fewer questions than they do now. Sometimes Maggie reads to me. She stumbles along good-naturedly but can't see well. She knows she is not bright. Like good looks and money, quickness passed her by. She will marry John Thomas (who has mossy teeth in an earnest face) and then I'll be free to sit here and I guess just sing church songs to myself. Although I never was a good singer. Never could carry a tune. I was always better at a man's job. I used to love to milk till I was hooked in the side in '49. Cows are soothing and slow and don't bother you, unless you try to milk them the wrong way.

I have deliberately turned my back on the house. It is three rooms, just like the one that burned, except the roof is tin; they don't make shingle roofs any more. There are no real windows, just some holes cut in the sides, like the portholes in a ship, but not round and not square, with rawhide holding the shutters up on the outside. This house is in a pasture, too, like the other one. No doubt when Dee sees it she will want to tear it down. She wrote me once that no matter where we "choose" to live, she will manage to come see us. But she will never bring her friends. Maggie and I thought about this and Maggie asked me, "Mama, when did Dee ever *have* any friends?"

She had a few. Furtive boys in pink shirts hanging about on washday after school. Nervous girls who never laughed. Impressed with her they worshiped the well-turned phrase, the cute shape, the scalding humor that erupted like bubbles in lye. She read to them.

When she was courting Jimmy T she didn't have much time to pay to us, but turned all her faultfinding power on him. He *flew* to marry a cheap city girl from a family

Everyday Use   545

of ignorant flashy people. She hardly had time to recompose herself.

When she comes I will meet—but there they are!

Maggie attempts to make a dash for the house, in her shuffling way, but I stay her with my hand. "Come back here," I say. And she stops and tries to dig a well in the sand with her toe.

It is hard to see them clearly through the strong sun. But even the first glimpse of leg out of the car tells me it is Dee. Her feet were always neat-looking, as if God himself had shaped them with a certain style. From the other side of the car comes a short, stocky man. Hair is all over his head a foot long and hanging from his chin like a kinky mule tail. I hear Maggie suck in her breath. "Uhnnnh," is what it sounds like. Like when you see the wriggling end of a snake just in front of your foot on the road. "Uhnnnh."

Dee next. A dress down to the ground, in this hot weather. A dress so loud it hurts my eyes. There are yellows and oranges enough to throw back the light of the sun. I feel my whole face warming from the heat waves it throws out. Earrings gold, too, and hanging down to her shoulders. Bracelets dangling and making noises when she moves her arm up to shake the folds of the dress out of her armpits. The dress is loose and flows, and as she walks closer, I like it. I hear Maggie go "Uhnnnh" again. It is her sister's hair. It stands straight up like the wool on a sheep. It is black as night and around the edges are two long pigtails that rope about like small lizards disappearing behind her ears.

"Wa-su-zo-Tean-o!" she says, coming on in that gliding way the dress makes her move. The short stocky fellow with the hair to his navel is all grinning and he follows up with "Asalamalakim,[1] my mother and sister!" He moves to hug Maggie but she falls back, right up against the back of my chair. I feel her trembling there and when I look up I see the perspiration falling off her chin.

"Don't get up," says Dee. Since I am stout it takes something of a push. You can see me trying to move a second or two before I make it. She turns, showing white heels through her sandals, and goes back to the car. Out she peeks next with a Polaroid. She stoops down quickly and lines up picture after picture of me sitting there in front of the house with Maggie cowering behind me. She never takes a shot without making sure the house is included. When a cow comes nibbling around the edge of the yard she snaps it and me and Maggie *and* the house. Then she puts the Polaroid in the back seat of the car, and comes up and kisses me on the forehead.

Meanwhile Asalamalakim is going through motions with Maggie's hand. Maggie's hand is as limp as a fish, and probably as cold, despite the sweat, and she keeps trying to pull it back. It looks like Asalamalakim wants to shake hands but wants to do it fancy. Or maybe he don't know how people shake hands. Anyhow, he soon gives up on Maggie.

"Well," I say. "Dee."

"No, Mama," she says. "Not 'Dee,' Wangero Leewanika Kemanjo!"

"What happened to 'Dee'?" I wanted to know.

"She's dead," Wangero said. "I couldn't bear it any longer, being named after the people who oppress me."

"You know as well as me you was named after your aunt Dicie," I said. Dicie is my

---

1. **Asalamalakim:** *Salaam aleikhim* (sə-läm′ ä-lī′kōom′), a greeting used by Muslims. It means "Peace be with you." The origin of *salaam* is an Arabic word meaning "peace."

sister. She named Dee. We called her "Big Dee" after Dee was born.

"But who was *she* named after?" asked Wangero.

"I guess after Grandma Dee," I said.

"And who was she named after?" asked Wangero.

"Her mother," I said, and saw Wangero was getting tired. "That's about as far back as I can trace it," I said. Though, in fact, I probably could have carried it back beyond the Civil War through the branches.

"Well," said Asalamalakim, "there you are."

"Uhnnnh," I heard Maggie say.

"There I was not," I said, "before 'Dicie' cropped up in our family, so why should I try to trace it that far back?"

He just stood there grinning, looking down on me like somebody inspecting a Model A car. Every once in a while he and Wangero sent eye signals over my head.

"How do you pronounce this name?" I asked.

"You don't have to call me by it if you don't want to," said Wangero.

"Why shouldn't I?" I asked. "If that's what you want us to call you, we'll call you."

"I know it might sound awkward at first," said Wangero.

"I'll get used to it," I said. "Ream it out again."

Well, soon we got the name out of the way. Asalamalakim had a name twice as long and three times as hard. After I tripped over it two or three times he told me to just call him Hakim-a-barber. I wanted to ask him was he a barber, but I didn't really think he was, so I didn't ask.

"You must belong to those beef-cattle peoples down the road," I said. They said "Asalamalakim" when they met you, too, but they didn't shake hands. Always too busy: feeding the cattle, fixing the fences, putting up salt-lick shelters, throwing down hay. When the white folks poisoned some of the herd the men stayed up all night with rifles in their hands. I walked a mile and a half just to see the sight.

Hakim-a-barber said, "I accept some of their doctrines, but farming and raising cattle is not my style." (They didn't tell me, and I didn't ask, whether Wangero (Dee) had really gone and married him.)

We sat down to eat and right away he said he didn't eat collards and pork was unclean. Wangero, though, went on through the chitlins and corn bread, the greens and everything else. She talked a blue streak over the sweet potatoes. Everything delighted her. Even the fact that we still used the benches her daddy made for the table when we couldn't afford to buy chairs.

"Oh, Mama!" she cried. Then turned to Hakim-a-barber. "I never knew how lovely these benches are. You can feel the rump prints," she said, running her hands underneath her and along the bench. Then she gave a sigh and her hand closed over Grandma Dee's butter dish. "That's it!" she said. "I knew there was something I wanted to ask you if I could have." She jumped up from the table and went over in the corner where the churn stood, the milk in it clabber[2] by now. She looked at the churn and looked at it.

"This churn top is what I need," she said. "Didn't Uncle Buddy whittle it out of a tree you all used to have?"

"Yes," I said.

"Uh huh," she said happily. "And I want the dasher,[3] too."

2. **clabber:** milk that is sour and thickly curdled.
3. **dasher:** the plunger of a butter churn.

Poplar-wood butter churn, c. 1885.

"Uncle Buddy whittle that, too?" asked the barber.

Dee (Wangero) looked up at me.

"Aunt Dee's first husband whittled the dash," said Maggie so low you almost couldn't hear her. "His name was Henry, but they called him Stash."

"Maggie's brain is like an elephant's," Wangero said, laughing. "I can use the churn top as a centerpiece for the alcove table," she said, sliding a plate over the churn, "and I'll think of something artistic to do with the dasher."

When she finished wrapping the dasher the handle stuck out. I took it for a moment in my hands. You didn't even have to look close to see where hands pushing the dasher up and down to make butter had left a kind of sink in the wood. In fact, there were a lot of small sinks; you could see where thumbs and

fingers had sunk into the wood. It was beautiful light yellow wood, from a tree that grew in the yard where Big Dee and Stash had lived.

After dinner Dee (Wangero) went to the trunk at the foot of my bed and started rifling through it. Maggie hung back in the kitchen over the dishpan. Out came Wangero with two quilts. They had been pieced by Grandma Dee and then Big Dee and me had hung them on the quilt frames on the front porch and quilted them. One was in the Lone Star pattern. The other was Walk Around the Mountain. In both of them were scraps of dresses Grandma Dee had worn fifty and more years ago. Bits and pieces of Grandpa Jarrell's Paisley shirts. And one teeny faded blue piece, about the size of a penny matchbox, that was from Great Grandpa Ezra's uniform that he wore in the Civil War.

"Mama," Wangero said sweet as a bird. "Can I have these old quilts?"

I heard something fall in the kitchen, and a minute later the kitchen door slammed.

"Why don't you take one or two of the others?" I asked. "These old things was just done by me and Big Dee from some tops your grandma pieced before she died."

"No," said Wangero. "I don't want those. They are stitched around the borders by machine."

"That'll make them last better," I said.

"That's not the point," said Wangero. "These are all pieces of dresses Grandma used to wear. She did all this stitching by hand. Imagine!" She held the quilts securely in her arms, stroking them.

"Some of the pieces, like those lavender

Quilt with Lone Star pattern.
Barbara Kirk/The Stock Market

ones, come from old clothes her mother handed down to her," I said, moving up to touch the quilts. Dee (Wangero) moved back just enough so that I couldn't reach the quilts. They already belonged to her.

"Imagine!" she breathed again, clutching them closely to her bosom.

"The truth is," I said, "I promised to give them quilts to Maggie, for when she marries John Thomas."

She gasped like a bee had stung her.

"Maggie can't appreciate these quilts!" she said. "She'd probably be backward enough to put them to everyday use."

"I reckon she would," I said. "God knows I been saving 'em for long enough with nobody using 'em. I hope she will!" I didn't want to bring up how I had offered Dee (Wangero) a quilt when she went away to college. Then she had told me they were old-fashioned, out of style.

"But they're *priceless*!" she was saying now, furiously; for she has a temper. "Maggie would put them on the bed and in five years they'd be in rags. Less than that!"

"She can always make some more," I said. "Maggie knows how to quilt."

Dee (Wangero) looked at me with hatred. "You just will not understand. The point is these quilts, *these* quilts!"

"Well," I said, stumped. "What would *you* do with them?"

"Hang them," she said. As if that was the only thing you *could* do with quilts.

Maggie by now was standing in the door. I could almost hear the sound her feet made as they scraped over each other.

"She can have them, Mama," she said, like somebody used to never winning anything, or having anything reserved for her. "I can 'member Grandma Dee without the quilts."

I looked at her hard. She had filled her bottom lip with checkerberry snuff and it gave her face a kind of dopey, hangdog look. It was Grandma Dee and Big Dee who taught her how to quilt herself. She stood there with her scarred hands hidden in the folds of her skirt. She looked at her sister with something like fear but she wasn't mad at her. This was Maggie's portion. This was the way she knew God to work.

When I looked at her like that something hit me in the top of my head and ran down to the soles of my feet. Just like when I'm in church and the spirit of God touches me and I get happy and shout. I did something I never had done before: hugged Maggie to me, then dragged her on into the room, snatched the quilts out of Miss Wangero's hands and dumped them into Maggie's lap. Maggie just sat there on my bed with her mouth open.

"Take one or two of the others," I said to Dee.

But she turned without a word and went out to Hakim-a-barber.

"You just don't understand," she said, as Maggie and I came out to the car.

"What don't I understand?" I wanted to know.

"Your heritage," she said. And then she turned to Maggie, kissed her, and said, "You ought to try to make something of yourself, too, Maggie. It's really a new day for us. But from the way you and Mama still live you'd never know it."

She put on some sunglasses that hid everything above the tip of her nose and her chin.

Maggie smiled; maybe at the sunglasses. But a real smile, not scared. After we watched the car dust settle I asked Maggie to bring me a dip of snuff. And then the two of us sat there just enjoying, until it was time to go in the house and go to bed.

Responding to the Selection
Everyday Use by Alice Walker

Identifying Facts

1. Describe the place where the narrator and Maggie live.
2. How has Dee changed her appearance?
3. What reason does Dee give for changing her name?
4. How does Dee plan to use the churn top and the hand-stitched quilts?
5. Find the passage that explains the title of the story.

Interpreting Meanings

1. The narrator tells about a dream in which she appears on TV as the "model" mother Dee would like her to be. What does this dream reveal about the conflict between mother and daughter?
2. What comic misunderstandings occur when Dee and her escort arrive?
3. Dee has left behind her rural Southern life and reinvented a name and a personality for herself. Why, then, does she want to have the churn and the quilts?
4. The **climax** of the story occurs when the mother-narrator gives the quilts to Maggie rather than to Dee. Dee accuses her mother and sister of not understanding their heritage. What do you think the word *heritage* means to Dee? What do you think it means to Maggie and her mother?
5. Contrast the sisters. Explain the difference

in their values as well as in their appearance.
6. What does the narrator realize about Maggie? Why do you suppose Maggie and her mother are happy at the end of the story?
7. This story focuses on the conflict between two ideas of a family's heritage. State that conflict in your own words. Think about the title and the dedication of the story in giving your answer.

Literary Elements

Relating Symbol to Theme

Theme is the main idea or basic meaning of a literary work. The theme of a story is revealed through all its elements, including symbols. "Everyday Use" is about the homecoming of a young woman who considers herself modern and fashionable, in contrast to her mother and sister, who she thinks are backward. In the course of the story, the meaning of the family's heritage comes to focus on some ordinary quilts.

Walker uses the quilts as a symbol that brings out conflicting ideas about the meaning of heritage. Dee, who has rejected her background by leaving home and by adopting a new personality, thinks of her heritage as things, like the quilts, that should be put on view. To Maggie and her mother, one's heritage is part of day-to-day life; its traditions link the present generation with the past. Maggie doesn't need to preserve the quilts because she "knows how to quilt." She can always make more. She is willing to give up the quilts because her memories are enough to create strong bonds with the past: "I can 'member Grandma Dee without the quilts," she says.

Identify some other symbols in the story and tell what connection they have with the story's theme. Here are some guidelines to follow in your search for symbols:

1. Look for an object that the author emphasizes. If the author has included dialogue or action involving the object, it might be considered a symbol.
2. Ask yourself how the object relates to the theme of the story. Does it stand for something important?

Language and Vocabulary

Recognizing Humorous Comparisons

Walker's language in this story is the language of everyday use, yet she is able to make this simple language very expressive. The narrator's comparisons often take a humorous turn:

> He just stood there grinning, looking down on me like somebody inspecting a Model A car.

The Ford Motor Company manufactured a motor car known as the Model T between 1909 and 1927. It was replaced by the Model A. By referring to herself as a

Model A, the narrator humorously implies that she is an early and outdated model.

Locate another humorous comparison in the story and explain its meaning.

Persuasive Writing

Stating an Opinion

At the end of the story, the narrator gives the quilts to Maggie rather than to Dee. Who do you think should have received the quilts? Write a letter to the author, agreeing or disagreeing with her decision to end the story as she does. You may wish to begin with a sentence stating your opinion. Then, list reasons and examples that support your position. Here is one plan you might follow.

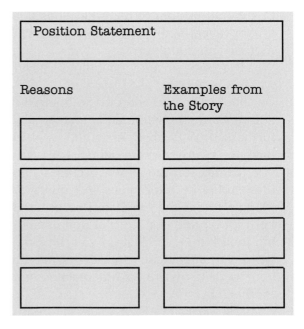

Position Statement

Reasons	Examples from the Story

Speaking and Listening

Improvising a Scene

When you **improvise**, you make up something without preparation. With a partner, improvise a short scene to follow the end of the story. You might invent a conversation between Maggie and her mother, or you might dramatize the reactions of Dee and her companion to the day's events. Take turns performing your scene with other student actors, and see how many different ideas emerge.

The Author Comments

In a well-known essay called "In Search of Our Mothers' Gardens," Alice Walker discusses the creative spirit that black women have inherited from their mothers. She describes a quilt she saw hanging in the Smithsonian Institution in Washington, D.C., "obviously the work of a person of powerful imagination and deep spiritual feeling." Walker has this to say about the unknown artist:

If we could locate this "anonymous" black woman from Alabama, she would turn out to be one of our grandmothers— an artist who left her mark in the only materials she could afford, and in the only medium her position in society allowed her to use.

Reread the description of the quilts in Walker's story. How do they represent a similar creativity?

About the Author

Reginald McKnight (b. 1955)

© Miriam Berkley

McKnight says that only recently did he begin to think of himself as a writer. "It's difficult to accept that title because my roots are in the working class, and I always reserved the word 'writer' for people who had the money, time and leisure for that pursuit. And it's also partly because I never knew how long the writing would go on."

McKnight was born in Fürstenfeldbruck, Germany. His father was a sergeant in the Air Force. He has lived in various places in the United States, including New York, California, Colorado, Texas, and Louisiana. He had the urge to write at an early age and wrote his first book, *The Littlest Dragon,* when he was eight. After graduation from high school, McKnight served in the United States Marine Corps. He attended Pikes Peak Community College and went on to take a degree in African literature at Colorado State College. He won a Watson Foundation Fellowship and traveled to Senegal, in West Africa, where he taught English. He now teaches at the University of Maryland.

McKnight's work has appeared in many literary journals. His book of stories, *Moustapha's Eclipse,* won the Drue Heinz Award in 1988. "The Kind of Light That Shines on Texas," the story that is reprinted here, first appeared in *The Kenyon Review.* It received the Kenyon Review Award for Fiction (1989) and was chosen for inclusion in *Prize Stories 1990: The O. Henry Awards. I Get on the Bus,* a novel based on his experiences in Africa, was published in 1990.

Before You Read

The Kind of Light That Shines on Texas

Using What You Know

A bully is someone who enjoys frightening or hurting someone who is smaller or weaker. Why do bullies single out timid or defenseless people? What kinds of tactics do they use to harass people? How can one stand up to a bully? Consider your own experiences as you read McKnight's story.

Literary Focus: Total Effect

The **total effect,** or impact, of a story depends on the interaction of the various elements you have studied. The **plot** of a story is the plan of events. **Conflict** may be **internal** or **external,** and in many stories, the major **character** experiences both kinds. Every story is told from a particular **point of view.** Sometimes, the **narrator** is a character in the story; at other times, the narrator stands outside the story as an observer. Every story has a **setting,** the time and place of action. The **tone** of a story shows the writer's attitude toward characters as well as toward readers. Frequently, tone is a key to the writer's purpose. Many stories express a **theme**—some idea or insight into human experience.

The **total effect** of the story is the result of all these elements working together.

Setting a Purpose

As you read, see how well you can put together all the elements of the short story.

Reginald McKnight   555

The Kind of Light That Shines on Texas

Reginald McKnight

I never liked Marvin Pruitt. Never liked him, never knew him, even though there were only three of us in the class. Three black kids. In our school there were fourteen classrooms of thirty-odd white kids (in '66, they considered Chicanos provisionally[1] white) and three or four black kids. Primary school in primary colors.[2] Neat division. Alphabetized. They didn't stick us in the back, or arrange us by degrees of hue, apartheidlike.[3] This was real integration, a ten-to-one ratio as tidy as upper-class landscaping. If it all worked, you could have ten white kids all to yourself. They could talk to you, get the feel of you, scrutinize you bone deep if they wanted to. They seldom wanted to, and that was fine with me for two reasons. The first was that their scrutiny was irritating. How do you comb your hair—why do you comb your hair—may I please touch your hair—were the kinds of questions they asked. This is no way to feel at home. The second reason was

1. **provisionally** (prə-vĭzh′ə-nə-lē): for the time being.
2. **Primary . . . colors:** The author is punning on different meanings of *primary*. *Primary school* refers to the first three or four grades. The *primary colors* are red, green, and blue, which can be mixed to make all colors. Here, *primary* seems to be used in the sense of "most fundamental."
3. **apartheidlike** (ə-pärt′hīt′līk): like the policy of racial segregation in South Africa.

Marvin. He embarrassed me. He smelled bad, was at least two grades behind, was hostile, dark skinned, homely, closemouthed. I feared him for his size, pitied him for his dress, watched him all the time. Marveled at him, mystified, astonished, uneasy.

He had the habit of spitting on his right arm, juicing it down till it would glisten. He would start in immediately after taking his seat when we'd finished with the Pledge of Allegiance, "The Yellow Rose of Texas," "The Eyes of Texas Are upon You," and "Mistress Shady."[4] Marvin would rub his spit-flecked arm with his left hand, rub and roll as if polishing an ebony pool cue. Then he would rest his head in the crook of his arm, sniffing, huffing deep like old folks huff 3-for-a-dollar fruit at the Piggly-Wiggly. After ten minutes or so, his eyes would close, heavy. He would sleep till recess. Mrs. Wickham would let him.

There was one other black kid in our class, a girl they called Ah-so. I never learned what she did to earn this name. There was nothing Asian about this big-shouldered girl. She was the tallest, heaviest kid in school. She was quiet, but I don't think any one of us was subtle or sophisticated enough to nickname our classmates according to any but physical attributes. Fat kids were called Porky or Butterball; skinny ones were called Stick or Ichabod.[5] Ah-so was big, thick, and African. She would impassively sit, sullen, silent as Marvin. She wore the same dark blue pleated skirt every day, the same ruffled white blouse every day. Her skin always shone as if worked by Marvin's palms and fingers. I never spoke one word to her, nor she to me.

Of the three of us, Mrs. Wickham called only on Ah-so and me. Ah-so never answered one question, correctly or incorrectly, so far as I can recall. She wasn't stupid. When asked to read aloud she read well, seldom stumbling over long words, reading with humor and expression. But when Wickham asked her about Farmer Brown and how many cows, or the capital of Vermont, or the date of this war or that, Ah-so never spoke. Not one word. But you always felt she could have answered those questions if she'd wanted to. I sensed no tension, embarrassment, or anger in Ah-so's reticence. She simply refused to speak. There was something unshakable about her, some core so impenetrably solid, you got the feeling that if you stood too close to her she could eat your thoughts like a black star eats light. I didn't despise Ah-so as I despised Marvin. There was nothing malevolent about her. She sat like a great icon[6] in the back of the classroom, tranquil, guarded, sealed up, watchful. She was close to sixteen, and it was my guess she'd given up on school. Perhaps she was just obliging the wishes of her family, sticking it out till the law could no longer reach her.

There were at least half a dozen older kids in our class. Besides Marvin and Ah-so there was Oakley, who sat behind me, whispering threats into my ear; Varna Willard with the woman's body; Eddie Limon, who played bass for a high school rock band; and Lawrence Ridderbeck, whom everyone said had a kid and a wife. You couldn't expect me to know anything about Texan educational practices of the 1960s, so I never knew why there were so many older kids in my sixth grade class. After all, I was just a boy and had trans-

---

4. **"The Yellow Rose . . . Shady":** well-known songs.
5. **Ichabod** (ĭk′ə-bŏd): after a character in "The Legend of Sleepy Hollow," who is extremely tall and thin.

6. **icon** (ī′kŏn): an object such as an idol.

The Kind of Light That Shines on Texas   557

ferred into the school around midyear. My father, an air force sergeant, had been sent to Viet Nam. The air force sent my mother, my sister Claire, and me to Connolly Air Force Base, which during the war housed "unaccompanied wives." I'd been to so many different schools in my short life that I ceased wondering about their differences. All I knew about the Texas schools is that they weren't afraid to flunk you.

Yet though I was only twelve then, I had a good idea why Wickham never once called on Marvin, why she let him snooze in the crook of his polished arm. I knew why she would press her lips together, and narrow her eyes at me whenever I correctly answered a question, rare as that was. I knew why she badgered Ah-so with questions everyone knew Ah-so would never even consider answering. Wickham didn't like us. She wasn't gross about it, but it was clear she didn't want us around. She would prove her dislike day after day with little stories and jokes. "I just want to share with you all," she would say, "a little riddle my daughter told me at the supper table th'other day. Now, where do you go when you injure your knee?" Then one, two, or all three of her pets would say for the rest of us, "We don't know, Miz Wickham," in that skin-chilling way toadies speak, "where?" "Why, to Africa," Wickham would say, "where the knee grows."

The thirty-odd white kids would laugh, and I would look across the room at Marvin. He'd be asleep. I would glance back at Ah-so. She'd be sitting still as a projected image, staring down at her desk. I, myself, would smile at Wickham's stupid jokes, sometimes fake a laugh. I tried to show her that at least one of us was alive and alert, even though her jokes hurt. I toadified, too, I suppose.

But I wanted her to understand more than anything that I was not like her other nigra children, that I was worthy of more than the nonattention and the negative attention she paid Marvin and Ah-so. I hated her, but never showed it. No one could safely contradict that woman. She knew all kinds of tricks to demean, control, and punish you. And she could swing her two-foot paddle as fluidly as a big league slugger swings a bat. You didn't speak in Wickham's class unless she spoke to you first. You didn't chew gum, or wear "hood" hair. You didn't drag your feet, curse, pass notes, hold hands with the opposite sex. Most especially, you didn't say anything bad about the Aggies, Governor Connolly, LBJ, Sam Houston, or Waco.[7] You did the forbidden and she would get you. It was that simple.

She never got me, though. Never gave her reason to. But she could have invented reasons. She did a lot of that. I can't be sure, but I used to think she pitied me because my father was in Viet Nam and my uncle A.J. had recently died there. Whenever she would tell one of her racist jokes, she would always glance at me, preface the joke with, "Now don't you nigra children take offense. This is all in fun, you know. I just want to share with you all something Coach Gilchrest told me th'other day." She would tell her joke, and glance at me again. I'd giggle, feeling a little queasy. "I'm half Irish," she would chuckle, "and you should hear some of those Irish jokes." She never told any, and I never really expected her to. I just

7. **Aggies . . . Waco:** *Aggies* are students enrolled in agricultural programs; Governor John B. Connolly was wounded by the assassin who killed President John F. Kennedy in 1963; Lyndon B. Johnson (LBJ) served as President of the United States from 1963 to 1969; Sam Houston was first president of the Republic of Texas; Waco (wā′kō), where the story takes place, is in central Texas.

did my Tom-thing. I kept my shoes shined, my desk neat, answered her questions as best I could, never brought gum to school, never cursed, never slept in class. I wanted to show her we were not all the same.

I tried to show them all, all thirty-odd, that I was different. It worked to some degree, but not very well. When some article was stolen from someone's locker or desk, Marvin, not I, was the first accused. I'd be second. Neither Marvin, nor Ah-so nor I were ever chosen for certain classroom honors—"Pledge leader," "flag holder," "noise monitor," "paper passer outer," but Mrs. Wickham once let me be "eraser duster." I was proud. I didn't even care about the cracks my fellow students made about my finally having turned the right color. I had done something that Marvin, in the deeps of his never-ending sleep, couldn't even dream of doing. Jack Preston, a kid who sat in front of me, asked me one day at recess whether I was embarrassed about Marvin. "Can you believe that guy?" I said. "He's like a pig or something. Makes me sick."

"Does it make you ashamed to be colored?"

"No," I said, but I meant yes. Yes, if you insist on thinking us all the same. Yes, if his faults are mine, his weaknesses inherent in me.

"I'd be," said Jack.

I made no reply. I was ashamed. Ashamed for not defending Marvin and ashamed that Marvin even existed. But if it had occurred to me, I would have asked Jack whether he was ashamed of being white because of Oakley. Oakley, "Oak Tree," Kelvin "Oak Tree" Oakley. He was sixteen and proud of it. He made it clear to everyone, including Wickham, that his life's ambition was to stay in school one more year, till he'd be old enough to en-

list in the army. "Them slopes[8] got my brother," he would say. "I'mna sign up and git me a few slopes. Gonna kill them monkeys deader'n hell." Oakley, so far as anyone knew, was and always had been the oldest kid in his family. But no one contradicted him. He would, as anyone would tell you, "snap yer neck jest as soon as look at you." Not a boy in class, excepting Marvin and myself, had been able to avoid Oakley's pink bellies, moon pie punches, or worse. He didn't bother Marvin, I suppose, because Marvin was closer to his size and age, and because Marvin spent five-sixths of the school day asleep. Marvin probably never crossed Oakley's mind. And to say that Oakley hadn't bothered me is not to say he had no intention of ever doing so. In fact, this haphazard sketch of hairy fingers, slash of eyebrow, explosion of acne, elbows, and crooked teeth, swore almost daily that he'd like to kill me.

Naturally, I feared him. Though we were about the same height, he outweighed me by no less than forty pounds. He talked, stood, smoked, and swore like a man. No one, except for Mrs. Wickham, the principal, and the coach, ever laid a finger on him. And even Wickham knew that the hot lines she laid on him merely amused him. He would smile out at the classroom, goofy and bashful, as she laid down the two, five, or maximum ten strokes on him. Often he would wink, or surreptitiously[9] flash us the thumb as Wickham worked on him. When she was finished, Oakley would walk so cool back to his seat you'd think he was on wheels. He'd slide into his chair, sniff the air, and say, "Somethin's burnin. Do y'all smell smoke? I swanee, I smell smoke and fahr back here."

8. **slopes:** an offensive name for Oriental people.
9. **surreptitiously** (sûr′əp-tĭsh′əs-lē): secretly.

The Kind of Light That Shines on Texas   559

If he had made these cracks and never threatened me, I might have grown to admire Oakley, even liked him a little. But he hated me, and took every opportunity during the six-hour school day to make me aware of this. "Some Sambo's gittin his butt broke open one of these days," he'd mumble. "I wanna fight somebody. Need to keep in shape till I git to Nam."

I never said anything to him for the longest time. I pretended not to hear him, pretended not to notice his sour breath on my neck and ear. "Yep," he'd whisper. "Coonies keep ya in good shape for slope killin." Day in, day out, that's the kind of thing I'd pretend not to hear. But one day when the rain dropped down like lead balls, and the cold air made your skin look plucked, Oakley whispered to me, "My brother tells me it rains like this in Nam. Maybe I oughta go out at recess and break your butt open today. Nice and cool so you don't sweat. Nice and wet to clean up the blood." I said nothing for at least half a minute, then I turned half right and said, "Thought you said your brother was dead." Oakley, silent himself, for a time, poked me in the back with his pencil and hissed, "Yer dead." Wickham cut her eyes our way, and it was over.

It was hardest avoiding him in gym class. Especially when we played murderball. Oakley always aimed his throws at me. He threw with unblinking intensity, his teeth gritting, his neck veining, his face flushing, his black hair sweeping over one eye. He could throw hard, but the balls were squishy and harmless. In fact, I found his misses more intimidating than his hits. The balls would whizz by, thunder against the folded bleachers. They rattled as though a locomotive were passing through them. I would duck, dodge, leap as if he were throwing grenades. But he always hit me, sooner or later. And after a while I noticed that the other boys would avoid throwing at me, as if I belonged to Oakley.

One day, however, I was surprised to see that Oakley was throwing at everyone else but me. He was uncommonly accurate, too; kids were falling like tin cans. Since no one was throwing at me, I spent most of the game watching Oakley cut this one and that one down. Finally, he and I were the only ones left on the court. Try as he would, he couldn't hit me, nor I him. Coach Gilchrest blew his whistle and told Oakley and me to bring the red rubber balls to the equipment locker. I was relieved I'd escaped Oakley's stinging throws for once. I was feeling triumphant, full of myself. As Oakley and I approached Gilchrest, I thought about saying something friendly to Oakley: Good game, Oak Tree, I would say. Before I could speak, though, Gilchrest said, "All right boys, there's five minutes left in the period. Y'all are so good, looks like, you're gonna have to play like men. No boundaries, no catch outs,[10] and you gotta hit your opponent three times in order to win. Got me?"

We nodded.

"And you're gonna use these," said Gilchrest, pointing to three volleyballs at his feet. "And you better believe they're pumped full. Oates, you start at that end of the court. Oak Tree, you're at th'other end. Just like usual, I'll set the balls at mid-court, and when I blow my whistle I want y'all to haul your cheeks to the middle and th'ow for all you're worth. Got me?" Gilchrest nodded at our nods, then added, "Remember, no boundaries, right?"

I at my end, Oakley at his, Gilchrest blew

10. **catch outs:** catching balls before they hit the ground.

his whistle. I was faster than Oakley and scooped up a ball before he'd covered three quarters of his side. I aimed, threw, and popped him right on the knee. "One-zip!" I heard Gilchrest shout. The ball bounced off his knee and shot right back into my hands. I hurried my throw and missed. Oakley bent down, clutched the two remaining balls. I remember being amazed that he could palm each ball, run full out and throw left-handed or right-handed without a shade of awkwardness. I spun, ran, but one of Oakley's throws glanced off the back of my head. "One-one!" hollered Gilchrest. I fell and spun on my butt as the other ball came sailing at me. I caught it. "He's out!" I yelled. Gilchrest's voice boomed, "No catch outs. Three hits. Three hits." I leapt to my feet as Oakley scrambled across the floor for another ball. I chased him down, leapt, and heaved the ball hard as he drew himself erect. The ball hit him dead in the face, and he went down flat. He rolled around, cupping his hands over his nose. Gilchrest sped to his side, helped him to his feet, asked him whether he was OK. Blood flowed from Oakley's nose, dripped in startlingly bright spots on the floor, his shoes, Gilchrest's shirt. The coach removed Oakley's T-shirt and pressed it against the big kid's nose to stanch the bleeding. As they walked past me toward the office I mumbled an apology to Oakley, but couldn't catch his reply. "You watch your filthy mouth, boy," said Gilchrest to Oakley.

The locker room was unnaturally quiet as I stepped into its steamy atmosphere. Eyes clicked in my direction, looked away. After I was out of my shorts, had my towel wrapped around me, my shower kit in hand, Jack Preston and Brian Nailor approached me. Preston's hair was combed slick and plastic looking. Nailor's stood up like frozen flames.

Nailor smiled at me with his big teeth and pale eyes. He poked my arm with a finger. "You screwed up," he said.

"I tried to apologize."

"Won't do you no good," said Preston.

"I swanee," said Nailor.

"It's part of the game," I said. "It was an accident. Wasn't my idea to use volleyballs."

"Don't matter," Preston said. "He's jest lookin for an excuse to fight you."

"I never done nothing to him."

"Don't matter," said Nailor. "He don't like you."

"Brian's right, Clint. He'd jest as soon kill you as look at you."

"I never done nothing to him."

"Look," said Preston, "I know him pretty good. And jest between you and me, it's cause you're a city boy—"

"Whadda you mean? I've never—"

"He don't like your clothes—"

"And he don't like the fancy way you talk in class."

"What fancy—"

"I'm tellin him, if you don't mind, Brian."

"Tell him then."

"He don't like the way you say 'tennis shoes' instead of sneakers. He don't like coloreds. A whole bunch a things, really."

"I never done nothing to him. He's got no reason—"

"*And,*" said Nailor, grinning, "*and,* he says you're a stuck-up rich kid." Nailor's eyes had crow's-feet, bags beneath them. They were a man's eyes.

"My dad's a sergeant," I said.

"You chicken to fight him?" said Nailor.

"Yeah, Clint, don't be chicken. Jest go on and git it over with. He's whupped pert near ever'body else in the class. It ain't so bad."

"Might as well, Oates."

"Yeah, yer pretty skinny, but yer jest

about his height. Jest git im in a headlock and don't let go."

"Damn," I said, "he's got no reason to—"

Their eyes shot right and I looked over my shoulder. Oakley stood at his locker, turning its tumblers. From where I stood I could see that a piece of cotton was wedged up one of his nostrils, and he already had the makings of a good shiner. His acne burned red like a fresh abrasion. He snapped the locker open and kicked his shoes off without sitting. Then he pulled off his shorts, revealing two paddle stripes on his backside. They were fresh red bars speckled with white, the white speckles being the reverse impression of the paddle's suction holes. He must not have watched his filthy mouth while in Gilchrest's presence. Behind me, I heard Preston and Nailor pad to their lockers.

Oakley spoke without turning around. "Somebody's gonna git his skinny black behind kicked, right today, right after school." He said it softly. He slipped his jock off, turned around. I looked away. Out the corner of my eye I saw him stride off, his hairy nakedness a weapon clearing the younger boys from his path. Just before he rounded the corner of the shower stalls, I threw my toilet kit to the floor and stammered, "I—I never did nothing to you, Oakley." He stopped, turned, stepped closer to me, wrapping his towel around himself. Sweat streamed down my rib cage. It felt like ice water. "You wanna go at it right now, boy?"

"I never did nothing to you." I felt tears in my eyes. I couldn't stop them even though I was blinking like mad. "Never."

He laughed. "You busted my nose, boy."

"What about before? What'd I ever do to you?"

"See you after school, Coonie." Then he turned away, flashing his acne-spotted back like a semaphore.[11] "Why?" I shouted. "Why you wanna fight me?" Oakley stopped and turned, folded his arms, leaned against a toilet stall. "Why you wanna fight *me*, Oakley?" I stepped over the bench. "What'd I do? Why me?" And then unconsciously, as if scratching, as if breathing, I walked toward Marvin, who stood a few feet from Oakley, combing his hair at the mirror. "Why not him?" I said. "How come you're after *me* and not *him*?" The room froze. Froze for a moment that was both evanescent[12] and eternal, somewhere between an eye blink and a week in hell. No one moved, nothing happened; there was no sound at all. And then it was as if all of us at the same moment looked at Marvin. He just stood there, combing away, the only body in motion, I think. He combed his hair and combed it, as if seeing only his image, hearing only his comb scraping his scalp. I knew he'd heard me. There's no way he could not have heard me. But all he did was slide the comb into his pocket and walk out the door.

"I got no quarrel with Marvin," I heard Oakley say. I turned toward his voice, but he was already in the shower.

I was able to avoid Oakley at the end of the school day. I made my escape by asking Mrs. Wickham if I could go to the restroom.

"'Restroom,'" Oakley mumbled. "It's a damn toilet, sissy."

"Clinton," said Mrs. Wickham. "Can you *not* wait till the bell rings? It's almost three o'clock."

"No ma'am," I said. "I won't make it."

"Well, I should make you wait just to teach you to be more mindful about . . . hygiene . . . uh things." She sucked in her cheeks, squinted. "But I'm feeling charitable today.

11. **semaphore** (sĕm′ə-fôr′): a device for sending signals.
12. **evanescent** (ĕv′ə-nĕs′ənt): fleeting.

You may go." I immediately left the building, and got on the bus. "Ain't you a little early?" said the bus driver, swinging the door shut. "Just left the office," I said. The driver nodded, apparently not giving me a second thought. I had no idea why I'd told her I'd come from the office, or why she found it a satisfactory answer. Two minutes later the bus filled, rolled and shook its way to Connolly Air Base.

When I got home, my mother was sitting in the living room, smoking her Slims, watching her soap opera. She absently asked me how my day had gone and I told her fine. "Hear from Dad?" I said.

"No, but I'm sure he's fine." She always said that when we hadn't heard from him in a while. I suppose she thought I was worried about him, or that I felt vulnerable without him. It was neither. I just wanted to discuss something with my mother that we both cared about. If I spoke with her about things that happened at school, or on my weekends, she'd listen with half an ear, say something like, "Is that so?" or "You don't say?" I couldn't stand that sort of thing. But when I mentioned my father, she treated me a bit more like an adult, or at least someone who was worth listening to. I didn't want to feel like a boy that afternoon. As I turned from my mother and walked down the hall I thought about the day my father left for Viet Nam. Sharp in his uniform, sure behind his aviator specs, he slipped a cigar from his pocket and stuck it in mine. "Not till I get back," he said. "We'll have us one when we go fishing. Just you and me, out on the lake all day, smoking and casting and sitting. Don't let Mamma see it. Put it in y' back pocket." He hugged me, shook my hand, and told me I was the man of the house now. He told me he was depending on me to take

good care of my mother and sister. "Don't you let me down, now, hear?" And he tapped his thick finger on my chest. "You almost as big as me. Boy, you something else." I believed him when he told me those things. My heart swelled big enough to swallow my father, my mother, Claire. I loved, feared, and respected myself, my manhood. That day I could have put all of Waco, Texas, in my heart. And it wasn't till about three months later that I discovered I really wasn't the man of the house, that my mother and sister, as they always had, were taking care of me.

For a brief moment I considered telling my mother about what happened at school that day, but for one thing, she was deep down in the halls of "General Hospital," and never paid you much mind till it was over. For another thing, I just wasn't the kind of person—I'm still not, really—to discuss my problems with anyone. Like my father I kept things to myself, talked about my problems only in retrospect. Since my father wasn't around, I consciously wanted to be like him, doubly like him, I could say. I wanted to be the man of the house in some respect, even if it had to be in an inward way. I went to my room, changed my clothes, and laid out my homework. I couldn't focus on it. I thought about Marvin, what I'd said about him or done to him—I couldn't tell which. I'd done something to him, said something about him; said something about and done something to myself. *How come you're after* me *and not* him? I kept trying to tell myself I hadn't meant it that way. *That* way. I thought about approaching Marvin, telling him what I really meant was that he was more Oakley's age and weight than I. I would tell him I meant I was no match for Oakley. *See, Marvin, what I meant was that he wants to fight*

The Kind of Light That Shines on Texas   563

a colored guy, but is afraid to fight you cause you could beat him. But try as I did, I couldn't for a moment convince myself that Marvin would believe me. I meant it *that* way and no other. Everybody heard. Everybody knew. That afternoon I forced myself to confront the notion that tomorrow I would probably have to fight both Oakley and Marvin. I'd have to be two men.

I rose from my desk and walked to the window. The light made my skin look orange, and I started thinking about what Wickham had told us once about light. She said that oranges and apples, leaves and flowers, the whole multi-colored world, was not what it appeared to be. The colors we see, she said, look like they do only because of the light or ray that shines on them. "The color of the thing isn't what you see, but the light that's reflected off it." Then she shut out the lights and shone a white light lamp on a prism.[13] We watched the pale splay of colors on the projector screen; some people ooohed and aaahed. Suddenly, she switched on a black light and the color of everything changed. The prism colors vanished, Wickham's arms were purple, the buttons of her dress were as orange as hot coals, rather than the blue they had been only seconds before. We were all very quiet. "Nothing," she said after a while, "is really what it appears to be." I didn't really understand then. But as I stood at the window, gazing at my orange skin, I wondered what kind of light I could shine on Marvin, Oakley, and me that would reveal us as the same.

I sat down and stared at my arms. They were dark brown again. I worked up a bit of saliva under my tongue and spat on my left arm. I spat again, then rubbed the spittle into it, polishing, working till my arm grew warm. As I spat, and rubbed, I wondered why Marvin did this weird, nasty thing to himself, day after day. Was he trying to rub away the black, or deepen it, doll it up? And if he did this weird nasty thing for a hundred years, would he spit-shine himself invisible, rolling away the eggplant skin, revealing the scarlet muscle, blue vein, pink and yellow tendon, white bone? Then disappear? Seen through, all colors, no colors. Spitting and rubbing. Is this the way you do it? I leaned forward, sniffed the arm. It smelled vaguely of mayonnaise. After an hour or so, I fell asleep.

I saw Oakley the second I stepped off the bus the next morning. He stood outside the gym in his usual black penny loafers, white socks, high water jeans, T-shirt and black jacket. Nailor stood with him, his big teeth spread across his bottom lip like playing cards. If there was anyone I felt like fighting, that day, it was Nailor. But I wanted to put off fighting for as long as I could. I stepped toward the gymnasium, thinking that I shouldn't run, but if I hurried I could beat Oakley to the door and secure myself near Gilchrest's office. But the moment I stepped into the gym, I felt Oakley's broad palm clap down on my shoulder. "Might as well stay out here, Coonie," he said. "I need me a little target practice." I turned to face him and he slapped me, one-two, with the back, then the palm of his hand, as I'd seen Bogart do to Peter Lorre in "The Maltese Falcon."[14] My heart went wild. I could scarcely breathe. I couldn't swallow.

"Call me a nigger," I said. I have no idea

13. **prism** (prĭz′əm): a glass object that breaks up white light into rainbow colors.

14. **"The Maltese Falcon"**: a film from 1941, now considered a classic, in which Humphrey Bogart played the role of Sam Spade, a hard-boiled detective.

what made me say this. All I know is that it kept me from crying. "Call me a nigger, Oakley."

"Shut up, boy." He slapped me again, scratching my eye. "I don't do what coonies tell me."

"Call me a nigger."

"Outside, Coonie."

"Call me one. Go ahead."

He lifted his hand to slap me again, but before his arm could swing my way, Marvin Pruitt came from behind me and calmly pushed me aside. "Git out my way, boy," he said. And he slugged Oakley on the side of his head. Oakley stumbled back, stiff-legged. His eyes were big. Marvin hit him twice more, once again to the side of the head, once to the nose. Oakley went down and stayed down. Though blood was drawn, whistles blowing, fingers pointing, kids hollering, Marvin just stood there, staring at me with cool eyes. He spat on the ground, licked his lips, and just stared at me, till Coach Gilchrest and Mr. Calderon tackled him and violently carried him away. He never struggled, never took his eyes off me.

Nailor and Mrs. Wickham helped Oakley to his feet. His already fattened nose bled and swelled so that I had to look away. He looked around, bemused, wall-eyed,[15] maybe scared. It was apparent he had no idea how bad he was hurt. He didn't even touch his nose. He didn't look like he knew much of anything. He looked at me, looked me dead in the eye in fact, but didn't seem to recognize me.

That morning, like all other mornings, we said the Pledge of Allegiance, sang "The Yellow Rose of Texas," "The Eyes of Texas Are upon You," and "Mistress Shady." The room stood strangely empty without Oakley, and without Marvin, but at the same time you could feel their presence more intensely somehow. I felt like I did when I'd walk into my mother's room and could smell my father's cigars, or cologne. He was more palpable, in certain respects, than when there in actual flesh. For some reason, I turned to look at Ah-so, and just this once I let my eyes linger on her face. She had a very gentle-looking face, really. That surprised me. She must have felt my eyes on her because she glanced up at me for a second and smiled, white teeth, downcast eyes. Such a pretty smile. That surprised me too. She held it for a few seconds, then let it fade. She looked down at her desk, and sat still as a photograph.

Henry Monroe/Black Star

15. **wall-eyed:** with his eyes wide and glaring.

The Kind of Light That Shines on Texas   565

Responding to the Selection

The Kind of Light That Shines on Texas by Reginald McKnight

Identifying Facts

1. Name the three African American students in the story.
2. How old is the narrator at the time of the story?
3. What is Kelvin Oakley's nickname?
4. How is Oakley injured in gym class?
5. Why is Marvin a good match for Oakley?

Interpreting Meanings

Plot

1. This story deals with several **conflicts**. What **external conflict** or **conflicts** does Clint Oates experience? What **internal conflicts** does he have?
2. Identify the **climax** of the story. Does it resolve the narrator's conflicts?
3. A situation is said to be **ironic** when the opposite of what is expected occurs. What ironic situations can you identify in the story?

Character

4. Why is it so important for Clint to show that he is different from the other black students? Do you feel that he succeeds in changing anyone's attitude?
5. How does the author make Oakley a repellent, but wholly believable, character?
6. In the locker room, Clint tries to get Oakley to fight Marvin Pruitt. After he thinks about this episode, he concludes: "I'd done something to him, said something about him . . . and done something to myself." What has Clint done to Marvin and what has he done to himself?
7. Why do you suppose Marvin Pruitt fights Clint's battle for him? What is the significance of the look that passes between them after Marvin knocks Oakley down?
8. To the narrator, both Marvin and Ah-so are puzzles. Do you feel you have a better understanding of these characters at the end of the story? Why do you think Ah-so smiles at Clint?

Setting

9. During the 1960s, schools in the South were being desegregated. How is setting important in this story?

Point of View

10. The story is told by a grown man looking back on events from his twelfth year. Find passages where he interprets his actions, thoughts, and feelings.

Tone

11. What do you think is the author's attitude toward his characters and events? Is he sympathetic toward his main character? Is he also critical?

Theme

12. Locate the passage that explains the title of the story. How is the lesson about the prism colors related to the racial conflicts in the story?

Literary Elements

Relating Dialogue to Character

The conversation between two or more characters is called **dialogue**. Dialogue can advance the plot of a story, and it can also help to reveal what the characters are like.

Oakley uses derogatory and offensive language in referring to African Americans and to Vietnamese. Why do you think McKnight has Oakley do this? Would Oakley have been as convincing a character if McKnight had omitted derogatory words entirely?

Writing About Literature

Responding to the Story

Imagine yourself in Clint's place when Oakley threatened him. How would you have reacted? Would you have reported Oakley's threats to the school authorities? Would you have taken someone into your confidence? Or would you have handled the situation as Clint did? After you have written your response, discuss your reactions with other students in the class.

Critical Thinking

Evaluating a Short Story

How do you judge a short story? What **criteria,** or standards, can you apply to evaluate the merits of a story? Here are some criteria you can use.

Plot

1. **Is the major conflict well developed?** Does the action of the story develop logically out of the conflict? Is the resolution acceptable or is it improbable?
2. **Is your interest sustained?** Are suspense and foreshadowing used skillfully?

Character

3. **Are the characters believable?** Are their motivations clear? Do they behave consistently? Are you prepared for any change in their actions or thoughts?
4. **Are the characters presented skillfully?** Are the characters revealed chiefly through description or through actions, thoughts, and dialogue? Are the characters clearly individualized?

Setting

5. **Is the setting an important part of the story?** Is the setting clearly connected to the plot? Does it help to create mood or to reveal characters' states of mind?

Point of View

6. **What point of view is used?** Is the point of view consistent? How does it affect your reactions to the characters and actions?

Tone

7. **What is the author's attitude toward the characters and toward the reader?** How does the tone of the story affect your interpretation of its meaning?

Theme

8. **Does the story provide insight into human experience?** How do all the other elements contribute to the theme?

Writing a Short Story

You have seen that the basic elements of a short story are **plot, character, setting, point of view, tone,** and **theme.** Short stories also contain many of the stylistic elements found in other forms of literature, such as **imagery** and **figures of speech.**

Ideas for short stories can come in a number of ways. Some stories are based on personal experience. Some writers get ideas for stories from newspaper articles. Some stories are inspired by other stories. For example, you might write a sequel to a story you have read, inventing new characters and incidents. You can even get ideas for a story from a photograph. Imagine one of the photographs in this book "coming to life." What would the characters say? What conflicts can you imagine?

Here are some suggestions to guide you in writing your own stories.

Prewriting Strategies

1. Choose an idea for a story. Write about what you know best. Remember that the main action should be about some kind of conflict or problem.
2. Invent characters, a setting, and incidents. Use the **5 W–How** questions (**Who? What? When? Where? Why?** and **How?**)
3. Once you have decided on the situation, the setting, and main characters, list the events that will grow out of the conflict. How will you begin your story? What will be the climax? How will the climax be resolved?
4. Decide on a point of view. Will the story be told by a character in the story or by an outside observer?
5. Use a diagram to plan your story.

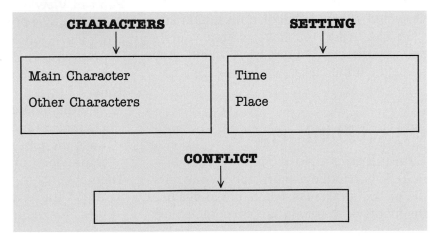

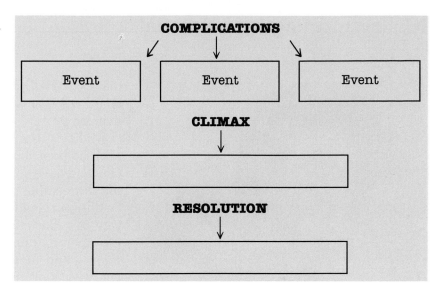

COMPLICATIONS

| Event | Event | Event |

CLIMAX

RESOLUTION

Writing a First Draft

1. Get your reader's attention by opening with an interesting sentence. Create a mood or establish the conflict at the beginning of the story.
2. Use **direct** and **indirect methods of characterization** to present your characters. Have characters reveal themselves chiefly through their own words, thoughts, and actions.
3. Make sure that the characters speak naturally.
4. Keep a consistent point of view.

Revision Checklist

1. Does the beginning catch the reader's interest?
2. Have you included a conflict?
3. Are the characters believable?
4. Does the story have a beginning, middle, and end?
5. Is the dialogue convincing? Is it written in correct style?
6. Is your point of view consistent?

Writing the Final Draft

1. Check your paper for errors in grammar, usage, and mechanics.
2. Prepare a final copy and check it for accuracy.

▶I. Interpreting New Material

Jerry Bauer/The Schomburg Center for Research in Black Culture/New York Public Library

Alice Childress (chĭl′drĕs) (1920–1994) was born in Charleston, South Carolina. She began her career in the theater as an actress and as a director. Her novel *A Hero Ain't Nothin' but a Sandwich* won many awards. It was named the Best Young Adult Book of 1975 by the American Library Association. In addition to novels and short stories, Childress wrote plays and screenplays.

A. Read the following story carefully before answering the questions.

The Pocketbook Game
Alice Childress

Marge . . . Day's work is an education! Well, I mean workin' in different homes you learn much more than if you was steady in one place. . . . I tell you, it really keeps your mind sharp tryin' to watch for what folks will put over on you.

What? . . . No, Marge, I do not want to help shell no beans, but I'd be more than glad to stay and have supper with you, and I'll wash the dishes after. Is that all right? . . .

Who put anything over on who? . . . Oh yes! It's like this. . . . I been working for Mrs. E . . . one day a week for several months and I notice that she has some peculiar ways. Well, there was only one thing that really bothered me and that was her pocketbook habit. . . . No, not those little novels. . . . I mean her purse—her handbag.

Marge, she's got a big old pocketbook with two long straps on it . . . and whenever I'd go there, she'd be propped up in a chair with her handbag double wrapped tight around her wrist, and from room to room she'd roam with that purse hugged to her bosom. . . . Yes, girl! This happens every time! No, there's *nobody* there but me and her. . . . Marge, I couldn't say nothin' to her! It's her purse, ain't it? She can hold onto it if she wants to!

I held my peace for months, tryin' to figure out how I'd make my point. . . . Well, bless Bess! *Today was the day!* . . . Please, Marge, keep shellin' the beans so we can eat! I know you're listenin', but you listen with your ears, not your hands. . . . Well, anyway, I was almost ready to go home when she steps in the room hangin' onto her bag as usual and says, "Mildred, will you ask the super to come up and fix the kitchen faucet?" "Yes, Mrs. E . . . ," I says, "as soon as I leave." "Oh, no," she says, "he may be gone by then. Please go now." "All right," I says, and out the door I went, still wearin' my Hoover apron.

I just went down the hall and stood there a few minutes . . . and then I rushed back to the door and knocked on it as hard and frantic as I could. She flung open the door sayin', "What's the matter? Did you see the super?" . . . "No," I says, gaspin' hard for breath, "I was almost downstairs when I remembered . . . *I left my pocketbook!*"

With that I dashed in, grabbed my purse and then went down to get the super! Later, when I was leavin' she says real timid-like, "Mildred, I hope that you don't think I distrust you because . . . " I cut her off real quick. . . . "That's all right, Mrs. E . . . , I un-

derstand. 'Cause if I paid anybody as little as you pay me, I'd hold my pocketbook too!"

Marge, you fool . . . lookout! . . . You gonna drop the beans on the floor!

1. This short story is a **monologue,** a speech by a single character. Even though Marge doesn't speak, how does the speaker indicate that they are good friends?
2. What do you learn about Mildred? What do you learn about Mrs. E?
3. What does the "pocketbook game" refer to? Who wins the game?
4. Interpret what happens in the last line of the story.

B. **Using "The Pocketbook Game" as a model, relate an experience in which you felt someone was misjudging you. Write this as a monologue or as a dialogue between you and your best friend.**

▶▶II. For Discussion

Which of the stories in this unit did you prefer? Is there one character that you liked above all others? Discuss your responses to the experiences you have read about.

▶▶▶III. For Writing

This unit is about change—change that results from some dramatic event. In "Marigolds," a young girl gains painful insight into herself after she destroys an old woman's flower garden. In "Neighbors," a family is forced to make a crucial decision after they are terrorized by a bomb blast. Consider some of the stories you have read and how characters are affected both externally and internally by their experiences. In an essay, discuss the subject of change in one or more selections. If you wish, choose two characters or two situations for comparison and contrast.

The African American Novel

David Adams Leeming
Formerly at
University of Connecticut

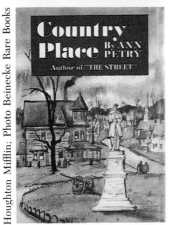

The Tradition of the African American Novel

In less than one hundred and forty years, African American culture has developed a tradition in the novel that most nations would envy. This tradition spans many approaches to fiction, from historical romance and social realism to diverse and experimental forms. The names most often associated with the tradition are among the giants of American literature. No study of the American novel can ignore James Baldwin, Ralph Ellison, Toni Morrison, Alice Walker, or Richard Wright. Works such as *Go Tell It on the Mountain, Invisible Man, Beloved, The Color Purple,* and *Native Son* are American classics.

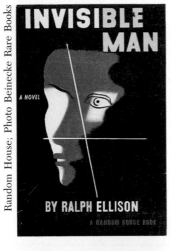

The Isolation of African Americans

If most Americans have never heard of Ann Petry's *Country Place* or Claude Brown's *Manchild in the Promised Land* or Ishmael Reed's *Mumbo Jumbo,* it is because African Americans have been culturally and socially isolated in the dominant European-American culture of our country. African Americans have had to create a literature on their own that reflects their isolated condition in the American experience.

In the African American novel, we find the popular American fictional themes: the quest for freedom, the individual confronting a vast frontier landscape, and the rags-to-riches hope. But these themes are treated from the point of view of a people denied freedom, individuality, and financial success for racial reasons. In short, the African American novel has almost always reflected the bicultural aspect of African American life, the fact that African Americans have been not only Americans, but also "colored," "Negro," or "black" Americans. The African American novel asks the question, "What does it mean to be African American?" In *The Afro-American Novel and Its Tradition* (1987), Bernard W. Bell writes:

> . . . the tradition of the Afro-American novel is dominated by the struggle for freedom from all forms of oppression and by the personal odyssey to realize the full potential of one's complex bicultural identity as an Afro-American (page 341).

The Sources of the African American Novel

The African American novel emerged from the cultural experience of the African slaves in America. The tradition of oral narrative, stories passed down by word of mouth, was important in Africa, and it continued to be important in America. Although the slaves were from many ethnic groups with many different languages, they quickly developed an African American language. It was based on the language they found in America but was shaped by their own needs and by their particular condition, and it retained African language structures. The oral narratives that took form in that language were based at first on the myths, legends, and folk tales of Africa, embellished later by folk tales and literary traditions already in existence in America. Since the slaves were denied education and, therefore, the art of writing, they were dependent on the common oral language to pass along what they considered to be necessary knowledge and values.

Musical traditions brought from Africa were also important vehicles for creativity and information. Over the years these traditions, too, were affected by the peculiar circumstances of slavery in America. Songs could be used to express the agony of separation, the hope for freedom. They would eventually be combined with stories from the Bible, especially the Old Testament stories of the struggles for freedom from captivity, the stories of longing for the Promised Land. Such musical forms as jazz and the blues and gospel would grow out of these early interminglings of the African and African American experiences.

These various elements—folklore, storytelling, musical practices, and linguistic forms—were instrumental in the development of the African American novel. They continue to affect the tradition to this day, long after the written word has taken precedence over the spoken word. When in the mid-nineteenth century slave narratives, such as *Narrative of the Life of Frederick Douglass* (1845) and *The Life of Josiah Henson* (1849), were added to the earlier traditions, the foundation was ready for the emergence of the African American novel itself.

The African American Novel Before the Civil War

The first novel by an African American was *Clotel; or The President's Daughter: A Narrative of Slave Life in the United States* (1853) by William Wells Brown (1814–1884), a well-known fugitive slave. In this romance about his own escape from slavery and the plight of a young slave who is said to be Thomas Jefferson's daughter, Brown demonstrates the dehumanizing aspect of slav-

The Creation of the Animals, *quilt by Harriet Powers, c. 1895–1898.* Bequest of Maxim Karolik, Courtesy, Museum of Fine Arts, Boston

(Left) *African musician playing an instrument made of gourds.*
General Commission on Archives and History, The United Methodist Church/ Photo by George Goodwin

(Right) *Lionel Hampton playing a vibraphone.*
Michael Ochs Archives/ Venice, CA

ery. Ironically, Brown's novel was published in England rather than in the United States.

Other significant novelists of this early period are Harriet Wilson (born c. 1828), Martin R. Delany (1812–1885), and Frank Webb (born c. 1830). Webb's *The Garies and Their Friends* (1857) and Wilson's *Our Nig* (1859) treat the subject of prejudice in the North. Delany was the most radical of the early black abolitionists. He is best known for his novel *Blake; or The Huts of Africa* (1859).

Novels Between the Civil War and World War I

The two most important black writers of the post–Civil War period were Charles W. Chesnutt (1858–1932), who felt that his mission was to free white people of the burden of prejudice, and Paul Laurence Dunbar (1872–1906), who brought black folklore closer to the mainstream of American literature. Chesnutt's greatest work is probably *The Marrow of Tradition* (1901), in which he demonstrates some of the irony and subtlety that would later mark fictional treatments of race by such writers as James Baldwin and Ralph Ellison. Dunbar was better known for his poems and short stories than for his novels, although his *The Sport of the Gods*

The African American Novel   575

(1902) follows Chesnutt toward a more realistic treatment of the African American condition. In this development, African American literature seems to move closer to the mainstream of American literature, where in the late 1890s and early 1900s the realism and naturalism of Stephen Crane, Frank Norris, and Theodore Dreiser were the order of the day.

Two important figures who bring us up to the period of the First World War are W. E. B. Du Bois (1868–1963) and James Weldon Johnson (1871–1938). Du Bois was better known as an intellectual and social activist than as a novelist. He did advance the cause of realism in five novels, however. Johnson was primarily a poet and song writer, but his *The Autobiography of an Ex-Coloured Man* (1912), which deals with a black man "passing" for white, has been called the first attempt to treat racial issues in modern psychological terms.

The Harlem Renaissance

After the First World War, New York's Harlem became a center for a blossoming of black culture that has been called the **Harlem Renaissance.** Some of the major figures of the Renaissance were Claude McKay (1889–1948), Zora Neale Hurston (1891–1960), Jean Toomer (1894–1967), Langston Hughes (1902–1967), Arna Bontemps (1902–1973), and Countee Cullen (1903–1946). These writers had in common a sense of pride in their ethnic identity and a desire to experiment with the language and literary traditions that had been passed down to them through their African American heritage.

Jean Toomer was not, strictly speaking, a novelist, but his *Cane* (1923) is a collection of narratives that make use of folk and music traditions to convey the African American experience. Toomer, like so many writers of the period, was experimenting with new forms and was searching for originality in the use of the black idiom. Claude McKay, who wrote *Home to Harlem* (1928), was another writer to make full use of the black idiom. Arna Bontemps wrote three novels, the most important of which was *Black Thunder* (1936), a historical romance about a failed slave revolt in Virginia. Bontemps's work marks the continued interest in the slave narratives as models for the continuing black search for real freedom.

Several woman novelists emerged during the Harlem Renaissance, among them Jessie Fauset (1882–1961), Nella Larsen (1893–1963), and Zora Neale Hurston, one of the greatest of Afri-

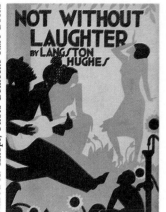

can American writers. Hurston made poetry of African American idiom. She was deeply influenced by African American and American folklore. Her best work is *Their Eyes Were Watching God* (1937), a novel that points to later feminist trends in its treatment of a black woman's search for identity in a relationship.

Countee Cullen and Langston Hughes were poets rather than novelists, but both also wrote fiction. Hughes's novels were *Not Without Laughter* (1930) and *Tambourines to Glory* (1958). Like other writers of the Harlem Renaissance, Hughes was drawn to the poetic possibilities of the black idiom. Countee Cullen's only novel was *One Way to Heaven* (1932), a satire on aspects of Harlem life.

The Great Tradition: Richard Wright to James Baldwin

During the period of the Great Depression and World War II, African American writers became less lyrical and more somber. Like their white colleagues, they turned to realism to convey the complicated social issues of their time.

Richard Wright (1908–1960) was the first universally recognized "giant" of African American literature. The product of a tragic childhood and extreme poverty, Wright for a while embraced Marxism as a surer path to improvement than pride in black culture. In *Native Son* (1940), he created Bigger Thomas, a disturbing character who is perhaps the most famous protagonist in African American literature. Bigger Thomas is a thoroughly naturalistic figure; that is, he is the predictable product of his heredity and environment, a living symbol of the dehumanizing power of racism and social injustice. He is the broken black psyche, the representative of Wright's anger and his belief that black culture cannot save itself.

Chester Himes (1909–1984), like his friend Richard Wright, was influenced in his writing by a tumultuous personal past. Like Wright, he chose the path of psychological naturalism to reveal the effects of racism on the black psyche, as in *If He Hollers Let Him Go* (1945). Himes is best known for his Harlem-based novels and his two black detectives, "Coffin" Ed and "Grave Digger."

The work of Ann Petry (b. 1911) stands in contrast to the pessimism of Wright and Himes. Her novels, *The Street* (1946), *Country Place* (1947), and *The Narrows* (1953), are sensitive explorations of characters as individuals rather than as naturalistic symbols.

The African American Novel 577

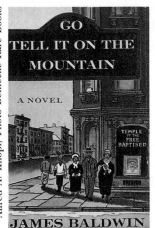

Ralph Ellison (1914–1994) completed one novel, *Invisible Man* (1952), arguably the "great African American novel." It is one of the most important novels to emerge from any culture in our time. The protagonist's social "invisibility" symbolizes the invisibility or isolation of the black American in his own country. His epic search for an identity represents the ongoing quest of the black American. But more than that, the invisible man is a universal modernist hero, a black version of the alienated individual in a modern world that seems to have no place for individuals.

A logical descendant of Ralph Ellison is James Baldwin (1924–1987), whose version of the invisible man is indicated in such essay titles as "Nobody Knows My Name," "Stranger in the Village," and "No Name in the Street." Baldwin's best-known novels are *Go Tell It on the Mountain* (1953), an autobiographical treatment of his childhood; *Giovanni's Room* (1956); and *Another Country* (1962). In each of his novels, an alienated protagonist seeks desperately for identity and fulfillment in love relationships. In the course of his career, culminating in *Just Above My Head* (1979), Baldwin uses the rhythms and sounds of the Bible and of gospel and blues music and couches it all in some of the most elegant prose in American fiction.

Honolulu Academy of Arts. Gift of Geraldine P. Clark, 1977. Photograph by Tibor Franyo. Courtesy Estate of Romare Bearden/The Romare Howard Bearden Foundation, NY

The Blues, *collage by Romare Bearden, from the series* **Of the Blues,** *1974.*

The African American Novel 579

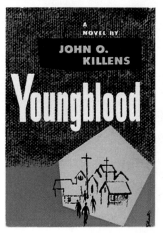

The Contemporary African American Novel

The last twenty-five years have seen an explosion in the production of African American novels. It is no exaggeration to suggest
that the African American novel has become a dominant factor in
contemporary American literature as a whole. Beginning with
Baldwin and Ellison, the number of highly acclaimed black novelists is so large, in fact, that just a few of the most important names
can be given here. John O. Killens, John A. Williams, Clarence
Major, John Wideman, Ishmael Reed, Frank Yerby, Ernest Gaines,
William Kelley, and Charles Wright have all given voice to the painful experience of the African American in today's world, often with
great technical originality. Reed's *Yellow Back Radio Broke-Down*
(1969), for example, is a highly innovative satire that makes use of
parody and the black oral tradition to expose many foibles of our
society. Gaines, in *The Autobiography of Miss Jane Pittman*
(1971), a work that was made into a television show, uses the story
of a slave woman's life to reexamine the history of black America
from the 1850s to our time. All of these writers are necessarily
concerned with racism and its destructive results, even as they
experiment with forms of narrative that place them firmly in the
forefront of modern literature.

Alfred A. Knopf; Photo Beinecke Rare Books

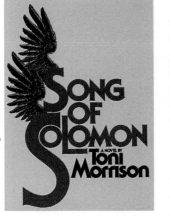

Among the most significant contributions to the history of African American fiction in particular and American literature in general during the past ten years have been those of women. The promise of such pioneers as Harriet Wilson and Zora Neale Hurston has been more than fulfilled by such contemporary figures as J. California Cooper, Paule Marshall, Toni Cade Bambara, Gloria Naylor, Terry McMillan, and especially Alice Walker and Toni Morrison. Walker gained international fame with *The Color Purple* (1982), the moving story of a woman's struggle to achieve identity and maintain integrity against a background of poverty, abuse, and oppression. Toni Morrison's *Beloved* (1987), a passionate masterpiece of great psychological depth and historical insight, is about a woman who struggles with the ghosts of slavery in an attempt to maintain sanity and dignity.

It seems likely that the foremost achievement of the contemporary African American novel is to have broken down once and for all the wall of isolation behind which William Wells Brown wrote the first African American novel in 1853. When writers of the stature of Alice Walker and Toni Morrison and Ishmael Reed publish novels today, the whole world takes note.

(Left) *Alice Walker.*
Thomas Victor/Time Magazine
(Right) *Toni Morrison.*
Wide World Photos

582 CONTEMPORARY NONFICTION

Contemporary Nonfiction

Nonfiction is prose that deals with real events and people rather than with imagined events and people. Three forms of nonfiction are included in this unit: **biography, essay,** and **speech.**

Biography (a classification that includes **autobiography**) is a narrative of events in someone's life. If the narrative is told by the person who is the subject, it is called autobiography. If it is told by someone other than the subject, it is called biography. In this textbook, you may have read excerpts from these outstanding autobiographies by African Americans: *Narrative of the Life of Frederick Douglass* (page 173); *Up from Slavery,* by Booker T. Washington (page 214); *Black Boy,* by Richard Wright (page 412); and *I Know Why the Caged Bird Sings,* by Maya Angelou (page 33).

Related to the autobiography are **memoirs, diaries,** and **letters.** In an autobiography, the emphasis is on the author's own development as an individual. The memoir emphasizes the people and events the author has known. The diary or journal is generally a private record of day-to-day experiences. The letter is a form intended for a single reader rather than for a wider audience. A fine example of the letter as persuasive writing is Benjamin Banneker's Letter to Thomas Jefferson (page 159).

An **essay** is any short prose composition that deals with its subject in a limited way and expresses a particular point of view. The word *essay* comes from the French word *essai,* which means "attempt." An essayist literally "tries out" ideas on the reader. The purpose of an essay may be to entertain, to discuss a subject informatively, to argue a position, or to persuade readers to follow some course of action.

Little Oba's Heritage, crib quilt for her cousin's son by Wini McQueen, 1987. In Yoruba, Oba means "king." The quilt combines personal family images with African emblems to show Little Oba's heritage.
Collection Ryan Kelly

The writers Amiri Baraka and Maya Angelou dance at a ceremony marking the eighty-ninth birthday of Langston Hughes and the beginning of Black History Month. The ceremony was held in the auditorium of the Schomburg Center for Research in Black Culture, located in Harlem.
Chester Higgins, Jr./NYT Pictures

Essays may be **formal** or **informal**. The **formal essay** is usually impersonal and serious in tone. The **informal essay,** also called the **familiar essay,** is personal and often light or humorous in tone.

A **speech** is generally intended for a specific audience. Some speeches, like Lincoln's Gettysburg Address, are masterpieces of prose and are read for their style as well as for their content. You may have read Sojourner Truth's famous speech "Ain't I a Woman?" (page 169), which was delivered at a women's rights convention in Ohio.

The line between fiction and nonfiction is not always easy to draw. Writers of nonfiction use many of the same literary devices used by writers of fiction, as you will find in reading the selections in this unit.

About the Author
Dorothy West (1907–1998)

 Dorothy West was born in Boston, where her father ran a fruit company. She began writing stories when she was seven. She won several *Boston Post* prizes while she was in her teens. After entering an *Opportunity* writing contest, she decided to settle in New York City. *Opportunity* published West's story "The Typewriter" in 1926. This story was included in *The Best Short Stories of 1926.*

In New York, West became acquainted with many writers of the Harlem Renaissance, including Zora Neale Hurston and Langston Hughes. In the early thirties, she founded *Challenge,* a magazine that helped introduce younger writers to readers. Another magazine, *New Challenge,* published the work of such writers as Richard Wright and Ralph Ellison.

After her magazine ventures failed, West took a job as a welfare investigator in Harlem and then joined the Federal Writers' Project. She became a contributor to the *New York Daily News,* which published many of her stories.

In 1945, West left for Martha's Vineyard, where she wrote her first novel, *The Living Is Easy* (1948). For the rest of her life, she lived in Oak Bluffs, Massachusetts, where she continued to write. Her other publications include *The Richer, the Poorer: Stories, Sketches, and Reminiscences* (1995) *and The Wedding* (1995), a novel.

Stephen Rose

Dorothy West   585

Before You Read

Rachel

Using What You Know

In his autobiography *Up from Slavery,* Booker T. Washington tells us that his mother was ambitious for her children and helped him in every way that she could: "If I have done anything in life worth attention, I feel sure that I inherited the disposition from my mother" (page 216). Think of instances in literature or in life where women have encouraged children through their own example.

Literary Focus: Memoir

Like an autobiography, the **memoir** is a form of personal recollection, but its emphasis is different. Whereas the autobiography generally focuses on the writer's growth and development, the memoir deals with events and people the writer has known. West's memoir of her mother includes scenes of family life, anecdotes, and conversations.

Setting a Purpose

As you read, what impression do you get of the writer's mother? What might have been Dorothy West's purpose in writing this memoir?

Rachel

Dorothy West

When my mother died, we who had sparred with her over the years of our growth and maturity said with relief, well, we won't have her intruding herself in our lives again. Our saying it may have been a kind of swaggering, or maybe we were in shock, trying to hide what was really inside us.

My mother had often made the declaration that she was never going to die. She knew what was here, she would say with a laugh, but she didn't know what was there. Heaven was a long way from home. She was staying right here.

So we just accepted it as fact that she would be the death of us instead. When her own death came first, we didn't know what to make of it. There was a thinness in the air. There was silence where there had been sound and fury. There was no longer that beautiful and compelling voice bending us to her will against our own.

The house that I grew up in was four-storied, but we were an extended family, continuously adding new members, and the perpetual joke was, if we lived in the Boston Museum, we'd still need one more room. Surrounded by all these different personalities, each one wanting to be first among equals, I knew I wanted to be a writer. Living with them was like living inside a story.

My mother was the dominant figure by the force of her vitality, and by the indisputable fact that she had the right to rule the roof that my father provided. She was a beautiful woman, and there was that day when I was grown, eighteen or so, ready to go off on my own, sure that I knew everything, that I said to her, "Well, your beauty was certainly wasted on you. All you did with it was raise children and run your sisters' lives."

My mother had done what she felt she had to do, knowing the risks, knowing there would be no rewards, but determined to build a foundation for the generations unborn. She had gathered us together so that the weakness of one would be balanced by her strength, and the loneliness of another eased by her laughter, and someone else's fears tempered by her fierce bravado, and the children treated alike, no matter what their degree of lovability, and her eye riveting mine if I tried to draw a distinction between myself and them.

We who had been the children under her command, and then the adults, still subject to her meddling in our intimate affairs, were finally bereaved, free of the departed, and in a rush to divorce ourselves from any resemblance to her influence.

When one of us said something that

In the Wind, *marble sculpture by Otto Neals.* Collection of the artist

Mother might have said, and an outraged chorus shouted, "You sound just like her," the speaker, stung with shame and close to tears, shouted back, "I do not!"

Then as time passed, whoever forgot to watch her language and echoed some sentiment culled from my mother responded to the catcalls with a cool, "So what?"

As time increased its pace, although there were diehards who would never relent, there were more of us shifting positions, examining our ambivalent feelings, wondering if the life force that had so overwhelmed our exercise of free will, and now no longer had to be reckoned with, was a greater loss than a relief.

When a newborn disciple recited my mother's sayings as if they were gospel, the chiding came from a scattered chorus of uninspired voices.

Then there was the day when someone said with wonder, "Have you noticed that those of us who sound just like her are the ones who laugh a lot, love children a lot, don't have any hangups about race or color, and never give up without trying?"

"Yes, I've noticed," one of us answered, with the rest of us adding softly, "Me, too."

I suppose that was the day and the hour of our acknowledgment that some part of her was forever imbedded in our psyches,[1] and we were not the worse for it.

But I still cannot put my finger on the why of her. What had she wanted, this beautiful

1. **psyches** (sī′kēz): souls.

588 DOROTHY WEST

woman? Did she get it? I would look at her face when it was shut away, and I would long to offer her a penny for her thoughts. But I knew she would laugh and say, "I was just thinking it's time to start dinner," or something equally far from her yearning heart.

I don't think she ever realized how often she made the remark, "Speech was given man to hide his thoughts." At such times I would say to myself, she will die with her secrets. I had guessed a few, but they had been only surface deep, easy to flush out. I know that the rest went with her on her flight to heaven.

Responding to the Selection
Rachel by Dorothy West

Identifying Facts

1. Why was the family's house never big enough?
2. Why did Dorothy West want to be a writer?
3. Why did she once believe that her mother's beauty was wasted?
4. What mystery about her mother was the author unable to solve?

Interpreting Meanings

1. How does the word *sparred* in the very first sentence emphasize the conflicts between Rachel West and her children? How does the phrase "bending us to her will against our own" help to characterize Rachel West?
2. The author says that her mother was "determined to build a foundation for the generations unborn." How did she treat her children? Why did they resent her influence?
3. Dorothy West says that the feelings of the family were *ambivalent*. What does she mean? How did these feelings shift with time? What accounted for the changing attitudes of the family?
4. "Speech was given man to hide his thoughts." How does this remark apply to Rachel West?
5. What might have been Dorothy West's purpose in creating this portrait of her mother?

Literary Elements
Understanding a Writer's Purpose
A writer's purpose affects the way a subject is handled. For example, the writer who wishes chiefly to entertain readers will choose amusing incidents and use a conver-

sational or light style. The writer who is interested in giving information will include specific facts and write in a serious, straightforward style. The writer who wishes to persuade readers to adopt a particular position or course of action will offer opinions, reasons, and evidence and will probably choose a formal style. Sometimes a piece of writing has more than one purpose.

Dorothy West's description tells us how the family viewed their mother. It reveals the complex, divided feelings the children shared. What do you think is the author's purpose in focusing on these ambivalent, or conflicting, feelings?

Language and Vocabulary

Recognizing Precise Meanings

In her opening sentence, West uses the word *sparred* as a **metaphor** to describe the encounters between the children and their mother. *Sparring* is a type of practice boxing that uses very light, skillful blows. Verbal sparring is the exchanging of words in an argument. Suppose West had chosen to use *fought* instead of *sparred.* How would the meaning have changed? Why is *sparred* a more precise word than *fought?*

Locate the words *swaggering* and *chiding* in the selection. How does each word convey specific meaning? Check your answers by looking at the entries for *swagger* and *chide* in a college or an unabridged dictionary.

Creative Writing

Writing a Memoir

Think of someone who has had a strong influence on you. In two or three paragraphs, create a portrait that brings that person to life.

Prewriting Suggestions

1. Identify the person and give a brief description of memorable characteristics: voice, manner of dress, sense of humor, and the like.
2. Note specific scenes or anecdotes that show your interaction with that person.
3. Report conversations that reveal the personality of the individual.
4. Tell how that person influenced you.

Speaking and Listening

Responding to the Selection

Comment on this remark: "Speech was given man to hide his thoughts." How can one use language to hide one's thoughts and feelings? Can you give instances of this in your own experience?

About the Author
Ralph Ellison (1914–1994)

Ralph Waldo Ellison was born in Oklahoma City, where he spent a happy childhood. He grew up in an atmosphere of freedom and openness. An interest in reading was encouraged by his father, who introduced him to books when he was very young. His interest in social and political affairs may have been fostered by his mother, who was politically active.

When he entered Tuskegee Institute, he was intent on a musical career. During his second year, he began to immerse himself in books.

In 1936, Ellison needed money to continue his studies and left for New York City in order to find summer work. He never returned to Tuskegee. In New York he met Langston Hughes and then Richard Wright, who asked him to contribute to a Harlem literary magazine. Between 1938 and 1944, Ellison had a number of short stories and essays published. Two stories from this period that are often anthologized are ''Flying Home'' and ''King of the Bingo Game.''

Near the end of World War II, Ellison began work on *Invisible Man.* He completed it seven years later, in 1952. Many critics consider this novel to be the greatest work of fiction by an African American writer. It received the National Book Award in 1953. The title of the book refers to the main character, whose invisibility is a metaphor for the black American experience. The protagonist undergoes a long and difficult journey to discover his identity.

Bob Adelman/Magnum Photos

Shadow and Act (1964), Ellison's second book, is a collection of essays dealing with literature and folklore, with jazz and the blues, and with the relationship of black and white cultures. *Going to the Territory* (1986), a second collection of essays, contains ''An Extravagance of Laughter,'' part of which is reprinted here. This essay deals with Ellison's trip to New York City in 1936. *Flying Home and Other Stories* was published posthumously in 1996.

Ralph Ellison   591

Before You Read

from An Extravagance of Laughter

Using What You Know

Ellison, who had been at school in Alabama, arrived in New York City in 1936 and began to make his way around the city by public transportation. In this selection, he gives his observations about New York's subways and buses.

Have you ever taken a subway or a railroad that runs underground? How does this form of transportation differ from other forms you are familiar with?

Literary Focus: Humor

The purpose of an essay may be to entertain, to inform, to explain, or to persuade. Often, an essay has a combination of purposes. In this selection, Ellison mixes his amusement over comic oddities with his observations about the North.

Humor often results from some comic exaggeration or from the joining together of unlikely things in order to create an unexpected or ridiculous situation. One such example is giving a slow-moving creature such as a turtle the name "Speedy."

Setting a Purpose

As you read, note how Ellison keeps to his purpose of comparing Southern styles with Northern styles at the same time that he diverts the reader.

An Extravagance of Laughter

Ralph Ellison

Beyond the borders of Harlem's brier patch—which seemed familiar because of my racial and cultural identification with the majority of its people and the lingering spell that had been cast nationwide by the music, dance, and literature of the so-called Harlem Renaissance—I viewed New Yorkers through the overlay of my Alabama experience. Contrasting the whites I encountered with those I had observed in the South, I weighed class against class and compared Southern styles with their Northern counterparts. I listened to diction and noted dress, and searched for attitudes in inflections, carriage, and manners. And in pursuing this aspect of my extracurricular education, I explored the landscape.

I crossed Manhattan back and forth from river to river and up, down, and around again, from Spuyten Duyvil Creek to the Battery,[1] looking and listening and gadding about; rode streetcar and el,[2] subway and bus; took a hint from Edna Millay[3] and spent an evening riding back and forth on the Staten Island Ferry. For given my Oklahoma-Alabama perspective, even New York's forms of transportation were unexpected sources of education. From the elevated trains I saw my first penthouses with green trees growing atop tall buildings, caught remote glimpses of homes, businesses, and factories while moving above the teeming streets, and felt a sense of quiet tranquillity despite the bang and clatter. Yes, but the subways were something else again.

In fact, the subways were utterly confusing to my Southern-bred idea of good manners, and especially the absence of a certain gallantry that men were expected to extend toward women. Subway cars appeared to be underground arenas in which Northern social equality took the form of an endless shoving match in which the usual rules of etiquette were turned upside down—or so I

1. **Spuyten Duyvil** (spīt′ən dī′vəl) **Creek:** a narrow channel that separates Manhattan Island from the mainland; **Battery:** a park at the southern tip of Manhattan.
2. **el:** an elevated railway, part of the city's transportation system.

3. **Edna Millay:** Edna St. Vincent Millay (1892–1950), an American poet who describes the romance and enchantment of riding the ferry in her poem "Recuerdo."

concluded after watching a five-o'clock foot race in a crowded car.

The contest was between a huge white woman who carried an armful of bundles, and a small Negro man who lugged a large suitcase. At the time I was standing against the track-side door, and when the train stopped at a downtown station I saw the two come charging through the opening doors like race horses leaving the starting gate at Belmont.[4] And as they spied and dashed for the single empty seat, the outcome appeared up for grabs,[5] but it was the woman, thanks to a bustling, more ruthless stride (and more subway know-how) who won—though but by a hip and a hair. For just as they reached the seat she swung a well-padded hip and knocked the man off stride, thus causing him to lose his balance as she turned, slipped beneath his reeling body, and plopped into the seat. It was a maneuver which produced a startling effect—at least on me.

For as she banged into the seat it caused the man to spin and land smack-dab into her lap—in which massive and heaving center of gravity he froze, stared into her face nose-tip to nose, and then performed a springlike leap to his feet as from a red-hot stove. It was but the briefest conjunction,[6] and then, as he reached down and fumbled for his suitcase, the woman began adjusting her bundles, and with an elegant toss of her head she looked up into his face with the most ladylike and triumphant of smiles. . . .

But for all their noise and tension, it was not the subways that most intrigued me. For although a pleasant way to explore the city, my rides in New York buses soon aroused questions about matters that I had hoped to leave behind. And yet the very fact that I encountered little on Northern buses that was distressing allowed me to face up to a problem which had puzzled me down South: the relationship between Southern buses and racial status. In the South you occupied the back of the bus, and nowhere *but* the back, or so help you God. So being in the North and encouraged by my anonymity, I experimented by riding all *over* New York buses, excluding only the driver's seat—front end, back end, right side, left side, sitting or standing as the route and flow of passengers demanded. *And*, since those were the glorious days of double-deckers, both enclosed and open, I even rode *top*side.

Thus having convinced myself that no questions of racial status would be raised by where I chose to ride, I asked myself whether a seat at the back of the bus wasn't actually more desirable than one at the front. For not only did it provide more leg room, it offered a more inclusive perspective on both the interior and exterior scenes. I found the answer obvious and quite amusing, but then, as though to raise to consciousness more serious questions that I had too long ignored, the buses forced a more troubling contradiction upon my attention. Now that I was no longer forced by law and compelled by custom to ride at the back and to surrender my seat to any white who demanded it, what was more desirable—the possibility of exercising what was routinely accepted in the North as an abstract, highly symbolic (even trivial) form

4. **Belmont:** a racetrack.
5. **up for grabs:** a slang expression meaning "available to the most aggressive person."
6. **conjunction:** union; association.

of democratic freedom, or the creature comfort which was to be had by occupying a spot from which more of the passing scene could be observed? And in my own personal terms, what was more important—my own individual comfort, or the exercise of the democratic right to be squeezed and jostled by strangers? The highly questionable privilege of being touched by anonymous whites—not to mention reds, browns, blacks, and yellows—or the minor pleasure afforded by having a maximum of breathing space? Such questions were akin to that of whether you lived in a Negro neighborhood because you were forced to do so, or because you preferred living among those of your own background. Which was easy to answer, because having experienced life in mixed neighborhoods as a child, I preferred to live where people spoke my own version of the American language,

and where misreadings of tone or gesture were less likely to ignite lethal conflict. Segregation laws aside, this was a matter of personal choice, for even though class and cultural differences existed among Negroes, it was far easier to deal with hostilities arising between yourself and your own people than with, say, Jeeter Lester[7] or, more realistically, Lester Maddox.[8] And that even though I would have found it far better to be Lestered by Jeeter than mattock-handled by Maddox, that most improbable governor of a state that I had often visited!

7. **Jeeter Lester:** a white Southern sharecropper who is a famous character in Erskine Caldwell's *Tobacco Road*.
8. **Lester Maddox:** He resisted attempts at integration. Rather than serve African Americans, he closed his restaurant in Atlanta. In 1967, he was elected governor of Georgia by the state legislature because no candidate had received 50 percent of the votes.

Responding to the Selection
from An Extravagance of Laughter by Ralph Ellison

Identifying Facts

1. What are the five means of public transportation Ellison uses to get around the city?
2. How does Ellison get his first glimpse of penthouses?
3. Which mode of transportation does he find most confusing?
4. Which one holds the most fascination for him?

Interpreting Meanings

1. A *brier patch* consists of thorny, prickly shrubs. What literary associations might this phrase have for Ellison? Why do you think he refers to Harlem as a "brier patch"?
2. In the first paragraph, Ellison states the purpose of his observations. What does his "education" consist of? Does the word *landscape* refer only to scenery?
3. What does he discover about manners in

the subway? How does the conflict he witnesses demonstrate "Northern social equality"? Which details did you find most humorous?

4. Ellison concludes that the back of the bus is the best place to sit. Given the fact that in the South at this time, African Americans had no choice about where they could sit, why is this conclusion ironic? Why does Ellison's realization cause a conflict?

5. Why does Ellison say he prefers living among his own people, even though he is not compelled to do so? Do you feel that his argument is sound?

6. What do you think is Ellison's purpose in mentioning the fictional character Jeeter Lester, an ignorant white Southern farmer who is ruined by the Depression, and the real-life Lester Maddox, a segregationist who became governor of Georgia?

Literary Elements

Recognizing Humorous Techniques

One way Ralph Ellison creates humor is through **metaphor.** In describing the struggle between the people in the subway, he compares the contest first to "a five o'clock foot race" and then to a horse race:

> I saw the two come charging through the opening doors like race horses leaving the starting gate at Belmont.

Another technique Ellison uses is **exaggeration,** as when he compares the woman's lap to a "massive and heaving center of gravity."

Find other examples of these techniques in the passage.

Developing Sentence Sense

Achieving Sentence Variety

The usual order of sentences in English is **subject** followed by **predicate.** In the following sentence, the subject is *I.* The predicate is made up of a verb, *explored,* and an object, *the landscape:*

> I explored the landscape.

If every sentence were written in this pattern, however, one's writing would become boring.

Note the different ways Ellison begins his sentences in order to achieve variety. Sometimes he begins with **prepositional phrases:**

> Beyond the borders of Harlem's brier patch . . .

Sometimes he begins with **participial phrases:**

> Contrasting the whites I encountered . . .

He may begin with a **subordinate construction:**

An Extravagance of Laughter 597

And, since those were the glorious days of double-deckers . . .

Choose one passage in the selection and examine the structure of its sentences. How does Ellison vary the openings of his sentences?

LANGUAGE WORKSHOP

LW 9 Ch 6 & 7
LW 10 Ch 6 & 7
Phrases and
Clauses
Sentences

Expository Writing

Explaining Rules

As part of his education, Ellison studied the manners of New Yorkers and found that they could be quite different from what he was used to in the South. Think of the unwritten rules for good manners that affect you in public places: the school bus, the cafeteria, the line at a movie theater or fast-food restaurant, the check-out counter in a supermarket, and so on. How would you explain these rules to someone from another land?

If you wish, compare the manners you have observed in different places. For instance, have you noted differences in driving etiquette? Do the rules of the road differ for drivers in small towns and in big cities?

Speaking and Listening

Relating a Humorous Incident

Humor often stems from recognizing and describing peculiarities and absurdities in a situation. Ellison creates a picture with a cartoon quality when he describes two characters scrambling for the same seat in the subway—a large woman loaded down with bundles and a small man lugging a big suitcase.

Think of a humorous incident that you have been involved in or have heard about. Practice telling the incident as a comedian might, using voice, gesture, and timing to get laughs. Then deliver your story to a group or to the class.

About the Author

James Baldwin (1924–1987)

 James Arthur Baldwin, whose biography appears on page 471, is one of the greatest essayists this country has ever produced. His passion and eloquence as a spokesperson for human dignity and worth and justice for his race—indeed, for all people—have earned him a prominent place in American literature of the twentieth century.

Notes of a Native Son (1955), Baldwin's first volume of essays, alludes in its title to the famous novel by Richard Wright, whom Baldwin admired greatly. *Nobody Knows My Name: More Notes of a Native Son* (1961) and *The Fire Next Time* (1963), were best-sellers that brought him a large audience. His collected essays are available in *The Price of the Ticket: Collected Nonfiction 1948–1985* (1985).

Baldwin has been highly praised for both his style and his ideas. Many critics have noted that Baldwin's service as a preacher in his father's church affected the style of his prose, which has been described as a "spoken" prose.

His essays are both personal and analytical. One of his recurrent themes is the injustice he finds in American society. Baldwin once explained his own aims by saying that you write "in order to change the world, knowing perfectly well that you probably can't, but also knowing that literature is indispensable to the world. In some way, your aspirations and concern for a single man in fact do begin to change the world."

Sygma

Baldwin's concern for the welfare of the individual is reflected in the moving essay that is reprinted here. Originally published in *The Progressive* as "A Letter to My Nephew," in December 1962, it was retitled "My Dungeon Shook" and collected in *The Fire Next Time.*

James Baldwin 599

Before You Read

My Dungeon Shook

Using What You Know

One of the ideals that has been associated with our country from its earliest days has been equality of opportunity. How did the Emancipation Proclamation, signed in 1863, affirm our nation's best ideals? Consider Baldwin's reasons for writing this letter/essay on the anniversary of the Emancipation Proclamation.

Literary Focus: Organization

Some forms of nonfiction, such as biographies, diaries, and journals, tend to be narratives and thus follow a chronological sequence. Since the focus of an essay may be the analysis of an idea or the presentation of an argument, its **organization** may not be obvious at first. An essay may be organized to dramatize contrasts; it may progress from specific observations to generalization; its ideas may be presented in order of importance. Even when topics seem to be discussed in random order, there is usually a plan.

Setting a Purpose

As you read, note how Baldwin organizes his material. Watch how he connects ideas so that his writing flows easily.

My Dungeon Shook

James Baldwin

Dear James:

I have begun this letter five times and torn it up five times. I keep seeing your face, which is also the face of your father and my brother. Like him, you are tough, dark, vulnerable, moody—with a very definite tendency to sound truculent[1] because you want no one to think you are soft. You may be like your grandfather in this, I don't know, but certainly both you and your father resemble him very much physically. Well, he is dead, he never saw you, and he had a terrible life; he was defeated long before he died because, at the bottom of his heart, he really believed what white people said about him. This is one of the reasons that he became so holy. I am sure that your father has told you something about all that. Neither you nor your father exhibit any tendency toward holiness: you really are of another era, part of what happened when the Negro left the land and came into what the late E. Franklin Frazier[2] called "the cities of destruction." You can only be destroyed by believing that you really are what the white world calls a *nigger*. I tell you this because I love you, and please don't you ever forget it.

1. **truculent** (trŭk'yə-lənt): eager to fight.
2. **E. Franklin Frazier:** a sociologist appointed to investigate the riots in Harlem during the Depression.

I have known both of you all your lives, have carried your Daddy in my arms and on my shoulders, kissed and spanked him and watched him learn to walk. I don't know if you've known anybody from that far back; if you've loved anybody that long, first as an infant, then as a child, then as a man, you gain a strange perspective on time and human pain and effort. Other people cannot see what I see whenever I look into your father's face, for behind your father's face as it is today are all those other faces which were his. Let him laugh and I see a cellar your father does not remember and a house he does not remember and I hear in his present laughter his laughter as a child. Let him curse and I remember him falling down the cellar steps, and howling, and I remember, with pain, his tears, which my hand or your grandmother's so easily wiped away. But no one's hand can wipe away those tears he sheds invisibly today, which one hears in his laughter and in his speech and in his songs. I know what the world has done to my brother and how narrowly he has survived it. And I know, which is much worse, and this is the crime of which I accuse my country and my countrymen, and for which neither I nor time nor history will ever forgive them, that they have destroyed and are destroying hun-

Steve Schapiro/Black Star

dreds of thousands of lives and do not know it and do not want to know it. One can be, indeed one must strive to become, tough and philosophical concerning destruction and death, for this is what most of mankind has been best at since we have heard of man. (But remember: *most* of mankind is not *all* of mankind.) But it is not permissible that the authors of devastation should also be innocent. It is the innocence which constitutes the crime.

Now, my dear namesake, these innocent and well-meaning people, your countrymen, have caused you to be born under conditions not very far removed from those described for us by Charles Dickens[3] in the London of more than a hundred years ago. (I hear the chorus of the innocents screaming, "No! This is not true! How *bitter* you are!"—but I am writing this letter to *you*, to try to tell you something about how to handle *them*, for most of them do not yet really know that you exist. I *know* the conditions under which you were born, for I was there. Your countrymen were *not* there, and haven't made it yet.

3. **Charles Dickens:** English novelist (1812–1870), whose books exposed the dismal living conditions of the poor in nineteenth-century London.

Your grandmother was also there, and no one has ever accused her of being bitter. I suggest that the innocents check with her. She isn't hard to find. Your countrymen don't know that she exists, either, though she has been working for them all their lives.)

Well, you were born, here you came, something like fourteen years ago; and though your father and mother and grandmother, looking about the streets through which they were carrying you, staring at the walls into which they brought you, had every reason to be heavyhearted, yet they were not. For here you were, Big James, named for me—you were a big baby, I was not— here you were: to be loved. To be loved, baby, hard, at once, and forever, to strengthen you against the loveless world. Remember that: I know how black it looks today, for you. It looked bad that day, too, yes, we were trembling. We have not stopped trembling yet, but if we had not loved each other none of us would have survived. And now you must survive because we love you, and for the sake of your children and your children's children.

This innocent country set you down in a ghetto in which, in fact, it intended that you should perish. Let me spell out precisely what I mean by that, for the heart of the matter is here, and the root of my dispute with my country. You were born where you were born and faced the future that you faced because you were black and *for no other reason.* The limits of your ambition were, thus, expected to be set forever. You were born into a society which spelled out with brutal clarity, and in as many ways as possible, that you were a worthless human being. You were not expected to aspire to excellence: you were expected to make peace with mediocrity. Wherever you have turned, James, in your short time on this earth, you have been told where you could go and what you could do (and *how* you could do it) and where you could live and whom you could marry. I know your countrymen do not agree with me about this, and I hear them saying, "You exaggerate." They do not know Harlem, and I do. So do you. Take no one's word for anything, including mine—but trust your experience. Know whence[4] you came. If you know whence you came, there is really no limit to where you can go. The details and symbols of your life have been deliberately constructed to make you believe what white people say about you. Please try to remember that what they believe, as well as what they do and cause you to endure, does not testify to your inferiority but to their inhumanity and fear. Please try to be clear, dear James, through the storm which rages about your youthful head today, about the reality which lies behind the words *acceptance* and *integration.* There is no reason for you to try to become like white people and there is no basis whatever for their impertinent assumption that *they* must accept *you.* The really terrible thing, old buddy, is that *you* must accept *them.* And I mean that very seriously. You must accept them and accept them with love. For these innocent people have no other hope. They are, in effect, still trapped in a history which they do not understand; and until they understand it, they cannot be released from it. They have had to believe for many years, and for innumerable reasons, that black men are inferior to white men. Many of them, indeed, know better, but, as you will discover, people find it very difficult to act on what they know. To act is to be committed, and to be committed is to be in

4. **whence:** from where.

danger. In this case, the danger, in the minds of most white Americans, is the loss of their identity. Try to imagine how you would feel if you woke up one morning to find the sun shining and all the stars aflame. You would be frightened because it is out of the order of nature. Any upheaval in the universe is terrifying because it so profoundly attacks one's sense of one's own reality. Well, the black man has functioned in the white man's world as a fixed star, as an immovable pillar: and as he moves out of his place, heaven and earth are shaken to their foundations. You, don't be afraid. I said that it was intended that you should perish in the ghetto, perish by never being allowed to go behind the white man's definitions, by never being allowed to spell your proper name. You have, and many of us have, defeated this intention: and, by a terrible law, a terrible paradox,[5] those innocents who believed that your imprisonment made them safe are losing their grasp of reality. But these men are your brothers—your lost, younger brothers. And if the word *integration* means anything,

this is what it means: that we, with love, shall force our brothers to see themselves as they are, to cease fleeing from reality and begin to change it. For this is your home, my friend, do not be driven from it; great men have done great things here, and will again, and we can make America what America must become. It will be hard, James, but you come from sturdy, peasant stock, men who picked cotton and dammed rivers and built railroads, and, in the teeth of the most terrifying odds, achieved an unassailable and monumental dignity. You come from a long line of great poets, some of the greatest poets since Homer.[6] One of them said, "The very time I thought I was lost, My dungeon shook and my chains fell off."

You know, and I know, that the country is celebrating one hundred years of freedom one hundred years too soon. We cannot be free until they are free. God bless you, James, and Godspeed.

YOUR UNCLE,
James

---

5. **paradox** (păr′ə-dŏks′): a statement that appears to be self-contradictory but is nonetheless true.

6. **Homer:** an ancient Greek poet, who is thought to have lived around 850 B.C. He is credited with creating two great epic poems, the *Iliad* and the *Odyssey*.

Responding to the Selection

My Dungeon Shook by James Baldwin

Identifying Facts

1. According to Baldwin, why was his father defeated in life?
2. What is Baldwin's "dispute" with his country?
3. What does Baldwin tell his nephew to trust?
4. In Baldwin's view, what is the danger that most white Americans experience?

Interpreting Meanings

1. In the first two paragraphs of his letter, Baldwin recalls his nephew's father and grandfather. Why do you think he opens his essay by referring to these two men?
2. In paragraphs 3 and 4, Baldwin deals with the circumstances of his nephew's birth. How does Baldwin emphasize the importance of love in surviving these conditions?
3. Paragraph 5, the longest paragraph in the essay, contains the central meaning of Baldwin's essay. What is his advice to his nephew? According to Baldwin, what is the reality behind the words *acceptance* and *integration*? Why does he say that it is necessary for his nephew to accept white people with love? What does he mean by *integration*?
4. Who are the "innocents" Baldwin refers to? Is his use of this word ironic?

5. Baldwin is noted for dealing with the complexities of interracial relations. In this essay, he is concerned with what racism does not only to the oppressed but to the oppressor. Why does he believe that racial hatred destroys those who are guilty of it?
6. Toward the end of his essay, Baldwin speaks of a dungeon and chains. What kind of "imprisonment" is he referring to? What does he mean when he says, "We cannot be free until they are free"?
7. This letter was written on the one-hundredth anniversary of the Emancipation Proclamation. At that time, the Civil Rights Movement was well under way. Where in the essay does Baldwin make you aware of the goals of the movement?
8. Baldwin was described as an angry young man by some critics when he wrote this letter. Would you agree that the **tone** of this letter is angry, or is the tone one of hope? Support your answer with examples from the letter.

Literary Elements

Recognizing Parallelism

One characteristic of Baldwin's style is **parallelism**—the use of phrases, clauses, or sentences that are similar in structure or in meaning. Parallelism can create emphasis through repetition; it can also create contrast. It can be used as a technique for reinforcing connections between ideas.

Baldwin writes of loving his brother "first as an infant, then as a child, then as a man." Note how these phrases, which are similar in structure, seem to balance and echo each other.

Baldwin also uses parallelism to emphasize contrast: "Let him laugh and I see a cellar . . . Let him curse and I remember him . . . ."

Locate some other examples of parallelism in the essay. Read these lines aloud and note their rhythmic effect.

Writer's Journal

Defining One's Identity

Baldwin advises his nephew, "Know whence you came. If you know whence you came, there is really no limit to where you can go." Why does Baldwin believe it is important to understand and accept one's heritage?

In your journal, write an entry in response to the question, "Who am I?" Attempt to define your own identity.

Prewriting Strategies

Make a list of various things that make you who and what you are. You may want to include, but are not limited to, the following:

family and traditions
ethnic background
physical characteristics
goals and values
education
tastes in music and foods
neighborhood
friends

Use natural language. After you have listed your details, select those that you feel best define your identity. Write a paragraph or two that might introduce you to a stranger. If you wish, plan a letter that you might send to a pen pal in another country.

Speaking and Listening

Listening to Spirituals

Baldwin's writing often reflects the profound influence of spirituals. Although he left preaching, he never rejected the basic messages of the spirituals: love, patience, forbearance, and hope. Listen to recordings of "Go Tell It on the Mountain," "Just Above My Head," "Every Time I Feel the Spirit," or any other spirituals, including those on pages 189–190. Listen closely to the lyrics and then explain why you think these songs provided inspiration and comfort to Baldwin.

About the Author
Malcolm X (1925–1965)

 In the 1950s, Malcolm X gained prominence as a spokesperson for black separatism. His public appearances inspired many people in the African American community, but they also produced a chilling effect on many others who heard him. His rhetoric about violence—"the ballot or the bullet" alienated many black Americans who sided with the nonviolence teachings of Martin Luther King, Jr. Toward the end of his life, Malcolm X accepted the possibility of a "worldwide multiracial brotherhood." At the time of his assassination, he was working to unite blacks throughout the world.

Malcolm X was born Malcolm Little in Omaha, Nebraska. His father, a Baptist minister and organizer for the Marcus Garvey movement, was killed under suspicious circumstances. Malcolm's mother became ill and the children were separated and sent to foster homes.

After eighth grade, Malcolm went to Roxbury, Massachusetts, to live with an older sister. He slipped into a life of crime. Before he was twenty-one, he was arrested for robbery and sentenced to ten years in prison. In the penitentiary, he became converted to the Black Muslim religion. It was through his desire to communicate with Elijah Muhammad, founder and leader of the Black Muslims, that Malcolm began his program of education. He denounced his Christian surname and took the name Malcolm X.

After his release, he became a minister at a mosque in Harlem. He rose in rank and in-

John Launois/Black Star

fluence. Malcolm X became increasingly critical, however, of Elijah Muhammad. On a tour of Mecca, he experienced a profound conversion. He renamed himself El-Hajj Malik El-Shabazz and decided to work for unity and harmony among all blacks. He founded his own Muslim association, the Organization of Afro-American Unity.

Although he knew that his life was in danger, he continued to speak out for his views. On February 21, 1965, while he was addressing an audience in the Audubon Ballroom in Harlem, he was gunned down.

He left a legacy of recorded speeches. *The Autobiography of Malcolm X* was completed, with the assistance of Alex Haley, just before his death.

Before You Read

from The Autobiography of Malcolm X

Using What You Know

Throughout this book, you have seen examples of African Americans who endured great hardships in order to obtain an education. Recall the experiences of Booker T. Washington (page 212) and Richard Wright (page 410), for example.

Imagine what your life would be like if you could not read and write. List five things you would be unable to do. What problems might you have in finding and keeping a job? Put yourself in Malcolm X's place as he describes his "homemade education."

Literary Focus: Autobiography

In an **autobiography,** the narrator is also the central character. The autobiographer has many reasons for looking back over his or her life: to preserve memories of certain people; to express feelings about specific incidents and situations; to clarify reasons for actions; to explain why life turned out as it did; and, in the case of a noteworthy individual, to trace the influences and events that shaped a career. Like the essayist, the autobiographer has a point of view toward the material and toward the reader.

Setting a Purpose

The following excerpt from the *Autobiography* appears in a chapter called "Saved." After you have read the selection, determine why Malcolm X used this title.

The Autobiography of Malcolm X

It was because of my letters that I happened to stumble upon starting to acquire some kind of a homemade education.

I became increasingly frustrated at not being able to express what I wanted to convey in letters that I wrote, especially those to Mr. Elijah Muhammad.[1] In the street, I had been the most articulate hustler out there—I had commanded attention when I said something. But now, trying to write simple English, I not only wasn't articulate, I wasn't even functional. How would I sound writing in slang, the way I would *say* it, something such as, "Look, daddy, let me pull your coat about a cat, Elijah Muhammad—"

Many who today hear me somewhere in person, or on television, or those who read something I've said, will think I went to school far beyond the eighth grade. This impression is due entirely to my prison studies.

It had really begun back in the Charlestown Prison, when Bimbi[2] first made me feel envy of his stock of knowledge. Bimbi had always taken charge of any conversation he was in, and I had tried to emulate him. But

1. **Elijah Muhammad:** the Black Muslims' founder and leader.
2. **Bimbi:** a fellow inmate he met in 1947, at Charlestown State Prison.

every book I picked up had few sentences which didn't contain anywhere from one to nearly all of the words that might as well have been in Chinese. When I just skipped those words, of course, I really ended up with little idea of what the book said. So I had come to the Norfolk Prison Colony still going through only book-reading motions. Pretty soon, I would have quit even these motions, unless I had received the motivation that I did.

I saw that the best thing I could do was get hold of a dictionary—to study, to learn some words. I was lucky enough to reason also that I should try to improve my penmanship. It was sad. I couldn't even write in a straight line. It was both ideas together that moved me to request a dictionary along with some tablets and pencils from the Norfolk Prison Colony school.

I spent two days just riffling uncertainly through the dictionary's pages. I'd never realized so many words existed! I didn't know *which* words I needed to learn. Finally, just to start some kind of action, I began copying.

In my slow, painstaking, ragged handwriting, I copied into my tablet everything printed on that first page, down to the punctuation marks.

I believe it took me a day. Then, aloud, I

The Autobiography of Malcolm X   609

**Malcolm Speaks for Us,
*linocut by Elizabeth Cat-
lett, 1969.***
Collection of Dr. Samella Lewis.
© 1998 Elizabeth Catlett/
Licensed by VAGA,
New York, NY

read back, to myself, everything I'd written on the tablet. Over and over, aloud, to myself, I read my own handwriting.

I woke up the next morning, thinking about those words—immensely proud to realize that not only had I written so much at one time, but I'd written words that I never knew were in the world. Moreover, with a little effort, I also could remember what many of these words meant. I reviewed the words whose meanings I didn't remember. Funny thing, from the dictionary first page right now, that "aardvark" springs to my mind. The dictionary had a picture of it, a long-tailed, long-eared, burrowing African mammal, which lives off termites caught by sticking out its tongue as an anteater does for ants.

610 MALCOLM X

I was so fascinated that I went on—I copied the dictionary's next page. And the same experience came when I studied that. With every succeeding page, I also learned of people and places and events from history. Actually the dictionary is like a miniature encyclopedia. Finally the dictionary's A section had filled a whole tablet—and I went on into the B's. That was the way I started copying what eventually became the entire dictionary. It went a lot faster after so much practice helped me to pick up handwriting speed. Between what I wrote in my tablet, and writing letters, during the rest of my time in prison I would guess I wrote a million words.

I suppose it was inevitable that as my word-base broadened, I could for the first time pick up a book and read and now begin to understand what the book was saying. Anyone who has read a great deal can imagine the new world that opened. Let me tell you something: from then until I left that prison, in every free moment I had, if I was not reading in the library, I was reading on my bunk. You couldn't have gotten me out of books with a wedge. Between Mr. Muhammad's teachings, my correspondence, my visitors—usually Ella and Reginald[3]—and my reading of books, months passed without my even thinking about being imprisoned. In fact, up to then, I never had been so truly free in my life.

The Norfolk Prison Colony's library was in the school building. A variety of classes was taught there by instructors who came from such places as Harvard and Boston universities. The weekly debates between inmate teams were also held in the school building. You would be astonished to know how worked up convict debaters and audiences would get over subjects like "Should Babies Be Fed Milk?"

Available on the prison library's shelves were books on just about every general subject. Much of the big private collection that Parkhurst[4] had willed to the prison was still in crates and boxes in the back of the library—thousands of old books. Some of them looked ancient: covers faded, old-time parchment-looking binding. Parkhurst, I've mentioned, seemed to have been principally interested in history and religion. He had the money and the special interest to have a lot of books that you wouldn't have in general circulation. Any college library would have been lucky to get that collection.

As you can imagine, especially in a prison where there was heavy emphasis on rehabilitation, an inmate was smiled upon if he demonstrated an unusually intense interest in books. There was a sizable number of well-read inmates, especially the popular debaters. Some were said by many to be practically walking encyclopedias. They were almost celebrities. No university would ask any student to devour literature as I did when this new world opened to me, of being able to read and *understand*.

I read more in my room than in the library itself. An inmate who was known to read a lot could check out more than the permitted maximum number of books. I preferred reading in the total isolation of my own room.

When I had progressed to really serious reading, every night at about ten P.M. I would be outraged with the "lights out." It always seemed to catch me right in the middle of something engrossing.

3. **Ella and Reginald:** his sister and brother.

4. **Parkhurst:** a millionaire interested in the prison rehabilitation program.

The Autobiography of Malcolm X   611

Fortunately, right outside my door was a corridor light that cast a glow into my room. The glow was enough to read by, once my eyes adjusted to it. So when "lights out" came, I would sit on the floor where I could continue reading in that glow.

At one-hour intervals the night guards paced past every room. Each time I heard the approaching footsteps, I jumped into bed and feigned sleep. And as soon as the guard passed, I got back out of bed onto the floor area of that light-glow, where I would read for another fifty-eight minutes—until the guard approached again. That went on until three or four every morning. Three or four hours of sleep a night was enough for me. Often in the years in the streets I had slept less than that.

Responding to the Selection
from **The Autobiography of Malcolm X**

Identifying Facts

1. What motivated Malcolm X to begin a program of self-education?
2. Why did he envy Bimbi?
3. What were his two reasons for wanting a dictionary?
4. What did he learn from the dictionary besides the meanings of words?
5. How did he continue reading after "lights out" each night?

Interpreting Meanings

1. What does Malcolm X mean when he says that he wasn't even "functional" in English?
2. Describe his system of "homemade education." What role did the dictionary play? How important was the prison library?

3. What changes did he notice in himself when the world of books opened to him?
4. After he learned to read, Malcolm X says he felt more truly free than he had ever been in his life. Explain what he means.
5. Why is the title "Saved" appropriate for this chapter?

Literary Elements

Understanding the Narrator

In an autobiography, the narrator is the main character, who tells his or her story from the first-person point of view. What is your impression of Malcolm X from the account he gives of himself in this selection? What adjectives would you use to describe him: determined? honest? intelligent? Does he gain your sympathy? Does he give indications here of the great figure he was to become within a few years? Do you think his description of his own rehabilitation is meant to inspire other young people who have made mistakes?

Language and Vocabulary

Recognizing Levels of Language
Malcolm X realizes that he cannot use "street language" in writing to Elijah Muhammad. **Slang**—highly informal language that is outside standard usage—can add life and color to speech, but it is not appropriate for all occasions. For instance, slang should not be used in a formal essay or letter.

Here are some slang terms. Give the standard English word or phrase for each one.

chicken	rip off
dough	sharp
hangout	washout
lid	

Writing About Literature

Interpreting a Quotation
Richard Lovelace, an English poet who was imprisoned by his king, once wrote these lines:

> Stone walls do not a prison make,
>   Nor iron bars a cage.

These lines express a **paradox**. A paradox is a statement that seems to be self-contradictory, yet reveals a kind of truth. Think about the meaning of these lines. How is it possible to be free within a prison? Then apply the quotation to what Malcolm X says. Why did he no longer feel imprisoned once he gained the power to read? Write a brief explanation. Refer to details in the selection in your discussion.

Speaking and Listening

Giving a Report
Malcolm X had no formal education beyond the eighth grade, yet he became one of the most sought-after speakers on college campuses during the 1960s. Plan a talk about other famous individuals who were self-taught and who became great speakers, such as Frederick Douglass and Abraham Lincoln.

About the Author

Martin Luther King, Jr. (1929–1968)

Laffont/Sygma

 In February 1957, a cover story in *Time* magazine referred to the Reverend Martin Luther King, Jr., as a scholarly Baptist minister "who in a little more than a year has risen from nowhere to become one of the nation's remarkable leaders of men." The "nowhere" was Montgomery, Alabama, where in December 1955, a black woman named Rosa Parks was arrested for refusing to give up her seat on a bus to a white passenger. King was elected president of the Montgomery Improvement Association, a group formed to protest the arrest.

After the success of the Montgomery boycott, King was elected president of the Southern Christian Leadership Conference, whose goals were to increase black voter registration in the South and to eliminate all forms of segregation. King was thrust into national and world prominence as a champion for civil rights. He led campaigns for voter registration in the cities of Birmingham and Selma, and he helped organize the massive march on Washington, D.C., in 1963.

King was born in Atlanta, Georgia, and nurtured in the Christian ideas of his father, a Baptist minister. King earned a bachelor's degree from Morehouse College (1948) and a doctorate in theology from Boston University (1955). The most notable element of King's leadership was his commitment to the philosophy of nonviolent resistance, first learned from the Christian faith and then from the teachings of Mahatma Gandhi. Especially dedicated to King's cause were young people—even children—who withstood attacks by dogs, firehoses, bombs, and club-wielding police. Images of these brutalities, broadcast by the media, stung the conscience of the nation and helped to bring about the overthrow of Southern segregation laws and passage of the Civil Rights Act of 1964.

King's struggle for human dignity earned him many awards, including the Nobel Peace Prize in 1964 and the Presidential Medal of Freedom, posthumously, in 1977.

King was assassinated in Memphis, Tennessee, on April 4, 1968. Robert Kennedy said of him, "Martin Luther King dedicated his life to love and to justice for his fellow human beings, and he died because of that effort." In honor of his memory, King's birthday has been established as a national holiday.

Before You Read

I Have a Dream

Using What You Know _____

What is meant by the phrase "the American dream"? What does it say about our country's ideals of social and political equality? Why do so many Americans feel that they have failed to achieve the American dream?

Background _____

On August 28, 1963, a quarter of a million Americans gathered in Washington, D.C., to urge Congress to pass President Kennedy's civil rights legislation. The **March on Washington** marked the hundredth anniversary of the signing of the Emancipation Proclamation. This is the speech that Dr. King delivered on that momentous day.

Literary Focus: Techniques of Emphasis _____

In his speech, King uses a variety of literary techniques for emphasis. One technique is that of **repetition,** which stresses key words and also serves to connect ideas. Note, for example, how the recurrent phrase "I have a dream" unifies parts of the speech.

Another technique King uses is **parallelism,** in which he arranges for emphasis phrases, clauses, and sentences that are similar in structure and meaning.

A particular kind of parallelism is **antithesis,** which is used for contrast. For example, King balances the phrase "desolate valley of segregation" against the "sunlit path of racial justice."

Setting a Purpose _____

As you read King's stirring speech, note how the eloquence of his ideas is enhanced by his skillful use of language.

I Have a Dream   615

I Have a Dream

Martin Luther King, Jr.

I am happy to join with you today in what will go down in history as the greatest demonstration for freedom in the history of our nation.

Five score years ago, a great American, in whose symbolic shadow we stand today, signed the Emancipation Proclamation. This momentous decree came as a great beacon light of hope to millions of Negro slaves, who had been seared in the flames of withering injustice. It came as a joyous daybreak to end the long night of their captivity. But one hundred years later, the Negro still is not free. One hundred years later, the life of the Negro is still sadly crippled by the manacles of segregation and the chains of discrimination.

One hundred years later, the Negro lives on a lonely island of poverty in the midst of a vast ocean of material prosperity. One hundred years later, the Negro is still languished in the corners of American society and finds himself an exile in his own land. So we've come here today to dramatize a shameful condition.

In a sense we have come to our nation's capital to cash a check. When the architects of our republic wrote the magnificent words of the Constitution and the Declaration of Independence, they were signing a promissory note[1] to which every American was to fall heir.

This note was a promise that all men, yes, black men as well as white men, would be guaranteed the unalienable[2] rights of life, liberty, and the pursuit of happiness.

It is obvious today that America has defaulted on this promissory note insofar as her citizens of color are concerned. Instead of honoring this sacred obligation, America has given the Negro people a bad check; a check which has come back marked "insufficient funds."

But we refuse to believe that the bank of justice is bankrupt. We refuse to believe that there are insufficient funds in the great vaults of opportunity of this nation. So we have come to cash this check, a check that will give us upon demand the riches of freedom and the security of justice.

We have also come to this hallowed spot to remind America of the fierce urgency of Now. This is no time to engage in the luxury of cooling off or to take the tranquilizing drug of gradualism. Now is the time to make real the promises of democracy. Now is the time

---

1. **promissory note:** a written pledge to pay a sum of money at a specified time.
2. **unalienable** (ŭn-āl′yən-ə-bəl): that cannot be taken away.

Martin Luther King, Jr., speaking during the March on Washington demonstration in August 1963.

Francis Miller/Life Magazine
© Time, Inc.

to rise from the dark and desolate valley of segregation to the sunlit path of racial justice. Now is the time to lift our nation from the quicksands of racial injustice to the solid rock of brotherhood. Now is the time to make justice a reality for all of God's children.

It would be fatal for the nation to overlook the urgency of the moment. This sweltering summer of the Negro's legitimate discontent will not pass until there is an invigorating autumn of freedom and equality. Nineteen sixty-three is not an end but a beginning. Those who hope that the Negro needed to blow off steam and will now be content will have a rude awakening if the nation returns to business as usual.

There will be neither rest nor tranquility in America until the Negro is granted his citizenship rights. The whirlwinds of revolt will continue to shake the foundations of our nation until the bright day of justice emerges.

But there is something that I must say to my people who stand on the warm threshold which leads into the palace of justice. In the process of gaining our rightful place we must not be guilty of wrongful deeds.

Let us not seek to satisfy our thirst for freedom by drinking from the cup of bitterness and hatred. We must ever conduct our struggle on the high plane of dignity and discipline. We must not allow our creative protest to degenerate into physical violence. Again and again we must rise to the majestic

I Have a Dream   617

heights of meeting physical force with soul force.

The marvelous new militancy which has engulfed the Negro community must not lead us to a distrust of all white people, for many of our white brothers, as evidenced by their presence here today, have come to realize that their destiny is tied up with our destiny. They have come to realize that their freedom is inextricably bound to our freedom. We cannot walk alone.

And as we walk, we must make the pledge that we shall always march ahead. We cannot turn back. There are those who are asking the devotees of civil rights, "When will you be satisfied?" We can never be satisfied as long as the Negro is the victim of the unspeakable horrors of police brutality.

We can never be satisfied as long as our bodies, heavy with the fatigue of travel, cannot gain lodging in the motels of the highways and the hotels of the cities. We cannot be satisfied as long as a Negro in Mississippi cannot vote and a Negro in New York believes he has nothing for which to vote.

No, no, we are not satisfied and we will not be satisfied until justice rolls down like waters and righteousness like a mighty stream.

I am not unmindful that some of you have come here out of great trials and tribulations. Some of you have come fresh from narrow jail cells. Some of you have come from areas where your quest for freedom left you battered by the storms of persecution and staggered by the winds of police brutality. You have been the veterans of creative suffering. Continue to work with the faith that unearned suffering is redemptive.

Go back to Mississippi, go back to Alabama, go back to South Carolina, go back to Georgia, go back to Louisiana, go back to the slums and ghettos of our northern cities, knowing that somehow this situation can and will be changed.

Let us not wallow in the valley of despair. I say to you today, my friends, so even though we face the difficulties of today and tomorrow. I still have a dream. It is a dream deeply rooted in the American dream.

I have a dream that one day this nation will rise up and live out the true meaning of its creed—we hold these truths to be self-evident that all men are created equal.

I have a dream that one day on the red hills of Georgia the sons of former slaves and the sons of former slave owners will be able to sit down together at the table of brotherhood.

I have a dream that one day even the state of Mississippi, a state sweltering with the heat of injustice, sweltering with the heat of oppression, will be transformed into an oasis of freedom and justice.

I have a dream that my four little children will one day live in a nation where they will not be judged by the color of their skin but by the content of their character.

I have a dream today.

I have a dream that one day, down in Alabama, with its vicious racists, with its governor[3] having his lips dripping with the words of interposition and nullification;[4] one day right down in Alabama little black boys and black girls will be able to join hands with little white boys and white girls as sisters and brothers.

I have a dream today.

3. **Alabama . . . governor:** George Wallace, who was a segregationist. In 1963, he stood in the doorway of the University of Alabama to block the enrollment of black students.
4. **interposition** (ĭn′tər-pə-zĭsh′ən): the doctrine that a state may reject a federal order that it considers to be trespassing on its rights; **nullification** (nŭl′ə-fĭ-kā′shən): the refusal of a state to recognize or enforce a federal law that it considers a violation of its sovereignty.

I have a dream that one day every valley shall be exalted, and every hill and mountain shall be made low, the rough places will be made plain and the crooked places will be made straight and the glory of the Lord shall be revealed and all flesh shall see it together.[5]

This is our hope. This is the faith that I will go back to the South with. With this faith we will be able to hew out of the mountain of despair a stone of hope. With this faith we will be able to transform the jangling discords of our nation into a beautiful symphony of brotherhood. With this faith we will be able to work together, to pray together, to struggle together, to go to jail together, to stand up for freedom together, knowing that we will be free one day.

This will be the day, this will be the day when all of God's children will be able to sing with new meaning "My country 'tis of thee, sweet land of liberty, of thee I sing. Land where my fathers died, land of the Pilgrim's pride, from every mountainside, let freedom ring!" And if America is to be a great nation this must become true.

And so let freedom ring from the prodigious hilltops of New Hampshire.

Let freedom ring from the mighty mountains of New York.

Let freedom ring from the heightening Alleghenies of Pennsylvania.

Let freedom ring from the snow-capped Rockies of Colorado.

Let freedom ring from the curvaceous peaks of California.

But not only that.

Let freedom ring from Stone Mountain of Georgia.

Let freedom ring from Lookout Mountain of Tennessee.

Let freedom ring from every hill and mole hill of Mississippi, from every mountainside, let freedom ring!

And when this happens, when we allow freedom to ring, when we let it ring from every village and every hamlet, from every state and every city, we will be able to speed up that day when all of God's children, black men and white men, Jews and Gentiles, Protestants and Catholics, will be able to join hands and sing in the words of the old Negro spiritual, "Free at last, free at last. Thank God Almighty, we are free at last."[6]

---

5. Compare Isaiah 40:4–5:
    Every Valley shall be exalted, and every mountain and hill shall be made low: and the crooked shall be made straight, and the rough places plain:
    And the glory of the Lord shall be revealed, and all flesh shall see it together: for the mouth of the Lord hath spoken *it*.

6. "Free at last.": See page 190.

Responding to the Selection

I Have a Dream by Martin Luther King, Jr.

Identifying Facts

1. What three American documents associated with liberty does King refer to?
2. What does King advocate as a countermeasure to physical force?
3. Give three specific examples of injustice that King cites.
4. Where in his speech does King acknowledge the presence of white supporters?
5. What different groups of people does King include in his vision of brotherhood?

Interpreting Meanings

1. King spoke from the steps of the Lincoln Memorial. Where in the speech does King refer to Lincoln? What conclusion does he come to about the Emancipation Proclamation?
2. King uses **figurative language** throughout the speech. Explain the "bank" metaphor. Why is this metaphor effective?
3. What metaphor does King use to emphasize the separation of blacks from the rest of American society?
4. What does King identify as the problem the nation faces? What solution does he present?
5. In the famous "I have a dream" passage, King quotes from the Declaration of Independence, the Bible, and a well-known patriotic song. What emotional response might he wish to elicit from his audience?
6. What evidence is there in the speech that King intends for his dream to include the whole nation?
7. King quotes from a spiritual at the end of his speech. Why is this an effective technique?

Literary Elements

Identifying Devices Used for Emphasis

Locate three examples of **repetition** of words and phrases in King's speech. What idea is emphasized in each case?

Give three examples of **parallelism**. Explain the similarity in content or in structure.

Cite three examples of **antithesis**. Explain the contrasting ideas in each example.

Analyzing Metaphor

Locate each of the following **metaphors** in King's speech. Explain why each metaphor is effective.

"bank of justice"
"great vaults of opportunity"
"sunlit path of racial justice"
"storms of persecution"
"winds of police brutality"
"mountain of despair"
"stone of hope"
"symphony of brotherhood"

Language and Vocabulary

Explaining Connotations

Denotation refers to the exact, literal meaning of a word as given in a dictionary. Words have meanings beyond the definitions given in a dictionary. Words can evoke emotional responses because of their associations and suggestions. For example, during the 1950s, the word *Red* took on certain unpleasant overtones because of its association with radicals and communists. **Connotation** refers to these associated and suggested meanings.

Explain the connotations of each of the italicized words in the following phrases. Use a dictionary or a thesaurus to find synonyms for these words. Do the synonyms evoke feelings similar to those evoked by King's own choices? Explain.

"*manacles* of segregation"
"*defaulted* on this promissory note"
"*hallowed* spot"
"*sweltering* summer"
"*unspeakable* horrors"

Writing About Literature

Comparing Styles

Both James Baldwin and Martin Luther King, Jr., were trained for careers in the ministry. Both writers show the effect of **oratory**—the art of public speaking—in their work.

Reread "My Dungeon Shook" (page 601) and the "I Have a Dream" speech. Compare the techniques used by both writers to engage and influence their readers.

Prewriting Strategies

How does each author use connotative meanings to evoke certain associations and emotions?

How does each author make effective use of metaphor?

What devices of emphasis, such as repetition and parallelism, does each writer use?

Organize your findings into a brief essay.

Speaking and Listening

Preparing a Speech

If Martin Luther King, Jr., were alive today, would he find his dream in the process of becoming reality, or would he find his dream too idealistic for the real world? Prepare a two-minute speech presenting your position. Then deliver your speech to a group of students or to the class.

About the Author

Ishmael Reed (b. 1938)

Costa Manos/Magnum Photos

 Ishmael Reed considers himself as much a publisher as a novelist and poet. During the sixties, in New York City, he cofounded the *East Village Other,* an unconventional newspaper that achieved national circulation. In 1971, in California, he helped to found the Yardbird Publishing Company to bring out works of different ethnic groups. Reed's publishing interests have expanded into the Reed, Cannon, and Johnson Communications Company. This company not only publishes novels, but also produces *The Steve Cannon Show,* an audio-cassette magazine containing interviews, jazz concerts, "soap operas," and poetry.

Reed's own writing ranges over several genres. His novels include *The Free-Lance Pallbearers* (1967), *Yellow Back Radio Broke-Down* (1969), *Mumbo Jumbo* (1972), *The Last Days of Louisiana Red* (1974), *Flight to Canada* (1976), and *Japanese by Spring* (1993). Essays are collected in *Writin' Is Fightin': Thirty-seven Years of Boxing on Paper* (1988). Among his books of poetry are *Conjure: Selected Poems* (1972); *Chattanooga: Poems* (1973); and *New and Collected Poetry* (1988).

Reed spent the first four years of his life in Chattanooga, Tennessee. In 1942, he and his mother moved to Buffalo, New York. Reed attended the State University of New York at Buffalo, and during his second year there he began to write. After withdrawing from the university in 1960, he worked for a newspaper and served as cohost of a radio program that aired controversial views.

Reed moved to New York City in 1962, where he was active in political and cultural organizations. In 1967, he left for Berkeley, California, to take a teaching job at the University of California. He has since taught and lectured at various universities.

Reed is one of the most innovative and controversial writers of his generation. His novels, unusual in both style and content, are known for their sharp satire. Nothing Americans hold sacred is safe from his pen. He challenges literary forms and conventions. In his work, he combines Western literary forms with elements of African American traditions.

Before You Read

America: The Multinational Society

Using What You Know

We often take for granted the contributions made to our everyday lives by different cultures. Consider, for example, the foods that many Americans eat: spaghetti, corn, tacos, chow mein, pita bread. What cultures introduced these foods into our diet? How are our lives enriched by the presence of different ethnic groups in our communities?

Literary Focus: Argument

In writing a persuasive essay, you take a position on some debatable issue and then defend your stand with specific evidence. The statement of your viewpoint, along with supporting facts and reasons, is your **argument.** The purpose of argument is to win the reader's **assent,** or agreement, to a belief or opinion. The more tightly reasoned your thinking is, the more likely you are to convince others to accept your ideas. In his essay, Reed presents a case for America as a multinational, or "many-nation," society. Note the kinds of evidence he uses in developing his position.

Setting a Purpose

Reed views the United States as a **microcosm,** a little world representing the larger world: "The world has been arriving at these shores for at least ten thousand years from Europe, Africa, and Asia." Reed claims that our culture is not just European but a "unique" blend of all cultures. As you read, determine whether or not he convinces you to agree with him.

America: The Multinational Society

Ishmael Reed

At the annual Lower East Side[1] Jewish Festival yesterday, a Chinese woman ate a pizza slice in front of Ty Thuan Duc's Vietnamese grocery store. Beside her a Spanish-speaking family patronized a cart with two signs: "Italian Ices" and "Kosher[2] by Rabbi Alper." And after the pastrami ran out, everybody ate knishes.[3]

(*New York Times*, 23 June 1983)

On the day before Memorial Day, 1983, a poet called me to describe a city he had just visited. He said that one section included mosques,[4] built by the Islamic people who dwelled there. Attending his reading, he said, were large numbers of Hispanic people, forty thousand of whom lived in the same city. He was not talking about a fabled city located in some mysterious region of the world. The city he'd visited was Detroit.

A few months before, as I was leaving Houston, Texas, I heard it announced on the radio that Texas's largest minority was Mexican-American, and though a foundation recently issued a report critical of bilingual education, the taped voice used to guide the passengers on the air trams[5] connecting ter-minals in Dallas Airport is in both Spanish and English. If the trend continues, a day will come when it will be difficult to travel through some sections of the country without hearing commands in both English and Spanish; after all, for some western states, Spanish was the first written language and the Spanish style lives on in the western way of life.

Shortly after my Texas trip, I sat in an auditorium located on the campus of the University of Wisconsin at Milwaukee as a Yale professor—whose original work on the influence of African cultures upon those of the Americas has led to his ostracism from some monocultural intellectual circles—walked up and down the aisle, like an old-time southern evangelist, dancing and drumming the top of the lectern, illustrating his points before some serious Afro-American intellectuals and artists who cheered and applauded his performance and his mastery of information.

1. **Lower East Side:** a section of Manhattan.
2. **Kosher:** fit to eat according to Judaic dietary laws.
3. **knishes:** pieces of rolled dough filled with potatoes or meat and baked.
4. **mosques** (mŏsks): Muslim houses of worship.
5. **air trams:** cars drawn by overhead cables.

The professor was "white." After his lecture, he joined a group of Milwaukeeans in a conversation. All of the participants spoke Yoruban,[6] though only the professor had ever traveled to Africa.

One of the artists told me that his paintings, which included African and Afro-American mythological symbols and imagery, were hanging in the local McDonald's restaurant. The next day I went to McDonald's and snapped pictures of smiling youngsters eating hamburgers below paintings that could grace the walls of any of the country's leading museums. The manager of the local McDonald's said, "I don't know what you boys are doing, but I like it," as he commissioned the local painters to exhibit in his restaurant.

Such blurring of cultural styles occurs in everyday life in the United States to a greater extent than anyone can imagine and is probably more prevalent than the sensational conflict between people of different backgrounds that is played up and often encouraged by the media. The result is what the Yale professor, Robert Thompson, referred to as a cultural bouillabaisse,[7] yet members of the nation's present educational and cultural Elect[8] still cling to the notion that the United States belongs to some vaguely defined entity they refer to as "Western civilization," by which they mean, presumably, a civilization created by the people of Europe, as if Europe can be viewed in monolithic terms. Is Beethoven's Ninth Symphony, which includes Turkish marches, a part of Western civilization, or the late nineteenth- and twentieth-century French paintings, whose creators were influenced by Japanese art? And what of the cubists,[9] through whom the influence of African art changed modern painting, or the surrealists,[10] who were so impressed with the art of the Pacific Northwest Indians that, in their map of North America, Alaska dwarfs the lower forty-eight in size?

Are the Russians, who are often criticized for their adoption of "Western" ways by Tsarist dissidents[11] in exile, members of Western civilization? And what of the millions of Europeans who have black African and Asian ancestry, black Africans having occupied several countries for hundreds of years? Are these "Europeans" members of Western civilization, or the Hungarians, who originated across the Urals[12] in a place called Greater Hungary, or the Irish, who came from the Iberian Peninsula?[13]

Even the notion that North America is part of Western civilization because our "system of government" is derived from Europe is being challenged by Native American historians who say that the founding fathers, Benjamin Franklin especially, were actually influenced by the system of government that had been adopted by the Iroquois[14] hundreds of years prior to the arrival of large numbers of Europeans.

6. **Yoruban** (yō′rōo-bän): the Kwa language of the Yoruba, a West African people.
7. **bouillabaisse** (bōo′yə-bäs′): a stew made up of different kinds of fish and shellfish.
8. **Elect:** in theology, those selected for salvation. Reed is using the word ironically for people who insist on the primacy of Western civilization.
9. **cubists** (kyōo′bĭsts): a school of twentieth-century painters and sculptors who represented objects as abstract and geometric structures.
10. **surrealists** (sə-rē′ə-lĭsts′): twentieth-century artists who attempted to express the workings of the subconscious.
11. **dissidents:** those who are in disagreement with the official policy of the government.
12. **Urals** (yōor′əlz): the Ural Mountains, forming the boundary between Europe and Asia.
13. **Iberian** (ī-bîr′ē-ən) **Peninsula:** in southwest Europe, now comprising Spain and Portugal.
14. **Iroquois** (îr′ə-kwoi′): a confederation of Indian peoples in upstate New York.

Western civilization, then, becomes another confusing category like Third World,[15] or Judeo-Christian culture, as man attempts to impose his small-screen view of political and cultural reality upon a complex world. Our most publicized novelist recently said that Western civilization was the greatest achievement of mankind, an attitude that flourishes on the street level as scribbles in public restrooms: "White Power," or "Hitler was a prophet," the latter being the most telling, for wasn't Adolf Hitler the archetypal monoculturalist who, in his pigheaded arrogance, believed that one way and one blood was so pure[16] that it had to be protected from alien strains at all costs? Where did such an attitude, which has caused so much misery and depression in our national life, which has tainted even our noblest achievements, begin? An attitude that caused the incarceration[17] of Japanese-American citizens during World War II, the persecution of Chicanos and Chinese-Americans, the near-extermination of the Indians, and the murder and lynchings of thousands of Afro-Americans.

Virtuous, hardworking, pious, even though they occasionally would wander off after some fancy clothes, or rendezvous in the woods with the town prostitute, the Puritans are idealized in our schoolbooks as "a hardy band" of no-nonsense patriarchs whose discipline razed the forest and brought order to the New World (a term that annoys Native American historians). Industrious, responsible, it was their "Yankee ingenuity" and practicality that created the work ethic. They were simple folk who produced a number of good poets, and they set the tone for the American writing style, of lean and spare lines, long before Hemingway.[18] They worshiped in churches whose colors blended in with the New England snow, churches with simple structures and ornate lecterns.

The Puritans were a daring lot, but they had a mean streak. They hated the theater and banned Christmas. They punished people in a cruel and inhuman manner. They killed children who disobeyed their parents. When they came in contact with those whom they considered heathens or aliens, they behaved in such a bizarre and irrational manner that this chapter in the American history comes down to us as a late-movie horror film. They exterminated the Indians, who taught them how to survive in a world unknown to them, and their encounter with the calypso culture of Barbados resulted in what the tourist guide in Salem's Witches' House refers to as the Witchcraft Hysteria.

The Puritan legacy of hard work and meticulous accounting led to the establishment of a great industrial society; it is no wonder that the American industrial revolution began in Lowell, Massachusetts, but there was the other side, the strange and paranoid attitudes toward those different from the Elect.

The cultural attitudes of that early Elect continue to be voiced in everyday life in the United States: the president of a distinguished university, writing a letter to the *Times*, belittling the study of African civilizations; the television network that promoted its show on the Vatican[19] art with the boast

15. **Third World:** referring to the developing countries of the world.
16. **blood . . . pure:** a reference to the racist doctrines of the Nazis, who viewed themselves as the "Master Race."
17. **incarceration** (ĭn-kär′sə-rā′shən): confinement in detention camps.

18. **Hemingway:** Ernest Hemingway (1899–1961), a twentieth-century writer known for his concise, deceptively simple style.
19. **Vatican** (văt′i-kən): referring to the pope's residence in Rome.

that this art represented "the finest achievements of the human spirit." A modern up-tempo state of complex rhythms that depends upon contacts with an international community can no longer behave as if it dwelled in a "Zion Wilderness"[20] surrounded by beasts and pagans.

When I heard a schoolteacher warn the other night about the invasion of the American educational system by foreign curriculums, I wanted to yell at the television set, "Lady, they're already here." It has already begun because the world is here. The world has been arriving at these shores for at least ten thousand years from Europe, Africa, and Asia. In the late nineteenth and early twentieth centuries, large numbers of Europeans arrived, adding their cultures to those of the European, African, and Asian settlers who were already here, and recently millions have been entering the country from South America and the Caribbean, making Yale Professor Bob Thompson's bouillabaisse richer and thicker.

One of our most visionary politicians said that he envisioned a time when the United States could become the brain of the world, by which he meant the repository of all of the latest advanced information systems. I thought of that remark when an enterprising poet friend of mine called to say that he had just sold a poem to a computer magazine and that the editors were delighted to get it because they didn't carry fiction or poetry. Is that the kind of world we desire? A humdrum homogeneous world of all brains and no heart, no fiction, no poetry; a world of robots with human attendants bereft of imagination, of culture? Or does North America deserve a more exciting destiny? To become a place where the cultures of the world crisscross. This is possible because the United States is unique in the world: The world is here.

20. **"Zion Wilderness"**: The Puritans believed that America was appointed by God to be a "city upon a hill." The New Testament refers to Zion as the New Jerusalem, the heavenly city.

Responding to the Selection

America: The Multinational Society by Ishmael Reed

Identifying Facts

1. What example does Reed use as an introduction to his essay to show the everyday "blurring of cultural styles" in the United States?
2. How are some Native American historians challenging traditional views about the American system of government?
3. Who does Reed claim is responsible for our negative attitudes toward different cultures?
4. According to Reed, what was the Puritans' contribution to our industrial society?
5. What destiny does Reed envision for our continent?

Interpreting Meanings

1. In the first four paragraphs of his essay, Reed gives examples of the "blurring of cultural styles" in the United States. What does he mean by this phrase? How does he support his point?
2. Reed attacks "Western civilization" as a vague and confusing term that obscures the many complex influences that have contributed to our culture. What arguments does he offer in paragraphs 5–7 to show that our culture is not derived exclusively from Europe? In your opinion, are these arguments equally strong?

3. What does Reed mean by the "strange and paranoid" attitudes of the Puritans? According to Reed, how do these attitudes show themselves today?
4. Do you think Reed argues forcefully that America is a multinational society?

Literary Elements

Understanding Inductive and Deductive Reasoning

Induction and **deduction** are methods of reasoning. When you reason *inductively,* you begin by observing specific kinds of evidence and then drawing a conclusion based on the evidence. When you reason *deductively,* you begin with a generalization and then use the generalization to arrive at a conclusion about a specific case.

If you were to discover that you had no electricity coming into your house, then found that your neighbor and the people on the next street had none, you might conclude *inductively* that electricity in your area had been cut off. Induction allows for a fair sampling of evidence without total proof.

On the other hand, if you were on vacation and heard on the radio that there had been a generator failure in your home town, you might reason *deductively* that there is no electricity in your house.

The most common kind of inductive reasoning is the **argument from analogy**. In this form of reasoning, you compare two things that share a number of similarities. Your purpose is to show that what holds true for one thing holds true for the thing to which it is compared. A common analogy compares the human heart to a pump.

A formal deductive argument is constructed in three steps called a **syllogism** (sĭl'ə-jĭz'əm). A syllogism begins with a **major premise,** which is a general statement; then goes to its **minor premise,** which is a specific example; and moves toward its **conclusion,** which is logically drawn from the first two statements:

Major Premise	All reptiles are cold-blooded.
Minor Premise	Snakes are reptiles.
Conclusion	Snakes are coldblooded.

What method of reasoning does Reed use to develop his argument? What evidence does he present? What conclusion does he come to?

Language and Vocabulary

Learning Prefixes Used in Measurement

A number of prefixes stand for amounts or numbers. For example, the prefix **multi–** in the word *multinational* means "many."

Using a college or an unabridged dictionary, find the meanings of these prefixes: **bi–, tri–, quadri–, semi–, mono–.** List words that contain these prefixes and give their meanings.

Persuasive Writing

Taking a Position

Decide whether or not you agree with the following statement from Reed's essay:

> . . . blurring of cultural styles occurs in everyday life in the United States to a greater extent than anyone can imagine and is probably more prevalent than the sensational conflict between people of different backgrounds that is played up and often encouraged by the media.

Gather evidence that you might use to support your position. Refer to pages 637–638 in planning and developing your paper.

Critical Thinking

Distinguishing Fact from Opinion

In reading and in writing, it is important to distinguish fact from opinion. A **fact** is something that can be proved. An **opinion** states a belief or a judgment. Even though an opinion may be sound, it cannot be proved.

In evaluating an argument, you need to know whether the writer is supporting a statement with facts or stating an opinion. Reed tells about the paintings he sees displayed in a local restaurant. It is a **fact** that the paintings are there, but it is Reed's **opinion** that these paintings might be hung on museum walls. Identify other examples of facts and opinions in Reed's essay.

About the Author

Henry Louis Gates, Jr. (b. 1950)

Oxford University Press

 As he tells us in his essay "A Giant Step," Henry Louis Gates, Jr., grew up in Piedmont, West Virginia. He spent a year at a junior college before applying to Yale. After graduating *summa cum laude* (with highest honors), he received a fellowship to Cambridge University. There he met the Nigerian writer Wole Soyinka, who encouraged him to study African American literature. Gates wrote his doctoral dissertation on the critical reception of early black literature. After he completed his Ph.D., he received an appointment to Yale. He is now at Harvard, where he is the W. E. B. Du Bois Professor of Humanities, Chair of the Afro-American Studies Department, and Director of the W. E. B. Du Bois Institute for Afro-American Research.

Gates has received many awards, including a Ford Foundation National Fellowship and the Zora Neale Hurston Society Award for Cultural Scholarship, and grants from the National Endowment for the Humanities and from the MacArthur Foundation.

Gates has achieved a reputation as a "literary archaeologist." While he was looking at books in a Manhattan bookstore, he came across a copy of *Our Nig,* written in 1859 by a free black woman named Harriet E. Wilson. Gates investigated and was able to show that this was the first novel published by a black person in the United States. He has written extensively on the black vernacular. His publications include *Figures in Black: Words, Signs, and the Racial Self,* a collection of essays (1987); *The Signifying Monkey: A Theory of Afro-American Literary Criticism* (1988), which won an American Book Award; *Loose Canons: Notes on the Culture Wars* (1992); *Colored People: A Memoir* (1994); and *The Future of the Race* (1996) with Cornel West. He is also general editor of the *Norton Anthology of African-American Literature* and series editor of *The Schomburg Library of Nineteenth-Century Black Women Writers.*

Before You Read

A Giant Step

Using What You Know

Think about figures of speech that are used when a person overcomes obstacles or succeeds in some undertaking. One such expression is "to come off with flying colors," which draws a comparison to unfurled flags waving in the air. What other phrases can you list? What does it mean "to take a giant step"?

Literary Focus: Tone

Tone—the attitude a writer takes in his or her work—may be humorous or solemn, lighthearted or bitter, warm or distant, and the like. A writer's tone can affect our entire view of a situation. A writer can make us laugh at something most people take very seriously; a writer can create enthusiasm for a subject that is not of general interest.

Tone is created through the choice of words and details. Language that is formal often gives writing a dignified tone. Informal language tends to give writing a more relaxed and less serious tone.

Setting a Purpose

Consider the author's tone as you read. What is his attitude toward his physical problem? What is his attitude toward the reader?

A Giant Step

Henry Louis Gates, Jr.

"What's this?" the hospital janitor said to me as he stumbled over my right shoe.

"My shoes," I said.

'That's not a shoe, brother," he replied, holding it to the light. "That's a brick."

It *did* look like a brick, sort of.

"Well, we can throw these in the trash now," he said.

"I guess so."

We had been together since 1975, those shoes and I. They were orthopedic[1] shoes built around molds of my feet, and they had a 2¼-inch lift. I had mixed feelings about them. On the one hand, they had given me a more or less even gait for the first time in 10 years. On the other hand, they had marked me as a "handicapped person," complete with cane and special license plates. I went through a pair a year, but it was always the same shoe, black, wide, weighing about four pounds.

It all started 26 years ago in Piedmont, W.Va., a backwoods town of 2,000 people. While playing a game of touch football at a Methodist summer camp, I incurred a hairline fracture. Thing is, I didn't know it yet. I was 14 and had finally lost the chubbiness of my youth. I was just learning tennis and be-

ginning to date, and who knew where that might lead?

Not too far. A few weeks later, I was returning to school from lunch when, out of the blue, the ball-and-socket joint of my hip sheared apart. It was instant agony, and from that time on nothing in my life would be quite the same.

I propped myself against the brick wall of the schoolhouse, where the school delinquent found me. He was black as slate, twice my size, mean as the day was long and beat up kids just because he could. But the look on my face told him something was seriously wrong, and—bless him—he stayed by my side for the two hours it took to get me into a taxi.

"It's a torn ligament in your knee," the surgeon said. (One of the signs of what I had—a "slipped epithysis"[2]—is intense knee pain, I later learned.) So he scheduled me for a walking cast.

I was wheeled into surgery and placed on the operating table. As the doctor wrapped my leg with wet plaster strips, he asked about my schoolwork.

"Boy," he said, "I understand you want to be a doctor."

1. **orthopedic** (ôr′thə-pē′dĭk): for the correction of defects in the skeletal system.

2. **epithysis** (ĕp′ə-thī′sĭs).

I said, "Yessir." Where I came from, you always said "sir" to white people, unless you were trying to make a statement.

Had I taken a lot of science courses?

"Yessir. I enjoy science."

"Are you good at it?"

"Yessir, I believe so."

"Tell me, who was the father of sterilization?"

"Oh, that's easy, Joseph Lister."

Then he asked who discovered penicillin. Alexander Fleming.

And what about DNA?

Watson and Crick.

The interview went on like this, and I thought my answers might get me a pat on the head. Actually, they just confirmed the diagnosis he'd come to.

He stood me on my feet and insisted that I walk. When I tried, the joint ripped apart and I fell on the floor. It hurt like nothing I'd ever known.

The doctor shook his head. "Pauline," he said to my mother, his voice kindly but amused, "there's not a thing wrong with that child. The problem's psychosomatic.[3] Your son's an overachiever."

Back then, the term didn't mean what it usually means today. In Appalachia, in 1964, "overachiever" designated a sort of pathology:[4] the overstraining of your natural capacity. A colored kid who thought he could be a doctor—just for instance—was headed for a breakdown.

What made the pain abate was my mother's reaction. I'd never, ever heard her talk back to a white person before. And doctors, well, their words were scripture.

Not this time. Pauline Gates stared at him

for a moment. "Get his clothes, pack his bags—we're going to the University Medical Center," which was 60 miles away.

Not great news: the one thing I knew was that they only moved you to the University Medical Center when you were going to die. I had three operations that year. I gave my tennis racket to the delinquent, which he probably used to club little kids with. So I wasn't going to make it to Wimbledon.[5] But at least I wasn't going to die, though sometimes I wanted to. Following the last operation, which fitted me for a metal ball, I was confined to bed, flat on my back, immobilized by a complex system of weights and pulleys. It was six weeks of bondage—and bedpans. I spent my time reading James Baldwin, learning to play chess and quarreling daily with my mother, who had rented a small room—which we could ill afford—in a motel just down the hill from the hospital.

I think we both came to realize that our quarreling was a sort of ritual. We'd argue about everything—what time of day it was—but the arguments kept me from thinking about that traction system.

I limped through the next decade—through Yale and Cambridge . . . as far away from Piedmont as I could get. But I couldn't escape the pain, which increased as the joint calcified and began to fuse over the next 15 years. My leg grew shorter, as the muscle atrophied[6] and the ball of the ball-and-socket joint migrated into my pelvis. Aspirin, then Motrin, heating pads and massages, became my traveling companions.

Most frustrating was passing store windows full of fine shoes. I used to dream about walking into one of those stores and buying a

---

3. **psychosomatic** (sī′kō-sō-măt′ĭk): bodily symptoms caused by emotional or mental problems.
4. **pathology** (pă-thŏl′ə-jē): abnormal condition.

5. **Wimbledon:** in England, where an international lawn tennis tournament is held each year.
6. **atrophied** (ăt′rə-fēd′): withered; wasted away.

pair of shoes. "Give me two pairs, one black, one cordovan," I'd say. "Wrap 'em up." No six-week wait as with the orthotics[7] in which I was confined. These would be real shoes. Not bricks.

In the meantime, hip-joint technology progressed dramatically. But no surgeon wanted to operate on me until I was significantly older, or until the pain was so great that surgery was unavoidable. After all, a new hip would last only for 15 years, and I'd already lost too much bone. It wasn't a procedure they were sure they'd be able to repeat.

This year, my 40th, the doctors decided the time had come.

I increased my life insurance and made the plunge.

The nights before my operations are the longest nights of my life—but never long enough. Jerking awake, grabbing for my watch, I experience a delicious sense of relief as I discover that only a minute or two have passed. You never want 6 A.M. to come.

And then the door swings open. "Good morning, Mr. Gates," the nurse says. "It's time."

The last thing I remember, just vaguely, was wondering where amnesiac[8] minutes go in one's consciousness, wondering if I experienced the pain and sounds, then forgot them, or if these were somehow blocked out, dividing the self on the operating table from the conscious self in the recovery room. I didn't like that idea very much. I was about to protest when I blinked.

"It's over, Mr. Gates." says a voice. But how could it be over? I had merely blinked. "You talked to us several times," the surgeon had told me, and that was the scariest part of all.

Twenty-four hours later, they get me out of bed and help me into a "walker." As they stand me on my feet, my wife bursts into tears. "Your foot is touching the ground!" I am afraid to look, but it is true: the surgeon has lengthened my leg with that gleaming titanium and chrome-cobalt alloy[9] ball-and-socket-joint.

"You'll need new shoes," the surgeon says. "Get a pair of Dock-Sides; they have a secure grip. You'll need a ¾-inch lift in the heel, which can be as discreet as you want."

I can't help thinking about those window displays of shoes, those elegant shoes that, suddenly, I will be able to wear. Dock-Sides and sneakers, boots and loafers, sandals and brogues. I feel, at last, a furtive sympathy for Imelda Marcos,[10] the queen of soles.

The next day, I walk over to the trash can, and take a long look at the brick. I don't want to seem ungracious or unappreciative. We have walked long miles together. I feel disloyal, as if I am abandoning an old friend. I take a second look.

Maybe I'll have them bronzed.

---

7. **orthotics** (ôr-thŏt′ĭks): containing supports for weak muscles.
8. **amnesiac** (ăm-nē′zhē-ăk′): referring to the memory gap caused by loss of consciousness during surgery.

9. **alloy** (ăl′oi′): mixture of metals.
10. **Imelda Marcos**: wife of Philippine president Ferdinand Marcos, who was driven out of power in 1986. Her extravagant collection of shoes was ridiculed in tabloid newspapers.

Responding to the Selection

A Giant Step by Henry Louis Gates, Jr.

Identifying Facts

1. How did the author injure his hip?
2. According to the first surgeon, what was Gates's problem?
3. Why did he need special shoes?
4. What did he find most frustrating?
5. Why were surgeons reluctant to operate on his hip?

Interpreting Meanings

1. The author does not comment directly on the surgeon who called him an "over-achiever" except to note that his voice was "kindly but amused." What do you think is his attitude toward this doctor?
2. What impression do you get of Gates's mother?
3. Why does the author change his mind about keeping his "brick" shoes?
4. Although the author experienced pain, frustration, and fear for many years, his essay is not somber but filled with touches of humor. How do these humorous touches affect the tone of the essay?
5. What does the title refer to?

Literary Elements

Understanding the Informal Essay

Essays are generally classified as **informal** (or **familiar** or **personal**) and **formal**. The in-formal essay often reveals the writer's personality. Its style tends to be conversational.

Look back at Gates's essay. What impression do you get of the writer? Does he have a sense of humor about himself?

What characteristics in his style give the essay a conversational tone? Where, for example, does he use short phrases rather than complete sentences, as one might do in everyday conversation? Where does he share his feelings with the reader?

Language and Vocabulary

Learning Words that Come from Greek

The word *psychosomatic* is made up of two parts: *psycho* and *somatic*. *Psycho* comes from a Greek word meaning "spirit" or "soul" and is found in many English words having to do with the mind. *Somatic* comes from a Greek word meaning "body." When these meanings are combined, we get the definition of *psychosomatic,* which refers to something that begins in the mind but causes physical symptoms.

The word *pathology* is also made up of two parts. The first part comes from a Greek word meaning "suffering" or "feeling." The second part is the combining form **–logy,** which now generally carries the meaning of "the study of" or "the science of," as in the words *biology* and *geology. Pathology* is the branch of medicine that deals with the causes and progress of disease.

The word *orthopedic* comes from two Greek words, one meaning "right" or "straight," and the other meaning "child." Originally, the word *orthopedic* referred to the correction of children's deformities. Now it refers to the correction of deformities in bones and joints.

In a college or an unabridged dictionary, look up the meanings of the following words. Find out how they are related to their Greek origins.

orthodontics   psychobiography
orthography   psychology
pathogenic

Descriptive Writing
Describing an Object
When Gates looks at his shoes, he has mixed feelings about them. The shoes helped him in walking, but they also called attention to his physical handicap. He feels a certain attachment to them, and at the end of his essay, he reveals that he is reluctant to throw them out.

Think of some possession to which you have become attached, even if it is no longer useful. In an essay, give the "history" of that object—how it came into your life, how you used it, and how you now feel about it. For suggestions on developing your paper, see pages 193–195.

Speaking and Listening
Recalling a Giant Step
Consider some of the times in your own life when you had to take "a giant step." Perhaps it was the day you took the training wheels off your bicycle. It may have been the first time you traveled somewhere on your own. Recall your feelings. Share your recollections with your classmates.

Writing a Persuasive Essay

A persuasive essay is written in order to convince someone to accept your opinion or to follow a certain course of action. You begin by choosing an **issue**—some topic that is debatable. For example, the following topics all represent issues that can be debated. Some people might argue *for* them, and others might argue *against* them:

> The school year should be extended to twelve months.
> Rent control laws should be adopted for all new residential and commercial buildings.
> Students should be required to do community service.

When you write a persuasive essay, you begin with a statement of your **position**. This statement is sometimes called a **proposition** or a **position statement.**

After you have a clear statement of your opinion, you build your argument with **rea-sons** and **evidence.** The more reasons you have, the stronger your argument will be. Your reasons must be relevant and they must be distinct.

In order to back up your reasons, you need to supply evidence. Evidence includes facts, incidents, and quotations from authorities. Your evidence should be gathered from reliable sources.

In writing a persuasive essay, it is often most effective to present your reasons in the order of importance. By beginning with the least important reason and building up to the most important one, you achieve a conclusion that has impact. Sometimes, however, you may feel that it is better to start with your strongest reason and then give the lesser reasons that support it.

Select a subject that has been an issue in your school, among your friends, in the community, or in the country. Write a persuasive essay presenting your position.

Prewriting Strategies

1. In choosing a topic, consider whether you will be able to find background information and supporting evidence.
2. Take into account the audience you wish to convince. There is no point arguing a position if your audience is already in agreement with you.
3. Write a statement of your position. Most position statements contain the words *should* or *should not.*
4. Choose reasons and evidence. You should have a minimum of three different reasons. List the items of evidence that are directly related to your reasons.
5. Outline your argument, following this plan:

Writing a Persuasive Essay

> **Position Statement** _____
>   **Reason** _____
>   **Evidence** _____

Writing a First Draft

1. Begin with an introductory paragraph that states the topic and makes clear your position.
2. Develop each reason in a separate paragraph. To make your argument stronger, discuss the opposing point of view and present reasons against it.
3. Summarize your argument in your concluding paragraph by restating your position and supporting reasons.

Evaluating and Revising

1. Does your paper clearly express a position on the topic?
2. Is your opinion supported by at least three separate reasons?
3. Have you used supporting evidence for each reason?
4. Are your reasons arranged in an effective order?
5. Have you used transitional expressions to connect ideas?
6. Have you summarized your argument?

Writing a Final Draft

1. Read your revised essay carefully to catch any errors in grammar, usage, or mechanics. Use the dictionary to check any doubtful spellings.
2. Ask a classmate to help you proofread your paper.
3. After proofreading, write your final version and check once more for copying errors.

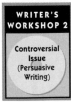

WRITER'S WORKSHOP 2

Controversial Issue (Persuasive Writing)

►I. Interpreting New Material

Photo by Jeffrey/The Schomburg Center for Research in Black Culture/New York Public Library

This excerpt is from a collection of memoirs in which the author describes many people she has known throughout her life, particularly the members of her family. In Swahili, *Itabari* means "an esteemed person." *Njeri* is Kikuyu for "worthy of a warrior."

A. Read the selection carefully before answering the questions.

from **Every Good-bye Ain't Gone**
Itabari Njeri

It was the Fourth of July, Louis Armstrong's birthday, and tar was bubbling between the cracks in the city pavement. It had been one of the hottest summers on record in New York. Aunt Rae had decided to forgo her usual urban summer holiday barbecue on a rooftop or under a bridge, preferably the George Washington, and journey to the sticks[1]—Brooklyn. My mother was holding a big family cookout in the backyard.

Aunt Rae would have made a great professional cook, despite her hoofing[2] ambitions or family expectations that she'd be an attorney because she was so smart and combative. She made a mean, mustard-based barbecue sauce, jars of which were ready to be transported to my mother's.

We rose early that holiday morning and began carrying the sauce, ribs, chicken, potato salad and six-packs of Champale to the first floor. It was four steep flights from the apartment to the narrow, ground-floor hallway where we waited for the car.

Despite her mastery of mass transit survival techniques, Aunt Rae avoided the subway whenever she could. No matter how great the distance from borough to borough, she preferred the often circuitous route of buses to being underground. But Flatbush[3] was too far from the South Bronx, the day too sweltering and the load too heavy for the bus. She arranged for us to go by car.

1. **the sticks:** an area far from a city or town; here, used ironically for the borough of Brooklyn, which is some distance from the Bronx.
2. **hoofing:** professional dancing (slang).
3. **Flatbush:** a section in Brooklyn, New York City.

Willie, Aunt Rae, Karen and several other cousins stood in the tight tenement hallway waiting. When the car came, one of us was to get my grandmother, who never let a week go by without reminding us of the flotilla[4] of servants she'd had in Jamaica—much to Aunt Rae's annoyance: "Mama, no body wants to hear that. That's why people don't like you West Indians, always bragging about what you had before you got here." Of course, the cultural subtext[5] for my aunt's proclaimed disgust was African-American resentment of West Indian highhandedness. And she, like the children of most immigrants, wanted to be accepted by her peers, most of whom were African-Americans.

I stepped from the hallway to the cracked front stoop to see if the car was coming. It was early in the morning and blindingly bright. In the middle of the block, a vast, junk-heaped lot held tons of smashed glass and crushed aluminum cans that reflected the powerful sunlight, making them glitter like precious things they were not. It resembled the poverty of the tropics, where the unrelenting sun sears the ugliness into your eyes.

A car turned slowly into our block, rolling past all the other walk-ups before ours. Willie got Grandma.

The chauffeur got out of the long, black limousine and tipped his hat to my seventy-year-old grandmother, who was smiling girlishly. "Madam," he said, "my name is Clarence." He helped her into the limo, where

4. **flotilla** (flō-tĭl′ə): a fleet of ships, here used figuratively.
5. **subtext**: implied meaning.

she sat in the front next to him. My cousins and I, Willie and my privilege-eschewing[6] aunt piled into the back.

With the raw ribs and chicken, potato salad, Champale and barbecue sauce loaded in the trunk, we rolled across the potholed street with barely a bounce, passing the glitter in the junk-heaped lot.

When my mother saw us roll to her door and unload the rattling jars of barbecue sauce, she shook her head and muttered, "No fools, no fun."

6. **eschewing** (ĕs-choo′ĭng): shunning.

1. How does Aunt Rae arrange for the family to get to the big cookout in Brooklyn?
2. What impression do you get of Aunt Rae from this excerpt?
3. Aunt Rae's mother, the narrator's grandmother, has a habit of bragging about her life in Jamaica. Why does Aunt Rae object to these reminders?
4. What images does Njeri use to give a sense of how the city looks and feels on a hot summer day?
5. When the narrator's mother sees the limousine pull up to the door, she says, "No fools, no fun." What do you think this expression means?

B. **Using Njeri's narrative as an example, write about an outing or another experience you have had with friends or family. Use descriptive details and dialogue to reveal the personalities of the people involved.**

▶▶II. For Discussion

A number of selections in this unit deal with the concept of *freedom.* What different perspectives are offered by Ralph Ellison, James Baldwin, Malcolm X, and Martin Luther King, Jr., in their respective works? Share your ideas with your classmates.

▶▶▶III. For Writing

In reading an essay or other work of nonfiction, we are aware not only of the writer's subject but also of the writer's personality. The words chosen, the incidents selected, the tone taken toward the material and toward the reader all contribute to an impression of the particular writer.

Select several writers whose work is represented in this unit. Give your impression of them as writers and as individuals.

Bruce Davidson/Magnum Photos

Wheel in Wheel, *oil and acrylic on canvas by John Biggers, 1986.*
Dr. and Mrs. William R. Harvey. Used with permission of the artist. Photo courtesy of the Dallas Museum of Art

642   CONTEMPORARY POETRY

Contemporary Poetry

A PERSONAL ESSAY BY **Mari Evans**

The Continuity of a Literary Tradition

The contemporary poetry in this unit is part of a tradition of written African letters that is over five thousand years old. It began with the invention, by Africans, of several forms of writing. One form, developed in South Central Africa, had twenty-three letters, which consisted of seventeen consonants, four vowels, and two syllabic signs, and used spaces between words. It was a form of writing that preceded Egyptian hieroglyphics.

Records indicate that approximately 1,350 years before the birth of Christ, the Black Egyptian pharaoh King Akhenaton wrote an elegant poem entitled "Hymn to the Sun" (see page 80). It was his attempt to convince his people to worship a single god instead of many gods. He saw that god as the sun, a nurturing giver of life. Akhenaton ordered a new city to be built. It would be devoted to the arts; he called it Tel El Amarna.

Writing flourished in many places in Africa, and even private libraries were not uncommon. One individual, Es Sadi, is reputed to have owned sixteen hundred volumes.

With the introduction of the African slave trade, things changed. From that time it would be difficult for persons of African descent to continue their creative contributions to the vast body of written African letters that was their heritage.

The captured Africans, branded, chained, and humiliated, brought no material possessions with them on the cramped and fetid ships. They did, however, bring much that was precious, that

Akhenaton, *fragment from a temple column.*
Scala/Art Resource, NY

Jug, rendering by Alfred Parys, c. 1935.
Index of American Design, © 1996 Board of Trustees, National Gallery of Art, Washington

was intrinsic: their history of having been a people with strong moral codes, their physical prowess—an incredible strength and agility without which they could never have survived slavery's brutality—a quick intelligence, and creative abilities of all kinds. These became their legacy to their descendants, a legacy from which African Americans today draw heavily as they demonstrate excellence in all areas of scholarship, in athletics, and in the arts.

Despite the horrors of the middle passage, and despite laws that for decades made it illegal to teach the enslaved African people to read or to write, in time they did both. Motivated by a desire to learn, they triumphed, and African Americans gradually began, on these shores, the production of an extraordinary body of literature.

By 1912, only forty-seven years after physical slavery ended for most African Americans, Daniel Murray had documented over six thousand books and pamphlets and five thousand musical scores written by African Americans. A Black literature, pulsed by the experience of Africans and their descendants in the United States, was well on its way. It evolved, it thrived, and it continues to make significant contributions to the body of American letters and to world literatures.

The Distinctiveness of African American Poetry

Traditionally, poetry has been the essence of a people's culture, saying who they are, the ways they feel, the ways in which they respond to one another, the ways they interact with and view the world.

We are the sum and substance of all that is past. Racial and ethnic identities and histories have significantly shaped the climates in which we presently move, determining not only how we appear physically, but why we live as we do and, most importantly, why we think as we do. To go full circle, we think as we do because of our past histories, and those histories have been significantly affected by our racial and ethnic identities. All of this becomes our foundation, part of our culture.

Who we are, then, becomes a complexity of past and present, and when we go in search of ourselves, we often find the keys to ourselves in the poetry that reflects the culture of our people. Poetry may well be a universal language, but it sings in different keys. African American poetry has a music of its own, a music everyone can hear, regardless of the instrumentation.

Freedmen's school.
Charles Phillips, Life Magazine
© Time, Inc.

Stephen Henderson, an African American educator, scholar, and literary critic, maintains that when Black poetry is most distinctive, "it derives its form from two basic sources, Black speech and Black music." He suggests that to appreciate the poet's craftsmanship the reader must have a sensitivity to "and understanding of the entire range of Black spoken language in America. This includes the techniques and timbres of the sermon and other forms of oratory, the dozens, the rap, the signifying, and the oral folktale," the living speech of the Black community, urban and rural. He thinks that there is no adequate way of representing its rhythmic variety or its incredible energy.

Stylistic Devices

We expect to find the poet using stylistic devices such as **oxymoron,** which joins together words that have opposite or contradictory meanings. Gwendolyn Brooks on one occasion used the phrase "a tied hurricane" to describe the energy of an actress. Other stylistic devices often used are **satire, internal** and **end** rhyming, and **metaphor** (which is the transfer of meaning, such as calling a shrewd person a fox). Metaphor expands the meaning of a poem by adding the excitement of colorful and imaginative detail. There will also be **description,** to provide information we have not had access to previously. There will be **imagery,** to provide for the recovery of experience, that is, to allow the reader to recall tastes, sounds, smells, sights, and textures he or she once knew.

The Poet's Choice of Words

The Black writer is comfortably bilingual, moving easily between the English used in mass communication and the semi-private idiom of the national African American community, seeing neither as right or wrong, seeing each as different, as optional, and both as useful.

Diction, or word choice, is vital to successful crafting. The poet must select a language that fits the poem, the situation, and the poem's speaker. The beauty of Robert Frost's classic lines "But I have promises to keep,/And miles to go before I sleep . . ." would have been lost to us had he been less skillful, had he been content with "it's going to be a long time before I finish and get home to bed." Black poets, keeping in mind time, place, and speaker, make the same careful choices. Sometimes the poet will choose to use **idiom.** Idiom should not be confused with **dialect.**

Dialect, as it has been construed, is disrespectful, a distortion of Black speech. It has been used to portray the speaker as a buffoon, as a ridiculous caricature, an ignorant or witless creature. Idiom, on the other hand, is as accurate a reproduction of Black speech patterns as possible. It is easy to recognize idiom. The writer (or speaker) chooses to arrange ordinary words in ways that seem unusual. Sometimes word endings or entire words are omitted. In her classic poem "We Real Cool" (page 667), Gwendolyn Brooks has omitted the word *are.* The speaker, as Brooks intuitively knows, has decided to set style, to reinvent the language according to his sense of what "works" for this situation and what would not work. These pool players could say, if they chose, "We decided we would no longer attend school; that we would, in the future, devote ourselves to this recreational activity." They would not, however, so choose, and Brooks, with a careful selection of words, sensitively suggests both their language and their view of the world, and ours.

Festival of Negro Poets, Jackson, Mississippi, October 1952. Standing from left: Arna Bontemps, Melvin Tolson, Jacob Reddix, Owen Dodson, and Robert Hayden. Seated from left: Sterling Brown, Ruth Dease, Margaret Walker, and Langston Hughes.
By permission of the Tolson family

The poet often uses fewer words than we might use in ordinary speech. He or she chooses with great care the words that will finally be used in the poem, retaining the few that will most affect us when we read. The best poets try for fresh expressions, and African American poets feel a challenge to reinvent the language to meet the special situations they encounter.

Poetry Touches Our Emotions

Good poetry touches our emotions, makes us feel something when we read or hear it. The poet knows how we feel, for he or she has felt the same way. Robert Hayden knows the truth about a house too cold to move in without shivering. In "Those Winter Sundays" (page 652), he tells us how it feels to lie in bed, hoping the heat will come, waiting to hear "the cold splintering, breaking." He also knows what it is like to be whipped. More importantly, he has written a "healing" poem by sharing with us some insight about the person who inflicts punishment. He reminds us that each of us is the sum of all that is past and suggests that meanness and violence are often the results of having experienced violent, hurtful things in one's past.

His poem "The Whipping" (page 653) is a healing poem because it allows us to share the child's pain and terror, and it forces us to conclude that the old woman has confused her unhappy life with what she should do to the child. This might well be seen as a teaching poem because what we feel, as a result of reading it, is that to seek relief from one's own hurt by inflicting pain or violence on another is unworthy of us. We find that behavior objectionable and vow not to be guilty of it in our own future.

Each of Hayden's poems is different in style and in tone. His "Runagate Runagate" (page 654) is so vivid that from the first stanza we see the escaping slaves and we feel their tension as clearly as if they were on a television screen. This suggests that we can expect stylistic and structural versatility in poetry. This many-sidedness also speaks to the range of poetry's concerns.

New Dimensions in African American Poetry

To appreciate literature better, it is often useful to understand what the writer sees as his or her mission. Black women writers, shaped by race and gender, often address issues and make major observations that are rarely touched on by men. Consequently, their work expands the body of African American literature by adding important new dimensions. Listen to the edge in Julia Fields's voice in "High on the Hog" (page 690) as she says she has had enough of living her "wretched life/Between domestic rats/And foreign wars." Rita Dove, in quite another mood, talks to us about the love-bond that exists between sisters despite their quarrels (page 719). Alice Childress, in an essay called "A Candle in a Gale Wind," says, "I continue to write about those who come in second, or not at all." Other issues that Black women poets seem to address more often than men are child abuse, abortion, mother-daughter relationships, aspects of making a home, and alienation from loved ones.

This is a time when African American women writers, already recognized historically as a creative group with a mission, have examined what has been written about them and are determined to set the record straight. They approach the business of defining Black womanhood in ways that are healing, nurturing, and revealing. They attack head-on the large issues of social concern.

The Black female poet is not only poignant and reflective; she is strong, resistant, and as given to jazz riffs as to ancient chants. Together, she and the Black male poet make a harmonious music.

Black writers, therefore, are reaching for the connective currents that nod Black heads from Maine to Mississippi to Montana—

reaching for the common denominator, the shared moments of language or event or situation. Black poets do not have to wait for "inspiration." Nor do they need to invent scenarios; drama is part of the very texture of their lives.

In a poem entitled "Note on Commercial Theatre," Langston Hughes once wondered who would write the many African American poems and stories waiting to be told. "I reckon," he stated with obvious pride, "it'll be/Me, myself!/Yes, it'll be me."

There is energy, excitement, and substance in Black poetry. If you're not ready for all of that, "Do not," Ishmael Reed might caution, "read this poem" (page 698).

Sun Offering,
oil by Gaylord Hassan,
1982.
Collection of the artist.
© 1998 Gaylord Hassan/
Licensed by VAGA,
New York, NY

About the Author

Robert Hayden (1913–1980)

Timothy D. Franklin/The Schomburg Center for Research in Black Culture/New York Public Library

 When asked to define poetry, Robert Hayden said it is "the art of saying the impossible." Hayden was born and raised in Detroit, Michigan. He earned his B.A. from Wayne University and his M.A. from the University of Michigan. In 1946, Hayden joined the English faculty at Fisk University and he taught there until 1968. He then accepted a post teaching English at the University of Michigan, a crowning achievement after his graduate school days when he could barely afford to live in a segregated rooming house. During his years as a professor, Hayden once said that he was "a poet who teaches in order to earn a living so that he can write a poem or two now and then."

In the 1930s, working for the Federal Writers' Project in Detroit, Hayden researched and studied the history of black people from their roots in Africa to the present day. His elegant and formal poems about black history have won him many awards. He wrote about such figures as Harriet Tubman, Nat Turner, Malcolm X, and Frederick Douglass.

While much of Hayden's poetry concerns African American history and the black experience, it is informed by a larger vision. As a follower of the Baha'i faith, which teaches the spiritual unity of all humankind, Hayden rejected narrow racial categorizations—both for himself and his work.

Hayden's poetry ranges from formal diction and traditional verse forms to informal diction and free verse. His best-known collections of poetry include *Heart-Shape in the Dust* (1940), *The Lion and the Archer* (1948), *Figure of Time: Poems* (1955), *Words in the Mourning Time* (1970), and *The Night-Blooming Cereus* (1972). In 1976, Hayden became the first African American to serve as Poetry Consultant to the Library of Congress.

Before You Read

Those Winter Sundays; The Whipping; Runagate Runagate

Using What You Know

Identifying the **speaker** in a poem is an aid to understanding its meaning. The speaker in a poem is often the poet, but may be someone or something other than the poet. For example, who is the speaker in "The Creation" (page 285)? in "Mother to Son" (page 327)? Can you name any poem in which the speaker is an animal or a nonliving object that has been given a voice?

A poem may also have more than one speaker. In "Runagate Runagate," for instance, you will find several different voices. Knowing who the speaker (or speakers) may be can also help you understand other things, such as the **setting** and **tone** of a poem.

Literary Focus: Free Verse

Hayden's style as well as his subject matter has a wide range. He uses **free verse** extensively. Free verse is "free" in that there is no fixed pattern of rhyme, meter, line length, or stanza form. Sometimes, free verse also ignores standard punctuation and traditional line arrangements. Even though free verse does not use certain conventions of poetic structure, however, it tends to emphasize others, such as **alliteration, repetition,** and **parallel constructions**. Many poets are able to capture the natural rhythms of speech in their free verse.

Setting a Purpose

As you read, note the speakers of these poems. What voices can you hear? Where do you recognize the voice of the poet speaking of his own feelings? Where has he created characters with their own voices?

Breadwinner, *lithograph by* *John Wilson, 1942.* Museum of the National Center of Afro-American Artists, Inc.

Those Winter Sundays

Robert Hayden

Sundays too my father got up early
and put his clothes on in the blueblack cold,
then with cracked hands that ached
from labor in the weekday weather made
banked fires blaze. No one ever thanked him.   5

I'd wake and hear the cold splintering, breaking.
When the rooms were warm, he'd call,
and slowly I would rise and dress,
fearing the chronic angers of that house,

Speaking indifferently to him,   10
who had driven out the cold
and polished my good shoes as well.
What did I know, what did I know
of love's austere and lonely offices?

The Whipping

Robert Hayden

The old woman across the way
   is whipping the boy again
and shouting to the neighborhood
   her goodness and his wrongs.

Wildly he crashes through elephant ears,°
   pleads in dusty zinnias,
while she in spite of crippling fat
   pursues and corners him.

She strikes and strikes the shrilly circling
   boy till the stick breaks
in her hand. His tears are rainy weather
   to woundlike memories:

My head gripped in bony vise
   of knees, the writhing struggle
to wrench free, the blows, the fear
   worse than blows that hateful

Words could bring, the face that I
   no longer knew or loved . . . .
Well, it is over now, it is over,
   and the boy sobs in his room,

And the woman leans muttering against
   a tree, exhausted, purged—
avenged in part for lifelong hidings
   she has had to bear.

5

10

15

20

5. elephant ears: a plant with large heart-shaped leaves, also called *elephant's ear.*

Runagate Runagate°

Robert Hayden

I.

Runs falls rises stumbles on from darkness into darkness
and the darkness thicketed with shapes of terror
and the hunters pursuing and the hounds pursuing
and the night cold and the night long and the river
to cross and the jack-muh-lanterns beckoning beckoning   5
and blackness ahead and when shall I reach that somewhere
morning and keep on going and never turn back and keep on going

       Runagate
           Runagate
                Runagate   10

Many thousands rise and go
many thousands crossing over

                 O mythic North
           O star-shaped yonder Bible city

Some go weeping and some rejoicing   15
some in coffins and some in carriages
some in silks and some in shackles

      Rise and go or fare you well

No more auction block for me
no more driver's lash for me   20

    If you see my Pompey, 30 yrs of age,
    new breeches, plain stockings, negro shoes;
    if you see my Anna, likely young mulatto
    branded E on the right cheek, R on the left,
    catch them if you can and notify subscriber.   25
    Catch them if you can, but it won't be easy.
    They'll dart underground when you try to catch them,
    plunge into quicksand, whirlpools, mazes,
    turn into scorpions when you try to catch them.

° **Runagate:** a runaway or fugitive.

654   ROBERT HAYDEN

Canada Bound (*illustration for* Harriet and the Promised Land)
by Jacob Lawrence, 1967.

And before I'll be a slave   30
I'll be buried in my grave

    North star and bonanza gold
    I'm bound for the freedom, freedom-bound
    and oh Susyanna don't you cry for me

           Runagate   35

         Runagate

II.
Rises from their anguish and their power,

        Harriet Tubman,

        woman of earth, whipscarred,
        a summoning, a shining   40

        Mean to be free

Runagate Runagate   655

And this was the way of it, brethren° brethren,
way we journeyed from Can't to Can.
Moon so bright and no place to hide,
the cry up and the patterollers° riding,   45
hound dogs belling in bladed air.
And fear starts a-murbling, Never make it,
we'll never make it. *Hush that now,*
and she's turned upon us, levelled pistol
glinting in the moonlight: 50
Dead folks can't jaybird-talk, she says;
you keep on going now or die, she says.

Wanted   Harriet Tubman   alias The General
alias Moses   Stealer of Slaves
In league with Garrison   Alcott   Emerson   55
Garrett   Douglass   Thoreau   John Brown°

Armed and known to be Dangerous

Wanted   Reward   Dead or Alive

Tell me, Ezekiel, oh tell me do you see
mailed Jehovah coming to deliver me?°   60

Hoot-owl calling in the ghosted air,
five times calling to the hants° in the air.
Shadow of a face in the scary leaves,
shadow of a voice in the talking leaves:

Come ride-a my train   65

Oh that train, ghost-story train
through swamp and savanna movering movering,
over trestles of dew, through caves of the wish,
Midnight Special on a sabre track movering movering,
first stop Mercy and the last Hallelujah.   70

Come ride-a my train

Mean mean mean to be free.

---

42. **brethren** (bre*th*'rən): brothers (chiefly in religious use). 45. **patterollers:**
patrollers, slave catchers. 55–56. **Garrison . . . Brown:** individuals active in the
movement to abolish slavery. 59–60. **Ezekiel . . . me:** In the Bible, God appears to
the prophet Ezekiel in glowing metal (here, the word *mailed* means "armored"). Ezekiel was commissioned by God to comfort the Israelites in captivity (Ezekiel 1:26–28;
2:1–10). 62. **hants:** variant of *haunts,* or spirits.

Responding to the Selections
Three Poems by Robert Hayden

Interpreting Meanings

Those Winter Sundays

1. The speaker in this poem is an adult who now understands things he didn't understand as a child. What are his most vivid memories of winter Sundays? Why are these memories both tender and sad?
2. An **image** represents something that you can experience through your senses. Most images appeal to the sense of sight, but images can also appeal to the senses of hearing, touch, taste, and smell. Which images in the poem appeal to more than one sense?
3. What is the significance of the word *too* in line 1? Why is the detail of his father polishing the child's "good shoes" so touching?
4. Many children take for granted their parents' expressions of love. Where does the speaker refer to his own attitudes? What do you think is meant by the "chronic angers of that house" (line 9)?
5. The poem ends with a question, in which the speaker seems to be reproaching himself. What do you think might have happened to make him realize that the duties performed as acts of love are often thankless tasks?

The Whipping

1. Why do you think the speaker never tells us how the old woman and the boy are related?
2. At what point does the speaker identify with the boy? What do you think he means when he refers to fear as "worse than blows" (lines 15–16)?
3. How does the speaker show sympathy for both the boy and the old woman?
4. Mari Evans, herself a celebrated poet, refers to this as a "healing poem" (see page 647). How do you think it helps us to deal with our own experiences of frustration or abuse?

Runagate Runagate

1. In this poem, Hayden creates a *collage* in words, using phrases from hymns, spirituals, antislavery songs, posters, voices of slaves and slaveowners, and the voice of Harriet Tubman. Identify these various elements in the poem.
2. In Part I, how does the poet re-create the drama of the fugitive slave's escape to freedom? How does he convey the fear and the determination of the runaway?
3. Who might be speaking in lines 21–29?
4. In Part II, the poet refers to the Underground Railroad and to one of its greatest leaders—Harriet Tubman. Who might be speaking in lines 42–52? Why was it necessary to keep runaway slaves from going back?
5. Many spirituals invite people to board the "glory train," which is actually a call to have faith in God. Lines 65–71 allude to this spiritual train. What other meaning might this train have?

Literary Elements

Recognizing Characteristics of Free Verse

Free verse does not use regular patterns of rhyme, meter, or line length, but it does depend on other devices. One of these is **alliteration**—the repetition of similar sounds, usually consonants, in a group of related words. Alliteration is often used to gain emphasis. In "Runagate Runagate," Hayden uses **initial alliteration** in lines 16–17:

some in coffins and some in carriages
some in silks and some in shackles

Note how the alliteration helps to set up a contrast between the parts of each line.

Another poetic device that is used as a unifying element in free verse is **repetition** of words. How does Hayden use repetition in lines 1–10 of "Runagate Runagate"?

In "Runagate Runagate," Hayden arranges his words in unusual ways to achieve certain effects. Where in the poem do the words look like they are running? How does the break in lines 11–14 actually create an image of "crossing over"?

Language and Vocabulary

Learning the Origin of a Word

Look up the word *runagate* in an unabridged dictionary. Find out its history. What other words in English is it related to?

Writer's Journal

Responding to the Poems

In your journal, briefly write your response to the poems by Hayden. Did these poems cause you to relive any experiences in your own life? Did his treatment of events in African American history give you a new viewpoint on things that have been familiar through your readings elsewhere?

Descriptive Writing

Describing a Season

Reread "Those Winter Sundays" and examine the poet's use of imagery. Choose a season and write a descriptive poem or short essay. Use images that appeal to more than one sense.

Speaking and Listening

Presenting a Group Reading

Form a small group to present an oral interpretation of "Runagate Runagate." What speakers will you need? Reread the poem to distinguish the different voices. When you read aloud, be sure to follow the movement of the poem. For example, the first lines would probably be read quickly, but other sections of the poem might be intended for a slower delivery. The lines from spirituals and songs might be chanted or sung.

About the Author

Dudley Randall (b. 1914)

 Dudley Randall was four years old when he wrote his first poem, and thirteen when he had poems published in the *Detroit Free Press.* After working in a foundry for five years and serving in the army, he earned a master's degree in library science from the University of Michigan, and became the reference librarian for Wayne County. Randall also learned Russian and has translated many Russian poems into English.

Randall's poems are not his only contribution to African American poetry. The Broadside Press, which he established in 1963, served for many years as a forum for such emerging black poets as Etheridge Knight, Haki R. Madhubuti (formerly Don L. Lee), Nikki Giovanni, and Sonia Sanchez.

Randall's work has been recognized as a bridge between the work of earlier black writers and that of the generation of the sixties. He is influenced by classical traditions, but, as one critic put it, "he also gives his energetic support to modern originality." He has explained his literary philosophy in *Negro Digest:* "Precision and accuracy are necessary for both white and black writers ... what we tend to overlook is that our common humanity makes it possible to write a love poem, for instance, without a word of race, or to write a nationalistic poem that will be valid for all humanity."

Randall's early books of poetry are *Poem Counterpoem* (with Margaret Danner); *Cities Burning,* which reflects the political climate

Layle Silbert

of the time; and *More to Remember: Poems of Four Decades,* which treats universal themes and shows his artistic breadth. His later collections, *After the Killing* (1973) and *A Litany of Friends: New and Selected Poems* (1981), display his skill and craftsmanship. He edited the anthology *The Black Poets* (1971), and in 1975 coauthored *A Capsule Course in Black Poetry Writing* (with Gwendolyn Brooks, Keorapetse Kgositsile, and Haki R. Madhubuti).

Before You Read

George

Using What You Know

Before joining the army, Dudley Randall worked in a foundry, a place where metal is melted down and poured into molds. The first part of his poem "George" is set in a foundry. If you have seen pictures of foundries, you may recall that the *founding,* or casting, is often done in large pits in the floor. Overhead cranes are used to lift and carry the molds and the castings. Some foundries turn out engine blocks. What other products do they make? What precautions would have to be taken by the workers in a foundry?

Literary Focus: Simile

A **simile,** like all **figures of speech,** helps us to see things in new and vivid ways. A simile uses a word of comparison, such as *like* or *as,* in order to draw a comparison between two unlike things. We use similes in our everyday speech when we say someone is "as smart as a whip" or has "a mind like a steel trap." Note how Randall uses simile in both familiar and unexpected ways.

Setting a Purpose

As you read, see how effectively Randall develops the relationship between the two men. How does he show the speaker's feelings for George?

George

Dudley Randall

When I was a boy desiring the title of man
And toiling to earn it
In the inferno of the foundry knockout,
I watched and admired you working by my side,
As, goggled, with mask on your mouth and shoulders bright
    with sweat,   5
You mastered the monstrous, lumpish cylinder blocks,
And when they clotted° the line and plunged to the floor
With force enough to tear your foot in two,
You calmly stepped aside.

One day when the line broke down and the blocks reared up 10
Groaning, grinding, and mounted like an ocean wave
And then rushed thundering down like an avalanche,
And we frantically dodged, then braced our heads together
To form an arch to lift and stack them,
You gave me your highest accolade:°   15
You said: "You not afraid to sweat. You strong as a mule."

Now, here, in the hospital,
In a ward where old men wait to die,
You sit, and watch time go by.
You cannot read the books I bring, not even   20
Those that are only picture books,
As you sit among the senile wrecks,
The psychopaths,° the incontinent.

One day when you fell from your chair and stared at the air
With the look of fright which sight of death inspires,   25
I lifted you like a cylinder block, and said,
"Don't be afraid
Of a little fall, for you'll be here
A long time yet, because you're strong as a mule."

7. **clotted:** formed a jumbled mass.

15. **accolade** (ăk'ə-lād): praise.

23. **psychopaths** (sī'kə-păths'): people suffering from mental disorders.

Responding to the Selection

George by Dudley Randall

Interpreting Meanings

1. Which details in the poem show the author's familiarity with the work in a foundry? Which **similes** emphasize the dangers of the workplace?
2. What impression of George is created in the first part of the poem? How do you know that the comparison "strong as a mule" in line 16 is meant as a compliment?
3. How is George presented in lines 17–25?
4. Which details show that the younger man has remained loyal? At the end of the poem, how has the relationship of the two men changed?
5. Do you find the concluding lines of the poem sad or uplifting? Give reasons for your response.

Language and Vocabulary

Recognizing Connotative Meanings

Diction, or word choice, is very important in poetry. A poet chooses words carefully in order to control the reader's response. In line 3, Randall could have written "In the *hot* foundry knockout." Instead he uses the word *inferno,* meaning "hell, or a place character- ized by great heat or flames." The word *inferno* has **connotations,** or suggestions, of great suffering as well as unbearable heat. How does this word add to the atmosphere of the setting?

Describe the effect of the word *monstrous* in line 6. Why is it a better choice than the word *huge?*

Creative Writing

Writing a Poem

Write a short poem about someone whom you admire very much. Think of at least two similes to describe that person. If you wish, follow this plan.

Prewriting Strategies

Begin with a chart. Jot down as many comparisons as you can think of and then include the ones you like best in your poem. Here is an example.

Person I Admire	Qualities	Similes
My brother	Fast runner	He flew down the track like a bird in flight.

About the Author

Gwendolyn Brooks (b. 1917)

Gwendolyn Brooks, whose poetry has earned her many honors and awards, is one of America's most imaginative and accomplished poets. Born in Topeka, Kansas, Brooks moved to Chicago at an early age, and still lives in the core of that city's black community.

Brooks's poetic talents were apparent from a young age. Her early poems were influenced by the work of Emily Dickinson, John Keats, and Percy Bysshe Shelley. While still a teenager, she mastered traditional forms. Only in her twenties did she make "a systematic and concentrated raid upon the storehouse of modern poetic techniques."

Brooks's first volume of poetry, *A Street in Bronzeville,* was published in 1945. The subjects of the poems were generally the black urban poor. Throughout the 1950s, Brooks continued to write about the thousands of African Americans who had fled the rural South for Northern cities. She discovered that there was little difference between the two regions in terms of racism. Brooks received the Pulitzer Prize for poetry in 1950 for the collection *Annie Allen.* She was the first African American ever to be awarded this prize. In 1985, she became the first black woman ever to be appointed Poetry Consultant to the Library of Congress.

With her fourth volume of poetry, *The Bean Eaters* (1960), Brooks's poetry began to change in response to the radical movements of that time. Her poems became more political in content, freer in style, and more

Wide World Photos

colloquial in language. In 1967 she said she had successfully escaped from close rhyme "because it just isn't natural."

Though best known for her poetry, Brooks has also published a novel, *Maud Martha* (1953), and has edited two poetry collections, *A Broadside Treasury* and *Jump Bad: A New Chicago Anthology* (1971).

Brooks continues to be active in writing poetry and encouraging young people to do the same. In 1991 she published *Very Young Poets* and *Winnie,* a short book of poetry inspired by Winnie Mandela. She has also recently published *Report from Part Two* (1996), the sequel to her autobiography, *Report from Part One* (1972).

Gwendolyn Brooks 663

Before You Read

the sonnet-ballad; The Bean Eaters; We Real Cool

Using What You Know

Poets have a wide range of **forms** available to them. Some traditional forms, such as the **sonnet,** have a tightly controlled structure and rhyme scheme. Other forms, such as **free verse,** allow for variations in line length and rhythm. Many poets are comfortable in a range of styles and will choose the poetic forms that are appropriate for particular subjects.

Identify some of the poems you have read in this book that are written in traditional and nontraditional forms. Which ones have uniform stanzas and regular rhyme schemes? Consider "For My People" (page 442) and "Runagate Runagate" (page 654). How is the form of each poem appropriate for its subject?

Literary Focus: The Lyric

Some poems, like "John Henry" (page 259), are **narrative** poems. They tell a story. Many **ballads** are narrative poems. Some other poems, like those you are about to read, are examples of the **lyric** form. Lyric poetry is usually fairly short and expresses the personal thoughts and feelings of the speaker. Some types of lyric poetry are **sonnets, songs, odes,** and **elegies.**

Setting a Purpose

As you read, note that in each poem Brooks is using a different form. How is the form of each poem suitable for its subject?

the sonnet-ballad

Gwendolyn Brooks

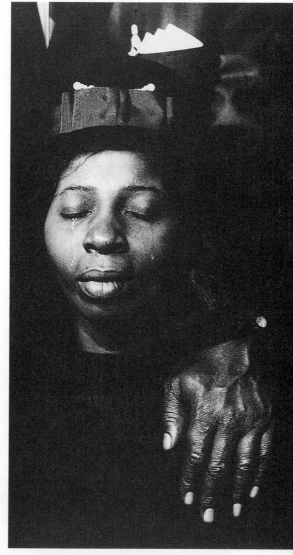

Oh mother, mother, where is happiness?
They took my lover's tallness off to war,
Left me lamenting. Now I cannot guess
What I can use an empty heart-cup for.
He won't be coming back here any more.   5
Some day the war will end, but, oh, I knew
When he went walking grandly out that door
That my sweet love would have to be untrue.
Would have to be untrue. Would have to court
Coquettish° death, whose impudent and strange   10
Possessive arms and beauty (of a sort)
Can make a hard man hesitate—and change.
And he will be the one to stammer, "Yes."
Oh mother, mother, where is happiness?

10. **Coquettish** (kō-kĕt'ĭsh): flirtatious.

The Bean Eaters

Gwendolyn Brooks

They eat beans mostly, this old yellow pair.
Dinner is a casual affair.
Plain chipware on a plain and creaking wood,
Tin flatware.

Two who are Mostly Good.   5
Two who have lived their day,
But keep on putting on their clothes
And putting things away.

And remembering . . .
Remembering, with twinklings and twinges,   10
As they lean over the beans in their rented back room that
        is full of beads and receipts and dolls and cloths,
        tobacco crumbs, vases and fringes.

**The Ghosts of
Third Street,** *photo by
Ronald Corbin, 1986.*
Ronald Corbin

We Real Cool

Gwendolyn Brooks

THE POOL PLAYERS.
SEVEN AT THE GOLDEN SHOVEL.

We real cool. We
Left school. We

Lurk late. We
Strike straight. We

Sing sin. We
Thin gin. We

Jazz June. We
Die soon.

Responding to the Selections

Three Poems by Gwendolyn Brooks

Interpreting Meanings

the sonnet-ballad

1. Why is the speaker unhappy? Why does she believe her love will have to be untrue?
2. **Personification** is a figure of speech in which a nonhuman thing is talked about as if it were human. How does Brooks personify death in this poem?
3. What view of war does the poem present?
4. This poem is called a **sonnet-ballad**. What elements does it have of both forms?

The Bean Eaters

1. Which details in the poem make you realize that the people are poor?
2. What do you think the poet means by *chipware* (line 3)?
3. What different kinds of memories are suggested by "twinklings and twinges"?
4. What do you think is the poet's attitude toward the couple?
5. Although this couple has few material possessions, do you think they have something that is more important? Explain your answer.

We Real Cool

1. How does Brooks identify the speakers in this poem?
2. What does the phrase "real cool" mean?
3. How does the boasting mood of the poem change abruptly in the last line?
4. **Irony** points up the contrast between appearance and reality. What irony is expressed by this poem?
5. Reread the comments on the language of this poem on page 646. Do you agree that the speakers' language shows their view of the world? How does the use of **rhyme** emphasize the character of the speakers?

Literary Elements

Analyzing Rhyme

Rhyme in poetry tends to give pleasure. The repetition of sounds contributes to the musical quality of the lines. Rhyme also functions as a unifying device. It can help to tie together ideas and emphasize meaning.

Rhyme can be **exact** or **partial**. **Exact rhyme** uses identical vowel and consonant sounds: *stand/band.* In **partial** (or **approximate**) **rhyme,** the sounds of the words are similar but not identical: *luck/stock.*

If rhyme occurs at the end of lines, it is called **end rhyme**. If it occurs within a line, it is called **internal rhyme.**

Find examples of end rhyme and internal rhyme in Brooks's poems. Describe the **rhyme scheme,** or pattern of rhymes, in "the sonnet-ballad."

Creative Writing

Answering a Poem's Question

In "the sonnet-ballad," the speaker asks her mother twice "where is happiness?" Pretend that you are the speaker's mother and answer her question. How would you comfort the speaker? What advice would you give her?

Describing the Characters in a Poem

Describe either the bean-eating couple or the people who are "real cool." Make up their story.

Why do the bean eaters live in a back room? Where did the beads, receipts, and other objects come from? How do the people spend their days?

Who are the "cool" ones? Are they the pool players that Brooks mentions at the beginning of the poem? Does Brooks believe the speakers are "cool"? Explain why the speakers say "We/Die soon."

Speaking and Listening

Preparing an Oral Reading

Prepare each of these poems for an oral reading. Try to read with feeling and expression by keeping in mind the tone of each poem.

About the Author
Derek Walcott (b. 1930)

Derek Alton Walcott was born in Saint Lucia, in the West Indies, where a French / English *patois* (păt'wä'), or local dialect, is spoken. He has used the mixed French and English language of his native island in his plays. He learned English as a second language and has become highly skilled in its use, as his many works show.

Walcott attended St. Mary's College in Saint Lucia and the University of the West Indies in Kingston, Jamaica. He has taught in Saint Lucia, in Grenada, in Jamaica, and at several universities in the United States. He is the founding director of the Trinidad Theatre Workshop. He has won many awards for his poetry and drama.

Walcott's work deals with a divided allegiance to European and to Carribbean culture and ancestry. He was raised in a colonial society and educated as a subject of Great Britain. At the same time, he absorbed the folk literature handed down through the oral culture of his ancestors. Walcott's work reflects this dual heritage.

Critics have noted that Walcott is closest to his island culture in his plays. In *Ti-Jean and His Brothers* (1958), Walcott introduces animals and a devil as characters. His plays are filled with the fables and superstitions of folk culture. One of his folk dramas, *Dream on Monkey Mountain,* won an Obie Award when it was presented in New York City in 1971.

Walcott tends to use traditional forms of English poetry, and his verse contains classi-

Thomas Victor/Time Magazine

cal allusions, complicated metaphors, and complex rhyme schemes. His volumes of poetry include *In a Green Night* (1962), *The Castaway* (1965), *The Gulf* (1970), *The Star-Apple Kingdom* (1979), *The Fortunate Traveller* (1981), *Midsummer* (1984), *The Arkansas Testament* (1987), *Omeros* (1990), and *Antilles: Fragments of Epic Memory* (1993). In 1992 he was awarded the Nobel Prize in Literature.

Before You Read

from **Omeros**

Using What You Know

Recall what you have learned about the **middle passage,** the voyage in which African slaves were transported across the Atlantic. Refer to the excerpt from Equiano's autobiography (pages 150–154) and to other sources you have read. Why did so many of the enslaved Africans die before reaching the Caribbean islands?

Background

Omeros is a long poem in seven books. Critics and scholars have called it an **epic poem** inspired by the *Iliad* and *Odyssey* of Homer, the ancient Greek poet. A number of characters in Walcott's poem, such as Achille, Helen, and Hector, recall figures in Homer's epics, but Walcott is not retelling Homer's stories of the Trojan War and its aftermath. Walcott has said that the poem is meant to capture "the whole experience of the people of the Caribbean."

Achille, the central figure, starts out on a fishing expedition from Saint Lucia, Walcott's own birthplace in the West Indies. He is carried back to the home of his ancestors on the West African coast. In the following episode from Chapter 28, a griot narrates the tragic events of African enslavement.

Setting a Purpose

As you read, determine who the different speakers are.

Omeros

Derek Walcott

Now he heard the griot° muttering his prophetic song
of sorrow that would be the past. It was a note, long-drawn
and endless in its winding like the brown river's tongue:

"We were the colour of shadows when we came down
with tinkling leg-irons to join the chains of the sea,   5
for the silver coins multiplying on the sold horizon,

and these shadows are reprinted now on the white sand
of antipodal° coasts, your ashen ancestors
from the Bight of Benin,° from the margin of Guinea.

There were seeds in our stomachs, in the cracking pods   10
of our skulls on the scorching decks, the tubers
withered in no time. We watched as the river-gods

changed from snakes into currents. When inspected,
our eyes showed dried fronds in their brown irises,
and from our curved spines, the rib-cages radiated   15

like fronds from a palm-branch. Then, when the dead
palms were heaved overside, the ribbed corpses
floated, riding, to the white sand they remembered,

to the Bight of Benin, to the margin of Guinea.
So, when you see burnt branches riding the swell,°   20
trying to reclaim the surf through crooked fingers,

1. **griot** (grē′ō): a professional historian, who may also be a poet, genealogist, teacher, musician, and storyteller.

8. **antipodal** (ăn-tĭp′ə-dəl): situated on opposite sides of the earth.
9. **Bight of Benin**: bay in northern section of the Gulf of Guinea.

20. **swell**: a long wave that moves steadily without breaking.

Autobiography: Water/ Ancestors/Middle Passage/Family Ghosts, *mixed media by Howardena Pindell, 1988.* Wadsworth Atheneum, Hartford. The Ella Gallup Sumner and Mary Catlin Sumner Collection Fund. © Howardena Pindell

after a night of rough wind by some stone-white hotel,
past the bright triangular passage of the windsurfers,
remember us to the black waiter bringing the bill."

But they crossed, they survived. There is the epical splendour.   25
Multiply the rain's lances, multiply their ruin,
the grace born from subtraction as the hold's° iron door

27. **hold:** the interior part of a ship, where cargo is kept.

rolled over their eyes like pots left out in the rain,
and the bolt rammed home its echo, the way that thunder-
claps perpetuate their reverberation.   30

So there went the Ashanti° one way, the Mandingo° another,
the Ibo° another, the Guinea. Now each man was a nation
in himself, without mother, father, brother.

31. **Ashanti** (ə-shăn′tē, ə-shän′-): a people from a region in central Ghana. **Mandingo** (măn-dĭng′gō): a people from the region of the upper Niger River in western Africa.
32. **Ibo** (ē′bō): a people of Nigeria.

Responding to the Selection
from **Omeros** by Derek Walcott

Interpreting Meanings

1. Who is speaking in lines 4–24?
2. In lines 10–18, Walcott uses the imagery of vegetation to describe the enslaved Africans. What does the phrase "dead palms" refer to?
3. How does Walcott convey the suffering of the slaves? What metaphors does he use to show their longing for their native lands?
4. In line 20, the slave-ancestors address their unborn descendants. What memory do they wish to have associated with the sea? What do you think is the meaning of the reference to the black waiter in line 24?
5. In lines 31–33, the narrator refers to the dispersion of African peoples during their enslavement. How does Walcott convey the terrible isolation endured by these displaced people? What is the "epical splendour" of their suffering?

About the Author

Mari Evans

Derek Phemster

Mari Evans, educator, writer, musician, resides in Indianapolis. Formerly Distinguished Writer and Assistant Professor, ASRC, Cornell University, she has taught at Indiana University, Purdue University, Northwestern University, Washington University, St. Louis, the State University of New York at Albany, the University of Miami at Coral Gables, and at Spelman College, Atlanta, over the past twenty years. Author of numerous articles, four children's books, several performed theater pieces, two musicals, and four volumes of poetry, including *I Am a Black Woman, Nightstar,* and *A Dark and Spendid Mass* (1991), she edited the highly acclaimed *Black Women Writers (1950–1980): A Critical Evaluation.* Her work has been widely anthologized in collections and textbooks.

Before You Read

If There Be Sorrow; The Rebel

Using What You Know

On page 647, Mari Evans says, "Good poetry touches our emotions, makes us feel something when we read or hear it. The poet knows how we feel, for he or she has felt the same way." What poems have you read that have moved you? Which poets have written about experiences that are like yours?

Literary Focus: Tone

Tone is the attitude a writer takes toward a subject or toward the reader. Tone shows the emotion behind words. All the elements in a poem contribute to its tone. **Diction,** or choice of words, influences tone. The word *cool* in Brooks's poem "We Real Cool" (page 667) carries a different tone than the word *calm* or *nonchalant* does. The **imagery** in a poem can affect its tone. The image of "tin flatware" in "The Bean Eaters" (page 666) carries a tone different from that of "sterling silverware." Even the sounds of words can affect tone.

Setting a Purpose

Listen to the speaker's voice in these poems. How would you describe the tone in each work?

Two Poems by Mari Evans 675

If There
Be Sorrow

Mari Evans

If there be sorrow
let it be
for things undone . . .
undreamed
   unrealized
     unattained
to these add one;
Love withheld . . .
. . . restrained

The Rebel

Mari Evans

When I
die
I'm sure
I will have a
Big Funeral . . .   5
Curiosity
seekers . . .
coming to see
if I
am really   10
Dead . . .
or just
trying to make
Trouble. . . .

Funeral Procession
by Ellis Wilson (1946),
32.5 × 31" oil on
masonite.
Aaron Douglas Collection
Amistad Research Center,
Tulane University

Two Poems by Mari Evans 677

Responding to the Selections

If There Be Sorrow; The Rebel by Mari Evans

Interpreting Meanings

If There Be Sorrow

1. What advice does the speaker offer for dealing with the experiences of life?
2. What do you think the speaker would consider the source of one's greatest happiness?
3. Do you consider the speaker a *realist,* who emphasizes the practical side of life, or a *romantic,* who emphasizes the possibilities of experience? Give reasons for your answer.
4. How does the poet use **rhyme** and **repetition** to reinforce ideas?
5. Despite the word *sorrow* in the title, do you consider the **tone** of this poem sad?

The Rebel

1. How does the title of this poem give you a clue to the speaker's personality?
2. Although the subject of the poem is the speaker's death, the tone is not at all serious or sad. How would you describe it?

Critical Thinking

Analyzing Tone

The following poem, by Samuel Allen (Paul Vesey), is about baseball's Satchel Paige, the legendary pitcher who played in the black leagues for nearly thirty years. He was still pitching when other men his age had retired from baseball. He was finally admitted to the American League in 1948. He is supposed to have said that he would die while winding up for a pitch at the mound.

How would you describe the **tone** of this poem? How does the **diction** of the poem contribute to its tone?

Leandre Jackson

American Gothic
To Satch
Samuel Allen (Paul Vesey)

Sometimes I feel like I will *never* stop
Just go on forever
'Til one fine mornin'
I'm gonna reach up and grab me a
   handfulla stars
Swing out my long lean leg
And whip three hot strikes burnin' down
   the heavens
And look over at God and say
How about that!

About the Author
Amiri Baraka (LeRoi Jones) (b. 1934)

 Amiri Baraka was born Everett LeRoi Jones in Newark, New Jersey. He changed his name as part of his rejection of white establishment values. He adopted the Bantuized Muslim name Imamu ("spiritual leader") Ameer ("blessed") Baraka ("prince"), which he later shortened to Amiri Baraka.

Although Baraka began his literary career as an avant-garde Beat poet, greatly influenced by white avant-garde artists such as Allen Ginsberg and Frank O'Hara, a trip to Cuba in 1960 radicalized his political stance and led to his identification with Third World artists. Not only did Baraka see his African American identity as central to his art, but he also dared to bring radical politics into the world of literature. Baraka rejected traditional poetic forms, saying, "I'm not interested in writing sonnets, sestinas or anything . . . only poems."

Throughout the 1960s, Baraka became more radical, rejecting white culture and searching for "the dark gods of the black soul." He became well-known in 1964 for his play *Dutchman,* which won the *Village Voice*'s Obie Award. Baraka was influential in black theater, establishing the Black Arts Repertory Theater and School in Harlem in 1965. This school inspired black theaters throughout the country.

In addition to his poetry, plays, and essays, Baraka researched and wrote a comprehensive study of black music in America. *Blues People: Negro Music in White America* (1963) deals with the development of black

Bert Andrews

music from the time of slavery up until the present.

In 1967, Baraka published two volumes: *Black Magic* and *Tales.* These encouraged African Americans to create an identity separate from the world of white culture. Baraka's poem "Black Art" announced his view that all black artistic expression should aim to achieve social, moral, and political revolution.

In 1974, however, Baraka reversed his black nationalist stance, calling it racist. He became a Third World Socialist and his poems reflected his new Marxist philosophy.

Amiri Baraka remains a major and controversial writer. As one of the primary architects of the Black Arts Movement, he has significantly affected the course of African American literary culture.

Before You Read

Preface to a Twenty Volume Suicide Note; SOS

Using What You Know

Informally, one speaks about a depressed, unhappy feeling as "the blues." Have you ever been lifted out of a sad mood by the kindness of a friend or by the sight of something beautiful, such as a child's smile? Have you ever befriended a depressed person and helped raise his or her spirits? Try to imagine the feelings of the speaker in each of these poems.

Literary Focus: Overstatement

We frequently use **overstatement,** or exaggeration, in everyday speech, in such expressions as "This suitcase weighs a ton" and "I haven't seen you in a month of Sundays." The technical term for overstatement is **hyperbole** (hī-pûr′bə-lē). Poets sometimes use hyperbole for humorous effect. They also use it for emphasis. In love poetry, the speakers often use overstatement to express their emotions.

Setting a Purpose

How does the speaker in each of these poems convey his state of mind? What examples of overstatement can you find?

Preface to a Twenty Volume Suicide Note

(For Kellie Jones, born 16 May 1959)

Amiri Baraka

Rewards, *collage by*
Phoebe Beasley.

Lately, I've become accustomed to the way
The ground opens up and envelops me
Each time I go out to walk the dog.
Or the broad edged silly music the wind
Makes when I run for a bus . . .   5

Things have come to that.

And now, each night I count the stars,
And each night I get the same number.
And when they will not come to be counted,
I count the holes they leave.   10

Nobody sings anymore.

And then last night, I tiptoed up
To my daughter's room and heard her
Talking to someone, and when I opened
The door, there was no one there . . .   15
Only she on her knees, peeking into

Her own clasped hands.

Prophet #1 *by Charles White, 1975.*

SOS

Amiri Baraka

Calling black people
Calling all black people, man woman child
Wherever you are, calling you, urgent, come in
Black People, come in, wherever you are, urgent, calling
you, calling all black people
calling all black people, come in, black people, come
on in.

Responding to the Selections

Two Poems by Amiri Baraka

Interpreting Meanings

Preface to a Twenty Volume Suicide Note

1. In "Preface to a Twenty Volume Suicide Note," how does the poet use **overstatement,** or exaggeration, in line 2? What do you think the poet means by this line?
2. What does the word *that* represent in line 6?
3. Can you really count holes that the stars leave? What does the poet convey with this image?
4. Whom is the daughter talking to?
5. What larger idea is expressed in the line "Nobody sings anymore"?
6. How do the words "And then" in line 12 tell you that the **tone** of the poem is changing? What is the new tone?

SOS

1. How does the lack of punctuation in "SOS" imitate the code that SOS distress signals are transmitted in?
2. What do you think the poet means by urging black people to "come on in"?

Speaking and Listening

Reading Aloud

The poem "SOS" has very little punctuation. Create your own rhythm and read the poem out loud to the class. You could give it a chantlike quality, or make it into a rap song. You'll probably have to experiment with different rhythms before you hit on one that works.

About the Author

Sonia Sanchez (b. 1934)

Leandre Jackson

 "I write to tell the truth about the Black condition as I see it. Therefore I write to offer a Black woman's view of the world." With these words, Sonia Sanchez defines and explains her work, which includes poetry, short stories, children's stories, and plays.

Born in Birmingham, Alabama, Sanchez studied at New York University and at Hunter College in New York City. She currently teaches at Temple University in Philadelphia, Pennsylvania.

Sanchez strongly espouses the use of the urban African American vernacular in writing. She explains that she and a number of other black poets decided "to tell the truth in poetry by using the language, dialect, idioms, of the folks we believed our audience to be." Sanchez directs her poetry to African Americans, concentrating on themes of black identity and pride. Her first volume of poetry, *Homecoming* (1969), introduced her use of the black idiom. *We a BaddDDD People* was published the next year. *A Blues Book for Blue Black Magical Women* (1973) focuses on the roles and struggles of black women. Sanchez won the American Book Award, Before Columbus Foundation, for her poetry collection *homegirls & handgrenades* (1984).

Sanchez has often spoken out against sexism as well as against racism. She has warned that "If we're not careful, the animosity between black men and women will destroy us." To avoid this fate, she believes women must refuse to adopt the posture of victims. Throughout her work, Sanchez has affirmed the value of strong family relationships and lashed out against all forms of racism, sexism, classism, and ignorance.

Before You Read

Graduation Notes

Using What You Know _____

If you have read "For My People" (page 442), you will recall that Margaret Walker organizes her poem into free verse paragraphs that function as stanzas. Contemporary poets have taken many liberties with traditional poetic forms. Can you name any works you have read in this anthology or in other books that use experimental or innovative poetic forms?

Literary Focus: The Prose Poem _____

A **prose poem** is a composition that is written in the form of prose yet contains many elements of poetry, such as **imagery, figurative language, alliteration, rhythm,** and **rhyme.**

Setting a Purpose _____

In reading this prose poem, note how the writer combines elements of prose and poetry.

Graduation Notes:

*for Mungu, Morani, Monica and
Andrew and Crefeld seniors:*

Sonia Sanchez

So much of growing up is an unbearable waiting. A constant
longing for another time. Another season.

I remember walking like you today down this path. In love with
the day. Flesh awkward. I sang at the edge of adolescence and the
scent of adulthood rushed me and I thought I would suffocate. But   5
I didn't. I am here. So are you. Finally. Tired of tiny noises your eyes
hum a large vibration.

I think all journeys are the same. My breath delighting in the
single dawn. Yours. Walking at the edge. Unafraid. Anxious for the
unseen dawns are mixing today like the underground rhythms   10
seeping from your pores.

At this moment your skins living your eighteen years suspend all
noises. Your days still half-opened, crackle like the fires to come.
Outside. The earth. Wind. Night. Unfold for you. Listen to their
sounds. They have sung me seasons that never abandoned me. A   15
dance of summer rain. A ceremony of thunder waking up the earth
to human monuments.

Facing each other I smile at your faces. Know you as young
heroes soon to be decorated with years. Hope no wars dwarf you.
Know your dreams wild and sweet will sail from your waists to   20
surround the non-lovers. Dreamers. And you will rise up like
newborn armies refashioning lives. Louder than the sea you come
from.

Responding to the Selection

Graduation Notes by Sonia Sanchez

Interpreting Meanings

1. This poem is addressed to a graduating class. What is the journey the poet refers to in line 8?
2. What advice does she give to the seniors?
3. Why does the poet refer to young people as "heroes"?
4. Are these "notes" written just for the Crefeld seniors or are they intended for all young people? Explain.

Creative Writing

Writing a Prose Poem

Write a letter to someone you know in the form of a prose poem. Decide first what thoughts you want to express. Then think about some images that would help to convey those thoughts. You might want to begin by jotting down some images.

Towards Identity,
oil by Nelson Stevens.
Collection of the artist

About the Author

Julia Fields (b. 1938)

 When Julia Fields had her first two poems published in 1962, she commented: "I have one ambition: to be a poet." The road toward that goal has not always been smooth, but today Fields is a respected poet and teacher. She is one of the few contemporary African American poets to live in and write about the South.

Born in the rural community of Perry County, Alabama, Fields grew up in a large family. She graduated from Knoxville College, in Tennessee, in 1961. The next year, two of her poems were published in an anthology of black literature, *Beyond the Blues* (1962). Encouraged by this success, she continued to write poetry and short stories while teaching high school in Birmingham, Alabama. She has held positions at several colleges and universities.

Her first volume of poetry, *Poems* (1968), was well-received. It included "High on the Hog," the poem reprinted here. This poem is generally acknowledged by critics to be "a masterpiece of irony in its daring to defy the defiance of the 1960s movement." Like Langston Hughes, whom she greatly admires, Fields clothes the serious criticism in her poems with humor and irony.

Although Fields emerged as a poet during the turbulent 1960s, she never identified with any particular group, movement, or philosophy. But she too probes the political, social, and moral status of black people. Her poems are saturated with the language, sensibilities, values, rituals, and myths of African Americans.

Fields's second volume of poetry, *East of Moonlight* (1973), captures and reflects the folk spirit in black life. In these poems it is clear that Fields has a genuine respect for the folk values of older people who provide strength and security for the younger generation. *A Summoning: A Shining* (1976) develops the themes of the previous poems. Some critics view *Slow Coins* (1981) as Fields's finest book of poetry.

Fields has said that "the black experience seems the most intense experience in the modern world." She continues to examine and convey this through her poetry.

Before You Read

High on the Hog

Using What You Know

What are the traditional foods known as "soul food"? How does soul food provide a link between African Americans and their heritage? What **connotations,** or associations, does the phrase "soul food" evoke? Compare your responses with those in **The Author Comments** on page 694.

Literary Focus: Diction

The term **diction** refers to a writer's choice of words, especially for clarity and effectiveness. A writer's diction can be formal and elegant, or it can be informal, even slangy. In choosing precise words, a writer must think of what is appropriate for both subject and audience.

Poets depend upon both the **denotative,** or literal, meanings and the **connotative,** or suggested, meanings of words. Imagine, for example, that Julia Fields had called her poem "Living Well" instead of "High on the Hog." What would have been lost?

Setting a Purpose

As you read, note how Fields uses words that arouse strong feelings. How does she use language to present serious political and social themes with humor?

High on the Hog

Julia Fields

Take my share of Soul Food—
I do not wish
To taste of pig
    Of either gut
        Or Grunt   5
        From bowel
           Or jowl

I want caviar°
Shrimp soufflé°
Sherry   10
    Champagne

        And not because
These are the
Whites' domain
But just because   15
I'm entitled—

For I've been
        V.d.'d enough
        T.b.'d° enough
    and   20
Hoe-cake° fed Knock-Knee'd enough
Spindly leg bloodhound tree'd° enough
        To eat
        High on the Hog

I've been   25
        Hired last
        Fired first enough

8. **caviar** (kă′vē-är′): the salted eggs of certain fish, eaten as a delicacy.
9. **soufflé** (soo-flā′): a light and puffy dish, made with eggs and other ingredients, such as cheese or shrimp.

19. **T.b.**: tuberculosis, a disease that chiefly affects lungs.
21. **Hoe-cake**: a thin cornmeal cake.
22. **bloodhound tree'd**: forced to climb a tree to escape from bloodhounds. Dogs were used in the pursuit of runaway slaves.

I've sugar-watered my
        Thirst enough—

Been lynched enough   30
        Slaved enough
        Cried enough
        Died enough

Been deprived—
        Have survived enough   35
                To eat
        High on the Hog.

Keep the black-eyed peas
And the grits,
The high blood-pressure chops   40
And gravy sops

I want aperitifs° supreme
        Baked Alaska°—
        Something suave, cool
        For I've been considered faithful fool   45
        From 40 acres and a mule° . . .

I've been
        Slighted enough
        Sever-righted° enough
        And up tighted enough   50
And I want
        High on the Hog

For dragging the cotton sack
        On bended knees
        In burning sun   55
        In homage to the
                Great King cotton
        For priming the money-green tobacco
                And earning pocket-change

        For washing in iron pots   60
        For warming by coal and soot
        For eating the leavings from
                Others' tables

42. **aperitifs** (ä-pĕr′ə-tēfs′):
drinks served before a meal.
43. **Baked Alaska:** a fancy
dessert made with cake and
ice cream.
46. **40 acres and a mule:**
During Reconstruction, the
efforts to give land to
each black family came to
nothing.

49. **Sever-righted:** a play on
"civil righted."

I've lived my wretched life
　　Between domestic rats　　　　　　　65
　　And foreign wars
　　Carted to my final rest
　　In second-hand cars

But I've been leeched° enough
　　Dixie-peached° enough　　　　　　70
　　Color bleached enough

　　And I want
　　High on the Hog!

Oh, I've heard the Mau Mau°
　　Screaming　　　　　　　　　　　75

　　Romanticizing Pain
　　I hear them think
　　They go against the Grain

But I've lived in shacks
　　Long enough　　　　　　　　　　80
　　Had strong black beaten
　　Backs long enough

And I've been
　　Urban-planned
　　　　Been moynihanned°　　　　　85
　　Enough
　　And I want
　　High on the Hog

69. **leeched:** preyed upon, as by a parasite.
70. **Dixie-peached:** a reference to heavy oil used for the hair.

74. **Mau Mau** (mou mou): a secret society of Africans who wanted to end colonial rule in Kenya.

85. **moynihanned:** Senator Daniel Patrick Moynihan, a leading sociologist, later a United States Senator from New York.

Responding to the Selection

High on the Hog by Julia Fields

Interpreting Meanings

1. What foods are contrasted in lines 1–11? Why does the speaker reject soul food?
2. Where in the poem do you first realize that the speaker is not talking only about personal experiences? What is the reason for including allusions to African American history?
3. What does the speaker mean by being "Urban-planned" enough (line 84)?
4. **Free verse,** as you have seen, does not use regular patterns of rhyme, meter, or line length. It does use devices such as **alliteration, repetition,** and **parallelism.** Find examples of each device in the poem and tell what effect it creates in the poem.
5. The poet uses words such as *gut* and *grunt* that are usually not associated with poetry. Why is this informal **diction** appropriate in the poem?
6. The phrase "high on the hog" is used as a **refrain**—a phrase that is repeated throughout the poem as a constant reminder of the poet's theme. Does the phrase here refer just to eating or does it have a broader significance?

Literary Elements

Understanding the Role of Diction
Fields discusses serious subjects in "High on the Hog"—poverty, slavery, and discrimination—yet the tone of the poem is not somber or depressing. To a great extent, her **diction**—her choice of words and manner of expression—is responsible for the poem's witty effect.

What is the difference in **connotation** between the word *pork* and the word *pig,* which Fields chooses to use in line 3? What if she had used *leftovers* instead of *leavings* in line 62?

Sometimes poets take liberties with language. They make up new words, run words together, or use unusual word order. Examine lines 83–88. The sentence "I'm tired of liberal politicians trying unsuccessfully to improve my environment" is not as clever and effective as "I've been/Urban-planned/Been moynihanned/Enough."

Find other examples of language used in creative ways in the poem.

Creative Writing

Writing a Humorous Poem
Think about the foods that you would like to eat. What foods have you "had enough of"? Write a humorous poem, in the style of "High on the Hog." You might start by adapting Fields's opening line ("Take my share of Cafeteria Food").

Prewriting Strategies
Complete a chart showing the contrast in foods. Select words that are appropriate in tone. Include reasons for your choices.

The Author Comments

"High on the hog" is a common expression used to describe living in an extravagant or luxurious way. In some parts of the country, the expression is "high off the hog."

During the 1960s, the words "soul food" were on the lips of many people who used them to make a statement of black American cultural unity. As a native of the South, I was somewhat wary of this. For as long as black people have been in America, those in the South, in the main, have subsisted on staples that included cornmeal, molasses, rice, and pork. In some instances, there were meal and bread and little animal flesh. As a Southerner, I was glad to see the first "meat and bread" place open in North Carolina—Hardee's. It offered meat, bread, salad, a little of "something sweet," and a beverage—to stay or to go.

Needless to say, this was not happening to soul food. Beef was not pork, and it could not be handled in the same way. Beef was "high." Chitterlings, pig's feet, pig tails, and pig ears were considered "sorrow food." For those who had no land, no access to mediating institutions, and no return tickets to their place of origin—with its abundance of fish, kangaroo, turtle, and other foods—it was too early to treat soul food as a symbol of triumphant survival.

Even *The Wall Street Journal* lent its pages to a serious consideration for the future possibilities of soul food. My poem was begun a few minutes after reading that issue of the paper. I finished the poem while going up a steep hill in North Carolina. It helped that I was passing many farms, many people tending to their hogs, cattle, and some horses. The poem has no period at the end. I thought that other people and younger people would extend it, keeping open for discussion the questions in it regarding diet and nutrition, freedom of choices, housing, government policies of health, employment, and forms of inflicted brutalities.

I first read the poem at Saint Augustine's College in Raleigh, North Carolina. People responded enthusiastically. Some wanted to know where copies could be bought. I was too ashamed to tell them that my copy was hot off a mangled last page in an old composition tablet.

The next time I read the poem, I was at another school. At this school, I was told by a member of the audience that they wanted to hear Nikki Giovanni's poetry. Since they had brought some copies of her book, I read from it to them. It was my way to read selections by various poets whenever I was invited to read. And I either recited or read from the Bible because young people are curious about it and they expect any presentation in language to have a reference to something "serious" from their background.

"High on the Hog" was published in book form by Charlene Swansea, a pioneer publisher, founder of *The Red Clay Reader.* In magazine format, it was published in *Negro Digest* in September of 1969.

It was recorded for *Soul!* by Anna Marie Horsford of the television show *Amen.* The record was lost somewhere. I have no doubt that there is a copy waiting for me to claim it—in New York or, these days, even in Dallas or Mobile!!!

—Julia Fields

About the Author
Ishmael Reed (b. 1938)

Costa Manos/Magnum Photos

Ishmael Reed is the author of nine novels, four volumes of poetry, two collections of essays, and editor and publisher of several anthologies. His biography can be found on page 622.

Although Reed is known primarily as a novelist and essayist, he began his literary career as a poet. He participated in the Umbra Workshop, a black writers' group that was one of the forces behind the flowering of African American poetry. In his introduction to *19 Necromancers from Now* (1970), Reed criticizes black poets who have given up their unique voices to write "sonnets, iambic pentameter, ballads, [and] every possible Western gentleman's form."

Reed's first volume of poetry, *Conjure* (1972), was nominated for the National Book Award. Poems from this volume as well as from *Chattanooga* (1973) and *A Secretary to the Spirits* (1978) have appeared in many anthologies and literary magazines. In his poetry, Reed often uses satire and parody to attack the vices, excesses, and other failings of the middle and upper classes. His satires often reveal his revulsion at both the victims and perpetrators of economic exploitation.

Although he is obviously concerned with racism, sexism, and economic exploitation, Reed cannot be categorized simply as a social and political activist. The prime target for his satires and parodies is often literary convention itself. He has said of his writing, "I try to do what has never been done before."

Ishmael Reed   695

Before You Read

.05; Beware: Do Not Read This Poem

Using What You Know

Think of the titles of poems you have read in this anthology and elsewhere. How does a title prepare you for the subject and tone of a poem? What would you expect of a poem with the title "Beware: Do Not Read This Poem"?

Literary Focus: Poetic License

Poets often take liberties with language. They change the natural word order; they invent words; they omit punctuation; they deliberately misspell words. Recall, for example, the word *chipware* in "The Bean Eaters" (page 666), which combines two familiar words to create a new word. Recall the form and style of "Runagate Runagate" (page 654), where the poet uses verbs without subjects in his opening line.

This disregard of conventional rules of form and style is known as **poetic license**. What examples have you seen so far in this unit?

Setting a Purpose

How does Ishmael Reed play with words in the following poems? Can you suggest reasons for the liberties he takes with traditional forms and language?

.05

Ishmael Reed

If i had a nickel
For all the women who've
Rejected me in my life
I would be the head of the
World Bank with a flunkie   5
To hold my derby as i
Prepared to fly chartered
Jet to sign a check
Giving India a new lease
On life   10

If i had a nickel for
All the women who've loved
Me in my life i would be
The World Bank's assistant
Janitor and wouldn't need   15
To wear a derby
All i'd think about would
Be going home

**Crying Ain't Gonna Help
None Baby or Don't Shed
Your Tears on My Rug,**
*lithograph by
Margo Humphrey, 1971.*
Collection of the artist

Beware: Do Not Read This Poem

Ishmael Reed

tonite, *thriller* was
abt an ol woman, so vain she
surrounded herself w/
   many mirrors

It got so bad that finally she   5
locked herself indoors & her
whole life became the
   mirrors

one day the villagers broke
into her house, but she was too   10
swift for them, she disappeared
    into a mirror
each tenant who bought the house
after that, lost a loved one to
    the ol woman in the mirror: 15
    first a little girl
    then a young woman
    then the young woman/s husband

the hunger of this poem is legendary
it has taken in many victims   20
back off from this poem
it has drawn in yr feet
back off from this poem
it has drawn in yr legs
back off from this poem   25
it is a greedy mirror
you are into this poem, from
   the waist down
nobody can hear you can they?
this poem has had you up to here   30
     belch
this poem aint got no manners
you cant call out frm this poem
relax now & go w/this poem
move & roll on to this poem   35

    do not resist this poem
    this poem has yr eyes
    this poem has his head
    this poem has his arms
    this poem has his fingers   40
    this poem has his fingertips

this poem is the reader & the
    reader this poem

statistic: the us bureau of missing persons reports
    that in 1968 over 100,000 people disappeared   45
    leaving no solid clues
       nor trace   only
 a space   in the lives of their friends

Responding to the Selections

.05; Beware: Do Not Read This Poem by Ishmael Reed

Interpreting Meanings

.05

1. You have seen that **hyperbole,** or exaggeration, is often used in a humorous way. What kind of exaggeration is the speaker making in this poem?
2. Do you think the speaker would rather be rich or loved?
3. Why do you suppose the pronoun *I* is written with a small letter instead of a capital letter?
4. The speaker could have said plainly, "I've had bad luck with women." Why is the humorous treatment of this idea more effective than a direct statement?

Beware: Do Not Read This Poem

1. What did you feel when you read the title of this poem?
2. What is the parallel between the mirror that swallows people and the poem? Why does the speaker call the poem a "greedy mirror" in line 26?
3. Why do you think the speaker says "this poem is the reader & the/reader this poem"? Do you agree?
4. Do Reed's unusual spellings of words and his unconventional approach to language make you think about poetry in a new way?

Writing About Literature

Interpreting a Statement

Mari Evans says that "African American poets feel a challenge to reinvent the language to meet the special situations they encounter" (page 647). How does Reed reinvent the language? Refer to the poems in your anthology and other poems by Reed, if you wish.

About the Author
Al Young (b. 1939)

Lee Phillips

 Al Young has been called "a gifted stylist and a keen observer of the human comedy." He was born in Ocean Springs, Mississippi, and was educated at the University of Michigan and the University of California, Berkeley. Young spent the years between the ages of eighteen and twenty-five playing the guitar and flute and singing professionally throughout the United States. Since then he has been a disc jockey, a writing teacher, a language consultant, and a screenwriter. His first novel, *Snakes* (1970), is about a black jazz musician in New York City and, as one critic said, "offers some alternative to hopelessness." Young seeks to write about the human experience, as well as about specific African American concerns. His collections of poetry include *Dancing: Poems* (1969), *Some Recent Fiction* (1974), *The Blues Don't Change: New and Selected Poems* (1982), and *Heaven: Collected Poems* (1988).

Before You Read

For Poets

Using What You Know

You have probably heard the phrase "to commune with nature." The word *commune* has several meanings. It can mean "to be close to"; it can mean "to exchange thoughts and feelings privately"; it can mean "to be in harmony with." How is it possible to *commune* with nature?

Literary Focus: Assonance

A poet can achieve musical effects by using **assonance** (ăs'ə-nəns), the repetition of similar vowel sounds in a group of related words. The words *town* and *down* rhyme exactly. The vowel sound and the end consonant sound are the same in both words. The words *down* and *underground* are not an exact rhyming pair. They illustrate **assonance**. They contain a similar vowel sound, but the final consonant sounds are different. Like **alliteration,** assonance is a form of repetition. In addition to giving pleasure to the ear, it emphasizes the words in which the sounds are repeated.

Setting a Purpose

As you read, note how the author uses devices of sound to emphasize ideas.

702   AL YOUNG

For Poets

Al Young

Stay beautiful
but dont stay down underground too long
Dont turn into a mole
or a worm
or a root   5
or a stone

Come on out into the sunlight
Breathe in trees
Knock out mountains
Commune with snakes   10
& be the very hero of birds

Dont forget to poke your head up
& blink
Think
Walk all around   15
Swim upstream

Dont forget to fly

Two in the Shade, *pastel by Sharon Wilson.*
Collection of the artist

Responding to the Selection
For Poets by Al Young

Interpreting Meanings

1. In the first stanza, who or what is being compared to a mole, worm, root, or stone? Why do you think the poet chooses to list these things in this order?

2. In stanza 2, what does the speaker advise? Of course one can't "breathe in trees" or "knock out mountains." What do you think the poet means here?

3. The third stanza and last line of the poem contain **implied metaphors.** What animals is the speaker advising poets to act like?

4. It is much easier to swim downstream than upstream against the current. What do you think the speaker means by the command "Swim upstream"?

5. Find examples of **assonance** in the poem. How does it link ideas?

About the Author

Alice Walker (b. 1944)

Brian Lanker

Alice Walker has been called one of America's finest novelists. She is also an accomplished poet and essayist. The dominant themes of her writing are the effects of racism and sexism, and her central characters are almost always black women. She explains this choice by saying that "The black woman is one of America's greatest heroes. . . . Not enough credit has been given to the black woman who has been oppressed beyond recognition." For general biographical material, see page 541.

Walker has published five volumes of poetry. The first, *Once* (1968), deals with the Civil Rights Movement. *Revolutionary Petunias and Other Poems* (1973) is more personal and analyzes the relationship between love and change. *Good Night, Willie Lee, I'll See You in the Morning* (1979) examines the community of black women, while *Horses Make a Landscape Look More Beautiful* (1984) invokes some of Walker's environmental concerns. In 1991 her collected poems, *Her Blue Body Everything We Know: Earthling Poems: 1965–1990* was published.

In all of her poetry, Walker focuses on the struggle of blacks, especially black women, to claim their own lives. The poems themselves tend to be spare. Each word is carefully chosen and placed to give the maximum meaning and effect.

Alice Walker 705

Before You Read

Women by Alice Walker

Using What You Know

In 1955, Rosa Parks was arrested in Montgomery, Alabama, because she would not give up her seat on a bus to a white man. Her arrest led to the Montgomery Bus Boycott. Think of some other women who have been active in the struggle for equal rights. Keep them in mind as you read Alice Walker's tribute to the women of her mother's generation.

Literary Focus: Types of Metaphor

A **metaphor** points out the similarities between two unlike things. In these lines, Langston Hughes draws a specific comparison between life and a bird:

> Life is a broken-winged bird
> That cannot fly.

Sometimes a metaphor is not stated directly but is suggested. Then it is called an **implied metaphor.**

> Life's wings are clipped.

This line does not directly say that life is a bird, but the comparison is implied in the word *wings.*

Sometimes a poet will extend a metaphor through several lines or through an entire poem. Hughes does this in ''Mother to Son'' (page 327), where he compares life to a staircase. Such a metaphor is called an **extended metaphor.**

Setting a Purpose

As you read, note the poem's central metaphor. Do you think this is an effective metaphor for the poem's subject?

Women Wiping Up the World *by Jane Evershed.*

Women   Alice Walker

They were women then
My mama's generation
Husky of voice—Stout of
Step
With fists as well as   5
Hands
How they battered down
Doors
And ironed
Starched white   10
Shirts
How they led
Armies
Headragged Generals
Across mined   15
Fields
Booby-trapped
Ditches
To discover books
Desks   20
A place for us
How they knew what we
Must know
Without knowing a page
Of it   25
Themselves.

Responding to the Selection

Women by Alice Walker

Interpreting Meanings

1. What is the central **metaphor** in the poem?
2. Which words in the poem emphasize the strength of the women?
3. Which words are normally used to talk about warfare? Are these words appropriate for the "battles" fought by the women?
4. In lines 22–24, the poet repeats some form of the verb *know* three times. What is the effect of this emphasis?

Writer's Journal

Writing a Tribute

Alice Walker has said that she wrote "Women" as a tribute to her mother "and all our mothers who were not famous." Write about someone "not famous" whom you admire. Be specific about the aspects or qualities you respect. If you wish, turn your journal entry into a poem.

Speaking and Listening

Interpreting a Poem

"Women" contains little punctuation. How should the lines be phrased? Which words should be emphasized? Practice reading the poem aloud. Vary the pace and the tone of your voice. Decide where you should pause. After you have experimented with a number of interpretations, choose the one you like the best and read the poem to the class in that way.

About the Author
Ntozake Shange (b. 1948)

Born Paulette Williams in Trenton, New Jersey, Ntozake Shange (ĕn-tō-zä′kē shän′gä) was raised in a comfortably middle-class family. Her father was a surgeon and her mother was a social worker and educator. Although her childhood was filled with music, literature, and art, she was unhappy. She felt that nobody really expected anything of her because she was black and a woman. When her career choices of jazz musician or war correspondent were dismissed as "no good for a woman," she decided to become a writer.

Shange became not only a writer, but a teacher, performer, and director as well. All of her work draws heavily on her personal experiences and centers on the difficulties and frustrations of being a black woman in America. Shange adopted her African name in 1971 as a way of affirming her strength and determining her own identity. The name means "she who comes with her own things" and she "who walks like a lion."

Shange first received national recognition for her "choreopoem," *For Colored Girls Who Have Considered Suicide/When the Rainbow Is Enuf.* This combination of poetry, music, dance, and drama took the theater world by storm in 1975. It concerns the trials and tribulations of a young black girl growing up.

Shange has published collections of poetry, including *Nappy Edges* (1978); *Ridin' the Moon in Texas: Word Paintings* (1987); and *I Live in Music: Poem* (1995). She has also written two novels, *Sassafras, Cypress,*

Wide World Photos

and Indigo (1983), and *Betsey Brown* (1985). *See No Evil: Prefaces, Essays and Accounts, 1976–1983* was published in 1984.

Ntozake Shange 709

Before You Read

senses of heritage

Using What You Know

Note that the poet uses the plural word *senses* in her title. What might be the different meanings of "senses of heritage"? Does the plural word imply that there is more than one kind of sense? Discuss the possible meanings of the phrase.

Literary Focus: Irony

Irony has several different functions. It can be used by the satirist to attack some vice or folly. It can be used, in a lighter vein, to bring a smile to the reader's face, and it can also bring out the tragic or cruel distance between appearance and reality. Sometimes, irony functions as a comment on a general situation.

Setting a Purpose

Think about the meaning of the title as you read. What senses might have been neglected as the speaker was growing up?

senses of heritage

Ntozake Shange

my grandpa waz a doughboy° from carolina
the other a garveyite from lakewood°
i got talked to abt the race & achievement
bout color & propriety/
nobody spoke to me about the moon   5

daddy talked abt music & mama bout christians
my sisters/we
always talked & talked
there waz never quiet
trees were status symbols   10

i've taken to fog/
the moon still surprisin me

1. **doughboy:** a United States infantryman in World War I.
2. **garveyite:** a follower of Marcus Garvey (see page 274); **lakewood:** a town in New Jersey.

Responding to the Selection
senses of heritage by Ntozake Shange

Interpreting Meanings

1. The speaker says there was always a great deal of talk in her family. What subjects were discussed? What was *not* discussed?
2. What can you infer from the speaker's statement in line 3 that she "got talked to"?
3. Explain why people might think that the more trees they have on their property, the more status they have. Do you agree?
4. The phrase "to take to" means "to develop an affection for." Why do you think the speaker might "take to" fog and the moon? How is this preference ironic?
5. The speaker never mentions the word *heritage* in the poem. What, then, does it mean in the title?

About the Author

Safiya Henderson (b. 1950)

Mel Wright

 Safiya Henderson-Holmes is currently Associate Professor of Creative Writing/Poetry at Syracuse University in New York. Her work has appeared in magazines and journals such as *Black Creations, Journal of New African Literature and Art, The Black Scholar, Essence, Women's News,* and in the anthologies *Confirmation* (1985) and *Art Against Apartheid* (1986).

Henderson received a B.A. degree in Physiotherapy from New York University, and for several years she worked as a physiotherapist in New York City hospitals. In 1982, she received an M.A. degree in Creative Writing from City College of New York. She has taught English at Touro College in Brooklyn, and poetry at Sarah Lawrence College in Bronxville, New York. In 1986, she served as United States Cultural Delegate at the World Peace Congress in Copenhagen.

Henderson is the recipient of two New York Foundation for the Arts fellowships. *Madness and a Bit of Hope* (1990), her first book of poetry, won the William Carlos Williams Award for Poetry from the Poetry Society of America. Henderson performs her poetry all over the world.

Before You Read

harlem/soweto

Using What You Know

You have seen that poets draw on the **denotative,** or literal, meanings of words and their **connotative,** or suggested, meanings. Poets also use **allusions,** or references, that call up specific associations. In this poem, the author uses place names that have particular significance for Africans and African Americans. Think, for example, of your associations with the name *Harlem* in the phrase "Harlem Renaissance." What other associations does the name call up? Consider how the poet draws on the ideas of community and identity in this poem.

Background

Zimbabwe is a country northeast of South Africa (see the map on page 74). *Bantustans,* a product of the former institution of apartheid, were territories set aside for black Africans. Soweto is a black township in South Africa. In 1976, police in Soweto brutally crushed a peaceful demonstration by black students. This event triggered uprisings around the country. In the United States, a number of violent protests took place in 1965. One of them, in Watts, Los Angeles, was suppressed by the National Guard.

Literary Focus: Theme

Theme is the underlying idea in a literary work. The theme of a work is not the same thing as its subject. The subject of a poem may be the experiences of black people in Africa and in the United States, but its theme will present some insight about those experiences.

Setting a Purpose

How does the title of the poem express its theme?

harlem / soweto

Safiya Henderson

zimbabwe
and we
are one

there is no separation

one stone hammered   5
by foreign hands
my sons have your physique
muscles pulled
taut
over of ice   10
and steel

here my wrist
there your hand

fingers knotted
around one stick   15

you say bantustans
we say harlem
you say soweto
we say watts
you sweat coal   20
we burn steel
you're locked on lands
we're locked indoors

my body smells of your nights
lips cracked with your hurt   25
one bruised back
no broken spirits

714 SAFIYA HENDERSON

we are woven
inseparable as sky
with one sun   30
    one moon
    one tongue
    rolled to spit
    in one
    eye . . .   35

Gold miners in Johannesburg,
South Africa, 1950.
Margaret Bourke-White,
Life Magazine © Time, Inc.

Responding to the Selection
harlem/soweto by Safiya Henderson

Interpreting Meanings

1. This poem expresses the idea of unity. What different **metaphors** in the poem draw comparisons between Africans and African Americans?
2. In line 5, the poet uses the word *stone* as a **metaphor** for the human body. To whom do the "foreign hands" belong? In what way has the stone been hammered?
3. What is the **implied metaphor** in lines 28–29?
4. How does the title of the poem express its theme?

Writing About Literature
Analyzing Tone
Tone is the attitude a writer takes toward a subject or audience. What feelings does the poet convey in "harlem/soweto"? In a paragraph, identify the tone and support your answer by referring to words and details in the poem. Be sure to account for the associated meanings as well as the literal meanings of words.

Speaking and Listening
Interpreting a Poem
Practice reading the poem aloud. Think about how the poet meant each line to be read. Will you use just one tone of voice in reading the poem, or will your tone vary? Ask a friend or a partner to listen to your reading before you present your interpretation to a group or to the class.

About the Author

Rita Dove (b. 1952)

 Rita Dove was born in Akron, Ohio, earned her B.A. at Miami University in Ohio, and went on to study in West Germany, on a grant from the International Working Period for Authors Fellowship for West Germany. She has lived and traveled in Israel and southern Europe. Dove has been called a quiet poet, one who is concerned with race issues but one who writes about many other subjects as well. She says, "Obviously, as a black woman, I am concerned with race. . . . But certainly not every poem of mine mentions the fact of being black. They are poems about humanity, and sometimes humanity happens to be black. I cannot run from, I *won't* run from any kind of truth."

She is well known for her collection of poems called *Thomas and Beulah* (1986), which present the story of her grandparents' lives. As Dove says, "It's not a dramatic story—nothing absolutely tragic happened in my grandparents' life. . . . But I think these are the people who often are ignored and lost." Other collections of her poems include *The Yellow House on the Corner* (1980), *Museum* (1983), *The Other Side of the House* (1988), and *Grace Notes* (1989). In her most recent collection, *Mother Love* (1995), Dove incorporates Greek mythology into her poetry. She has also written a collec-

Wide World Photos

tion of short stories called *Fifth Sunday* (1985) and a novel, *Through the Ivory Gate* (1992). Dove received the Pulitzer Prize for *Thomas and Beulah* in 1987.

In 1993 Rita Dove was named United States Poet Laureate. She was the first black poet to be named to the position and also the youngest to be chosen. She is now Commonwealth Professor of English at the University of Virginia.

Before You Read

Sisters

Using What You Know

People who keep photograph albums will often share these pictures with friends and relatives. Think of some of your favorite photographs. Which of them are particularly dear to you? What memories do these pictures call up?

Literary Focus: Dramatic Poetry

Some poems are like scenes in a play. The speaker is in a specific place, talking to someone whose presence is understood, even if he or she doesn't speak. These poems are called **dramatic poems**. Many **narrative poems** are also dramatic poems that contain dialogue between speakers. A special kind of dramatic poem is the **dramatic monologue** or **dramatic lyric**.

Setting a Purpose

What does the speaker reveal about herself and her relationship with her sister? What has evoked these memories?

Sisters

for Robin Dove Waynesboro

Rita Dove

This is the one we called
Bird of the Dead, Double Bird
Who Feeds on Carrion. Dark
with a red organdy dress
for her third birthday,   5
she cried and cried,
snap-eyed imp whose brow sprouted horns
whenever she screwed up her face.

Sisters, *lithograph by Ernest Crichlow.*   Cinque Gallery, New York City

"Buzzard!" we shrieked
and when that was forbidden: 10
"Schmawk Schmawk Bird!" after the local radio
personality. Several beatings later
the first literary effort appeared, a story
called "Blank the Buzzard,"
for which I claimed the First Amendment.   15
It was confiscated° and shredded.

I can't believe she's taller
than me now, that my smile
lines sag where her Indian cheekbones soar.
This is my home, my knothole   20
we're posing in front of. The palm tree
throws a boa° across our shoulders.
Light seals the cracks.

16. **confiscated** (kŏn′fĭs-kāt′ĕd) seized or taken away by authorities.

22. **boa** (bō′ə): a long, fluffy scarf made of fur, feathers, or other soft material.

Responding to the Selection
Sisters by Rita Dove

Interpreting Meanings

1. Which lines tell you that the speaker is looking at photographs? What do the photographs show?
2. What inference can you draw about the *we* in line 1?
3. How did the speaker taunt her sister when they were children? After she was punished, how did she continue to tease her sister?
4. The First Amendment of the Constitution protects freedom of speech. Why does the speaker claim the First Amendment for her "first literary effort"?
5. How have the speaker's feelings about her sister changed over the years? Is this change believable?
6. In lines 21–22, the palm tree doesn't throw an actual scarf over the women's shoulders. What does the **metaphor** mean?
7. In the last line of the poem, what might the light **symbolize**? What might the "cracks" that the light seals stand for?

Language and Vocabulary

Recognizing Connotative Meanings

We can create a favorable or unfavorable impression about someone by using words that are "emotionally loaded." For example, think of the difference between referring to someone as "weak" or "ineffective" and referring to that person as "a wimp." In the poem, the speaker calls her sister a number of names that have negative **connotations**. What are the connotations of the word *buzzard?* of *carrion?* of *imp?*

Create the opposite effect. Substitute words with positive connotations that would flatter and praise a small child.

Writer's Journal

Recalling a Relationship

Recall your relationship with someone in your family or a close friend. Imagine yourself, like the speaker in the poem, showing some treasured photographs to a spouse or to a friend. Tell which memories these photographs evoke.

The Author Comments

"Schmawk Schmawk Bird" has its origins in a local radio (in this case, Akron, Ohio) disc jockey's patter; the bird was his own creation and was characterized by its raucous cry. In the poem, however, the bird is simply a mythical bird created by the siblings—in order to taunt the younger sister. A nonsense bird with a visual and aural name ("Schmawk Schmawk Bird" sounds yucky, loud, and goofy) is more effective.

—Rita Dove

Writing a Poem

Constance Burts Jackson

Learning to write poetry in some ways is like learning to play a musical instrument. Like the aspiring musician, the young poet can improve through constant practice.

Do not worry about feeling awkward or uncomfortable when you first begin to write. This feeling will pass with practice. Just use your powers of observation and let your inspiration grow.

Choosing a Subject

1. Choose a subject that interests you.
2. Search through newspapers, pamphlets, and magazines for ideas.
3. Interview a relative as the subject of a poem.
4. Write a poem celebrating an event.
5. Write about an object that you value or fear.
6. Write about an animal.
7. Write about the birth or death of a loved one.
8. Write about a place you remember with strong emotions.

Choosing a Form

1. One short form for beginners is the **couplet**. A couplet consists of a pair of rhyming lines:

   Twilight drags its shadows over the countryside
   Creating quilted patches covering fields wide.

2. Another short form is the **quatrain**. A quatrain consists of four lines. Quatrains have different rhyme patterns. In this quatrain, the rhyme occurs in the second and fourth lines:

   Leaves dance on morning's breeze
   In meadows drenched with dew
   Water lily-pad clouds
   Wave sunrise into view.

3. Another form for beginners is **haiku** (hī′kōō). Haiku is a Japanese lyric form. The subject matter is usually drawn from nature. Haiku always presents a picture. No emotion is expressed,

but the reader is invited to react emotionally to the imagery. A haiku consists of seventeen syllables arranged in three lines. There are five syllables in the first line, seven syllables in the second, and five syllables in the third line.

Sullen clouds scudding
Across the Michigan sky
Burst into sad tears.

4. A **monometer** (mə-näməd′ər) is a line of verse consisting of one poetic foot. An **iambic** (ī-ăm′bĭk) foot follows the pattern of one unstressed and one stressed syllable, as in the word *rĕ port.* A **trochaic** (trō-kā′ĭk) foot follows the pattern of one stressed and one unstressed syllable, as in the word *réa sŏn.* A **dactylic** (dăk-tĭl′ĭk) foot has one stressed syllable followed by two unstressed syllables, as in the word *pó ĕ trў.* Monometer poems are easy to write. You may want to create an interesting visual form, as in this dactylic example:

Africa
    Dusty gem
        Sun painted

Suggestions for Writing

1. If you use a cliché in your poem (an overused phrase like "peaceful as a dove"), cross it out and replace it with something more original.
2. Use rhyme if you like, but don't let rhyme use you.
3. Do not overuse alliteration.
4. Use fresh, vivid language and sensory details.
5. Use figurative language.
6. Use precise verbs.
7. Avoid a monotonous or mechanical effect.
8. Do not use more words than are necessary.

▶I. Interpreting New Material

James Hinton

The following poem is by **Larry Neal** (1937–1981), who was a folklorist, playwright, film-maker, editor, and teacher as well as a poet. He was also an influential theorist, interpreter, and spokesperson of the Black Arts Movement. He and Amiri Baraka coedited *Black Fire: An Anthology of Afro-American Writing* in 1968.

A. Read the following poem carefully before answering the questions.

The Middle Passage and After
Larry Neal

Decked, stacked, pillaged from
their homes
packed bodies on bodies rock in the belly
of death.

sea blood, sea blood churns   5
production for the West's dying
machine; commodities for profit—
stuffed empires with spices;
moved history closer to our truth—
death's prophecy—in the sea their   10
screams and the salt smell on our
faces pressed against one another,
hands push stiffward, push for air
     room.

Our nightmares are tight compacted
whitenesses, smotherings of babies,   15
jammed into drunken limits.
our souls are open skies and children
zooming across green places;
open clearings, rhythms bursting
sea-shell prisons; are things heard   20
in between tropical blasts of wind;
are ancestor-wisdom making itself
known in every black face born or
     about to be.

1. The poem speaks about the inhuman, crowded conditions aboard the slave ships that carried African captives to the New World. How do the language and the compression of ideas help to convey the physical and emotional horrors of the voyage?
2. What is the ''ancestor-wisdom'' referred to in line 22?
3. What does the word *After* in the title mean?

4. Choose some of the most powerful words and phrases in the poem. Explain their meanings and the feelings they evoke.
5. According to this poem, what is the legacy of the middle passage?

B. Choose one of these assignments for a short essay.
1. Consider what you have learned about the middle passage in this textbook and elsewhere. How has this poem broadened your understanding of historical events?

2. Sometimes a work leaves you with the feeling that there is more to tell. Imagine that you are one of the following people on board the ship and write a passage in prose or in verse, giving your impressions of the voyage.

a captured African man, woman, or child
the ship's captain
a member of the crew

▶▶II. For Discussion _____

Which of the poems you have read in this unit or in other units of the anthology would you like to share with a close friend? Discuss your preferences with others in the class.

Determine the criteria you would use in putting together an anthology of favorite poems.

▶▶▶III. For Writing _____

Several poems in this unit deal with the subject of African American heritage. Some of these poems are "Runagate Runagate" (page 654), "High on the Hog" (page 690), "harlem/soweto" (page 714), and "The Middle Passage and After" (page 724). Choose one or more of these poems for analysis. If you wish, compare the works you have chosen with poems you have read in earlier units, such as "Song of the Son" (page 309), "A Black Man Talks of Reaping" (page 396), and "For My People" (page 442).

WRITER'S WORKSHOP 2

Interpretation (Expository Writing)

The Piano Lesson, *lithograph by Romare Bearden, 1984.*

Contemporary Drama

Ira Aldridge as Mingo, slave of a West Indian planter, in The Padlock, *1827.*
Research Center for the Performing Arts/New York Public Library at Lincoln Center

The Beginnings of African American Drama

In the early 1820s, a group of black actors under the direction of James Hewlett provided entertainment at the African Grove, a tea garden in lower Manhattan. They performed many of Shakespeare's plays, and Hewlett, a West Indian, became the first black performer to play the part of Othello. Previously, the role had been played only by white actors, despite the fact that this famous Shakespearean character is a black man. The African Grove lasted for only a few years, but it was the first attempt by African Americans at performing in traditional theater. The African Grove Theater was where Ira Aldridge got his start. Now famous in theater history, Aldridge performed throughout Europe, often before royalty, and received numerous honors for his work. He and Hewlett established the tradition of black actors playing the role of Othello.

The first African American to publish plays was William Wells Brown, an escaped slave who became a lecturer and abolitionist and also the first published black novelist. Brown wrote two anti-slavery plays, the second of which was published in 1858. They were never performed on stage; Brown read them aloud in lecture halls.

Despite these early attempts at working in legitimate theater, African Americans for a long time would find acceptance and success more in light entertainment than in serious drama, and would participate in the theater as actors rather than as playwrights. There was no demand by the American theater audience for realistic plays about the lives and concerns of African Americans, and success and fame were possible only in the musical comedy and variety shows of commercial theater.

Introduction 727

The Minstrel Show

From the 1840s until the turn of the century, the American stage was dominated by the minstrel show. Minstrelsy, the first truly American theater form, began on the Southern plantations, where groups of slave entertainers would sing, dance, play musical instruments, and perform comedy routines. These shows grew out of the African dramatic tradition, in which mime, dance, music, and storytelling had played important roles in community life.

In the early nineteenth century, white performers began to blacken their faces with burnt cork, paint their lips red or white, and imitate the slave performances. These minstrel shows developed into grotesque and offensive caricatures as time went on. The shows followed a formula that included a comedy routine, music and dancing, and short skits and plays. The formula grew stale and unimaginative after a number of years, but black entertainers, permitted on the minstrel stage after the Civil War, added freshness and vitality to the shows. They had to perform in the traditional blackface and to promote the demeaning stereotypes and caricatures (it was, as one writer put it, "an imitation of an imitation of plantation life"), but African Americans first gained professional stage experience on the minstrel stage.

The Development of Musical Comedy

Toward the end of the nineteenth century, black musicians, singers, and actors with backgrounds in minstrelsy wanted to gain more control of theater production and to break with the minstrel tradition. Working together to produce a new type of show, they developed the musical play. Bob Cole's *A Trip to Coontown* (1898) was the first musical comedy as well as the first show to be written, produced, directed, and managed by African Americans. Later that year came *Clorindy—The Origin of the Cakewalk,* with music by Will Marion Cook and lyrics by Paul Laurence Dunbar. *In Dahomey,* the first show by African Americans to open on Broadway, starred Bert Williams and George Walker, a popular comedy team who went on to produce other successful shows. Musical comedy by blacks reached its height in 1921 with *Shuffle Along,* a production by the team of Flourney E. Miller, Aubrey Lyles, Eubie Blake, and Noble Sissle. Tunes from this show became hits around the world. Musical plays by black writers would remain popular with theatergoers through the early 1940s.

The Crisis, *collage by Phoebe Beasley.* Crisis *magazine sponsored an annual playwriting contest.*
Collection of the artist

The Rise of Serious Drama

After the closing of the African Grove in the early 1820s, there were no theaters where African American playwrights and actors with an interest in serious drama could develop their craft, until early in the twentieth century. Then the rising black population in major cities around the country supported local community theaters. Black theater troupes were formed, such as the Pekin Players in Chicago and the Lafayette Theatre Stock Players and the Lincoln Theatre Troupe in Harlem. Their purpose was to perform serious drama, but they soon had to turn to musical plays and variety shows, which were in much greater demand.

Although overshadowed by the popular and commercially successful Broadway musicals, a number of serious plays by African Americans were written and performed from the early 1900s through the Harlem Renaissance of the 1920s. Black playwrights pursuing serious theater received encouragement from the NAACP (National Association for the Advancement of Colored People). W. E. B. Du Bois, the NAACP's Director of Publicity and Research, insisted that there should be a theater by, for, about, and near black people. *Crisis* magazine, which he edited, not only pro-

Charles Gilpin as the Emperor Jones.
The Schomburg Center for Research in Black Culture/New York Public Library

Paul Robeson as the Emperor Jones, 1933.
International Museum of Photography at George Eastman House. Bequest of Edward Steichen by direction of Joanna T. Steichen. Reprinted with permission of Joanna T. Steichen

vided a place for African American writers to publish their work, but also sponsored an annual playwriting contest. Many black playwrights received support from the NAACP's Drama Committee of Washington, D.C., which was responsible for the opening of many black theaters between 1910 and 1930.

One of the plays produced by the drama committee was Angelina Weld Grimké's *Rachel* (1916). A strong denunciation of lynching, it was highly praised as the first successful play by an African American. Some other important plays of the 1920s were *The Chip Woman's Fortune,* by Willis Richardson; *A Sunday Morning in the South,* by Georgia Douglas Johnson; *Appearances,* by Garland Anderson, which played briefly on Broadway; and *Harlem,* by Wallace Thurman and William Jourdan Rapp. In 1926, W. E. B. Du Bois organized the Krigwa Players to perform plays by and about African Americans. Their production of *The Fool's Errand,* by Eulalie Spence, won a prize in a theater tournament, and the group provided a model for other black theater groups.

Most major theater roles for black actors, however, were found in the work of white playwrights. Most were not true portrayals of the experience of African Americans, but they established the careers of many black actors. Charles Gilpin and Paul Robeson, for example, rose to fame in the plays of Eugene O'Neill.

The Federal Theater and Other Projects

During the late 1930s, aspiring black playwrights and actors found an outlet for their talent through the Federal Theater Project. The FTP was created in 1935 to provide work for theater people who were unemployed as a result of the Great Depression. At the suggestion of the popular actress Rose McClendon, separate black theater units were established in large cities throughout the country. One of the FTP's goals was to bring serious, realistic drama to the masses, which commercial theater had seldom done. A further purpose of the black units was to end discrimination in the theater and to ban the use of blackface.

The black theater units produced various types of shows—comedies, classics, historical plays, works of current white writers, and some original material. Critics were impressed with the high quality of most of the productions. The Chicago unit ran Theodore Ward's *Big White Fog,* which, like several other Federal Theater plays, dealt with such problems as discrimination, poverty, and unemployment. *Stevedore,* which played in Seattle and Boston,

(Left) *A scene from Hall Johnson's* Run Little Chillun, *1933.*
White Collection/Research Center for the Performing Arts/New York Public Library at Lincoln Center

(Top right) *A scene from Rudolph Fisher's* Conjur Man Dies, *at the Lafayette Theater.*
Research Center for the Performing Arts/New York Public Library at Lincoln Center

(Bottom right) *A scene from* Macbeth, *at the Lafayette Theater, 1936.*
Research Center for the Performing Arts/New York Public Library at Lincoln Center

was about united black and white dock workers. The Lafayette Theater in Harlem, the most successful of the black units, produced Hall Johnson's *Run Little Chillun,* Frank Wilson's *Brother Mose* and *Walk Together Chillun,* and Rudolph Fisher's *Conjur Man Dies.* The most spectacular production was an adaptation of Shakespeare's *Macbeth.* The setting was changed from Scotland to Haiti, and the show was a huge success. The Federal Theater Project, which might have brought significant progress to African American drama, was terminated in 1939 because its radical themes made some in Congress suspicious about ties with communism. During its brief life, however, it did provide a much-needed forum for black actors and playwrights. And many of the themes of the Federal

Introduction 731

A scene from Philip Yordan's **Anna Lucasta,** *1944.*
Fred Fehl/Research Center for the Performing Arts/New York Public Library at Lincoln Center

Theater plays would resurface in the socially and politically conscious black theater of the 1950s and 1960s.

During the late thirties, Langston Hughes had many of his plays produced by small theater groups that he established around the country. *Don't You Want to Be Free?* (1938) had a long run at his Harlem Suitcase Theater. *Mulatto* (1935) was the longest running Broadway play by a black writer until *A Raisin in the Sun* appeared in the late fifties.

In 1939, the American Negro Theater was established. It produced *On Striver's Row* and *Walk Hard* by Abram Hill, *Natural Man* (about John Brown) by Theodore Browne, and *The Garden of Time* by Owen Dodson. Its most successful endeavor, an adaptation of a play by the white playwright Philip Yordan called *Anna Lucasta,* ran for more than 900 performances on Broadway. The American Negro Theater began as an experimental theater, but by the middle of the 1940s it produced only "safe" plays by white writers, and was seen by aspiring actors as a step to Broadway.

New Attitudes

After World War II, black drama became confrontational, challenging the white establishment. Among the earliest plays exemplifying this new attitude were two works of social realism produced in

(Left) *A scene from Lorraine Hansberry's* A Raisin in the Sun, *1959.*
Friedman Abeles/Research Center for the Performing Arts/New York Public Library at Lincoln Center

(Right) *A scene from Ossie Davis's* Purlie Victorious, *1961.*
Friedman Abeles/Research Center for the Performing Arts/New York Public Library at Lincoln Center

the 1940s. One was an adaptation of Richard Wright's controversial novel *Native Son.* The other, Theodore Ward's *Our Lan'* (1947), which deals with the injustice suffered by slaves freed after the Civil War, parallels the experience of African American soldiers returning home after World War II.

During the 1950s, William Branch, Loften Mitchell, and Alice Childress saw their plays produced in small theaters in New York City. In *A Medal For Willie,* by Branch, a black mother whose son was killed in the Korean War criticizes the hypocrisy of the townspeople trying to honor him. Mitchell's *A Land Beyond the River* and Childress's *Trouble in Mind* deal with issues between whites and blacks.

Two commercially successful ventures took a milder approach. *A Raisin in the Sun,* by Lorraine Hansberry, which ran on Broadway and won the New York Drama Critics Circle Award in 1959, is about a black ghetto family looking for a better life. The comedy

Diana Sands as Juanita in James Baldwin's **Blues for Mr. Charlie**, *1964.*
Research Center for the Performing Arts/New York Public Library at Lincoln Center

Ntozake Shange, 1989.

(Below) *Amiri Baraka.*

Wide World Photos

Leandre Jackson

Purlie Victorious, by Ossie Davis, opened on Broadway in 1961. Davis uses satire and stereotypes to convey his message about the ridiculousness of racism and prejudice.

An attempt at bringing theater back to the people was the Free Southern Theater, established in 1963 in the impoverished Mississippi Delta region. This politically oriented theater sought not only to train theater people, but also to educate the audience. It began as an integrated theater, but soon adopted a separatist approach. In search of a dramatic form that could be considered truly black, it experimented successfully with staged poetry readings.

By the mid-1960s, a trend toward militancy and separatism had become widespread among African Americans. In the theater, this trend was emphasized in the work of such writers as James Baldwin and Amiri Baraka. Baldwin's *Blues for Mr. Charlie* is based on the killing of a young black man by white Southerners. The most radical change was brought about by Baraka (known until the late 1960s as LeRoi Jones). Like W. E. B. Du Bois, Baraka envisioned a theater that would be exclusively by and for black people. His work and philosophy were part of the Black Arts Movement of the sixties. Baraka received a great deal of attention for three off-Broadway plays produced between 1963 and 1964—*Dutchman,* which won an Obie Award, *The Toilet,* and *The Slave.*

New Directions

During the 1970s, there were more black musical plays on Broadway than at any time since the Harlem Renaissance. One serious play by an African American that made it to the Broadway stage was *For Colored Girls Who Have Considered Suicide/When the Rainbow Is Enuf.* Its writer, Ntozake Shange, whose style is experimental, calls it a "choreopoem."

Playwright Ed Bullins was among those writers influenced by Amiri Baraka. He got his start with the Black Arts Movement, and during the seventies he became a major figure in African American theater. Bullins uses nontraditional forms for a realistic portrayal of ghetto life. Ron Milner, another important voice in contemporary African American theater, writes about the black middle class. Other important plays by African Americans during these years include *Ceremonies in Dark Old Men,* by Lonne Elder III, and *No Place to Be Somebody,* by Charles Gordone, which received the 1970 Pulitzer Prize for drama.

Martha Swope © Time, Inc.

Bert Andrews

(Above) *A scene from Ntozake Shange's* **For Colored Girls Who Have Considered Suicide/ When the Rainbow Is Enuf,** *1976.*

(Below) *A scene from Charles Fuller's* **A Soldier's Play,** *1982.*

Current African American playwrights are turning to history as a source of inspiration. *The Brownsville Raid,* by Charles Fuller, is based on an event from the past. Fuller's *A Soldier's Play,* set at an army base in Louisiana during World War II, won the Pulitzer Prize for drama in 1982. August Wilson is writing a series of plays, one for each decade of the twentieth century. They are part of a trend in literature toward the celebration of the life and culture of African Americans.

Introduction   735

About the Author

August Wilson (b. 1945)

David Burnett/Woodfin Camp

 "All those awards, all that stuff, I take them and I hang them on my wall," says August Wilson. "But then I turn around, and my typewriter's sitting there, and it doesn't know from awards." Wilson, who finishes one play and doesn't get up until he has the idea for the next, has seen five of his plays produced on the Broadway stage: *Ma Rainey's Black Bottom, Fences, Joe Turner's Come and Gone, The Piano Lesson,* and *Seven Guitars.* Four of these plays have won the New York Drama Critics Circle Award for best new play. Two of the plays—*Fences* and *The Piano Lesson*—were awarded the Pulitzer Prize. In addition, Wilson received the Whit-

ing Writers Award for *Ma Rainey;* the American Theater Critics Play Award, the Tony Award, and the Outer Critics Circle Award for *Fences;* and the John Gassner Award for *Joe Turner.* In 1987, Wilson was named Artist of the Year by the *Chicago Tribune.*

Wilson grew up in Pittsburgh, Pennsylvania. He was reading by the age of five. He quit school at sixteen, and while working at menial jobs, wrote poems which were accepted by black publications at the University of Pittsburgh. While in his twenties, Wilson embraced the ideas of Malcolm X and Amiri Baraka. In 1968 he founded the Black Horizons Theatre Company in St. Paul, Minnesota.

Wilson began his writing career as a poet, but when his first play, *Jitney,* was accepted for production in 1982 at the O'Neill Theatre Center's National Playwrights Conference, he decided to pursue playwriting. A number of his plays have been developed at the O'Neill Conference and have premiered at the Yale Repertory Theater.

A self-proclaimed "cultural nationalist," Wilson uses theater to raise the consciousness of black people. Since the early 1980s, Wilson has been writing a series of plays about the lives of African Americans, incorporating elements of their history and culture. Each play is set in a different decade. *Ma Rainey's Black Bottom* takes place in the twenties. *Fences* is set in the fifties, *Joe Turner's Come and Gone* in 1911, *The Piano Lesson* in the thirties, and *Two Trains Running* in the sixties. Wilson's latest play, *Seven Guitars* (1996), is set in the forties.

Before You Read

Using What You Know

A *legacy* is something passed on from one generation to the next. Sometimes what is handed down becomes a source of conflict between family members. In "Everyday Use" (page 543), for example, the conflict centers on some quilts that connect the present generation with the past. Have you read any stories or watched any television shows where relatives quarrel over an inheritance? Do you know of any real-life examples?

Background

A work by Romare Bearden called *The Piano Lesson* (see page 726) provided the inspiration for this play. Wilson saw the woman in his play as a character trying to deny her past in order to gain a sense of self-worth. In all of his plays, Wilson stresses the importance of connecting with your past in order to understand your relation to society.

Literary Focus: Drama

Like other forms of creative writing, **drama** has such literary elements as **characterization, setting, theme,** and **plot.** Unlike the plot of a short story or a novel, however, the plot of a play is advanced chiefly by **dialogue,** the conversations held by the characters. **Stage directions** tell the actors how to move and how to deliver certain lines.

Setting a Purpose

Two very good arguments are developed in the play. As you read, consider the strong points for each argument. Are there also weaknesses?

The Piano Lesson

August Wilson

Seven members from the New York production of **The Piano Lesson,** *1990. From left: Tommy Hollis (Avery), Lisa Gay Hamilton (Grace), Lou Myers (Wining Boy), S. Epatha Merkerson (Berniece), Charles S. Dutton (Boy Willie), Carl Gordon (Doaker), Rocky Carroll (Lymon).*
All photos of stage production by Gerry Goodstein

THE SETTING

The action of the play takes place in the kitchen and parlor of the house where **Doaker Charles** lives with his niece, **Berniece,** and her eleven-year old daughter, **Maretha.** The house is sparsely furnished, and although there is evidence of a woman's touch, there is a lack of warmth and vigor. **Berniece** and **Maretha** occupy the upstairs rooms. **Doaker**'s room is prominent and opens onto the kitchen. Dominating the par-

lor is an old upright piano.[1] On the legs of the piano, carved in the manner of African sculpture, are mask-like figures resembling totems.[2] The carvings are rendered with a grace and power of invention that lifts them out of the realm of craftsmanship and into the realm of art. At left is a staircase leading to the upstairs.

1. **upright piano:** a piano with a vertical frame and strings, in contrast to a grand piano, which has a horizontal frame and strings.
2. **totems:** carved or painted emblems or symbols revered by a family or a clan.

ACT ONE

Scene 1

[*The lights come up on the Charles household. It is five o'clock in the morning. The dawn is beginning to announce itself, but there is something in the air that belongs to the night. A stillness that is a portent,[1] a gathering, a coming together of something akin to a storm. There is a loud knock at the door.*]

Boy Willie: (*off stage, calling*) Hey, Doaker . . . Doaker! (*He knocks again and calls.*) Hey, Doaker! Hey, Berniece! Berniece!

[DOAKER *enters from his room. He is a tall, thin man of forty-seven, with severe features, who has for all intents and purposes retired from the world though he works full-time as a railroad cook.*]

Doaker: Who is it?
Boy Willie: Open the door, nigger! It's me . . . Boy Willie!
Doaker: Who?
Boy Willie: Boy Willie! Open the door!

[DOAKER *opens the door and* BOY WILLIE *and* LYMON *enter.* BOY WILLIE *is thirty years old. He has an infectious grin and a boyishness that is apt for his name. He is brash and impulsive, talkative and somewhat crude in speech and manner.* LYMON *is twenty-nine.* BOY WILLIE*'s partner, he talks little, and then with a straightforwardness that is often disarming.*]

Doaker: What you doing up here?

---
1. **portent** (pôr′tĕnt′): omen or sign of something to come.

Boy Willie: I told you, Lymon. Lymon talking about you might be sleep. This is Lymon. You remember Lymon Jackson from down home? This my Uncle Doaker.
Doaker: What you doing up here? I couldn't figure out who that was. I thought you was still down in Mississippi.
Boy Willie: Me and Lymon selling watermelons. We got a truck out there. Got a whole truckload of watermelons. We brought them up here to sell. Where's Berniece? (*Calls.*) Hey, Berniece!
Doaker: Berniece up there sleep.
Boy Willie: Well, let her get up. (*Calls.*) Hey, Berniece!
Doaker: She got to go to work in the morning.
Boy Willie: Well she can get up and say hi. It's been three years since I seen her. (*Calls.*) Hey, Berniece! It's me . . . Boy Willie.
Doaker: Berniece don't like all that hollering now. She got to work in the morning.
Boy Willie: She can go on back to bed. Me and Lymon been riding two days in that truck . . . the least she can do is get up and say hi.
Doaker: (*looking out the window*) Where you all get that truck from?
Boy Willie: It's Lymon's. I told him let's get a load of watermelons and bring them up here.
Lymon: Boy Willie say he going back, but I'm gonna stay. See what it's like up here.
Boy Willie: You gonna carry me down there first.
Lymon: I told you I ain't going back down there and take a chance on that truck breaking down again. You can take the train. Hey, tell him Doaker, he can take the train back. After we sell them watermelons he have enough money he can buy him a whole railroad car.

Doaker: You got all them watermelons stacked up there no wonder the truck broke down. I'm surprised you made it this far with a load like that. Where you break down at?

Boy Willie: We broke down three times! It took us two and a half days to get here. It's a good thing we picked them watermelons fresh.

Lymon: The first time was just as soon as we got out of Sunflower.[2] About forty miles out she broke down. We got it going and got all the way to West Virginia before she broke down again.

Boy Willie: We had to walk about five miles for some water.

Lymon: It got a hole in the radiator but it runs pretty good. You have to pump the brakes sometime before they catch. Boy Willie have his door open and be ready to jump when that happens.

Boy Willie: Lymon think that's funny. I told the nigger I give him ten dollars to get the brakes fixed. But he thinks that funny.

Lymon: They don't need fixing. All you got to do is pump them till they catch.

[BERNIECE *enters on the stairs. Thirty-five years old, with an eleven-year-old daughter, she is still in mourning for her husband after three years.*]

Berniece: What you doing all that hollering for?

Boy Willie: Hey, Berniece. Doaker said you was sleep. I said at least you could get up and say hi.

Berniece: It's five o'clock in the morning and you come in here with all this noise. You can't come like normal folks. You got to bring all that noise with you.

Boy Willie: Hell, I ain't done nothing but come in and say hi. I ain't got in the house good.

Berniece: That's what I'm talking about. You start all that hollering and carry on as soon as you hit the door.

Boy Willie: Aw hell, woman, I was glad to see Doaker. You ain't had to come down if you didn't want to. I come eighteen hundred miles to see my sister I figure she might want to get up and say hi. Other than that you can go back upstairs. What you got, Doaker? Where your bottle? Me and Lymon want a drink. (*to* BERNIECE) This is Lymon. You remember Lymon Jackson from down home.

Lymon: How you doing, Berniece. You look just like I thought you looked.

Berniece: Why you all got to come in hollering and carrying on? Waking the neighbors with all that noise.

Boy Willie: They can come over and join the party. We fixing to have a party. Doaker, where your bottle? Me and Lymon celebrating. The Ghosts of the Yellow Dog[3] got Sutter.

Berniece: Say what?

Boy Willie: Ask Lymon, they found him the next morning. Say he drowned in his well.

Doaker: When this happen, Boy Willie?

Boy Willie: About three weeks ago. Me and Lymon was over in Stoner County when we heard about it. We laughed. We thought it was funny. A great big old three-hundred-and-forty-pound man gonna fall down his well.

Lymon: It remind me of Humpty Dumpty.

Boy Willie: Everybody say the Ghosts of the Yellow Dog pushed him.

Berniece: I don't want to hear that nonsense. Somebody down there pushing them people in their wells.

2. **Sunflower:** a county in western Mississippi.

3. **Yellow Dog:** a popular name for the Yazoo Delta railroad. It is used in many blues songs [*Author's note*].

Doaker: What was you and Lymon doing over in Stoner County?

Boy Willie: We was down there working. Lymon got some people down there.

Lymon: My cousin got some land down there. We was helping him.

Boy Willie: Got near about a hundred acres. He got it set up real nice. Me and Lymon was down there chopping down trees. We was using Lymon's truck to haul the wood. Me and Lymon used to haul wood all around them parts. (*to* BERNIECE) Me and Lymon got a truckload of watermelons out there.

[BERNIECE *crosses to the window in the parlor.*]

Doaker, where your bottle? I know you got a bottle stuck up in your room. Come on, me and Lymon want a drink.

[DOAKER *exits into his room.*]

Berniece: Where you all get that truck from?

Boy Willie: I told you it's Lymon's.

Berniece: Where you get the truck from, Lymon?

Lymon: I bought it.

Berniece: Where he get that truck from, Boy Willie?

Boy Willie: He told you he bought it. Bought it for a hundred and twenty dollars. I can't say where he got that hundred and twenty dollars from . . . but he bought that old piece of truck from Henry Porter. (*to* LYMON) Where you get that hundred and twenty dollars from, nigger?

Lymon: I got it like you get yours. I know how to take care of money.

[DOAKER *brings a bottle and sets it on the table.*]

Boy Willie: Aw hell, Doaker got some of that good whiskey. Don't give Lymon none of that. He ain't used to good whiskey. He liable to get sick.

The Piano Lesson   Act One   741

Lymon: I done had good whiskey before.

Boy Willie: Lymon bought that truck so he have him a place to sleep. He down there wasn't doing no work or nothing. Sheriff looking for him. He bought that truck to keep away from the sheriff. Got Stovall looking for him too. He down there sleeping in that truck ducking and dodging both of them. I told him come on let's go up and see my sister.

Berniece: What the sheriff looking for you for, Lymon?

Boy Willie: The man don't want you to know all his business. He's my company. He ain't asking you no questions.

Lymon: It wasn't nothing. It was just a misunderstanding.

Berniece: He in my house. You say the sheriff looking for him, I wanna know what he looking for him for. Otherwise you all can go back out there and be where nobody don't have to ask you nothing.

Lymon: It was just a misunderstanding. Sometimes me and the sheriff we don't think alike. So we just got crossed on each other.

Berniece: Might be looking for him about that truck. He might have stole that truck.

Boy Willie: We ain't stole no truck, woman. I told you Lymon bought it.

Doaker: Boy Willie and Lymon got more sense than to ride all the way up here in a stolen truck with a load of watermelons. Now they might have stole them watermelons, but I don't believe they stole that truck.

Boy Willie: You don't even know the man good and you calling him a thief. And we ain't stole them watermelons either. Them old man Pitterford's watermelons. He give me and Lymon all we could load for ten dollars.

Doaker: No wonder you got them stacked up out there. You must have five hundred wa-

termelons stacked up out there.

Berniece: Boy Willie, when you and Lymon planning on going back?

Boy Willie: Lymon say he staying. As soon as we sell them watermelons I'm going on back.

Berniece: *(starts to exit up the stairs)* That's what you need to do. And you need to do it quick. Come in here disrupting the house. I don't want all that loud carrying on around here. I'm surprised you ain't woke Maretha up.

Boy Willie: I was fixing to get her now. *(Calls.)* Hey, Maretha!

Doaker: Berniece don't like all that hollering now.

Berniece: Don't you wake that child up!

Boy Willie: You going up there . . . wake her up and tell her her uncle's here. I ain't seen her in three years. Wake her up and send her down here. She can go back to bed.

Berniece: I ain't waking that child up . . . and don't you be making all that noise. You and Lymon need to sell them watermelons and go on back.

[BERNIECE *exits up the stairs.*]

Boy Willie: I see Berniece still try to be stuck up.

Doaker: Berniece alright. She don't want you making all that noise. Maretha up there sleep. Let her sleep until she get up. She can see you then.

Boy Willie: I ain't thinking about Berniece. You hear from Wining Boy? You know Cleotha died?

Doaker: Yeah, I heard that. He come by here about a year ago. Had a whole sack of money. He stayed here about two weeks. Ain't offered nothing. Berniece asked him for three dollars to buy some food and he got mad and left.

Lymon: Who's Wining Boy?

Boy Willie: That's my uncle. That's Doaker's

brother. You heard me talk about Wining Boy. He play piano. He done made some records and everything. He still doing that, Doaker?

Doaker: He made one or two records a long time ago. That's the only ones I ever known him to make. If you let him tell it he a big recording star.

Boy Willie: He stopped down home about two years ago. That's what I hear. I don't know. Me and Lymon was up on Parchman Farm[4] doing them three years.

Doaker: He don't never stay in one place. Now, he been here about eight months ago. Back in the winter. Now, you subject not to see him for another two years. It's liable to be that long before he stop by.

Boy Willie: If he had a whole sack of money you liable never to see him. You ain't gonna see him until he get broke. Just as soon as that sack of money is gone you look up and he be on your doorstep.

Lymon: (*noticing the piano*) Is that the piano?

Boy Willie: Yeah . . . look here, Lymon. See how it's carved up real nice and polished and everything? You never find you another piano like that.

Lymon: Yeah, that look real nice.

Boy Willie: I told you. See how it's polished? My mama used to polish it every day. See all them pictures carved on it? That's what I was talking about. You can get a nice price for that piano.

Lymon: That's all Boy Willie talked about the whole trip up here. I got tired of hearing him talk about the piano.

Boy Willie: All you want to talk about is women. You ought to hear this nigger, Doaker. Talking about all the women he

gonna get when he get up here. He ain't had none down there but he gonna get a hundred when he get up here.

Doaker: How your people doing down there, Lymon?

Lymon: They alright. They still there. I come up here to see what it's like up here. Boy Willie trying to get me to go back and farm with him.

Boy Willie: Sutter's brother selling the land. He say he gonna sell it to me. That's why I come up here. I got one part of it. Sell them watermelons and get me another part. Get Berniece to sell that piano and I'll have the third part.

Doaker: Berniece ain't gonna sell that piano.

Boy Willie: I'm gonna talk to her. When she see I got a chance to get Sutter's land she'll come around.

Doaker: You can put that thought out your mind. Berniece ain't gonna sell that piano.

Boy Willie: I'm gonna talk to her. She been playing on it?

Doaker: You know she won't touch that piano. I ain't never known her to touch it since Mama Ola died. That's over seven years now. She say it got blood on it. She got Maretha playing on it though. Say Maretha can go on and do everything she can't do. Got her in an extra school down at the Irene Kaufman Settlement House. She want Maretha to grow up and be a schoolteacher. Say she good enough she can teach on the piano.

Boy Willie: Maretha don't need to be playing on no piano. She can play on the guitar.

Doaker: How much land Sutter got left?

Boy Willie: Got a hundred acres. Good land. He done sold it piece by piece, he kept the good part for himself. Now he got to give that up. His brother come down from Chicago for the funeral . . . he up there in Chicago got

4. **Parchman Farm:** a state penitentiary in Mississippi.

some kind of business with soda fountain equipment. He anxious to sell the land, Doaker. He don't want to be bothered with it. He called me to him and said cause of how long our families done known each other and how we been good friends and all, say he wanted to sell the land to me. Say he'd rather see me with it than Jim Stovall. Told me he'd let me have it for two thousand dollars cash money. He don't know I found out the most Stovall would give him for it was fifteen hundred dollars. He trying to get that extra five hundred out of me telling me he doing me a favor. I thanked him just as nice. Told him what a good man Sutter was and how he had my sympathy and all. Told him to give me two weeks. He said he'd wait on me. That's why I come up here. Sell them watermelons. Get Berniece to sell that piano. Put them two parts with the part I done saved. Walk in there. Tip my hat. Lay my money down on the table. Get my deed[5] and walk on out. This time I get to keep all the cotton. Hire me some men to work it for me. Gin my cotton. Get my seed. And I'll see you again next year. Might even plant some tobacco or some oats.

Doaker: You gonna have a hard time trying to get Berniece to sell that piano. You know Avery Brown from down there don't you? He up here now. He followed Berniece up here trying to get her to marry him after Crawley got killed. He been up here about two years. He call himself a preacher now.

Boy Willie: I know Avery. I know him from when he used to work on the Willshaw place. Lymon know him too.

Doaker: He after Berniece to marry him. She keep telling him no but he won't give up. He keep pressing her on it.

5. **deed:** a legal document showing property ownership.

Boy Willie: Avery think all white men is bigshots. He don't know there some white men ain't got as much as he got.

Doaker: He supposed to come past here this morning. Berniece going down to the bank with him to see if he can get a loan to start his church. That's why I know Berniece ain't gonna sell that piano. He tried to get her to sell it to help him start his church. Sent the man around and everything.

Boy Willie: What man?

Doaker: Some white fellow was going around to all the colored people's houses looking to buy up musical instruments. He'd buy anything. Drums. Guitars. Harmonicas. Pianos. Avery sent him past here. He looked at the piano and got excited. Offered her a nice price. She turned him down and got on Avery for sending him past. The man kept on her about two weeks. He seen where she wasn't gonna sell it, he gave her his number and told her if she ever wanted to sell it to call him first. Say he'd go one better than what anybody else would give her for it.

Boy Willie: How much he offer her for it?

Doaker: Now you know me. She didn't say and I didn't ask. I just know it was a nice price.

Lymon: All you got to do is find out who he is and tell him somebody else wanna buy it from you. Tell him you can't make up your mind who to sell it to, and if he like Doaker say, he'll give you anything you want for it.

Boy Willie: That's what I'm gonna do. I'm gonna find out who he is from Avery.

Doaker: It ain't gonna do you no good. Berniece ain't gonna sell that piano.

Boy Willie: She ain't got to sell it. I'm gonna sell it. I own just as much of it as she does.

Berniece: (offstage, hollers) Doaker! Go on get away. Doaker!

Doaker: (calling) Berniece?

[DOAKER *and* BOY WILLIE *rush to the stairs,* BOY WILLIE *runs up the stairs, passing* BERNIECE *as she enters, running.*]

Doaker: Berniece, what's the matter? You alright? What's the matter?

[BERNIECE *tries to catch her breath. She is unable to speak.*]

Doaker: That's alright. Take your time. You alright. What's the matter? (*He calls.*) Hey, Boy Willie?

Boy Willie: (*offstage*) Ain't nobody up here.

Berniece: Sutter . . . Sutter's standing at the top of the steps.

Doaker: (*Calls.*) Boy Willie!

[LYMON *crosses to the stairs and looks up.* BOY WILLIE *enters from the stairs.*]

Boy Willie: Hey Doaker, what's wrong with her? Berniece, what's wrong? Who was you talking to?

Doaker: She say she seen Sutter's ghost standing at the top of the stairs.

Boy Willie: Seen what? Sutter? She ain't seen no Sutter.

Berniece: He was standing right up there.

Boy Willie: (*entering on the stairs*) That's all in Berniece's head. Ain't nobody up there. Go on up there, Doaker.

Doaker: I'll take your word for it. Berniece talking about what she seen. She say Sutter's ghost standing at the top of the steps. She ain't just make all that up.

Boy Willie: She up there dreaming. She ain't seen no ghost.

Lymon: You want a glass of water, Berniece? Get her a glass of water, Boy Willie.

Boy Willie: She don't need no water. She ain't seen nothing. Go on up there and look. Ain't nobody up there but Maretha.

Doaker: Let Berniece tell it.

Boy Willie: I ain't stopping her from telling it.

Doaker: What happened, Berniece?

Berniece: I come out my room to come back down here and Sutter was standing there in the hall.

Boy Willie: What he look like?

Berniece: He look like Sutter. He look like he always look.

Boy Willie: Sutter couldn't find his way from Big Sandy to Little Sandy.[6] How he gonna find his way all the way up here to Pittsburgh? Sutter ain't never even heard of Pittsburgh.

Doaker: Go on, Berniece.

Berniece: Just standing there with the blue suit on.

Boy Willie: The man ain't never left Marlin County when he was living . . . and he's gonna come all the way up here now that he's dead?

Doaker: Let her finish. I want to hear what she got to say.

Boy Willie: I'll tell you this. If Berniece had seen him like she think she seen him she'd still be running.

Doaker: Go on, Berniece. Don't pay Boy Willie no mind.

Berniece: He was standing there . . . had his hand on top of his head. Look like he might have thought if he took his hand down his head might have fallen off.

Lymon: Did he have on a hat?

Berniece: Just had on that blue suit . . . I told him to go away and he just stood there looking at me . . . calling Boy Willie's name.

Boy Willie: What he calling my name for?

Berniece: I believe you pushed him in the well.

Boy Willie: Now what kind of sense that

6. **Big Sandy to Little Sandy:** rivers in Kentucky that empty into the Ohio River.

The Piano Lesson   Act One   745

make? You telling me I'm gonna go out there and hide in the weeds with all them dogs and things he got around there . . . I'm gonna hide and wait till I catch him looking down his well just right . . . then I'm gonna run over and push him in. A great big old three-hundred-and-forty-pound man.

Berniece: Well, what he calling your name for?

Boy Willie: He bending over looking down his well, woman . . . how he know who pushed him? It could have been anybody. Where was you when Sutter fell in his well? Where was Doaker? Me and Lymon was over in Stoner County. Tell her, Lymon. The Ghosts of the Yellow Dog got Sutter. That's what happened to him.

Berniece: You can talk all that Ghosts of the Yellow Dog stuff if you want. I know better.

Lymon: The Ghosts of the Yellow Dog pushed him. That's what the people say. They found him in his well and all the people say it must be the Ghosts of the Yellow Dog. Just like all them other men.

Boy Willie: Come talking about he looking for me. What he come all the way up here for? If he looking for me all he got to do is wait. He could have saved himself a trip if he looking for me. That ain't nothing but in Berniece's head. Ain't no telling what she liable to come up with next.

Berniece: Boy Willie, I want you and Lymon to go ahead and leave my house. Just go on somewhere. You don't do nothing but bring trouble with you everywhere you go. If it wasn't for you Crawley would still be alive.

Boy Willie: Crawley what? I ain't had nothing to do with Crawley getting killed. Crawley three time seven. He had his own mind.

Berniece: Just go on and leave. Let Sutter go somewhere else looking for you.

Boy Willie: I'm leaving. Soon as we sell them watermelons. Other than that I ain't going nowhere. Hell, I just got here. Talking about Sutter looking for me. Sutter was looking for that piano. That's what he was looking for. He had to die to find out where that piano was at . . . If I was you I'd get rid of it. That's the way to get rid of Sutter's ghost. Get rid of that piano.

Berniece: I want you and Lymon to go on and take all this confusion out of my house!

Boy Willie: Hey, tell her, Doaker. What kind of sense that make? I told you, Lymon, as soon as Berniece see me she was gonna start something. Didn't I tell you that? Now she done made up that story about Sutter just so she could tell me to leave her house. Well, hell, I ain't going nowhere till I sell them watermelons.

Berniece: Well, why don't you go out there and sell them! Sell them and go on back!

Boy Willie: We waiting till the people get up.

Lymon: Boy Willie say if you get out there too early and wake the people up they get mad at you and won't buy nothing from you.

Doaker: You won't be waiting long. You done let the sun catch up with you. This the time everybody be getting up around here.

Berniece: Come on, Doaker, walk up here with me. Let me get Maretha up and get her started. I got to get ready myself. Boy Willie, just go on out there and sell them watermelons and you and Lymon leave my house.

[BERNIECE *and* DOAKER *exit up the stairs.*]

Boy Willie: (*calling after them*) If you see Sutter up there . . . tell him I'm down here waiting on him.

Lymon: What if she see him again?

Boy Willie: That's all in her head. There ain't no ghost up there. (*Calls.*) Hey, Doaker . . . I told you ain't nothing up there.

Lymon: I'm glad he didn't say he was looking for me.

Boy Willie: I wish I would see Sutter's ghost. Give me a chance to put a whupping on him.

Lymon: You ought to stay up here with me. You be down there working his land . . . he might come looking for you all the time.

Boy Willie: I ain't thinking about Sutter. And I ain't thinking about staying up here. You stay up here. I'm going back and get Sutter's land. You think you ain't got to work up here. You think this the land of milk and honey. But I ain't scared of work. I'm going back and farm every acre of that land.

[DOAKER *enters from the stairs.*]

I told you there ain't nothing up there, Doaker. Berniece dreaming all that.

Doaker: I believe Berniece seen something. Berniece level-headed. She ain't just made all that up. She say Sutter had on a suit. I don't believe she ever seen Sutter in a suit. I believe that's what he was buried in, and that's what Berniece saw.

Boy Willie: Well, let her keep on seeing him then. As long as he don't mess with me.

[DOAKER *starts to cook his breakfast.*]

I heard about you, Doaker. They say you got all the women looking out for you down home. They be looking to see you coming. Say you got a different one every two weeks. Say they be fighting one another for you to stay with them. (*to* LYMON) Look at him, Lymon. He know it's true.

Doaker: I ain't thinking about no women. They never get me tied up with them. After Coreen I ain't got no use for them. I stay up on Jack Slattery's place when I be down there. All them women want is somebody with a steady payday.

Boy Willie: That ain't what I hear. I hear every two weeks the women all put on their dresses and line up at the railroad station.

Doaker: I don't get down there but once a month. I used to go down there every two weeks but they keep switching me around. They keep switching all the fellows around.

Boy Willie: Doaker can't turn that railroad loose. He was working the railroad when I was walking around crying. My mama used to brag on him.

Doaker: I'm cooking now, but I used to line track. I pieced together the Yellow Dog stitch by stitch. Rail by rail. Line track all up around there. I lined track all up around Sunflower and Clarksdale.[7] Wining Boy worked with me. He helped put in some of that track. He'd work it for six months and quit. Go back to playing piano and gambling.

Boy Willie: How long you been with the railroad now?

Doaker: Twenty-seven years. Now, I'll tell you something about the railroad. What I done learned after twenty-seven years. See, you got North. You got West. You look over here you got South. Over there you got East. Now, you can start from anywhere. Don't care where you at. You got to go one of them four ways. And whichever way you decide to go they got a railroad that will take you there. Now, that's something simple. You think anybody would be able to understand that. But you'd be surprised how many people trying to go North get on a train going West. They think the train's supposed to go where they going rather than where it's going.

Now, why people going? Their sister's sick. They leaving before they kill somebody . . . and they sitting across from somebody who's leaving to keep from getting killed. They leaving cause they can't get satisfied. They going to meet someone. I wish I had a dollar for every time that someone wasn't at the station to meet them. I done seen that a lot. In between the time they sent the telegram and the time the person get there . . . they done forgot all about them.

They got so many trains out there they have a hard time keeping them from running into each other. Got trains going every whichaway. Got people on all of them. Somebody going where somebody just left. If everybody stay in one place I believe this would be a better world. Now what I done learned after twenty-seven years of railroading is this . . . if the train stays on the track . . . it's going to get where it's going. It might not be where you going. If it ain't, then all you got to do is sit and wait cause the train's coming back to get you. The train don't never stop. It'll come back every time. Now I'll tell you another thing . . .

Boy Willie: What you cooking over there, Doaker? Me and Lymon's hungry.

Doaker: Go on down there to Wylie and Kirkpatrick to Eddie's restaurant. Coffee cost a nickel and you can get two eggs, sausage, and grits for fifteen cents. He even give you a biscuit with it.

Boy Willie: That look good what you got. Give me a little piece of that grilled bread.

Doaker: Here . . . go on take the whole piece.

Boy Willie: Here you go, Lymon . . . you want a piece?

[*He gives* LYMON *a piece of toast.* MARETHA *enters from the stairs.*]

Boy Willie: Hey, sugar. Come here and give me a hug. Come on give Uncle Boy Willie a hug. Don't be shy. Look at her, Doaker. She done got bigger. Ain't she got big?

Doaker: Yeah, she getting up there.

Boy Willie: How you doing, sugar?

---

7. **Clarksdale:** a city in northwest Mississippi, a trade and shopping center for cotton.

Maretha: Fine.

Boy Willie: You was just a little old thing last time I seen you. You remember me, don't you? This your Uncle Boy Willie from down South. That there's Lymon. He my friend. We come up here to sell watermelons. You like watermelons?

[MARETHA *nods.*]

We got a whole truckload out front. You can have as many as you want. What you been doing?

Maretha: Nothing.

Boy Willie: Don't be shy now. Look at you getting all big. How old is you?

Maretha: Eleven. I'm gonna be twelve soon.

Boy Willie: You like it up here? You like the North?

Maretha: It's alright.

Boy Willie: That there's Lymon. Did you say hi to Lymon?

Maretha: Hi.

Lymon: How you doing? You look just like your mama. I remember you when you was wearing diapers.

Boy Willie: You gonna come down South and see me? Uncle Boy Willie gonna get him a farm. Gonna get a great big old farm. Come down there and I'll teach you how to ride a mule. Teach you how to kill a chicken, too.

Maretha: I seen my mama do that.

Boy Willie: Ain't nothing to it. You just grab him by his neck and twist it. Get you a real good grip and then you just wring his neck and throw him in the pot. Cook him up. Then you got some good eating. What you like to eat? What kind of food you like?

Maretha: I like everything . . . except I don't like no black-eyed peas.

Boy Willie: Uncle Doaker tell me your mama got you playing the piano. Come on play something for me.

[BOY WILLIE *crosses over to the piano followed by* MARETHA.]

Show me what you can do. Come on now. Here . . . Uncle Boy Willie give you a dime . . . show me what you can do. Don't be bashful now. That dime say you can't be bashful.

[MARETHA *plays. It is something any beginner first learns.*]

Here, let me show you something.

[BOY WILLIE *sits and plays a simple boogie-woogie.*[8]]

See that? See what I'm doing? That's what you call the boogie-woogie. See now . . . you can get up and dance to that. That's how good it sound. It sound like you wanna dance. You can dance to that. It'll hold you up. Whatever kind of dance you wanna do you can dance to that right there. See that? See how it go? Ain't nothing to it. Go on you do it.

Maretha: I got to read it on the paper.

Boy Willie: You don't need no paper. Go on. Do just like that there.

Berniece: Maretha! You get up here and get ready to go so you be on time. Ain't no need you trying to take advantage of company.

Maretha: I got to go.

Boy Willie: Uncle Boy Willie gonna get you a guitar. Let Uncle Doaker teach you how to play that. You don't need to read no paper to play the guitar. Your mama told you about that piano? You know how them pictures got on there?

Maretha: She say it just always been like that since she got it.

Boy Willie: You hear that, Doaker? And you

---

8. *boogie-woogie:* a style of playing jazz on the piano in which there is a repeated pattern of rhythm and melody in the bass.

sitting up here in the house with Berniece.

Doaker: I ain't got nothing to do with that. I don't get in the way of Berniece's raising her.

Boy Willie: You tell your mama to tell you about that piano. You ask her how them pictures got on there. If she don't tell you I'll tell you.

Berniece: Maretha!

Maretha: I got to get ready to go.

Boy Willie: She getting big, Doaker. You remember her, Lymon?

Lymon: She used to be real little.

[*There is a knock on the door.* DOAKER *goes to answer it.* AVERY *enters. Thirty-eight years old, honest and ambitious, he has taken to the city like a fish to water, finding in it opportunities for growth and advancement that did not exist for him in the rural South. He is dressed in a suit and tie with a gold cross around his neck. He carries a small Bible.*]

Doaker: Hey, Avery, come on in. Berniece upstairs.

Boy Willie: Look at him . . . look at him . . . he don't know what to say. He wasn't expecting to see me.

Avery: Hey, Boy Willie. What you doing up here?

Boy Willie: Look at him, Lymon.

Avery: Is that Lymon? Lymon Jackson?

Boy Willie: Yeah, you know Lymon.

Doaker: Berniece be ready in a minute, Avery.

Boy Willie: Doaker say you a preacher now. What . . . we supposed to call you Reverend? You used to be plain old Avery. When you get to be a preacher, nigger?

Lymon: Avery say he gonna be a preacher so he don't have to work.

Boy Willie: I remember when you was down there on the Willshaw place planting cotton.

You wasn't thinking about no Reverend then.

Avery: That must be your truck out there. I saw that truck with them watermelons, I was trying to figure out what it was doing in front of the house.

Boy Willie: Yeah, me and Lymon selling watermelons. That's Lymon's truck.

Doaker: Berniece say you all going down to the bank.

Avery: Yeah, they give me a half day off work. I got an appointment to talk to the bank about getting a loan to start my church.

Boy Willie: Lymon say preachers don't have to work. Where you working at, nigger?

Doaker: Avery got him one of them good jobs. He working at one of them skyscrapers downtown.

Avery: I'm working down there at the Gulf Building running an elevator. Got a pension and everything. They even give you a turkey on Thanksgiving.

750 AUGUST WILSON

Lymon: How you know the rope ain't gonna break? Ain't you scared the rope's gonna break?

Avery: That's steel. They got steel cables hold it up. It take a whole lot of breaking to break that steel. Naw, I ain't worried about nothing like that. It ain't nothing but a little old elevator. Now, I wouldn't get in none of them airplanes. You couldn't pay me to do nothing like that.

Lymon: That be fun. I'd rather do that than ride in one of them elevators.

Boy Willie: How many of them watermelons you wanna buy?

Avery: I thought you was gonna give me one seeing as how you got a whole truck full.

Boy Willie: You can get one, get two. I'll give you two for a dollar.

Avery: I can't eat but one. How much are they?

Boy Willie: Aw, nigger, you know I'll give you a watermelon. Go on, take as many as you want. Just leave some for me and Lymon to sell.

Avery: I don't want but one.

Boy Willie: How you get to be a preacher, Avery? I might want to be a preacher one day. Have everybody call me Reverend Boy Willie.

Avery: It come to me in a dream. God called me and told me he wanted me to be a shepherd for his flock. That's what I'm gonna call my church . . . The Good Shepherd Church of God in Christ.

Doaker: Tell him what you told me. Tell him about the three hobos.

Avery: Boy Willie don't want to hear all that.

Lymon: I do. Lots of people say your dreams can come true.

Avery: Naw. You don't want to hear all that.

Doaker: Go on. I told him you was a preacher. He didn't want to believe me. Tell him about the three hobos.

Avery: Well, it come to me in a dream. See . . . I was sitting out in this railroad yard watching the trains go by. The train stopped and these three hobos got off. They told me they had come from Nazareth and was on their way to Jerusalem. They had three candles. They gave me one and told me to light it . . . but to be careful that it didn't go out. Next thing I knew I was standing in front of this house. Something told me to go knock on the door. This old woman opened the door and said they had been waiting on me. Then she led me into this room. It was a big room and it was full of all kinds of different people. They looked like anybody else except they all had sheep heads and was making noise like sheep make. I heard somebody call my name. I looked around and there was these same three hobos. They told me to take off my clothes and they give me a blue robe with gold thread. They washed my feet and combed my hair. Then they showed me these three doors and told me to pick one.

I went through one of them doors and that flame leapt off that candle and it seemed like my whole head caught fire. I looked around and there was four or five other men standing there with these same blue robes on. Then we heard a voice tell us to look out across this valley. We looked out and saw the valley was full of wolves. The voice told us that these sheep people that I had seen in the other room had to go over to the other side of this valley and somebody had to take them. Then I heard another voice say, "Who shall I send?" Next thing I knew I said, "Here I am. Send me." That's when I met Jesus. He say, "If you go, I'll go with you." Something told me to say, "Come on. Let's go." That's when I woke up. My head still felt like it was on fire . . . but I had a peace about myself that was hard to explain. I knew right then that I had been filled with the Holy Ghost and called to be a servant of the Lord. It took me a while before I could accept that. But then a lot of little ways God showed me that it was true. So I became a preacher.

Lymon: I see why you gonna call it the Good Shepherd Church. You dreaming about them sheep people. I can see that easy.

Boy Willie: Doaker say you sent some white man past the house to look at that piano. Say he was going around to all the colored people's houses looking to buy up musical instruments.

Avery: Yeah, but Berniece didn't want to sell that piano. After she told me about it . . . I could see why she didn't want to sell it.

Boy Willie: What's this man's name?

Avery: Oh, that's a while back now. I done forgot his name. He gave Berniece a card with his name and telephone number on it, but I believe she throwed it away.

[BERNIECE *and* MARETHA *enter from the stairs.*]

Berniece: Maretha, run back upstairs and get my pocketbook. And wipe that hair grease off your forehead. Go ahead, hurry up.

[MARETHA *exits up the stairs.*]

How you doing, Avery? You done got all dressed up. You look nice. Boy Willie, I thought you and Lymon was going to sell them watermelons.

Boy Willie: Lymon done got sleepy. We liable to get some sleep first.

Lymon: I ain't sleepy.

Doaker: As many watermelons as you got stacked up on that truck out there, you ought to have been gone.

Boy Willie: We gonna go in a minute. We going.

Berniece: Doaker. I'm gonna stop down there on Logan Street. You want anything?

Doaker: You can pick up some ham hocks if you going down there. See if you can get the smoked ones. If they ain't got that get the fresh ones. Don't get the ones that got all that fat under the skin. Look for the long ones. They nice and lean. (*He gives her a dollar.*) Don't get the short ones lessen they smoked. If you got to get the fresh ones make sure that they the long ones. If they ain't got them smoked then go ahead and get the short ones. (*Pause*). You may as well get some turnip greens while you down there. I got some buttermilk . . . if you pick up some cornmeal I'll make me some cornbread and cook up them turnip greens.

[MARETHA *enters from the stairs.*]

Maretha: We gonna take the streetcar?[9]

Berniece: Me and Avery gonna drop you off at the settlement house. You mind them people down there. Don't be going down there showing your color. Boy Willie, I done told you what to do. I'll see you later, Doaker.

Avery: I'll be seeing you again, Boy Willie.

Boy Willie: Hey, Berniece . . . what's the name of that man Avery sent past say he want to buy the piano?

Berniece: I knew it. I knew it when I first seen you. I knew you was up to something.

Boy Willie: Sutter's brother say he selling the land to me. He waiting on me now. Told me he'd give me two weeks. I got one part. Sell them watermelons get me another part. Then we can sell that piano and I'll have the third part.

___

9. **streetcar:** a trolley, an electric passenger car that runs on rails set into the street.

Berniece: I ain't selling that piano, Boy Willie. If that's why you come up here you can just forget about it. *(to* DOAKER*)* Doaker, I'll see you later. Boy Willie ain't nothing but a whole lot of mouth. I ain't paying him no mind. If he come up here thinking he gonna sell that piano then he done come up here for nothing.

[BERNIECE, AVERY, *and* MARETHA *exit the front door.*]

Boy Willie: Hey, Lymon! You ready to go sell these watermelons.

[BOY WILLIE *and* LYMON *start to exit. At the door* BOY WILLIE *turns to* DOAKER.]

Hey, Doaker . . . if Berniece don't want to sell that piano . . . I'm gonna cut it in half and go on and sell my half.

[BOY WILLIE *and* LYMON *exit.*]

[*The lights go down on the scene.*]

Scene 2

[*The lights come up on the kitchen. It is three days later.* WINING BOY *sits at the kitchen table. There is a half-empty pint bottle on the table.* DOAKER *busies himself washing pots.* WINING BOY *is fifty-six years old.* DOAKER*'s older brother, he tries to present the image of a successful musician and gambler, but his music, his clothes, and even his manner of presentation are old. He is a man who looking back over his life continues to live it with an odd mixture of zest and sorrow.*]

Wining Boy: So the Ghosts of the Yellow Dog got Sutter. That just go to show you I believe I always lived right. They say every dog gonna have his day and time it go around it sure come back to you. I done seen that a thousand times. I know the truth of that. But I'll tell you outright . . . if I see Sutter's ghost I'll be on the first thing I find that got wheels on it.

Doaker: Wining Boy!

Wining Boy: And I'll tell you another thing . . . Berniece ain't gonna sell that piano.

Doaker: That's what she told him. He say he gonna cut it in half and go on and sell his half. They been around here three days trying to sell them watermelons. They trying to get out to where the white folks live but the truck keep breaking down. They go a block or two and it break down again. They trying to get out to Squirrel Hill and can't get around the corner. He say soon as he can get that truck empty to where he can set the piano up in there he gonna take it out of here and go sell it.

Wining Boy: What about them boys Sutter got? How come they ain't farming that land?

Doaker: One of them going to school. He left down there and come North to school. The other one ain't got as much sense as that frying pan over yonder. That is the dumbest white man I ever seen. He'd stand in the river and watch it rise till it drown him.

Wining Boy: Other than seeing Sutter's ghost how's Berniece doing?

Doaker: She doing alright. She still got Crawley on her mind. He been dead three years but she still holding on to him.

[*Pause.*]

Wining Boy: You know Cleotha died.

Doaker: Yeah, I heard that last time I was down there. I was sorry to hear that.

Wining Boy: One of her friends wrote and told me. I got the letter right here. (*He takes the letter out of his pocket.*) I was down in Kansas City and she wrote and told me Cleotha had died. Name of Willa Bryant. She say she know cousin Rupert. (*He opens the letter and reads.*) Dear Wining Boy: I am writing this letter to let you know Miss Cleotha Holman passed on Saturday the first of May she departed this world in the loving arms of her sister Miss Alberta Samuels. I know you would want to know this and am writing as a friend of Cleotha. There have been many hardships since last you seen her but she survived them all and to the end was a good woman whom I hope have God's grace and is in His Paradise. Your cousin Rupert Bates is my friend also and he give me your address and I pray this reaches you about Cleotha. Miss Willa Bryant. A friend.

(*He folds the letter and returns it to his pocket.*) They was nailing her coffin shut by the time I heard about it. I never knew she was sick. I believe it was that yellow jaundice.[1] That's what killed her mama.

Doaker: Cleotha wasn't but forty-some.

Wining Boy: She was forty-six. I got ten years on her. I met her when she was sixteen. You remember I used to run around there. Couldn't nothing keep me still. Much as I loved Cleotha I loved to ramble. Couldn't nothing keep me still. We got married and we used to fight about it all the time. Then one day she asked me to leave. Told me she loved me before I left. Told me, Wining Boy, you got a home as long as I got mine. And I believe in my heart I always felt that and that kept me safe.

Doaker: Cleotha always did have a nice way about her.

Wining Boy: Man, that woman was something. I used to thank the Lord. Many a night I sat up and looked out over my life. Said, well, I had Cleotha. When it didn't look like there was nothing else for me, I said, thank God, at least I had that. If ever I go anywhere in this life I done known a good woman. And that used to hold me till the next morning. (*Pause.*) What you got? Give me a little nip. I know you got something stuck up in your room.

Doaker: I ain't seen you walk in here and put nothing on the table. You done sat there and drank up your whiskey. Now you talking about what you got.

Wining Boy: I got plenty money. Give me a little nip.

[DOAKER *carries a glass into his room and returns with it half-filled. He sets it on the table in front of* WINING BOY.]

---

1. **jaundice** (jôn′dĭs): a disease affecting the liver.

[*The door opens and* BOY WILLIE *and* LYMON *enter.*]

Boy Willie: Aw hell . . . look here! We was just talking about you. Doaker say you left out of here with a whole sack of money. I told him we wasn't going to see you till you got broke.

Wining Boy: What you mean broke? I got a whole pocketful of money.

Doaker: Did you all get that truck fixed?

Boy Willie: We got it running and got halfway out there on Centre and it broke down again. Lymon went out there and messed it up some more. Fellow told us we got to wait till tomorrow to get it fixed. Say he have it running like new. Lymon going back down there and sleep in the truck so the people don't take the watermelons.

Lymon: Lymon nothing. You go down there and sleep in it.

Boy Willie: You was sleeping in it down home, nigger! I don't know nothing about sleeping in no truck.

Lymon: I ain't sleeping in no truck.

Boy Willie: They can take all the watermelons. I don't care. Wining Boy, where you coming from? Where you been?

Wining Boy: I been down in Kansas City.

Boy Willie: You remember Lymon? Lymon Jackson.

Wining Boy: Yeah, I used to know his daddy.

Boy Willie: Doaker say you don't never leave no address with nobody. Say he got to depend on your whim. See when it strike you to pay a visit.

Wining Boy: I got four or five addresses.

Boy Willie: Doaker say Berniece asked you for three dollars and you got mad and left.

Wining Boy: Berniece try and rule over you too much for me. That's why I left. It wasn't about no three dollars.

Boy Willie: Where you getting all these sacks of money from? I need to be with you. Doaker say you had a whole sack of money . . . turn some of it loose.

Wining Boy: I was just fixing to ask you for five dollars.

Boy Willie: I ain't got no money. I'm trying to get some. Doaker tell you about Sutter? The Ghosts of the Yellow Dog got him about three weeks ago. Berniece done seen his ghost and everything. He right upstairs. (*Calls.*) Hey Sutter! Wining Boy's here. Come on, get a drink!

Wining Boy: How many that make the Ghosts of the Yellow Dog done got?

Boy Willie: Must be about nine or ten, eleven or twelve. I don't know.

Doaker: You got Ed Saunders. Howard Peterson. Charlie Webb.

Wining Boy: Robert Smith. That fellow that shot Becky's boy . . . say he was stealing peaches . . .

Doaker: You talking about Bob Mallory.

Boy Willie: Berniece say she don't believe all that about the Ghosts of the Yellow Dog.

Wining Boy: She ain't got to believe. You go ask them white folks in Sunflower County if they believe. You go ask Sutter if he believe. I don't care if Berniece believe or not. I done been to where the Southern[2] cross the Yellow Dog and called out their names. They talk back to you, too.

Lymon: What they sound like? The wind or something?

Boy Willie: You done been there for real, Wining Boy?

Wining Boy: Nineteen thirty. July of nineteen thirty I stood right there on that spot. It didn't look like nothing was going right in my life. I said everything can't go wrong all the

2. **Southern:** a railroad.

time . . . let me go down there and call on the Ghosts of the Yellow Dog, see if they can help me. I went down there and right there where them two railroads cross each other . . . I stood right there on that spot and called out their names. They talk back to you, too.

Lymon: People say you can ask them questions. They talk to you like that?

Wining Boy: A lot of things you got to find out on your own. I can't say how they talked to nobody else. But to me it just filled me up in a strange sort of way to be standing there on that spot. I didn't want to leave. It felt like the longer I stood there the bigger I got. I seen the train coming and it seem like I was bigger than the train. I started not to move. But something told me to go ahead and get on out the way. The train passed and I started to go back up there and stand some more. But something told me not to do it. I walked away from there feeling like a king. Went on and had a stroke of luck that run on for three years. So I don't care if Berniece believe or not. Berniece ain't got to believe. I know cause I been there. Now Doaker'll tell you about the Ghosts of the Yellow Dog.

Doaker: I don't try and talk that stuff with Berniece. Avery got her all tied up in that church. She just think it's a whole lot of nonsense.

Boy Willie: Berniece don't believe in nothing. She just think she believe. She believe in anything if it's convenient for her to believe. But when that convenience run out then she ain't got nothing to stand on.

Wining Boy: Let's not get on Berniece now. Doaker tell me you talking about selling that piano.

Boy Willie: Yeah . . . hey, Doaker, I got the name of that man Avery was talking about. The man what's fixing the truck gave me his name. Everybody know him. Say he buy up anything you can make music with. I got his name and his telephone number. Hey, Wining Boy, Sutter's brother say he selling the land to me. I got one part. Sell them watermelons get me the second part. Then . . . soon as I get them watermelons out that truck I'm gonna take and sell that piano and get the third part.

Doaker: That land ain't worth nothing no more. The smart white man's up here in these cities. He cut the land loose and step back and watch you and the dumb white man argue over it.

Wining Boy: How you know Sutter's brother ain't sold it already? You talking about selling the piano and the man's liable to sold the land two or three times.

Boy Willie: He say he waiting on me. He say he give me two weeks. That's two weeks from Friday. Say if I ain't back by then he might gonna sell it to somebody else. He say he wanna see me with it.

Wining Boy: You know as well as I know the man gonna sell the land to the first one walk up and hand him the money.

Boy Willie: That's just who I'm gonna be. Look, you ain't gotta know he waiting on me. I know. Okay. I know what the man told me. Stovall already done tried to buy the land from him and he told him no. The man say he waiting on me . . . he waiting on me. Hey, Doaker . . . give me a drink. I see Wining Boy got his glass.

[DOAKER *exits into his room.*]

Wining Boy, what you doing in Kansas City? What they got down there?

Lymon: I hear they got some nice-looking women in Kansas City. I sure like to go down there and find out.

Wining Boy: Man, the women down there is something else.

[DOAKER *enters with a bottle of whiskey. He sets it on the table with some glasses.*]

Doaker: You wanna sit up here and drink up my whiskey, leave a dollar on the table when you get up.

Boy Willie: You ain't doing nothing but showing your hospitality. I know we ain't got to pay for your hospitality.

Wining Boy: Doaker say they had you and Lymon down on the Parchman Farm. Had you on my old stomping grounds.[3]

Boy Willie: Me and Lymon was down there hauling wood for Jim Miller and keeping us a little bit to sell. Some white fellows tried to run us off of it. That's when Crawley got killed. They put me and Lymon in the penitentiary.

Lymon: They ambushed us right there where that road dip down and around that bend in the creek. Crawley tried to fight them. Me and Boy Willie got away but the sheriff got us. Say we was stealing wood. They shot me in my stomach.

Boy Willie: They looking for Lymon down there now. They rounded him up and put him in jail for not working.

Lymon: Fined me a hundred dollars. Mr. Stovall come and paid my hundred dollars and the judge say I got to work for him to pay him back his hundred dollars. I told them I'd rather take my thirty days but they wouldn't let me do that.

Boy Willie: As soon as Stovall turned his back, Lymon was gone. He down there living in that truck dodging the sheriff and Stovall. He got both of them looking for him. So I brought him up here.

3. **stomping grounds:** a place where a person spends a great deal of time.

Lymon: I told Boy Willie I'm gonna stay up here. I ain't going back with him.

Boy Willie: Ain't nobody twisting your arm to make you go back. You can do what you want to do.

Wining Boy: I'll go back with you. I'm on my way down there. You gonna take the train? I'm gonna take the train.

Lymon: They treat you better up here.

Boy Willie: I ain't worried about nobody mistreating me. They treat you like you let them treat you. They mistreat me I mistreat them right back. Ain't no difference in me and the white man.

Wining Boy: Ain't no difference as far as how somebody supposed to treat you. I agree with that. But I'll tell you the difference between the colored man and the white man. Alright. Now you take and eat some berries. They taste real good to you. So you say I'm gonna go out and get me a whole pot of these berries and cook them up to make a pie or whatever. But you ain't looked to see them berries is sitting in the white fellow's yard. Ain't got no fence around them. You figure anybody want something they'd fence it in. Alright. Now the white man come along and say that's my land. Therefore everything that grow on it belong to me. He tell the sheriff, "I want you to put this nigger in jail as a warning to all the other niggers. Otherwise first thing you know these niggers have everything that belong to us."

Boy Willie: I'd come back at night and haul off his whole patch while he was sleep.

Wining Boy: Alright. Now Mr. So and So, he sell the land to you. And he come to you and say, "John, you own the land. It's all yours now. But them is my berries. And come time to pick them I'm gonna send my boys over. You got the land . . . but them berries, I'm gonna keep them. They mine." And he go and fix it with the law that them is his berries. Now that's the difference between the colored man and the white man. The colored man can't fix nothing with the law.

Boy Willie: I don't go by what the law say. The law's liable to say anything. I go by if it's right or not. It don't matter to me what the law say. I take and look at it for myself.

Lymon: That's why you gonna end up back down there on the Parchman Farm.

Boy Willie: I ain't thinking about no Parchman Farm. You liable to go back before me.

Lymon: They work you too hard down there. All that weeding and hoeing and chopping down trees. I didn't like all that.

Wining Boy: You ain't got to like your job on Parchman. Hey, tell him, Doaker, the only one got to like his job is the waterboy.

Doaker: If he don't like his job he need to set that bucket down.

Boy Willie: That's what they told Lymon. They had Lymon on water and everybody got mad at him cause he was lazy.

Lymon: That water was heavy.

Boy Willie: They had Lymon down there singing: *(Sings.)*

O Lord Berta Berta O Lord gal oh-ah
O Lord Berta Berta O Lord gal well

[LYMON *and* WINING BOY *join in.*]

Go 'head marry don't you wait on me
    oh-ah
Go 'head marry don't you wait on me
    well
Might not want you when I go free oh-ah
Might not want you when I go free well

Boy Willie: Come on, Doaker. Doaker know this one.

[As DOAKER *joins in the men stamp and clap*

to keep time. They sing in harmony with great fervor and style.]

O Lord Berta Berta O Lord gal oh-ah
O Lord Berta Berta O Lord gal well

Raise them up higher, let them drop on
    down oh-ah
Raise them up higher, let them drop on
    down well
Don't know the difference when the sun
    go down oh-ah
Don't know the difference when the sun
    go down well

Berta in Meridan and she living at ease
    oh-ah
Berta in Meridan and she living at ease
    well
I'm on old Parchman, got to work or
    leave oh-ah
I'm on old Parchman, got to work or
    leave well

O Alberta, Berta, O Lord gal oh-ah
O Alberta, Berta, O Lord gal well

When you marry, don't marry no farming
    man oh-ah
When you marry, don't marry no farming
    man well
Everyday Monday, hoe handle in your
    hand oh-ah
Everyday Monday, hoe handle in your
    hand well

When you marry, marry a railroad man,
    oh-ah
When you marry, marry a railroad man,
    well
Everyday Sunday, dollar in your hand
    oh-ah
Everyday Sunday, dollar in your hand
    well

O Alberta, Berta, O Lord gal oh-ah
O Alberta, Berta, O Lord gal well

Boy Willie: Doaker like that part. He like that railroad part.

Lymon: Doaker sound like Tangleye.[4] He can't sing a lick.

Boy Willie: Hey, Doaker, they still talk about you down on Parchman. They ask me, "You Doaker Boy's nephew?" I say, "Yeah, me and him is family." They treated me alright soon as I told them that. Say, "Yeah, he my uncle."

Doaker: I don't never want to see none of them niggers no more.

Boy Willie: I don't want to see them either. Hey, Wining Boy, come on play some piano. You a piano player, play some piano. Lymon wanna hear you.

Wining Boy: I give that piano up. That was the best thing that ever happened to me, getting rid of that piano. That piano got so big and I'm carrying it around on my back. I don't wish that on nobody. See, you think it's all fun being a recording star. Got to carrying that piano around and man did I get slow. Got just like molasses. The world just slipping by me and I'm walking around with that piano. Alright. Now, there ain't but so many places you can go. Only so many road wide enough for you and that piano. And that piano get heavier and heavier. Go to a place and they find out you play piano, the first thing they want to do is give you a drink, find you a piano, and sit you right down. And that's where you gonna be for the next eight hours. They ain't gonna let you get up! Now, the first three or four years of that is fun. You can't get enough whiskey and you can't get enough women and you don't never get tired

of playing that piano. But that only last so long. You look up one day and you hate the whiskey, and you hate the women, and you hate the piano. But that's all you got. You can't do nothing else. All you know how to do is play that piano. Now, who am I? Am I me? Or am I the piano player? Sometime it seem like the only thing to do is shoot the piano player cause he the cause of all the trouble I'm having.

Doaker: What you gonna do when your troubles get like mine?

Lymon: If I knew how to play it, I'd play it. That's a nice piano.

Boy Willie: Whoever playing better play quick. Sutter's brother say he waiting on me. I sell them watermelons. Get Berniece to sell that piano. Put them two parts with the part I done saved . . .

Wining Boy: Berniece ain't gonna sell that piano. I don't see why you don't know that.

Boy Willie: What she gonna do with it? She ain't doing nothing but letting it sit up there and rot. That piano ain't doing nobody no good.

Lymon: That's a nice piano. If I had it I'd sell it. Unless I knew how to play like Wining Boy. You can get a nice price for that piano.

Doaker: Now I'm gonna tell you something, Lymon don't know this . . . but I'm gonna tell you why me and Wining Boy say Berniece ain't gonna sell that piano.

Boy Willie: She ain't got to sell it! I'm gonna sell it! Berniece ain't got no more rights to that piano than I do.

Doaker: I'm talking to the man . . . let me talk to the man. See, now . . . to understand why we say that . . . to understand about that piano . . . you got to go back to slavery time. See, our family was owned by a fellow named Robert Sutter. That was Sutter's grandfather. Alright. The piano was owned

---

4. **Tangleye:** the nickname of an actual prisoner on Parchman Farm in the 1930s [*Author's note*].

by a fellow named Joel Nolander. He was one of the Nolander brothers from down in Georgia. It was coming up on Sutter's wedding anniversary and he was looking to buy his wife . . . Miss Ophelia was her name . . . he was looking to buy her an anniversary present. Only thing with him . . . he ain't had no money. But he had some niggers. So he asked Mr. Nolander to see if maybe he could trade off some of his niggers for that piano. Told him he would give him one and a half niggers for it. That's the way he told him. Say he could have one full grown and one half grown. Mr. Nolander agreed only he say he had to pick them. He didn't want Sutter to give him just any old nigger. He say he wanted to have the pick of the litter. So Sutter lined up his niggers and Mr. Nolander looked them over and out of the whole bunch he picked my grandmother . . . her name was Berniece . . . same like Berniece . . . and he picked my daddy when he wasn't nothing but a little boy nine years old. They made the trade off and Miss Ophelia was so happy with that piano that it got to be just about all she would do was play on that piano.

Wining Boy: Just get up in the morning, get all dressed up and sit down and play on that piano.

Doaker: Alright. Time go along. Miss Ophelia got to missing my grandmother . . . the way she would cook and clean the house and talk to her and what not. And she missed having my daddy around the house to fetch things for her. So she asked to see if maybe she could trade back that piano and get her niggers back. Mr. Nolander said no. Said a deal was a deal. Him and Sutter had a big falling out about it and Miss Ophelia took sick to the bed. Wouldn't get out of the bed in the morning. She just lay there. The doc-tor said she was wasting away.

Wining Boy: That's when Sutter called our granddaddy up to the house.

Doaker: Now, our granddaddy's name was Boy Willie. That's who Boy Willie's named after . . . only they called him Willie Boy. Now, he was a worker of wood. He could make you anything you wanted out of wood. He'd make you a desk. A table. A lamp. Anything you wanted. Them white fellows around there used to come up to Mr. Sutter and get him to make all kinds of things for them. Then they'd pay Mr. Sutter a nice price. See, everything my granddaddy made Mr. Sutter owned cause he owned him. That's why when Mr. Nolander offered to buy him to keep the family together Mr. Sutter wouldn't sell him. Told Mr. Nolander he didn't have enough money to buy him. Now . . . am I telling it right, Wining Boy?

Wining Boy: You telling it.

Doaker: Sutter called him up to the house and told him to carve my grandmother and my daddy's picture on the piano for Miss Ophelia. And he took and carved this . . . (DOAKER *crosses over to the piano.*) See that right there? That's my grandmother, Berniece. She looked just like that. And he put a picture of my daddy when he wasn't nothing but a little boy the way he remembered him. He made them up out of his memory. Only thing . . . he didn't stop there. He carved all this. He got a picture of his mama . . . Mama Esther . . . and his daddy, Boy Charles.

Wining Boy: That was the first Boy Charles.

Doaker: Then he put on the side here all kinds of things. See that? That's when him and Mama Berniece got married. They called it jumping the broom. That's how you got married in them days. Then he got here when my daddy was born . . . and here he got Mama Esther's funeral . . . and down here he got Mr. Nolander taking Mama Berniece and my daddy away down to his place in Georgia. He got all kinds of things what happened with our family. When Mr. Sutter seen the piano with all them carvings on it he got mad. He didn't ask for all that. But see . . . there wasn't nothing he could do about it. When Miss Ophelia seen it . . . she got excited. Now she had her piano and her niggers too. She took back to playing it and played on it right up till the day she died. Alright . . . now see, our brother Boy Charles . . . that's Berniece and Boy Willie's daddy . . . he was the oldest of us three boys. He's dead now. But he would have been fifty-seven if he had lived. He died in 1911 when he was thirty-one years old. Boy Charles used to talk about that piano all the time. He never could get it off his mind. Two or three months go by and he be talking about it again. He be talking about taking it out of Sutter's house. Say it was the story of our whole family and as long as Sutter had it . . . he had us. Say we was still in slavery. Me and Wining Boy tried to talk him out of it but it wouldn't do any good. Soon as he quiet down about it he'd start up again. We seen where he wasn't gonna get it off his mind . . . so, on the Fourth of July, 1911 . . . when Sutter was at the picnic what the county give every year . . . me and Wining Boy went on down there with him and took that piano out of Sutter's house. We put it on a wagon and me and Wining Boy carried it over into the next county with Mama Ola's people. Boy Charles decided to stay around there and wait until Sutter got home to make it look like business as usual.

Now, I don't know what happened when Sutter came home and found that piano gone. But somebody went up to Boy Charles's house and set it on fire. But he

wasn't in there. He must have seen them coming cause he went down and caught the 3:57 Yellow Dog. He didn't know they was gonna come down and stop the train. Stopped the train and found Boy Charles in the boxcar with four of them hobos. Must have got mad when they couldn't find the piano cause they set the boxcar afire and killed everybody. Now, nobody know who done that. Some people say it was Sutter cause it was his piano. Some people say it was Sheriff Carter. Some people say it was Robert Smith and Ed Saunders. But don't nobody know for sure. It was about two months after that that Ed Saunders fell down his well. Just upped and fell down his well for no reason. People say it was the ghost of them men who burned up in the boxcar that pushed him in his well. They started calling them the Ghosts of the Yellow Dog. Now, that's how all that got started and that why we say Berniece ain't gonna sell that piano. Cause her daddy died over it.

Boy Willie: All that's in the past. If my daddy had seen where he could have traded that piano in for some land of his own, it wouldn't be sitting up here now. He spent his whole life farming on somebody else's land. I ain't gonna do that. See, he couldn't do no better. When he come along he ain't had nothing he could build on. His daddy ain't had nothing to give him. The only thing my daddy had to give me was that piano. And he died over giving me that. I ain't gonna let it sit up there and rot without trying to do something with it. If Berniece can't see that, then I'm gonna go ahead and sell my half. And you and Wining Boy know I'm right.

Doaker: Ain't nobody said nothing about who's right and who's wrong. I was just telling the man about the piano. I was telling him why we say Berniece ain't gonna sell it.

Lymon: Yeah, I can see why you say that now. I told Boy Willie he ought to stay up here with me.

Boy Willie: You stay! I'm going back! That's what I'm gonna do with my life! Why I got to come up here and learn to do something I don't know how to do when I already know how to farm? You stay up here and make your own way if that's what you want to do. I'm going back and live my life the way I want to live it.

[WINING BOY *gets up and crosses to the piano.*]

Wining Boy: Let's see what we got here. I ain't played on this thing for a while.

Doaker: You can stop telling that. You was playing on it the last time you was through here. We couldn't get you off of it. Go on and play something.

[WINING BOY *sits down at the piano and plays and sings. The song is one which has put many dimes and quarters in his pocket, long ago, in dimly remembered towns and way stations.[5] He plays badly, without hesitation, and sings in a forceful voice.*]

Wining Boy: (*singing*)
I am a rambling gambling man
I gambled in many towns
I rambled this wide world over
I rambled this world around
I had my ups and downs in life
And bitter times I saw
But I never knew what misery was
Till I lit on old Arkansas.

I started out one morning
to meet that early train
He said, "You better work for me
I have some land to drain.
I'll give you fifty cents a day,
Your washing, board and all
And you shall be a different man
In the state of Arkansas."

I worked six months for the rascal
Joe Herrin was his name
He fed me old corn dodgers[6]
They was hard as any rock
My tooth is all got loosened

---

5. *way stations:* intermediate stations between main stations.
6. **corn dodgers:** cakes made of cornmeal.

And my knees begin to knock
That was the kind of hash I got
In the state of Arkansas.

Traveling man
I've traveled all around this world
Traveling man
I've traveled from land to land
Traveling man
I've traveled all around this world
Well it ain't no use
writing no news
I'm a traveling man.

[*The door opens and* BERNIECE *enters with* MARETHA.]

Berniece: Is that . . . Lord, I know that ain't Wining boy sitting there.

Wining Boy: Hey, Berniece.

Berniece: You all had this planned. You and Boy Willie had this planned.

Wining Boy: I didn't know he was gonna be here. I'm on my way down home. I stopped by to see you and Doaker first.

Doaker: I told the nigger he left out of here with that sack of money, we thought we might never see him again. Boy Willie say we wasn't gonna see him till he got broke. I looked up and seen him sitting on the door-step asking for two dollars. Look at him laughing. He know it's the truth.

Berniece: Boy Willie, I didn't see that truck out there. I thought you was out selling watermelons.

Boy Willie: We done sold them all. Sold the truck too.

Berniece: I don't want to go through none of your stuff. I done told you to go back where you belong.

Boy Willie: I was just teasing you, woman. You can't take no teasing?

Berniece: Wining Boy, when you get here?

Wining Boy: A little while ago. I took the train from Kansas City.

Berniece: Let me go upstairs and change and then I'll cook you something to eat.

Boy Willie: You ain't cooked me nothing when I come.

Berniece: Boy Willie, go on and leave me alone. Come on, Maretha, get up here and change your clothes before you get them dirty.

[BERNIECE *exits up the stairs, followed by* MARETHA.]

Wining Boy: Maretha sure getting big, ain't she, Doaker. And just as pretty as she want to be. I didn't know Crawley had it in him.

[BOY WILLIE *crosses to the piano.*]

Boy Willie: Hey, Lymon . . . get up on the other side of this piano and let me see something.

Wining Boy: Boy Willie, what is you doing?

Boy Willie: I'm seeing how heavy this piano is. Get up over there, Lymon.

Wining Boy: Go on and leave that piano alone. You ain't taking that piano out of here and selling it.

Boy Willie: Just as soon as I get them watermelons out that truck.

Wining Boy: Well, I got something to say about that.

Boy Willie: This my daddy's piano.

Wining Boy: He ain't took it by himself. Me and Doaker helped him.

Boy Willie: He died by himself. Where was you and Doaker at then? Don't come telling me nothing about this piano. This is me and Berniece's piano. Am I right, Doaker?

Doaker: Yeah, you right.

Boy Willie: Let's see if we can lift it up, Lymon. Get a good grip on it and pick it up on your end. Ready? Lift!

The Piano Lesson   Act One   763

[*As they start to move the piano, the sound of* SUTTER'S GHOST *is heard.* DOAKER *is the only one to hear it. With difficulty they move the piano a little bit so it is out of place.*]

Boy Willie: What you think?
Lymon: It's heavy . . . but you can move it. Only it ain't gonna be easy.
Boy Willie: It wasn't that heavy to me. Okay, let's put it back.

[*The sound of* SUTTER'S GHOST *is heard again. They all hear it as* BERNIECE *enters on the stairs.*]

Berniece: Boy Willie . . . you gonna play around with me one too many times. And then God's gonna bless you and West is gonna dress you. Now set that piano back over there. I done told you a hundred times I ain't selling that piano.
Boy Willie: I'm trying to get me some land, woman. I need that piano to get me some money so I can buy Sutter's land.
Berniece: Money can't buy what that piano cost. You can't sell your soul for money. It won't go with the buyer. It'll shrivel and shrink to know that you ain't taken on to it. But it won't go with the buyer.
Boy Willie: I ain't talking about all that, woman. I ain't talking about selling my soul. I'm talking about trading that piece of wood for some land. Get something under your feet. Land the only thing God ain't making no more of. You can always get you another piano. I'm talking about some land. What you get something out the ground from. That's what I'm talking about. You can't do nothing with that piano but sit up there and look at it.
Berniece: That's just what I'm gonna do. Wining Boy, you want me to fry you some pork chops?

Boy Willie: Now, I'm gonna tell you the way I see it. The only thing that make that piano worth something is them carvings Papa Willie Boy put on there. That's what make it worth something. That was my great-grandaddy. Papa Boy Charles brought that piano into the house. Now, I'm supposed to build on what they left me. You can't do nothing with that piano sitting up here in the house. That's just like if I let them watermelons sit out there and rot. I'd be a fool. Alright now, if you say to me, Boy Willie, I'm using that piano. I give out lessons on it and that help me make my rent or whatever. Then that be something else. I'd have to go on and say, well, Berniece using that piano. She building on it. Let her go on and use it. I got to find another way to get Sutter's land. But Doaker say you ain't touched that piano the whole time it's been up here. So why you wanna stand in my way? See, you just looking at the sentimental value. See, that's good. That's alright. I take my hat off whenever somebody say my daddy's name. But I ain't gonna be no fool about no sentimental value. You can sit up here and look at the piano for the next hundred years and it's just gonna be a piano. You can't make more than that. Now I want to get Sutter's land with that piano. I get Sutter's land and I can go down and cash in the crop and get my seed. As long as I got the land and the seed then I'm alright. I can always get me a little something else. Cause that land give back to you. I can make me another crop and cash that in. I still got the land and the seed. But that piano don't put out nothing else. You ain't got nothing working for you. Now, the kind of man my daddy was he would have understood that. I'm sorry you can't see it that way. But that's why I'm gonna take that piano out of here and sell it.

Berniece: You ain't taking that piano out of my house. (*She crosses to the piano.*) Look at this piano. Look at it. Mama Ola polished this piano with her tears for seventeen years. For seventeen years she rubbed on it till her hands bled. Then she rubbed the blood in . . . mixed it up with the rest of the blood on it. Every day that God breathed life into her body she rubbed and cleaned and polished and prayed over it. "Play something for me, Berniece. Play something for me, Berniece." Every day. "I cleaned it up for you, play something for me, Berniece." You always talking about your daddy but you ain't never stopped to look at what his foolishness cost your mama. Seventeen years' worth of cold nights and an empty bed. For what? For a piano? For a piece of wood? To get even with somebody? I look at you and you're all the same. You, Papa Boy Charles, Wining Boy, Doaker, Crawley . . . you're all alike. All this thieving and killing and thieving and killing. And what it ever lead to? More killing and more thieving. I ain't never seen it come to nothing. People getting burned up. People getting shot. People falling down their wells. It don't never stop.

Doaker: Come on now, Berniece, ain't no need in getting upset.

Boy Willie: I done a little bit of stealing here and there, but I ain't never killed nobody. I can't be speaking for nobody else. You all got to speak for yourself, but I ain't never killed nobody.

Berniece: You killed Crawley just as sure as if you pulled the trigger.

Boy Willie: See, that's ignorant. That's downright foolish for you to say something like that. You ain't doing nothing but showing your ignorance. If the nigger was here I'd whup him for getting me and Lymon shot at.

Berniece: Crawley ain't knew about the wood.

Boy Willie: We told the man about the wood. Ask Lymon. He knew all about the wood. He seen we was sneaking it. Why else we gonna be out there at night? Don't come telling me Crawley ain't knew about the wood. Them fellows come up on us and Crawley tried to bully them. Me and Lymon seen the sheriff with them and give in. Wasn't no sense in getting killed over fifty dollars' worth of wood.

Berniece: Crawley ain't knew you stole that wood.

Boy Willie: We ain't stole no wood. Me and Lymon was hauling wood for Jim Miller and keeping us a little bit on the side. We dumped our little bit down there by the creek till we had enough to make a load. Some fellows seen us and we figured we better get it before they did. We come up there and got Crawley to help us load it. Figured we'd cut him in. Crawley trying to keep the wolf from his door . . . we was trying to help him.

Lymon: Me and Boy Willie told him about the wood. We told him some fellows might be trying to beat us to it. He say let me go back and get my thirty-eight. That's what caused all the trouble.

Boy Willie: If Crawley ain't had the gun he'd be alive today.

Lymon: We had it about half loaded when they come up on us. We seen the sheriff with them and we tried to get away. We ducked around near the bend in the creek . . . but they was down there too. Boy Willie say let's give in. But Crawley pulled out his gun and started shooting. That's when they started shooting back.

Berniece: All I know is Crawley would be alive if you hadn't come up there and got him.

Boy Willie: I ain't had nothing to do with Crawley getting killed. That was his own fault.

Berniece: Crawley's dead and in the ground and you still walking around here eating. That's all I know. He went off to load some wood with you and ain't never come back.

Boy Willie: I told you, woman . . . I ain't had nothing to do with . . .

Berniece: He ain't here, is he? He ain't here! (BERNIECE *hits* BOY WILLIE.) I said he ain't here. Is he?

[BERNIECE *continues to hit* BOY WILLIE, *who doesn't move to defend himself, other than back up and turning his head so that most of the blows fall on his chest and arms.*]

Doaker: (*grabbing* BERNIECE) Come on,

Berniece . . . let it go, it ain't his fault.

Berniece: He ain't here, is he? Is he?

Boy Willie: I told you I ain't responsible for Crawley.

Berniece: He ain't here.

Boy Willie: Come on now, Berniece . . . don't do this now. Doaker get her. I ain't had nothing to do with Crawley . . .

Berniece: You come up there and got him!

Boy Willie: I done told you now. Doaker, get her. I ain't playing.

Doaker: Come on. Berniece.

[MARETHA *is heard screaming upstairs. It is a scream of stark terror.*]

Maretha: Mama! . . . Mama!

[*The lights go down to black. End of Act One.*]

ACT TWO

Scene 1

[*The lights come up on the kitchen. It is the following morning.* DOAKER *is ironing the pants to his uniform. He has a pot cooking on the stove at the same time. He is singing a song. The song provides him with the rhythm for his work and he moves about the kitchen with the ease born of many years as a railroad cook.*]

Doaker:
> Gonna leave Jackson Mississippi
> and go to Memphis
> and double back to Jackson
> Come on down to Hattiesburg
> Change cars on the Y.D.[1]
> coming through the territory to Meridian
> and Meridian to Greenville
> and Greenville to Memphis
> I'm on my way and I know where
>
> Change cars on the Katy[2]
> Leaving Jackson
> and going through Clarksdale
> Hello Winona!
> Courtland!
> Bateville!
> Como!
> Senitobia!
> Lewisberg!
> Sunflower!
> Glendora!

Sharkey!
And double back to Jackson
Hello Greenwood
I'm on my way Memphis
Clarksdale
Moorhead
Indianola
Can a highball[3] pass through?
Highball on through sir
Grand Carson!
Thirty First Street Depot
Fourth Street Depot
Memphis!

[WINING BOY *enters carrying a suit of clothes.*]

Doaker: I thought you took that suit to the pawnshop?
Wining Boy: I went down there and the man tell me the suit is too old. Look at this suit. This is one hundred percent silk! How a silk suit gonna get too old? I know what it was he just didn't want to give me five dollars for it. Best he wanna give me is three dollars. I figure a silk suit is worth five dollars all over the world. I wasn't gonna part with it for no three dollars so I brought it back.
Doaker: They got another pawnshop up on Wylie.
Wining Boy: I carried it up there. He say don't take no clothes. Only thing he takes is guns and radios. Maybe a guitar or two. Where's Berniece?
Doaker: Berniece still at work. Boy Willie went down there to meet Lymon this morning. I guess they got that truck fixed, they been out there all day and ain't come back yet. Maretha scared to sleep up there now. Berniece don't know, but I seen Sutter before she did.

---

1. **Y.D.:** The Yazoo Delta, called "Yellow Dog."
2. **Katy:** the nickname of a railroad, probably one near Kansas City. It is used in many songs, such as "She caught the Katy and left me a mule to ride" [*Author's note*].
3. **highball:** a fast train.

Wining Boy: Say what?

Doaker: About three weeks ago. I had just come back from down there. Sutter couldn't have been dead more than three days. He was sitting over there at the piano. I come out to go to work . . . and he was sitting right there. Had his hand on top of his head just like Berniece said. I believe he broke his neck when he fell in the well. I kept quiet about it. I didn't see no reason to upset Berniece.

Wining Boy: Did he say anything? Did he say he was looking for Boy Willie?

Doaker: He was just sitting there. He ain't said nothing. I went on out the door and left him sitting there. I figure as long as he was on the other side of the room everything be alright. I don't know what I would have done if he had started walking toward me.

Wining Boy: Berniece say he was calling Boy Willie's name.

Doaker: I ain't heard him say nothing. He was just sitting there when I seen him. But I don't believe Boy Willie pushed him in the well. Sutter here cause of that piano. I heard him playing on it one time. I thought it was Berniece but then she don't play that kind of music. I come out here and ain't seen nobody, but them piano keys was moving a mile a minute. Berniece need to go on and get rid of it. It ain't done nothing but cause trouble.

Wining Boy: I agree with Berniece. Boy Charles ain't took it to give it back. He took it cause he figure he had more right to it than Sutter did. If Sutter can't understand that . . . then that's just the way that go. Sutter dead and in the ground . . . don't care where his ghost is. He can hover around and play on the piano all he want. I want to see him carry it out the house. That's what I want to see. What time Berniece get home? I don't

see how I let her get away from me this morning.

Doaker: You up there sleep. Berniece leave out of here early in the morning. She out there in Squirrel Hill cleaning house for some bigshot down there at the steel mill. They don't like you to come late. You come late they won't give you your carfare. What kind of business you got with Berniece?

Wining Boy: My business. I ain't asked you what kind of business you got.

Doaker: Berniece ain't got no money. If that's why you was trying to catch her. She having a hard enough time trying to get by as it is. If she go ahead and marry Avery . . . he working every day . . . she go ahead and marry him they could do alright for themselves. But as it stands she ain't got no money.

Wining Boy: Well, let me have five dollars.

Doaker: I just give you a dollar before you left out of here. You ain't gonna take my five dollars out there and gamble and drink it up.

Wining Boy: Aw, nigger, give me five dollars. I'll give it back to you.

Doaker: You wasn't looking to give me five dollars when you had that sack of money. You wasn't looking to throw nothing my way. Now you wanna come in here and borrow five dollars. If you going back with Boy Willie you need to be trying to figure out how you gonna get train fare.

Wining Boy: That's why I need the five dollars. If I had five dollars I could get me some money. (DOAKER *goes into his pocket.*) Make it seven.

Doaker: You take this five dollars . . . and you bring my money back here too.

[BOY WILLIE *and* LYMON *enter. They are happy and excited. They have money in all of their pockets and are anxious to count it.*]

Doaker: How'd you do out there?

Boy Willie: They was lining up for them.

Lymon: Me and Boy Willie couldn't sell them fast enough. Time we got one sold we'd sell another.

Boy Willie: I seen what was happening and told Lymon to up the price on them.

Lymon: Boy Willie say charge them a quarter more. They didn't care. A couple of people give me a dollar and told me to keep the change.

Boy Willie: One fellow bought five. I say now what he gonna do with five watermelons? He can't eat them all. I sold him the five and asked him did he want to buy five more.

Lymon: I ain't never seen nobody snatch a dollar fast as Boy Willie.

Boy Willie: One lady asked me say, "Is they sweet?" I told her say, "Lady, where we grow these watermelons we put sugar in the ground." You know, she believed me. Talking about she had never heard of that before. Lymon was laughing his head off. I told her, "Oh, yeah, we put the sugar right in the ground with the seed." She say, "Well, give me another one." Them white folks is something else . . . ain't they, Lymon?

Lymon: Soon as you holler watermelons they come right out their door. Then they go and get their neighbors. Look like they having a contest to see who can buy the most.

Wining Boy: I got something for Lymon.

[WINING BOY *goes to get his suit.* BOY WILLIE *and* LYMON *continue to count their money.*]

Boy Willie: I know you got more than that. You ain't sold all them watermelons for that little bit of money.

Lymon: I'm still looking. That ain't all you

got either. Where's all them quarters?

Boy Willie: You let me worry about the quarters. Just put the money on the table.

Wining Boy: (*entering with his suit*) Look here, Lymon . . . see this? Look at his eyes getting big. He ain't never seen a suit like this. This is one hundred percent silk. Go ahead . . . put it on. See if it fit you.

[LYMON *tries the suit coat on.*]

Look at that. Feel it. That's one hundred percent genuine silk. I got that in Chicago. You can't get clothes like that nowhere but New York and Chicago. You can't get clothes like that in Pittsburgh. These folks in Pittsburgh ain't never seen clothes like that.

Lymon: This is nice, feel real nice and smooth.

Wining Boy: That's a fifty-five-dollar suit. That's the kind of suit the bigshots wear. You need a pistol and a pocketful of money to wear that suit. I'll let you have it for three dollars. The women will fall out their windows they see you in a suit like that. Give me three dollars and go on and wear it down the street and get you a woman.

Boy Willie: That looks nice, Lymon. Put the pants on. Let me see it with the pants.

[LYMON *begins to try on the pants.*]

Wining Boy: Look at that . . . see how it fits you? Give me three dollars and go on and take it. Look at that, Doaker . . . don't he look nice?

Doaker: Yeah . . . that's a nice suit.

Wining Boy: Got a shirt to go with it. Cost you an extra dollar. Four dollars you got the whole deal.

Lymon: How this look, Boy Willie?

Boy Willie: That look nice . . . if you like that kind of thing. I don't like them dress-up kind of clothes. If you like it, look real nice.

Wining Boy: That's the kind of suit you need for up here in the North.

Lymon: Four dollars for everything? The suit and the shirt?

Wining Boy: That's cheap. I should be charging you twenty dollars. I give you a break cause you a homeboy. That's the only way I let you have it for four dollars.

Lymon: (*going into his pocket*) Okay . . . here go the four dollars.

Wining Boy: You got some shoes? What size you wear?

Lymon: Size nine.

Wining Boy: That's what size I got! Size nine. I let you have them for three dollars.

Lymon: Where they at? Let me see them.

Wining Boy: They real nice shoes, too. Got a nice tip to them. Got pointy toe just like you want.

[WINING BOY *goes to get his shoes.*]

Lymon: Come on, Boy Willie, let's go out tonight. I wanna see what it looks like up here. Maybe we go to a picture show. Hey, Doaker, they got picture shows up here?

Doaker: The Rhumba Theater. Right down there on Fullerton Street. Can't miss it. Got the speakers outside on the sidewalk. You can hear it a block away. Boy Willie know where it's at.

[DOAKER *exits into his room.*]

Lymon: Let's go to the picture show, Boy Willie. Let's go find some women.

Boy Willie: Hey, Lymon, how many of them watermelons would you say we got left? We got just under a half a load . . . right?

Lymon: About that much. Maybe a little more.

Boy Willie: You think that piano will fit up in there?

Lymon: If we stack them watermelons you

can sit it up in the front there.

Boy Willie: I'm gonna call that man tomorrow.

Wining Boy: *(returns with his shoes)* Here you go . . . size nine. Put them on. Cost you three dollars. That's a Florsheim shoe. That's the kind Staggerlee[4] wore.

Lymon: *(trying on the shoes)* You sure these size nine?

Wining Boy: You can look at my feet and see we wear the same size. Man, you put on that suit and them shoes and you got something there. You ready for whatever's out there. But is they ready for you? With them shoes on you be the King of the Walk. Have everybody stop to look at your shoes. Wishing they had a pair. I'll give you a break. Go on and take them for two dollars.

[LYMON *pays* WINING BOY *two dollars.*]

4. **Staggerlee:** a character in a folk ballad, also called *Stack-alee.*

Lymon: Come on, Boy Willie . . . let's go find some women. I'm gonna go upstairs and get ready. I'll be ready to go in a minute. Ain't you gonna get dressed?

Boy Willie: I'm gonna wear what I got on. I ain't dressing up for these city niggers.

[LYMON *exits up the stairs.*]

That's all Lymon think about is women.

[DOAKER *enters from his room.*]

Look like you ready to railroad some.

Doaker: Yeah, I got to make that run.

[LYMON *enters from the stairs. He is dressed in his new suit and shoes, to which he has added a cheap straw hat.*]

Lymon: How I look?

Wining Boy: You look like a million dollars. Don't he look good, Doaker? Come on, let's play some cards. You wanna play some cards?

Boy Willie: We ain't gonna play no cards with you. Me and Lymon gonna find some women. Hey, Lymon, don't play no cards with Wining Boy. He'll take all your money.

Wining Boy: (to LYMON) You got a magic suit there. You can get you a woman easy with that suit . . . but you got to know the magic words. You know the magic words to get you a woman?

Lymon: I just talk to them to see if I like them and they like me.

Boy Willie: Come on, I'm ready. You ready, Lymon? Come on, let's go find some women.

Wining Boy: Here, let me walk out with you. I wanna see the women fall out their window when they see Lymon.

[*They all exit and the lights go down on the scene.*]

Scene 2

[*The lights come up on the kitchen. It is late evening of the same day.* BERNIECE *has set a tub for her bath in the kitchen. She is heating up water on the stove. There is a knock at the door.*]

Berniece: Who is it?

Avery: It's me, Avery.

[BERNIECE *opens the door and lets him in.*]

Berniece: Avery, come on in. I was just fixing to take my bath.

Avery: Where Boy Willie? I see that truck out there almost empty. They done sold almost all them watermelons.

Berniece: They was gone when I come home. I don't know where they went off to. Boy Willie around here about to drive me crazy.

Avery: They sell them watermelons . . . he'll be gone soon.

Berniece: What Mr. Cohen say about letting you have the place?

Avery: He say he'll let me have it for thirty dollars a month. I talked him out of thirty-five and he say he'll let me have it for thirty.

Berniece: That's a nice spot next to Benny Diamond's store.

Avery: Berniece . . . I be at home and I get to thinking you up here an' I'm down there. I get to thinking how that look to have a preacher that ain't married. It makes for a better congregation if the preacher was settled down and married.

Berniece: Avery . . . not now. I was fixing to take my bath.

Avery: You know how I feel about you, Berniece. Now . . . I done got the place from Mr. Cohen. I get the money from the bank and I can fix it up real nice. They give me a ten cents a hour raise down there on the job . . . now Berniece, I ain't got much in the way of comforts. I got a hole in my pockets near about as far as money is concerned. I ain't never found no way through life to a woman I care about like I care about you. I need that. I need somebody on my bond side. I need a woman that fits in my hand.

Bernice: Avery, I ain't ready to get married now.

Avery: You too young a woman to close up, Berniece.

Berniece: I ain't said nothing about closing up. I got a lot of woman left in me.

Avery: Anytime I get anywhere near you . . . you push me away.

Berniece: I got enough on my hands with Maretha. I got enough people to love and take care of.

Avery: Who you got to love you? Can't nobody get close enough to you. Doaker can't half say nothing to you. You jump all over Boy Willie. Who you got to love you, Berniece?

Berniece: You trying to tell me a woman can't be nothing without a man. But you alright, huh? You can just walk out of here without me—without a woman—and still be a man. That's alright. Ain't nobody gonna ask you, "Avery, who you got to love you?" That's alright for you. But everybody gonna be worried about Berniece. "How Berniece gonna take care of herself? How she gonna raise that child without a man? Wonder what she do with herself. How she gonna live like that?" Everybody got all kinds of questions for Berniece. Everybody telling me I can't be a woman unless I got a man. Well, you tell me, Avery—you know—how much woman am I?

Avery: It wasn't me, Berniece. You can't blame me for nobody else. I'll own up to my own shortcomings. But you can't blame me for Crawley or nobody else.

Berniece: I ain't blaming nobody for nothing. I'm just stating the facts.

Avery: How long you gonna carry Crawley with you, Berniece? It's been over three years. At some point you got to let go and go on. Life's got all kinds of twists and turns. That don't mean you stop living. That don't mean you cut yourself off from life. You can't go through life carrying Crawley's ghost with you. Crawley's been dead three years. Three years, Berniece.

Berniece: I know how long Crawley's been dead. You ain't got to tell me that. I just ain't ready to get married right now.

Avery: What is you ready for, Berniece? You just gonna drift along from day to day. Life is more than making it from one day to another. You gonna look up one day and it's all gonna be past you. Life's gonna be gone out

of your hands—there won't be enough to make nothing with. I'm standing here now, Berniece—but I don't know how much longer I'm gonna be standing here waiting on you.

Berniece: Avery, I told you . . . when you get your church we'll sit down and talk about this. I got too many other things to deal with right now. Boy Willie and the piano . . . and Sutter's ghost. I thought I might have been seeing things, but Maretha done seen Sutter's ghost, too.

Avery: When this happen, Berniece?

Berniece: Right after I came home yesterday. Me and Boy Willie was arguing about the piano and Sutter's ghost was standing at the top of the stairs. Maretha scared to sleep up there now. Maybe if you bless the house he'll go away.

The Piano Lesson   Act Two   773

Avery: I don't know, Berniece. I don't know if I should fool around with something like that.

Berniece: I can't have Maretha scared to go to sleep up there. Seem like if you bless the house he would go away.

Avery: You might have to be a special kind of preacher to do something like that.

Berniece: I keep telling myself when Boy Willie leave he'll go on and leave with him. I believe Boy Willie pushed him in the well.

Avery: That's been going on down there a long time. The Ghosts of the Yellow Dog been pushing people in their wells long before Boy Willie got grown.

Berniece: Somebody down there pushing them people in their wells. They ain't just upped and fell. Ain't no wind pushed nobody in their well.

Avery: Oh, I don't know. God works in mysterious ways.

Berniece: He ain't pushed nobody in their wells.

Avery: He caused it to happen. God is the Great Causer. He can do anything. He parted the Red Sea.[1] He say I will smite my enemies. Reverend Thompson used to preach on the Ghosts of the Yellow Dog as the hand of God.

Berniece: I don't care who preached what. Somebody down there pushing them people in their wells. Somebody like Boy Willie. I can see him doing something like that. You ain't gonna tell me that Sutter just upped and fell in his well. I believe Boy Willie pushed him so he could get his land.

Avery: What Doaker say about Boy Willie selling the piano?

Berniece: Doaker don't want no part of that piano. He ain't never wanted no part of it. He blames himself for not staying behind with Papa Boy Charles. He washed his hands of that piano a long time ago. He didn't want me to bring it up here—but I wasn't gonna leave it down there.

Avery: Well, it seems to me somebody ought to be able to talk to Boy Willie.

Berniece: You can't talk to Boy Willie. He been that way all his life. Mama Ola had her hands full trying to talk to him. He don't listen to nobody. He just like my daddy. He get his mind fixed on something and can't nobody turn him from it.

Avery: You ought to start a choir at the church. Maybe if he seen you was doing something with it—if you told him you was gonna put it in my church—maybe he'd see it different. You ought to put it down in the church and start a choir. The Bible say "Make a joyful noise unto the Lord." Maybe if Boy Willie see you was doing something with it he'd see it different.

Berniece: I done told you I don't play on that piano. Ain't no need in you to keep talking this choir stuff. When my mama died I shut the top on that piano and I ain't never opened it since. I was only playing it for her. When my daddy died seem like all her life went into that piano. She used to have me playing on it . . . had Miss Eula come in and teach me . . . say when I played it she could hear my daddy talking to her. I used to think them pictures came alive and walked through the house. Sometime late at night I could hear my mama talking to them. I said that wasn't gonna happen to me. I don't play that piano cause I don't want to wake them spirits. They never be walking around in this house.

Avery: You got to put all that behind you, Berniece.

---

1. **Red Sea:** When Pharaoh's army pursued the Israelites, the Lord parted the Red Sea to make a path for their escape (Exodus 14:21–30).

Berniece: I got Maretha playing on it. She don't know nothing about it. Let her go on and be a schoolteacher or something. She don't have to carry all of that with her. She got a chance I didn't have. I ain't gonna burden her with that piano.

Avery: You got to put all of that behind you, Berniece. That's the same thing like Crawley. Everybody got stones in their passway. You got to step over them or walk around them. You picking them up and carrying them with you. All you got to do is set them down by the side of the road. You ain't got to carry them with you. You can walk over there right now and play that piano. You can walk over there right now and God will walk over there with you. Right now you can set that sack of stones down by the side of the road and walk away from it. You don't have to carry it with you. You can do it right now. (AVERY *crosses over to the piano and raises the lid.*) Come on, Berniece . . . set it down and walk away from it. Come on, play "Old Ship of Zion." Walk over here and claim it as an instrument of the Lord. You can walk over here right now and make it into a celebration.

[BERNIECE *moves toward the piano.*]

Berniece: Avery . . . I done told you I don't want to play that piano. Now or no other time.

Avery: The Bible say, "The Lord is my refuge . . . and my strength!" With the strength of God you can put the past behind you, Berniece. With the strength of God you can do anything! God got a bright tomorrow. God don't ask what you done . . . God ask what you gonna do. The strength of God can move mountains! God's got a bright tomorrow for you . . . all you got to do is walk over here and claim it.

Berniece: Avery, just go on and let me finish my bath. I'll see you tomorrow.

Avery: Okay, Berniece. I'm gonna go home. I'm gonna go home and read up on my Bible. And tomorrow . . . if the good Lord give me strength tomorrow . . . I'm gonna come by and bless the house . . . and show you the power of the Lord. (AVERY *crosses to the door.*) It's gonna be alright, Berniece. God say he will soothe the troubled waters. I'll come by tomorrow and bless the house.

[*The lights go down to black.*]

Scene 3 takes place several hours later. BOY WILLIE *returns with* GRACE, *whom he has just met while out with* LYMON. *They accidentally knock over a lamp and wake* BERNIECE, *who promptly kicks them out. Soon* LYMON *returns.* BERNIECE *is still up, and the two chat.* LYMON *talks about his plans for the future—staying up North, finding the right woman, and settling down. He pulls from his pocket a small bottle of perfume he had planned to give to whichever woman he would meet that night, and in a gesture of tenderness, gives it to* BERNIECE *as she exits upstairs.*

Scene 4

[*It is late the next morning. The lights come up on the parlor.* LYMON *is asleep on the sofa.* BOY WILLIE *enters the front door.*]

Boy Willie: Hey, Lymon! Lymon, come on get up.

Lymon: Leave me alone.

Boy Willie: Come on, get up, nigger! Wake up, Lymon.

Lymon: What you want?

Boy Willie: Come on, let's go. I done called the man about the piano.

Lymon: What piano?

Boy Willie: (*dumps* LYMON *on the floor*) Come on, get up!

Lymon: Wining Boy seen Sutter's ghost last night.

Boy Willie: Wining Boy's liable to see anything. I'm surprised he found the right house. Come on, I done called the man about the piano.

Lymon: What he say?

Boy Willie: He say to bring it on out. I told him I was calling for my sister, Miss Berniece Charles. I told him some man wanted to buy it for eleven hundred dollars and asked him if he would go any better. He said yeah, he would give me eleven hundred and fifty dollars for it if it was the same piano. I described it to him again and he told me to bring it out.

Lymon: Why didn't you tell him to come and pick it up?

Boy Willie: I didn't want to have no problem with Berniece. This way we just take it on out there and it be out the way. He want to charge twenty-five dollars to pick it up.

Lymon: You should have told him the man was gonna give you twelve hundred for it.

Boy Willie: I figure I was taking a chance with that eleven hundred. If I had told him twelve hundred he might have run off. Now I wish I had told him twelve-fifty. It's hard to figure out white folks sometimes.

Lymon: You might have been able to tell him anything. White folks got a lot of money.

Boy Willie: Come on, let's get it loaded before Berniece come back. Get that end over there. All you got to do is pick it up on that side. Don't worry about this side. You wanna stretch you' back for a minute?

Lymon: I'm ready.

Boy Willie: Get a real good grip on it now.

[*The sound of* SUTTER'S GHOST *is heard. They do not hear it.*]

Lymon: I got this end. You get that end.

Boy Willie: Wait till I say ready now. Alright. You got it good? You got a grip on it?

Lymon: Yeah, I got it. You lift up on that end.

Boy Willie: Ready? Lift!

[*The piano will not budge.*]

Lymon: Man, this piano is heavy! It's gonna take more than me and you to move this piano.

Boy Willie: We can do it. Come on—we did it before.

Lymon: Nigger—you crazy! That piano weighs five hundred pounds!

Boy Willie: I got three hundred pounds of it! I know you can carry two hundred pounds! You be lifting them cotton sacks! Come on lift this piano!

[*They try to move the piano again without success.*]

Lymon: It's stuck. Something holding it.

Boy Willie: How the piano gonna be stuck? We just moved it. Slide you' end out.

Lymon: Naw—we gonna need two or three more people. How this big old piano get in the house?

Boy Willie: I don't know how it got in the house. I know how it's going out though! You get on this end. I'll carry three hundred and fifty pounds of it. All you got to do is slide your end out. Ready?

[*They switch sides and try again without success.* DOAKER *enters from his room as they try to push and shove it.*]

Lymon: Hey, Doaker . . . how this piano get in the house?

Doaker: Boy Willie, what you doing?

Boy Willie: I'm carrying this piano out the house. What it look like I'm doing? Come on, Lymon, let's try again.

Doaker: Go on let the piano sit there till Berniece come home.

Boy Willie: You ain't got nothing to do with this, Doaker. This my business.

Doaker: This is my house, nigger! I ain't gonna let you or nobody else carry nothing out of it. You ain't gonna carry nothing out of here without my permission!

Boy Willie: This is my piano. I don't need your permission to carry my belongings out of your house. This is mine. This ain't got nothing to do with you.

Doaker: I say leave it over there till Berniece come home. She got part of it too. Leave it set there till you see what she say.

Boy Willie: I don't care what Berniece say. Come on, Lymon. I got this side.

Doaker: Go on and cut it half in two if you want to. Just leave Berniece's half sitting over there. I can't tell you what to do with your piano. But I can't let you take her half out of here.

Boy Willie: Go on, Doaker. You ain't got nothing to do with this. I don't want you starting nothing now. Just go on and leave me alone. Come on, Lymon. I got this end.

[DOAKER *goes into his room.* BOY WILLIE *and* LYMON *prepare to move the piano.*]

Lymon: How we gonna get it in the truck?

Boy Willie: Don't worry about how we gonna get it on the truck. You got to get it out the house first.

Lymon: It's gonna take more than me and you to move this piano.

Boy Willie: Just lift up on that end, nigger!

The Piano Lesson Act Two 777

[DOAKER *comes to the doorway of his room and stands.*]

Doaker: (*quietly with authority*) Leave that piano set over there till Berniece come back. I don't care what you do with it then. But you gonna leave it sit over there right now.

Boy Willie: Alright . . . I'm gonna tell you this, Doaker. I'm going out of here . . . I'm gonna get me some rope . . . find me a plank and some wheels . . . and I'm coming back. Then I'm gonna carry that piano out of here . . . sell it and give Berniece half the money. See . . . now that's what I'm gonna do. And you . . . or nobody else is gonna stop me. Come on, Lymon . . . let's go get some rope and stuff. I'll be back, Doaker.

[BOY WILLIE *and* LYMON *exit. The lights go down on the scene.*]

Scene 5

[*The lights come up.* BOY WILLIE *sits on the sofa, screwing casters on a wooden plank.* MARETHA *is sitting on the piano stool.* DOAKER *sits at the table playing solitaire.*[1]]

Boy Willie: (*to* MARETHA) Then after that them white folks down around there started falling down their wells. You ever seen a well? A well got a wall around it. It's hard to fall down a well. You got to be leaning way over. Couldn't nobody figure out too much what was making these fellows fall down their well . . . so everybody says the Ghosts of the Yellow Dog must have pushed them. That's what everybody called them four men what got burned up in the boxcar.

1. *solitaire* (sŏl′ə-târ′): a card game for one player.

Maretha: Why they call them that?

Boy Willie: Cause the Yazoo Delta railroad got yellow boxcars. Sometime the way the whistle blow sound like an old dog howling so the people call it the Yellow Dog.

Maretha: Anybody ever see the Ghosts?

Boy Willie: I told you they like the wind. Can you see the wind?

Maretha: No.

Boy Willie: They like the wind you can't see them. But sometimes you be in trouble they might be around to help you. They say if you go where the Southern cross the Yellow Dog . . . you go to where them two railroads cross each other . . . and call out their names . . . they say they talk back to you. I don't know, I ain't never done that. But Uncle Wining Boy he say he been down there and talked to them. You have to ask him about that part.

[BERNIECE *has entered from the front door.*]

Berniece: Maretha, you go on and get ready for me to do your hair.

[MARETHA *crosses to the steps.*]

Boy Willie, I done told you to leave my house. (*to* MARETHA) Go on, Maretha.

[MARETHA *is hesitant about going up the stairs.*]

Boy Willie: Don't be scared. Here, I'll go up there with you. If we see Sutter's ghost I'll put a whupping on him. Come on, Uncle Boy Willie going with you.

[BOY WILLIE *and* MARETHA *exit up the stairs.*]

Berniece: Doaker—what is going on here?

Doaker: I come home and him and Lymon was moving the piano. I told them to leave it over there till you got home. He went out

Apryl R. Foster as Maretha and Charles S. Dutton as Boy Willie.

and got that board and them wheels. He say he gonna take that piano out of here and ain't nobody gonna stop him.

Berniece: I ain't playing with Boy Willie. I got Crawley's gun upstairs. He don't know but I'm through with it. Where Lymon go?

Doaker: Boy Willie sent him for some rope just before you come in.

Berniece: I ain't studying Boy Willie or Lymon—or the rope. Boy Willie ain't taking that piano out this house. That's all there is to it.

[BOY WILLIE *and* MARETHA *enter on the stairs.* MARETHA *carries a hot comb and a can of hair grease.* BOY WILLIE *crosses over and continues to screw the wheels on the board.*]

Maretha: Mama, all the hair grease is gone. There ain't but this little bit left.

Berniece: (*gives her a dollar*) Here . . . run across the street and get another can. You come straight back, too. Don't you be play-

ing around out there. And watch the cars. Be careful when you cross the street.

[MARETHA *exits out the front door.*]

Boy Willie, I done told you to leave my house.

Boy Willie: I ain't in you' house. I'm in Doaker's house. If he ask me to leave then I'll go on and leave. But consider me done left your part.

Berniece: Doaker, tell him to leave. Tell him to go on.

Doaker: Boy Willie ain't done nothing for me to put him out of the house. I told you if you can't get along just go on and don't have nothing to do with each other.

Boy Willie: I ain't thinking about Berniece. (*He gets up and draws a line across the floor with his foot.*) There! Now I'm out of your part of the house. Consider me done left your part. Soon as Lymon come back with that rope, I'm gonna take that piano out of here and sell it.

Berniece: You ain't gonna touch that piano.

Boy Willie: Carry it out of here just as big and bold. Do like my daddy would have done come time to get Sutter's land.

Berniece: I got something to make you leave it over there.

Boy Willie: It's got to come better than this thirty-two-twenty.

Doaker: Why don't you stop all that! Boy Willie, go on and leave her alone. You know how Berniece get. Why you wanna sit there and pick with her?

Boy Willie: I ain't picking with her. I told her the truth. She the one talking about what she got. I just told her what she better have.

Berniece: That's alright, Doaker. Leave him alone.

Boy Willie: She trying to scare me. Hell, I ain't scared of dying. I look around and see people dying every day. You got to die to make room for somebody else. I had a dog that died. Wasn't nothing but a puppy. I picked it up and put it in a bag and carried it up there to Reverend C. L. Thompson's church. I carried it up there and prayed and asked Jesus to make it live like he did the man in the Bible. I prayed real hard. Knelt down and everything. Say ask in Jesus' name. Well, I must have called Jesus' name two hundred times. I called his name till my mouth got sore. I got up and looked in the bag and the dog still dead. It ain't moved a muscle! I say, "Well, ain't nothing precious." And then I went out and killed me a cat. That's when I discovered the power of death. See, a nigger that ain't afraid to die is the worse kind of nigger for the white man. He can't hold that power over you. That's what I learned when I killed that cat. I got the power of death too. I can command him. I can call him up. The white man don't like to see that. He don't like for you to stand up and look him square in the eye and say, "I got it too." Then he got to deal with you square up.

Berniece: That's why I don't talk to him, Doaker. You try and talk to him and that's the only kind of stuff that comes out his mouth.

Doaker: You say Avery went home to get his Bible?

Boy Willie: What Avery gonna do? Avery can't do nothing with me. I wish Avery would say something to me about this piano.

Doaker: Berniece ain't said about that. Avery went home to get his Bible. He coming by to bless the house see if he can get rid of Sutter's ghost.

Boy Willie: Ain't nothing but a house full of ghosts down there at the church. What Avery look like chasing away somebody's ghost?

[MARETHA *enters the front door.*]

Berniece: Light that stove and set that comb over there to get hot. Get something to put around your shoulders.

Boy Willie: The Bible say an eye for an eye, a tooth for a tooth, and a life for a life.[2] Tit for tat. But you and Avery don't want to believe that. You gonna pass up that part and pretend it ain't in there. Everything else you gonna agree with. But if you gonna agree with part of it you got to agree with all of it. You can't do nothing halfway. You gonna go at the Bible halfway. You gonna act like that part ain't in there. But you pull out the Bible and open it and see what it say. Ask Avery. He a preacher. He'll tell you it's in there. He the Good Shepherd. Unless he gonna shepherd you to heaven with half the Bible.

---

2. **eye . . . life:** The phrase in the Bible reads: "Eye for eye, tooth for tooth, hand for hand, foot for foot" (Exodus 21:24).

Berniece: Maretha, bring me that comb. Make sure it's hot.

[MARETHA *brings the comb.* BERNIECE *begins to do her hair.*]

Boy Willie: I will say this for Avery. He done figured out a path to go through life. I don't agree with it. But he done fixed it so he can go right through it real smooth. Hell, he liable to end up with a million dollars that he done got from selling bread and wine.

Maretha: OWWWWWW!

Berniece: Be still, Maretha. If you was a boy I wouldn't be going through this.

Boy Willie: Don't you tell that girl that. Why you wanna tell her that?

Berniece: You ain't got nothing to do with this child.

Boy Willie: Telling her you wished she was a boy. How's that gonna make her feel?

Berniece: Boy Willie, go on and leave me alone.

Doaker: Why don't you leave her alone? What you got to pick with her for? Why don't you go on out and see what's out there in the streets? Have something to tell the fellows down home.

Boy Willie: I'm waiting on Lymon to get back with that truck. Why don't you go on out and see what's out there in the streets? You ain't got to work tomorrow. Talking about me . . . why don't you go out there? It's Friday night.

Doaker: I got to stay around here and keep you all from killing one another.

Boy Willie: You ain't got to worry about me. I'm gonna be here just as long as it takes Lymon to get back here with that truck. You ought to be talking to Berniece. Sitting up there telling Maretha she wished she was a boy. What kind of thing is that to tell a child? If you want to tell her something tell her about that piano. You ain't even told her about that piano. Like that's something to be ashamed of. Like she supposed to go off and hide somewhere about that piano. You ought to mark down on the calendar the day that Papa Boy Charles brought that piano into the house. You ought to mark that day down and draw a circle around it . . . and every year when it come up throw a party. Have a celebration. If you did that she wouldn't have no problem in life. She could walk around here with her head held high. I'm talking about a big party!

Invite everybody! Mark that day down with a special meaning. That way she know where she at in the world. You got her going out here thinking she wrong in the world. Like there ain't no part of it belong to her.

Berniece: Let me take care of my child. When you get one of your own then you can teach it what you want to teach it.

[DOAKER *exits into his room.*]

Boy Willie: What I want to bring a child into this world for? Why I wanna bring somebody else into all this for? I'll tell you this . . . If I was Rockefeller[3] I'd have forty or fifty. I'd make one every day. Cause they gonna start out in life with all the advantages. I ain't got no advantages to offer nobody. Many is the time I looked at my daddy and seen him staring off at his hands. I got a little older I know what he was thinking. He sitting there saying, "I got these big old hands but what I'm gonna do with them? Best I can do is make a fifty-acre crop for Mr. Stovall. Got these big old hands capable of doing anything. I can take and build something with these hands. But where's the tools? All I got is these hands. Unless I go out here and kill me

---

3. **Rockefeller:** a well-known family of millionaires.

somebody and take what they got . . . it's a long row to hoe for me to get something of my own. So what I'm gonna do with these big old hands? What would you do?"

See now . . . if he had his own land he wouldn't have felt that way. If he had something under his feet that belonged to him he could stand up taller. That's what I'm talking about. Hell, the land is there for everybody. All you got to do is figure out how to get you a piece. Ain't no mystery to life. You just got to go out and meet it square on. If you got a piece of land you'll find everything else fall right into place. You can stand right up next to the white man and talk about the price of cotton . . . the weather, and anything else you want to talk about. If you teach that girl that she living at the bottom of life, she's gonna grow up and hate you.

Berniece: I'm gonna teach her the truth. That's just where she living. Only she ain't got to stay there. (*to* MARETHA) Turn you' head over to the other side.

Boy Willie: This might be your bottom but it ain't mine. I'm living at the top of life. I ain't gonna just take my life and throw it away at the bottom. I'm in the world like everybody else. The way I see it everybody else got to come up a little taste to be where I am.

Berniece: You right at the bottom with the rest of us.

Boy Willie: I'll tell you this . . . and ain't a living soul can put a come back on it. If you believe that's where you at then you gonna act that way. If you act that way then that's where you gonna be. It's as simple as that. Ain't no mystery to life. I don't know how you come to believe that stuff. Crawley didn't think like that. He wasn't living at the bottom of life. Papa Boy Charles and Mama Ola wasn't living at the bottom of life. You ain't never heard them say nothing like that.

They would have taken a strap to you if they heard you say something like that.

(DOAKER *enters from his room.*)

Hey, Doaker . . . Berniece say the colored folks is living at the bottom of life. I tried to tell her if she think that . . . that's where she gonna be. You think you living at the bottom of life? Is that how you see yourself?

Doaker: I'm just living the best way I know how. I ain't thinking about no top or no bottom.

Boy Willie: That's what I tried to tell Berniece. I don't know where she got that from. That sound like something Avery would say. Avery think cause the white man give him a turkey for Thanksgiving that makes him better than everybody else. That's gonna raise him out of the bottom of life. I don't need nobody to give me a turkey. I can get my own turkey. All you have to do is get out my way. I'll get me two or three turkeys.

Berniece: You can't even get a chicken let alone two or three turkeys. Talking about get out your way. Ain't nobody in your way. (*to* MARETHA) Straighten your head, Maretha! Don't be bending down like that. Hold your head up! (*to* BOY WILLIE) All you got going for you is talk. You' whole life that's all you ever had going for you.

Boy Willie: See now . . . I'll tell you something about me. I done strung along and strung along. Going this way and that. Whatever way would lead me to a moment of peace. That's all I want. To be as easy with everything. But I wasn't born to that. I was born to a time of fire.

The world ain't wanted no part of me. I could see that since I was about seven. The world say it's better off without me. See, Berniece accept that. She trying to come up to where she can prove something to the world. Hell, the world a better place cause of me. I don't see it like Berniece. I got a heart that beats here and it beats just as loud as the next fellow's. Don't care if he black or white. Sometime it beats louder. When it beats louder, then everybody can hear it. Some people get scared of that. Like Berniece. Some people get scared to hear a nigger's heart beating. They think you ought to lay low with that heart. Make it beat quiet and go along with everything the way it is. But my mama ain't birthed me for nothing. So what I got to do? I got to mark my passing on the road. Just like you write on a tree, "Boy Willie was here."

That's all I'm trying to do with that piano. Trying to put my mark on the road. Like my daddy done. My heart say for me to sell that piano and get me some land so I can make a life for myself to live in my own way. Other than that I ain't thinking about nothing Berniece got to say.

[*There is a knock at the door.* BOY WILLIE *crosses to it and yanks it open thinking it is* LYMON. AVERY *enters. He carries a Bible.*]

Boy Willie: Where you been, nigger? Aw . . . I thought you was Lymon. Hey, Berniece, look who's here.

Berniece: Come on in, Avery. Don't you pay Boy Willie no mind.

Boy Willie: Hey . . . Hey, Avery . . . tell me this . . . can you get to heaven with half the Bible?

Berniece: Boy Willie . . . I done told you to leave me alone.

Boy Willie: I just ask the man a question. He can answer. He don't need you to speak for him. Avery . . . if you only believe on half the Bible and don't want to accept the other half . . . you think God let you in heaven? Or do you got to have the whole Bible? Tell Ber-

niece . . . if you only believe in part of it . . . when you see God he gonna ask you why you ain't believed in the other part . . . then he gonna send you straight to Hell.

Avery: You got to be born again. Jesus say unless a man be born again he cannot come unto the Father and who so ever heareth my words and believeth them not shall be cast into a fiery pit.

Boy Willie: That's what I was trying to tell Berniece. You got to believe in it all. You can't go at nothing halfway. She think she going to heaven with half the Bible. (*to* BERNIECE) You hear that . . . Jesus say you got to believe in it all.

Berniece: You keep messing with me.

Boy Willie: I ain't thinking about you.

Doaker: Come on in, Avery, and have a seat. Don't pay neither one of them no mind. They been arguing all day.

Berniece: Come on in, Avery.

Avery: How's everybody in here?

Berniece: Here, set this comb back over there on that stove. (*to* AVERY) Don't pay Boy Willie no mind. He been around here bothering me since I come home from work.

Boy Willie: Boy Willie ain't bothering you. Boy Willie ain't bothering nobody. I'm just waiting on Lymon to get back. I ain't thinking about you. You heard the man say I was right and you still don't want to believe it. You just wanna go and make up anythin'. Well there's Avery . . . there's the preacher . . . go on and ask him.

Avery: Berniece believe in the Bible. She been baptized.

Boy Willie: What about that part that say an eye for an eye a tooth for a tooth and a life for a life? Ain't that in there?

Doaker: What they say down there at the bank, Avery?

Avery: Oh, they talked to me real nice. I told

Berniece . . . they say maybe they let me borrow the money. They done talked to my boss down at work and everything.

Doaker: That's what I told Berniece. You working every day you ought to be able to borrow some money.

Avery: I'm getting more people in my congregation every day. Berniece says she gonna be the Deaconess. I get me my church I can get married and settled down. That's what I told Berniece.

Doaker: That be nice. You all ought to go ahead and get married. Berniece don't need to be by herself. I tell her that all the time.

Berniece: I ain't said nothing about getting married. I said I was thinking about it.

Doaker: Avery get him his church you all can make it nice. (*to* AVERY) Berniece said you was coming by to bless the house.

Avery: Yeah, I done read up on my Bible. She asked me to come by and see if I can get rid of Sutter's ghost.

Boy Willie: Ain't no ghost in this house. That's all in Berniece's head. Go on up there and see if you see him. I'll give you a hundred dollars if you see him. That's all in her imagination.

Doaker: Well, let her find that out then. If Avery blessing the house is gonna make her feel better . . . what you got to do with it?

Avery: Berniece say Maretha seen him too. I don't know, but I found a part in the Bible to bless the house. If he is here then that ought to make him go.

Boy Willie: You worse than Berniece believing all that stuff. Talking about . . . if he here. Go on up there and find out. I been up there I ain't seen him. If you reading from that Bible gonna make him leave out of Berniece imagination, well, you might be right. But if you talking about . . .

Doaker: Boy Willie, why don't you just be quiet? Getting all up in the man's business. This ain't got nothing to do with you. Let him go ahead and do what he gonna do.

Boy Willie: I ain't stopping him. Avery ain't got no power to do nothing.

Avery: Oh, I ain't got no power. God got the power! God got power over everything in His creation. God can do anything. God say, "As I commandeth so it shall be." God said, "Let there be light," and there was light. He made the world in six days and rested on the seventh. God's got a wonderful power. He got power over life and death. Jesus raised Lazareth[4] from the dead. They was getting ready to bury him and Jesus told him say, "Rise up and walk." He got up and walked and the people made great rejoicing at the power of God. I ain't worried about him chasing away a little old ghost!

[*There is a knock at the door.* BOY WILLIE *goes to answer it.* LYMON *enters carrying a coil of rope.*]

Boy Willie: Where you been? I been waiting on you and you run off somewhere.

Lymon: I ran into Grace. I stopped and bought her drink. She say she gonna go to the picture show with me.

Boy Willie: I ain't thinking about no Grace nothing.

Lymon: Hi, Berniece.

Boy Willie: Give me that rope and get up on this side of the piano.

Doaker: Boy Willie, don't start nothing now. Leave the piano alone.

Boy Willie: Get that board there, Lymon. Stay out of this, Doaker.

[BERNIECE *exits up the stairs.*]

---

4. **Lazareth:** Lazarus, a brother of Mary and Martha, raised from the dead (John 11:1–44).

Doaker: You just can't take the piano. How you gonna take the piano? Berniece ain't said nothing about selling that piano.

Boy Willie: She ain't got to say nothing. Come on, Lymon. We got to lift one end at a time up on the board. You got to watch so that the board don't slide up under there.

Lymon: What we gonna do with the rope?

Boy Willie: Let me worry about the rope. You just get up on this side over here with me.

[BERNIECE *enters from the stairs. She has her hand in her pocket where she has Crawley's gun.*]

Avery: Boy Willie . . . Berniece . . . why don't you all sit down and talk this out now?

Berniece: Ain't nothing to talk out.

Boy Willie: I'm through talking to Berniece. You can talk to Berniece till you get blue in the face, and it don't make no difference. Get up on that side, Lymon. Throw that rope around there and tie it to the leg.

Lymon: Wait a minute . . . wait a minute, Boy Willie. Berniece got to say. Hey, Berniece . . . did you tell Boy Willie he could take this piano?

Berniece: Boy Willie ain't taking nothing out of my house but himself. Now you let him go ahead and try.

Boy Willie: Come on, Lymon, get up on this side with me.

[LYMON *stands undecided.*]

Come on, nigger! What you standing there for?

Lymon: Maybe Berniece is right, Boy Willie. Maybe you shouldn't sell it.

Avery: You all ought to sit down and talk it out. See if you can come to an agreement.

Doaker: That's what I been trying to tell them. Seem like one of them ought to respect the other one's wishes.

Berniece: I wish Boy Willie would go on and leave my house. That's what I wish. Now, he can respect that. Cause he's leaving here one way or another.

Boy Willie: What you mean one way or another? What's that supposed to mean? I ain't scared of no gun.

Doaker: Come on, Berniece, leave him alone with that.

Boy Willie: I don't care what Berniece say. I'm selling my half. I can't help it if her half got to go along with it. It ain't like I'm trying to cheat her out of her half. Come on, Lymon.

Lymon: Berniece . . . I got to do this . . . Boy Willie say he gonna give you half of the money . . . say he want to get Sutter's land.

Berniece: Go on, Lymon. Just go on . . . I done told Boy Willie what to do.

Boy Willie: Here, Lymon . . . put that rope up over there.

Lymon: Boy Willie, you sure you want to do this? The way I figure it . . . I might be wrong . . . but I figure she gonna shoot you first.

Boy Willie: She just gonna have to shoot me.

Berniece: Maretha, get on out the way. Get her out the way, Doaker.

Doaker: Go on, do what your mama told you.

Berniece: Put her in your room.

[MARETHA *exits to Doaker's room.* BOY WILLIE *and* LYMON *try to lift the piano. The door opens and* WINING BOY *enters. He has been drinking.*]

Wining Boy: Man, these niggers around here! I stopped down there at Seefus . . . These folks standing around talking about

Patchneck Red's[5] coming. They jumping back and getting off the sidewalk talking about Patchneck Red this and Patchneck Red that. Come to find out . . . you know who they was talking about? Old John D. from up around Tyler! Used to run around with Otis Smith. He got everybody scared of him. Calling him Patchneck Red. They don't know I whupped the nigger's head in one time.

Boy Willie: Just make sure that board don't slide, Lymon.

Lymon: I got this side. You watch that side.

Wining Boy: Hey, Boy Willie, what you got? I know you got a pint stuck up in your coat.

Boy Willie: Wining Boy, get out the way!

Wining Boy: Hey, Doaker. What you got? Gimme a drink. I want a drink.

Doaker: It look like you had enough of whatever it was. Come talking about "What you got?" You ought to be trying to find somewhere to lay down.

Wining Boy: I ain't worried about no place to lay down. I can always find me a place to lay down in Berniece's house. Ain't that right, Berniece?

Berniece: Wining Boy, sit down somewhere. You been out there drinking all day. Come in here smelling like an old polecat. Sit on down there, you don't need nothing to drink.

Doaker: You know Berniece don't like all that drinking.

Wining Boy: I ain't disrespecting Berniece. Berniece, am I disrespecting you? I'm just trying to be nice. I been with strangers all day and they treated me like family. I come in here to family and you treat me like a stranger. I don't need your whiskey. I can buy my own. I wanted your company, not your whiskey.

Doaker: Nigger, why don't you go upstairs and lay down? You don't need nothing to drink.

Wining Boy: I ain't thinking about no laying down. Me and Boy Willie fixing to party. Ain't that right, Boy Willie? Tell him. I'm fixing to play me some piano. Watch this.

[WINING BOY *sits down at the piano*]

Boy Willie: Come on, Wining Boy, get up! Get up, Wining Boy! Me and Lymon's fixing to move the piano.

Wining Boy: Naw . . . Naw . . . you ain't gonna move this piano!

Boy Willie: Get out the way, Wining Boy.

[WINING BOY, *his back to the piano, spreads his arms out over the piano.*]

Wining Boy: You ain't taking this piano out the house. You got to take me with it!

Boy Willie: Get on out the way, Wining Boy! Doaker get him!

[*There is a knock on the door.*]

Berniece: I got him, Doaker. Come on, Wining Boy. I done told Boy Willie he ain't taking the piano.

[BERNIECE *tries to take* WINING BOY *away from the piano.*]

Wining Boy: He got to take me with it!

[DOAKER *goes to answer the door.* GRACE *enters.*]

Grace: Is Lymon here?

Doaker: Lymon.

Wining Boy: He ain't taking that piano.

Berniece: I ain't gonna let him take it.

Grace: I thought you was coming back. I ain't gonna sit in that truck all day.

5. **Patchneck Red:** the name of a gambler in Pittsburgh. It is rumored he had the largest funeral of any black in Pittsburgh. He was a lightskinned man and got his name from an identifying birthmark on his neck [*Author's note*].

Lymon: I told you I was coming back.

Berniece: Lymon, you got to take your company someplace else.

Lymon: Berniece, this is Grace. That there is Berniece.

Grace: Nice to meet you. (*to* LYMON) I ain't gonna sit out in that truck all day. You told me you was gonna take me to the movie.

Lymon: I told you I had something to do first. You supposed to wait on me.

Berniece: Lymon, just go on and leave. Take Grace or whoever with you. Just go on get out my house.

Boy Willie: You gonna help me move this piano first, nigger!

Lymon: (*to* GRACE) I got to help Boy Willie move the piano first.

[*Everybody but* GRACE *suddenly senses* SUTTER'S *presence.*]

Grace: I ain't waiting on you. Told me you was coming right back. Now you got to move a piano. You just like all the other men. (GRACE *now senses something.*) Something ain't right here. I knew I shouldn't have come back up in this house.

[GRACE *exits.*]

Lymon: Hey, Grace! I'll be right back, Boy Willie.

Boy Willie: Where you going, nigger?

Lymon: I'll be back. I got to take Grace home.

Boy Willie: Come on, let's move the piano first!

Lymon: I got to take Grace home. I told you I'll be back.

[LYMON *exits.* BOY WILLIE *exits and calls after him.*]

Boy Willie: Come on, Lymon! Hey . . . Lymon! Lymon . . . come on!

[*Again, the presence of* SUTTER *is felt.*]

Wining Boy: Hey, Doaker, did you feel that? Hey, Berniece . . . did you get cold? Hey, Doaker . . .

Doaker: What you calling me for?

Wining Boy: I believe that's Sutter.

Doaker: Well, let him stay up there. As long as he don't mess with me.

Berniece: Avery, go on and bless the house.

Doaker: You need to bless that piano. That's what you need to bless. It ain't done nothing but cause trouble. If you gonna bless anything go on and bless that.

Wining Boy: Hey, Doaker, if he gonna bless something let him bless everything. The kitchen . . . the upstairs. Go on and bless it all.

Boy Willie: Ain't no ghost in this house. He need to bless Berniece's head. That's what he need to bless.

Avery: Seem like that piano's causing all the trouble. I can bless that. Berniece, put me some water in that bottle.

[AVERY *takes a small bottle from his pocket and hands it to* BERNIECE, *who goes into the kitchen to get water.* AVERY *takes a candle from his pocket and lights it. He gives it to* BERNIECE *as she gives him the water.*]

Hold this candle. Whatever you do make sure it don't go out.

O Holy Father we gather here this evening in the Holy Name to cast out the spirit of one James Sutter. May this vial of water be empowered with thy spirit. May each drop of it be a weapon and a shield against the presence of all evil and may it be a cleansing and blessing of this humble abode.

Just as Our Father taught us how to pray so He say, "I will prepare a table for you in the midst of mine enemies," and in His

hands we place ourselves to come unto his presence. Where there is Good so shall it cause Evil to scatter to the Four Winds.

[*He throws water at the piano at each commandment.*]

Avery: Get thee behind me, Satan! Get thee behind the face of Righteousness as we Glorify His Holy Name! Get thee behind the Hammer of Truth that breaketh down the Wall of Falsehood! Father. Father. Praise. Praise. We ask in Jesus' name and call forth the power of the Holy Spirit as it is written. . . .

[*He opens the Bible and reads from it.*]

I will sprinkle clean water upon thee and ye shall be clean.[6]

6. **I will . . . clean:** The Lord promises to cleanse the captive Israelites when they turn from sin and idolatry (Ezekiel 36:25).

Boy Willie: All this old preaching stuff. Hell, just tell him to leave.

[AVERY *continues reading throughout* BOY WILLIE's *outburst.*]

Avery: I will sprinkle clean water upon you and you shall be clean: from all your uncleanliness, and from all your idols, will I cleanse you. A new heart also will I give you, and a new spirit will I put within you: and I will take out of your flesh the heart of stone, and I will give you a heart of flesh. And I will put my spirit within you, and cause you to walk in my statutes, and ye shall keep my judgments, and do them.

[BOY WILLIE *grabs a pot of water from the stove and begins to fling it around the room.*]

Boy Willie: Hey Sutter! Sutter! Get out of this house! Sutter! Come on and get some of this water! You done drowned in the well, come on and get some more of this water!

(BOY WILLIE *is working himself into a frenzy as he runs around the room throwing water and calling* SUTTER's *name.* AVERY *continues reading.*)

Boy Willie: Come on, Sutter! (*He starts up the stairs.*) Come on, get some water! Come on, Sutter!

[*The sound of* SUTTER'S GHOST *is heard. As* BOY WILLIE *approaches the steps he is suddenly thrown back by the unseen force, which is choking him. As he struggles he frees himself, then dashes up the stairs.*]

Boy Willie: Come on, Sutter!
Avery: (*continuing*) A new heart also will I give you and a new spirit will I put within you: and I will take out of your flesh the heart of stone, and I will give you a heart of flesh. And I will put my spirit within you, and cause you to walk in my statutes, and ye shall keep my judgments, and do them.

[*There are loud sounds heard from upstairs as* BOY WILLIE *begins to wrestle with* SUTTER'S GHOST. *It is a life-and-death struggle fraught[7] with perils and faultless terror.* BOY WILLIE *is thrown down the stairs.* AVERY *is stunned into silence.* BOY WILLIE *picks himself up and dashes back upstairs.*]

Avery: Berniece, I can't do it.

[*There are more sounds heard from upstairs.* DOAKER *and* WINING BOY *stare at one another in stunned disbelief. It is in this moment, from somewhere old, that* BERNIECE *realizes what she must do. She crosses to the piano. She begins to play. The song is found piece by piece. It is an old urge to song that is both a commandment and a plea. With each*

repetition it gains in strength. It is intended as an exorcism[8] and a dressing for battle. A rustle of wind blowing across two continents.]

Berniece: (*singing*)
I want you to help me
I want you to help me
I want you to help me
I want you to help me
I want you to help me
I want you to help me
Mama Berniece
I want you to help me
Mama Esther
I want you to help me
Papa Boy Charles
I want you to help me
Mama Ola
I want you to help me

I want you to help me
I want you to help me
I want you to help me
I want you to help me
I want you to help me
I want you to help me
I want you to help me
I want you to help me

[*The sound of a train approaching is heard. The noise upstairs subsides.*]

Boy Willie: Come on, Sutter! Come back, Sutter!
Berniece: (*begins to chant*)
Thank you.
Thank you.
Thank you.

[*A calm comes over the house.* MARETHA *enters from* DOAKER's *room.* BOY WILLIE *en-*

---

7. *fraught* (frôt): full of.

8. *exorcism* (ĕk′sôr-sĭz′əm): the act of casting out an evil spirit.

ters on the stairs. He pauses a moment to watch BERNIECE at the piano.]

Berniece:
Thank you.
Thank you.
Boy Willie: Wining Boy, you ready to go back down home? Hey, Doaker, what time the train leave?
Doaker: You still got time to make it.

[MARETHA crosses and embraces BOY WILLIE.]

Boy Willie: Hey Berniece . . . if you and Maretha don't keep playing on that piano . . . ain't no telling . . . me and Sutter both liable to be back. (*He exits.*)
Berniece: Thank you.

[*The lights go down to black.*]

Responding to the Selection

from **The Piano Lesson** by August Wilson

Act One
Identifying Facts

1. Where did Boy Willie and Lymon begin their trip?
2. How does Boy Willie plan to raise the money to buy Sutter's land?
3. Who was Sutter?
4. Which member of the Charles family did the carving on the piano?
5. What incident from the past is a source of conflict and resentment between Boy Willie and Berniece?

Interpreting Meanings

1. Berniece has not seen Boy Willie for three years. How does she feel about seeing him again? Describe their relationship.

2. How does Boy Willie explain Sutter's falling down the well? How does Berniece explain the people falling down their wells?
3. Reread the passage on page 743 where Boy Willie begins, ''Got a hundred acres . . . '' Why does Boy Willie feel that owning land is an advantage?
4. How does Berniece explain the appearance of Sutter's ghost? Although Boy Willie does not believe that there really is a ghost, what explanation does he offer?
5. Why was it so important to Boy Charles to get the piano back?
6. Why does Berniece refuse to sell the piano?
7. How does Boy Willie justify selling the piano?

Act Two
Identifying Facts

1. Why doesn't Doaker tell Berniece that he has seen Sutter's ghost?
2. Why is Maretha now afraid to sleep upstairs?
3. What is Berniece doing as Avery knocks on the door?
4. Why doesn't Boy Willie have the man purchasing the piano come to pick it up?
5. How does Avery try to get rid of Sutter's ghost?

Interpreting Meanings

1. Doaker and Wining Boy do not interfere with Berniece and Boy Willie's decision about the piano, but they do reveal their opinions to each other. How does Doaker feel about having the piano in the house? What does Wining Boy say about the piano?
2. The scene in which Wining Boy sells the clothes to Lymon is an example of **dramatic irony**. Lymon thinks that Wining Boy is generously selling him a ''magic suit'' for a bargain, but the audience knows that Wining Boy is just desperate for gambling money. Why is Lymon so pleased with the suit? Why do you think the author included the scene?
3. When did Berniece stop playing the piano? What explanation does she give?
4. Why has Berniece chosen not to tell Maretha about the history of the piano? Why does she insist that Maretha play the piano?
5. The piano is a **symbol** of the Charles family's heritage, yet it holds different meanings for Berniece and Boy Willie. What does the piano represent for Berniece? What is Boy Willie's attitude toward the piano?
6. What are Lymon's reasons for wanting to stay up North? Why is Boy Willie determined to return to the South? How are their personalities reflected in their choices?
7. Sutter's ghost is a presence throughout the play. What do you think is his purpose in visiting the Charles household?
8. Berniece and Boy Willie have different attitudes toward their *heritage,* a family history of slavery, that has an effect on their lives in the present. They are in **conflict** over their *legacy,* the unusual piano handed down from a slave ancestor. Recall the argument each has presented throughout the play concerning the piano. How is the conflict resolved? What do you think is the **theme** of *The Piano Lesson?*

Literary Elements
Understanding Dramatic Structure
The short story and the novel are forms of **narrative**; the story is *told* from a particular

voice, or **point of view.** In **drama,** the story is *acted out* by actors and actresses taking the parts of the characters. Important background information, the **exposition,** is either established at the beginning of the play, or revealed during the course of the play, as the audience needs information. The characters are engaged in **conflict,** either a battle with an outside force or a struggle among themselves. Most plays have a **climax,** a point of great emotional intensity or suspense. The **turning point,** sometimes called the **crisis,** determines the **resolution,** or outcome of the events.

Do we learn important background information right at the start of the play, or as the play develops? At what point do we fully understand the situation?

What is the main **conflict** in the play? Are there any other conflicts going on? Does the play have a **climax?** What would you say is the **turning point?** Describe the **resolution** of the play.

Language and Vocabulary

Understanding African American Speech

Wilson has said, "I find in black life a very elegant kind of logical language, based on the logical order of things . . . When you ask a question, you get . . . ideas . . . opinions about everything, a little explanation." When asked by Lymon about the safety of the elevators (Act One, Scene 1), Avery responds:

That's steel. They got steel cables hold it up. It take a whole lot of breaking to break that steel. Naw, I ain't worried about nothing like that. It ain't nothing but a little old elevator. Now, I wouldn't get in none of them airplanes. You couldn't pay me to do nothing like that (page 751).

How does Avery's answer illustrate Wilson's statement?

Writing About Literature

Comparing Treatments of a Theme

The short story "Everyday Use" (page 543) also deals with the **theme** of heritage. Compare the attitudes of the characters in the story with those of the characters in *The Piano Lesson.* Which characters would be in agreement? What do the story and the play suggest about the "use" of one's heritage? Write an essay discussing your response to these questions. Refer to specific episodes, scenes, and passages of dialogue.

Discussing a Character's Action

Boy Charles believed that as long as Sutter owned the piano, he owned the family. Boy Charles was killed as he tried to retrieve the piano from Sutter. Do you agree with his belief? Was his principle worth risking his life for? Or is freedom more a state of mind? In a few paragraphs, summarize Boy Charles's situation, and explain whether or not you agree with his belief and action.

Speaking and Listening

Presenting an Argument

Choose two classmates to perform the scene that might have followed if Sutter's ghost had not intervened, and Berniece and Boy Willie took their case to small claims court. If you choose to act the part of either Berniece or Boy Willie, plan your argument carefully. If you will be playing the part of the judge, think of the questions you will need to ask.

The Author Comments

I saw a painting by Romare Bearden called "The Piano Lesson." . . . So I got the idea from the painting that there would be a woman and a little girl in the play. And I thought that the woman would be a character who was trying to acquire a sense of self-worth by denying her past. And I felt that she couldn't do that. She had to confront the past, in the person of her brother, who was going to sweep through the house like a tornado coming from the South, bringing the past with him. . . .

When it came to the piano, I knew there was a story behind it. What I didn't know was what was carved. And as I wrote, everything sort of came together. It was the idea of linkage. It provided a link to the past, to Africa, to who these people are. And then the question became, What do you do with your legacy? How do you best put it to use? . . .

In all my plays, I always point toward making that connection, toward reconnecting with the past. You have to know who you are, and understand your history in America over more than 300 years, in order to know what your relation is to your society.

From a *New York Times* interview
April 15, 1990

Writing a Play

Short stories and plays have many elements in common. The major difference between the two literary forms is that a play is not told from a single point of view. In a play, the story is revealed mainly through the dialogue and actions of the characters. A playwright sometimes makes use of stage directions that specify gestures and movements and indicate how certain lines should be read. For the most part, however, you must infer characters' motivations, thoughts, and feelings from what they say or what they *don't* say but imply through their silences or through their actions.

Dialogue in a play can serve many ends. It can reveal a character's inner feelings. It can provide information about what has already happened. It can tell where and when the action is happening. Examine the following dramatic speech from the opening scene of *The Piano Lesson.* How does it advance the plot? What does it reveal about the speaker?

> **Boy Willie:** Sutter's brother selling the land. He say he gonna sell it to me. That's why I come up here. I got one part of it. Sell them watermelons and get me another part. Get Berniece to sell that piano and I'll have the third part.

Writing a Play

Ideas for plays can come from any number of sources. Wilson says that he got the idea for *The Piano Lesson* from a painting by Romare Bearden. You might choose an incident or event from your own experience, or you might prefer to make something up. You could adapt one of the short stories, folk tales, or biographical excerpts in this book.

Prewriting Strategies

1. Begin with a situation that presents a **conflict**. Will this situation be serious or comic? Will it be suspenseful?
2. Decide who the **characters** will be. What are their personalities like? What do they want?
3. Plan the **plot**. What will happen in the beginning? in the middle? at the end? Where will the **climax** occur? What will the **resolution** be?
4. Choose the **setting** of the play—where and when the events occur. What **props** will be needed?
5. What **symbols,** if any, will you use?
6. What is the **theme,** or underlying idea, of your play?
7. Use a diagram to map out your play.

Situation	_____
Setting	_____
Cast of Characters	_____
Plot	_____
Event	_____
Event	_____
Climax/ Turning Point	_____
Resolution	_____

Writing a First Draft

1. As you write, imagine the characters speaking. Make sure that the dialogue is consistent with the characters and that it reveals the conflict.
2. Add stage directions to show how the characters speak and move.
3. Include a series of actions that lead logically to a resolution.
4. Give your play an appropriate title.

Revision Checklist

1. Is the conflict clear?
2. Is there a cause-and-effect sequence leading from the first event to the last?
3. Is the dialogue natural? Is the dialogue appropriate for individual characters?
4. Have you provided the necessary stage directions?

Writing the Final Draft

1. Check your paper for errors in style and mechanics.
2. Prepare a final copy and check it for accuracy. Choose student actors to present your play to the class.

►I. Interpreting a Dramatic Speech

A *monologue* is a lengthy speech in which a character's thoughts and feelings are revealed directly. Here are two such speeches by Boy Willie. The first appears in Act One (page 764); the second appears in the last scene of the play (pages 782–783).

Boy Willie: Now, I'm gonna tell you the way I see it. The only thing that make that piano worth something is them carvings Papa Willie Boy put on there. That's what make it worth something. That was my great-grandaddy. Papa Boy Charles brought that piano into the house. Now, I'm supposed to build on what they left me. You can't do nothing with that piano sitting up here in the house. That's just like if I let them watermelons sit out there and rot. I'd be a fool. Alright now, if you say to me, Boy Willie, I'm using that piano. I give out lessons on it and that help me make my rent or whatever. Then that be something else. I'd have to go on and say, well, Berniece using that piano. She building on it. Let her go on and use it. I got to find another way to get Sutter's land. But Doaker say you ain't touched that piano the whole time it's been up here. So why you wanna stand in my way? See, you just looking at the sentimental value. See, that's good. That's alright. I take my hat off whenever somebody say my daddy's name. But I ain't gonna be no fool about no sentimental value. You can sit up here and look at the piano for the next hundred years and it's just gonna be a piano. You can't make more than that. Now I want to get Sutter's land with that piano. I get Sutter's land and I can go down and cash in the crop and get my seed. As long as I got the land and the seed then I'm alright. I can always get me a little something else. Cause that land give back to you. I can make me another crop and cash that in. I still got the land and the seed. But that piano don't put out nothing else. You ain't got nothing working for you. Now, the kind of man my daddy was he would have understood that. I'm sorry you can't see it that way. But that's why I'm gonna take that piano out of here and sell it.

Boy Willie: See now . . . I'll tell you something about me. I done strung along and strung along. Going this way and that. Whatever way would lead me to a moment of peace. That's all I want. To be as easy with everything. But I wasn't born to that. I was born to a time of fire.

The world ain't wanted no part of me. I could see that since I was about seven. The world say it's better off without me. See, Berniece accept that. She trying to come up to where she can prove something to the world. Hell, the world a better place cause of me. I don't see it like Berniece. I got a heart that beats here and it beats just as loud as the next fellow's. Don't care if he black or white. Sometime it beats louder. When it beats louder, then everybody can hear it.

Some people get scared of that. Like Berniece. Some people get scared to hear a nigger's heart beating. They think you ought to lay low with that heart. Make it beat quiet and go along with everything the way it is. But my mama ain't birthed me for nothing. So what I got to do? I got to mark my passing on the road. Just like you write on a tree, "Boy Willie was here."

That's all I'm trying to do with that piano. Trying to put my mark on the road. Like my daddy done. My heart say for me to sell that piano and get me some land so I can make a life for myself to live in my own way. Other than that I ain't thinking about nothing Berniece got to say.

1. How do these speeches reveal Boy Willie's hopes for a better life?
2. What does Boy Willie mean when he says he was "born to a time of fire"?
3. How does Boy Willie think selling the piano will help him put his "mark on the road"?

▶▶II. For Discussion

How does August Wilson individualize his characters, that is, give each one certain personal characteristics so that he or she comes alive? How does he contrast Boy Willie with Lymon? with Doaker? with Avery? How are the brothers Doaker and Wining Boy differentiated? How does Wilson show different aspects of Boy Willie in his speeches to Berniece, to Maretha, and to Lymon?

▶▶▶III. For Writing

In speaking about his play, August Wilson says, "You have to know who you are, and understand your history in America over more than 300 years, in order to know what your relation is to your society" (page 793). How does he deal with these connections in *The Piano Lesson?* Refer to specific scenes and speeches in your essay.

Portrait sculpture of Soweto-based musician Paul Ndlovu, enamel paint on wood by Johannes Maswanganyl, 1987.
Gavin Younge

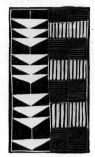

Contemporary African Literature

INTRODUCTION BY **Alice A. Deck**

University of Illinois at Urbana/Champaign

Africa as a Symbol to African Americans

In a poem called "Heritage," written during the 1920s, Countee Cullen asked himself, "What is Africa to me?" Cullen, who had never been to Africa, reflected the Western conceptions about Africa that were popular during his day. He imagined "strong bronzed men," "regal black women," "wild barbaric birds," "massive jungle herds," "heathen gods," and "great drums throbbing through the air."

For many African Americans writing since the 1920s, Africa is more than a series of romantic images. These writers have traveled to Africa to experience it firsthand. The poet Gwendolyn Brooks devotes one section of her 1972 autobiography, *Report from Part One,* to memories of her trip to East Africa. In 1983 the novelist Marita Golden published her autobiography, *Migrations of the Heart: A Personal Odyssey,* in which a large segment focuses on her life in West Africa with her Nigerian husband. In both books we see travelers seeking an answer to the question first posed by Cullen—What is Africa to me?—only to realize during the course of their travels that many Africans living on the continent were asking themselves the same question!

Modern African culture consists of ancient tribal practices (animistic religious rituals, extended family kinship systems that include "living-dead" ancestors, folk tales and "talking drums"). It also consists of Western institutions first introduced during the nineteenth century by European colonizers (Christianity, the nu-

Modern Africans in traditional dress.
[*Left*] Abbas/Magnum Photos
[*Right*] Marc & Evelyne Bernheim/Woodfin Camp

clear family, recorded music, cinemas, and automated forms of transportation). Many African people see themselves as living at a crossroads between these vastly different worlds. They recognize the need for health care facilities and the technological training and inventions widely available in the West. They also recognize, however, the risk of losing touch with traditional African practices crucial to the survival of their particular ethnic groups. This problem gives rise to conflicting opinions among modern Africans, both the traditional and westernized groups, on workable directions for the future development of Africa.

In spite of its cultural complexities and economic and political instabilities in some places, Africa stands as a meaningful symbol to many African Americans. Historically, Africa represents the beginnings of black culture in America. Since the 1960s, when individual African nations began to declare independence from European colonial rule, African Americans have looked to Africa as a symbol of black resilience and self-determination.

Background of Contemporary African Literature

The contemporary African selections in this unit reflect the cultural and political complexity of the continent. Contemporary literature from sub-Saharan Africa exists in many languages. There are two broad categories of literature. One includes literature written in any of the European languages introduced during the colonial period: English, French, Spanish, and Portuguese. The other includes literature written in native African languages: Anlo-Ewe, Hausa, Gikuyu, Yoruba, Sotho, Xhosa, and Swahili. These two categories of literature, which address two different audiences, originated during two different historical periods.

"Displaced" Africans

The first Africans to write poetry, plays, and personal narratives in one of the European languages were those "displaced" from their homeland by the trans-Atlantic slave trade. Most were born in Africa, and while some retained their original West African names, most took the surnames of their European "owners." These men and women were products of eighteenth-century Europe's "experiment" to test whether Africans could be educated. All of their literary productions were intended for European and European-American (including Latin American) readers.

Francis Williams of Jamaica, for example, was selected for such training by the Duke of Montagu. He attended English schools in Jamaica and then went on to Cambridge University, in England. In 1758 he wrote a poem in Latin celebrating the inaugural of the governor of Jamaica. Another African, born on a slave ship and named Ignatius Sancho by his owners, became a protégé and butler to the Duke of Montagu. In 1782 he published a collection of his letters, which were recognized for their literary merit. Abrasu Hannibal, an Abyssinian African slave educated at the court of Czar Peter the Great, became a famous military figure in Russia and was the grandfather of Alexander Pushkin, the renowned Russian poet.

Two other writers of this period were Phillis Wheatley and Olaudah Equiano (Gustavus Vassa). Wheatley was born in Senegal, West Africa, and brought to Boston as a slave in 1761 when she was a child. She was taught to read and write English by her owners. By age seventeen, she was famous in and around Boston as a literary prodigy and the author of many popular poems. She traveled to London in 1773, where a collection of her poems was published. One of Wheatley's most famous poems, "On Being Brought from Africa to America," reflects her early Methodist training. Her idea that Africa was pagan and that its people were in need of Christian salvation represented the common thought of white Americans and Europeans at that time (see page 166).

William Loren Katz

GUSTAVUS VASSA,
OR
Olaudah Equiano.

NARRATIVE
OF THE
LORD's wonderful DEALINGS
WITH
JOHN MARRANT,
A BLACK,
(Now going to Preach the GOSPEL in Nova-Scotia)
Born in New-York, in North-America.

Taken down from his own Relation,
Arranged, Corrected, and Published
By the Rev. Mr. ALDRIDGE.

THE SECOND EDITION.

THY PEOPLE SHALL BE WILLING IN THE DAY
OF THY POWER, Pſa. cx. 3.

DECLARE HIS WONDERS AMONG ALL PEOPLE,
Pſa. xcvi. 3.

LONDON:
Printed by Gilbert and Plummer, No. 13, Cree-
Church-Lane, 1785;
And ſold at the Chapel in Jewry-Street,—Price 6d.

Library of Congress

In contrast, Equiano's narrative of his life expresses a nostalgia for his African culture and the utmost respect for its practices. Born in Essaka, Nigeria, to the Igbo, or Ibo, people, Equiano was captured and sold into slavery when he was about eleven. He was carried first to the West Indies and then to Virginia, where he was eventually sold to a British naval officer. He became a skilled seaman and was able to buy his freedom. His autobiography, *The Interesting Narrative of the Life of Olaudah Equiano, or Gustavus Vassa, the African, Written by Himself,* appeared in 1789. Equiano's book recalls travel-adventure books such as *Gulliver's Travels,* by Jonathan Swift, and *Robinson Crusoe,* by Daniel Defoe. It is also an impressive example of the slave narrative and is considered the first great black autobiography (see page 146).

Other "displaced" Africans writing in English during the eighteenth century included Briton Hammon, from Massachusetts; John Marrant, a sailor; and Jupiter Hammon, a lyric poet from Long Island. Several Africans in the Portuguese colony of Brazil were chosen to be educated at Coimbra University, in Portugal, between 1773 and 1776. They then returned to Brazil with advanced degrees and assumed prominent roles as poets.

African Literature in Native Languages

The beginnings of literature written in indigenous African languages can be traced to the late nineteenth and early twentieth centuries. Early in the nineteenth century, Christian missionary institutions in sub-Saharan Africa began to translate the Bible and Christian hymnbooks into African languages. A spelling system was needed for translation. Working with Christian converts from the various ethnic groups, the missionaries developed a method of spelling based on the Roman alphabet. This was a laborious process but resulted in many African language dictionaries and grammars that have not yet been surpassed. The Bible, hymnbooks, and John Bunyan's *Pilgrim's Progress* were translated into several West African languages. By the end of the nineteenth century, these same works were translated into southern African languages.

Nineteenth-century Africans attending missionary schools acquired the religion and culture of Europe, and they often acquired literacy in their native languages. In turn, they helped to convert their people to Christianity.

Glossary of Names

Ashanti (ə-shăn′tē, ə-shan′-) or **Asante:** 1. A people of Ashanti, a region in central Ghana. 2. A language spoken in western Africa.

Duala or **Douala** (do͞o-ä′lə): A city of Cameroon, a country on the Bight of Biafra, an inlet of the Gulf of Guinea.

Ewe (ā′vā, ā′wā): 1. A people of Togo, Ghana, and parts of Dahomey. 2. The language of this people.

Gikuyu or **Kikuyu** (kĭ-ko͞o′yo͞o): 1. A Bantu (băn′to͞o) people of Kenya. 2. The Bantu language of the Gikuyu. **Bantu** is a family of languages, which includes Swahili and Zulu.

Hausa (hou′sə, -zə): 1. A people of the Sudan and northern Nigeria. 2. The language of this people.

Igbo or **Ibo** (ē′bō): 1. A people of Nigeria.

2. The Kwa language spoken by these people.

Sotho (sō′thō): 1. A people of southern Africa. 2. A group of Bantu languages spoken in South Africa.

Swahili (swä-hē′lē): 1. A Bantu language in eastern and central Africa. 2. A Bantu people of Zanzibar and the neighboring mainland who speak this language.

Xhosa (kō′sä): 1. A Bantu people of the Cape of Good Hope Province in South Africa. 2. A Bantu language related to Zulu.

Yoruba (yō′ro͞o-bä): 1. A West African people living in southwestern Nigeria. 2. The language of this people, which is a branch of the **Kwa** language family.

Zulu (zo͞o′lo͞o): 1. A people of a Bantu nation in southeastern Africa. 2. The Bantu language spoken by these people.

A few novels and plays written by Africans in African languages appeared in the early years of the twentieth century. These works reflect the missionary beliefs and teachings that tribal culture was pagan and satanic and that European culture, coming from a Christian base, was enlightened. Thomas Mofolo, a Sotho speaker, who worked as a proofreader in the press of the Paris Evangelical Mission in Morija, published his *Moeti oa Bochabela (The Pilgrim for the East)* in 1906. This novel tells the story of an African who converts to Christianity and, upon his return to Africa after receiving a European education, becomes a missionary and teacher among his own people. In 1908 Mofolo wrote *Chaka,* a historical novel that attacked what he saw as the paganism of the Zulu people. His third novel, *Pitseng,* portrays two Christian youths achieving happiness under the benign wings of the church. Lechesa Segote, another Sotho writer of Mofolo's time, wrote *Monomo ke moholi ke mouoane (Riches Are Only Mist).* It resembles the conversion story of Paul the Apostle, on the road to Damascus.

During the late eighteenth century in South Africa, Joseph Williams, of the London Missionary Society, converted the Xhosa Prince Ntsikana to Christianity. Following his work, the Scottish Mission established a college at Lovedale in Cape Province, South Africa. Several of the Xhosa and Zulu converts to Christianity who attended Lovedale wrote novels in these languages. The first Xhosa novel was written by Henry Ndawo in 1909. His *U Hambo Luk a Gboboka (A Journey Toward Conversion)* resembles Mofolo's *Pilgrim for the East* in that both authors borrowed heavily from Bunyan's *Pilgrim's Progress.* In their writings, Samuel Mgayi and Enoch Guima, both Christian converts, followed the same thematic pattern of extolling Christian virtue. The style of this early literature was didactic and moralistic. All of these writers ignored the oral literatures of their people, which they had been taught to believe were satanic.

During the early twentieth century in West Africa, missionaries provided spelling systems for such indigenous languages as Anlo and Ewe. Ewe writers of this period primarily wrote hymns, but at the start of World War I, when the Bremen (German) missionaries had to leave Africa, these writers (Torsu, Banini, Aku, and Kwami) took over the mission work themselves. They helped to disseminate Ewe translations of the Bible as well as pamphlets on treating snakebites, gathering honey, farming, raising animals, and civics. One difference between the early Ewe writers and those writing in Sotho and Xhosa is that they did not denounce their indigenous culture as pagan and satanic. They were, in fact, very interested in Ewe culture and in their writings tried to explain it to European colonizers.

One Ewe writer in particular, Kwasi Fiawoo, was among the first West Africans to be educated in the United States by the African Methodist Episcopal Church. He received degrees from Johnson C. Smith University, a predominantly black institution in North Carolina, and from Roosevelt University in Chicago. In 1937 he published his play *Toko Atolia (The Fifth Landing Stage),* which is now recognized as a classic of Ewe literature because it attempts to explore an indigenous way of life without apologizing for it. The play dramatizes how crimes were punished among the Anlo-Ewe of the southeast coast of what is now Ghana. There were no police, no prisons, and no soldiers in that area at the time. The people punished criminal youths by fines, by selling some into slavery, or, in extreme cases, by executions. The author's point was that the Ewe youth of his day, whether Christian or "pagan," needed to heed their ancestors' lessons regarding the survival of the group and its traditions.

The Négritude Movement

At this point, the history of African literature in European languages resumes. During the early 1930s, a small group of French-speaking blacks who were studying in Paris coined the term **Négritude** for their determination to affirm the dignity and value of African culture. Three students were the principal architects of this concept: Aimé Césaire, of Martinique, French West Indies; Léopold Sédar Senghor, of Senegal, West Africa; and Léon Damas, of Guyane (French Guiana), South America.

Césaire, Senghor, and Damas shared feelings of isolation from the citizens of France. African and West Indian blacks under French rule were expected to develop into citizens of France. In dress,

Léopold Sédar Senghor at the ceremony making him a member of the Académie Française, 1984.
Wide World Photos

Place du Tertre, *oil by*
Loïs Mailou Jones, 1932.
© The Phillips Collection,
Washington, D.C.

speech, and manners, they were expected to reflect the culture and customs of the French people. Their education was French. This meant that history was taught from the perspective that colonialism was a blessing to blacks fortunate to have the French for colonial masters. Furthermore, the French colonials (like their British counterparts) tried to convince blacks that they did not have a great culture or a history prior to colonization.

Also in Paris at that time were African American students who had brought with them collections of poetry by Sterling Brown, Countee Cullen, Langston Hughes, and Claude McKay. The Africans and West Indians were immediately attracted to this body of literature because it dealt with themes related to black life. They had been taught that poetry should deal only with themes related to European culture and thought. African American poetry reflected an interest in Africa (Cullen and Hughes), concern over the life of the Southern farmer (Brown), anger at the lynching of black men and women (McKay and Brown), and a fascination with life in Harlem, New York City. The language of this poetry reflected African American speech as well as its various forms of music, especially blues and jazz. The images in African American poetry mirrored the multicultural lifestyle of black America. Some of it celebrated the beauty of the black woman. This poetry, as well as fiction by such writers as Wallace Thurman, Jean Toomer, and Eric Walrond, inspired Africans and West Indians to reclaim the black African and black West Indian cultures they had been taught to despise.

Themes in Contemporary African Literature

The central themes of Négritude poetry are all related to the reclamation of African ancestry and an African view of humanity and its relationship to nature. Birago Diop's poem "Souffles" ("Breath") reflects the African belief that the spirits of the dead ancestors are watching over the lives of those still living in the tangible world. "The dead are not gone forever . . . They are in the rustling tree, / In the murmuring wood, / The flowing water . . . in the crowd . . . The dead are never dead." One idea central to the philosophy of Négritude, and adopted by contemporary African writers, is the interdependence between nature and human beings.

While some African writers from the French colonies built their work around the theme of reclaiming an African ancestry, others rejected the Négritude themes as too idealistic and highly romanticized. Nigerian and black South African writers are more concerned with demonstrating how difficult it is to reconstruct a precolonial African culture free of Westernization. Chinua Achebe's short story "Dead Men's Path" resembles Birago Diop's "Souffles" in showing that among some of the native people, traditional African beliefs in ancestral spirits were not entirely discarded when the missionaries arrived on the continent. Those westernized Africans in Achebe's story who disregard traditional beliefs in their efforts to build Western-style schools are taught an important lesson in coexistence with tribal beliefs.

Chinua Achebe.
Marc & Evelyne Bernheim/
Woodfin Camp

Farthest removed from the Négritude themes of a glorious African past are the writings of black South African writers. Most of them are concerned with the disastrous economic and psychological effects of racism on "colored" and black families, especially the children. "The Park," by James Matthews, shows how a child is denied access to a playground reserved for "whites only." This rejection breeds a hatred in the child for the entire world.

Several contemporary African writers are concerned with the plight of black Africans living abroad in an industrial, mechanized Europe. There they must deal with feelings of alienation because of lingering racist attitudes toward blacks and because of the overcrowded, urban setting. The poem "Telephone Conversation," by Wole Soyinka, exposes the racist attitudes of whites in London. The speaker in the poem anticipates the final rejection, but his humiliation by it is poignant nevertheless.

Black African women writers have been concerned with the changing role of women as they emerge from traditional tribal positions to assume new places in society and new relationships to men. Buchi Emecheta, who has achieved an international reputation, has written a number of autobiographical novels dealing with the impact of Western values on the culture and attitudes of village life. Of particular concern to Emecheta and most contemporary African women writers are traditional expectations that all women will marry and bear children and the problems that arise for young women who choose to do otherwise.

*Wole Soyinka, shortly
after winning the Nobel
Prize in Literature, 1986.*
Wide World Photos

About the Author
Léopold Sédar Senghor (b. 1906)

Léopold Sédar Senghor (lā-ô-pôld' sā-där' säN-gôr') is ranked among the best-known West African poets and is one of the leading advocates of Négritude. Négritude, as Senghor defined and illustrated it in his poetry, asserts the values and the spirit of black African civilizations.

Senghor was born in Joal, an old Portuguese coastal settlement in Senegal, West Africa. His parents were Serer but had converted to Christianity. His father was a wealthy, highly respected merchant. He encouraged his son to pursue his education at a French lycée (secondary school) in Dakar, the capital of Senegal. Senghor then went on to Paris. There he attended the Lycée Louis-le-Grand, a prestigious school, where one of his classmates was Georges Pompidou, later to become President of France. In Paris Senghor met Aimé Césaire, with whom he founded the magazine *L'Étudiant Noir (Black Student)*. Its first issue, published in 1934, put forth the principles of Négritude. After completing advanced studies in Paris, Senghor became the first black African to be appointed a professor in a secondary school in France.

During World War II, Senghor served in the French army. He was captured by the Germans and imprisoned in a concentration camp. He later wrote the poem "Camp 1940" about his experiences as a prisoner. After he was released, in 1942, he joined the French Resistance. Senghor became increasingly active politically. He was elected a Senegal-

William Campbell/Sygma

ese representative to the National Constituent Assembly in Paris, which drew up the constitution for France's Fourth Republic. In addition to his political responsibilities, Senghor worked on two journals, *Condition Humaine* and *Présence Africaine.*

Senghor was elected President of the Federal Assembly of Mali in 1959. Then, in 1960, after Senegal withdrew from the Federation, he was elected the first President of the Republic of Senegal. He held that office until 1980, when he retired.

"Be Not Amazed" is from *Nocturnes* (1963), which won the *Grand Prix International de Poésie,* a prestigious prize awarded by the Society of Poets and Artists of France. He was elected to France's highest cultural body, the Académie Francaise, in 1984.

Léopold Sédar Senghor 809

Before You Read

Be Not Amazed

Using What You Know

Many poems are intended to be sung. "Lift Every Voice and Sing" (page 293) is one example. What other poems that you have read in this anthology are often sung? Can you name additional poems that are songs?

Literary Focus: Lyric

A **lyric** is a poem expressing a mood or the speaker's thoughts and feelings. The word *lyric* can be traced back to the Greek word *lyra,* a musical instrument used by ancient poets. In *Nocturnes,* Senghor often indicates that his poetry is written for a specific African musical instrument and is meant to be sung. "Be Not Amazed" is written for the *khalam,* a four-stringed guitar.

Senghor's poem is a love lyric that has elements of the **elegy,** another kind of lyric. An elegy is a poem of mourning that is sometimes a reflection on the passing of time and life.

Setting a Purpose

As you read, note the variety of feelings in the poem. How does the poet celebrate the beauty of his beloved? How does he also show an acceptance of pain and death?

Be Not Amazed

Léopold Sédar Senghor

Be not amazed, beloved, if sometimes my song grows dark.
If I exchange the lyrical reed° for the Khalam° or the tama°
And the green scent of the ricefields, for the swiftly galloping
    war drums.
I hear the threats of ancient deities, the furious cannonade of
    the god.
Oh, tomorrow perhaps, the purple voice of your bard° will be
    silent for ever.
That is why my rhythm becomes so fast, that the fingers bleed
    on the Khalam.
Perhaps, beloved, I shall fall tomorrow, on a restless earth
Lamenting your sinking eyes, and the dark tom-tom of the
    mortars below.
And you will weep in the twilight for the glowing voice that
    sang your black beauty.

2. **reed:** instrument associated with poets. **Khalam:** a four-stringed guitar. **tama:** a small drum carried under the arm.

5. **bard:** poet.

Responding to the Selection

Be Not Amazed by Léopold Sédar Senghor

Interpreting Meanings

1. The speaker is a poet who believes that war may come soon and he imagines his own death. How is his "song," or poetry, affected by these thoughts?

2. How does he imagine the reaction of his beloved to news of his death?

3. Senghor once defined poetry as the "expression by images and rhythm of profound feelings." Do you think that is a good description of this poem?

Mask from Dakar Negro Art Festival, Senegal.
René Burri/Magnum Photos

Birago Diop (1906–1989)

Birago Diop (dē′ŏp) was born in Dakar, Senegal, which at that time was part of French West Africa. His family was Wolof (wō′lŏf′), one of the ethnic groups found in the Sudanese plains of West Africa. Diop attended the Lycée Faidherbe in Saint-Louis (săn-lo͞o-ē′), a port on the Senegal River. After completing studies at this school, Diop traveled to France, where he studied at the University of Toulouse and became a veterinary surgeon. In Paris, he met Léopold Sédar Senghor and the Caribbean writers who founded the Négritude movement. Upon his return to West Africa, Diop worked for many years as a government veterinary officer in various locations throughout the French colonies of Senegal, Côte d'Ivoire, and Burkina Faso.

While traveling in connection with his job, Diop observed that French colonialism was eroding traditional Wolof life. He wanted to preserve as much of the traditional folklore as he could before it was completely forgotten. Diop transcribed into French many of the Wolof tales he heard while traveling and working in the rural regions of Senegal. In 1947, he published *The Tales of Amadou Koumba,* the first of two collections of these tales. The second volume, *The New Tales of Amadou Koumba,* was published in 1958. His book of poetry, *Lures and Lights,* appeared in 1960, and in 1963, Diop published a third collection of folk tales, *Tales and Commentaries.*

Diop was appointed Senegalese ambassador to Tunisia in 1960. He was a member of

Layle Silbert

the cabinet of independent Senegal.

The poem "Souffles" (so͞o′fəlz) was first published in 1960. Its theme—the need for modern Africans to pay attention to the culture of their ancestors—is a central theme of the Négritude movement. The African American folk singers who call themselves "Sweet Honey in the Rock" rendered Birago Diop's poem "Souffles" (which they translate as "Breaths") into music in 1980.

Birago Diop   813

Before You Read

Souffles

Using What You Know

In Native American literature, there is a deep reverence for nature. The human and natural worlds are closely related. The natural world is considered sacred.

If you have read "The Hymn to the Aton" (page 80), you will recall that this ancient Egyptian poem praises the benevolence of the sun god. What other works have you read that express a spirit of reverence for nature?

Background

Many westernized black Africans of Diop's generation continue to believe in the importance of their ancestral culture. This culture teaches that the world consists of a tangible and an intangible realm—that which can be seen and that which is invisible. When an individual dies, he or she becomes an ancestral spirit. Ancestors are viewed as part of the extended family and as guardians of the living. Diop is urging his readers to accept this belief because it provides a spiritual base.

Setting a Purpose

As you read, note the different sounds that the speaker describes. Determine what he means by "the breath of the ancestors."

Souffles°

(It is the breath of the ancestors)

Birago Diop   TRANSLATED BY **Samuel Allen**

Listen more often to things than to beings
   Hear the fire's voice,
   Hear the voice of water.
   Hear, in the wind, the sobbing of the trees.
It is the breath of the ancestors.   5

The dead are not gone forever
They are in the paling shadows,
They are in the darkening shadows.
The dead are not beneath the ground,
They are in the rustling tree,   10

°**Souffles** (soo͞′fəlz): soft murmuring sounds.

In the murmuring wood,
The flowing water,
The still water,
In the lonely place, in the crowd;
The dead are never dead.   15

Listen more often to things than to beings.
    Hear the fire's voice.
    Hear the voice of water.
    In the wind hear the sobbing of the trees.
    It is the breath of the ancestors.   20
    They are not gone
    They are not beneath the ground
    They are not dead.

The dead are not gone forever.
    They are in a woman's breast,   25
    A child's cry, a glowing ember.
    The dead are not beneath the earth,
    They are in the flickering fire,
    In the weeping plant, the groaning rock,
    The wooded place, the home.   30
    The dead are never dead.

Listen more often to things than to beings
    Hear the fire's voice,
    Hear the voice of water.
    Hear, in the wind, the sobbing of the trees.   35
    It is the breath of the ancestors.

Responding to the Selection

Souffles by Birago Diop

Interpreting Meanings

1. **Personification** is a figure of speech in which some nonliving thing is given human characteristics. How does Diop personify nature in the first stanza?

2. Diop believes that the supernatural exists everywhere and must be respected. How does the presence of ancestors continue to be felt in the world?

3. What is "the breath of the ancestors"?

About the Author
Amos Tutuola (1920–1997)

Amos Tutuola (tōō-tōō-ō'lä) was born in Abeokuta, a small town in the Yoruba section of Nigeria, sixty miles north of the capital city, Lagos. Tutuola's father was a relatively wealthy farmer. For the first six years of his life, Tutuola attended the Salvation Army primary school in Abeokuta. He then attended Lagos High School, where he studied the blacksmith trade for two years. During World War II, Tutuola served in the West African Air Force (a branch of the British Royal Air Force) as a coppersmith. After the war, he worked as a messenger in the Department of Labor in Lagos.

When Tutuola's first novel, *The Palm-Wine Drinkard,* was published in London in 1952, it attracted large numbers of readers because of its language (a representation of English as it is spoken in West Africa) and its combination of Yoruba mythology with Tutuola's own imaginative exaggerations. Many black West Africans were embarrassed by Tutuola's novel because they were afraid Europeans and Americans would assume that all West Africans spoke and wrote like Tutuola. After Nigeria gained its independence from Great Britain in 1960, black Nigerian writers such as Chinua Achebe and Wole Soyinka began to reevaluate Tutuola's skill in manipulating the "Queen's English" to reflect black West African imagination and speech patterns.

The Palm-Wine Drinkard is a quest story. The Drinkard's search for his tapster leads him to many strange adventures. The book

Grove/Atlantic, Inc.

has been compared with such classic works as the *Odyssey* and *Gulliver's Travels.* Dylan Thomas, a well-known lyric poet who reviewed the book, found it to be a "brief, thronged, grisly and bewitching story."

Each of Tutuola's novels is based on one of the many Yoruba folk tales he heard as a child. These novels include *My Life in the Bush of Ghosts* (1954), *Simbi and the Satyr of the Dark Jungle* (1955), *The Brave African Huntress* (1958), *The Feather Woman of the Jungle* (1962), *Ajaiyi and His Inherited Poverty* (1967), *The Witch-Herbalist of the Remote Town* (1981), and *Pauper, Brawler, and Slanderer* (1987).

Amos Tutuola   817

Before You Read

from **The Palm-Wine Drinkard**

Using What You Know _____

Recall what you learned about the African oral tradition in Unit Two. What do you remember about professional storytellers such as the griot? What is the relationship between storytellers and their audiences? Think of some of the narratives you have read. How do such elements as magic, charms, and disguises play an important role in folk tales and legends?

Literary Focus: Oral Tradition _____

Tutuola is the first major African writer to use traditional tales in his fiction. Some critics have noted that he represents the transition from an oral to a written literature. One characteristic associated with the oral tradition of storytelling is the repetition of certain details. Another characteristic is a childlike imagination that creates fantastic and incredible creatures. Note these elements in Tutuola's story of "Wraith-Island."

Setting a Purpose _____

Those who find fault with Tutuola's use of language consider his writing ungrammatical and unconventional. Those who admire his use of language praise his faithfulness to the oral tradition. Read this prose excerpt aloud. Then see what you think.

The Palm-Wine Drinkard

Amos Tutuola

Not Too Small to Be Chosen

There were many wonderful creatures in the olden days. One day, the king of the "Wraith[1]-Island" town chose all the people, spirits and terrible creatures of the Island to help him to clear his corn field which was about 2 miles square. Then one fine morning, we gathered together and went to the corn field, and cleared it away, after that, we returned to the king and told him that we had cleared his corn field, he thanked us, and gave us food and drinks.

But as a matter of fact none of the creatures is too small to choose for a help. We did not know that immediately we left the field, a tiny creature who was not chosen with us by the king went to the field and commanded all the weeds that we had cleared to grow up as if they were not cleared.

He was saying thus:—"THE KING OF THE 'WRAITH-ISLAND' BEGGED ALL THE CREATURES OF THE 'WRAITH-ISLAND' AND LEFT HIM OUT, SO THAT, ALL THE CLEARED-WEEDS RISE UP; AND LET US GO AND DANCE TO A BAND AT THE 'WRAITH-ISLAND'; IF BAND COULD NOT SOUND, WE SHOULD DANCE WITH MELODIOUS MUSIC."

1. **Wraith** (rāth): ghost or apparition.

But at the same time that the tiny creature commanded the weeds, all rose up as if the field was not cleared for two years. Then early in the morning of the second day that we had cleared it, the king went to the field to visit his corn, but to his surprise, he met the field uncleared, then he returned to the town and called the whole of us and asked that why did we not clear his field? We replied that we had cleared it yesterday, but the king said no, we did not clear it. Then the whole of us went to the field to witness it, but we saw the field as if it was not cleared as the king said. After that we gathered together and went to clear it as before, then we returned to the king again and told him that we had cleared it. But when he went there, he found it uncleared as before and came back to the town and told us again that we did not clear his field, then the whole of us ran to the field and found it uncleared. So we gathered together for the third time and went to clear it, after we had cleared it, we told one of us to hide himself inside a bush which was very close to the field, but before 30 minutes that he was watching the field, he saw a very tiny creature who was just a baby of one day of age and he commanded the weeds to rise up as he was commanding before. Then that one of us who hid himself inside the bush and was watching him tried all his efforts and caught him, then he brought him to the king; when the king saw the tiny creature, he called the whole of us to his palace.

After that, the king asked him who was commanding the cleared-weeds of his field to rise up after the field had been cleared: The tiny creature replied that he was commanding all the weeds to rise up, because the king chose all the creatures of the "Wraith-Island" town but left him out, although he was the smallest among all, but he had the power to command weeds etc. which had been cleared to grow up as if it was not cleared at all. But the king said that he had just forgotten to choose him with the rest and not because of his small appearance.

Then the king made excuses to him, after that he went away. This was a very wonderful tiny creature.

Responding to the Selection
from **The Palm-Wine Drinkard** by Amos Tutuola

Interpreting Meanings

1. Why is the tiny creature offended by the king's action? Do you know of any fairy tales or folk tales that make use of a similar theme?
2. Small creatures who possess special powers appear in folklore of many different cultures. Name some examples. Why do you think small creatures are often associated with mischief?
3. Read aloud the tiny creature's complaint, printed in capital letters. What is unusual about the language?
4. How is the tiny creature discovered? Why do you think the king does not punish him?

Creative Writing

Writing a Tale
Think of some tiny creatures that have become famous in folklore. Tom Thumb, for example, is a well-known hero in English folk tales. Thumbelisa, a character in a fairy tale by Hans Christian Andersen, is an inch in height and sleeps in a walnut shell.

Write an original story with the title "Not Too Small to Be Chosen." You can base your story on some actual event, or you can invent an imaginary creature, as Tutuola has done.

About the Author
Camara Laye (1928–1980)

Camara Laye was born in Kouroussa (ko͞o-ro͞o′sä), a town in Guinea (gĭn′ē), at that time a territory of French West Africa. Laye received his formal education in French. He attended a technical high school in Conakry (kän′ə-krē), the capital, and then went to Paris to study automotive engineering. He returned to Guinea in 1956 and after his nation received its independence in 1958, he served as a diplomat to several African nations. In 1965 Laye left Guinea because of political difficulties and went into exile, first to Côte d'Ivoire and then to Senegal.

While Laye was living in Paris and feeling homesick, he began *The Dark Child* (its French title is *L'Enfant noir*). This autobiographical novel, which appeared in 1953, tells the story of a boy growing up in an African village. The book brought Laye international recognition. Many readers consider it the most famous African novel in French, and it has been called a major example of the Négritude movement, a literary movement among French-speaking black Africans that affirmed the values of black African culture. Laye's other works include *The Radiance of the King* (1954) and *A Dream of Africa* (1966). Before his death he wrote *The Guardian of the Word* (1978), an epic novel about Sundiata Keita, the first emperor of Mali. Laye based his story on the oral accounts of Guinea's griots.

Before You Read

from **The Dark Child**

Using What You Know

Almost every society has certain *initiation* rites, ceremonies in which someone becomes a member of a group or achieves a special position. Do you know of any religious ceremonies that are held when young people reach the age of duty and responsibility? How do fraternities, sororities, clubs, and other social organizations admit new members? Do any of these experiences require passing a difficult test of character or courage? What personal experiences have you had with initiation ceremonies?

Literary Focus: Suspense and Foreshadowing

To build your interest in his narrative, the author uses certain techniques of **suspense**. Suspense makes a reader wonder about the outcome of events. It makes the reader ask, "What will happen next?" Often a writer will hint at what is to come by dropping clues. This method of building suspense is called **foreshadowing**.

Setting a Purpose

In the narrative you will read here, the young boys of an African village must undergo a special kind of initiation before they can be admitted into adulthood. As you read, note how the author gets you interested in the narrative and prepares you for its outcome.

The Dark Child

Camara Laye

TRANSLATED BY **James Kirkup and Ernest Jones**

I was growing up. The time had come for me to join the society of the uninitiated. This rather mysterious society—and at that age it was very mysterious to me, though not very secret—comprised all the young boys, all the uncircumcised, of twelve, thirteen and fourteen years of age, and it was run by our elders, whom we called the big *Kondéns*. I joined it one evening before the feast of Ramadan.[1]

As soon as the sun had gone down, the tom-tom had begun to beat. Even though it was being played in a remote part of the concession,[2] its notes had roused me at once, had struck my breast, had struck right at my heart, just as if Kodoké, our best player, had been playing for me alone. A little later I had heard the shrill voices of boys accompanying the tom-tom with their cries and singing. Yes, the time had come for me.

It was the first time I had spent the feast of Ramadan at Kouroussa. Until this year, my grandmother had always insisted on my spending it with her at Tindican. All that morning and even more so in the afternoon,

I had been in a state of great agitation, with everyone busy preparing for the festival, bumping into and pushing each other and asking me to help. Outside, the uproar was just as bad. Kouroussa is the chief town of our region, and all the canton[3] chiefs, attended by their musicians, make it a custom to gather here for the festival. From the gateway to the concession I had watched them pass by, with their companies of praise-singers, balaphonists[4] and guitarists, drum and tom-tom players. Until now I had only been thinking of the festival and of the sumptuous feast that awaited me—but now there was something quite different in the wind.

The screaming crowd that surrounded Kodoké and his famous tom-tom was getting nearer. Going from one concession to another, the crowd would stop where there was a boy of an age, to join the society, and take him away. That is why it was so slow in coming, yet so sure, so ineluctable.[5] As sure, as ineluctable as the fate that awaited me.

1. **Ramadan** (răm'ə-dän'): the ninth month of the Islamic year. Fasting is observed daily from dawn to sunset.
2. **concession:** here, household.

3. **canton** (kăn'tən,-tŏn'): district.
4. **balaphonists** (bă'lə-fō'nĭsts): muscians who play the *balaphon*, a West African xylophone using gourds as resonators.
5. **ineluctable** (ĭn'ĭ-lŭk'tə-bəl): unable to be avoided.

Ramadan procession, Kano, Nigeria.
Peter Marlow/Magnum Photos

What fate? My meeting with Kondén Diara!

Now I was not unaware of who Kondén Diara was. My mother had often talked of him, and so at times had my uncles and whoever else had authority over me. They had threatened me only too often with Kondén Diara, that terrible bogeyman, that "lion that eats up little boys." And here was Kondén Diara—but was he a man? Was he an animal? Was he not rather half-man, half-animal? My friend Kouyaté believed he was more man than beast—here was Kondén Diara leaving the dim world of hearsay, here he was taking on flesh and blood, yes, and roused by Kodoké's tom-tom was prowling around the town! This night was to be the night of Kondén Diara.

Now I could hear the beating of the tom-tom very plainly—Kodoké was much nearer—I could hear perfectly the chanting and the shouts that rose into the dark. I could make out almost as distinctly the rather hollow, crisp, well-marked beats of the *coros* that are a kind of miniature canoe, and are beaten with a bit of wood. I was standing at the entrance to the concession, waiting. I, too, was holding my *coro*, ready to play it with the stick clutched nervously in my hand. I was waiting, hidden by the shadow of the hut. I was waiting, filled with a dreadful anxiety, my eyes searching the blackness.

"Well?" asked my father.

He had crossed the workshop without my hearing him.

"Are you afraid?"

"A little," I replied.

He laid his hand on my shoulder.

"It's all right. Don't worry."

He drew me to him, and I could feel his warmth; it warmed me, too, and I began to feel less frightened; my heart did not beat so fast.

"You mustn't be afraid."

"No."

I knew that whatever my fear might be I must be brave. I wasn't to show fright or to run off and hide. Still less was I to resist or cry out when my elders carried me off.

"I, too, went through this test," said my father.

"What happens to you?" I asked.

"Nothing you need really be afraid of, nothing you can not overcome by your own will power. Remember: you have to control your fear; you have to control yourself. Kondén Diara will not take you away. He will roar. But he won't do more than roar. You won't be frightened, now, will you?"

"I'll try not to be."

"Even if you are frightened, do not show it."

He went away, and I began waiting again, and the disturbing uproar came nearer and nearer. Suddenly I saw the crowd emerging from the dark and rushing towards me. Kodoké, his tom-tom slung over one shoulder, was marching at their head, followed by the drummers.

I ran back quickly into the yard, and, standing in the middle of it, I awaited the awful invasion with as much courage as I could manage. I did not have long to wait. The crowd was upon me. It was spreading tumultuously all around me, overwhelming me with shouts and cries and beating tom-toms, beating drums. It formed a circle, and I found myself in the center, alone, curiously isolated, still free and yet already captive. Inside the circle, I recognized Kouyaté and others, many of them friends of mine who had been collected as the crowd moved on, collected as I was to be, as I already was; and it seemed to me they were none of them looking very happy—but was I any more happy than they? I began to beat my *coro,* as they were doing. Perhaps I was beating it with less confidence than they.

At this point young girls and women joined the circle and began to dance; young men and adolescents, stepping out of the crowd, moved into the circle too and began to dance facing the women. The men sang, the women clapped their hands. Soon the only ones left to form the circle were the uncircumcised boys. They too began to sing— they were not allowed to dance—and, as they sang, sang in unison, they forgot their anxiety. I too sang with them. When, having formed a circle again, the crowd left our concession, I went with it, almost willingly, beating my *coro* with great enthusiasm. Kouyaté was on my right.

Toward the middle of the night our tour of the town and the collection of uncircumcised boys were finished. We had arrived at the farthest outskirts of the concessions, and in front of us lay only the brush. Here the women and young girls left us. Then the grown men left. We were alone with the older boys, or should I say "delivered over" to them—for I remember the often rather disagreeable natures and rarely pleasant manners of those older ones.

The women and young girls now hurried back to their dwellings. Actually, they can

Tribesman from Kankan, a town in Upper Guinea.

year the initiation takes place. The place is well known: it is situated under an enormous bombax[6] tree, a hollow at the junction of the river Komoni and the river Niger. At normal times it is not forbidden to go there; but certainly it has not always been so, and some emanation[7] from the past I never knew still seems to hover around the huge trunk of the bombax tree. I think that a night such as the one we were going through must certainly have resurrected a part of that past.

We were walking in silence, closely hemmed in by our elders. Perhaps they were afraid we might escape? It looked like it. I do not think, however, that the idea of escape had occurred to any of us. The night, and that particular night, seemed impenetrable. Who knew where Kondén Diara had his lair? Who knew where he was prowling? But was it not right here, near the hollow? Yes, it must be here. And if we had to face him—and certainly we had to face him—it would surely be better to do so in a crowd, in this jostling group that seemed to make us all one, and seemed like a last refuge from the peril that was approaching.

Yet for all our nearness to one another and for all the vigilance of our elders, our march—so silent after the recent uproar—through the wan moonlight, far from the town, frightened us. And we were filled with terror at the thought of the sacred place toward which we were going, and the hidden presence of Kondén Diara.

Were our elders marching so closely beside us only to keep watch over us? Perhaps. But it is likely that they too felt something of the terror which had seized us. They too

not have been any more at ease than we were. I know for a fact that not one of them would have ventured to leave town on this night. Already, they found the town and the night sinister. I am certain that more than one who went back to her concession alone was to regret having joined the crowd. They took courage only after they had shut the gates of their concessions and the doors of their huts. Meanwhile, they hurried on and from time to time cast unquiet looks behind them. In a short while, when Kondén Diara would begin to roar, they would not be able to stop shaking with fright; they would all shake uncontrollably. Then they would run to make sure the doors were all properly barred. For them, as for us, though in a much less significant way, this night would be the night of Kondén Diara.

As soon as our elders had made sure that no intruder was present to disturb the mysteriousness of the ceremony, we left the town behind and entered the bush by a path which leads to a sacred place where each

6. **bombax** (băm′băks′): a tree that has showy flowers and leaves with fingerlike divisions.
7. **emanation** (ĕm′ə-nā′shən): something that comes forth or is emitted from a source.

826 CAMARA LAYE

found the night and the silence disturbing. And for them, as for us, marching close together was a means of allaying terror.

Just before we reached the hollow we saw flames leap from a huge wood fire previously hidden by bushes. Kouyaté squeezed my arm, and I knew he was referring to the fire. Yes, there was a fire. There too was Kondén Diara, the hidden presence of Kondén Diara. But there was also a reassuring presence in the depth of the night: a great fire! My spirits rose—at least they rose a little—and I squeezed Kouyaté's arm in return. I quickened my steps—we all quickened our steps—and the crimson radiance of the fire enveloped us. We had a harbor now, this kind of haven from the night: a huge blaze, and, at our backs, the enormous trunk of the bombax tree. Oh! It was a precarious[8] haven! But, however poor, it was infinitely better than the silence and the dark, the sullen silence of the dark. We assembled beneath the bombax tree. The ground beneath had been cleared of reeds and tall grasses.

Our elders suddenly shouted: "Kneel!"

We at once fell to our knees.

"Heads down!"

We lowered our heads.

"Lower than that!"

We bent our heads right to the ground, as if in prayer.

"Now hide your eyes!"

We didn't have to be told twice. We shut our eyes tight and pressed our hands over them. For would we not die of fright and horror if we should see, or so much as catch a glimpse of the Kondén Diara? Our elders walked up and down, behind us and in front of us, to make sure that we had all obeyed their orders to the letter. Woe to him who

8. **precarious** (prĭ-kâr′ē-əs): insecure; uncertain.

would have the audacity to disobey! He would be cruelly whipped. It would be a whipping all the more cruel because he would have no hope of redress, for he would find no one to listen to his complaint, no one to transgress against custom. But who would have the audacity to disobey?

Now that we were on our knees with our foreheads to the ground and our hands pressed over our eyes, Kondén Diara's roaring suddenly burst out.

We were expecting to hear this hoarse roar, we were not expecting any other sound, but it took us by surprise and shattered us, froze our hearts with its unexpectedness. And it was not only a lion, it was not only Kondén Diara roaring: there were ten, twenty, perhaps thirty lions that took their lead from him, uttering their terrible roars and surrounding the hollow; ten or twenty lions separated from us by a few yards only and whom the great wood fire would perhaps not always keep at bay; lions of every size and every age—we could tell that by the way they roared—from the very oldest ones to the very youngest cubs. No, not one of us would dream of venturing to open an eye, not one! Not one of us would dare to lift his head from the ground; he would rather bury it in the earth. And I bent down as far as I could; we all bent down further; we bent our knees as much as we could; we kept our backs as low as possible. I made myself—we all made ourselves—as small as we could.

"You mustn't be afraid!" I said to myself. "You must master your fear! Your father has commanded you to!"

But how was I to master it? Even in the town, far away from this clearing, women and children trembled and hid themselves in their huts. They heard the growling of Kondén Diara, and many of them stopped their

The Dark Child 827

ears to keep it out. The braver arose—that night it took courage to leave one's bed—and went again and again to check the doors and see that they were shut tight. How was I to stave off fear when I was within range of the dread monster? If he pleased, Kondén Diara could leap the fire in one bound and sink his claws in my back!

I did not doubt the presence of the monster, not for a single instant. Who could assemble such a numerous herd, hold such a nocturnal revel, if not Kondén Diara?

"He alone," I said to myself, "he alone has such power over lions. . . . Keep away, Kondén Diara! Keep away! Go back into the bush! . . ." But Kondén Diara went on with his revels, and sometimes it seemed to me that he roared right over my head, right into my own ears. "Keep away, I implore you, Kondén Diara!"

What was it my father had said? "Kondén Diara roars; but he won't do more than roar; he will not take you away . . ." Yes, something like that. But was it true, really true?

There was also a rumor that Kondén Diara sometimes pounced with fearsome claws on someone or other and carried him far away, far, far away into the depths of the bush; and then, days and days afterwards, months or even years later, quite by chance a huntsman might discover some whitened bones.

And do not people also die of fright? Ah! how I wished this roaring would stop! How I wished I was far away from this clearing, back in the concession, in the warm security of the hut! Would this roaring never cease?

"Go away, Kondén Diara! Go away! Stop roaring." Oh! those roars! I felt as if I could bear them no longer.

Whereupon, suddenly, they stopped! They stopped just as they had begun, so suddenly, in fact, that I felt only reluctant relief.

A rain forest in Guinea.

Marc & Evelyne Bernheim/Woodfin Camp

Was it over? Really over? Was it not just a temporary interruption? No, I dared not feel relieved just yet. And then suddenly the voice of one of the older boys rang out: "Get up!"

I heaved a sigh of relief. This time it was really over. We looked at one another: I looked at Kouyaté and the others. If there were only a little more light. . . . But the light from the fire was sufficient: great drops of sweat were still beading our foreheads; yet the night was chill. . . . Yes, we were afraid. We were not able to conceal our fear.

A new command rang out, and we sat down in front of the fire. Now our elders began our initiation. For the rest of the night they taught us the chants sung by the uncircumcised. We never moved. We learned the words and tunes as we heard them. We were attentive as if we had been at school, entirely attentive and docile.

When dawn came, our instruction was at an end. My legs and arms were numb. I worked my joints and rubbed my legs for a while, but my blood still flowed slowly. I was worn out, and I was cold. Looking around me, I could not understand why I had shaken with fear during the night: the first rays of dawn were falling so gently, so reassuringly, on the bombax tree, on the clearing. The sky looked so pure! Who would have believed that a few hours earlier a pack of lions led by Kondén Diara in person had been raging fiercely in the high grass and among the reeds, and that they had been separated from us only by a wood fire which had just now gone out as dawn came? No one. I would have doubted my own senses and set it all down as a nightmare if I had not noticed more than one of my companions casting an occasional fearful glance in the direction of the highest grass.

Responding to the Selection

from **The Dark Child** by Camara Laye

Identifying Facts

1. What signal gathers the village boys together for the ceremony of Kondén Diara?
2. What instruments do the boys carry and play?
3. Where does the initiation rite take place?
4. When they reach the sacred place, what are the boys commanded to do by the elders?
5. After the roaring stops, what instruction do the boys receive?

Interpreting Meanings

1. Describe the mood in the village when the sun goes down and the people get ready for the ceremony. What effect do the drums have?
2. What roles are played by the elders, by the older boys, and by the women and girls?
3. What mystery is associated with Kondén Diara? How does the setting where the ceremony takes place add to the suspense and mystery?
4. When does the ceremony reach its **climax,** or most exciting point? What terrors

does the narrator imagine during Kondén Diara's revels?

5. In your opinion, what is the purpose of the ceremony of Kondén Diara?

6. Does the father's advice (see page 825) indirectly explain why all the boys in the village are made to undergo this test?

Literary Elements

Understanding Suspense and Foreshadowing

We have all seen movies and television programs where a character is trapped in a dangerous situation—swimming in shark-infested waters, racing to defuse a time bomb, piloting a disabled aircraft. Such situations keep us on the edge of our seats, wondering how things will turn out.

Suspense is a sense of uncertainty about the outcome of events. In a narrative, suspense keeps us in a state of high interest so that we read on to find out what will happen. A skillful writer knows how to intensify our suspense so that as we read our own fear and uncertainty increase.

Suspense works hand in hand with **foreshadowing**. Foreshadowing refers to the use of clues that hint at what is to come. Foreshadowing builds suspense by preparing the reader for the outcome. The planting of clues can also help to create a mood of doubt and anxiety.

In the opening paragraph of the selection, the narrator describes the society of the un-initiated as *mysterious.* How does this word create suspense?

On page 823, the narrator says

Until now I had only been thinking of the festival and of the sumptuous feast that awaited me—but now there was something quite different in the wind.

What does this statement foreshadow?

How do the sounds—of the drums, of chanting and shouting—add to the narrative's suspense?

Read the passage on page 826 where the boys are taken to the sacred place for the ceremony. How does the description arouse suspense? Which words in particular heighten your interest?

Language and Vocabulary

Recognizing Denotative and Connotative Meanings

The literal (or "dictionary") definition of a word is called its **denotation. Connotation** refers to the emotions and associations that a word arouses. For example, the word *crimson* literally means "of a deep-red color." The word is often used, however, to describe something violent or lurid ("a crimson past") or to refer to someone's embarrassment or anger ("he turned crimson"). In Camara's phrase "the crimson radiance of the fire" (page 827), the word suggests vividness and intensity.

Writers use the connotative meanings of words to build mood. Consider the meanings of the word *wan* on page 826:

Word	Denotation	Connotation
wan	pale or colorless	weak or sickly

Using this chart as a model, give the denotative and connotative meanings of the italicized words in the following excerpts from the selection. Use a dictionary.

> We had a harbor now, this kind of *haven* from the night (page 827).
> . . . it was infinitely better than the silence and the dark, the *sullen* silence of the dark (page 827).
> We were attentive as if we had been at school, entirely attentive and *docile* (page 829).

Narrative Writing

Relating a Personal Experience
Narrative, as you know, is another word for *story.* A narrative relates a series of events, usually in **chronological order,** or the order in which they happen.

Write a narrative based on some test of your personal courage, telling how you over-

came your fears of something or someone. In your narrative discuss your feelings about the experience.

Prewriting Strategies
A good narrative deals with one main action and has a beginning, a middle, and an end.

Make a list of the actions you will include in your narrative. Make sure that your narrative answers the **5W–How?** questions **(Who? What? When? Where? Why?** and **How?).** Arrange the events in chronological order.

Begin with a sentence that will get your reader's attention. Vary your sentences so that not all of them begin in the same way. Connect ideas with transitional words such as *then, next, by this time,* and so on.

Evaluate your first draft by using the **Guide** on pages 65–66. Proofread the revised paper and prepare a final copy.

Speaking and Listening

Reporting on a Festival
Report on a particular holiday or festival that is celebrated by your family or in your community, or locate information about some special occasion, such as the Mardi Gras preceding Lent. For example, you might look into the Jonkonnu, or Junkeroo, holiday, which is a masquerade blending African and Caribbean customs.

About the Author

James Matthews (b. 1929)

The Schomburg Center for Research in Black Culture/New York Public Library

James Matthews was born in Cape Town, South Africa. He attended local schools for blacks but had to work as a newsboy, messenger, and telephone operator to support himself. He devoted his free time to writing for *Drum,* the leading journal open to black writers in South Africa.

Matthews has written short stories, novels, and poetry. Two of his books were translated into Swedish in the early sixties: *Azikwelwa,* a collection of short stories, in 1962, and *Mary, Bill, Cyril, John and Joseph,* a novel, in 1963. Four of his short stories were included in Richard Rive's anthology *Quartet: New Voices from South Africa,* which was published in 1965. In the stories in *Azikwelwa* and *Quartet,* Matthews satirized what was at the time South Africa's official policy of racial segregation.

During the 1970s, Matthews published two collections of poetry that more openly attacked the government: *Cry Rage* (1972) and *Pass Me a Meatball* (1977). The second collection contains poems written while he was held in detention in 1976. The poems in *Images* (1980), a third volume, depict the tragedy of life in South Africa.

Before You Read

The Park

Using What You Know

Many public parks have a playground area set aside for children, where there may be swings, a seesaw, a slide, and other equipment for recreation. Recall your own experiences in playgrounds when you were younger. Which activities did you enjoy most—sliding down the chute, using the swings, climbing the monkey bars? Compare your memories with those of your classmates.

Literary Focus: Flashback

The plot of a short story usually moves in **chronological order**. The events are presented as they occur in time. Sometimes, however, a writer interrupts the action to tell about something that happened earlier. A **flashback** is a scene in a narrative that "flashes back" to a past event in a character's life. A flashback often makes the present action clearer.

Often, but not always, a writer will signal when a flashback occurs. You need to pay close attention to find the point where the narrative is interrupted and where the action resumes.

Setting a Purpose

As you read, look for the flashbacks that tell you what happened at an earlier time. How do these flashbacks help you understand the boy's feelings and actions?

The Park

James Matthews

1

He looked longingly at the children on the other side of the railings; the children sliding down the chute, landing with feet astride on the bouncy lawn; screaming as they almost touched the sky with each upward curve of their swings; their joyful, demented shrieks at each dip of the merry-go-round. He looked at them and his body trembled and itched to share their joy—buttocks to fit board, and hands and feet to touch steel. Next to him, on the ground, was a bundle of clothing, washed and ironed, wrapped in a sheet.

Five small boys, pursued by two bigger ones, ran past, ignoring him. One of the bigger boys stopped. "What are you looking at, you brown ape?" he said, stooping to pick up a lump of clay. He recognized him. The boy was present the day he was put out of the park. The boy pitched the lump, shattering it on the rail above his head and the fragments fell on to his face.

He spat out the particles of clay clinging to the lining of his lips, eyes searching for an object to throw at the boys separated from him by the railings. More boys joined the one in front of him and he was frightened by their number.

834 JAMES MATTHEWS

Without a word he shook his bundle free from the clay and raised it to his head and walked away.

As he walked he recalled his last visit to the park. Without hesitation he had gone through the gates and got on to the nearest swing. Even now he could feel that pleasurable thrill which travelled the length of his body as he rocketed himself higher, higher, until he felt that the swing would up-end him when it reached its peak. Almost leisurely he had allowed it to come to a halt, like a pendulum shortening its stroke, and then ran towards the see-saw. A white boy, about his own age, was seated opposite him. Accordion-like, their legs folded to send the see-saw jerking from the indentation it pounded in the grass. A hand pressing on his shoulder stopped a jerk. He turned around to look into the face of the attendant.

"Get off!" The skin tightened between his eyes. "Why must I get off? What have I done?" He held on, hands clamped on to the iron hoop attached to the wooden see-saw. The white boy jumped off from the other end and stood—a detached spectator. "You must get off!" the attendant spoke in a low voice so that it would not carry to the people who were gathering.

"The council says," he continued, "that we coloureds must not use the same swings as the whites. You must use the park where you stay." His voice apologizing for the uniform he wore which gave him the right to be in the park to watch that the little whites were not hurt while playing.

"There's no park where we stay." He waved a hand in the direction of a block of flats. "There's a park on the other side of town but I don't know where it is." He walked past them. The mothers with their babies—pink and belching—cradled in their arms, the children lolling on the grass, his companion from the see-saw, the nurse girls—their uniforms their badges of indemnity[1]—pushing prams.[2] Beside him walked the attendant. At the entrance, the attendant pointed an accusing finger at a notice board.

"There you can read for yourself." Absolving himself of any blame. He struggled with the red letters on the white background.

"Blankes Alleen, Whites Only." He walked through the gates and behind him the swings screeched, the see-saw rattled, and the merry-go-round rumbled.

He walked past the park as on each occasion after that he had been forced to walk past it.

He shifted the bundle to a more comfortable position, easing the pain biting into his shoulder muscles. What harm would I be doing if I were to use the swings? Would it stop the swings from swinging? Would the chute collapse? The bundle pressed deeper and the pain became an even line across his shoulders and he had no answer to his reasoning.

The park itself, with its wide lawns and flower-beds and rockeries and dwarf trees, meant nothing to him. It was the gaily painted tubing, the silver chains and brown boards, transport to never-never land, which gripped him.

Only once, long ago, and then almost as if by mistake, had he been on something to beat it. He was taken by his father, in one of those rare moments when they were taken anywhere, to a fair ground. He had stood captivated by the wooden horses with their gilded reins and scarlet saddles dipping in time to the music as they whirled by.

1. **badges of indemnity** (ĭn-dĕm′nə-tē): Their uniforms allow them to come and go freely in the park.
2. **prams:** baby carriages.

For a brief moment he was astride one and he prayed it would last for ever, but the moment lasted only the time it took him to whisper the prayer. Then he was standing, clutching his father's trousers, watching the other riders astride the dipping horses.

Another shifting of the bundle and he was at the house where he delivered the clothing his mother had washed in a round tub, filled with boiling water, the steam covering her face with a film of sweat. Her voice, when she spoke, was as soft and clinging as the steam enveloping her.

He pushed the gate open and walked around the back, watching for the aged lap-dog[3] which, at his entry, would rush out to wheeze asthmatically around his feet and nip with blunt teeth at his ankles.

A round-faced African girl, her blackness heightened by the white, starched uniform she wore, opened the kitchen door to let him in. She cleared the table and placed the bundle on it.

"I will call madam." She said the words spaced and highly pitched as if she had some difficulty in uttering the syllables in English. Her buttocks bounced beneath the tight uniform and the backs of her calves shone with fat.

"Are you sure you've brought everything?" was the greeting he received each time he brought the bundle, and each time she checked every item and always nothing was missing. He looked at her and lowered his voice as he said, "Everything's there, madam."

What followed had become a routine between the three of them.

"Have you had anything to eat?" she asked him.

He shook his head.

"Well, we can't let you go off like that." Turning to the African woman in the white, starched uniform, "What have we got?"

The maid swung open the refrigerator door and took out a plate of food. She placed it on the table and set a glass of milk next to it.

When he was seated the white woman left the kitchen and he was alone with the maid.

His nervousness left him and he could concentrate on what was on the plate.

A handful of peas, a dab of mashed potato, a tomato sliced into bleeding circles, a sprinkling of grated carrots, and no rice.

White people are funny, he told himself. How can anyone fill himself with this? It doesn't form a lump, like the food my mama makes.

He washed it down with milk.

"Thank you, Annie," he said as he pushed the glass aside.

Her teeth gleamed porcelain-white as she smiled.

He sat fidgeting, impatient to be outside, away from the kitchen with its glossy, tiled floor and steel cupboards Duco-ed[4] a clinical white to match the food-stacked refrigerator.

"I see you have finished." The voice startled him. She held out an envelope containing the ten-shilling note[5]—payment for his mother's weekly struggle over the wash tub. "This is for you." A sixpence was dropped into his hand, a long fingernail raking his palm.

"Thank you, madam." His voice barely audible.

"Tell your mother I'm going away on holi-

---

3. **lap-dog:** a small dog that easily fits in one's lap.

4. **Duco-ed:** Duco is a trademark for a kind of lacquer.
5. **ten-shilling note:** The shilling was a monetary unit in countries that were in the British Commonwealth. A sixpence was a coin worth six pennies.

day for about a month and I will let her know when I'm back."

Then he was dismissed and her high heels tapped out of the kitchen. He nodded his head at the African maid who took an apple from the bowl which was bursting with fruit, and handed it to him.

Her smile bathed her face in light.

As he walked down the path he finished off the apple with big bites.

Before he reached the gate the dog was after him, its hot breath warming his heels. He turned and poked his toes into its face. It barked hoarsely in protest, a look of outrage on its face.

He laughed delightedly at the expression which changed the dog's features into those of an old man.

Let's see you do that again. He waved his foot in front of the pug-nose. The nose retreated and made an about-turn, waddling away with its dignity deflated by his affront.

As he walked he mentally spent his sixpence.

I'll buy a penny drops, the sour ones which taste like limes; a penny bull's eyes, a packet of sherbet with the licorice tube at the end of the packet; and a penny star toffees, red ones, which colour your tongue and turn your spittle into blood.

His glands were titillated[6] and his mouth filled with saliva. He stopped at the first shop and walked inside.

Trays were filled with expensive chocolates and sweets of a type never seen in jars on the shelves of the Indian shop at the corner where he stayed. He walked out, not buying a thing.

His footsteps lagged as he reached the park.

6. **titillated** (tĭt'ə-lāt'əd): excited; stimulated.

The nurse girls with their babies and prams were gone, their places occupied by old men, who, with their hands holding up their stomachs, were casting disapproving eyes over the confusion and clatter confronting them.

A ball was kicked perilously close to one old man, and the boy who ran after it stopped as the old man raised his stick, daring him to come closer.

The rest of them called to the boy to get the ball. He edged closer and made a grab at it as the old man swung his cane. The cane missed him by more than a foot and he swaggered back, the ball held under his arm. Their game was resumed.

From the other side of the railings he watched them; the boys kicking the ball; the children cavorting on the grass; even the old men, senile on the seats; but most of all, the children enjoying themselves with what was denied him; and his whole body yearned to be part of them.

"Damn it!" He looked over his shoulder to see if anyone had heard him. "Damn it!" he said louder. "Damn on them! Their park, the grass, the swings, the see-saw. Everything! Damn it! Damn it!"

His small hands impotently shook the tall railings towering above his head.

It struck him that he would not be seeing the park for a whole month, that there would be no reason for him to pass it.

Despair filled him. He had to do something to ease his anger.

A bag filled with fruit peelings was on top of the rubbish stacked in a waste-basket fitted to a pole. He reached for it and frantically threw it over the railings. He ran without waiting to see the result.

Out of breath three streets farther, he slowed down, pain stabbing beneath his

heart. The act had brought no relief, only intensified the longing.

He was oblivious of the people passing, the hoots of the vehicles whose path he crossed without thinking. Once, when he was roughly pushed aside, he did not even bother to look and see who had done it.

2

The familiar shrieks and smells told him he was home.

The Indian shop could not draw him out of his melancholy mood and he walked past it, his sixpence unspent, in his pocket.

A group of boys were playing on the pavement.

Some of them called to him but he ignored them and turned into a short side-street.

He mounted the flat stoep[7] of a double-storey house with a façade[8] that must have been painted once but had now turned a nondescript grey with the red brick underneath showing through.

Beyond the threshold the room was dim. He walked past the scattered furniture with a familiarity that did not need guidance.

His mother was in the kitchen, hovering above a pot perched on a pressure stove.

He placed the envelope on the table. She

7. **stoep** (sto͞op): a raised platform at the front or on the sides of a house.
8. **façade** (fə-säd′): front part.

put aside the spoon and stuck a finger under the flap of the envelope, tearing it in half. She placed the ten-shilling note in a spout-less teapot on the shelf.

"Are you hungry?"

He nodded his head.

She poured him a cup of soup and added a thick slice of brown bread.

Between bites of bread and sips of the soup which scalded his throat he told her that there wouldn't be any washing coming during the week.

"Why? What's the matter? What have I done?"

"Nothing. Madam says she's going away for a month and she'll let mama know when she gets back."

"What am I going to do now?" Her voice took on a whine and her eyes strayed to the teapot containing the money. The whine hardened to reproach as she continued. "Why didn't she let me know she was going away? I could have looked for another madam."

She paused. "I slave away and the pain never leaves my back, and it's too much for her to let me know she's going away. The money I get from her just keeps us nicely steady. How am I going to cover the hole?"

As he ate, he wondered how the ten shillings he had brought helped to keep them nicely steady. There was no change in their meals. It was, as usual, not enough and the only time they received new clothes was at Christmas.

"There's the burial to pay and I was going to ask Mr. Lemonsky to bring some lino[9] for the front room. I'm sick of seeing boards where the lino's worn through, but it's no use asking him to bring it now. Without

money you have as much hope as getting wine on a Saturday."

He hurried his eating to get away from the words wafting towards him, before they could soak into him, trapping him in the chair to witness his mother's miseries.

Outside, they were still playing with their tyres.[10] He joined them half-heartedly. As he rolled the tyre, his spirit was in the park on the swings. There was no barrier to his coming and he could do as he pleased. He was away from the narrow streets and squawking children and speeding cars. He was in a place of green grass and red tubing and silver steel. The tyre rolled past him. He made no effort to grab it.

"Go get the tyre." . . . "Are you asleep?" . . . "Don't you want to play any more?" He walked away, ignoring their cries.

Rage boiled up inside him. Rage against the houses with their streaked walls and smashed panes filled by too many people; the overflowing garbage pails outside doors; the alleys and streets; and a law he could not understand; a law that shut him out of the park.

He burst into tears. He swept his arms across his cheeks to check his weeping.

He lowered his hands to peer at the boy confronting him.

"I'm not crying, damn you. Something's gone into my eye and I was rubbing it."

"I think you're crying."

He pushed past and continued towards the shop. "Crying doll!" the boy's taunt rang after him.

The shop's sole, iron-barred window was crowded. Oranges were mixed with writing paper and dried figs were strewn on school slates; clothing and crockery collected dust.

9. **lino:** linoleum, used as a floor covering.

10. **tyres:** British spelling for *tires.*

Across the window a cockroach made its leisurely way, antennae on the alert.

Inside, the shop was as crowded as the window. Bags covered the floor, leaving a narrow path to the counter. "Yes, boy?" He showed teeth scarlet with betel.[11]

"Come'n, boy. What you want? No stand here all day." His jaws worked at the betel-nut held captive by his stained teeth.

He ordered penny portions of his selections.

Transferring the sweets to his pocket he threw the torn container on the floor and walked out. Behind him the Indian murmured grimly, jaws working faster.

One side of the street was in shadow. He sat with his back against the wall, savouring the last of the sun.

Bull's-eye, peppermint, a piece of licorice —all lumped together in his cheek. For the moment, the park was forgotten.

He watched the girl advance without interest.

"Mama says you must come 'n eat." She stared at his bulging cheek, one hand rubbing the side of her nose. "Gimme." He gave her a bull's-eye which she dropped into her mouth between dabs at her nose.

"Wipe your snot!" he ordered her, showing his superiority. He walked past. She followed, sucking and sniffing.

When they entered the kitchen their father was already seated at the table.

"Why must I always send somebody after you?" his mother said.

He slipped into his seat and then hurriedly got up to wash his hands before his mother could find fault with yet another point.

Supper was a silent affair except for the scraping of spoon across plate and an occa-

sional sniff from his sister.

Almost at the end of the meal a thought came to mind. He sat, spoon poised in the air, shaken by its magnitude. Why not go to the park after dark? After it had closed its gates on the old men, the children, the nurses with their prams. There would be no one to stop him. He couldn't think further. He was light-headed with the thought of it. His mother's voice, as she related her day to his father, was not the steam which stung but a soft breeze wafting past him, leaving him undisturbed. Qualms troubled him. He had never been in that part of town at night. A band of fear tightened across his chest, contracting his insides, making it hard for him to swallow his food. He gripped his spoon more tightly, stretching the skin across his knuckles.

I'll do it! I'll go to the park as soon as we're finished eating. He controlled himself with difficulty. He swallowed what was left on his plate and furtively checked to see how the others were faring. Hurry it up! Hurry it up!

When his father pushed the last plate aside and lit a cigarette, he hastily cleared the table and began washing up.

Each piece of crockery washed, he passed on to his sister whose sniffing kept pace with their combined operation.

The dishes done, he swept the kitchen and carried out the garbage bin.

"Can I go out and play, mama?"

"Don't let me have to send for you again."

His father remained silent, buried behind his newspaper.

"Before you go," his mother stopped him, "light the lamp and hang it in the passage."

He filled the lamp with paraffin, turned up its wick and lit it. The light glimmered weakly through the streaked glass.

11. **betel** (bēt′əl): the fruit of the betel palm.

Struan Robertson/Magnum Photos

3

The moon to him was a fluorescent ball—light without warmth—and the stars, fragments chipped off it. Beneath street lights card games were in session. As he walked past, he sniffed the nostril-prickling smell of dagga.[12] Dim doorways could not conceal couples clutching at each other.

Once clear of the district he broke into a jog-trot. He did not slacken his pace as he passed through downtown with its wonderland shop windows. As he neared the park

12. **dagga** (dăg′ă): an herb that is smoked like tobacco.

his elation seeped out and his footsteps dragged.

In front of him was the park with its gate and iron railings. Behind the railings stood impaled the notice board. He could see the swings beyond. The sight strengthened him.

He walked over, his breath coming faster. There was no one in sight. A car turned the corner and came towards him and he started at the sound of its engine. The car swept past, the tyres softly licking the asphalt.

The railings were icy-cold to his touch and the shock sent him into action. He extended his arms and with monkey-like movements pulled himself up to perch on top of the railings, then dropped on the newly-turned earth.

The grass was damp with dew and he swept his feet across it. Then he ran and the wet grass bowed beneath his bare feet.

He ran from the swings to the merry-go-round, see-saw to chute, hands covering the metal.

Up the steps to the top of the chute. He stood outlined against the sky. He was a bird, an eagle. He flung himself down on his stomach, sliding swiftly. Wheeeeeeeeh! He rolled over when he slammed on to the grass. He was looking at the moon for an instant, then propelled himself to his feet and ran for the steps of the chute to recapture that feeling of flight. Each time he swept down the chute he wanted the trip never to end, to go on sliding, sliding, sliding.

He walked reluctantly past the see-saw, consoling himself with pushing at one end to send it whacking on the grass.

"Damn it!" he grunted as he strained to set the merry-go-round in motion. Thigh tensed, leg stretched, he pushed. The merry-go-round moved. He increased his exertion and jumped on, one leg trailing at

The Park   841

the ready, to shove if it should slow down. The merry-go-round dipped and swayed. To keep it moving, he had to push more than he rode. Not wanting to spoil his pleasure he jumped off and raced for the swings.

Feet astride, hands clutching silver chains, he jerked his body to gain momentum. He crouched like a runner, then violently straightened. The swing widened its arc. It swept higher, higher, higher. It reached the sky. He could touch the moon. He plucked a star to pin to his breast. The earth was far below him. No bird could fly as high as he. Upwards and onwards he went.

A light switched on in the hut at the far side of the park. It was a small patch of yellow on a dark square. The door opened and he saw a dark figure in the doorway, then the door was shut and the figure strode towards him. He knew it was the attendant. A torch glinted brightly in the moonlight, as it swung at his side.

He continued swinging.

The attendant came to a halt in front of him, out of reach of the swing's arc, and flashed his torch. The light caught him in mid-air.

"Dammit!" the attendant swore, "I've told you before you can't get on the swings."

The rattle of chains when the boy shifted his feet was the only answer he received.

"Why did you come back?"

"The swings, I came back for the swings."

The attendant catalogued the things denied them because of their colour. Even his job depended on their goodwill.

"Blerry whites! They got everything."

All his feelings urged him to leave the boy alone, to let him continue to enjoy himself. But the fear that someone might see them hardened him.

"Get off! Go home!" he screamed, his voice harsh, his anger directed at the system that drove him against his own. "If you don't get off, I'll go for the police. You know what they'll do to you."

The swing raced back and forth.

The attendant turned and raced towards the gate.

"Mama. Mama." His lips trembled, wishing himself safe in his mother's kitchen sitting next to the still-burning stove with a comic spread across his knees. "Mama. Mama." His voice mounted, wrenching from his throat, keeping pace with the soaring swing as it climbed to the sky. Voice and swing. Swing and voice. Higher. Higher. Higher. Until they were one.

At the entrance to the park the notice board stood tall, its shadow elongated, pointing towards him.

Responding to the Selection
The Park by James Matthews

Identifying Facts

1. What is the boy carrying when he stops at the park?
2. What message is he told to give his mother?
3. How does the boy spend his sixpence?
4. Why does the boy return to the park at night?

Interpreting Meanings

1. While the boy watches the children in the playground, he recalls an earlier visit to the park. What happened when he got on the seesaw? What reason was he given for being excluded from the park?
2. In a second **flashback,** the boy remembers being taken to a fair ground. Why has this memory made such an impression on him?
3. What contrasts are drawn between the child's home and the home where he delivers his bundle? How do you know that the payment for his mother's work is very little money?
4. When the boy passes the park on his way home, how does he show his frustration?
5. How does the boy finally satisfy his longing? Why do you think he defies the attendant?
6. What do you think will happen to the boy at the end of the story?

Literary Elements
Understanding Flashback

The term **flashback** refers to a scene in a short story, novel, play, or poem that interrupts the action to tell what happened earlier. Locate the first flashback in the story. How does the author signal this flashback? At what point does the flashback end and the present action resume?

Where does the second flashback occur? How is it signaled? Where does it end? How do both flashbacks help you understand what the boy thinks and feels?

Language and Vocabulary
Recognizing British Spellings

In this story, the word Americans spell *tire* is spelled *tyre,* which is the British spelling of the word. American spellings differ from British spellings in several ways. For example, we use **–or** where the British normally use **–our.** We write **color** and **neighbor,** whereas the British write **colour** and **neighbour.**

Using a dictionary if necessary, find the American spellings for each of these words:

theatre
centre
pretence
organise
connexion

Writer's Journal

Responding to the Story

The biographical introduction states that Matthews believes children are the worst victims of racial segregation. How does Matthews make the little boy in the story a sympathetic character? Do you feel you understand his rage and unhappiness? Discuss your reaction to the story. Share your response with others, if you wish.

Speaking and Listening

Comparing Characters

If you have read the excerpt from *Tell Freedom* (page 55), compare the experiences of the boy in that novel with those of the boy in Matthews's story. What do they have in common? How does each character rebel against racial oppression?

About the Author
Chinua Achebe (b. 1930)

Chinua Achebe (ä-chä′bē), one of Nigeria's leading writers, was born in Ogidi, a large village of the Igbo, or Ibo (ē′bō), people in eastern Nigeria. In the early twentieth century, the Anglican Church established one of its first missionary institutions at Ogidi, where it coexisted peacefully with the local culture. As a young child, Achebe attended the local missionary school. He then got a scholarship to Government College in Umuahia. In 1948 Achebe was among the first students admitted to University College at Ibadan (ē-bäd′ən), in western Nigeria, the traditional territory of the Yoruba (yō′rō͞o-bä) people. He had intended to study medicine but decided instead to study English literature, history, and religion. He received his B.A. in 1953.

Between 1954 and 1957, Achebe produced radio talk shows for the Nigerian Broadcasting Corporation in Lagos (lä′gōs), the capital city. During this period he wrote his first novel, *Things Fall Apart* (1958), which received international acclaim. He continued a dual career as a broadcaster and a novelist in Lagos until 1966. He published three more novels in rapid succession: *No Longer at Ease* (1960), *Arrow of God* (1964), and *A Man of the People* (1966). Then he left broadcasting and Lagos to return home, where civil war was looming. The Eastern Region, traditional territory of the Igbo people, made an unsuccessful attempt to declare itself an independent nation, Biafra (bē-ä′frä), and fought a war against the Nigerian govern-

Wide World Photos

ment, known as the Nigerian civil war, from 1967 to 1970. Achebe was one of the Igbo intellectuals who supported the move for independence.

During his thirty-year career, Achebe has traveled the world on lecture tours and teaching assignments. He has also edited or coedited collections of fiction and poetry by modern African writers. His recent publications include a novel, *Anthills of the Savannah* (1987), and a collection of essays, *Hopes and Impediments* (1988).

Achebe writes in English but transforms the language to reflect the African oral tradition. He uses Igbo proverbs, not only to give the flavor of Nigerian talk, but also to focus on the values of his people's cultural heritage.

Chinua Achebe   845

Before You Read

Dead Men's Path

Using What You Know

You sometimes have to choose between two courses of action or support one position rather than another. Sometimes you are asked for your advice where two friends or relatives disagree. Do you ever feel that both sides are "right"? What do you do if you believe that neither position is completely right? Think of a recent experience and consider how you handled it. Would you handle it the same way again?

Literary Focus: Conflict

The term **conflict** refers to the struggle between two opposing forces. Conflict may take place between two or more characters; it may occur between a character and society; it may happen between a character and some natural force. These forms of conflict are **external**. Conflict that takes place within a character's mind is **internal**. In a long narrative or a play, there may be several interrelated conflicts. In a short story there is generally one major conflict.

Setting a Purpose

As you read, note how Achebe handles the controversy. Does he force you to take sides, or does he give you a balanced picture of both sides?

Dead Men's Path

Chinua Achebe

Michael Obi's hopes were fulfilled much earlier than he had expected. He was appointed headmaster of Ndume[1] Central School in January 1949. It had always been an unprogressive school, so the Mission authorities decided to send a young and energetic man to run it. Obi accepted this responsibility with enthusiasm. He had many wonderful ideas and this was an opportunity to put them into practice. He had had sound secondary school education which designated him a "pivotal teacher" in the official records and set him apart from the other headmasters in the mission field. He was outspoken in his condemnation of the narrow views of these older and often less-educated ones.

"We shall make a good job of it, shan't we?" he asked his young wife when they first heard the joyful news of his promotion.

"We shall do our best," she replied. "We shall have such beautiful gardens and everything will be just *modern* and delightful . . ." In their two years of married life she had become completely infected by his passion for "modern methods" and his denigration of "these old and superannuated[2]

1. **Ndume** (n-d$\overline{oo}$′mē).
2. **superannuated** (s$\overline{oo}$′pər-ăn′y$\overline{oo}$-ā′tĭd): too old to be useful.

Dead Men's Path   847

people in the teaching field who would be better employed as traders in the Onitsha[3] market." She began to see herself already as the admired wife of the young headmaster, the queen of the school.

The wives of the other teachers would envy her position. She would set the fashion in everything . . . Then, suddenly, it occurred to her that there might not be other wives. Wavering between hope and fear, she asked her husband, looking anxiously at him.

"All our colleagues are young and unmarried," he said with enthusiasm which for once she did not share. "Which is a good thing," he continued.

"Why?"

"Why? They will give all their time and energy to the school."

Nancy was downcast. For a few minutes she became sceptical about the new school; but it was only for a few minutes. Her little personal misfortune could not blind her to her husband's happy prospects. She looked at him as he sat folded up in a chair. He was stoop-shouldered and looked frail. But he sometimes surprised people with sudden bursts of physical energy. In his present posture, however, all his bodily strength seemed to have retired behind his deep-set eyes, giving them an extraordinary power of penetration. He was only twenty-six, but looked thirty or more. On the whole, he was not unhandsome.

"A penny for your thoughts, Mike," said Nancy after a while, imitating the woman's magazine she read.

"I was thinking what a grand opportunity we've got at last to show these people how a school should be run."

Ndume School was backward in every sense of the word. Mr. Obi put his whole life into the work, and his wife hers too. He had two aims. A high standard of teaching was insisted upon, and the school compound[4] was to be turned into a place of beauty. Nancy's dream-gardens came to life with the coming of the rains, and blossomed. Beautiful hibiscus and allamanda hedges in brilliant red and yellow marked out the carefully tended school compound from the rank neighbourhood bushes.

One evening as Obi was admiring his work he was scandalized to see an old woman from the village hobble right across the compound, through a marigold flower-bed and the hedges. On going up there he found faint signs of an almost disused path from the village across the school compound to the bush on the other side.

"It amazes me," said Obi to one of his teachers who had been three years in the school, "that you people allowed the villagers to make use of this footpath. It is simply incredible." He shook his head.

"The path," said the teacher apologetically, "appears to be very important to them. Although it is hardly used, it connects the village shrine with their place of burial."

"And what has that got to do with the school?" asked the headmaster.

"Well, I don't know," replied the other with a shrug of the shoulders. "But I remember there was a big row some time ago when we attempted to close it."

"That was some time ago. But it will not be used now," said Obi as he walked away. "What will the Government Education Officer think of this when he comes to inspect the school next week? The villagers might,

---

3. **Onitsha** (ō-nĭch′ə): a commercial center in Nigeria.

4. **compound:** an enclosed area for a group of buildings.

for all I know, decide to use the schoolroom for a pagan ritual during the inspection."

Heavy sticks were planted closely across the path at the two places where it entered and left the school premises. These were further strengthened with barbed wire.

Three days later the village priest of *Ani* called on the headmaster. He was an old man and walked with a slight stoop. He carried a stout walking-stick which he usually tapped on the floor, by way of emphasis, each time he made a new point in his argument.

"I have heard," he said after the usual exchange of cordialities, "that our ancestral footpath has recently been closed . . ."

"Yes," replied Mr. Obi. "We cannot allow people to make a highway of our school compound."

"Look here, my son," said the priest bringing down his walking-stick, "this path was here before you were born and before your father was born. The whole life of this village depends on it. Our dead relatives depart by it and our ancestors visit us by it. But most important, it is the path of children coming in to be born . . ."

Mr. Obi listened with a satisfied smile on his face.

"The whole purpose of our school," he said finally, "is to eradicate just such beliefs as that. Dead men do not require footpaths.

Shrine to the earth goddess Ane, Ibo country, Nigeria.
Marc & Evelyne Bernheim/Woodfin Camp

The whole idea is just fantastic. Our duty is to teach your children to laugh at such ideas."

"What you say may be true," replied the priest, "but we follow the practices of our fathers. If you reopen the path we shall have nothing to quarrel about. What I always say is: let the hawk perch and let the eagle perch." He rose to go.

"I am sorry," said the young headmaster. "But the school compound cannot be a thoroughfare. It is against our regulations. I would suggest your constructing another path, skirting our premises. We can even get our boys to help in building it. I don't suppose the ancestors will find the little detour too burdensome."

"I have no more words to say," said the old priest, already outside.

Two days later a young woman in the vil-lage died in childbed. A diviner[5] was immediately consulted and he prescribed heavy sacrifices to propitiate[6] ancestors insulted by the fence.

Obi woke up next morning among the ruins of his work. The beautiful hedges were torn up not just near the path but right round the school, the flowers trampled to death and one of the school buildings pulled down . . . That day, the white Supervisor came to inspect the school and wrote a nasty report on the state of the premises but more seriously about the "tribal-war situation developing between the school and the village, arising in part from the misguided zeal of the new headmaster."

---

5. **diviner:** one who interprets omens or foretells the future.
6. **propitiate** (prō-pĭsh′ē-āt′): to regain the good will of or pacify (the ancestor).

Responding to the Selection

Dead Men's Path by Chinua Achebe

Identifying Facts

1. Who appoints Michael Obi headmaster of the Ndume Central School?
2. Why is his wife at first disappointed?
3. What two aims does Obi bring to his work?
4. Why do the villagers use the old path from the village to the bush?
5. How do the villagers take revenge?

Interpreting Meanings

1. Michael Obi's name is partly European and partly African. What significance does this have for the story?
2. How does Obi treat the beliefs of the villagers?
3. How does the village priest try to avoid controversy? What is the meaning of the proverb he recites to the headmaster?
4. A situation is said to be **ironic** when the outcome is the opposite of what was ex-

pected. In light of Obi's ambitions, why is the conclusion of the story ironic?

5. Is the major conflict in this story a conflict between characters, between generations, or between ideas? Explain.

Literary Elements

Relating Conflict to Plot

Plot is the sequence of events that make up a story. The chief element in a plot is **conflict.** Most stories end when the conflict is **resolved.** In other words, the main character either succeeds or fails, or one side wins out over the other. Some stories do not have a **resolution.** They end without a definite conclusion.

The events in a story often build toward a **climax,** the point at which the outcome of the story is decided. Which episode is the climax of "Dead Men's Path"?

Sometimes the term **dénouement** (dā-nōo'män) is used for the final revelation or outcome of the plot. How does the supervisor's report clarify the outcome?

Language and Vocabulary

Recognizing Compound Words

Some words in our language are **compound words.** They consist of two or more independent words that have been joined to form new words. The word *headmaster,* for example, or *headmistress* is composed of two independent words. Locate other compound words in the story. Then see how many more words of this kind you can name.

Narrative Writing

Relating the Story of a Conflict

Recall a "tribal-war situation" in your own experience. This might be a conflict in the community, for instance, an attempt to get elders to change a traditional way of thinking or to accept an unfamiliar form of behavior or dress.

Develop your narrative, following the **Writer's Guide** on pages 65–66. Share your narratives with other members of the class.

Speaking and Listening

Suggesting Alternative Action

Could Michael Obi have been successful by using a different approach? Consider the advice you might give him if you were a parent, a member of the school board, or a village elder reviewing his case. How would you take advantage of his enthusiasm and dedication? Try your ideas on some students before presenting your position to the class.

About the Author

Wole Soyinka (b. 1934)

 Wole Soyinka (wō'lĕ shô-yĭn'kä) is one of Africa's greatest writers. He is known primarily for his drama, but he has also written poetry, novels, essays, and autobiographies.

Abeokuta, Soyinka's birthplace, is one of six western provinces inhabited by the Yoruba people, the largest tribal group in Nigeria. Soyinka's parents were Christian converts who raised their children on a missionary compound; nevertheless, the Yoruba culture that thrived just beyond the compound walls had a profound influence on their son Wole's imagination.

Wole Soyinka attended universities in Ibadan and Lagos in Nigeria. He then went to Leeds University in England, where he earned a degree with honors in 1959. He became involved with theatrical productions while he was a student. After graduation, he taught for a while in London and worked for the Royal Court Theatre, where one of his plays was produced in 1958. Two early plays, *The Swamp Dwellers* and *The Lion and the Jewel,* were staged at the Ibadan Arts Theater in 1959. In 1960, his verse play, *A Dance of the Forests,* was produced to celebrate Nigerian independence.

Until his arrest and detention during the Nigerian civil war (1967–1970), Soyinka actively promoted the development of drama that combined Yoruba mythology, Christian Bible stories, and Greek and Roman legends. Since his release from prison, Soyinka's writings reflect his deep concern for modern

J. Langevin/Sygma

Nigerian society, specifically, how valuable aspects of traditional life can coexist with Westernization. This theme is prominent in *Aké: The Years of Childhood* (1981), an autobiography dealing with Soyinka's early years in the village of Aké. He tells how he was influenced by both Yoruban and European cultures.

As an editor of modern African poetry anthologies, Soyinka has been instrumental in introducing American and European audiences to African literature. In 1986, Soyinka became the first black African to receive the Nobel Prize in Literature for his outstanding achievements.

Before You Read

Using What You Know

In this excerpt from his autobiography, the author takes us back to his third year and re-creates the world as he experienced it at that early age. Try to recall your earliest memories. Do you remember your first birthday party? your first day in nursery school? Which experiences were difficult for you to understand? Keep these recollections in mind as you share Wole's view of events.

Literary Focus: Points of View

The autobiographer has many reasons for looking back over his or her life: to preserve fond memories of certain people, to explain why life turned out as it did, or to describe what life was like to an audience unfamiliar with the writer's culture. The most difficult task facing an autobiographer is to recall and describe accurately how it felt to be a child. At the same time that the impressions of childhood are being re-created for the reader, the writer tries to explain and evaluate the experiences of the past. The writer must be skillful in keeping the **points of view** of the child and of the adult narrator separated.

Setting a Purpose

Look for clues that help you understand the point of view of Wole, as a very young child, reacting to new experiences.

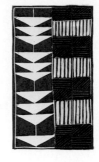

Aké
The Years of Childhood
Wole Soyinka

Marc Riboud/Magnum Photos

Every morning before I woke up, Tinu[1] was gone. She returned about midday carrying a slate with its marker attached to it. And she was dressed in the same khaki uniform as the hordes of children, of different sizes, who milled around the compound from morning till afternoon, occupied in a hundred ways.

At a set hour in the morning one of the bigger ones seized the chain which dangled from the bell-house, tugged at it with a motion which gave the appearance of a dance and the bell began pealing. Instantly, the various jostling, tumbling, racing and fighting pupils rushed in different directions around the school buildings, the smaller in size towards the schoolroom at the further end of the compound where I could no longer see them. The bigger pupils remained within sight, near the main building. They split into several groups, each group lined up under the watchful eye of a teacher. When all was orderly, I saw father[2] appear from nowhere at the top of the steps. He made a

1. **Tinu:** Wole's older sister.
2. **father:** Wole's father, also called Essay, is headmaster, or principal, of the school.

speech to the assembly, then stood aside. One member of the very biggest group stepped forward and raised a song. The others took it up and they marched into the school-building in twos, to the rhythm of the song.

The song changed every day, chosen from the constant group of five or six. That I came to have a favourite among them was because this was the same one which they sang with more zest than others. I noticed that on the days when it was the turn of this tune, they danced rather than marched. Even the teachers seemed affected, they had an indulgent smile on their faces and would even point out a pupil who on a certain charged beat in the tune would dip his shoulders in a most curious way, yet march without breaking the rhythm. It was an unusual song too, since the main song was in English but the chorus was sung in Yoruba:[3] I could only catch the words of the latter:

B'ina njo ma je'ko
B'ole nja, ma je'ko
Eni ebi npa, omo wi ti're[4]

I never heard any such lively singing from the other school, indeed that group simply vanished from sight, yet this was where my sister went. I never saw her anywhere among the marching group; in any case, there was nobody her size in that section. My curiosity grew every day. She sensed this and played on it, refusing to answer my questions or else throwing off incomplete fragments which only fed my curiosity.

3. **Yoruba** (yō'rōō-bä): a language spoken by the people in southwestern Nigeria.
4. **B'ina . . . ti're**: The author's own translation reads:
    If the house is on fire, I must eat
    If the house is being robbed, I must eat
    The child who is hungry, let him speak.

"I am going to school," I announced one day. It became a joke to be passed from mouth to mouth, producing instant guffaws. Mother appeasingly said, "Wait till you are as old as your sister."

The hum of voices, once the pupils were within the buildings, took mysterious overtones. Through the open windows of the schoolroom I saw heads in concentration, the majestic figure of a teacher who passed in and out of vision, mumbling incantations over the heads of his attentive audience. Different chants broke out from different parts of each building, sometimes there was even direct singing, accompanied by a harmonium.[5] When the indoor rites were over, they came out in different groups, played games, ran races, they spread over the compound picking up litter, sweeping the paths, clipping lawns and weeding flower-beds. They roamed about with hoes, cutlasses, brooms and sticks, retired into open workshop sheds where they wove baskets, carved bits of wood and bamboo, kneaded clay and transformed them into odd-shaped objects.

Under the anxious eyes of "Auntie" Lawanle, I played by myself on the pavement of our house and observed these varied activities. The tools of the open air were again transformed into books, exercise books, slates, books under armpits, in little tin or wooden boxes, books in raffia bags, tied together with string and carried on the head, slung over shoulders in cloth pouches. Directly in front of our home was the lawn which was used exclusively by girls from the other school. They formed circles, chased one another in and out of the circles, struggled for a ball and tossed it through an iron hoop stuck on a board. Then they also van-

5. **harmonium** (här-mō'nē-əm): an organlike instrument.

Aké 855

ished into classrooms, books were produced and they commenced their own observances of the mystery rites.[6]

Tinu became even more smug. My erstwhile[7] playmate had entered a new world and, though we still played together, she now had a new terrain to draw upon. Every morning she was woken earlier than I, scrubbed, fed and led to school by one of the older children of the house. My toys and games soon palled but the laughter still rankled, so I no longer demanded that I join Tinu in school.

Instead, I got up one morning as she was being woken up, demanded my bath at the same time, ate, selected the clothing which I thought came closest to the uniforms I had seen, and insisted on being dressed in them. I had marked down a number of books on father's table but did not yet remove them. I waited in the front-room. When Tinu passed through with her escort, I let them leave the house, waited a few moments, then seized the books I had earlier selected and followed them. Both parents were still in the dining-room. I followed at a discreet distance, so I was not noticed until we arrived at the infant school. I waited at the door, watched where Tinu was seated, then went and climbed on to the bench beside her.

Only then did Lawanle, Tinu's escort that day, see me. She let out a cry of alarm and asked me what I thought I was doing. I ignored her. The teachers heard the commotion and came into the room. I appeared to be everybody's object of fun. They looked at me, pointed and they held their sides, rocked forwards and backwards with laughter. A man who appeared to be in charge of

the infant section next came in, he was also our father's friend and came often to the house. I recognized him, and I was pleased that he was not laughing with the others. Instead he stood in front of me and asked,

"Have you come to keep your sister company?"

"No. I have come to school."

Then he looked down at the books I had plucked from father's table.

"Aren't these your father's books?"

"Yes. I want to learn them."

"But you are not old enough, Wole."

"I am three years old."

Lawanle cut in, "Three years old *wo?* Don't mind him sir, he won't be three until July."

"I am nearly three. Anyway, I have come to school. I have books."

He turned to the class-teacher and said, "Enter his name in the register." He then turned to me and said, "Of course you needn't come to school everyday—come only when you feel like it. You may wake up tomorrow morning and feel that you would prefer to play at home. . . ."

I looked at him in some astonishment. Not feel like coming to school! The coloured maps, pictures and other hangings on the walls, the coloured counters, markers, slates, inkwells in neat round holes, crayons and drawing-books, a shelf laden with modelled objects—animals, human beings, implements—raffia and basket-work in various stages of completion, even the blackboards, chalk and duster. . . . I had yet to see a more inviting playroom! In addition, I had made some vague, intuitive connection between school and the piles of books with which my father appeared to commune so religiously in the front room, and which had constantly to be snatched from me as soon as

---

6. **mystery rites:** Wole refers figuratively to secret ceremonies, such as those practiced by ancient religious cults.
7. **erstwhile** (ûrst′hwīl′): former.

my hands grew long enough to reach them on the table.

"I shall come everyday," I confidently declared.

Mr. Olagbaju's bachelor house behind the school became a second lunch-hour home. His favourite food appeared to be the pounded yam, *iyan,* at which I soon became his keen accomplice. Through the same *iyan,* I made my first close school friend, Osiki, simply by discovering that he was an even more ardent lover of the pounded yam than either Mr. Olagbaju or I. It seemed a simple matter of course that I should take him home or to Mr. Olagbaju's whenever the meal was *iyan;* moreover, Mr. Olagbaju was also teaching me to play *ayo,*[8] and this required a partner to play with. It was with some surprise that I heard my mother remark:

"This one is going to be like his father. He brings home friends at meal-times without any notice."

I saw nothing to remark in it at all; it was the most natural thing in the world to bring a friend home at his favourite meal-time. So Osiki became an inseparable companion and a regular feature of the house, especially on *iyan* days. One of the house helps composed a song on him:

Osiki oko oniyan
A ti nwa e, a ko ri e[9]

which she began singing as soon as we appeared, hand in hand, on the path leading from the school. But the pounded yam was also to provide the first test of our friendship.

8. *ayo:* a game played on a wooden board, using seeds.
9. **Osiki . . . ri e:** The author's translation is
Osiki, lord of the pounded-yam seller
We have sought you everywhere but failed to find you.

Child playing pebble game.
Struan Robertson/Magnum Photos

There were far too many aspects of the schoolroom and the compound to absorb in the regular school hours, moreover, an empty schoolroom appeared to acquire a totally different character which changed from day to day. And so, new discoveries began to keep me behind at lunch-time after everyone had gone. I began to stay longer and longer, pausing over objects which became endowed with new meanings, forms, even dimensions as soon as silence descended on their environment. Sometimes I simply wandered off among the rocks intending merely to climb a challenging surface when no one was around. Finally, Osiki lost patience. He would usually wait for me at home even while Tinu had her own food. On this day however, being perhaps more hungry than usual, Osiki decided not to wait. Afterwards he tried to explain that he had only meant to eat half of the food but had been unable to stop himself. I returned home to encounter empty dishes and was just in time to see Osiki disappearing behind the croton bush in the backyard, meaning no doubt to escape through the rear gate. I rushed through the parlour and the front room, empty dishes in hand, hid behind the door until he came past, then pelted him with the dishes. A chase followed, with Osiki instantly in front by almost the full length of the school compound while I followed doggedly, inconsolable at the sight of the increasing gap, yet unable to make my legs emulate Osiki's pace.

Finally, I stopped. I no longer saw Osiki but—Speed, Swiftness! I had not given any thought before then to the phenomenon of human swiftness and Osiki's passage through the compound seemed little short of the magical. The effect of his *dansiki*[10] which flowed like wings from his sides also added to the illusion of him flying over the ground. This, more than anything else, made it easy enough for the quarrel to be settled by my mother. It was very difficult to cut oneself off from a school friend who could fly at will from one end of the compound to the other. Even so, some weeks elapsed before he returned to the pounded-yam table, only to follow up his perfidy by putting me out of school for the first time in my career.

There was a birthday party for one of the Canon's[11] children. Only the children of the parsonage were expected but I passed the secret to Osiki and he turned up at the party in his best *buba*.[12] The entertainments had been set up out of doors in front of the house. I noticed that one of the benches was not properly placed, so that it acted like a see-saw when we sat on it close to the two ends. It was an obvious idea for a game, so with the help of some of the other children, we carried it to an even more uneven ground, rested its middle leg on a low rock outcrop and turned it into a proper see-saw. We all took turns to ride on it.

For a long time it all went without mishap. Then Osiki got carried away. He was a bigger boy than I, so that I had to exert a lot of energy to raise him up, lifting myself on both hands and landing with all possible weight on my seat. Suddenly, while he was up in his turn, it entered his head to do the same. The result was that I was catapulted up very sharply while he landed with such force that the leg of the bench broke on his side. I was flung in the air, sailed over his head and saw, for one long moment, the Canon's square residence rushing out to meet me.

It was only after I had landed that I took much notice of what I had worn to the party. It was a yellow silk *dansiki*, and I now saw with some surprise that it had turned a bright crimson, though not yet entirely. But the remaining yellow was rapidly taking on the new colour. My hair on the left side was matted with blood and dirt and, just before the afternoon was shut out and I fell asleep, I wondered if it was going to be possible to squeeze the blood out of the *dansiki* and

---

10. *dansiki:* a loose-fitting shirt, open at the sides.

11. **Canon:** a clergyman.
12. ***buba:*** a shirt with tailored sleeves.

pump it back through the gash which I had located beneath my hair.

The house was still and quiet when I woke up. One moment there had been the noise, the shouts and laughter and the bumpy ride of the see-saw, now silence and semi-darkness and the familiar walls of mother's bedroom. Despite mishaps, I reflected that there was something to be said for birthdays and began to look forward to mine. My only worry now was whether I would have recovered sufficiently to go to school and invite all my friends. Sending Tinu seemed a risky business, she might choose to invite all her friends and pack my birthday with girls I hardly even knew or played with. Then there was another worry. I had noticed that some of the pupils had been kept back in my earlier class and were still going through the same lessons as we had all learnt during my first year in school. I developed a fear that if I remained too long at home, I would also be sent back to join them. When I thought again of all the blood I had lost, it seemed to me that I might actually be bed-ridden for the rest of the year. Everything depended on whether or not the blood on my *dansiki* had been saved up and restored to my head. I raised it now and turned towards the mirror; it was difficult to tell because of the heavy bandage but, I felt quite certain that my head had not shrunk to any alarming degree.

The bedroom door opened and mother peeped in. Seeing me awake she entered, and was followed in by father. When I asked for Osiki, she gave me a peculiar look and turned to say something to father. I was not too sure, but it sounded as if she wanted father to tell Osiki that killing me was not going to guarantee him my share of *iyan*. I studied their faces intently as they asked me how I felt, if I had a headache or a fever and if I would like some tea. Neither would touch on the crucial question, so finally I decided to put an end to my suspense. I asked them what they had done with my *dansiki*.

"It's going to be washed," mother said, and began to crush a half-tablet in a spoon for me to take.

"What did you do with the blood?"

She stopped, they looked at each other. Father frowned a little and reached forward to place his hand on my forehead. I shook my head anxiously, ignoring the throb of pain this provoked.

"Have you washed it away?" I persisted.

Again they looked at each other. Mother seemed about to speak but fell silent as my father raised his hand and sat on the bed, close to my head. Keeping his eyes on me he drew out a long, "No-o-o-o-o."

I sank back in relief. "Because, you see, you mustn't. It wouldn't matter if I had merely cut my hand or stubbed my toe or something like that—not much blood comes out when that happens. But I saw this one, it was too much. And it comes from my head. So you must squeeze it out and pump it back into my head. That way I can go back to school at once."

My father nodded agreement, smiling. "How did you know that was the right thing to do?"

I looked at him in some surprise. "But everybody knows."

Then he wagged his finger at me, "Ah-ha, but what you don't know is that we have already done it. It's all back in there, while you were asleep. I used Dipo's[13] feeding-bottle to pour it back."

I was satisfied. "I'll be ready for school tomorrow" I announced.

13. **Dipo:** the youngest child.

I was kept home another three days. I resumed classes with my head still swathed in a bandage and proceeded to inform my favourite classmates that the next important event in the parsonage was going to be my birthday, still some months away. Birthdays were not new. I had shared one with Tinu the previous year and even little Dipo had had his first year of existence confirmed a few weeks before the fateful one at the Canon's house. But now, with the daily dressing of my head prolonging the aura of the last, the Birthday acquired a new status, a special and personal significance which I assumed was recognized by everyone. Indeed I thought that this was a routine knowledge into which one entered in the normal way of growing up. Understanding the functioning of the calendar became part of the order of birthdays and I dutifully watched Essay cancel one date after the other on the IBUKUN OLU STORES 1938 Almanac alias The Blessed Jacob, the alias of which was printed, for some reason, in a slanting form, rather like my father's handwriting.

All was ready on the thirteenth of July. I headed home after school with about a dozen of the favoured friends, led by Osiki. They all stacked their slates in the front room and took over the parlour. On the faces of the guests, everyone on his best behaviour, was a keen anticipation of food and drinks, of some music from the gramophone[14] and games and excitement. Now that they were home, I became a little uncertain of my rôle as celebrant and host; still, I took my place among the others and awaited the parade of good things.

We had settled down for a while before I noticed the silence of the house. Essay was still at school, mother was obviously at her shop with Dipo who would probably be strapped to the back of Auntie Lawanle. But where were the others? Come to think of it I had expected mother to be home to welcome my friends even if she had to go back to the shop to attend to her customers. It occurred to me also that Tinu had not come home at all, perhaps she went straight to the shop— she was considered old enough by now to do this on her own. That looked promising; any moment now I expected our mother to rush through the doors, making up for the delay with all sorts of unexpected delights.

I went out to the backyard, expecting to find at least one of our cousins or detect signs of preparations for the Birthday. There was nobody. The kitchen was empty and there was no aroma from recent cooking. I called out, announcing that I was home with guests and where was everybody? Really puzzled now, I returned to the dining-room, inspected the cupboards, the table—beyond the usual items there was nothing at all, no jars of *chin-chin*, no *akara*, no glasses or mugs obviously set aside, no pan-cakes, jollof rice . . . there was simply nothing out of the ordinary. This was not how Birthdays normally behaved but, there did not seem to be any cause for alarm. I checked the date on Ibukun Olu Stores once more, satisfied myself that there was no mistake, then settled down with my guests to wait for Birthday to happen.

My mother rushed in not long afterwards. Dipo strapped to her back, Auntie Lawanle and others following, carrying the usual assorted items which accompanied them to the shop every morning. This was impressive because it meant that the shop had been closed for the day and it was still early afternoon—obviously Birthday was really about

14. **gramophone:** a record player.

to happen in earnest. But she came in shaking her head and casting up her eyes in a rather strange manner. She stopped in the parlour, took a long look at my friends, looked at me again, shook her head repeatedly and passed through to the kitchen from where I heard her giving rapid orders to the welcome ring of pots and pans and the creak of the kitchen door. I nodded with satisfaction to the guests and assured them.

"The Birthday is beginning to come."

A moment later Tinu came in to say I was wanted by mother in the kitchen. I found her with her arms elbow deep in flour which she was kneading as if possessed. Without taking her eye off the dough she began,

"Now Wole, tell me, what have your friends come for?"

It was a strange question but I replied, "We've come to eat Birthday."

"You came to eat Birthday" she repeated. For some reason, Lawanle and the others had already burst out laughing. Mother continued, "Do you realize that you and your friends would still be sitting in that parlour, waiting to 'eat your birthday' if Tinu hadn't come and told me?"

"But today is my birthday" I pointed out to her.

Patiently she explained, "No one is denying that. I had planned to cook something special tonight but . . . look, you just don't invite people home without letting us know. How was I to know you were bringing friends? Now look at us rushing around, your friends have been sitting there, nearly starving to death, and you say you've brought them to eat birthday. You see, you have to let people know. . . ."

The Birthday proved to be all that was expected once it had got over the one disappointing limitation—Birthday did not just happen but needed to be reminded to happen. That aspect of its character bothered me for a while, it was a shortcoming for which I tried to find excuses, without success. The Birthday lost a lot in stature after this, almost as if it had slid down from the raised end of that fateful see-saw to the lower end and landed in a heap, among other humdrum incidents in the parsonage. Still, it had added the calendar to my repertoire of knowledge. When it came to my turn to entertain the gathering, I sang:

Ogbon'jo ni September
April, June ati November
February ni meji din l'ogbon
Awon iyoku le okan l'ogbon[15]

The others took it up, Osiki supplying a ko-ko-ti-ko-ko . . . ko-ko-ti-ko-ko beat on the table so fluently that my mother asked him jokingly if he had been drumming for the masqueraders. To everybody's surprise he said, Yes. Their *agbole*,[16] he revealed, even possessed its own mask which paraded the town with others at the yearly festival of the *egúngún*. When Osiki promised to lead their *egúngún* on a visit to our house at the next festival, I could not help feeling that the Birthday had more than made up for its earlier shortcoming. I had watched them before over the wall of the backyard, seated on Joseph's shoulders. I knew that the *egúngún* were spirits of the dead. They spoke in guttural voices and were to be feared even more than kidnappers. And yet I had noticed that many of them were also playful and would

15. **Ogbon . . . l'ogbon:** The saying is similar to
       Thirty days hath September
       April, June, and November
       All the rest have thirty-one
       Except for February.
16. *agbole:* family compound.

Aké 861

Yoruban musicians performing on drums and calabash rhythm gourds, near Ogbomosho, Nigeria.
Marc & Evelyne Bernheim/Woodfin Camp

joke with children. I had very nearly been startled off Joseph's shoulders once when one of them passed directly beneath the wall, looked up and waved, calling out in the familiar throaty manner,

"Nle o, omo Tisa Agba."[17]

But Joseph explained that it was only natural that the dead should know all about the living ones. After all, they once lived like us and that friendly one might even have been in the compound before. Now, discovering that Osiki had an *egúngún* which emerged from their compound every year was almost the same as if we also had one of our own.

17. **Nle . . . Agba:** Greetings, son of the Senior Teacher.

We crowded round him and I asked if he knew which of his dead ancestors it was.

He shook his head. "I only know it is one of our ancient people."

"Are you actually there when he emerges from the bottom of the earth?"

He nodded yes. "Any of us can watch. As long as you are male of course. Women mustn't come near."

"Then you must come and call me the next time" I said. "I want to watch."

"You want to what?" It was mother, her voice raised in alarm. "Did I hear you say you want to go and watch *egúngún* in his compound?"

"Osiki will take me" I said.

"Osiki is taking you nowhere. Better not even let your father hear you."

"Why not?" I said, "he can come too. Osiki, we can take him can't we? He is not like Mama, he is a man too."

My mother gave a sigh, shook her head and left us to listen to Osiki's tales of the different kinds of *egúngún*, the dangerous ones with bad charms who could strike a man with epilepsy and worse, the violent ones who had to be restrained with powerful ropes, the *opidan* with their magical tricks. They would transform themselves into alligators, snakes, tigers and rams and turn back again into *egúngún*. Then there were the acrobats—I had seen those myself over the wall, performing in a circle of spectators near the cenotaph.[18] They did forward and backward somersaults, doubled up their limbs in the strangest manner, squeezed their lower trunks into mortars and then bounced up and down in the mortar along short distances as if they were doing a mortar race. Apart from Giro, the crippled contortionist to whose performance we had once been taken in the palace compound, only these *egúngún* appeared to be able to tie up their limbs in any manner they pleased.

"Can I come back as an *egúngún* if I die?" I asked Osiki.

"I don't think so" he said. "I've never heard of any Christian becoming an *egúngún*."

"Do they speak English in the *egúngún* world?" I now wanted to know.

Osiki shrugged. "I don't know. Our own *egúngún* doesn't speak English."

It seemed important to find out. The stained-glass windows behind the altar of St.

Peter's church displayed the figures of three white men, dressed in robes which were very clearly *egúngún* robes. Their faces were exposed, which was very unlike our own *egúngún*, but I felt that this was something peculiar to the country from which those white people came. After all, Osiki had explained that there were many different kinds of *egúngún*. I sought his opinion on the three figures only to have Tinu interrupt.

"They are not *egúngún*" she said, "those are pictures of two missionaries and one of St. Peter himself."

"Then why are they wearing dresses like *egúngún*?"

"They are Christians, not masqueraders. Just let Mama hear you."

"They are dead aren't they? They've become *egúngún*, that is why they are wearing those robes. Let's ask Osiki."

Osiki continued to look uncertain. "I still haven't heard of any Christian becoming *egúngún*. I've never heard of it." Then he suddenly brightened. "Wait a minute, I've just remembered. My father told me that some years ago, they carried the *egúngún* of an *ajele*, you know, the District Officer who was here before."

I rounded on Tinu triumphantly. "You see. Now I can speak to those *egúngún* in the church window whenever they come. I am sure they only speak English."

"You don't know what you are talking about. You are just a child." She turned scornfully away and left us alone.

"Don't mind her" I told Osiki. "She knows I've always liked the one in the middle, the St. Peter. I've told her before that he is my special *egúngún*. If I come first to your compound, perhaps we can go next to the church cemetery and make him come out of the ground in the same way."

---

18. **cenotaph** (sĕn′ə-tăf′): a monument for someone who is buried elsewhere.

Egúngún festival.
John Pemberton III

"With his face bared like that?" Osiki sounded scandalized.

"Of course not" I assured him. "That is only his picture. When he comes out of the ground he will be properly dressed. And I'll be able to talk to him."

Osiki looked troubled. "I don't know. I don't really know if he will be a real *egúngún*."

"But you've just said that the *egúngún* of the District Officer came out in procession before."

"It is not the same thing. . . ." Osiki tried to explain, but finally admitted that he did not really understand. Somehow, it was not going to be possible but, why it should be that way, he didn't know. I reminded him that the District Officer was both white and Christian, that St. Peter's had the advantage because he was near a cemetery. In addition, anyone with eyes could see that he was already in his *egúngún* robes, which meant that he had joined in such festivals before. Osiki continued to be undecided, to my intense disappointment. Without his experience, I did not even know how to begin to bring out *egúngún* St. Peter without whom, from then on, the parade of ancestral masquerades at Aké would always seem incomplete.

When I again lay bleeding on the lawns of the infant school, barely a year later, I tried to see myself as a one-eyed masquerade, led by Osiki along the paths of the parsonage to visit my old home and surprise Tinu and Dipo by calling out their names. The accident occurred during a grass-cutting session by the bigger boys. The rest of us simply played around the school grounds or went home for the rest of the day. Osiki should have been cutting grass with the others but he had become my unofficial guardian, taking me home or to Mr. Olagbaju's house after school or fetching me from home, as if I had not walked to school all by myself nearly two years before. On that afternoon we were playing together, he chasing me round and round the infant school building. I was already developing a sense of speed, nothing to match his, but could dodge faster than he could turn whenever his arms reached out to grab me. I had just rounded the corner of the schoolroom when I saw, through the corner of my eye, the upward flash of a blade. Beneath it was a crouching form, its back turned towards me. That was all I had time to see. The next instant I felt the blade bite deep into the corner of my eye, the day was blotted out in a flush of redness and I collapsed forward on my face, blinded. I heard screams from everywhere. When I rolled over and put my hands to my face they were

Chapel at Ibadan University. Panels by Lamidi Fakeye.
Marc & Evelyne Bernheim/Woodfin Camp

instantly drenched in the same warm thick flood which had accompanied my somersault in the Canon's garden.

I lay still, unaware of any pain. My only thought was that if I did not remain like that, on my back, my eye would fall out on to the ground. Then I thought perhaps I would actually die this time; since I had obviously lost an eye. I tried to recall if I had ever seen a one-eyed masquerade among the *egúngún* whom we watched over the wall. There were sounds of heavier feet running towards me. I

recognized the voices of teachers, felt myself raised up and carried into the schoolroom, then laid on a table. I heard Mr. Olagbaju send someone to fetch my father.

Through the noise and confusion I gathered that I had run straight into the upward stroke of a cutlass wielded by a pupil who was busy cutting grass, his back turned to me. I heard the confused boy calling on God to save him from the stigma of becoming a murderer in his lifetime. One of the teachers told him to shut up and eventually pushed him out. When I heard my father's voice, it occurred to me to open the undamaged eye—I had not, until then, acted on the fact that I was only hit in one eye, not both. Wiping the blood from the left eye, I blinked it open. Standing round the table was a semi-circle of teachers, looking at me as if I was already a masquerade, the *opidan* type, about to transform himself into something else. I touched myself to ensure that this had not already happened, so strangely watchful were all the pairs of eyes.

"How did it happen?" my father demanded even as he examined the wound. A babble of voices rose in explanation.

I asked him, "Am I blind?"

Everyone shouted at once, "Keep still, Wole. Don't move!"

I repeated my question, feeling now that I was not dying but wondering if I would be obliged to become a beggar like those blind men who sometimes came into the parsonage, led by a small child, sometimes no bigger than I. It occurred to me then that I had never seen a small child leading a blind child.

Someone asked, "Where is that Osiki?"

But Osiki was gone. Osiki, when I was struck down, had simply continued running in the direction which he was facing at the time. He ran, I was sure, at a speed which surpassed even his usual phenomenal swiftness. Some of the bigger boys had tried to catch him—why, I did not know—but Osiki outstripped them running lean and light in the wind. I could see him, and the sight brought a smile to my face. It also made me open the injured eye and, to my surprise, I could see with it. There were loud gasps from the anxious faces who now crowded closer to see for themselves. The skin was split right into the corner of the eye but the eyeball itself was unscathed. Even the bleeding appeared to have stopped. I heard one teacher breathe "Impossible!" while another shouted, "Olorun ku ise!"[19] My father simply stood back and stared, his mouth agape in disbelief.

And then I felt very tired, a mist appeared to cover my eyes, and I fell asleep.

19. **Olorun ku ise:** God's work be praised.

Responding to the Selection

from **Aké** by Wole Soyinka

Identifying Facts

1. Which school song does Wole like best?
2. How does Wole get ready to go to school?
3. How is Wole injured at the birthday party?
4. Who are the *egúngún*?
5. Why does Wole think that the figures in the Christian church are masqueraders?

Interpreting Meanings

1. What is your impression of Wole as a child?
2. Soyinka describes events from the point of view of a young child. Where does he show the contrast between an adult's view of events and Wole's understanding of them?
3. Soyinka's autobiography gives us a vivid picture of the village and community life in Nigeria where he grew up. How is the school in Wole's village different from the elementary schools you attended?
4. One of the important events in village life is the yearly festival of the *egúngún.* What are the beliefs associated with the *egúngún*?

Narrative Writing

Using the Autobiographer's Method
Soyinka's method as an autobiographer is to keep us aware of his reaction to events as a child. At the same time, he provides an interpretation of these events from the adult's point of view.

Try to imitate his method. Choose a vivid recollection from childhood. Re-create your experience of that event as you remember it in the past and as you now see it.

Prewriting Strategies
You might begin by listing your details in three columns:

Facts	**Then**	**Now**

In the first column, list the details as objectively as you can. Answer the **5 W–How?** questions. In the second column, recall your reaction to the events as a child. In the third column, give your present interpretation of what happened. Write a short narrative of one or two paragraphs.

WRITER'S
WORKSHOP 2

Autobiographical
Incident
(Narrative
Writing)

Before You Read

Telephone Conversation

Using What You Know

The following poem reports a telephone conversation between two people who have never met. Their impressions of each other are formed by what is revealed during the conversation. How much can you learn about someone by listening to that person's tone of voice and telephone manners?

Literary Focus: Satire

Satire is a kind of writing that holds up to ridicule the weaknesses of individuals or of human beings in general. Satire can be lighthearted or it can be bitter. If you have read the excerpt from *Crick Crack, Monkey* (page 48), you may recall the satirical portrait of Sir.

Setting a Purpose

We tend to think in fragments and impressions rather than in complete thoughts. As you read, distinguish the words that are actually spoken during the telephone conversation from the speaker's thoughts and sensations.

Telephone Conversation

Wole Soyinka

The price seemed reasonable, location
Indifferent. The landlady swore she lived
Off premises. Nothing remained
But self-confession. "Madam," I warned,
"I hate a wasted journey—I am African."   5
Silence. Silenced transmission of
Pressurized good-breeding. Voice, when it came,
Lipstick coated, long gold-rolled
Cigarette-holder pipped. Caught I was, foully.
"HOW DARK?" . . . I had not misheard . . . ."ARE YOU LIGHT 10
OR VERY DARK?" Button B. Button A. Stench
Of rancid breath of public hide-and-speak.
Red booth. Red pillar-box.° Red double-tiered
Omnibus° squelching tar. It *was* real! Shamed
By ill-mannered silence, surrender   15
Pushed dumbfoundment to beg simplification.
Considerate she was, varying the emphasis—
"ARE YOU DARK? OR VERY LIGHT?" Revelation came.
"You mean—like plain or milk chocolate?"
Her assent was clinical,° crushing in its light   20
Impersonality. Rapidly, wave-length adjusted,
I chose. "West African sepia"°—and as afterthought,
"Down in my passport." Silence for spectroscopic
Flight of fancy,° till truthfulness clanged her accent
Hard on the mouthpiece. "WHAT'S THAT?" conceding   25
"DON'T KNOW WHAT THAT IS." "Like brunette."
"THAT'S DARK, ISN'T IT?" "Not altogether.
Facially, I am brunette, but madam, you should see
The rest of me. Palm of my hand, soles of my feet
Are a peroxide blonde. Friction, caused—   30
Foolishly madam—by sitting down, has turned
My bottom raven black—One moment madam!"—sensing
Her receiver rearing on the thunderclap
About my ears—"Madam," I pleaded, "wouldn't you rather
See for yourself?"   35

13. **Red pillar-box:** mailbox.

13–14. **double-tiered / Omnibus:** a bus having two decks (tiers) for passengers.

20. **clinical:** impersonal; detached.

22. **sepia** (sē′pē-ə): a dark-brown color.

23–24. **spectroscopic** (spĕk′trə-skŏp′ĭk) . . . **fancy:** referring to a range of ideas or notions.

Responding to the Selection

Telephone Conversation by Wole Soyinka

Interpreting Meanings

1. The speaker has never seen the landlady to whom he is speaking, yet he has a distinct impression of her. What does he tell you about her in lines 6–7? How does he imagine her in lines 8–9?
2. The speaker is placing his call from a public telephone box in Britain. How does he describe the setting in lines 13–14?
3. How does the speaker react to the landlady's blunt question? What do the words *stench* and *rancid* suggest about his thoughts and feelings? What do you think is the "revelation" that comes in line 18?
4. Why do you think the speaker chooses to use humor rather than anger in dealing with the landlady's prejudice? Is this approach more effective? How do you know?

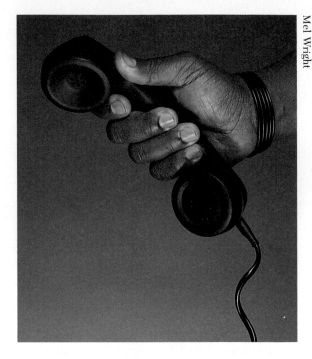

Mel Wright

About the Author
Ngugi wa Thiong'o (b. 1938)

At his birth to Christian parents in Limuru, Kenya, Ngugi (n-gōō′gē) was named James Thiong'o Ngugi. He used this as his official name for the first thirty-two years of his life. His three earliest novels, *Weep Not, Child* (1964), *The River Between* (1965), and *A Grain of Wheat* (1967), were published under the name James T. Ngugi. Then, in 1970, he announced that he would change his name to Ngugi wa Thiong'o ("Ngugi, son of Thiong'o"). This change symbolized his desire to link himself with the Gikuyu people and the traditional culture of his ancestors. In 1977, Ngugi announced his intention to write in Gikuyu or in Swahili, not in English, having decided that he wanted to write for the people of Kenya rather than for an American or European audience.

Ngugi attended primary and secondary schools in Kenya from 1947 to 1959. He entered Makerere University College in Kampala, Uganda, in 1959, where he earned a B.A. in English. He left Kenya in 1964 to attend the University of Leeds, in England, but returned four years later to serve as lecturer in the Department of English at University College in Nairobi. He resigned his teaching post in 1969 in protest against the Kenyan government's interference with academic freedom at the university. After a year at Northwestern University, in the United States, he returned to Nairobi as a lecturer in the literature department of the university.

In his novels, essays, and plays, Ngugi explores a number of themes common to

© Carrie Craig/Heinemann International

modern African literature: the clashing of traditional and Western cultures, the economic exploitation of the African continent by European settlers, the continued economic exploitation of African people in recent years by African heads of state, and the importance of both formal and informal education.

Ngugi was arrested and detained without a trial in 1978, following the staging of his play *I Will Marry When I Want* in his hometown of Limuru. His novel *Petals of Blood,* a harsh criticism of the Kenyan government, had just been published in England. Ngugi was released from prison one year later, but he had lost his professorship at the university. In his novel *Detained: A Writer's Prison Diary* (1981), he describes his prison experiences. In 1982 he left Kenya to live in England.

Ngugi wa Thiong'o   871

Before You Read

The Return

Using What You Know

Soldiers who return to civilian life after leaving the service often find the adjustment difficult. Think of some veterans you know or recall some films and books that have dealt with this subject. Why is coming home not always easy? Think of people who are forcibly detained as hostages and political prisoners. What kind of changes might they find in others upon their return? What changes might they find in themselves?

Literary Focus: Setting

A short story, like a photograph or a painting, has a foreground and a background. The main characters and actions form the foreground, the part of the scene closest to you. The background of the story—the time and place of events and the circumstances surrounding the events—is called its **setting.**

Setting is an important element in many stories where the action depends upon the physical background. Writers often create a setting that is true to a specific time and place.

Setting a Purpose

As you read, note how the author makes the setting convincing. What details give you a sense of time and place? Does the setting also help to create a mood?

The Return

Ngugi wa Thiong'o

The road was long. Whenever he took a step forward, little clouds of dust rose, whirled angrily behind him, and then slowly settled again. But a thin train of dust was left in the air, moving like smoke. He walked on, however, unmindful of the dust and ground under his feet. Yet with every step he seemed more and more conscious of the hardness and apparent animosity of the road. Not that he looked down; on the contrary, he looked straight ahead as if he would, any time now, see a familiar object that would hail him as a friend and tell him that he was near home. But the road stretched on.

He made quick, springing steps, his left hand dangling freely by the side of his once white coat, now torn and worn out. His right hand, bent at the elbow, held onto a string tied to a small bundle on his slightly drooping back. The bundle, well wrapped with a cotton cloth that had once been printed with red flowers now faded out, swung from side to side in harmony with the rhythm of his steps. The bundle held the bitterness and hardships of the years spent in detention camps.[1] Now and then he looked at the sun on its homeward journey. Sometimes he darted quick side-glances at the small hedged strips of land which, with their sickly-looking crops, maize, beans, and peas, appeared much as everything else did— unfriendly. The whole country was dull and seemed weary. To Kamau, this was nothing new. He remembered that, even before the Mau Mau emergency,[2] the overtilled Gikuyu[3] holdings wore haggard looks in contrast to the sprawling green fields in the settled area.

A path branched to the left. He hesitated for a moment and then made up his mind. For the first time, his eyes brightened a little as he went along the path that would take him down the valley and then to the village. At last home was near and, with that realization, the faraway look of a weary traveler seemed to desert him for a while. The valley and the vegetation along it were in deep contrast to the surrounding country. For here green bush and trees thrived. This could only mean one thing: Honia River still flowed. He quickened his steps as if he could scarcely believe this to be true till he had actually set his eyes on the river. It was there; it still flowed. Honia, where so often

1. **detention camps:** where political prisoners were confined.

2. **Mau Mau** (mou'mou') **emergency:** a conflict between whites and blacks over land ownership in the 1950s.
3. **Gikuyu** (kĭ-kōō'yōō): an agricultural people of Kenya, also called *Kikuyu*.

Mau Mau detention center, Nairobi, 1954.

he had taken a bath, plunging stark naked into its cool living water, warmed his heart as he watched its serpentine movement around the rocks and heard its slight murmurs. A painful exhilaration passed all over him, and for a moment he longed for those days. He sighed. Perhaps the river would not recognize in his hardened features that same boy to whom the riverside world had meant everything. Yet as he approached Honia, he felt more akin to it than he had felt to anything else since his release.

A group of women were drawing water. He was excited, for he could recognize one or two from his ridge. There was the middle-aged Wanjiku, whose deaf son had been killed by the Security Forces just before he himself was arrested. She had always been a

darling of the village, having a smile for everyone and food for all. Would they receive him? Would they give him a "hero's welcome?" He thought so. Had he not always been a favorite all along the ridge? And had he not fought for the land? He wanted to run and shout: "Here I am. I have come back to you." But he desisted. He was a man.

"Is it well with you?" A few voices responded. The other women, with tired and worn features, looked at him mutely as if his greeting was of no consequence. Why! Had he been so long in the camp? His spirits were damped as he feebly asked: "Do you not remember me?" Again they looked at him. They stared at him with cold, hard looks; like everything else, they seemed to be deliberately refusing to know or own him. It was

Wanjiku who at last recognized him. But there was neither warmth nor enthusiasm in her voice as she said, "Oh, is it you, Kamau? We thought you—" She did not continue. Only now he noticed something else— surprise? fear? He could not tell. He saw their quick glances dart at him and he knew for certain that a secret from which he was excluded bound them together.

"Perhaps I am no longer one of them!" he bitterly reflected. But they told him of the new village. The old village of scattered huts spread thinly over the ridge was no more.

He left them, feeling embittered and cheated. The old village had not even waited for him. And suddenly he felt a strong nostalgia for his old home, friends and surroundings. He thought of his father, mother and— and—he dared not think about her. But for all that, Muthoni, just as she had been in the old days, came back to his mind. His heart beat faster. He felt desire and a warmth thrilled through him. He quickened his step. He forgot the village women as he remembered his wife. He had stayed with her for a mere two weeks; then he had been swept away by the colonial forces. Like many others, he had been hurriedly screened and then taken to detention without trial. And all that time he had thought of nothing but the village and his beautiful woman.

The others had been like him. They had talked of nothing but their homes. One day he was working next to another detainee from Muranga. Suddenly the detainee, Njoroge, stopped breaking stones. He sighed heavily. His worn-out eyes had a faraway look.

"What's wrong, man? What's the matter with you?" Kamau asked.

"It is my wife. I left her expecting a baby. I have no idea what has happened to her."

Kikuyu women.
Hans Leuenberger/Black Star

Another detainee put in: "For me, I left my woman with a baby. She had just been delivered. We were all happy. But on the same day, I was arrested . . ."

And so they went on. All of them longed for one day—the day of their return home. Then life would begin anew.

Kamau himself had left his wife without a child. He had not even finished paying the bride price.[4] But now he would go, seek work in Nairobi,[5] and pay off the remainder

4. **bride price:** It is customary for the husband-to-be to pay money or give property to the bride's family.
5. **Nairobi** (nī-rō′bē): capital of Kenya.

to Muthoni's parents. Life would indeed begin anew. They would have a son and bring him up in their own home. With these prospects before his eyes, he quickened his steps. He wanted to run—no, fly to hasten his return. He was now nearing the top of the hill. He wished he could suddenly meet his brothers and sisters. Would they ask him questions? He would, at any rate, not tell them all: the beating, the screening and the work on roads and in quarries with an askari[6] always nearby ready to kick him if he relaxed. Yes. He had suffered many humiliations, and he had not resisted. Was there any need? But his soul and all the vigor of his manhood had rebelled and bled with rage and bitterness.

One day these wazungu would go!

One day his people would be free! Then, then—he did not know what he would do. However, he bitterly assured himself no one would ever flout his manhood again.

He mounted the hill and then stopped. The whole plain lay below. The new village was before him—rows and rows of compact mud huts, crouching on the plain under the fast-vanishing sun. Dark blue smoke curled upward from various huts, to form a dark mist that hovered over the village. Beyond, the deep, blood-red sinking sun sent out fingerlike streaks of light that thinned outward and mingled with the gray mist shrouding the distant hills.

In the village, he moved from street to street, meeting new faces. He inquired. He found his home. He stopped at the entrance to the yard and breathed hard and full. This was the moment of his return home. His father sat huddled up on a three-legged stool.

He was now very aged and Kamau pitied the old man. But he had been spared—yes, spared to see his son's return—

"Father!"

The old man did not answer. He just looked at Kamau with strange vacant eyes. Kamau was impatient. He felt annoyed and irritated. Did he not see him? Would he behave like the women Kamau had met by the river?

In the street, naked and half-naked children were playing, throwing dust at one another. The sun had already set and it looked as if there would be moonlight.

"Father, don't you remember me?" Hope was sinking in him. He felt tired. Then he saw his father suddenly start and tremble like a leaf. He saw him stare with unbelieving eyes. Fear was discernible in those eyes. His mother came, and his brothers too. They crowded around him. His aged mother clung to him and sobbed hard.

"I knew my son would come. I knew he was not dead."

"Why, who told you I was dead?"

"That Karanja, son of Njogu."

And then Kamau understood. He understood his trembling father. He understood the women at the river. But one thing puzzled him: he had never been in the same detention camp with Karanja. Anyway he had come back. He wanted now to see Muthoni. Why had she not come out? He wanted to shout, "I have come, Muthoni; I am here." He looked around. His mother understood him. She quickly darted a glance at her man and then simply said:

"Muthoni went away."

Kamau felt something cold settle in his stomach. He looked at the village huts and the dullness of the land. He wanted to ask many questions but he dared not. He could

6. **askari** (äs′kä-rē): an African soldier who works for a European power.

A Kikuyu village.
Marc Riboud/Magnum Photos

not yet believe that Muthoni had gone. But he knew by the look of the women at the river, by the look of his parents, that she was gone.

"She was a good daughter to us," his mother was explaining. "She waited for you and patiently bore all the ills of the land. Then Karanja came and said that you were dead. Your father believed him. She believed him too and keened[7] for a month. Karanja constantly paid us visits. He was of your Rika, you know. Then she got a child. We could have kept her. But where is the land? Where is the food? Ever since land consolidation, our last security was taken away. We let Karanja go with her. Other women had done worse—gone to town. Only the infirm and the old have been left here."

He was not listening; the coldness in his stomach slowly changed to bitterness. He felt bitter against all, all the people including his father and mother. They had betrayed him. They had leagued against him, and Karanja had always been his rival. Five years was admittedly not a short time. But why did she go? Why did they allow her to go? He wanted to speak. Yes, speak and denounce everything—the women by the river, the village and the people who dwelled there. But he could not. This bitter thing was choking him.

---

7. **keened:** lamented.

"You—you gave my own away?" he whispered.

"Listen, child, child . . ."

The big yellow moon dominated the horizon. He hurried away bitter and blind, and only stopped when he came to the Honia River.

And standing at the bank, he saw not the river, but his hopes dashed on the ground instead. The river moved swiftly, making ceaseless monotonous murmurs. In the forest the crickets and other insects kept up an incessant buzz. And above, the moon shone bright. He tried to remove his coat, and the small bundle he had held on to so firmly fell.

It rolled down the bank and before Kamau knew what was happening, it was floating swiftly down the river. For a time he was shocked and wanted to retrieve it. What would he show his—Oh, had he forgotten so soon? His wife had gone. And the little things that had so strangely reminded him of her and that he had guarded all those years, had gone! He did not know why, but somehow he felt relieved. Thoughts of drowning himself dispersed. He began to put on his coat, murmuring to himself, "Why should she have waited for me? Why should all the changes have waited for my return?"

Responding to the Selection

The Return by Ngugi wa Thiong'o

Identifying Facts

1. How long has Kamau been away from his village?
2. What kind of work was he forced to do at the detention camp?
3. How has Kamau been betrayed?
4. Where has Kamau's wife gone?
5. What does the small bundle that Kamau loses contain?

Interpreting Meanings

1. What impression do you get of the setting at the opening of the story? How does the setting change as Kamau approaches his own village?
2. What memories does Kamau associate with the river? In light of what happens later on in the story, why are these memories ironic?
3. Why does Kamau receive a cold reception from the villagers?
4. Why does Kamau accuse his parents of giving away what was his?
5. At the end of the story, Kamau returns to the river in bitter dejection. What has he decided to do? Why does he change his mind?
6. What contrast in mood occurs when Kamau reaches the river? Which details in setting reflect the change in him?

Literary Elements

Understanding the Role of Setting

The overall mood or feeling in a work is called its **atmosphere**. Atmosphere is most often produced by descriptions of setting. Ngugi creates a powerful emotional feeling through his descriptions of the countryside.

Reread the description of the new village. How does the description of "the deep, blood-red sinking sun" foreshadow Kamau's disillusion?

Language and Vocabulary

Understanding Denotation and Connotation

All words have **denotations,** which are their literal, dictionary meanings. Many words also have **connotations,** feelings and associations that exist in addition to their strict dictionary meanings.

Read the following excerpts from "The Return." Explain why the author selected each of the italicized words rather than the synonym which appears beside it in parentheses.

"For here green bush and trees *thrived* (grew)."

". . . fingerlike streaks of light that thinned outward and mingled with the gray mist *shrouding* (covering) the distant hills."

"The big yellow moon *dominated* (ruled) the horizon."

Creative Writing

Describing a Setting

Most of Ngugi's details give us visual images of the countryside, but some appeal to other senses as well—our sense of touch (heat and cold) and our sense of hearing.

In one or more paragraphs, create a setting through the use of details that appeal to one or more of the senses. Convey to your readers the look and feel of the place.

Use the form distributed by your teacher or a separate sheet of paper.

Prewriting Strategies

1. Jot down details that will create a vivid picture for the reader. Choose details that appeal to the senses.
2. Arrange the details in a logical sequence, spatial or some other order.
3. Write a topic sentence that gives the main impression of the setting.

After writing a draft, ask another student to help you evaluate and revise your paper. Then proofread and prepare a final copy.

Speaking and Listening

Reporting on Historical Background

Locate information about the Mau Mau Emergency in an encyclopedia or a history textbook. Prepare to give a short oral report on the background of this event. Use the information you obtain to draw connections with the events described in "The Return."

Writing a Comparison/Contrast Essay

In your analysis of literature, you will frequently find that you wish to **compare** or **contrast** two things, such as ideas, characters, techniques, or complete works. When you *compare,* you point out likenesses. When you *contrast,* you point out differences. Sometimes the term *compare* implies both comparison and contrast.

This approach to literature often helps to cast light on an individual work, a pair of works, or even a group of works by one or more authors. In writing a paper of comparison (or contrast), it is important to have a clear basis for comparison.

There are two general methods for organizing the essay of comparison or contrast. One method is called the **block method.** All the ideas about one topic are presented first. Then all the ideas about the second topic are presented. The second method is called the **alternating method.** The two works or features are examined point by point.

Certain transitional expressions are used to point up comparison or contrast. The essay of comparison uses such transitional expressions as *also, and, besides, both, in the same way,* and *similarly.* The essay of contrast uses such expressions as *although, but, by contrast, however,* and *whereas.*

Prewriting Strategies

1. If you are asked to choose a topic for a comparison/contrast essay, consider selections that lend themselves to this kind of analysis. For example, one belief that recurs in contemporary African literature is that the spirits of dead ancestors continue to affect the living. This idea might be explored in such works as "Souffles" (page 815), "Dead Men's Path" (page 847), and *Aké* (page 854).

2. Use two columns to list the similarities and differences you find. If you prefer, use a Venn diagram to record likenesses and differences. Differences are listed in the outer portions of the ellipses. Similarities are listed in the overlapping area.

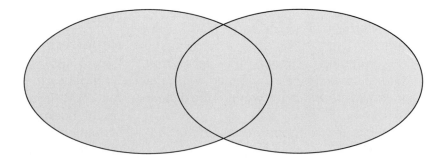

Writing the First Draft

1. In your opening paragraph, identify the works by title and author. Include a sentence that states your **thesis,** or controlling idea.
2. Determine how many key ideas you will develop. If there are several significant similarities and differences, you might devote one paragraph to the similarities and one to the differences.

Evaluating and Revising

Use the **Checklist** on page 68 to evaluate and revise your paper.

Writing the Final Draft

Ask a classmate to check your revision for accuracy. Prepare a final copy and proofread it carefully.

▶I. Interpreting New Material

Michael Kienitz/Picture Group

Niyi Osundare (nē'yē ō-shōōn-där'ĕ) was born in Ikere-Ekiti, Ondo State, Nigeria, in 1947. He attended schools in Ibadan, Nigeria, and in England and Canada. He has written plays as well as poetry and is a frequent contributor to such publications as *Opon Ifa* and *West Africa.* He has lectured at Ibadan University in Nigeria and at colleges in the United States.

A. Read the following poem carefully before answering the questions.

I Sing of Change
Niyi Osundare

Sing on: somewhere, at some new moon,
We'll learn that sleeping is not death,
Hearing the whole earth change its tune.
                                    W. B. YEATS.

I sing
of the beauty of Athens
without its slaves

Of a world free
of kings and queens   5
and other remnants
of an arbitrary past

Of earth
with no
sharp north   10
or deep south
without blind curtains
or iron walls

of the end
of warlords and armouries   15
and prisons of hate and fear

Of deserts treeing
and fruiting
after the quickening rains

Of the sun   20
radiating ignorance
and stars informing
nights of unknowing

I sing of a world reshaped

The Author Comments

I wrote the first draft of "I Sing of Change" in 1980, and its final version provided the rallying vision for *Songs of the Marketplace,* my first collection of poems, published in 1983. This poem is very close to the social and aesthetic center of my poetic career. The poem is a kind of reaction to historical as well as contemporary injustices: "civilizations" whose power and wealth are built upon enslavement and exploitation; warmongers who define their strength in bloody ventures and conquests; the dungeons and prisons of tyrants where men and women of conscience suffer and die; a world ripped apart into exploiting North and exploited South . . .

I envision an end to all this, just as I celebrate the possibility of hope—all in keeping with my belief in the transformative power of art in the creation of a *truly* democratic and humane world.

—Niyi Osundare

1. Although noted for their democracy, the ancient Athenians kept slaves. Explain the allusion in lines 2–3.
2. The word *arbitrary* can mean "dictatorial." What does the phrase "arbitrary past" (line 7) suggest?

3. What is meant by "blind curtains" and "iron walls" (lines 12–13)?

B. Osundare contrasts the images of an imperfect world and "a world reshaped." Write an essay examining his ideas.

▶▶II. For Discussion

One central theme that runs through contemporary African literature is the need for modern-day Africans to pay attention to the culture of their ancestors. Choose several selections in this unit that focus on the importance of ancestral culture. How does each of the works you have chosen deal with this theme?

▶▶▶III. For Writing

This unit has introduced you to some contemporary African writers and to some of the themes in their writing. Which selections have had the most meaning for you? Write an essay in which you give your personal response to the literature in this unit.

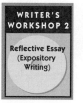

WRITER'S WORKSHOP 2

Reflective Essay (Expository Writing)

A Human and a Spirit Wrestling (Orakpo Voreinrbin), *deep etching by Bruce Onobrakpeya, 1984.*

Drs. David and Lynn McKinley-Grant; Photo by Steven Tuttle

Unit Twelve

The Novel
The Wrestling Match

INTRODUCTION BY **David Dorsey**
Clark Atlanta University

The Wrestling Match is a story about things most teenagers in America experience: the rivalry between "our guys" and "their guys," the courtship between a popular boy and an attractive girl, and the conflicts that occur between teenagers and their parents. The story, however, takes place far from the United States—in an Igbo village in Nigeria. *The Wrestling Match* challenges those who are not Nigerian or Igbo to consider another way of living. The story is like a window; in reading it we can see into another country and another culture. We will find both similarities and differences between Igbo culture and our own. The similarities show that all over the world human beings face the same basic needs. The differences teach us how critically each culture shapes the way its members see and respond to those needs.

Nigeria has over one hundred million citizens. Each person belongs to one of more than fifty ethnic groups, each with its own language and customs. Communication is not a problem since most people speak English and one or two of their neighbors' languages as well as their own. Nigerians now have a strong sense of national unity. When they won their independence from Great Britain in 1960, however, ethnic rivalry and mistrust were so strong that one of the largest ethnic groups, the Igbo people, decided to form a separate nation, Biafra. They fought and lost a civil war (1967–1970), but are now fully reintegrated into Nigerian life.

In addition to being a story about young people, *The Wrestling Match* is a comment on the civil war. The novel suggests that although the causes of the war were serious, the motives of the two sides were ill-considered. The novel also suggests what has proved to be true—that from the disaster of the conflict, the "children of the Biafran War" can rise to a new, higher level of wisdom, cooperation, and unity.

The characters of *The Wrestling Match* and Buchi Emecheta herself are Igbo. Many details of the novel reflect Igbo values and customs. Every society has social structures that are strange to outsiders, but not hard to understand when they are explained. Consider, for example, a few aspects of Igbo society: hospitality, education, family, competition and achievement, and government.

Every society has its own rituals of hospitality. Usually they include offering food to any guest. In many parts of West Africa, the kola nut is the symbolic item of welcome. A host or guest will offer it soon after the first greetings. The nut is opened, split apart, and distributed in a ceremonial fashion. As in America, hospitality among adult males often involves offering an alcoholic beverage. In West Africa, the most traditional beverage is palm wine, which is made from the sap of palm trees.

In most of Africa, especially in the countryside, schools are not free. Often a family cannot afford to educate all or any of its children in schools. But those who do not go to school get a different education at home, learning farming and crafts such as blacksmithing and medicine, or even arts such as carving religious masks. It is no surprise that rivalries develop between the group that is educated at home and the group that goes to school.

The traditional Igbo family was sometimes polygamous. This means that, often with his wife's blessing, a husband could choose to add a second or third wife to the family. Most children grew up with more than one mother and with some sisters and brothers who had a different mother. If you wanted to say that two people had the same father *and mother,* you would have to use a long, awkward phrase like "brother born of the same mother and father." A man was expected to marry his widowed sister-in-law and adopt her children. That is why in *The Wrestling Match* Okei's uncle is called his "father." As a gesture of love, unity, and mutual respect, a mother may call any of her husband's sons "my little husband." In the ideal cases, the whole polygamous family is just as close-knit and loving as a monogamous family in America.

***Teacher and student in a
Nigerian primary school.***
Marc & Evelyne Bernheim/
Woodfin Camp

Igbo society, like American society, encourages competition and
individual achievement. Individuals are judged by what they can
accomplish through hard work and determination. Unlike some
competitions in America, Igbo competition is community oriented.
A person can win envy but no respect for achievements if the rewards are not shared with the community. This competitive drive
and community spirit are illustrated in the favorite sport of the
Igbo, wrestling.

The champion wrestler is a glorious hero. Each wrestler com-
petes as a representative of his school or village or some other
group. The community does everything possible to help the wrestler, because if he wins, they have won. The ceremonies leading up

to the match involve the whole community. The group competitions in costumes, songs, dances, and eloquence are as important as the wrestling itself. Wrestling matches are so central to Igbo life that communities have to agree on a holiday to conduct them. Everyone wants to be present!

The Igbo respect for personal achievement and for services to one's community mean that Igbo society is stratified—people are classified by the level of their achievement. Yet Igbo society remains essentially egalitarian. Children cannot inherit their parents' respect and influence. Theoretically, each person begins from the same level and has the same obligations to achieve and excel on his or her own merit. The roles of women, however, are subordinate to men's roles in some real and some symbolic ways.

The emphasis on equality is reflected in Igbo government. Governmental issues are addressed in community discussions and decisions are reached by the entire membership. All adult men participate in a sort of council or town meeting to reach decisions. Women have similar councils for their affairs. As much as possible, Igbo organizations follow this democratic ideal of direct participation rather than representative government or monarchy. In *The Wrestling Match* this way of making decisions is evident not only in how the older generation leads, but also in the way the young boys form and execute their plans and in the girls' deliberations and actions. In Igbo society, a person earns respect by suggesting successful plans and having enough persuasive eloquence to get these plans adopted. *The Wrestling Match* shows young people unconsciously practicing these skills.

In any culture, children become adults by learning why and how they must act within the laws and guidelines of their society. Through the action of *The Wrestling Match,* the young people learn to appreciate the values of the older generation. Yet the author and the older characters take great pains to encourage the children's independence and initiative.

The Wrestling Match presents an opportunity for us to compare ourselves to the characters in the story and to learn from the comparison. It is also an exciting, suspenseful story of romance, sports, and growing up.

About the Author
Buchi Emecheta (b. 1944)

Buchi Emecheta (bōō′chē ĕm′ə-chĕt-ə) was born in Lagos, Nigeria. When she was sixteen, she entered a marriage that was arranged to save her from poverty. The next year she bore the first of her five children. In 1962, she joined her husband in England and helped support him while he studied there. During this time, Emecheta developed an interest in writing and in educating herself. She pursued these new interests while remaining busy as a wife and mother. Her ambitions, however, alienated her husband. She soon found herself a single parent and college student, working to support her children in a foreign land.

Emecheta's first novel, *In the Ditch* (1972), portrays the lives of mothers living in a London tenement. The novel was so factual and analytical that it served as her master's thesis in sociology. In 1975, her second novel, *Second-Class Citizen,* appeared. It is a fictional account of her youth, marriage, and migration to England. Emecheta has written over a dozen more novels. Some, like *The Wrestling Match* (1981), were written especially for young people. Emecheta has also worked as an essayist, lecturer, and occasionally as a university professor. She lives in England.

One of the most versatile and interesting writers of African fiction today, Emecheta has written inspiring accounts of her own life and portrayed the conditions of people, especially women, in traditional African vil-

The Schomburg Center for Research in Black Culture/New York Public Library

lages, in English tenements, and in African colleges and businesses. In all of her writing, Emecheta exposes the unconscious beliefs and values that govern people's lives. She also shows that people can grow and slough off ideas or rules that stifle freedom.

Emecheta's main characters often find themselves in unfair or painful situations, such as arranged marriages, slavery, or poverty. They manage to extricate themselves through courage and cleverness, and come to see that the ideas of their families or societies are not always wise or true. Even in her stories that defend traditional values, Emecheta encourages an enlightened, moral independence in everyone, male and female, young and old.

Buchi Emecheta 889

GUIDE TO PRONUNCIATION OF IGBO WORDS

In *The Wrestling Match,* you will meet a number of Igbo words. This guide will help you pronounce those words. Although it is not possible to pronounce Igbo words accurately by using only the sounds of English, you can get reasonably close by following these instructions.

1. Pronounce each vowel, using this key. When two vowels occur together, pronounce each one separately.

Vowel	English Word	Written on the Chart as	Example	
a pronounced as in	*pat*	a	aya	
e	*pet, net*	e	Eke	
i	*peat, neat*	ee	Obi	o-bee
o	*Poe, no*	o	Olie	o-lee-e
u	*do, new*	ou	Uche	ou-che

Sometimes, however, the nearest vowel in English is different, and some texts mark the difference with **diacritical marks**, especially:

i̱ pronounced as in   *pit*
o̱   *pot, not*
u̱   *put*

2. Most syllables consist of a vowel plus a consonant, a consonant plus a vowel, or just a vowel.
3. As in English, sometimes one consonant is written with two letters.

Consonant	English Word	Example
ch pronounced as	**ch** in *chicken*	u-chi
kw	**qu** in *quick*	Kwu-te-lu
ng	**ng** in *doing*	Ng-wu-ru
sh	**sh** in *should*	O-bo-shi

The following cases indicate a sound that English does *not* use in forming words. Therefore the English pronunciation would not be correct in Igbo. Follow these instructions:

gb pronounce as	**b**	
gh	**g** in *get*	
gw	**gw** in *Gwendolyn*	
kp	**p**	
nw	**nw** in *bet 'n win*	
ny	**n** in Spanish *jalapeño*	

4. The consonants **m** and **n** can each occur as a whole syllable. Try not to add a vowel
   sound before or after the **m** or **n** if none is printed.

   Example: Pronounce **ndu** as n-doo.

5. Accent the next-to-last syllable of a word.

   Example: Pronounce **abada** as a-ba'da.

Igbo Word	Pronunciation Guide	Igbo Word	Pronunciation Guide
abada	a-ba-da	Nkwo	n-quo
Adaobi	a-da-o-bee	Nne Ojo	n-ne o-jo
Afo	a-fo	Nwogbu	n-wo-bou
Akpei	ak-pay-ee	Obi Agiliga	o-bee a-gee-lee-ga
Akwete	a-kwe-te	Obi Uju	o-bee ou-jou
Awolowo	a-wo-lo-wo	Obi Uwechue	o-bee ou-we-chou-e
Benin	ben-een	Oboshi	o-bo-shee
Eke	e-ke	Ogbeukwu	o-be-ou-quou
Igbo	ee-bo	Okei	o-ke-ee
Igbuno	ee-bou-no	Olie	o-lee-e
Ilorin	ee-lo-rin	Onuoha	o-nou-o-ha
koboz	ko-boz	otuogwu	o-tou-o-gwu
Kwutelu	quou-te-lou	Uche	ou-che
Mbekwu	m-be-quou	Umu aya Biafra	ou-mou a-ya bee-a-fra
Nduka	n-dou-ka	Yoruba	yo-rou-ba

Before You Read

The Wrestling Match

Using What You Know

Some people tend to use stereotypes or generalizations when they talk about others. Older people sometimes say that the younger generation is lazy, while younger people sometimes say their elders are old-fashioned or boring. Ethnic and regional groups are also subject to stereotyped images.

If you stop to think of individuals within a particular age or ethnic group, you will generally find more differences than similarities. Think of a person who does not fit the conventional pattern of his or her age group. Tell the class about this person and how he or she is different.

Literary Focus: The Novel

The **novel** is usually defined as any extended fictional prose narrative. It consists of the same basic elements as the short story: **plot, character, setting, point of view,** and **theme**. Because of the novel's greater length, however, these elements tend to be more complex. A novel generally has major and minor characters, a detailed setting, and a complex theme. It may also have **subplots** that are secondary, but closely related, to the main plot.

Setting a Purpose

As you read, note the opinions that the various groups have of one another. What do the elders and the Umu aya Biafra (the children born during the war) think of each other? What do the villagers in Akpei and Igbuno think of each other? What do the young people who have gone to school think of those who haven't?

Do their opinions change by the end of the novel? How?

The Wrestling Match

Buchi Emecheta

1

It was during that quiet part of the evening when all the buyers and sellers of the Eke market[1] had gone home. It was not yet time for the noises of children playing in the moonlight to be heard; they were all on the mud verandahs around their thatched huts, eating their evening meal. It was the time for the swishes of the fronds of the coconut-palms to be heard; it was the time for the fire-insects of the night to hiss through the still air. It was the time for the frogs in the nearby ponds to croak to their mates, as if to say that they should now seek shelter because night was fast approaching.

But this quiet did not last long. In the compound of Obi Agiliga, his senior wife Nne Ojo was already murmuring. Soon the murmuring exploded into an outcry. "Look," she shouted, holding a piece of pounded yam she was about to swallow. "Look, if you are not satisfied with the best your family can do for you, go and live elsewhere. I don't care

what anybody says. I am doing my best with you. If you are not satisfied . . . ."

"Now what is all that noise about? Not Okei again?" thundered Obi Agiliga, struggling into his outer otuogwu cloth and seething with anger. "What am I going to do about you? I did not ask those federal soldiers to kill your parents. I have told you this so many times. Are you the only boy who had lost his parents during the civil war?"[2]

A young figure uncurled himself from the verandah where he had been sitting and eating with the others. He got up slowly, taking his time and almost stepping on the bowls of fish soup that stood on the mud floor. He extracted himself from the family, and was about to walk out of the compound when he changed his mind and said insultingly: "Oh, Uncle, we have heard that before. Why don't you think of something new to say?"

Obi Agiliga's wife could take no more. "You dare insult your father like that, you ungrateful boy? Every evening you have to eat badly, wading your dirty fingers in the

---

1. **Eke market:** The traditional Igbo week consists of four days: Oye (= Olie), Afo, Nkwo, and Eke. Frequently, neighboring villages choose a different day of the week on which each one will hold its market.

2. **civil war:** From May 30, 1967, to January 15, 1970, there was a civil war in Nigeria, in which the Igbo people tried to form a separate, independent nation called Biafra. They were unsuccessful.

soup-bowl as if you provided the food. If you don't stop this attitude, I will get boys of your age to beat you up."

"Boys of my age . . . ha, I'd like to see you do that!"

Nne Ojo was a quick-tempered woman. She threw the pounded yam she had been rolling in her hand on to Okei's shoulder. And he laughed again in derision.

"The way he behaves, one would have thought that I have never been young before," Obi Agiliga said, going back to his disrupted meal. "Go and find something to do. Go with us to the farm, or even try and catch those friends of yours who have been stealing things from old people, or go and fight a wrestling match. Do anything to prove that you're a man, Okei. Not sit here arguing over soup with my wives. Go and be a man, just as I was when I was your age."

"Yeah, when I was your age, when I was your age. . . . I was not there to prove your claim, was I . . . when I was your age. . . ."

He strolled out of the compound with the angry voices of his uncle's wives still cutting the night air.

Immediately outside his uncle's compound, Okei was greeted with an easy laughter from two of his friends. They had been outside the compound waiting for him to finish his evening meal.

"The usual night song, I see," remarked Nduka. He was sixteen years old, the same age as Okei; but whilst Okei was thin and lanky, Nduka was stocky and short. He had a very sharp tongue as well. Okei was not given to much talking, but when he lost his temper he really lost it.

The third boy, Uche, was nicknamed Mbekwu—the easy-going tortoise. He had the irritating habit of laughing at everything and at everybody. He was a year younger than the other two, but they all belonged to the same age-group, Umu aya Biafra:[3] babies born around the civil war.

The ripple of the great civil war started around 1964 and culminated in the creation of a new nation of Biafra in May 1967. But the children born at the very beginning of the political deadlock, and all those born during the war, and those born towards the end of the war were all called Umu aya Biafra, because it was the greatest happening that had ever occurred in Nigeria. It was a civil war, which started among the politicians; the army stepped in to keep the peace, then the military leaders started to quarrel among themselves, and one created a new state, taking his followers with him. That state was Biafra. It was a civil war that did cost Nigeria dear. Almost a million lives were lost, not just on the losing side; those who won the war lost thousands of people too—showing that in any war, however justified its cause, nobody wins.

But that was a long time ago. Now Uche was giggling at Okei's anger. The other two simply ignored him and went on talking as if he was not there.

"Did you hear what my uncle was saying—that some members of our age-group were stealing from old people? That cannot be true, can it?"

"Trouble with these old men is that they say things simply to hurt, without any proof," Nduka said, watching a group of children coming out of their huts into the open air to play.

"I don't know, but he has been saying this for the past few market days, and it's becoming boring. I hope they don't think I am one of the thieves!"

3. **Umu aya Biafra:** [The] children [of the] Biafra War.

"Yes, that is the trouble. If a member of our age-group steals, the adults will say that we all steal. And what annoys me is that the thief gets all the attention and publicity and we get nothing."

"We get the nagging to go to the farm, to prove our manhood," laughed Uche.

"You won't prove your manhood like that when you laugh and eat all the time like a woman," snapped Okei. "This is not a laughing matter. I wish I knew what to do. I sometimes wish I hadn't gone out into the back yard when these soldiers came and killed my family. Sometimes I wish I had died with them. Listening to these women every evening . . . hm . . . I'm getting really fed up with life."

"Oh come on!" said Nduka. "Life is only just beginning for us. It's not as bad as that. We've called on you to go to Akpei[4] with us, to meet Josephine and her friends. They are on their way from the market there."

"You're really crazy about this girl, aren't you, Nduka?"

Nduka shrugged his shoulders, "Well, what else is there for me to do? Sit on our verandah and listen to my father telling me that I am hopeless, and that since my elder brother has been killed in the army there's no hope for our family line any more?"

"Does your father say that to you too?" Okei asked, incredulous.

Uche started to laugh uncontrollably.

"What have I said to make you go mad like that? One of these days I'm going to show you that I don't like people who laugh when others are trying to be serious."

"There is nothing to be serious about. You think you are the only one being nagged at?

The Compound

The traditional Igbo home consists of a small plot of land with several separate structures, each with one or two rooms. One such building is the father's **obi**, where the family receives guests formally, and where the father eats, sleeps, and does indoor work, such as writing letters, reading, and mending tools. Each wife and mother has her own building where she does her indoor work, receives women guests informally, and prepares the food, which will be cooked outdoors. Here she and her children usually sleep and eat. Outside, but within the compound, she also has a small vegetable garden, which helps to feed the family all year. Sometimes the garden produces enough vegetables for the family to sell some at the weekly market. Each parent also has a farm. The compounds of a village are located together.

Well, you are wrong. The only good boys of our age-group are those who did not go to school at all—you know, who've been going to the farm with their parents all the four market days of the week—all through Eke, Olie, Nkwo, and Afo,[5] and back again on another Eke day—since they took their first steps, and who will remain like that until their dying day. Those of us who went to school are no good."

"Come on, let's go and meet the girls," said Nduka, finishing the argument. "At least they will be happy to see us."

And they trotted into the darkening night on their way to Akpei.

4. **Akpei:** the village nearest the Ogbuno, where most of the characters in this story live. There is a friendly rivalry between the two villages.

5. **Eke . . . Afo:** the four days of the traditional Igbo week.

The Wrestling Match   895

Age Groups

All the children born in a certain period belong to the same "age group." In Igbo villages, the age group usually has a range of three years, and each age group is named for an important event that took place during the period when its children were born. The civil war to form an independent Biafra lasted two years and eight months. All the children born then were placed in an age group called "the children of Biafra." In African villages, children mostly play, work, and study with other children in their own age group. Therefore, each age group has very strong feelings of loyalty and unity, like a lifelong team.

The Farm

The compounds of a village are collected together, but the lands assigned to each man for cultivating mainly yams, and to each woman for cassava, are scattered all around the village. Most people cultivate farmland so far from their compounds that they set out before dawn and do not return until dusk. Generally, each person has only as much land as one individual can cultivate, but the person may have help from children, visiting relatives, and even a few hired hands. Because each person works in a separate area, it is hard to summon everyone during the daytime if there is an emergency. Of course, grandparents and small children usually do not go to the farm.

By the time Okei and his friends got to the little hill that bordered the Oboshi stream, the moon had risen full and clear. It illuminated the sands, highlighting their silvery colour the more. The silver path through which the boys walked was thickly edged by dense evergreen bushes. Here they came to a clearing in which there was a cluster of cottages, most of them thatched but one or two roofed with corrugated iron sheets that glistened in the moonlight. There was an open clearing in which children and old people sat, telling stories and singing by the moonlight. The night was airy, and the young people on their way to Akpei enjoyed the feel of it all. There was no need for much conversation.

"We will have to run down the slope to the stream. I always enjoy doing that," Uche announced.

"Everybody enjoys that," Okei cut in. "I'll like to see you run up on your way back."

"You can't run up, though," Nduka compromised, "because in most cases you're carrying something from the market or the stream."

"Wait a minute. Why is it that Josephine and her friends had to go to Akpei to sell plantain[1] on an Eke day, when there is a big market here in Igbuno?" asked Okei.

"You don't know our girls, you don't know them at all," Nduka said, looking wise. "They claim that in Akpei people are willing to pay more and that they are nicer."

"So they walk all these miles for a few kobos?"

"Well," Uche put in, "going to meet them at least gives us something to do. Isn't that

---

1. **plantain** (plăn′tĭn): a nutritious bananalike fruit. It is a staple in the diet of people in many tropical countries.

what the adults have been accusing us of? That we are idle?" And he got ready to run down the slope.

"Hm . . . maybe you are right, Uche," said Okei. "But I am going to Akpei this night to accompany a friend and age-mate, not to meet any silly, giggling girl."

"So am I," laughed Uche.

"All right, all right, it is my own fault. But you cannot deny that it is a lovely evening, too lovely to stay indoors or sit by old women listening to their old-fashioned stories. Let us run down. I am sure we shall not reach Akpei, because the girls will have left the market a long time ago."

They tore down the slope, enjoying the wind whistling in their ears. At the bottom of the hill they all stopped short. They could hear voices. The voices of a group of girls.

"They are early. They must have left earlier than they normally do," remarked Nduka.

"I know what's happened," Okei said in a low voice. "I think they have had a good market and sold their plantain very quickly. You did say that they are eager for Igbuno plantain in Akpei. Lazy people, the people of Akpei. Can't they grow their own plantain?"

"They are singing again," laughed Uche.

"Sh . . . sh . . . we do not want them to know that we are here," Nduka said. "Otherwise they will not have their bath—and they won't thank us for that. So we just have to sit here quietly until they have finished washing, then we will surprise them with our presence."

Nobody contradicted him. They all flopped themselves down by the low bush near the stream. They lay on their backs, watching the slow movements of the moon whilst the voices of the chattering girls reached them distinctly.

The girls splashed and sang as they washed themselves. Then a voice said clear and loud: "You know, if I could afford it I would never go to Akpei again, not after today. Who do they think they are, that's what I'd like to know. They are playing the big people just because we take plantain to their villages. God, and their boys . . . aren't they annoying?"

"There is no smoke without fire, though. Maybe there is some truth in what they were saying."

"Well, if their accusations were true, should they not go to our young men and say it to them face to face? Why make all these innuendoes[2] . . . and to us? We did not mug their old people, we did not break into the houses of our elders. If all those things had happened at all, only boys could have done them. Our elders make sure we girls are too busy to have time for such things."

"You know, the boys in our age-group are all capable of many things. Because they have been to school they do not wish to farm any more. And they are not educated enough to take up big jobs in the cities."

"They can be houseboys, though."

"Houseboys? These boys? Can you imagine a bighead like Okei being anybody's houseboy?"

There was a peal of laughter.

"Oh, I don't know. If there is any truth in all this, I won't be surprised if they were led by our Okei."

The girls laughed again, and went on splashing so much water that their voices were drowned by the sheer noises of their movements.

"If I lay my hands on that girl . . ." Okei growled from where he was sitting. He had

2. **innuendoes** (ĭn′yōo-ĕn′dōz): indirect or vague accusations instead of direct statements.

sat bolt upright when he heard his name mentioned.

"Please, Okei, don't do anything rash," begged Nduka. "They are only girls, and don't forget that they were told this by those young people from Akpei."

"But why me? Why me? I have nothing to do with it. My uncle was making such insinuations earlier on. Why me?"

"Because, Okei, you are taller than any of us. You are more polished. You know, you were born into a little wealth and you started life richer than any of us. All that has given you the makings of a leader. So you are the uncontested leader of our age-group. You get blamed for things like this. I must talk to Josephine, though. She should watch her tongue."

"You better make sure you do. As for those Akpei weak-livered boys, we will deal with them. What do old people have that I'd like to take? Some of them are so poor."

"We can do something, though. We can arrange a meeting of all our age-group, and take it in turns to police the areas where these thieves operate," Uche suggested, giggling at Okei's anger.

"But that's a good suggestion, Uche. Please don't spoil it by your stupid laughter. At least they will not accuse us of doing nothing. As for those people in Akpei . . . ."

"No," Nduka said, "leave those people until we all meet, then we will decide how to deal with them."

The girls, with their wares delicately balanced on their heads, walked out of the stream still talking of this and that, until they saw Okei and his friends. They stopped short, not at first knowing what to do.

Josephine stepped forward in a brave attempt to cover their confusion. "Have you been waiting here long?"

"No," said Nduka hurriedly, "we were just coming from the village. You must have left Akpei very early today, or we were late in leaving. You normally are not here by the time we meet you."

"Yes, we sold our plantains very quickly today, didn't we?" her friends agreed, but one small girl started to laugh.

"And why do you want to know if we have been waiting here long or not?" growled Okei. "Have you been saying sly things about us?"

"Oh, Okei!" shouted an elegant girl of seventeen, Kwutelu. She was the oldest of all the girls, the most sophisticated and the one that the others modelled their behaviour by. "I didn't know you were here with the others! You are really beginning to care for us, coming to meet us on our way from Akpei. Thank you very much."

"I did not come to meet you, Kwutelu. I only accompany my friend Nduka here," Okei snarled. "And am I so indistinct that you cannot see me in this clear moon?"

"Ahem, let us share your wares," Nduka said quickly. "Josephine, give me half of your things, I'll relieve you of the load." The others stood there and watched enviously as Nduka took all the heavy things from Josephine's basket and slung them across his thick shoulder.

Uche, not to be left out, took bits from each of the other five girls. But Okei was unmoved by all this show of affection. He was hurt and he was angry. He was dying to know more about the gossip from Akpei, but pride would not let him ask the girls. And the girls did not wish to pursue the conversation. Some of them had a suspicion that they had been overheard.

As they walked home the girls concentrated on being girls, being nice and being

Girls carrying plantains.

Kryn Taconis/Magnum Photos

feminine. They brought out the roasted cashew nuts they had bought, and distributed them among themselves. They sang, made light conversation, and laughed just as Igbuno girls were expected to do.

Okei did not say a word, amidst all this show.

They parted at the market square. "You, Uche, go round and make the announcements. We must all meet tomorrow by the moonlight, in front of my uncle Obi Agiliga's compound," Okei said as he walked away very quickly, leaving the group to wonder about him.

"I don't like that young man very much," Kwutelu remarked.

"You don't have to like him. He does not go for girls like you," Uche said, sniggering.

"And what type of girls does he go for?" snapped Kwutelu.

"College girls, not gossip market girls from Akpei market. Here, take your stuff, I am going home. The moon is waning too," Uche said, half in joke and half in seriousness, confusing his listeners.

People never knew whether to take Uche seriously or not.

3

The sun was very high in the sky and the heat was almost unbearably intense. All the leaves along the footpaths drooped from lack of moisture. All the bush animals had sought for shelter in the shades of trees and the giant grass. Even the ever-chattering wood-parrots were silent. So hot was the afternoon. Obi Agiliga knew that it was time for him and his farm-hands to have a rest. It was time for him to go into the cool shed on his farm and lie on the beaten floor to smoke his pipe.

His paid helpers saw him and wordlessly followed his example. They all ambled into different parts of the bush in search of shelter.

"If only I could have more hands on this farm. Then I could be sure that all the yams would be harvested before the yam festival," Obi Agiliga moaned as he stretched his tall body on the cool floor. "Onuoha, go to the stream and get some water. We must have something to eat before we go on. This sun can burn life out of any man."

"I'll be back in no time at all, Father," said Onuoha, his twelve-year-old son. "Are you not happy about the progress of the harvesting?"

"Hmm, I am not too happy. When the sun is so hot it burns out all the moisture from the yams. So we will have to hurry."

"I wish you could make Okei come to the farm sometimes to help. He is very strong, yet he does not like coming to the farm at all."

"I know, but he is troubled about something, Onuoha. We don't know what it is. And he did not dream that he would ever be asked to come and work on the farm. That Awolowo free education has given him and his age-group airs. They will grow, never mind. They all will grow."

Father and son stopped talking as they listened carefully, knowing that a group of people were approaching their shed. Onuoha peeped into the bush-path, and the fear and curiosity in his young face were transformed and became a trusting and joyous glow.

"Father, you have visitors. It's Obi Uwechue from Akpei. I must run to the stream to get you all something to drink." So saying, he dashed into the bush-path, his young and determined feet crackling the dry fallen leaves as he went.

"It must be an important matter that brought you to my farm in this heat and at this time of year. Please sit down, sit down. The floor is cool at least."

"The matter is very urgent indeed, my friend," said Obi Uwechue. "And I do not want to come to your compound, because the women would interfere. How is your family?"

They all sat down and distributed kola nuts, and drank some cool palm-wine which Obi Uwechue had brought. Onuoha soon arrived from the stream and, with the help of his father's helpers, made a bush-meat soup which they all ate with pounded yam. Obi Agiliga studied his visitor all the time, wondering why he had come at such an odd time. But he was soon relieved of his suspense.

"My friend, you have a troublesome age-group in your village in Igbuno. We have the same in ours. I have never come across such stubborn young men. In Akpei it is now becoming difficult for women to walk down a footpath on moonless nights, a thing which we have never heard of before. Yesterday we had to send your girls away home early because they started picking quarrels with them. They say that your young men are equally bad. And of course a fight almost broke out. But during the argument, the name of your nephew was being mentioned all the time. . . ."

Obi Uwechue paused and looked around the farm hut, and laughed gently. "I was even hoping that I might find him on your farm today, since it is harvest-time."

"You are hoping for the moon, my friend," Obi Agiliga replied. "That boy is driving us all mad. And he is setting a very bad example for my younger sons. Onuoha here admires his strength. What shall we do, my friend? This must stop."

"Last Nkwo day, for example, some of your boys came into our stream to fish, when they know quite well that it is forbidden. They did not just fish, they muddled all the cassava[1] pulp which our women were soaking in the stream."

"Funny, I did not hear of all this, and my nephew did not say a word," Obi Agiliga remarked reflectively.

They were silent for a while, then as if on cue they both started to laugh. Obi Uwechue was the first one to speak.

"You remember what our fathers used to say, that when young men are idle the elders must give them something to worry about. I think we will have to create a big worry for our young men. By the time they have finished solving that problem they will be wiser."

"I was thinking of the same thing. The girls will be very useful. Women always have sharp tongues. Encourage your girls to start talking . . . you know, making pungent songs . . . and leave the rest to me," Obi Agiliga said with a knowing wink.

4

Uche got up very early the following morning and rushed to the stream. This was very

---

1. **cassava** (kə-sä′və): a tuber crop that has mostly starch and little protein. Among Igbos, it is grown mainly by women. It is a very hard root, so it must be cooked a long time or pounded and soaked (as here). It is cheap and plentiful, even when drought or economic conditions make all other food scarce.

unusual, and his family thought that maybe he was having a change of heart. They hoped that he would probably be going to the farm with the rest of the men in the family.

He ran down the slope leading to the stream, as usual, and looked uncertainly at the clear water as it tumbled over tiny rocks and then formed a deep pool at the bottom of the stream. There were very few people about, one or two early risers. He did not say anything to them. He stood there scowling at the water. It was a chilly morning, and the thought of dipping into the stream took some courage. He was feeling the water with his feet when he heard his friend and age-mate whistling as he ran down the slope.

"Ah," sneered Nduka, "someone is feeling the water like an old woman."

"No I am not. I was only thinking," replied Uche, holding his breath and ready for a compulsory plunge. He knew that if he did not get into the water by himself his friend would push him in, and he would laugh at him as well. So before Nduka could reach him he threw his shorts on the nearby rocks and dashed into the water.

"You know I would have helped you to make up your mind," laughed Nduka.

"Well, I have cheated you of your fun. You are early. Going to Akpei with your Josephine?"

"She is not my Josephine. She is just a friend. And people don't go to Akpei on Olie day. They go on Eke days to sell. I want to have my bath early in order to start the announcements for our gathering this night."

"So do I," Uche said. "And look, I have a big gourd here to take home enough water to last my family the whole day. But they will not talk of that. They will only talk of the fact that I did not go to the farm."

"Hmm, I would have gone to the farm today myself, but this gathering is more important to me. I am taking home a lot of water too."

"Listen, Nduka, how are we going to make the announcements? Okei did not say . . . maybe he expects us to beat a drum. . . ." Uche started to laugh.

"Use whatever method you like, but make sure all our age-group in your area hear about it."

"All our age-group—what of those who did not go to school, those who are playing at being good boys and go to the farms with their fathers? Should we not leave them out?"

Both boys did not know how to deal with this situation. Before their time, an age-group was an age-group. Now they had the educated ones and the uneducated ones. Should the uneducated ones be left out? Nduka was thinking of writing out the announcements for the meeting, instead of using a gong as people normally did. But if he wrote it out, would those of them who were illiterate get the message? He said reflectively: "I think we better include them. If they feel they cannot understand us, then they can absent themselves."

"Suppose we start speaking in English?" asked Uche, showing off.

"How many English words have you mastered? You are silly sometimes. Do you forget that we have many age-mates who are already in colleges? How would you feel if they exclude you in our age-gathering just because you stopped at Primary Six?"[1]

Uche gobbled his morning meal and waited for his people to leave for the farm, before he ransacked his mother's hut for a gong. He was not going to write the announcement. Nduka was right. He did not command enough English language for such a task. He started to beat the gong.

"All the males belonging to the Umu aya Biafra age-group are to meet in front of Obi Agiliga's compound when the moon is out this evening. All the males belonging . . . ."

A group of girls going to the stream saw him and wondered what the troublesome age-group had got to say to each other. "After all the trouble they have been causing. Go to your father's farm and help!" shouted one bold girl.

Uche ignored them and went on with his announcements. He would beat the going three times to arrest attention, then deliver his message, and beat the gong three times more to emphasize the end of his announcement.

Nduka took up the other side of Igbuno. But he copied out his message in shaky, large letters and distributed them by hand. He had to use plain sheets from his old school exercise book, because the age-group did not have much money. If we claim to be educated we must do things the way educated people do their things, he said to himself in justification for his action.

Okei enlisted the help of the young children in his uncle's compound and they swept the front of the compound leading to the footpath.

He was quiet and sullen, and the wives in the compound knew that something was on his mind. They teased him into anger, knowing that he would explode at the least provocation, but he seemed unaware of them. He was the more determined not to argue with anybody, when he noticed that his uncle Obi

---

1. **Primary Six:** In African countries that were once ruled by Great Britain, elementary school is called *primary school* and has six grades, often called *forms*, from Primary One to Primary Six. As in the United States, each grade lasts one year.

Agiliga was staying longer than usual on the farm.

"The Obi must be working so hard today. It is always like this during yam harvest time. Poor Obi. So much work," his senior wife Nne Ojo remarked pointedly.

The other, younger wives agreed, and all expressed the view that another pair of male hands would have been such a welcome gift to Obi Agiliga.

Okei knew that they were referring to his pair of idle hands. But he said nothing. If he picked a quarrel with any of them, the story would be repeated differently to his absent uncle.

By the time they had finished their evening meal many of the young people were already gathering. The meeting soon started.

Just as Okei had expected, he was elected as the leader of the age-group. Even though he himself doubted whether he had been a good choice, yet the cheers with which the election was greeted showed him that his age-mates had confidence in him. They went through all the allegations[2] that had been blamed on them, and nobody seemed to have done any of them. But towards the tail-end Uche, of all people, got up. He coughed and twiddled his ears for a time and then confessed:

"I got so fed up with all the lies told about us that last Nkwo day I went to Akpei to fish. Well, I must give them something to talk about. I did that on purpose with three of my younger half-brothers. It will not happen again."

"To think that you of all people should do a think like that," Okei shouted. "Were you very hungry? Can't your father feed you?

2. **allegations** (ăl´ĭ-gā´shənz): charges, accusations, or even just outspoken suspicions, but without proof or evidence.

You disgrace us. Does the group think we have to punish him?"

"No," was the unanimous answer.

"He is silly and he has promised not to do so again. I will keep an eye on him," finished Nduka.

It was then decided that all the other insults heaped upon them from the young people of Akpei would be settled in a wrestling match. "It will be a friendly one, just like a play, but it will settle our superiority once and for all," Okei said.

This was greeted cheerfully too.

The match would be played strictly according to the wrestling rules. They would select their best wrestlers, and the Akpei young people would select theirs. They would not invite the elders from the two villages to decide the better of the two. The young men of Igbuno were quite sure of their winning, because they felt they had been wrongly accused.

"How come they started to accuse us in the first place?" asked Nduka.

"Because they hear our elders talking of our faults in the open, washing our dirty linen outside under the very noses of those chicken-livered Akpei boys," explained one farmer's boy from Obi Ogbeukwu's compound. "Never mind, we will teach them, we will teach them."

Well, he talked sense, thought Okei as he sat there on the silvery sand, watching his friends. To think that that farmer's boy never spent a day in school. Aloud he said: "But what are we going to do about this farming business?"

"How can we farm using the old, old method which our great-great-grandparents had used?" Nduka said. "Look at our fathers. They spend four days out of every five, from sunrise to sundown on the farm. What do

Man watering a paprika plot in Sokoto, Nigeria.

Abbas/Magnum Photos

they have to show for it? Only enough yams to feed each family, and during dry season we almost starve. And what do we get from yams? Only starch. They taught us this much at school. I am not going to throw my life away working on such a farm. I am still thinking of a way of avoiding it, if I am to stay in this village and be a farmer. I think we should let the elders know this." He heaved his hefty chest in anger.

And he too was cheered. But the boys who had never been to school did not know what their friends and age-mates were saying. They knew their limitations though, so they cheered with the rest.

It was amidst this cheering and comradeship that Obi Agiliga came from his farm, tired out after such a long day. "What is happening in front of my compound?" he roared. "Clear out, all of you lazy lot! Clear out, you lazy, good-for-nothing pilferers of fishes and muggers of the old. . . ."

"Come in, come in, come in!" begged his senior wife, Nne Ojo. "The Umu Biafra age-group are holding a meeting in front of your compound, that is all." Here she laughed a little. "Our future leaders and town planners . . . ."

Obi Agiliga allowed himself to be led in, and said in a low voice: "They should think of

904 BUCHI EMECHETA

how to fill their bellies first. I must eat quickly. I have a word or two to say to the elders of Igbuno. This state of affairs must not go on."

The young people hurried over their deliberations and dispersed noisily. Okei and Nduka were to practise their wrestling skills, and the farmer's boy from Ogbeukwu was to go to Akpei the following day and throw the challenge to the loud mouths from Akpei.

"We will show them," Okei boasted in encouragement. "The wrestling match will decide who was in the wrong, and it will settle all the bickering and gossips once and for all."

Much later that evening Obi Agiliga went to see a few friends in their compound. He returned very late, when the moon was so clear and the footpaths so silent that the whole area looked like man-made glass. The air was so cool and light, the trees so clear in their thickness, that one was tempted to stay outside. But a mischievous smile played on the sealed lips of Obi Agiliga.

"These boys thought they were the only people who have ever been young. They will learn, sure they will learn," he murmured as he made his way to his own compound.

5

Okei, at the age of sixteen, knew what was expected of him as a leader. He worried over it most of the night, but there was one thing he was determined on: the leadership was not going to be taken from him. He had been told stories of failed leaders when he was very little. Such ideas were woven into the native fables told to children by their grannies on moonlight nights. He was going to be a good leader, and would live up to the expectations of those who had elected him.

He got up early the next day. He ran up and down the incline that led to the stream, in order to toughen his feet. He knew that as a result of this kind of exercise his feet would not give way easily for his opponent to fell him in wrestling.

"Ah, you have started already?" greeted Nduka, who had come to the spot for his toughening-up and practising with Okei.

"Yes, I have to do this part of it early to avoid the curious," Okei said as he panted.

"Oh, we can never prevent them from asking questions. Did you tell your uncle—I mean your little father, as you are expected to say—that you have been elected the leader of your age-group?"

"No. Whatever for? It won't interest him."

"I am sure it will. They say he was a great wrestler during his time."

"He never lets us forget it."

They ran up and down the slope many more times, until they were completely exhausted. Okei flopped on the nearby low bush, breathing hard. "I think all our age-group should toughen themselves up. You never know. I may lose the fight, and it could become an open one."

"There are rules to these wrestling matches, you know," Nduka said. "In any case, all our age-mates do wrestle for fun in their different compounds."

"That may be so, but I still would like it to become the accepted thing. They should all practise, not just the two of us."

"Ah, you are now talking as a leader," laughed Nduka.

"You all nominated me. . . . Come on, let us wrestle."

They moved to a sandier area and started to practise their wrestling. They both sweated profusely. People on their way to the stream soon started to pass them. Some gave them their praise-names in form of greetings, others just stared, encouraging this one against that one. It was all done in a lighthearted mood. The people of Igbuno loved such sports.

Soon a lighter, noisier group was approaching them. The wrestlers could tell that they were young people by the sounds their water-cans made against their carrier trays. They knew that they were girls. Then the approaching crowd saw them and stopped.

"Should we stop wrestling?" Nduka asked, uncertain.

"But why? They are going to the stream and we are wrestling. Just ignore them," Okei admonished[1] his friend hoarsely.

But the two young men could see from the corner of their eyes that the girls were led by Kwutelu, and they both knew that she could be very provoking. They saw that she started to whisper something to the other girls, and this unnerved the wrestlers.

Then all of a sudden the girls burst out laughing. Kwutelu covered her mouth in amusement, and walked on her toes in an annoying manner towards Okei and Nduka.

"Oh, so you are wrestling?" she asked in suppressed laughter.

"What is bad in wrestling? Or are you frightened we might floor your friends from Akpei?" Nduka snapped.

"Why don't you keep quiet, for God's sake?" Okei shouted at his friend. But Nduka was not the one to be silenced. He cared for and respected Josephine, but not that arrogant Kwutelu. He did not hate her, only he did not so much as care for her.

"Why should we let her get away with her saucy remarks? Yes, we are practising in order to challenge your friends from Akpei. Go and tell them. Come on, let's go, Okei. We've had enough for one morning anyway."

"Oh . . . so all this ballyhoo is for the Akpei boys," Kwutelu said. "Do you want to hear more of what they have been saying? They said you even pinch little sprats from their streams, and steal from our old people." She looked in amusement towards the other girls, who were laughing at it all and encouraging her.

"Look, enough is enough, do you hear me?" Okei said menacingly. "Stop that nonsense. You know that there is no truth in all that. If you were a boy you wouldn't stand there saying all that to us. You are hiding behind the fact that you are a girl. But don't annoy me, because I can still beat girls up." He was showing his anger now. He was very tired from their early practise, and that made him rather vulnerable.

"So you have now come so low as to talk to ordinary girls like us? I thought you go for college girls. And how come you are wrestling? I thought you have become too civilized for that, Okei the son of Agiliga."

"There is no need in replying to you," Nduka said. "If you have retained anything you learnt at school you will remember that every nation on earth wrestles, even the white people."

"Well, that is nice to hear, but I hope you go and practise your prowess on the sneaking thieves that lurk in the bushes at night, and not on innocent boys from Akpei. After all, all they did was to complain about your stealing fish from their stream . . . ."

"I wish I knew who the thieves were. And if I did, I would encourage them to come and burgle your father's compound. And that, I

---

1. **admonished** (ăd-mŏn'ĭshd): gave warning; criticized.

think, would put your poisonous tongue in check."

"Oh, Okei, so you are threatening our compound now? You try it. My father will wait for you. And as for you and the boys from Akpei, you know what they say in our native fables, that the guilty person always loses in such an open fight. So you have to practise hard, to prove your innocence."

Okei made a move toward her, but Nduka held him back. "They will go and say that we are waylaying[2] innocent girls. Don't do it, let us go."

Then the girls burst into a song:

"Umu aya Biafra.
Stealer of sprats from the streams,
Molester of innocent girls by the streams,
They will never go to the farms,
They will never help in the house.
Akpei boys will teach them a lesson, a lesson. . . ."

Okei was so angry that he did not bother to go to the stream to wash himself. He simply walked home with his friend, hoping to go back to the stream later on.

"Who is going to marry that chatterbox of a girl, Kwutelu?" he asked all of a sudden.

"I don't know him personally. They say he is on government service in Ilorin,[3] one of the Yoruba[4] towns in the west."

"God help that man."

Nduka laughed. "I know what you mean. I wonder why she is going out of her way to

---

Praise Names

In many societies, persons can win one or more special names because of something outstanding that they have done. Athletic performance, heroism, eloquence, beauty, or some particular achievement may earn the name. By the time they have reached early adulthood, most people have praise names. The praise name can be used at any time, but especially on ceremonial occasions. In the United States, we use epithets as praise names. For example, George Washington is known as "The Father of His Country"; Abraham Lincoln is called "The Great Emancipator"; Joe Louis is remembered as "The Brown Bomber."

---

annoy us, as if she had been set up into doing it. She was going to goad you into fighting her, and you know what that means. Her future parents-in-law and her real parents and their families would all go against us. That was why I was holding you."

"Thank you. But I will teach her a lesson one of these days if she continues this way. I don't think she was set up against us. I have never heard that girl utter a polite word to anybody."

"She is always cheeky, but not this far," Nduka maintained.

6

As soon as Kwutelu got home from the stream, she felt it was her business to go and tell her friend Josephine all that had happened. Josephine did not go to the stream that early because she had to help in getting

---

2. **waylaying:** hiding beside a road and attacking unsuspecting travelers as they pass.
3. **Ilorin:** a southwestern city and district of Nigeria, far from the villages in the novel.
4. **Yoruba** (yō′roō-bä): an ethnic group of people who, like the Igbo, live in Nigeria. The Yoruba culture and religion have been more influential in shaping the culture of the Western Hemisphere than any other African culture.

ready bits and pieces for the labourers who were going to help her father harvest the yams.

"This is the part of yam festivals that I hate most," she moaned to Kwutelu. "But how come you are not doing some work in your compound?"

"I am supposed to be claying the huts really, and my mother thought I was out in one of the groves getting the claying things. But I've just got to tell you this."

She went into a great detail of all that took place that morning. How she had successfully ruffled Okei's feathers; how he was so angry that he almost struck her. But thank goodness, Nduka was there to hold him back. She told Josephine how amused they were and how they had laughed. "Do you know, they really want to beat the Akpei boys in wrestling. What a big fun we are going to have watching them. Was it not a good thing that we started talking about it, eh?"

"I don't know, Kwutelu, if I like it all so much. I heard from my father this morning that they, the Umu Biafra, had a meeting last night. And the stupid boys had it in the open, and all the Agiliga household heard their deliberations."

"I did not hear that one. What have they decided to do? Kill us all on our sleeping-mats?"

"Oh, Kwutelu, you tend to dramatize everything. They are only going to wrestle with the boys from Akpei, and I heard my father saying that things were changing. He said that during his time young boys came of age with dancing and songs, but this group are coming of age with wrestling."

"Well, wrestling is a kind of sport, just like football the college boys play. At least Okei told me that much, this morning."

"Hm, if it is taken to be a friendly sport it will be nice. But this one is starting with a gossip. I wish we did not start it, Kwutelu. That boy Okei is very intense."

"Did your father tell you that we have done wrong?" Kwutelu asked.

"No, that's the funny part of it. I think the elders want us to goad them into anger. If you ask me, the elders from Akpei are doing the same," Josephine said reflectively.

They both laughed, and agreed that it could not be true. Though they would like some of those proud Igbuno boys, who thought they were going to be young for ever, taught a lesson.

"I am glad Okei did not beat you up. That would have been bad for you."

"And for him too."

When Kwutelu's father, Obi Uju, returned from the farm, his pet daughter Kwutelu told him of Okei's threats. Her father became angry and asked, "Can't our girls go to the stream without being molested? I must see his uncle Obi Agiliga. If he has to tie that nephew of his with a string to his door-post, I am going to make sure that I make him do so. If he wishes to practise wrestling, why choose the pathway to the stream, just to be seen by everybody? If he threatens you again, just let me know. Since when have we stopped young girls from singing provoking songs? Is that not what women are made for, to provoke men? I don't understand these young people any more."

Obi Uju did not feel like going out that evening. Few callers came to see him, and after they had all gone he felt he would retire early. He would have to get up early the following day to go and work on his farm with the few paid labourers he could afford. Labourers, especially paid ones, would look for any reasons to dodge the work they were paid to do. The master had to be on the alert all the time. He must work hard himself, setting a good example. This was even more imperative with Obi Uju, because he could only get three workers and could only afford to pay them for four days. Four days, which he calculated would be just enough to finish the toughest part of his harvesting. He must make sure the workers worked for every kobo he paid them. He called his daughter to fill his evening pipe for him.

"You are retiring early," Kwutelu remarked indulgently. She was well loved by her father. She was always close to him, and he spoilt her. Many of Obi Uju's youngest wives resented this, but they all now took consolation in that she would be going away to her husband soon after the yam festival. Meanwhile Kwutelu knew that she was free to sleep in her father's sleeping-house[1] or her mother's hut.[2] Her father's house had spare inner rooms. She liked these better than her mother's thatched hut. When teased about it she used to say: "I like sleeping under corrugated iron sheets." Her listeners would smile indulgently, knowing full well that her future husband worked as a sales manager in one of the Nigerian companies in Ilorin.

She filled the pipe for her father, and with the youngest wife in the family swept and got ready his sleeping-place. Clean goatskins were spread on a wooden bed and a feather-filled pillow was placed on a wooden head-rest.

"I think you have guests," the young wife told Kwutelu.

"Oh," she gasped as she listened to the

1. **father's sleeping-house:** the part of the family compound that contains the father's reception and sleeping room, and his special storage room.
2. **mother's hut:** the part of the compound that contains the mother's working and sleeping room, storage area, and outside hearth.

noises that were coming into the inner room from the compound. "Yes, you are right. I can hear my future brothers-in-law whistling. I must go. I will entertain them in the compound. Father is too tired tonight to receive any more guests."

"Yes, he is dozing already. These harvests, they are men-killers."

"I know," Kwutelu said as she made her way out into the compound. She glanced at her father on her way and said casually: "I am in the compound, father, if you want anything."

"No, daughter, go and be nice to your future brothers. They are growing impatient, I can tell by the wonkiness of their whistle."

Kwutelu laughed lightly as she dashed out to welcome her fiancé's brothers. They were happy to see her. They had heard that Okei had waylaid her on her way to the stream, and had come to find out why. Kwutelu told them all that happened in a lighthearted way, because she did not wish to start trouble for her future in-laws. That, she knew, would give her a bad name. They were both farmers, very traditional, and would take no nonsense from anybody. By the time she had finished her story they were all laughing at the naïvety of the young people born around the civil war.

"They are so proud about being partly educated," Kwutelu emphasized. "They are like bats, neither birds nor animals. After all, people like your big brother were educated in this village. They did not burn our huts down."

She went into her mother's hut and brought them some nuts. They all ate, and they talked and kept her company till the moon had really gone pale. They wished her goodnight, and warned her to be a good girl because she was already their wife. Kwutelu knew all that on the day her bride-price was paid. She promised to be good, and they saw her make her way to her father's house.

She did not like going to her mother's hut tonight, because she would wake up and tell her how late she was. Yes, all the young children playing outside had gone to sleep, but she was only chatting. She could hear her mother warning her against making herself cheap by over-exposure to her future in-laws, and these warnings had begun to get on her nerves. So she made her way to her father's sleeping-house. He would say nothing, nothing at all.

Obi Uju, Kwutelu's father, was deep in sleep, his tired body relaxed on the cool goatskins that had been lovingly laid out for him in his inner room by his daughter and youngest wife. He opened his eyes suddenly, not because the first bout of tiredness had ebbed away as a result of his retiring early but because he sensed that somebody was moving outside his outer door. He had got up earlier on, when it was very dark and when he guessed that his family were all asleep, and had hooked the heavy catch that held in the heavy wooden door. So he probably was dreaming.

Then he heard the sound again. This time he sat bolt upright. No, he was not dreaming. There was a determined rattling and pushing noise going on. The person was being careful not to wake the household. But for Obi Uju, whose well-trained ears were accustomed to hearing the slightest hiss of a snake, the noise at the door was loud enough. Then he remembered the threat Kwutelu told him that Okei had made to her earlier in the day.

"So, that stupid boy Okei thought he would carry out his threat? What is the world coming to? In the olden days one would have been justified in killing a thief like this one. But things have changed now. And I do not want to get involved in any unnecessary law-suits over so silly a boy, and at this time of year too. But the boy must be taught a lesson, a lesson he will always remember for the rest of his life. He must learn never to defy and laugh at his elders. He must learn the fact that we, the older ones, have seen greater things happen than young people of his age."

He got up and soundlessly padded his way to the shelf by his head and took out a small cutlass[3] which he used for cutting young corn. He crept quietly towards the door. "Sorry, son, that I have to teach you a lesson which you refused to learn from your uncle, and sorry that I have to teach you in this ghastly way. But you will live," Obi Uju thought. "This cutlass will scar you for life, but will not kill or break any bones of your body. To be threatened by such a tiny boy. What an insult!"

The pushing of the wooden door became stronger and Obi Uju helped the thief outside by unhinging the door from the inside. The door gave way slightly with a whining noise.

The moon had waned, but the distinct shape of a young person's shoulder was visible in the dark. This fired the anger in Obi Uju's mind. "To think that I am even older than your father . . . you threatening me . . . ." With that he aimed the cutlass at the shoulder, making sure to control the force with which it would land on the silly thief. The person outside instinctively dodged it, and instead of scratching the shoulder-blade as Obi Uju had calculated, it

3. **cutlass** (kŭt'lăs): a short sword or long knife with a flat, wide, and slightly curved blade.

A compound in northern Nigeria.

Marc & Evelyne Bernheim/Woodfin Camp

landed on the side of the head, cutting a young ear neatly off.

Then a scream rang out, piercing and painful like that of a goat being killed. "Oh, Father . . . Father . . . why do you want to kill me? Father, it's only me, your daughter Kwutelu."

Obi Uju dropped the knife, looked at his own hands, and then stretched them both out to catch the sagging body of his beloved daughter before she hit the hard floor.

Then he took up the cry, but his was heavy with anguish and bitterness. "Wake up, wake up, everybody. Come and see the abomination,[4] an abomination which has never hap-

> ### Bride-price
> In some societies, the family of each bride pays a "dowry" to the groom's family. In many other societies, the family of the bride receives a contribution from the groom's family to show how much they appreciate her leaving her own family to join them. A marriage is not complete and official until the agreed bride-price is paid, and if there later is a divorce, the bride-price must be returned.

pened in our village. I have killed my own daughter, with my own hands, all because of Umu aya Biafra. Wake up, wake up . . . an abomination . . . an abomination . . . ."

4. **abomination** (ə-bŏm′ə-nā′shən): a crime or any other action so terrible that gods punish the offender and even his or her whole community.

The Wrestling Match 911

7

The cry of "Umu aya Biafra, Umu aya Biafra" echoed from one end of Igbuno to the other. The cries cut through the otherwise still night like the sharp edges of so many shooting swords. The sounds seemed to give even the very still, dark leaves of trees bordering every footpath and open place a life of their own. They all seemed to quiver with the intensity of it all.

At first all the members of Obi Agiliga's compound were justly sleeping like everybody else. Obi Agiliga's house was in the innermost part of the compound. His wives' huts were built on both sides, and the whole set of buildings was surrounded with thatched walls made of very young, strong palm-fronds. A big gate sealed the whole compound from the rest of the village.

Nne Ojo's hut was the first one on the right. Because she was the nearest to the gate, she was always the first to hear shouts and gong announcements.

On this night, she could not believe her ears. "Umu aya Biafra—what have they been up to now?" she wondered. She sat up in the dark and would not wake her husband in the big house until she was quite sure what the trouble was. The noise grew louder and nearer. So she came out of the hut, and the words "Death, abomination, death, Umu aya Biafra" reached her. This was serious.

She wrapped her night waist-cloth around her and ran, shouting: "Obi Agiliga, wake up, they say that Umu aya Biafra have killed somebody, wake up." As she shouted and ran across the compound she went straight to the spare hut which the boys of the compound shared. She breathed a sigh of relief when she saw Okei, spread out in sleep next to his cousin Onuoha. "So

whatever it is, we have nothing to do with it."

"What is it now, what are you shouting for?" Obi Agiliga shouted at his first wife.

"Just listen, listen to the whole Igbuno. They are saying that Umu aya Biafra have killed and burgled somebody—I don't know who."

"Oh my God, oh my God. These young boys. What of our son?" asked the Obi, now surrounded by most of the males in the compound.

"He is there, still sleeping."

"Then he has nothing to do with it. Wake him up. I must find out from him first."

Okei was still drowsy with sleep when he was led into Obi Agiliga's courtyard. "Now, I want to know everything. Don't leave anything behind. You know what our people say, that the day of blood relatives, friends would go?[1] This night is the night of blood relatives. If we are going into a knife-fight to defend this compound, we must know the truth first. Who have you sent to go and kill somebody, Okei?"

Okei wanted to be sarcastic as usual, but he sensed the seriousness and urgency of the occasion. He shook his head violently, anger giving him strength. "I don't know anything about it. I did not send anybody to burgle or steal or kill . . . ."

"But they say that you are the leader. You did not feel us important enough to hear it from your own lips, but I know. So if you are the leader and an abomination has been committed in the name of your age-group, you should be the first to know. I believe you did not do it"—here Agiliga smiled a little— "and I believe you have nothing to do with it.

1. **day of blood relatives . . . go:** When the welfare of blood relatives is critical, even friendships may have to be sacrificed.

No son of Agiliga would tell a lie to his own people."

"I am sorry, Father, I did not tell you about my nomination. I did not know that such a thing would interest you. I thought you would laugh at me."

"A leader is a leader, son, and this harvest-time is your coming-of-age time, and it is an important age in any man's life. But let all that be. Who could have done this, and for what reason?" Okei's mind went to giggling Uche, who had to muddle the Akpei stream just to annoy people—but killing a person? No, he did not think Uche could do such a thing. He did not have such a courage. Again Okei shrugged his shoulders and shook his head. "I don't know, really I don't know."

"You had a gathering a few nights ago. You did not discuss anything like that?" Agiliga persisted.

"Discuss a thing like what?" Nne Ojo asked. "I was there in my hut, and I could hear all that they said. How I laughed about it all. They were just boys, groping their way to life. They discussed many things—wrestling, announcing this and that—but not killing or stealing. I can swear for my little husband Okei. But who would do a thing like this, to discredit a group of innocent boys, for God's sake?"

"All right, woman. Say no more until we know the full story. We know where we stand now."

So saying, he changed his sleeping-loin-cloth and put on a pair of shorts which he covered with an outer otuogwu cloth. He frightened his family when he took out two curved knives and a cutlass and slung them around his waist. Nne Ojo started to cry when she saw them.

"But Okei did not do anything, Agiliga!"

"People do not know that now. They may know later, but meanwhile some stupid people may take it upon themselves to revenge on the leader of the age-group. You see, son, why it's no easy thing being a leader. I must go and find out."

"I am going with you," Okei said, standing out.

"That is good, son, but you can't and you won't. This time, you will obey me. I am your father's brother, born of the same parents. I am your father alive. You must do what I say. Nne Ojo, take the boy and hide him in your hut. No respectable man would search the wife of an Obi, to say nothing of the hut of his senior wife. You and the others just keep awake, and if anybody asks for me and Okei say we have gone to find out what is happening in Igbuno."

"Oh, father, suppose they attack you in anger, when you have nothing to do with it? I will go with you to prove our innocence," Okei begged, near tears.

"No son of Agiliga cries in the presence of the women in his compound. If you must do that, go and do it in private."

With that he left his family. And Nne Ojo's grip on Okei's wrist tightened as she led him into her hut.

Obi Agiliga had scarcely left when two angry young men burst into his compound, demanding to have a word with Okei. But Nne Ojo had hidden him in the darkest part of her hut, where he could hear nothing from the outside. She sat in her front room, peeping at the two men. "Only two people? Well, we can cope with those." She did not come out, but allowed the hired labourers who were still staying in the compound to deal with them. She could hear every word that was being uttered and could see them all too clearly.

"They have gone to the centre of Igbuno to

see why everybody was shouting 'Murder, murder'," said the labourers in their imperfect Igbo.

"They? Who are they?" asked one of the young men.

"Oh, the two people you are looking for. Obi Agiliga and his nephew Okei."

"Are all members of this family dead, then? How come we can only have a word with hired labourers who can scarcely understand us?" one of the men asked in a loud voice of insolence.

Obi Agiliga's youngest wife was pregnant. She knew that they would not dare do any harm to her, and she could not stand there in the shadow and hear her compound insulted. Nne Ojo, she knew, was watching her and keeping an eye on Okei. So she came out from the corner of the compound, rubbing her eyes as if she had been woken from sleep. "What do we owe that you should come and visit us this time of night? Anyway, welcome. Our father has gone out, so we can't give you kola nut and palm-wine."

"Are you the only compound in Igbuno that has not heard all that has been going on for the past hours?"

"What has been going on?" the young wife demanded, stressing her innocence by opening her eyes wide.

"Have you not heard that Obi Uju has almost killed his beloved daughter Kwutelu, all because of a son of this compound?"

"Almost killed her? She is alive, then?"

"Do you want her dead? My brother in Ilorin has paid for her bride-price, and now she has only one ear. Her father has sliced the other one off."

"Oh dear, oh dear. And what has our Okei got to do with it?"

"What has he got to do with it? He threatened Kwutelu this morning by the stream that he would burgle her father's compound. So when she came in late her father thought it was your Okei, and cut her ear by mistake."

"I am sorry you are going to marry a young bride with only one ear . . ." the young wife began, but she could not help laughing, and all the others who had been listening to the conversation started with a ripple of laughter and then laughed out loud.

Nne Ojo knew that it was time for her to take over. Thank goodness the girl was still alive, she thought.

She welcomed the two angry men again and expressed her sorrow. It was a very nasty accident, and they should take it so. The Europeans could fix a new ear for their wife. They could use a piece of brown rubber; it would look like a brand new ear. "It's no use crying for revenge. Okei could have threatened to burgle Obi Uju's compound but he has not done it. And don't forget that Kwutelu is also of the same age-group. So you two come here to fight a small boy of sixteen? I am sure you are older than him by at least ten years. I am sorry for what has happened, though. But you all know how our people settle such things, by wrestling openly for the truth."

"Who will wrestle with that ninny? I'll break his bones in pieces."

"You see, we are saying the same thing. Okei is just a baby, and you two come here to revenge your wife-to-be's ear with knives . . . ."

"We haven't got any knives on us. We are not murderers."

"Then please go back to your compound and sleep off your anger. I am sorry about your wife's ear."

The two young men left shamefacedly. And Nne Ojo tried very hard to hush the laughter that would have overtaken all the members of Obi Agiliga's compound. She went back to her hut and said to Okei: "Go back to sleep. All is well."

When Obi Agiliga returned to his compound some time later, he and his senior wife stayed in the middle of their compound and went through the whole episode. They both agreed that Obi Uju had been a bit high-handed. "Suppose he had killed his daughter, all because she had an argument with Okei, and an argument which she started," Obi Agiliga wondered.

The Obi asked Nne Ojo whether she had told Okei anything. She said she had not, because she hid him in the darkest part of her hut. "But," she added, "the boy is sleeping now. I think he is beginning to trust us at last. He knew that you would take care of everything."

"Yes, let him sleep. I can see the faces of those mischievous boys in the morning. They say that Kwutelu has been a pain in the neck to them. Most of them did not like her very much. She is very cheeky."

"Oh, Obi Agiliga, the poor girl does not deserve to lose an ear just because she was cheeky," Nne Ojo said.

She made her way back to her hut, and slept soundly till morning.

8

Okei woke up and for a time wondered where he was. Then the happenings of the night came flooding through his mind. He wondered at the whole set-up and would have liked to know exactly what had taken place. No one would tell him. In any case, it was too early for people to get up from their sleeping-places. He had now become used to getting up early, so he crept out of Nne Ojo's hut and jogged down to the stream's incline, hoping to have covered several rounds of his daily running exercises before Nduka arrived. Once or twice an eel of fear wriggled in his stomach, but he calmed himself by remembering what Nne Ojo had said to him before his going to sleep. Had she not said, "Go back to sleep, all is well" to him? He knew that Nne Ojo, being the senior wife, would never make a statement like that for fun. All must be well.

As he ran up and down the incline breathing heavily, feeling the strength building up in his young, thin but strong legs, a kind of confidence was gradually building inside him as well. In a wrestling match a contender was on the lose if he allowed his opponent to floor him. But if one had a pair of very strong legs that could stand the pushing and thumping and still be on one's feet, then that one was bound to win. He sometimes wondered who his opponent was going to be.

During his runs he disturbed many little animals who had been sleeping in peace before his arrival on the scene. Here he heard one angry bird singing croakily out of tune, as if in protest to his being there. There he saw a bush rabbit scurrying away into safety, no doubt wondering why such a person as Okei should take it upon himself to disturb them so. All the animals could not help hearing him, because the fallen, yellowing, dry leaves made loud crackling noises on his approach, like corn popping in an open fire. Never mind, little animals. The fight will be towards the end of the harvest, and then you will not see me again here to come and disturb your peace.

Then he stopped short. He heard a laughter that sounded more like that of a bush monkey than that of any human he had known. "Surely this part of the forest is too close to human habitation for monkeys to come this close," Okei thought as he looked around him, wondering whether he had imagined it. Then he heard the laughter again, this time closer to him, and with this second bout of uncontrollable, unnecessary laughter Uche, his friend and age-mate, emerged from that part of the forest that jutted itself into the pathway. He had been crouching there, watching him no doubt.

"I was not expecting to see you here this morning. Since when have you decided to come and exercise with me?" said Okei angrily.

"I know you were expecting Nduka, but I come early because I wish to congratulate you for what happened last night."

"What happened?"

"Have they not told you? They thought we cut Kwutelu's ear. It is so funny." Uche started to laugh again.

Okei was not amused, but was willing to wait for Uche to control himself before asking him for the full story. Uche was only too happy to comply. He told the story, dancing his demonstrations, making this funny sound and that silly one, just as if he had been there when Obi Uju was sharpening the knife with which he had accidentally sliced his daughter's ear. Okei had to laugh loud as Uche mimicked Obi Uju's cries of agony when he realized his mistake.

". . . And of course early this morning I decided to go and see and show my sympathy to Kwutelu. But when I saw her, I could not laugh. Eh, you know something, that girl is really sick now. I saw her ear in a calabash[1] bowl. They had to tie her hair with bandages and a scarf. They are taking her to the big

hospital in Benin.[2] Her father is still crying and cursing us all, especially you. I told them how sorry we are, and do you know, Kwutelu could not talk . . . ."

"Who could not talk?" Nduka asked as he sprang on them from the part of the forest that jutted into the pathway.

"Kwutelu!" Okei replied in astonishment. "Have you ever heard of a thing like that before? That Kwutelu could not talk?"

"I can't believe it. I think her father did a nasty job. I think he ought to have cut her tongue or even her lips, instead of her innocent ear. Her future husband would not thank him for the loss of her ear, but he would thank him for the loss of her abusive tongue."

"Oh, but we are awful," Okei said, becoming thoughtful as his mood changed. "We should really be sorry for the poor soul, not making fun of her like this."

"But that sharpened knife was meant for you, Okei," Uche pointed out.

"You did not believe for a moment that I was going there to steal anything? What I said was that if I had known those who did the burgling I would gladly tell them to come and burgle her father's compound. But of course she changed the story, to sensationalize it for her father. And now he has overreacted . . . . Pity. Come, let's go on with our wrestling practice."

"You don't need to do that too seriously any more. This incident has shown that God is on our side," Uche said, wanting to back out from the rigorous exercise.

"Have you not heard that heavens help those who help themselves? God will not

1. **calabash** (kăl′ə-băsh′): a gourdlike fruit that is used as a bowl or a cup.

2. **Benin** (bĕ-nĕn′): a city in Nigeria named after a Nigerian ethnic group who are famed for the unique bronze sculptures of their ancient kingdom. A neighboring country in West Africa is also named Benin.

come down and wrestle with the Akpei boys for us. We will have to do it. He may help us if he wished, but the Akpei boys will be praying to him too," Okei said.

"That sounds like what one of my teachers used to say," Nduka replied. "He claimed to have known somebody who had been a prisoner on both sides of the last war. He said that the person said that each side prayed to God to be on their side."

"The man who had known another who had been in the great war said that somebody said—Gosh, you make me dizzy," laughed Uche. "That may be so, but I am not going to kill myself running and wrestling. I am going to the market-place to watch Kwutelu go to the big hospital in Benin. The mammy lorry[3] will be there soon. And in particular I want to watch a crying Obi and a dumb Kwutelu. I wouldn't miss that scene for all the wrestling matches in the world."

He left his two friends and faced the path towards home. Then he added for a good measure: "I will tell you all about it when I see you later in the day."

"Yes, and all garnished and spiced to your taste," Nduka said, and Okei laughed.

Uche went back into the village, and Okei asked Nduka if he had told the others to practice wrestling as he had advised them to do. Nduka had already done so and this pleased Okei. With that they went into the hard work of catching each other's legs and thumbing one another's arms and stomach to toughen all their young muscles.

At that moment, Obi Uwechue paid an early visit to Obi Agiliga on the farm. He had heard rumours of knifing, he said, and he wanted to know whether it was true that

Umu aya Biafra had started it all.

"How news flies," marvelled Obi Agiliga.

He soon told his friend from Akpei how it all happened, and they were both sorry, because they knew that indirectly they had encouraged the girls to goad the boys into anger. They agreed that the accident could have been worse. "Suppose Obi Uju had killed his daughter outright?" Obi Uwechue pondered aloud.

After a pause, he went on: "There is one good thing that is arising from all this—we do not have boys molesting anyone in the footpath any more. They are all busy practising their wrestling and getting angry at the insults the other party is heaping on them."

"Have you noticed that in Akpei too? But for the last night's incident, the aya Biafra boys in Igbuno had been busy holding meetings and getting themselves toughened."

"Well, that is the whole point of the whole exercise, isn't it?" asked Obi Uwechue.

"You are right, my friend, after this incident they will learn to think a little like adults. Even my nephew is beginning to look at me as if I am somebody at last. Before, I was just an old man to be shouted at."

The two elders chuckled knowingly at their cleverness. They had successfully created problems for the "know-all" youngsters.

9

It was another Eke market. There was much excitement in the air, and the girls of Igbuno were determined to make the best of the few Eke markets left. They would sell their heavy load of plantain as expensively as they possibly could; they would need the money to buy the latest colourful outfits. The relation between them and the boys was still uncertain, but a few boys had already made

3. **mammy lorry:** In some countries, pick-up trucks with a canvas cover over the bed or mini-vans are used as the cheapest form of transportation from one town to another.

Plantains on sale at a market.
Kryn Taconis/Magnum Photos

it up with some of their girl-friends. Even Kwutelu had started to exchange polite praise-greetings.

"Lord, your neck will sink into your chest with that big bunch of bananas," Josephine's mother observed. "It is too heavy. Why don't you sell them here? You will make some profit with such a big bunch."

"But I will make even more profit in Akpei. All my friends are going there this

Eke market with as big a bunch as they can carry. I am not the only one."

"These modern girls and their love for money," Josephine's mother said, shaking her head.

Josephine balanced the bunch on the piece of old cloth she had coiled, and placed it all on her head. Yes, it was heavy, but the picture of the latest abada cloth she was going to wear on the day of the wrestling match was already imprinted in her mind. She had to work hard and save the money.

At the main crossing she saw some of her friends waiting for her. They all carried much heavier bunches than usual.

"I hope the Akpei people will buy all your plantain," said an old woman cynically, looking at them with contempt.

"I don't know why some people won't mind their business," said Josephine in a low voice.

"Well, if they all do mind their business, they won't be the people of Igbuno," Kwutelu said. She then looked around her enviously and continued: "My bunch is the size of a small girl's. I don't know why that old woman did not make any remark about that."

"Don't talk like that, Kwutelu. When you were well we all know that you used to carry the biggest bunches of plantain of any of us. You must not carry anything big now, because it gives you headache," said Josephine consolingly.

Kwutelu sighed and was silent. This was the new attitude people noticed about her since the accident. Some thought that maybe she stopped being abusive because she was frightened in case people would call her "rubber ear." Because, as Nne Ojo had foretold on the night of the accident, an artificial ear had been glued to her head.

The spirit of the girls soon became light as they jogged their way to Akpei. They chattered about empty nothings as they climbed the steep hill that led to Akpei.

They arrived there very early as usual, hoping that by so doing they would sell their wares and leave for home early. After waiting for a while for the market to get full, they noticed that nobody from Akpei had come to ask them for their plantain. "Maybe they

have stopped eating plantain," Josephine said with a nervous giggle.

"It's still early yet," Kwutelu said confidently.

The market became full and people started going home, yet all the Igbuno girls stood there staring at their unsold plantain.

"Do you think they are doing this on purpose?" a little girl of fourteen asked Kwutelu.

"But I don't know either. Maybe they too are going off food in order to save for their yam festival and the wrestling match," Kwutelu replied.

"It will be funny and humiliating if we have to go back home still carrying our bunches of plantain," Josephine remarked.

Kwutelu and the others were thinking of the same thing. They would be disappointed, to say nothing of the shame of it. Still, they all agreed to stay a little longer.

"I am so hungry," cried one girl in despair.

"You are not the only one," Josephine replied to her.

Normally by this time they would have almost finished selling and would have some food for themselves. But this afternoon they still had their plantain untouched by any customer, so there was no money to buy food.

Then came an old woman. She was in dark-patterned abada cloth and was walking with a stick, peering this way and that way critically as some old people do. She stopped in front of the girls and, having appraised them, advised them to give their plantain away to poor old people like herself. That way the bunches of plantain would be useful. "If you stand here all day and night, nobody will buy your plantain."

"But why, why?" Kwutelu cried.

"You ask me why?" she asked as she shook her stick in the air. "I shall tell you. Our Umu aya Biafra are planning a friendly wrestling match with your boys, and what do you think your boys are doing by turning the whole thing upside down?"

"Turning it upside down? What is she talking about?" the girls asked one another.

But the woman did not answer. Her mind went on to other things. "If you carry a bunch of your plantain to my hut, I will always bless you. If you take all your wares home, they will go rotten on you. If you think you are going to sell them here in Akpei, you will wait for ever." She went down the market square, still peering this way and that.

"What are we going to do?" cried Josephine. "If I have to carry that bunch back all the way to Igbuno I will never recover from the shame. Do you think we should ask them why they are boycotting[1] our part of the market, Kwutelu?"

"And be insulted into the bargain? No, Josephine the daughter of Nwogbu, we won't stoop that low. We can dump some of the plantain in the bush on our way home if they are too heavy, but if not we must take them back to Igbuno with us. Can't you see what is happening, the way those people are looking at us slyly and laughing? All this was not accident. I know that we are hungry and tired, but we must go. And as far as I am concerned, I will always support my own people. I will always sell my plantain in our own Eke market, not come to a place like this and be insulted. You remove that woebegone look from your face, it is not the end of the world." Kwutelu finished addressing the latter part of her speech to the youngest girl, Adaobi, who had previously complained of hunger.

They packed their plantain again and

1. **boycotting:** a group's refusing to do business with some other group or organization.

helped each other into putting them on their heads, then went down the road leading to Igbuno, forcing themselves to make light jokes as if this type of thing happened to them every market day. They could hear people, one or two knots of gossip loungers, laughing out loudly. But the girls went on with determined steps.

When they knew that they were far from Akpei, they did away with their mask of pretence.

"Goodbye to my dream abada material," Josephine moaned.

"And welcome to our village pride. From now on we will have to boost the ego of our boys, not deflect it. The people of Akpei have turned a harmless joke into something serious." Kwutelu was quiet for a while, realizing that all these rumours had almost cost her her life. So it must be serious.

Halfway between Akpei and Igbuno some of the girls threw away their plantain because they knew that they had a lot at home and it could not keep very long. They were all tired and could scarcely carry themselves, to say nothing of taking home heavy bundles of plantain which seemed to have become doubly weighty.

"It does not matter very much if we appear at the wrestling-square in our old abada cloth," said Kwutelu. "After all, the way the Akpei people are going about it, I don't think it is going to be all that friendly."

"Yes, that will be a good idea. Let us make it an old abada cloth day. Those silly Akpei girls will come in their very best, then we can pick up quarrel with them and mess their new outfits. Yes, that will teach them," said Josephine mischievously.

They all laughed, despite their failure to sell their plantain.

They were still laughing when they came

to the hill bordering the Igbuno stream. They were met by a larger group of people, because many of the parents were anxious about them. It was a moonless night and very dark. But the friends and relatives met them with lamps and hand-torches.

The girls poured out their story and the young men became really incensed, determined to win the match.

But when the male elders heard it all later in the night, they all smiled with a conspiratorial wink.

10

The next gathering of the Umu aya Biafra was held on a moonless night. The night was dark and forbidding. All the familiar trees and everyday shapes acquired greater solidity. Some trees even seemed to be moving when the night breeze fanned the landscape. The age-group carried hurricane lamps, and some modern and well-to-do boys brought powerful hand-torches.

This time they decided not to meet in the open, after their experience of the last meeting. They were moody almost to the last person. The insults, jibes, and abuses of the young men and women of Akpei had aroused the anger of the mildest member. Even Uche, who was always thought to be easygoing, had taken it almost as a personal insult that the Igbuno girls were shunned in Akpei market. So they met in an old abandoned hut at the corner of Akpuenu. This hut was large and used for occasional dance-practices. The boys did not know who owned it, but they knew that they would not be chased away.

The matter of Kwutelu's ear was mentioned briefly. Some still found it funny, but many were beginning to feel sorry for Kwutelu, especially as she had now changed for the better.

Everybody was then allowed to display the tricks of wrestling they had mastered since their last gathering. They had fun with this, because there were those who were born to be non-wrestlers. Uche, for example, was always looking for a nice, soft place to fall instead of defending himself. "Oh, Uche, you wrestle like a pregnant woman," Okei shouted at the top of the laughter.

There was a big hush when Okei chose Nduka as a partner. The others were intrigued by the quickness of the two wrestlers, their lightness of touch, and the clever way with which they were polite to each other. It was a kind of wrestling, but a wrestling with an art. It was beautiful to watch. But the farmer boys among them started to grumble. The grumble became loud, and Okei had to stop the wrestling.

"And what is your problem, farmer's boy from Ogbeukwu?" he asked.

The so-addressed disregarded the insolent tone and answered sharply. "This is like a white man's wrestling, you two dancing about each other as if you are playing hide and seek. It is beautiful to watch, it is amusing. But it will not do for those Akpei people. Remember that I had to take message of the wrestle to them. I saw the spirit with which my news was received. They were determined. This type of dancing will win nothing for us."

"So how do you want us to wrestle?" asked Okei, panting with anger and breathless.

"The way real wrestlers wrestle."

Others applauded the statement from the farmer's boy. "After all, we elected you to be our leader. You should do your best to retain the post."

"I am not afraid of the leadership being taken away from me . . . ." Okei began.

"Ahem, ahem," Uche butted in. "I like the dance, as you said, but where can we learn to improve it? Okei is very fast and strong, but if we can help him to be better it will be much more helpful than arguing about it." Then he started to laugh.

"You have made a good contribution," said the farmer's boy, "but I don't know why you are laughing. I saw the Akpei boys consulting with their elders even whilst I was still there. Okei can consult his uncle. They say that he was a good heavy wrestler in his time. Why can't we use his knowledge? I am sure he will be willing to teach us."

"No! No! This is our war, this is our problem. We don't want the elders to nose into our business. So keep him out of it. I won't like to consult with him for anything." Okei yelled, his voice echoing round the hushed gathering as if he were the only person there.

"But the Akpei young people are being helped by their elders," Nduka put in pointedly. "Why can't we use their knowledge too?"

"Because we are doing our thing our own way. We don't want their ways. They are old-fashioned, and as for my uncle . . . well, he is not bad for an uncle, but I don't like consulting him for anything."

"Then we are fighting a losing battle," the farmer's boy said, "because the young people of Akpei are bound to come out on top. And listen, Okei, are you going to do without the wrestling dance too? You know you will have to dance round the circle in a certain way. None of us here knows the wordings of the song, to say nothing of the way to dance it. Your uncle is a master at it. Are you going to do without that too?"

Wrestling Contests

Among the Igbo, wrestling is an extremely important sport. Wrestling contests are major holiday occasions. The wrestlers represent their age group and village. The ceremonies include the song and dance that the village age group performs as the wrestlers are led to the wrestling ring. There is also a victory dance. Each village tries to compose the most spectacular show.

Okei looked at him in the dim light for a long time. Had they made a mistake in allowing those who had never sat behind desks at school to come and join them? Could they not do without the dance? A wrestling match without its dance was half a show, he knew. He must give in.

". . . We need our elders," the farmer's boy continued. "After all, they are our fathers, and they cannot direct us wrong. This is going to be a friendly match, and I hope it remains so. But suppose it should go out of hand?"

"All right, you have made your point. I'll see what help he can give us, to polish up our way of wrestling. I suppose one has to look up to one's elders."

"A village that has no elders has no future. I hope we will always have elders," Nduka said prayerfully.

11

It was easy for Okei's age-mates to suggest that he should seek advice from his uncle, Obi Agiliga. He saw the point of his not making the mistakes which the elders had made

Members of the council of elder men and women known as Osugbo among the Ijebu Yoruba and Ogboni in the Oyo area have hereditary titles. These Osugbo/Ogboni titled male elders are seated in their lodge, iledi, *in Ibese, Nigeria.*

Professor Henry J. Drewal

before him. But until now it had never occurred to him that he and his age-mates could make mistakes at all. "Blast those Akpei boys! Why should they take it upon themselves to seek advice from their elders?" How was he going to start telling his troubles to his uncle? A man he had looked upon with tolerance, that type of tolerance that had to exist because there was no way out for him, because he had no other place to live. He feared that his uncle would feel proud and would hint, "I have always thought you would come to me to ask for advice."

"It is that humiliating part that I resent so much," he confessed to Nduka the second day. "I would have liked us to do without the likes of my uncle completely."

"Well, we can't, and we won't. We need the likes of him. What is wrong with his feeling proud about our seeking his advice? You never know, in a few years time it will be your turn to advise his young sons. You will be the elder in your family then. Would it be wrong of you to feel proud then? I don't know what you are worrying about."

"I resented my parents' death and maybe his staying alive. Maybe if he had been my

The Wrestling Match   923

father and not my uncle, I would have been able to go to him naturally."

"Well, he cannot help staying alive, can he? It's not his fault your parents were killed. It was a war, and you and I know that in such wars, the innocent suffer. Don't lose the match for us because of your pride and stubbornness. I shall come with you, if you so desire."

"Thank you very much. I think that this is a family matter. I shall deal with it alone. Come on, let us run down the slope one more time."

Obi Agiliga was surprised to see Okei sitting in his courtyard in the evening. He was behaving in the normal traditional way, of sitting around in the evening after the day's work had been done and listening to the conversations of the adults and learning lessons from them. Agiliga glanced at him uneasily once or twice, and wondered what had come upon him. But he controlled himself from asking him any questions.

Okei helped in serving the adults the ever-present kola nuts and palm-wine, betraying no emotion but being extremely polite. One or two of Agiliga's friends who knew Okei's reputation arched their brows in a question, and Obi Agiliga simply shrugged his shoulders. He did not know the reason for this change of heart.

Okei started clearing and tidying up when the visitors had left. Agiliga watched him as he smoked his last pipe before retiring for the night. Then he asked: "What is it, Okei? What is worrying you?"

Okei looked up at his uncle and smiled. "It is the wrestling match," he replied promptly.

"You want to learn the songs and the style we used. Our style."

Okei would have liked to find out how his uncle knew exactly what he wanted, but he was so taken in by its suddenness that he nodded enthusiastically.

Then his uncle—who was also a tall man, but whose tallness was less pronounced because of his thickened body—got out from his sitting-place and took two simple but cunning steps towards Okei, and by the time he realized what he was doing Okei found himself lying on the floor.

He got up and glared at his uncle. Obi Agiliga roared with laughter and said, "That is not a very fair way to treat your wrestling opponent. But if everything fails, it is a useful art to master. I will teach you that first."

Obi Agiliga did not stop with teaching him how to take his opponent unawares, especially if the person became violent; he taught him how to give his audience pleasure by luring his opponent round and round and then suddenly confronting him. "Most opponents are not prepared for this sudden halt, and you have to use their unpreparedness to floor them. You know that if an opponent's back reaches the ground, then you have won."

"I know that, uncle," Okei said with his mouth full of laughter at this Obi who in his enthusiasm had been transformed into an agile young man. He worked up his body into lumps and hooks, displaying many methods of trapping an opponent. It looked for a while as if the Obi was simply displaying his art only for himself. He became completely unaware of Okei's presence. Okei's respect for his uncle really soared high.

When it came to the words of the wrestling song, Obi Agiliga became supple and almost soft as a woman. He would jump into the air, and just as you thought he was going to land flatly on his back, you would see him touching the ground as lightly as a fallen dry leaf. Then like a cat he would tread softly on the balls of his feet, singing and moving to the rhythm of his own music.

He was thus preoccupied when his senior wife Nne Ojo came in. Okei made a sign for her to be quiet, and the two of them watched Obi Agiliga perform. It was only when he had danced to his heart's content that he said, "Now I have to teach you all that."

Nne Ojo laughed with tears in her eyes. "I used to see you in the wrestling circle performing like that. To think that you were that young once."

"Yes, that was a long time ago," the Obi said with some confusion. "I have to teach it all to this young man here. It is his turn now. My turn has come and gone."

"It was a lovely time, when we were always young," Nne Ojo said, and walked across the courtyard, making for the door leading into one of the rooms.

"Don't go, my senior wife. I was the leader of the wrestling group of my age, but not the leader of my age-group. But Okei here is the leader of his age-group and is required to defend their reputation. So it will be a big occasion for this family. Could you let him borrow one of your red Akwete[1] cloths to use as a kind of cloak? I want him to come out in style to beat those crude Akpei boys. It is not always that a wrestling leader is also elected as the leader of his age-group. You will get the whole compound ready as well."

"We have done all the preparation in secret, hoping that one day our Okei will ask for your help. Now he has done it, we will all be behind him."

"Yes, that is right. The Akpei people and the whole of Igbuno will not forget the year

1. **Akwete:** highly esteemed and valuable cloth among Igbo women.

in which Okei the son of Agiliga came of age," Obi Agiliga said proudly.

Nne Ojo soon left them and the two men, one middle-aged, the other a youth, practised the art and songs of wrestling till late at night.

12

The people of Igbuno, in their fever of excitement, started to count the days by saying that the day of the great wrestling match had only two market days to go. Then they started to count the days. It would be in four days' time, then three, then two, eventually the day after tomorrow.

Okei and his friend Nduka had become village heroes. As they practised in the early morning they now had a large group of young enthusiasts who came to watch them. It was during the school holidays, and those boys who went to the farms were all free because the yams had been harvested. They cheered as the two boys punched each other mercilessly. They applauded as they danced in their art. They ran up and down the incline with them until they were out of breath. It was a time of great hope.

All the boys of that age went to a special barber, who had to cut their hair in a certain style called the Appian Way.[1] So they were easily recognizable. The old, the young men, and the women prayed for them to win the wrestling match.

"Our own age-group has got an original touch," boasted Uche as he trotted and puffed like a dog behind Okei and Nduka.

1. **Appian Way:** The original Appian Way was the main road into Rome when Rome ruled the whole Mediterranean Sea. Nigerian children learn about it in school. The haircut probably had a big, main separation (a "part") along the middle and several smaller parts.

The Wrestling Match 925

"What master touch?" Okei asked.

"All age-groups until now usually come out with some lousy dances. But we are wrestling our way into manhood."

"Maybe because we saw the gunning down and killing of many people in our baby-hood."

"But that is true, though," Okei put in to enlighten his friend Nduka. "I keep wondering why it never occurred to us to dance our way out."

"It never occurred to us," said Nduka.

"But why since that would have been the normal thing?"

"I don't know. Don't ask me," Uche replied with a sickening giggle.

At home in Agiliga's compound, Okei was being treated to a place of honour. He was always being invited to eat with the Obi. He was no longer ordered to go and eat with the women, so Nne Ojo could not complain about his nasty eating manner. Once he started to eat with the elders, he began to behave himself.

Amidst the excitement and expectation, Okei asked Obi Agiliga one evening: "Suppose, father, I lose the contest?"

"In the first place, you will not lose. In the second place, even if you lost, it won't be a complete loss because you would have added a new art to the game of wrestling, and you would have taken part and done your best. Don't you think it is better to think on those lines, Okei the son of Agiliga?"

"You are right, father."

They had just finished their evening meal, the day before the official yam festival day, when they were suddenly forced to listen to a group of dancers coming towards the Agiliga's compound. As they drew nearer, the words of their songs became more distinct.

They were singing:

"Akpei people bumkum,[2]
The world bumkum, we don't care.
Why should we care?
When we have heroes like Okei . . . .
Heroes like Okei the son of Agiliga
In our midst."

They came to the front gate of the compound and made a circle. The dancers were the very girls who only a few months ago had been against the boys of Umu aya Biafra.

Kwutelu and another girl led the singing in turns. The rest of the group answered, shaking their beaded gourds in the air. They were so organized that the circle was never crowded. There were never more than two girls in the circle at the same time. Their male guide had a mock whip in his hands, ready to chase any unwanted dancer who was not invited to join in. So great was the happiness and excitement that everybody wished to display their own special dance. They kept on and on calling Okei to come out and dance for them. He would not. And people thought he was shy.

"I will dance for him," said the senior wife of the family, Nne Ojo. Her dance was a little comical, and it was clear that she was putting it on on purpose. She knew she could not crouch and jump as quickly and as gracefully as the young girls, so she overdid her stiff back. She placed one hand on her hip, and walked round the circle in imitation of the girls. She made faces at them, until the drummers and singers all collapsed in laughter.

"You must go and make a few dancing steps, Okei, at least to show your apprecia-

---

2. **bumkum:** *bunkum*, empty, unsupported claims. Here, the song claims that the people of Akpei can make only false claims to glory, since Igbuno has a truly glorious wrestler.

tion for all the girls' efforts," Obi Agiliga advised.

"I can't believe Kwutelu is singing my praises. She used to laugh at me."

"Everyone loves a winner," his uncle said wisely.

Okei eventually sprinted into the circle, dancing lightly as if he were a bird in flight. When he crouched slightly to the music, he looked like a bird pecking some food with its beak and then taking flight. He was so light. He was so agile, and they loved him.

The dancers were entertained, and they sang their way to other compounds. Everybody knew that the yam festival had started.

13

The wrestling match day did arrive at last. The dawn was misty, but it was clear even from that early morning mist that it was going to be a sunny and dry day. No one expected it to rain at this time of year, but one could never tell for sure, especially as it was possible for some people who were not well disposed to the wrestling to intone[1] to the skies and make it rain.

Okei was awakened by the drums of Igbuno. The special drummers knew how to make their drums talk and convey messages. This used to be a common thing a very, very long time ago. But now, these drums were used only on important occasions like this.

The doubt still lingered in Okei's mind. He had never been beaten in wrestling before, in Igbuno. But he did not know the style the opponents from Akpei would use. He did not let anybody know of his fear though, but he was determined to take his uncle's advice and do his best. And if he should lose, to accept it gallantly.

1. **intone:** to speak as if singing, especially when praying aloud.

He was not left on his sleeping-mat long. Excited voices rang round the compound as young mothers called their children for the stream and their morning bath. The smell of roasted yams wafted all over the compound and the whole village. Smoke from wood fires rose from here and there and everywhere. On yam festival wrestling match days, even the poorest widow could afford to dip a whole yam into the open fire. When roasted, they were dipped in palm-oil and slightly salted and peppered. The crust of that roasted yam was a great treat for both children and adults. Okei knew that at least on this his great day, the crust of the yams would be left for him. At the thought of this, it looked to him as if the aroma of the food was strengthened especially for his nose. He got up and walked into the open compound.

"Oh, my strong little husband will come to my hut and eat my roasted yam?" Obi Agiliga's youngest wife asked hopefully.

Unfortunately for her, Nne Ojo was not too far away. She gave the young woman such a look that sent her scurrying like a squirrel into her own hut. "You must be careful of what you eat and where you eat today, Okei," she said.

Okei had to suppress the urge to show his eagerness. He was dying to have a taste, but he said manfully: "I must go to the stream to have a bath first."

"Well, don't stay too long and don't practise any more," Obi Agiliga shouted from the verandah of his house. He had heard all that Nne Ojo and his youngest wife had been saying. "When you return, your yam, specially prepared for you, will be here, hot and waiting."

At the stream many people wished Okei luck from afar. He acknowledged them all with a nod. Meeting Nduka at the men's area relaxed him a little.

"Did you see Kwutelu and the others last night?" Nduka asked.

"Yes, they came to our compound, and she was singing my praises," Okei said with a laugh.

"Did you not notice that all the girls were wearing their headscarves like a band, to cover their ears and display their hairdos?"

"I thought that was their latest fashion or something," Okei said naïvely.

"Well, it could become fashionable. But Kwutelu started it, to cover her damaged ear, and she willed the style so strongly on the other girls that it was accepted as part of their dancing outfit."

Both boys laughed conspiratorially.

"Poor Kwutelu," Okei said in sympathy.

"We have to hurry home, and good luck to you. The Akpei people are taking this very seriously, I heard," Nduka said.

"As far as we are concerned, it is a friendly match between the same age-groups. The adults can come and watch, but they must not interfere. We will choose our own judges and referees from both sides. They will be of the same age as all of us. Nothing to do with the adults and nothing at all that serious."

"Well, you'll have to warn the Igbuno girls. They see this wrestling match as a way of revenging the bad treatment they received over their plantain issue."

"That was their fault," said Okei. "We have an Eke market here in Igbuno. Why go all that way just to sell them? Yes, I know they make a few pennies extra. But if for any reason they have to go by a car or a bus of some kind, that money would be eroded."

"Anyway, few cars run that road. And they have stopped going to Akpei now. Yet they still want to use this match to get even with them."

Okei shrugged his shoulders. The two boys soon parted, each to his own compound to go and get ready for the wrestling.

By the afternoon there were drums being beaten in every big compound in Igbuno. People put on their best clothes, and went round to relatives' houses to eat yams and exchange gifts of yams. Everything and everybody was yammy. There would still be many dances for the rest of the season, but on wrestling match day the excitement was at its highest.

"Ah, I can hear a different kind of drum from ours," Obi Agiliga remarked. "And I think it is the Akpei people. They must be nearing our hill." He watched Nne Ojo, his senior wife, put the last touches on the Akwete cloak Okei was going to wear.

Okei, who had been lying on the mud couch in the courtyard, sat and listened carefully. Yes, he could hear a faint rhythm, different from the other, nearer ones. It was so faint that he had to strain his ears to hear it. Then he smiled at his uncle and said: "You have been expecting that sound, have you not?"

Obi Agiliga nodded, puffing confidently at his pipe. "Are you boys not having any elders there to see to the smooth running of things?"

"No, father, we are boys of a new breed. We want to do most of the whole things by ourselves. But since the Akpei boys consulted their elders to give them some tips, I had to come to you to teach me the tricky bits of wrestling and the dance to it. But you have helped us this far, I think we can now go on by ourselves. You all are invited to come and watch, though."

Obi Agiliga smiled into the smoke from his pipe. "You don't invite people to watch anything in Igbuno. We just go. And as far back as I can remember, the yam festival was always climaxed by boys on the verge of manhood entertaining everybody with a dance of some sort. But in your case, you want to celebrate yours with a fight."

"Not a fight, father. A sport."

"Well that may be so. But some people are not so good at losing. You must remember that. In any case, the whole village will be there."

The other people in the compound gave a shout of delight and cried, "We will show them, we will show them."

"They have heard the Akpei drums too. They are talking drums, and are saying that their wrestlers are the greatest and fastest wrestlers in the whole of Nigeria," explained Obi Agiliga.

"Is that what they are saying? I must get ready. We must go and meet them in style."

The men in the compound helped Okei to dress up. He only wore a plain pair of shorts and a pair of colourful plimsolls[2] to match. But on top of this, he had several charms slung round his neck. One of them was made with crocodile teeth, to prevent him from becoming breathless. Another was from nut kernels, to harden him like nuts which are hard to crack. His face had to be washed with waters mixed with many herbs, so that no evil eye would penetrate beyond his face to his heart. After all that, Okei was forced to drink a mixture which was supposed to get rid of any shyness he had.

The drink worked like a miracle. He started to sway to the drums of the Akpei people who were fast approaching the centre

2. **plimsolls:** rubber-soled, canvas shoes, like tennis shoes.

Jubilee—Ghana Harvest Festival, *mixed media on canvas by John Biggers, 1959.*

of the village. He laughed loudly when he heard the thin voices of Igbuno girls going to meet the new arrivals. People told him that Kwutelu and the others were singing his praises to the Akpei people, and this was annoying the girls who came with them. Okei then shouted: "That is it. That is the spirit."

They soon finished dressing him up and getting him emotionally ready. Then the drums all stopped as if on cue. Their places were taken by the biggest drum of all, that of the age-group dancers. This drum was beaten only once a year, at every yam festival season. It boomed, and its sound seemed to shake the very earth. Okei leapt into the air, and all the members of Agiliga's compound and all the members of the nearby com-

pounds ran out, some carrying their locally made guitars, some carrying beer bottles and teaspoons to make music with. Children got empty tins and their covers. These musical instruments were all kept in secret before, waiting for the time they thought the spirit of the yam harvest and the coming of age would descend upon Okei. He led the crowd on, leaping and whirling in the air, until he neared the open place called Kumbi, where he knew that the Akpei contestants would be waiting. Someone had to stop him, because it was said that if he saw his opponent first he would not live to be an old man.

Four young men got hold of him and held him, forcing him to lean against the mud wall of Obi Uju's compound. Even Obi Uju, Kwutelu's father, came out and said prayers for Okei that he should bring glory to Igbuno.

All the other young Umu aya Biafra came and went into the square with their own relatives and friends, singing their praise-names and dancing with them. The other people, young members of the age-group, were slightly more sober than Okei. They too had been given the mixture, but not as strong as Okei's. Nduka too came with a big crowd. He was to take the place of Okei if he had an accident or got beaten. He was to be kept in reserve.

The Umu aya Biafra drum boomed from Obi Uju's compound, where the drummers had been hidden. The wordings of the drums were very clear: "We will show you, we will show you."

The farmer's boy from Ogbeukwu went into the circle and welcomed the people of Akpei, reminding them that it was he who had come to them to ask them for this match, a friendly one. He welcomed them again and showed them the pile of food and drinks which the parents of those coming of age had prepared. He introduced them to the girls who would be ready to get them anything they wanted. He then told them to choose a judge, and someone to act as a referee: the Igbuno boys had already chosen theirs. Whatever decisions these four people made would be final.

The Akpei spokesman, a young man of the same age-group, thanked the Igbuno people and hoped that after this kind of friendly match a greater bond of friendship would exist between the two villages.

The elders, Obi Agiliga, Obi Uju, and Obi Uwechue, and many others watched the proceedings from afar. They listened to the glowing speeches. One or two of them coughed a little and winked at the other.

They all smiled and shook their heads knowingly.

14

The occasion started in a friendly way. The Igbuno dancers came and sang round the circle, they demonstrated their beautiful bodies and their agility. They were cheered and there was even great applause when girls performed acrobatic feats that took the breaths of the onlookers away. Josephine, Nduka's friend, was the leader of the acrobatic group. In acknowledging the cheers, they arranged themselves into such a pattern that they looked like the waters of Igbuno streams tumbling down the rocks into the valley beyond. The fact that the girls were not dressed in the latest abada cloth did not bother them. They came in tunics which they had made themselves. After the acrobatics, they threw loose lappas round themselves and danced their way out of the circle, followed by the great cheers of so many people.

There was hardly any living person left in Igbuno who was not at Kumbi that late afternoon. The sun was going down and it was nearing the cool of the evening. The cool breezes fanned the people from the surrounding coconut and oil palms.

The Akpei dancers were so well dressed that they could not move so quickly. People admired their outfits and hairdos, but their dance was nothing compared to the determined performance of the Igbuno girls. They did not receive so loud a cheer as the other group, and one could see frowns beginning to form themselves on the faces of the young men. Even some of the older women who came with them were murmuring behind the back of their hands. They were not given much time to grumble, because the big drum that was in Obi Uju's compound had been quietly moved nearer to the square. Then it boomed, so loud and so resonant that those people nearest to the drummers jumped and almost ran away from the circle. They quickly came back though, because they knew that if they did not they would lose their places. The crowd was ten to twelve people thick, like an impenetrable wall surrounding this circle.

As the drum boomed faster and faster Nduka jumped into the circle, ran fast round it, and dropped his cloak in the centre as a challenge to the Akpei people. The symbolic cloak was picked up by one of the referees. The drums beat even faster, and the circle was filled with all the boys of Igbuno born in and around the civil war. They had identical lappas, and their hair was cut in the same way. They were young, most of them slim and tall. They were proud and they showed it. Even the elders inched closer to admire the handsomeness of these young people who would take over the running of things when they were gone. They did a few light steps, and moved out of the circle.

Then the Akpei drummers took over, and their people were likewise shown. When the drums of the Igbuno people boomed again the four men holding Okei let him go. He danced into the square amidst the loudest cheer of that afternoon. He danced, and his young body pulsated in the cool of the evening. The Igbuno girls burst into song, praising him. His opponent watched him from his own side. Then at a sign from the referee, Okei threw his Akwete cloak on the ground and shouted: "Come out, whoever you are."

A young man, who was the same age as Okei but looked thicker and older somehow, leapt into the circle. And the wrestling started. The Akpei contestant kept looking for a way to pin down Okei, but he had been taught to wrestle like a dancer. He would leap here, run there, and dodge at the other place. They both sweated and panted, and Okei came closer only when he thought he had given his audience enough cheering and yelling for the afternoon. Okei was floored, almost at the very first close encounter. But he thanked his uncle in his heart. He used one of the surprise tactics he was taught, and his opponent was flat on the ground. He jumped on the boy from Akpei before he had time to recover from the shock, and held his arms in the air. Okei had won.

The excitement was terrific. The Igbuno people jumped and screamed in the air. But when the noise died down the Akpei people made it clear that an annual contest like that would not rest just on one wrestling match between two people only. They pushed in another boy, who floored Okei in no time at all. Arguments then started. The girls of Igbuno claimed that it was not fair for the Akpei people to have two contestants. So Nduka came in and the boy from Akpei floored him too. The Igbuno people became bitter and Okei could see that his people were becoming abusive, so he volunteered to wrestle the same boy again. He did this, and he won.

Kwutelu was so excited that she jumped into the circle and started to wipe Okei's face with one of the handkerchiefs she was carrying. Then a shout came from one of the Akpei girls: "Why don't you use that handkerchief to wipe your rubber ear!"

Nobody knew who hit the other person first, but every Igbuno boy found himself wrestling and fighting a boy from Akpei. The confusion became so intense that younger

people screamed, as the adults called on the fighters to stop. But fists were in the air, and all the bottled anger of the past months was let loose.

"I think they will need us now," said Obi Agiliga to the other Obis. They made their way into the confusion, and it took them a long time to disentangle the drumsticks from one of the drummers. They beat the drums as if they would burst, and shouted with their voices as well. Many of the fighters stopped unwillingly, as each was determined to get the better of the other.

Okei was grateful for the drums because two boys were really beating him without mercy. They asked him how he dared floor their best wrestlers. By the time the whole fight stopped blood was gushing down his nose, and both his feet felt like lead.

"This has been a very successful fight," said Obi Agiliga. "It has ended well . . . I mean the way we knew it would end. You have to stop punishing yourselves now. You all have to go home. We thank the girls for fanning the rumours and even taking part in fighting for their villages on this day. You can see for yourselves that you were all good wrestlers and fighters. And in all good fights, just like wars, nobody wins. You were all hurt and humiliated. I am sure you will always remember this day."

"What is he talking about?" asked Kwutelu

of Josephine, as she tried to tie her headscarf properly.

"He said that we should be thanked for fanning the rumours. But did we fan the rumours, Kwutelu? Did the elders use us to organize this wrestling match?"

"But why?" asked Kwutelu.

"Just to keep the boys busy. They were getting on everybody's nerves a few months ago. I think we have been used. What actually started the quarrel between us and the Akpei Umu Biafra?" asked Josephine.

"That's the trouble, I can't even remember."

The two girls went back to their huts, very, very thoughtful.

Obi Agiliga and the other elders sat down to big kegs of palm-wine. "It has all gone well, has it not?" Obi Uwechue asked.

The others nodded and drank a toast to the elders of any land.

"My nephew told me this morning that we would not be needed. If we had not appeared there on time, those Akpei boys would have torn him into pieces. I am glad they have got the message—in a good war, nobody wins."

Responding to the Selection

The Wrestling Match by Buchi Emecheta

Identifying Facts

Chapters 1–7

1. What is the conflict between Okei and his uncle at the beginning of the novel?
2. Why does Okei live with his uncle rather than with his parents?
3. Who are Nduka and Uche? Josephine and Kwutelu?
4. Why do the Igbuno girls go to Akpei to sell their plantain?
5. Who is elected leader of the Umu aya Biafra age group?

Interpreting Meanings

Chapters 1–7

1. An important element of a novel's **setting** is its time frame. Emecheta often refers to the effects of the recent civil war. How did this war affect Okei? his parents? his uncle? his whole generation?
2. Emecheta uses both **direct** and **indirect** **characterization**. Nne Ojo is characterized directly as "a quick-tempered woman." Okei is characterized indirectly. The reader must draw conclusions about his personality from his words, actions, and thoughts, and from the responses of other characters. After reading the first chapter, what was your impression of Okei? Find the passages that led you to your impression.

3. Does Okei take his position as the group's leader seriously? How do you know? How has he learned about the responsibilities of a leader?
4. The **complications** of a plot are the events that move the story toward its **climax**. The girls talking at the stream in Chapter 2 and the conversation between the two elders in Chapter 3 are such complications. How do these episodes advance the plot?
5. At the first meeting of the Umu aya Biafra, Uche admits that he muddied the stream. What does the group decide to do about his behavior? Do you think it was a good decision? Why or why not?
6. When Okei proposes a wrestling match against the Akpei boys, he says it will be a "friendly match." Soon, however, it takes on a greater significance. What is this greater meaning? In addition to the strength of the contestants, what will the outcome of the match determine?
7. When Kwutelu's father is awakened by the sound of someone trying to enter his hut, who does he assume the intruder is? When does he realize he has made a mistake? Whom does he blame? Do you think his blame is fairly placed?
8. The main character, or **protagonist,** of a novel is usually a **dynamic character** who changes during the action of the novel. On the night that Kwutelu is injured, Okei "wanted to be sarcastic as usual," but instead answers his uncle seriously and truthfully. What has caused this change in Okei's character?

Identifying Facts

Chapters 8–14

1. What happens the second time the Igbuno girls go to the Eke market in the Akpei village?
2. Why do the girls begin wearing their headscarves a new way?
3. How do the village men prepare Okei for the wrestling match?
4. Which girls dance better before the match?
5. Who wins each of the matches?

Interpreting Meanings

Chapters 8–14

1. In the first part of the novel, Okei feels superior to the uneducated village boys. Gradually, he changes his mind. Find passages in later chapters that show this change.
2. Why do the two elders feel partly responsible for Kwutelu's accident? Why do they nevertheless feel satisfied with themselves and their actions at the end of Chapter 8?
3. How is the girls' song in the second half of the story different from their song in the first half? What causes the change?
4. What does Obi Agiliga teach Okei? What is Agiliga's advice when Okei says he is worried about losing? Do you think this is good advice?
5. How is Okei able to pin his opponent? Do you think he would have won if he had not asked his uncle for help?
6. In a story, the narrator or a character may make a general observation or statement about life or human nature. This is generally an indication of one of the **themes** of the story. The theme of a novel is its controlling idea, the central insight that it gives about life or human behavior. Do you think that Obi Agiliga's final words, "in a good war, nobody wins," indicate a theme of this novel? Support your opinion with references to the text.
7. What do the elders think they have taught the younger generation? Do you think the younger people have learned that lesson? Have they learned any other lessons?

Literary Elements

Understanding Plot Structure

The **plot** of a novel is the series of events that make up the story. A traditional plot structure includes **exposition, conflict, climax,** and **dénouement.**

The first chapter of this novel provides the **exposition**—the setting and background information. Do you have a clear picture of the village from the details in the first paragraph? Why does the narrator provide a paragraph of historical information about the great civil war? Describe ways in which the historical setting influences events in the plot.

The major element in most plots is **conflict**. As you have seen in previous selections, conflicts can be **external** (against the forces of nature, against another person, or against society), or **internal** (within the character). Identify at least one external and one internal conflict in this novel. What is the main conflict in *The Wrestling Match?*

The **climax** of a novel is the most exciting or dramatic point. It generally occurs when the main conflict is resolved. Where do you think the climax of *The Wrestling Match* occurs?

The **turning point** is the moment in a story when you know what the outcome will be. It may or may not coincide with the **climax**. Where do you think the turning point occurs in this novel?

The **dénouement** refers to action that occurs after the **turning point**. While in short stories the dénouement is usually very short, it may be longer in novels, since it takes more time to unravel the more complex plot.

Although Emecheta chose a traditional plot structure for *The Wrestling Match,* many contemporary writers now use more experimental plot structures.

Language and Vocabulary

Recognizing Figurative Language

Figurative language is especially important in poetry, but prose writers also turn to it when they want to present something in a fresher, more vivid way. Emecheta's use of figurative language helps bring the setting and characters to life.

On page 905, Emecheta uses figurative language to describe the evening. Instead of simply saying that the night was cool and clear, she writes that "the moon was so clear and the footpaths so silent that the whole area looked like man-made glass." Does this simile make the scene more real in your mind?

Figurative language is also used in characterizations. At the beginning of Chapter 6, Emecheta says that Kwutelu "had successfully ruffled Okei's feathers." Later in this chapter, on page 909, Kwutelu uses a simile to describe the boys who have been to college. What does she say? Do you think it is a good image?

What is the metaphor that Emecheta uses to describe Okei's feeling in the first paragraph of Chapter 8?

Writer's Journal

Responding to a Theme

Young people often feel that they have nothing to learn from the older generation. Okei was persuaded to ask his uncle to teach him some wrestling techniques only after his friend Nduka warned him that his pride and stubbornness could make him lose the wrestling match. Nduka also reminded Okei that in a few years he would be an elder and would want to advise his young sons.

Write a paragraph describing an incident

in which you advised a younger child or classmate or in which you received advice from a friend or relative who is older.

Speaking and Listening

Creating a Tune and Rhythm for a Song

Toward the end of Chapter 5, the girls sing a song that makes fun of the Umu aya Biafra boys. Did you imagine how this song would sound as you read it?

In small groups, work out a rhythm and tune for the song. After you have rehearsed it, present it to the class.

Critical Thinking

Understanding Cause-and-Effect Relationships

In short story or a novel, a single act often leads to a chain of events. The cause in a cause-and-effect relationship may be a person, situation, event, reason, or motive. The effect may be an action, an attitude, or a realization. This effect often becomes the cause for another effect and a long chain of events may occur. A plot in fiction or drama usually depends on these cause-and-effect relationships. Recognizing these relationships helps you follow the action and helps you understand the characters' motivations—the reasons for their actions.

In *The Wrestling Match,* Emecheta includes many cause-and-effect relationships in the plot. In the second paragraph of the novel, we are presented with an effect—Nne Ojo has exploded in anger at someone. The third paragraph provides some of the causes. We learn that Okei has been complaining, that he complains because he is unhappy and frustrated, that he feels this way because his parents were killed, and that they were killed because there was a civil war.

In Chapters 5 and 6, there is a series of cause-and-effect events that lead up to an accident. Trace these events on a sheet of paper or on the form that your teacher provides. You may need to add more boxes.

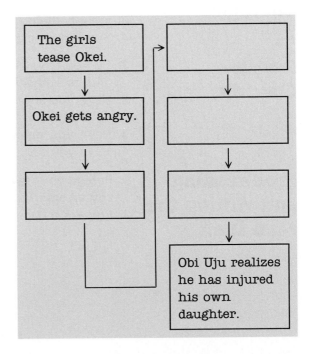

The girls tease Okei.

↓

Okei gets angry.

↓

Obi Uju realizes he has injured his own daughter.

Writing a Critical Review

You are probably familiar with movie reviews carried in newspapers and on television. The reviewer usually tells you what the movie is about and briefly discusses its merits or faults.

A critical review of a novel is different from a popular review of a movie. A good critical review is actually a search for the deeper meanings in a work of literature.

The first part of your critical review should summarize the content of the novel. You should briefly describe the main action and the main conflict. How does the novel begin? What is important about the setting? Who are the major characters? How do their personalities contribute to the conflict?

In the second part of your critical review, evaluate the novel and give your opinion of it. Your opinion is more than a simple judgment such as, "I did/did not like this novel." You should be specific about what aspects of the novel you did or didn't like and support your opinion with specific reasons and references to the novel. Are characters and actions described vividly? Did the author keep your interest throughout the story? Would you like to read another book by the same author?

Prewriting Strategies

1. Jot down the ideas you want to include.
2. Decide how you will organize your ideas.
3. Identify the novel and author in the first sentence of the review.
4. Support your opinions with examples from the text.

Revision Checklist

1. Do you have an introductory sentence that identifies the novel and its author? (Remember that titles are always underlined.)
2. Have you summarized the main action of the novel and mentioned the main characters and conflicts?
3. Have you given your opinion of the novel and supported it?
4. Have you told what the novel means to you and why?

Proofreading and Writing the Final Draft

1. Reread your review or have a friend read it to find and correct any errors in grammar, usage, and mechanics.
2. Prepare a final copy and check it once again for accuracy.

WRITER'S WORKSHOP 2

Evaluation (Persuasive Writing)

UNIT REVIEW

►I. For Discussion

You have seen that certain works of literature are still enjoyed many years after they were first composed. That quality in a work of art that gives it continuing appeal down through the ages is called **universality**. Although *The Wrestling Match* takes place in an Igbo vil-lage in Nigeria, the story appeals to readers in many different cultures. What aspects of human nature and behavior does the book focus on? Discuss the quality of universality in the novel.

►►II. For Writing

Consider this statement about *The Wrestling Match:*

> The story is like a window; in reading it we can see into another country and another culture. We will find both similarities and differences between Igbo culture and our own. The similarities show that all over the world human beings face the same basic needs. The differences teach us how critically each culture shapes the way its members see and respond to those needs.

In an essay, identify some of the key similarities and differences. What have you learned about Igbo culture from the novel?

Sharpening Your Test-Taking Skills in Reading and Writing

Throughout your school career, you will probably be asked to take tests that evaluate your growth and development as a reader and as a writer. These tests, which are used as an assessment of your abilities, may be called **proficiency tests**. This unit is designed to reinforce the reading and writing skills you have already learned and to give you practice in applying these skills. The questions and exercises presented in this unit will better prepare you for all forms of testing in both reading and writing.

Responding to Reading-Assessment Questions

One reads for different purposes, and a proficient reader possesses the skills that can be used for a range of needs: gathering information, drawing conclusions from different kinds of evidence, inferring the main idea of a work, evaluating evidence, or interpreting a theme, for example. An assessment of your reading proficiency would ask you to demonstrate not only the ability to take meaning off the page but also the ability to think critically about a text. A test might ask you to consider a group of related passages or selections. In some tests you might also be directed to write a response to the readings.

On the following pages you will find two practice tests that contain some of the types of selections and questions used in actual reading proficiency tests. Each test includes three selections that are related to a common theme. Each selection is accompanied by a set of multiple-choice questions, and each group of selections is followed by a set of cross-text questions based on two or more of the readings. With practice, you should become adept at responding to these types of questions. After you have read the selections and answered the questions, you will be asked to write a response that is related to the readings.

Reading for Meaning

Writing Prompts
To prepare yourself for the readings that follow, choose one of these exercises.

Writing Exercise 1
Write about an incident in your life that had an important effect on you or that changed you in some way.

Writing Exercise 2
Freewrite about why it might be important for people to remember their pasts, both as individuals and as a society or race.

Focus Question
The three selections that follow deal with the theme of personal growth and development. As you read the selections, keep in mind this focus question:

How do life's experiences help shape our attitudes and values and help us better understand ourselves and others?

Back to School (ESSAY)

Andrea Lee

A couple of weeks ago, I paid a visit to the girls' preparatory school outside of Philadelphia where, about thirty years ago, I entered as one of the first two black students. It wasn't my first return trip, but it was one that had a peculiarly definitive feeling: this time, I was going back to look at classes with my daughter, who is eleven—exactly the age I was when I first put on a blue-and-white uniform and walked in the front entrance of an institution where black people had always used the back door. My daughter, who was born in Europe, and who views the civil-rights struggles of the sixties as an antique heroic cycle not much removed in drama and time frame from the Iliad, sees her mother's experiences as a singularly tame example of integration. There were, after all, no jeering mobs, no night riders, no police dogs or fire hoses—just a girl going to school and learning with quiet thoroughness the meaning of isolation.

The air inside the schoolhouse smelled exactly as it used to on rainy April days—that mysterious school essence of damp wood and ancient chalk dust and pent-up young flesh. For an instant, I relived precisely what it felt like to walk those halls with girls who never included me in a social event, with teachers and administrators who regarded me with bemused incomprehension—halls where the only other black faces I saw were those of maids and cooks, and where I never received the slightest hint that books had been written and discoveries made by people whose skin wasn't white. I remembered the defensive bravado that I once used as a cover for a constant and despairing sense of worthlessness, born and reinforced at school.

As I delivered my daughter to the sixth-grade classroom where she would spend the day, I saw that in the intervening time not only had the school sprouted a few glossy modern additions—an art wing, science and computer facilities, and a new lower school—but the faculty and student body had also been transformed. Black and Asian girls mingled in the crowd of students rushing back and forth between classrooms and playing fields, giddy with excitement over the impending Easter and Passover weekend. A black teacher with braids strode out of the room where long ago I'd conjugated Latin verbs. Posters celebrating African-American artists and scientists hung on the walls, and the school's curriculum included dozens of works by black, Native American, and Hispanic writers. The director of the middle school was, miracle of miracles, a young black woman—a woman who combined an old-fashioned headmistress's unflappable good sense with a preternatural sensitivity to the psychology of culture and identity. She explained to me that she herself had once been a student at a mostly white East Coast prep school. When I asked who on her staff, in particular, was responsible for the self-esteem of minority students, she said firmly, "Every person who works here."

That day, I finally forgave my old school. I'd held a touchy rancor toward it through much of my adult life, like someone heaping blame on a negligent parent, and had taken the institution rather churlishly to task during a Commencement address I gave there some years ago. The changes I saw now disarmed and delighted me. Watching my daughter run by with a group of girls, I realized with envy how different her experience would be from mine if she were enrolled there. "Just think, I used to dream of burning the place down," I remarked to her, as we drove away, along the school's winding drive. She looked at me impatiently. "Can't you just forget all that?" she asked. The sound of her voice—half childish and half adolescent—made it clear to me that I wouldn't do any such thing. Wounds that have healed bring a responsibility to avoid repeating the past. The important thing is to pardon, even with joy, when the time comes—but never, I thought, driving on in silence, to forget.

Constructing Meaning

Literal Comprehension

1. Why did this visit to the preparatory school have special meaning for the writer?
    a. It was her first trip back since she had been a student there.
    b. She was accompanied by her daughter, who was the same age the writer was when she first entered the school.
    c. She was asked to evaluate the changes that had taken place since she attended the school.
    d. She was going to give the commencement address.

Understanding Cause and Effect

2. Which of the following statements best describes the effect that the visit had on the writer?
    a. It caused her to become angry.
    b. It caused her to remember old friends.
    c. It caused her to reflect on the past.
    d. It caused her to consider teaching as a career.

Literal Comprehension
To comprend, or understand, a passage, you must be attentive to the details presented by the writer.

In the first paragraph, Andrea Lee explains the significance of this visit to the school. She states that this was not her first return trip, so answer **a** is incorrect. Answer **c** may sound correct because Lee does evaluate many changes that have taken place; however, she does not say that she was asked to do so. Answer **d** is incorrect because Lee had given a commencement address several years earlier. The answer to the question is found in the phrase that begins "I was going back to look at classes with my daughter . . ." Answer **b** is correct.

Understanding Cause and Effect
In an essay or story, one event triggers another event, which in turn triggers another, and so on. This is called a chain of **cause and effect**.

As she walked the halls of her old school, Andrea Lee was reminded of her time there as a student. The visit directly caused her to reflect on her past experiences. Therefore, answer **c** is the correct choice.

Using Context Clues

3. In paragraph 3 the word *transformed* means
   a. moved to a different location.
   b. noticeably changed.
   c. given more powers.
   d. increased.

Making Inferences (Drawing Conclusions)

4. The essay contains enough evidence to support the statement that
   a. the daughter has little understanding of the struggles faced by members of her mother's generation.
   b. there are more African-American, Native American, and Hispanic writers today than there were in the past.
   c. a number of schools are including works by minority writers in their curriculums.
   d. the writer is eager to forget the events of the past.

Identifying the Main Idea

5. The main idea of the essay is that
   a. it is important to forgive and forget.
   b. the schools of today celebrate the lives and works of people from many cultures.
   c. change is slow yet inevitable.
   d. it is important to remember the past.

Using Context Clues

In the course of your reading, you probably encounter words that are unfamiliar to you. In many cases, you can determine the meaning of a word by its *context*, the words and sentences surrounding the unfamiliar word.

After describing something about the school building, Lee says that the student body had *also* been transformed. Apparently, whatever happened to the school happened to the students as well. Since the school had new additions and new facilities, it had *changed*. Thus, the student body had changed also. The correct answer is **b.**

Making Inferences

Sometimes a writer makes a point without stating it directly. When this is the case, it is necessary for the reader to make **inferences**, or draw conclusions, about the writer's meaning. Lee says that her daughter viewed the civil-rights struggles as remote and in the distant past, that the girl lost no time in making friends, and that she was impatient with her mother's remembrance of the past. Since the girl's experience is so different from her mother's, we can infer that she does not understand the difficulties that her mother faced. The correct answer is **a.**

Identifying the Main Idea

If you understand the meaning of a work, or the author's purpose for writing it, you understand the **main idea.** Answer **c** sounds like it might be correct since Lee does describe changes that took place over time. However, she does not say that change is inevitable. In fact, she says that the changes "disarmed and delighted" her; she had not expected them. Answer **c** is therefore incorrect.

Throughout the essay, Lee refers to her days as a student at the preparatory school. She compares her experience in the past with her observations of the present. She concludes her essay by explaining the importance of remembering the past. The correct answer is **d.**

FROM ———

Integrity (NONFICTION)

Stephen L. Carter

My first lesson in integrity came the hard way. It was 1960 or thereabouts and I was a first-grader at P.S. 129 in Harlem. The teacher had us all sitting in a circle, playing a game in which each child would take a turn donning a blindfold and then trying to identify objects by touch alone as she handed them to us. If you guessed right, you stayed in until the next round. If you guessed wrong, you were out. I survived almost to the end, amazing the entire class with my abilities. Then, to my dismay, the teacher realized what I had known, and relied upon, from the start: my blindfold was tied imperfectly and a sliver of bright reality leaked in from outside. By holding the unknown object in my lap instead of out in front of me, as most of the other children did, I could see at least a corner or a side and sometimes more—but always enough to figure out what it was. So my remarkable success was due only to my ability to break the rules.

Fortunately for my own moral development, I was caught. And as a result of being caught, I suffered, in front of my classmates, a humiliating reminder of right and wrong: I had cheated at the game. Cheating was wrong. It was that simple.

I do not remember many of the details of the "public" lecture that I received from my teacher. I do remember that I was made to feel terribly ashamed; and it is good that I was made to feel that way, for I had something to be ashamed of. The moral opprobrium that accompanied that shame was sufficiently intense that it has stayed with me ever since, which is exactly how shame is supposed to work. And as I grew older, whenever I was even tempted to cheat—at a game, on homework—I would remember my teacher's stern face and the humiliation of sitting before my classmates, revealed to the world as a cheater.

That was then, this is now. Browsing recently in my local bookstore, I came across a book that boldly proclaimed, on its cover, that it contained instructions on how to *cheat*—the very word occurred in the title—at a variety of video games. My instincts tell me that this cleverly chosen title is helping the book to sell very well. For it captures precisely what is wrong with America today: we care far more about winning than about playing by the rules.

Consider just a handful of examples, drawn from headlines of the mid-1990s: the winner of the Miss Virginia pageant is stripped of her title after officials determine that her educational credentials are false; a television network is forced to apologize for using explosives to add a bit of verisimilitude to a tape purporting to show that a particular truck is unsafe; and the authors of a popular book on management are accused of using bulk purchases at key stores to manipulate the *New York Times* best-seller list. Go back a few more years and we can add in everything from a slew of Wall Street titans imprisoned for violating a bewildering variety of laws in their frantic effort to get ahead, to the women's Boston Marathon winner branded a cheater for spending part of the race on the subway. But cheating is evidently no big deal: some 70 percent of college students admit to having done it at least once.

This, in a nutshell, is America's integrity dilemma: we are all full of fine talk about how desperately our society needs it, but, when push comes to shove, we would just as soon be on the winning side. A couple of years ago as I sat watching a televised football game with my children, trying to explain to them what was going on, I was struck by an event I had often noticed but on which I had never reflected. A player who failed to catch a ball thrown his way hit the ground, rolled over, and then jumped up, celebrating as though he had caught the pass after all. The referee was standing in a position that did not give him a good view of what had happened, was fooled by the player's pretense, and so moved the ball down the field. The player rushed back to the huddle so that his team could run another play before the officials had a chance to review the tape. (Until 1992, National Football League officials could watch a television replay and change their call, as long as the next play had not been run.) But viewers at home did have the benefit of the replay, and we saw what the referee missed: the ball lying on the ground instead of snug in the receiver's hands. The only comment from the broadcasters: "What a heads-up play!" Meaning: "Wow, what a great liar this kid is! Well done!"

Let's be very clear: that is exactly what they meant. The player set out to mislead the referee and succeeded; he helped his team to obtain an advantage in the game that it had not earned. It could not have been accidental.

He knew he did not catch the ball. By jumping up and celebrating, he was trying to convey a false impression. He was trying to convince the officials that he had caught the ball. And the officials believed him. So, in any ordinary understanding of the word, he lied. And that, too, is what happens to integrity in American life: if we happen to do something wrong, we would just as soon have nobody point it out.

Now, suppose that the player had instead gone to the referee and said, "I'm sorry, sir, but I did not make the catch. Your call is wrong." Probably his coach and teammates and most of his team's fans would have been furious: he would not have been a good team player. The good team player lies to the referee, and does so in a manner that is at once blatant (because millions of viewers see it) and virtually impossible for the referee to detect. Having pulled off this trickery, the player is congratulated: he is told that he has made a heads-up play. Thus, the ethic of the game turns out to be an ethic that rewards cheating. (But I still love football.) Perhaps I should have been shocked. Yet, thinking through the implications of our celebration of a national sport that rewards cheating, I could not help but recognize that we as a nation too often lack integrity, which might be described, in a loose and colloquial way, as the courage of one's convictions. . . .

A couple of years ago I began a university commencement address by telling the audience that I was going to talk about integrity. The crowd broke into applause. Applause! Just because they had heard the word *integrity*—that's how starved for it they were. They had no idea how I was using the word, or what I was going to say about it, or, indeed, whether I was for it or against it. But they knew they liked the idea of simply talking about it. This celebration of integrity is intriguing: we seem to carry on a passionate love affair with a word that we scarcely pause to define. . . .

When I refer to integrity, I have something very simple and very specific in mind. Integrity, as I will use the term, requires three steps: (1) *discerning* what is right and what is wrong; (2) *acting* on what you have discerned, even at personal cost; and (3) *saying openly* that you are acting on your understanding of right from wrong. The first criterion captures the idea of integrity as requiring a degree of moral reflectiveness. The second brings in the ideal of an integral person as steadfast, which includes the sense of keeping commitments. The third reminds us that a person of integrity is unashamed of doing the right.

The word *integrity* comes from the same Latin root as *integer* and historically has been understood to carry much the same sense, the sense of *wholeness*: a person of integrity, like a whole number, is a whole person, a person somehow undivided. The word conveys not so much a single-mindedness as a completeness; not the frenzy of a fanatic who wants to remake all the world in a single mold but the serenity of a person who is confident in the knowledge that he or she is living rightly. The person of integrity need not be a Gandhi but also cannot be a person who blows up buildings to make a point. A person of integrity

lurks somewhere inside each of us: a person we feel we can trust to do right, to play by the rules, to keep commitments. Perhaps it is because we all sense the capacity for integrity within ourselves that we are able to notice and admire it even in people with whom, on many issues, we sharply disagree.

Indeed, one reason to focus on integrity as perhaps the first among the virtues that make for good character is that it is in some sense prior to everything else: the rest of what we think matters very little if we lack essential integrity, the courage of our convictions, the willingness to act and speak in behalf of what we know to be right. In an era when the American people are crying out for open discussion of morality—of right and wrong—the ideal of integrity seems a good place to begin. No matter what our politics, no matter what causes we may support, would anybody really want to be led or followed or assisted by people who *lack* integrity? People whose words we could not trust, whose motives we didn't respect, who might at any moment toss aside everything we thought we had in common and march off in some other direction?

The answer, of course, is no: we would not want leaders of that kind, even though we too often get them. The question is not only what integrity is and why it is valuable, but how we move our institutions, and our very lives, closer to exemplifying it.

Constructing Meaning

Literal Comprehension

6. Which of the following is not mentioned by Carter in his definition of integrity?
   a. Treating others with respect
   b. Understanding right and wrong
   c. Doing what is right
   d. Explaining your actions

Literal Comprehension
This type of question requires only that you read the text carefully, with an eye for detail. All the answers may seem to relate to the theme of integrity, but Carter mentions only three of them. You may recall that Carter mentions the ideas in answers **b**, **c**, and **d**. Although he would most likely agree with it, he never mentions the idea in answer **a**.

Distinguishing Fact from Opinion

7. Which of the following claims made by the writer is a fact rather than an opinion?
   a. Everybody agrees that our nation needs more integrity.
   b. Each of us has the capacity for integrity.
   c. Seventy percent of college students admit to having cheated at least once.
   d. We do not want leaders who lack integrity.

Distinguishing Fact from Opinion
As you become a more proficient reader, you learn to distinguish facts from opinions. A fact is something that can be proved to be true by concrete information. An opinion represents the belief of one or more individuals and cannot be proven true. Carter claims that seventy percent of college students have admitted to having cheated at least once; this statement is a fact based on research. The other statements represent Carter's opinions. Answer **c** is correct.

Making Inferences

8. The writer would probably agree that a person with integrity would do all of the following except
   a. whatever is necessary to earn more money.
   b. fail an examination rather than pass by cheating.
   c. admit to having made a mistake.
   d. inform a cashier that he or she had received too much change.

Making Inferences
After reading Carter's essay, you should be fairly familiar with his concept of integrity. You are now ready to make **inferences**, or educated guesses, about things that Carter does not mention specifically in the essay. Since Carter values honesty and decency, he would probably not agree with statement **a**. The phrase "whatever is necessary" implies that the person might have to resort to dishonest or unethical methods to make more money, a policy of which Carter would most likely disapprove.

Sharpening Your Test-Taking Skills 949

Recognizing Supporting Facts and Details

9. The author provides evidence to support his statement that
   a. we rarely pause to define the word *integrity*.
   b. A person with integrity is not ashamed to do the right thing.
   c. Americans care more about winning than about playing by the rules.
   d. everybody has an inner sense of integrity.

Identifying the Main Idea

10. Which of the following statements best summarizes the author's main idea?
    a. We need a better understanding of what integrity is and how to integrate it into our public and private lives.
    b. We need to do something about the dishonesty among our leaders in business and government.
    c. Our government and our schools are sorely in need of leaders with integrity.
    d. Organized sports are being corrupted by players who are willing to win at any cost.

Recognizing Supporting Facts and Details
This type of question requires that you pay attention to the methods a writer uses to support his or her argument. Certain statements a writer makes will be supported by details, examples, and reasons that he or she chooses to include. Carter provides evidence to support his statement that Americans care more about winning than about playing by the rules. He describes specific instances in which cheating took place, such as the incidents from the Miss Virginia pageant and from the televised football game. Therefore, answer **c** is the correct choice.

Identifying the Main Idea
The **main idea** of an essay is the most important point that the writer is trying to get across. Although answers **b**, **c**, and **d** are all mentioned in Carter's essay, they are all too specific to be considered the main idea. Answer **a**, however, contains many of Carter's ideas in one general statement.

Zami: A New Spelling of My Name (ESSAY)

Audre Lorde

I learned how to read from Mrs. Augusta Baker, the children's librarian at the old 135th Street branch library, which has just recently been torn down to make way for a new library building to house the Schomburg Collection on African-American History and Culture. If that was the only good deed that lady ever did in her life, may she rest in peace. Because that deed saved my life, if not sooner, then later, when sometimes the only thing I had to hold on to was knowing I could read, and that that could get me through.

My mother was pinching my ear off one bright afternoon, while I lay spreadeagled on the floor of the Children's Room like a furious little brown toad, screaming bloody murder and embarrassing my mother to death. I know it must have been spring or early fall, because without the protection of a heavy coat, I can still feel the stinging soreness in the flesh of my upper arm. There, where my mother's sharp fingers had already tried to pinch me into silence. To escape those inexorable fingers I had hurled myself to the floor, roaring with pain as I could see them advancing toward my ears again. We were waiting to pick up my two older sisters from story hour, held upstairs on another floor of the dry-smelling quiet library. My shrieks pierced the reverential stillness.

Suddenly, I looked up, and there was a library lady standing over me. My mother's hands had dropped to her sides. From the floor where I was lying, Mrs. Baker seemed like yet another mile-high woman about to do me in. She had immense, light, hooded eyes and a very quiet voice that said, not damnation for my noise, but "Would you like to hear a story, little girl?"

Part of my fury was because I had not been allowed to go to that secret feast called story hour since I was too young, and now here was this strange lady offering me my own story.

I didn't dare to look at my mother, half-afraid she might say no, I was too bad for stories. Still bewildered by this sudden change of events, I climbed up upon the stool which Mrs. Baker pulled over for me, and gave her my full attention. This was a new experience for me and I was insatiably curious.

Mrs. Baker read me *Madeline*, and *Horton Hatches the Egg*, both of which rhymed and had huge lovely pictures which I could see from behind my newly acquired eyeglasses, fastened around the back of my rambunctious head by a black elastic band running from earpiece to earpiece. She also read me another storybook about a bear named Herbert who ate up an entire family, one by one, starting with the parents. By the time she had finished that one, I was sold on reading for the rest of my life.

I took the books from Mrs. Baker's hands after she was finished reading, and traced the large black letters with my fingers, while I peered again at the beautiful bright colors of the pictures. Right then I decided I was going to find out how to do that myself. I pointed to the black marks which I could now distinguish as separate letters, different from my sisters' more grown-up books, whose smaller print made the pages only one grey blur for me. I said, quite loudly, for whoever was listening to hear, "I want to read."

My mother's surprised relief outweighed whatever annoyance she was still feeling at what she called my whelpish carryings-on. From the background where she had been hovering while Mrs. Baker read, my mother moved forward quickly, mollified and impressed. I had spoken. She scooped me up from the low stool, and to my surprise, kissed me, right in front of everybody in the library, including Mrs. Baker.

This was an unprecedented and unusual display of affection in public, the cause of which I did not comprehend. But it was a warm and happy feeling. For once, obviously, I had done something right.

My mother set me back upon the stool and turned to Mrs. Baker, smiling.

"Will wonders never cease to perform!" Her excitement startled me back into cautious silence.

Not only had I been sitting still for longer than my mother would have thought possible, and sitting quietly. I had also spoken rather than screamed, something that my mother, after four years and a lot of worry, had despaired that I would ever do. Even one intelligible word was a very rare event for me. And although the doctors at the clinic had clipped the little membrane under my tongue so I was no longer tongue-tied, and had assured my mother that I was not retarded, she still had her terrors and her doubts. She was genuinely happy for any possible alternative to what she was afraid might be a dumb child. The ear-pinching was forgotten. My mother accepted the alphabet and picture books Mrs. Baker gave her for me, and I was on my way.

Constructing Meaning

Literal Comprehension

11. Which statement cannot be supported by details from the story?
    a. As a young girl, the writer frequently found herself getting into trouble.
    b. The girl was determined and strong-willed.
    c. The experience in the library made a lasting impression on the writer.
    d. The writer had enjoyed listening to stories as far back as she could remember.

Literal Comprehension
The writer, who was four years old when the incident took place, makes it clear that the experience of listening quietly to a story was a new one for her. Therefore, answer **d** is correct.

Literal Comprehension

12. Which word best explains what caused the writer to calm down and attend to the story?

 a. Anger

 b. Curiosity

 c. Fear

 d. Guilt

Making Inferences

13. On the basis of this passage, we can draw the conclusion that

 a. the writer would face some type of hardships later on in life.

 b. the writer would probably have learned to read soon on her own.

 c. the writer's older sisters treated her unfairly.

 d. the librarian wanted to quiet the girl so that she wouldn't disturb others.

Using Context Clues

14. In paragraph 5 the word *bewildered* means

 a. inspired.

 b. confused.

 c. worried.

 d. angered.

Recognizing the Author's Point of View and Purpose

15. The author's purpose in this passage is to

 a. show that stories have the power to change our emotions.

 b. explain why she disliked her older sisters.

 c. prove that children can learn to read at an early age.

 d. describe an incident that changed her life.

Literal Comprehension

The writer's anger at not being allowed to attend the story hour was the cause of her furious outburst, and she then feared that her mother would not allow her to listen to the story. Thus, answers **a** and **c** are incorrect. Since nothing is said about guilt, answer **d** is also incorrect. The writer states that she was "insatiably curious" when she climbed on the stool; answer **b** is correct.

Making Inferences

The writer says near the beginning of the passage that her ability to read "saved my life, if not sooner, then later," indicating that reading helped her to withstand some hardships she later encountered. Therefore, answer **a** is correct. Answer **d**, while it might be true, is not borne out by the librarian's behavior.

Using Context Clues

The writer states that she was "still bewildered by this sudden change of events." Because the writer was excited and pleased at the prospect of being read aloud to, she would be neither worried (answer **c**) nor angered (answer **d**). Although she might have eventually been inspired (answer **a**) by the incident, at the moment it occurred she was merely confused. Therefore, answer **b** would be the most logical choice: *bewildered* means "confused."

Recognizing the Author's Point of View and Purpose

The writer does not try to prove that children can learn to read at an early age (answer **c**). Although the writer is angry that her sisters were old enough to attend the story hour and she was not, there is no evidence in the passage that she disliked her sisters (answer **b**). Although Lorde might agree that stories have the power to change our emotions (answer **a**), she does not address this issue. Her main purpose in the passage is to describe an incident that changed her life. She makes this clear through the emphasis on the newness of the experience, on the change that came over her as a result of it, and on the lasting impact of the experience on her life. Therefore, answer **d** is the correct choice.

Making Cross-Text Connections

Questions 16–20 relate to "Back to School" by Andrea Lee and the excerpts from *Integrity* by Stephen L. Carter and *Zami: A New Spelling of My Name* by Audre Lorde.

Constructing Meaning

Comparing and Contrasting

16. What do the selections by Andrea Lee, Stephen L. Carter, and Audre Lorde have in common?
    a. They contain reflections about childhood experiences.
    b. They discuss ways of getting along in our society.
    c. They show that you can accomplish anything as long as you have courage and determination.
    d. They describe people who act on their understanding of right and wrong.

17. Both Audre Lorde and Stephen L. Carter had childhood experiences that
    a. made them ashamed.
    b. had a profound effect on the course of their lives.
    c. made them angry.
    d. cheered them up.

Recognizing the Author's Point of View and Purpose

18. Which word best describes the attitude of Carter and Lorde toward the experiences they have written about?
    a. Gratitude
    b. Bitterness
    c. Humor
    d. Pride

Comparing and Contrasting
The skill of **comparing and contrasting** requires that you evaluate the similarities and differences between two or more texts, characters, or ideas. Carter and Lee make comments about our society, but they do not discuss specific ways of getting along in it. Lorde makes no mention of society. Answer **b** is therefore incorrect. None of the writers discusses the idea of accomplishment or describes people who act on their understanding of right and wrong, so answers **c** and **d** are incorrect. All three contain reflections about childhood experiences, so answer **a** is the correct choice.

In question 17, you are asked to compare only two of the passages. Both passages begin in a similar way. Lorde and Carter both describe a childhood incident, then go on to explain the impact that the incident had on the course of their lives. Answer **b** is the correct choice.

Recognizing the Author's Point of View and Purpose
Both Lorde and Carter make it clear that they are intensely grateful for the experiences that shaped them. Lorde is thankful that Mrs. Baker, the librarian, took the time to read to her and to teach her the power of books. Carter is thankful that his teacher caught him cheating and gave him his first lesson in integrity. Answer **a**, *gratitude*, is the correct choice.

Making Inferences

19. Which statement would Andrea Lee and Stephen L. Carter be most likely to disagree with?

a. We must do whatever is necessary to make a point or bring about change.

b. Thinking about the way you behave will help you become a person of integrity.

c. Not all ways of expressing oneself are appropriate.

d. We have a responsibility to avoid repeating the mistakes of the past.

Making Generalizations

20. The librarian in the passage by Lorde and the director in the passage by Lee both appear to be concerned with

a. keeping students quiet and busy.

b. the way young people feel about themselves.

c. making sure that students follow the rules.

d. providing young people with works by writers of various backgrounds.

Making Inferences
Andrea Lee and Stephen Carter seem to share certain views, so you can make **inferences** about how both writers would respond to a statement. You might first decide which statements the two would agree upon. Both might agree that thinking about the way we behave is important, as well as acknowledging our responsibility to be better people and avoid repeating the mistakes of the past. Both might agree that only certain ways of acting or reacting to events are appropriate. For example, Lee has feelings of anger toward her old school, but she is able to recognize and deal with these feelings rather than seek revenge for slights in the past. Lee would be likely to disagree with the statement that "We must do whatever is necessary to make a point or bring about change." Similarly, Carter would probably disagree with such a statement, since "doing whatever is necessary" might involve corrupt or dishonest behavior that would contradict his definition of integrity. Therefore, answer **a** is the correct choice.

Making Generalizations
When you make a **generalization**, you are analyzing the whole picture. A generalization does not have to be exact or specific, but it should contain a general idea of what is occurring in a scene or an entire work. In the selections by Lorde and Lee, both the librarian and the school director make an effort to improve the self-esteem of young people. The librarian has consideration for the child's feelings; she does not condemn the girl's noise but speaks quietly and offers the youngster her own story. The director declares that "every person who works" at the school is responsible for the self-esteem of its minority students. Answer **b** is the best choice.

Writing a Response to Readings

You can improve your writing significantly if you make a habit of evaluating your writing efforts. Learn to recognize your strengths and weaknesses and to revise your work with the assistance of others as well as independently.

In general, the purpose of a writing proficiency test is to assess how well you can communicate meaning. Although it is important that you avoid errors in grammar and usage, your writing will be judged mainly on the effectiveness of your content and style—the way you present your ideas. The material on the following pages is intended to help you with those aspects of the writing process that can make you a more effective communicator: clarifying purpose and audience; exploring approaches to a topic; developing a focus; generating ideas; organizing material; evaluating drafts; using revision techniques; and polishing manuscripts.

Your examiner will very likely use a scoring guide to evaluate your paper. One example of such a guide appears on the right.

The selections on pages 943–952 deal with the theme of growth and change. Recall the **focus question** that was asked before you read the selections: **How do life's experiences help shape our attitudes and values and help us understand ourselves and others?** For the writer of each selection, the examination of significant life experiences led to personal growth and development.

As you read the following scenario, think about how the incident described relates to the selections you have just read. You may wish to go back and reread part of these

Scoring Guide
1. **Focus on Clarity**   Does the paper have a main idea? Is the purpose of the writing clear? Does the writer stick to the topic?
2. **Structure**   Are ideas developed logically in an introduction, body, and conclusion? Are major ideas supported by sufficient details, examples, or reasons? Are transitions used to connect sentences?
3. **Style**   Are sentences varied? Does the writer use capitalization, punctuation, and spelling correctly? Does the writer use vivid and specific words?

selections and discuss them with a small group of classmates. Then write a thoughtful response to the scenario question. You may make notes or list ideas before you begin writing. Draw on your own ideas and experiences as well as on the ideas presented in the selections in order to support your position. Be sure to refer to all three selections in your answer.

Scenario

While in high school, Roger and Dennis had parallel careers. They both belonged to the debate team, the basketball team, and the French club. Both made the honor roll every semester. Although they were equally successful, Roger always felt that he was losing ground to Dennis in the competition for top honors. He tried to have Dennis excluded from parties and social events. When both boys decided to run for class president, Roger spread a rumor about Dennis cheating on a math exam. Dennis believed that Roger's smear campaign cost him the election.

Several years have passed. Dennis is working for an engineering firm. His supervisors are trying to fill a key position. Dennis discovers that Roger has applied for the job. The company's personnel director finds out that Dennis and Roger were classmates and Dennis is asked if he would recommend Roger for the job. Dennis realizes that he and Roger will again be placed in competition. Remembering his past bitterness, Dennis is tempted to reject his former rival to even the score. However, after a careful review of all the candidates, Dennis sees that Roger is clearly the best qualified for the job.

Scenario Question

What should Dennis do, and why?

Before responding to this question, review the stages of the **writing process: prewriting, writing, evaluating and revising, proofreading**, and **publishing.** For a discussion of the process, see the **Writer's Guide** that begins on page 65.

Prewriting

In the **prewriting** stage, you gather and organize ideas and plan your response. You can gather ideas by jotting down words and phrases and listing the points you want to make. It is also helpful to draft a **thesis statement,** which contains the main idea of your paper. This statement will be refined as you evaluate and revise your paper.

When responding to a writing prompt, you first need to determine which type of writing the prompt is calling for: **expressive, informative, persuasive,** or **imaginative.** The type of writing used in a passage is

governed by the writer's primary purpose. In responding to the scenario question, you need to convince your reader that a particular course of action is the best one. Thus, your essay will be **persuasive.**

The chart below lists the features of each of four types of writing.

Types of Writing
Expressive
Style: Usually informal
Purpose: To describe thoughts and feelings
Examples: Journal entries, memoirs, reflective essays
Informative
Style: Usually formal
Purpose: To inform; present information
Examples: Business letters, memorandums, reports, news articles, pamphlets
Persuasive
Style: Usually formal
Purpose: To persuade; present an argument
Examples: Editorials, campaign literature, proposals, letters to the editor, literary analyses
Imaginative
Style: Formal or informal
Purpose: To entertain; convey a message
Examples: Poems, stories, stage plays, screen plays, advertisements

For a response to the question about the action Dennis should take, here is a set of prewriting notes.

What is the connection between the three passages and the situation Dennis is facing?

Dennis is reflecting on his past experience

Dennis's past experience is having an effect on his decision

Carter's definition of integrity applies to Dennis's situation
—Dennis has to figure out right and wrong
—honesty, responsibility toward employer v. desire for revenge

Andrea Lee's article—forgiving mistakes from the past
—Apply to Dennis's situation

I teased Lisa in the fifth grade—now we are good friends

Maybe Roger doesn't behave that way any more—people change
—Understanding of others

Andrea Lee—change in attitude
Audre Lorde—her experience changed the course of her life

Thesis statement: Dennis needs to act with integrity and understanding and recommend Roger for the job.

When you have finished gathering ideas, you can begin to organize them and plan your essay. You will probably find that your words and phrases can be put into groups, each of which expresses a different idea or argument. Each of the ideas can be developed into a paragraph.

At this point, you should begin to think about your introductory and closing paragraphs. In this case, your introductory paragraph should explain how the passages you have read can be applied to the scenario you are writing about. Your closing paragraph should summarize your main points.

Here is a plan that has been developed from the prewriting notes.

Paragraph 1: **Introduction**

Present relationship between the ideas in the passages and Dennis's dilemma

Dennis is reflecting on his past experience

Dennis's past experience is having an effect on his decision

Dennis needs to act with integrity and understanding and recommend Roger for the job

Paragraph 2: **Body / Supporting details**

Carter's definition of integrity applies to Dennis's situation
—Dennis has to figure out right and wrong
—honesty, responsibility toward employer v. desire for revenge

Andrea Lee's article—forgiving mistakes from the past
—Apply to Dennis's situation

I teased Lisa in the fifth grade—now we are good friends

Paragraph 3: **Body / Supporting details**

Maybe Roger won't act the same way—people change
Understanding of others

Andrea Lee—change in attitude
Audre Lorde—her experience changed the course of her life

Paragraph 4: **Conclusion**
Summarize main ideas, state answer

Thesis statement: Dennis needs to act with integrity and understanding and recommend Roger for the job.

Writing

After you have organized your ideas and your essay is taking shape, you can begin writing a rough draft. Remember that when responding to a question that relates to passages you have read, you need to refer to those passages in your essay and identify titles and authors.

Evaluating and Revising

After you have written the rough draft of your essay, you need to **evaluate** it. Evaluation involves reading your essay over carefully and examining it for content, structure, and style. At this stage, you make sure that the question has been answered, that supporting details have been included, and that ideas are organized logically and related clearly to one another.

Once you have identified the strengths and weaknesses of your essay, you can begin **revising** it. Writers generally revise their work by using the following techniques:

- adding, cutting, or rearranging words and ideas
- combining and restructuring sentences
- replacing unclear words and phrases
- rephrasing sentences to make them clearer

You may wish to use the **Checklist for Evaluation** shown below.

Checklist for Evaluation
• Do I grab the reader's attention in the introduction?
• Do I make my position clear?
• Do I make references to the selections?
• Do I include details about my own ideas and experiences?
• Is my organization clear?
• Have I used a variety of sentences and precise words?

A revised draft of the essay might look like this:

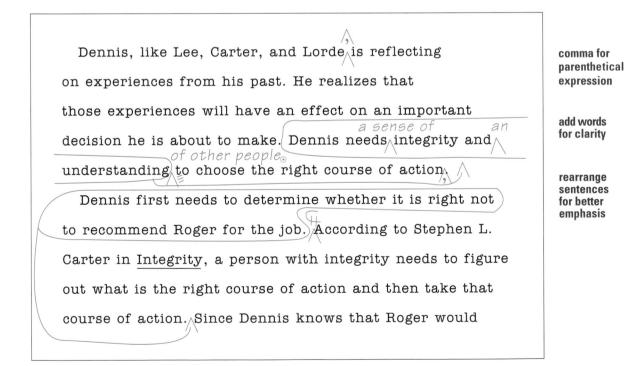

probably be right for the job, it would be dishonest for him to say otherwise. As a responsible employee, he will speak the truth despite the "personal cost." Dennis should also see that it is wrong to hold a grudge for so long. *I remember that* When Lisa and I were in fifth grade, I often embarrassed her by making fun of her ugly eyeglasses. If she had held a grudge against me, we wouldn't be the close friends we are today. I agree with the point Andrea Lee makes *in "Back to School"* you don't have to forget the past, but when the time comes, you have to forgive.

Dennis also needs to have an understanding of others: people sometimes change over time. After spending a day at her old school, Andrea Lee ~~'s attitude changed~~ *experienced a change in attitude toward the institution.* In the excerpt from <u>Zami: A New Spelling of My Name</u>, Audre Lorde describes a brief encounter that changed the course of her life. Dennis has to remember that he and Roger have not seen each other in years; in that span of time, Roger may have changed, too.

In the situation described, Dennis should act with integrity and take the course of action that he knows is right. Dennis has to give an honest answer, he needs to be willing to forgive, and he should allow for the possibility that Roger might not behave as he did in the past. I believe that Dennis should recommend Roger for the job.

transition

include title

run-on sentence

dangling phrase

spelling

comma for intro- ductory phrase

Proofreading and Publishing

After you have revised your essay, you **proofread** it to find any errors in spelling, grammar, and usage. You then make any necessary corrections and prepare a final version.

The revised, corrected version of the essay is as follows:

> Dennis, like Lee, Carter, and Lorde, is reflecting on experiences from his past. He realizes that those experiences will have an effect on an important decision he is about to make. To choose the right course of action, Dennis needs a sense of integrity and an understanding of other people.
>
> According to Stephen L. Carter in Integrity, a person with integrity needs to figure out what is the right course of action and then take that course of action. Dennis first needs to determine whether it is right not to recommend Roger for the job. Since Dennis knows that Roger would probably be right for the job, it would be dishonest for him to say otherwise. As a responsible employee, he will speak the truth despite the "personal cost." Dennis should also see that it is wrong to hold a grudge for so long. I remember that when Lisa and I were in fifth grade, I often embarrassed her by making fun of her ugly eyeglasses. If she had held a grudge against me, we wouldn't be the close friends we are today. I agree with the point Andrea Lee makes in "Back to School": you don't have to forget the past, but when the time comes, you have to forgive.
>
> Dennis also needs to have an understanding of others: people sometimes change over time. After spending a day at her old school, Andrea Lee experienced a change in attitude toward the institution. In the excerpt from Zami: A New Spelling of My Name, Audre Lorde describes one brief encounter that changed the course of her life. Dennis has to remember that he and Roger have not seen each other in years; in that span of time, Roger may have changed, too.
>
> In the situation described, Dennis should act with integrity and take the course of action that he knows is right. Dennis has to give an honest answer, he needs to be willing to forgive, and he should allow for the possiblity that Roger might not behave as he did in the past. I believe that Dennis should recommend Roger for the job.

With the first practice test, you were given the correct answer to each question, and you were given reasons for that choice. You were also guided step by step in forming a written response to a question that was related to the selections you had read.

For the following test, you will have to use your own thinking and reasoning skills to answer the multiple-choice questions and to develop a written response to the scenario question on page 971. Be sure to place your answers on a separate sheet of paper.

Focus Question

As you read the following three selections, keep in mind this focus question:

> How can understanding different forms of communication help us become better members of the human community?

FROM ———————————————

A Call to Assembly (AUTOBIOGRAPHY)

Willie Ruff

In those preadolescent days, the delicious pleasures of my ear—the music and the stylish spoken language of our world—got out of hand and developed into serious distractions that caused me no end of problems at home. For a time, Mama Minnie insisted I was close to being retarded and a little "off." I was too much a listener. Impossible for me to concentrate on anything else if there was an ear diversion close by. I'd get stuck, for instance, at the barber shop for hours, listening to Doc Long and Wonderful C. Hill and Bitsy Pillar weaving the most colorful and engrossing stories. And when Tab and Ice-Truck Raymond came in, woofing with their boastful lying, I'd totally forget myself and linger for hours. Then suddenly I would realize I had a country skinning coming when I got back home, because Mama Minnie had ordered, "You get that head cut and get yourself back home and scrub that kitchen floor and sweep the front yard." It would be worse if I'd pass the railroad tracks and the hobo jungle on an errand and be pulled into it by the soulful strains of a traveling tramp's fiddle, or a mouth organ and a banjo, and forget the errand. Music and the spoken language of our world, which sounded like music, were taking over my life.

I was a slave to my ear and in love with my shackles.

But then I had a chance encounter with an altogether different kind of language, full of another kind of color, and it sucked me into its sphere and turned my impressionable ten-year-old mind completely upside down: it was sign language—talking with hands—the language of the deaf.

It happened when I went to work in a shoe repair shop, replacing a young black man who'd decided to go on to better things. This was a job that Mama Minnie was enthusiastic about, because it was an opportunity to learn a good trade while earning a little coin. The work was not hard to learn, and Mr. Steele, the owner, was a good teacher even though he could be touchy and sharp.

He started me off on the basics of nailing and gluing leather and rubber soles and heels, polishing and dyeing shoes, and making deliveries on the shop's new Elgin bicycle—the absolute best part of the job for me. He kept me away from the big sewing machines, power cutters, and polishers, saying that when I got bigger he would teach me to use them safely. His wife worked the cash register. Mrs. Steele was a kind, quiet woman, whose presence in the shop took the edge off the old man's occasional abrasiveness. If, for instance, she went out to get him and herself a Coca-Cola, she'd bring me one, and she was polite enough to call me by my name and not "boy" all the time, as Mr. Steele did.

One day a man came into the shop and started rattling off talk on his hands with Mr. Steele. I was amazed that the boss could give it right back to this deaf fellow. Such expressive agility in his big shoemaker's dirty fingers made me wonder. He looked perfectly at home signing and even laughed out loud a couple of times with the deaf man before he left. Then I asked Mr. Steele, "Where did you learn to talk on your hands?"

"I was raised and taught my trade by my older brother," he said. "He was deaf, and he taught me shoemaking and the sign language. It ain't hard." After that, I kind of regarded the boss as a man of some mysterious inner substance, for I'd never heard or seen a real conversation in a foreign language before. This shoemaker speaking that silent secret code was an intoxicatingly exotic curiosity: "a white man with a language mojo," I told myself.

A few days later, Mr. Steele called me over to his workbench and said, "You remember that deaf man who was in here? Well, in a couple of weeks we're going to have company in the shop; a deaf boy is coming from the Talladega School for the Deaf and Blind to apprentice with me." He added a warning: "You got to learn how to talk to him. It'll be for your own good. You have to be careful working around deaf people, because they can sometimes be dangerous." I was confused. "Why are they dangerous?" I asked. Mr. Steele said, "Well, it's aggravating for them if they can't make you understand them or if they can't understand you. Then they're liable to hurt you. But I can teach you to talk on your hands in no time." That news provoked mixed feelings; I wanted desperately to learn to talk on my hands, but I wasn't looking forward to courting danger in the bargain.

We began my lessons that same day. In slack moments in the shop or during our rest breaks, he'd show me finger spelling. He'd been right about the ease of it; and it got to be fun saying the ABCs on my fingers. In a couple of days I could form all twenty-six letters without mistakes, and we began spelling out most of our conversation. Then, because I'd practiced at home and got pretty good showing off for Mama and the neighborhood, Mr. Steele said we'd not talk anymore at all, just spell. But I had trouble figuring out where one word ended and the next began, he spelled so quickly; I got better when he slowed down. Then he started teaching me real signs.

"Look here, boy," he said. "You can say a lotta things with one or two motions of your hands. You can do it real quick and with practically no fuss." . . .

When he told me that much of the sign language we use came from the American Indians, I felt proud of the Choctaw and Cherokee blood Mama said I had in me.

This, my very first foreign language, was starting to absorb me in its nonverbalness and its direct reference to thought and explicit meanings. I was falling in love with the magic of the live symbols shaped in the air between people doing all that communicating. Not suddenly, but gradually, I started to appreciate that these expressive hand shapes represented concepts that seemed bigger than just words to me, and I couldn't wait to learn as many as I could take in.

Constructing Meaning

Literal Comprehension

1. When the writer says that the pleasures of music and spoken language developed into serious distractions, he means that
   a. when listening to music and conversation, he would forget about what he was supposed to be doing.
   b. he found himself irritated by excess noise and loud conversation.
   c. he enjoyed making conversation with others.
   d. he wanted to take banjo lessons.

Interpreting Figurative Language

2. When Ruff writes "I was a slave to my ear and in love with my shackles," he uses figurative language to suggest
   a. an escape from a dull existence.
   b. the loss of will power.
   c. the wonders of unspoken language.
   d. an intense fascination with sound.

Making Inferences

3. The excerpt contains enough evidence to support the statement that
   a. Mr. Steel was not a skillful shoe-maker.
   b. everyone should learn sign language.
   c. when the writer was interested in something, he could pursue it with passion and intensity.
   d. the writer learned sign language only to avoid problems with a future coworker.

Understanding Cause and Effect

4. According to Ruff, learning how to sign
   a. increased his respect for deaf people.
   b. gave him a powerful form of communication.
   c. made him forget his interest in music.
   d. taught him to better appreciate spoken language.

Recognizing the Author's Point of View and Purpose

5. In this passage, the writer's purpose is to show
   a. that it is not good to let your interests and hobbies take over your life.
   b. that everyone should learn how to use sign language.
   c. how it was important for him to be able to communicate with all kinds of people.
   d. how he became fascinated not only by the sound of language but also by its concepts and meanings.

ABC (ESSAY)

Faith Adiele

I was eight years old before I realized music existed. It was the summer of 1971, and I was staying with my grandparents on our farm in eastern Washington State. My mother was away at summer school in Seattle where she wrote to us regularly from a rented room. A few weeks into the summer she sent a package.

I had been playing outside in the yard when Grandma went to get the mail from the big mailbox across the road. The red flag was down, indicating that the mailman had come and gone, zigzagging his way across country roads from right-hand boxes to left-hand boxes like drunken farm boys on a Saturday night. On the times I was allowed to cross the road to get the mail with Grandma, I surveyed the distance in both directions, noting with satisfaction that our mailbox was the largest one for as far as I could see. When the county rezoned all the rural routes and we were upgraded from Route 1 to Route 2, Grandpa took the opportunity to buy a new mailbox. I sat on a stool in his workshop while he painted the huge box a light, pearly silver and handlettered our new address on the side: *Hansson, Route 2, Box 2704.*

That particular day Grandma came running down the gravel driveway, a thin cardboard package in her hand, calling that my mother had sent me a present. I jumped up and tore open the box. Inside was a letter and a record album by a group called the Jackson Five. My mother's letter explained that she had come across it while searching a used bookstore for textbooks.

I stared at the album cover. Except for my old Disney storybook records, I had never had a record of my own before. To be honest, I had never particularly wanted one. I was surrounded by music—from Grandpa's country western radio out in the woodshed, to the music my grandparents played on Saturday nights before going squaredancing; from the musical comedies my mother sang along to when she cleaned house, to the stacks of classical albums she put on the stereo each night to help her sleep—but paid it little attention. At that moment, however, studying the record sleeve in my hands, its psychedelic red and yellow splotches fairly quivering with big-city excitement, I realized that I had been missing something. My mother's letter claimed that all the young black kids in Seattle were listening to the Jackson Five.

Mine had been a childhood spent waiting for information and clues in the mail. Periodically my father, an African who lived in Africa, sent letters about our family. My only other link to black life was through my mother's subscriptions to *Ebony, Essence,* and *Jet.* Each month these magazines arrived, a bit worn and battered, from New York City, a place that seemed as mythic and faraway as Africa. And now there was this, a letter from my white mother informing me that the Jackson Five were sweeping the nation without me. *All the young black kids in Seattle are listening to them.*

Heart pounding, I carefully slipped the white inner sleeve out of the cardboard cover and opened it. A heavy record—broken into three neat pieces—slid into my hands.

The next few weeks dragged. My mother had promised to send another record once she had some extra money, but I was inconsolable. I read the liner notes over and over, learning that this was the group's third album and that the Jackson Five were wildly successful. Using Super Glue, I tried to resurrect the record. The break lines were so clean and the circle of plastic fit together so perfectly that I wouldn't believe it could not be saved. I played the album—with its three ridges of hardened glue—anyway, spending hours hunched over my grandparents' large stereo console, trying to decipher the pained gurgles of sound trickling from the speakers, trying to imagine what the real Jackson Five sounded like. What the rest of the black world was hearing.

Finally another package arrived. Grandma and I hugged each other with relief: the record inside was unharmed. I ran to put it on the stereo. *"Stop!"* a voice on the album commanded and I froze, aghast. A loud terrible noise flooded out of the speakers and filled the room: the sound of boys yelling and screaming and howling in the street. "Hey!" they shouted. "Oh! Oh!" Occasionally the crash of cymbals could be heard over the terrible racket. This wasn't music! I looked to Grandma for guidance, but she appeared equally horrified. I thought I had chosen the wrong speed and adjusted it to 45 rpm. The screaming sped up; I switched to 78, it slowed down.

"Whatever was your mother thinking?" my grandmother muttered, going back into the kitchen. I remained in the living room, staring at the record as it spun on the turntable. I sat down on the floor directly in front of the built-in cloth speakers and listened hard. The noise was fast, disturbing, and confusing. I studied the album cover carefully. Five young black boys, dressed in wide pants with bright striped and flowered shirts like the ones in *Ebony* magazine, climbed out of giant letters on a bright blue cover. The pastel letters spelled *ABC;* it was their first major album. Maybe it was good that the other record had been broken in the mail, I thought. I liked the symmetry of having my first album be their first.

When the record finished, I restarted it, and suddenly all the screaming, all the terrible noises were gone. *"Stop!"* young Michael sang this time. "The love you save may be your own." I jumped up from the floor and stared at the turntable. Somehow, without having done anything, there was now music where before there had been only noise. The album looked exactly the same. I checked the controls; the settings were the same. I settled gingerly on the floor, afraid to break the spell.

The music was like nothing I had ever heard. There were high and low voices harmonizing against a rhythmic, infectious beat. Some of the lyrical melodies were peppy, others were more soothing. The voices bubbled up happy and excited like a party was going on inside the stereo. "Let me show you what it's all about," they beckoned. I realized that they were not yelling in chaos or anger; they were singing, chanting. "2-4-6-8. Who do you appreciate? *Hey!*" The shouts punctuated their emotions.

The exhilarating sounds spoke to me like my family's music had never done. The words were simple, the emotions honest; when the drum beat I could feel it throbbing against my neck. "Hey girl," Michael's clear voice called to me. "I'm-ma gonna teach you all about melody. Sit yourself down and take a seat. All you gotta do is repeat after me." I felt as if I were learning a new way of communicating. "A-B-C—it's as easy as 1-2-3, as simple as do-re-mi. Baby you and me."

My grandmother popped her head back into the room, surprised to hear me replaying "that noise." She stared at me with curiosity. I stared back, equally confused. Didn't she notice how sound had transformed? How noise had become music? What I had learned to hear? *"Listen,"* I urged her. "Can't you hear the change?" She couldn't. To her the Jackson Five remained noise.

Excited as I was, I could sense something was wrong. What, I didn't know. I didn't know that I had started to speak a new language, with new sounds, that this music promised an entire world somewhere else, a black world.

Constructing Meaning _____

Literal Comprehension

6. The writer had never wanted a record of her own because
   a. she disliked music.
   b. she hadn't heard any type of music that interested her.
   c. she was busy exploring her other interests.
   d. she had never been exposed to good music.

Making Predictions

7. After this incident took place, the author probably
   a. tried to find out more about the new "world" she had discovered.
   b. apologized to her grandmother.
   c. decided to learn more about classical music
   d. went to live in Seattle

Using Context Clues

8. In paragraph seven the word *decipher* means
   a. hear.
   b. repair.
   c. enjoy thoroughly.
   d. make meaning of.

Distinguishing Fact from Opinion

9. Which of the following statements is an opinion rather than a fact?
   a. The music on the Jackson Five album was more interesting than the music played by the writer's family.
   b. The writer had received the Jackson Five's third album.
   c. To the writer, New York City seemed as remote as Africa.
   d. The music on the album was meaningful to the writer.

Identifying the Main Idea

10. Which of the following statements best summarizes the main idea of the essay?
    a. All people are moved by music.
    b. Music is a "language" that can help you make a connection with your cultural heritage.
    c. Young people need to learn to communicate with their elders.
    d. The meaning of a passage of music or literature is not always apparent at first.

Seeds (POEM)

Carolyn M. Rodgers

words are not what people
read
and yet they are.
there are feelings, a symmetry
a complexity of emotions   5
thoughts, heart communications
and spirit conversations,

that press
through the word
and elevate the bareness of a page   10

words are not what people are
nor read, nor need . . .
and yet,
they are.

Constructing Meaning _____

Literal Comprehension

11. According to the first seven lines of the poem, words communicate all of the following except
   a. ideas
   b. interrelated feelings
   c. affections
   d. wishes

Interpreting Poetic Language

12. When the poet says that "words are not what people/ read/ and yet they are," she means that
   a. many people do not enjoy reading.
   b. people do not always understand what they read.
   c. it is usually necessary to "read between the lines" to understand a poem.
   d. words are much more than symbols on a page.

13. According to the poet, the "bareness of a page" is elevated when
   a. people read with enthusiasm.
   b. the words on a page convey a great deal of thought and emotion.
   c. the text deals with an exciting topic.
   d. people get together to discuss what they are reading.

Making Inferences

14. The writer may have called the poem "Seeds" because
    a. seeds often symbolize new beginnings.
    b. the word brings pleasant images to mind.
    c. the poem is really about nature.
    d. she is drawing a comparison between seeds and words.

Recognizing the Author's Point of View and Purpose

15. In this poem the author's purpose is to explain
    a. the importance of reading.
    b. that words are more important to us than we might realize.
    c. why it is important for people to express their true feelings.
    d. why it is helpful to understand what you read.

Making Cross-Text Connections

Questions 16–20 relate to the excerpt from "*A Call to Assembly* by Willie Ruff," "ABC" by Faith Adiele, and "Seeds" by Carolyn M. Rodgers.

Comparing and Contrasting

16. What do the selections by Willie Ruff, Faith Adiele, and Carolyn M. Rodgers have in common?
    a. They show how communication is an important part of the human experience.
    b. They describe experiences of learning to appreciate music.
    c. They discuss the power of spoken language.
    d. They list ways in which people can improve their ability to communicate.

17. Adiele and Rodgers both speak of emotions that
    a. go beyond words printed on a page.
    b. every person feels at some point.
    c. are easily captured by the written word.
    d. are shared by members of their family.

Making Inferences

18. Ruff and Rodgers would probably agree that
    a. there is a similarity between music and spoken language.
    b. the ideas that words can represent can be far greater than the words themselves.
    c. ideas can be expressed without words.
    d. nothing can match the effectiveness of spoken language.

Understanding Cause and Effect

19. Both Ruff and Adiele had experiences that caused them to
    a. understand why they enjoyed music.
    b. become eager to explore a new "language."
    c. want to learn more about their cultural heritage.
    d. make a decision about what to do with their lives.

Making Generalizations

20. Ruff, Adiele, and Rodgers would most likely agree with the statement that
    a. music is an effective tool for communication.
    b. people need to learn to communicate better.
    c. language is more than just words on a page.
    d. everyone should learn a new "language."

Writing a Response to Readings

Recall the **focus question** that precedes the selections on pages 963–969: **How can understanding different forms of communication help us become better members of the human community?** For the writers of the selections, learning a new language, or form of communication, helped them discover ways of better understanding themselves and others.

Read the following scenario and think about how it relates to the selections you have just read. Then get together with a peer group and read the scenario question. Discuss the ways in which the problem posed in the question can be solved. After you have exchanged ideas with the members of your group, respond to the scenario question in a well-planned essay.

Scenario

A new student named Petra, who has recently moved to this country, is in several of Tanya's classes. Petra has a friendly, inviting smile, but she cannot talk with her classmates because she speaks very little English. Tanya has noticed that Petra is alone most of the time and sometimes looks longingly at Tanya and her friends as they are laughing and walking out of class together.

Scenario Question

What can Tanya do to communicate with Petra and help her become part of the classroom community?

Reflecting on Your Own Writing

To determine how well you can evaluate your own writing, you may be asked to select examples from your portfolio or writing folder that you believe show your strengths as a writer. You may also be asked to explain why you think the writing demonstrates proficiency.

Before you choose pieces of your own writing to examine critically, read the following models and answer the questions that accompany each one. If you wish, work with a partner or a small group of classmates.

Reading the Dictionary

Most people go to a dictionary when they want to find the meaning of an unfamiliar word or when they need to check how something is spelled or pronounced. They don't realize how much additional information a standard desk dictionary holds. The dictionary is now my favorite research book and I am thinking about becoming a lexicographer (that's the person who writes the dictionary).

Take any entry, for example. What do you find? Besides all the definitions and parts of speech a word might have, the entry will tell you where the word comes from, will tell you if the word is slang, obsolete, or colloquial. It might also give you examples of current usage. I love learning how synonyms differ. Want to know the distinction between double-cross, bamboozle, and dupe? You can really learn to use English with precision by reading the dictionary.

Just take a look at the table of contents in any dictionary. Chances are you'll find a list of abbreviations and symbols for

---

chemical elements, a section on foreign words and phrases, birth and death dates for well-known people; information about countries, regions, and cities; even listings of colleges and universities. Some dictionaries even give you the signs and symbols used in different fields, such as mathematics and medicine. Lots of dictionaries will include a handbook of style and proofreading symbols. That can help you revise your own writing.

Some dictionaries contain illustrations. Want to know what a flying buttress looks like? or a tuatara? or a fez?

Do you want to know how to convert measures and weights to the metric system? Do you want to find out what the unit of money is in a particular country? Would you like to know the atomic number or weight of a chemical element? Start reading your dictionary today!

The opening of a paper states or implies the main idea, reveals the writer's purpose, and gets the reader's attention.

The body of a paper develops the main idea through details, examples, and reasons. Transitions are used to connect ideas. The writer does not stray from the topic.

The conclusion of a paper summarizes the writer's ideas or gives some new insight.

1. In your opinion, what are the strengths of this opening paragraph? What are its weaknesses? What changes would you make either in content or in style?

2. Are the ideas in each paragraph related to the main idea? Has the writer chosen good details, examples, reasons? Is all the material necessary? What changes would you recommend?

3. In your opinion, does the writer end on a strong note? How might the conclusion be improved?

How Bats See

Scientists once thought that bats had exceptionally good eyesight because they could fly and hunt in total darkness. There is no truth to the expression "blind as a bat" because most bats have eyesight. We now know the reason bats can fly in a completely dark room without bumping into walls has nothing to do with eyesight. Bats can use sound instead of light in a way that is just as efficient as sight is for other mammals. In effect, bats can see with sound.

Bats create "sound pictures" by sending out certain high-frequency sound pulses. When the sound hits an object, an echo of the bat's call comes back to the bat. The bat then builds up a picture of its surroundings from these reflected sound waves or echoes. Bats can tell size, shape, even the distance of objects from these echoes. The name for this process is echolocation. Echolocation allows the bat to detect its prey without its own presence detected.

It turns out that different species of bats have individual voices. This is how they can avoid confusion in sending and receiving messages. Bats have the ability to adjust the sounds they make when flying from one place to another. They can use echolocation when they are moving through the air or when they are on a perch.

The bat's external ears collect sounds. In order to locate sounds, bats move their ears. The bat then forms a picture of the

An **expository** or **informative** paper contains a clearly stated thesis.

Each paragraph should deal with one central idea expressed in a topic sentence or implied.

There should be adequate development of ideas through details, examples, and reasons.

The conclusion should flow naturally out of what has preceded it.

1. Locate the main idea or **thesis** of the paper. Is the central idea well stated or should it be rephrased more effectively?

2. Is each paragraph unified? Are there any sentences that don't belong? Are there wordy or repetitive passages?

3. Do any of the writer's statements need clarification or more development?

4. Does the paper end on a strong note? How might you improve it?

Choosing a Career

One of the most important decisions a high school student needs to make before graduation is what career to pursue. Many students leave high school without a realistic idea of what kind of work they are suited to do. Even college-bound students do not have a clear idea about the job market and how they can fit into it. I believe that our schools have the responsibility to help students make intelligent career choices.

Students need first of all to have a fair assessment of their own abilities. A student who flunks his chemistry course should think twice about a career in pharmacology. Knowing the truth about their strengths and their limitations can help students avoid unwise choices. Before the senior year, every student should be scheduled for a career-goal conference with a guidance counselor or adviser who is able to discuss the student's achievements and potential.

Schools need to institute a program that encourages students to visit work sites in the community and ask questions of prospective employers. Students need firsthand experience to appreciate what will be expected of them in the workplace. Students need opportunity to do internships to learn about possible employment opportunities. Schools should secure the cooperation of business and professional personnel to set up internships in museums, libraries, newspaper offices, laboratories, shops, hospitals, theaters, and other workplaces.

For their part, students need to pursue information about career choices more aggressively. They should form clubs that discuss the credentials needed for specific jobs and the availability of employment in the region. They should invite spokespersons from different companies to address the student body about the growth of particular industries and professions.

Career changes are inevitable, even for those who train carefully for a specific line of work. But there are bound to be fewer disappointments and job losses if young people are given better preparation for career choices.

A **persuasive** paper tries to convince the reader to agree with the writer or to take some specific action.

There should be a clear beginning, middle, and end.

The details, examples, and reasons presented must support the writer's position.

The issue should be appropriate to the audience.

1. Is the purpose of the paper clear? Where is the writer's position stated?

2. Is the paper well organized? Are ideas well developed and are sentences connected logically?

3. Has the writer presented enough evidence? Is the evidence convincing?

4. Is the content interesting? Is the subject suitable for its readers?

5. What advice would you give the writer to help improve content and style?

Now select two or more pieces of your own writing for evaluation. Answer these questions on your own or with the assistance of a partner.

1. What was your intention in the paper?
2. Which ideas or phrases do you think express your intention most effectively? Why?
3. Which sentences or passages do you consider weak? Why?
4. Rewrite any parts of the paper you feel need improvement.

Writing in Response to a Topic

At times you may be assigned a writing topic that is quite specific, as in the scenario question on page 957. Often, however, you may be given a more general topic and asked to develop your own focus. The kind of paper you write in response to such an assignment will be determined by your purpose and audience. Although different kinds of writing call for individual approaches, there are certain characteristics that all good compositions share. Most compositions will include a **thesis statement**—a sentence that expresses your main idea about the topic you have chosen. A well-written composition will have a clear structure—an introduction, a body, and a conclusion.

In some writing proficiency tests, you may be given a period of time to freewrite about a topic or to write a rough draft and have it evaluated by a peer group before you complete the formal essay assignment.

Sharpening Your Test-Taking Skills 977

Thinking About a Topic

Think for a few moments about the word *heritage.* Then think about the meaning of the following comments and the cartoon. Jot down your responses.

> Know whence you come. If you know whence you come, there is really no limit to where you can go.
> —James Baldwin
> "My Dungeon Shook"

> Guided by my heritage of a love of beauty and a respect for strength—in search of my mother's garden, I found my own.
> —Alice Walker
> "In Search of Our Mothers' Gardens"

> zimbabwe
> and we
> are one
>
> there is no separation
> —Safiya Henderson
> "harlem/soweto"

> In all my plays, I always point toward making that connection, toward reconnecting it with the past. You have to know who you are, and understand your history, in America over more than 300 years, in order to know what your relation is to your society.
> —August Wilson
> *New York Times* interview

"My mother is black, my father is African–American, and my grandfather is Negro. I can hardly wait to find out about me."

Drawing by Handelsman; © 1996 The New Yorker Magazine, Inc.

Now consider what the word *heritage* suggests to you. Explore your ideas by writing a response. Use techniques such as brainstorming and clustering to come up with ideas. Here is one impromptu response to the writing assignment.

There are many words that come to mind when I think about "heritage": roots, ancestors, lineage, traditions, values, identity. Heritage is what gets passed down from one's ancestors.

Some people think of heritage in terms of things. This is what the character Dee in "Everyday Use" thinks. She wants her family's quilts because they are objects she can show off as her cultural heritage. But Dee's mother and sister think of quiltmaking as a tradition that connects present and past generations.

Because there is so much diversity in our society, we have to get used to the idea of mixed heritage. Many of my friends have more than a single racial or national heritage.

If you're working with a partner or a group, you might spend some time commenting on one another's written work. Then think about the following questions and share your responses to the questions with a partner or with your peer group.

Do you believe that knowledge of and respect for one's heritage leads to a fuller and more responsible life?

Do you think that recognition of other-people's heritage can improve relationships between diverse groups in society?

Have you ever felt that you were at an advantage or disadvantage because of your cultural background?

Discussion of these questions will help prepare you for the formal writing assignment in which you are to develop a carefully thought-out paper.

Developing the Topic

You might be asked to develop a topic such as this:

People interpret the significance of their heritage in different ways. Write a paper in which you examine the role heritage plays in your life or in the lives of others. Your audience includes your teacher, classmates, and friends.

In order to give your paper a focus, here are some approaches you might use:

Examine how your ideas of heritage have been influenced not only by your experience but also by books and the media.

Explain how different cultural groups recognize and celebrate their customs and traditions.

Show what conflicts might be faced by people who are loyal to more than one country or culture.

The following essay is one response to the assignment. Using the Rating Scale on page 981, evaluate how successful the writer has been in responding to the topic. Then discuss other approaches that you might take to the assignment.

My Ideas About Heritage

Last spring our school held a "Celebrate Your Heritage" day. Instead of having regular classes, students shared some aspect of their family or cultural heritage with others. Some students came in costume; some brought letters from relatives in different countries; some played songs or demonstrated dances. In the lunchroom parents set up booths in which different ethnic foods could be sampled. For the first time I tasted a stuffed grape leaf and couscous. My own contribution was my grandparents' photograph album, showing photos of people I never knew but had heard about in family gatherings. By the end of the day, I had learned a lot about the meaning of "heritage." I discovered how important that link with the past was to all of us, no matter who our ancestors were.

One thing I became aware of was how many of my fellow students were of mixed backgrounds, like myself. Helen, for example, has a Greek father and a Lebanese mother. Her grandfather was born in Cypress and her grandmother in Italy. Because his father is from Mexico and his mother from Martinique, Octavio can speak both Spanish and French. We did a survey of the places of origin of our parents and found that in the junior class we could name 79 different countries. As a result, we all became interested in finding out as much as we could about our ancestors' ethnic or national origins.

I found myself paying more attention to issues of cultural values and tradition in my reading and in watching TV. I had read August Wilson's The Piano Lesson and thought it was great fun, but now I began to understand the conflict between Boy Willie and Berniece. To Boy Willie, the piano is a legacy that he can sell in order to buy some land, but to Berniece, the piano represents an important link to her family's past. I realized that on TV I was catching all kinds of cultural stereotypes about Asian Americans, African Americans, and Native Americans that had no relationship to the truth I was experiencing every day in my communication with people in the neighborhood and at school.

I also began to realize that there are problems in having a diverse ethnic background. The decision to hold on to one's native culture or to assimilate into a new culture is not simple. For example, I could see how language ties us to our roots. I could understand the problem Richard Rodriguez described in <u>Hunger of Memory</u> about growing up in a bilingual family.

I have to admit that I had never before given much thought to my background or to the customs of earlier generations. I, who had always been bored when stories about the family were told, now began pestering my parents to tell me more about my ancestry. I began studying the features of those people in the photograph album. Did I look at all like them? I began pulling out old recordings by Bessie Smith and Louis Armstrong and listening to the music my grandparents had listened to when they were my age. Doing that made me feel closer somehow to my origins.

Chiefly, though, I have found that learning to appreciate my own heritage has made me more tolerant of others. Instead of dismissing unfamiliar customs—as I used to do—I now want to know more about them. Words that once were just labels—like roots, tradition, identity—now mean something special to me.

Rating Scale

Good
Content is interesting. Paper has a main idea or focus. Paper is clearly organized with a beginning, middle, and end. Ideas are developed with sufficient details and examples. Writer uses a variety of sentence types and precise words. Writer uses transitions to connect ideas. Writer uses conventions such as capitalization, punctuation, and spelling fairly well. Literary works are identified by title and author.

Fair
Focus of paper is not sharp and writing is of uneven quality. Ideas are developed with some details and examples. There is evidence of disorganization. Not all paragraphs are developed logically. The vocabulary is limited and sentences are not varied. There are errors in capitalization, punctuation, or spelling that interfere with communication of ideas.

Weak
Paper has little focus or development. Paragaphs are not clearly and carefully organized. Ideas are not carefully thought out. Few details or examples are given to support ideas. Vocabulary is limited, and sentence structure is not varied.

Guide to Literary Terms and Techniques

ALLITERATION *The repetition of a sound in successive or closely associated words or syllables.* Usually the sound is a consonant or consonant cluster and is found at the beginning of words. Some common examples of this **initial alliteration** are "*st*icks and *st*ones" and *m*ind over *m*atter." When alliteration occurs within words, it is called **hidden alliteration** or **internal alliteration.**

The repetition of final consonant sounds, as in ba*ck*/thi*ck*, is generally called **consonance,** although some writers prefer to refer to any repetition of consonant sounds as *alliteration.* The term *consonance* is also used for a form of imperfect rhyme where the consonants are the same but the vowels are different: *look*/*lack*.

Alliteration is often found in poetry. The repetition of a sound adds emphasis to words and helps make images more memorable. It also serves to unify a passage or poem.

See **Assonance, Repetition.**
See also pages 247, 304, 658.

ALLUSION *An indirect reference to a work of literature or art or to a well-known person, place, or event.* Allusions are used to expand and enrich the meaning of a work. They do so by tapping into the reader's previous knowledge. The effectiveness of allusion rests on there being a common body of knowledge between writer and reader.

In African American literature, there are many allusions to the Bible and to historical events such as the Emancipation Proclamation. James Weldon Johnson's "The Creation" alludes to the Biblical story of Creation, building on the reader's knowledge of that text. Johnson's "O Black and Unknown Bards" contains allusions to spirituals that are themselves rich in Biblical allusions.

See pages 45, 188, 280, 284, 713.

ANALOGY *A comparison of two things that have certain similarities in order to illustrate a point or advance an argument.*

In his letter to Thomas Jefferson, Benjamin Banneker draws an analogy between the treatment of the American colonists by Britain and the treatment of black slaves by white American slaveholders. If the former was unjust, Banneker argues, then so is the latter.

Analogies can also be used to describe or explain an unfamiliar situation or object by comparing it to a familiar one.

See **Argument.**
See also pages 163, 628–629.

ANECDOTE *A short narrative, often humorous, detailing a single episode or incident.* An anecdote illustrates an idea or reveals something about a person, place, or thing. Writers of biography and autobiography often include anecdotes to bring their subject to life. In *Up From Slavery*, Booker T. Washington tells of turning back the hands of the clock so that he could get to school on time. From this anecdote, the reader learns of his zeal for learning.

See page 224.

ANTAGONIST *The person or force in fiction that opposes the **protagonist**, or main character.* The Greek root of this word means "to struggle against." Most fairy tales and folk tales have obvious antagonists—the evil stepmother in "Cinderella," the wicked witch in "Hansel and Gretel." The monster in the form of a hippopotamus is the antagonist in the African myth "Nana Miriam." In some short stories and novels, the antagonist may be a force of nature.

See **Protagonist.**

ANTHEM   *A song of praise, rejoicing, or reverence.* Originally, anthems were musical arrangements of Biblical passages, often from Psalms. Now anthems are also written to praise nations (national anthems) and people. James Weldon Johnson's "Lift Every Voice and Sing" has been called the "Negro National Anthem." It praises God, African American men and women, and the nation.

See **Hymn.**
See also page 292.

ANTITHESIS   *The balancing of two contrasting words, phrases, sentences, or ideas.*
See pages 615, 620.

APHORISM   *A concise statement of a principle, truth, or sentiment.* Politicians and other speechmakers often use aphorisms to make a point or to summarize an argument. In her speech "Ain't I a Woman?" Sojourner Truth uses an aphorism. She says, "If my cup won't hold but a pint, and yours holds a quart, wouldn't you be mean not to let me have my little half-measure full?"

See **Proverb.**
See also page 168.

APOSTROPHE   *A literary device in which a person or thing that is not present is addressed as if it were.* Paul Laurence Dunbar begins his poem "Douglass" with an apostrophe: "Ah, Douglass, we have fall'n on evil days." The Hymn to the Aton" speaks directly to the sun: "Thou appearest beautifully on the horizon of heaven . . . ." Hymns and prayers often begin with apostrophes.

See page 82.

ARCHAISM   *The use of words, phrases, or grammatical constructions that are no longer found in common speech.* Some writers use archaisms to re-create the atmosphere of the past or to create a reverential tone. Common archaisms are *thou* and *thine.*

See page 255.

ARGUMENT   *The reasons and evidence used to support a speaker's or writer's opinion or to disprove an opponent's opinion.* An argument seeks to lead the listener or reader to a specific conclusion.

An **argument from analogy** compares two things and concludes that because they are similar in certain ways, they are similar in some other way. Benjamin Banneker uses an argument from analogy in his letter to Thomas Jefferson by noting the similarities between the colonists' grievances against Britain and African Americans' grievances against slaveholders.

See **Analogy.**
See also pages 64, 158, 163, 623, 628–629.

ASSONANCE   *The repetition of similar vowel sounds in nearby words.* Langston Hughes uses assonance in "The Negro Speaks of Rivers": "I've kn*o*wn rivers *a*ncient as the world and *o*lder than the fl*ow* of human blood in human v*ei*ns."

Like **alliteration,** assonance is often used in poetry to emphasize particular words and to unify the poem. It differs from **rhyme** in that only the vowels, not the final consonants, are the same. *Light* and *tight* rhyme, while *light* and *tied* illustrate assonance. Like rhyme, assonance contributes to the music of the writing.

See **Alliteration, Repetition.**
See also pages 308, 702.

ATMOSPHERE   *The prevailing feeling or mood of a literary work.* Atmosphere is created primarily, but not exclusively, by the **setting.** It is also created by careful word choice and vivid descriptions. Arna Bontemps creates a disturbing atmosphere, one heavy with a brooding sense of finality, in "A Summer Tragedy."

See pages 484, 879.

AUTOBIOGRAPHY *A person's account of his or her own life.* The events are generally presented in chronological order. Autobiographies are different from memoirs, diaries, journals, and letters in that they present a unified life-story.

Most autobiographies are written by famous people, but ordinary citizens also write autobiographies. During the years preceding the Civil War, many freed and fugitive slaves wrote autobiographies that became known as **slave narratives.** The narratives of Olaudah Equiano, Harriet Jacobs, and many others helped to bring about the emancipation of the slaves. The autobiographies of Frederick Douglass, Booker T. Washington, Ida B. Wells, Zora Neale Hurston, Richard Wright, and Malcolm X are well-known examples of the genre.

See **Biography, Nonfiction.**
See also pages 145, 213, 411, 583, 608, 853.

BALLAD *A story told in verse, with a refrain, strong rhythm, and rhyme, usually meant to be sung.* Ballads usually present a dramatic or exciting episode, often about physical courage or love. Frequently, as in ''John Henry,'' the story ends tragically.

Folk ballads are anonymous compositions that have been preserved through the oral tradition. **Literary ballads** are narrative poems by known authors. They are generally not meant to be sung.

See **Refrain.**
See also pages 258, 261.

BARD *In present usage, any poet.* Originally, the word referred to a Celtic poet who recited verses glorifying the deeds of heroes and leaders. The ancient bards generally accompanied themselves on a harp.

See page 280.

BIOGRAPHY *A written account of a person's life.* This is one of the most popular forms of nonfiction. Biographies have been written about almost every famous person, contemporary or historical. The biographer chooses a particular person and then researches his or her background in detail to convey accurately both the personality and the historical significance of the person.

See **Autobiography.**
See also page 583.

BLACK ARTS MOVEMENT *A movement in the 1960s that emphasized black pride and sought to forge and define a black culture separate from mainstream white culture.* The movement led to another blossoming of art and literature by African Americans, similar to that of the Harlem Renaissance. This period, however, was more politically radical. One of the main figures of the movement was Amiri Baraka.

See pages 462, 679, 734.

BLANK VERSE *Unrhymed lines of iambic pentameter (lines of ten syllables each, where every second syllable is stressed).* The English language generally falls into iambic patterns. Many lines in the works of William Shakespeare, such as these from *Romeo and Juliet,* are written in blank verse.

> But, soft! What light through yonder window
> breaks?
> It is the east, and Juliet is the sun!

See **Iambic Pentameter, Meter.**

BLUES *A kind of vocal and instrumental music developed by African Americans.* The blues grew out of slave work songs and spirituals and have many elements of African **call-and-response** singing. They are characterized by their melancholy tone and their short (usually three-line) stanzas with the first two lines repeated. A typical example is the last stanza from ''Backwater Blues'' by Bessie Smith:

> (Moan) . . . . I can't move no more,
> (Moan) . . . . I can't move no more,
> There ain't no place for a poor old girl
> to go.

See **Call-and-Response.**
See also page 370.

CALL-AND-RESPONSE *A typically African pattern of exchange between a singer or storyteller and an audience.* This pattern, found in many African societies, is one of the elements that took root in African American culture. It can be heard most clearly between a black preacher and the congregation, between a jazz soloist and the ensemble, and in blues songs.

See **Blues.**
See also pages 86, 370.

CATALOG *A literary device that lists people, places, things, events, or attributes.* A catalog can establish a setting or a theme. Many ancient forms of literature contain extended catalogs. The **epic** uses a catalog of heroes, ships, armor, and the like. In modern poetry, the catalog has been used extensively by Walt Whitman, Carl Sandburg, Allen Ginsburg, and Vachel Lindsay. Margaret Walker's poem "For My People" is a catalog of the attributes of "all the adams and eves."

See page 441.

CHARACTERIZATION *The methods a writer uses to present a character's personality.* These methods can be direct or indirect. In **direct characterization,** the author tells the reader what the character is like. In **indirect characterization,** the character is revealed by his or her appearance, speech, private thoughts, and actions. Another important method of indirect characterization is showing how others react to the character. Writers generally use both direct and indirect characterization.

See **Characters.**
See also pages 3, 448.

CHARACTERS *The people, animals, or things presented as persons in a work of literature.* Characters may be described as dynamic or static, and as round or flat. **Dynamic characters** change in some fundamental way during the course of the story, while **static characters** remain the same. The main characters in a work of fiction are almost always dynamic. The mother and father in "Neighbors" by Diane Oliver change their minds about sending their son to a newly integrated school after they are sent hate mail and their house is bombed. In some stories, the minor characters are **flat characters.** They are one-sided and stereotypi-

cal. A **round character** is many-sided and more true to life. Main characters, like the narrator and her grandmother in "To Da-duh, in Memoriam," by Paule Marshall, are almost always round.

In **fables** and **folk tales** characters such as Ananse the Spider or Brer Rabbit are often animals.

See pages 3, 448, 498.

CLIMAX *The most exciting and tense part of a narrative.* It is also the point at which the outcome of the **conflict** becomes apparent. In Arna Bontemps's "A Summer Tragedy," the climax occurs when the reader realizes that the main characters intend to commit suicide.

In dramatic structure, the climax may precede, follow, or coincide with the **crisis,** or **turning point,** which is the moment when the plot turns to its final resolution.

See **Crisis, Drama, Plot.**
See also pages 792, 851, 938.

COMEDY *A light form of drama that has a happy ending and aims primarily to amuse the audience.* **Farce** is a form of low comedy. It has less sustained plot and less characterization than a comedy and more improbable situations and boisterous behavior.

COMPLICATION *The events in a drama or narrative that develop the conflict.* Complications are like knots, which are finally untied in the **resolution.** In Buchi Emecheta's *The Wrestling Match,* the elders' schemes provide many of the plot complications.

See **Conflict, Plot.**
See also page 569.

CONFLICT *The struggle between characters or forces in a play, novel, short story, narrative poem, or film.* Conflicts take many forms and may be external or internal. **External conflicts** can be against the forces of nature, against another person, or against society. **Internal conflicts** take place within the character.

Frederick Douglass's autobiography includes external conflicts (his fight with Covey and with a society that allows slavery), and internal conflicts (his decision to stand up for himself and become a man). In James Baldwin's "The Rockpile," both Roy and John have internal conflicts about following their mother's rules.

The presentation and development of conflict provide the elements of interest and **suspense** in most forms of fiction.

See **Plot**.
See also pages 172, 432, 472, 792, 846, 851, 938.

CONNOTATION *The emotional implications of a word or phrase.* This is distinct from the word's dictionary meaning, or **denotation**. Although *stingy* and *thrifty* both describe someone who is careful with money, *stingy* carries a negative connotation while *thrifty* has a positive connotation. Writers, particularly poets, pay careful attention to the connotations of the words they use.

See **Denotation**.
See also pages 247, 302, 329, 621, 662, 721, 830, 879.

COUPLET *Two lines of verse with similar end rhyme that usually express a complete thought.* Shakespearean sonnets always end in a couplet.

A **heroic couplet** is a couplet written in **iambic pentameter**.

See pages 165, 722.

CRISIS or **TURNING POINT** *The point at which the opposing forces in a **conflict** cause the **plot** to turn toward its ultimate **resolution**.* The crisis is a structural element of the plot and does not necessarily coincide with the **climax**, which is the moment of greatest emotional intensity.

See **Climax, Conflict, Plot**.
See also page 938.

DENOTATION *The exact meaning of a word (its dictionary meaning), independent of its connotative, or emotional meanings.* The denotation of *home* is simply a place where someone lives. The connotative meaning of the word, however, conveys feelings of warmth and love.

See **Connotation**.
See also pages 247, 302.

DÉNOUEMENT *The final unraveling of a plot in drama or fiction.* Novels sometimes have long, involved dénouements, while in short stories the dénouement is generally brief.

See pages 851, 938.

DESCRIPTION *Writing that creates the impression of a person, place, thing, or event by using sensory details.* Descriptive writing is most powerful when the images are concrete and clear. It is sometimes used as an end in itself, but it is most often found with the other forms of writing.

See **Imagery, Setting**.
See also pages 12, 82, 193.

DIALECT *The vocabulary, grammatical habits, and pronunciations of a particular regional, social, or cultural group.*

See pages 264, 390.

DIALOGUE *Conversation between two or more people as reproduced in writing.* Dialogue is used to reveal character, establish conflict, build suspense, and move the action of a plot forward. It is often used in fiction. Plays are usually constructed entirely out of dialogue.

See pages 64, 418, 794.

DICTION *A writer's or speaker's choice of words.* Diction can be formal or informal. Writers choose their level of diction according to their audience and the desired effect.

Benjamin Banneker uses formal diction in his letter to Thomas Jefferson, while Rudolph Fisher uses informal diction in "Miss Cynthie." Diction has a great effect on the **tone** of a piece of writing.

See **Tone**.
See also pages 255, 295, 445, 689, 693.

DRAMA *A narrative written to be acted on a*

stage. A playwright generally emphasizes **character, conflict,** and **action.**

Dialogue is used for characterization and to advance the plot. In addition to dialogue, some playwrights use **asides** and **soliloquies** to flesh out a character. An aside occurs when a character turns to the audience and says something that the other characters on stage do not hear. A soliloquy involves a character making an extended speech while alone on stage. The character usually thinks aloud and reveals his or her innermost feelings.

Staging involves all elements of the drama except dialogue. Common elements of staging include **scenery, costume, gesture, movement,** and **lighting. Stage directions** tell the actors how to move and speak. All entrances and exits and movements on the stage are spelled out in the stage directions. When a play is performed, the staging (or **stagecraft**) enhances the impact of the story. Drama is often said to be living literature since the same play is different each time it is performed by different actors or under different direction.

See pages 737, 791.

ELEGY *A formal, lyric poem about a solemn theme, usually someone's death.* Some elegies also mourn the passing of life and beauty. Walt Whitman's "O Captain! My Captain!" is an elegy mourning the death of President Lincoln.

See pages 257, 810.

EPIC *A long narrative poem that centers on an important character who embodies the values of a particular society.* In common usage, *epic* is used to describe anything that is huge in scope. The literary meaning of the term, however, implies a heroic character, an action of great importance, and a range of adventures. Some of the most ancient stories are epics. A well-known African epic is *Sundiata.*

See pages 118, 119, 670.

EPIGRAM *A pointed, concise poem that sums up a situation or a philosophy in a few lines.* Countee Cullen captures and comments on a woman's character in only four lines in "For a Lady I Know."

See page 339.

EPITHET *An adjective or adjective phrase that is regularly used to characterize a person, place, or thing.* Examples are "Catherine the Great," "Richard the Lion-Hearted," and "America the Beautiful." Some **praise names** found in African societies are epithets.

ESSAY *A brief prose discussion of a limited subject that presents a particular point of view.* The aim of the essay may be to educate or persuade, or perhaps just to entertain, the reader. There are both **formal** and **informal essays.**

See **Nonfiction.**
See also pages 583, 584, 600.

EXPLICATION *A type of literary analysis that involves close reading of a work, followed by an analysis of the words, images, structure, and techniques the author used.* In the explication of poetry, the reader looks closely at figurative language, rhythm, rhyme, stanza breaks, and other devices to show how all these techniques work together to create the meaning and feeling of the poem.

See page 374.

EXPOSITION *A type of writing that explains something or provides information.* Most nonfiction (newspaper and magazine articles, essays, reports, and biographies) is expository.

In some fictional works, exposition is the part of the plot that provides information about the setting and what has happened before the story opens.

See pages 262, 792, 937.

FABLE *A brief story, often originating in folklore, told to illustrate a moral point or point out human follies.* The characters in a fable are usually animals, but people and inanimate objects can also be central figures. Brer Rabbit is the best-known figure in African American fables.

See pages 96, 181.

FICTION *Narrative writing that comes from the imagination of the author, rather than from history or fact.* The term usually refers to short stories and novels.

Historical fiction uses actual events and people as the springboard for the imagination. Buchi Emecheta sets *The Wrestling Match* in Nigeria after the great civil war.

See **Nonfiction.**

FIGURATIVE LANGUAGE *Words and phrases that are used in a nonliteral sense.* Figurative language departs from the normal order and meaning of words and phrases to lend power, strength, or humor to verbal communication. **Metaphor, simile, personification,** and **symbol** are the most commonly used figures of speech in figurative language.

Instead of saying that the protagonist in *The Wrestling Match* was afraid, Buchi Emecheta writes that "an eel of fear wriggled in his stomach." Of course, there is no such thing as "an eel of fear," but the feeling of fear is conveyed vividly by this use of figurative language.

See pages 43, 324, 938.

FIGURE OF SPEECH *Any expression that uses language figuratively rather than literally.* Figures of speech such as **metaphor, simile,** and **personification** are used frequently in everyday conversation. When you say, "She's a peach" or "He was running around like a chicken with its head cut off," you are using a figure of speech.

See **Figurative Language.**

FLASHBACK *A presentation of scenes or incidents that occurred before the opening scene of a work of fiction, a play, or a film.* The flashback may take the form of a character's recollection, narration, dream, or reverie.

See pages 472, 833.

FOIL *A character (less frequently, a thing, place, or event) that contrasts strongly with another.* The term originally referred to the thin sheet of bright metal placed under a jewel to increase its brilliance. In "The Rockpile," the brothers Roy and John are foils.

FOLKLORE or **FOLK LITERATURE** *Traditional songs, myths, legends, fables, proverbs, riddles, and the like that are passed down from generation to generation.* The spirituals and the Brer Rabbit stories are examples of African American folklore.

See pages 181, 187.

FOLK TALE *A short narrative, passed down to succeeding generations through the oral tradition.* Most African folk tales feature animal characters and many of these tales were transplanted to America via the slave trade. Folk tales like "Osebo's Drum," which explains how the leopard got his spots, have counterparts in African American folk tales.

See pages 97, 181.

FORESHADOWING *The presentation of information that gives clues as to the final outcome of a work of fiction.* Foreshadowing is a way to draw readers into a work and to prepare them for the action to come.

The incident in which the Red Caps in "Miss Cynthie" laugh over her assumption that Dave is an undertaker is an example of foreshadowing. We now know that Dave has chosen some other profession, although we are not yet sure what it is.

See pages 356, 399, 472, 822, 830.

FREE VERSE *Poetry that does not have a fixed rhyme scheme, meter, line length, or stanza form.* It does, however, use poetic techniques such as **alliteration, figurative language,** and **parallelism.**

Much contemporary poetry is written in free verse. Margaret Walker uses alliteration in her free verse poem "For My People," which begins, "For my people everywhere *s*inging their slave songs repeatedly: their *d*irges and their *d*itties . . . ." James Weldon Johnson uses strong images and parallelism in his free verse poem "The Creation."

See pages 289, 441, 444, 651, 658.

GRIOT *A person who is skilled in storytelling.* Griots have many functions. They are poets, historians, teachers, singers, and entertainers. Griots have been very important members of African society because they have recorded and preserved history and tradition. Because of their great knowledge, griots were often called on to solve disputes and to advise their chiefs. Now most griots are professional musicians.

See pages 87, 119.

HARLEM RENAISSANCE *A creative outpouring by a group of African American writers, artists, and musicians in New York during the 1920s.* These talented people, part of the mass migration of African Americans to Northern cities, congregated in Harlem, making it the cultural and intellectual capital of black America. Blacks and whites alike were drawn to Harlem to observe or become a part of this movement. Langston Hughes, Arna Bontemps, and Zora Neale Hurston were a few of the African American writers of the Harlem Renaissance.

See pages 267–278, 313.

HYMN *A lyric poem expressing a religious theme or emotion, and generally meant to be sung.* One of the main forms of African poetic expression, the **praise song,** is a type of hymn.

See **Anthem.**

See also page 79.

HYPERBOLE *A figure of speech that uses overstatement or exaggeration to emphasize a point or to create a comic effect.* The title of Amiri Baraka's poem "Preface to a Twenty Volume Suicide Note" contains hyperbole.

See page 680.

IAMBIC PENTAMETER *A line of verse that contains five iambs.* An **iamb** consists of an

unaccented syllable followed by an accented syllable. Iambic pentameter is the most common rhythmic pattern for verse written in English. Countee Cullen uses it often, as in his poem "From the Dark Tower," which begins:

Wĕ sháll nŏt álwăys plánt whĭle óthĕřs reáp

Thĕ góldĕn íncrĕmént ŏf búrstĭng frúit,

See **Meter.**

See also pages 338, 723.

IDIOM *The use of words or grammatical constructions characteristic of a given language or dialect.* It is usuallly impossible to translate an idiomatic expression literally into another language and retain its meaning. For example, "to carry out" means to pick something up and actually carry it out of a place. Idiomatically, it means to see that something is done: "I carried out the instructions."

Idiom can also refer to the accurate reproduction of the speech patterns of a particular ethnic or regional group. Authors often use idiom in characterization. In Langston Hughes's Jesse B. Semple sketches, the reader can infer a great deal about the two characters from the way they speak. Zora Neale Hurston begins her story "How the 'Gator Got Black" by saying, "Ah'm tellin' dis lie on de 'gator." This use of idiom lends authenticity to the narrative.

See **Dialect, Regionalism.**

See also pages 518, 646.

IMAGERY *The use of words or phrases that create pictures (images) in a reader's mind.* Although visual imagery is the most common form of imagery, images may appeal to any of the five senses.

In this stanza from "Southern Mansion," Arna Bontemps describes a scene by using several images that appeal to our senses of sight and sound:

There is a sound of music echoing
Through the open door
And in the field there is
Another sound tinkling in the cotton:
Chains of bondmen dragging on the ground.

See pages 15, 341.

Guide to Literary Terms and Techniques   **989**

INVERSION *A reversal of word order in a phrase or sentence for poetic effect or emphasis.* Instead of saying "My heart will not tremble to meet its fate," Claude McKay wrote these lines in his poem "Baptism":

You will not note a flicker of defeat,
My heart shall tremble not its fate to meet.

This word order emphasizes the word *not* and creates a line of iambic pentameter that rhymes with the preceding line.
See page 283.

IRONY *A broad term referring to the recognition that reality is different from appearances or from what was expected.* Authors use irony to create effects that range from humorous to tragic. There are three main types of irony.

Verbal irony—a writer or speaker says one thing but means something quite different. ("Nice dog you have," Beth said as she came to the door trailing a ripped pant leg.)

Dramatic irony—the reader or audience realizes something that a character in the play or story does not. In August Wilson's *The Piano Lesson,* Wining Boy sells Lymon a "magic suit." Although Lymon believes him, the audience knows that it is just an old suit that Wining Boy is selling because he needs money.

Irony of situation, in which there is a discrepancy between the expected result of an action or situation and its actual result. The main character in Chinua Achebe's "Dead Men's Path" is a victim of irony of situation. As a modern teacher, Michael Obi refuses to respect the beliefs and traditions of the village elders. His actions result in severe criticism from his supervisor, rather than the praise he expected.
See pages 227, 236, 313, 710.

LYRIC POETRY *Poetry that expresses the thoughts or emotions of the speaker.* The emotion or thought is often implied rather than stated. Originally, lyric poems were sung to the accompaniment of a stringed instrument called the lyre. Types of lyric poetry include **sonnets, elegies, songs,** and **odes.**
See **Elegy, Sonnet.**
See also pages 250, 297, 664, 810.

METAMORPHOSIS *A striking change in physical form or substance, usually by supernatural means.* This transformation often happens to characters in myths and legends. In the story "Nana Miriam," the hippopotamus becomes a river.
See page 113.

METAPHOR *A comparison between two dissimilar things, in order to give added meaning to one of them.* Metaphor is one of the most important figures of speech used in poetry. A metaphor can arouse strong feelings and make an idea or emotion powerful and memorable.

When Langston Hughes writes that without dreams "Life is a broken-winged bird/That cannot fly," he makes the reader think of the pitiful, damaged, earthbound bird. At the same time, he brings into the reader's mind a vision of how life should be lived—with the freedom and grace of a bird soaring through the air.

An **extended metaphor** is one that is carried throughout several lines or an entire poem. The speaker in Hughes's "Mother to Son" uses an extended metaphor that compares the journey through life to climbing a staircase.

An **implied metaphor** suggests the comparison between one thing and another. In the sentence "Her words stung my pride," the implied comparison is between the words and a bee sting.
See **Figurative Language.**
See also pages 42–43, 256–257, 324, 328, 706.

METER *The recurrence of a regular pattern of stressed and unstressed syllables in lines of poetry.* The metric unit in a line is called a **foot.** A **metrical foot** usually has one stressed syllable and one or more unstressed syllables. In metrical analysis (**scansion**), a number of symbols are used. The sign (˘) means the syllable is not stressed, while the sign (˘) indicates that the syllable is stressed. The sign (/) is used to separate metrical feet.

Some poets write in a regular meter. Scansion of the first lines of "America" reveals that the poem is in iambic pentameter.

Ălthoúgh/sŏe feéds/me breád/

ŏf bít/tĕrnéss/

Aňd siňks/ĭntó/my thróat/

hĕr tí/geř's tóoth/

See **Iambic Pentameter, Rhythm.**
See also pages 336, 338, 723.

MINSTREL SHOW *A type of vaudeville show that included singing, dancing, storytelling, and comedy routines.* It originated on Southern plantations during the 1840s, but had its roots in the African traditions of mime, dance, music, and storytelling that were integral to life in African society. Because of the popularity of the slave minstrel shows, white performers put on blackface and began imitating them. When black entertainers returned to the stage after the Civil War, they were forced to wear blackface and perpetuate the demeaning stereotypes. Minstrel shows ended with the demise of vaudeville in the early 1900s.

See page 728.

MONOLOGUE *A long speech delivered by a single person.* It differs from a **soliloquy** in that it is spoken in the presence of one or more other characters.

See page 796.

MYTH *An anonymous story having its roots in the folk beliefs of a culture.* These stories often explain natural events.

See page 107.

NARRATION *A form of writing or speaking that tells about an event or series of events.* The events may be actual or fictional. The narrative tells what happened, when, and to whom. Narratives take many forms: ballads, fables, short stories, epics, and novels. Narrative episodes are also found in essays and biographies.

See pages 664, 791, 831.

NARRATOR *The person who narrates, or tells, a story.* If the story is told in the **first person,** the *I* character is the narrator. Lizabeth is the first-person narrator in Eugenia Collier's story "Marigolds." It is important not to mistake a first-person narrator in fiction for the author.

There are two types of **third-person narrators**—omniscient and limited. James Baldwin's story "The Rockpile" is told by a third-person omniscient (all-knowing) narrator. The narrator is not in the story at all, but can tell us about the thoughts and feelings of any of the characters. A third-person limited narrator can give the inner thoughts of only one of the characters in a narrative.

In order to understand a narrative, it is important to be aware of who the narrator is, what his or her attitudes are, and whether or not he or she is trustworthy.

See **Point of View.**
See also page 419.

NÉGRITUDE *A philosophy that asserts the independence and value of African culture, and stresses its vitality and beauty.* The writers who developed this philosophy were a group of Africans and West Indians living in Paris after World War I. The main proponents of Négritude were the poets Léopold Sédar Senghor and Aimé Césaire. Césaire coined the term and first used it in his poem "Return to My Native Land." The Négritude writers drew upon the wealth of African history and art to rehabilitate and dignify black culture in the eyes of the world. They sought to celebrate black civilizations and to increase unity among blacks worldwide.

See pages 805–809, 821.

NONFICTION *Prose that deals with real, rather than imagined, events and people.* The characters, settings, and actions in nonfiction must conform to what is true and cannot be manipulated by the writer.

Biography, autobiography, and the **essay** are some of the most popular forms of nonfiction. Other forms include newspaper and magazine articles, journals, diaries, and speeches.

Nonfiction uses all of the major forms of discourse: **description** gives sensory information; **narration** tells about events; **exposition** explains a process or situation; and **persuasion** or argument tries to change the way a reader acts or thinks about something.

See **Autobiography, Biography, Essay.**
See also pages 411, 583.

NOVEL *Any long, fictional prose narrative.* This term is applied to a wide variety of works, generally having many characters and a strong, often complex, plot. The novel is a relatively new form of literature, born in the eighteenth century.

See pages 572–581, 892.

OCTAVE *A group of eight lines.* The term usually refers to the first eight lines of the **Petrarchan** (Italian) **sonnet.** The octave is thought of as a unit because the lines develop a single subject or thought. The last six lines of the Italian sonnet are also thought of as a unit, called the **sestet.**

Claude McKay's "Baptism" is an example of a Petrarchan sonnet. The octave presents the speaker's thoughts about going into a metaphoric furnace. The sestet reveals the effects of the speaker's experience.

See **Petrarchan Sonnet.**
See also page 301.

ODE See **LYRIC POETRY.**

ONOMATOPOEIA *The use of words whose sound imitates or suggests their meanings.* Some onomatopoeic words are *hiss, splash, sizzle, buzz,* and *knock.* In poetry, onomatopoeia can create a musical effect and enhance meaning. In "Beehive," Jean Toomer uses obvious onomatopoeic words like "buzzing" and "lapping." He also makes the whole poem sound like an active beehive by including many sibilants (words with *s, sh,* and *z* sounds).

See page 305.

OXYMORON *The bringing together of two contradictory terms.* "Wise fool," "loving hate," and "eloquent silence" are oxymorons. Poets sometimes use oxymorons for emphasis.

See **Paradox.**
See also page 645.

PARADOX *A statement that seems contradictory or absurd, but is in fact true or reveals some truth.* A paradox can be used as a rhetorical device to attract the reader's attention or to emphasize a particular point. Paradoxes are often used in **epigrams** and poetry such as Paul Laurence Dunbar's "Life's Tragedy," which ends with the paradoxical idea that "We count our joys not by the things we have,/But by what kept us from the perfect thing."

See page 613.

PARALLELISM *The use of words, phrases, clauses, or sentences that are similar in structure or in meaning.* Parallelism is often used in poetry and in speeches to add rhythm and to emphasize words and meanings. Martin Luther King, Jr., was especially skilled in its use.

Parallelism is often found in the Bible and in poetry handed down in the oral tradition.

See pages 178, 444, 605, 615.

PARAPHRASE *A restatement of an idea or passage in a text for purposes of clarification or simplification.* A paraphrase differs from a summary in that it may be as long as or longer than the original text. Although a paraphrase aids understanding, it does not convey the atmosphere, style, and tone of the original.

See page 256.

PARODY *A comic imitation of a serious work of literature, music, or art.* The purpose of the parody may be to ridicule or criticize the original, or simply to amuse an audience.

PERSONIFICATION *A figure of speech in which human attributes are given to something that is not human.* In "Beware: Do Not Read This Poem," Ishmael Reed gives the poem characteristics of a ravenous person.
See **Figurative Language.**
See also pages 244, 324.

PERSUASION *Speech or writing for the purpose of influencing people's actions.* Newspaper editorials, essays, advertisements, and political speeches are all forms of persuasion.
See pages 158, 637.

PETRARCHAN SONNET *A fourteen-line lyric poem divided into an **octave** and a **sestet**.* Also known as the Italian sonnet, it is written in iambic pentameter and generally follows the rhyme scheme *abbaabba cdecde.* The octave establishes a proposition or problem and the sestet resolves it.
See **Octave, Sonnet.**
See also page 301.

PLOT *The sequence of related episodes that make up a story or drama.* A plot advances through cause-effect relationships. Plots may be very simple, as in sketches and some short stories, or they may be complex, with a major plot and a number of **subplots,** as in most novels.

Although some contemporary writers no longer follow traditional plot structure, it is still widely used and functions as a base for more experimental plots. A traditional plot includes **exposition** (background information), **conflict,** a **climax** where the conflict is resolved, and a **dénouement** that resolves the remaining complications of the plot. Chinua Achebe follows a traditional plot structure in "Dead Men's Path." The reader is introduced to the situation and characters in the exposition, and then engaged by the conflict between Michael Obi and the village priest, who represents ancient traditions and beliefs.
See pages 22, 472, 851, 937.

POETIC LICENSE *A writer's freedom to break conventional rules of language.* Poets often experiment with nonstandard word order, spelling, and punctuation in order to create mood or enhance meaning. Many contemporary poets use a great deal of poetic license.
See page 696.

POETRY *A literary form characterized by imagination, sensory impressions, and emotion.* It is difficult to define poetry, but easy to recognize it by its use of **imagery, figurative language,** and **rhythm.** Although traditional poetry is characterized by a regular rhythm and rhyme scheme, modern poetry often dispenses with these patterns and is written in **free verse.**

Poetry has been used in the ceremonies of most ancient civilizations. The first poetry was probably associated with music and dance, and chronicled important events in the lives of the people. There are many types of poetry: **dramatic poetry,** which presents characters who speak to others; **narrative poetry,** which tells a story and has characters, setting, and action; and **lyric poetry,** which is usually brief and expresses personal thoughts and feelings. Some of the traditional forms of poetry include the **ballad,** the **epic,** and the **sonnet.**
See pages 643–649.

POINT OF VIEW *The way in which a reader is presented with the action of a story.* The three most often used points of view are the omniscient, limited third-person, and first-person. A narrator who is "all-knowing" and not restricted to any time, place, or character is called **omniscient.** An author who tells a story from the vantage point of one character uses the **limited third-person point of view.** An author who has one of the characters tell the story in his or her own voice (from the "I" vantage point) uses the **first-person point of view.**
See **Narrator.**
See also pages 419, 430, 512, 517, 792, 853.

PROTAGONIST *The main character in a play, story, or film.* The character who opposes the protagonist is the **antagonist.**

See **Antagonist.**

PROVERB *A sentence or phrase which briefly and pointedly conveys some general truth about life.* Proverbs are usually about human relations and human weaknesses. They often use **metaphor** (A stitch in time saves nine), **parallelism** (Man proposes; God disposes), **rhyme** (When the cat is away, the mice will play), or **alliteration** (Speech is silver, but silence is golden).

Unlike most forms of literature, proverbs translate easily from one language and culture to another.

See **Aphorism.**
See also pages 92, 93.

QUATRAIN *Four lines of verse that are unified in thought and sometimes in rhyme.* The rhyme scheme of a quatrain is usually *abab, abba,* or *abcb.* A **Shakespearean sonnet** consists of three quatrains and a **couplet.**

See **Shakespearean Sonnet.**
See also page 722.

REALISM *The representation in literature of reality as it is.* Realism is often opposed to **romanticism.** Romantic literature presents life as more adventurous and heroic than it really is. The Realistic Period of American literature followed the Civil War (1865–1914). Mark Twain and Charles Chesnutt were major writers of realism. Many contemporary writers continue to write in this tradition.

See page 383.

REFRAIN *One or more words, phrases, or lines repeated at intervals in a poem, usually at the end of each stanza.* Many **ballads** and songs, particularly the **blues,** have refrains. Refrains serve to emphasize ideas or emotions.

See **Repetition.**
See also pages 247, 310.

REGIONALISM *The faithful re-creation of a particular geographical location in literature.* This involves the accurate representation of the region's habits, speech, manners, history, folklore, beliefs, and social structures.

A regionalism can also refer to a word or phrase used in a particular region. In Ernest Gaines's ''Robert Louis Stevenson Banks, aka Chimley,'' the characters use the regionalism *sackalay* for a kind of sunfish.

See **Dialect, Idiom.**
See also pages 512, 518.

REPETITION *A rhetorical device in which a word, phrase, or larger unit is repeated in a literary work.* Repetition is used to emphasize an idea and to create intensity. There are many kinds of repetition. **Parallelism** is used in both poetry and prose, while **refrain, rhyme, assonance,** and **alliteration** are used in poetry.

See **Alliteration, Assonance, Parallelism, Refrain, Rhyme.**
See also pages 247, 310, 615.

RESOLUTION *The events that follow the **climax** in a **plot.***

See pages 792, 851.

RHYME *The repetition of accented vowel sounds and all succeeding sounds in words or phrases that appear close together in a poem.*

One of the functions of rhyme is to contribute to the unity of a poem.

See **Rhyme Scheme.**
See also pages 247, 255, 310, 447, 668.

RHYME SCHEME *The pattern of rhymes in a stanza or poem.* Rhyme schemes are represented by using a small letter *a* for the first rhyme, *b* for the second, and so on.

See **Rhyme.**
See also pages 255, 310.

RHYTHM *In language, the pattern of stressed and unstressed syllables.* When the rhythm of words in a poem follows a regular pattern, it is called **meter.**

Rhythm is often used together with rhyme and contributes to the musicality of a poem. It can also contribute to the poem's meaning. The heavy accents that fall at the beginning of the lines of "Souffles" by Birago Diop emphasize the importance of listening. They also create a slow rhythm that is soothing and solemn.

> Listen more often to things than to beings
>> Hear the fire's voice,
>> Hear the voice of water.
>> Hear, in the wind, the sobbing of the trees.

See **Meter.**
See also page 336.

SATIRE *A literary style or work that uses criticism and wit to point out the faults or vices of individuals, groups, institutions, or society in general.* Satire is generally of two types: gentle and amusing, or forceful, bitter, even vicious.

In *Crick Crack, Monkey,* Merle Hodge uses satire to show that Sir is not only a bad teacher, but also a bully and a hypocrite.

Caricature is a type of satire generally used to attack personal qualities. It involves the exaggeration of characteristics, often to a ludicrous degree. Although this term is frequently used to describe drawings (cartoons) where certain features are exaggerated, it can also be used to describe writing that seizes upon certain aspects of a person and through exaggeration or distortion produces a ridiculous effect.

See pages 47, 51, 868.

SESTET *A group of six lines.* The term generally refers to the last six lines of a **Petrarchan** (Italian) **sonnet.** The sestet concludes or resolves the issue addressed in the first eight lines (**octave**). The sestet is generally in the rhyme scheme *cdecde.*

See **Petrarchan Sonnet.**
See also page 301.

SETTING *The time and place in which the action of a narrative takes place.* The setting is generally conveyed by **description.** In drama, it is established by the stage sets and through dialogue. Setting is often used to establish atmosphere or mood (the hot weather in "A Summer Tragedy") or to advance the plot (the recent civil war that is the backdrop of *The Wrestling Match*).

See **Atmosphere.**
See also pages 32, 484, 494, 872.

SHAKESPEAREAN SONNET *A lyric poem of fourteen lines of iambic pentameter, with three quatrains and a concluding couplet.* The rhyme scheme of the Shakespearean, or English, sonnet is usually *abab cdcd efef gg.* Each quatrain deals with a single thought, which is summed up or resolved in the **couplet.**

See **Sonnet.**
See also page 301.

SHORT STORY *A relatively brief fictional narrative in prose.* Because of its brevity, the short story is often limited to one main event and the development of one character or aspect of a character. Although the short story lacks the detail and complexity of the **novel,** it can still have a powerful impact through the compression of character and events.

See pages 469, 555, 567.

SIMILE *A figure of speech in which the similarity between two things is directly expressed by the use of words of comparison such as* like, as, than, such as, *or* resembles. Similes are frequently used in poetry and prose. They are also used in daily life. When you say, "Her fingers felt like ice," or "He was shaking like a leaf," you are using a simile.

See **Figurative Language, Metaphor.**
See also pages 42–43, 324, 509, 660.

SKETCH *A brief, simple composition that presents a single scene, character, and incident.* It lacks plot development and depth of characterization. Originally, the word meant preliminary work toward a short story or novel. Some, however, such as the "Simple" sketches by Langston Hughes, are finished products.

See page 330.

SLAVE NARRATIVES *Autobiographical accounts written by former slaves.* These narratives were sought out by abolitionist groups who used them to publicize the cruel treatment of the slaves and the inhumanity of the institution of slavery. Thousands of slave narratives were written. Among the most famous are those of Olaudah Equiano, Frederick Douglass, and Harriet A. Jacobs.

See **Autobiography.**
See also pages 138, 145.

SONNET *A lyric poem of fourteen lines, generally written in accordance with a given* **rhyme scheme** *and in* **iambic pentameter.** The most important sonnet forms are the Petrarchan (Italian) and Shakespearean (English). Examples include Paul Laurence Dunbar's "Douglass" (Petrarchan), and Claude McKay's "If We Must Die" (Shakespearean).

See **Octave, Petrarchan Sonnet, Sestet, Shakespearean Sonnet.**
See also pages 254–255, 297, 301.

SPEAKER *The voice in a poem.* Poets often speak in the voice of another person or an animal or inanimate object. Even when there is a first-person speaker (*I*), we cannot assume that the poet is speaking in his or her own voice. In Langston Hughes's "Mother to Son," the speaker is a woman.

See pages 321, 651.

SPIRITUALS *The religious folk songs of American slaves.* The rhythms of the spirituals reflect elements common in African music. These rhythms, as well as the **call-and-response** pattern, subsequently found their way into black secular music and became basic components of early blues and jazz.

See **Blues.**
See also page 187.

STAGE DIRECTIONS *A playwright's instructions telling the actors how to move and how to deliver certain lines.*

See **Drama.**
See also pages 737, 794.

STANZA *A group of lines that form a unit in a poem or song.* Some poets, such as Claude McKay, tend to write stanzas with a uniform length and rhyme scheme. Poems written in free verse, like Alice Walker's "For My Sister Molly Who in the Fifties," often use **variable stanzas.** Here the stanza divisions are dictated by content (each containing a unit of thought), rather than by the requirements of a given form.

See page 395.

STEREOTYPE *A commonly held, oversimplified mental picture or judgment of a group of people, an issue, or a kind of art.* Stereotypes are often based on racial, social, religious, or ethnic prejudices. In Dunbar's day, white readers expected stereotypes of African Americans as "happy darkies."

STYLE *The characteristic diction, sentence structure, and use of imagery and figurative language of a particular writer.* There are as many styles as there are writers. Styles range from serious to humorous, poetic to journalistic, formal to informal. Style can be thought of as a writer's signature. Just as no two signatures are alike, no two styles are alike.

See page 353.

SUBPLOT *A plot in a work of fiction that is secondary to the main plot.* In novels and dramas, there are sometimes several subplots. Subplots are usually closely related to the main plot and support one unified theme.

See **Plot.**

SUSPENSE *That quality in a story or drama that makes the reader wonder (or worry) about what will happen next.* Suspense is a major device for securing and maintaining a reader's interest. **Foreshadowing** is also used to create suspense.

See **Foreshadowing.**
See also pages 356, 399, 409, 822, 830.

SYMBOL *In a literary work, something which is itself and at the same time represents something else.* There are many common symbols: birds represent the spirit world; a rose is a symbol of love and beauty; a voyage is a symbol of the journey through life.

A writer lets the reader know through context when something should be interpreted as a symbol. Once we recognize a symbol, its greater meanings can resonate in our imaginations. The patchwork quilt in Alice Walker's story "Everyday Use" is a symbol of the family's ancestors and heritage.

See pages 324, 542, 551.

THEME *The central or dominating idea in a work of literature.* Theme usually involves some insight into life or human behavior. It is seldom expressed directly, but there are usually key passages in a work that indicate the theme. In longer works, such as novels and plays, there are often several interwoven themes.

Theme is different from subject. The subject of Chinua Achebe's "Dead Men's Path" is a young headmaster's progressive plans for his school. The theme involves reconciling progress toward the future with preservation of the past. Sometimes a theme will become apparent only after careful reading and thinking about a work.

See pages 54, 494, 526, 540, 551, 713.

TONE *The reflection of a writer's attitude, mood, and manner in his or her writing.* The counterpart in speech is tone of voice. Since you cannot hear the writer's voice, you must infer the tone from the words used and the way ideas are presented in the work. Tone may be warm or cool, serious or humorous, ironic or straightforward.

See pages 239, 346, 353, 520, 631, 675.

TRAGEDY *A form of literature that addresses a serious theme and usually ends with the death of the* **protagonist***.* Although tragedies may end with death and destruction, the audience is usually uplifted because the tragic hero or heroine has gained some wisdom from failure, and faces death with courage and dignity.

See page 399.

TRICKSTER *A character who uses cunning and trickery to outwit stronger enemies.* This character type is found in many African folk tales. He reappears in African American stories such as those featuring Brer Rabbit.

See pages 98, 181.

TURNING POINT See **CRISIS**.

See also page 938.

Glossary

This glossary is a short dictionary of words found in the selections in this textbook. Strictly speaking, the word *glossary* means a collection of technical, obscure, or foreign words used in a certain field of work. The words in this glossary are not "technical," "obscure," or "foreign," but some of them might present difficulty as you read this book.

The words are defined according to their meanings in the selections in this textbook. If you are interested in a more complete definition of a word, or in learning its history or other meanings, you should consult a college or an unabridged dictionary.

Words whose various forms are similar in meaning are listed together in one entry (**agile** and **agility**). Related words are listed separately when they generally appear that way in dictionaries or when their meanings are not quite the same (**apprehension** and **apprehensive**). Adverbs are listed after the definition of their adjective forms.

A pronunciation key appears at the bottom of the right column of every right-hand page.

The following abbreviations are used:

adj. adjective   *n.* noun   *v.* verb
adv. adverb   *n. pl.* noun plural

A

abandonment (ə-băn′dən-mənt) *n.* Unrestrained freedom of actions or emotions; surrender to one's impulses.

abate (ə-bāt′) *v.* To lessen.

abatement (ə-bāt′mənt) *n.* Reduction in intensity.

abeyance (ə-bā′əns) *n.* Temporary inactivity or suspension.

abhorrence (ab-hôr′əns) *n.* Loathing; disgust.

abject (ăb′jĕkt′) *adj.* **1.** Lacking in self-respect. **2.** Miserable; wretched.

abode (ə-bōd′) *n.* Dwelling place.

abrasion (ə-brā′zhən) *n.* A scraped area.

abrupt (ə-brŭpt′) *adj.* Sudden.—**abruptly** *adv.*

absolve (ăb-zŏlv′) *v.* To relieve of guilt.

absorbed (əb-zôrbd′) *adj.* Greatly interested; wholly occupied.

abusive (ə-byōō′sĭv, -zĭv) *adj.* Insulting; scolding.

accommodate (ə-kŏm′ə-dāt′) *v.* To provide a service or lodging for someone.

accomplice (ə-kom′plis) *n.* Partner in crime.

accumulate (ə-kyōōm′yə-lāt′) *v.* To pile up.

acknowledge (ăk-nŏl′ĭj) *v.* To recognize or take notice of.

adjoining (ə-joi′nĭng) *adj.* Next to.

admonish (ăd-mŏn′ĭsh) *v.* To scold.

adversity (ăd-vûr′sə-tē) *n.* Misfortune.

affliction (ə-flĭk′shən) *n.* A condition of pain or suffering.

affluent (ăf′lōō-ənt) *adj.* Rich; wealthy.

afford (ə-fôrd′) *v.* To give; provide.

affront (ə-frŭnt′) *n.* Insult or offense.

agape (ə-gāp′) *adv.* Wide open.

aggravate (ăg′rə-vāt′) *v.* To make worse.

agile (ăj′əl) *adj.* Capable of doing something quickly and easily.—**agility** (ə-jĭl′ə-tē) *n.*

agitate (ăj′ə-tāt′) *v.* To debate; arouse interest in.

agitation (ăj′ə-tā′shən) *n.* Emotional disturbance.

akin (ə-kĭn′) *adj.* Similar.

alien (ā′lē-ən, āl′yən) *adj.* Strange or different; foreign.

allay (ə-lā′) *v.* To reduce or relieve.

alleviate (ə-lē′vē-āt′) *v.* To relieve.

allusion (ə-lōō′zhən) *n.* Indirect mention.

alternation (ôl′tər-nā′shən) *n.* Change from one thing to another and back again.

alternative (ôl-tûr′nə-tĭv) *n.* A choice between two or more things.

ambivalent (ăm-bĭv′ə-lənt) *adj.* Wavering between conflicting emotions.

amble (ăm′bəl) *v.* To walk unhurriedly.

amends (ə-mĕndz′) *n.* Payment; reparation.

ample (ăm′pəl) *adj.* Of large size or amount; abundant.

anemia (ə-nē′mē-ə) *n.* A blood condition that leaves the victim weak and listless.

anguish (ăng′gwĭsh) *n.* Suffering, as from grief or pain; agony.

animosity (ăn′ə-mos′ə-tē) *n.* Hostility; hatred.

anonymity (ăn′ə-nĭm′ə-tē) *n.* Condition of being unknown.

antic (ăn′tĭk) *n.* A playful, silly, or ludicrous act; caper.

anticipation (ăn-tĭs′ə-pā′shən) *n.* Expectation.

antithesis (ăn-tĭth′ə-sĭs) *n.* A contrast or opposition.

aperture (ăp′ər-cho͝or′) *n.* Opening.

appall (ə-pôl′) *v.* To fill with dread or dismay.— **appalling** *adj.*

appease (ə-pēz′) *v.* To soothe; satisfy.— **appeasing** *adj.*—**appeasingly** *adv.*

appraise (ə-prāz′) *v.* To decide the worth of.

apprehension (ăp′rĭ-hĕn′shən) *n.* An anxious feeling of foreboding; dread.

apprehensive (ăp′rĭ-hĕn′sĭv) *adj.* Uneasy; fearful.

appropriate (ə-prō′prē-āt′) *v.* To take possession of.—(ə-prō′prē-ĭt) *adj.* Suitable.

apt (ăpt) *adj.* Unusually well suited.

archetypal (är′kə-tī′pəl) *adj.* Used as a model or pattern.

ardent (är′dənt) *adj.* Enthusiastic.

arid (ăr′ĭd) *adj.* Dry.

armoury (är′mər-ē) *n.* **1.** A storehouse for arms. **2.** An arms factory. A variant of *armory.*

array (ə-rā′) *v.* To arrange in an orderly manner.

arrogance (ăr′ə-gəns) *n.* Haughtiness; pride.— **arrogant** *adj.*

articulate (är-tĭk′yə-lĭt) *adj.* Able to speak clearly and expressively.

ascend (ə-sĕnd′) *v.* To go up.

ascribe (ə-skrīb′) *v.* To attribute to a specific cause.

aspiration (ăs′pə-rā′shən) *n.* Goal or high ambition.

assailant (ə-sā′lənt) *n.* Attacker.

assert (ə-sûrt′) *v.* To state one's position; claim.

asthma (ăz′mə) *n.* A chronic disease marked by coughing and difficulty in breathing.

asthmatic (az-mat′ik) *adj.* Having the characteristics of asthma.—**asthmatically** (ăz-măt′ĭk-lē) *adv.*

astride (ə-strīd′) *adj.* With legs wide apart.

atmospheric (ăt′məs-fîr′ĭk) *adj.* Filled with atmosphere; rich in mood.

atone (ə-tōn′) *v.* To make amends for wrongdoing.

attest (ə-tĕst′) *v.* To demonstrate.

attribute (ăt′rə-byo͞ot′) *n.* Characteristic.— (ə-trĭb′yo͞ot) *v.* To assign or ascribe to a particular cause.

audacity (ô-dăs′ə-tē) *n.* Boldness.

audible (ô′də-bəl) *adj.* Loud enough to be heard.

aura (ôr′ə) *n.* A particular atmosphere or quality surrounding a person or a place.

austere (ô-stîr′) *adj.* Severe; simple.

avail (ə-vāl′) *v.* To help; be of use.

avarice (ăv′ə-rĭs) *n.* Greed for wealth.

B

baffle (băf′əl) *v.* To confuse.

balk (bôk) *v.* To stop short and refuse to proceed.

barren (băr′ən) *adj.* Producing little or no vegetation; desolate.

beacon (bē′kən) *n.* A signal or guide.

beckon (bĕk′ən) *v.* To signal to someone by waving or nodding; summon.

beguile (bĭ-gīl′) *v.* To charm or please.

ă cat	ĭ sit	o͝o hook	oi soil
ā cane	ī kite	o͞o cool	ou mouse
â fare	ŏ mop	ŭ fun	ng king
ä calm	ō code	û turn	th think
ĕ set	ô for	yo͞o fumes	*th* that
ē me			zh fusion
			N *Fr.* mon

ə = { a in *cobra* e in *novel* i in *recipe* o in *concern* u in *awful* }

belittle (bĭ-lĭt′l) v. To speak of slightingly or as if of no importance.

bell (bĕl) n. The baying cry of certain animals; bellowing.

bemused (bĭ-myoozd′) adj. Bewildered; confused.

benediction (bĕn′ə-dĭk′shən) n. A blessing.

benevolent (bə-nĕv′ə-lənt) adj. Kindly.

benighted (bĭ-nī′tĭd) adj. Unenlightened.

bequeath (bĭ-kwēth′) v. To hand down.

bereaved (bĭ-rēvd′) adj. Deprived of by death.

bereft (bĭ-rĕft′) adj. Without; deprived of.

beset (bĭ-sĕt′) v. To harass; trouble.

bestow (bĭ-stō′) v. To give; present.

bicker (bĭk′ər) v. To squabble.

bilingual (bī-lĭng′gwəl) adj. In two languages.

bizarre (bĭ-zär′) adj. Extremely odd or strange.

bodice (bŏd′ĭs) n. The part of a dress extending from the shoulder to the waist.

bog (bôg, bŏg) n. Marsh.

boisterous (boi′stər-əs) adj. Loud; noisy.

boll (bōl) n. The rounded seed pod of certain plants such as cotton or flax.

bonanza (bə-nǎn′zə) n. A source of great wealth or prosperity.

booming (boo′mĭng) adj. Loud and deep.

bouquet (bō-kā′) n. A cluster of flowers.

brash (brǎsh) adj. 1. Impudent 2. Tactless.

bravado (brə-vä′dō) n. A show of false courage or defiance.

brazen (brā′zən) adj. Impudent; showing no shame.

brimstone (brĭm′stōn′) n. Sulfur (obsolete).

brisk (brĭsk) adj. Lively.—**briskly** adv.

brogue (brōg) n. A laced shoe with perforations.

brute (broot) adj. Without reason or feeling; cruel.

C

cabaret (kǎb′ə-rā′) n. A restaurant featuring floorshows.

calamitous (kə-lǎm′ə-təs) adj. Disastrous; causing great loss and sorrow.

calamity (kə-lǎm′ə-tē) n. Disaster.

calcify (kǎl′sə-fī′) v. To become hard because of calcium salts deposits.

cannonade (kǎn′ə-nād′) n. Bombardment; heavy attack.

caper (kā′pər) n. 1. A leap. 2. A prank.

caprice (kə-prēs′) n. A sudden change of mind; whim.

captivate (kǎp′tə-vāt′) v. To fascinate.

carbide (kär′bīd′) n. A carbon compound.

carrion (kǎr′ē-ən) n. Decaying flesh of a carcass, used as food by scavenging animals.

cart (kärt) v. To carry or transport, usually by force.

cascade (kǎs-kād′) v. To fall from one level to another.

cast (kǎst) n. Complexion; color.

catapult (kǎt′ə-pŭlt′) v. To leap or spring up suddenly.

catcall (kǎt′kôl′) n. Derisive whistles; boos.

cavernous (kǎv′ər-nəs) adj. Like a cavern; vast.

cavort (kə-vôrt′) v. To jump or prance about merrily.

celebrant (sĕl′ə-brənt) n. A person who performs or observes a religious ceremony.

chant (chǎnt) n. A rhythmic call or shout.

chaotic (kā-ŏt′ĭk) adj. Confused; disordered.

chary (châr′ē) adj. Not giving freely.

chasten (chā′sən) v. To punish.

chauffeur (shō′fər) n. Hired driver of a private automobile.

cheeky (chē′kē) adj. Rude; saucy; disrespectful.

chide (chīd) v. To scold; reprove.

chronic (krŏn′ĭk) adj. Constant; continuing for a long time.

churn (chûrn) v. To shake or stir violently.

circuitous (sər-kyoo′-ə-təs) adj. Roundabout; indirect.

clamber (klǎm′bər) v. To climb on all fours.

clime (klīm) n. Region.

clod (klŏd) n. 1. A lump or mass of earth or clay. 2. A dull or stupid person.

cloddish (klŏd′ĭsh) adj. Dull; ignorant.

clout (klout) n. A blow with the fist.

collard (kŏl′ərd) n. A type of leafy green vegetable.

collide (kə-līd′) v. To clash.

colloquialism (kə-lō′kwē-ə-lĭz′əm) n. A conversational or casual expression.

colossal (kə-lŏs′əl) adj. Gigantic.

combative (kəm-bǎt′ĭv) adj. Eager to fight.

commence (kə-měns') *v.* To begin.

commentative (kŏm'ən-tā'tĭv) *adj.* Of or relating to comments.

commissary (kŏm'ə-sĕr'ē) *n.* A store at a lumber camp, army camp, etc., providing food and supplies.

commission (kə-mĭsh'ən) *v.* To order or request something.

commodious (kə-mō'dē-əs) *adj.* Roomy; spacious.

commodity (kə-mŏd'ə-tē) *n.* An article that has commercial value.

commune (kə-myōōn') *v.* **1.** To converse in a close, intimate manner. **2.** To be in close rapport with.

compact (kŏm'păkt') *adj.* Dense; closely put together.—(kəm-pakt') *v.* To pack tightly.

compassion (kəm-păsh'ən) *n.* Feeling for the sufferings of others.

compel (kəm-pěl') *v.* To force to do something.

compelling (kəm-pěl'ĭng) *adj.* Forceful; requiring submission.

compensation (kŏm'pən-sā'shən) *n.* Payment or reward.

complacent (kəm-plā'sənt) *adj.* Self-satisfied; smug.

comply (kəm-plī') *v.* To act in agreement with someone's request or wish.

composure (kəm-pō'zhər) *n.* Calmness of mind or manner; self-possession.

comprehend (kŏm'prĭ-hěnd') *v.* To understand.

comprise (kəm-prīz') *v.* To include.

compromise (kŏm'prə-mīz') *v.* To settle by making concessions.

compulsory (kəm-pŭl'sə-rē) *adj.* Required; obligatory.

concede (kən-sēd') *v.* To admit; acknowledge.

conceivable (kən-sēv'ə-bəl) *adj.* Capable of being understood or believed.

conceive (kən-sēv') *v.* To imagine.

conclusive (kən-klōō'sĭv) *adj.* Decisive; putting an end to uncertainty.—**conclusiveness** *n.*

concordance (kən-kôr'dəns) *n.* Agreement; harmony.

concurrent (kən-kûr'ənt) *adj.* In agreement.

condiment (kŏn'də-mənt) *n.* Something used to season food.

confine (kən-fīn') *v.* To keep within certain limits; restrict.

confirm (kən-fûrm') *v.* To establish as true; make certain.

confirmation (kŏn'fər-mā'shən) *n.* Verification or proof.

confront (kən-frŭnt') *v.* To come face to face with.

congenial (kən-jēn'yəl) *adj.* Agreeable.—**congenially** *adv.*

conscientious (kŏn'shē-ĕn'shəs) *adj.* Thorough and careful.—**conscientiousness** *n.*

consolation (kŏn'sə-lā'shən) *n.* Comfort.—**console** *v.*

conspiratorial (kən-spîr'ə-tôr'ē-əl, -tōr'ē-əl) *adj.* Indicating participation in a secret plot.

constable (kŏn'stə-bəl) *n.* Peace officer.

consternation (kŏn'stər-nā'shən) *n.* Great fear or bewilderment.

constitute (kŏn'stə-tōōt', -tyōōt') *v.* To compose; make up.

constrain (kən-strān') *v.* **1.** To force into; confine. **2.** To hold back by force; restrain.

constrained (kən-strānd) *adj.* Compelled; obliged; made to feel that it is necessary to do something.

consume (kən-sōōm', -syōōm') *v.* **1.** To destroy, as by fire; do away with. **2.** To use up; squander.

consumption (kən-sŭmp'shən) *n.* Tuberculosis.

contemplate (kŏn'təm-plāt') *v.* To look at intently.

contempt (kən-těmpt') *n.* Scorn.—**contemptuous** *adj.*

contend (kən-těnd') *v.* to strive; struggle.

contingency (kən-tĭn'jən-sē) *n.* Future emergency.

ă cat	ĭ sit	o͞o hook	oi soil
ā cane	ī kite	o͞o cool	ou mouse
â fare	ŏ mop	ŭ fun	ng king
ä calm	ō code	û turn	th think
ě set	ô for	yo͞o fumes	*th* that
ē me			zh fusion
			N *Fr.* mon

ə = { a in *cobra* e in *novel* i in *recipe* o in *concern* u in *awful* }

contravene (kŏn'trə-vēn') v. To oppose.

contrive (kən-trīv') v. To plan or invent.

conviction (kən-vĭk'shən) n. A strong belief.

copious (kō'pē-əs) adj. Plentiful.

cordial (kôr'jəl) adj. Courteous; friendly.

cordialities (kôr'jăl'ə-tēz) n. pl. Warm and friendly acts or remarks.

cordovan (kôr'də-vən) adj. A dark grayish red.

corrugated (kôr'ə-gā'tĭd) adj. Shaped in parallel grooves and ridges.

countenance (koun'tə-nəns) n. The look on a person's face that shows one's nature or feelings.

counteract (koun'tər-ăkt') v. To oppose; check.

counterpart (koun'tər-pärt') n. Something that closely resembles another.

court (kôrt) v. To try to win the love or attention of.

cower (kou'ər) v. To cringe; shrink away in fear.

crane (krān) v. To stretch one's neck in order to see something.

crescendo (krə-shĕn'dō) n. A gradual increase in loudness or intensity of music.

crevice (krĕv'ĭs) n. A narrow crack.

crimson (krĭm'zən) adj. Vivid red.

crockery (krŏk'ə-rē) n. Earthenware.

croon (krōōn) v. To sing softly.

crouch (krouch) v. To stoop with the legs pulled close to the body.

crude (krōōd) adj. Rough; vulgar; rude.—**crudely** adv.

cryptic (krĭp'tĭk) adj. Mysterious; difficult to understand.

cull (kŭl) v. To pick out something from an assortment of.

culminate (kŭl'mə-nāt') v. To result in.

cunning (kŭn'ĭng) adj. Arful; dexterous.

curing (kyōōr'ĭng) n. The process of preserving meat or fish, as by salting or smoking.

curry (kûr'ē) v. To groom a horse with a currycomb.

curt (kûrt) adj. Brief or abrupt in speech.

D

dais (dā'ĭs, dās) n. A raised platform at one end of a room or hall.

deadlock (dĕd'lŏk') n. A standstill between two opposing forces.

declaim (dĭ-klām') v. To speak or recite loudly and forcefully.

decorous (dĕk'ə-rəs, dĭ-kôr'əs) adj. Showing correct behavior.—**decorously** adv.

decree (dĭ-krē') n. An order which has the force of law.

decrepit (dĭ-krĕp'ĭt) adj. Broken down.

default (dĭ-fôlt') v. To fail to pay; to renege on a promise.

defer (dĭ-fûr') v. To put off something to a future time.

deflate (dĭ-flāt') v. To collapse.

deflect (dĭ-flĕkt') v. To turn aside.

degenerate (dĭ-jĕn'ə-rāt') v. To change for the worse; deteriorate.

degradation (dĕg'rə-dā'shən) n. Decline in dignity or self-respect; humiliation.

degrade (dĭ-grād') v. To reduce in dignity or prestige; disgrace; debase.

deity (dē'ə-tē) n. A god or goddess.

deliberation (dĭ-lĭb'ə-rā'shən) n. Discussion and debate about an issue.

delusion (dĭ-lōō'zhən, -lyōō') n. False belief.

demean (dĭ-mēn') v. To debase.

demented (dĭ-mĕn'tĭd) adj. Wild; mad.

denigration (dĕn'ĭ-grā'shən) n. Belittling of character or reputation.

denounce (dĭ-nouns') v. To condemn.

deplorable (dĭ-plôr'ə-bəl) adj. Wretched.

depot (dē'pō) n. A bus or train station.

derision (dĭ-rĭzh'ən) n. Contempt; ridicule.

derive (dĭ-rīv') v. To receive or obtain.

designate (dĕz'ĭg-nāt') v. To point out.

desist (dĭ-zĭst') v. To stop.

desolation (dĕs'ə-lā'shən) n. Ruin.

detainee (dĭ-tān'ē) n. One who is kept in custody.

devastate (dĕv'ə-stāt') v. To ruin or waste.

devastation (dĕv'ə-stā'shən) n. Destruction.

devious (dē'vē-əs) adj. **1.** Roundabout; not direct. **2.** Dishonest.

devoid (dĭ-void') adj. Without; lacking (used with of).

devotee (dĕv'ə-tē', -tā') n. A believer in and devoted follower of.

devour (dĭ-vour') v. To swallow or eat up greedily.

diabolic (dī'ə-bŏl'ĭk) *adj.* Characteristic of the devil; satanic.

diagnosis (dī'əg-nō'sĭs) *n.* Analysis of an illness through examination.

diehard (dī'härd') *n.* One who stubbornly refuses to give in or change.

diffusion (dĭ-fyōo'zhən) *n.* Spreading out; dispersion.

dirge (dûrj) *n.* Lament or funeral song.

disarming (dĭs-är'mĭng) *adj.* Pleasing.

discernible (dĭ-sûr'nə-bəl) *adj.* Able to be made out or recognized.

disciple (dĭ-sī'pəl) *n.* One who follows and spreads the teachings of another.

discord (dĭs'kôrd') *n.* Harsh disagreement which prevents unified action.

discourse (dĭs'kôrs') *n.* Talk; speech.— (dĭs-kôrs') *v.* To speak at length.

discredit (dĭs-krĕd'ĭt) *v.* To cast doubt on the reputation of.

discreet (dĭs-krēt') *adj.* **1.** Careful. **2.** Modest; not showy.

disdain (dĭs-dān') *n.* Scorn; contempt.

disembarkation (dĭs-ĭm'bär'kā'shən) *n.* Going ashore from a ship.

dispense (dĭs-pĕns') *v.* To deal out.

disperse (dĭs-pûrs') *v.* To scatter.

dispirited (dĭs-pîr'ĭt-ĭd) *adj.* Dejected; low in spirits.

disport (dĭs-pôrt') *v.* To play; frolic.

dispose (dĭs-pōz') *v.* **1.** To arrange. **2.** To put in a mood for; make willing.

disposed (dĭs-pōzd') *adj.* Tending toward.

disposition (dĭs'-pə-zĭsh'ən) *n.* One's nature or temperament.

dispossessed (dĭs'pə-zĕsd') *adj.* Deprived of property.

dispraise (dĭs-prāz') *n.* Censure; reproach.

dispute (dĭs-pyōot') *n.* Debate.

disrupt (dĭs-rŭpt') *v.* **1.** To create disorder; break apart. **2.** To disturb; interrupt the progress of.

dissension (dĭ-sĕn'shən) *n.* Conflict; disagreement.

dissonant (dĭs'ə-nənt) *adj.* Harsh or unpleasant-sounding.

distort (dĭs-tôrt') *v.* **1.** To twist into a strained expression. **2.** To misrepresent.

distraction (dĭs-trăk'shən) *n.* Great distress.

ditty (dĭt'ē) *n.* Simple song.

docile (dŏs'əl, -sīl') *adj.* Submissive.

dog (dôg, dŏg) *v.* To hunt or track persistently.

dogged (dô'gĭd, dŏg'ĭd) *adj.* Persistent; stubborn.—**doggedly** *adv.*

dominant (dŏm'ə-nənt) *adj.* Most influential.

draught (drăft) *n.* A British variant of *draft.*

drone (drōn) *v.* To make a low, continuing sound.

drove (drōv) *n.* A large number, driven or moving along as a group.

dumbfoundment (dŭm'found'mənt) *n.* Amazement.

dupe (dōop, dyōop) *v.* To trick or fool someone who is easily deceived.

duration (dōo-rā'shən, dyōo-) *n.* The time something lasts.

E

edifice (ĕd'ə-fĭs) *n.* A building, especially a large, impressive one.

elate (ĭ-lāt') *v.* To make very happy or proud.

elation (ĭ-lā'shən) *n.* Exalted feeling; high spirits.

elite (ĭ-lēt', ā-lēt') *n.* A small, privileged group.

elongated (ĭ-lŏng'gāt'-əd) *adj.* Stretched out.

elude (ĭ-lōod') *v.* To avoid; escape from.

elusive (ĭ-lōo'sĭv) *adj.* Hard to describe or identify.

emanate (ĕm'ə-nāt') *v.* To come forth; issue.

embassy (ĕm'bə-sē) *n.* Ambassador and his staff.

emissary (ĕm'ə-sĕr'ē) *n.* Messenger.

ă cat	ĭ sit	ŏo hook	oi soil
ā cane	ī kite	ōo cool	ou mouse
â fare	ŏ mop	ŭ fun	ng king
ä calm	ō code	û turn	th think
ě set	ô for	yōo fumes	*th* that
ē me			zh fusion
			N *Fr.* mon

ə = { a in *cobra* e in *novel* i in *recipe*
      o in *concern* u in *awful*

emulate (ĕm′yə-lāt′) *v.* To imitate in an effort to equal.

encase (ĕn-kās′) *v.* To enclose; cover completely.

encore (äng′kôr) *n.* A demand, as by applause, for the repetition of a song or an act, or for an additional performance.

encounter (ĕn-koun′tər, ĭn-) *v.* To happen to meet.

endow (ĕn-dou′, ĭn-) *v.* To provide with; supply.

endowment (ĕn-dou′mənt, ĭn-) *n.* Natural ability or gift.

engross (ĕn-grōs′, ĭn-) *v.* To hold the attention of.—**engrossing** *adj.*

engulf (ĕn-gŭlf′, ĭn-) *v.* To overwhelm, as by a flood.

enlighten (ĕn-līt′n, ĭn-) *v.* To inform; instruct.

enlightenment (ĕn-līt′n-mənt, ĭn-) *n.* Knowledge that opens the mind and gives insight into some problem.

enterprising (ĕn′tər-prī-zĭng) *adj.* Imaginative; ready to try.

entity (ĕn′tə-tē) *n.* A unit or indivisible whole.

entreat (ĕn-trēt′) *v.* To ask for earnestly; plead.

envelop (ĕn-vĕl′əp, ĭn-) *v.* **1.** To enclose. **2.** To surround.

envision (ĕn-vĭzh′ən) *v.* To imagine; picture.

epical (ĕp′ĭ-kəl) *adj.* Impressive; heroic.

epitome (ĭ-pĭt′ə-mē) *n.* A person or thing that is representative of a whole class or type.

epoch (ĕp′ək, ē′pŏk′) *n.* A noteworthy period.

eradicate (ĭ-răd′ĭ-kāt′) *v.* To get rid of; wipe out.

erect (ĭ-rĕkt′) *adj.* Standing upright.

erode (ĭ-rōd′) *v.* To eat away; make disappear.

exalt (ĕg-zôlt′, ĭg-) *v.* To fill with pride or joy.

exasperate (ĕg-zăs′pə-rāt′, ĭg-) *v.* To make angry; irritate.

excursion (ĕk-skûr′zhən, ĭk-) *n.* Short journey.

exhilaration (ĕg-zĭl′ə-rā′shən, ĭg-) *n.* High spirits.

exile (ĕg′zīl′, ĕk′sīl′) *n.* Banishment from one's homeland.

exotic (ĕg-zŏt′ĭk, ĭg-) *adj.* Interestingly different; unusual and fascinating.

expectancy (ĕk-spĕk′tən-sē, ĭk-) *n.* The act or state of expecting; expectation.

expire (ĕk-spīr′, ĭk-) *v.* To die.

exploit (ĕks′ploit′) *n.* A heroic act or deed.

extract (ĕk-străkt′) *v.* To pull away from.

extracurricular (ĕk′strə-kə-rĭk′yə-lər) *adj.* Outside of or apart from formal schooling.

exult (ĕg-zŭlt′, ĭg-) *v.* To rejoice.

exultant (ĕg-zŭl′tənt, ĭg-) *adj.* Triumphant; jubilant.

F

facile (făs′əl) *adj.* Effortless; easy.

fatuity (fə-tyoo′ə-tē) *n.* Foolishness.

feign (fān) *v.* To pretend.

ferment (fûr′ment′) *n.* A state of unrest.

fervent (fûr′vənt) *adj.* Expressing great emotion.

fervor (fûr′vər) *n.* Intensity of feeling.

fester (fĕs′tər) *v.* To form pus.

fickle (fĭk′əl) *adj.* Not constant in loyalty or affection; changeable.

fidget (fĭj′ĭt) *v.* To behave restlessly.

fiscal (fĭs′kəl) *adj.* Pertaining to finances.

fitful (fĭt′fəl) *adj.* Irregular.

flail (flāl) *v.* To beat or thrash.

flaunt (flônt) *v.* To show off.

flicker (flĭk′ər) *n.* A flutter or brief movement.

flinch (flĭnch) *v.* To draw back suddenly, as from pain.

flinty (flĭn′tē) *adj.* Stern; unyielding.

flog (flŏg, flôg) *v.* To whip.

flounder (floun′dər) *v.* To move in confusion.

flourish (flûr′ĭsh) *v.* To flower; grow in a healthy way.

flout (flout) *v.* To show scorn for.

fluid (floo′ĭd) *adj.* Effortless.—**fluidly** *adv.*

fluster (flŭs′tər) *v.* To make nervous; confuse.

foliage (fō′lē-ĭj) *n.* Leaves and branches.

foreknowledge (fôr-nŏl′ĭj) *n.* Knowledge of something before it happens.

formality (fôr-măl′ə-tē) *n.* Something done for the sake of form or custom.

formidable (fôr′mə-də-bəl) *adj.* Awesome; fearful.

fortify (fôr′tə-fī′) *v.* To strengthen; reinforce.

fortitude (fôr′tə-tood′, tyood′) *n.* Courage.

fragile (frăj′əl) *adj.* Delicate.

frantic (frăn′tĭk) *adj.* Wild with pain or anger.—**frantically** *adv.*

frenzy (frĕn′zē) *n.* Agitation.

fruition (froo-ĭsh′ən) *n.* Accomplishment.

fumble (fŭm'bəl) v. To feel about for something awkwardly or clumsily.

functional (fŭngk'shən-əl) adj. Able to perform a task satisfactorily.

funereal (fyŏŏ-nîr'ē-əl) adj. Mournful.

furtive (fûr'tĭv) adj. Stealthy; sneaky.— **furtively** adv.

futile (fyŏŏt'l) adj. Without any effort.

gross (grōs) adj. Distasteful. *(Slang)*

grotesque (grō-tĕsk') adj. Strange or ugly in appearance.

grovel (grŏv'əl, grŭv'-) v. To creep face downward.

guile (gīl) n. Deceit; slyness.

guileless (gīl'lĭs) adj. Simple.

guttural (gŭt'ər-əl) adj. Coming from the throat.

G

gad (găd) v. To wander about in an aimless way.

gait (gāt) n. Way of walking or running.

gall (gôl) v. To irritate.

garnish (gär'nĭsh) v. To embellish; add decorative touches to.

garret (găr'ĭt) n. Attic.

ghastly (găst'lē, gäst'-) adj. Very unpleasant; horrid.

ghetto (gĕt'ō) n. A section of a city, usually a slum, occupied by a minority group.

gild (gĭld) v. To cover with a thin layer of gold.

gingerly (jĭn'jər-lē) adv. Carefully.

gingham (gĭng'əm) n. Cotton cloth woven in a pattern of stripes, checks, or plaids.

glare (glâr) v. To stare fixedly and angrily.

glean (glēn) v. To gather grain from a field that has been reaped.

glimmer (glĭm'ər) v. To flicker.

goad (gōd) v. To urge into action by teasing or bullying.

gospel (gŏs'pəl) n. Absolute truth, as from the Bible.

gouge (gouj) v. To dig out.

gourd (gôrd) n. The dried, hollowed-out shell of a fruit such as a pumpkin or calabash, used as a container.

grapple (grăp'əl) v. To struggle or wrestle.

grave (grāv) adj. Serious.—**gravely** adv.

Greco-Roman (grĕ'kō-rō'mən) adj. Influenced by Greece and Rome.

grievance (grē'vəns) n. Complaint.

grimace (grĭm'ĭs, grĭ-mās') n. An expression of pain or annoyance; a twisting of the face.

grimy (grī'mē) adj. Covered with dirt.

grizzly (grĭz'lē) adj. Grayish.

grope (grōp) v. To search uncertainly.

H

habitation (hăb'ə-tā'shən) n. Dwelling place.

haggard (hăg'ərd) adj. Worn.

hallow (hăl'ō) v. To make sacred; bless.

hammy (hăm'ē) adj. Characterized by overacting.

haphazard (hăp-hăz'ərd) adj. Without plan or order.

haste (hāst) n. Quickness; swiftness.

haven (hā'vən) n. Place of refuge.

headmaster (hĕd'măs'tər) n. Male principal of a school.

hearken (här'kən) v. To listen.

hedge (hĕj) v. To avoid giving a direct answer.

hefty (hĕf'tē) adj. Large; muscular.

helpmeet (hĕlp'mēt') n. Companion and helper; spouse.

hiding (hīd'ĭng) n. A whipping.

high-handed (hī'hăn'dĭd) adj. Acting without proper discretion or regard for others.

hind (hīnd) n. Female deer.

homage (hŏm'ĭj, ŏ'-) n. A public expression of honor or respect.

ă cat	ĭ sit	ŏŏ hook	oi soil
ā cane	ī kite	ōō cool	ou mouse
â fare	ŏ mop	ŭ fun	ng king
ä calm	ō code	û turn	th think
ĕ set	ô for	yŏŏ fumes	*th* that
ē me			zh fusion
			N *Fr.* mon

ə = { a in *cobra* e in *novel* i in *recipe*
      { o in *concern* u in *awful*

homogeneous (hō'mə-jē'nē-əs, -jēn'yəs, hŏm'ə-) *adj.* With all parts alike.

horde (hôrd) *n.* A swarm.

hound (hound) *v.* To pursue relentlessly; pester.

hover (hŭv'ər) *v.* **1.** To remain suspended in the air. **2.** To remain close beside or to linger near a place.

I

idol (īd'l) *n.* False god.

illusive (ĭ-lōō'sĭv) *adj.* Unreal; like an illusion.

imbue (ĭm-byōō') *v.* To fill with.

immemorial (ĭm'ə-môr'ē-əl) *adj.* Beyond recorded history.

imminence (ĭm'ə-nəns) *n.* Something about to occur.

immobile (ĭ-mō'bəl) *adj.* Fixed; motionless.

immobilize (ĭ-mō'bə-līz') *v.* To prevent movement.

imp (ĭmp) *n.* A mischievous child.

impale (ĭm-pāl') *v.* To pierce with something sharp.

impart (ĭm-pärt') *v.* To give.

impassive (ĭm-păs'ĭv) *adj.* Showing no emotion.—**impassively** *adv.*

impenetrable (ĭm-pĕn'ə-trə-bəl) *adj.* **1.** Not able to be entered or penetrated. **2.** Not capable of being understood.—**impenetrably** *adv.*

imperative (ĭm-pĕr'ə-tĭv) *adj.* Necessary; required.

impersonality (ĭm-pûr'sən-ăl'ĭ-tē) *n.* The state of being impersonal or detached.

impertinent (ĭm-pûrt'n-ənt) *adj.* Insolent; disrespectful; rude.

impious (ĭm'pē-əs, ĭm-pī') *adj.* Lacking respect or reverence for God.

implant (ĭm-plănt') *v.* To fix firmly.

implement (ĭm'plə-mənt) *n.* Tool or instrument.

implore (ĭm-plôr') *v.* To plead or beg.

import (ĭm'pôrt') *n.* Meaning.

impose (ĭm-pōz') *v.* To force upon someone or something.

imposing (ĭm-pō'zĭng) *adj.* Grand; impressive.

impotent (ĭm'pə-tənt) *adj.* Powerless.—**impotently** *adv.*

impoverish (ĭm-pŏv'ər-ĭsh) *v.* To make poor.

improbable (ĭm-prŏb'ə-bəl) *adj.* Unlikely; unbelievable.

improvident (ĭm-prŏv'ə-dənt) *adj.* Lacking foresight.

impudent (ĭm'pyə-dənt) *adj.* Bold and shameless.

impulsive (ĭm-pŭl'sĭv) *adj.* Acting on impulse.

incantation (ĭn'kăn-tā'shən) *n.* The chanting of magical words.

incense (ĭn-sĕns') *v.* To cause to become very angry.—**incensed** *adj.*

incessant (ĭn-sĕs'ənt) *adj.* Constant; continual.

incite (ĭn-sīt') *v.* To stir up.

incoherency (ĭn'kō-hîr'ən-sē) *n.* Something that lacks order or clear connections.

inconceivable (ĭn'kən-sē'və-bəl) *adj.* That which cannot be imagined or believed.

inconsolable (ĭn'kən-sō'lə-bəl) *adj.* Despondent; not capable of being comforted; brokenhearted.

incontinent (ĭn-kŏn'tə-nənt) *adj.* Unable to control bodily discharge, as of urine.

incredulous (ĭn-krĕj'ə-ləs) *adj.* Unwilling or unable to believe; doubting; skeptical.—**incredulously** *adv.*

incur (ĭn-kûr') *v.* To bring upon oneself.

indifference (ĭn-dĭf'ər-əns) *n.* The state of being unconcerned.

indifferent (ĭn-dĭf'ər-ənt) *adj.* **1.** Showing no interest. **2.** Insignificant; of no great importance.—**indifferently** *adv.*

indignant (ĭn-dĭg'nənt) *adj.* Angry at some unfairness or injustice.—**indignantly** *adv.*

indispensable (ĭn'dĭs-pĕn'sə-bəl) *adj.* Essential.

indisputable (ĭn'dĭs-pyōō'tə-bəl) *adj.* With no basis for argument or question.

indulge (ĭn-dŭlj') *v.* **1.** To yield to some desire. **2.** To grant as a kindness.

indulgent (ĭn-dŭl'jənt) *adj.* Easy-going; kind; lenient.—**indulgently** *adv.*

inevitable (ĭn-ĕv'ə-tə-bəl) *adj.* Certain; unavoidable.

inexplicable (ĭn-ĕk'splĭ-kə-bəl) *adj.* Not possible to explain.—**inexplicably** *adv.*

inextricable (ĭn-ĕk'strĭ-kə-bəl) *adj.* Without possibility of being separated from.—**inextricably** *adv.*

infectious (ĭn-fĕk'shəs) *adj.* Spreading rapidly from one source to others.

inferno (ĭn-fûr′nō) *n.* A place likened to hell, usually with heat and flames.

infirm (ĭn-fûrm′) *adj.* Weak; feeble.

inflexible (ĭn-flĕk′sə-bəl) *adj.* Not capable of being changed.

influx (ĭn′flŭks′) *n.* Coming in.

infuse (ĭn-fyōoz′) *v.* To fill with feeling; inspire.

ingenuity (ĭn′jə-nōo′ə-tē, -nyōo′ə-tē) *n.* Inventiveness; cleverness.

inglorious (ĭn-glôr′ē-əs) *adj.* Dishonorable.

inherent (ĭn-hîr′ənt) *adj.* Essential.

initiate (ĭ-nĭsh′ē-āt′) *v.* **1.** To begin. **2.** To admit as a member.

inordinate (ĭn-ôrd′n-ĭt) *adj.* Lacking restraint; excessive.

inscription (ĭn-skrĭp′shən) *n.* Something that is written, printed, or engraved to last.

insinuation (ĭn-sĭn′yōo-ā′shən) *n.* A sly hint or suggestion against someone.

insolence (ĭn′sə-ləns) *n.* Disrespect; rudeness.—**insolent** *adj.*—**insolently** *adv.*

instinctive (ĭn-stĭngk′tĭv) *adj.* Unthinking; spontaneous.—**instinctively** *adv.*

insupportable (ĭn-sə-pôr′tə-bəl) *adj.* Unbearable.

inter (ĭn-tûr′) *v.* To bury.

interminable (ĭn-tûr′mə-nə-bəl) *adj.* Endless.

interpose (ĭn′tər-pōz′) *v.* To place (oneself) between.

intersperse (ĭn′tər-spûrs′) *v.* To scatter.

interstice (ĭn-tûr′stĭs) *n.* Narrow space.

intertwine (ĭn′tər-twīn′) *v.* To interlace or join by twisting together.

intervene (ĭn′tər-vēn′) *v.* To come between.

intimate (ĭn′tə-mĭt) *adj.* Personal; private.—(ĭn′tə-māt′) *v.* To imply; hint.

intimidate (ĭn-tĭm′ə-dāt′) *v.* **1.** To make timid or afraid. **2.** To threaten.

intolerable (ĭn-tŏl′ər-ə-bəl) *adj.* Unbearable.—**intolerably** *adv.*

intone (ĭn-tōn′) *v.* To speak in a singing tone; chant.

intricate (ĭn′trĭ-kĭt) *adj.* Complex; elaborate.

intriguing (ĭn-trēg′ĭng) *adj.* Arousing interest or curiosity.

intrinsic (ĭn-trĭn′zĭk, -sĭk) *adj.* Essential; characteristic.

intuitive (ĭn-tōo′ə-tĭv, ĭn-tyōo′-) *adj.* Not based on conscious reasoning but on inner feeling.—**intuitively** *adv.*

invariable (ĭn-vâr′ē-ə-bəl) *adj.* Unchanging.—**invariably** *adv.*

invest (ĭn-vĕst′) *v.* To endow with power or influence.

invigorate (ĭn-vĭg′ə-rāt′) *v.* To give energy or life to.—**invigorating** *adj.*

involuntary (ĭn-vŏl′ən-tĕr′ē) *adj.* **1.** Not done of one's free will. **2.** Automatic.—**involuntarily** *adv.*

irascible (ĭ-răs′ə-bəl) *adj.* Easily angered.

irrational (ĭ-răsh′ən-əl) *adj.* Unreasonable; illogical.

irreverent (ĭ-rĕv′ər-ənt) *adj.* Disrespectful.

Islamic (ĭs-läm′ĭk) *adj.* Belonging to the religion of Islam.

J

jagged (jăg′ĭd) *adj.* Ragged; having a rough surface.

jamboree (jăm′bə-rē′) *n.* A noisy party or celebration.

jaunty (jôn′tē) *adj.* Carefree; sprightly; perky.—**jauntily** *adv.*

javelin (jăv′ə-lĭn) *n.* A light spear.

jeer (jîr) *n.* A sarcastic or derisive comment.

jellied (jĕl′ēd) *adj.* Thick; like jelly.

jest (jĕst) *n.* A playful, joking manner.

jibe (jīb) *n.* Taunt.

joist (joist) *n.* A horizontal beam supporting the boards of a floor or ceiling.

jostle (jŏs′əl) *v.* To push or shove.

ă cat	ĭ sit	ŏŏ hook	oi soil
ā cane	ī kite	ōō cool	ou mouse
â fare	ŏ mop	ŭ fun	ng king
ä calm	ō code	û turn	th think
ĕ set	ô for	yōo fumes	*th* that
ē me			zh fusion
			N *Fr.* mon

ə = { a in *cobra* e in *novel* i in *recipe* o in *concern* u in *awful* }

jowl (joul) *n.* **1.** The jawbone. **2.** The meat from the cheeks of a hog.

jubilant (jōō′bə-lənt) *adj.* Joyful.

jubilee (jōō′bə-lē′) *n.* Celebration.

junction (jŭngk′shən) *n.* The place where two things join.

justification (jŭs′tə-fĭ-kā′shən) *n.* Good reason for.

K

kinsman (kĭnz′mən) *n.* A relative.

knot (nŏt) *n.* A small group of people or things.

L

lacerate (lăs′ə-rāt′) *v.* To tear.

lag (lăg) *v.* To slow up; fall behind.

lair (lâr) *n.* Den of a wild animal.

languish (lăng′gwĭsh) *v.* To grow weak and feeble.—**languishing** *adj.*

latent (lā′tənt) *adj.* Present but inactive.

laud (lôd) *v.* To praise.

lay (lā) *adj.* Not associated with the church; secular.

league (lēg) *n.* An informal alliance, as in the phrase *in league with.*

lectern (lĕk′tərn) *n.* A reading stand on which a speaker can keep notes or books.

leech (lēch) *n.* Parasite.

legacy (lĕg′ə-sē) *n.* Something handed down from predecessors or from the past.

lethal (lē′thəl) *adj.* Deadly; fatal.

listless (lĭst′lĭs) *adj.* Without energy or enthusiasm.

livery (lĭv′ə-rē) *n.* Dress or appearance.

loam (lōm) *n.* Soil containing sand, clay, and humus.

loath (lōth) *adj.* Unwilling.

loathing (lō′thĭng) *n.* Intense dislike; hatred.

loathsome (lōth′səm) *adj.* Disgusting.—**loathsomeness** *n.*

loiter (loi′tər) *v.* To spend time in idleness.

loom (lōōm) *v.* To appear in a threatening or imposing way.

loophole (lōōp′hōl′) *n.* **1.** A small hole or slit. **2.** A means of getting out of some difficulty.

lumber (lŭm′bər) *v.* To move clumsily.

luminous (lōō′mə-nəs) *adj.* Filled with light; glowing.

lunge (lŭnj) *v.* To move forward suddenly.

lurch (lûrch) *v.* To roll suddenly to one side, as if losing balance.

lush (lŭsh) *adj.* Thriving; luxuriant.

lyrical (lîr′ĭk-əl) *adj.* Of poetry.

M

magnitude (măg′nĭ-tōōd′, tyōōd′) *n.* Greatness.

malevolence (mə-lĕv′ə-ləns) *n.* Malice.

malevolent (mə-lĕv′ə-lənt) *adj.* Evil.

malicious (mə-lĭsh′əs) *adj.* Spiteful.

manacle (măn′ə-kəl) *n.* A chain or handcuff; something used to hold back or restrain.

manifest (măn′ə-fĕst′) *v.* To show.

mantle (măn′təl) *n.* Cloak.

marl (märl) *n.* A mixture of clay and shells.

martial (mär′shəl) *adj.* Connected with war or the military profession.

massive (măs′ĭv) *adj.* Large and solid.

mediocrity (mē′dē-ŏk′rə-tē) *n.* Mediocre or ordinary state of affairs or performance.

meticulous (mə-tĭk′yə-ləs) *adj.* Very careful.

mien (mēn) *n.* Expression.

migrate (mī′grāt′) *v.* To move from one position within the body to another.

millennium (mĭ-lĕn′ē-əm) *n.* A hoped-for period of happiness and prosperity.

misconstrue (mĭs′kən-strōō′) *v.* To misunderstand.

misguided (mĭs-gīd′əd) *adj.* Led astray.

mishap (mĭs′hăp′) *n.* Unlucky accident.

mobile (mō′bəl, -bīl′) *adj.* Moveable.

mockery (mŏk′ə-rē) *n.* Ridicule or derision.

mode (mōd) *n.* **1.** Manner. **2.** Form; variety.

moderate (mŏd′ər-ĭt) *adj.* Calm.

modulate (mŏj′ōō-lāt′) *v.* To change or vary tone.

momentous (mō-mĕn′təs) *adj.* Having great significance.

momentum (mō-mĕn′təm) *n.* Driving force.

monarch (mŏn′ərk, -ärk′) *n.* Sole ruler.

monocultural (mŏn′ə-kŭl′chər-əl) *adj.* Concerning only one culture.

monolithic (mŏn′ə-lĭth′ĭk) *adj.* As a unified mass.

monotonous (mə-nŏt′n-əs) *adj.* Repetitiously dull; boring.—**monotonously** *adv.*

monstrous (mŏn′strəs) *adj.* Huge; enormous.

monumental (mŏn′yə-mĕn′təl) *adj.* Impressive.

mortal (môrt′l) *adj.* Fatal; deadly.

motley (mŏt′lē) *adj.* Having a mixture of elements.

mouth (mouth) *v.* To speak in an insincere way.

multinational (mŭl′tē-năsh′ən-əl, -năsh′nəl) *adj.* Including many countries.

muster (mŭs′tər) *v.* To collect or gather.

musty (mŭs′tē) *adj.* Stale; worn out; antiquated.

mystical (mĭs′tĭ-kəl) *adj.* Having spiritual significance.

mythic (mĭth′ĭk) *adj.* **1.** Having the nature of a myth. **2.** Imaginary; fanciful.

N

naivety (nä-ēv′ə-tē) *n.* Childlike foolishness; simplicity.

namesake (nām′sāk′) *n.* A person given the same name as someone else.

nautical (nô′tĭ-kəl) *adj.* Having to do with sailors, ships, or navigation.

nocturnal (nŏk-tûr′nəl) *adj.* Occuring at night.

nondescript (nŏn′dĭ-skrĭpt′) *adj.* Having no distinctive or individual features.

nostalgia (nŏ-stăl′jə, nə-) *n.* **1.** Homesickness. **2.** A longing for the past.

O

obdurate (ŏb′dyo͞o-rĭt) *adj.* Unyielding; hardhearted.

oblivion (ə-blĭv′ē-ən) *n.* State of being completely forgotten.

oblivious (ə-blĭv′ē-əs) *adj.* Unmindful or unaware (usually with *to* or *of*).

obscure (ŏb-skyo͞or′, əb-) *v.* To conceal; hide from view.

obsession (əb-sĕsh′ən, ŏb-) *n.* An idea or thought that is impossible to get rid of.

obstinate (ŏb′stə-nĭt) *adj.* Stubborn; difficult to control.

obstruct (əb-strŭkt′, ŏb-) *v.* To block; get in the way.

officiate (ə-fĭsh′ē-āt′) *v.* To perform official functions.

omen (ō′mən) *n.* Sign of some future event.

ominous (ŏm′ə-nəs) *adj.* Sinister; threatening.

omniscient (ŏm-nĭsh′ənt) *adj.* Knowing everything.—**omnisciently** *adv.*

oppress (ə-prĕs′) *v.* To crush or persecute.

oppressive (ə-prĕs′ĭv) *adj.* Burdensome.

ordain (ôr-dān′) *v.* To determine beforehand.

ordeal (ôr-dēl′) *n.* Difficult or painful experience.

organdy (ôr′gən-dē) *n.* A transparent fabric used for light dresses and curtains.

ornate (ôr-nāt′) *adj.* Overly decorated; showy.

ostracism (ŏs′trə-sĭz′əm) *n.* The condition of being excluded from.

outlandish (out-lăn′dĭsh) *adj.* Very odd; bizarre; absurd.

overhaul (ō′vər-hôl′, ō′vər-hôl′) *v.* To overtake; catch up with.

overlay (ō′vər-lā′) *n.* A usually transparent covering laid over something.

P

pagan (pā′gən) *n.* Someone without religion. *adj.* Not Christian, Moslem, or Jewish.

pageant (păj′ənt) *n.* A dramatic production.

palate (păl′ĭt) *n.* Roof of the mouth.

pall (pôl) *v.* To become boring.

pallet (păl′ĭt) *n.* A straw-filled mattress or a narrow, hard bed.

palpable (păl′pə-bəl) *adj.* Capable of being touched.

panama (păn′ə-mä′) *n.* A straw hat.

ă cat	ĭ sit	o͝o hook	oi soil
ā cane	ī kite	o͞o cool	ou mouse
â fare	ŏ mop	ŭ fun	ng king
ä calm	ō code	û turn	th think
ĕ set	ô for	yo͞o fumes	*th* that
ē me			zh fusion
			ɴ *Fr.* mon

ə = { a in *cobra* e in *novel* i in *recipe*
o in *concern* u in *awful* }

pandemonium (păn′də-mō′nē̵-um) *n.* Wild disorder; noise and confusion.

paranoia (păr′ə-noi′ə) *n.* Unreasonable distrust and suspicion.

paranoid (păr′ə-noid′) *adj.* Unreasonably suspicious and distrustful.

parasol (păr′ə-sôl′) *n.* A lightweight umbrella.

parish (păr′ĭsh) *n.* **1.** The members of the congregation of a church. **2.** The district in which members of a congregation live.

parsonage (păr′sən-ĭj) *n.* The dwelling of a parson.

partiality (păr′shē-ăl′ə-tē) *n.* Tendency to favor unfairly.

patriarch (pā′trē-ärk′) *n.* The father of a long line of descendants.

patronize (pā′trə-nīz′, păt′rə) *v.* To buy from; be a customer of.

pedigree (pĕd′ə-grē′) *n.* Ancestry.

peevish (pē′vĭsh) *adj.* Ill-tempered.

penance (pĕn′əns) *n.* Punishment for wrongdoing or sin.

pendulum (pĕn′jōō-ləm) *n.* Something that swings back and forth, such as an object used to regulate the movements of a clock.

penetrate (pĕn′ə-trāt′) *v.* To find a way into.

penitentiary (pĕn′ə-tĕn′-shə-rē) *n.* A state or federal prison.

perennial (pə-rĕn′ē-əl) *adj.* Perpetual.

perfidy (pûr′fə-dē) *n.* Treachery.

permeate (pûr′mē-āt′) *v.* To flow or spread throughout.

peroxide (pə-rŏk′sīd′) *n.* A chemical compound used to bleach hair.

perpetual (pər-pĕch′ōō-əl) *adj.* Continuous; of long duration.

perpetuate (pər-pĕch′ōō-āt′) *v.* To cause to continue.

perplexed (pər-plĕkst′) *adj.* Confused.

perplexity (pər-plĕk′sə-tē) *n.* Bewilderment; confusion.

persistent (pər-sĭs′tənt, -zĭs′-) *adj.* Repeated; continued.—**persistently** *adv.*

perspective (pər-spĕk′tĭv) *n.* Point of view; outlook.

pervasive (pər-vā′sĭv) *adj.* Tending to spread throughout.

perverse (pər-vûrs′) *adj.* Contrary; wicked.

pestilential (pĕs′tə-lĕn′shəl) *adj.* **1.** Causing infection. **2.** Harmful. **3.** Widespread and deadly.

petty (pĕt′ē) *adj.* Unimportant; trivial.

phenomenon (fĭ-nŏm′ə-nŏn′) *n.* Extraordinary occurrence.

physique (fĭ-zēk′) *n.* The shape, strength, and general appearance of a body.

piazza (pē-ăz′ə) *n.* Porch.

pigmentation (pĭg′mən-tā′shən) *n.* Coloration of tissues.

pilferer (pĭl′-fər-ər) *n.* Petty thief.

pillage (pĭl′ĭj) *v.* To be seized or taken forcefully, especially during war.

pillar (pĭl′ər) *n.* Column that is a main support.

pious (pī′əs) *adj.* Devoutly religious.

pivotal (pĭv′ət-əl) *adj.* Essential; central.

placid (plăs′ĭd) *adj.* Calm.—**placidly** *adv.*

plaintiff (plān′tĭf) *n.* The person who begins a suit in court.

plaintive (plān′tĭv) *adj.* Sad; mournful.

pluck (plŭk) *v.* To pull out.

plumed (plūmd) *adj.* Decorated, as with feathers.

plunge (plŭnj) *n.* Fall.

ply (plī) *v.* To keep supplying or offering (as gifts, food, drinks, etc.).

poignant (poin′yənt) *adj.* Moving; painful to the feelings.—**poignantly** *adv.*

poise (poiz) *v.* To hover or hold in balance.

ponder (pŏn′dər) *v.* To think about carefully.

poplar (pŏp′lər) *n.* A type of tree.

possessive (pə-zĕs′ĭv) *adj.* Characterized by a desire to own or control.

potent (pōt′nt) *adj.* Powerful.

precedent (prĕs′ə-dənt) *n.* A legal decision that establishes a custom.

preface (prĕf′ĭs) *n.* A statement that introduces a book or speech and explains its purpose.—*v.* To introduce.

premature (prē′mə-tyŏŏr′, -chŏŏr′) *adj.* Unexpectedly early.

preoccupied (prē-ŏk′yə-pīd′) *adj.* Absorbed in thought; concerned with something.

prescribe (prĭ-skrīb′) *v.* To establish or set down as a rule; to order.

presumably (prĭ-zōō′mə-blē) *adv.* Probably.

presume (prĭ-zōōm′) *v.* To dare.

presumption (prĭ-zŭmp′shən) *n.* Attitude or belief; assumption.

prevail (prĭ-vāl′) *v.* To win out.

prevalent (prĕv′ə-lənt) *adj*. Common; widely occurring or existing.

prima donna (prē′mə dŏn′ə) *n*. Principal female singer in an opera company.

prime (prīm) *v*. To prepare; make ready.

probe (prōb) *v*. To search or explore.

procession (prə-sĕsh′ən) *n*. A group moving forward in an orderly way.

procure (prō-kyoor′, prə-) *v*. To obtain; acquire.

prodigious (prə-dĭj′əs) *adj*. Very large and impressive.

prodigy (prŏd′ə-jē) *n*. An unusually gifted child.

profess (prə-fĕs′) *v*. To declare; claim.

profound (prə-found′) *adj*. Deep; thorough; far-reaching.—**profoundly** *adv*.

profuse (prə-fyoos′, prō-) *adj*. Plentiful; abundant; excessive.—**profusely** *adv*.

progression (prə-grĕsh′ən) *n*. A sequence.

prolong (prə-lông′, -lŏng′) *v*. To lengthen.

prominent (prŏm′ə-nənt) *adj*. **1.** Standing out; conspicuous. **2.** Widely known.

prompt (prŏmpt) *adj*. Without delay.

pronounced (prə-nounst′) *adj*. Strongly and clearly spoken.

prop (prŏp) *v*. To support.

propel (prə-pĕl′) *v*. To cause something to move.

prophet (prŏf′ĭt) *n*. One who can foretell the future.

prophetic (prə-fĕt′ĭk) *adj*. Having the ability to foretell the future.

proprietor (prə-prī′ə-tər) *n*. Owner of a business establishment.

propriety (prə-prī′ə-tē) *n*. The quality of being proper or appropriate.

prospect (prŏs′pĕkt) *n*. Something expected.

prosperity (prŏs-pĕr′ə-te) *n*. Financial success.

protestation (prŏt′ĭs-tā′shən, prō′tĭs-) *n*. Protest; disapproval.

protract (prō-trăkt′) *v*. To draw out.

Providence (prŏv′ə-dəns, -dĕns′) *n*. God.

providential (prŏv′ə-den′shəl) *adj*. Opportune; happening as if by divine providence.

provocation (prŏv′ə-kā′shən) *n*. Cause for annoyance.

prowess (prou′ĭs) *n*. Skill; ability.

psych (sīk) *v*. To use psychological pressure to outwit or control others. *(Slang)*

pulsate (pŭl′sāt′) *v*. To vibrate rhythmically.

pungent (pŭn′jənt) *adj*. Stimulating; biting; clever.

purge (pûrj) *v*. To cleanse or purify.

purloin (pər-loin′, pûr′loin′) *v*. To steal.

Q

quail (kwāl) *v*. To lose courage; shrink back in fear.

qualm (kwäm) *n*. **1.** Pang of conscience. **2.** Uneasiness.

quarry (kwôr′ē, kwŏr′ē) *n*. Prey that is hunted.

quarter (kwôr′tər) *n*. Source or region.—*v*. To be lodged.

queasy (kwē′zē) *adj*. Uneasy.

quest (kwĕst) *n*. Search.

quibble (kwĭb′əl) *v*. To argue over unimportant details.

quicksilver (kwĭk′sĭl′vər) *n*. Another name for mercury, a metal that moves quickly in its liquid form.

R

rake (rāk) *v*. To scrape.

rampart (răm′pärt) *n*. Fortification with a low protective wall.

ramshackle (răm′shăk′əl) *adj*. Rickety; ready to fall apart.

rancid (răn′sĭd) *adj*. Stale; offensive.

random (răn′dəm) *adj*. Haphazard; chosen without pattern or order.

rank (răngk) *adj*. Growing excessively.

rankle (răng′kəl) *v*. To cause resentment.

ă cat	ĭ sit	o͞o hook	oi soil
ā cane	ī kite	o͞o cool	ou mouse
â fare	ŏ mop	ŭ fun	ng king
ä calm	ō code	û turn	th think
ĕ set	ô for	yo͞o fumes	*th* that
ē me			zh fusion
			N *Fr.* mon

ə = { a in *cobra* e in *novel* i in *recipe*
       o in *concern* u in *awful*

ransack (răn′săk′) v. To search thoroughly.

rapt (răpt) adj. Deeply absorbed.

rationalize (răsh′ən-əl-īz′) v. To give reasons.

ravenous (răv′ən-əs) adj. Extremely hungry.

raze (rāz) v. To destroy by tearing down.

readily (rĕd′ə-lē) adv. Willingly.

reaffirm (rē′ə-fûrm′) v. To restate or declare that something is true.

realm (rĕlm) n. **1.** Kingdom. **2.** Area; domain.

recessional (rĭ-sĕsh′ən-əl) n. A hymn or other piece of music sung or played during the exit of clergy and choir after a church service.

reckless (rĕk′lĭs) adj. Foolhardy; daring.

reckon (rĕk′ən) v. To deal with; consider.

reclaim (rĭ-klām′) v. To recover.

recoil (rĭ-koil′) v. **1.** To spring back. **2.** To shrink back in fear.

recompose (rē′kəm-pōz′) v. To calm.

reconcile (rĕk′ən-sīl′) v. To bring together; settle or resolve.

rector (rĕk′tər) n. Clergyman in charge of a parish.

redeem (rĭ-dēm′) v. **1.** To fulfill a promise; pay off. **2.** To save from sinfulness.

redemptive (rĭ-dĕmp′tĭv) adj. Offering the possibility of making amends for.

redouble (rē-dŭb′əl) v. To become twice as great.

redoubtable (rĭ-dou′tə-bəl) adj. Commanding respect.

redress (rĭ-drĕs′, rē′-) n. Satisfaction or amends for wrongdoing.

reflective (rĭ-flĕk′tĭv) adj. Thoughtful.— **reflectively** adv.

relapse (rĭ-lăps′) v. To slip back.

relay (rē′lā′, rĭ-lā′) v. To pass along.

relent (rĭ-lĕnt′) v. To soften; yield.

relinquish (rĭ-lĭng′kwĭsh) v. To give up; abandon.

relish (rĕl′ĭsh) n. Great pleasure; enthusiastic enjoyment; zest.

reluctant (rĭ-lŭk′tənt) adj. Unwilling.— **reluctantly** adv.

remnant (rĕm′nənt) n. What is left from the past; a remainder.

remote (rĭ-mōt′) adj. **1.** Distant; far off. **2.** Distant in manner; aloof.

renaissance (rĕn′ə-säns′, -zäns′) n. New birth; rebirth.

render (rĕn′dər) v. **1.** To cause to become; make. **2.** To make available. **3.** To represent; depict.

rendezvous (rän′dā-vōō′, rän′də-) n. Prearranged meeting.

renege (rĭ-nĭg′, -nĕg′) v. To fail to carry out a promise or an agreement.

repertoire (rĕp′ər-twär′) n. Stock of roles or works for performance.

repository (rĭ-pŏz′ə-tôr′ē) n. **1.** Place for safekeeping; storehouse. **2.** A person who receives things for safekeeping.

reprimand (rĕp′rə-mănd′) n. A severe or formal rebuke, especially by a person in authority.

reproach (rĭ-prōch′) n. Blame.

reprove (rĭ-prōōv′) v. To scold.

resolute (rĕz′ə-lōōt′) adj. Determined.— **resolutely** adv.

resolve (rĭ-zŏlv′) v. To make a decision.

resonant (rĕz′ə-nənt) adj. Vibrating with increasing intensity.

resound (rĭ-zound′) v. To be filled with sound.

respiration (rĕs′pə-rā′shən) n. Breathing.

respite (rĕs′pĭt) n. Short interval.

responsive (rĭ-spŏn′sĭv) adj. Reacting easily or quickly.

resume (rĭ-zōōm′) v. To continue after interruption.

resurrect (rĕz′ə-rĕkt′) v. To bring back into use.

resurrection (rĕz′ə-rĕk′shən) n. Revival; renewal.

reticence (rĕt′ə-səns) n. Reserve; hesitance about speaking.

retort (rĭ-tôrt′) v. To reply.

retreat (rĭ-trēt′) n. A private place or refuge.

retribution (rĕt′rə-byōō′shən) n. Punishment.

retrieve (rĭ-trēv′) v. To recover.

retrospect (rĕt′rə-spĕkt′) n. Review of the past.

revel (rĕv′əl) n. Noisy festivity.

reverberation (rĭ-vûr′bə-rā′shən) n. A resounding or echoing of sound.

reverie (rĕv′ər-ē) n. Daydreaming.

revue (rĭ-vyōō′) n. A type of musical show, with skits, songs, and dances, often satirizing current topics and personalities.

riffle (rĭf′əl) v. To turn pages by shuffling or thumbing through them.

rifle (rī′fəl) v. To ransack.

rigid (rĭj′ĭd) adj. **1.** Stiff; inflexible. **2.** Not moving.

rigorous (rĭg'ər-əs) *adj*. Very difficult or strenous.

rill (rĭl) *n*. A small brook.

riotous (rī'ət-əs) *adj*. Loud; exuberant.

rite (rīt) *n*. A ceremony, especially a religious ceremony.

ritual (rĭch'oo-əl) *n*. An observance or ceremony.

rivet (rĭv'ĭt) *v*. To secure or fasten.

riveting (rĭv'ĭt-ĭng) *adj*. Holding the attention.

roguish (rō'gĭsh) *adj*. Mischievous.

romanticize (rō-măn'tə-sīz') *v*. To hold dreamy, romantic ideas.

rout (rout) *v*. To drive out.

rowdy (rou'dē) *adj*. Disorderly.

ruddy (rŭd'ē) *adj*. Reddish.

rummage (rŭm'ĭj) *v*. To search hastily.

rumpus (rŭm'pəs) *n*. Noisy or violent disturbance; uproar.

ruthless (rooth'lĭs) *adj*. Relentless.

S

sable (sā'bəl) *adj*. Black or dark.

sallow (săl'ō) *adj*. Of a sickly, pale-yellowish complexion.

salutation (săl'yə-tā'shən) *n*. Greeting.

salvage (săl'vĭj) *v*. To save or rescue (property).

savanna (sə-văn'ə) *n*. Flat, treeless grassland.

savour (sā'vər) *v*. To enjoy; relish. Also spelled *savor*.

sceptical (skĕp'tĭ-kəl) *adj*. Disbelieving; doubting. Variant of **skeptical**.

scintillate (sĭn'tə-lāt') *v*. To flash; sparkle.

scowl (skoul) *v*. To frown angrily.

scraggly (skrăg'lē) *adj*. Messy; ragged.

scrawny (skrô'nē) *adj*. Bony and thin.

scruple (skroo'pəl) *n*. Uneasiness; doubt.

scrutinize (skroot'n-īz) *v*. To inspect carefully.

scrutiny (skroot'n-ē) *n*. Careful and close examination.

seethe (sēth) *v*. To be greatly disturbed.—**seething** *adj*.

semblance (sĕm'bləns) *n*. Outward form or appearance; likeness.

senile (sē'nīl') *adj*. Of old age, especially when characterized by mental impairment such as confusion and memory loss.

sensationalize (sĕn-sā'shən-əl-īz') *v*. To use vivid, dramatic language with the intent to shock or startle.

sepulchral (sə-pŭl'krəl) *adj*. Gloomy; sad.

serpentine (sûr'pən-tīn') *adj*. Twisting and coiling.

servile (sûr'vīl') *adj*. Suitable to a slave; submissive.

sexton (sĕks'tən) *n*. Someone who takes care of church property.

shackle (shăk'əl) *n*. A metal fastening for the wrists or ankles, usually one of a pair, for confining a prisoner.

shamefaced (shām'fāst') *adj*. Looking embarrassed or ashamed.—**shamefacedly** *adv*.

shear (shîr) *v*. To divide.

sheathe (shēth) *v*. To enclose.

sheen (shēn) *n*. Brightness; shininess.

shrine (shrīn) *n*. A place of worship.

shun (shŭn) *v*. To avoid contact with.

singular (sĭng'gyə-lər) *adj*. Extraordinary; uncommon.

sinuous (sĭn'yoo-əs) *adj*. Graceful and supple in movement.

skein (skān) *n*. Yarn wound in a coil.

skulk (skŭlk) *v*. To move stealthily so as to avoid notice.

slick (slĭk) *adj*. Smooth and glossy.

smite (smīt) *v*. To destroy.

snigger (snĭg'ər) *v*. To laugh in a sly, derisive way.

sod (sŏd) *n*. Grass-covered soil.

solemnity (sə-lĕm'nə-tē) *n*. Seriousness.

solicitous (sə-lĭs'ə-təs) *adj*. Concerned.

solidity (sə-lĭd'ə-tē) *n*. Thickness and denseness in appearance.

ă cat	ĭ sit	oo hook	oi soil
ā cane	ī kite	oo cool	ou mouse
â fare	ŏ mop	ŭ fun	ng king
ä calm	ō code	û turn	th think
ĕ set	ô for	yoo fumes	th that
ē me			zh fusion
			N *Fr.* mon

ə = { a in *cobra* e in *novel* i in *recipe* o in *concern* u in *awful* }

sophisticated (sə-fĭs′tĭ-kā′tĭd) *adj.* Worldly-wise.

spacious (spā′shəs) *adj.* Open; wide.

spangle (spăng′gəl) *v.* To set sparkling.

spar (spär) *v.* To argue.

sparse (spärs) *adj.* Meager; thinly spread or scattered.—**sparsely** *adv.*

speculate (spĕk′yə-lāt′) *v.* To reflect.

spent (spĕnt) *adj.* Worn out; exhausted.

spontaneity (spŏn′tə-nē′ĭ-tē) *n.* Quality of naturalness, as something that is done from impulse.

sprint (sprĭnt) *v.* To leap or dash at full speed.

spry (sprī) *adj.* Full of life; active.

squalor (skwŏl′ər) *n.* Extreme disarray and dirtiness.

squelch (skwĕlch) *v.* **1.** To crush; squash. **2.** To silence or suppress.

staccato (stə-kä′tō) *adj.* Abrupt and emphatic; disconnected.

stalk (stôk) *v.* To walk angrily.

stanch (stänch, stănch) *v.* To stop the flow of blood.

stark (stärk) *adj.* **1.** Sharply outlined. **2.** Bare. **3.** Unsoftened; grim.

station (stā′shən) *n.* Social position; rank.

stature (stăch′ər) *n.* Height.

status (stā′təs) *n.* Social standing or position.

statute (stăch′o͞ot) *n.* Law.

stave off (stāv ôf) *v.* To keep off; repel.

steed (stēd) *n.* A spirited horse.

stem (stĕm) *v.* To stop or hold back.

sterile (stĕr′əl) *adj.* Unfruitful.

stifle (stī′fəl) *v.* **1.** To smother or suffocate. **2.** To suppress; hold back.

stifling (stī′flĭng) *adj.* Suffocating; suppressed.

stigma (stĭg′mə) *n.* Disgrace.

stiletto (stĭ-lĕt′ō) *n.* A dagger with a slender blade.

stilted (stĭl′tĭd) *adj.* Artificially dignified; not natural.

stimulus (stĭm′yə-ləs) *n.* Incentive.

stock (stŏk) *n.* An accumulated supply.

strain (strān) *n.* **1.** Descendants from a common blood line. **2.** A tune; musical passage.

stupor (sto͞o′pər, styo͞o′-) *n.* A dazed state.

suave (swäv) *n.* Smoothly polite; refined.

subtlety (sŭt′l-tē) *n.* Something that is a fine point or a clever distinction.

suffice (sə-fīs′) *v.* To satisfy a need.

sulk (sŭlk) *v.* To withdraw in resentment.

sullen (sŭl′ən) *adj.* Gloomy.

sumptuous (sŭmp′cho͞o-əs) *adj.* Lavish; extravagant.

sundry (sŭn′drē) *adj.* Various.

supercilious (so͞o′pər-sĭl′ē-əs) *adj.* Disdainful or contemptuous; haughty.

superficial (so͞o′pər-fĭsh′əl) *adj.* Near the surface.

supple (sŭp′əl) *adj.* Able to bend and twist nimbly.

suppress (sə-prĕs′) *v.* To restrain; hold back.

surge (sûrj) *v.* **1.** To move in waves. **2.** To increase suddenly.

surname (sûr′nām′) *n.* Family name.

surpass (sər-păs′) *v.* To exceed; go beyond.

susceptibility (sə-sĕp′tə-bĭl′ə-tē) *n.* Sensitivity.

swagger (swăg′ər) *n.* A bold, arrogant, or lordly stride; strut.—*v.* To act in an uncaring or insolent manner.

swath (swäth) *n.* A broad strip.

swelter (swĕl′tər) *v.* To feel faint and sick from heat.

sweltering (swĕl′tər-ĭng) *adj.* Uncomfortably hot and humid.

swill (swĭl) *n.* A mixture of liquid and food, as table scraps, fed to animals.

symbolic (sĭm-bŏl′ĭk) *adj.* Representing something other than itself.

symbolize (sĭm′bə-līz′) *v.* To represent.

T

taboo (tă-bo͞o′) *adj.* Prohibited by tradition.

tactful (tăkt′fəl) *adj.* Considerate.—**tactfully** *adv.*

tam (tăm) *n.* A tam-o′-shanter, a cap with a round flat top and a pompom.

taunt (tônt) *n.* Jeer or scornful remark.

taut (tôt) *adj.* Pulled or stretched tightly.

tedious (tē′dē-əs) *adj.* Wearisome; tiresome; boring.

temper (tĕm′pər) *v.* To moderate; lessen.

tempest (tĕm′pĭst) *n.* A violent storm.

terrain (tə-rān′) *n.* A stretch of land.

terse (tûrs) *adj.* Concise.

testimony (tĕs′tə-mō′nē) *n.* Proof.

thong (thông, thŏng) *n.* A strip of leather.

thoroughfare (thûr′ō-fâr′) *n.* Main road.

tolerance (tŏl′ər-əns) *n.* The ability to put up with someone not especially liked.

tolerate (tŏl′ə-rāt) *v.* To put up with.

torrent (tôr′ənt) *n.* Raging flood.

tote (tōt) *v.* To carry.

totter (tŏt′ər) *v.* **1.** To appear ready to collapse. **2.** To walk unsteadily.

tragicomic (trăj′ĭ-kŏm′ĭk) *adj.* Both sad and funny.

transact (trăn-săkt′, zăkt′) *v.* To manage or carry out.

transgression (trăns-grĕsh′ən, trănz-) *n.* The act of overstepping or breaking (a law, commandment, etc.).—**transgress** *v.*

transmission (trăns-mĭsh′ən, trănz-) *n.* The act of passing on or conveying something.

travesty (trăv′ĭs-tē) *n.* A crude, distorted, or ridiculous representation of something.

tread (trĕd) *n.* Step; footprint.

trek (trĕk) *n.* A slow, difficult journey.

tremulous (trĕm′yə-ləs) *adj.* Vibrating; trembling.

trespass (trĕs′pəs, trĕs′păs′) *v.* To go beyond what is considered right or proper.

trestle (trĕs′əl) *n.* A support consisting of a bar held up by two pairs of legs.

truculent (trŭk′yə-lənt) *adj.* Defiant.

trusty (trŭs′tē) *adj.* Dependable.

tuber (tōō′bər, tyōō′-) *n.* A short, thickened underground stem, as in a potato.

tumultuous (tə-mŭl′chōō-əs) *adj.* Wild and noisy; disorderly.—**tumultuously** *adv.*

tunic (tōō′nĭk, tyōō′-) *n.* A loose-fitting garment reaching to the hips or below.

U

ultimate (ŭl′tə-mĭt) *adj.* Final; highest.

unaccountable (ŭn′ə-koun′tə-bəl) *adj.* Not able to be explained or accounted for; mysterious.

unalterable (ŭn-ôl′tər-ə-bəl) *adj.* Not capable of being changed.

unassailable (ŭn′ə-sāl′ə-bəl) *adj.* Too strong to be attacked.

undermine (ŭn′dər-mīn′) *v.* **1.** To wear away a base or foundation. **2.** To weaken or injure gradually.

undertone (ŭn′dər-tōn′) *n.* Low tone of voice.

unerring (ŭn-ĕr′ĭng) *adj.* **1.** Free from error. **2.** Not missing or failing; exact.

unfetter (ŭn-fĕt′ər) *v.* To free.

unison (yōō-nə-sən, -zən) *n.* Complete agreement.

unprogressive (ŭn′prə-grĕs′ĭv) *adj.* Not stressing reform.

unrelenting (ŭn′rĭ-lĕn′tĭng) *adj.* Hard; stern; unyielding.

untempered (ŭn′tĕm′pərd) *adj.* Not modified or softened.

upheaval (ŭp′hē′vəl) *n.* Violent disturbance.

upper crust (ŭp′ər krŭst′) *n.* The highest social class.

uproarious (ŭp′-rôr′ē-əs) *adj.* Hilarious.—**uproariously** *adv.*

upstartedness (ŭp′stärt′əd-nəs) *n.* Presumption; self-importance.

utterance (ŭt′ər-əns) *n.* Something that is spoken.

V

valiant (văl′yənt) *adj.* Brave; courageous.

valid (văl′ĭd) *adj.* Sound; logical.

ventriloquist (vĕn-trĭl′ə-kwĭst′) *n.* A person who can produce sounds that seem to come from another speaker.

venture (vĕn′chər) *v.* To dare; risk.

veracity (və-răs′ə-tē) *n.* Truthfulness.

verandah (və-răn′də) *n.* A partly enclosed porch, usually with a roof.

verbiage (vûr′bē-ĭj) *n.* Wordiness.

ă cat	ĭ sit	ōō hook	oi soil
ā cane	ī kite	ōō cool	ou mouse
â fare	ŏ mop	ŭ fun	ng king
ä calm	ō code	û turn	th think
ĕ set	ô for	yōō fumes	*th* that
ē me			zh fusion
			N *Fr.* mon

ə = { a in *cobra* e in *novel* i in *recipe* o in *concern* u in *awful* }

verge (vûrj) *n.* The beginning or brink of.

verve (vûrv) *n.* Vitality.

vial (vī'əl) *n.* A small bottle for liquids.

victuals (vĭt'əlz) *n. pl.* Food.

vigilance (vĭj'ə-ləns) *n.* Watchfulness.

vile (vīl) *adj.* **1.** Wretched. **2.** Unpleasant.

virtuosity (vûr'chōō-ŏs'ə-tē) *n.* Great technical skill in some fine art, especially in the performance of music.

vise (vīs) *n.* A clamp, usually of two jaws that can be closed together with a screw or lever, for grasping and holding something.

vitality (vī-tăl'ə-tē) *n.* Liveliness; energy.

vittle (vĭt'l) *n.* (nonstandard for victual) Food.

vogue (vōg) *n.* **1.** Fashion (often with *the*). **2.** Popularity.

volley (vŏl'ē) *n.* A burst of words or sounds.

voluminous (və-lōō'mə-nəs) *adj.* Full; large; bulky.

voodoo (vōō'dōō) *n.* A religion that originated in Africa, characterized by a belief in the power of charms and witchcraft.

vulgar (vŭl'gər) *n.* Common people.

vulgarity (vŭl'-găr'ə-tē) *n.* Coarseness; lack of taste.

vulnerable (vŭl'nər-ə-bəl) *adj.* Open to attack or injury; without defenses.

W

waft (wäft, wăft) *v.* To float lightly through the air.

wallow (wŏl'ō) *v.* To flounder around in.

wan (wŏn) *adj.* Pale.

wane (wān) *v.* To decrease in visible illumination.

wanton (wŏn'tən) *n.* An immoral person, especially a loose or unrestrained woman.

wary (wâr'ē) *adj.* Watchful.—**warily** *adv.*

waver (wā'vər) *v.* To sway.

wayward (wā'wərd) *adj.* Disobedient; willful.

wean (wēn) *v.* To give up a habit.

well (wĕl) *v.* To rise to the surface, as if ready to flow.

wheeze (hwēz) *v.* To breathe with difficulty.

whim (hwĭm, wĭm) *n.* A sudden idea or fancy.

whimper (hwĭm'pər, wĭm'-) *v.* To whine.

whit (hwĭt) *n.* A small bit or amount (usually with *not a*).

wield (wēld) *v.* To handle.

wince (wĭns) *v.* To flinch, as in pain or distress.

winding (wīn'dĭng) *n.* A series of turns.

woebegone (wō'bĭ-gôn', -gŏn') *adj.* Sorrowful; miserable.

wrath (răth, räth) *n.* Rage; fury.

writhe (rīth) *v.* To twist as in pain.

Y

yawning (yôn'ĭng) *adj.* Wide open.

yonder (yŏn'dər) *adj.* Distant.

Z

zeal (zēl) *n.* Intense enthusiasm; passion.

zest (zĕst) *n.* Keen enjoyment.

Index of Skills

Page numbers in italics refer to entries in the **Guide to Literary Terms and Techniques.**

LITERARY ELEMENTS

Alliteration 247, 304, 310, 444, 658, 702, *942*
Allusion 45, 188, 280, 713, *942*
   Biblical Allusion 284
Analogy *942*
   Argument from Analogy 163, 628–629
   Word Analogies 29, 369
Anecdote 224, *942*
Antagonist *942*
Anthem 292, *943*
Antithesis 615, 620, *943*
Aphorism 168, *943*
Apostrophe 82, *943*
Archaism 255, *943*
Argument 64, 158, 623, 628, *943*
Assonance 308, 310, 702, *943*
Atmosphere 484, 879, *943*
Autobiography 145, 213, 411, 583, 608, 853, *944*
Autobiographical Narrative 67–68
Ballad 664, *944*
   Folk Ballad 258, 261
   Literary Ballad *944*
Bard 280, *944*
Biography 583, *944*
Blank Verse *944*
Blues 370, *944*
Call-and-Response 86, 370, *944*
Catalog 441, *945*
Characterization 3, 11, 448, *945*
   Direct and Indirect 3, 11, 448, 509, 936
Characters 448, 469, 494, 498, 509, 555, 566, 567, *945*
   Flat and Round 509
   Static and Dynamic 498, 509, 936
Climax 178, 472, 551, 566, 792, 829, 851, 936, 938, *945*
Comedy *945*
Complication 936, *945*

Conflict 172, 178, 432, 438, 472, 481, 555, 792, 846, 851, 938, *945*
   External and Internal 172, 178, 432, 438, 472, 566, 846, 938
Connotation 247, 302, 329, 445, 621, 662, 689, 693, 721, 830, 879, *946*
Couplet 165, 301, 395, 722, *946*
Crisis *946*
Denotation 329, 621, 830–831, *946*
Dénouement 851, 938, *946*
Description *946*
Dialect 264, 390, *946*
Dialogue 567, 737, 794, *946*
Diction 295, 445, 646, 662, 675, 689, 693, *946*
Drama 737, 791, 794, *946*
Dramatic Poetry 718
Elegy 250, 257, 664, 810, *947*
Epic 118, 119, 125, 670, *947*
Epigram 339, *947*
Epithet *947*
Essay 583, 592, 600, 637, *947*
   Formal and Informal 584, 635
Explication 374, *947*
Exposition 126, 262, *947*
   In Drama 792
   In the Novel 937
Fable 96, 181, *947*
Fiction 469, *948*
Figurative Language 42–43, 324, 341, 374, 620, 938, *948*
Figure of Speech 660, *948*
Flashback 472, 833, 843, *948*
Foil *948*
Folk Literature 187, *948*
Folklore 181, *948*
Folk Tale 97, 181, *948*
Foreshadowing 178, 261, 356, 399, 409, 472, 822, 830, *948*
Free Verse 289, 441, 444, 651, 658, 664, 693, *948*
Griot 87, 119, *949*
Haiku 722–723
Humor 592, 597
Hymn 79, 250, *949*

Index of Artists

Artists Unknown

Akhenaton, temple fragment, 643
Akhenaton and Sun-god Aton, relief, 81
Asante Spokesman's Staff, 131
Ashanti turtle, 111
Belt mask of ivory, 507
Benin archer, bronze relief, 102
Benin horn player, bronze, 72
Benjamin Banneker, frontispiece, 157
Book of the Dead, scroll, 78
Douglass Flogged by Covey, engraving from an almanac, 174
Egyptian god Thoth, relief, 83
Figure of wood, brass, glass, beads, cowrie shells, and cloth, 94
The First Vote, engraving, 203
Frederick Douglass speaking at an abolitionist meeting, 177
Galla Boy, illustration from *Dr. Prichard's Natural History of Man, 1885,* 146
Head of an Oba, bronze, 105
Hippopotamus mask, painted wood, 115
List of Sumerian kings, cuneiform clay block, 76
Log Cabin Quilt, silk appliqué, 403
Lone Star Quilt, 549
Man from Ancient Jenné, terra-cotta statue, 121
Monkey, glazed earthenware, 97
Negro Exodus, print, 205
The Oba of Benin in Divine Aspect, bronze, 110
Olaudah Equiano, oil, 144
Painted relief from tomb of Queen Nefertari of Thebes, 76
Phillis Wheatley, frontispiece, 164
Rider on Horseback, terra cotta, 123
Scribes holding scrolls of papyrus, bas-relief, 77
Sojourner Truth and Abraham Lincoln, painting, 170
Statue of leopard, bronze, 109
Yoruba Gelede mask, 92

Fine Art Photographers

Allen, James Latimer, 296, 383
Bourke-White, Margaret, 715
Cook, Huestis P., 218
Corbin, Ronald, 666
Davidson, Bruce, 641
Jones, Brent, 458, 556
Lange, Dorothea, 396
Lanker, Brian, 705
Parks, Gordon, 410
Rothstein, Arthur, 486
Shahn, Ben, 36
Simpson, Coreen, 461
Siskind, Aaron, 381
Van Der Zee, James, 359, 362
Van Vechten, Carl, 294, 345, 440

About the Contributors _____

William L. Andrews is E. Maynard Adams Professor of English at the University of North Carolina at Chapel Hill. He is the author of *To Tell a Free Story: The First Century of Afro-American Autobiography 1760–1865* and *The Literary Career of Charles W. Chesnutt*. He is general editor of the Wisconsin Studies in American Autobiography series. He is a coeditor of *The Norton Anthology of African American Literature* and the *Oxford Companion to African American Literature*. Professor Andrews wrote the introductions for Unit Three, "The Beginnings of African American Literature," and Unit Four, "From Reconstruction to Renaissance." He also reviewed materials for this textbook.

Barbara Bowen Coulter was formerly Director of Communication Arts for the Detroit Public Schools. She has been a teacher, reading specialist, and reading supervisor with the Detroit Public Schools, a university instructor in language arts, and an author and consultant for language arts textbooks. Dr. Coulter has served on various committees for reading and education. She led the committee of teachers and supervisors that worked with editors in outlining objectives and developing a structure for this textbook.

Carole Boyce Davies is Professor with joint appointments in English, Afro-American and African Studies, and Comparative Literature at the State University of New York at Binghamton. Her research and teaching interests span African, Caribbean, and African American literatures with special focus on women writers and the relationships between oral and written literary traditions. Her published works include *Black Women, Writing and Identity: Migrations of the Subject*. Dr. Boyce Davies serves on the editorial boards of a number of scholarly journals and has edited two volumes of criticism: *Ngambika: Studies of Women in African Literature* and *Out of the Kumbla: Caribbean Women and Literature*. She is coeditor of the two-volume *Moving Beyond Boundaries: International Dimensions of Black Women's Writing*. She has served on the African Literature Association Executive Board and has also been Secretary of the Association. Dr. Boyce Davies reviewed materials for this textbook.

Alice A. Deck is Associate Professor of English and Afro-American Studies at the University of Illinois at Urbana/Champaign. She teaches courses in Modern African fiction and drama, Afro-American literature, and the American novel. She is interested in literature by women of color from Africa and the United States, particularly women's autobiographies. She is currently completing a book entitled *Against the Tyrannies of Silence: Black Women's Autobiography in Africa and the United States,* which will be published by Indiana University Press. She has written articles for *Black American Literature Forum, Women's Studies International Forum,* and *Explorations in Ethnic Studies*. Professor Deck wrote the introduction to Unit Eleven, "Contemporary African Literature," in this textbook.

David Dorsey is Professor of English Linguistics and African Literature at Clark Atlanta University. Before coming to Atlanta, he taught Latin and Greek at Howard and New York universities. As a 1970–1971 Ford Foundation Fellow, he spent a year studying the evolution of the humanities disciplines at the universities of Uganda (Makerere) and Kenya (Nairobi). In 1984, he directed the first College Teachers' Summer Seminar on the subject of African literature for the National Endowment for the Humanities. He is also the author of numerous essays on African and African American literature. Professor Dorsey wrote the introduction and notes for Unit Twelve, "The Novel," and also reviewed materials for this textbook.

Mari Evans has written articles, books for children, theater pieces, two musicals, and several volumes of poetry, including *I Am a Black Woman, Nightstar,* and *A Dark and Splendid Mass.* She edited *Black Women Writers,* a highly acclaimed collection of essays. She has taught at universities and colleges for the past twenty years and has received many awards, including the Black Academy of Arts and Letters first annual Poetry Award (1970) and the National Endowment for the Arts Creative Writing Award (1981). Ms. Evans wrote the special essay that appears in Unit Nine of this textbook, "Contemporary Poetry."

Robert E. Fox is Associate Professor of American and African American Literature at Southern Illinois University at Carbondale. From 1985 to 1991 he was a member of the English Department and Director of the Collection of Afro-American Literature at Suffolk University in Boston. From 1978 to 1985 he taught at the University of Ife in Nigeria. He serves on the board of advisory editors of the journal *Black American Literature Forum.* He is the author of *Conscientious Sorcerers,* a study of black American postmodernist fiction, and a collection of essays on black literature and aesthetics entitled *Masters of the Drum.* He was awarded a fellowship from the American Council of Learned Societies and a position as Visiting Scholar for 1991–1992 at the W. E. B. Du Bois Institute for Afro-American Research at Harvard University. Professor Fox wrote the introductory material to Unit Two, "The African Literary Tradition," and also reviewed materials for this textbook.

Henry Louis Gates, Jr., is W. E. B. Du Bois Professor of Humanities, Chair of the Afro-American Studies Department, and Director of the W. E. B. Du Bois Institute for Afro-American Research at Harvard. Before coming to Harvard he taught at Yale, Cornell, and Duke universities. He is the general editor of the *Norton Anthology of African American Literature* and the editor of Oxford's 30-volume series, *The Schomburg Library of Nineteenth Century Black Women Writers.* His publications include *Figures in Black: Words, Signs, and the Racial Self; The Signifying Monkey: A Theory* of *Afro-American Literary Criticism* (which won the American Book Award); *Loose Canons: Notes on the Culture Wars; Colored People: A Memoir;* and *The Future of the Race* with Cornel West. Professor Gates served as an adviser for this textbook.

Constance Burts Jackson teaches at Communication and Media Arts High School in Detroit. She has published several volumes of her poetry. She served on the committee that assisted in the planning of this textbook, and she prepared instructional materials for Unit Nine, "Contemporary Poetry." She has used some of her own poems to illustrate techniques of writing in the special feature "How to Write a Poem."

Sterling C. Jones, Jr., who has served as Supervisor of High School English for the Detroit Public Schools, is currently Program Supervisor of Academic Task Force/Gifted and Talented Education. He has edited a syllabus for the anthology *Voices from the Black Experience.* He served on the committee that assisted in planning this textbook and he prepared instructional materials for Unit Five, "The Harlem Renaissance."

Yvonne Robinson Jones is Associate Professor in the Department of Languages and Literature at Shelby State Community College in Memphis, Tennessee. She has received several awards for her work in the humanities, including a National Endowment for the Humanities Fellowship. In 1993 she won a Fulbright Fellowship that allowed her to study a year in Egypt. Her publications include articles and essays in African American literature. She is a contributing author to the *Oxford Companion to African American Literature* and has also contributed several poems to *Homespun Images: An Anthology of Black Memphis Writers and Artists.* She has done extensive research on Richard Wright. Professor Jones prepared instructional materials for Unit Six of this textbook, "From Renaissance to Mid-Forties."

David Adams Leeming was formerly Professor of English and Comparative Literature at the University of Connecticut in Storrs. He has published an authorized biography of James Baldwin. He wrote the essay on the African American novel and also reviewed materials for this textbook.

Jewel Lenard formerly taught English at Cooley High School in Detroit. She has donated research projects to the Wayne State Archives of Black Folklore. She has edited a volume of poetry, *More Magic,* and is working on her first book of poetry, *Ebony Jewels.* She was a member of the committee that assisted in planning this textbook.

Barbara Smith Palmer teaches at Locke High School in Los Angeles, California. She helped to develop and implement the California Model Curriculum Standards and the English/Language Arts and History/Social Science Frameworks. She has conducted workshops, seminars, and summer institutes for teachers. She has been a regular in-studio guest on the Educational Television Network. Dr. Palmer has received many awards for her contributions to education and has been named finalist for California Teacher of the Year. She has helped to develop, write, and edit a number of curriculum guides. She has been a teacher-leader of the California Literature Project and of the UCLA Writing Project. The titles of some of her publications reflect her commitment to educational reform: *English, An Alternate Course of Study; Experimental English; Uhuru; Literature for All Students: A Sourcebook for Teachers.* Dr. Palmer prepared instructional materials for Unit Three of this textbook, "The Beginnings of African American Literature," and Unit Nine, "Contemporary Poetry."

Viola Palmer is English Department Head at Cass Technical High School in Detroit. She served on a central committee that developed a syllabus for the anthology *Voices from the Black Experience.* She was a member of the committee that assisted in planning this textbook.

Phil W. Petrie formerly taught classes in writing and literature at the Frederick Douglass Creative Arts Center in New York City. He has edited the work of a number of African American writers, including Amiri Baraka, Ed Bullins, Mari Evans, and Nikki Giovanni. He has also worked as a free-lance writer, contributing more than fifty feature articles to magazines. He prepared instructional materials for Unit Seven of this textbook, "Contemporary Short Stories."

Arnold Rampersad is Woodrow Wilson Professor of Literature and Director of the Program in African-American Studies at Princeton. Before coming to Princeton he taught English at the University of Virginia, and at Stanford, Rutgers, and Columbia universities. His books include *The Art and Imagination of W. E. B. Du Bois* and the two-volume biography *The Life of Langston Hughes.* His collection of Hughes's poems is considered definitive, and he has edited the works of Richard Wright for the Library of America. Professor Rampersad wrote the introduction to "Contemporary African American Literature" and also served as a critical reader, reviewer, and adviser for this textbook.

John Edgar Tidwell teaches English at Miami University in Oxford, Ohio. He has contributed a number of critical essays, book reviews, interviews, and bibliographies to scholarly journals, books, and anthologies of African American literature. Among his several honors and awards are fellowships from the American Council of Learned Societies and the National Endowment for the Humanities. He has edited *Livin' the Blues: Memoirs of a Black Journalist and Poet.* Professor Tidwell wrote the introduction to Unit Six, "From Renaissance to Mid-Forties," and also reviewed materials for this textbook.

Nancy Timmons is Assistant Superintendent of Administrative Services for the Fort Worth Independent School District, Fort Worth, Texas. She has been a teacher of secondary English language arts and United States history and has served as Supervisor for English Language Arts and Social Studies. Dr. Timmons is the author of the *Reader's Response Journal,* a supplement to the first edition of *Elements of Literature* for Grades Seven and Eight. She developed materials for the special writing features in this textbook.

Shirley W. Tinsley taught English at Northwestern High School in Detroit for twenty-two years. She prepared instructional materials for Unit Eight, "Contemporary Nonfiction," and she also served as a member of the committee that assisted in planning this textbook.

Mary Toskos was Assistant Principal and Supervisor of the English Department at Flushing High School in New York City. She has been an adjunct professor at the Queens campus of St. John's University and at the Brooklyn campus of Long Island University. She has cowritten several curriculum guides for the New York City Board of Education and has chaired conferences for the New York City Teachers of English, the New York

City Association of Assistant Principals, and other educational organizations. Ms. Toskos prepared instructional materials for Unit Four of this textbook, "From Reconstruction to Renaissance."

Christopher van Wyk lives in Johannesburg, South Africa. He works at SACHED (South African Committee for Higher Education), which publishes innovative and self-instructional books for secondary school students. He has had several poems published in literary journals and newspapers. His first book of poetry, *It Is Time to Go Home,* was published in 1979. Mr. van Wyk reviewed materials for this textbook.

Cheryl A. Wall is Associate Professor of English at Rutgers University. She is the author of *Women of Letters of the Harlem Renaissance* and the editor of *Changing Our Own Words: Essays on Criticism, Theory, and Writing by Black Women.* She has also edited the novels and stories of Zora Neale Hurston for the Library of America. Professor Wall wrote the introduction to Unit Five, "The Harlem Renaissance," and also served as an adviser for this textbook.

Acknowledgments_____

For permission to reprint copyrighted material, grateful acknowledgment is made to the following sources:

Addison Wesley Longman Ltd.: From "Krina" and from "The Words of the Griot Mamadou Kouyaté" from *Sundiata: An Epic of Old Mali* by D. T. Niane, translated by G. D. Pickett. Copyright © 1965 by Longman Group Ltd.

Africa World Press: "Graduation Notes" from *Under A Soprano Sky* by Sonia Sanchez. Copyright © 1987 by Sonia Sanchez.

Margaret Walker Alexander: "Childhood," "For My People," and "Lineage" from *This Is My Century, New and Collected Poems* by Margaret Walker. Copyright © 1942, 1989 by Margaret Walker. Published by the University of Georgia Press, 1989.

Samuel W. Allen: "American Gothic" by Samuel Allen (Paul Vesey) from *I Am the Darker Brother,* edited by Arnold Adoff. "Souffles" by Birago Diop, translated by Samuel Allen from *Poems from Africa,* selected by Samuel Allen. Copyright © 1973 by Samuel Allen.

James Baldwin Estate: "My Dungeon Shook: Letter to My Nephew on the One Hundredth Anniversary of the Emancipation" by James Baldwin. Copyright © 1962 and renewed © 1990 by The Estate of James Baldwin. Originally published in the *Progressive.* Collected in *The Fire Next Time,* published by Vintage Books. "The Rockpile" from *Going to Meet the Man* by James Baldwin. Copyright © 1965 and renewed © 1993 by The Estate of James Baldwin. Published by Vintage Books.

Basic Books, a division of HarperCollins Publishers, Inc.: From "The Rules About the Rules" from *(integrity)* by Stephen L. Carter. Copyright © 1996 by Stephen L. Carter.

Beacon Press: From "ABC" by Faith Adiele from *Testimony: Young African-Americans on Self-Discovery and Black Identity,* edited by Natasha Tarpley. Copyright © 1995 by Natasha Tarpley.

Black Orpheus, University of Lagos Press Ltd.: "Be Not Amazed" by Léopold Sédar Senghor from *Black Orpheus.*

BOA Editions Ltd., 260 East Ave., Rochester, NY 14604: "in the inner city" from *good woman: poems and a memoir 1969–1980* by Lucille Clifton. Copyright © 1987 by Lucille Clifton.

George Braziller, Inc.: *The Wrestling Match* by Buchi Emecheta. Copyright © 1980 by Oxford University Press, UK. Published in the United States by George Braziller, Inc., 1983.

Broadside Press: "Booker T. and W.E.B." and "George" from *Poem Counterpoem* by Margaret Danner and Dudley Randall. Copyright © 1969 by Margaret Danner and Dudley Randall.

Gwendolyn Brooks: "The Bean Eaters," "the sonnet ballad," and "We Real Cool" from *Blacks* by Gwendolyn Brooks. Copyright © 1991 by Gwendolyn Brooks. Published by Third World Press, Chicago, 1991.

Cambridge University Press: "Song for the Sun that Disappeared Behind the Rainclouds" from *African Poetry,* translated and edited by Ulli Beier. Copyright © 1966 by Cambridge University Press.

Eugenia Collier: "Marigolds" by Eugenia Collier from *Negro Digest,* November 1969. Copyright © 1969 by Johnson Publishing Company, Inc. Comment about "Marigolds" by Eugenia Collier. Copyright © 1992 by Eugenia Collier.

Crisis Publishing Co. Inc.: From a review of Langston Hughes' *The Weary Blues: A Book of Verse* by Jessie Fauset from *The Crisis,* March 1926. Copyright 1926 by The Crisis.

The Crossing Press: From *Zami: A New Spelling of My Name* by Audre Lorde. Copyright © 1982 by Audre Lourde.

Crown Publishers, Inc.: "The Park" by James Matthews from *Quartet: New Voices from South Africa,* edited by Richard Rive. Copyright © 1963 by Crown Publishers, Inc.

Andre Deutsch Ltd.: From *Crick Crack, Monkey* by Merle Hodge. Copyright © 1970 by Merle Hodge.

Doubleday, a division of Bantam Doubleday Dell Publishing Group, Inc.: "Dead Men's Path" from *Girls at War and Other Stories* by Chinua Achebe. Copyright © 1972, 1973 by Chinua Achebe. "Brother Carlyle" from *Dancers on the Shore* by William Melvin Kelley. Copyright © 1956 by William Melvin Kelley.

Rita Dove: Comment about "Sisters" by Rita Dove. Copyright © 1992 by Rita Dove.

Rita Dove and W. W. Norton & Company, Inc.: "Sisters" from Grace Notes by Rita Dove. Copyright © 1989 by Rita Dove.

Dutton Signet, a division of Penguin Books USA Inc.: From The Piano Lesson by August Wilson. Copyright © 1988, 1990 by August Wilson.

Mari Evans: "If There Be Sorrow" and "The Rebel" from I Am a Black Woman by Mari Evans. Copyright © 1970 by Mari Evans. Published by William Morrow & Co., 1970.

Faber and Faber Limited: From Tell Freedom by Peter Abrahams. Copyright © 1954, 1981 by Peter Abrahams.

Farrar, Straus & Giroux, Inc.: From Omeros by Derek Walcott. Copyright © 1990 by Derek Walcott.

The Feminist Press: "To Da-Duh, In Memoriam" from Reena and Other Stories by Paule Marshall. Copyright © 1983 by Paule Marshall. Published by The Feminist Press at The City University of New York, 1983.

Flannery, White & Stone: "The Kind of Light That Shines on Texas" by Reginald McKnight. Copyright © 1989 by Reginald McKnight. First published in The Kenyon Review, New Series, vol. XI, no. 3, Summer 1989.

Greenwood Press, an imprint of Greenwood Publishing Group, Inc., Westport, CT: "Miss Cynthie" from The Short Fiction of Rudolph Fisher, edited by Margaret Perry. Copyright © 1987 by Margaret Perry.

GRM Associates, Inc., Agents for the Estate of Ida M. Cullen: "For a Lady I Know," "Incident," "Tableau," and "Yet Do I Marvel" from Color by Countee Cullen. Copyright © 1925 by Harper & Brothers; copyright renewed 1953 by Ida M. Cullen. "From the Dark Tower" from Copper Sun by Countee Cullen. Copyright 1927 by Harper & Brothers; copyright renewed © 1955 by Ida M. Cullen.

Grove/Atlantic, Inc.: From "Not too Small to Be Chosen" from The Palm-Wine Drinkard by Amos Tutuola. Copyright © 1953 by George Braziller.

Harcourt Brace & Company: "Everyday Use" from In Love & Trouble: Stories of Black Women by Alice Walker. Copyright © 1973 by Alice Walker. "For My Sister Molly Who in the Fifties" and "Women" from Revolutionary Petunias & Other Poems by Alice Walker. Copyright © 1970, 1972 by Alice Walker.

HarperCollins Publishers, Inc.: "Strange Legacies" from Southern Road by Sterling A. Brown. Copyright 1932 by Harcourt Brace & Co.; copyright renewed © 1960 by Sterling Brown. Included in The Collected Poems of Sterling A. Brown, selected by Michael S. Harper. Copyright © 1980 by Sterling A. Brown. From Dust Tracks on a Road: An Autobiography by Zora Neale Hurston. Copyright 1942 by Zora Neale Hurston; copyright renewed © 1970 by John C. Hurston. "How the Gator Got Black," "How Jack O'Lanterns Came to Be," "How the Possum Lost the Hair Off His Tail," and "How the Snake Got Poison" from Mules and Men by Zora Neale Hurston. Copyright 1935 by Zora Neale Hurston; copyright renewed © 1963 by John C. Hurston and Joel Hurston. From Black Boy by Richard Wright. Copyright 1937, 1942, 1944, 1945 by Richard Wright; copyright renewed © 1973 by Ellen Wright.

Harvard University Press: From "The Loophole of Retreat" from Incidents in the Life of a Slave Girl Written by Herself by Harriet A. Jacobs, edited by Jean Fagan Yellin. Copyright © 1987 by the President and Fellows of Harvard College. Published by Harvard University Press, Cambridge, Mass.

Safiya Henderson-Holmes: "harlem/soweto" by Safiya Henderson-Holmes. Copyright © 1988 by Safiya Henderson-Holmes.

Hill and Wang, a division of Farrar, Straus & Giroux, Inc.: From "I've Known Rivers" and "When the Negro Was in Vogue" from The Big Sea: An Autobiography by Langston Hughes. Copyright © 1940 by Langston Hughes; copyright renewed © 1968 by Arna Bontemps and George Houston Bass. "Seeing Double" and "Two Sides Not Enough" from The Best of Simple by Langston Hughes. Copyright © 1962 by Langston Hughes; copyright renewed © 1989 by George Houston Bass. From The Dark Child by Camara Laye. Copyright © 1954 and renewed © 1982 by Camara Laye.

Lawrence Hill Books, an imprint of Chicago Review Press, Inc.: "The Return" from Secret Lives by Ngugi wa Thiong'o. Copyright © 1975 by Ngugi wa Thiong'o.

Henry Holt and Company, Inc.: From "Stopping by Woods on a Snowy Evening" from The Poetry of Robert Frost, edited by Edward Connery Lathem. Copyright 1923, © 1969 by Henry Holt and Co., Inc.; copyright © 1951 by Robert Frost.

John Hopkins & Associates: "The Man Who Was Almost a Man" from Eight Men by Richard Wright, foreword by David Bradley. Copyright © 1940, 1961 by Richard Wright; copyright © 1987 by the Estate of Richard Wright. Published by Chatto & Windus.

International Creative Management, Inc.: From The Bluest Eye by Toni Morrison. Copyright © 1970 by Toni Morrison.

The Heirs to the Estate of Martin Luther King, Jr., c/o Writers House, Inc. as agent for the proprietor: "I Have a Dream" by Martin Luther King, Jr. Copyright © 1963 by Martin Luther King, Jr.; copyright renewed © 1991 by Coretta Scott King.

Alfred A. Knopf, Inc.: "Robert Louis Stevenson Banks, a.k.a. Chimley" from *A Gathering of Old Men* by Ernest J. Gaines. Copyright © 1983 by Ernest J. Gaines. "Dreams" from *The Dream Keeper and Other Poems* by Langston Hughes. Copyright 1932 by Alfred A. Knopf, Inc.; copyright renewed © 1960 by Langston Hughes. "Dream Deferred" ("Harlem") from *The Panther and the Lash* by Langston Hughes. Copyright 1951 by Langston Hughes. "I Too," "Mother to Son" and "The Negro Speaks of Rivers" from *Selected Poems* by Langston Hughes. Copyright 1926 by Alfred A. Knopf, Inc.; copyright renewed 1954 by Langston Hughes.

Liveright Publishing Corporation: "Beehive," "November Cotton Flower," "Reapers," and "Song of the Son," from *Cane* by Jean Toomer. Copyright 1923 by Boni & Liveright; copyright renewed 1951 by Jean Toomer. "Runagate, Runagate," "Those Winter Sundays," and "The Whipping" from *Collected Poems of Robert Hayden*, edited by Frederick Glaysher. Copyright © 1966 by Robert Hayden.

Sterling Lord Literistic, Inc.: From "Black Art" by Amiri Baraka/LeRoi Jones from *Black Magic Poetry 1961–1967*. Copyright © 1969 by Amiri Baraka. "Preface to a Twenty Volume Suicide Note" and "SOS" from *Selected Poetry of Amiri Baraka/LeRoi Jones*. Copyright © 1979 by Amiri Baraka.

Lowenstein Associates Inc.: "Beware: Do Not Read This Poem" from *Catechism of a Neo-American Hoodoo Church* by Ishmael Reed. Copyright © 1968 by Ishmael Reed. ".05" from *Chattanooga* by Ishmael Reed. Copyright © 1973 by Ishmael Reed. "America: The Multinational Society" from *Writin' Is Fightin'* by Ishmael Reed. Copyright © 1988 by Ishmael Reed.

Edward B. Marks Music Company: "Lift Every Voice and Sing" by James Weldon Johnson and J. Rosamond Johnson.

The Archives of Claude McKay, Carl Cowl, Administrator: "America," "Baptism," "If We Must Die," and "The Tropics in New York" from *Selected Poems of Claude McKay*. Copyright 1953 by Bookman Associates, Inc.

Evelyn W. Neal: "The Middle Passage and After" from *Black Boogaloo (Notes on Black Liberation)* by Larry Neal. Copyright © 1969 by Larry Neal.

The New York Times Co.: "A Giant Step" by Henry Louis Gates, Jr., from "About Men" section of *The New York Times*, December 9, 1990. Copyright © 1990 by The New York Times Company. From "Round Five for a Theatrical Heavyweight" by Mervyn Rothstein from *The*

New York Times, April 15, 1990. Copyright © 1990 by The New York Times Company.

The New Yorker: "Back to School" by Andrea Lee from *The New Yorker*, April 29 & May 6, 1996. Copyright © 1996 by The New Yorker Magazine Inc.

Northwestern University Press: "Spider's Bargain with God" from *West African Folk Tales,* collected and translated by Jack Berry, edited and with an introduction by Richard Spears. Copyright © 1991 by Northwestern University Press.

Harold Ober Associates: "A Black Man Talks of Reaping" and "Southern Mansion" by Arna Bontemps from *American Negro Poetry*, edited by Arna Bontemps. Copyright © 1963 by Arna Bontemps. "A Summer Tragedy" by Arna Bontemps. Copyright © 1933 by Arna Bontemps.

Niyi Osundare: "I Sing of Change" from *Songs of the Marketplace* by Niyi Osundare. Copyright © 1983 by Niyi Osundare.

Pantheon Books, a division of Random House, Inc.: "Nana Miriam" from *The Stolen Fire* by Hans Baumann, translated by Stella Humphries. Copyright © 1974 by Random House, Inc.

Peter Pauper Press, Inc.: 42 proverbs from *African Proverbs*, compiled by Charlotte and Wolf Leslau. Copyright © 1962, 1985 by Peter Pauper Press, Inc.

Princeton University Press: From "The Hymn to the Aton" by Pharaoh Akhenaton, translated by John A. Wilson from *Ancient Near Eastern Texts: Relating to the Old Testament, 3rd Edition with Supplement,* edited by James B. Pritchard. Copyright © 1969 by Princeton University Press.

Random House, Inc.: From *I Know Why the Caged Bird Sings* by Maya Angelou. Copyright © 1969 by Maya Angelou. "Raymond's Run" from *Gorilla, My Love* by Toni Cade Bambara. Copyright © 1972 by Toni Cade Bambara. From "An Extravagance of Laughter" from *Going to the Territory* by Ralph Ellison. Copyright © 1986 by Ralph Ellison. From *Aké: The Years of Childhood* by Wole Soyinka. Copyright © 1981 by Wole Soyinka. From *The Autobiography of Malcolm X* by Alex Haley and Malcolm X. Copyright © 1964 by Alex Haley and Malcolm X; copyright © 1965 by Alex Haley and Betty Shabazz.

Marian Reiner for Julia Fields: "High on the Hog" by Julia Fields. Copyright © 1968 by Julia Fields. "High on the Hog" appeared originally in *Celebrations*, edited by Arnold Adoff. Comment about "High on the Hog" by Julia Fields. Copyright © 1992 by Julia Fields.

Flora Roberts, Inc.: "The Pocketbook Game" from *Like One of the Family* by Alice Childress. Copyright © 1956 and renewed © 1984 by Alice Childress.

Russell & Volkening, Inc., as agents for Ann Petry: From *The Street* by Ann Petry. Copyright © 1946 and renewed © 1974 by Ann Petry.

The Sewanee Review and Diane Oliver's agent: "Neighbors" by Diane Oliver from *The Sewanee Review,* vol. 74, no. 2, Spring 1966. Copyright © 1966 by the University of the South.

Wole Soyinka: "Telephone Conversation" by Wole Soyinka from *Reflections: Nigerian Prose and Verse,* edited by Frances Ademola.

St. Martin's Press, Incorporated: "senses of heritage" from *nappy edges* by Ntozake Shange. Copyright © 1972, 1974, 1975, 1976, 1977, 1978 by Ntozake Shange.

The Roslyn Targ Literary Agency, Inc.: "Black Laughter" from *Black on Blacks* by Chester Himes. Copyright © 1946, 1973 by Chester Himes.

Times Books, a division of Random House, Inc.: From "No Fools, No Fun" from *Every Good-bye Ain't Gone* by Itabari Njeri. Copyright © 1982, 1983, 1984, 1986, 1990 by Itabari Njeri.

The University of Chicago Press: From *Crusade for Justice: The Autobiography of Ida Wells,* edited by Alfreda M. Duster. Copyright © 1970 by The University of Chicago.

University of North Carolina Press: "John Henry" from *John Henry: Tracking Down a Negro Legend* by Guy B. Johnson. Copyright © 1929 by the University of North Carolina Press.

Vanguard Press, a division of Random House, Inc.: "Talk" from *African Voices: An Anthology of Native African Writings,* edited by Peggy Rutherford. Copyright © 1958 by Vanguard Press.

Viking Penguin, a division of Penguin Books USA Inc.: "The Creation" and from "Preface" from *God's Trombones* by James Weldon Johnson. Copyright 1927 by The Viking Press, Inc.; copyright renewed © 1955 by Grace Nail Johnson. From *A Call to Assembly: The Autobiography of a Musical Storyteller* by Willie Ruff. Copyright © 1991 by Willie Ruff.

Dorothy West: "My Mother, Rachel West" from *The Living Is Easy* by Dorothy West. Copyright 1948 by Dorothy West.

Al Young: "For Poets" by Al Young. Copyright © 1968 by Al Young.

We would like to thank the following people for their assistance in obtaining fine art, photographs, and other illustrative materials for this textbook:

Shola Akintolaya of Saana International, NYC; **Deirdre Bibby,** Art and Artifacts Manager, The Schomburg Center for Research in Black Culture, New York Public Library; **George Calderaro,** Public Relations Director, The Studio Museum in Harlem; **Johanna Cooper,** The Center for African Art, NYC; **Dorothy Davis,** Curator, The Studio Museum in Harlem; **Edmund Barry Gaither,** Director, The National Center of Afro-American Artists, Inc., Boston, MA; **Dr. Christraud Geary,** Curator, The National Museum of African Art, Washington, D.C.; **Jim Huffman,** Reference Librarian, The Schomburg Center for Research in Black Culture, New York Public Library; **Mary Lou Hultgren,** Curator, Hampton University Museum, Hampton, VA; **Ruth Jett,** Cinque Gallery, NYC; **Loïs Mailou Jones,** Artist; **Bill Karg,** Contemporary African Art, NYC; **Diane Lefer,** Writer; **Dr. Samella Lewis,** Artist and Art Historian; **Michelle Lowery,** Coordinator, Role Model Experiences, St. Louis Public Schools; **Frank Matson,** Office of Special Collections, Henry W. and Albert A. Berg Collection, New York Public Library; **Patricia Middleton,** Reference Librarian, The Beinecke Rare Books and Manuscripts Library, Yale University; **Naomi Nelson,** Archivist, The Studio Museum in Harlem; **Myron Schwartzman,** Writer; **Norman Skinner,** Norman Skinner Enterprises, NYC; **Edward Smith,** Director, The Art of Raymond Lark, Los Angeles, CA; The Time Life Photo Lab; **Steve Vallillo,** TheatResearch, NYC; **Katheryn White,** Picture Research Assistant; **Beth Zarcone,** Director, Time Inc. Magazines Picture Collection; **Jeanne Zeidler,** Director, Hampton University Museum, Hampton, VA.

PHOTO CREDITS

Page 572, From *Invisible Man* by Ralph Ellison. Copyright © 1951 by Ralph Ellison, Reprinted by permission of Random House, Inc.; 576, "Cover of original 1923 edition," from *Cane* by Jean Toomer. Copyright 1923 by Boni & Liveright, renewed 1951 by Jean Toomer. Reprinted by permission of Doubleday, a division of Bantam Doubleday Dell Publishing Group, Inc. Photo Beinecke Rare Books; 577, From *If He Hollers Let Him Go* (Jacket Cover) by Chester B. Himes. Copyright. Used with permission of Doubleday, a division of Bantam Doubleday Dell Publishing Group, Inc. Photo Beinecke Rare Books.

General Index